CHEMISTRY

For Advanced Level

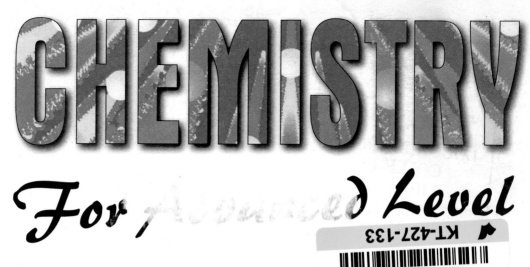

Fourth Edition

Ted Lister
and Janet Renshaw

Stanley Thornes Publishers Ltd

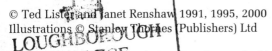

First published in 1991

Third edition published in 2000 by:

Stanley Thornes (Publishers) Ltd
Ellenborough House
Wellington Street
Cheltenham
GL50 1YW

00 01 02 03 04 / 10 9 8 7 6 5 4 3 2 1

A catalogue record of this book is available from the British Library.

ISBN 0 7487 3958 0

Book plus Course Study Guide
ISBN 0 7487 4463 0

Book plus Course Study Guide (Trade Edition)
ISBN 0 7487 4464 9

Course Study Guide
ISBN 0 7487 4465 7

STRUCTURES of CHEMISTRY for Advanced Level CD-ROM
Single- and Multi-user versions available
Free sample available on request
Please contact the publisher at the address given above
or telephone customer services on 01242 267273

Throughout this book a CD-ROM icon is used to indicate where links exist to the CD-ROM. The CD-ROM provides additional support described on the back cover of this book to further aid your understanding of the topic.

Typeset by Tech Set, Gateshead, Tyne & Wear.

Printed in Italy by Vincenzo Bona, Turin.

Contents

PART A: FOUNDATIONS

PART B: FUNDAMENTALS

PART C: FURTHER CHEMISTRY

Acknowledgements

The authors and publishers would like to thank the following people and organisations.

The following examination boards granted permission to reproduce questions from recent examination papers:

Associated Examining Board (AEB)
London Examinations, A Division of Edexcel (L)
Northern Examinations and Assessment Board (NEAB)
Northern Ireland Council for the Curriculum Examinations and Assessment (NI)
University of Cambridge Local Examinations Syndicate (incorporating University of Oxford Delegacy of Local Examinations)
Welsh Joint Education Committee (WJEC)

The following granted permission to reproduce photographs:

Allsport: 496 (top – Agence Vandystadt/Jean-Marc Loubat); Ann Ronan Picture Library: 12 (top), 38, 411 (top); Argonaut Technologies: 619; Axon Images: 464 (middle – John M. Bailey); BASF: 1 (top), 586; Bass Brewers: 138 (bottom right); Biophoto Associates: 117 (bottom), 205 (middle), 319 (bottom), 338 (top): British Library: 338; Camera Press: 322; Cephas: 295 (left); Collections: 492 (top – John Wender); David Hoffman: 450; Du Pont: 260; Ecoscene: 415 (Gryniewicz), 445 (bottom – Sally Morgan); Food and Drug Administration: 408 (bottom); FORD: 560 (bottom); Great Lakes UK: 208 (bottom); Groupal Ltd: 361; Hewlett Packard: 325 (bottom), 567; Hulton Getty: 506; IBM: 35; Image Bank: 530 (background); Image Select: 2 (Fragment Collection/Petr Placek); J. Allen Cash Photo Library: 126, 440; Leslie Garland Picture Library: 342 (Andrew Lambert), 487 (top); Mary Evans Picture Library: 124 (top), 410 (bottom), 411 (right), 575 (bottom); Martyn Chillmaid: 1 (middle), 12 (bottom), 14, 16 (bottom), 17, 29, 32, 74, 95, 117 (middle), 120, 127, 138 (top and middle), 145 (bottom), 148, 153, 160, 161, 162, 190 (middle), 200 (top right and bottom right), 205 (top and bottom), 208 (top), 212, 213, 225, 234, 241, 251 (top and bottom), 260 (middle), 263, 268, 269, 278, 290, 295 (right), 300, 308, 313, 323, 333, 341, 353, 356, 359, 388 (right), 389, 399, 400, 408 (top), 441, 442 (top), 444, 446 (bottom), 452, 474, 476, 483, 487 (bottom), 504, 510, 516, 523, 532, 537, 539 (top and bottom), 544 (top and bottom), 545, 553 (top), 555 (left and right), 558, 569, 575 (middle), 578, 581, 590 (top), 594, 604, 608, 612 (left and right), 613, 640; Mountain Camera: 321 (John Cleare); NIH: 171; Oxford Scientific Films: 145 (top – Densey Clyne), 369 (Kim Westerskov), 393 (Jonathon Watts and Peter Parks), 534 (Scott Camazine); PA News: 382; Panos Pictures: 311; Perkin Elmer Ltd: 44, 416; Pilkington Technology: 439; PPL: 489 (British Steel); Raychem: 599; Robert Harding Picture Library: 530 (J. Florea); Royal Society: 177 (left); Royal Society of Chemistry: 177 (right); Science Museum/Science and Society Picture Library: 446 (top), 496 (bottom); Science Photo Library: 1 (bottom), 37, 40, 56 (top – Gregory Scott, middle – Dick Rowan), 79 (John Mead), 117 (top – Will and Deni McIntyre), 133, 135 (Martin Bond), 138 (bottom left – Dr Kari Lounatmaa), 175, 190 (bottom – Chris Bjornberg), 194 (David Taylor and Jerry Mason), 219 (Simon Fraser), 320 (Charles D. Winters), 325 (top – TEK IMAGE), 378 (Volker Steger), 410 (top – Philippe Plailly), 413 (James Holmes/Fulmer Research), 421 (Geoff Tompkinson), 423 (Mehan Kulyk), 429 (top – Klaus Guldbransen, bottom left – Geoff Tompkinson), 437 (Mike McNamee), 438 (bottom left – Phillip Hayson), 442 (bottom – Alfred Pasieka), 445 (middle – Dr Jeremy Burgess), 500, 518, 560 (Charles D. Winters), 575 (top), 606 (Clive Freeman/The Royal Institution); Still Pictures: 172 (Andre Maslennikov); Telegraph Colour Library: 553 (bottom – J. Cummins); Tony Stone Images: 464 (top – Andy Sacks); Topham Picturepoint: 56 (bottom), 124 (bottom – ASAP), 143, 200 (left); West Midlands Fire Brigade: 591 (bottom).

Whilst every effort has been made to contact copyright holders the publishers would like to apologise if any have been overlooked.

Three-dimensional figures of graphite, diamond, buckminsterfullerene and silicon dioxide were supplied by Alex Renshaw from the program Crystallographica®.

Dr Michael Taylor made valuable comments during the development of this book.

Preface

The structure of all A-level courses has changed as a result of the introduction of new AS-level (Advanced Subsidiary) syllabuses (now called specifications) examined at a level midway between GCSE and A-level standard. All AS-level and A-level chemistry specifications have a core of common topics based on the Subject Criteria and this book is built around these. The compulsory topics of every specification are covered in this book as well as most of the optional topics and modules. AS-level courses have effectively half the content of the full A-level course and are set at a standard expected of candidates who have completed the first half of a full A-level qualification. This can be a qualification in its own right or a stepping-stone to the second year (A2 specification) and a full A-level. As well as suiting AS-level and A-level courses this book will also be useful for Advanced GNVQ Science, Scottish Higher Grade and the International Baccalaureate. We have tried to make this book colourful, highly visual and readable.

The book is arranged in three sections:

● Foundations (colour-coded green). This will help you bridge the gap between GCSE Science Double Award or Science: Chemistry and post-sixteen studies and literally give your chemistry a firm foundation.

● Fundamentals (colour-coded brown). This section builds on Foundations and covers the basic ideas required for further study of chemistry. It broadly corresponds to the AS-level core, although the details vary between specifications.

● Further chemistry (colour-coded dark green) develops some of the ideas in Fundamentals and also includes some completely new topics. This section broadly corresponds to the content required for a full A-level.

How to use this book

Each chapter in the Fundamentals and Further Chemistry sections of the book has the same structure.

● 'Chemistry Now' gives an insight into how some ideas in the chapter relate to our lives;

● An introductory box lists the ideas that will be developed in the chapter;

● A 'Concept Checkpoint' box lists the basic ideas which you need to be confident about before starting the chapter. It guides you to the chapters in the book where you can look these up.

Most chapters contain boxes of two sorts. At a first reading it should be possible to follow the chapter without reference to these. Boxes labelled 'Further Focus' contain extension material or reference material. Boxes labelled 'Chemistry Around Us' contain interesting and up-to-date applications of chemistry.

In the margin there are hints and questions. Hints contain helpful tips and also pitfalls to avoid. The questions are designed to develop your understanding of the text. They are the sort that your teacher might ask you during a lesson, to keep you on your toes. They are well worth trying as you read the text and in most cases can be done very quickly. The answers to these are at the foot of the page.

Each chapter has a summary of the key ideas. These are set out in two columns so that you can cover the right-hand one and test yourself.

At the end of each chapter are selections of two further types of questions. Practice questions develop, rather than just test, your understanding of the ideas in the chapter. The answers to these questions are at the end of the book. Examination questions have been selected from the most recent papers of all the major Examination Boards. There are more examination questions at the very end of the book.

The *Course Study Guide* which accompanies this book contains specimen answers to the first exam question of each chapter of the Fundamentals section, along with notes to help you.

The complete package

New Understanding Chemistry has two further components to help you fulfil your potential at chemistry: a *Course Study Guide* and *Structures of Chemistry for Advanced Level CD-ROM*.

The *Course Study Guide*

This supports the main text and helps you make the most effective use of it while developing your chemistry skills. These include practical and mathematical skills, and how to use information and communication technology (ICT) in your course.

It also covers revision and examination techniques, and in particular, how to tackle different types of examination questions.

STRUCTURES of CHEMISTRY for Advanced Level CD-ROM

One of the most important facts about chemical structures is that they are three-dimensional and this may sometimes be difficult to appreciate on a flat piece of paper. *Structures of Chemistry CD-ROM* allows you to examine some key structures of chemistry in three-dimensional representation on a computer screen and lets you rotate them so that you can view them from any angle.

There is a database of information about these structures. Also on the CD-ROM is an interactive Periodic Table with information on each element. For those of you that are online, it contains links to other sites of chemical interest on the Internet.

We hope you will enjoy your chemistry.

Ted Lister and Janet Renshaw

Introduction

The importance of chemistry

Chemistry is the branch of science which is concerned with materials of every description. It is often called the central science because it overlaps with both biology and physics. On the one hand, chemists unravel the chemical reactions that are responsible for life, and on the other, they investigate new materials with exciting and potentially useful properties such as 'remembering' their shapes, contracting when they are heated or conducting electricity in one direction only. Chemistry is also concerned with how to change one substance into another. Indeed chemistry evolved from the work of the early alchemists who tried to turn so-called base metals into gold. Although they failed they learned a lot of chemistry on the way.

Modern chemists are concerned with equally dramatic changes, turning, for example, crude oil into a whole range of useful and diverse products, such as nylon, aspirins, paint, adhesives and petrol. Other spectacular transformations include sand into glass and silicon chips, and nitrogen from the air into fertilisers and explosives. In fact we use very few materials which have *not* been changed in some way by a chemist. Even wood is likely to be treated by fungicides to prevent rot, and then painted or varnished.

All this means that chemistry is big business. The UK chemical business is the nation's fourth largest industry and its biggest export earner. It is the fifth largest chemical industry in the world. Over one person in 20 in the UK is employed by the chemical industry.

Chemistry is not without problems: there have been well-publicised chemical disasters, pollution problems such as acid rain and the ozone hole, and many people are concerned about the long-term risks to health of food additives.

What is undeniable, however, is that chemistry affects the lives of each and every one of us.

2 Atomic structure and bonding

2.1 Inside the atom

The quest to find out what an atom was made of started when radioactive elements, whose atoms naturally break up and reveal their contents, were discovered. The search is not finished and subatomic particles are still being discovered. However, we can use quite a simple picture to explain the patterns of the Periodic Table (see Chapter 3) and why elements react with each other.

The structure of the atom

The most surprising feature is that an atom is mostly space. The mass is concentrated in the middle, in the **nucleus,** which is positively charged. Orbiting round this nucleus, but a long way from it, are very light, negatively charged particles called **electrons.** So it is the attraction between positive charge and negative charge that holds the electrons in place round the atom. The nucleus is composed of two sorts of subatomic particles, **protons**, which each have a positive charge, and **neutrons** which have the same mass as protons but are neutral (see **Figure 2.1** and **Table 2.1**).

Figure 2.1 The arrangement of subatomic paricles in the atom (not to scale)

The atomic number, *Z*

Table 2.1 Main subatomic particles

	Proton	Neuton	Electron
Position	nucleus	nucleus	orbiting nucleus
Mass (atomic mass units)	1	1	$\frac{1}{1840}$
Charge (relative)	1+	0	1−

The number of protons in an atom is equal to the number of electrons and thus the atom is neutral. The number of protons is called the **atomic number** of the element and it is unique for the element. It is usually given the symbol *Z*. If you look at the Periodic Table you will see that each element has two numbers.

For example: beryllium

$$9 \longleftarrow \text{relative atomic mass}$$
$$\text{Be}$$
$$3 \longleftarrow \text{atomic number}$$

The smaller number is the atomic number and in most versions of the table it is written at the bottom. Elements are arranged in the Periodic Table in order of the number of protons, starting with hydrogen, which has one proton, and ending (at present) with meitnerium, which has one hundred and nine. There are no numbers missing.

In 1869, when Dmitri Mendeleev arranged the elements that were known at the time into the Periodic Table, he had no knowledge of protons, so his achievement was really astonishing.

The relative atomic mass, *A*_r

The larger number, the **relative atomic mass**, A_r, tells us the average mass of an atom of an element compared with the mass of an atom of

Dmitri Mendeleev – father of the Periodic Table

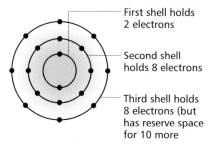

First shell holds 2 electrons

Second shell holds 8 electrons

Third shell holds 8 electrons (but has reserve space for 10 more

Figure 2.2 Electron shells

hydrogen (whose relative atomic mass is taken as 1). So a helium atom, with a relative atomic mass of 4, is four times more massive than a hydrogen atom.

Mass number, *A*

For a single atom we sometimes refer to the **mass number.** This is *not* an average. The mass number is the total number of protons and neutrons in a given atom.

The number of neutrons, *N*, in an atom can be found by taking the atomic number from the mass number:

$$N = A - Z$$

7 protons + neutrons

For example   lithium   Li

3 protons

has $7 - 3 = 4$ neutrons in its nucleus.

Isotopes

Some elements have atoms with different numbers of neutrons, which means that some atoms of that element will be slightly more massive than others. These slightly different atoms of the same element are called **isotopes.** The relative atomic mass, A_r, is the *average* mass of all the isotopes of the element.

For example, chlorine has two isotopes in the ratio of about three to one:

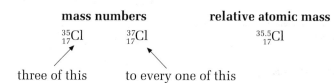

mass numbers   relative atomic mass

$^{35}_{17}$Cl $^{37}_{17}$Cl $^{35.5}_{17}$Cl

three of this   to every one of this

so that their average mass is 35.5, as shown below.

mass of four atoms = 35 + 35 + 35 + 37 = 142
average mass = 142 / 4 = 35.5

The arrangement of the electrons

Again we can use a simple picture.

The electrons orbit the nucleus in a series of 'shells' which become bigger and bigger as they get further and further from the nucleus.

Each shell can hold only a given number of electrons (**Figure 2.2**).

● The first shell, which is always filled first, is closest to the nucleus and can only hold two electrons.
● The second shell is full when it has eight electrons in it.
● The third shell will also hold eight, but has reserve room for a further ten which fills up when we reach the transition elements. There will be more about this in Chapter 7.

Table 2.2 shows the electron arrangements from hydrogen to calcium.

Looking for a pattern

If we write the elements in the same groups together, we can see a pattern:

Table 2.2 Electron arrangements of the first 20 elements

Element	Shell			
	First	Second	Third	Fourth
$_1$H	1			
$_2$He	2			
$_3$Li	2	1		
$_4$Be	2	2		
$_5$B	2	3		
$_6$C	2	4		
$_7$N	2	5		
$_8$O	2	6		
$_9$F	2	7		
$_{10}$Ne	2	8		
$_{11}$Na	2	8	1	
$_{12}$Mg	2	8	2	
$_{13}$Al	2	8	3	
$_{14}$Si	2	8	4	
$_{15}$P	2	8	5	
$_{16}$S	2	8	6	
$_{17}$Cl	2	8	7	
$_{18}$Ar	2	8	8	
$_{19}$K	2	8	8	1
$_{20}$Ca	2	8	8	2

Group I	Group II	Group III	Group 0
H 1	He 2		
Li 2,1	Be 2,2	B 2,3	Ne 2,8
Na 2,8,1	Mg 2,8,2	Al 2,8,3	Ar 2,8,8
K 2,8,8,1	Ca 2,8,8,2		

All Group I elements have one electron in the outer shell, Group II elements have two electrons in the outer shell, Group III have three and so on, until we get to the noble gases in Group 0. These all have a full outer shell.

From these patterns we can infer that:

● It is having the same number of electrons in the *outer* shell that makes elements have similar chemical properties.
● A full outer shell of electrons makes an atom chemically inert.
● The electrons are all-important in the chemical behaviour of atoms. We might expect this anyway, since electrons are on the outside of the atom.

Electron diagrams

Atoms can be represented as flat circles as in **Figure 2.3**. This is not accurate, but gives a simple picture of the electrons, which is helpful for showing how atoms bond together.

In these diagrams it is useful to show electrons as having four positions on the circle. These four positions are first filled singly, then filled up as pairs. For example, **Figure 2.4**:

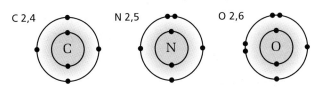

Figure 2.4 The electron arrangements of carbon, nitrogen and oxygen

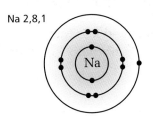

Figure 2.3 The electron arrangement of sodium

Q An atom has 13 electrons. Using only this information say what group it is in.

2.2 Bonding

Atoms bond together to become more stable, which means they will be less reactive when bonded. Noble gases are very unreactive. They have full outer shells. This leads to the idea that a full outer shell results in stability and that atoms bond together to get a full outer shell. There are three types of strong chemical bonds: **ionic**, **covalent**, and **metallic**. Chapter 9 develops the theories of bonding in more depth.

Ionic bonding

This occurs between metals and non-metals, for example in sodium fluoride (**Figure 2.5**).

The outer electron from sodium moves into the outer shell of the fluorine atom.

An electron is *transferred* (**Figure 2.6**). Each outer shell is now full, and both sodium and fluorine have a noble gas electron structure.

This means that the two particles left are no longer neutral. The sodium will be positively charged, because it has lost a negative electron. The fluorine will be negatively charged, because it has

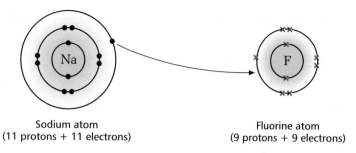

Figure 2.5 A dot-cross diagram to illustrate the transfer of an electron from a sodium atom to a fluorine atom (remember that electrons are all identical whether shown by a dot or a cross)

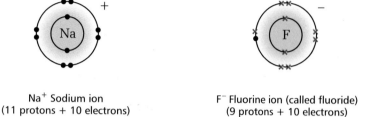

Figure 2.6 The ions that result from electron transfer

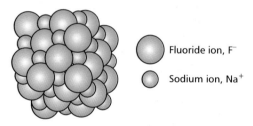

Figure 2.7 The sodium fluoride structure. This is an example of a **giant structure**. The strong bonding extends throughout the compound, and because of this it will be difficult to melt

gained an extra electron. These charged particles are called **ions**. They are attracted to each other and to other ions in the compound and it is this attraction of positive for negative that makes the bond between atoms. The attraction extends throughout the compound (**Figure 2.7**).

We can also say that the formula of sodium fluoride is NaF, because we know that one sodium atom is required for each fluorine atom.

More examples:

1. Magnesium oxide

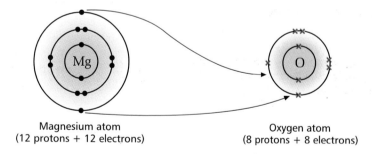

This time two electrons from the magnesium atom move to the outer shell of the oxygen atom.

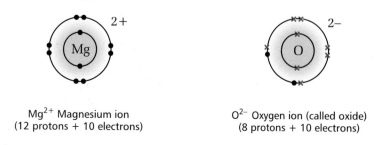

The magnesium atom has lost two electrons and has a 2+ charge. The oxygen atom has gained two electrons and has a 2− charge. The formula of magnesium oxide will be MgO.

2. **Calcium chloride**

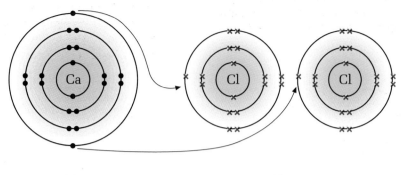

Calcium
(20 protons + 20 electrons)

Chlorine
(17 protons + 17 electrons)

This time we need *two* chlorine atoms for each calcium atom because the calcium atom has two electrons in its outer shell to give away, but each chlorine atom can receive only one electron.

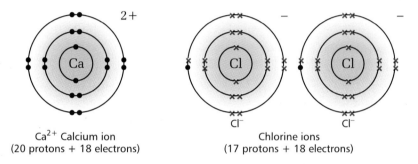

Ca^{2+} Calcium ion
(20 protons + 18 electrons)

Chlorine ions
(17 protons + 18 electrons)

The formula of calcium chloride is $CaCl_2$.

Properties of compounds with ionic bonding

- Ionic compounds are solids that have high melting temperatures.
- They will not conduct electricity when solid. (The bonding is too strong for the ions to separate.)
- If they are melted, i.e. liquid, they will conduct electricity. (The charged ions are then free to move and carry a current.) Those that dissolve in water produce solutions that will conduct electricity. (Again the ions are free to move.)

Covalent bonding

This occurs between non-metal atoms, for example fluorine gas, F_2:

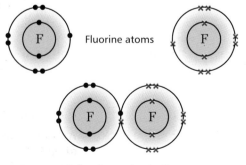

Fluorine atoms

A fluorine molecule, F_2

In this sort of bonding the atoms move close together and **share** a pair of electrons. Each atom then has a full outer shell.

Q Use dot-cross diagrams to work out the formula for sodium oxide.

Hint: Other words which mean melted are **molten** and **fused**.

Hint: If a substance is liquid, it means that it is a melted state and not that it is dissolved in water. The latter is called an aqueous solution.

Answer: Na_2O

Hint: You can check that both atoms have a full outer shell by covering each atom in turn, as in **Figure 2.8**.

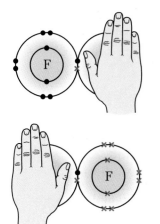

Figure 2.8 Each fluorine atom has eight electrons

F—F

Figure 2.9 Displayed formula for F_2

Hint: Remember that hydrogen completes the outer shell with two electrons (rather than 8) as it is the first shell. It gains the same structure as the noble gas helium.

Use dot-cross diagrams to work out the formula of hydrogen fluoride.

How would (a) oxygen, (b) nitrogen be written in displayed formulae?

Answer: HF

Answer: (a) O=O, (b) N≡N

A small group of covalently bonded atoms is called a **molecule**. The formula in this case is F_2.

We can represent one pair of shared electrons in a covalent bond by a line. Formulae drawn using lines to show all the bonds are called **displayed formulae** (see **Figure 2.9**).

Other examples:

1. **Water, H_2O**

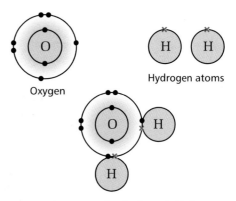

A water molecule, formula H_2O

2. **Oxygen, O_2**

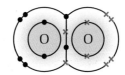

Here we have *two* pairs of shared electrons: a double bond.

3. **Nitrogen, N_2**

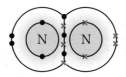

Here we have *three* pairs of shared electrons: a triple bond.

Notice that in the examples above we have formed neutral molecules. These are not strongly attracted to each other, so the resulting substances have low melting and boiling temperatures. They are examples of **molecular covalent structures.**

Giant covalent compounds

Another example of covalent bonding occurs in, for example, silicon dioxide (the main substance in sand). Silicon dioxide, SiO_2, is a covalently bonded compound with a very *high* melting temperature. This is because, instead of forming small molecules, silicon dioxide is a giant structure, where a network of covalent bonds extend throughout the compound (**Figure 2.10**).

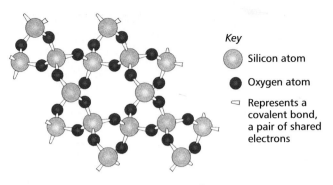

Key

⬤ Silicon atom

⬤ Oxygen atom

▷ Represents a covalent bond, a pair of shared electrons

Figure 2.10 The structure of silicon dioxide

Properties of compounds with covalent bonding

Molecular covalent compounds:

- Molecular covalent compounds will be gases, liquids or solids with low melting temperatures. (The strong bonds are *between* the atoms *within* the molecules and do not extend throughout the compound so that the molecules can easily be given the energy to move apart).
- They are poor conductors of electricity. (There are no charged particles to carry the current.)
- If they dissolve in water, the solution is a poor conductor of electricity. (Again there are no charged particles.)

Giant covalent compounds:

- Giant covalent compounds will have high melting temperatures. (They have a giant structure.)
- They are poor conductors of electricity.
- They do not normally dissolve in water.

Metallic bonding

This bonding is present in metals or alloys of metals. For example, magnesium metal, Mg:

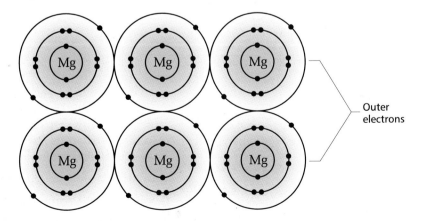

Outer electrons

The two electrons from the outer shell of each magnesium metal are free to move around all the atoms. Thus the outer electrons form a general pool. The atoms remain neutral, but the electrons are free. This pool is often referred to as a 'sea of electrons', and it is this 'sea' that gives the metals their unique properties.

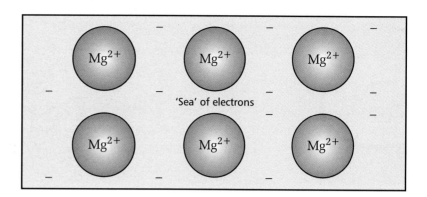

Hint: The melting temperature tells you about *structure*. The pattern of conductivity tells you *the type of bonding*.

Q Predict the bonding and structure in the following:
(a) calcium oxide, (b) ammonia gas, NH_3, (c) brass (copper/zinc alloy), (d) diamond (carbon).

Properties of materials with metallic bonding

- They have high melting temperatures because they have giant structures.
- They conduct electricity as solids or liquids.
- They are shiny, malleable (can be beaten into shape) and ductile (can be pulled into thin wires).

Summary of properties

These are shown in **Table 2.3**.

Table 2.3 Properties of elements and compounds according to type of bonding

	Melting temperature T_m	Structure	Bond	Conductivity		
				Solid	Liquid	Aqueous solution
	High	Giant	Ionic	No	Yes	Yes
	High	Giant	Covalent	No	No	No
	Low	Molecular	Covalent	No	No	No
	High	Giant	Metallic	Yes	Yes	— (does not dissolve)

Answer: (a) ionic, giant (compound of a metal and a non-metal), (b) covalent, molecular (compound of two non-metals, and it is a gas), (c) metallic, giant (it consists of two metals), (d) covalent, giant (non-metal, high melting temperature).

The Periodic Table

3.1 The arrangement of the Periodic Table

An element was originally defined as a substance that could not be broken down into anything simpler, but this definition is not a fundamental one. All atoms of a given element have the same number of protons in their nuclei, and this number is unique to the element and defines it. This is the atomic number of the element (see Chapter 2).

The Periodic Table is a list of all the elements in order of their atomic numbers. There is a copy of the Periodic Table at the end of the book.

Groups

The Periodic Table is arranged so that similar elements fall into vertical columns forming chemical 'families' called **groups.**

So H, Li, Na, K, Cs, Rb form Group I; Be, Mg, Ca, Sr, Ba, Ra form Group II, and so on.

Periods

Horizontal rows of elements are called **periods**. So H and He form Period 1; Li, Be, B, C, N, O, F, Ne form Period 2, and so on.

Hint: A group is usually numbered using Roman numerals, while a period uses ordinary numerals.

Some areas of the Periodic Table are given names as shown in Figure 3.1.

Q Name the element in (a) Group I, Period 2, (b) Group IV, Period 4, (c) Group VII, Period 5. (You will need to use the Periodic Table at the end of the book.)

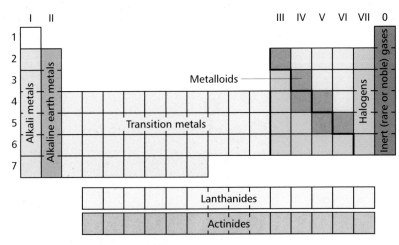

Figure 3.1 Named areas of the Periodic Table

Metals and non-metals

The heavy line, sometimes called the 'staircase' line, in Figure 3.1 divides metals (on its left) from non-metals (on its right). Elements

Answer: (a) lithium, (b) germanium, (c) iodine

Did you know? When 'doped' with other elements silicon conducts electricity in one direction only. This is the basis of many microelectronic devices such as personal computers.

close to this line, like silicon, have properties intermediate between those of metals and non-metals. These elements are called **metalloids** or **semi-metals**.

The Periodic Table should really look like **Figure 3.2**. The conventional way of drawing it simply saves space.

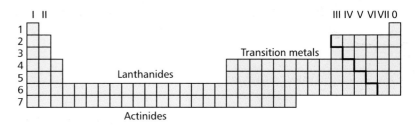

Figure 3.2 The full form of the Periodic Table

3.2 Using the Periodic Table

The Periodic Table can be used to predict how any element behaves, by looking at its position in the table. The overall pattern of the Periodic Table can be seen by considering just a few groups.

Group I: the alkali metals

Although hydrogen is usually (but not always) included in Group I, it is not a typical member of the group and is not included as an alkali metal, though in the solid state (at very low temperature) it has the appearance of a shiny red metal.

The alkali metals are soft and shiny in appearance. Some physical properties are set out in **Table 3.1**

The density generally increases as we go down the group, while the melting and boiling temperatures decrease. Thus, caesium is much denser than water (density $1\,\mathrm{g\,cm^{-3}}$), but would be a liquid on a very hot day (temperature 303 K).

Francium is a very rare radioactive metal and not enough of it has been isolated for long enough to know its properties for certain, but from Table 3.1 there are trends which would allow us to predict the values in the gaps.

Q Estimate the values in the gaps in Table 3.1 for francium, by looking at the values for the other elements.

Table 3.1 Properties of the alkali metals

Atomic number	Metal	Electron arrangement	Density/ $\mathrm{g\,cm^{-3}}$	Melting temperature/K	Boiling temperature/K
3	Li	1, 1	0.53	454	1615
11	Na	2, 8, 1	0.97	371	1156
19	K	2, 8, 8, 1	0.86	336	1033
37	Rb	2, 8, 18, 8, 1	1.53	312	959
55	Cs	2, 8, 18, 18, 8, 1	1.88	302	942
87	Fr	2, 8, 18, 32, 18, 8, 1	?	?	?

Answer: Approximately: density $2.3\,\mathrm{g\,cm^{-3}}$, T_m 290 K, T_b 940 K

Humphry Davy discovered sodium and potassium during electrolysis experiments on moistened salts

From left to right: lithium, potassium and sodium reacting with water

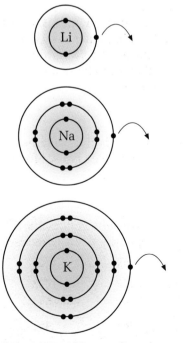

Figure 3.3 Loss of the outer electron becomes easier as we go down the group in Group I metals

Chemical properties and trends

These metals are very reactive indeed and, for example, have to be stored carefully to prevent them from reacting with air.

Reaction in air

They all react immediately with air to form oxides.
The oxides then react with the water in the air to form strongly **alkaline** hydroxides.

For example:

$$4Li(s) \quad + \quad O_2(g) \quad \longrightarrow \quad 2Li_2O(s)$$
lithium   oxygen   lithium oxide

$$Li_2O(s) \quad + \quad H_2O(l) \quad \longrightarrow \quad 2LiOH(aq)$$
lithium oxide   water   lithium hydroxide

Reaction with water

They all react with water to form **alkaline** solutions of the hydroxides, and hydrogen is given off.

For example:

$$2Li(s) \quad + \quad 2H_2O(l) \quad \longrightarrow \quad 2LiOH(aq) \quad + \quad H_2(g)$$
lithium   water   lithium hydroxide   hydrogen

Trends

The reactivity of the metals *increases* as we go down the group. A good example is the reaction with water. Lithium fizzes gently, sodium more so, potassium catches fire and from then on the reaction becomes more and more explosive.

If we look at the electronic structures of the elements, we can try to explain this trend.

Group I metals all react by giving away their single outer electron to form an ion with a single positive charge, and a full outer shell of eight electrons.

$$\text{metal} \longrightarrow \text{metal}^+ + \text{electron}^-$$

The attraction for the positively charged nucleus is what holds the negatively charged electrons to it.

As we go down the group, the outer electron gets further away from the nucleus (**Figure 3.3**), so it can leave the atom more easily. This is partly why the elements are more reactive as we go down the group. This topic is developed further in Chapter 9.

Group II metals: the alkaline earth metals

These are similar in many ways to Group I metals, though they are less reactive. This time, the atoms all have two electrons in their outer shell and *both* these are given away when the elements react to form a doubly charged metal ion:

$$\text{metal} \longrightarrow \text{metal}^{2+} + 2 \text{ electrons}^-$$

Loss of two electrons is more difficult than loss of one, so any Group II metal is less reactive than the Group I metal in the same period.

The reactivity of the elements increases as we go down the group in the same way as before and for the same reason.

> **Q** Estimate the value of the melting and boiling temperatures of astatine.

Group VII non-metals: the halogens

Again there is a pattern of general similarity of the elements with trends in both physical properties and chemical reactivity (**Table 3.2**).

While the appearances of the elements are not similar, their smells are. All have a characteristic 'swimming pool' smell. Chlorine is used to sterilise the water in swimming pools, though the amounts are carefully controlled, since chlorine, like the other halogens, is harmful to us.

Chemical properties and trends

The elements exist as covalently bonded molecules, X_2, where X represents any halogen atom, and all are reactive. They react with metals by gaining one electron per atom and form ions with one negative charge in these compounds:

$$X_2 \quad + \quad \text{2 electrons}^- \longrightarrow \quad 2X^-$$

halogen   (from the metal)   halogen ions (called **halide** ions)

For example:

$$2Na(s) \quad + \quad Cl_2(g) \longrightarrow \quad 2NaCl(s)$$

sodium   chlorine   sodium chloride
(sodium chloride exists
as Na^+Cl^-)

They all react with sodium hydroxide to form bleaches. For example:

$$2NaOH(aq) \; + \; Cl_2(g) \longrightarrow NaOCl(aq) \; + \; NaCl(aq) \; + \; H_2O(l)$$

sodium   chlorine   sodium   sodium   water
hydroxide   chlorate(ı)   chloride

> **Did you know?** Sodium chlorate(ı), which used to be called sodium hypochlorite, is the main ingredient in household bleach.

Trends

The halogens get more reactive as we go *up* the group, so that fluorine is a remarkably reactive gas and will attack (combine with) almost all of the elements, even including some noble gases. Many of the reactions take place at room temperature.

Again, electron structures help to explain this (see **Figure 3.4**). All the halogens are one electron short of having a full outer shell and this time, unlike the Group I and Group II metals, the *nearer* the outer shell is to the nucleus, the more readily it can attract an electron. Chapter 9 explains the other factors involved.

The transition metals

This block of elements is neither a group nor a period. It contains most of the familiar, everyday metals. Many have been known for a long time.

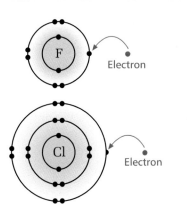

Figure 3.4 Electron gain by halogen atoms

Table 3.2 Properties of the halogens

Atomic number	Element	Electron arrangement	Appearance	Melting temperature/K	Boiling temperature/K
9	F	2,7	colourless gas	53	85
17	Cl	2,8,7	yellow/green gas	172	238
35	Br	2,8,18,7	brown liquid	266	332
53	I	2,8,18,18,7	black solid	387	457
85	At	2,8,18,32,18,7	?	?	?

Uses of transition metals

Properties of transition elements

These are hard, dense, rather similar metals, which are good conductors of electricity.

Compared with the metals in Groups I and II, they are unreactive, which makes them useful. They often form coloured compounds such as blue copper(II) sulphate or brown iron(III) sulphate. Transition metals are often used in catalysts.

The reason for their similarities is again due to their electron structures. In these elements, the atoms usually have two electrons in their outer shell, and the inner shells are not complete. This is dealt with in Chapter 31.

Did you know? The paint used for 'No Parking' lines contains compounds of chromium which gives them their yellow colour.

3.3 Trends across a period

A number of trends occur as we go across a period, for example from sodium to argon. The most obvious is the gradual change in properties from metallic to non-metallic, but there are other trends that we can notice and they are shown in **Table 3.3** for Period 3,

Points to notice

- From left to right we move from metals, through semi-metals, to non-metals.
- Metals form positive ions by loss of one, two or three electrons.
- At silicon the loss of 4 electrons is too difficult and it forms covalent bonds only.
- The other non-metals can form negative ions by gain of one, two or three electrons.
- Argon has no tendency to lose, gain or share electrons.
- The oxides go from strongly basic to strongly acidic as we move from left to right. Aluminium is **amphoteric**. It can display both acidic and basic properties.
- There is a general trend in both elements and compounds from giant structures on the left to molecular structures on the right (except for the noble gas argon, which is atomic).

Group	I	II	III	IV	V	VI	VII	0
Element	Na	Mg	Al	Si	P	S	Cl	Ar
		Metals		Semi-metal		Non-metals		(Noble gas)
		less reactive →				← less reactive		
Structure of element		Giant metallic		Giant covalent		Molecular		(Atomic)
Ion	Na^+	Mg^{2+}	Al^{3+}	None	P^{3-}	S^{2-}	Cl^-	none
Oxide	Na_2O	MgO	Al_2O_3	SiO_2	P_4O_{10} (P_4O_6)	SO_2 (SO_3)	Cl_2O (Cl_2O_7 etc.)	none
		Strongly basic	Amphoteric			Acidic		
Structure of oxide		Giant ionic		Giant covalent		Molecular		None

Table 3.3 Trends across Period 3

3.4 Predicting formulae of simple ionic compounds

The list below shows the charges on the ions for the period Na to Ar.

Group	I	II	III	IV	V	VI	VII	0
	Na^+	Mg^{2+}	Al^{3+}		P^{3-}	S^{2-}	Cl^-	

These charges will tend to be the same for all the elements in the same group. For example, sodium forms an ion with a single positive charge and so do all the rest of the Group I metals.

Compounds are always electrically neutral, so we can predict the formulae of simple ionic compounds. For example,

1. **Magnesium fluoride**
   Mg is in Group II and will form Mg^{2+} ions.
   F is in Group VII and will form F^- ions.

To form a neutral compound, two F^- ions are needed to balance the charge on the Mg^{2+}, so the formula will be MgF_2.

2. **Aluminium oxide**
   Al in Group III forms Al^{3+}.
   O in Group VI forms O^{2-}.

The simplest formula for a neutral compound is Al_2O_3 ($2Al^{3+} + 3O^{2-}$).

Complex ions

Some common ions contain more than one atom. They are called **complex** ions. Some common ions are:

Some common ions	
Name	**Formula and charge**
sulphate	SO_4^{2-}
carbonate	CO_3^{2-}
nitrate	NO_3^-
phosphate	PO_4^{3-}
hydroxide	OH^-
ammonium	NH_4^+

To find the formula of a compound containing complex ions the method of balancing the charges can still be used if we know the charges on the ions. For example, we might want to find the formula of magnesium phosphate, which contains the ions Mg^{2+} and PO_4^{3-}. To get the charges to balance we need:

$$Mg^{2+} \quad Mg^{2+} \quad Mg^{2+} \qquad PO_4^{3-} \quad PO_4^{3-}$$

So the formula must be $Mg_3(PO_4)_2$ (i.e. $3Mg^{2+} + 2PO_4^{3-}$).

Q Work out the formulae for the following:

magnesium oxide, sodium fluoride, calcium sulphide, sodium phosphide.

Q Work out the formulae for the following: sodium carbonate, calcium hydroxide, ammonium sulphate.

Answer: MgO, NaF, CaS, Na_3P

Answer: Na_2CO_3, $Ca(OH)_2$, $(NH_4)_2SO_4$

4 Moles

4.1 Counting atoms

An atom is too small to be seen by even the most powerful microscope and impossible to weigh individually. When chemists need to know how many atoms are involved they must count by weighing large numbers. This is similar to the normal method of counting coins in a bank: a large numbers of coins are weighed together.

4.2 Relative atomic mass, A_r

The relative atomic mass, A_r, shows how heavy an atom of an element is compared with an atom of hydrogen. We can find A_r from the Periodic Table.

For example, an atom of helium, He, which has $A_r = 4$, is *four* times heavier than an atom of hydrogen, H, and an atom of lithium, Li, which has $A_r = 7$, is *seven* times as heavy as an atom of hydrogen.

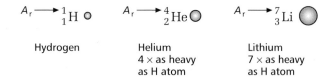

$A_r \longrightarrow {}^{1}_{1}H$ ○	$A_r \longrightarrow {}^{4}_{2}He$ ○	$A_r \longrightarrow {}^{7}_{3}Li$ ○
Hydrogen	Helium 4 × as heavy as H atom	Lithium 7 × as heavy as H atom

A 1p coin weighs 3.5 g and a 2p coin 7 g

Suppose we could weigh out 1 g of hydrogen atoms. Then, to get *the same number* of atoms of helium, we would have to weigh out 4 g of helium, because each atom of helium is four times as heavy as each atom of hydrogen. In the same way, to get the same number of lithium atoms we would have to weigh out 7 g of lithium, because each atom of lithium is seven times as heavy as each atom of hydrogen.

350 g   700 g

Coins can be counted by weighing. Each stack has the same number of coins. How many is that?

4.3 Relative molecular mass, M_r

The relative molecular mass, M_r, is the mass of a molecule (small group of atoms covalently bonded together) compared with the mass of an *atom* of hydrogen. It is found from the formula, by adding together the relative atomic masses of the elements present. The term relative molecular mass is also used for compounds that are not molecular. Calcium nitrate, for example, has a giant ionic structure. In this case M_r refers to the simplest formula unit, which is called an **entity**. The term 'entity' is useful because it includes all types of structure such as ions, atoms and molecules.

For example:

	Element	A_r		Number present		Total
Water H_2O	H	1	×	2	=	2
	O	16	×	1	=	16
				M_r	=	18
Calcium nitrate $Ca(NO_3)_2$	Ca	40	×	1	=	40
	N	14	×	2	=	28
	O	16	×	6	=	96
				M_r	=	164

So one entity of water is 18 times as heavy as an *atom* of hydrogen, and one entity of calcium nitrate is 164 times as heavy as an *atom* of hydrogen. To get the *same number* of entities as there are in 1 g of hydrogen, we need to weigh out 18 g of water or 164 g of calcium nitrate.

> **Q** Work out M_r for (a) calcium oxide, CaO, (b) ammonia, NH_3, (c) calcium hydroxide, $Ca(OH)_2$. (A_r's: Ca = 40, O = 16, N = 14, H = 1.)

4.4 The mole

The number of atoms or other entities we get when we weigh out the relative atomic mass or the relative molecular mass in grams is enormous. It is called the Avogadro constant and is approximately equal to 6×10^{23}. The amount of substance that contains this number of atoms or other entities is called a **mole**.

Whenever we weigh out the relative atomic mass of an element in grams we have a mole of atoms. Similarly, the relative molecular mass in grams gives a mole of entities.

(Although the mole is defined in terms of an *amount* of substance, it is more useful to treat it as meaning a huge *number* with a special name, just as a dozen or a score is a number with a special name).

> **Hint:** 6×10^{23} is a shorthand way of writing 6 followed by 23 zeros. If you are not sure about numbers expressed in this way, see section 6.5.

For example:

a mole of carbon atoms, C, has a mass of 12 g
a mole of copper atoms, Cu, has a mass of 63.5 g
a mole of hydrogen atoms, H, has a mass of 1 g
BUT note a mole of hydrogen *molecules*, H_2, has a mass of 2 g.
a mole of calcium nitrate, $Ca(NO_3)_2$, entities has a mass of 164 g.

To avoid ambiguity, it is best to give the formula of the entity you are referring to. (The symbol for 'mole' is mol. M is sometimes used to stand for mol dm^{-3} and should not be used as an abbreviation for mole.)

A mole of carbon (left) and a mole of copper (right). Each has the same number of atoms

> **Q** What is the mass of (a) 2 moles of methane, CH_4, (b) 0.5 moles of ethane, C_2H_6, (c) 0.01 moles of copper atoms? (A_r's: C = 12, H = 1, Cu = 63.5.)

Number of moles

We can find out how many moles of substance are present in a given mass of substance if we know its formula.

$$\text{number of moles} = \frac{\text{mass in g}}{\text{mass of 1 mole in g}}$$

Answer: (a) 56, (b) 17, (c) 74

Answer: (a) 32 g, (b) 15 g, (c) 0.635 g

How many moles of atoms or entities (state which) are there in:

(a) 23 g of sodium, Na, (b) 2 g of hydrogen, H_2, (c) 1 g of calcium carbonate, $CaCO_3$? (A_r's: Na = 23, H = 1, Ca = 40, C = 12.)

Hint: 'mol dm^{-3}' is a way of writing 'moles per cubic decimetre' or 'mol/dm^3'. If you are not sure about units expressed like this, see Chapter 6.

Hint: A solution of concentration 1 mol dm^{-3} used to be called (and still may be called) 1 molar (1M). Similarly 2 mol dm^{-3} is 2 molar (2M) and so on.

Hint: One cubic decimetre (1 dm^3) is the same as 1 litre (1 l or 1 L)

(a) How many moles of sodium hydroxide are there in 25 cm^3 of a 0.2 mol dm^{-3} solution?
(b) How many grams of copper sulphate ($CuSO_4.5H_2O$) would be dissolved in 100 cm^3 of a 2 mol dm^{-3} solution?

For example, in 0.09 g of water, H_2O ($M_r = 18$, so 1 mole has a mass of 18 g):

$$\text{number of moles} = \frac{0.09}{18} = 0.005$$

Moles and solutions

Concentrations of solutions are measured in moles per cubic decimetre (mol dm^{-3}). (One *cubic* decimetre = 1000 cm^3, because 1 decimetre = 10 cm.)

1 mol dm^{-3} means there is 1 mole per cubic decimetre of solution. 2 mol dm^{-3} means there are 2 moles per cubic decimetre of solution, and so on.

Number of moles in a given volume of solution

It is often necessary to work out how many moles are present in a solution. For example:

How many moles are there in 20 cm^3 of a solution of concentration 0.5 mol dm^{-3}?

From the definition,

1000 cm^3 of a solution of 1 mol dm^{-3} contains 1 mole
So 1000 cm^3 of a solution of 0.5 mol dm^{-3} contains 0.5 mole.

So 1 cm^3 of a solution of 0.5 mol dm^{-3} contains $\dfrac{0.5}{1000}$ mole

So 20 cm^3 of a solution of 0.5 mol dm^{-3} contains $\dfrac{0.5 \times 20}{1000} =$ 0.01 mole.

In general, in a solution of concentration M mol dm^{-3} and volume V cm^3:

$$\text{number of moles} = \frac{M \times V}{1000}$$

Moles and gases

A mole of any gas has the same volume under the same conditions of temperature and pressure. At room temperature and pressure this volume is approximately 24 000 cm^3 (24 dm^3). Thus a mole of carbon dioxide gas, CO_2 (mass 44 g), has the same volume as a mole of hydrogen gas, H_2 (mass 2 g).

This may seem unlikely at first, but a gas particle (even quite a heavy one) is extremely small compared with the space in between the particles. Think of four people running around a large hall, and imagine the space between them. It wouldn't make any noticeable difference to this space if the people were fat or thin. In the same way, the space *between* the gas molecules is what accounts for the volume of a gas. The size of the gas molecules themselves is negligible compared with this.

For example:

How many moles of methane gas (CH_4) are present in a volume of 240 cm^3 at room temperature and pressure? What is the mass of this volume of gas? (A_r's: C = 12, H = 1.)

A mole of CH_4 has a volume of 24 000 cm^3, so

$$\text{number of moles in 240 cm}^3 = \frac{240}{24\,000} = 0.01 \text{ moles}$$

Answer: (a) 1 mole of atoms, (b) 1 mole of entities, or 2 moles of atoms, (c) 0.01 mole of entities

Answer: (a) 0.005 mol, (b) 50 g

(a) How many moles of hydrogen molecules are present in a volume of 480 cm³ at room temperature and pressure? What is the mass of this volume of gas?
(b) What would be the volume at room temperature and pressure of 22 g of carbon dioxide gas?
(c) What mass of water, H_2O, would be present in 240 dm³ of steam?

Hint: Learn and be able to use the following:
- number of moles
$$= \frac{\text{mass in grams}}{\text{mass of 1 mole in grams}}$$
- number of moles of solute in a
solution $= \dfrac{M \times V}{1000}$,
where
M = concentration in mol dm⁻³,
V = volume of solution in cm³
- A mole of any gas has a volume of approximately 24 dm³ (24 000 cm³) at room temperature and pressure.

What is the volume of 0.50 moles of mercury, density 13.6 g cm⁻³? ($A_r(Hg) = 201$.)

Hint: The simplest formula (also called the empirical formula) need not be the actual formula. It is the simplest ratio of the elements present in the compound. For example, ethene, C_2H_4, would have an empirical formula of CH_2.

Hint: The final ratio of atoms is normally written in whole numbers, i.e. 0.5 : 1 is 1 : 2.
Use the simplest ratio, i.e 2 : 4 is 1 : 2.

Find the simplest formula of the following:
(a) 2.39 g of lead sulphide containing 2.07 g of lead.
(b) 22 g of a gas containing 6 g of carbon and 16g of oxygen.
(c) 5 g of calcium carbonate containing 2 g of calcium, 0.6 g of carbon and the rest oxygen.
(A_r's: Pb = 207, S = 32, C = 12, O = 16, Ca = 40.)

Answer: (a) 0.02 mol, 0.04 g, (b) 12 000 cm³, (c) 180 g
Answer: 7.4 cm³
Answer: (a) PbS, (b) CO_2, (c) $CaCO_3$

1 mole of CH_4 has a mass of 16 g, so 0.01 moles has a mass of $16 \times 0.01 = 0.16$ g

Moles of liquids

It is often more convenient to measure a mole of liquid by volume, rather than by weighing. This is easy to do if we know the density of the liquid, because we can use the formula:
$$\text{density, } \rho = \text{mass/volume}$$
(If you think of the units of density, g cm⁻³, it is easier to remember this formula.)

For example:
What is the volume of 0.10 moles of ethanol, C_2H_5OH, density 0.80 g cm⁻³?
mass of 1 mole of ethanol = 46 g, so mass of 0.10 mole = 4.6 g
$$\text{density} = \frac{\text{mass}}{\text{volume}}$$
So
$$\text{volume} = \frac{\text{mass}}{\text{density}}$$
$$\text{volume} = \frac{4.6}{0.8} \text{ cm}^3$$
$$\text{volume} = 5.75 \text{ cm}^3$$
$$= 5.8 \text{ cm}^3 \text{ (to 2 s.f.)}$$

4.5 Moles and formulae

To find the formula of a compound, we need to know the number of moles of each element which combine together. To do this we must first know the combining masses of the elements.

One way to find the formula of, for example, magnesium oxide is to weigh some magnesium, burn it (i.e. make it combine with oxygen) and weigh the magnesium oxide formed.

For example:
0.24 g of magnesium ribbon burns to form 0.40 g of magnesium oxide. (A_r's: Mg = 24, O = 16.)
mass of magnesium = 0.24 g
number of moles of magnesium = 0.24/24 = 0.01
mass of oxygen combined with the magnesium = 0.40 − 0.24
$$= 0.16 \text{ g}$$
number of moles of oxygen = 0.16/16 = 0.01
So
ratio of magnesium moles to oxygen moles = 0.01 : 0.01
$$= 1 : 1$$
The simplest formula of magnesium oxide is therefore MgO.

Another example:
9.8 g of an oily liquid was found to contain 0.2 g of hydrogen, 3.2 g of sulphur and 6.4 g of oxygen. (A_r's: H = 1, S = 32, O = 16.)
number of moles of hydrogen = 0.2/1 = 0.2
number of moles of sulphur = 3.2/32 = 0.1
number of moles of oxygen = 6.4/16 = 0.4
ratio of hydrogen : sulphur : oxygen in moles
= 0.2 : 0.1 : 0.4
= 2 : 1 : 4
The formula is therefore H_2SO_4.

Equations

5.1 Chemical change

When a chemical change takes place, chemical bonds are broken and atoms are rearranged to form new substances.

The substances we start with are called **the reactants** and these rearrange to form the **products**. Equations are used to represent what is happening in a chemical reaction.

5.2 Word equations

Hint: Writing an equation in itself does not mean that the reaction can happen. Equations should always be based on experimental evidence.

A word equation states the reactants and products.

For example, when magnesium is burnt in air the word equation would be:

$$\text{magnesium} + \text{oxygen} \longrightarrow \text{magnesium oxide}$$

5.3 Symbol equations

In a symbol equation, reactants and products are represented by their formulae.

State symbols

These are letters in brackets which can be added to say what state the reactants and products are in: (s) means solid; (l) means liquid; (g) means gas; (aq) means aqueous solution (dissolved in water).

Hint: Equations do not say how fast a reaction happens. Conditions (heat, pressure, etc.) may be shown on arrows.

For example: $\xrightarrow{\text{heat}}$

Balanced symbol equations

A balanced symbol equation is useful because it tells us not only what happens in a reaction but also the *quantities* that react together and how much of the products we should get from a given amount of reactants. 'Balanced' means that there are the same number of each atom on both sides of the arrow. Equations must balance because atoms cannot be made or destroyed in chemical reactions, just rearranged.

It is very important to start with the correct formulae.

For example:

$$\text{magnesium} + \text{copper sulphate} \longrightarrow \text{magnesium sulphate} + \text{copper}$$
$$\text{Mg(s)} + \text{CuSO}_4\text{(aq)} \longrightarrow \text{MgSO}_4\text{(aq)} + \text{Cu(s)}$$

This is a balanced symbol equation because the number of atoms of each element is the same on both sides of the arrow.

Writing balanced equations

We know that when magnesium burns in air it forms magnesium oxide. We can build up a balanced symbol equation from this:

1. Write the word equation:

$$\text{magnesium} + \text{oxygen} \longrightarrow \text{magnesium oxide}$$

2. Write in the correct formulae:

$$Mg + O_2 \longrightarrow MgO$$

This is not balanced because there are 2 oxygen atoms on the side of the reactants (left-hand side) but only 1 on the side of the products (right-hand side).

Hint: It is very tempting to change the formula of magnesium oxide to MgO_2 at this stage, which would indeed balance the equation, or to write O for the formula of oxygen but you must **never change the correct formulae.** These have been established by experiment and cannot be changed at your convenience! All we can do is change the number of entities involved.

3. Multiply the MgO by 2 to get 2 oxygen atoms on the right:

$$Mg + O_2 \longrightarrow 2MgO$$

This is still not balanced because now we have ended up with two magnesium atoms on the side of the products (right-hand) side and only one on the side of the reactants (left-hand) side. If we now multiply the Mg by 2, the equation will be balanced:

$$2Mg + O_2 \longrightarrow 2MgO$$

Hint: Check by counting the atoms of each element on each side of the arrow. The numbers should be the same.

We can say from this that 2 atoms of magnesium react with 1 molecule of oxygen to produce 2 entities of magnesium oxide. So that 2 moles of magnesium atoms react with 1 mole of oxygen molecules to give 2 moles of magnesium oxide entities.

At this point we can put in the state symbols and also work out the masses that will react together according to our equation:

$$\begin{array}{ccc} 2Mg(s) & + & O_2(g) & \longrightarrow & 2MgO(s) \\ \text{2 moles} & & \text{1 mole} & & \text{2 moles} \\ 48\,g & & 32\,g & & 80\,g \end{array}$$

Note that the total mass is the same on both sides, which is a good way of checking whether the equation is balanced.

An analogy to balancing an equation might be the task of buying batteries for torches. Suppose torches each take three batteries, and batteries are sold in twos. The task is to buy enough torches and enough batteries to fit them with none left over.

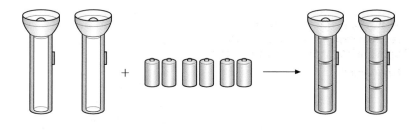

$$\begin{array}{ccc} \text{torch} + \text{batteries} & \longrightarrow & \text{working torch} \\ 2T \quad + \quad 3B_2 & \longrightarrow & 2TB_3 \end{array}$$

So the steps to writing a balanced symbol equation are:

1. Write a word equation.
2. Put in the correct formulae.

3. Add large numbers (called 'coefficients') in front of the formulae where necessary to get the same number of atoms of each element on both sides. A coefficient multiplies the whole of the formula that follows it. *Do not change the formulae.*
4. Check the equation is balanced by counting the atoms on each side.

We then know the number of moles that react and the masses can be worked out.

Another example:

Write a balanced symbol equation for the reaction that occurs when aluminium burns in air.

1. Word equation:

$$\text{aluminium} + \text{oxygen} \longrightarrow \text{aluminium oxide}$$

2. Correct formulae:

$$Al \quad + \quad O_2 \quad \longrightarrow \quad Al_2O_3$$

3. Balancing:

(i)	tackling Al	$2Al$	$+ \quad O_2$	$\longrightarrow$	Al_2O_3
(ii)	now the O	$2Al$	$+ \quad 3O_2$	$\longrightarrow$	$2Al_2O_3$
(iii)	back to Al	$4Al$	$+ \quad 3O_2$	$\longrightarrow$	$2Al_2O_3$
(iv)	add state symbols	$4Al(s)$	$+ \quad 3O_2(g)$	$\longrightarrow$	$2Al_2O_3(s)$
		4 moles	3 moles		2 moles
		108 g	96 g		204 g

Check: Is there the same number of atoms of each element on both sides? Do the masses add up?

5.4 Using the balanced symbol equation

Predicting quantities

As we have seen, we can predict the quantities produced during a reaction if we have a balanced symbol equation. For example, the reaction between calcium carbonate and hydrochloric acid produces carbon dioxide gas (see **Figure 5.1**). (A_r's: C = 12, Ca = 40, O = 16, H = 1.)

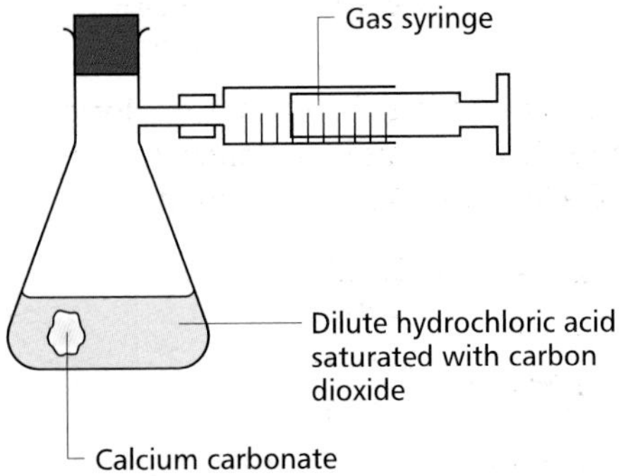

1. How much gas is produced by 1 g of calcium carbonate and excess acid?

First write the balanced symbol equation, and then the numbers of moles that react:

calcium carbonate	+	hydrochloric acid	$\longrightarrow$	calcium chloride	+	water	+	carbon dioxide

$CaCO_3(s) +$		$2HCl(aq)$	$\longrightarrow$	$CaCl_2(aq) +$	$H_2O(l) +$	$CO_2(g)$
1 mole		2 moles		1 mole	1 mole	1 mole

So 1 mole of $CaCO_3$ produces 1 mole of CO_2, which has a volume of 24 000 cm³ (1 mole of *any* gas has a volume of 24 000 cm³ at room temperature and pressure.)

But 1 mole of $CaCO_3$ has a mass of 100 g because $M_r = 100$.

So 1 g of $CaCO_3$ (0.01 mole) produces 0.01 moles CO_2, which has a volume of 240 cm³.

Q Write a balanced symbol equation for the reaction between lithium, Li, and oxygen, O_2, and hence find how many grams of lithium oxide, Li_2O, would be formed from 0.7 g of lithium. (A_r's: Li = 7, O = 16.)

Figure 5.1 Apparatus for collecting carbon dioxide gas

Labels: Gas syringe; Dilute hydrochloric acid saturated with carbon dioxide; Calcium carbonate

Hint: 'Excess' acid means more than enough acid to react with all the carbonate.

Answer: $4Li + O_2 \longrightarrow 2Li_2O$, 1.5 g

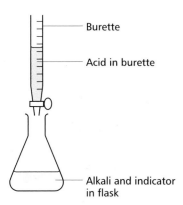

Burette

Acid in burette

Alkali and indicator in flask

Figure 5.2 Apparatus for a titration

2. How much gas would be produced by a large lump (excess) of calcium carbonate in 25 cm³ of 0.2 mol dm⁻³ HCl?

From the above balanced symbol equation we can see that 2 moles of HCl will produce 1 mole of CO_2.

$$\text{number of moles in solution} = \frac{M \times V}{1000}$$

where M is concentration in mol dm⁻³ and V is volume in cm³ (see section 4.4).

So   number of moles of HCl $= \dfrac{0.2 \times 25}{1000} = 0.005$

0.005 moles of HCl will produce 0.0025 moles of CO_2.

volume of 0.0025 moles of gas = 24 000 × 0.0025 cm³ = 60 cm³

Therefore the volume of carbon dioxide produced is 60 cm³.

Finding concentrations

The technique of finding the concentration of a solution is important. An example is the reaction between an acid and an alkali when:

(a) the equation for the reaction is known
(b) the concentration of one of the reactants is known.

Usually a **titration** is done using the apparatus in **Figure 5.2**. An accurately measured amount of alkali is added to the conical flask with a few drops of a suitable indicator, and acid is run in from the burette until the colour just changes, showing that the solution in the conical flask is now neutral.

For example:

10 cm³ of a 2 mol dm⁻³ solution of sodium hydroxide were neutralised by 25 cm³ of hydrochloric acid. What is the concentration of the acid?

First write a balanced symbol equation for the reaction between hydrochloric acid and sodium hydroxide:

$$\text{NaOH(aq)} + \text{HCl(aq)} \longrightarrow \text{NaCl(aq)} + \text{H}_2\text{O(l)}$$

sodium hydroxide   hydrochloric acid   sodium chloride   water

So 1 mole of sodium hydroxide reacts with 1 mole of hydrochloric acid to give 1 mole of sodium chloride and 1 mole of water. In other words, equal numbers of moles of acid and alkali are needed.

$$\text{number of moles in a solution} = \frac{M \times V}{1000}$$

So   number of moles of NaOH $= \dfrac{2 \times 10}{1000}$

Let the concentration of acid be Y mol dm⁻³.

$$\text{number of moles of HCl} = \frac{Y \times 25}{1000}$$

Since we know there must be an equal number of moles of sodium hydroxide and hydrochloric acid for neutralisation, we can say:

number of moles of NaOH = number of moles of HCl

So $\dfrac{2 \times 10}{1000} = \dfrac{Y \times 25}{1000}$

Answer: Mg + 2HCl $\longrightarrow$ MgCl₂ + H₂
(a) 120 cm³, (b) 150 cm³

What is the concentration of sodium hydroxide if 25 cm³ of it was neutralised by 10 cm³ of hydrochloric acid of concentration 0.15 mol dm⁻³?

From this

$$Y = 0.8$$

and the concentration of the acid is 0.8 mol dm⁻³.

Another example:

25 cm³ of sodium hydroxide were neutralised by 10 cm³ of sulphuric acid of concentration 0.1 mol dm⁻³. What is the concentration of the sodium hydroxide?

First write the balanced symbol equation:

$$2NaOH(aq) \ + \ H_2SO_4(aq) \ \longrightarrow \ Na_2SO_4(aq) \ + \ 2H_2O(l)$$

2 moles   1 mole   1 mole   2 moles

From the balanced equation we can see that two moles of sodium hydroxide are required to neutralise every mole of sulphuric acid.

$$\text{number of moles of acid} = \frac{0.1 \times 10}{1000} = 0.001$$

From the balanced equation , the number of moles of sodium hydroxide must be twice this, i.e. 0.002. Let Y be the concentration of NaOH in mol dm⁻³.

$$\text{number of moles of sodium hydroxide} = \frac{Y \times 25}{1000}$$

and this number must be equal to 0.002.

Then

$$0.002 = \frac{Y \times 25}{1000}$$

and from this

$$Y = 0.08$$

so the concentration of the sodium hydroxide is 0.08 mol dm⁻³.

Q 20 cm³ of 0.1 mol dm⁻³ sodium hydroxide were neutralised by 25 cm³ of sulphuric acid. What is the concentration in mol dm⁻³ of the acid?

5.5 Equations using ions

Ionic compounds (such as sodium chloride) break up into ions when they dissolve in water. Many reactions that take place in aqueous solution can be represented using ions. Ions have charge: negatively charged ions are called **anions**; positively charged ions are called **cations**. Just as an equation must balance, the charges on both sides of the equation must balance.

Here are some examples:

Displacement reactions

$$Mg(s) + CuSO_4(aq) \ \longrightarrow \ MgSO_4(aq) + Cu(s)$$

Since copper sulphate exists as ions when dissolved in water we can write:

$$Mg(s) + Cu^{2+}(aq) + \cancel{SO_4^{2-}(aq)} \ \longrightarrow \ Mg^{2+}(aq) + \cancel{SO_4^{2-}(aq)} + Cu(s)$$

If we cancel out any ions(s) that are on both sides we end up with:

$$Mg(s) + Cu^{2+}(aq) \ \longrightarrow \ Mg^{2+}(aq) + Cu(s)$$

Q Zinc, which also forms a 2+ ion, reacts with copper chloride in a similar way. Write the ionic equation.

Answer: 0.06 mol dm⁻³

Answer: 0.04 mol dm⁻³

Answer: $Zn(s) + Cu^{2+}(aq) \longrightarrow Zn^{2+}(aq) + Cu(s)$

Q Write the ionic equation for the reaction of zinc with sulphuric acid.

Acid reactions

$$\text{magnesium} + \text{hydrochloric acid} \longrightarrow \text{magnesium chloride} + \text{hydrogen}$$

$$\text{Mg(s)} + \text{2HCl(aq)} \longrightarrow \text{MgCl}_2\text{(aq)} + \text{H}_2\text{(g)}$$

Since magnesium chloride and hydrochloric acid exist as ions in solution we can write:

$$\text{Mg(s)} + 2\text{H}^+\text{(aq)} + 2\text{Cl}^-\text{(aq)} \longrightarrow \text{Mg}^{2+}\text{(aq)} + 2\text{Cl}^-\text{(aq)} + \text{H}_2\text{(g)}$$

Cancelling the ions common to both sides:

$$\text{Mg(s)} + 2\text{H}^+\text{(aq)} \longrightarrow \text{Mg}^{2+}\text{(aq)} + \text{H}_2\text{(g)}$$

Notice that the charge is the same on both sides.

Answer: $\text{Zn(s)} + 2\text{H}^+\text{(aq)} \longrightarrow \text{Zn}^{2+}\text{(aq)} + \text{H}_2\text{(g)}$

Physics and mathematics background

6.1 Ideas from mathematics and physics

This chapter contains some of the important ideas from physics which you should be familiar with in order to understand some areas of chemistry fully. There are also some mathematical techniques that you will find useful.

6.2 Waves

(Used in Chapter 7, Atomic and nuclear structure, section 19.4, Radical chain reactions, Chapter 29, Structure determination, Chapter 38, Identifying organic compounds.)

Waves are disturbances in a **medium** which carry energy through the medium without the medium itself moving from place to place. A good example is dropping a stone into a pond (**Figure 6.1**). Energy is transferred from the stone to the toy boat (which moves up and down) via the water which is the medium. The water does not move from place to place: it merely moves up and down as the wave passes.

Waves have two important measurements associated with them:

Stone

λ

ν (number of complete up and down vibrations per second)

Figure 6.1 Water waves

- **Wavelength** is the distance between two neighbouring peaks (or troughs). This is given the Greek letter λ (lambda) as its symbol. The usual units are metres.

- **Frequency** is the number of complete up-and-down vibrations per second. This is also given a Greek symbol, ν (nu). The usual units are s^{-1}. These are sometimes called hertz (Hz).

Hint: Velocity is speed in a given direction.

Q The wavelength of a radio wave is 1500 m. What is the frequency of the wave if its velocity is 300 000 000 m s⁻¹ (3 × 10⁸ m s⁻¹)?

Frequency and wavelength are related by the equation:

$$v = \nu\lambda$$

where v is the velocity with which the wave travels along. Waves have two important and interesting properties: **diffraction** and **interference**.

Diffraction

When waves pass through a gap comparable in size with their wavelength, they spread out as shown in **Figure 6.2(a)**, rather than as you might expect in **Figure 6.2(b)**.

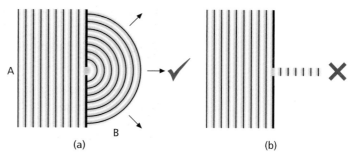

Figure 6.2 Diffraction

This is called **diffraction**. It is the reason that you can hear someone in another room talking even though they are not in line with the door. The sound waves are diffracted as they pass through the door. Someone standing at B would hear sound from A but would be quite safe from a stream of bullets, which would not be diffracted.

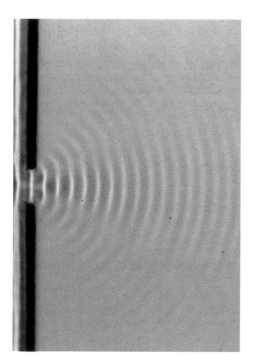

Diffraction of water waves in a ripple tank

Interference

This occurs when two waves meet. Think about water waves. If two peaks coincide, an extra-large peak will result. Similarly, if two troughs coincide, an extra-deep trough will occur. This is called **constructive interference**. However, if a trough and a peak coincide, the two will cancel out and undisturbed water will result. This is called **destructive interference**. (See **Figure 6.3**.) The two effects are illustrated in the photograph.

Interference of water waves produced by two vibrators in a ripple tank

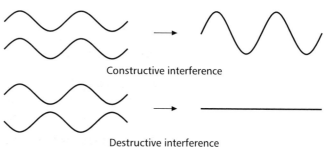

Constructive interference

Destructive interference

Answer: 2 × 10⁵ s⁻¹

Figure 6.3 Interference

Hint: The symbol *c* is used for the velocity of light and other electromagnetic radiation.

Electromagnetic radiation

(Used in section 7.2, Line spectra and section 19.1, Radical chain reactions.)

Electromagnetic radiation is an exception to the rule that waves travel through a medium. Electromagnetic radiations are able to travel through a vacuum as, for example, sunlight reaching the Earth from the Sun. Different types of electromagnetic radiation have different wavelengths and frequencies but they all travel through a vacuum at the same speed: 'the speed of light', 300 000 000 m s^{-1}. Examples include radio waves, infra-red (heat), visible light, ultraviolet (which causes tanning and possible skin damage) and X-rays.

6.3 Electricity

(Used in Chapter 7, Atomic and nuclear structure, Chapter 8, Energetics, Chapter 16, The s-block elements, Chapter 25, Further redox: Electrochemical cells.)

Experiments show that there are two types of electric charge: positive (+) and negative (−). Like charges repel one another while opposite charges attract.

Q What is the size of the charge that passes if a current of 10 A flows for 20 minutes?

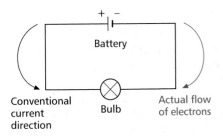

Conventional current direction

Battery

Bulb

Actual flow of electrons

Figure 6.4 Electric current

Hint: Remember that the unit of energy is the joule (J).

Q How much energy is given out by a 10 V battery if it supplies a current of 0.1 A for 1 minute?

Answer: 12 000 C. Did you remember to multiply by 60 for seconds?

Answer: 60 J

Current

The size of an electric charge is given the symbol Q and is measured in units called **coulombs** (symbol C). An electric **current** (symbol I) is a flow of electric charge, usually through a wire. The current is the rate at which the charge flows and is measured in units called **amperes** (often abbreviated to 'amps', symbol A). One amp is a rate of flow of charge of one coulomb per second. So the number of coulombs of charge, Q, which flow through a circuit in a given time, t, is current × time.

$$Q = I \times t$$

Usually an electric current is visualised as a flow of positive charge from the positive to the negative terminal, although we now know that a current is actually a flow of negatively charged electrons from negative to positive (**Figure 6.4**). The coulomb is a rather large unit of charge. The electron has a charge of only 1.6×10^{-19} coulombs.

Voltage

The force that drives the charge through the circuit is provided by the **voltage**, V, (more properly called **potential difference**) of the battery. The voltage of the supply is measured in **volts** (symbol V). Voltage can also be interpreted as the **amount of energy** given to each unit of charge by the supply. One volt means one joule per coulomb: each coulomb of charge is given an energy of one joule by a 1 V supply. This energy will be given up by the charge on its journey through the circuit. It may be changed into light energy by a bulb, heat energy by a heater, movement (or kinetic energy) by a motor, and so on.

6.4 Force, pressure and momentum

(Used in deriving the ideal gas equation, Chapter 27, Gases.)

Force

A force is a push or pull which moves or tends to move something. Force is measured in units called **newtons**, (symbol N), after Isaac Newton. One newton is approximately the force needed to lift 100 g on the Earth's surface. This is roughly the force needed to lift an average-sized apple.

Pressure

In chemistry we more often come across the idea of pressure. This is the force per unit area.

$$\text{pressure, } P = \frac{\text{force}}{\text{area}}$$

$$= \frac{F}{A}$$

The units of pressure are newtons per square metre (N m^{-2}). These are also called pascals (Pa).

In chemistry, we use pressure in connection with gases. Gases exert a pressure on the walls of their container because their molecules constantly bombard them. This is what keeps a balloon inflated and holds up the plunger of the syringe (see **Figure 6.5**).

Momentum

The impact of a particle in a collision depends on its momentum, the product of its mass, m, and velocity, v.

$$\text{momentum} = mv$$

The units are therefore kg m s^{-1}. The more massive the particle the harder it hits and the faster the particle, the harder it hits. Newton's second law of motion says that the force exerted in a collision is equal to the rate of change of momentum.

Imagine a tennis ball colliding with a wall (see **Figure 6.6**). The ball will rebound with the same speed as before *but in the opposite direction*. So its velocity has changed from $+v$ to $-v$, and the change of momentum is from $+mv$ (in one direction) to $-mv$ (in the opposite direction), a change of $2mv$.

The effect of a force applied over a small area is greater than when it is applied over a large area

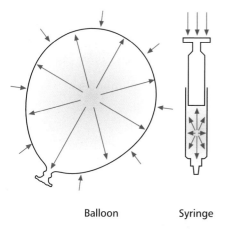

Balloon   Syringe

Figure 6.5 Some effects of pressure

> **Q** What is the pressure of a gas acting with force of 200 000 N on an area of 2 m²?

> **Q** What is the momentum of a car of mass 1000 kg travelling at 30 m s⁻¹ (about 67 mph)?

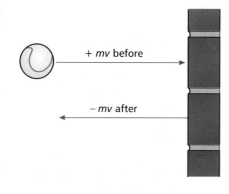

Answer: 100 000 N m⁻² (This is about the normal pressure of the atmosphere.)

Answer: 30 000 kg m s⁻¹.

Figure 6.6 Tennis ball colliding with a wall

6.5 Mathematics

Indices

The number 100 is ten squared and so can be written 10^2, 1000 can be written 10^3, 10 000 as 10^4 and so on. The power to which ten is raised, i.e. the 2 in 10^2, the 3 in 10^3, etc., is called the **index** (plural **indices**). When *multiplying* numbers, we *add* the indices. For example:

$$100 \times 1000 = 100\,000$$

or using indices,

$$10^2 \times 10^3 = 10^{2+3} = 10^5$$

On *dividing* we *subtract* the indices. For example:

$$1000 \div 10 = 100$$
$$10^3 \div 10^1 = 10^{3-1} = 10^2$$

In this system 1 is written 10^0. We can use negative indices to represent numbers less than 1. For example:

$$\frac{1}{100} = 1 \div 100 = 10^0 \div 10^2 = 10^{0-2} = 10^{-2}$$

> **Q** Work out the following using indices to help you:
> (a) $0.0001 \times 1\,000\,000$, (b) $1 \div 0.001$, (c) 0.001×0.001

Standard form

(Used whenever we have very large or very small numbers.)

In standard form, a number is written as a number between 1 and 10 multiplied by 10 raised to the appropriate power.

For example:

$$387\,000 = 3.87 \times 100\,000 = 3.87 \times 10^5$$

To get 3.87 from 387 000.0 we had to move the decimal point 5 places, so the index is 5.

Similarly, 0.00387 could be written 3.87×10^{-3}.

> **Hint:** Remember that when you divide a larger number by a positive number that is less than 1 the answer will be larger than the larger number!

Units

Indices can be applied to units too. For example, the units of area, square metres, are written as m^2. A pressure in newtons per square metre can be written as $N\,m^{-2}$.

$$\begin{array}{ccc} \text{pressure} & = & \text{force} \div \text{area} \\ (N\,m^{-2}) & & (N) \quad (m^2) \end{array}$$

> **Q** Write the following numbers in standard form: (a) 300 000 000 (the speed of light in $m\,s^{-1}$), (b) 0.000 000 000 000 000 000 16 (the charge on an electron in coulombs), (c) 0.000 000 000 1 (the radius of an atom in metres).

Other examples include:

Quantity	Unit		
speed	m/s	$m\,s^{-1}$	metres per second
voltage	J/C	$J\,C^{-1}$	joules per coulomb
ΔH	J/mole	$J\,mol^{-1}$	joules per mole

Manipulating units

When quantities are multiplied or divided, then the units are also multiplied or divided, to give the units of the resulting quantity. An example of this is the units for specific heat capacity, c. This is defined by the equation:

$$H = m \times c \times \Delta T$$

> **Hint:** It is useful to know that 'per' any value means divide by it. For example:
>
> pressure = force *per* unit area
>
> implies
>
> pressure = force ÷ area

Answer: (a) $10^{-4} \times 10^6 = 10^2$, (b) $10^0 \div 10^{-3} = 10^3$, (c) $10^{-3} \times 10^{-3} = 10^{-6}$

Answer: (a) 3×10^8, (b) 1.6×10^{-19}, (c) 1×10^{-10}

where H is the heat supplied in joules to a mass m in kilograms, to give a temperature change of ΔT in °C.

Rearranging this equation,

$$c = \frac{H}{m \times \Delta T}$$

So putting in the units,

$$c = \frac{J}{kg \times °C}$$

So, the units of c are J per kg per °C, or $J\,kg^{-1}\,°C^{-1}$.

Logarithms

(Used in Chapter 12, Acids and bases.)

The **logarithm** (or '**log**') of a number is the power to which some other number (the **base**) must be raised to give the original number. One common base is ten. Such logarithms are written '$\log_{10}$' or just 'log' or sometimes 'lg'. So, for example, what is log 1000?

$$1000 \text{ is } 10^3$$

so $\log 1000 = 3$

Similarly, $\log 100\,000 = 5$

When we want to *multiply* numbers, we *add* their logs:

$$1000 \times 100\,000 = 100\,000\,000$$
$$\log 1000 + \log 100\,000 = 3 + 5 = 8$$
$$8 \text{ is the log of } 100\,000\,000.$$

We say that the **antilogarithm** (or **antilog** or **inverse log**) of 8 is 100 000 000. Antilogs can be found using the INV LOG or 10^x functions on a calculator.

So multiplication of two numbers can be carried out by adding their logs, and division by subtracting their logs, followed by taking the antilog of the result in each case.

For example:

$$1000 \div 100$$

Taking logs, $\log 1000 - \log 100 = 3 - 2 = 1$

$$\text{antilog of } 1 = 10$$

so $1000 \div 100 = 10$

It is easy to see what the log is of numbers like 10, 100, 1000, etc. Other numbers are more difficult but they can be worked out. Tables are available and calculators have a log function. For example, check these using your calculator:

$$\log 3.142 = 0.4972$$
$$\log 483.1 = 2.6840$$

One use of logs is to help scaling on graphs. The numbers 10, 1000, 100 000 would be difficult to fit on the same scale on a graph but their logs: 1, 3 and 5 will fit easily.

This display would be written 6×10^{-12}

Natural logarithms

(Used in Chapter 26, Further kinetics.)

An alternative base for logs is the number 2.718, called 'e'. Such logs are called **natural** logs and the symbol **ln** is used. They have certain mathematical advantages and are more often used in science than logs to the base 10. The rules for their manipulation are the same as for logs to the base ten:

To multiply two numbers add their logs, then take the antilog.
To divide two numbers subtract their logs, then take the antilog.
To raise a number to the power n, multiply its log by n, then take the antilog.

Use of a calculator

Efficient use of a calculator will be vital both during your course and in exams. You will need log, ln, cos, sin, tan, $\sqrt{}$, square functions and brackets, as well as $+$, $-$, $\times$, and $\div$. Calculators vary, so learn how to use your calculator effectively.

Q Use your calculator to find the answers to the examples in the table.

Function	Example	First key	Second key	Third key	Fourth key
x^n	6^3	6	x^y	3	$=$
$1/x$	$1/45$	45	$1/x$		
$\sqrt{x}$	$\sqrt{62}$	62	$\sqrt{}$		
$\log_{10} x$	$\log_{10} 6$	6	log		

Watch out for these common mistakes:

1. When entering numbers like 3.8×10^8, enter
$$3.8 \text{ EXP } 8,$$
$$not \ 3.8 \times 10 \text{ EXP } 8.$$
(The EXP function means '$\times 10$ to the power'. The extra '10' is not needed.)

Hint: Check for this error if you keep getting calculations wrong by a factor of 10.

2. When calculating a fraction like $\dfrac{8 \times 4}{3 \times 16}$ enter
$$8 \times 4 \div 3 \div 16 \text{ or } 8 \times 4 \div (3 \times 16)$$
$$not \ 8 \times 4 \div 3 \times 16, \text{ which would give } \dfrac{8 \times 4}{3} \times 16.$$

Q Work out the value of the fraction
$$\dfrac{8 \times 4}{3 \times 16}$$

Hint: Calculator displays often show numbers in standard form in shorthand, so that 6×10^{-12} is written 6. −12. This is not an acceptable way to write numbers and could lead to confusion. It will certainly lose you marks in an exam.

Significant figures

3.0 g and 3.00 g do not have the same meaning: 3.0 g implies we have used a balance which can weigh to the nearest 0.1 g whereas 3.00 g implies we have used a more accurate balance, which can weigh to the nearest 0.01 g. So the number of figures after the decimal point in this case tells us about the accuracy of the measurement.

After a calculation using your calculator, you often end up with a long string of numerals, such as 17.893456. It is important that you use only the number of figures that match the accuracy of your data. You cannot get a number out of a calculation that is more accurate than the data you put in.

Hint: Writing the whole of a long number on your calculator display, rather than an appropriate number of significant figures really upsets examiners!

Significant figures are counted starting from the first non-zero of any number and working towards the right.

For example, the number 543 has three significant figures: 5 is the first (and most) significant figure, 4 the second and 3 the third. The number 4.572 has 4 significant figures.

Answer: 216, 0.022, 7.87, 0.778

Answer: 0.667 (to 3 significant figures: see the next section)

Q How many significant figures are there in the following numbers?
(a) 3456, (b) 03.45, (c) 345.12

Hint: Sometimes to prevent confusion we need to say how many significant figures we are using. For example, there is no way of telling if 3450 is to 3 significant figures or 4 unless we specify.

Q Express the following to three significant figures:
(a) 410.05 ,(b) 0.044 26, (c) 34.543

Hint: When using significant figures in calculations, identify the quantity used in the calculation that has the *least* number of significant figures. Do not quote your answer to more significant figures than this. It is useful to write the number of significant figures in brackets after the answer, for example 6.2 (to 2 s.f.).

Writing a number to a specified number of significant figures

Starting from the left, write down the numerals until the required number of significant figures is reached. There may have to be zeros to show the size of the number. For example:

- 5671 to three significant figures is 5670.
- 56 055.34 to three significant figures is 56 100. (We round up the last significant figure if it is followed by 5 or more.)
- For numbers such as 0.021 43, the first significant number is 2 and not 0, so to three significant figures this would be 0.0214.

Graphs

(Used throughout, but particularly in Chapter 14, Kinetics and Chapter 26, Further kinetics.)

Straight line graphs

If you plot a graph of two variables, and end up with a straight line, it means that the variables are **proportional** to each other: a regular increase in one produces a regular increase in the other.

The equation of a straight line (**Figure 6.7**) is always $y = mx + c$, where m is the **gradient** of the line and c the **intercept** with the y axis (the value of y where the line crosses the y axis).

The gradient, m, is positive if the line slopes upwards from left to right and negative if the line slopes downwards from left to right.

If c is 0, the line goes through the origin (0,0) and in this case the variables are **directly proportional**. This means that doubling (or halving) one doubles (or halves) the other, etc.

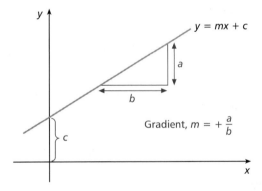

Figure 6.7 Straight line graph

Q Find the gradient m of line CD on **Figure 6.8**.

Q Write down the equation for a line which is parallel to CD but which cuts the y axis at the point $y = 6$.

Answer: (a) 4, (b) 3, (c) 5

Answer: (a) 410, (b) 0.0443, (c) 34.5

Answer: 0.5

Answer: $y = 0.5x + 6$

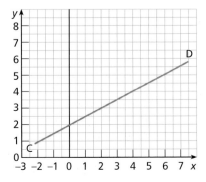

Figure 6.8

Tangents

A tangent is a line that touches a curve. **Figure 6.9** shows a typical reaction rate curve, with the amount of gas given off each minute decreasing as the reactants are used up. We can find the gradient at any point by drawing a tangent. From the gradient of the tangent we find the gradient of the curve at that point.

> **Q** Work out the gradient of the curve at C.

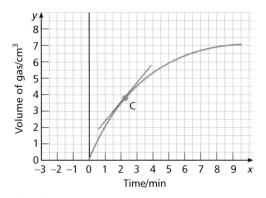

Figure 6.9 A tangent to a curve at point C

Rearranging equations

This is a vital skill in chemistry, and involves applying what you have learnt in algebra to letters that stand for real quantities. For example, pressure = force/area:

$$P = \frac{F}{A}$$

You know P and A, and need to find F, so F must stand alone on one side of the equation.

F is divided by A, so if you multiply F by A this will leave F on its own.

$$\cancel{A} \times \frac{F}{\cancel{A}}$$

> **Q** Rearrange the following equations:
> (a) density = mass/volume to find (i) mass, (ii) volume
> (b) $H = m \times c \times \Delta T$ to find c
> (c) no. of moles in solution
> $$= \frac{\text{concentration} \times \text{volume}}{1000}$$
> to find concentration
> (d) Use this expression to find the concentration in mol dm⁻³ of a solution containing 0.5 moles of solute in 100 cm³ of solution.
>
> **Hint:** ΔT is a single term. Δ means 'change in'.

But if we multiply one side of the equation we must do the same to the other side, so:

$$F = P \times A$$

Another example:

$$\text{kinetic energy, } E = \tfrac{1}{2}mv^2$$

where m is mass and v is velocity. Suppose you want to find the velocity of a moving mass, when you know its energy and its mass.

$$E = \tfrac{1}{2}mv^2$$

Step 1: Multiply *both* sides by 2 to remove the 2 that is dividing v.

$$2 \times E = \cancel{2} \times \tfrac{1}{\cancel{2}}mv^2 = mv^2$$

Step 2: Divide *both* sides by m to remove the m that is multiplying v.

$$\frac{2 \times E}{m} = \frac{\cancel{m}v^2}{\cancel{m}}$$

$$= v^2$$

Answer: 1.0 cm³ min⁻¹

Answer: (a) (i) mass = density × volume,
         (ii) volume = mass/density,

   (b) $C = \dfrac{H}{m \times \Delta T}$

   (c) concentration =
   $$\frac{\text{no. of moles in solution} \times 1000}{\text{volume}},$$

   (d) concentration = 5 mol dm⁻³

Step 3: Take the square root of *both* sides to remove the square on v.

$$\sqrt{\frac{2 \times E}{m}} = v$$

7 Atomic and nuclear structure

C H E M I S T R Y   N O W

Can we see atoms?

Today everybody has heard of atoms and we all accept that everything is made of these minute particles that are themselves mostly empty space.

It was not always so: even in the early years of the twentieth century a number of well-respected scientists, such as Nobel prize-winner Friedrich Ostwald, believed that the idea of atoms was no more than a useful model. Part of the reason was probably because it is not possible to see atoms.

IBM scientists 'wrote' this logo with separate atoms of xenon on a nickel surface

This is not because microscopes are not powerful enough. It will never be possible to see atoms directly using the visible light to which our eyes are sensitive. Light is a form of wave motion and waves are only affected by objects that are larger than their own wavelength. Atoms are smaller than the wavelength of visible light: a typical atom is 0.2 nm across and the wavelength of visible light is about 600 nm. So, light waves pass atoms without being affected, as if the atoms are not there.

Atoms were first located by X-ray diffraction (see Chapter 29). The wavelength of X-rays is comparable to the size of atoms. Thus X-rays 'bounce off' atoms and can be detected.

More recently, Scanning Tunnelling Electron Microscopy (STEM) has allowed us to 'see' atoms even more directly and provides remarkable pictures such as that in the photograph above. STEM works by moving a metal probe less than one nanometre above a surface and applying a low voltage between the probe and the surface. Electrons jump (or tunnel) across the gap between the probe and the surface. This causes a current whose size depends on the distance between the probe and the surface. The probe is scanned across the surface and is moved up and down in such a way that the current remains constant. This technique is sensitive enough to produce a contour map showing individual atoms.

In a variation of the technique, the probe can be used to 'push' individual atoms across a surface and place them where required. This is how IBM scientists produced the 'commercial' above. Each dot in the letter is a single atom.

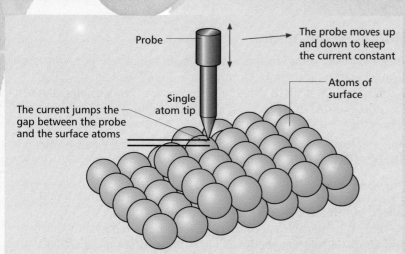

Probe

The probe moves up and down to keep the current constant

Atoms of surface

Single atom tip

The current jumps the gap between the probe and the surface atoms

STEM: the probe moves above the surface mapping the shape

In this chapter we will be looking at:
- subatomic particles: electrons, protons and neutrons
- the arrangement of electrons in s, p and d orbitals
- line spectra: the light given out by atoms
- ionisation energy: removing electrons from atoms
- isotopes
- the mass spectrometer: finding the masses of atoms
- the ^{12}C scale of atomic masses

Introduction

Atoms are the basic building bricks of chemistry. In order to understand how they bond together we must have an idea of their structure. This chapter builds on the simple picture of the atom given in Chapter 2 to give a more detailed and sophisticated model. Some of the key experiments which led to the working out of the atom's structure are described but the whole story, while fascinating, is too long for this book. The unravelling of the structure of the atom is still going on. It is rather like doing a jigsaw puzzle: as each piece fits in, it confirms that all the others were in the right place and the whole picture is slowly revealed.

CONCEPT CHECKPOINTS

The following basic ideas are used in this chapter. You may revise some of these topics elsewhere in the book.
- the behaviour of positive and negative electric charges (section 6.3)
- the electromagnetic spectrum (section 6.2)
- relative atomic mass (section 4.2)

Did you know? The word 'atom' comes from the Greek word *atomos* meaning indivisible!

Did you know? In 1932 the positron was discovered. It has the same mass as the electron but has a positive charge. It is called the anti-particle of the electron.

7.1 Subatomic particles

The electron

The idea of matter being made up of atoms was first proposed in relatively modern times by John Dalton in 1803, but it was not until the end of the nineteenth century that it became clear that particles smaller than atoms existed.

The first to be identified was the electron, a negatively charged particle which seemed to exist in all atoms. Electrons, then called 'cathode rays', were first detected in discharge tubes used to investigate the conduction of electricity by gases at low pressure.

The proton

Shortly afterwards, 'positive rays' were discovered in the same type of experiment. These turned out to be charged particles with a variety of masses, the smallest of which were what we now know as protons, the fundamental positively charged particle. Protons were found to be about two thousand times more massive than electrons. They were later detected directly by Ernest Rutherford when he bombarded nuclei with alpha particles.

Models of the atom

These discoveries led to speculation about how these particles might be arranged to form neutral atoms. One theory was the so-called 'plum pudding' atom in which electrons were seen as being dotted about like plums in a positively charged pudding. This is shown in **Figure 7.1**.

Rutherford's nuclear atom

The 'plum pudding' idea was disproved by Ernest Rutherford, Hans Geiger and Ernst Marsden's famous alpha scattering experiment carried out in 1911 (see the box 'The nucleus'). They used fast-moving alpha particles as 'bullets' which they fired at thin sheets of gold atoms. A very few bounced back, indicating that the mass and positive charge of the gold atom must be concentrated in a dense core or nucleus. Mathematical analysis of the detailed scattering

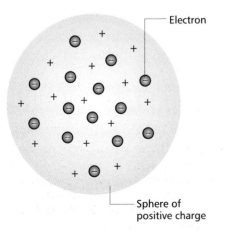

Electron

Sphere of positive charge

Figure 7.1 The plum pudding model of the atom – electrons dotted about within a sphere of positive charge

The discovery of the electron

By the last two decades of the nineteenth century it was known that there was some connection between atoms and electricity because of the formation of positive and negative ions which moved during electrolysis.

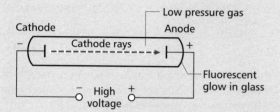

During experiments on the conduction of electricity by gases at low pressure in gas discharge tubes like that above, a glow was noted at the anode end of the tube. Metal objects placed in the tube caused a 'shadow' and the glow seemed to be caused by rays of some sort coming from the cathode, hence the name 'cathode rays'. The rays could be deflected towards the positive plate in an electric field, showing that they carried a negative charge.

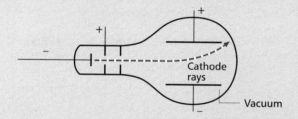

Cathode rays were investigated by the British scientist J. J. Thomson, who deflected them with magnetic and electric fields and demonstrated that they were charged particles by measuring their charge/mass ratio.

The deflection depends both on the mass and the charge, so only the ratio could be determined. Thomson found that cathode rays always had the same charge/mass ratio whatever the material of the cathode (or if any other

details of the experiment were changed). He had discovered a fundamental constituent of all matter: the first subatomic particle, called the electron.

Joseph John Thomson — discoverer of the electron. He was always known as 'J J'

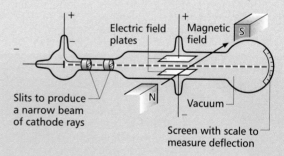

J.J. Thomson's apparatus for measuring the charge/mass ratio of cathode rays. The charge of the electron was measured by Millikan some years later

The discovery of the proton

The discovery of the electron left the question of what constituted the positive part of the atom, since atoms are electrically neutral. It also left a question about the mass of the atom, as electrons were known to have a mass of around 1/2000 of the lightest atom, hydrogen.

Further experiments with gas discharge tubes led to the discovery of positive rays travelling in the opposite

direction to cathode rays. These had a variety of masses, but the smallest had the same mass as a hydrogen atom (assuming they carried one unit of electric charge). These were named protons. Protons were observed directly in 1914 by Rutherford, who produced them by bombarding various nuclei with alpha particles.

patterns enabled them to estimate that the diameter of the nucleus was less than one ten-thousandth of that of the whole atom. Scaled up, this corresponds to a nucleus the size of a pinhead in an atom the size of a house. The 'house' is occupied only by the electrons, which are very light. This means that the nucleus is exceptionally dense: approximately $6 \times 10^{10} \, \text{kg cm}^{-3}$ so that a matchbox full of nuclei would weigh around 60 million tonnes!

The nucleus

How were the positive and negative parts of the atom arranged? By 1906, a new tool existed for probing the structure of the atom. It had been discovered that some radioactive elements gave off alpha particles: positively charged particles with the mass of a helium atom. The New Zealander Ernest Rutherford, one of the greatest experimental scientists ever, and his collaborators Hans Geiger and Ernst Marsden used alpha particles as a sort of nuclear 'artillery'. They fired them at gold foil just a few atoms thick and investigated how they were scattered by observing scintillations (flashes of light) as the alpha particles hit a zinc sulphide screen.

The scattering pattern showed that the vast majority of alpha particles passed almost undeflected through the foil. This is what would have been expected if the plum pudding model was correct, because in it the mass and positive charge are well spread out. However, in fact a few alpha particles were deflected through large angles and a very few even bounced back. The plum pudding model could *not* explain this. These results suggested that the gold atoms were mostly empty space occupied by the

electrons (which were not massive enough to deflect an alpha particle) while most of the mass and positive charge was concentrated in a small core, the nucleus.

Note that a collision between an alpha particle and a gold nucleus involves repulsion between the two positively charged entities. Mathematical analysis of the scattering pattern allowed the charge and size of the gold nucleus to be estimated.

The experiment is rather like finding and measuring the size of a cannon-ball hidden in a bale of hay by firing machine gun bullets at the bale.

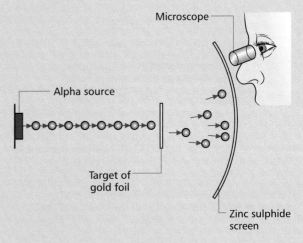

Schematic diagram of the alpha scattering experiment

Ernest Rutherford. His nuclear model of the atom forms the basis of current atomic structure

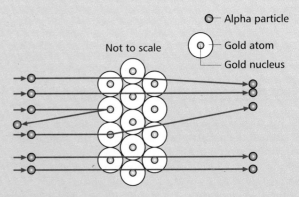

The process of alpha scattering

FURTHER FOCUS

The neutron

At the time when the proton and electron were the only subatomic particles known, it was believed that nuclei must contain both protons and electrons. This was necessary to account for their known charges and masses. For example He ($A_r = 4$, $Z = 2$) was thought to consist of four protons and two electrons in the nucleus, protons having a mass of one unit each and the electrons negligible mass. The nucleus was orbited by two electrons. It was not until 1934 that James Chadwick found evidence for neutral particles within the nucleus, although Rutherford had proposed this some years earlier. Chadwick bombarded beryllium with alpha particles and detected no resulting particles. However, on placing a wax screen close to the beryllium, protons were detected.

He explained this result by supposing that the alpha particles ejected neutral particles from the beryllium, which in turn knocked protons out of the wax. Neutrons, being uncharged, were not detectable by methods then in use.

This led to a model of the nucleus made up of protons and neutrons both of mass 1 unit. Both contributed to the mass, but only the protons to the charge. So a helium atom would be made up of two protons and two neutrons in the nucleus, surrounded by two electrons. Protons and neutrons are both referred to as nucleons.

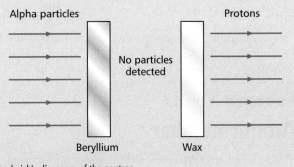

Chadwick's discovery of the neutron

Q If the nucleus were the size of a marble (approximately 1 cm in diameter), how big would an atom be?

Exactly what was in the nucleus was a puzzle for a number of years until a neutral particle of the same mass as a proton was discovered by James Chadwick in 1934. It was named the **neutron**. Being neutral, it was more difficult to detect than charged particles, which was why it had escaped detection for so long. This led to a model of the atom consisting of protons and neutrons packed closely together in the nucleus surrounded by electrons orbiting at a considerable distance.

The strong nuclear force

Clearly nuclei must be held together by a very powerful force to hold many protons close together against their electrostatic repulsion. The force that does so is called the **strong nuclear force.** It is much stronger than the electrostatic forces that hold electrons and protons together in the atom, but it operates only at very short range: within the nucleus. It is this force which gives rise to the large amounts of energy that are released in nuclear reactions such as in the atom bomb and nuclear reactors.

The idea of a small positive nucleus led to the idea of electrons orbiting the nucleus like planets in the solar system, their orbital motion counteracting the electrostatic attraction of the nucleus, and preventing them from being dragged inwards.

Atomic number

The atomic number was originally merely the number of an element's position in the Periodic Table and was not thought to be of fundamental significance. However, in 1914 Henry Moseley discovered that on bombarding metallic elements with electrons, X-rays were produced, and that the frequency of X-rays produced

Answer: About 100 m in diameter: about the size of a soccer stadium.

> **Hint:** The total number of protons and neutrons in an atom is sometimes called the nucleon number.

was related to the atomic number of the bombarded element. This suggested that the atomic number represented a fundamental property of the atom. It is in fact the number of protons in an atom, and so the atomic number is now often called the proton number. It is usually given the symbol Z.

Thus by the Second World War, atomic structure was well enough understood to allow nuclear reactions to be brought about, resulting in the atomic bombs used at Hiroshima and Nagasaki and, later, the controlled use of nuclear energy. Atoms were by then known to consist of a small, dense nucleus containing protons and neutrons held together by the strong nuclear force. The diameter of the nucleus is of the order of 10^{-14} m compared with that of the atom of 10^{-10} m. The nucleus was visualised as being surrounded by orbiting electrons whose arrangement will be considered next.

FURTHER FOCUS

Atomic number

When metals are bombarded with a stream of electrons (called cathode rays), in the apparatus shown below, X-rays, which are a form of high energy electromagnetic radiation, are given off.

In 1913 Henry Moseley measured the frequency of the X-rays emitted by different metals. There seemed to be a relationship between the square root of the frequency, ν,

and the relative atomic mass. However, an even better straight line is obtained if $\sqrt{\nu}$ is plotted against the atomic number, the order in which the elements appear in the Periodic Table.

This suggests that the atomic number represents something more fundamental than just the element's position in an arbitrary list. Moseley proposed that the atomic number represented the number of protons in the nucleus. This connection between a real physical quantity and position in the Periodic Table made it possible to know for sure whether any elements in the Periodic Table were missing. This technique also made it possible to identify any element with certainty. The mechanism for the emission of characteristic X-rays is similar to that for the production of line spectra in the visible region (see main text).

Henry Moseley. His work demonstrated the significance of atomic number as the number of protons in the nucleus. He was killed fighting in the First World War

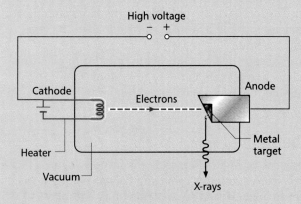

Moseley's apparatus

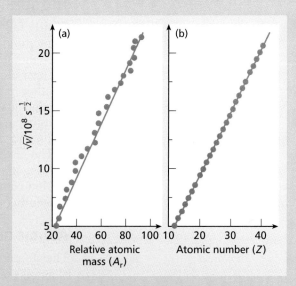

Graphs of $\sqrt{\nu}$ for characteristic X-rays of various elements. Note the much better straight line when plotted against Z rather than A_r

Summary of subatomic particles

This is given in **Table 7.1**.

Table 7.1 Summary of subatomic particles

Name	Mass number	Mass/kg	Relative charge	Charge/coulomb
proton	1	1.673×10^{-27}	+1	$+1.6 \times 10^{-19}$
neutron	1	1.675×10^{-27}	0	0
electron	0	0.911×10^{-30}	−1	-1.6×10^{-19}

Note that the accurate masses of the proton and neutron are not exactly the same. The charges on the proton and the electron *are* exactly the same. The **mass number** is simply the number of nucleons (protons and neutrons) in an atom.

7.2 The arrangement of electrons in atoms

The evidence for the way that electrons are arranged in atoms comes largely from the study of light and other types of electromagnetic radiation given out and absorbed by atoms.

The electromagnetic spectrum

Electromagnetic radiation is energy that can travel through a vacuum. The most familiar form is light, but other types include heat (infra-red), radio waves and X-rays. Electromagnetic radiation can be thought of as a wave and therefore like all waves has a wavelength (λ), the distance between two successive peaks, and a frequency (ν), the number of vibrations per second. See section 6.2.

Wavelength and frequency are linked by the equation:

$$c = \nu\lambda$$

where c is the velocity of the electromagnetic radiation (the velocity of light, approximately 3×10^8 m s^{-1}). The different types of electromagnetic radiation have different frequencies and wavelengths. Notice that in **Figure 7.2** high frequency radiation has a short wavelength and low frequency radiation has a long wavelength. The boundaries between different types are approximate.

Electromagnetic radiation may also be thought of as coming in individual 'packets' called **quanta** (often called photons, especially for quanta of visible light). Each quantum carries an amount of energy that depends on its frequency and is given by the equation:

$$E = h\nu$$

where h is a constant called Planck's constant, having the value 6.6×10^{-34} J s. So a photon of yellow visible light of frequency 6×10^{14} s^{-1} has an energy of $6.6 \times 10^{-34} \times 6 \times 10^{14}$ J $= 3.96 \times 10^{-19}$ J per quantum. This idea of electromagnetic radiation having some properties of both waves and particles is sometimes called **wave–particle duality**. It was once regarded as a contradiction in terms by scientists but now the two views are seen as complementary.

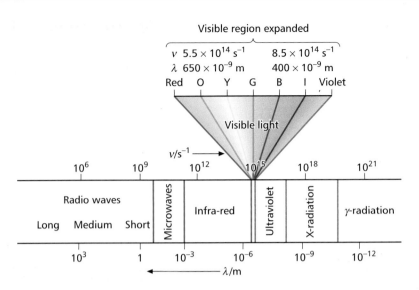

Figure 7.2 The electromagnetic spectrum

Line spectra

When atoms have been **excited** (given extra energy) they give out light and other forms of electromagnetic energy. Excitation may be brought about in a variety of ways. One of the simplest is to heat the substance in a Bunsen flame; another is to pass an electric discharge through the vapour using the apparatus shown in **Figure 7.3**. This will produce a glow.

If the light is observed through a spectroscope (a device which splits light into its component wavelengths or frequencies) each element will be seen to produce a pattern of **lines**. Part of the spectrum of hydrogen is shown in **Figure 7.4**

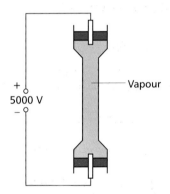

Figure 7.3 A discharge lamp

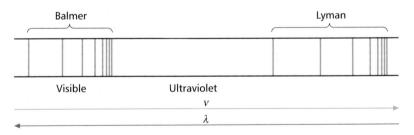

Figure 7.4 Part of the line spectrum of hydrogen showing two of the groups of lines

Notice how the lines fall in groups and that the lines in each group get closer together or **converge** towards the high frequency (high energy) end of the spectrum. Each element produces a completely individual pattern of lines that can be used to identify it.

Spectral lines

All elements are found to have several series of lines, each fitting a formula similar to the one below for hydrogen.

$$\nu = cR \left(\frac{1}{n_1{}^2} - \frac{1}{n_2{}^2} \right)$$

where

ν = frequency of line
c = velocity of light
R = constant (the Rydberg constant)
n_1 and n_2 are whole numbers, $n_2 > n_1$

For hydrogen the groups of lines have been given the names of their discoverers. They are listed in **Table 7.2**.

Table 7.2 Named series of lines in the hydrogen spectrum

Lyman	$n_1 = 1$, $n_2 = 2, 3, 4$, etc	found in the ultraviolet region
Balmer	$n_1 = 2$, $n_2 = 3, 4, 5$, etc	found in the visible region
Paschen	$n_1 = 3$, $n_2 = 4, 5, 6$, etc	
Brackett	$n_1 = 4$, $n_2 = 5, 6, 7$, etc	found in the infra-red region
Pfund	$n_1 = 5$, $n_2 = 6, 7, 8$, etc	

An interpretation of these line spectra was proposed by the Danish scientist Niels Bohr in 1913. He suggested that electrons could occupy only certain fixed energy levels around the nucleus. These energy levels can be visualised as orbits of increasing radius (see **Figure 7.5**). Orbits of larger radius have higher energy.

Even in hydrogen, which has only one electron, an infinite number of levels exists even though only one is occupied at any one time. The situation is rather like a set of shelves with only one object. The object can only be placed on a shelf (not in the gaps between) and the shelves still exist even if they have no object on them. When an electron moves from one orbit to another, it absorbs (if going to a higher level) or emits (if dropping to a lower level) a **single quantum** of energy equal in size to the energy gap (ΔE) between the two levels.

So the line spectrum of hydrogen is explained as follows:

- When hydrogen is excited in a discharge tube, the electron is promoted from the lowest level (the ground state), which it normally occupies, to a higher level.
- It then drops back to the lowest level, either directly or via a series of steps.
- At each drop in level, it gives out a quantum of energy equal to the difference in levels ΔE.
- Because of the relationship $E = h\nu$, each quantum has a different frequency and therefore contributes one line to the line spectrum, as shown in **Figure 7.6**.
- Electrons dropping into level 1 give rise to the Lyman series of lines, those dropping into level 2 the Balmer series (of overall lower energy) and so on.

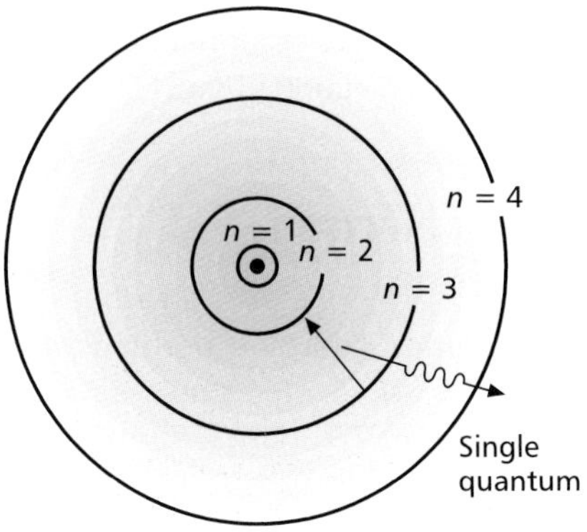

Figure 7.5 The first four Bohr orbits of hydrogen showing a transition between level 3 and level 2. The quantum of radiation would produce a line in the Balmer series

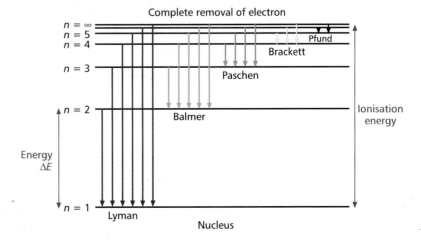

Figure 7.6 Energy levels in hydrogen. Note how this fits in with Figure 7.5. In Figure 7.5, the *radii* are drawn roughly to scale. Here the *energies* are drawn to scale. Also the energy levels are drawn as straight lines rather than as circles

Ionisation energy

As the energy levels get further from the nucleus, they get closer together. Eventually they are effectively 'touching' and they merge together. When an electron has reached this level, it has effectively been completely removed from the atom. This is called **ionisation.** The amount of energy required to do this is called the **ionisation energy** (strictly enthalpy of ionisation: see section 8.1). A value of 1312 kJ mol^{-1} is found for hydrogen.

The method described in the first box on page 45 can be used to find the ionisation energy of any atom. Also the energy gaps between the various electronic levels can be found. This can be done by measuring ionisation energies from levels 1, 2, 3, etc. and finding the differences. For example, the ionisation energy of hydrogen from level 1 is 1312 kJ mol^{-1} and from level 2 it is 362 kJ mol^{-1}, so the energy gap between levels 1 and 2 must be $1312 - 326 = 986$ kJ mol^{-1}.

Measuring ionisation energies by electron bombardment

An alternative method of measuring ionisation energy is by using a beam of fast-moving electrons as 'bullets' to knock electrons out of the atom, using the apparatus shown in **Figure 7.7**, which shows the method being used for argon gas.

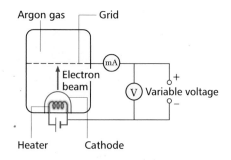

Figure 7.7 Apparatus for measuring the ionisation energy of argon by electrical bombardment

Flame emission spectrophotometry

This powerful analytical technique has become very important in recent years for the qualitative ('what's there?') and quantitative ('how much is there?') analysis of trace amounts of elements. It is used in pharmaceutical, metallurgical, medical, geological and forensic work. For example, the concentration of sodium ions in blood can be measured. It depends on the fact that every element produces a unique set of spectral lines. A solution containing the sample is sprayed into a flame and the spectral lines identified using a spectrometer. Quantities are measured by comparing the intensity of the lines with a standard. Modern instruments are computer-controlled and can produce a print-out of results in seconds. (This is vital in quality control work, where stopping a production line to await analysis results could be very costly.) A further advantage of the method is that only very small amounts of sample are required. The method is a much more sophisticated version of flame testing which you may have carried out to identify metals (sodium yellow, potassium lilac, etc).

Atomic absorption spectroscopy

A related technique is called atomic absorption spectroscopy. It depends on the absorption of light by a vapour which contains atoms of the sample. It is very good for the quantitative analysis of, for example, metals. A source of light is chosen which contains the element whose concentration is to be measured. For example, to measure sodium concentration, we must use a sodium light. In this way the light source produces exactly the wavelengths which will be absorbed by the sample. Then, the amount of light absorbed is proportional to the concentration of the element absorbing it. (This is called the Beer–Lambert law.)

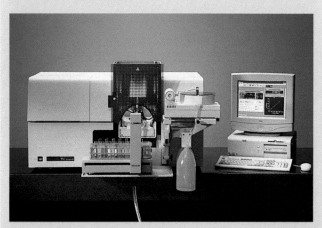

Flame emission spectrophotometer

FURTHER FOCUS

Measuring the ionisation energy of hydrogen from its line spectrum

It is possible to determine graphically the frequency at which the spectral lines 'merge' (which corresponds to ionisation).

A graph is plotted of the *difference* in frequency of successive lines ($\Delta\nu$) of one series against the frequency and extrapolated to find when $\Delta\nu$ is zero. This frequency is called the **convergence limit** of the series of lines. When this is done for the Lyman lines of hydrogen, a convergence limit of 3.283×10^{15} s^{-1} is found.

Using
$$E = h\nu$$
$$E = 6.626 \times 10^{-34} \times 3.283 \times 10^{15} \text{ J}$$
$$E = 2.186 \times 10^{-18} \text{ J per atom}$$

For one mole of atoms,
$$E = 2.175 \times 10^{-18} \times 6 \times 10^{23} \text{ J mol}^{-1}$$
$$E = 1\,312\,000 \text{ J mol}^{-1} \text{ (to 4 s.f.)}$$

In more familiar units, $E = 1312$ kJ mol^{-1}. This is the energy required to remove an electron from the lowest energy level of hydrogen, the **ground state** and is called the **ionisation energy**.

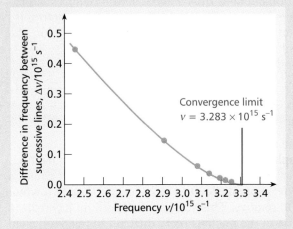

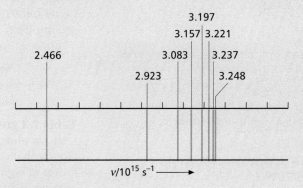

The Lyman lines in the hydrogen spectrum

FURTHER FOCUS

Calculating ionisation energy from electron bombardment experiments

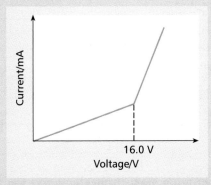

The voltage is equal to the energy of the bombarding electrons in joules per coulomb. So when the current jumps,

number of joules per electron
$$= 16.0 \times \text{charge on electron}$$
$$= 16.0 \times 1.60 \times 10^{-19} \text{ J}$$
$$= 2.56 \times 10^{-18} \text{ J}$$

Ionisation energies are usually quoted per mole, so
$$\text{IE} = 2.56 \times 10^{-18} \times 6.02 \times 10^{23}$$
$$= 1\,541\,120 \text{ J mol}^{-1}$$
$$= 1540 \text{ kJ mol}^{-1} \text{ (to 3 s.f.)}$$

Remember: The first ionisation energy is ΔH for the process
$$\text{Ar(g)} \longrightarrow \text{Ar(g)}^+ + \text{e}^-.$$

Electrons are attracted from the heated cathode by the positively charged grid. A current flows and is detected by the milliammeter. As the voltage increases, so does the current. Eventually, a voltage is reached at which the electrons have enough energy to knock out an electron from an argon atom if they collide with it:

$$Ar(g) + e^- \longrightarrow Ar^+(g) + 2e^-$$

so three charged particles replace the original one. The current thus jumps. The ionisation energy of argon can be calculated from the voltage at which the jump in current starts (see the second box on page 45).

The numbers of electrons in different orbits

The energies required to remove the electrons one by one from an atom with many electrons can be measured. These are usually called successive ionisation energies (IEs). Each electron requires more energy than the previous one. This is because the first electron is being removed from a neutral atom, the second from a 1+ ion, the second from a 2+ ion and so on.

For example, sodium:

$$Na(g) \longrightarrow Na^+(g) + e^- \quad \text{first IE}$$
$$Na^+(g) \longrightarrow Na^{2+}(g) + e^- \quad \text{second IE}$$
$$Na^{2+}(g) \longrightarrow Na^{3+}(g) + e^- \quad \text{third IE and so on}$$

Table 7.3 gives the successive IEs for sodium.

If we plot a graph of the figures in Table 7.3 we get **Figure 7.8**. Notice that one electron is relatively easy to remove, then comes a group of eight rather more difficult to remove, and then two which are very difficult to remove. This suggests that sodium has two electrons very close to the nucleus (very difficult to remove), eight further out (easier to remove) and one further away still (easy to remove). So it is possible to work out the number of electrons in each shell or orbit. A closer look at the figures shows that the group of eight electrons is in fact split into a group of two and a group of six although the difference in energy is small and is not noticeable in Figure 7.8.

> **Hint:** Notice that the second IE is *not* the energy change for
> $$Na(g) \longrightarrow Na^{2+}(g) + 2e^-$$
> The energy for this process would be the first IE plus the second IE.

Table 7.3 Successive ionisation energies of sodium/kJ mol^{-1}

1	496
2	4563
3	6913
4	9544
5	13 352
6	16 611
7	20 115
8	25 491
9	28 934
10	141 367
11	159 079

> **Q** Use Table 7.3 to work out the energy required to form (a) Na^{2+}(g) and (b) Na^{3+}(g) from Na(g). Why does sodium not usually form Na^{2+} ions?

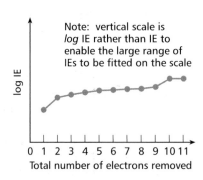

Note: vertical scale is *log* IE rather than IE to enable the large range of IEs to be fitted on the scale

log IE

0 1 2 3 4 5 6 7 8 9 10 11
Total number of electrons removed

Figure 7.8 Successive ionisation energies of sodium

Answer: (a) 5059 kJ mol^{-1}, (b) 11 972 kJ mol^{-1}. It requires about ten times as much energy to form a doubly charged ion as a singly charged ion.

Orbitals

For a more complete description of electrons in atoms we must turn to a theory called **quantum mechanics**. This considers the electron as a wave (wave–particle duality again) and describes the atom with an equation (the Schrödinger equation). The solutions to this equation give the *probability* of finding an electron in a given volume

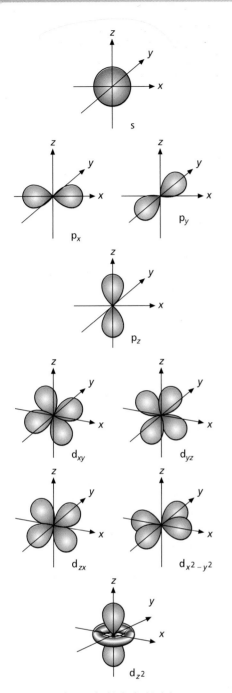

Figure 7.9 Shapes of orbitals. f orbitals have more complex shapes still. These shapes represent a volume of space in which there is a 95% probability of finding an electron

Hint: Any single orbital can hold a maximum of two electrons

Did you know? The labels for the orbitals s, p, d and f come from the descriptions of lines in the spectra of atoms: sharp, principal, diffuse and fine.

of space, rather than its exact location at any time. Think of the electron as a cloud of negative charge which may fill a volume in space called its **orbital**. The solutions to the equation tell us the distance from the nucleus and hence the energy of an electron, and these solutions correspond to the shell numbers 1, 2, 3, etc. The shapes of the orbitals are described by the letters s, p, d and f. These shapes are shown in **Figure 7.9**.

- s orbitals can hold up to two electrons.
- p orbitals can hold up to two electrons each, but always come in groups of three of the same energy to give a total of six electrons.
- d orbitals can hold up to two electrons each, but come in groups of five of the same energy to give a total of 10 electrons.
- f orbitals can hold up to two electrons each, but come in groups of seven of the same energy to give a total of 14 electrons.

The energy level diagram in **Figure 7.10** shows the orbitals for the first few elements of the Periodic Table. Notice that 4s is actually of slightly lower energy than 3d. Also notice that level 1 has only an s orbital, level 2 has s and p orbitals, level 3 has s, p and d, and so on. Each 'box' in Figure 7.10 represents an orbital of the appropriate shape which can hold up to two electrons.

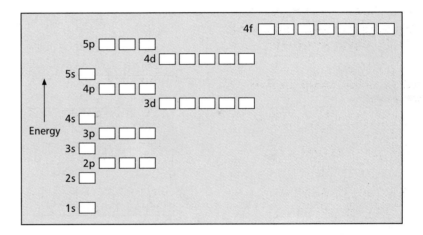

Figure 7.10 The energy levels of the first few atomic orbitals

Spin

Electrons also have the property of **spin**. Two electrons in the same orbital must have opposite spins. This is usually represented by arrows pointing up or down to represent the different directions of spin.

The rules for allocating electrons to orbitals state that the orbitals of lower energy are filled first. Since electrons repel one another, some energy is needed to pair them in the same orbital. So orbitals of the same energy fill singly before pairing starts. The electron diagrams for the elements hydrogen to sodium are shown in **Figure 7.11**.

There is a shorthand way of writing electronic structures, sometimes called electron arrangements or configurations. For example, for sodium, which has 11 electrons, this is:

$$1s^2 \quad 2s^2 2p^6 \quad 3s^1$$
$$2 \qquad 8 \qquad 1$$

Q Work out the electron configuration of an Na$^+$ ion. Which *element* has the same electron configuration?

Q Write down the shorthand electron arrangement for (a) magnesium (12 electrons), (b) potassium (19 electrons).

Note how this corresponds with the simpler 2, 8, 1.
Calcium, with 20 electrons, would be:

$$1s^22s^22p^63s^23p^64s^2$$

and argon with 18 electrons would be:

$$1s^22s^22p^63s^23p^6$$

Sometimes it simplifies things to refer back to the previous noble gas structure. So the electron arrangement of calcium, Ca, could be written [Ar]4s^2 as a shorthand for $1s^22s^22p^63s^23p^64s^2$, since $1s^22s^22p^63s^23p^6$ is the electron arrangement of argon.

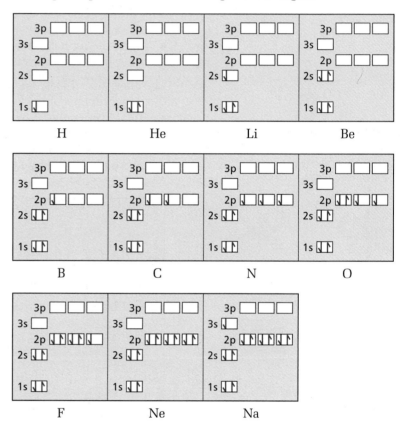

Figure 7.11 The electron arrangements for the elements hydrogen to sodium

7.3 Nuclides and isotopes

Any combination of protons and neutrons forming the nucleus of an atom is called a **nuclide**.

However, it is the number of protons in the nucleus (called the atomic number, or proton number) that identifies an element. This governs the number of electrons and thus the chemical reactivity of the element. The number of neutrons in a nucleus of a particular element may vary.

Nuclides with the same number of protons, but different numbers of neutrons, are called isotopes. Different isotopes *of the same element* will react in the same way as one another chemically, although they will have slightly different masses and may have different radioactive properties. For example, carbon has three common isotopes. All have six protons and they have six, seven and eight neutrons respectively.

Answer: 2,8; neon.

Answer: (a) [Ne]3s^2, (b) [Ar]4s^1

Nuclides can be symbolised with the following shorthand:

$$^{\text{mass number}}_{\text{atomic number}} \text{Chemical symbol}$$

So the isotopes of carbon are:

$$^{12}_{6}\text{C} \quad ^{13}_{6}\text{C} \quad ^{14}_{6}\text{C}$$

The first two are stable but $^{14}_{6}\text{C}$ (carbon-14) is radioactive.

The relative atomic mass of an element, A_r, is the average relative atomic mass of all its isotopes, taking into account their abundances (see section 7.4).

7.4 The mass spectrometer

Hint: There is more about the mass spectrometer and its uses in Chapters 29, Structure determination and 38, Identifying organic compounds.

An early form of this instrument was used by Francis Aston in 1920 to detect for the first time the existence of isotopes. Now it is one of the most useful instruments in the chemist's 'armoury' for accurate measurements of relative atomic and molecular masses and for structure determination, especially in organic chemistry. A form of the instrument is shown in **Figure 7.12**.

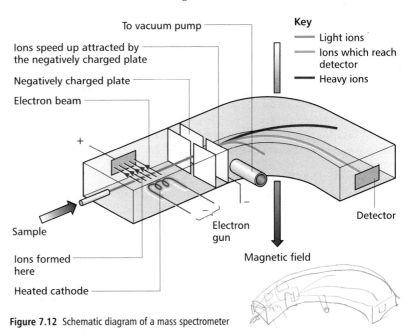

Figure 7.12 Schematic diagram of a mass spectrometer

What happens in a mass spectrometer?

● The sample to be investigated is injected directly, if a gas or a volatile liquid, or else vaporised first in an oven.
● A beam of electrons from an 'electron gun' (see the first box on page 50) then knocks out electrons from molecules of the sample to form positive ions. These are then accelerated towards plates that are held at a negative potential.
● Some ions pass through a pair of slits, which form them into a beam. The speed they reach depends on their mass. The less massive ions are moving faster.
● The beam then moves into a magnetic field at right angles to its direction of travel. This deflects the ions into an arc of a circle.

FURTHER FOCUS

The electron gun

The electron gun is a vital part of a number of pieces of apparatus. Its function is to produce a beam of electrons. This beam may be used to ionise a sample as in the mass spectrometer or in the apparatus used to measure ionisation energies (see section 7.2), or to bombard a target as in an X-ray tube (see the box 'Atomic number' in this chapter).

An anode and cathode are sealed into an apparatus from which the air has been removed. This is necessary as collisions with air molecules would stop the electron beam. The cathode is heated by a low voltage heater. This gives the mobile electrons in the metal extra kinetic energy to enable them to escape from the metal surface.

This is often referred to as 'boiling off' electrons. These electrons are attracted by the positive charge of the anode producing a high-speed beam.

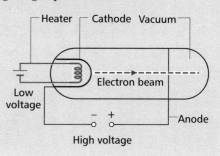

FURTHER FOCUS

Other types of mass spectrometer

The mass spectrometer described in the main text is called an 'electron ionisation magnetic sector' instrument. These terms describe the methods of producing the ions and deflecting them respectively. Other methods can be used for ionising the sample. One of these is to bombard the sample with fast-moving atoms of a noble gas such as xenon. Another is to use a laser to vaporise the surface of a solid sample. Yet another is to use an electric discharge. These techniques are useful for dealing with involatile samples (ones that do not vaporise easily) and they can also be used to control the amount of fragmentation.

Not all mass spectrometers use a magnet to deflect the ions. Time-of-flight machines measure how long different ions take to fly (undeflected) through the machine, more massive ions moving more slowly than lighter ones. Quadrupole mass spectrometers 'filter' ions of different masses using four electrodes, which carry oscillating electric fields.

To analyse mixtures, mass spectrometers are often connected directly to a gas chromatograph (GCMS) or a high performance liquid chromatograph (LCMS) (see Chapter 23, Further equilibrium). As each component of the mixture comes off the chromatograph, it is fed directly into the mass spectrometer for identification. The identification can be performed by using a computer to match the spectrum of each component with a database of spectra of known compounds.

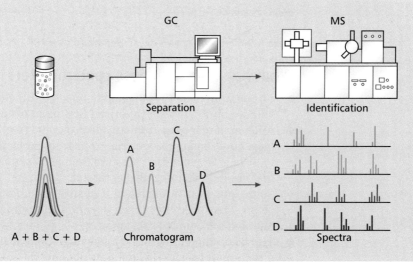

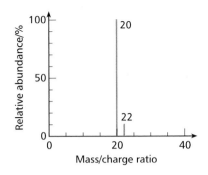

Figure 7.13 The mass spectrum of neon

The deflection depends on (a) mass (the most massive ions are deflected the least) and (b) the magnetic field strength (the stronger the field, the greater the deflection).
● The magnetic field is gradually increased so that ions of increasing mass enter the detector, which produces a signal proportional to the number of ions reaching it.

Notice that the instrument detects individual ions so that isotopes of different mass are detected separately. The output is normally presented as a graph of abundance of ions present against mass number (strictly the mass/charge ratio, but since virtually all the ions have one unit of positive charge, the two are effectively the same). For example, neon would give the trace shown in **Figure 7.13**. This shows that neon has two isotopes of mass numbers 20 and 22, present in the approximate ratio 9 : 1. Hence neon has an average relative atomic mass of:

$$[(9 \times 20) + (1 \times 22)]/10 = 20.2$$

Note that the peak height gives the *abundance* of each isotope and the horizontal scale gives the *atomic mass* of each isotope. They are often confused.

Mass spectrometry is the main method for determining relative molecular masses of compounds. During their time of flight through the mass spectrometer, some of the ions of many compounds break up or **fragment**, as the bonds have been weakened by the loss of an electron during ionisation. The fragments that are charged also appear in the mass spectrum and give useful clues to the structure of the compound. Structure determination is covered in more detail in Chapters 29, Structure determination and 38, Identifying organic compounds.

Hint: When calculating the average relative atomic mass of an element, you must take account of the abundances of the isotopes. The average relative atomic mass of neon is not 21, because there are far more atoms of the lighter isotope.

Q What is the average relative atomic mass of chlorine, which has two isotopes: ^{35}Cl (abundance 75%) and ^{37}Cl (abundance 25%)?

7.5 The ^{12}C scale of atomic masses

You are probably used to using relative atomic and molecular masses (sometimes called relative formula masses) on the scale based on the mass of a hydrogen atom as 1. Since 1961, relative atomic, and therefore molecular, masses have been based on a scale on which the mass of one atom of the isotope ^{12}C is defined as exactly 12.

The isotope ^{12}C is the only nuclide with a relative atomic mass that is exactly a whole number. For carbon itself, the relative atomic mass is 12.0111, as this is an average of several isotopes of different relative atomic masses and abundances.

On the ^{12}C scale neither the relative mass of the proton nor that of the neutron is exactly 1 (see **Table 7.4**).

Table 7.4 Relative masses of subatomic particles

Particle	A_r on ^{12}C scale
proton	1.0072
neutron	1.0086
electron	0.000 548

Thus the relative masses of other atoms are not exact whole numbers. However, the difference between the H = 1 and the ^{12}C = 12 scales is small and for many purposes relative atomic masses rounded to the nearest whole number will do for calculations.

Answer: 35.5

7.6 Summary

● Atoms consist of a dense nucleus containing	protons and neutrons (nucleons).
● Any atom with a given number of protons and neutrons is called	a nuclide.
● Nuclides are written:	$\substack{\text{mass number}\\\text{atomic number}}$ Chemical symbol
● The mass number is	the total number of nucleons (protons and neutrons).
● The atomic number or proton number is	the total number of protons.
● The atomic number governs	the chemical identity of the atom.
● The nucleus is surrounded by	electrons (clouds of negative charge).
● Electrons exist in	orbitals.
● Orbitals define	the volume of space in which an electron is likely to be found.
● Orbitals are described by	a number and a letter.
● The orbital number gives	the distance from the nucleus and hence the energy level.
● The letters s, p, d and f define	the shape of the orbital.
● Level 1 contains Level 2 contains Level 3 contains Level 4 contains	s only. s and p. s, p and d. s, p, d and f.
● Each orbital can hold up to	two electrons.
● Two electrons in the same orbital must have	opposite spins.
● The s orbital in a given level can hold	a pair of electrons.
The p orbitals in a given level can hold	three pairs of electrons.
The d orbitals in a given level can hold	five pairs of electrons.
The f orbitals in a given level can hold	seven pairs of electrons.
● When an electron jumps from one orbital to another it emits or absorbs	a single quantum of electromagnetic radiation.
● This is equal in energy to	the gap between the levels.
● This gives rise to	line spectra.
● The frequency of the lines is given by the equation	$E = h\nu$
● The convergence limit of a line spectrum allows us to find	the ionisation energy of the atom.
● The first ionisation energy for an element E is the energy change (ΔH) for	$E(g) \longrightarrow E^{+}(g) + e^{-}$

- The second ionisation energy is the energy change (ΔH) for · · · $E^+(g) \longrightarrow E^{2+}(g) + e^-$
- All ionisation energies are · · · endothermic.
- Line spectra tell us about · · · the existence of energy levels.
- Successive ionisation energies tell us · · · how many electrons are in each energy level.
- The modern instrument for measuring relative atomic masses, A_r, and relative molecular masses, M_r, is · · · the mass spectrometer.
- This can measure · · · the masses of individual isotopes.
- Relative atomic and molecular masses are now measured on · · · the ^{12}C scale.
- The relative mass of an atom of the ^{12}C isotope is defined as · · · exactly 12.

7.7 Practice questions

Use the following data as necessary:

$$h = 6.6 \times 10^{-34}\,\text{J s}$$
$$c = 3.0 \times 10^8\,\text{m s}^{-1}$$
$$\text{Avogadro constant} = 6.0 \times 10^{23}\,\text{mol}^{-1}$$

1. The electron arrangement of fluorine may be written $1s^2 2s^2 2p^5$, or more simply 2, 7. Using each of these shorthands write the electron arrangements of the elements carbon, oxygen, aluminium and potassium.

2. $^{40}_{20}V$, $^{13}_{6}W$, $^{42}_{20}X$, $^{15}_{7}Y$, $^{19}_{9}Z$
   (a) How many protons, neutrons and electrons do each of the nuclides above have?
   (V, W, X, Y, Z are not their real symbols.)
   (b) Which two are a pair of isotopes?

3. The mass spectrum of copper is given. Calculate the average relative atomic mass, A_r, of copper.

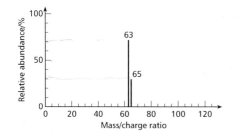

4. (a) Calculate the energy of a quantum of the following types of electromagnetic radiation:
   visible light $\lambda = 1.00 \times 10^{-6}\,\text{m}$
   ultraviolet $\nu = 1.00 \times 10^{16}\,\text{s}^{-1}$
   infra-red $\nu = 1.00 \times 10^{14}\,\text{s}^{-1}$
   γ-radiation $\lambda = 1.00 \times 10^{-14}\,\text{m}$
   (b) Calculate the energy of a mole of each type of quantum.

5. The successive ionisation energies (IEs) of sodium, Na, and magnesium, Mg, are given in kJ mo1^{-1}.

   Na: 496, 4563, 6913, 9544, 13 352, 16 611, 20 115, 25 491, 28 934, 141 367, 159 079
   Mg: 738, 1451, 7733, 10 541, 13 629, 17 995, 21 704, 25 657, 31 644, 35 463, 169 996, 189 371

   (a) What is the total energy required to form an Mg^{3+} ion from a magnesium atom, Mg?
   (b) Use the figures to explain why Mg usually forms Mg^{2+} and Na usually forms Na$^+$.
   (c) Why is each successive IE greater than the previous one?
   (d) Why is the last IE of Mg higher than the last IE of Na?

6. The first five IEs of an element are given in kJ mol^{-1}:

   578, 1817, 2745, 11 578, 14 831

   In which group of the Periodic Table would you expect it to be? Explain your answer.

7. The table gives the frequencies for lines in the Balmer series in the spectrum of hydrogen.

Line number	Frequency $\nu/10^{14}\,s^{-1}$
1	4.568
2	6.167
3	6.907
4	7.309
5	7.551
6	7.709
7	7.817
8	7.894

$\Delta\nu$ for lines 1 and 2 is $1.599 \times 10^{14}\,s^{-1}$.
Calculate $\Delta\nu$ for all the other pairs of lines, i.e. 2 and 3, 3 and 4, etc.
Plot a graph of $\Delta\nu$ against the smaller frequency of each pair of lines. Use the graph to find the frequency of the convergence limit for this series of lines (i.e. the frequency when $\Delta\nu = 0$). Using the equation $E = h\nu$, what ionisation energy does this correspond to:
(a) in joules per atom
(b) in kJ mol^{-1}?
In the Balmer series, electrons fall back to level 2. The ionisation energy from level 1 is 1312 kJ mol^{-1}. What is the energy difference between levels 1 and 2 in the hydrogen atom?

8. Use the equation $\nu = cR(1/n_1^2 - 1/n_2^2)$ where $R = 1.09 \times 10^7\,m^{-1}$, to calculate the frequency of the spectral line produced when an electron drops from level 4 to level 3 in the hydrogen atom. In which of the named series of lines does this appear?

9. The radius of a ^{238}U nucleus is 74×10^{-15} m. What is the volume of the nucleus? Remembering that it contains 238 nucleons (each of mass approximately 1.7×10^{-27} kg), what is the density of the uranium nucleus in kg m^{-3}? Compare this with the density of uranium metal (1.9×10^4 kg m^{-3}).

10. Chlorine has two isotopes, ^{35}Cl and ^{37}Cl.
(a) What three values of M_r are possible for the molecule Cl_2?
(b) Bearing in mind that the molecule might fragment, give the mass numbers of five peaks that might be expected in the mass spectrum of chlorine.

11. A quantum of electromagnetic radiation has an energy of 1×10^{-20} J. Calculate:
(a) its frequency
(b) its wavelength.
(c) Use Figure 7.2 to decide what type of electromagnetic radiation it represents.

7.8 Examination questions

1. Potassium was discovered and named in 1807 by the British chemist Sir Humphry Davy. The mass spectrum of a sample of potassium is shown below.

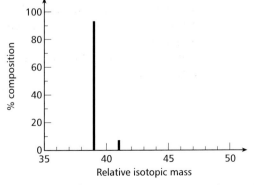

(a) (i) Use the mass spectrum to estimate the percentage composition of potassium isotopes in the sample.

Copy and complete the table below to show the percentage composition and atomic structure of each potassium isotope.

Isotope	Percentage composition	Protons	Neutrons	Electrons
^{39}K				
^{41}K				

(ii) The relative atomic mass of the potassium sample can be determined from its mass spectrum.
Explain what you understand by the term *relative atomic mass*.
(iii) Calculate the relative atomic mass of the potassium sample

(b) Complete the electronic configuration of a potassium atom.

$1s^2$

(c) The first and second ionisation energies of potassium are shown in the table below.

Ionisation	1st	2nd
Ionisation energy/kJ mol^{-1}	419	3051

(i) Explain what you understand by the term *first ionisation energy* of potassium.

(ii) Why is there a large difference between the first and the second ionisation energy of potassium?

[O & C 1997, specimen]

2. (a) Lithium, sodium and potassium all give characteristic emission spectra when their compounds are placed in a fierce, non-luminous Bunsen flame.
Account for the origin of these emission spectra.

(b) (i) Sketch the arrangement of the lines in the visible emission spectrum for atomic hydrogen.

(ii) Explain the meaning of the frequency of the convergence limit in the spectrum of atomic hydrogen.

(iii) Explain how the ionisation energy of the hydrogen atom may be derived from its atomic spectrum.

[WJEC 1997, part question]

3. (a) (i) On a copy of the diagram below, sketch the path that a beam of electrons would follow when passed through an applied electric field.

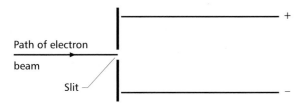

(ii) Explain the difference(s) which would be observed if the electron beam were replaced by a beam were replaced by a beam of protons passing through the applied electric field under the same conditions.

(b) Geiger and Marsden bombarded gold foil with alpha particles, which are nuclei of helium atoms, $_2^4\text{He}^{2+}$.

(i) Predict, with reasons, what happens when a rapidly moving alpha particle approaches the stationary nucleus of a gold atom.

(ii) Explain why the majority of alpha particles would pass straight through the gold foil.

(iii) Explain what is meant by *1 mole* of alpha particles.

[Oxford 1997]

4. (a) Copy and complete the table below, giving the name, relative mass and relative charge of each of the fundamental sub-atomic particles.

Particle	Relative mass	Relative charge
	1.0	
neutron		
		−1

(b) The element magnesium (atomic number 12) has three isotopes of mass numbers 24, 25 and 26, having abundances of 78.6%, 10.1% and 11.3%, respectively.
Explain the meaning of the terms:
(i) *atomic number*
(ii) *isotopes.*

(c) Before magnesium atoms can be deflected in a mass spectrometer, they must be ionised and then accelerated.
(i) Briefly explain why the atoms need to be ionised.
(ii) By what method are the ions accelerated?
(iii) By what means are the ions deflected?

(d) Define the term *relative atomic mass.*

(e) Use the information given in (b) to:
(i) calculate the relative atomic mass of magnesium, giving your answer to two decimal places;
(ii) draw the mass spectrum for magnesium on graph paper.

[AEB 1996]

8 Energetics

Living light

Chemical reactions are almost always accompanied by energy changes. One unusual way in which this energy is given out is called bioluminescence or 'living light'. This is the light given out by living organisms. You might have heard of, or even seen, fireflies and glow-worms flashing, but there are many other organisms that emit light. For example, there are bacteria, fungi, jellyfish, molluscs, crustaceans and fish which bioluminesce.

Organisms use bioluminescence to:

- attract mates
- lure their prey
- defend themselves by alarming predators

Some strange results of bioluminescence include:

- tree branches which glow when broken because of bacteria
- rotting meat and fish which give out light from a surface cover of bacteria
- swimmers glowing eerily as they strike millions of minute light-emitting organisms
- trees lit up by fireflies synchronising their flashes

Bioluminescence is unusual because almost no heat is given out in the process and so it is often described as 'cold light'. It is the result of a chemical reaction. The light-emitting organism contains a chemical such as luciferin, which reacts with oxygen in the presence of an enzyme catalyst. The product of this reaction is formed in a high-energy state (called an excited state: see section 7.2) and when it drops back to the ground state, light is given out.

A similar reaction is used in light sticks. These consist of a plastic tube containing a chemical called a phenyloxalate ester and a glass vial containing hydrogen peroxide. Bending the outer tube breaks the glass vial and the chemicals mix. The resulting reaction gives out light for several hours. Light sticks can be used to provide illumination in situations where heat might be dangerous and electricity is not available.

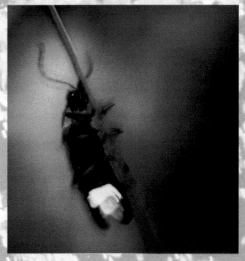

Fireflies use bioluminescence to attract their mates

Phosphorescence on the ocean is caused by bioluminescent organisms

Light sticks

Introduction

When a chemical reaction takes place, chemical bonds break and new ones are formed. Energy must be *put in* to break bonds and energy is *given out* when bonds are formed, so most chemical reactions involve an energy change. The energy may be given out or taken in.
The energy involved may be in different forms, light, electrical or most usually heat.

Studying heat changes is called **thermochemistry** and is important for both practical and theoretical reasons. Practical applications include measuring the energy values of fuels, and determining energy requirements of industrial processes. Theoretical considerations include working out the energy to break particular bonds, calculating energy changes for hypothetical reactions and predicting whether a particular reaction can take place or not: its **feasibility**.

CONCEPT CHECKPOINTS

The following basic ideas are used in this chapter. You may revise some of these topics elsewhere in the book.
- energy as the ability to do work
- the joule, J, and kilojoule, kJ, as units of energy
- balanced symbol equations (section 5.3)
- the covalent bond represented by — (section 2.2)

Did you know? Many rockets, such as those that propel the US space shuttle are powered by the exothermic reaction between hydrogen and oxygen.

8.1 What is energy?

Energy is defined as 'the ability to do work', work being the moving of a force through a distance, for example lifting a load. This is the basis of the unit of energy (and work), the joule.

One joule is the energy required to move a force of one newton through one metre in the direction of the force.

To get a feel for the size of this unit, consider that it is approximately the energy required to lift a medium-sized apple one metre vertically. To boil the water for a cup of tea requires about 80 000 J (joules), which is 80 kJ (kilojoules) in the units more usually used by chemists. Anything that can directly or indirectly move a force has energy. Heat, for example, could be used to produce steam which will drive a turbine and lift a load, electricity could turn a motor to lift a load and so on.

Enthalpy

The type of energy of most importance to chemistry is heat. The precise amount of heat given out or taken in by a reaction varies with the conditions: temperature, pressure, concentration of solutions, etc. Therefore if different experimental results are to be compared, chemists must agree on the conditions under which measurements are made. For example, we normally measure heat changes at constant pressure. This makes practical sense as it means that flasks open to the atmosphere are used, which is normal practice.

To illustrate how pressure can affect heat change, think of a reaction in which a gas is given off, such as:

$$CaCO_3(s) + 2HCl(aq) \longrightarrow CaCl_2(aq) + H_2O(l) + CO_2(g)$$

calcium carbonate   hydrochloric acid   calcium chloride   water   carbon dioxide

If the reaction is carried out in an open flask, the gas that is evolved has to push back the air in the atmosphere, thus doing work

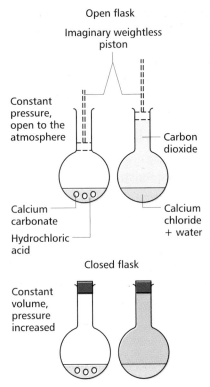

Figure 8.1 Comparison between a reaction taking place at constant pressure and the same reaction at constant volume

Hint: Sometimes an older convention for the standard pressure is still used: 101.325 kPa. This makes very little difference.

and using energy. This becomes clear if we imagine a weightless 'piston' placed across the neck of the flask, as shown in **Figure 8.1**.

In the closed flask, the pressure inside the vessel increases but there is no work done to push back the atmosphere. The total heat output, called the internal energy change, will therefore be greater in this case, since no energy is lost in pushing back the atmosphere.

However, the energy difference between these two situations is usually quite small, typically no more than a few per cent of the total energy change for the reaction.

A heat change measured at constant pressure is called an enthalpy change. Enthalpy changes are given the symbol ΔH. The Greek letter Δ (delta) is used to indicate a change in any quantity. The standard conditions for measuring enthalpies are:

pressure of 100 kPa (approximately normal atmospheric pressure)
temperature of 298 K (around normal room temperature 25 °C).

Points to watch out for

- The symbol $\Delta H_m^{\ominus}(298\text{ K})$ is used to represent an enthalpy change per mole measured under these conditions. Substances that appear in the equations will be in the states in which they exist at standard temperature (298 K) and pressure (100 kPa). For example, the equation:

$$2H_2(g) \; + \; O_2(g) \; \longrightarrow \; 2H_2O(l) \quad \Delta H_m^{\ominus}(298\text{ K}) = -572\text{ kJ mol}^{-1}$$
hydrogen   oxygen   water

refers to the formation of water as a liquid (not as steam, which would give a different value).
- Occasionally allotropes (different forms of the same element, such as graphite and diamond, which are allotropes of carbon) will be encountered. The most stable of these, which in the case of carbon is graphite, is the standard state. Graphite is given the special state symbol (gr).
- The subscript 'm', meaning molar (i.e. per mole), is often dropped, as the units of ΔH are generally stated as kJ mol^{-1}.
- The 298 K in brackets is also frequently omitted. The symbol '$\ominus$' (called 'standard') is taken to imply a pressure of 100 kPa *and* a temperature of 298 K, unless otherwise stated.
- It is important when stating enthalpy changes that the equation to which the measurement refers is given. For example, the statement 'the enthalpy change of atomisation of hydrogen is 218 kJ mol^{-1}' is ambiguous because it could refer to:

$$H_2(g) \; \longrightarrow \; 2H(g)$$
or
$$\tfrac{1}{2}H_2(g) \; \longrightarrow \; H(g)$$

The figure given actually represents the latter. The former would be 436 kJ mol^{-1}. So the equation needs to be given.

It may seem odd to refer to heat changes taking place at a constant temperature, when a heat change inevitably leads to a temperature change. The best way to regard this is to imagine the reactants starting at 298 K (see **Figure 8.2**). In this reaction, heat is given out.

The reaction is not considered to be complete *until the products have cooled back to 298 K.* The heat transferred to the surroundings while cooling is the enthalpy change for the reaction. This sort of reaction is called **exothermic**, and the convention is that ΔH **is given a negative sign.**

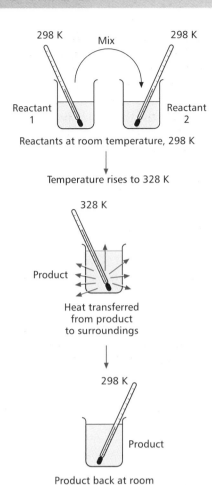

Figure 8.2 A reaction giving out heat at 298 K

Hint: When writing enthalpy changes always put in the + and − signs.

If energy needs to be absorbed in order for a reaction to take place, the reaction is called **endothermic**, and **ΔH is given a positive sign**. Endothermic reactions which take place in aqueous solution can absorb heat from the water and cool it down quite dramatically. As in the exothermic example, the reaction is not considered to be complete until the products have returned to the temperature at which they started, but in this case the solution has to absorb heat from the surroundings to do this. Unless you remember this, it can seem strange that a reaction that is absorbing heat can get cold.

> Exothermic reaction, heat given out: ΔH is negative.
> Endothermic reaction, heat taken in: ΔH is positive.

Enthalpy diagrams (energy level diagrams)

Enthalpy changes may be presented on enthalpy diagrams (see **Figure 8.3**), often called energy level diagrams. The vertical axis represents enthalpy while the horizontal axis represents the extent of reaction: the percentage change from reactants to products. Often we are interested only in the extremes: 100% reactants and 100% products (0% reactants), so the axis is left unlabelled.

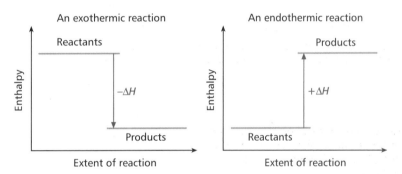

Figure 8.3 Enthalpy diagrams

CHEMISTRY AROUND US

Photosynthesis

This process is the origin of the energy used by living systems.

In green plants the following overall reaction takes place:

$$6CO_2(g) + 6H_2O(l) \longrightarrow C_6H_{12}O_6(s) + 6O_2(g)$$
$$\text{glucose}$$
$$\Delta H^\ominus = +2820 \text{ kJ mol}^{-1}$$

This is an endothermic reaction, i.e. energy is absorbed. The energy comes from light, absorbed by the green pigment in plants, chlorophyll. Glucose acts as an energy store, later releasing energy by the reverse of the reaction above. Some of the released energy appears in a molecule called adenosine triphosphate (ATP) which fuels many reactions in living cells, including protein synthesis and muscular movement.

Photosynthesis is the original source of the energy in fossil fuels.

Sunlight was the original source of energy for the charcoal in this barbecue

Q How much heat is needed to heat 300 g of water from 20 °C to 100 °C? This is approximately the energy needed to make a cup of tea.

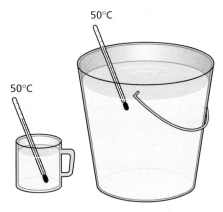

50°C

50°C

Figure 8.4 The water in the bucket has the same temperature as that in the cup but the water in the bucket has more heat

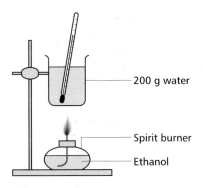

200 g water

Spirit burner

Ethanol

Figure 8.5 A simple calorimeter

A temperature rise of 8 K is the same as a temperature rise of 8 °C because both units are the same size. Only the zeros of the scales differ.

Answer: 10.1 kJ

8.2 Measurement of enthalpy changes: calorimetry

Before tackling this, we must be clear about the difference between heat and temperature. These words are often used interchangeably in daily conversation but as scientific terms they are quite distinct.

Essentially, temperature represents the *average* kinetic energy of the particles in a system, and is independent of the *number* present.

Heat is a measure of the *total* energy in a given amount of substance. It *does* depend on how much of the substance is present.

For example two buckets of hot water at 50 °C have twice as much *heat* as one bucketful although both have the *same temperature.* Temperature is measured by a thermometer, which takes no account of the amount of substance present. It would give the same reading in a mugful or a bucketful of the same water (see **Figure 8.4**).

Heat always flows from high to low temperature, so heat will flow from a red hot nail into a bucket full of lukewarm water, even though the total heat content of the water is greater than that of the nail.

To measure heat we must take into account the temperature, the mass of the substance and the type of substance itself, because some substances take more heat to raise their temperatures than others.

The amount of heat needed to raise the temperature of 1 g of substance by 1 K is called the **specific heat capacity,** c.

For water the specific heat capacity is 4.2 J g^{-1} K^{-1}, an unusually high figure.

There is no instrument which measures heat directly. We have to arrange for the heat we wish to measure to be transferred into a known mass of a substance (usually water) and then we must measure the temperature rise. The heat is then given by the expression:

$$\text{Heat} = \text{mass of water} \times \text{specific heat capacity} \times \text{temperature rise}$$
$$\text{Heat} = m \times c \times \Delta T$$

The apparatus used is called a **calorimeter** (from the Latin *calor*, meaning 'heat').

The simple calorimeter

Figure 8.5 shows the simplest form of calorimeter being used to measure the enthalpy change of combustion (ΔH_c) of ethanol:

$$C_2H_5OH(l) + 3O_2(g) \longrightarrow 2CO_2(g) + 3H_2O(l)$$

If 0.46 g (0.010 mol) of ethanol is burned, a temperature rise of the water of 8.0 K is found.

$$\text{Heat} = m \times c \times \Delta T$$
$$= 200 \times 4.2 \times 8 = 6720 \text{ J}$$

0.01 mol gives   6720 J
1 mol would give   672 000 J or 672 kJ
$$\Delta H_c = 670 \text{ kJ mol}^{-1} \text{ (to 2 s.f.)}$$

As the experiment was not necessarily done under standard conditions, the symbol '$\ominus$' should not, strictly speaking, be used, but the difference will be small.

FURTHER FOCUS

Definition of terms

$\Delta H^\ominus$, the enthalpy change of reaction, is the general name for the enthalpy change for any reaction. Some commonly used enthalpy changes are given names, though it is always better to give an equation for the reaction to avoid ambiguity. Some enthalpy changes that have particular definitions follow. Note that the word 'molar' is used to mean 'per mole', rather than ' moles per dm³'. All values are corrected to standard conditions (298 K, 100 kPa).

1. **Standard molar enthalpy change of formation, $\Delta H_f^\ominus$**
   The enthalpy change for the formation of one mole of a compound from its elements.
   For example:

   $$H_2(g) + \tfrac{1}{2}O_2(g) \longrightarrow H_2O(l) \qquad \Delta H_f^\ominus = -286 \text{ kJ mol}^{-1}$$

   Note that the elements and compounds are all in the state (gas, liquid or solid) that they are in under standard conditions (298 K, 100 kPa) even though the reaction may not actually take place under these conditions.

2. **Standard molar enthalpy change of combustion, $\Delta H_c^\ominus$**
   The enthalpy change when one mole of substance is completely burned in oxygen.
   For example:

   $$CH_4(g) + 2O_2(g) \longrightarrow CO_2(g) + 2H_2O(l)$$
   $$\Delta H_c^\ominus = -890 \text{ kJ mol}^{-1}$$

3. **Standard molar enthalpy change of atomisation, $\Delta H_{at}^\ominus$**
   The enthalpy change when one mole of a substance decomposes completely into gaseous atoms.
   For example:

   $$\tfrac{1}{2}Cl_2(g) \longrightarrow Cl(g) \qquad \Delta H_{at}^\ominus = +121 \text{ kJ mol}^{-1}$$

   Note that this is given per mole of chlorine atoms and not per mole of chlorine molecules. It is particularly important to have an equation to refer to for this type of enthalpy change.

4. **Standard molar enthalpy change of lattice formation (often called lattice energy or LE), $\Delta H_L^\ominus$**
   The enthalpy change when one mole of ionic compound is formed from its gaseous ions.
   For example:

   $$Na^+(g) + Cl^-(g) \longrightarrow NaCl(s) \qquad \Delta H_L^\ominus = -780 \text{ kJ mol}^{-1}$$

5. **Standard molar enthalpy change of first ionisation (first ionisation energy, 1st IE)**
   The enthalpy change when one mole of gaseous atoms is converted into singly positively charged ions.
   For example:

   $$Na(g) \longrightarrow Na^+(g) + e^- \qquad \Delta H^\ominus = +496 \text{ kJ mol}^{-1}$$

   Note: The molar enthalpy change of second ionisation (second ionisation energy, 2nd IE) refers to the loss of a mole of electrons from a mole of singly positively charged ions.
   For example:

   $$Na^+(g) \longrightarrow Na^{2+}(g) + e^- \qquad \Delta H^\ominus = +4563 \text{ kJ mol}^{-1}$$

6. **Standard molar enthalpy change of electron gain (electron affinity, EA, or first electron affinity)**
   The enthalpy change when a mole of gaseous atoms is converted to a mole of singly negatively charged ions.
   For example:

   $$O(g) + e^- \longrightarrow O^-(g) \qquad \Delta H^\ominus = -141 \text{ kJ mol}^{-1}$$

   Note that the second electron affinity refers to the addition of a mole of electrons to a mole of singly negatively charged ions.
   For example:

   $$O^-(g) + e^- \longrightarrow O^{2-}(g) \qquad \Delta H^\ominus = +798 \text{ kJ mol}^{-1}$$

7. **Standard molar enthalpy change of bond dissociation (bond dissociation energy)**
   This refers to a specific bond in a specific compound, in molar amounts as specified by an equation.
   For example:

   $$CH_4(g) \longrightarrow CH_3(g) + H(g) \qquad \Delta H^\ominus = +425 \text{ kJ mol}^{-1}$$

8. **Mean standard molar enthalpy change of bond dissociation (mean molar bond dissociation energy)**
   This refers to the average molar enthalpy change of bond dissociation of all the same bonds in the same molecule.
   For example:

   $$\tfrac{1}{4}CH_4(g) \longrightarrow C(g) + 4H(g)) \qquad \Delta H^\ominus = +416 \text{ kJ mol}^{-1}$$

   Average bond energies in tables refer to an average of the mean molar bond dissociation energy of several compounds for the bond under consideration. These are referred to as 'tabulated bond enthalpies (or energies)'.

9. **Standard molar enthalpy change of neutralisation, $\Delta H_{neut}^\ominus$**
   The enthalpy change when one mole of acid reacts with one mole of base to form one mole of water.
   For example:

   $$HCl(aq) + NaOH(aq) \longrightarrow NaCl(aq) + H_2O(l)$$
   $$\Delta H_{neut}^\ominus = -58 \text{ kJ mol}^{-1}$$

10. **Standard molar enthalpy change of dissolution $\Delta H_{solution}^\ominus$**
    The enthalpy change when one mole of a substance is dissolved in sufficient solvent to make one dm³ of solution.
    For example:

    $$NaCl(s) + aq \longrightarrow NaCl(aq) \qquad \Delta H_{solution}^\ominus = +1 \text{ kJ mol}^{-1}$$

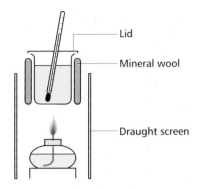

Figure 8.6 An improved calorimeter

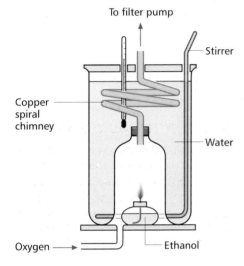

Figure 8.7 A flame calorimeter

This value is about half the 'accepted' value. It is such a poor approximation because:

● some heat never enters the calorimeter, because of draughts, for example
● heat is lost from the top and sides of the calorimeter
● heat goes into the material of the beaker rather than the water
● incomplete combustion occurs. In a restricted supply of oxygen, some of the ethanol will not burn completely, giving carbon and carbon monoxide rather than carbon dioxide. Soot (carbon) on the bottom of the beaker will show whether this has happened.

Despite these disadvantages, the simple calorimeter may be satisfactory for comparing the ΔH_c values of a series of similar compounds, as the errors will be comparable.

Improvements may be made to this simple calorimeter by insulating the sides of the beaker, using a lid and providing a draught screen as shown in **Figure 8.6**.

The flame calorimeter

This is a more sophisticated version of the simple calorimeter. It is shown in **Figure 8.7**. The chimney is made of copper, to conduct heat from the combustion products to the water. The flame is enclosed, to reduce heat loss. Oxygen is supplied to ensure complete combustion.

The heat output may be calculated in one of three ways :

1. As before (i.e. heat = $m \times c \times \Delta T$). We need to do a separate calculation for each of the materials of the calorimeter (copper, glass, rubber) as well as the water.

2. The **heat capacity** of the whole apparatus may be measured by burning in the apparatus a substance whose molar enthalpy change of combustion, $\Delta H_c^{\ominus}$, we know. The heat capacity of the apparatus is the heat needed to raise the temperature of the whole apparatus by 1 K, so:

heat capacity of the calorimeter = heat change/temperature change

Since heat losses will be similar for both the calibration and the experiment, these will tend to cancel out and be eliminated.

Benzenecarboxylic acid ($M_r = 122$) – sometimes called benzoic acid – is often used to calibrate calorimeters as its molar enthalpy change of combustion, $\Delta H_c^{\ominus}$, is accurately known and the compound can be obtained very pure.

The following example shows how to determine the heat capacity of a calorimeter and then use it for further enthalpy determinations.

1.22 g (0.0100 mol) of benzenecarboxylic acid was burned in a flame calorimeter and gave a temperature rise of 10.00 K. $\Delta H_c^{\ominus}$ for benzenecarboxylic acid is 3230 kJ mol^{-1}, so burning 0.010 mol benzenecarboxylic acid would produce 32.3 kJ of heat. This raises the temperature of the calorimeter by 10.00 K.

But as we have seen above, the heat capacity of the calorimeter = heat change/temperature change, so heat capacity = 32.3/10.00 kJ K^{-1} = 3.23 kJ K^{-1}

0.460 g (0.0100 mol) of ethanol was burned in the same calorimeter producing a temperature rise of 4.00 K.

heat produced by the ethanol = heat capacity × temperature change

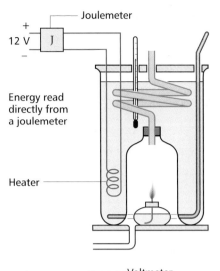

Joulemeter

+
12 V   J
−

Energy read
directly from
a joulemeter

Heater

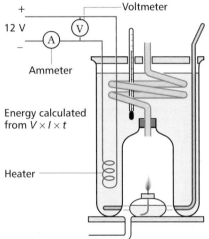

Voltmeter

+
12 V
−   A   V

Ammeter

Energy calculated
from $V \times I \times t$

Heater

Figure 8.8 Electrical methods for determining enthalpy change of combustion

$$= 4.00 \, \text{K} \times 3.23 \, \text{kJ K}^{-1}$$
$$= 12.9 \, \text{kJ}$$

0.01 mol ethanol produces   12.9 kJ
1 mol ethanol produces   1290 kJ
ΔH_c of ethanol $= -1290 \, \text{kJ mol}^{-1}$ (to 3 s.f.)

Note the difference between this value and that determined by a simple calorimeter.

3. An electrical method may be used. After burning the ethanol, the calorimeter is refilled with water and a small electric immersion heater placed in it. This is switched on until the same temperature rise is produced as was produced by burning the ethanol. Again the heat losses in both experiments will cancel out. The heat produced by the heater can be measured by an electrical joulemeter, which records the energy directly. It can also be determined by measuring the voltage, V, and current, I, of the heater and the time, t, for which it ran. Then the following expression is used:

$$\text{energy} = V \times I \times t$$

where V = voltage of heater, I = current, t = time in seconds. Both set-ups are shown in **Figure 8.8**

Measuring enthalpy changes of reactions in solution

The methods already described dealt with combustion reactions. The situation is simpler with reactions that take place in solution. The heat is generated in the solutions themselves and merely has to be kept in the calorimeter. Such experiments are often carried out in expanded polystyrene beakers. These are good insulators and have a low heat capacity and thus absorb little heat. We usually take the specific heat capacity of dilute solutions to be the same as that of water, $4.2 \, \text{J g}^{-1} \text{K}^{-1}$.

Neutralisation reactions

For example, to find the standard molar enthalpy change of reaction, $\Delta H^{\ominus}$, for

$$\text{HCl(aq)} \quad + \quad \text{NaOH(aq)} \quad \longrightarrow \quad \text{NaCl(aq)} \quad + \quad \text{H}_2\text{O(l)}$$

hydrochloric   sodium   sodium   water
acid   hydroxide   chloride

50.0 cm³ of 1.00 mol dm⁻³ hydrochloric acid and 50.0 cm³ of 1.0 mol dm⁻³ sodium hydroxide solution were mixed in an expanded polystyrene beaker. The temperature rose by 6.6 K.

The total volume of the mixture is 100 cm³ which has a mass of approximately 100 g.

$$\text{heat produced} = m \times c \times \Delta T$$
$$= 100 \times 4.2 \times 6.6$$
$$= 2772 \, \text{J}$$

This is produced by $\dfrac{50.0 \times 1}{1000} = 0.05 \, \text{mol}$

so   1 mol would give $\dfrac{2772}{0.05} \, \text{J}$

$$= 55\,440 \, \text{J}$$
$$= 55 \, \text{kJ (to 2 s.f.)}$$
$$\Delta H^{\ominus} = -55 \, \text{kJ mol}^{-1} \quad \text{(negative as heat is given out)}$$

Hint: Remember to use the total volume of the mixture, 100 cm³. A common mistake would be to use 50 cm³.

FURTHER FOCUS

The bomb calorimeter

This is the most accurate method for measuring enthalpies of combustion and it is how accurate 'Data Book' values are determined.

The actual 'bomb' is a thick stainless steel pressure vessel into which the sample is placed in a crucible. A 'wick' leads from the sample to an electrical ignition coil. The bomb is filled with oxygen at a pressure of several atmospheres, sealed and placed in a calorimeter full of water which itself sits in a water-filled tank. The sample is ignited electrically and as the heat passes into the calorimeter, a thermostat and heater ensure that the water in the outer tank is kept at the same temperature as the water in the calorimeter. This eliminates heat loss from the calorimeter as its surroundings are always at its own temperature. The heat capacity of the calorimeter is calibrated by the combustion of benzenecarboxylic acid as in the flame calorimeter. The mass of the sample is determined to within 0.0001 g and the temperature measured to three places of decimals using a platinum resistance thermometer.

Since the reaction takes place in a sealed container, the energy change measured is not in fact the enthalpy change. However, there is a simple relationship between the measured energy change and the enthalpy change.

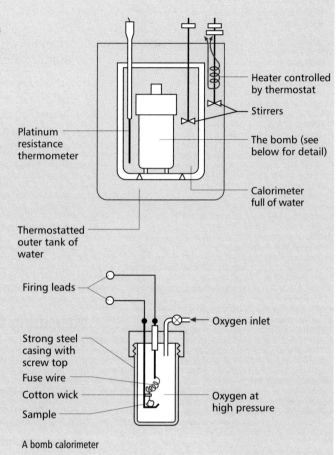

A bomb calorimeter

For more accurate work a vacuum flask can replace the polystyrene beaker and the electrical compensation method as described above can be used. This has the advantage that the specific heat capacity of the solution does not need to be known.

For example, to find the standard molar enthalpy change of

$$\underset{\text{nitric acid}}{HNO_3(aq)} \;+\; \underset{\text{sodium hydroxide}}{NaOH(aq)} \longrightarrow \underset{\text{sodium nitrate}}{NaNO_3(aq)} \;+\; \underset{\text{water}}{H_2O(l)}$$

100 cm^3 of 1 mol dm^{-3} nitric acid solution and 100 cm^3 of 1 mol dm^{-3} sodium hydroxide solution were mixed in a vacuum flask. A temperature rise of 6.8 K was noted. The solutions were allowed to cool back to room temperature and next heated with an electrical immersion heater connected to a joulemeter. 5600 J were required to produce the same temperature rise as before.

So 5600 J was produced by $\dfrac{100 \times 1}{1000}$ mol $= \frac{1}{10}$ mol

So 1 mol would produce 56 000 J
$$= 56 \text{ kJ}$$
So $\Delta H^{\ominus} = -56 \text{ kJ mol}^{-1}$ (negative as heat is given out)

The close agreement between the results of this experiment and the last one is no coincidence. If we look at the reactions ionically, we see that the Cl^-, NO_3^-, and Na^+ ions take no part in the reactions:

they are **spectator ions**. Eliminating these from the reactions shows that both reactions are the same.

1. $H^+(aq) + Cl^-(aq) + Na^+(aq) + OH^-(aq)$
   $\longrightarrow H_2O(l) + Cl^-(aq) + Na^+(aq)$
   which leaves $H^+(aq) + OH^-(aq) \longrightarrow H_2O(l)$

2. $H^+(aq) + NO_3^-(aq) + Na^+(aq) + OH^-(aq)$
   $\longrightarrow H_2O(l) + NO_3^-(aq) + Na^+(aq)$
   which leaves $H^+(aq) + OH^-(aq) \longrightarrow H_2O(l)$ once more

In fact *all* neutralisation reactions involving a strong acid and a strong base (see Chapter 12) have the same standard molar enthalpy change.

> **Q** Write the ionic equation for the reaction between sulphuric acid and sodium hydroxide and show that this neutralisation will have the same value of $\Delta H^\ominus$ per mole of H^+ ions as the reactions in 1. and 2.

8.3 Hess's law

Hess's law states that the total energy (or enthalpy) change for a chemical reaction is the same, whatever route is taken. It is the outcome of a vast number of measurements of energy changes. It is also a consequence of a more general physical law: the Law of Conservation of Energy, sometimes called the First Law of Thermodynamics, which states that energy can never be created or destroyed. To see what Hess's law means, let us take an example.

Ethyne reacts with two moles of hydrogen molecules to give ethane:

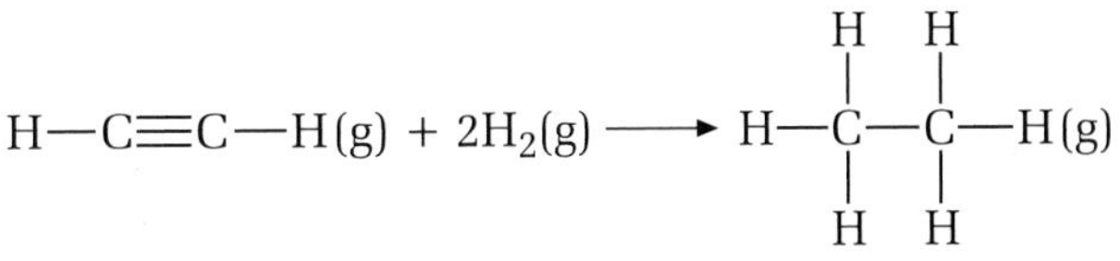

ethyne   ethane

> **Did you know?** Of the two allotropes of carbon, graphite and diamond, graphite is lower in energy by 2 kJ mol^{-1}. This means that diamond is actually less stable than graphite, which may surprise those with diamond jewellery!

> **Did you know?** The combustion of ethyne is of great practical importance. The non-systematic name for ethyne is acetylene and its combustion provides the heat for oxy-acetylene welding and cutting torches.

This reaction could take place directly *or* ethyne could react first with one mole of hydrogen molecules to give ethene, which could then react with a second mole of hydrogen to give ethane.

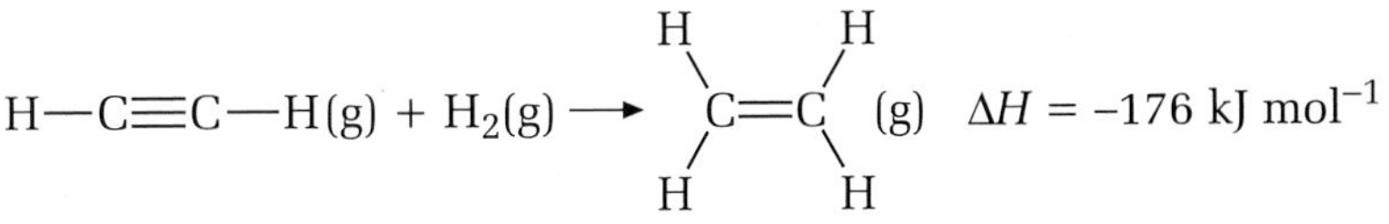

ethyne   ethene

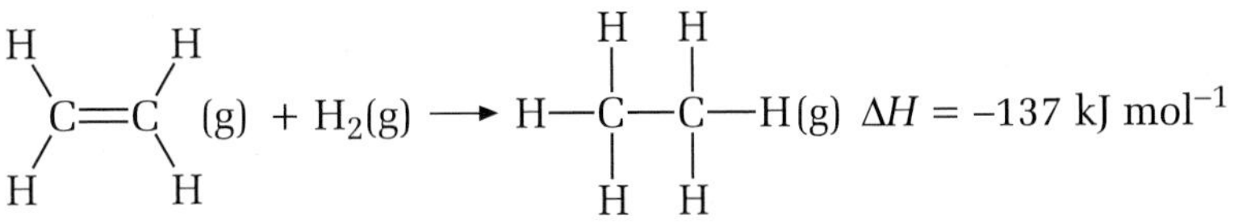

ethane

Answer: $2H^+(aq) + SO_4^{2-}(aq) + 2Na^+(aq) + 2OH^-(aq)$
$\longrightarrow 2H_2O(l) + SO_4^{2-}(aq) + 2Na^+(aq)$
which leaves $2H^+(aq) + 2OH^-(aq)$
$\longrightarrow 2H_2O$, or $H^+(aq) + OH^-(aq) \longrightarrow H_2O(l)$

Hess's law states that the total energy change is the same whichever route is taken, direct or via ethene (or, in fact, any other route).

$$\text{H}-\text{C}\equiv\text{C}-\text{H(g)} + 2\text{H}_2\text{(g)} \xrightarrow[1.]{\Delta H_1 \ (?)} \text{H}-\underset{\underset{\text{H}}{|}}{\overset{\overset{\text{H}}{|}}{\text{C}}}-\underset{\underset{\text{H}}{|}}{\overset{\overset{\text{H}}{|}}{\text{C}}}-\text{H(g)}$$

$\Delta H_2\ (-176\ \text{kJ mol}^{-1})$ 2.   3. $\Delta H_3\ (-137\ \text{kJ mol}^{-1})$

$$\underset{\text{H}}{\overset{\text{H}}{\diagdown}}\text{C}=\text{C}\underset{\text{H}}{\overset{\text{H}}{\diagup}}\text{(g)}$$

$$+\ \text{H}_2\text{(g)}$$

Hess's law tells us that $\Delta H_1 = \Delta H_2 + \Delta H_3$

The actual figures are:

$$\Delta H_2 = -176\ \text{kJ mol}^{-1}$$
$$\Delta H_3 = -137\ \text{kJ mol}^{-1}$$
So $\Delta H_1 = -176 + -137 = -313\ \text{kJ mol}^{-1}$

Another alternative route might be via the elements carbon and hydrogen, i.e. ethyne is converted to its elements, carbon and hydrogen, which then can react to form ethane.

$$\text{H}-\text{C}\equiv\text{C}-\text{H(g)} + 2\text{H}_2\text{(g)} \xrightarrow[1.]{\Delta H_1 \ (?)} \text{H}-\underset{\underset{\text{H}}{|}}{\overset{\overset{\text{H}}{|}}{\text{C}}}-\underset{\underset{\text{H}}{|}}{\overset{\overset{\text{H}}{|}}{\text{C}}}-\text{H(g)}$$

ΔH_4 4.   5. ΔH_5

$$2\text{C(gr)} + 3\text{H}_2\text{(g)}$$

Hess"s law tells us that $\Delta H_1 = \Delta H_4 + \Delta H_5$

ΔH_5 is the enthalpy of formation of ethane, $\Delta H_f^{\ominus}$, while reaction 4 is the *reverse* of the formation of ethyne. Another consequence of Hess's law is that the **reverse of a reaction has the negative of its ΔH value.**

The values we need are $\Delta H_f^{\ominus}(\text{C}_2\text{H}_2) = +228\ \text{kJ mol}^{-1}$
and $\Delta H_f^{\ominus}(\text{C}_2\text{H}_6) = -85\ \text{kJ mol}^{-1}$

So $\Delta H_4 = -228\ \text{kJ mol}^{-1}$
(Remember to change the sign.)
$$\Delta H_5 = -85\ \text{kJ mol}^{-1}$$

Thus $\Delta H_1 = -228 + -85$
$$= -313\ \text{kJ mol}^{-1}$$

which was the result we got from the previous method, as we should expect from Hess's law.

You may have noticed that in reaction 4 there are two moles of hydrogen 'spare' as only one of the three moles of hydrogen is involved.

$$\text{H}-\text{C}\equiv\text{C}-\text{H(g)} \longrightarrow 2\text{C(gr)} + \text{H}_2\text{(g)}$$

is the reaction we are considering , but we have:

$$\text{H}-\text{C}\equiv\text{C}-\text{H(g)} + 2\text{H}_2\text{(g)} \longrightarrow 2\text{C(gr)} + 3\text{H}_2\text{(g)}$$

However, this makes no difference. The 'extra' hydrogen *is not involved in the reaction* and there is no ΔH to consider. We could

Hint: Remember the special state symbol (gr) for graphite. Graphite, not diamond, is the standard state of carbon.

have added any amount of any other substance which is not involved and the same would be true. This point comes up again in the next example, which is a third way of calculating the enthalpy change for the original reaction.

This time we will go via the enthalpy changes of combustion of the starting material and product. This is of particular importance since all three substances involved, ethyne, hydrogen and ethane, burn readily, which means their enthalpy changes of combustion can be easily measured.

Hints:
1. Both reactions 6 *and* 7 have to occur to get from the starting materials to the combustion products. Do not forget the hydrogen.
2. In this case there are two moles of hydrogen, so we need *twice* the value of ΔH_c, which refers to one mole of hydrogen.
$$\Delta H_c^{\ominus}(C_2H_2) = -1301 \text{ kJ mol}^{-1}$$
$$\Delta H_c^{\ominus}(H_2) = -286 \text{ kJ mol}^{-1}$$
$$\Delta H_c^{\ominus}(C_2H_6) = -1560 \text{ kJ mol}^{-1}$$

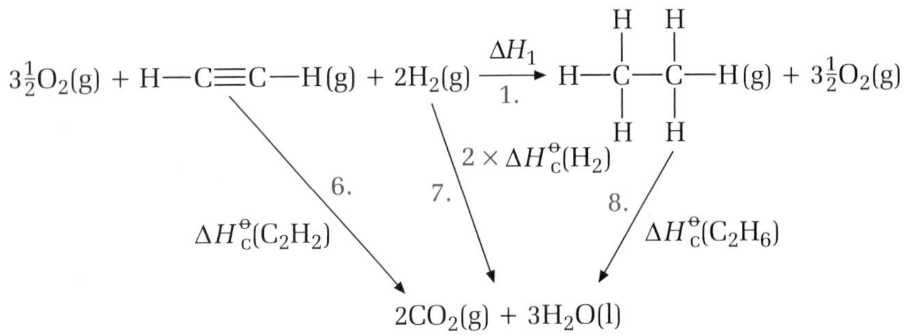

Putting in the figures:

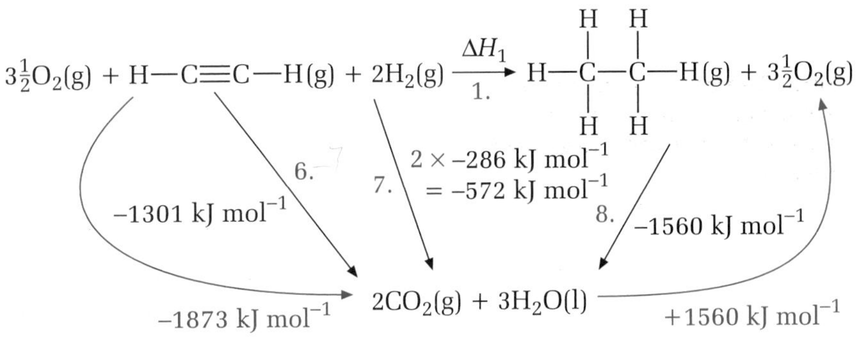

If we want the enthalpy change for reaction 1 we must go round the cycle in the direction of the red arrows. We are dealing with the reverse of reaction 8 and so its sign must change.

So

$$\Delta H_1 = -1873 + 1560 \text{ kJ mol}^{-1}$$
$$\Delta H_2 = -313 \text{ kJ mol}^{-1}$$

again, the same answer as before.

Notice that in reaction 1 there are $3\frac{1}{2}$ moles of oxygen on either side of the equation. They take no part in the reaction and do not affect the value of ΔH.

The above instances are examples of **thermochemical cycles** and show how we use Hess's law to calculate ΔH's which cannot be measured directly either because the reaction does not take place at all, does not take place under the required conditions (298 K, 100 kPa) or cannot easily or safely be carried out in a calorimeter.

Lattice energies (see section 9.1) refer to reactions which cannot be brought about at all. So, these *can only* be calculated using Hess's law.

Enthalpy diagrams

It is often useful to put thermochemical cycles, like those above, on enthalpy diagrams. These show the relative energy levels of different species (including reactants and products) on a vertical scale of increasing energy. This allows us to compare their relative energies. If a species is of lower energy than another, it is said to be energetically more stable.

Hint: This convention means that the standard state of oxygen, for example, is O_2 and not separate O atoms.

So far, all the data we have considered have been enthalpy *changes*, not absolute values. When drawing enthalpy diagrams it is useful to have a zero to work from.

By convention, the enthalpies of elements in their standard states (i.e. at 298 K and 100 kPa) are taken as zero.

Here are some further examples of thermochemical cycles presented both as cycles and as enthalpy diagrams.

Example 1

What is $\Delta H^{\ominus}$ for the change from methoxymethane to ethanol (the compounds are a pair of isomers, i.e. they have the same formula but different structures)?

$$
\begin{array}{cc}
\begin{array}{ccc}
 & \text{H} & \text{H} \\
 & | & | \\
\text{H}-\text{C}-\text{O}-\text{C}-\text{H} \\
 & | & | \\
 & \text{H} & \text{H}
\end{array}
&
\begin{array}{ccc}
\text{H} & \text{H} & \\
| & | & \\
\text{H}-\text{C}-\text{C}-\text{O}-\text{H} \\
| & | & \\
\text{H} & \text{H} &
\end{array}
\\
\text{methoxymethane} & \text{ethanol}
\end{array}
$$

The standard molar enthalpy changes of formation of the two compounds are:

$$
\begin{array}{lll}
CH_3OCH_3 & \Delta H_f^{\ominus} = -184 \text{ kJ mol}^{-1} \\
C_2H_5OH & \Delta H_f^{\ominus} = -277 \text{ kJ mol}^{-1}
\end{array}
$$

Using a thermochemical cycle

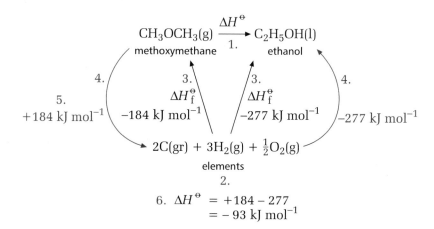

$$
\begin{aligned}
\text{6. } \Delta H^{\ominus} &= +184 - 277 \\
&= -93 \text{ kJ mol}^{-1}
\end{aligned}
$$

1. Write an equation for the reaction.
2. Write down the elements in the two compounds with the correct quantities of each.
3. Put in the $\Delta H_f^{\ominus}$ values with arrows showing the direction, i.e. *from* elements *to* compounds.
4. Put in the arrows to go from starting materials to products via the elements (the red arrows).
5. Reverse the sign of $\Delta H_f^{\ominus}$ if the red arrow is in the reverse direction to the black arrow.
6. Go round the cycle in the direction of the red arrows and add up the ΔH values as you go (taking account of the signs).

Hess's law tells us that this is the same as $\Delta H^{\ominus}$ for the direct reaction.

Using an enthalpy diagram

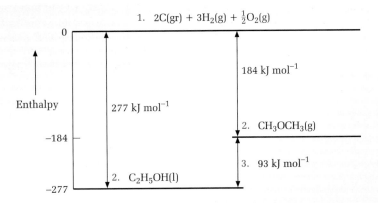

1. 2C(gr) + 3H$_2$(g) + $\frac{1}{2}$O$_2$(g)

184 kJ mol^{-1}

277 kJ mol^{-1}

2. CH$_3$OCH$_3$(g)

3. 93 kJ mol^{-1}

2. C$_2$H$_5$OH(l)

Enthalpy

0

−184

−277

1. Draw a line at level 0 to represent the elements.
2. Look up the values of $\Delta H_f^{\ominus}$ for each compound and enter these on the enthalpy diagrams, taking account of the signs: negative values are below 0, positive values are above.
3. Find the difference in levels between the two compounds. This represents the difference in their enthalpies.
4. $\Delta H^{\ominus}$ is the difference in levels, taking account of the direction of change. Up is positive and down negative. From methoxymethane to ethanol is *down*, so the sign is negative, i.e.:

$$CH_3COCH_3(g) \longrightarrow CH_3CH_2OH(l) \qquad \Delta H^{\ominus} = -93 \text{ kJ mol}^{-1}$$

Example 2

To find $\Delta H^{\ominus}$ for the reaction:

$$NH_3(g) + HBr(g) \longrightarrow NH_4Br(s)$$

The standard molar enthalpy changes of formation of the compounds are:

NH$_3$	$\Delta H_f^{\ominus} = -46$ kJ mol^{-1}
HBr	$\Delta H_f^{\ominus} = -36$ kJ mol^{-1}
NH$_4$Br	$\Delta H_f^{\ominus} = -271$ kJ mol^{-1}

Using a thermochemical cycle

1.

$$NH_3(g) + HBr(g) \xrightarrow{\Delta H^{\ominus}} NH_4Br(s)$$

3. $\Delta H_f^{\ominus}$ −46 kJ mol^{-1}

3. $\Delta H_f^{\ominus}$ −36 kJ mol^{-1}

3. $\Delta H_f^{\ominus}$ −271 kJ mol^{-1}

4.

4.

+82 kJ mol^{-1} $\frac{1}{2}$N$_2$(g) + 2H$_2$(g) + $\frac{1}{2}$Br$_2$(g)   −271 kJ mol^{-1}

2.

$$\Delta H^{\ominus} = +46 + 36 + -271 \text{ kJ mol}^{-1}$$
$$\Delta H^{\ominus} = -189 \text{ kJ mol}^{-1}$$

1. Write an equation for the reaction.
2. Write down the elements.
3. Put in the $\Delta H_f^{\ominus}$ values with arrows showing the direction, i.e. *from* elements *to* compounds.
4. Put in the arrows to go from the starting materials to products via the elements (the red arrows).

5. Reverse the sign of $\Delta H^{\ominus}$ if the red arrow is in the opposite direction to the black arrow.
6. Go round the cycle in the direction of the red arrows and add up the values of $\Delta H^{\ominus}$ as you go.

Using an enthalpy diagram

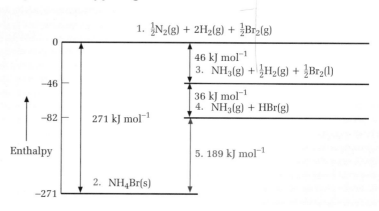

Hint: When drawing enthalpy diagrams use a rough scale, e.g. one line on lined paper ≈ 50 kJ mol^{-1}.

1. Draw a line at level 0 to represent the elements.
2. Draw in NH_4Br 271 kJ mol^{-1} below this.
3. Draw a line representing ammonia 46 kJ mol^{-1} below the level of the elements. There is still $\frac{1}{2}H_2$ and $\frac{1}{2}Br_2$ left unused.
4. Draw a line 36 kJ mol^{-1} below ammonia. This represents hydrogen bromide.
5. Find the difference in levels between the NH_3 + HBr line and the NH_4Br one. This represents $\Delta H^{\ominus}$ for the reaction. As the change from NH_3 + HBr to NH_4Br is 'downhill', $\Delta H^{\ominus}$ must be negative, i.e.:

$$NH_3(g) + HBr(g) \longrightarrow NH_4Br(s) \qquad \Delta H^{\ominus} = -189 \text{ kJ mol}^{-1}$$

8.4 Bond enthalpies

Did you know? The upper limit of bond energies is about 1000 kJ mol^{-1}. The C≡O bond in carbon monoxide has a bond energy of 1077 kJ mol^{-1}.

The idea of bond enthalpies, often called bond energies, is to apportion an amount of enthalpy to each covalent bond in a molecule. This energy has to be *put in* to break the bond and is *given out* when the bond is formed.

The **standard molar enthalpy change of bond dissociation (bond dissociation energy)** refers to a specific bond in a specific molecule. So methane, CH_4, has four different bond dissociation enthalpies.

$$
\begin{aligned}
CH_4(g) &\longrightarrow CH_3(g) + H(g) & \Delta H^{\ominus} &= +424 \text{ kJ mol}^{-1} \\
CH_3(g) &\longrightarrow CH_2(g) + H(g) & \Delta H^{\ominus} &= +480 \text{ kJ mol}^{-1} \\
CH_2(g) &\longrightarrow CH(g) + H(g) & \Delta H^{\ominus} &= +425 \text{ kJ mol}^{-1} \\
CH(g) &\longrightarrow C(g) + H(g) & \Delta H^{\ominus} &= +335 \text{ kJ mol}^{-1}
\end{aligned}
$$

The average of these corresponding to:

$$\tfrac{1}{4}(CH_4(g) \longrightarrow C(g) + 4H(g)) \qquad \Delta H^{\ominus} = +416 \text{ kJ mol}^{-1}$$

is called the **mean molar bond dissociation enthalpy** and is an average for the bonds in the specific compound methane.

The mean molar bond dissociation enthalpy will vary slightly for C—H bonds in other compounds and the average of these over several compounds is often used: the '**tabulated' bond enthalpy** or just **bond enthalpy**. It is often just called bond energy.

As bond energies are only averages, calculations done by applying bond energies to specific compounds can give only approximate answers. Nevertheless, they are useful and are quick and easy to use. A thermochemical cycle can be used to calculate the mean bond dissociation enthalpy.

$$CH_4(g) \xrightarrow{\Delta H^\ominus} C(g) \quad + \quad 4H(g)$$

$\Delta H_f^\ominus$ -75 kJ mol^{-1}

$\Delta H_{at}^\ominus$ $+717 \text{ kJ mol}^{-1}$

$4 \times \Delta H_{at}^\ominus$ $4 \times +218 \text{ kJ mol}^{-1}$ $= +872 \text{ kJ mol}^{-1}$

$$C(gr) \quad + \quad 2H_2(g) \xrightarrow{\hspace{3cm}} +1589 \text{ kJ mol}^{-1}$$

$+75 \text{ kJ mol}^{-1}$

$$\Delta H^\ominus = +75 + 1589 \text{ kJ mol}^{-1}$$
$$\Delta H^\ominus = +1664 \text{ kJ mol}^{-1}$$

$\Delta H_{at}^\ominus$: the subscript 'at' stands for atomisation.

Mean bond dissociation enthalpy $= +1664/4 = +416 \text{ kJ mol}^{-1}$

Using bond energies

The usefulness of bond enthalpies is shown by the following example, calculating the enthalpy change of the reaction:

$$C_2H_6(g) + Cl_2(g) \longrightarrow C_2H_5Cl(g) + HCl(g)$$

The steps are as follows:
1. First draw out the molecules showing all the bonds.

Hint: Formulae drawn to show all the bonds are called displayed formulae.

$$H-\underset{\underset{H}{|}}{\overset{\overset{H}{|}}{C}}-\underset{\underset{H}{|}}{\overset{\overset{H}{|}}{C}}-H(g) + Cl-Cl(g) \longrightarrow H-\underset{\underset{H}{|}}{\overset{\overset{H}{|}}{C}}-\underset{\underset{H}{|}}{\overset{\overset{H}{|}}{C}}-H(g) + H-Cl(g)$$

Imagine all the bonds in the reactants break leaving separate atoms.
2. Add the bond enthalpies up to give the total energy which must be *put in* to do this.
3. Now imagine the separate atoms reassemble to give the products. Add the bond enthalpies of the bonds that form to find the total enthalpy *given out* by the bonds forming. The difference is the approximate enthalpy change of the reaction.

Table 8.1 Tabulated bond enthalpies

The tabulated bond energies required for the above examples are given in **Table 8.1**.

Bond	Bond enthalpy
C—H	413 kJ mol^{-1}
C—C	347 kJ mol^{-1}
Cl—Cl	243 kJ mol^{-1}
C—Cl	346 kJ mol^{-1}
Cl—H	432 kJ mol^{-1}

← Note: Not exactly the same C—H in methane, as the tabulated bond enthalpy is an average over many compounds

kJ mol^{-1}

We need to *break* these bonds:

$6 \times$ C—H $\quad 6 \times 413 = 2478$
$1 \times$ C—C $\quad 1 \times 347 = 347$
$1 \times$ Cl—Cl $\quad 1 \times 243 = 243$
$\overline{3068}$

So 3068 kJ mol^{-1} must be *put in*.

kJ mol^{-1}

We need to *make* these bonds:

$5 \times$ C—H $\quad 5 \times 413 = 2065$
$1 \times$ C—C $\quad 1 \times 347 = 347$
$1 \times$ C—Cl $\quad 1 \times 346 = 346$
$1 \times$ Cl—H $\quad 1 \times 432 = 432$
$\overline{3190}$

So 3190 kJ mol^{-1} is *given out*.

The difference is $\qquad$ $3190 - 3068 = 122 \text{ kJ mol}^{-1}$

More enthalpy is given out than put in, so the reaction is exothermic. So

$$\Delta H^{\ominus} = -122 \text{ kJ mol}^{-1}$$

We could in fact have shortened this calculation:

$$\underset{\substack{| \ \ | \\ \text{H H}}}{\overset{\substack{\text{H H} \\ | \ \ |}}{\text{H—C—C—H}}}(g) + \text{Cl—Cl}(g) \longrightarrow \underset{\substack{| \ \ | \\ \text{H H}}}{\overset{\substack{\text{H H} \\ | \ \ |}}{\text{H—C—C—H}}}(g) + \text{H—Cl}(g)$$

Only the bonds drawn in red make or break during the reaction, so

We need to break $\qquad$
$$\begin{array}{ll} & \text{kJ mol}^{-1} \\ 1 \times \text{C—H} & = 413 \\ 1 \times \text{Cl—Cl} & = \underline{243} \\ & 656 \end{array}$$

We need to make $\qquad$
$$\begin{array}{ll} & \text{kJ mol}^{-1} \\ 1 \times \text{C—Cl} = & 346 \\ 1 \times \text{H—Cl} = & \underline{432} \\ & 778 \end{array}$$

> **Hint:** You can use either method. The first is longer, but there is less risk of forgetting any bonds.

The difference is $\qquad$ $778 - 656 = 122 \text{ kJ mol}^{-1}$

More energy is given out than taken in so,

$$\Delta H^{\ominus} = -122 \text{ kJ mol}^{-1} \text{ (as before)}$$

> **Q** Use bond energies to find ΔH for the similar reaction between methane and chlorine.

This is only an approximate value because the tabulated bond energies do not refer to the specific compounds used. An accurate value can be found using a thermochemical cycle (see below).

Remember $\text{Cl}_2(g)$ is an element, so no $\Delta H_f^{\ominus}$ value is needed.

$$\Delta H^{\ominus} = 85 - 229 \text{ kJ mol}^{-1}$$

$\Delta H^{\ominus} = -144 \text{ kJ mol}^{-1}$ (compared with -122 kJ mol^{-1} calculated from tabulated bond energies.) This discrepancy is typical of what may be expected using tabulated bond energies. The answer obtained from the thermochemical cycle is the 'right' one as all the $\Delta H_f^{\ominus}$ values have been obtained from the actual compounds involved.

Predicting bond-breaking

Another use of bond energies is to predict which bonds might be expected to break during reactions.

For example, look at the formula of diethyl peroxide:

Answer: -122 kJ mol^{-1}. The bonds actually broken and made are exactly the same as in the reaction with ethane.

$$H-\underset{\underset{H}{|}}{\overset{\overset{H}{|}}{C}}-\underset{\underset{H}{|}}{\overset{\overset{H}{|}}{C}}-O-O-\underset{\underset{H}{|}}{\overset{\overset{H}{|}}{C}}-\underset{\underset{H}{|}}{\overset{\overset{H}{|}}{C}}-H$$

The tabulated bond energies are

	kJ mol^{-1}
C—H	413
C—O	358
O—O	144
C—C	347

> **Did you know?** Compounds like diethyl peroxide are used as initiators for chain reactions in fibreglass resins, used in making canoes and repairing car bodies. The O—O bond breaks to give two highly reactive fragments called free **radicals**, which initiate the setting reaction.

The O—O bond is by far the weakest (requires the least energy to break it). We could predict that this molecule might react by cleavage of the O—O bond. This actually occurs.

8.5 Why do chemical reactions take place?

Chemists use the terms **feasible** or **spontaneous** to describe reactions which could take place of their own accord. The terms take no account of the rate of the reaction, which could be so slow as to be unmeasurable at room temperature.

   You may have noticed that many of the reactions that occur of their own accord are exothermic. For example, if we add magnesium to copper sulphate solution, the reaction to form copper and magnesium sulphate takes place and the solution gets hot. It is tempting to think that all spontaneous reactions are exothermic and that this is the driving force which makes reactions go. However, this is only part of the story.

Randomness or entropy

Many processes which take place of their own accord involve mixing or spreading out: for example, liquids evaporating, solids dissolving, gases mixing (see **Figure 8.9**). The second factor which drives processes is a tendency towards mixing or disorder.

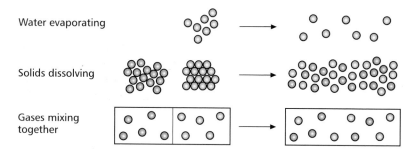

Water evaporating

Solids dissolving

Gases mixing together

Figure 8.9 Spontaneous processes

   Indeed the reverse of the last process would be quite extraordinary. We should be most surprised if the oxygen and the nitrogen in the air were to unmix and give, say, a room with all the oxygen on one side and all the nitrogen on the other!

Processes which involve 'spreading out', randomising or disordering the arrangement of molecules tend to happen of their own accord because they happen by chance alone.

So endothermic reactions can be spontaneous if they involve 'spreading out', randomising or disordering.

For example, the following reaction, which occurs spontaneously, is endothermic:

$$C_6H_8O_7(aq) + 3NaHCO_3(aq) \longrightarrow Na_3C_6H_5O_7(aq) + 3H_2O(l) + 3CO_2(g)$$

| citric acid | sodium hydrogencarbonate | sodium citrate | water | carbon dioxide |

The randomness of a system, expressed mathematically, is called the **entropy** of the system and is given the symbol S.

So *two* factors govern the feasibility of a chemical reaction:

the **enthalpy change** ΔH which should be **negative**

the **entropy change** ΔS which should be **positive** for the reaction to be spontaneous.

We can now classify four types of reactions.

1. $+ \Delta H$ cannot
   $- \Delta S$ 'go'
	2. $- \Delta H$ might
	   $- \Delta S$ 'go'

3. $+ \Delta H$ might
   $+ \Delta S$ 'go'
	4. $- \Delta H$ must
	   $+ \Delta S$ 'go'

Reaction corresponding to area 4 with a negative ΔH and an increase in entropy or randomness would be sure to be spontaneous. An area 1 reaction will not happen spontaneously. Reactions in areas 2 and 3 might go, depending on the relative importance of enthalpy and entropy changes.

However, there are still complications. How do we measure randomness and thus give a value to an entropy change, and how do we decide on the relative importance of the entropy and enthalpy changes when they predict opposite outcomes? These problems will be tackled in Chapter 28.

Kinetic factors

Neither enthalpy changes nor entropy changes tell us anything about how quickly or slowly a reaction is likely to go. We might predict that a certain reaction should occur spontaneously because of enthalpy and entropy changes, but the reaction might take place so slowly that for practical purposes it does not occur at all.

Carbon gives an interesting example:

$$C(gr) + O_2(g) \longrightarrow CO_2(g) \qquad \Delta H = -394 \text{ kJ mol}^{-1}$$

The entropy increases as we go from an ordered solid to a disordered gas, and the enthalpy change is negative, so we would expect the reaction to 'go' on both counts. However, experience with graphite (the 'lead' in pencils) tells us that the reaction does not take place at room temperature, although it will take place at higher temperatures. At room temperature the reaction is too slow.

Since the branch of chemistry dealing with enthalpy and entropy changes is called **thermodynamics**, and that dealing with rates is called **kinetics**, graphite is said to be thermodynamically unstable but kinetically stable, when exposed to oxygen, as in air.

This reaction takes place on your tongue when you eat sherbet. You can feel your tongue getting cold!

Hint: Entropy measures *disorder*, so a positive value of ΔS means the system becomes *more* random.

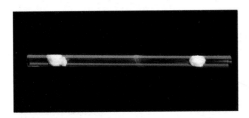

The white ring produced from the reaction of ammonia and hydrogen chloride

---

Q You have probably seen the spontaneous reaction below, shown in the photograph.

$$NH_3(g) + HCl(g) \longrightarrow NH_4Cl(s)$$

It is the reaction which produces the white ring in diffusion experiments. Work out into which of the areas in the table it fits.

Did you know? Until fairly recently, chemists measured energy in calories rather than joules.

1 calorie is the amount of heat energy needed to raise the temperature of 1 g of water by 1 °C (1 K).

So 1 calorie = 4.2 J.

Answer: Area 2. The solid is more ordered than the gaseous reactants, as we know more precisely where the atoms are, so ΔS is negative. Since the reaction is spontaneous, ΔH must be negative.

8.6 Summary

- Energy is the   ability to do work.

- It is measured in   joules.

- The enthalpy change ΔH of a chemical reaction is   the energy given out or taken in.

- It is measured under conditions of   constant pressure (100 kPa) and temperature (298 K).

- To avoid ambiguity,   the equation of the reaction should always be given.

- Enthalpy changes are often represented on   enthalpy diagrams (energy level diagrams).

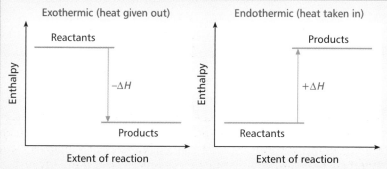

Figure 8.10 Enthalpy diagrams

- ΔH is negative for an   exothermic reaction.

- ΔH is positive for an   endothermic reaction.

- Enthalpy changes are measured by   transferring the heat into a container of water (a calorimeter).

- The equation to know is   heat change = mass of water × specific heat capacity of water × temperature change

- Sometimes the heat capacity of the whole apparatus is found by a separate experiment or electrical calibration. In this case: heat = heat capacity × temperature change

- The most accurate determinations are made with   a bomb calorimeter.

- Hess's law states that   the overall heat change of a chemical change is independent of the route by which the change occurs.

- This enables heat changes of reactions to be calculated using .... thermochemical cycles.

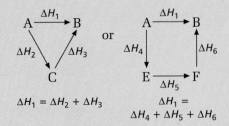

$$\Delta H_1 = \Delta H_2 + \Delta H_3 \qquad \Delta H_1 = \Delta H_4 + \Delta H_5 + \Delta H_6$$

Figure 8.11 Enthalpy cycles

- Reversing a reaction means .... the sign of ΔH is reversed.

- Changes may also be represented on enthalpy diagrams using the convention that .... elements in their standard states have an enthalpy of zero.

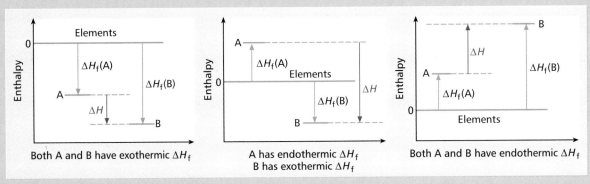

Figure 8.12 Enthalpy diagrams – some examples

- Tabulated bond enthalpy is .... the enthalpy required to break a particular bond averaged over many compounds.

- Tabulated bond enthalpies can be used to calculate approximate enthalpy changes for reactions by .... working out the difference between enthalpies to break all the bonds in the reactants and make all the bonds in the products.

- Tabulated bond enthalpies may also suggest .... which bonds might break in a given molecule.

- Entropy is a measure of .... the degree of disorder or randomness of a system.

- Two factors which govern the feasibility of reactions are .... the enthalpy change, ΔH, and the entropy change, ΔS.

- The factors which favour reaction are:
  Negative enthalpy change ($-\Delta H$) which denotes .... an exothermic reaction.
  Positive entropy change ($+\Delta S$) which means .... an increase in disorder.

8.7 Practice questions

1. 50 cm^3 of 2.0 mol dm^{-3} sodium hydroxide and 50 cm^3 of 2.0 mol dm^{-3} hydrochloric acid were mixed in an expanded polystyrene beaker. The temperature rose by $11 \,°C$.
   (a) Calculate $\Delta H^{\ominus}$ for the reaction in kJ mol^{-1}.
   (b) How will this value compare with the accepted value for this reaction? Explain your answer.
   (c) What value of $\Delta H^{\ominus}$ would you expect if 50 cm^3 of 2.0 mol dm^{-3} potassium hydroxide and 50 cm^3 of 2.0 mol dm^{-3} nitric acid were mixed in the same apparatus? Explain your answer.

2. A bomb calorimeter was calibrated by burning a pellet of benzenecarboxylic acid ($C_7H_6O_2$) of mass 0.7934 g. The temperature rise was $2.037 \,°C$. $\Delta H_c^{\ominus}$ for benzenecarboxylic acid is $-3227.0 \text{ kJ mol}^{-1}$.
   (a) What fraction of a mole of benzenecarboxylic acid was used?
   (b) Calculate the heat capacity of the calorimeter using the relationship

   heat given out = heat capacity $\times$ temperature rise

   The calorimeter was then used to calculate $\Delta H_c^{\ominus}$ for other compounds and the following results were obtained.

Compound	M_r	Mass used/g	Temperature rise/K
propan-1-ol	60.10	0.7563	2.445
butan-1-ol	74.10	0.8233	2.860
pentan-1-ol	88.20	0.8378	3.059

   (c) Calculate $\Delta H_c^{\ominus}$ for each alcohol using the following steps:
   (i) What fraction of a mole was used?
   (ii) How much heat has been produced?
   (iii) How much heat would be produced by a mole?

3. Use the following tabulated bond energies to calculate the standard enthalpy change of atomisation of methanol.

   $CH_3OH(g) \longrightarrow C(g) + 4H(g) + O(g)$

   $C—H = 413 \text{ kJ mol}^{-1}$, $C—O = 358 \text{ kJ mol}^{-1}$,
   $O—H = 464 \text{ kJ mol}^{-1}$

4. Use a thermochemical cycle to calculate $\Delta H^{\ominus}$ for the following reactions using the values of $\Delta H_f^{\ominus}$ given below. Represent each reaction on an enthalpy diagram.

   (a) $CH_3COCH_3(l) + H_2(g) \longrightarrow CH_3—\overset{\displaystyle H}{\underset{\displaystyle OH}{\overset{|}{\underset{|}{C}}}}—CH_3(l)$

   (b)

   (c)

   (d) $Zn(s) + CuO(s) \longrightarrow ZnO(s) + Cu(s)$
   (e) $Pb(NO_3)_2(s) \longrightarrow PbO(s) + 2NO_2(g) + \frac{1}{2}O_2(g)$

Compound	$\Delta H_f^{\ominus}/\text{kJ mol}^{-1}$	Compound	$\Delta H_f^{\ominus}/\text{kJ mol}^{-1}$
$CH_3COCH_3(l)$	-248	$CuO(s)$	-157
$CH_3CH(OH)CH_3(l)$	-318	$ZnO(s)$	-348
$C_2H_4(g)$	$+52$	$Pb(NO_3)_2(s)$	-452
$C_2H_4Cl_2(l)$	-165	$PbO(s)$	-217
$HCl(g)$	-92	$NO_2(g)$	$+33$
$CH_3CH_2Cl(g)$	-137		

5. For the following reactions say whether you would expect an increase or decrease in entropy.
   (a) $NaNO_3(s) \longrightarrow NaNO_2(s) + \frac{1}{2}O_2(g)$
   (b) $H_2O(l) \longrightarrow H_2O(g)$
   (c) $Na(s) + \frac{1}{2}Cl_2(g) \longrightarrow NaCl(s)$
   (d) $Ca^{2+}(aq) + CO_3^{2-}(aq) \longrightarrow CaCO_3(s)$

6. For the reaction:

   Calculate $\Delta H^{\ominus}$ by using tabulated bond energies. ($C—H$ 413 kJ mol^{-1}, $C=C$ 612 kJ mol^{-1}, $H—Cl$ 432 kJ mol^{-1}, $C—C$ 347 kJ mol^{-1}, $C—Cl$ 346 kJ mol^{-1}.)

7.

   Calculate $\Delta H^{\ominus}$ for the reaction by thermochemical cycles:
   (a) via $\Delta H_f^{\ominus}$ values
   (b) via $\Delta H_c^{\ominus}$ values

	$\Delta H_f^{\ominus}/\text{kJ mol}^{-1}$	$\Delta H_c^{\ominus}/\text{kJ mol}^{-1}$
CH_3CHO	-192	-1167
H_2	—	-286
CH_3CH_2OH	-277	-1367

   Comment on the two answers.

8.8 Examination questions

1. (a) In $\Delta H^{\ominus}$, what does the symbol $^{\ominus}$ indicate?
   (b) Some mean bond enthalpies are given below.

Bond	C—C	H—H	Cl—Cl	C—H
Mean bond enthalpy/kJ mol^{-1}	348	436	242	412

   (i) Write the equation for the reaction used to define the bond enthalpy of a chlorine-chlorine bond. Include state symbols.
   (ii) Why is the term *mean bond enthalpy* used in the table instead of just *bond enthalpy*?
   (iii) Use the data above to predict what happens first when a sample of propane, C_3H_8, is cracked in the absence of air and explain your prediction.
   (c) Use the following data to calculate the standard enthalpy of formation of propane.

$$C_3H_8(g) + 5O_2(g) \longrightarrow 3CO_2(g) + 4H_2O(l)$$
$$\Delta H^{\ominus} = -2220 \text{ kJ mol}^{-1}$$
$$H_2(g) + \tfrac{1}{2}O_2(g) \longrightarrow H_2O(l)$$
$$\Delta H^{\ominus} = -286 \text{ kJ mol}^{-1}$$
$$C(s) + O_2(g) \longrightarrow CO_2(g)$$
$$\Delta H^{\ominus} = -394 \text{ kJ mol}^{-1}$$

[NEAB 1998]

2. (a) Define the term *standard molar enthalpy change of formation*.
   (b) State *Hess's law*.
   (c) The equation below shows the reaction between ammonia and fluorine.

$$NH_3(g) + 3F_2(g) \longrightarrow 3HF(g) + NF_3(g)$$

   (i) Use the standard molar enthalpy change of formation ($\Delta H_f^{\ominus}$) data in the table below to calculate the molar enthalpy change for this reaction.

Compound	NH$_3$	HF	NF$_3$
$\Delta H_f^{\ominus}$/kJ mol^{-1}	−46	−268	−114

   (ii) Use the average bond enthalpy data in the table below to calculate a value for the molar enthalpy change for the same reaction between ammonia and fluorine.

$$NH_3(g) + 3F_2(g) \longrightarrow 3HF(g) + NF_3(g)$$

Bond	N—H	F—F	H—F	N—F
Average bond enthalpy/kJ mol^{-1}	388	158	562	272

   (d) The answer you have calculated in (c)(i) is regarded as being the more reliable value. Suggest why this is so.

[AEB 1997]

3. (a) Define the term *standard enthalpy of formation*.
   (b) The standard enthalpies of combustion of ethene, carbon and hydrogen are −1411, −393 and −286 kJ mol^{-1} respectively. Calculate the standard enthalpy of formation of ethene.
   (c) The standard enthalpy of neutralisation for hydrochloric acid with sodium hydroxide is −58 kJ mol^{-1}. The value for ethanoic acid with sodium hydroxide is −56 kJ mol^{-1}. Suggest an explanation for this difference.

[London 1997, AS]

4. (a) State Hess's law.
   (b) (i) Write an equation, the enthalpy change for which would be the enthalpy of formation of zinc sulphide, ZnS.
       (ii) In the smelting of zinc ores, the following reaction occurs:

$$ZnS(s) + 1\tfrac{1}{2}O_2(g) \longrightarrow ZnO(s) + SO_2(g)$$
$$\Delta H^{\ominus} = -441 \text{ kJ mol}^{-1}$$

   Use this, together with the data below, to calculate a value for the enthalpy of formation of ZnS.

Data: $Zn(s) + \tfrac{1}{2}O_2(g) \longrightarrow ZnO(s)$
$$\Delta H^{\ominus} = -348 \text{ kJ mol}^{-1}$$
$$S(s) + O_2(g) \longrightarrow SO_2(s)$$
$$\Delta H^{\ominus} = -297 \text{ kJ mol}^{-1}$$

[London 1997, part question]

9 Bonding and structure

C H E M I S T R Y   N O W

Balls of carbon

Until a few years ago chemistry textbooks used to state that the element carbon had two allotropes: diamond and graphite. Now they have all had to be rewritten – including this one – because several new allotropes have been discovered. Allotropes are forms of a pure element that differ in the way that the atoms are arranged and therefore they have different properties. Diamond and graphite form a classic example. Diamond is hard, transparent and doesn't conduct electricity while graphite is soft, grey and does conduct. The carbon atoms in diamond are arranged in triangular pyramids, while those in graphite are arranged in layers built up of hexagons.

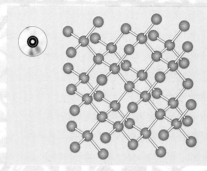

Arrangement of carbon atoms in diamond

In the 1980s, several research teams around the world pieced together the discovery of a third allotrope – buckminsterfullerene, C_{60}, molecules of carbon in the form of spheres. The molecules were arranged as though a layer of graphite had curled into a ball. The researchers were puzzled as to how this could happen until they realised that some pentagons in the array of hexagons would do the trick. One group asked the mathematics department at their

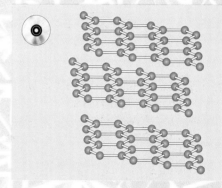

Arrangement of carbon atoms in graphite

university if they had heard of this geometrical shape, only to realise that it was exactly the pattern of the panels on a soccer ball!

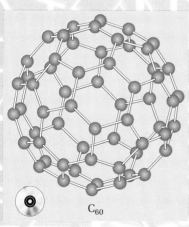

C_{60}

Buckminsterfullerene

The molecule was christened buckminsterfullerene after the geodesic domes designed by the architect Richard Buckminster Fuller. Other related molecules have been found including C_{70} in the shape of a rugby ball and also tube-shaped molecules.

Although they look odd, these molecules can undergo normal chemical reactions and chemists are beginning to make derivatives of them and look for uses of these new allotropes.

Geodesic dome

Introduction

When nylon first came on the market in 1928, the public was told it was made of 'coal, air and water'. This is true in as much as the elements in nylon – carbon, oxygen, hydrogen and nitrogen – do indeed come from these materials. However, it is the way the atoms are held together (bonding) and how they are arranged in space (structure) that accounts for the quite different properties of these different substances.

Chapter 2 describes three types of bonding – ionic, covalent and metallic – which involve respectively transfer, sharing and pooling of electrons between atoms, and two types of structure – giant and molecular. These types of bonding are extremes: the character of most bonds is somewhere between them. Some weaker types of bond are described in Chapter 10, Intermolecular forces. This chapter uses the ideas of atomic structure in Chapter 7 to develop a more sophisticated picture of bonding – in particular the idea of energy being involved. Finally, it shows how bonding ideas can explain the shapes of molecules and the geometries of some giant structures.

CONCEPT CHECKPOINTS

The following basic ideas are used in this chapter. You may revise some of these topics elsewhere in the book.
▢ the behaviour of positive and
  negative electric charges (section 6.3)
▢ ionisation energies (section 7.2)
▢ Hess's law (section 8.3)
▢ electron arrangements (section 7.2)
▢ dot-cross diagrams (section 2.2)
▢ electronic orbitals (section 7.2)
▢ bond energies (section 8.4)

9.1 **Bonding**

Ionic bonding

In a simple model of ionic bonding electrons are transferred from metal atoms to non-metal atoms so that the resulting charged ions each gain a full outer shell of electrons. However, this is a considerable oversimplification. In fact removal of electrons from, for example, alkali metals requires energy to be put in. Why, then, do ionic compounds form so readily and exothermically? To answer this question we need to look much more carefully at the energy changes that occur when ionic compounds are formed.

Energy changes on forming ionic compounds: the Born–Haber cycle

Note that all energies in this chapter are measured at or converted to 298 K and 100 kPa and are therefore enthalpies. However, most chemists still refer to ionisation *energies* and lattice *energies* and we shall use these terms.

If a cleaned piece of solid sodium is placed in a gas jar containing chlorine gas, a rapid exothermic reaction takes place, forming solid sodium chloride.

$$Na(s) + \tfrac{1}{2}Cl_2(g) \longrightarrow (Na^+ + Cl^-)(s) \qquad \Delta H_f^{\ominus} = -411 \text{ kJ mol}^{-1}$$

Let us examine the enthalpy changes that take place.

At some stage the sodium atom must give up an electron to form Na^+. The energy change for the process:

$$Na(g) \longrightarrow Na^+(g) + e^-$$

is the **first ionisation energy** of sodium and is $+496 \, kJ \, mol^{-1}$, i.e. energy must be *put in* for this process to occur.

At some stage a chlorine atom must gain an electron:

$$Cl(g) + e^- \longrightarrow Cl^-(g)$$

The energy change for this process of electron *gain* is called the **first electron affinity.** The first electron affinity for the chlorine atom is $-349 \, kJ \, mol^{-1}$, i.e. energy is given out when this process occurs.

However, this is not the whole story. The reaction we are considering involves *solid* sodium, not gaseous, and chlorine *molecules*, not separate atoms, so we must consider the energy changes for the processes below:

$$Na(s) \longrightarrow Na(g) \qquad \Delta H_{at}^{\ominus} = +108 \, kJ \, mol^{-1}$$

$$\tfrac{1}{2}Cl_2(g) \longrightarrow Cl(g) \qquad \Delta H_{at}^{\ominus} = +122 \, kJ \, mol^{-1}$$

These energy values are called **atomisation energies**. Notice that energy has to be *put in* to 'pull apart' the atoms (ΔH is positive).

There is a further energy change to be considered. At room temperature sodium chloride exists as a solid lattice of alternating positive and negative ions and not as separate gaseous ions. If oppositely charged ions are allowed to come together into a solid lattice, energy is given out, owing to the attraction of the ions. This is called the **lattice energy** and it refers to the process:

$$Na^+(g) + Cl^-(g) \longrightarrow (Na^+ + Cl^-)(s) \qquad LE = -788 \, kJ \, mol^{-1}$$

So we have five processes which lead to the formation of NaCl(s) from its elements. These are listed below:

- atomisation of Na:
$$Na(s) \longrightarrow Na(g) \qquad \Delta H_{at}^{\ominus} = +108 \, kJ \, mol^{-1}$$

- atomisation of Cl:
$$\tfrac{1}{2}Cl_2(g) \longrightarrow Cl(g) \qquad \Delta H_{at}^{\ominus} = +122 \, kJ \, mol^{-1}$$

- ionisation (e^- loss) of Na:
$$Na(g) \longrightarrow Na^+(g) + e^- \qquad \text{first IE} = +496 \, kJ \, mol^{-1}$$

- gain of e^- by Cl:
$$Cl(g) + e^- \longrightarrow Cl^-(g) \qquad \text{first EA} = -349 \, kJ \, mol^{-1}$$

- formation of lattice:
$$Na^+(g) + Cl^-(g) \longrightarrow (Na^+ + Cl^-)(s) \qquad LE = -787 \, kJ \, mol^{-1}$$

- formation of NaCl(s) from its elements
$$Na(g) + \tfrac{1}{2}Cl_2(g) \longrightarrow (Na^+ + Cl^-)(s) \qquad \Delta H_f^{\ominus} = -411 \, kJ \, mol^{-1}$$

Hess's law (see Chapter 8) tells us that the sum of the first five energy changes is equal to the enthalpy change of formation of sodium chloride. If we put all the changes together, we get a thermochemical cycle called a **Born–Haber cycle** (the same Haber as in the Haber process). We can calculate any of the quantities, provided all the others are known.

Hint: Do not confuse ionisation energy, which refers to electron *loss*, with electron affinity, which refers to electron *gain*.

Ionisation energies and electron affinities

It is interesting to see why the ionisation energy of sodium is positive (energy is put in), while the electron affinity of chlorine is negative (energy is given out).

If we look at a sodium atom with 11 protons and 11 electrons:

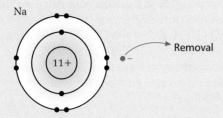

the electron which is being removed is attracted to the positive charge of the nucleus and therefore energy must be put in to pull it away. It does not 'feel' the full 11+ charge of the nucleus because there are 10 electrons in inner shells which shield the nuclear charge. It therefore feels $11 - 10$, i.e. an effective nuclear of charge of 1+. This is approximate because the inner electrons do not shield the nucleus perfectly.

In the case of chlorine (17 protons and 17 electrons):

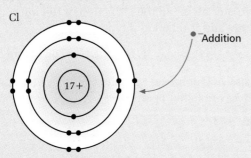

the electron which is being added 'feels' the nuclear charge of 17+ shielded by 10 electrons in inner shells, i.e. an effective nuclear charge of approximately 7+. It is therefore attracted by the nucleus and energy is given out in the process.

Addition of a second electron would require energy to be put in, as the original ion would now have an overall negative charge. Forcing the two negatively charged entities together requires energy to be put in. For example, adding the first electron in the formation of O^{2-}:

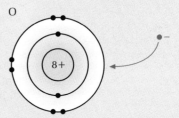

The added electron is attracted by an effective charge of $8 - 2 = 6+$.

$$\text{first electron affinity} = -141 \text{ kJ mol}^{-1}$$

Adding the second electron:

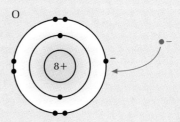

Although the added electron still feels a shielded charge of $6+$, the O^- ion has an overall negative charge and repels the electron.

$$\text{second electon affinity} = +798 \text{ kJ mol}^{-1}$$

The overall process is the sum of these two:

$O(g) + e^- \longrightarrow O^-(g)$	$\Delta H = -141 \text{ kJ mol}^{-1}$	
$O^-(g) + e^- \longrightarrow O^{2-}(g)$	$\Delta H = +798 \text{ kJ mol}^{-1}$	
$O(g) + 2e^- \longrightarrow O^{2-}(g)$	$\Delta H = +657 \text{ kJ mol}^{-1}$	

The cycle is constructed by starting with the elements in their standard states, which have zero energy. Then each step is added as shown in **Figure 9.1**, positive changes going upwards and negative ones downwards. When drawing Born–Haber cycles pay attention to the following points:

● Devise a rough scale, e.g. one line of lined paper to 100 kJ mol⁻¹. This will enable you to see which energy changes are the most significant and give you the correct relative levels.

● Allow plenty of space and plan out roughly first to avoid going off the top or bottom of the paper.

● It is better not to put signs in on the diagram, because if you do you can easily count them twice. If you go 'uphill' from a lower

$$Na(g) + \tfrac{1}{2}Cl_2(g)$$

$\Delta H_{at}^{\ominus}$ (Na) = 108

$$Na(s) + \tfrac{1}{2}Cl_2(g)$$

1. Elements in their standard states. This is the energy zero of the diagram

2. Add in the atomisation of sodium. This is positive, so it is drawn 'uphill'

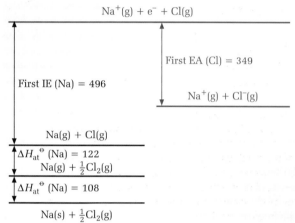

3. Add in the atomisation of chlorine. This too is positive and so drawn 'uphill'

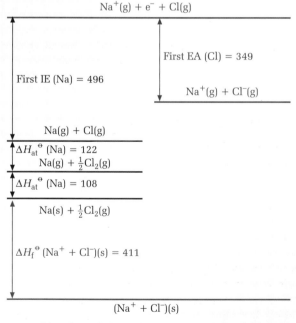

4. Add in the ionisation of sodium, also positive and so drawn 'uphill'

5. Add in the electron affinity of chlorine. This is a negative energy change and so is drawn 'downhill'

6. Add in the enthalpy of formation of sodium chloride, also negative and drawn 'downhill'

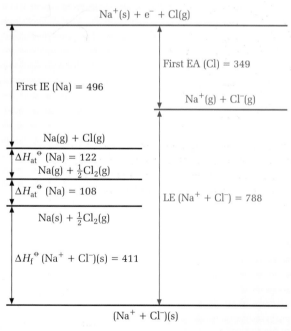

7. The final unknown quantity is the lattice energy of sodium chloride. The size of this is 788 kJ mol^{-1} from the diagram. The definition of lattice energy is the change from separate ions to solid lattice and we must therefore go 'downhill', so LE (Na$^+$ + Cl$^-$)(s) = –788 kJ mol^{-1}

The complete Born–Haber cycle for sodium chloride, NaCl

Figure 9.1 Stages in the construction of the Born–Haber cycle for sodium chloride, NaCl. All energies are in kJ mol^{-1}

line to a higher line, the energy change is positive (endothermic: energy put in); if you go 'downhill', from a higher line to a lower line, the energy change is negative (exothermic: energy given out), so the quantities can be given signs after you have calculated their sizes. For example, the lattice energy refers to the change *from* separate gaseous ions *to* crystalline solid (downhill) so that the lattice energy of sodium chloride is

$$-788 \text{ kJ mol}^{-1}.$$

Using a Born–Haber cycle we can see why the formation of an ionic compound from its elements is an exothermic process, principally because the large amount of energy given out when the lattice is formed outweighs the energy which has to be put in to form the positive ions.

There are more examples of Born–Haber cycles in **Figures 9.2–4**, together with notes on their construction.

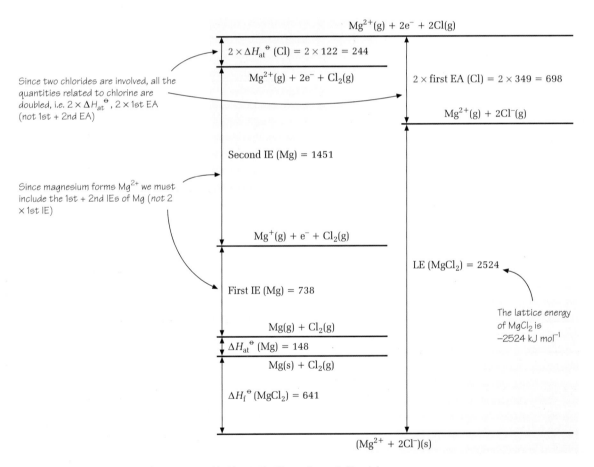

Figure 9.2 The Born–Haber cycle for magnesium chloride, $MgCl_2$. All energies are in kJ mol^{-1}

Hint: First electron affinities of most elements are negative because the added electron is attracted by the nuclear charge. Second (and subsequent) electron affinities are always positive because a negatively charged electron is being added to an already negatively charged ion.

Notice how in each case the cycles are dominated by the ionisation energy and the lattice energy terms. These are the largest terms and each gets larger with more highly charged ions.

There are trends in lattice energies related to the charge and size of the ions involved in the compound. These are illustrated in **Tables 9.1** and **9.2**.

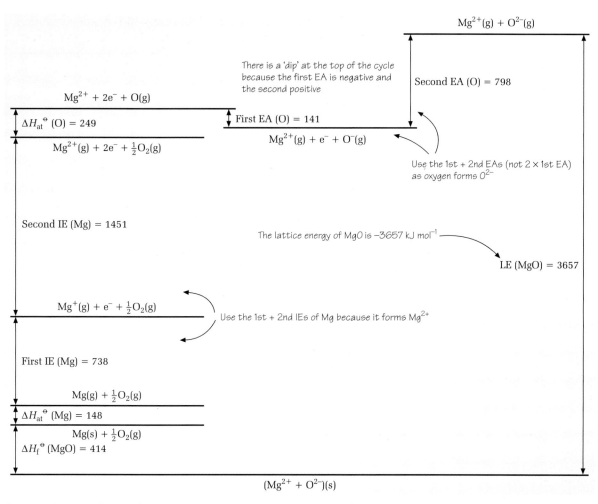

Figure 9.3 The Born–Haber cycle for magnesium oxide, MgO. All energies are in kJ mol^{-1}

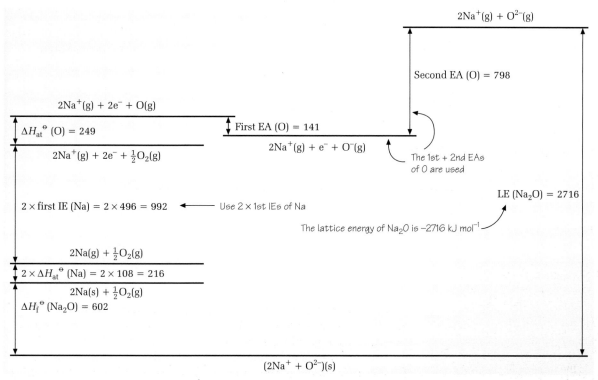

Figure 9.4 The Born–Haber cycle for sodium oxide. All energies are in kJ mol^{-1}

Table 9.1 Lattice energies in kJ mol^{-1} for M$^+$X$^-$

		Larger negative ions (anions)			
		F$^-$	Cl$^-$	Br$^-$	I$^-$
Larger positive ions (cations)	Li$^+$	−1031	−848	−803	−759
	Na$^+$	−918	−780	−742	−705
	K$^+$	−817	−711	−679	−651
	Rb$^+$	−783	−685	−656	−628
	Cs$^+$	−747	−661	−635	−613

Table 9.2 Lattice energies in kJ mol^{-1} for M^{2+}X^{2-}

		Larger anions	
		O^{2-}	S^{2-}
Larger cations	Be^{2+}	−4443	−3832
	Mg^{2+}	−3791	−3299
	Ca^{2+}	−3401	−3013
	Sr^{2+}	−3223	−2843
	Ba^{2+}	−3054	−2725

Notice these two relationships:

1. Larger ions have smaller lattice energies – this is because large ions cannot approach as closely as small ones, so less energy is given out when the lattice forms.
2. More highly charged ions produce *much* larger lattice energies than singly charged ones of approximately the same size. Compare Li$^+$F$^-$ and Be^{2+}O^{2-}. Doubling both charges increases the lattice energy more than fourfold.

Both these relationships illustrate the **Born–Mayer equation** (see the box below), a formula for calculating the lattice energy from the sizes and charges of the ions and a knowledge of the geometry of the lattice which is formed. This formula has been derived assuming pure ionic bonding, i.e. complete transfer of electrons from metal to non-metal.

Hypothetical compounds

Born–Haber cycles can be used to investigate $\Delta H_f^{\ominus}$'s of hypothetical compounds to see if they might be expected to exist. The cycles in **Figure 9.5** are for CaF (Ca$^+$ + F$^-$), CaF$_2$ (Ca^{2+} + 2F$^-$), and CaF$_3$ (Ca^{3+} + 3F$^-$). Only CaF$_2$ actually exists, so intelligent guesses have to be made about the geometries of the lattices of CaF and CaF$_3$ in order to make an estimate of their lattice energies via the Born–Mayer equation.

FURTHER FOCUS

The Born–Mayer equation

The Born–Mayer equation is derived from the theory of electric charges and states that the lattice energy is proportional to the product of the charges on each ion, and is inversely proportional to the distance between the centres of the ions. It also includes a factor related to the geometry of the crystal lattice. The equation is:

$$\text{lattice energy} = \frac{LMz^+z^-e^2}{4\pi\varepsilon_0 r}\left(\frac{1-\rho}{r}\right)$$

where L is the Avogadro constant
  M is the Madelung constant (which depends on the geometry of the crystal lattice)
  z^+ is the number of charges on each positive ion
  z^- is the number of charges on each negative ion

e is the charge on the electron
r is the distance between the centres of the ions
ρ is a constant which takes account of the repulsion between the electron shells of adjacent ions
ε_0 is a constant called the permittivity of space, which governs the strength of electrostatic forces

You will not be expected to remember this equation for Advanced level.

For many ionic compounds the lattice energy, as determined from experimental values via a Born–Haber cycle, agrees extremely well with that calculated by the Born–Mayer expression, giving further confirmation of the correctness of the ionic model.

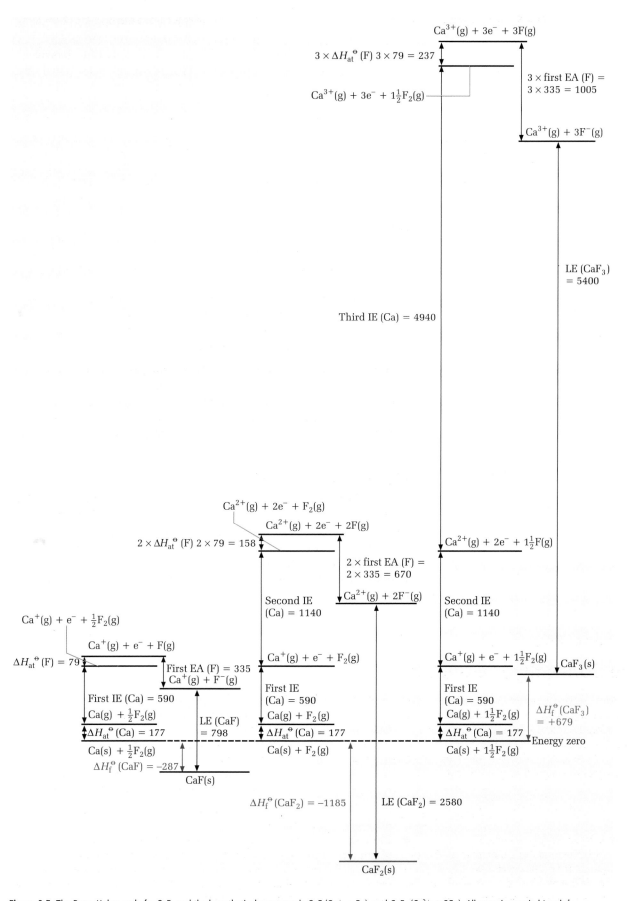

Figure 9.5 The Born–Haber cycle for CaF_2 and the hypothetical compounds CaF ($Ca^+ + F^-$), and CaF_3 ($Ca^{3+} + 3F^-$). All energies are in kJ mol^{-1}

Look at the $\Delta H_f^{\ominus}$'s. A large amount of energy would have to be put in to form CaF_3. CaF's formation would give out energy, but not as much as that of CaF_2. This helps to explain why only CaF_2 has ever been prepared as a stable compound. This is a much more satisfying explanation than that 'calcium only needs to lose two electrons for a full outer shell'.

Polarisation

For many ionic compounds there is excellent agreement – within 1% – between experimental values of the lattice energies and those calculated from the Born–Mayer expression, which assumes pure ionic bonding. For some compounds, however, the discrepancy is large. Zinc selenide ($Zn^{2+} + Se^{2-}$) has an experimental lattice energy of $-3611 kJ\,mol^{-1}$. The value of the lattice energy calculated by the Born–Mayer expression is $-3305\ kJ\,mol^{-1}$, a difference of almost 10%. As the experimental lattice energy is greater than the theoretical one, this implies some extra bonding is present. What has happened is this. The ion Zn^{2+} is relatively small and has a high positive charge while Se^{2-} is relatively large and has a high negative charge. The small Zn^{2+} can approach closely to the electron clouds of the Se^{2-} and distort them by attracting them towards it. The Se^{2-} is fairly easy to distort because its large size means the electrons are far from the nucleus and its double charge means there is plenty of negative charge to distort. This distortion means there are more electrons than expected concentrated *between* the Zn and Se nuclei and it represents a degree of electron sharing or covalency which accounts for the lattice energy discrepancy. The Se^{2-} ion is said to be **polarised**. This is shown in **Figure 9.6**.

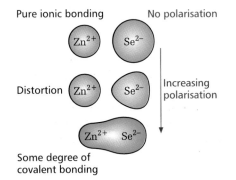

Pure ionic bonding   No polarisation

Distortion

Increasing polarisation

Some degree of covalent bonding

Figure 9.6 Polarisation in zinc selenide

The factors that increase polarisation are:

- positive ion (cation): small size, high charge   } These are called
- negative ion (anion): large size, high charge   } Fajans' rules

So pure ionic bonding can be seen as one extreme of a continuum from pure ionic to pure covalent.

Properties of ionically bonded compounds

- The main property of ionic compounds is that they conduct electricity when molten but not when solid. This is because the ions that carry the charge are not free to move in the solid state, but are in the liquid state.
- When a molten ionic compound does conduct electricity, it is decomposed at the electrodes. Aqueous solutions of ionic compounds also conduct electricity.
- To melt an ionic compound, the lattice energy (which is high) must be supplied and therefore ionic compounds have high melting points.
- Many ionic compounds dissolve in water. The energy required to break up the lattice is supplied by hydration by water molecules (see Chapter 10, Intermolecular forces). The water molecules also get between the ions and reduce the strength of their electrostatic attraction.
- Ionic compounds tend to be brittle, i.e. they shatter easily when given a firm blow. This is because they form a lattice of alternating positive and negative ions. A blow in the direction shown in **Figure 9.7** may move the ions sufficiently to produce contact between ions with like charges. This shattering occurs along planes of ions and is often called 'cleavage'.

Hint: You might not think of a 2+ or 2− ion as having a high charge. However, since the most highly charged simple ions have three units of charge, this is a reasonable description.

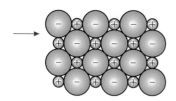

A small displacement causes contact between like charged ions....

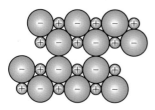

...and the structure shatters

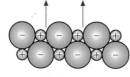

Shatters

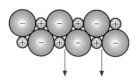

Figure 9.7 Breaking an ionic lattice

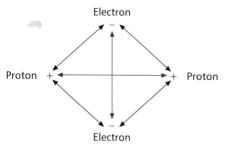

Figure 9.8 Electrostatic forces within the hydrogen molecule. The red arrows show repulsion and the black ones attraction

Covalent bonding

A simple picture of covalent bonding involves atoms sharing a pair or pairs of electrons in such a way that each atom obtains a full outer electron shell. It is most simply described by 'dot-cross' diagrams.

For example, water:

$$H \overset{\times}{\underset{\bullet}{\cdot}} O \overset{\times}{\underset{\bullet}{\cdot}} H$$

(Only the outer electrons are drawn, as is usual.) This simple picture does not at first sight explain how the bond holds the atoms together. It also gives the impression that the electrons are always equally shared between the atoms and that molecules are flat and two-dimensional: neither of which is always true. This section develops a more sophisticated model of covalent bonding, which will explain the distribution of electrons in molecules and also the molecules' shapes. It also deals with the strength of covalent bonds in terms of the energy needed to pull atoms apart.

How are atoms held together in molecules?

Atoms are held together by electrostatic attraction within the molecule. The simplest example is hydrogen. The hydrogen molecule consists of two protons held together by a pair of electrons. The electrostatic forces are shown in **Figure 9.8**. The attractive forces are in black and the repulsive forces in red. These forces just balance when the nuclei are a particular distance apart called the **bond length**.

Dative covalent bonding

We have used the idea that atoms share electrons in order to attain a full outer shell. However, this is not always possible.

For example, the dot-cross diagrams for the compounds beryllium chloride, $BeCl_2$, and boron trifluoride, BF_3 are shown below:

The beryllium atom in beryllium chloride has only four electrons in its outer shell and the boron atom in boron trifluoride has six. These are sometimes called **electron-deficient compounds.**

One way in which species like this can obtain a full outer shell is by accepting a pair of electrons from a species with an unshared pair (or **lone pair**) of electrons. Ammonia, NH_3, is a good example:

Single, e.g. F—F

Double, e.g. O=O

Triple, e.g. N≡N

Figure 9.9 Representing single, double and triple bonds

This type of bonding is called **dative** or **coordinate** bonding. 'Ordinary' covalent bonds are represented by a short line as a shorthand for an electron pair (**Figure 9.9**). Dative bonds are represented by an arrow showing the direction of donation:

$$\begin{array}{ccc} H & & F \\ | & & | \\ H—N & \rightarrow & B—F \\ | & & | \\ H & & F \end{array}$$

However, this is simply 'book-keeping'. Once established, a dative bond is identical in all respects to ordinary bonds between the same two atoms. In the ammonium ion, for example, the nitrogen atom uses its lone pair to form a dative bond to an H⁺ ion (a 'bare' proton with no electrons at all):

$$\begin{array}{ccc} H & & H \\ | & & | \\ H—N:\!\rightarrow\!H^+ & & \left[H—N\rightarrow H \right]^+ \\ | & & | \\ H & & H \end{array} \text{ ammonium ion}$$

The ammonium ion is completely symmetrical and all the bonds are identical in strength and length. It is also an example of a species with *covalently* bonded atoms, but with an overall charge, and is therefore an ion. Such species are often called **complex ions**. The OH⁻ ion is another example.

Dative bonds can also form part of a multiple bond as in carbon monoxide:

The extra electron • has come from the formation of a positive ion.

Hint: The word *species* can be used to refer to an ion, molecule or atom.

Because of their importance in the chemistry of many species, lone pairs are often drawn on the formula as above.

Further examples of dot-cross diagrams

Despite more sophisticated descriptions of bonding (see later), dot-cross diagrams are still very useful. Some examples are given below which include dative and multiple bonding. Only outer electrons are shown. This is acceptable because inner electrons are not involved in bonding.

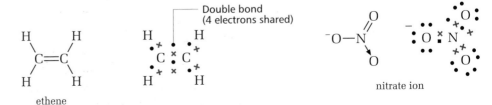

ethanol

Each atom has a full outer shell (hydrogen only needs 2 electrons)

Unshared pairs

Double bond (4 electrons shared)

ethene

nitrate ion

The extra electron, represented as a square dot in the nitrate ion, is the negative charge on the ion and came originally from the creation of a positive ion from a neutral species, e.g. Na ⟶ Na⁺. Since all electrons are identical *it could appear anywhere*.

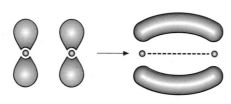

The two square dots represent the extra electrons gained when a positive ion is formed. They could be anywhere, since all electrons are identical.

carbonate ion

Molecular orbitals

A more sophisticated picture of covalent bonding considers **orbitals**. Remember that an orbital is a volume of space where an electron charge is likely to be found. This model of covalent bonding uses the idea that an orbital from one atom overlaps an orbital from another atom to form a new **molecular orbital**.

> **Hint:** s, p and d describe the shapes of atomic orbitals (see Chapter 7).

The shape of the molecular orbital is formed by combining the shapes of the atomic orbitals from which it is formed. A bond is formed when electrons fill one or more molecular orbitals. As with atomic orbitals, a molecular orbital can hold up to two electrons.

σ (sigma) orbitals

In hydrogen, H_2, for example, the two 1s orbitals can overlap, as in **Figure 9.10**. The new orbital shows a significant electron density *between* the nuclei. Notice that the new orbital has rotational symmetry about a line joining the nuclei (**Figure 9.11**). Such molecular orbitals are called σ (sigma) orbitals.

σ orbitals may also be formed by overlap of an s and a p orbital as in hydrogen fluoride, HF (**Figure 9.12**).

A pair of p orbitals can also overlap to give a σ orbital as in fluorine, F_2 (**Figure 9.13**).

Note that a σ orbital is always formed when two p orbitals approach along the line joining the nuclei of their atoms.

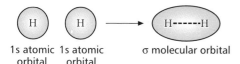

1s atomic orbital   1s atomic orbital   σ molecular orbital

Figure 9.10 A molecular orbital picture of the hydrogen molecule, H_2

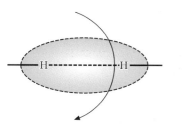

Figure 9.11 The shape of a σ orbital is unaffected by rotation about the axis joining the nuclei

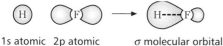

1s atomic orbital   2p atomic orbital   σ molecular orbital

Figure 9.12 A molecular orbital picture of the bonding in hydrogen fluoride, HF

2p atomic orbital   σ molecular orbital

Figure 9.13 A molecular orbital picture of the bonding in fluorine, F_2

π (pi) orbitals

A pair of p orbitals at right angles to the line joining the nuclei overlap in a different way (**Figure 9.14**). Here the new orbital is called a π (pi) orbital.

π orbitals produce electron density above and below the line joining the nuclei.

They only form where there is already a σ orbital.

Bonds formed from electrons in π orbitals are less effective at holding the atoms together than σ orbitals. The σ + π combination is usually less than twice as strong as the σ alone.

p atomic orbitals   π molecular orbital

Figure 9.14 Formation of a π molecular orbital

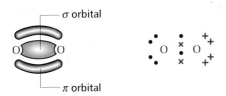

Figure 9.15 σ and π molecular orbitals in oxygen, O_2

Double bonds are composed of $\sigma + \pi$ bonds as in oxygen, O_2 (**Figure 9.15**).

It is possible to form a triple bond – a σ and two π orbitals – as in nitrogen, N_2 (**Figure 9.16**). Notice that there are orbitals holding electron pairs that take no part in the bonding. These pairs of electrons are **lone** or **unshared pairs** and exist in non-bonding orbitals.

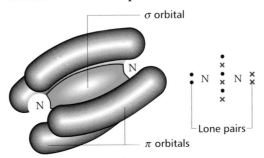

Figure 9.16 Nitrogen, N_2, has one σ and two π molecular orbitals

FURTHER FOCUS

Hybridisation

This description of bonding starts by considering that on any atom orbitals of similar energy, e.g. 2s and 2p, can 'mix together' to produce the same number of new orbitals of a different shape. These **hybrid orbitals** can then form bonds by overlapping with orbitals on other atoms. This model helps to explain the shapes of the molecules that result.

For example, in carbon, where the orbitals involved in bonding are the 2s and 2p orbitals, they may mix in three ways.

(a) $s + 3 \times p \longrightarrow 2 \times sp + 2 \times p$
(b) $s + 3 \times p \longrightarrow 3 \times sp^2 + 1 \times p$
(c) $s + 3 \times p \longrightarrow 4 \times sp^3$

Notice that the original four orbitals always give rise to four new ones.

The shapes are shown below:

The new hybrid orbitals are identified by the symbols sp, sp^2, and sp^3, which indicate the proportions of s and p orbitals from which they were formed.

The angles between the hybridised orbitals are important because they help to explain the shapes of molecules. The sp orbitals are at 180° to one another, the sp^2 orbitals are at 120° and the sp^3 orbitals point to the corners of a tetrahedron (109.5°). This is particularly important in organic chemistry (see section 18.2).

Hint: sp^2 is pronounced 'ess pee two' not 'ess pee squared'.

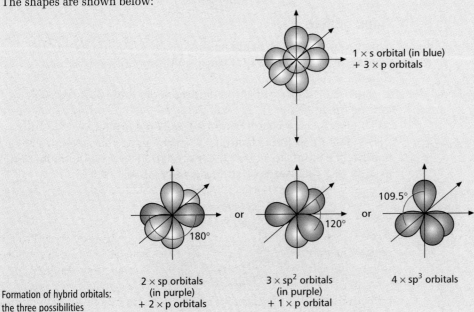

Formation of hybrid orbitals: the three possibilities

These alternative explanations – 'dot-cross' diagrams, and molecular orbitals (and hybridisation) – are not contradictory. They represent different levels of sophistication. Chemists tend to use the simplest model that is adequate to deal with a particular situation. Thus we shall frequently use the 'dot-cross' method.

Bond polarity

In a molecule like fluorine, F_2, where both atoms are the same (a **homonuclear diatomic** molecule), the electrons in the bond *must* be shared equally.

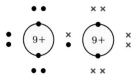

> **Q** Which of the following molecules are 'homonuclear diatomic': hydrogen, water, ozone (O_3), hydrogen fluoride, oxygen?

Both nuclei have a charge of 9+ but the inner electrons tend to shield or screen the nuclear charge so that the **effective nuclear charge** which is felt by the shared electrons is $9 + -2 = +7$.

So both 'feel' an effective nuclear charge (also called a **shielded** nuclear charge) of $+7$ ($9 - 2$ inner electrons). However, in a diatomic molecule with *different* atoms, the sharing of electrons will not be equal. In hydrogen fluoride, HF, the shared electrons 'feel' one positive charge from the hydrogen (no shielding) and 7 from the fluorine.

> **Q** Why is this calculation of effective nuclear charge an approximation?

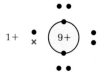

> **Q** Why is the nuclear charge not shielded in hydrogen?

The shared electrons will be attracted closer to the fluorine than to the hydrogen, or to express it another way, the electron charge cloud or molecular orbital will be distorted towards the fluorine. This makes the fluorine end of the molecule relatively negative and the hydrogen end relatively positive. This may be represented:

showing the charge cloud distorted towards the fluorine, or more usually:

$$\delta+ H—F^{\delta-}$$

'+' or '−' represent one 'electron's worth of charge'; '$\delta+$' and '$\delta-$' represent a small charge of less than one 'electron's worth'. Molecules like this are said to be **polar** or to have a **dipole**. Another way of looking at this is to say that the H—F bond is covalent, but has some ionic character. Compare this with the situation described earlier of ionic bonds with some covalent character.

H—F has been calculated to have 45% ionic character.

Electronegativity

> **Hint:** Think of electronegative atoms as having more 'electron-pulling power'.

Because of its greater electron-attracting ability, fluorine is said to be more **electronegative** than hydrogen. Electronegative atoms are those whose outer electrons 'feel' a large nuclear charge after allowing for the shielding effect of the inner electrons. As we go across a period in the Periodic Table, the shielded nuclear charge increases from Group I to Group VII (see **Table 9.3**).

Answer: Hydrogen and oxygen

Answer: The inner electrons do not shield the nucleus completely.

Answer: There is no inner electron shell.

Table 9.3 Effective nuclear charge increases across a period

	Li	Be	B	C	N	O	F	
Nuclear charge	3	4	5	6	7	8	9	All have a shielding factor of 2 (2 electrons
Effective nuclear charge	1	2	3	4	5	6	7	in the inner shell)

—increasing electronegativity→

On descending a group in the Periodic Table the effective nuclear charge remains the same but the outer electrons get further away from the nucleus, so electronegativity decreases.

Thus the most electronegative atoms are found at the top right-hand corner of the Periodic Table (ignoring the noble gases which form few compounds). The most electronegative atoms are fluorine, oxygen and nitrogen, followed by chlorine.

A scale of electronegativity values has been developed by the American chemist Linus Pauling. The greater the number, the more electronegative the atom. Some examples are shown in **Table 9.4**.

> **Q** Work out the effective nuclear charge (the charge felt by the outer electron) in sodium and potassium to show that it is the same as in lithium.

Table 9.4 Trends in electronegativity

Increasing electronegativity →							
Li	Be	B	C	N	O	F	
1.0	1.5	2.0	2.5	3.0	3.5	4.0	
						Cl	Increasing electronegativity
						3.0	
						Br	
						2.8	

It is the *difference* in electronegativities of two atoms that tells us how polar the bond between them is. A difference of zero corresponds to pure covalent bonding. A difference of more than 2.1 is usually considered to be ionic bonding.

For example, in lithium fluoride, Li^+F^-, the difference is $4.0 - 1.0 = 3.0$: clearly an ionic bond.

Between 0 and 2.1, the bonds are considered to be polar covalent bonds, i.e. covalent with some percentage of ionic character.

For example, in hydrogen fluoride the difference is $4.0 - 2.1 = 1.9$: a highly polar bond. But in an H—C bond the difference is only $2.5 - 2.1 = 0.4$, and relatively non-polar.

Dipole moment

Polarity is the property of a particular bond. Molecules as a whole may have a **dipole moment**. This means that if the molecules are placed in an electric field, they will flip, as shown in **Figure 9.17** until they lie with their negative ends towards the positive plate and their positive ends towards the negative plate.

However, in molecules with more than one polar bond, the effects of each bond may cancel, to leave a molecule with no dipole moment.

For example, carbon dioxide is a linear molecule and the dipoles cancel:

$$\overset{\delta-}{O}=\overset{\delta+}{C}=\overset{\delta-}{O}$$

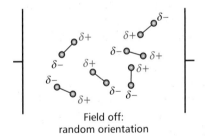

Field off:
random orientation

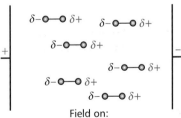

Field on:
molecules line up parallel to field

Figure 9.17 The effect of an electric field on molecules with dipoles

Answer: Sodium: nuclear charge, 11; less inner shells of (2 + 8). Effective nuclear charge is 1. Potassium: nuclear charge, 19; less inner shells of (2 + 8 + 8). Effective nuclear charge is 1.

Hint: The symbols '$\delta-$' and '$\delta+$' tell us the sign of the charges but not their size. In a water molecule, for example, $\delta-$ is twice the size of $\delta+$, because the molecule is neutral overall.

Q What can you say about the size of $\delta+$ and $\delta-$ in tetrachloromethane?

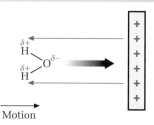

Motion

Figure 9.18 A water molecule is attracted by a charged rod

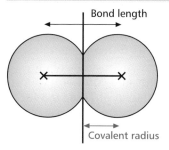

A stream of water is deflected by a charged plastic rod

Q Would you observe anything different if a negatively charged rod were used?

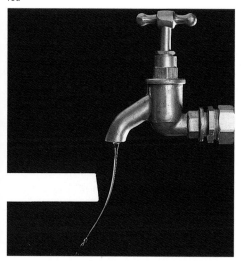

Figure 9.19 Bond length and covalent radius

Answer: $\delta+$ is four times the size of $\delta-$.

Answer: No, because the molecules would flip so that their positive ends are towards the rod.

Likewise in tetrachloromethane the dipoles cancel:

In water, however, the dipoles do not cancel:

The dipole moment of water explains why a stream of water bends when a plastic rod, charged by being rubbed, is brought near it (see **Figure 9.18** and photograph). The rod is charged positively by friction. The water molecules flip, so that their negative ends are towards the rod. Now since the negative ends, which are attracted, are closer to the rod than the positive ends, which repel, the attraction outweighs the repulsion, and the molecules move towards the rod.

Bond lengths

It is not easy to measure the sizes of atoms. Electron clouds are so diffuse (spread out) that it is difficult to say where the atom stops. Furthermore, isolated atoms are not easy to come by. What *can* be measured accurately is the distance between two nuclei: the centres of the atoms which are covalently bonded together. This distance is usually called the **bond length.** Bond lengths are usually in the range 0.1–0.2 nm. When two identical atoms are covalently bonded together, half the bond length is called the **covalent radius** shown in **Figure 9.19**.

Bond length and bond order

The **order** of a bond means whether it is single, double or triple. In the case of atoms that can form multiple bonds, there is a relationship between the bond length and bond order for bonds between the same atoms. This is shown by **Table 9.5** for carbon–carbon bonds.

This shows that multiple bonds are shorter. The extra attraction caused by more electrons being shared pulls the atoms closer before the repulsion of the electron clouds intervenes. This relationship allows bond orders to be determined experimentally.

Delocalisation

If we attempt to draw a dot-cross diagram of the bonding of nitric acid, HNO_3, whose *skeleton* is shown (the dashed lines showing simply which atom is bonded to which):

we get this result:

i.e. using the usual conventions

Table 9.5 Relationship between bond length and bond order for carbon–carbon bonds

Bond order	Bond length/nm
1 C—C	0.154
2 C=C	0.134
3 C≡C	0.120

However, we could just as easily have drawn:

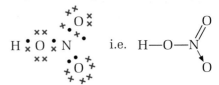

i.e.

Studies of the nitric acid molecule have measured the following bond lengths:

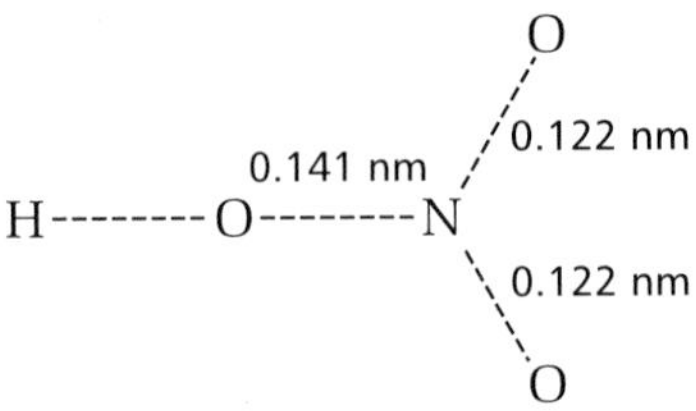

The usual N—O bond length is 0.136 nm and that for N=O is 0.114 nm. Thus the N—OH bond is approximately the expected length for a single bond, but neither of the others seems to be a double bond. In fact, both bonds have a length midway between that expected for a double and a single bond and they are identical in length, and therefore in bond order.

This can be explained if we think about the orbitals. The skeleton of the molecule is held together by σ orbitals. The nitrogen atom and the two oxygen atoms in question each have a p orbital, as shown in **Figure 9.20**. Since both oxygen atoms are identical, there is no reason for overlap to occur with one rather than the other, and overlap occurs with *both*. This produces a π-type orbital that extends across all three atoms. This is a **delocalised** π orbital, shown in **Figure 9.21**.

Although it covers three atoms, there are only two electrons in this orbital. Thus the two N—O bonds are neither double nor single, but somewhere in between, as the bond lengths indicate. This type of delocalisation is shown on structural formulae as in **Figure 9.22**. Whenever delocalisation occurs, the resulting molecule is always more stable (of lower energy) than either of the alternative structures with a double and a single bond.

Predict the approximate bond order for the two identical N—O bonds in the nitric acid molecule.

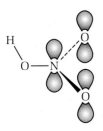

Figure 9.20 The p orbitals in nitric acid

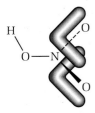

Figure 9.21 The delocalised π orbital in nitric acid

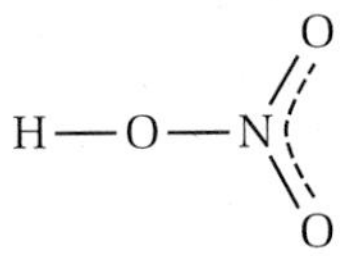

Figure 9.22 Representation of delocalised π bonding on the structural formula of nitric acid

Bond energies

How strong are covalent bonds? Their strengths are measured by the amount of energy which must be put in to completely separate the two atoms concerned. For example:

$$H_2(g) \longrightarrow 2H(g) \qquad \Delta H^{\ominus} = +436 \text{ kJ mol}^{-1}$$

The bond energies given in tables of data are averages taken from a number of compounds which may have slightly different energies. Thus C—H is usually given as +413 kJ mol^{-1}.

There is a relationship between bond energy and bond order in bonds between the same two atoms. This is shown in **Table 9.6** for carbon–carbon bonds.

Table 9.6 Bond order, bond length and bond energy for carbon–carbon bonds

Bond	Order	Length/nm	Energy/kJ mol^{-1}
C—C	1	0.154	+347
C=C	2	0.134	+612
C≡C	3	0.120	+838

Answer: About 1.5. The actual bond length is almost half-way for that predicted for N—O and N=O.

Hint: Another example of delocalisation is the benzene ring, C_6H_6, which is dealt with in Chapter 32.

Q Why is the π bond weaker than the σ?

Q Work out the difference in energy between $C\equiv C$ and $C=C$. What does this represent?

Did you know? At very low temperatures metals conduct electricity perfectly, i.e. their electrical resistance falls to zero. This is called superconductivity.

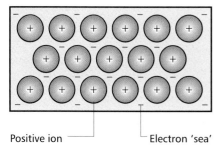

Positive ion — — Electron 'sea'

Figure 9.23 Metallic bonding

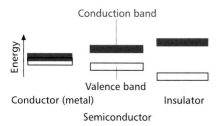

Conduction band

Energy

Valence band

Conductor (metal)   Insulator

Semiconductor

Figure 9.24 The valence and conduction bands in conductors, semiconductors and insulators

Answer: The electrons in the π bond are not directly between the nuclei.

Answer: Difference 226 kJ mol^{-1}. This represents the second π component of the bond.

Notice:

1. The relationship between length and energy. Shorter bonds are stronger.
2. A double bond is not twice as strong as a single bond. A single bond is a σ bond and a double a $\sigma + \pi$ bond, so the difference in energy represents the π bond energy: $612 - 347 = 265$ kJ mol^{-1}, significantly less than the σ bond energy.

It is important to note that it is easier to break the π component of a double bond than it is to break a single bond, so organic compounds with carbon–carbon double bonds (alkenes) are more reactive than those with single bonds only (alkanes); see Chapter 20.

Properties of covalently bonded compounds

Covalently bonded compounds are poor conductors of electricity, whatever their state. They tend not to dissolve in or mix with water unless they have relatively polar bonds as in sugars for example.

Metallic bonding

A simple picture of metallic bonding will be given here. Metals are all elements that can easily lose up to three electrons, thus forming positive ions. For example:

Na $\quad 1s^2 2s^2 2p^6 3s^1$ or 2,8,1 $\qquad$ Al $\quad 1s^2 2s^2 2p^6 3s^2 3p^1$ or 2,8,3

Transition metals have more complex electronic structures but still tend to give away electrons easily.

Metals consist of a lattice of positive ions existing in a freely moving 'sea' or 'cloud' of electrons. This is shown in **Figure 9.23**. The number of electrons in the 'sea' depends on how many electrons have been lost by each metal atom. Think of this 'sea' as a giant orbital, delocalised over the whole metal structure. This sea of mobile electrons is responsible for the good electrical conduction of metals: an electron from the negative terminal of the supply may join the electron cloud at one end of a metal wire and at the same time a different electron leaves the wire at the positive terminal.

Conductors, semiconductors and insulators

A molecular orbital picture of solids leads to the idea that there are two groups of energy levels or orbitals. The lower is called the **valence band** and the higher, the **conduction band** (see **Figure 9.24**). If the conduction band is partly filled with electrons, the electrons can move throughout the crystal (this is the electron 'sea' in metals). The difference between conductors, semiconductors and insulators depends on the energy gap between the two bands. In conductors, the two bands overlap, so the conduction band is always partly filled. In semiconductors, the bands are close together so that a few high-energy electrons can jump into the conduction band. In insulators the gap between the bands is large and no electrons exist in the conduction band.

Increasing the temperature of a semiconductor improves its conductivity as more electrons are able to reach the conduction band, but increasing the temperature of a metal conductor *decreases* its conductivity because vibrations of the lattice of ions impede the free movement of the electrons in the conduction band.

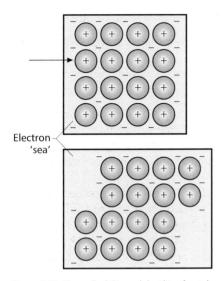

Electron 'sea'

Figure 9.25 The malleability and ductility of metals

Metallic radius

The distance between metal atoms in a solid metallic lattice can be measured accurately by X-ray diffraction (see section 29.1). Half of this distance is called the **metallic radius** and is a measure of the size of the metal atoms.

Properties of metals

Metals are good conductors of electricity because of their 'sea' of electrons. These electrons are also responsible for the high thermal conductivities of metal, i.e. they conduct heat well also.

In addition the metallic lattice explains the strength, ductility (ability to be drawn out into a wire) and malleability (the ability to be dented) of metals. The last two properties are illustrated in **Figure 9.25**. After a small distortion, each metal ion is still in exactly the same environment as before, so the new shape is retained. Contrast this with the brittleness of ionic compounds (see pages 88–9).

9.2 Structure

This section is concerned with the geometries of the arrangement of atoms in covalent molecules, giant covalent structures, giant ionic structures and metals.

Hint: To understand this section thoroughly, you probably need to build some structures. Molecular models would be ideal but you could improvise with Plasticine. Even coins might be helpful.

In a metal, all the units that make up the lattice are the same size, which simplifies the geometries considerably. X-ray diffraction (see section 29.1) shows that the ions are spherical.

Note about diagrams

When drawing diagrams of structures, it is difficult to represent three-dimensional structures in two dimensions. Two main types of diagrams are used: 'space-filling' as in **Figure 9.33(a)** and 'expanded' as in **Figure 9.33(b)**. The space-filling diagrams are better representations but expanded diagrams often make it easier to see geometries. In expanded diagrams some of the lines are to make the geometry clearer and do not represent covalent bonds.

The structures of metals
Close packing

In many metals, the ions pack as closely together as they possibly can. This of course still leaves some gaps, as you will realise if you think about a box of tennis balls.

In two dimensions a sphere can be surrounded by six spheres, which touch it as shown in **Figure 9.26**. Extending to three dimensions, a second layer can be placed *below* this one as shown in blue in **Figure 9.27(a)**.

Figure 9.26 Close packing of spheres in two dimensions

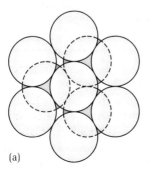

(a)

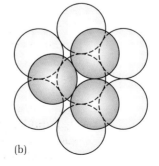

(b)

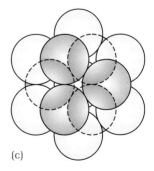

(c)

Figure 9.27 (a) Adding another close-packed layer below the first layer (b) The ABA arrangement (c) The ABC arrangement

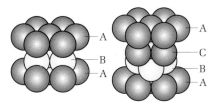

(a) ABA arrangement (b) ABC arrangement

Figure 9.28 The two close-packed arrangements

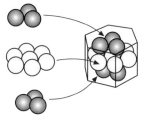

(a) ABA – hexagonal close packing

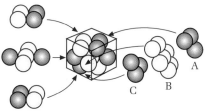

(b) ABC – cubic close packing

Figure 9.29 The two close-packed arrangements, showing hexagonal and cubic shapes

> **Q** Count up the number of atoms in the unit cell of a face-centred cubic close-packed arrangement. (Refer to Figure 9.31(a) on the next page.)

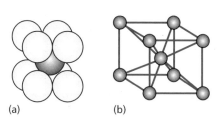

(a)   (b)

Figure 9.30 The body-centred cubic structure: (a) space-filling and (b) expanded

Answer: 4. The 6 atoms in the centres of the faces count as $\frac{1}{2}$ each and the 8 atoms at the corners count as $\frac{1}{8}$ each.

There are now *two* ways of placing a layer *above* the original one:

1. Directly above the second one. This is called an ABA arrangement (**Figure 9.27(b)**).
2. Twisted 60° from the position of the second one. This is called an ABC arrangement (**Figure 9.27(c)**).

Both are shown in **Figure 9.28**. In both ABA and ABC arrangements the central sphere is surrounded by 12 spheres that touch it (called **nearest neighbours**). Both arrangements are said to have a **coordination number** of 12. In both cases the spheres occupy 74% of the space.

The first arrangement, ABA, is called **hexagonal close packing** and the second arrangement, ABC, is called **face-centred cubic close packing**. or just **cubic close packing**. The hexagonal and cubic aspects of the symmetry can be seen in **Figure 9.29** but look at models if you can. Around fifty metals crystallise in one or other of these arrangements.

The body-centred cubic structure

This is the other common packing geometry for metals. It is not a close-packed arrangement, only 68% of the space being filled. It is best visualised by thinking of a sphere situated in the centre of a cube. Now imagine the sphere is surrounded by eight other spheres, one at each corner of the cube (**Figure 9.30**). The coordination number is 8. The alkali metals have this structure.

Unit cells

The unit cell of a structural arrangement is the smallest unit of it which contains enough information to generate the whole structure by repeating itself. **Figure 9.31** shows some unit cells.

The easiest way to visualise this repeating process is to imagine unit cells as in Figure 9.31 being stacked together like bricks. Notice that only fractions of the atoms on the edges, corners and faces are present in the unit cell.

Density

The density (mass per unit volume) of a metal depends on three factors: the atomic mass, the size of the atom, i.e. the metallic radius, and the type of packing. Smaller atoms, heavier atoms and closer packing all lead to a higher density.

The structures of ionic compounds

The situation here is more complex than in metals because in any ionic compound there are at least two ions of opposite charges and of different sizes. These may be in the ratio 1 : 1, 1 : 2, 2 : 1, etc. Only 1 : 1 compounds will be considered here in any detail.

The particular geometry which is adopted depends on the relative sizes or **radius ratio** of the cations (+) to anions (−). The essential point to grasp is that positive ions will be surrounded by as many negative ions as possible and vice versa. It is worth remembering that in general positive ions, which have *lost* electrons are smaller than negative ions, which have *gained* them. Ionic compounds that are 1 : 1 essentially adopt one of three structures, which are referred to by the names of representative compounds. These are:

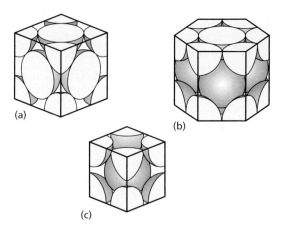

Figure 9.31 Some unit cells: (a) face-centred cubic close-packed unit cell, (b) hexagonal close-packed unit cell, (c) body-centred cubic unit cell

1. The **caesium chloride** structure, in which each cation is surrounded by eight anions and each anion by eight cations. This is referred to as 8 : 8 coordination.
2. The **sodium chloride** structure in which each cation is surrounded by six anions and vice versa. This is 6 : 6 coordination.
3. The **zinc blende** structure. This is 4 : 4 coordination.

The caesium chloride structure

This is illustrated in **Figure 9.32**. Notice the similarity between this and the body-centred cubic structure. Think of the Cs^+ ion as being at the centre of a cube. This is surrounded by eight Cl^- ions situated at the corners of that cube. The expanded diagram shows the geometry, but the space-filling one is more realistic because it shows the positive and negative ions touching.

This structure is quite stable because the negative ions do not touch each other owing to the large size of the Cs^+ ion. Imagine the positive ion shrinking. The structure would remain stable until the negative ions started to touch. If the positive ion then shrank further, fewer than eight negative ions could fit round the positive ion and it would be likely that a different structure would be adopted – one in which fewer negative ions surrounded the positive ion.

The sodium chloride structure

Here each cation is surrounded by six anions and vice versa as shown in **Figure 9.33**. The negative ions form an octahedron with the positive ion at the centre. Again, imagine the positive ion shrinking until the negative ions touch, at which point the structure starts to become unstable, and a different structure has to be adopted, with fewer anions around the cation.

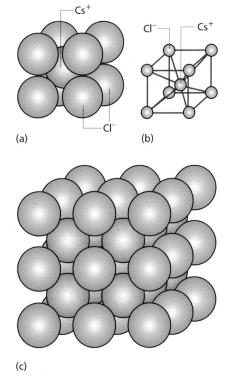

Figure 9.32 The caesium chloride structure: (a) space-filling, (b) expanded, (c) showing a larger section

Hint: An octahedron is so named because it has eight faces. Here we are interested in its six *points*.

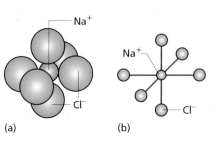

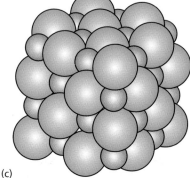

Figure 9.33 The sodium chloride structure

Hint: A tetrahedron is a triangle-based pyramid. It has four points.

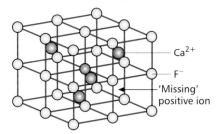

Figure 9.34 The zinc blende structure

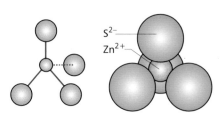

Figure 9.35 The fluorite structure

Hint: The electron pair repulsion theory is sometimes called VSEPR, short for Valence Shell Electron Pair Repulsion theory.

The CD-ROM that is available with this book enables you to see these shapes in different representations and to rotate them.

In three-dimensional representations of molecules ◢ is used to represent a bond coming out of the paper and a dashed line to represent one going into the paper, away from the reader.

The zinc blende structure

Zinc blende is a form of zinc sulphide, $Zn^{2+}S^{2-}$. Here the anion is at the centre of a tetrahedron of cations as shown in **Figure 9.34** (and vice versa).

The fluorite structure

Fluorite is calcium fluoride $Ca^{2+}2F^-$. This is a 2 : 1 structure. It can be thought of as being based on the caesium chloride structure but with half of the positive ions missing (see **Figure 9.35**). Look at the central F^- ion (shaded red). You should be able to see four nearest neighbour Ca^{2+} ions (shaded blue) arranged around it at the corners of a tetrahedron of which it is the centre. Each Ca^{2+} is the centre of a cube with an F^- ion (shaded pink) at each corner (totalling eight nearest neighbours), i.e. in exactly the same environment as a Cs^+ ion in Cs^+Cl^-. The structure is therefore sometimes referred to as 8 : 4 coordination.

Shapes of covalent molecules

Shapes of simple molecules can be predicted by the electron pair repulsion theory. The essential idea is that groups of electrons around an atom (such as a pair of electrons in the same orbital) will repel each other and therefore take up positions in space as far apart as possible.

A 'group' of electrons may be:

● a shared pair forming a single bond
● a set of four in a double bond
● a set of six forming a triple bond
● an unshared pair (often called a lone pair)

The shapes of the molecules depends on the number of groups of electrons surrounding a central atom.

Two groups

If there are two groups of electrons, as for example in beryllium chloride, which is covalent despite being a metal–non-metal compound, they will be 180° apart, forming a **linear** molecule.

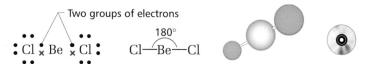

Three groups

Three groups of electrons, for example in boron trifluoride, will arrange themselves at 120° to each other. The resulting molecule is flat and described as **trigonal planar** in shape.

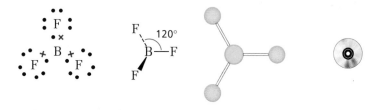

The shapes of BeCl$_2$, BF$_3$ and CH$_4$ represent the angles of sp, sp^2 and sp^3 hybrid orbitals (see page 92).

Four groups

Four groups of electrons as in methane, for example, will arrange themselves **tetrahedrally** (pointing towards the four corners of a tetrahedron). The angle here is 109.5°. Remember this is a three-dimensional, not flat arrangement.

For elements in Period 3, there may be more than eight electrons (four pairs) in the outer shell.

Five groups

Five groups of electrons lead to a **trigonal bipyramid** (**Figure 9.36**).

Six groups

Six groups of electrons lead to an **octahedral** shape in which all angles are 90° (**Figure 9.37**).

Lone pairs

Molecules with unshared pairs of electrons need care. The lone pairs affect the shape but do not have an atom associated with them. Water is a good example:

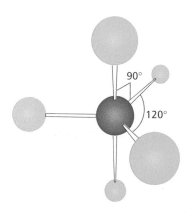

Figure 9.36 Five groups of electrons give a trigonal bipyramidal shape, e.g. PCl$_5$

There are four groups of electrons, so the shape is based on a tetrahedron, but two of the 'arms' of the tetrahedron are lone pairs which have no atoms and the resulting molecule is V-shaped, described as **angular**:

If you draw the lone pairs in, you are less likely to forget them. The angle of a perfect tetrahedron is 109.5° but the lone pairs are closer to the oxygen than the shared pairs (which are also attracted by the other nucleus). Therefore lone pairs repel more effectively than shared pairs, and 'squeeze' the hydrogens together, reducing the H—O—H angle. An approximate rule of thumb is 2° per lone pair, so the bond angle in water is approximately 105°.

In ammonia four groups of electrons mean the shape is based on a tetrahedron but with only three 'arms':

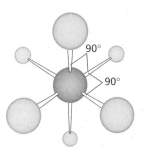

Figure 9.37 Six groups give an octahedral shape, e.g. SF$_6$

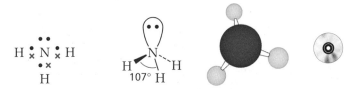

The bond angles are approximately 107°. The shape is often described as **pyramidal**.

Multiple bonds

These also need care. For example, in methanal:

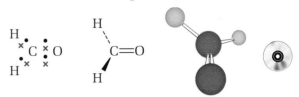

three groups of electrons mean that the shape is based on trigonal planar (the double bond counts as *one* group). However the group of four electrons in the double bond repels more than the groups of two in the single bonds, thus squeezing down the H—C—H angle to less than the 120° of a perfect trigonal shape.

In carbon dioxide, there are two groups of four electrons: therefore the molecule is linear.

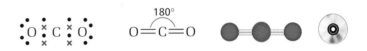

More complex molecules

This treatment can be extended to molecules with more than one centre by treating each separately. For example, in methanol:

the carbon, which has four groups of electrons, is tetrahedral. There are also four groups of electrons around the oxygen atom, but as two of these are lone pairs, the shape is angular with the C—O—H angle rather less than 109.5°.

Giant covalent structures

Giant covalent structures differ from giant ionic and metallic ones in that covalent bonds are directional and act between specific atoms, while the electrostatic forces that hold together the other structures act equally in all directions.

Diamond

This is a three-dimensional giant structure. Diamond is a form of pure carbon, in which the carbon atom forms four covalent bonds pointing to the corners of a tetrahedron. The resulting three-dimensional structure (**Figure 9.38**) is very rigid, leading to diamond being one of the hardest substances known. Diamond also has a very high melting point of around 4000 K. Both its hardness and high melting point are caused by the need to break many covalent bonds to disrupt the structure. As well as their use in jewellery, diamonds are used industrially to tip drills because of their great hardness. Synthetic industrial diamonds can be made from graphite (see below) using temperatures of 1500 K and pressures of 10^7 kPa (see the box 'Artificial diamonds', section 30.1)

Diamond – pure carbon

Graphite

This is a two-dimensional structure. Graphite is also a form of pure carbon, differing from diamond only in the arrangement of atoms. The two are **allotropes**. The contrasting properties of diamond and graphite provide a dramatic illustration of the effects of structure on physical properties. The carbon atoms in graphite each form three σ bonds in the same plane. This leads to two-dimensional layers of atoms (**Figure 9.39**). The p orbitals at right angles to this plane also provide a delocalised π bonding system spreading over each layer. This means that graphite conducts electricity well along the layers, but not so well at right angles to them. The bonding *between* the layers is weak (van der Waals: see section 10.1), allowing the layers to slide easily across one another. This leads to the use of graphite as a non-oily lubricant. It is also familiar as pencil 'lead', the layers flaking off onto the paper.

Pencil lead is graphite – also pure carbon

Did you know? In 1772 The French chemist Antoine Lavoisier demonstrated that a diamond burned to form carbon dioxide, thus showing that diamond was a form of carbon.

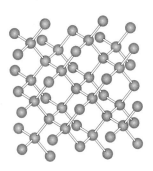

Figure 9.38 The structure of diamond

Figure 9.39 The structure of graphite

Summary

● Born–Haber cycles summarise	the energy terms involved in the formation of ionic compounds from their elements.
The most significant terms are (a)	the ionisation energy: $M(g) \longrightarrow M^+(g) + e^-$ $\Delta H^\ominus = IE$
and (b)	lattice energy: $M^+(g) + X^-(g) \longrightarrow (M^+ + X^-)(s)$ $\Delta H^\ominus = LE$
● Lattice energies are greater for (a) and (b)	smaller ions more highly charged ions
● Polarisation causes some ionic compounds to have a degree of	covalency.
● This is increased by (a) and (b)	small highly charged positive ions large highly charged negative ions.
● Covalent bonding may be described in terms of (a) or (b)	dot-cross diagrams by overlap of atomic orbitals to form molecular orbitals.

● σ molecular orbitals have electron density concentrated	along the line joining the nuclei.
● π orbitals have electron density	above and below the line joining the nuclei.
● π bonds only occur where	a σ bond already exists.
● In dative bonds, both shared electrons come from	one atom.
● Where a bond is between two different atoms, it will be polar if	the atoms differ in electronegativity (electron-attracting power).
● Bond energy is the energy required to	separate the two atoms in the bond. $X_2 \longrightarrow 2X$ $\Delta H^{\ominus}$ = bond energy
● Delocalisation involves a system of	π bonds spread over more than two atoms.
● Delocalisation results in	greater stability for the molecule than would be predicted without it.
● Metallic bonding involves	metal ions held together by a delocalised 'sea' of electrons.
● Metallic bonding allows the structure to	conduct both electricity and heat well.
● Metals have one of the following structures: (a) or (b) or (c)	hexagonal close-packed (ABA) face-centred cubic close-packed (ABC) structure. (both of coordination number 12) body-centred cubic (with coordination number 8)
● 1 : 1 ionic compounds adopt one of the following structures: (a) (b) or (c)	the CsCl (8 : 8), NaCl (6 : 6) ZnS (4 : 4) structure
● The structure adopted depends on	the relative radii of their cations and anions.
● The shapes of covalent molecules may be predicted by	electron pair repusion theory.
● This says that	the groups of electrons around a central atom will adopt positions as far away from each other as possible owing to their repulsion.
● This can lead to the following basic shapes: two groups: three groups: four groups: five groups: six groups:	 linear, trigonal planar, tetrahedral, trigonal bipyramidal, octahedral.

9.4 Practice questions

1. Draw dot-cross diagrams for the following compounds:

Ionic	Covalent
LiCl	H_2S
CaO	$C\equiv N^-$ ion
CaF_2	CF_4
Li_2O	

2. Predict the shapes of the following molecules or ions. You will need to draw a dot-cross diagram first.

   (a) F_2O, (b) $H—C\equiv N$, (c) NH_3, (d) NH_4^+,
   (e) NH_2^-, (f) PF_5, (g) PH_3, (h) SF_6, (i) CF_4,

   (j)   (k)

   (l)

3. Draw Born–Haber cycles for formation of the following, using the data below:

   $$NaBr\ (Na^+Br^-),\ CaCl_2\ (Ca^{2+}2Cl^-),$$
   $$CaO\ (Ca^{2+}O^{2-}),\ Li_2O\ (2Li^+O^{2-})$$

   Calculate the lattice energy in each case.

	$\Delta H_{at}^{\ominus}$	1st IE	2nd IE	1st EA	2nd EA	$\Delta H_f^{\ominus}$
Li	+159.4	+520	+7298			NaBr −361.1
Na	+107.3	+496	+4563			$CaCl_2$ −795.8
Ca	+178.2	+590	+1145			CaO −635.1
Br	+111.9	+1140	+2100	−324.6		Li_2O −597.9
Cl	+121.7	+1251	+2297	−348.8		
O	+249.2	+1314	+3388	−141.1	+798	

4. Indicate the polarity of the following molecules by drawing $\delta+$ and $\delta-$ on the appropriate atoms.

   (a) $H—Cl$ (b) $C\equiv O$ (c) $F—Cl$ (d)

   (e) $O=C=O$ (f) (g)

   Which two will have no overall dipole moment? Explain your answer.

5. (a) For each of the following atoms, calculate the approximate shielded nuclear charge felt by one of the outer electrons.

   $$Mg,\ Ca,\ F,\ Cl,\ N,\ O,\ H$$

   (b) Use your answer to explain why HF is a polar molecule.

6. Why is fluorine the most electronegative atom? What do you expect to be the most electropositive atom (the one that will give away electron(s) most readily)?

7. Draw a Born–Haber cycle for the hypothetical compound XeF (Xe^+F^-) using the value of the lattice energy of CsF $(-747\ kJ\ mol^{-1})$. Calculate $\Delta H_f^{\ominus}$ for XeF.

   $$\Delta H_{at}^{\ominus}(F) = +79.0\ kJ\ mol^{-1}$$
   $$\text{1st IE(Xe)} = +1170\ kJ\ mol^{-1}$$
   $$\text{1st EA(F)} = -328.0\ kJ\ mol^{-1}$$

   Why is $\Delta H_{at}^{\ominus}$ of Xe not given (or needed)? Explain why XeF does not exist. Comment on the validity of using the lattice energy of CsF.

8. The carbonate ion CO_3^{2-} is trigonal planar with the carbon atom in the centre. All bond angles are exactly 120° and all the bond lengths are 0.129 nm. The bond length C—O is 0.143 nm and that for C=O is 0.116 nm. What does this suggest about the bonding? Draw a dot-cross diagram of the bonding and sketch the orbitals involved.

9. Explain these trends in bond energies in $kJ\ mol^{-1}$ in terms of nuclear charge and size.

	Increase	
N—H	O—H	F—H
391	464	568
		Cl—H
		432
		Br—H
		366
		I—H
		298

   Increase ↑

10. Which of the following compounds would you expect to show the greatest degree of covalency? Explain.

BeF_2,	LiF,	NaF
$BeCl_2$,	LiCl,	NaCl
BeI_2,	LiI,	NaI

9.5 Examination questions

1. (a) (i) Using the data provided. construct a Born-Haber cycle for magnesium chloride, $MgCl_2$, and from it determine the electron affinity of chlorine.

	$\Delta H/kJ\ mol^{-1}$
Enthalpy of atomisation of chlorine	$+122$
Enthalpy of atomisation of magnesium	$+148$
First ionisation energy of magnesium	$+738$
Second ionisation energy of magnesium	$+1451$
Lattice enthalpy of magnesium chloride	-2526
Enthalpy of formation of magnesium chloride	-641

(ii) The theoretically calculated value for the lattice enthalpy of magnesium chloride is $-2326\ kJ\ mol^{-1}$. Explain the difference between the theoretically calculated value and the experimental value given in the data in (a)(i), in terms of the bonding of magnesium chloride.

[London Nuffield 1998]

2. (a) A Born–Haber cycle for the formation of calcium oxide is shown below.

(i) Identify the change which represents the lattice enthalpy of CaO.
(ii) Use the data above to calculate ΔH_5.
(iii) Use this value of ΔH_5 to calculate the first electron affinity of oxygen, given that the second electron affinity of oxygen is $+844\ kJ\ mol^{-1}$.

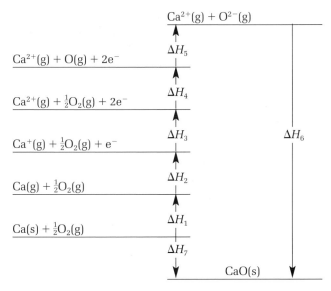

Data $\Delta H/kJ\ mol^{-1}$:
$\Delta H_1 = +193$; $\Delta H_2 = +590$; $\Delta H_3 = +1150$;
$\Delta H_4 = +248$; $\Delta H_6 = -3513$; $\Delta H_7 = -635$.

(b) (i) What enthalpy change does the value ΔH_2 represent?
(ii) Would the value of ΔH_2 be larger or smaller for magnesium than it is for calcium?
(iii) Explain your answer in (b)(ii).

[London 1997, part]

3. (i) State the shapes of the following molecules. Using the VSEPR (Valence-Shell Electron Pair Repulsion) principle explain how the shapes of these simple molecules arise (diagrams are not required):

BF_3; CH_4; SF_6.

(ii) The bond angle $H\hat{N}H$ in NH_4^- is 109°;
The bond angle $H\hat{N}H$ in NH_3 is 107°;
The bond angle $H\hat{O}H$ in H_2O is 104.5°.

Explain these differences in bond angles in terms of repulsion between the different types of electron pairs.

(iii) Use the VSEPR principle to predict the shapes of the following molecules:

$BeCl_2$; BrF_5.

[WJEC 1996, part]

4. Use the following data to answer parts (b) and (c) of this question.

$F_2(g) \longrightarrow 2F(g)$		$\Delta H_1^{\ominus} = +158\ kJ\ mol^{-1}$
$Ag^+(g) + F^-(g) \longrightarrow AgF(s)$		$\Delta H_2^{\ominus} = -969\ kJ\ mol^{-1}$
$Ag(s) \longrightarrow Ag(g)$		$\Delta H_3^{\ominus} = +278\ kJ\ mol^{-1}$
$Ag^+(g) + F^-(g)$		
$\quad\longrightarrow Ag^+(aq) + F^-(aq)$		$\Delta H_4^{\ominus} = -991\ kJ\ mol^{-1}$
$Ag(s) + \frac{1}{2}F_2(g) \longrightarrow AgF(s)$		$\Delta H_5^{\ominus} = -203\ kJ\ mol^{-1}$
$Ag(g) \longrightarrow Ag^+(g) + e^-$		$\Delta H_6^{\ominus} = +731\ kJ\ mol^{-1}$

(a) Explain what is meant by the term *standard enthalpy change* and write equations to illustrate the meaning of the terms *electron affinity* and *second ionisation enthalpy*.
(b) Calculate the enthalpy of solution of silver fluoride.
(c) (i) Construct a Born–Haber cycle for the formation of silver fluoride.
(ii) Use your cycle and the data given opposite to calculate the value of the electron affinity of fluorine.

[NEAB 1998]

10 Intermolecular forces: liquids and solutions

CHEMISTRY NOW

Stick to it – the chemistry of paint

Did you know that just one of the Dulux® paint ranges has 1600 colours and that the world's largest paint manufacturer, ICI, makes 700 million litres of paint per year? Have you ever wondered what makes paint stick to surfaces? The answer is 'intermolecular forces'. Overall, atoms are electrically neutral – they have as many electrons as protons – but these electrons and protons are not necessarily evenly distributed. If one end of a molecule has more than its share of electrons, then the molecule has a dipole and will attract other molecules that have dipoles. Dipoles *always* attract: even if they approach with like charged ends towards one another, they will 'flip' and attract. These attractive forces are what makes paint stick.

Art or vandalism? Whatever you think, the paint sticks because of intermolecular forces

Individually, these forces are weak (much weaker than covalent bonds), but all everyday objects have billions of particles at their surfaces. For example, a pinhead has 10 million million atoms on its surface. The effect of all these forces adds up. The situation is rather like Velcro®. Each individual hook-and-eye link is weak but the combined effect makes a strong join.

However, there is a little more to it. If you tried to 'paint' a Teflon-coated frying pan with water, the water wouldn't stick: it would form droplets on the surface. Ironically this is because the intermolecular forces in water are *too* strong. Water molecules attract each other much more than they attract Teflon. The paint technologist must tailor paint molecules so that they attract the surface more than they attract each other. This is why surface preparation is so important when painting.

Sanding the surface to be painted has another important effect that helps paint to stick. It roughens the surface causing microscopic cavities into which the wet paint runs. When it dries, the paint is mechanically locked into position.

Of course adhesion is not the only essential property of paint, which must also have the right colour and ability to scatter light, dry quickly enough to prevent runs (but not so fast that brush-marks can't be removed), and keep its colour for several years.

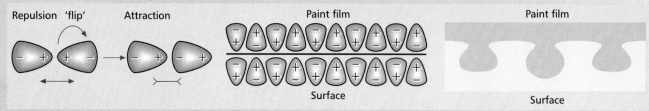

Repulsion 'flip'   Attraction

Dipoles always attract one another

Paint film

Surface

Paint sticks to surfaces by dipole–dipole attraction

Paint film

Surface

Microscopic surface cavities help to lock the paint film in place

Introduction

Chapter 9 describes the different bonds which hold atoms together:- covalent, ionic and metallic. For example, the water molecule has two atoms of hydrogen covalently bonded to an atom of oxygen. However, there must be other forces that hold one water molecule to the next: otherwise the water molecules would not hold together to form a liquid, and water would exist only as a gas. These **intermolecular forces** are the subject of this chapter. Do not confuse the intermolecular forces between the molecules with the covalent bonds between atoms *within* the molecules. Covalent bonds are much stronger than the intermolecular forces. For example, water only needs to be heated to 100°C (373 K) to break the intermolecular forces and separate the molecules, but much higher temperatures are needed to break apart the hydrogen atoms from the oxygen atoms.

Intermolecular forces exist between all molecules and atoms. Even the separate atoms of the noble gases can form liquids. There are three distinct types of intermolecular forces, called hydrogen bonding, dipole–dipole bonding and van der Waals bonding. The first two act only between certain types of molecules. van der Waals forces act between all atoms and molecules.

Intermolecular forces are responsible for the existence of the liquid state and also govern the processes of mixing, dissolving and boiling.

10.1 Intermolecular forces

Dipole–dipole forces

In the hydrogen chloride molecule (**Figure 10.1**), the hydrogen and chlorine atoms differ in electronegativity.

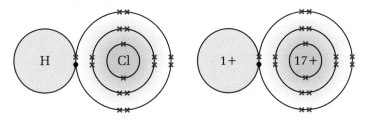

Figure 10.1 Dot-cross diagrams for hydrogen chloride

The shared electrons 'feel' one proton attracting them to the hydrogen atom and seven (after allowing for shielding) to the chlorine atom (see section 9.1). Thus the electrons are unequally shared, being pulled towards the chlorine atom rather than the hydrogen atom. The molecule is therefore written:

$$H^{\delta+}Cl^{\delta-}$$

and is said to have a **dipole**.

N 3.0	O 3.5	F 4.0	
	S 2.5	Cl 3.0	
		Br 2.8	
		I 2.5	

Figure 10.2 The most electronegative elements

Electronegative elements are found in the areas of the Periodic Table marked in **Figure 10.2**:

The electronegativity values are given: the larger the number, the more electronegative is the element.

Two molecules which both have dipoles will attract one another (**Figure 10.3**).

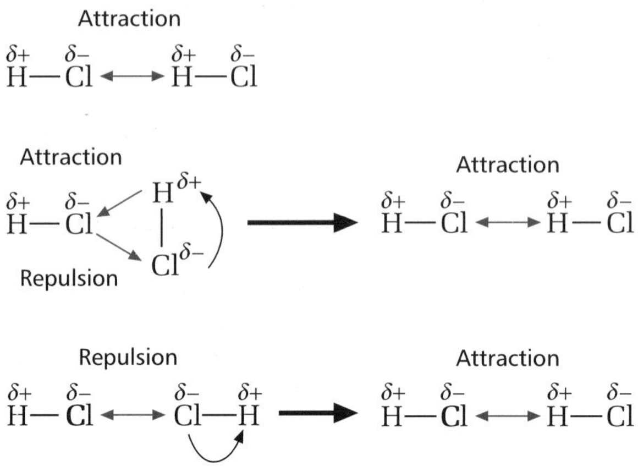

Attraction

$$\overset{\delta+}{H}\!-\!\overset{\delta-}{Cl} \longleftrightarrow \overset{\delta+}{H}\!-\!\overset{\delta-}{Cl}$$

Attraction   Attraction

$$\overset{\delta+}{H}\!-\!\overset{\delta-}{Cl} \quad \overset{H^{\delta+}}{\underset{Cl^{\delta-}}{|}} \quad \longrightarrow \quad \overset{\delta+}{H}\!-\!\overset{\delta-}{Cl} \longleftrightarrow \overset{\delta+}{H}\!-\!\overset{\delta-}{Cl}$$

Repulsion

Repulsion   Attraction

$$\overset{\delta+}{H}\!-\!\overset{\delta-}{Cl} \longleftrightarrow \overset{\delta-}{Cl}\!-\!\overset{\delta+}{H} \quad \longrightarrow \quad \overset{\delta+}{H}\!-\!\overset{\delta-}{Cl} \longleftrightarrow \overset{\delta+}{H}\!-\!\overset{\delta-}{Cl}$$

Figure 10.3 Two polar molecules, such as hydrogen chloride, will always attract one another

Whatever their original orientation, the molecules will 'flip' to give the first arrangement, where the two molecules attract.

Other examples of molecules that exhibit dipole–dipole attraction include:

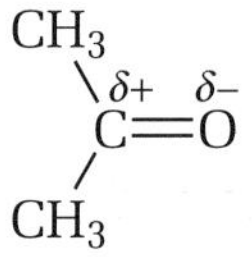

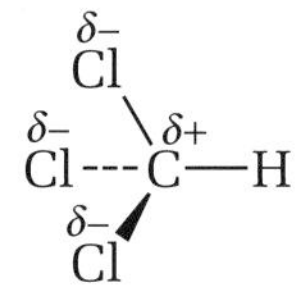

$$\begin{array}{c} CH_3 \\ \diagdown \overset{\delta+}{} \overset{\delta-}{} \\ C\!=\!O \\ \diagup \\ CH_3 \end{array} \quad \text{propanone}$$

$$\overset{\delta-}{Cl} \quad \overset{\delta-}{Cl}\text{---}\overset{\delta+}{C}\!-\!H \quad \text{trichloromethane} \\ \overset{\delta-}{Cl}$$

Q (a) Which of the following molecules are likely to have a dipole? (b) Which cannot have a dipole? H_2, N_2, CO, NO, HF

van der Waals forces

A helium atom has two positive charges on its nucleus and two negatively charged electrons. The atom is electrically neutral, but at any instant its charge distribution may not be symmetrical. Any of the arrangements in **Figure 10.4** could occur *at any instant* (or their equivalents with the electrons being thought of as 'charge clouds'). Any of the arrangements in Figure 10.4 mean the atom has a dipole at that moment. An instant later, the dipole may be in a different direction or even not exist, but the overwhelming likelihood is that at any point in time the atom *will* have a dipole. This instantaneous dipole can affect the electron distribution in nearby molecules, so that they too are distorted (**Figure 10.5**).

The result of this is to induce dipoles in nearby atoms, which will be *attracted* to the original dipoles. As the electron distribution of the original molecule changes, it will induce new dipoles in the atoms around it, but they will always be attracted to the original one. These forces are sometimes called **instantaneous dipole-induced dipole** forces, but this is rather a mouthful. The more usual name is van der Waals forces.

These forces are very weak but act between *all* atoms or molecules, in addition to any other intermolecular forces. The ease of distortion of the electron cloud, and therefore the size of the van der Waals forces, increases with the number of electrons present. This is why

Hint: van der Waals really is spelt with a small 'v', even at the beginning of a sentence.

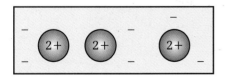

Figure 10.4 Possible arrangements of the electrons in helium

Answer: (a) CO, NO, HF. The two atoms differ in electronegativity.

(b) H_2, N_2. The two atoms have the same electronegativity.

Did you know? van der Waals forces are named after the Dutch physicist Johannes van der Waals who was awarded the Nobel Prize in 1910.

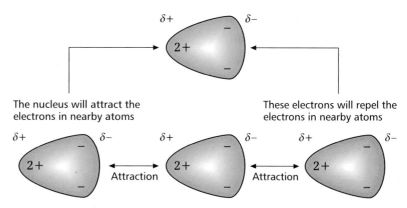

Figure 10.5 Instantaneous dipoles induce dipoles in nearby atoms

the boiling temperatures of the noble gases increase with their atomic numbers (**Figure 10.6**). It is also the reason for the increase in boiling temperatures with increased chain length for hydrocarbons, where the greater number of electrons increases the van der Waals forces.

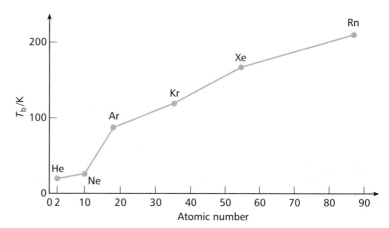

Figure 10.6 Graph of boiling temperature against atomic number for the noble gases. The increased boiling temperatures are caused by the greater number of electrons, and hence greater van der Waals forces

Did you know? Intermolecular forces are what stop you falling through your chair. When a piece of wood or most plastics break, it is the forces *between* the molecules, not the covalent bonds *within* them, which break.

Hydrogen bonding

Think of the water molecule, H_2O. Oxygen is much more electronegative than hydrogen and so water is polar.

Hint: The signs $\delta+$ and $\delta-$ do not indicate the size of the charges, only their signs. In water, for example, the $\delta-$ on the oxygen must be twice the size of the $\delta+$ on the hydrogens, because the molecule is neutral overall.

We should expect dipole–dipole attractions as shown. However, in this case, there is more to it than that, for two reasons:

Hint: Remember that the radius of a proton is between 10^4 and 10^5 times smaller than the radius of an atom.

1. The oxygen atoms have lone pairs of electrons.
2. The hydrogen atom has almost lost both the shared electrons to the oxygen to which it is covalently bonded. This leaves it almost bare of electrons.

The exposed proton that remains is *very* small. This means that a lone pair from the oxygen atom of another water molecule can approach very close to it and is therefore strongly attracted. This

Answer: Hexane is a larger molecule with more electrons and therefore strong enough van der Waals forces to hold the molecules together as a liquid.

oxygen atom can begin to form a dative covalent bond with the hydrogen atom, using this lone pair (see Chapter 9).

$$\underset{\substack{\delta+ \\ H}}{\overset{\substack{\delta- \\ \ddot{O} - H \; \delta+}}{}} \quad \underset{\substack{\delta+ \\ H}}{\overset{\substack{\delta- \\ \ddot{O} \; \delta+}}{}}$$

The new bond which is formed is called a **hydrogen bond**. It is considerably stronger than simple dipole–dipole interaction, although significantly weaker than a 'proper' covalent bond. Hydrogen is the only atom that can take part in this type of bonding: effectively acting as a bridge between two very electronegative atoms. This is because the bonding depends on the small size of the bare proton.

Hydrogen bonding only occurs between a very electronegative atom and a hydrogen covalently bonded to an electronegative atom. The only atoms electronegative enough are fluorine, oxygen and nitrogen, although chlorine is a borderline case.

One exception to the rule is the group:

$$\overset{\substack{\delta- \\ Cl}}{\underset{\substack{\delta- \\ Cl}}{Cl---\overset{\delta+}{C}}}-$$

The combined effect of the three chlorine atoms, all quite electronegative, makes this group almost as electronegative as a nitrogen, oxygen or fluorine atom, so that trichloromethane can form hydrogen bonds with, for example, propanone.

$$\underset{\substack{| \\ Cl \; \delta-}}{\overset{\substack{\delta- \\ Cl \\ |}}{Cl - C - H - - \overset{\delta-}{O} = C}} \overset{\substack{CH_3 \\ \delta+}}{\underset{CH_3}{}}$$

Hydrogen bond

A hydrogen bond forms between water, H_2O, and ammonia, NH_3.

$$\underset{\substack{\delta+/ \\ H}}{\overset{\delta-}{O}} - H - - \overset{\substack{\delta+ \\ H \\ \delta-/ \\ N}}{\underset{\substack{\backslash \delta+ \\ H}}{}} \overset{\delta+}{H}$$

Hydrogen bonds are usually represented by three dashes: – – –. As fluorine is the most electronegative atom, the hydrogen bonds formed with it as the electronegative atom are the strongest. The hydrogen bond between two molecules of HF has a bond energy of $125 \, kJ \, mol^{-1}$. Average hydrogen bond energies are around $25 \, kJ \, mol^{-1}$. Compare this with $300–400 \, kJ \, mol^{-1}$ for typical covalent bonds (see **Table 10.1**).

Examples of hydrogen bonding

Hydrogen bonds are very important. On several counts, life as we know it would not exist but for hydrogen bonding.

Hint: The three elements that are electronegative enough to take part in hydrogen bonding are fluorine, oxygen and nitrogen: 'the big three'.

Q Hydrogen bonds are normally linear, i.e. the two electronegative atoms and the hydrogen are in a straight line. Try to explain why this is.

Answer: The hydrogen is surrounded by two electron pairs which repel one another as far away as possible.

Table 10.1 Strengths of intermolecular forces compared with covalent bonds

Type of bond	Typical bond energy/kJ mol^{-1}	Acts between
hydrogen bonding	approx. 25 (max. 125)	an electronegative atom and a hydrogen atom which is covalently bonded to an electronegative atom
dipole–dipole	between these	two molecules, both with permanent dipoles
van der Waals	less than 1	all the above
[covalent	typically 300–400	atoms within molecules]

Hint: Hydrides are compounds of elements with hydrogen only.

Boiling points of hydrides

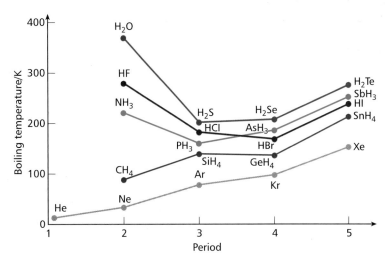

Figure 10.7 Graph of boiling temperatures against period numbers for some hydrides and the noble gases

The graph above (**Figure 10.7**) shows the boiling temperatures of the noble gases and the hydrides of elements of Groups IV, V, VI and VII plotted against the period number. The noble gases and the Group IV hydrides show a gradual decrease in boiling point going from Period 5 to Period 1 as we should expect.

These substances have van der Waals forces only: there is no hydrogen bonding because none of the elements is electronegative enough for this to take place. The same trend is observed for most of the Group V, VI and VII hydrides but hydrogen fluoride, water and ammonia show a marked deviation from the trend. This is because these three hydrides *can* form hydrogen bonds, making them much more difficult to boil (boiling involves separating the molecules and thus breaking the intermolecular bonds). Simple extrapolation of the graph predicts the boiling point of water to be about 200 K without hydrogen bonding, compared with the actual value of 373 K. But for hydrogen bonding, water would be a gas at room temperature.

There are two other points of interest on the graph. Firstly, the boiling point of water shows a greater deviation from the predicted value than that of hydrogen fluoride. This seems odd, since fluorine is more electronegative than oxygen and we might have expected the hydrogen bonding in hydrogen fluoride to be stronger than in water.

The explanation is simple: to form a hydrogen bond, we need a hydrogen atom *and* a lone pair. It is the number of these that is significant.

$$\text{HF gas, } T_b = 293 \text{ K} \quad \ddot{\underset{\cdot\cdot}{:F}}\text{—H}$$

On average, hydrogen fluoride can form only one hydrogen bond per molecule because it has only one hydrogen atom.

$$\text{H}_2\text{O liquid, } T_b = 373 \text{ K} \quad :\overset{\displaystyle \overset{\textstyle H}{\diagup}}{\underset{\diagdown}{\ddot{O}}}$$
$$\text{H}$$

Water, on the other hand, can on average form two hydrogen bonds per molecule because it has two hydrogen atoms and two lone pairs.

$$\text{NH}_3 \text{ gas, } T_b = 240 \text{ K} \quad :\overset{\displaystyle \overset{\textstyle H}{\diagup}}{\underset{\diagdown}{N}}\text{—H}$$
$$\text{H}$$

Ammonia, however, can on average form only one hydrogen bond per molecule because it has only one lone pair. So water can form more hydrogen bonds than either hydrogen fluoride or ammonia, leading to a three-dimensional network of water molecules.

Take a second look at the graph for the Group VII hydrides. Hydrogen chloride's boiling temperature is slightly greater than hydrogen bromide's. This suggests that chlorine is almost electronegative enough to form hydrogen bonds. In fact, we usually think of hydrogen chloride as having strong dipole–dipole bonds, but it is a borderline case.

The structure and density of ice

The oxygen atoms in water can form two hydrogen bonds per molecule as well as its two covalent bonds. In the liquid state, the hydrogen bonds, being relatively weak, break easily because the molecules are moving about. When water freezes, the water molecules are no longer free to move about and the hydrogen bonds form permanently. The resulting three-dimensional structure resembles the structure of diamond (**Figure 10.8**).

In order to fit into this structure, the molecules are slightly less closely packed than in liquid water. So ice is less dense than water and forms on top of ponds rather than at the bottom. This insulates the ponds and enables fish to survive through the winter and must have helped life to continue in the relative warmth of the water under the ice during the Ice Ages of the past.

The viscosity of alcohols

Viscosity is a measure of the 'treacliness' of liquids – how resistant they are to flowing. When liquids flow, the intermolecular bonds between their molecules are broken. The more hydrogen bonding between comparable molecules, the more viscous the liquid will be. Propan-1-ol, C_3H_7OH, has just one hydrogen bonding group per molecule, because only the hydrogen atom bonded to the oxygen atom can form a hydrogen bond:

Icebergs float because ice is less dense than water. This is because, unusually, in the solid state the molecules are less closely packed than in liquid water. Fish can survive in frozen lakes because the ice on the surface insulates the water from further freezing

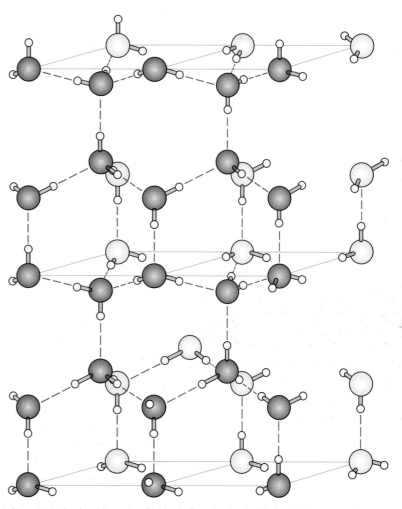

Propane-1,2-diol (an ingredient of car anti-freeze) is more viscous because it has two hydrogen bonding groups per molecule:

Figure 10.8 The three-dimensional network of covalent bonds (blue) and hydrogen bonds (pink) in ice

Q Explain why the hydrogens bonded to the carbon atoms in propan-1-ol, propane-1,2-diol and propane-1,2,3-triol cannot form hydrogen bonds.

Propane-1,2,3-triol (glycerine) has three hydrogen bonding groups per molecule and can therefore form three-dimensional hydrogen bonded networks of molecules. It is about as viscous as treacle.

Dimerisation

Hint: The word 'dimer' comes from the same Greek root as 'polymer'. A dimer has two units (di- meaning 'two'), a polymer 'many'.

If the relative molecular mass of ethanoic acid is measured in the gas phase, by the method described in Chapter 27, a value of 120 is found, while a measurement of relative molecular mass of the acid in aqueous solution (by, for example, titrating a weighed amount with standard sodium hydroxide solution) gives a value of 60. The molecules seem to have formed pairs or **dimers** in the gas phase. Two hydrogen bonds can form as shown:

$$CH_3-C \begin{array}{c} O---H-O \\ \\ O-H---O \end{array} C-CH_3$$

Their combined effect holds the molecules together as a pair.

Dimers are also formed when carboxylic acids are dissolved in solvents such as hexane, which cannot form hydrogen bonds. When the acids are dissolved in water, the water molecules form hydrogen bonds to the acid as shown:

$$CH_3-C \begin{array}{c} O---H-O \\ \\ O-H---O \end{array} \begin{array}{c} H \\ \\ H \\ \\ H \end{array}$$

Since there are far more water molecules than acid molecules, dimer formation is unlikely.

DNA and replication

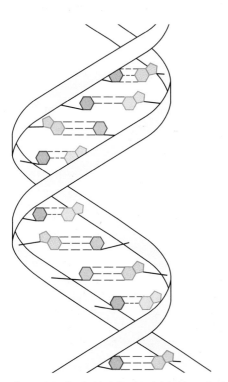

Figure 10.9 The double helix of DNA is held together by hydrogen bonds

DNA (deoxyribonucleic acid) is the molecule that stores the genetic information that makes offspring resemble their parents. The molecule exists as a double-stranded helix, the two chains being linked by hydrogen bonds (**Figure 10.9**). When cells divide, or replicate, the two strands of the double helix separate, and each strand adds on smaller chain units in the same pattern as before, thus building a new helix identical to the first. The weakness of the hydrogen bonds relative to the covalent bonds allows them to break easily in conditions which do not damage the rest of the molecule.

Answer: They are not bonded to an electronegative atom.

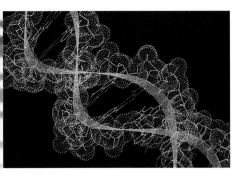

A computer-generated image of DNA, 'the molecule of life'. The double helix is held together by hydrogen bonding. This structure was first proposed in the 1950s by Francis Crick, Rosalind Franklin, James Watson and Maurice Wilkins working in London and Cambridge. You can read the exciting story of their discovery in *The Double Helix* by James Watson (Penguin)

Surface tension allows a needle to 'float' on water.

Hint: Hint: The symbol 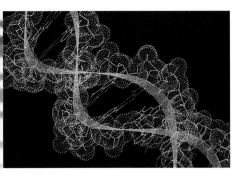 is a shorthand for a benzene ring, a hexagonal ring of six carbon atoms with a special type of bonding (see Chapter 32).

Pond skaters use the 'skin' caused by the high surface tension of water to walk on the surface to catch their prey

Surface tension

Surface tension is the 'skin' effect on the surface of liquids. The surface tension of water is unusually large, enabling a needle to be supported by the water surface, if it is lowered onto it carefully. The high surface tension of water is caused by hydrogen bonding, which holds together very strongly the molecules on the surface of the water. Liquids with high surface tension tend to form droplets with a small surface area rather than spread out and wet surfaces.

Intramolecular hydrogen bonds

'Intra-' means 'within'. Intramolecular hydrogen bonds form between atoms within the same molecule. This can affect the properties of the molecule considerably. The molecules 4-nitrophenol and 2-nitrophenol are a good example (**Figure 10.10**).

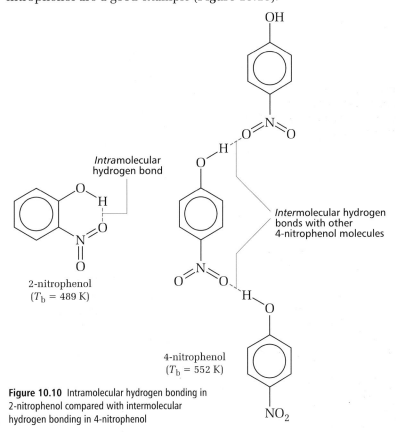

2-nitrophenol
(T_b = 489 K)

*Intra*molecular hydrogen bond

*Inter*molecular hydrogen bonds with other 4-nitrophenol molecules

4-nitrophenol
(T_b = 552 K)

Figure 10.10 Intramolecular hydrogen bonding in 2-nitrophenol compared with intermolecular hydrogen bonding in 4-nitrophenol

In 2-nitrophenol, an **intra**molecular hydrogen bond forms as shown. This means the hydrogen is not free to form hydrogen bonds with other 2-nitrophenol molecules. The OH group in 4-nitrophenol is not close enough to the oxygen atoms of the —NO_2 group to form hydrogen bonds with them. In this molecule, **inter**molecular hydrogen bonds form, so 4-nitrophenol is more soluble than 2-nitrophenol, because it can form hydrogen bonds with water while 2-nitrophenol cannot. Also, 2-nitrophenol, with weaker bonds between the molecules, melts at a lower temperature than 4-nitrophenol.

10.2 Mixtures and solutions

A mixture contains two or more components in any proportions. Some things can mix at a molecular level. These include:

● gases and gases

● gases and liquids
● liquids and liquids (liquids which do this are called **miscible**)
● solids and liquids, if the solid dissolves

In each case the resulting mixture is called a solution.

Since molecules are in constant random motion, substances tend to mix at the molecular level by chance alone. The arrangement of particles in a mixture is more disordered than in the separate components, so mixing involves a positive entropy change (see section 8.5).

Mixtures of liquids
Why don't all liquids mix?

A very general rule to predict which liquids are miscible is 'like mixes with like'. *Like* really refers to the type of intermolecular forces between the molecules. Liquids with similar intermolecular forces will mix. For example:

● Ethanol and water mix. They both form hydrogen bonds.
● Hexane and tetrachloromethane mix. They are both held together by van der Waals forces alone.
● But water will not mix with either hexane or tetrachloromethane.

The explanation is to do with energy changes. To form a mixture, the molecules of both components must first separate and then reassemble as a mixture. Imagine the process in **Figure 10.11** occurring as a mixture forms:

Hint: The process does not literally happen as shown, but Hess's law (Chapter 8) tells us that the route we take makes no difference to the overall energy change.

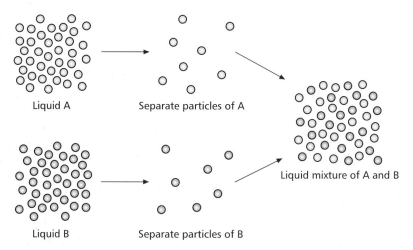

Figure 10.11 A possible way of making a mixture

Now apply this to trying to make a mixture of water and hexane. In order to separate water molecules, we must supply energy to break fairly strong hydrogen bonds between the molecules.

In order to separate hexane molecules, we must supply much less energy to break relatively weak van der Waals bonds.

The only bonds which could form between water and hexane in a mixture are weak van der Waals bonds. Thus to form a mixture of water and hexane would require an input of a lot of energy. So water and hexane do not mix.

In the case of alcohol and water, strong hydrogen bonds must be broken to separate both ethanol molecules and water molecules but bonds of comparable strength form between water and ethanol. So

Hint: It is an important general rule that processes which give out energy tend to happen of their own accord, i.e. low energy states are favoured.

there is little or no energy barrier to this process and water and ethanol do mix.

When we try to mix hexane and tetrachloromethane, weak van der Waals bonds in the pure liquids break, and on mixing, bonds of comparable strength form. So hexane and tetrachloromethane do mix.

Enthalpy changes on mixing

When a pair of liquids is mixed, there is often an enthalpy change, i.e. heat is taken in or given out. The observed enthalpy change is the difference between the enthalpy that has to be *put in* to break the intermolecular bonds in the separate liquids and the enthalpy *given out* when new intermolecular bonds are formed in the mixture.

Did you know? In some cases we add a third liquid, called a co-solvent, to get two immiscible liquids to mix.

Substances with dipole–dipole bonds tend to be intermediate between hydrogen bonded liquids and van der Waals bonded ones. They will often mix with both hydrogen bonded or van der Waals bonded substances. Propanone is a good example. It will mix quite well both with water and with hexane.

The effect of size

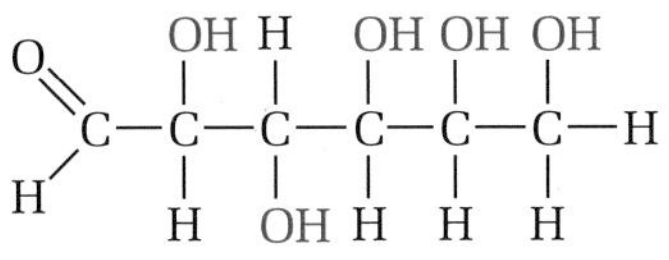

Figure 10.12 Glucose has five —OH groups and is very soluble in water

The size of a molecule may have an effect on how well it mixes. For example, the alcohols methanol, CH_3OH, ethanol C_2H_5OH and propanol, C_3H_7OH, all mix completely with water because of hydrogen bonding between the —OH group of the alcohol and water molecules. But longer-chain alcohols mix less well with water because their behaviour is dominated by the hydrocarbon chain, which cannot form hydrogen bonds. However, the addition of a second polar group may improve the solubility once more, so glucose, for example, with six carbon atoms, is very soluble because it has five —OH groups (**Figure 10.12**).

Solid–liquid mixtures: solutions

A similar rule – 'like dissolves like' – applies here. Solids that form hydrogen bonds dissolve in hydrogen-bonding solvents, so urea, $CONH_2$, (the main component of urine) dissolves in water. Iodine (I_2) molecules, which are held together by van der Waals forces, dissolve poorly in water but well in non-polar solvents such as hexane.

Solubility of ionic compounds

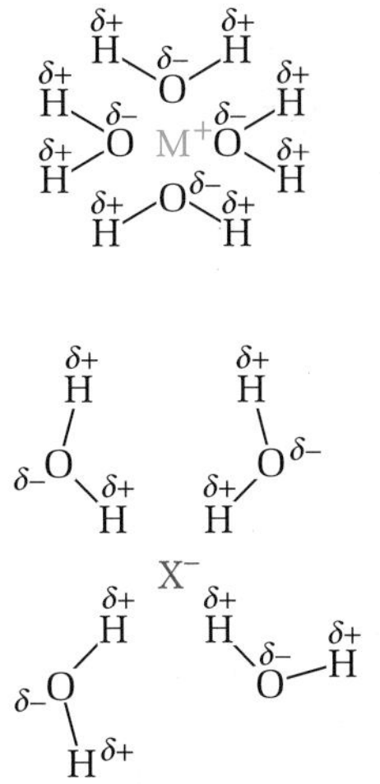

Figure 10.13 Solvation of cations, M^+, and anions, X^-, by water molecules

At room temperature ionic compounds can only dissolve well in polar liquids. In order to dissolve an ionic compound the lattice must be broken up. This requires the lattice energy (see section 9.1) to be put in. The separate ions are then **solvated** by solvent molecules. These cluster around the ions (see **Figure 10.13**):

- Positive ions are surrounded by the negative ends of the dipoles of the solvent molecules.
- Negative ions are surrounded by the positive ends of the dipoles of the solvent molecules.

This is called **hydration** when the solvent is water and **solvation** for any other solvent. Solvation (or hydration) *gives out* energy as opposite charges come together. This energy change is called the enthalpy change of hydration (or solvation) and given the symbol $\Delta H^{\ominus}_{\text{hydration}}$ or $\Delta H^{\ominus}_{\text{solvation}}$.

Enthalpy changes of hydration are approximately the same size as lattice energies for most ionic compounds and the process of

Stain removal and dry cleaning

Removing stains from clothes is sometimes considered an art, and a folklore of tips and remedies exists advising how to remove particular stains from different materials. The chemistry of stain removal is straightforward. To dissolve out a stain we need to find a solvent which forms stronger intermolecular forces with the stain than the stain does with the material. This is just an application of the 'like dissolves like' rule. So greasy stains are usually removable by treatment with a non-polar solvent like 1,1,1-trichloroethane and tar comes off by dabbing it with petrol, a hydrocarbon. Stains made by polar or ionic materials will be best removed by hydrogen bonding solvents such as water or methylated spirits (ethanol with added methanol and dye to make it unsuitable for drinking).

The type of cloth will also affect the ease of stain removal. Wool, for example, is a protein containing many N—H and C=O groups to which hydrogen bonds can form. Other materials may have few polar groups. For example, poly(propene), from which cheap carpets may be made, has only non-polar C—H bonds. Some methods of stain removal involve chemical reactions, like bleaching with various oxidising agents such as hydrogen peroxide or sodium chlorate(I) (sodium hypochlorite – household

bleach). Another interesting tip is to use salt on red wine stains. This seems to work by osmosis: water moving from the cloth to the salt and taking the stain with it.

Many materials shrink in water. For these, dry cleaning is used. Here a non-polar solvent is used, which will dissolve grease directly without the use of a detergent. Small quantities of water are added to remove polar stains like salt and sugar but the quantities used are too small to cause shrinkage of fabrics.

Commercial stain removers work on the 'like dissolves like' rule

dissolving can be represented on an enthalpy diagram (**Figure 10.14**). For example, for sodium chloride:

$$\text{lattice energy} = +771 \text{ kJ mol}^{-1}$$

and

$$\Delta H^{\ominus}_{\text{hydration}} = -770 \text{ kJ mol}^{-1}$$

Na$^+$(g) + Cl$^-$(g) + (aq)

$\Delta H^{\ominus}_{\text{hydration}}$ (Na$^+$ + Cl$^-$)
770 kJ mol^{-1}

Enthalpy

LE (NaCl)
771 kJ mol^{-1}

Na$^+$(aq) + Cl$^-$(aq)

$\Delta H^{\ominus}_{\text{solution}}$ (NaCl)
1 kJ mol^{-1}

NaCl(s) + (aq)

(Not to scale)

Figure 10.14 Enthalpy diagram for the dissolution of sodium chloride in water

$\Delta H^{\ominus}_{\text{hydration}}$ depends on the same factors as the lattice energy (i.e. both are larger for more highly charged ions and for smaller-sized ions). Since the enthalpy change for the process depends on the difference between the two, there is often only a small enthalpy change of solution for ionic compounds. It may be either positive or negative.

In the actual process of dissolving, the solvent molecules do two things. Firstly, they solvate the ions as described above. Secondly, they come between the positive and negative ions and weaken the forces of attraction between them.

10.3 Summary

● The three types of intermolecular forces are	hydrogen bonding, dipole–dipole forces and van der Waals forces
● Hydrogen bonding acts between	a hydrogen atom covalently bonded to a nitrogen, oxygen or fluorine atom *and* a nitrogen, oxygen or fluorine atom.
● Dipole–dipole bonding acts between	two molecules with permanent dipoles.
● van der Waals forces act between	all atoms.
● The strength of van der Waals forces depends on	the total number of electrons in a molecule.
● Intermolecular forces are responsible for	the existence of the liquid state.
● Mixtures of liquids form if	molecules of the two liquids are able to form bonds of comparable strength to the bonds in the pure liquids.
● The general rule is	'like mixes with like'.
● For solutions of solids in liquids the rule	'like dissolves like' applies.
● Ionic compounds will dissolve in	polar liquids.
● $\Delta H^{\ominus}_{\text{solution}}$ for ionic compounds in polar liquids is	small because…
● $\Delta H^{\ominus}_{\text{solution}}$ is the difference between	the lattice energy of the ionic crystal and $\Delta H^{\ominus}_{\text{solvation}}$, which are approximately the same size.

10.4 Practice questions

1. What type of intermolecular forces will predominate in the following liquids?
   (a) ammonia, NH_3
   (b) octane, C_8H_{18}
   (c) argon, Ar

   (d) propanone,
$$H-\overset{\overset{\displaystyle H}{|}}{\underset{\underset{\displaystyle H}{|}}{C}}-\overset{\overset{\displaystyle O}{||}}{C}-\overset{\overset{\displaystyle H}{|}}{\underset{\underset{\displaystyle H}{|}}{C}}-H$$

   (e) methanol,
$$H-\overset{\overset{\displaystyle H}{|}}{\underset{\underset{\displaystyle H}{|}}{C}}-O-H$$

2. Propanone, CH_3COCH_3, propan-1-ol, $CH_3CH_2CH_2OH$ and butane, $CH_3CH_2CH_2CH_3$, have very similar relative molecular masses. List them in the expected order of increasing boiling point. Explain your answer.

3. Explain the following as fully as possible.

   Ethanol,
$$H-\overset{\overset{\displaystyle H}{|}}{\underset{\underset{\displaystyle H}{|}}{C}}-\overset{\overset{\displaystyle H}{|}}{\underset{\underset{\displaystyle H}{|}}{C}}-OH,\text{ and propanoic}$$

   acid,
$$H-\overset{\overset{\displaystyle H}{|}}{\underset{\underset{\displaystyle H}{|}}{C}}-\overset{\overset{\displaystyle H}{|}}{\underset{\underset{\displaystyle H}{|}}{C}}-C\overset{\displaystyle O}{\underset{\displaystyle O-H}{\diagup}},\text{ are both miscible}$$

   with water in all proportions but ethyl

   propanoate,
$$H-\overset{\overset{\displaystyle H}{|}}{\underset{\underset{\displaystyle H}{|}}{C}}-\overset{\overset{\displaystyle H}{|}}{\underset{\underset{\displaystyle H}{|}}{C}}-\overset{\overset{\displaystyle O}{||}}{C}-O-\overset{\overset{\displaystyle H}{|}}{\underset{\underset{\displaystyle H}{|}}{C}}-\overset{\overset{\displaystyle H}{|}}{\underset{\underset{\displaystyle H}{|}}{C}}-H,$$

   is only slightly miscible with water.

10.5 Examination questions

1. The boiling points of four compounds which have hydrogen bonds between their molecules are shown below:

Compound	Formula	Molar mass /g mol^{-1}	Boiling point /°C
Water	H_2O	18	100
Methanol	CH_3OH	32	65
Ethanol	C_2H_5OH	46	79
Butan-1-ol	C_4H_9OH	74	117

(a) Draw a diagram showing the position of a hydrogen bond between two molecules of methanol.

(b) By considering the structures and intermolecular forces involved, explain:
(i) why water has a higher boiling point than ethanol
(ii) why methanol has a lower boiling point than ethanol.

(c) Butan-1-ol has an isomer named ethoxyethane, $C_2H_5OC_2H_5$.
Explain why there are no hydrogen bonds between ethoxyethane molecules.

(d) Iodine is almost insoluble in water but is more soluble in ethoxyethane.
(i) What type of force is present between molecules of iodine in a crystal?
(ii) Explain why iodine is more soluble in ethoxyethane than in water.

[London (Nuffield) 1997]

2. (a) (i) By using the symbols δ+ and δ−, indicate the polarity of the covalent bonds shown below.

$$H_3C-Cl \quad Cl-F \quad CH_3CH_2N\begin{smallmatrix}H\\ \\H\end{smallmatrix}$$

(ii) Explain the term *electronegativity*.
(b) The figure below shows the structure of ethanoic acid when dissolved in benzene.

$$H_3C-C\begin{smallmatrix}O\text{------}H-O\\ \\O-H\text{------}O\end{smallmatrix}C-CH_3$$

(i) Calculate the apparent relative molecular mass of ethanoic acid when dissolved in benzene.

(ii) Give the name of the type of bonding shown by the dashed lines in the figure and explain how it arises.
(iii) When ethanoic acid is dissolved in water the relative molecular mass is slightly less than half the value calculated in (b)(i). Explain this observation by referring to the bonding shown in the figure.

[AEB 1997]

3. (a) van der Waals forces are relatively unimportant in water but in poly(ethene) they are much more significant.
(i) What feature of poly(ethene) molecules makes these forces so significant?
(ii) Suggest one physical property of poly(ethene) which results from its strong van der Waals forces.
(iii) What are the strongest intermolecular forces present in water?
(iv) Explain the **origin** of these strong forces in water. You may find it helpful to draw a diagram.
(v) Explain, in terms of intermolecular forces, why poly(ethene) is insoluble in water.

(b) Ionic solids such as sodium chloride often dissolve readily in water. Copy and complete the following diagram to show how the dissolving process takes place and what is produced.
You may find it helpful to use (+ −) to represent a water molecule.

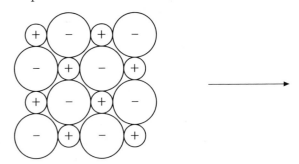

(c) The Hess cycle at the top of the next page can be used to calculate the enthalpy change of solution of lithium chloride.
(i) Insert the chemical symbols and the appropriate state symbols into a copy of the three boxes in the Hess cycle.
(ii) Calculate the enthalpy change of solution of lithium chloride, including its sign and units.
(iii) Will the temperature rise or fall when lithium chloride dissolves in water?

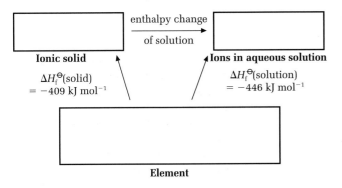

Ionic solid
$\Delta H_f^{\ominus}(\text{solid})$
$= -409 \text{ kJ mol}^{-1}$

Ions in aqueous solution
$\Delta H_f^{\ominus}(\text{solution})$
$= -446 \text{ kJ mol}^{-1}$

Element

Explain the rise or fall in terms of the making and breaking of bonds.

[London (Nuffield) 1998]

4. (i) Explain what is meant by the term *hydrogen bonding*.
   (ii) Icebergs float on water and are a danger to shipping due to their hardness. Relate these two facts to the nature (bonding and structure) of liquid water and ice.
   (iii) Deoxyribonucleic acid (DNA) exists as a double helix with individual strands being composed of *covalent bonds* and the strands being held together by *hydrogen bonding*.

DNA double helix

Covalent bonding within strands

Individual strands

H-bonding

I.   Which of the two bonding types is stronger?
II. Considering your answer to I, suggest reasons why arranging the two strands in a double helix produces such a stable structure.

[WJEC 1996, part question]

5. Some data relating to propane, ethanol and methanoic acid are given in the table.

Compound	Relative molecular mass	Boiling point /°C
Propane	44	−42.2
Ethanol	46	78.5
Methanoic acid	46	101.0

(a) (i) State what is meant by the term *polar bond* and explain how one can arise within a molecule.
    (ii) Draw the graphical formula for each of the compounds in the table and clearly show the polarity of any polar bonds present.
(b) (i) State the type of intermolecular force present in propane and explain why it has a low boiling point.
    (ii) State the main type of intermolecular force present in both pure ethanol and pure methanoic acid. Draw diagrams to show clearly this force in each of the compounds. Suggest a reason for the higher boiling point of methanoic acid.

[AEB 1998]

6. (b) The figure below shows a graph of melting temperature against relative molecular mass for the hydrides shown in line **A** and **B**.

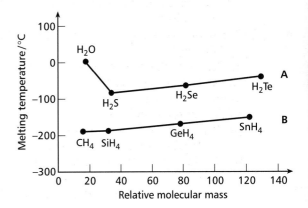

   (i) Explain the trend in the melting temperatures of the hydrides represented by line **B**.
   (ii) Explain why the first hydride in the group represented by line **A** has a higher melting temperature than the others.

(c) Bonding between peptide chains is very important biologically. The structure of a peptide chain is shown below.

$$\overset{+}{H_3}N—CH—\overset{\overset{O}{\|}}{C}—\overset{H}{N}—CH—\overset{\overset{O}{\|}}{C}—\overset{H}{N}—CH—\overset{\overset{O}{\|}}{C}—O^-$$
$$\quad\ \ \ |\qquad\qquad\qquad |\qquad\qquad\qquad |$$
$$\quad\ CH_2SH\qquad\quad (CH_2)_4\overset{+}{N}H_3\qquad CH_2CO_2^-$$

Give **two** features of this peptide chain which can result in bonding *between* chains.

[WJEC 1996, part question]

11

Equilibrium

C H E M I S T R Y   N O W

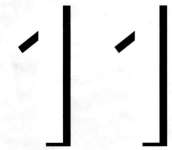

Chemistry in the trenches: Fritz Haber and the First World War

Fritz Haber (1868–1934) is remembered for devising the process named after him for making ammonia, the starting material for manufacturing nitric acid for fertilisers, explosives and a wide variety of other chemicals. At the heart of the process is the reversible reaction:

$$N_2 + 3H_2 \rightleftharpoons 2NH_3$$

This may look like a simple piece of chemistry and perhaps the most obvious way of making ammonia, but under most conditions, nitrogen and hydrogen obstinately refuse to combine in useful quantities. Haber found a way round this and now 140 million tonnes of ammonia are made each year around the world by his process.

Haber's work on the ammonia reaction was completed just before the First World War and probably helped to prolong this conflict. Before the Haber process, nitric acid was made from nitrates imported to Europe from South America. During the First World War, the British naval blockade denied these imports to Germany. Without nitrates, before Haber's process, Germany would have been unable to make fertilisers to help feed her people and manufacture explosives to continue the fighting. The raw materials for the Haber process are nitrogen (from the air) and hydrogen (which can be obtained from water) – freely available to all.

Haber used his chemical skills to help his country's war effort in another way. As an army captain, he developed the use of chlorine and phosgene as poison gases in the hope that they would prove to be war-winning weapons. In fact gas was ineffective because of its reliance on the prevailing wind and, in any case, the British and French soon retaliated in kind. Clearly Haber was not the only chemist thinking along these lines. Haber was awarded the 1918 Nobel prize for his work on ammonia but this award, so soon after the war, caused great offence to French scientists.

After the war, Haber tried to extract gold from seawater in order to repay German war debts imposed by the victors. He was unsuccessful: the sea contains a lot of gold but in a tiny concentration.

Haber had to flee Germany in 1933 because of the rise of Nazi anti-Semitism.

A gas mask in 1915

In this chapter we will be looking at:
- how we know a chemical equilibrium exists
- some examples of chemical equilibria
- the mathematics of chemical equilibria
- calculations involving chemical equilibria (the equilibrium law)
- the effect of changing conditions on chemical equilibria (Le Châtelier's principle)
- industrial examples

Introduction

The definition of equilibrium in the dictionary is 'balance or harmony of opposing forces'. Chemical equilibrium is also about balance – between the forward and back directions of reversible reactions. Chemical reactions, in principle, are all reversible, though many reactions appear to go to completion. But there are reactions that are obviously reversible and it is to these that we apply the idea of an equilibrium. Equilibrium is one of the key ideas of chemistry. Understanding the principles of equilibrium is essential to the appreciation of acid–base and redox chemistry and to the control of many industrial processes.

    The ideas behind chemical equilibrium are applicable in other fields like biology, physics and even economics.

CONCEPT CHECKPOINTS

The following basic ideas are used in this chapter. You may revise some of these topics elsewhere in the book.
- the use of chemical equations to represent the quantities of reactants and products involved in a reaction (Chapter 5)
- the idea of concentration (section 4.4)
- exothermic and endothermic reactions (section 8.1)
- using ΔH to express the enthalpy change in a reaction (section 8.1)

11.1 The characteristics of equilibrium

Imagine a puddle of water. Some of the water molecules at the surface will move fast enough to escape the liquid and evaporate. If the puddle of water is outside, it is unlikely that many of the water molecules will ever return to it, so evaporation will continue until the water is gone.

    However, if some water is placed into a closed container the situation will be quite different (see **Figure 11.1**).

    Evaporation will occur as before, but now the water molecules in the vapour are unable to escape and some will collide with the water surface and return to liquid, i.e. condense.

    At first, the rate of condensation will be small, as there will be few molecules in the vapour. So evaporation will continue at a greater rate than condensation. Therefore the volume of liquid water will shrink and the number of molecules in the vapour will increase.

    The increased number of molecules in the vapour phase makes it more likely that vapour molecules will collide with, and thus rejoin, the liquid.

    Eventually, the rate of evaporation and the rate of condensation will become equal. The level of the water will then stay the same, as will the number of molecules in the vapour and hence its pressure (the **vapour pressure**). The properties of the system will now remain constant but the evaporation and condensation are still going on *at the same rate*. This situation is called a **dynamic equilibrium** and is one of the key ideas of this topic.

    It is important to realise that equilibrium can be set up only in a **closed system**. If the container had a leak, which allowed the water vapour to escape, the equilibrium would not be set up. Eventually all the water would evaporate and escape. A 'closed system' means a system in which nothing is added or taken away, and does not have to be *literally* closed. For example, for an equilibrium between a solid

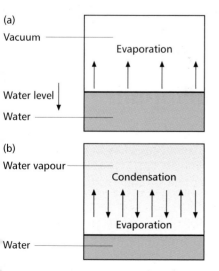

Figure 11.1 (a) Water will evaporate into an empty container. Eventually the rates of evaporation and condensation will become equal. **(b)** Equilibrium is set up

and its solution, an open beaker could provide a closed system, if the solvent did not evaporate.

We used the fact that the water level stayed the same to show that an equilibrium had been reached. Another property we could have monitored is the pressure exerted by the vapour. In fact the properties of any system do not change once equilibrium has been reached. This is an important characteristic of equilibrium.

Alternatively, we could have started by injecting the same mass of water in the form of water vapour into the empty container and allowing it to condense. We would have reached the same equilibrium position. This is a further characteristic of equilibrium: it can be approached from either 'reactants' (in this case liquid water) or 'products' (in this case water vapour) and the same equilibrium mixture results.

This particular example of equilibrium is called a **phase equilibrium** because it involves two **phases** (gas and liquid) of the same substance. The term **phase** refers to parts of a system which are physically separated from each other, e.g. solid, liquid, gas (or vapour) or solution. Although the system we have used is a very simple one, we can pick out four conditions that are applicable to *all* equilibria:

- Equilibria can only be set up in a closed system (one where no components can escape).
- Equilibrium has been reached when the properties of the system do not change with time – strictly, when properties that do not depend on the total quantity of matter (**intensive properties**) do not change. Such properties include density, concentration, colour and pressure.
- Equilibrium can be approached from either direction (in the above example, liquid or vapour) and the final equilibrium position will be the same.
- Equilibrium is a dynamic process: it occurs when the rates of two opposing processes (in this case evaporation and condensation) are the same.

A reversible reaction that can reach equilibrium is denoted by the symbol $\rightleftharpoons$. For example:

$$\text{liquid water} \rightleftharpoons \text{water vapour}$$

or

$$H_2O(l) \rightleftharpoons H_2O(g)$$

Did you know? Dynamic equilibria are quite common in many areas of life. A steady population of animals occurs when births are equal to deaths, and a steady bank balance means that spending is equal to income.

Hint: In this example, at equilibrium, evaporation and condensation both continue at the same rate, i.e. the number of molecules evaporating per second is the same as the number condensing.

11.2 Chemical equilibrium

Many chemical reactions are obviously reversible. For example ethanol, C_2H_5OH, will react with ethanoic acid, CH_3CO_2H, to produce some of the ester ethyl ethanoate, $CH_3CO_2C_2H_5$, and water. However, mixing the ester and water will produce some ethanol and ethanoic acid.

$$\underset{\text{ethanol}}{C_2H_5OH} + \underset{\text{ethanoic acid}}{CH_3CO_2H} \longrightarrow \underset{\substack{\text{ethyl ethanoate} \\ \text{(an ester)}}}{CH_3CO_2C_2H_5} + \underset{\text{water}}{H_2O}$$

$$\underset{\text{ethyl ethanoate}}{CH_3CO_2C_2H_5} + \underset{\text{water}}{H_2O} \longrightarrow \underset{\text{ethanol}}{C_2H_5OH} + \underset{\text{ethanoic acid}}{CH_3CO_2H}$$

Inside a sealed bottle garden, liquid water and water vapour are at equilibrium

If ethanol and ethanoic acid are mixed in a flask (stoppered to prevent evaporation) and left, a mixture is eventually obtained in which *all four* substances are present. (A strong acid catalyst is required if this is to occur within a reasonable length of time.) The system has reached equilibrium and we can write:

$$C_2H_5OH \; + \; CH_3CO_2C_2H_5 \; \rightleftharpoons \; CH_3CO_2C_2H_5 \; + \; H_2O$$

ethanol   ethanoic acid   ethyl ethanoate   water

The mixture may be analysed by titrating the ethanoic acid with standard alkali (allowing for the catalyst). This gives the number of moles of ethanoic acid, from which the number of moles of the other components can be worked out, and hence their concentration, if the total volume of the mixture is known. (see the box 'Equilibrium calculations example' on the next page).

If several experiments are done with different quantities of starting materials, it is always found that the ratio:

$$\frac{[CH_3CO_2C_2H_5]_{eqm} \, [H_2O]_{eqm}}{[CH_3CO_2H]_{eqm} \, [C_2H_5OH]_{eqm}}$$

Hint: A square bracket around a formula is shorthand for 'concentration of that substance in mol dm^{-3}'

has a constant value, provided the experiments are done at the same temperature. The value obtained using the figures in the box is 3.5 (no units – they cancel out). This ratio is called the **equilibrium constant** and is given the symbol K_c. The subscript 'c' indicates that it is a ratio of *concentrations*. The subscript 'eqm' means that the concentrations have been measured when equilibrium has been reached.

For the reaction below, which takes place in ethanol solution :

$$CH_3COCH_3 \; + \quad HCN \qquad \rightleftharpoons \qquad CH_3C(CN)(OH)CH_3$$

propanone   hydrogen cyanide   2-hydroxy-2-methylpropanenitrile

we find that the expression:

$$\frac{[CH_3C(CN)(OH)CH_3]_{eqm}}{[CH_3COCH_3]_{eqm}[HCN]_{eqm}}$$

is constant at constant temperature.

The equilibrium law

Both the above expressions are examples of a general law: the **equilibrium law**. This is expressed as follows. For a reaction:

$$aA + bB + cC \rightleftharpoons xX + yY + zZ$$

the expression:

$$\frac{[X]_{eqm}{}^x \, [Y]_{eqm}{}^y \, [Z]_{eqm}{}^z}{[A]_{eqm}{}^a \, [B]_{eqm}{}^b \, [C]_{eqm}{}^c}$$

has a constant value, provided the temperature is constant. The constant is called the **equilibrium constant**, K_c. The units of K_c vary, and you must work them out for each example by cancelling out the units of each term. For example:

$$A + B \rightleftharpoons C \qquad K_c = \frac{[C]^1}{[A]^1 \, [B]^1}$$

Titrating the ethanoic acid to investigate the equilibrium position

Q Work out the units of the equilibrium constant for the reaction above of propanone and hydrogen cyanide to give 2-hydroxy-2-methylpropanenitrile

Units are
$$\frac{\text{mol dm}^{-3}}{\text{mol dm}^{-3} \times \text{mol dm}^{-3}} = \text{dm}^3 \, \text{mol}^{-1}$$

Answer: dm^3 mol^{-1}

FURTHER FOCUS

Equilibrium calculations example

4.6 g (0.10 mol) of ethanol and 12.0 g (0.20 mol) of ethanoic acid were mixed in a flask with 20 cm³ of 1 mol dm⁻³ hydrochloric acid as catalyst at room temperature (20 °C, 293 K). The contents of the flask were left for a week, to reach equilibrium, and then titrated with 1.0 mol dm⁻³ sodium hydroxide. 137 cm³ were required, but 20 cm³ of these were used to react with the hydrochloric acid catalyst:

$$HCl(aq) + NaOH(aq) \longrightarrow NaCl(aq) + H_2O(l)$$

The rest (117 cm³) reacted 1 : 1 with the ethanoic acid which remained at equilibrium:

$$NaOH(aq) + CH_3CO_2H(aq) \longrightarrow CH_3CO_2Na(aq) + H_2O(l)$$

So number of moles NaOH = number of moles CH_3CO_2H

$$\text{Number of moles} = \frac{M \times V}{1000}$$

$$= \frac{1 \times 117}{1000}$$

$$= 0.117$$

Amount of ethanoic acid present at equilibrium = 0.117 mol

We can now calculate the number of moles of all the other components, from the equation and the number of moles of reactants that we started with.

Always set out problems of this type as follows:

1. Write the equation.

2. Below it write the number of moles of each component at the start.

3. Below this write the number of moles of each component known to be present at equilibrium.

4. Work out from 3 the number of moles of the other components of the equation, and write these amounts into your equation.

1. Equation: $CH_3CO_2H + C_2H_5OH \rightleftharpoons CH_3CO_2C_2H_5 + H_2O$

2. Start: 0.20 mol   0.10 mol   0 mol   0 mol

3. At eqm: 0. 117 mol   ?   ?   ?

Therefore $0.20 - 0.117 = 0.083$ mol of ethanoic acid has been used.

The equation tells us that each mole of ethanoic acid which reacts, also takes with it 1 mole of ethanol and produces 1 mole of each of the products.

So 0.083 mol of ethanol is *used* and $(0.10 - 0.083)$ = 0.017 mol is left.

0.083 mol each of ethyl ethanoate and water is formed. So we can now fill in the ?'s above.

4. $CH_3CO_2H + C_2H_5OH \rightleftharpoons CH_3CO_2C_2H_5 + H_2O$
   At equilibrium:
     0.117 mol   0.017 mol   0.083 mol   0.083 mol

If we know the volume of the whole mixture at equilibrium we can work out the concentrations at equilibrium. The volume was 37.3 cm³ or 0.0373 dm⁻³ including the catalyst which makes it an aqueous solution.

So
$$[CH_3CO_2H(aq)]_{eqm} = 0.117 \text{ mol}/0.0373 \text{ dm}^3$$
$$= 3.1 \text{ mol dm}^{-3}$$
$$[C_2H_5OH(aq)]_{eqm} = 0.017 \text{ mol}/0.0373 \text{ dm}^3$$
$$= 0.46 \text{ mol dm}^{-3}$$
$$[CH_3CO_2C_2H_5(aq)]_{eqm} = 0.083 \text{ mol}/0.0373 \text{ dm}^3$$
$$= 2.22 \text{ mol dm}^{-3}$$
$$[H_2O(aq)]_{eqm} = 0.083 \text{ mol}/0.0373 \text{ dm}^3$$
$$= 2.22 \text{ mol dm}^{-3}$$

$$K_c = \frac{[CH_3CO_2C_2H_5(aq)]_{eqm} \, [H_2O(aq)]_{eqm}}{[CH_3CO_2H(aq)]_{eqm} \, [C_2H_5OH(aq)]_{eqm}}$$

$$= \frac{2.22 \times 2.22}{3.1 \times 0.45} = 3.53 \text{ (no units)}$$

$$= 3.5 \text{ (to 2 s.f.)}$$

Position of equilibrium

A reaction that has reached equilibrium may contain more reactants than products, more products than reactants or comparable amounts of both. The size of the equilibrium constant gives an indication of the composition of the equilibrium mixture. The equilibrium law expression is always of the general form products/reactants. So if the equilibrium constant is much greater than 1, products predominate over reactants. We usually say that the equilibrium is over to the right. If the equilibrium constant is much less than 1, reactants predominate, and the equilibrium position is over to the left. Reactions where the equilibrium constant is greater than 10^{10} are usually regarded as going to completion while those with an equilibrium constant of less than 10^{-10} are regarded as not taking place at all.

Calculations using the equilibrium law expressions

What use is the equilibrium law? It enables us to calculate the composition of a reaction mixture that has reached equilibrium, and is therefore useful if we are preparing a 'target compound' via a reversible reaction.

Example 1

Let us go back to the reaction of ethanol and ethanoic acid:

$$C_2H_5OH(aq) + CH_3CO_2H(aq) \rightleftharpoons CH_3CO_2C_2H_5(aq) + H_2O(aq)$$

$$K_c = \frac{[CH_3CO_2C_2H_5(aq)]_{eqm}\,[H_2O(aq)]_{eqm}}{[C_2H_5OH(aq)]_{eqm}\,[CH_3CO_2H(aq)]_{eqm}}$$

Suppose that $K_c = 4$ at the temperature of our experiment and we want to know how much ethyl ethanoate we could produce by mixing 1 mol of ethanol and 1 mol of ethanoic acid. Set out the information as shown below:

Equation:

$$C_2H_5OH(aq) + CH_3CO_2H(aq) \rightleftharpoons CH_3CO_2C_2H_5(aq) + H_2O(aq)$$

Start:　　1 mol　　　　1 mol　　　　　　　0 mol　　　　0 mol

At equilibrium:

　　　$(1 - x)$ mol　　$(1 - x)$ mol　　　　　x mol　　　　x mol

We do not know how many moles of ethyl ethanoate will be produced, so we call this x. The equation tells us that x mol of water will also be produced and in doing so x mol of both ethanol and ethanoic acid will be used up. So the amount of each of these remaining at equilibrium is $(1 - x)$ mol.

These figures are in moles, but we need concentrations in mol dm^{-3} to substitute in the equilibrium law expression. Suppose the volume of the system at equilibrium was V dm^{-3}. Then:

$$[C_2H_5OH(aq)]_{eqm} = \frac{(1 - x)}{V} \text{ mol dm}^{-3}$$

$$[CH_3CO_2H(aq)]_{eqm} = \frac{(1 - x)}{V} \text{ mol dm}^{-3}$$

$$[CH_3CO_2C_2H_5(aq)]_{eqm} = \frac{x}{V} \text{ mol dm}^{-3}$$

$$[H_2O(aq)]_{eqm} = \frac{x}{V} \text{ mol dm}^{-3}$$

Hint: The volume of the reaction mixture will cancel for all systems with equal numbers of moles of products and reactants, so V is sometimes omitted. It is always better to include V and cancel it out later, so you will not forget it for systems where the V's do not cancel out.

These figures may now be put into the expression for K_c :

$$K_c = \frac{x/V \times x/V}{(1 - x)/V \times (1 - x)/V}$$

The V's cancel, so *in this case* we do not need to know the actual volume of the system.

$$4 = \frac{x \times x}{(1 - x) \times (1 - x)}$$

$$4 = \frac{x^2}{(1 - x)^2}$$

Taking the square root of both sides, we get:

$$2 = \frac{x}{(1-x)}$$
$$2(1-x) = x$$
$$2 - 2x = x$$
$$2 = 3x$$
$$x = \tfrac{2}{3}$$

So $\tfrac{2}{3}$ mol of ethyl ethanoate and $\tfrac{2}{3}$ mol of water are produced if the reaction reaches equilibrium, and the composition of the equilibrium mixture would be: ethanol $\tfrac{1}{3}$ mol, ethanoic acid $\tfrac{1}{3}$ mol, ethyl ethanoate $\tfrac{2}{3}$ mol, water $\tfrac{2}{3}$ mol.

Example 2

Alternatively, we can use K_c to find the amount of a reactant that will give a required amount of product.

For the following reaction in ethanol solution, $K_c = 30.0 \ dm^3 \ mol^{-1}$:

CH_3COCH_3	+	HCN	$\rightleftharpoons$	$CH_3C(CN)(OH)CH_3$
propanone		hydrogen cyanide		2-hydroxy-2-methylpropanenitrile

$$K_c = \frac{[CH_3C(CN)(OH)CH_3]_{eqm}}{[CH_3COCH_3]_{eqm} \ [HCN]_{eqm}} = 30.0 \ dm^3 \ mol^{-1}$$

Suppose we are carrying out this reaction in $2.00 \ dm^3$ of ethanol. How much hydrogen cyanide is required to produce 1.00 mol of product if we start with 4.00 mol of propanone? Set out as before with the quantities at the start and at equilibrium.

At equilibrium, we want 1.00 mol of product. Let x be the number of moles of HCN required.

Equation:	CH_3COCH_3	+	HCN	$\rightleftharpoons$	$CH_3C(CN)(OH)CH_3$
Start:	4.00 mol		x mol		0 mol
At equilibrium:	$(4.00 - 1.00)$ mol		$(x - 1.00)$ mol		1.00 mol

These are the numbers of moles and we need the concentrations to put in the equilibrium law expression. The volume of the solution is $2.00 \ dm^3$ and we need the concentration in $mol \ dm^{-3}$, so we next divide each quantitiy by $2.00 \ dm^3$.

So at equilibrium
$$[CH_3COCH_3]_{eqm} = \tfrac{3.00}{2.00} \ mol \ dm^{-3}$$
$$[HCN]_{eqm} = \tfrac{x - 1.00}{2.00} \ mol \ dm^{-3}$$
$$[CH_3C(CN)(OH)CH_3]_{eqm} = \tfrac{1.00}{2.00} \ mol \ dm^{-3}$$

Putting the figures into the equilibrium law expression:

$$30.0 \ dm^{-3} \ mol^{-1} = \frac{\tfrac{1.00}{2.00} \ mol \ dm^{-3}}{\tfrac{3.00}{2.00} \ mol \ dm^{-3} \times \tfrac{x - 1.00}{2.00} \ mol \ dm^{-3}}$$

$$30.0 \left(\tfrac{3.00}{2.00}\right)\left(\tfrac{x - 1.00}{2.00}\right) = \tfrac{1.00}{2.00}$$
$$45.0(x - 1.00) = 1.00$$
$$45.0x = 46.0$$
$$x = \tfrac{46.0}{45.0} = 1.02 \ mol \ \text{(to 3 s.f.)}$$

So, to obtain 1 mol of product we must start with 1.02 mol hydrogen cyanide, if the volume of the system is $2.00 \ dm^3$.

In this example the volume of the system *does* make a difference, because this reaction does not have the same number of moles of products and reactants.

> **Q** Try reworking the problem with the reactant dissolved in a volume of 1 dm³ of ethanol.

Answer: $x = 1.01 \ mol$

11.3 The effect of changing conditions on equilibria

Hint: The yield here means the amount of substance we obtain, divided by the amount of substance we could have obtained if the reaction had gone to completion. It is usually expressed as a percentage.

Once an equilibrium has been established, the composition of the equilibrium mixture can be changed by varying the temperature, the concentration of species involved and the pressure (in the case of reactions involving gases). This is important if we are making a target compound, either in the laboratory or industrially. It is useful to be able to choose conditions that will give the best yield of the target compound.

Le Châtelier's principle

This is a useful principle which makes it easier to predict what will happen to the position of equilibrium when the conditions of an equilibrium mixture are changed. It states that **if a system at equilibrium is disturbed the equilibrium moves in the direction which tends to reduce the disturbance.** Le Châtelier's principle tells us about the direction in which the position of equilibrium moves but does not tell us how far, so we cannot predict the *quantities* involved.

Changing concentrations

If we increase the concentration of one of the reactants, Le Châtelier's principle says that the equilibrium will shift in the direction that tends to reduce the concentration of this reactant. Look at the reaction:

$$A(aq) + B(aq) \rightleftharpoons C(aq) + D(aq)$$

Q What would happen if we removed C as it was formed?

Suppose we add some extra A without changing the volume. This would increase the concentration of A. The only way that this system can reduce the concentration of A is by A reacting with B (thus forming more C and D). So adding more A uses up more B and moves the equilibrium to the right. We end up with greater amounts of the products in the reaction mixture than there were before we added A.

Changing pressure

Hint: Increasing the pressure of a gas means that there are more molecules of it in a given volume. It is equivalent to increasing the concentration of a solution.

This only applies to reactions involving gases. An example of a gas reaction that reaches equilibrium is:

$$\underset{\substack{\text{dinitrogen tetraoxide} \\ \text{1 mole}}}{N_2O_4(g)} \rightleftharpoons \underset{\substack{\text{nitrogen dioxide} \\ \text{2 moles}}}{2NO_2(g)}$$

If we increase the pressure on this system, Le Châtelier's principle predicts that the equilibrium will move so as to try and decrease the pressure. The equilibrium will move left to do this (fewer molecules will exert less pressure).

Q Dinitrogen tetraoxide is a colourless gas and nitrogen dioxide is brown. How could you tell if the equilibrium moved to the right?

However, if there are the same number of moles on both sides of the equation, then pressure has no effect on the equilibrium position. For example:

$$\underset{\text{2 moles}}{H_2(g)} + \underset{}{Cl_2(g)} \rightleftharpoons \underset{\text{2 moles}}{2HCl(g)}$$

Answer: The equilibrium would move right to produce more C (and D).

Answer: The colour of the mixture would get browner.

The equilibrium position will not change in this reaction when the pressure is changed, so the proportions of H_2, Cl_2 and HCl will stay the same.

Hint: Reversible reactions that are exothermic in one direction are endothermic in the other direction.

Q How would an increase in pressure affect the yield of sulphur trioxide, SO_3, in this reaction?

In Chapter 23 we will work out how this is done for gas reactions and for reactions with a mixture of solids, solutions and gases (called heterogeneous reactions).

Hint: Notice that in both cases, the number of moles of ethanoic acid and water are the same. This is not a coincidence: the equation for the reaction tells us that for every mole of ethyl ethanoate formed a mole of water is also formed.

Hint: You could calculate the amounts of product formed from any amounts of reactants using the expression for K_c. However, in most cases you will need to solve a quadratic equation. You will not be asked to do this in an AS or A-level exam.

Hint: Notice that changing the temperature changes the value of K_c, whereas changing the concentration does not.

Did you know? Henri Le Châtelier also invented the oxy-acetylene torch.

Answer: Increase it.

Changing temperature

Suppose we increase the temperature of an equilibrium mixture that is exothermic in the forward direction. An example would be:

$$2SO_2(g) + O_2(g) \rightleftharpoons 2SO_3(g) \qquad \Delta H^\ominus = -197 \text{ kJ mol}^{-1}$$

Le Châtelier's principle predicts that the equilibrium moves in the direction which cools the system down. To do this is will move in the direction which absorbs heat (is endothermic), i.e. to the left.

Catalysts

Catalysts have no effect on the position of equilibrium. They work in such a way that they affect both the forward and reverse reactions equally (see Chapter 14). Therefore they speed up the rate at which equilibrium is set up but do not alter the composition of the equilibrium mixture.

Why does Le Châtelier's principle work?
The effect of changing concentration

We can use the equilibrium law expression to work out the actual quantities involved when we change the concentrations of an equilibrium mixture involving solutions. Provided the temperature does not change, the equilibrium constant remains the same.

Earlier we calculated the equilibrium composition for the reaction below, for which $K_c = 4$.

$$C_2H_5OH(aq) + CH_3CO_2H(aq) \rightleftharpoons CH_3CO_2C_2H_5(aq) + H_2O(aq)$$

Starting with 1 mole of ethanoic acid and 1 mole of ethanol:

$$[C_2H_5OH]_{eqm} = 0.33 \text{ mol}$$
$$[CH_3CO_2H]_{eqm} = 0.33 \text{ mol}$$
$$[CH_3CO_2C_2H_5]_{eqm} = 0.67 \text{ mol}$$
$$[H_2O]_{eqm} = 0.67 \text{ mol}$$

Starting with 3 moles of ethanol and 1 mole of ethanoic acid we get:

$$[C_2H_5OH]_{eqm} = 2.1 \text{ mol}$$
$$[CH_3CO_2H]_{eqm} = 0.1 \text{ mol}$$
$$[CH_3CO_2C_2H_5]_{eqm} = 0.9 \text{ mol}$$
$$[H_2O]_{eqm} = 0.9 \text{ mol}$$

Notice that adding more ethanol has used up more of the ethanoic acid and produced more moles of both products, as Le Châtelier's principle predicts.

The effect of changing temperature

Changing the temperature changes the value of the equilibrium constant. For an exothermic reaction, increasing the temperature decreases the equilibrium constant. For endothermic reactions, increasing the temperature increases the equilibrium constant. Equilibrium constants are always of the form:

$$K_c = \frac{\text{products}}{\text{reactants}}$$

so if, for example, K_c gets smaller, products must decrease and reactants must increase so that the value of the fraction decreases. **Table 11.1** summarises the other possibilities.

Again, these are as predicted by Le Châtelier's principle.

Table 11.1 The effect of changing temperature on equilibria

Type of reaction	Temperature change	Effect on K_c	Effect on products	Effect on reactants	Direction of change of equilibrium
endothermic	decrease	decrease	decrease	increase	moves left
endothermic	increase	increase	increase	decrease	moves right
exothermic	increase	decrease	decrease	increase	moves left
exothermic	decrease	increase	increase	decrease	moves right

Hint: Cover up the last four columns and test yourself on the result of changing temperature.

11.4 Measurements of equilibrium constant K_c

In principle this is straightforward. We simply have to let the system we are interested in reach equilibrium and measure the concentrations of one or more species – enough to calculate the concentrations of the rest. We can then substitute the values into the expression for K_c.

Any of the standard methods of measuring concentration may be used, with the one proviso that the method of measuring the concentration must not disturb the equilibrium. This might occur if a titration were used, for example, for the equilibrium mixture:

$$Ca(OH)_2(s) \rightleftharpoons Ca^{2+}(aq) + 2OH^-(aq)$$
calcium hydroxide   calcium ions   hydroxide ions

$[OH^-(aq)]_{eqm}$ could not be found by titration of the hydroxide ions with standard acid because, as the titration removed hydroxide ions, the equilibrium would move to the right (Le Châtelier's principle) and more calcium hydroxide would dissociate. If the titration continued, all the calcium hydroxide would eventually dissociate. Titration can only be used if the rate at which the equilibrium is set up is very slow compared with that of the titration reaction. An example of this is the equilibrium:

$$C_2H_5OH(aq) + CH_3CO_2H(aq) \rightleftharpoons CH_3CO_2C_2H_5(aq) + H_2O(aq)$$
ethanol   ethanoic acid   ethyl ethanoate   water

Here the acid could be titrated without disturbing the equilibrium, as the titration reaction is more or less instantaneous while the equilibrium takes several days to establish, even with a catalyst (see the box on page 128).

Another equilibrium which can be investigated by titration is:

$$2HI(g) \rightleftharpoons H_2(g) + I_2(g)$$
hydrogen iodide   hydrogen   ioddine

The equilibrium can be set up at high temperatures (over 500 K) and the mixture rapidly cooled to slow down the reaction rate and effectively 'freeze' the system in its equilibrium position. Either the hydrogen iodide (dissolved in water and therefore acidic) can be titrated with standard alkali or the iodine can be titrated with sodium thiosulphate. A colorimeter could also be used to measure the concentration of iodine, which is brown.

Henri Louis Le Châtelier, the French chemist who put forward his principle 'Loi de stabilité de l'equilibre chimique' in 1888

Hint:

Iodine/thiosulphate titrations

Iodine reacts with sodium thiosulphate according to the following equation:

$$I_2(aq) + 2Na_2S_2O_3(aq) \longrightarrow 2NaI(aq) + Na_2S_4O_6(aq)$$

i.e. in a 1:2 ratio.

To measure the concentration of a solution of iodine by titration, we add sodium thiosulphate from a burette until the brown colour of iodine has almost disappeared and the solution is the colour of lager. To make the end point easier to see, at this stage we add a few drops of starch, which forms a blue-black complex with the iodine. We now add thiosulphate solution a drop at a time until this colour has just disappeared.

If possible, concentrations should be measured by methods which do not disturb the system, e.g. colorimetry or E values (see Chapter 14 and the box 'The effect of concentration on E values' in section 25.2, page 366).

11.5 Industrial applications

The Haber process

Ammonia is a vital industrial chemical, current world production being in excess of 140 million tonnes annually. Around 80% is used to make fertilisers like urea, ammonium sulphate and ammonium nitrate. The rest is used in the manufacture of synthetic fibres including nylon, dyes, explosives and plastics like polyurethane.

Virtually all ammonia produced today is made by the Haber process, the key step of which is direct reaction of nitrogen and hydrogen via a reversible reaction:

$$N_2(g) + 3H_2(g) \rightleftharpoons 2NH_3(g) \qquad \Delta H^{\ominus} = -92 \text{ kJ mol}^{-1}$$

Application of Le Châtelier's principle to this equilibrium shows that high pressure and low temperature will both tend to move the equilibrium to the right and produce a larger proportion of ammonia in the equilibrium mixture. This is illustrated by the graph (**Figure 11.2**).

From the graph we might expect a low temperature and high pressure to be used: 600×10^2 kPa and 473 K would give close to 100% conversion. However, other economic and practical factors must also be considered such as:

- A high-pressure plant is expensive, both to build and to maintain.
- A low temperature means that equilibrium is reached slowly.
- Catalysts can be used to speed up the rate of attainment of equilibrium, but they do not last indefinitely, and lower temperatures prolong their life.
- Unreacted gases can be easily recycled through the reactor.

These factors lead to a 'compromise' set of conditions of around 200×10^2 kPa and 670 K in most plants. An iron catalyst is used to speed up the reaction to compensate for the relatively low temperature. Catalyst life is of the order of five years. These conditions would give an equilibrium conversion of about 40% but in fact the gases are not allowed to spend long enough in the reaction vessel to reach equilibrium, and the usual conversion is about 15%. The ammonia is removed by cooling, still under pressure, when it condenses to a liquid. The unconverted nitrogen and hydrogen are recycled back into the reaction vessel.

The raw materials for the process are air, to provide the nitrogen, and natural gas (methane CH_4) to provide the hydrogen by the following reaction:

$$CH_4(g) + H_2O(g) \longrightarrow CO(g) + 3H_2(g)$$

As and when supplies of natural gas are depleted, coal and water could replace the natural gas:

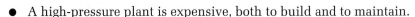

$$C(s) \quad + \quad H_2O(g) \quad \longrightarrow \quad CO(g) \quad + \quad H_2(g)$$

carbon   steam   carbon monoxide   hydrogen
monoxide

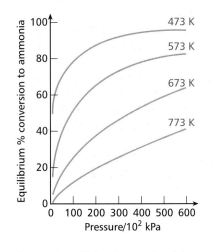

Figure 11.2 Equilibrium % conversion of nitrogen and hydrogen to ammonia under different conditions

A sulphuric acid plant. The conversion to sulphur trioxide takes place in the converter – the large vessel in the left foreground

The contact process

Sulphuric acid, H_2SO_4, is produced from sulphur, water and oxygen (from the air) by the contact process.

Sulphur is burnt to sulphur dioxide:

$$S(s) + O_2(g) \longrightarrow SO_2(g)$$

Sulphur dioxide is then converted to sulphur trioxide by reaction with more oxygen, using a catalyst of vanadium(V) oxide.

$$2SO_2(g) + O_2(g) \rightleftharpoons 2SO_3(g) \qquad \Delta H^{\ominus} = -197 \text{ kJ mol}^{-1}$$

However, this is a reversible reaction, so the yield of sulphur trioxide is dependent on the conditions of the reaction.

As the reaction is exothermic (in the forward direction), Le Châtelier's principle predicts that cooling will produce the maximum yield. In most plants the gas mixture is passed over three beds of catalyst and is cooled after each to remove the heat of reaction. This gives about 95% conversion to sulphur trioxide. This sulphur trioxide is then removed by being absorbed in very concentrated sulphuric acid solution. The remaining sulphur dioxide and oxygen are passed over a fourth catalyst bed and more sulphur trioxide is formed. The overall conversion is then 99.5%.

The cooling is aimed at keeping the catalyst at about 710 K. This is the best compromise between faster reaction at higher temperature and a lower conversion rate.

Le Châtelier's principle also predicts that increasing the pressure would drive the equilibrium to the right and give an even greater percentage conversion. Although this is done in some plants, the majority of plants operate at near atmospheric pressure as there is little to be gained from an extra 0.5% conversion.

The absorbed sulphur trioxide reacts with the water in the sulphuric acid solution to make more sulphuric acid so that the original acid becomes even more concentrated.

$$SO_3(g) + H_2O(l) \longrightarrow H_2SO_4(l)$$

Q What environmental problem is caused by any release of sulphur dioxide gas into the atmosphere?

Answer: Acid rain

11.6 Summary

• A chemical equilibrium may only be set up in	a closed system.
• Chemical equilibria can be approached from either	reactants or products.
• Chemical equilibria are reached when	the rates of the forward and back reactions are equal.
• Equilibrium mixtures have constant	physical properties.
• Chemical equilibria are dynamic because	the forward and back reactions continue after equilibrium is reached.

- The equilibrium law states that for a reaction:

$$aA + bB \rightleftharpoons cC + dD \qquad K_c = \frac{[C]_{eqm}{}^c [D]_{eqm}{}^d}{[A]_{eqm}{}^a [B]_{eqm}{}^b} \text{ (at constant temperature)}$$

- The concentrations may be expressed in $mol\,dm^{-3}$.

- Le Châtelier's principle says that if an equilibrium is disturbed | the position of equilibrium changes so as to reduce the disturbance.

- Equilibrium constants can be measured by normal analytical methods provided that or | (a) these do not disturb the equilibrium mixture (b) the analysis is completed before the system has time to react.

11.7 Practice questions

1. Write down the expression for K_c for the following equilibria in solution.
   (a) $2Fe^{3+}(aq) + 2I^-(aq) \rightleftharpoons 2Fe^{2+}(aq) + I_2(aq)$
   (b) $C_5H_{10} + CH_3CO_2H \rightleftharpoons CH_3CO_2C_5H_{11}$ (in ethanol)
   (c) $NH_4OH(aq) \rightleftharpoons OH^-(aq) + NH_4{}^+(aq)$
   (d) $NH_3(aq) + H^+(aq) \rightleftharpoons NH_4{}^+(aq)$
   (e) $Fe^{3+}(aq) + I^-(aq) \rightleftharpoons Fe^{2+}(aq) + \frac{1}{2}I_2(aq)$
   (f) $Cu^{2+}(aq) + 4NH_3(aq \rightleftharpoons Cu(NH_3)_4{}^{2+}(aq)$
   (g) $Fe^{3+}(aq) + NCS^-(aq \rightleftharpoons FeNCS^{2+}(aq)$
   (h) $Sn^{4+}(aq) + 2Fe^{2+}(aq) \rightleftharpoons Sn^{2+}(aq) + 2Fe^{3+}(aq)$
   (i) What mathematical relationship is there between K_c in (a) and in (e)?

2. Work out the units of the equilibrium constants in (a) to (h) above.

3. $CH_3CO_2H + C_2H_5OH \rightleftharpoons CH_3CO_2C_2H_5 + H_2O$
   0.10 mol of ethanol was mixed with 0.10 mol of ethanoic acid and allowed to reach equilibrium. At equilibrium, the remaining ethanoic acid was titrated with $1\,mol\,dm^{-3}$ sodium hydroxide. 33 cm³ were required.
   (a) How many moles of ethanoic acid remain at equilibrium?

   (b) What is the composition of the equilibrium mixture?
   (c) What is the value of K_c?
   (d) Explain why you do not have to know the volume of the mixture to calculate K_c.

4. Predict the effect on the equilibria below of:
   (a) increasing the temperature
   (b) increasing the pressure
   (i) $N_2O_4(g) \rightleftharpoons 2NO_2$
        $\Delta H = +58\,kJ\,mol^{-1}$
   (ii) $N_2(g) + 3H_2(g) \rightleftharpoons 2NH_3(g)$
        $\Delta H = -92\,kJ\,mol^{-1}$
   (iii) $H_2(g) + CO_2(g) \rightleftharpoons CO(g) + H_2O(g)$
        $\Delta H = +40\,kJ\,mol^{-1}$
   (iv) $KCl(s) \rightleftharpoons K^+(aq) + Cl^-(aq)$
        $\Delta H = +19\,kJ\,mol^{-1}$

5. Ethanoic acid will dissolve to some extent in hexane. Is it possible to titrate the acid with an aqueous solution of alkali which does not mix with hexane? Describe what would happen with regard to any equilibria that would occur.

11.8 Examination questions

1. Each of the equations **A**, **B**, **C** and **D** represents a dynamic equilibrium.

   A $N_2(g) + O_2(g) \rightleftharpoons 2NO(g)$ $\Delta H^{\ominus} = +180\ \text{kJ mol}^{-1}$

   B $N_2O_4(g) \rightleftharpoons 2NO_2(g)$ $\Delta H^{\ominus} = +58\ \text{kJ mol}^{-1}$

   C $3H_2(g) + N_2(g) \rightleftharpoons 2NH_3(g)$ $\Delta H^{\ominus} = -92\ \text{kJ mol}^{-1}$

   D $H_2(g) + I_2(g) \rightleftharpoons 2HI(g)$ $\Delta H^{\ominus} = -10\ \text{kJ mol}^{-1}$

   (a) Explain what is meant by the term *dynamic equilibrium*.

   (b) Explain why a catalyst does not alter the position of any equilibrium reaction.

   (c) The units of the equilibrium constant, K_c, for one of the above reactions are mol dm^{-3}. Identify the reaction **A**, **B**, **C** or **D** which has these units for K_c and write the expression for K_c for this reaction.

   (d) The graphs below show how the yield of product varies with pressure for three of the reactions **A**, **B**, **C** and **D** given above.

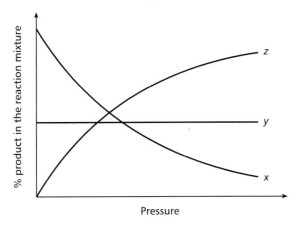

Pressure

   (i) Identify a reaction from **A**, **B**, **C** and **D** which would have the relationship between yield and pressure shown in graphs *x*, *y* and *z*.

   (ii) Explain why an industrial chemist would not use a very low pressure for the reaction represented in graph *x*.

   (iii) Explain why an industrial chemist may not use a very high pressure for the reaction represented in graph *z*.

   (iv) Add to a copy of the above graphs a line to show how the product yield would vary with pressure if the reaction which follows curve *z* was carried out at a temperature higher than that of the original graph.

   [NEAB 1998]

2. Consider the equilibrium

$$N_2O_4(g) \rightleftharpoons 2NO_2(g)$$

   (a) (i) Write an expression for K_c, indicating the units.

   (ii) 1 mol of dinitrogen tetroxide, N_2O_4, was introduced into a vessel of volume $10.0\ \text{dm}^3$ at a temperature of 70 °C. At equilibrium 50% had dissociated. Calculate K_c.

   (iii) Using the following data calculate the enthalpy change for the forward reaction.

	$\Delta H_f^{\ominus}/\text{kJ mol}^{-1}$
N_2O_4	+9.70
NO_2	+33.9

   (iv) If the same experiment is carried out at 100 °C, state qualitatively, giving your reasons, how the equilibrium composition will change.

   (b) Explain what you would do to increase the degree of dissociation of $N_2O_4(g)$ at constant temperature.

   (c) What is the effect of a catalyst on the following?
   (i) the value of K_c
   (ii) the equilibrium position
   (iii) the rate of attainment of equilibrium?

   (d) Suggest why the reaction

$$N_2 + 2O_2 \longrightarrow 2NO_2$$

   is not a very useful method of making NO_2.

   [London (Nuffield) 1998]

12 Acids and bases

Brewing up trouble

Did you know that the pH scale was first introduced by a brewer? In 1909, the Danish biochemist Søren Sørenson was working for the Carlsberg company studying the brewing of beer. (Probably the best job in the world?) Brewing requires careful control of acidity to produce conditions in which yeast (which aids the fermentation process) will grow but unwanted bacteria will not. The concentrations of acid with which Sørenson was working were very small, such as one ten-thousandth of a mole per litre and so he looked for a way to avoid using numbers such as 0.0001 (1×10^{-4}). Taking the $\log_{10}$ of this number gave -4 and for further convenience he took the negative of it giving 4. So the pH scale was born.

Beer is not the only drink for which acidity is important. Most wines are somewhat acidic which gives them their slightly sharp taste; the H^+ ion tastes sour. However, too much acidity causes problems. The ethanol (alcohol) in an opened bottle of wine will gradually be oxidised by oxygen in the air to form ethanoic acid, and eventually the wine will become so sour as to be undrinkable. Wine boxes avoid this problem because the collapsible bag inside the box protects the wine from the air.

The souring of milk also involves changes in acidity. Milk contains the sugar lactose. As milk goes 'off', bacteria called lactic bacilli convert lactose to lactic acid. Fresh milk's pH is about 6.6 (very slightly acidic). As it is stored, the pH decreases (it gets more acidic) and becomes sour, until its pH is about 4.4. This may not sound much of a difference until you remember that a decrease of 2 pH units represents a hundred-fold increase in acidity. UHT (ultra-high temperature) milk is preserved by heating it to about 140 °C for a few seconds. This destroys the bacteria which bring about this change and therefore the increase in acidity is slowed down considerably.

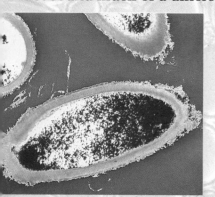

A lactobacillus

Brewing beer

Introduction

Acids were originally identified by their sour taste. Now they are recognised by the colour changes of dyes called indicators and by their reactions with metal oxides, hydroxides and carbonates and also with metals themselves. All of these reactions produce ionic compounds called salts.

Bases were originally identified by their slimy feel. Now they are recognised by their effect on indicators, and by the fact that they react with or neutralise acids. If a base dissolves in water it is called an alkali.

In this chapter we will be looking at:
- the reactions of acids and bases
- acids as proton donors and bases as proton acceptors
- the pH scale
- strong and weak acids and bases

CONCEPT CHECKPOINTS

The following basic ideas are used in this chapter. You may revise some of these topics elsewhere in the book.
- the formation of dative covalent bonds (Chapter 9)
- equilibrium between reactants and products in reversible reactions (Chapter 11)

Did you know? The German for oxygen is *Sauerstoff* (literally 'acid material') because it was once thought that all acids contained oxygen.

Hint: Make sure you are able to name the salts formed from different acids.

12.1 The reactions of acids

The three main types of acid reactions are:

1. With bases (metal oxides or hydroxides), for example:

$$2HNO_3(aq) \ + \ CaO(s) \ \longrightarrow \ Ca(NO_3)_2(aq) \ + \ H_2O(l)$$

     nitric acid   calcium oxide   calcium nitrate   water

$$H_2SO_4(aq) \ + 2NaOH(aq) \ \longrightarrow \ Na_2SO_4(aq) \ + \ 2H_2O(l)$$

     sulphuric acid   sodium hydroxide   sodium sulphate   water

2. With metal carbonates, for example:

$$2CH_3CO_2H(aq) + K_2CO_3(aq) \ \longrightarrow \ 2CH_3CO_2K(aq) + H_2O(l) + CO_2(g)$$

     ethanoic acid   potassium carbonate   potassium ethanoate   water   carbon dioxide

3. With reactive metals, for example:

$$2HCl(aq) \ + \ Zn(s) \ \longrightarrow \ ZnCl_2(aq) \ + \ H_2(g)$$

     hydrochloric acid   zinc   zinc chloride   hydrogen

In each case the hydrogen of the acid is replaced by the metal to form a compound called a salt.

12.2 Theories of acidity

Many theories of acidity have been proposed, including the following.

Lavoisier (1777)   proposed that all acids contain oxygen.
Davy (1816)   suggested that all contain hydrogen.
Liebig (1838)   defined acids as substances containing hydrogen which could be replaced by a metal.
Arrhenius (1887)   thought of acids as producing hydrogen ions (H^+).

FURTHER FOCUS

Lewis acids

Another theory (the **Lewis theory**) is also used to describe acids. This theory regards acids as electron pair acceptors and bases as electron pair donors in the formation of dative covalent bonds (see Chapter 9). For example:

$$F—B + :N—H \longrightarrow F—B{\leftarrow}N—H$$

boron trifluoride   ammonia

Here boron trifluoride is acting as a Lewis acid (electron pair acceptor) and ammonia as a Lewis base (electron pair donor). The Lewis definition of acids is wider than the Lowry–Brønsted one. Boron trifluoride contains no hydrogen and so cannot be an acid under the Lowry–Brønsted definition. H^+ ions can *only* form bonds by accepting on electron pair. For example:

$$H^+ + :O—H^- \longrightarrow H{\leftarrow}O—H$$

So all Lowry–Brønsted acids are also Lewis acids.

Hint: Positive ions are often called **cations**, because they move towards the cathode (negative electrode). Negative ions, which move towards the positive anode, are called **anions**. It is easy to get this the wrong way round.

You might like to consider how far each of these theories can go in explaining the properties of acids as you know them.

The **Lowry–Brønsted** description of acidity (developed in 1923 by Thomas Lowry and Johannes Brønsted independently) is the most generally useful current theory. This defines an acid as a substance which can donate a proton (an H^+ ion) and a base as a substance which can accept a proton.

Examples of proton transfer

$$HCl + NH_3 \longrightarrow Cl^- + NH_4^+$$

hydrogen   ammonia   chloride   ammonium
chloride   ion   ion

Here hydrogen chloride is acting as an acid by donating a proton to ammonia. Ammonia is acting as a base by accepting a proton. Acids and bases can only react in pairs: one acid and one base.

The Cl^- ion left after HCl has donated a proton is itself capable of accepting a proton (to go back to HCl) and is therefore a base. It is called the **conjugate base** of HCl. In the same way, the NH_4^+ ion is a acid because it can donate a proton to return to being NH_3. It is the **conjugate acid** of ammonia. So we have two conjugate acid–base pairs. These can be written either way round:

	HCl	and	Cl^-	or	HCl	and	Cl^-
	acid		conjugate base		conjugate acid		base

and

	NH_4^+	and	NH_3	or	NH_4^+	and	NH_3
	conjugate acid		base		acid		conjugate base

HCl is a much better acid (proton donor) than NH_4^+ because it is able to give away its proton and force NH_3 to accept it.

HCl can also donate a proton to water:

$$HCl + H_2O \longrightarrow H_3O^+ + Cl^-$$

Here water is acting as a base, H_3O^+ being its conjugate acid. H_3O^+ is called the **oxonium ion** but the names **hydronium** ion and **hydroxonium** ion are also used.

Water may also act as an acid. For example:

$$H_2O + NH_3 \longrightarrow OH^- + NH_4^+$$

Q Identify the conjugate acid/base pairs in:

$$HNO_3 + OH^- \longrightarrow NO_3^- + H_2O$$

Here OH^- is the conjugate base and H_2O the acid.

Acid and base reactions can be thought of as competitions for protons, the better base 'winning' the proton.

So in
$$HCl + NH_3 \longrightarrow NH_4^+ + Cl^-$$

ammonia must be a better base than the chloride ion, because it 'wins' the proton.

Bases and alkalis

Bases are substances which react with (neutralise) acids. Water-soluble bases are called alkalis and produce OH^- ions in aqueous solution.

The proton in aqueous solution

It is important to realise that an H^+ ion is just a proton. The hydrogen atom has only one electron and if this is lost all that remains is a proton (the hydrogen nucleus). This is about 1×10^{-15} m in diameter, compared with 1×10^{-10} m or more for any other chemical entity. This extremely small size and consequent intense electric field cause it to have unusual properties compared with other positive ions. It is never found isolated. In aqueous solutions it is always bonded to at least one water molecule to form the ion H_3O^+. Throughout this chapter, for simplicity, we shall represent a proton in an aqueous solution by $H^+(aq)$ rather than $H_3O^+(aq)$.

12.3 Measurement of acidity

The ionisation of water

Water is slightly ionised:

$$H_2O(l) \rightleftharpoons H^+(aq) + OH^-(aq)$$

or this may be written:

$$H_2O(l) + H_2O(l) \rightleftharpoons H_3O^+(aq) + OH^-(aq)$$

to emphasise that this is an acid–base reaction in which one water molecule donates a proton to another.

This equilibrium is established in water and all aqueous solutions.

$$H_2O(l) \rightleftharpoons H^+(aq) + OH^-(aq)$$

and we can write an equilibrium expression (see Chapter 11):

$$K = \frac{[H^+(aq)]_{eqm}[OH^-(aq)]_{eqm}}{[H_2O(l)]_{eqm}}$$

Hint: The important point to remember at this stage is that the product of $[H^+(aq)]_{eqm}$ and $[OH^-(aq)]_{eqm}$ is constant so that if one goes up, the other must go down proportionately.

The concentration of water, $[H_2O(l)]$, is constant and is incorporated into a modified equilibrium constant K_w (see Chapter 23).

$$K_w = [H^+(aq)]_{eqm}[OH^-(aq)]_{eqm}$$

Did you know?
$[H^+(aq)] = 10^{-7}$ mol dm^{-3} means that only 2 in every 1 000 000 000 water molecules is split up into hydrogen ions and hydroxide ions. To put this is context, 1 000 000 000 is the number of letters in 700 copies of this book!

K_w is called the **ionic product** of water and at 298 K it is equal to 1×10^{-14} mol^2 dm^{-6}. In pure water, each H_2O which dissociates (splits up) gives rise to one H^+ and one OH^-, so at 298 K:

$$[OH^-(aq)] = [H^+(aq)]$$

So
$$1 \times 10^{-14} = [H^+(aq)]^2$$
$$[H^+(aq)] = 1 \times 10^{-7} \text{ mol dm}^{-3} = [OH^-(aq)]$$

Answer: HNO_3 is an acid and NO_3^- its conjugate base. OH^- is a base and H_2O its conjugate acid.

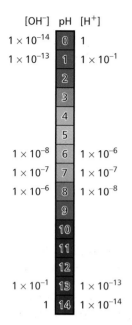

Figure 12.1 The pH scale. What is the concentration of hydrochloric acid in our stomachs, which has a pH of 2?

Hint: To find the log of a number, simply enter the number into your calculator and press the log button.

Did you know? Distilled water is usually slightly acidic because it has carbon dioxide dissolved in it.

Q The dissociation of water is endothermic and the value of K_w is 51×10^{-14} mol^2 dm^{-6} at 373 K. What is the pH of water at this temperature?

Q What is the pH of a 0.01 mol dm^{-3} solution of HCl at 298 K?

Answer: pH = 6.1; however, boiling water is still neutral as there are equal numbers of H$^+$ and OH$^-$ ions.

Answer: 2

The pH scale

The acidity of a solution depends on the concentration of H$^+$(aq) and is measured on the pH scale. The definition of pH is:

$$pH = -\log_{10}[H^+\,(aq)]$$

Although more complicated than simply stating the concentration of H$^+$(aq), it does away with awkward numbers like 1×10^{-13} etc. Using this definition, a difference of *one* pH number means a *ten-fold* difference in acidity, so that pH 2 is ten times as acidic as pH 3. Also, the *smaller* the pH, the *greater* the concentration of H$^+$(aq).

pH measures alkalinity as well as acidity, because as [H$^+$(aq)] goes up, [OH$^-$(aq)] goes down (see **Figure 12.1**). If a solution contains more H$^+$(aq) than OH$^-$(aq), its pH will be less than 7 and we call it acidic. If a solution contains more OH$^-$(aq) than H$^+$(aq), its pH will be greater than 7 and we call it alkaline.

Working with the pH scale

In practice we would measure the pH of a solution, using a pH meter (see the box 'The pH meter', section 25.2) or a suitable indicator (Chapter 24), but we can calculate the pH if we know the concentration of acid or alkali.

The basic method is to work out [H$^+$(aq)] (even if the solution is alkaline) and then use pH = $-\log_{10}$ [H$^+$(aq)].

The pH of pure water

In pure water,   [H$^+$(aq)] = 1×10^{-7} mol dm^{-3} (see above)

$$\log[H^+(aq)] = \log 10^{-7} = -7$$
$$-\log[H^+(aq)] = 7$$

So the pH of pure water is 7 at 298 K.

The pH of hydrochloric acid solutions

HCl dissociates completely in water to H$^+$(aq) ions and Cl$^-$(aq) ions, i.e. the reaction:

$$HCl(aq) \longrightarrow H^+(aq) + Cl^-(aq)$$

goes to completion.

So in 1 mol dm^{-3} HCl,   [H$^+$(aq)] = 1 mol dm^{-3}
$$\log[H^+(aq)] = \log 1 = 0$$
$$-\log[H^+(aq)] = 0$$
so   the pH of 1 mol dm^{-3} HCl = 0

In a 0.1 mol dm^{-3} solution of HCl,
$$[H^+(aq)] = 0.1 \text{ mol dm}^{-3}$$
$$\log[H^+(aq)] = \log 0.1 = -1$$
$$-\log[H^+(aq)] = 1$$
So   the pH of 0.1 mol dm^{-3} HCl = 1

In a 2 mol dm^{-3} solution of HCl,
$$[H^+(aq)] = 2 \text{ mol dm}^{-3}$$
$$\log[H^+(aq)] = \log 2 = 0.3$$
$$-\log[H^+(aq)] = -0.3$$
So   the pH of 2 mol dm^{-3} HCl = -0.3

Although pH numbers of less than zero and more than 14 are possible, zero and 14 are the practical limits of the scale, as in very concentrated solutions acids and alkalis tend not to be fully dissociated.

Hint: Diprotic acids were formerly called **dibasic** acids (and sometimes still are).

Q What is the pH of a 0.01 mol dm^{-3} solution of H$_2$SO$_4$?

Answer: 1.7

Diprotic acids

These are acids in which one molecule dissociates to give two protons, for example sulphuric acid, H_2SO_4. This dissociates more or less completely in dilute solutions.

$$H_2SO_4(aq) \longrightarrow 2H^+(aq) + SO_4^{2-}(aq)$$

In a 0.1 mol dm^{-3} solution:

$$[H^+(aq)] = 0.2 \text{ mol dm}^{-3}$$
$$\log[H^+(aq)] = \log 0.2 = -0.7$$
$$-\log[H^+(aq)] = 0.7$$
$$pH = 0.7$$

The pH of alkaline solutions

In alkaline solutions, the situation is slightly more complex. It is tempting to think that there are no H$^+$ ions in alkaline solutions but this is not the case.

At 298 K, the relationship $[H^+(aq)][OH^-(aq)] = 1 \times 10^{-14} \text{ mol}^2 \text{ dm}^{-6}$ applies to all aqueous solutions – acidic, alkaline or neutral. To find

---

CHEMISTRY AROUND US

Acid rain

Acid rain is by no means a new problem. In the early 1950s a series of 'smogs' (the word is a combination of 'smoke' and 'fog') brought London to a halt and caused many deaths through respiratory complaints. At the time, the smoke was the most obvious problem, but now it is thought that sulphuric acid was the main cause of deaths. The pH of smog has been estimated at less than 2.

Almost a century before this, the Norwegian playwright Ibsen wrote in the play *Brand*:

> Dimmer visions, worse foreboding
> Glare upon me through the gloom
> Britain's smoke-cloud sinks corroding
> On the land in noisome fumes...

London smog in the 1950s

Scandinavians are still complaining about acid pollution from Britain.

The precise causes of acid rain are the subject of fierce debate, but it is indisputable that the burning of sulphur-containing fuels leads to the formation of sulphur dioxide, which in the atmosphere reacts with air and water to produce sulphuric acid. British power stations are among the culprits and gradually 'flue gas desulphurisation' equipment is being fitted. This process involves passing the gaseous combustion products through a suspension of calcium hydroxide which reacts with any acidic gases to produce salts, mostly gypsum, calcium sulphate.

High-temperature combustion processes, such as the burning of petrol in car engines, cause some of the nitrogen in the air to combine with oxygen to form a mixture of nitrogen oxides, including NO and NO_2 (known collectively as NO_x). These react with oxygen and water in the air to form a solution of nitric acid.

The effects of acid pollution are many; two of the most important are the deaths of fish and trees. An increase in acidity of many streams and lakes has been observed in many areas. This kills fish both directly and also by leaching poisonous aluminium ions out of the soil and into the water. Trees are being killed by absorption of the acid both through their roots and directly through their leaves.

Did you know? Some cattle are thought to have survived the smogs because ammonia from their urine neutralised the acid gases.

the pH of an alkaline solution we must first calculate $[OH^-(aq)]$, then use:

$$[H^+(aq)] \, [OH^-(aq)] = 1 \times 10^{-14} \, mol^2 \, dm^{-6}$$

to calculate $[H^+(aq)]$, from which the pH can be calculated.

For example, to find the pH of $1 \, mol \, dm^{-3}$ sodium hydroxide solution:

Sodium hydroxide is fully dissociated in aqueous solution

$$NaOH(aq) \longrightarrow Na^+(aq) + OH^-(aq)$$

so
$$[OH^-(aq)] = 1 \, mol \, dm^{-3}$$

but
$$[OH^-(aq)][H^+(aq)] = 1 \times 10^{-14} \, mol \, dm^{-3}$$
$$1 \times [H^+(aq)] = 1 \times 10^{-14} \, mol \, dm^{-3}$$
$$\log [H^+(aq)] = -14$$
$$pH = 14$$

For example, to find the pH of $0.1 \, mol \, dm^{-3}$ sodium hydroxide solution:

$$[OH^-(aq)] = 1 \times 10^{-1} \, mol \, dm^{-3}$$
$$[OH^-(aq)] \, [H^+(aq)] = 1 \times 10^{-14} \, mol \, dm^{-3}$$
$$[H^+(aq)] \times 10^{-1} = 1 \times 10^{-14} \, mol \, dm^{-3}$$
$$[H^+(aq)] = 1 \times 10^{-13} \, mol \, dm^{-3}$$
$$\log [H^+(aq)] = -13$$
$$pH = 13$$

> **Q** Calculate the pH of $0.2 \, mol \, dm^{-3}$ sodium hydroxide.

Strong and weak acids and bases

Strong acids

The above examples have dealt with acids such as hydrochloric and sulphuric acids, which, when dissolved in water, dissociate completely into ions. Acids which completely dissociate into ions in aqueous solutions are called **strong** acids. The word 'strong' refers *only* to the extent of dissociation and *not in any way* to the concentration.

So it is perfectly possible to have a very dilute solution of a strong acid. It is vital to realise that strength and concentration are completely independent. Careful use of the two different words is most important.

Weak acids

> **Hint:** Although in the gas phase hydrogen chloride, HCl, is a covalent molecule, a solution of it in water is wholly ionic. To all intents and purposes, there are no covalently bonded HCl molecules remaining.

Many acids are not fully dissociated when dissolved in water. Ethanoic acid (the acid in vinegar, also known as acetic acid) is a typical example. In a $1 \, mol \, dm^{-3}$ solution of ethanoic acid, only about 4 in every thousand ethanoic acid molecules are dissociated into ions (so the **degree of dissociation** is 4/1000); the rest remain dissolved as wholly covalently bonded molecules. In fact an equilibrium is set up:

	$CH_3CO_2H(aq)$	$\rightleftharpoons$	$H^+(aq)$	+	$CH_3CO_2^-(aq)$
	ethanoic acid		hydrogen ions		ethanoate ions
before dissociation	1000		0		0
at equilibrium	996		4		4

Acids like this are called **weak acids**. Again note that 'weak' refers *only* to the degree of dissociation. In a $5 \, mol \, dm^{-3}$ solution, ethanoic acid is still a weak acid, while in a $1 \times 10^{-4} \, mol \, dm^{-3}$ solution, hydrochloric acid is still a strong acid.

Answer: 13.3

Formic acid (methanoic acid) is quite concentrated when used as a weapon by the stinging ant and although it is a weak acid, being sprayed with it can be a painful experience

Bases

The same arguments apply to bases. Strong bases are completely dissociated into ions in aqueous solutions, while weak bases are only partially split up. For example, sodium hydroxide is a strong base:

$$NaOH(aq) \longrightarrow Na^+(aq) + OH^-(aq)$$

Ammonium hydroxide (NH_4OH) is a weak base:

$$NH_4OH(aq) \rightleftharpoons NH_4^+(aq) + OH^-(aq)$$

In Chapter 24 we will look at how to calculate the pH of solutions of weak acids and bases using the equilibrium law.

CHEMISTRY AROUND US

Household acids and bases

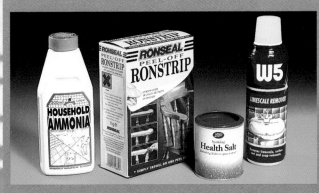

Various household acids and bases: paint stripper, limescale remover, household ammonia, health salts

Many common household substances contain acids or bases. Probably the best known is vinegar, a dilute solution of the weak acid ethanoic acid (acetic acid). Oranges, lemons and limes contain citric acid, a weak triprotic acid.

Citric acid (2-hydroxypropane-1,2,3-tricarboxylic acid). The acidic hydrogens (those lost on dissociation) are marked in red

The electrolyte in car batteries is a solution of the strong acid sulphuric acid, H_2SO_4.

Many powder types of lavatory cleaner contain sodium hydrogensulphate, $NaHSO_4$. This is called an acid salt and is produced when sulphuric acid, a diprotic acid, is half neutralised by sodium hydroxide, i.e. just one hydrogen atom is replaced:

$$H_2SO_4(aq) + NaOH(aq) \longrightarrow NaHSO_4(aq) + H_2O(l)$$

Sodium hydrogensulphate is a solid and therefore more convenient to package than a liquid or a solution. The acid salt dissociates to give $H^+(aq)$:

$$NaHSO_4(aq) \longrightarrow Na^+(aq) + H^+(aq) + SO_4^{2-}(aq)$$

This is used to dissolve hard water scale (mostly calcium carbonate) from the lavatory bowl.

$$2H^+(aq) + CaCO_3(s) \longrightarrow H_2O(l) + CO_2(g) + Ca^{2+}(aq)$$

However, care must be taken that this type of cleaner does not come into contact with other brands of cleaner containing bleach.

Bleach contains a mixture of chloride ions, Cl^-, and chlorate(I) ions, ClO^- (often still called hypochlorite ions). In the presence of acid the following reaction occurs:

$$2H^+(aq) + ClO^-(aq) + Cl^-(aq) \longrightarrow H_2O(l) + Cl_2(g)$$

producing chlorine, an irritant gas which is toxic at high concentrations.

Sulphamic acid, NH_2SO_3H, is used as a descaler for kettles and coffee machines.

Bases to be found around the home include ammonia, which is present in many heavy duty cleaners. Bases are particularly good at dissolving grease. Some types of paint-stripping products contain sodium hydroxide. Commercial paint strippers dip articles to be stripped in a large vat of sodium hydroxide solution which they refer to as 'caustic', after the common name for sodium hydroxide – caustic soda. In the garden, 'lime' or 'slaked lime' is used to treat acid soils. Lime is powdered calcium oxide, and slaked lime is calcium hydroxide.

A final piece of household acid–base chemistry is provided by effervescent 'liver salts'. These contain dry citric acid and sodium hydrogencarbonate. These do not react together when dry and can be kept indefinitely in a closed tin or sealed sachet, but both dissociate in water and react together to give off carbon dioxide, which causes the effervescence.

12.4 Summary

● Acids are substances which	donate protons (H^+ ions).
● Bases are substances which	accept protons (H^+ ions).
● Water can act as both	an acid and a base.
● The equation for the dissociation of water is	$H_2O(l) \rightleftharpoons H^+(aq) + OH^-(aq)$
● The dissociation constant for water, $K_w =$	$10^{-14}\ mol^2\ dm^{-6}$ (at 298 K).
● Acidity and alkalinity are measured on	the pH scale.
● pH =	$-\log[H^+(aq)]$
● In acid solutions the pH is	less than 7.
● The lower the pH the greater the	acidity.
● In alkaline solutions the pH is	greater than 7.
● The pH is 7 in	neutral solutions.
● In aqueous solution strong acids are	fully dissociated.
● For example, the strong acid hydrochloric acid dissociates:	$HCl(aq) \longrightarrow H^+(aq) + Cl^-(aq)$
● In aqueous solution weak acids are	partially dissociated.
● For example, the weak acid ethanoic acid dissociates:	$CH_3CO_2H(aq) \rightleftharpoons CH_3CO_2^-(aq) + H^+(aq)$
● In aqueous solution strong bases are	fully dissociated.
● For example, sodium hydroxide dissociates:	$NaOH(aq) \longrightarrow Na^+(aq) + OH^-(aq)$
● In aqueous solution weak bases are	partially dissociated.
● For example, ammonia dissociates	$NH_3(aq) + H_2O(l) \rightleftharpoons NH_4^+(aq) + OH^-(aq)$

12.5 Practice questions

1. Work out the acid–base conjugate pairs in the following reactions.
   (a) $HBr(aq) + H_2O(l) \longrightarrow Br^-(aq) + H_3O^+(aq)$
   (b) $H_2SO_4(aq) + OH^-(aq) \longrightarrow HSO_4^-(aq) + H_2O(l)$
   (c) $HSO_4^-(aq) + H_2O \longrightarrow SO_4^{2-}(aq) + H_3O^+(aq)$

2. Calculate the pH of the following.
   (a) hydrochloric acid, HCl, (a strong acid) of concentration:
       (i)   0.1 mol dm^{-3}
       (ii) 0.001 mol dm^{-3}
       (iii) 2 mol dm^{-3}

   (b) sulphuric acid, H_2SO_4 (a diprotic strong acid) of concentration:
       (i)   0.01 mol dm^{-3}
       (ii) 0.001 mol dm^{-3}
       (iii) 2 mol dm^{-3}
   (c) potassium hydroxide, KOH (a strong base) of concentration:
       (i)   0.01 mol dm^{-3}
       (ii) 0.001 mol dm^{-3}
       (iii) 2 mol dm^{-3}

12.6 Examination questions

1. A lake in Scotland had a pH of 4.2
   (a) State the relationship between pH and hydrogen ion concentration.
   (b) Calculate the hydrogen ion concentration of the lake in Scotland.
   (c) Explain, using suitable examples and equations, the difference between a strong acid and a weak acid.

   [Oxford 1997]

2. When the molar concentration of hydrogen ions and the molar concentration of hydroxide ions in a sample of water are multiplied together a value is obtained which is constant at a fixed temperature.
   (a) Name this constant.
   (b) State the value of this constant 298 K.
   (c) State qualitatively how the value of this constant changes when the temperature of the water is increased. Explain your answer.

   [NEAB 1998, part]

3. (a) Write an equation to represent the dissociation of water.
   (b) Give an expression for the *ionic product of water,* and show how it is related to the equilibrium constant for the reaction in (a).
   (c) Define pH.
   (d) The ionic product of water is 5.6×10^{-14} mol^2 dm^{-6} at 333 K. Calculate the pH of water at this temperature.

   (e) Given that at 298 K the pH of water is 7, state whether the dissociation of water is exothermic or endothermic. Give a reason for your answer.

   [AEB 1994]

4. The concentration of hydrochloric acid in the human stomach is approximately 0.1 mol dm^{-3}. Excess of this acid causes discomfort referred to as 'heartburn' or 'acid indigestion'. Remedies designed to neutralise some of this excess acid often contain compounds such as magnesium hydroxide, $Mg(OH)_2$, and sodium hydrogencarbonate, $NaHCO_3$.
   (a) The hydrogencarbonate ion, HCO_3^-, is capable of behaving as either an acid or a base. Write equations, with state symbols, to show the hydrogencarbonate ion acting as
       (i) an acid by reacting with water.
       (ii) a base by reacting with hydroxonium ions, $H_3O^+(aq)$, and giving off a gas.
   (b) Magnesium hydroxide reacts with hydrochloric acid according to the equation

   $$Mg(OH)_2(s) + 2HCl(aq) \longrightarrow MgCl_2(aq) + 2H_2O(l)$$

       (i) The molar mass of magnesium hydroxide is 58.0 g mol^{-1}. Calculate the number of moles of hydrochloric acid which can be neutralised by 1.00 g of magnesium hydroxide.
       (ii) Calculate the volume of 0.100 M HCl which can be neutralised by 1.00 g of magnesium hydroxide, giving your answer to 3 significant figures.

   [London (Nuffield) 1997]

13

Redox reactions

C H E M I S T R Y N O W

Chemistry in the kitchen

We live in a sea of air which contains 20% oxygen, so it is not surprising that oxidation reactions affect our daily lives. Some of the reactions which cause foods to go 'off' are oxidations. One example is that of fatty foods, which become rancid. This occurs to butter, cooking oil and especially to biscuits with a crumbly texture which exposes to the air a lot of the fat used in cooking.

Fats and oils are molecules called triglycerides. They are made from an alcohol with three —OH groups called glycerol (propane-1,2,3-triol) and three long-chain carboxylic acids called fatty acids.

$$
\begin{array}{ll}
\underset{\text{a typical fat}}{
\begin{array}{l}
\overset{\displaystyle O}{\overset{\|}{}}\\
CH_2-O-C(CH_2)_7CH{=}CH(CH_2)_7CH_3\\
\overset{\displaystyle O}{\overset{\|}{}}\\
CH-O-C(CH_2)_{16}CH_3\\
\overset{\displaystyle O}{\overset{\|}{}}\\
CH_2-O-C(CH_2)_7CH{=}CHCH_2CH{=}CH(CH_2)_4CH_3
\end{array}}
& \xrightarrow{+3H_2O}
\end{array}
$$

CH_2OH $HO-\overset{O}{\overset{\|}{C}}(CH_2)_7CH{=}CH(CH_2)_7CH_3$	(a)
$CHOH$ $HO-\overset{O}{\overset{\|}{C}}(CH_2)_{16}CH_3$	(b)
CH_2OH $HO-\overset{O}{\overset{\|}{C}}(CH_2)_7CH{=}CHCH_2CH{=}CH(CH_2)_4CH_3$	(c)

a typical fat   glycerol   free fatty acids

Free fatty acids can break off the fat molecule. If these are unsaturated (like (a) and (c)) they can further deteriorate by oxidation

Fats and oils go off in two ways. The fatty acids may break off from the glycerol stem. Free fatty acids have strong, often unpleasant, smells. Their non-systematic names may give this away. The acids with 6, 8 and 10 carbon atoms are called caproic, caprylic and capric acids respectively, from the Latin *caper*, meaning 'goat' (as in the star sign Capricorn). They all have unpleasant goat-like odours and are responsible for the smells of some of the more pungent cheeses.

The second method by which fats deteriorate is via oxidation. Unsaturated fats (those with carbon–carbon double bonds) react with oxygen via highly reactive intermediate compounds called free radicals. The end-products include compounds called aldehydes, which are also very smelly. Oxidation can be prevented by adding compounds that react with the free radicals and stop the reaction. Such antioxidants include vitamin E (which occurs naturally in oils and fats), butylated hydroxyanisole (BHA, E320) and butylated hydroxytoluene (BHT, E321). You may find these initials if you read the small print on food labels. These compounds merely delay the onset of rancidity: once they are used up, the fat goes off as fast as it would have without them.

The fats and oils in all these are liable to deteriorate by oxidation

In this chapter we will be looking at:

- oxidation as the addition of oxygen or removal of hydrogen
- reduction as the addition of hydrogen or the removal of oxygen
- oxidation as loss and reduction as gain of electrons
- oxidation numbers as a technique for keeping track of oxidation and reduction reactions
- oxidation numbers as a technique for balancing redox reactions
- the use of oxidation numbers to help in the naming of compounds

Introduction

The word 'redox' is a contraction of reduction–oxidation. Historically, oxidation was used to describe addition of oxygen. For example in the reaction:

$$Cu(s) + \tfrac{1}{2}O_2(g) \longrightarrow CuO(s)$$

the copper has been **oxidised** to copper oxide. Oxygen is the **oxidising agent** or **oxidant**. The reverse process, such as removing oxygen from a metal oxide to leave the metal, was called reduction. For example in the reaction:

$$CuO(s) + H_2(g) \longrightarrow Cu(s) + H_2O(l)$$

copper oxide has been reduced and hydrogen is the reducing agent or reductant.

As hydrogen was often used as a reductant, addition of hydrogen was also considered to be a reduction, and removal of hydrogen an oxidation. So in the reaction:

$$Cl_2(g) + H_2(g) \longrightarrow 2HCl(g)$$

chlorine is reduced.

Concept Checkpoints

The following basic ideas are used in this chapter. You may revise some of these topics elsewhere in the book.

- the formation of ions by loss or gain of electrons from the parent atom (section 2.2)
- ionic bonding (section 9.1)
- covalent bonding (section 9.1)
- balanced symbol equations (section 5.3)

Hint: The phrase **OIL RIG** makes the definitions of oxidation and reduction easy to remember.

13.1 Oxidation and reduction

A closer look at the oxidation and reduction reactions in the introduction shows that when a species is oxidised it has lost electrons, and when reduced it has gained electrons.

loss of 2 electrons

$$Cu(s) + \tfrac{1}{2}O_2(g) \longrightarrow (Cu^{2+} + O^{2-})(s) \text{ copper is oxidised}$$

$$(Cu^{2+} + O^{2-})(s) + H_2(g) \longrightarrow Cu(s) + H_2O(l) \text{ copper ions are reduced}$$

gain of 2 electrons

This is the basis of the modern definition of oxidation and reduction. **Oxidation Is Loss** of electrons. **Reduction Is Gain** of electrons.

So copper could equally well be oxidised by, for example, chlorine:

$$Cu(s) + Cl_2(g) \longrightarrow (Cu^{2+} + 2Cl^-)(s)$$

loss of 2 electrons

Look at the chlorine. It has gained electrons and has been reduced:

reduction
gain of electrons

$$Cu(s) + Cl_2(g) \longrightarrow (Cu^{2+} + 2Cl^-)(s)$$

loss of electrons
oxidation

> **Q** In the reaction
> $$Mg(s) + Br_2(l) \longrightarrow MgBr_2(s),$$
> what has been oxidised and what has been reduced?

Neither oxidation nor reduction can take place alone in a chemical reaction. If one species loses electrons (is oxidised), another must gain them (be reduced). An oxidising agent oxidises something else, but is itself reduced. In the same way, a reducing agent reduces, but is itself oxidised.

In Chapter 12 we thought of acid–base reactions as competitions for protons. Redox reactions are competitions for electrons and are often called **electron transfer** reactions.

13.2 Oxidation numbers

Oxidation numbers, sometimes called **oxidation states**, are a simple way of keeping track of redox reactions, so that it is easy to see which species has been oxidised and which reduced. They help in balancing equations for redox reactions and are used in the systematic naming system for inorganic compounds. They form the basis of chemical 'book keeping' for redox reactions. The abbreviation for oxidation number is Ox, though ON is also commonly used.

Ionic compounds

The oxidation number of each element in an ionic compound is the charge on the ion (including the sign). So in sodium chloride ($Na^+ + Cl^-$), the oxidation number of Na is +I and of Cl is −I. Oxidation numbers are written in Roman numerals.

Further examples of oxidation numbers in ionic compounds:

calcium chloride $\qquad$ $CaCl_2$, i.e. ($Ca^{2+} + 2Cl^-$)
oxidation number of Ca = +II, and of *each* Cl = −I
aluminium oxide $\qquad$ Al_2O_3, i.e. ($2Al^{3+} + 3O^{2-}$)
oxidation number of *each* Al = +III, and of *each* O = −II

Since all compounds are electrically neutral, **the sum of all the oxidation numbers in a compound is zero.**
So for Al_2O_3:

$$(2 \times +III) + (3 \times -II) = 0$$

Group I metals always form ions of charge +1, so they have a fixed oxidation number of +I in all compounds. Group II metals always form ions of charge +2, so they have a fixed oxidation number of +II in all compounds.

Table 13.1 Electronegativities of some elements

Element	Electronegativity
boron	2.0
hydrogen	2.1
carbon	2.5
nitrogen	3.0
chlorine	3.0
oxygen	3.5

Elements

As uncombined elements have no charge, their **oxidation number is zero.**

Covalent compounds

In a binary covalent compound (one with just two elements), the more electronegative element (section 9.1) has the negative oxidation number and the less electronegative element has the positive oxidation number (see **Table 13.1**). One way is to work as if the compound were ionic and predict the most likely charges of the ions. It is easier to see this from the following examples.

Answer: Mg has been oxidised and Br_2 reduced.

Boron trichloride, BCl_3

Chlorine is more electronegative than boron and so has the negative oxidation number. Chlorine often forms Cl^- ions as in sodium chloride ($Na^+ + Cl^-$), so in BCl_3:

$$\text{oxidation number of } Cl = -I.$$

This means that the oxidation number of B must be $+$ III to fit the rule that the sum of the oxidation numbers in a compound is zero.

Another alternative is to reason that boron (electron arrangement 2, 3) would be expected to form B^{3+} and chlorine (electron arrangement 2, 8, 7) to form Cl^-, which would give the same answer.

Ammonia, NH_3

Nitrogen is more electronegative than hydrogen and so has the negative oxidation number. Hydrogen usually forms H^+ ions, so its oxidation number is likely to be $+I$. This means that the oxidation number of nitrogen must be $-III$ to fit the rule that the sum of the oxidation numbers in a compound is zero.

Another alternative is to reason that nitrogen (electron arrangement 2, 5) would be expected to form N^{3-}, so its oxidation number is $-III$, which implies that hydrogen must be $+I$.

Methane, CH_4

Carbon is more electronegative than hydrogen and so has the negative oxidation number. Hydrogen usually forms H^+ ions, so its oxidation number is likely to be $+I$. This means that the oxidation number of carbon must be $-IV$ to fit the rule that the sum of the oxidation numbers in a compound is zero.

Carbon dioxide, CO_2

Hint: Notice that there are some elements, such as carbon, that can be assigned positive or negative oxidation numbers.

Carbon is less electronegative than oxygen and so has the positive oxidation number. Oxygen usually forms O^{2-} ions, so its oxidation number is likely to be $-II$. This means that the oxidation number of carbon must be $+IV$ to fit the rule that the sum of the oxidation numbers in a compound is zero.

Here the electron arrangement of carbon (2, 4) does not help. If carbon did form ions, the electron arrangement would suggest that positive or negative ions would be equally likely.

Complex ions

The final case is for compounds with complex ions. These are ions which have two or more atoms bonded covalently, but in which the whole group of atoms has a charge: for example, the ammonium ion, NH_4^+, in ammonium chloride, NH_4Cl ($NH_4^+ + Cl^-$). The whole ion has a positive charge, which must be supplied by the less electronegative element: in this case hydrogen.

Hydrogen usually forms H^+, so the oxidation number of $H = +I$.

Nitrogen would be likely to form N^{3-}, so the oxidation number of $N = -III$.

Chlorine often forms Cl^-, so the oxidation number of $Cl = -I$.

This fits the rule that the sum of the oxidation numbers $= 0$ ($-III + IV - I = 0$). We could think of the NH_4^+ ion itself. Here the sum of the oxidation numbers $=$ charge on the ion ($-III + IV = +I$).

Note that some oxidation numbers are so large that they could not possibly correspond to 'real' ionic charges. For example, in potassium dichromate, $K_2Cr_2O_7$, what is the oxidation number of Cr?

Rules for finding oxidation numbers

It is useful to remember the following rules for calculating oxidation numbers:

- The oxidation number of an uncombined element = 0
- The sum of the oxidation numbers of a neutral compound = 0
- The sum of the oxidation numbers of a complex ion = the charge on the ion
- Some elements always have the same oxidation numbers in their compounds:

    Group I metals: *always* +I.
    Group II metals: *always* +II.
    Al: *always* +III.
    H: +I, *except* in compounds with Group I or II metals (metal hydrides) where it is –I.
    F: *always* –I.
    O: –II, *except* in peroxides and compounds with F where it is –I, and superoxides where it is $-\frac{1}{2}$.

Cl: –I, *except* in compounds with F and O, where it has positive values.

These rules should help you to work out the oxidation number of almost any element in any compound. It is useful to remember the charges on some common complex ions as a short cut.

OH^-	hydroxide	NO_3^-	nitrate
SO_4^{2-}	sulphate	CO_3^{2-}	carbonate
NH_4^+	ammonium		

For example: What is the oxidation number of Cr in $Cr_2(SO_4)_3$?
    Since SO_4^{2-} contributes –II, the total negative oxidation number must be –VI. The total positive oxidation number must be +VI, which shared between two Cr's, gives the oxidation number of Cr = +III.

Q
What is the oxidation number of sulphur, S, in sodium thiosulphate, $Na_2S_2O_3$?

Using the rules:

Oxygen is always –II, so the O's contribute $7 \times -II = -14$
Potassium is always +I, so the K's contribute $2 \times +I = +2$

To make the sum of the oxidation numbers equal to zero, the two chromium atoms must contribute a total of +12, i.e. +6 each.
    So the oxidation number of Cr = +VI.
    Strict application of these rules can produce some oddities. For example, in the tetrathionate ion, $S_4O_6^{2-}$, the rules give each S atom an oxidation number of $+II\frac{1}{2}$. In fact there are two different types of S atom with oxidation numbers of 0 and +V respectively.

Hint: Practice is the key to working with oxidation numbers.

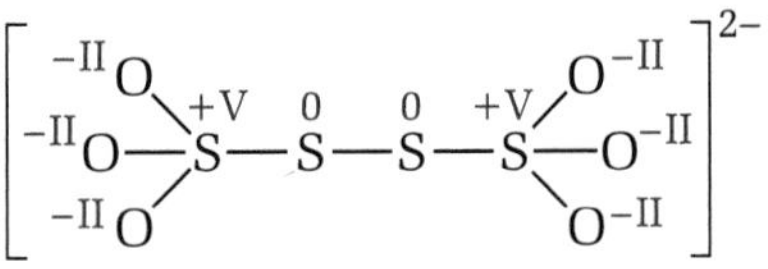

The *average* oxidation number of sulphur is $+II\frac{1}{2}$.

13.3 Uses of oxidation numbers

Naming inorganic compounds

The naming of inorganic compounds containing only two elements follows the simple rule of metal name first, followed by non-metal name with the end changed to '-ide'. However, this would not distinguish between, for example, CuO and Cu_2O. This is done by placing the oxidation number in brackets after the metal name:

CuO	copper(II) oxide
Cu_2O	copper(I) oxide
$PbCl_2$	lead(II) chloride
$PbCl_4$	lead(IV) chloride

Answer: +II

Copper(II) oxide is black whereas copper(I) oxide is red. Transition metals, such as copper, often show variable oxidation states in their compounds, which are often coloured

Q What is the full name of Cu_2SO_4?

Q What is the formula of iron(III) sulphate?

Compounds with three elements, one of which is oxygen, have the ending '-ate', to indicate the presence of oxygen. For example, sodium sulphate contains sodium, sulphur and oxygen. However, there are two compounds that contain these elements: Na_2SO_4 and Na_2SO_3. The ending '-ite' is often given to the compound with the lower amount of oxygen, so that Na_2SO_3 can be called sodium sulphite, but the compounds can also be distinguished by the use of oxidation numbers.

So Na_2SO_4 is sodium sulphate(VI) because here S has oxidation number $+VI$, and Na_2SO_3 is sodium sulphate(IV) because S has oxidation number $+IV$.

There is no need to include the oxidation numbers of elements whose oxidation numbers rarely change, like sodium (which is always $+I$) and oxygen (which is $-II$ except in peroxides, superoxides and fluorine compounds).

The full name for $CuSO_4$ is copper(II) sulphate(VI), but it is often abbreviated to copper sulphate when no confusion is likely.

The molecular compounds PCl_3 and PCl_5 are still usually called phosphorus trichloride and phosphorus pentachloride, rather than phosphorus(III) chloride and phosphorus(V) chloride and this applies to other molecular compounds.

It is more important to be able to work from the name to the formula than to be able to name a particular compound correctly. Some further examples are:

$KMnO_4$	potassium manganate(VII)
K_2MnO_4	potassium manganate(VI)
$CoCl_2$	cobalt(II) chloride
$CoCl_3$	cobalt(III) chloride

Keeping track of redox reactions

The use of oxidation numbers helps us to decide which element has been oxidised and which reduced in a redox reaction. By remembering that oxidation is loss of electrons ('OIL'), we can see that if an atom is oxidised, its oxidation number will go up:

$$Cu(s) + \tfrac{1}{2}O_2(s) \longrightarrow (Cu^{2+} + O^{2-})(s)$$

increase in oxidation number (loss of electrons) — $0 \rightarrow +II$

Similarly, when a substance is reduced, its oxidation number goes down. This includes an oxidation number becoming more negative ('RIG').

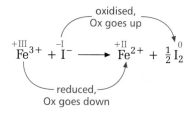

$$Fe^{3+} + I^- \longrightarrow Fe^{2+} + \tfrac{1}{2}I_2$$

oxidised, Ox goes up

reduced, Ox goes down

If we put in the oxidation numbers, it is easy to decide what has been oxidised and what reduced, even in fairly complicated equations.

Answer: Copper(I) sulphate

Answer: $Fe_2(SO_4)_3$

$$2IO_3^- + 5HSO_3^- \longrightarrow I_2 + 5SO_4^{2-} + 3H^+ + H_2O$$

All the other species have unchanged oxidation numbers.

Disproportionation

This happens in a reaction when some atoms *of the same element* from the same compound are oxidised and some are reduced.

e.g.

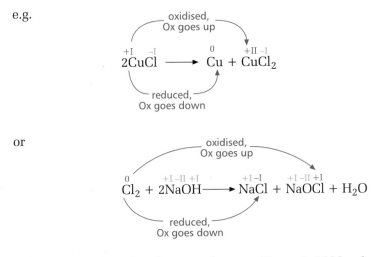

$$2CuCl \longrightarrow Cu + CuCl_2$$

or

$$Cl_2 + 2NaOH \longrightarrow NaCl + NaOCl + H_2O$$

This reaction is used in the manufacture of household bleach.

Balancing redox equations

If we know the starting materials and the products of a redox reaction, we can work out a balanced symbol equation for the reaction. Oxidation numbers can help us to balance redox reactions but they can only help us balance the redox change. Common sense and chemical intuition may allow us to do the rest. The key idea is that the *total* increase in oxidation number in one species must be balanced by the same *total* decrease in some other species. It is very important that you consider the *total* increase and decrease, not the increase and decrease per atom. For example, the equation:

> **Hint:** Always check that you have the correct formulae when balancing equations.

$$Zn + HCl \longrightarrow ZnCl_2 + H_2$$

is not balanced. How can we balance it? All the formulae are correct. First write the oxidation numbers of all the atoms:

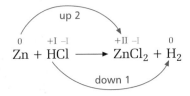

$$Zn + HCl \longrightarrow ZnCl_2 + H_2$$

Then identify those that change (marked in purple above).

The total upward change in oxidation number must be balanced by the same total downward change, so two H's must be involved.

$$Zn + 2HCl \longrightarrow ZnCl_2 + H_2$$

This was a straightforward example but here is a less familiar one where manganate(VII) ions oxidise iron(II) ions to iron(III) ions in acid solution:

$$\overset{+VII\ -II}{MnO_4^-} + \overset{+II}{Fe^{2+}} + \overset{+I}{H^+} \longrightarrow \overset{+II}{Mn^{2+}} + \overset{+III}{Fe^{3+}} + \overset{+I\ -II}{H_2O}$$

Again, the oxidation numbers of all the atoms are written down, with those that change in purple.

$$\overset{+VII\ -II}{MnO_4^-} + \overset{+II}{Fe^{2+}} + \overset{+I}{H^+} \longrightarrow \overset{+II}{Mn^{2+}} + \overset{+III}{Fe^{3+}} + \overset{+I\ -II}{H_2O}$$
$$\text{down 5}$$

The total downward change of the Mn must be balanced by the same upward change of the Fe. Each Fe changes by 1, so five Fe's must be involved.

$$\text{up 1 each} \times 5 = \text{up 5}$$
$$MnO_4^- + 5\overset{+II}{Fe^{2+}} + H^+ \longrightarrow Mn^{2+} + 5\overset{+III}{Fe^{3+}} + H_2O$$

Note that the process tells us nothing about the hydrogen or oxygen as their oxidation numbers do not change. However, to 'use up' all four oxygens of the MnO_4^-, 8 H's are needed and this will produce 4 H_2O's.

So the balanced equation is:

$$MnO_4^- + 5Fe^{2+} + 8H^+ \longrightarrow Mn^{2+} + 5Fe^{3+} + 4H_2O$$

In the next example sulphur dioxide (in solution) reduces aqueous bromine molecules to bromide ions:

$$\text{up 2}$$
$$\overset{+IV\ -II}{SO_2} + \overset{0}{Br_2} + \overset{+I\ -II}{H_2O} \longrightarrow \overset{+I}{H^+} + \overset{+VI\ -II}{SO_4^{2-}} + \overset{-I}{Br^-}$$

The total upward change of the sulphur is 2, so there must be a total downward change of 2. Each Br atom goes down by 1, so two of these are involved, i.e. one Br_2 molecule (not two molecules).

$$SO_2 + \overset{0}{Br_2} + H_2O \longrightarrow H^+ + SO_4^{2-} + 2\overset{-I}{Br^-}$$
$$\text{down 1 each} \times 2 = \text{down 2}$$

This is the redox balancing done. Again we are left with the task of 'sorting out' the O's and H's. Two extra O's are required to go from SO_2 to SO_4^{2-}, so there must be two H_2O molecules on the left and this means four H's on the right.

$$SO_2 + Br_2 + 2H_2O \longrightarrow 4H^+ + SO_4^{2-} + 2Br^-$$

Whenever you believe you have balanced an equation, check that:

1. The chemical balance is right, i.e. that there are the same number of atoms of each element left and right of the arrow.
2. That the charges balance, i.e. that the sum of the charges of all the ions on the left is equal to that on the right.

If either of these does not balance, you have made a mistake and will need to check back. Remember redox balancing can only help with those species whose oxidation numbers change.

13.4 Summary

● Redox reactions involve	electron transfer.
● A species has been oxidised if	it has lost electrons.
● A species has been reduced if	it has gained electrons.
● OIL RIG stands for	**oxidation is loss** and **reduction is gain** (of electrons).
● A species has been oxidised if its oxidation number	increases.
● A species has been reduced if its oxidation number	decreases.
● Oxidation number, abbreviated Ox, is	the charge on each ion in an ionic compound.
● Elements have Ox =	0.
● The sum of the Ox of each of all the atoms in a compound =	0.
● The sum of the Ox of each of all the atoms in an ionic species =	the charge of the ionic species.

13.5 Practice questions

1. What is the oxidation number of the underlined atom in the following?
   (a) $\underline{Co}Cl_3$, (b) $\underline{N}O_2$, (c) $\underline{N}_2O_4$, (d) $U\underline{F}_6$, (e) $Ca\underline{C}O_3$, (f) $\underline{Pb}$, (g) $\underline{Cl}^-$, (h) $\underline{N}H_4NO_3$, (i) $NH_4\underline{N}O_3$, (j) $P\underline{Cl}_3$, (k) $P\underline{Cl}_5$, (l) $H_2\underline{S}O_4$

2. Say whether the underlined atom is oxidised, is reduced, disproportionates or remains unchanged in the following reactions.
   (a) $\underline{Pb}Cl_2 + Cl_2 \longrightarrow PbCl_4$
   (b) $Na\underline{O}H + HCl \longrightarrow NaCl + H_2O$
   (c) $2\underline{I}O_3^- + 5HSO_3^- \longrightarrow I_2 + 5SO_4^{2-} + 3H^+ + H_2O$
   (d) $\underline{Cu} + \frac{1}{2}O_2 \longrightarrow CuO$
   (f) $3\underline{Cl}_2 + 6NaOH \longrightarrow 5NaCl + NaClO_3 + 3H_2O$

3. Name the following compounds using oxidation numbers where necessary.
   (a) $CoCl_3$, (b) H_2SO_4, (c) H_2SO_3, (d) $NaNO_3$, (e) PbO (f) PbO_2, (g) $NaClO_4$, (h) $NaClO_3$, (i) $NaClO$

4. Balance the following equations.
   (a) $Fe(s) + Fe^{3+}(aq) \longrightarrow Fe^{2+}(aq)$
   (b) $Al(s) + H^+(aq) \longrightarrow Al^{3+}(aq) + H_2(g)$
   (c) $Sn(s) + HNO_3(aq) \longrightarrow SnO_2(s) + NO_2(g) + H_2O(l)$

13.6 Examination questions

1. The stoichiometric equation for the catalytic oxidation of ammonia in an industrial process is:

$$4NH_3 + 5O_2 \longrightarrow 4NO + 6H_2O.$$

Name which elements here undergo a change in oxidation state and give the initial and final oxidation states.

[WJEC 1996]

2. (a) For **each** of the following reactions give the initial and final oxidation state(s) of the element specified.
   (i) $2Cu^{2+} + 4I^- \longrightarrow 2CuI + I_2$
       Copper.

   (ii) $3Cl_2 + 6NaOH \longrightarrow NaClO_3 + 5NaCl + 3H_2O$
        Chlorine.

   (b) State how gaseous chlorine reacts with water.

[WJEC 1997, part question]

3. Write down the oxidation states (numbers) of the elements in the following species:

I as I^-; Mn in MnO_4^-; O in H_2O; I in I_2; Mn in MnO_2.

[WJEC 1996]

14 Kinetics

Flixborough: plant explosion kills 29

Bhopal disaster: 200,000 affected

Chernobyl fall-out reaches UK

What do the above incidents have in common, apart from terrible loss of life? The answer is that they were all caused by chemical reactions that went out of control; they each went much faster than the operators had intended and the end result was an explosion. They are tragic examples of why we need to understand the factors that affect the rates of chemical reactions.

At a plant making nylon near Flixborough, a small town on Humberside, a cigarette ignited a cloud of flammable cyclohexane vapour, which had escaped from a leaking pipe. A tiny amount of energy from the cigarette was enough to start the reaction and release the vast amount of energy stored in the cyclohexane. This destroyed 100 houses and killed 29 people.

Many people misunderstand the causes of the Chernobyl incident which released a cloud of radioactive material into the atmosphere. The cause was chemical rather than nuclear. A series of operator errors produced steam inside the reactor. Zirconium metal reacted with the steam to release hydrogen which ultimately exploded and set fire to graphite (used to absorb neutrons in the reactor). The radioactive material was then released from the damaged reactor. Essentially this was a case of increased temperature increasing reaction rates. Estimates of the death toll vary widely because many people in the affected areas have died of cancers whose causes cannot always be pinned down with certainty. It is probably over 10 000.

At Bhopal, in India, an insecticide called carbamyl was being manufactured. The process involved several poisonous gases and one of these, methyl isocyanate, was the culprit. One theory is that a runaway reaction occurred between water and methyl isocyanate, causing a pressure build-up. This normally slow reaction could have been speeded up by sodium hydroxide (from a gas scrubbing system) acting as a catalyst. Because the manufacturing process used several toxic gases, there was confusion over which one was to blame and therefore what was the most appropriate treatment for victims. This may well have contributed to the number of casualties, which was over 2000.

In this chapter we will be looking at:
- factors which affect rates of chemical reactions
- the principles of measuring the rates of reactions
- experimental methods for measuring reaction rates
- the rate expression: a mathematical relationship showing how the concentrations of reactants affect reaction rates
- theories of reaction rates
- activation energy: the energy needed to start reactions
- catalysts and how they work

Did you know? The word 'kinetic' meaning 'moving' comes from the same root as the word 'cinema'.

Introduction

Chemical kinetics is the study of the rates of reactions and the factors that influence them. You will know from everyday experience that there is a very large variation in reaction rates from 'popping' a test tube full of hydrogen, which is over in a fraction of a second, to the complete rusting away of an iron nail, which could take several years. An everyday application of chemical kinetics is the use of low temperatures in a refrigerator to slow down spoilage reactions in food.

CONCEPT CHECKPOINTS

The following basic ideas are used in this chapter. You may revise some of these topics elsewhere in the book.
- concentration expressed in $mol\,dm^{-3}$ (section 4.4)
- the gradient (or slope) of a graph used to measure the rate at which something takes place (section 6.5)
- matter is made up of fast-moving particles

Q What is the surface area of a cube 2 cm × 2 cm × 2 cm? Imagine breaking this into 1 cm × 1 cm × 1 cm cubes. How many will you get? What will be the surface area of each? What will be the *total* surface area now?

14.1 Factors which affect the rate of chemical reactions

There are six factors that can affect the rate of chemical reactions.

Temperature

A rough rule of thumb which applies to many reactions at about room temperature is that a 10 K (10 °C) increase in temperature approximately doubles the rate of a chemical reaction.

Concentration

Increasing the concentration of some of the reactants increases the rate of reactions in solution.

Pressure

Increasing the pressure of a gas phase reaction increases the rate. Pressure, like concentration, increases the number of molecules, atoms or ions per cubic centimetre.

Surface area

Increasing the surface area of solid reactants increases the rate. For example, powdered zinc will react faster with acids than will zinc granules. The smaller the size of zinc particles, the greater the *total* surface area.

Light

Light affects the rate of certain reactions. For example, the reaction of bromine with alkanes proceeds quite quickly under a photoflood lamp but much more slowly in ordinary light. Some adhesives for sticking glass make use of this principle. The glue does not begin to react until exposed to sunlight.

Answer: 24 cm², 8, 6 cm², 48 cm²

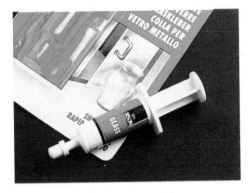

This adhesive sets on exposure to sunlight

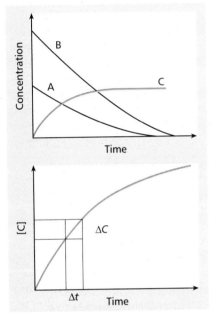

Figure 14.1 Changes of concentration

> **Hint:** Square brackets around a chemical symbol are used to indicate its concentration in mol dm^{-3}.

> **Hint:** Remember the use of the symbol Δ (delta) to mean a change in a quantity.

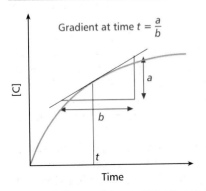

Figure 14.2 The rate of change of [C] at time t is the gradient of the concentration–time graph

Catalysts

Catalysts are substances that can change the rate of a chemical reaction without being chemically changed themselves. For example, addition of manganese(IV) oxide dramatically increases the rate of decomposition of hydrogen peroxide to oxygen and water. Catalysts are of great economic importance in industrial processes.

14.2 Measuring reaction rates

In the reaction:

$$A + 2B \longrightarrow C$$

the concentrations of the reactants A and B decrease with time and that of the product C increases as shown in **Figure 14.1**:

The average rate of the reaction with respect to C, during a period of time Δt is the change in concentration of C, $\Delta[C]$ divided by Δt.

$$\text{Rate of change of concentration of C} = \frac{\Delta[C]}{\Delta t}$$

so if in 10 seconds [C] changed from 1.0 mol dm^{-3} to 1.1 dm^{-3}

$$\text{Average rate of change of C} = \frac{1.1 - 1.0 \text{ mol dm}^{-3}}{10 \text{ s}}$$

$$= \frac{0.1}{10}$$

$$= 0.01 \text{ mol dm}^{-3}\text{ s}^{-1}$$

We are often interested in the rate of change of [C] *at a particular instant* in time rather than the *average* rate of change over a period of time. This rate of change at a particular instant is found from the gradient (slope) of the tangent to the curve at that time (**Figure 14.2**).

The mathematical notation for rate of change of [C] with time is d[C]/dt, (pronounced 'dee cee by dee tee'). So d[C]/dt = a/b. 'd' is used rather than Δ, to show that the change is taking place over a vanishingly small time. We will use this notation as it is shorter than writing out 'rate of change of [C] with time', although it means exactly the same.

The rate of change of concentration of different species may be different. As [C] is increasing, [A] is decreasing. As one molecule of A disappears, one of C appears, so

$$\frac{d[C]}{dt} = -\frac{d[A]}{dt}$$

As the equation tells us that 2 molecules of B are used up for every one of A, then

$$\frac{d[B]}{dt} = 2\frac{d[A]}{dt}$$

So when talking about the rate of a reaction, we must say which reactant or product we are referring to. We usually talk about 'the rate of reaction with respect to A' (or B or C).

14.3 Experimental methods for measuring reaction rates

To measure reaction rates, we need a method of measuring the concentration of one of the reactants or products as time goes on. The method chosen depends on the substance whose concentration is being measured and also the speed of the reaction. A method such as a titration which takes a few minutes to complete would be perfectly satisfactory for a reaction which takes over an hour to go to completion but not for one which is over in a few seconds.

Sampling and titration

The reaction mixture is sampled by pipette at suitable time intervals and the concentration of one of the reactants or products found by a suitable titration. If the reaction is relatively fast, it may be possible to stop or slow down the reaction in the sample, so that the titration can be carried out at leisure. For example, a reaction with an acid catalyst could be sampled and the sample run into an alkali to remove the catalyst and slow the reaction down. Alternatively, the sample can be cooled down rapidly, which will also slow down the reaction to give more time for titration. Either method is referred to as 'freezing' or 'quenching' the reaction. A reaction for which this would be suitable is:

$$I_2(aq) + CH_3COCH_3(aq) \xrightarrow[\text{catalyst}]{H^+} CH_2ICOCH_3(aq) + HI(aq)$$

iodine   propane   iodopropanone   hydrogen iodide

The reaction is complete in about 30 minutes depending on the concentrations. The reaction mixture can be sampled every five minutes or so and the sample run into a flask containing excess sodium hydrogencarbonate. This neutralises the acid catalyst, slowing the reaction considerably. The iodine remaining at this time can be titrated with sodium thiosulphate solution using starch at the end point.

$$I_2(aq) + 2Na_2S_2O_3(aq) \longrightarrow 2NaI(aq) + Na_2S_4O_6(aq)$$

Using a colorimeter

This method is only useful if one of the reactants or products is coloured. It is a more satisfactory method than titration for two reasons: firstly, no sampling is needed, and secondly, a reading can be taken almost instantaneously. So quite rapid reactions can be followed, especially if the colorimeter is interfaced to a data logger or computer which can plot a graph of concentration versus time as the reaction proceeds.

A colorimeter consists of a light source with filters to select a suitable colour (i.e. set of wavelengths) of light which is absorbed by the sample. (For example, a red-coloured sample transmits red light and therefore absorbs most of the other colours of light: see the box on the next page). The light passes through the sample onto a detector whose output goes to a meter or a recording device (**Figure 14.3**). This method could be used as an alternative for the investigation of the reaction above since iodine (brown) is the only coloured species involved in the reaction. The colorimeter will usually need to be calibrated to establish the relationship between its reading and the concentration of the species being observed.

Hint: Even if the sample is quenched, the main reaction mixture carries on reacting at its normal rate.

Q Why is it better to select a method which avoids sampling for following a reaction?

Colorimeter interfaced to a computer

Answer: Sampling is slow. It is possible to contaminate the reaction mixture while removing samples.

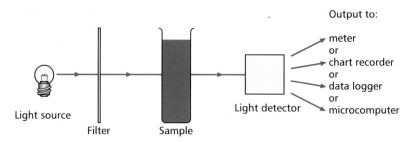

Light source   Filter   Sample   Light detector

Output to:

meter
or
chart recorder
or
data logger
or
microcomputer

Figure 14.3 Using a colorimeter to measure reaction rates

Q Why should we not start the reaction by dropping the zinc into the acid and replacing the bung?

The apparatus in Figure 14.4 interfaced to a computer

Answer: We would lose some hydrogen while replacing the bung.

Measuring the volume of gas given off

In the reaction:

$$Zn(s) + H_2SO_4(aq) \longrightarrow ZnSO_4(aq) + H_2(g)$$

we can follow the reaction by measuring the volume of hydrogen evolved at any time (see **Figure 14.4**). The reaction is started by shaking the zinc into the acid.

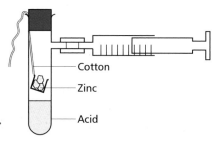

— Cotton

— Zinc

— Acid

Figure 14.4 Measuring gas volume to monitor reaction rates

By measuring the conductivity of a solution

This method (**Figure 14.5**) is suitable for reactions in which the number of ions in the solution changes.

Choice of filters for a colorimeter

This is a very simplified argument, which considers just the three primary colours: red, R, green, G, and blue, B.

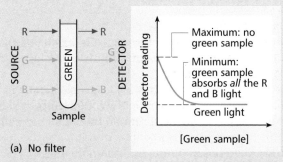

(a) No filter

A green sample lets green light through and absorbs some of the rest, the amount absorbed depending on the concentration of the green sample. So the meter reading can never drop to zero because there will always be green light passing through the sample unabsorbed, as well as some red and blue.

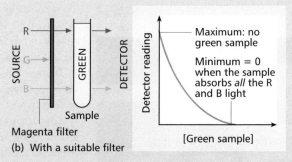

(b) With a suitable filter

A suitable filter absorbs green (the filter colour is called magenta – a purplish colour), allowing just red and blue through. Now if the green sample is concentrated enough, the meter reading can drop to zero because there is now none of the green light which always gets through without a filter. In practice, this means that we can use the meter on a more sensitive setting to measure how well the green solution absorbs red and blue.

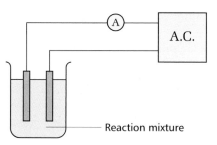

Figure 14.5 A conductivity meter can be used to measure the concentration of ionic species

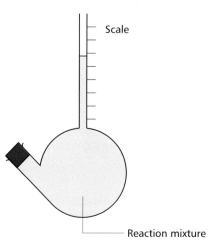

Figure 14.6 A dilatometer – used for measuring small volume changes during reactions

The more ions, the greater the conductivity and the bigger the ammeter reading. Alternating current is used to avoid electrolysing the solution. In the reaction below, neither of the reactants is ionic but one of the products is, so the conductivity should increase as the reaction proceeds.

$$C_4H_9Br + H_2O \longrightarrow C_4H_9OH + H^+ + Br^-$$

bromobutane   water   butanol   hydrogen ion   bromide ion

Using a dilatometer

Most reactions in solution involve small volume changes. These can be measured with a **dilatometer** (**Figure 14.6**). The narrow vertical tube means that small volume changes produce measurable changes in the liquid level.

Other methods

A variety of other methods can be used to measure rates. In fact any property of the reaction mixture which can be related to the concentration of one of the reactants or products can be used. Examples include pressure changes for gas reactions, and the rotation of the plane of polarisation for optically active compounds (see section 18.6).

14.4 The rate expression

The outcome of an experimental investigation of a reaction is a **rate expression**. This is an equation which describes how the rate of the reaction depends on the concentration of various species involved in the reaction. For example, the reaction:

$$X + Y \longrightarrow Z$$

might have the rate expression

$$\frac{d[Z]}{dt} \propto [X][Y]^2$$

which can be written:

$$\frac{d[Z]}{dt} = k[X][Y]^2$$

k is called the **rate constant** for the reaction.

The **order** of the reaction with respect to one of the species in the rate expression is the power to which the concentration of that species is raised in the rate expression.

In this case, the order with respect to X is one, so that doubling the concentration of X would double the rate. The order with respect to Y is two, so that doubling the concentration of Y would quadruple the rate.

The **overall order** of the reaction is the sum of the orders with respect to all the species that appear in the rate expression. In this case the overall order is three. So this reaction is said to be first order with respect to X, second order with respect to Y and third order overall.

The rate expression is entirely derived from the experimental evidence and *there is no way that it can be predicted from the chemical equation for the reaction*. Therefore it is quite unlike the equilibrium law expression (see Chapter 11) although it looks similar to it at first sight.

Species that do not appear in the chemical equation *may* appear in the rate expression and species which appear in the chemical equation do not necessarily appear in the rate equation.

For example, in the reaction:

$$CH_3COCH_3(aq) \ + \ I_2(aq) \xrightarrow{\text{H}^+ \text{ catalyst}} CH_2ICOCH_3(aq) \ + \ HI(aq)$$

propanone   iodine   iodopropanone   hydrogen iodide

the rate expression has been found to be:

$$-\frac{d[I_2(aq)]}{dt} = k[CH_3COCH_3(aq)][H^+(aq)]$$

Note that as I_2 is a reactant, its concentration decreases as the reaction proceeds, and there is a minus sign in the expression above. So the reaction is first order with respect to propanone, first order with respect to H^+ ions and second order overall.

The rate does not depend on $[I_2(aq)]$, so we can say the reaction is zero order with respect to iodine. The H^+ ions act as a catalyst in this reaction.

For the reaction:

$$BrO_3^-(aq) \ + \ 5Br^-(aq) \ + \ 6H^+(aq) \ \longrightarrow \ 3Br_2(aq) + 3H_2O(l)$$

bromate ions   bromide ions   hydrogen ions   bromine   water

the rate expression has been found to be:

$$-\frac{d[BrO_3^-(aq)]}{dt} = k[BrO_3^-(aq)][Br^-(aq)][H^+(aq)]^2$$

> **Q** What would happen to the rate if we doubled the concentration of (a) $BrO_3^-(aq)$, (b) $Br^-(aq)$, (c) $H^+(aq)$?

The reaction is:

first order with respect to $BrO_3^-(aq)$
first order with respect to $Br^-(aq)$
second order with respect to $H^+(aq)$
fourth order overall.

> **Hint:** The coefficient of a species in a chemical equation is the number which appears before it. If there is no number the coefficient is 1.

Notice that there is no relationship between the coefficients in the chemical equation and the powers in the rate expression.

Note that since $BrO_3^-(aq)$ is a reactant, $\dfrac{d[BrO_3^-(aq)]}{dt}$ is negative,

> **Q** What are the coefficients of $BrO_3^-(aq)$, $Br^-(aq)$, $H^+(aq)$, $Br_2(aq)$ and $H_2O(l)$ in the above equation?

hence the negative sign in the rate expression because all the other terms are positive numbers.

The rate constant, *k*

The units of the rate constant vary depending on the overall order of the reaction.

For a first order reaction where:

$$\frac{d[A]}{dt} = k[A]$$

the units of $d[A]/dt$ are $mol\ dm^{-3}\ s^{-1}$ and the units of $[A]$ are $mol\ dm^{-3}$, so by cancelling:

$$\cancel{mol}\ \cancel{dm^{-3}}s^{-1} = k\ \cancel{mol}\ \cancel{dm^{-3}}$$

Answer: (a) double, (b) double, (c) quadruple

Answer: 1, 5, 6, 3, 3

and the units of *k* are s^{-1}.

For a second order reaction where

$$\frac{d[B]}{dt} = k[A][C]$$

the units of $\frac{d[B]}{dt}$ are $mol\,dm^{-3}\,s^{-1}$ and the units of both [A] and [B] are $mol\,dm^{-3}$, so by cancelling:

$$mol\,dm^{-3}s^{-1} = k\,mol\,dm^{-3} \times mol\,dm^{-3}$$

the units of k are $dm^3\,mol^{-1}\,s^{-1}$. It is best to work out the units in each case rather than try to remember them.

It is perfectly possible to have orders of reaction which are not whole numbers, or are less than 1, although you are most unlikely to come across these at this level.

> **Q** Work out the units for the rate constant of a third order reaction.

> **Hint:** When writing out the units of quantities such as k, it is usual to list those with the positive indices first and s^{-1} at the end, though other orders are not wrong.

14.5 Theories of reaction rates

Any theory of kinetics must be able to explain why rates increase with increasing concentration or pressure and surface area of reactants and with increasing temperature. There are two theories, each stressing a different aspect of the process of a reaction. They are **collision theory** and **transition state theory**.

Collision theory

For a reaction to take place between two molecules A and B, they must collide. This explains why reaction rates increase with increased concentration or pressure. If there are more molecules per cubic centimetre, collisions will occur more frequently. Also increased surface area of a solid leads to more molecules of the solid being exposed to collisions with other reactants.

As molecules move faster when the temperature increases, there will be more collisions per second and the molecules will also hit each other harder (with more energy).

If we know the temperature (and therefore the speeds) of the reacting molecules and their concentrations, it is possible to calculate the number of collisions between them per second. When this is done, it is found that the actual rates of many reactions are less than those predicted by the collision rate by factors of around 10^{11}. So only a very small proportion of collisions actually result in a reaction. This is for two reasons:

1. For a collision to result in a reaction, the molecules must approach each other in the right orientation. This is sometimes called the **steric factor**. For example, OH^- ions react with bromobutane and replace the bromine:

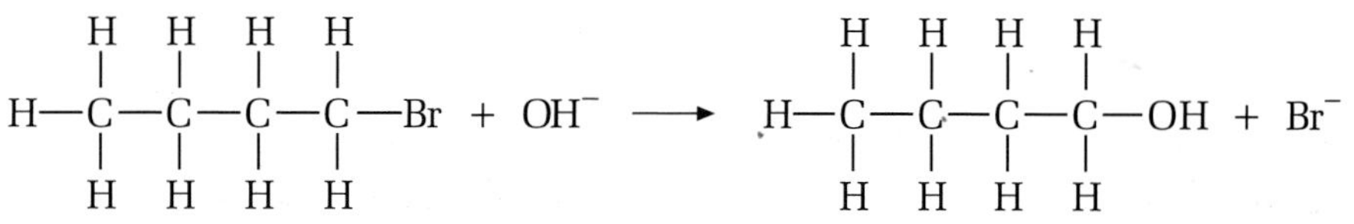

Answer: $dm^6\,mol^{-2}\,s^{-1}$

$$H-C-C-C-C-Br \longrightarrow H-C-C-C-C-Br$$

(with the H atoms shown above and below each C, and OH⁻ below each structure)

(a) Wrong orientation – no reaction

$$H-C-C-C-C-Br \longrightarrow H-C-C-C-C-OH$$

(with the H atoms shown above and below each C, OH⁻ approaching the Br end, and Br⁻ shown on the product side)

(b) Right orientation – reaction occurs

A collision of an OH⁻ ion with a bromobutane molecule is unlikely to result in a reaction if it hits the end of the molecule away from the Br. So only a small proportion of collisions result in a reaction for this reason.

2. If a collision is to result in a reaction, the molecules must have a certain minimum energy: enough to start breaking bonds. Otherwise they are unable to react. So again, many collisions will not lead to a reaction. This leads onto the second theory.

Transition state theory

This considers the details of the actual collision. When two molecules approach closely on a collision course, their electron clouds begin to repel. Unless they are moving very fast (i.e. have a lot of kinetic energy), this repulsion will push them apart before they get close enough for new bonds to form. If they get sufficiently close, rearrangement of the electrons in the outer shells can take place so that new bonds form and old ones break. The kinetic energy of the collision is converted into potential energy. The highly energetic and unstable species that exists briefly at the point of maximum potential energy is called the **transition state** or **activated complex**. In this species bonds are in the process of making and breaking. For example:

$$A—B + C \longrightarrow A + B—C$$

The transition state could be represented as:

$$A - - - B - - - C$$

where a dashed line represents bonds in the process of breaking and forming.

We can represent the reaction on an energy (enthalpy) diagram, sometimes called the **reaction profile** (see **Figure 14.7**).

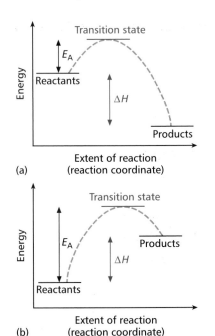

Figure 14.7 Reaction profile for (a) an exothermic reaction and (b) an endothermic reaction

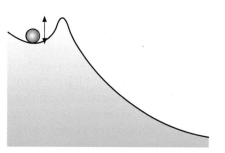

Figure 14.8 Ball on a mountainside model

The transition state is the highest point in this reaction profile. The energy gap between the reactants and the transition state is called the **activation energy**, E_A, for the reaction. If a pair of molecules collides with less energy than E_A, they cannot react. For an exothermic reaction, the situation is rather like a ball on a mountainside (**Figure 14.8**). A small amount of energy has to be supplied to lift the ball over the lip even though energy is given out overall when the ball rolls down the 'valley'.

14.6 Catalysts

Did you know? Inhibitors are added to the water in central heating systems and car radiators to slow down corrosion reactions.

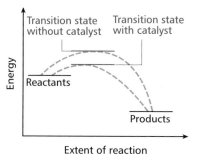

Figure 14.9 Reaction profiles for a catalysed and an uncatalysed reaction

Hint: Different **phases** are separated by a distinct boundary. For example, oil and water form two separate liquid phases.

Catalysts are substances that affect the rate of a chemical reaction without being chemically changed themselves. Normally we use the term catalyst to refer to substances that speed up reactions. The terms **negative catalyst** or **inhibitor** are used for ones which slow down reactions.

Positive catalysts work by reducing the activation energy of the reaction by allowing the reaction to go by a different pathway with a lower activation energy (**Figure 14.9**).

For example, for the breakdown of dinitrogen monoxide to nitrogen and oxygen:

$$2N_2O(g) \longrightarrow 2N_2(g) + O_2(g)$$
$$E_A = 240\ \text{kJ mol}^{-1}\ \text{(uncatalysed)}$$
$$E_A = 120\ \text{kJ mol}^{-1}\ \text{(with a gold catalyst)}$$

There is no single theory to explain catalysis and many catalysts were discovered simply by trial and error. They are usually divided into:

- **heterogeneous** catalysts (where the catalyst is in a different phase to the reactants – usually solid catalyst and liquid or gaseous reactants)
- **homogeneous** catalysts (where catalyst and reactants are in the same phase).

Some examples are given in **Table 14.1**.

Table 14.1 Examples of catalysts

Reaction	Catalyst	Type
$N_2(g) + 3H_2(g) \longrightarrow 2NH_3(g)$	Many metals, including Fe	heterogeneous
$SO_2(g) + \frac{1}{2}O_2(g) \longrightarrow SO_3(g)$	V_2O_5	heterogeneous
$H_2O_2(aq) \longrightarrow H_2O(l) + \frac{1}{2}O_2(g)$	MnO_2 + other metal oxides and enzymes	heterogeneous
$CH_3CO_2H(l) + CH_3OH(l) \longrightarrow CH_3CO_2CH_3(aq) + H_2O(l)$	H^+ or OH^-	homogeneous
$CH_3COCH_3(aq) + I_2(aq) \longrightarrow CH_2ICOCH_3(aq) + HI(aq)$	H^+	homogeneous

Heterogeneous catalysts

Transition metals frequently catalyse gas phase reactions. Transition metals have unfilled d orbitals (see section 31.1) and can use these to form new bonds. The gases are **adsorbed** on the surface of the metal,

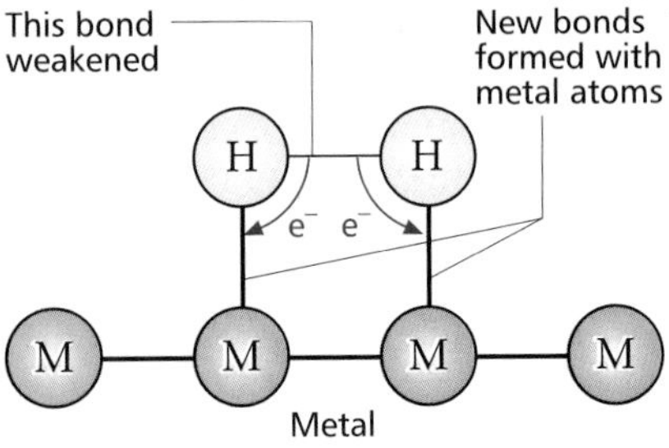

This bond weakened — New bonds formed with metal atoms

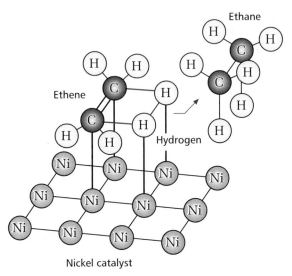

Metal

Figure 14.10 Adsorption of hydrogen onto a metal surface

i.e. they from weak bonds with the metal atoms. This adsorption may catalyse the reaction in one or both of two ways:

1. The formation of bonds with the metal may use some of the electrons in bonds within the gas molecule, thus weakening these bonds and allowing them to break more easily (see **Figure 14.10**).
2. The adsorbed gases may be held on the metal surface in just the right orientation for reaction to occur. This has the same effect as increasing the number of favourable collisions (see **Figure 14.11**).

Figure 14.11 Ethene and hydrogen adsorbed onto a nickel catalyst in the right orientation for new bonds (in red) to form

The strength of the adsorption of gases on the surface is critical. If it is too weak, little adsorption will occur. If it is too strong, the product molecules will tend to remain on the surface and block it for further catalysis. Impurities in the reaction mixture can sometimes adsorb more strongly than the reactants and 'poison' the catalyst. This is of critical importance in industrial processes, so the reaction mixtures need to be of a high purity. Closing down a plant to change the catalyst could be very expensive in terms of lost production.

The surface area of heterogeneous catalysts is important. In the Haber process for making ammonia, pea-sized lumps of iron are used rather than slabs to increase the total surface area.

Homogeneous catalysts

Many mechanisms are possible. We shall look at just two.

Acid-catalysed esterification

This is the reaction between a carboxylic acid like ethanoic acid and an alcohol to form an ester.

$$CH_3-\overset{\overset{O}{\|}}{C}-OH + CH_3OH \xrightarrow{H^+ \text{ catalyst}} CH_3-\overset{\overset{O}{\|}}{C}-O-CH_3 + H_2O$$

ethanoic acid   methanol   methyl ethanoate   water

Both ethanoic acid and methanol have dipoles (see Chapter 9):

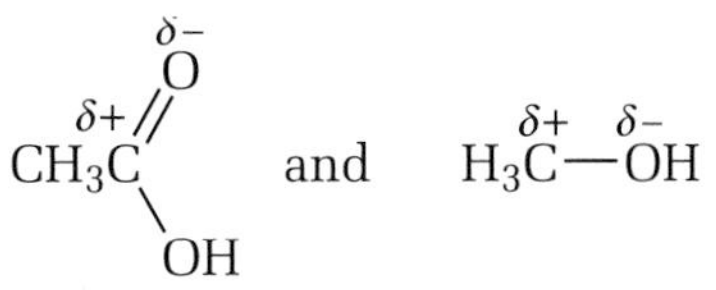

$$CH_3C \overset{\delta+}{\underset{\overset{\delta-}{O}}{\diagup\hspace{-0.3em}/}} \qquad \text{and} \qquad H_3\overset{\delta+}{C}\text{—}\overset{\delta-}{O}H$$

and the reaction occurs when the $O^{\delta-}$ on the methanol is attracted to the $C^{\delta+}$ on the acid to form a new bond.

Hint: Curved arrows, often called 'curly arrows' are used to show movement of electrons (see section 18.8).

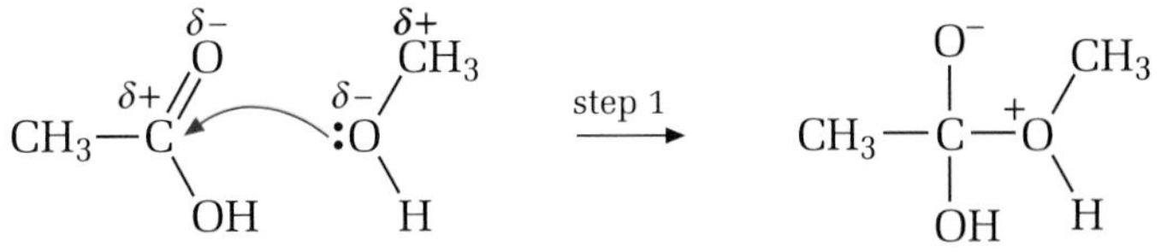

This is followed by the loss of water from the new species formed:

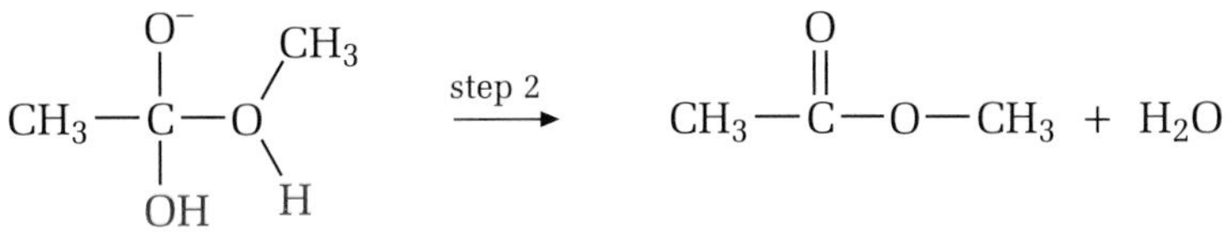

The first step is made easier if the $O^{\delta-}$ of the acid first accepts an H^+ ion (is protonated) from the catalyst:

Hint: An H^+ ion is a proton, so protonation is the addition of an H^+ ion.

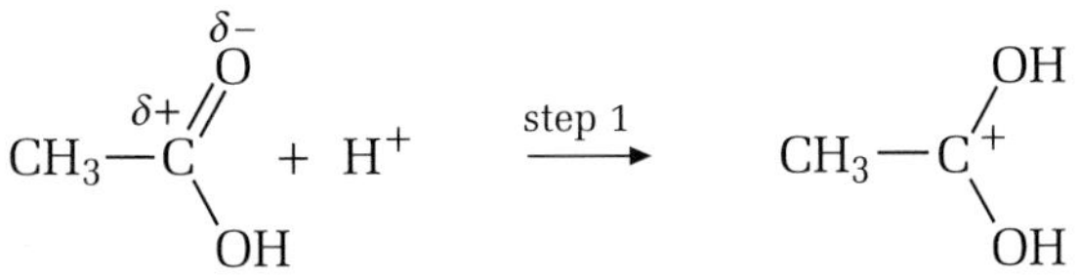

The protonated acid has more positive charge and is more easily attacked by the $O^{\delta-}$ on the methanol.

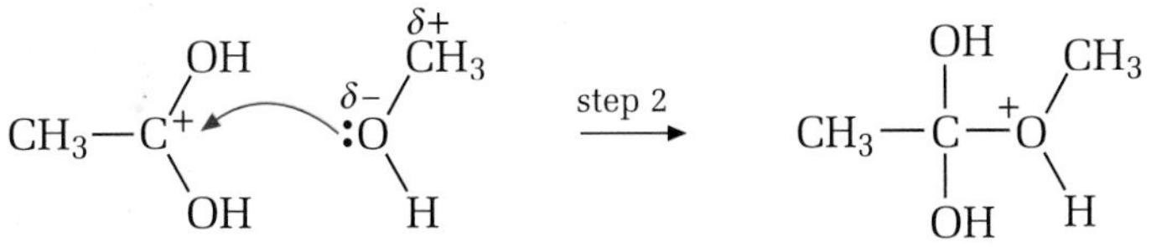

Water is lost as in the uncatalysed example. Finally, the H^+ ion is returned to the reaction mixture: it has not been changed in the reaction.

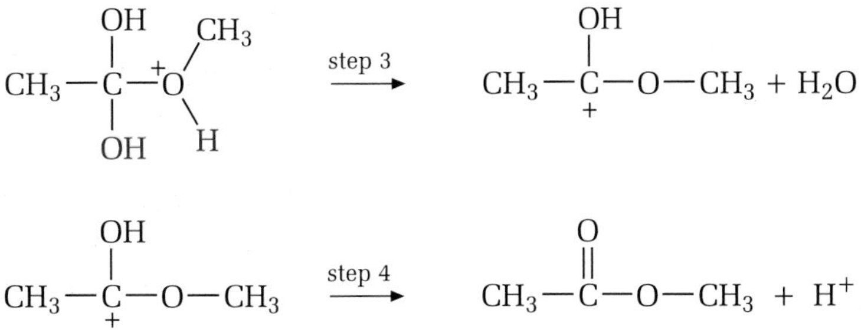

Even though there are two extra steps, the reaction goes faster because the key step (the attack by methanol), the 'rate determining step', is easier.

Similar mechanisms to this occur frequently in organic chemistry.

Hint: Do not be put off by unfamiliar chemical names (such as peroxodisulphate(VI) ions). Make sure you understand the *process* that they are used to illustrate.

Redox reactions catalysed by transition metals

Peroxodisulphate(VI) ions oxidise iodide ions to iodine. This reaction is catalysed by Fe^{2+} ions.

$$S_2O_8{}^{2-}(aq) + 2I^-(aq) \longrightarrow 2SO_4{}^{2-}(aq) + I_2(aq)$$

It is believed that the catalysed reaction takes place in two steps. First the peroxodisulphate ions oxidise iron(II) to iron(III):

$$S_2O_8{}^{2-}(aq) + 2Fe^{2+}(aq) \longrightarrow 2SO_4{}^{2-}(aq) + 2Fe^{3+}(aq)$$

The Fe^{3+} then oxidises the I^- to I_2, regenerating the Fe^{2+} ions so that none are used up in the reaction:

$$2Fe^{3+}(aq) + 2I^-(aq) \longrightarrow 2Fe^{2+}(aq) + I_2(aq)$$

The reaction profile would look something like **Figure 14.12**.

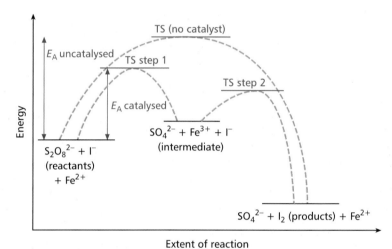

Figure 14.12 Possible reaction profile for the iodine/peroxodisulphate reaction. Note E_A for the catalysed reaction is the energy gap between the reactants and the higher of the two transition states in this reaction

Although there are two steps in the catalysed reaction, the overall activation energy is lower than that for the uncatalysed reaction. Part of the reason for this may be that the uncatalysed reaction takes place between two ions of the same charge (both negative). Both steps of the catalysed reaction involve reaction between pairs of oppositely charged ions.

Transition metals and their compounds frequently catalyse redox reactions in this sort of way because transition metals have variable oxidation numbers (see Chapter 31) and can act as a temporary 'warehouse' for electrons. In this case the iron first gives an electron to the peroxodisulphate and later takes one back from the iodide ions.

Q Fe^{3+} ions also catalyse this reaction. Can you work out how?

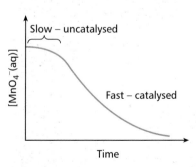

Figure 14.13 A concentration–time graph for an autocatalytic reaction

Autocatalysis

An interesting example of catalysis occurs when one of the products of the reaction is a catalyst for the reaction. Such a reaction starts slowly at the uncatalysed rate. As the concentration of the product (which is also the catalyst) builds up, the reaction speeds up to the catalysed rate. From then on it behaves like a normal reaction, gradually slowing down as the reactants are used up. This leads to an odd-looking rate curve (see **Figure 14.13**).

Answer: The two steps of the catalysed reaction take place in the reverse order.

Q Can you suggest another method of following the reaction?

The curve shown in Figure 14.13 is for the reaction:

$$2MnO_4^-(aq) + 16H^+(aq) + 5C_2O_4^{2-}(aq) \longrightarrow 2Mn^{2+}(aq) + 8H_2O(l) + 10CO_2(aq)$$

manganate(VII) ions   hydrogen ions   ethanedioate ions   manganese(II) ions   water   carbon dioxide

The catalyst is Mn^{2+} ions. The reaction can easily be followed using a colorimeter to measure the concentration of MnO_4^-, which is purple.

Answer: Sample and titrate the H^+ ions. The carbon dioxide is dissolved, so cannot be collected as a gas.

CHEMISTRY AROUND US

Enzymes and biotechnology

Enzymes are protein-based catalysts found in living things. They are extremely effective catalysts. They are also extremely specific: one enzyme normally catalyses one reaction of a single molecule (known as its **substrate**). Many enzymes convert their substrate so fast that the rate determining step is the diffusion of the substrate towards the enzyme. The reaction rates can be 1000 molecules of substrate per second per molecule of enzyme!

The shape of a protein molecule governs its catalytic activity. This shape is easily altered by relatively small changes in temperature or pH. When this happens the protein's efficiency as a catalyst is reduced and it is said to be **denatured**. Thus enzymes have an optimum temperature, often around body temperature (37 °C, 310 K). Up to this temperature the reaction rate increases with temperature in the usual way; above this temperature the rate decreases as the enzyme is denatured.

The human race has used enzymes for its own purposes for thousands of years, for example to ferment sugar into alcohol and turn milk into cheese and yoghurt. However, in the last twenty years vast strides have been made in this field, which is now called biotechnology. This includes the 'tailoring' of enzymes to catalyse particular processes with their usual super-efficiency. It is also possible to 'fix' enzyme molecules on a solid so that the enzyme can be retained for re-use rather than being mixed with the product and effectively lost after each batch is produced. The enzymes become effectively heterogeneous rather than homogeneous catalysts.

Many drugs especially are now synthesised by biotechnological processes, including insulin, the hormone required by diabetics and the drug interferon which has anti-viral and anti-cancer properties.

An enzyme called alkaline protease is an ingredient of many washing powders. It digests protein-based stains, such as blood, at low temperatures and in the slightly alkaline conditions of washing powder solutions. One drawback is that a number of people appear to be allergic to the enzyme. Lipases are also used in laundry products to digest fat stains.

The enzyme industry has grown because enzymes are so efficient. Not only can small quantities of enzymes convert large quantities of chemicals but they also do so at low temperatures and normal pressures. The idea of working with enzymes on a large scale was started by two British chemists, Malcolm Lilley and Peter Dunnill, working in a basement at University College, London.

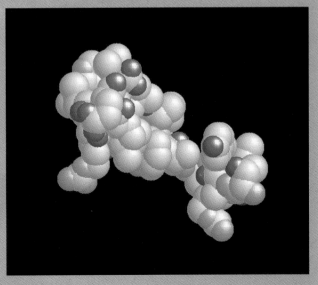

Haemophiliacs lack the clotting agent, factor VIII, in their blood, which means that small cuts bleed profusely. Synthetic factor VIII is made using enzymes. This avoids the possibility of haemophiliacs contracting AIDS from natural factor VIII obtained from contaminated blood

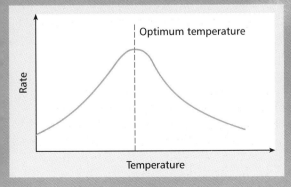

Catalytic converters for car exhausts

Motor vehicle exhausts are a major source of pollution and are responsible for significant amounts of carbon monoxide, hydrocarbons and nitrogen oxides (NO and NO_2 – often abbreviated to NO_x).

To comply with pollution regulations, most new cars are fitted with a catalytic converter in the exhaust system. This speeds up the reactions below, neatly removing the pollutants by getting them to react with one another to form harmless products.

carbon monoxide + nitrogen oxide
$\longrightarrow$ carbon dioxide + nitrogen

hydrocarbons + nitrogen oxide
$\longrightarrow$ carbon dioxide + nitrogen + water

The catalyst system consists of a ceramic honeycomb, coated with platinum and rhodium.

Catalytic converters have a number of drawbacks, however. They are not cheap, owing to the cost of the platinum and rhodium. The car must run on lead-free petrol or the catalyst will be 'poisoned' by the lead. The catalyst system is only effective at temperatures over 400 °C (673 K). On a short journey, the converter is inactive for much of the time as it does not reach the operating temperature.

Q Why is the catalyst coated onto a 'honeycomb'?

A catalytic converter

Answer: To provide a large surface area.

14.7 Summary

• Rates of chemical reactions can be affected by six factors. These are:	concentration of reactants, pressure (for gas phase reactants), temperature, surface area of solids, light and catalysts.
• Rates may be measured by monitoring any property of the reaction mixture which depends on	the concentration of a reactant or product.
• Common methods of determining rates include	quenching followed by a titration, colorimetry, conductivity measurement and measurement of volumes of gases involved.
• The rate expression is an equation that shows how	the reaction rate depends on the concentration of species present in the reaction mixture.
• The rate equation *cannot* be predicted from	the chemical equation.
• The order with respect to a particular species is	the power to which its concentration is raised in the rate expression.
• The overall order is	the sum of the orders with respect to each species.
• Collision theory says that reactions occur if	two molecules collide with the correct orientation and with at least a set minimum energy.

- The activation energy E_A is

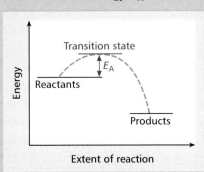

Figure 14.14 Reaction profile for an exothermic reaction

the energy required to reach a high-energy species called the transition state, the peak of the reaction profile (**Figure 14.14**).

- Catalysts

change the rate of a reaction without themselves being chemically changed.

- Homogeneous catalysts are

in the same phase as the reactants.

- Heterogeneous catalysts are

in a different phase from the reactants, usually solid catalyst and liquid or gaseous reactants.

- Catalysts work by

lowering the activation energy of the reaction in some way.

- Many reactions are catalysed by

acids or bases or transition metal compounds.

- Heterogeneous catalysts often work by

adsorbing the reactants onto their surface.

14.8 Practice questions

1. Suggest a method for measuring the rate of the following reactions.
   (a) $CaCO_3(s) + 2HCl(aq)$
       $\longrightarrow CaCl_2(aq) + H_2O(l) + CO_2(g)$
   (b) $CuSO_4(aq) + Zn(s) \longrightarrow ZnSO_4(aq) + Cu(s)$
   (c) $2NO(g) + O_2(g) \longrightarrow 2NO_2(g)$
   (d) $CH_3COCH_3(aq) + H^+(aq) + C\equiv N^-(aq)$
       $\longrightarrow CH_3C(OH)(C\equiv N)CH_3(aq)$
   (e) $BrO_3^-(aq) + 5Br^-(aq) + 6H^+(aq)$
       $\longrightarrow 3Br_2(l) + 3H_2O(l)$
   (f) $C_2H_5Br + NaOH \longrightarrow C_2H_5OH + NaBr$

2. In the reaction in (e) above, if the rate with respect to bromate ions is

   $$\frac{d[BrO_3^-]}{dt} = -10^{-3} \, \text{mol dm}^{-3} \, \text{s}^{-1}$$

   what will be:

   (a) the rate with respect to Br^- ions, $\dfrac{d[Br^-]}{dt}$?

   (b) the rate with respect to Br_2 molecules $\dfrac{d[Br_2]}{dt}$?

3. For the reaction:

   $$2H_2(g) + 2NO_2(g) \longrightarrow 2H_2O(l) + N_2(g)$$

   the following initial rates were determined:

Initial [NO] $/10^{-3}$ mol dm^{-3}	Initial [H$_2$] $/10^{-3}$ mol dm^{-3}	Initial rate $/10^{-3}$ mol dm^{-3} s^{-1}
6	1	3
6	2	6
6	3	9
1	6	0.5
2	6	2
3	6	4.5

   (a) What is the order of the reaction:
       (i)   with respect to NO?
       (ii) with respect to H$_2$?
       (iii) overall?
       Explain your reasoning for each answer.
   (b) Write the rate expression for the reaction.
   (c) Using values from the table above, determine the rate constant (with appropriate units).
   (d) What would the rate of the reaction be if [H$_2$] was 1×10^{-3} mol dm^{-3} and [NO$_2$] = 1×10^{-3} mol dm^{-3}?

14.9 Examination questions

1. The data below refer to the reaction

$$\mathbf{X} + \mathbf{Y} \longrightarrow \text{products}$$

Concentration of X/mol dm^{-3}	Concentration of Y/mol dm^{-3}	Rate /mol dm^{-3} s^{-1}
0.01	0.01	1.0×10^{-4}
0.01	0.02	2.0×10^{-4}
0.02	0.02	2.0×10^{-4}

Deduce the overall order of the reaction.

[WJEC 1997]

2. The equation for the reaction between bromine and nitrogen(II) oxide, in the gaseous state is;

$$Br_2(g) + 2NO(g) \longrightarrow 2NOBr(g)$$

The rate equation for the reaction is

$$\text{rate} = k[Br_2(g)][NO(g)]^2$$

Copy and complete the following table:

Experiment	Initial concentration/mol dm^{-3} [Br$_2$(g)]	[NO(g)]	Initial rate /mol dm^{-3} s^{-1}
A	0.1	0.1	5×10^{-4}
B	0.2	0.1	
C		0.2	40×10^{-4}

3. Hydrogen peroxide is a covalent compound which, in solution, can act as an oxidising or reducing agent.
   (a) It oxidises bromide ions according to the following ionic equation:

$$H_2O_2 + 2Br^- + 2H^+ \longrightarrow Br_2 + 2H_2O$$

The rate law for the reaction is:

$$\text{rate} = k[H_2O_2][H^+][Br^-]$$

   (i) What is the overall order of the reaction?
   (ii) What are the units of k?
   (iii) Suggest, without experimental detail, how the rate of the reaction may be determined.
   (iv) If the concentration of bromide was doubled, assuming all other factors were kept constant, what would be the effect on the rate?
   (v) Explain how raising the pH of the reaction mixture affects the rate.

[NI 1996, part question]

4. (a) The rate of the reaction between reactants **P** and **Q** can be represented by the equation

$$\text{rate} = k[P][Q]^2$$

Without giving practical details, outline the experiments you would perform to show that the reaction is first order with respect to **P** and second order with respect to **Q**. Given that the units of rate are mol dm^{-3} s^{-1}, deduce the units of the rate constant, k.
   (b) Give **three** ways in which you could increase the rate of reaction between a solid and a substance in solution other than by the addition of a catalyst. For each of your methods, explain why the rate of reaction increases.
   (c) Explain why an increase in pressure increases the rate of any reaction involving gases but has little effect on the rate of a reaction involving solids and solutions.

[NEAB 1998]

5. Chemical reactions can be affected by homogeneous or by heterogeneous catalysts.
   (a) Explain what is meant by the term *homogeneous* and suggest the most important feature in the mechanism of this type of catalysis when carried out by a transition-metal compound.
   (b) In aqueous solution, $S_2O_8^{2-}$ ions can be reduced to SO_4^{2-} ions.
      (i) Write an equation for this reaction.
      (ii) Suggest why the reaction has a high activation energy, making it slow in the absence of a catalyst.
      (iii) Iron salts can catalyse this reaction. Write two equations to show the role of the catalyst in this reaction.
   (c) Below is a sketch showing typical catalytic efficiencies of transition metals from Period 5 (Rb to Xe) and Period 6 (Cs to Rn) when used in heterogeneous catalysis.

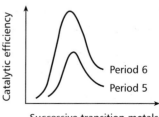

   (i) Identify two metals which lie at opposite ends of these curves and explain why they show rather low catalytic efficiency.
   (ii) Suggest why these curves pass through a maximum.

[NEAB 1998, part]

Periodicity

C H E M I S T R Y   N O W

What's in a name?

The Periodic Table is all about elements. Just over 100 of them make up the several million substances that chemists know about. You may be surprised to find that elements are still being discovered. This is done by using particle accelerators to smash together the nuclei of existing elements in the hope that they will 'stick together', i.e. that the strong nuclear force will hold the new nucleus together against the mutual repulsion of the protons. In fact the nuclei of such superheavy elements break apart very rapidly: they have extremely short half-lives.

Lise Meitner after whom element 109 is currently named. She shared in the discovery of nuclear fission wih Otto Hahn (also pictured) and her nephew Otto Frisch. Despite twelve nominations, she never won a Nobel prize.

For some years there has been controversy over the naming of these new elements and arguments have raged between rival research teams over who discovered which element and therefore who has the right to name it.

For a time, elements 104 onwards were given the names unnilquadium (Unq), unnilpentium (Unp) and so on. These were based on the Latin for '104-ium', '105-ium' etc. and were suggested by the International Union of Pure and Applied Chemistry (IUPAC), which deals with chemical naming, in order to prevent confusion. Recently, though, IUPAC has tried to adjudicate on the issue of definitive names but appeal and counter-appeal have caused controversy and led to some elements having several proposed names.

For example, element 106 has been suggested as seaborgium after Glenn T. Seaborg, a US scientist who discovered plutonium and several other elements. This was changed to rutherfordium (after Ernest Rutherford, the discoverer of the atomic nucleus) on the grounds that elements should not be named after living people. However, in the latest proposal seaborgium is back in favour.

The table summarises the present position for elements 104–109 but the situation may well have changed by the time you read these words.

Atomic number	Name(s) suggested previously	Name now proposed (1999)	Currently proposed name in honour of:
104	kurchatovium, dubnium	rutherfordium	Ernest Rutherford, who discovered the atomic nucleus
105	joliotium, hahnium	dubnium	Dubna in Russia, where the element was discovered
106	rutherfordium	seaborgium	Glenn T. Seaborg, who discovered nine artificial elements
107	nielsbohrium	bohrium	Niels Bohr, who proposed the idea of electron orbits
108	hahnium	hassium	Hesse, the German state where the element was discovered
109		meitnerium	Lise Meitner, the German scientist who helped to discover nuclear fission

Introduction

The Periodic Table is of central importance to chemistry. It provides a logical framework for recognising patterns in the properties of elements and their compounds. It also allows us to explain similarities and trends in properties in terms of the electronic structures of the elements. Without the Periodic Table, chemistry would be a hotch-potch of unrelated information about different substances. With it, we can see such data as part of a unified whole.

15.1 The structure of the Periodic Table

The Periodic Table has been written in many forms including pyramids and spirals. The one shown at the end of the book is the most usual and useful one.

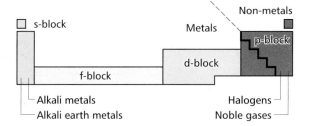

Figure 15.1 The Periodic Table. In most versions the f-block is placed below the d-block, as in Figure 15.2

FURTHER FOCUS

The history of the Periodic Table

Chemists have long searched for some order in their science. One of the first to make real progress was Antoine Lavoisier who in 1789 put forward a list of what we would now call elements. He divided these into sets on the basis of chemical similarities. His list looks decidedly odd now as he included light and heat (which we do not regard as chemical substances at all) and also several substances that we now know to be compounds such as 'alumina' (aluminium oxide) and 'magnesia' (magnesium oxide). The chemical techniques of the day were just not advanced enough to decompose these very stable compounds.

In 1817 a German, Johann Döbereiner noticed some sets of very similar elements: lithium, sodium and potassium;

calcium, barium and strontium; and chlorine, bromine and iodine. Not only did these 'triads', as he called them, have chemical similarities but the relative atomic mass of the middle one was approximately the average of those of the outer two. For example, A_r for Li = 7; K = 39; Na = 23 = (39 + 7)/2. Döbereiner had spotted sets of elements that we now recognise as members of the same chemical group.

By the 1860s more accurate methods of determining relative atomic masses had been developed. Three chemists discovered patterns in the then known elements when they were arranged in ascending order of atomic mass.

The English chemist John Newlands noticed that there were similarities between the first, eighth and fifteenth elements, the second, ninth and sixteenth and so on. He called this the 'law of octaves' and compared it with a musical scale. Partly because of this musical analogy but more seriously because he made no allowance for elements not then known, his ideas were ridiculed by some of his contemporaries.

and noted a repeating pattern. A modern version of his graph is shown in Figure 15.3.

The credit for the Periodic Table, however, goes firmly to the Russian Dimitri Mendeleev (see the photograph on page 2). His greatest achievement was to realise that there were probably elements remaining to be discovered (there were only around 60 then known). He not only left gaps in his table for them but predicted their properties by averaging the properties of the known elements above and below the gaps.

The table gives Mendeleev's predictions made in 1871 for the element between silicon and tin (which he called eka-silicon) and the element germanium discovered in 1886.

Eka-silicon	Germanium
Grey metal	Grey-white metal
Density 5.5 g cm^{-3}	Density 5.47 g cm^{-3}
A_r 73.4	A_r 72.6
$T_m > 1073$ K	$T_m = 1231$ K
Formula of oxide XO_2	Formula of oxide GeO_2
Density of oxide 4.7 g cm^{-3}	Density of oxide 4.7 g cm^{-3}
Formula of chloride XCl_4	Formula of chloride $GeCl_4$
Density of chloride 1.9 g cm^{-3}	Density of chloride 1.84 g cm^{-3}

Mendeleev also made departures from atomic mass order, placing tellurium (A_r 127.6) before iodine (A_r 126.9) so that these two should fall into the groups which fitted their properties (iodine has clear similarities to bromine and chlorine). We now know that it is atomic number, not atomic mass, that governs the positions in the Periodic Table. The significance of this was unknown to Mendeleev as this was many years before the structure of atoms was discovered. Mendeleev has been very appropriately honoured by having an element – number 101 – named after him.

Lavoisier's original list of 'elements'

Newlands' octaves. There is a striking similarity to the modern Periodic Table

H	Li	Be	B	C	N	O
F	Na	Mg	Al	Si	P	S
Cl	K	Ca	Cr	Ti	Mn	Fe

The noble gases had yet to be discovered in his day.

At around the same time, the German Julius Lothar Meyer had plotted a graph of what we would now call the volume of a mole of atoms against relative atomic mass

John Newlands

Notes

● Areas of the table are labelled s-block, p-block, d-block and f-block. Elements in the s-block have their highest energy electrons in s orbitals, e.g. Li ($1s^2\ 2s^1$). Elements in the p-block have their highest energy electrons in p orbitals, e.g. C ($1s^2\ 2s^2\ 2p^2$), and so on. These are shown in **Figure 15.1**.

● The periods are numbered starting from Period 1, containing just H and He. Period 2 contains the elements lithium to neon, and so on.

● The groups are traditionally numbered I–VII plus 0. However, it is becoming more common to number from 1–18 across the d-block, as shown in **Figure 15.2**.

● If the table were drawn out and in full it would look as in Figure 15.1.

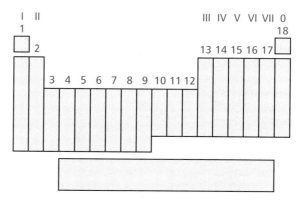

Figure 15.2 Alternative numbering systems for the groups in the Periodic Table

15.2 Periodicity of physical properties

The word 'periodic' means 'recurring regularly'. Most chemistry lessons are periodic as they occur regularly, on the same days of each week. One of the best ways of showing periodic behaviour of the properties of the elements is to plot graphs of the property against the atomic number.

Atomic sizes

One of the most obvious properties of an atom is its size. A plot of atomic volume (that is the volume of 1 mole of atoms of each element in the solid state) against atomic number for the first 60 elements is shown in **Figure 15.3**.

Two features are worth noting:

1. Atomic volume is clearly a periodic property: the graph always peaks at a Group I metal (except for He).
2. The Group I metals get larger as we descend the group.

The same two features are found on a plot of covalent radius against atomic number (**Figure 15.4**). We can explain these trends by looking at the electronic structures of the elements in a period, for example, lithium to neon, as illustrated in **Figure 15.5**.

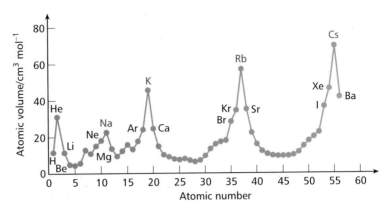

Figure 15.3 The periodicity of atomic volumes

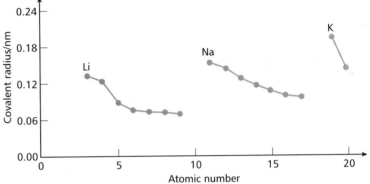

Hint: Atomic radii are measured in nanometres (nm) where $1\,nm = 10^{-9}\,m$.

Figure 15.4 The periodicity of covalent radii. The noble gases are not included on this graph because they do not form covalent bonds with one another. Even metals can form covalent molecules in the gas phase

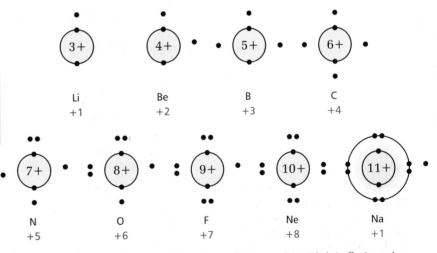

Hint: The effective nuclear charge is the atomic number (number of protons) minus the total number of electrons in *inner* shells.

Figure 15.5 The electronic structures of the elements lithium to sodium with their effective nuclear charges in red

Hint: It is a common mistake to believe that atoms get larger as we go across a period. In fact they get smaller.

As we go from lithium to neon we are adding electrons to the outer shell, the second shell. The charge on the nucleus is increasing from 3+ to 10+ (or 1+ to 8+ allowing for the shielding of the inner shell). This tends to pull the electrons in closer to the nucleus. So the size of the atom *decreases* as we go across the period. On moving from neon, where the second shell is full, to sodium, the extra electron goes into the third shell. The nuclear charge is 11+ but the shielding of the inner shells is 10 and the outer electron feels a shielded change of just $1+$. Thus for two reasons we get a sudden jump in size: firstly the outer electron in sodium is one shell further out than those in neon, and secondly it feels a shielded nuclear charge of $1+$ rather than $8+$.

The sizes of ions

Figure 15.6 shows roughly to scale the sizes of the covalent radii of the atoms sodium to chlorine (even metals can form covalent bonds in the gas phase). Below these are the sizes of the ions they form. You will see that *positive* ions (cations) are *smaller* than the parent atom because:

- The whole outer shell of electrons has been lost.
- The nuclear charge can pull the remaining electrons closer to the nucleus because there is now less electron–electron repulsion.

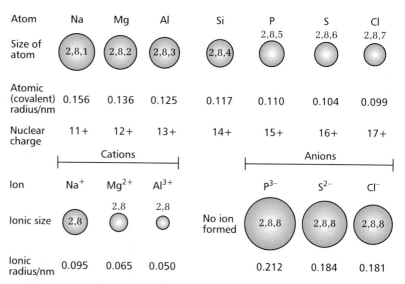

Atom	Na	Mg	Al	Si	P	S	Cl
					2,8,5	2,8,6	2,8,7
Size of atom	2,8,1	2,8,2	2,8,3	2,8,4			
Atomic (covalent) radius/nm	0.156	0.136	0.125	0.117	0.110	0.104	0.099
Nuclear charge	11+	12+	13+	14+	15+	16+	17+
	Cations				Anions		
Ion	Na$^+$	Mg^{2+}	Al^{3+}		P^{3-}	S^{2-}	Cl$^-$
		2,8	2,8				
Ionic size	2,8			No ion formed	2,8,8	2,8,8	2,8,8
Ionic radius/nm	0.095	0.065	0.050		0.212	0.184	0.181

Figure 15.6 The sizes of atoms and ions in Period 3

The *negative* ions (anions) are *larger* than the parent atoms as they have gained electrons, resulting in more electron–electron repulsion. The periodicity of atomic and ionic radii is shown in **Figure 15.7**. Notice that atomic radii peak at the Group I metals where a new shell starts, while ionic radii peak at the most negatively charged ion.

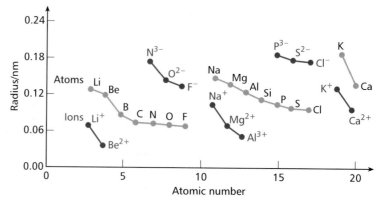

Figure 15.7 Graph of radius against atomic number for the elements helium to calcium

First ionisation energy

This is the energy required to convert a mole of isolated gaseous atoms into a mole of singly positively charged gaseous ions, i.e to remove one electron from each atom.

$$E(g) \longrightarrow E^+(g) + e^-$$

The periodicity of first ionisation energies is shown in **Figure 15.8**.

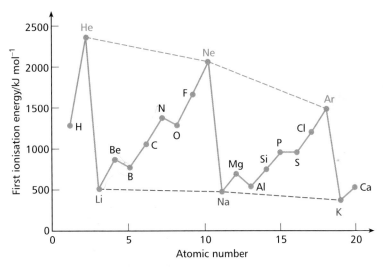

Figure 15.8 The periodicity of first ionisation energies

The alkali metals are at troughs and the noble gases at peaks. There is also a trend of decreasing first ionisation energy as we descend any group. Those for Group I and Group 0 are shown by the broken lines on the graph.

　　This graph can also be explained by looking at electronic structures. As we go along a period, electrons are being added to the same shell and the nuclear charge is increasing. So it gets increasingly difficult to pull an electron out of the atom (**Figure 15.9**). In neon, an outer electron feels an effective nuclear charge of 8+ and so neon has a high ionisation energy.

　　On moving to sodium, which has 11 protons in its nucleus (**Figure 15.10**), we start a new shell. The nuclear charge felt by the outer electron is shielded by 10 (2 + 8) inner electrons and it becomes much easier to remove the outer electron. In addition, the outer electron is in shell 3 rather than shell 2 and is thus already further

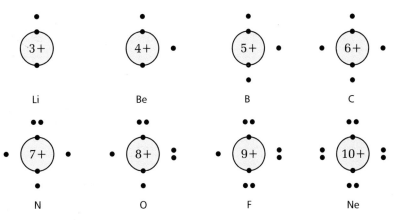

Figure 15.9 The electronic structures of the elements lithium to neon

Q What effective nuclear charge does the outer electron in lithium feel?

Figure 15.10 The electronic structure of sodium. The outer electron feels a nuclear charge of $(11 + -10 = 1+)$

away from the nucleus. As we go down a group, the shielding means that the outer electron(s) in each atom all feel the same effective nuclear charge (**Figure 15.11**). The outer electron gets easier to remove because it is further away from the nucleus.

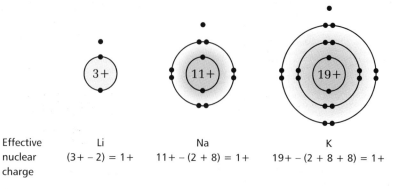

| Effective nuclear charge | Li $(3+ - 2) = 1+$ | Na $11+ - (2 + 8) = 1+$ | K $19+ - (2 + 8 + 8) = 1+$ |

Figure 15.11 The electronic structures of Group I elements

A closer look

Look at the graph of first ionisation energy against atomic number for the lithium to neon and sodium to argon periods. The rise in ionisation energy is not regular and the ionisation energy actually drops from beryllium to boron and from nitrogen to oxygen. The same thing happens with corresponding elements in Period 3. To explain this we must remember that the second shell of electrons is actually subdivided into 2s and 2p (**Figure 15.12**). The most easily removed electron in boron is that in the 2p orbital, higher in energy than the 2s electrons in beryllium. It therefore needs less energy for total removal than does the 2s electron of boron. This outweighs the effect of the increased nuclear charge of boron, which tends to make its outer electron harder to remove. A similar situation occurs with magnesium and aluminium in Period 3.

Comparing nitrogen and oxygen, the extra electron in oxygen has to be paired in one of the 2p orbitals while all three 2p electrons in nitrogen are unpaired (**Figure 15.13**).

An electron in a pair is easier to remove than one occupying an orbital alone owing to the repulsion of the other electron in the orbital. This outweighs the effect of the greater nuclear charge of oxygen. A similar situation occurs with phosphorus and sulphur in Period 3.

> **Hint:** Remember that the higher the energy level an electron is in, the easier it is to remove it.

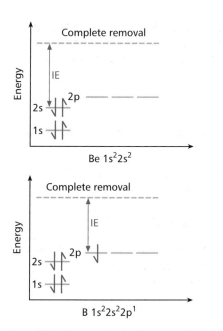

Figure 15.12 The energies of orbitals in beryllium and boron

> **Q** Suggest which element will have the lowest first ionisation energy.

The transition elements

Changes in atomic size and ionisation energy are much less marked on going across the transition elements than on going across the s and p blocks. This is because on moving along the transition series, the electrons are being added to an *inner* shell of electrons and this affects the properties less than electrons being added to the outer

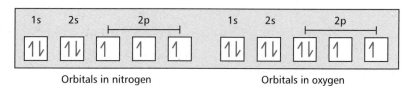

Orbitals in nitrogen   Orbitals in oxygen

Figure 15.13 Electron arrangements of nitrogen and oxygen

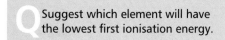

Answer: Francium: as it is Group I, the outer electron will feel a shielded nuclear charge of 1+ and francium's outer shell is the furthest from the nucleus.

Table 15.1 Electronic structures of the elements of the first transition series

Sc	[Ne] 3s² 3p⁶ 3d¹ 4s²
Ti	3d² 4s²
V	3d³ 4s²
Cr	3d⁵ 4s¹ *
Mn	3d⁵ 4s²
Fe	3d⁶ 4s²
Co	3d⁷ 4s²
Ni	3d⁸ 4s²
Cu	3d¹⁰ 4s¹ *
Zn	3d¹⁰ 4s² *

Note that the 3d⁵ and 3d¹⁰ arrangements seem to be preferred – half full and full shells seem to have extra stability which makes it worth transferring an electron from 4s. The 3d and 4s levels are very close in energy.

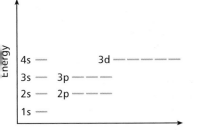

Figure 15.14 The energies of the orbitals up to 4s. Note that the 3d energy levels are slightly higher than the 4s

Hint: $E^{\ominus}$ is a measure of the oxidising/reducing power of the element. The more negative the value of $E^{\ominus}$, the better the element is as a reducing agent. The more positive the value of $E^{\ominus}$ the better the element is as an oxidising agent.

shell. The electron arrangements of the first transition series from scandium to zinc are shown in **Table 15.1**.

The electron arrangement of scandium is $1s^2\,2s^2\,2p^6\,3s^2\,3p^6\,3d^1\,4s^2$ which may be written [Ne] $3s^2\,3p^6\,3d^1\,4s^2$. The electrons are being added to the 3d shell while the outer shell (4s) is almost unchanged, because the 3d shell is higher in energy than the 4s (**Figure 15.14**).

Many other physical properties show periodicity, for example melting and boiling temperatures.

15.3 Periodicity of chemical properties

Detailed reactions of particular elements and compounds will be given in the relevant chapters. This section is devoted to more general trends in chemical properties. We have already seen in section 3.3. two trends in chemical properties on moving left to right across a period:

- a gradual change from metals to non metals.
- a gradual change from basic oxides to acidic oxides.

We can add to these the following trends.

Redox properties

A gradual change occurs from the element being a good reducing agent (on the left) to a powerful oxidising agent (on the right) shown by the values of $E^{\ominus}$ (see Chapter 25). Values of $E^{\ominus}$ in **Table 15.2** refer to aqueous solution.

Electronegativity

There is a gradual increase in electronegativity (electron attracting power) as we go from left to right:

	Na	Mg	Al	Si	P	S	Cl
electronegativity	0.9	1.2	1.5	1.8	2.1	2.5	3.0

increasing electronegativity →

A graph of electronegativity against atomic number (**Figure 15.15**) shows both the *increase* across a period and the *decrease* on descending a group (e.g. fluorine, chlorine, bromine, iodine).

Table 15.2 Redox properties of elements in Period 3

Na	Mg	Al	(Si, P)	S	Cl
$Na^+ + e^- \longrightarrow Na$	$Mg^{2+} + 2e^- \longrightarrow Mg$	$Al^{3+} + 3e^- \longrightarrow Al$		$S + 2e^- \longrightarrow S^{2-}$	$\frac{1}{2}Cl_2 + e^- \longrightarrow Cl^-$
$E^{\ominus}/V - 2.71$	-2.37	-1.66		-0.48	$+1.36$

→ [element is a stronger oxidising agent]

← [element is a stronger reducing agent]

element tends to give away electrons

element tends to accept electrons

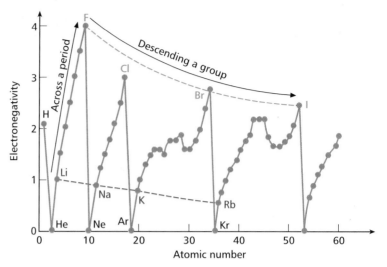

Figure 15.15 The periodicity of electronegativity values

Table 15.3 E—H bond energies/kJ mol^{-1}

IV	V	VI	VII
C—H	N—H	O—H	F—H
435	391	464	568
Si—H	P—H	S—H	Cl—H
318	321	364	432

Bond energies (bond enthalpies)

Table 15.3 shows element–hydrogen bond energies for the first two periods. (Typically elements in Groups I, II and III do not form covalent bonds with hydrogen).

Notice the overall increase across each period. This is due to the increased nuclear charge on successive elements, which holds the shared pair of electrons more strongly. For example, in methane carbon has an effective nuclear charge of $6+ - 2+ = 4+$.

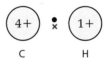

In hydrogen fluoride, fluorine has an effective nuclear charge of $9+ - 2+ = 7+$.

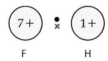

The decrease on descending the group is because the shared electrons become further from the nuclei.

Oxidation numbers

Hint: Remember that an oxidation number of +IV (or −IV) does not mean that a 4+ (or 4−) ion has been formed but that a compound has been formed with a more (or less) electronegative atom.

Figure 15.16 shows a plot of oxidation number in oxides, chlorides and hydrides against atomic number. A degree of periodicity is seen. The first three members of each group show only the positive oxidation number corresponding to loss of all their outer electrons. Group IV elements show oxidation numbers of both +IV and −IV. The last three members of the period show negative oxidation numbers corresponding to gaining sufficent electrons to form a full

Did you know? In the USA, sulphur is spelt 'sulfur'. This is in fact the recommended IUPAC spelling. We can't yet bring ourselves to spell it like this.

outer shell, although those in Period 3 (phosphorus, sulphur, chlorine) also show a number of positive oxidation numbers.

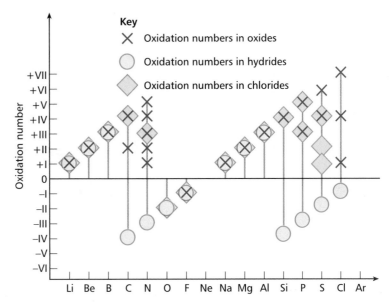

Figure 15.16 The variation of oxidation numbers with atomic number

Properties of elements in Periods 2 and 3

Table 15.4 shows melting temperature (T_m), boiling temperature (T_b) and enthalpy change of melting (ΔH_m) for elements of Periods 2 and 3. There is a clear break in the middle of the table between elements with giant structures (on the left) and those with molecular or atomic structures (on the right). The former have high melting temperatures, boiling temperatures and enthalpy changes of melting. The latter have low values for all these parameters.

Periodicity of properties of chlorides of elements in Periods 2 and 3

These are summarised in **Table 15.5**. A number of trends are apparent:

● On moving from left to right there is a change from giant ionic to molecular covalent structures.

Table 15.4 Melting and boiling temperatures and enthalpy changes of melting for elements of Periods 2 and 3

	Li	Be	B	C(gr)	N	O	F	Ne
T_m/K	454	1551	2573	3925	63	55	53	25
T_b/K	1615	3243	2823	5100	77	90	85	27
ΔH_m/kJ mol^{-1}	3.0	12.5	22.2		0.4	0.2	2.6	0.3

	Na	Mg	Al	Si	P (white)	S (monoclinic)	Cl	Ar
T_m/K	371	922	933	1683	317	392	172	84
T_b/K	1156	1380	2740	2628	553	718	238	87
ΔH_m/kJ mol^{-1}	2.6	9.0	10.7	46.4	0.6	1.4	3.2	1.2

- The behaviour in water shows a trend from dissociation into ions on the left to reaction to give acidic solutions on the right.
- The periodicity of the formulae can be seen with the ratio of Cl : E rising to a maximum in Group IV. Note that other chlorides of phosphorus and sulphur exist: PCl_5, S_2Cl_2 and SCl_4. Other oxides of chlorine also exist.

Anomalous properties of the elements of the lithium to neon period

It is generally true that elements in the same group of the Periodic Table have similar properties. However, the elements in the second period (lithium to neon) show many properties which are not typical of their group. For example, the compounds of lithium and beryllium show a degree of covalency which is not found in compounds of other s-block elements; nitrogen and oxygen form diatomic molecules while the other members of their groups form polyatomic molecules or chains. There are many other examples.

The reasons for these anomalies are:

1. These atoms are particularly small. This means that they have unusually high ionisation energies because electrons must be removed from close to the nucleus. This means it is harder to form ionic compounds. Their small size also makes them unusually electronegative, i.e. good at attracting electrons (when they form covalent bonds, the electrons in their bonds approach very close to the nucleus). Their small size also means that their positive ions have a high **charge density** and thus they can polarise negative ions very strongly (see section 9.1). These factors all lead to a greater degree of covalency of the metal compounds.

2. The elements of Period 2 can form bonds only through their 2s and 2p orbitals. The next available orbital, 3s, is of a much higher energy and it is most unlikely that an electron would be promoted

Table 15.5 Periodicity of chemical properties of the chlorides of elements in Periods 2 and 3

		I	II	III	IV	V	VI	VII
	Group	I	II	III	IV	V	VI	VII
	Formula	LiCl	$BeCl_2$	BCl_3	CCl_4	NCl_3	OCl_2	FCl
Period 2	Structure	Giant ionic	Covalent chain molecules	Molecular	Molecular	Molecular	Molecular	Molecular
	Effect of water	Dissolves to give ions $Li^+(aq) + Cl^-(aq)$	Hydrolyses to give $Be(OH)_2(s) + 2H^+(aq) + 2Cl^-(aq)$	Hydrolyses to give $B(OH)_3(s) + 3H^+(aq) + 3Cl^-(aq)$	Does not mix or react	Hydrolyses to give $NH_3(aq) + 3HClO(aq)$	Hydrolyses to give $HClO(aq)$	Hydrolyses to give $H^+(aq) + F^-(aq) + HClO(aq)$
	Formula	NaCl	$MgCl_2$	$AlCl_3$	$SiCl_4$	PCl_3	SCl_2	ClCl
Period 2	Structure	Giant ionic	Ionic layer lattice	Mainly covalent layer lattice	Molecular	Molecular	Molecular	Molecular
	Effect of water	Dissolves to give ions $Na^+(aq) + Cl^-(aq)$	Dissolves to give $Mg^{2+}(aq) + 2Cl^-(aq)$	Hydrolyses to give $Al(OH)_3(s) + 3H^+(aq) + 3Cl^-(aq)$	Hydrolyses to give $SiO_2(s) + 4H^+(aq) + 4Cl^-(aq)$	Hydrolyses to give $H_3PO_3(aq) + 3H^+(aq) + 3Cl^-(aq)$	Hydrolyses to to give S(s) + $H^+(aq) + Cl^-(aq)$	Partially hydrolyses to give $HClO(aq) + H^+(aq) + Cl^-(aq)$

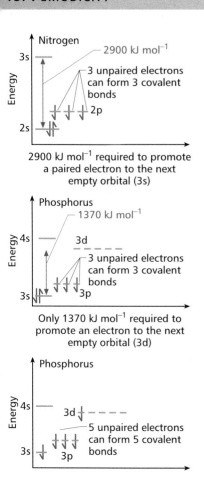

Figure 15.17 Nitrogen can form only three covalent bonds while phosphorus can form up to five

to it. The elements in Period 3 can more easily promote an electron because the 3d orbitals are available, being fairly close in energy to 3s and 3p. This allows them to form more covalent bonds. For example, nitrogen forms only NCl_3 while phosphorus forms both PCl_3 and PCl_5, as illustrated in **Figure 15.17**.

Diagonal relationships

The unusual electronegativity of lithium, beryllium and boron leads to what are called diagonal relationships: lithium is strikingly similar to magnesium, beryllium to aluminium and boron to silicon.

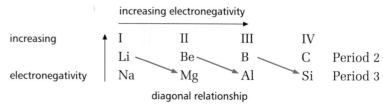

Electronegativity increases from left to right across a period. The untypically large electronegativities of Period 2 elements (caused by their small size) mean that they are in some ways more typical of elements one group to the right than to elements of their own group.

Examples of the diagonal relationship of lithium and magnesium are:

Lithium burns in air to form the 'normal' oxide Li_2O, while the other alkali metals form peroxides and superoxides (M_2O_2 and MO_2). Magnesium and the Group II elements form 'normal' oxides.

Lithium combines with nitrogen to form lithium nitride. The other Group I elements do not form nitrides. Magnesium does.

Lithium nitrate decomposes on heating to form the oxide, as do Group II nitrates. The other Group I nitrates decompose to form the metal nitrate(III) (nitrite).

Other examples will be found in Chapter 16.

15.4 Summary

• Areas of the Periodic Table are identified by the type of orbital which holds the highest energy electrons:	s-block, p-block, d-block and f-block.
• Many physical properties are periodic. Examples include	sizes of atoms and ions, first ionisation energies, electronegativies.
• Many periodic properties can be explained in terms of	the electron structures and the shielded nuclear charge felt by the outer electrons.

- Chemical properties of elements and their compounds are generally similar for | elements in the same group.
- The trends in properties that increase on crossing a period of s- and p-block elements, include | acidity of oxides, oxidising power of the element, electronegativity of the element, non-metal character of the element.
- d-block elements are similar to one another because | d electrons are being added to an inner shell.
- Elements in the Li–Ne period are often untypical of the rest of their group because of | their small size.

15.5 Practice questions

1. (a) Predict the order of the first ionisation energies of the elements Cl, Br, I. Explain your answer.
   (b) Predict the order of the size of covalent radius for the elements Si, P, S. Explain your answer.

2. The density of caesium (A_r 133) is 1.88 g cm^{-3}. Calculate its atomic volume, as plotted in Figure 15.3.

3. What shielded nuclear charge is felt by the outer electrons in (a) nitrogen, (b) silicon, (c) chlorine?

15.6 Examination questions

1. The atomic radii of elements in groups 1–7 of the Periodic Table are shown in the table below. Some radii have been omitted.

		Group						
		1	2	3	4	5	6	7
Period 2	element	Li	Be	B	C	N	O	F
	atomic radius/nm	0.134	0.125	0.090	0.077	0.075	0.073	0.071
Period 3	element	Na	Mg	Al	Si	P	S	Cl
	atomic radius/nm	0.154	0.145	0.130	0.118	0.110	0.110	0.099
Period 4	element	K	Ca	Ga	Ge	As	Se	Br
	atomic radius/nm	0.196	0.174		0.122	1.122	0.117	0.114

(a) (i) State the trend shown in atomic radius across a period.
   (ii) Explain this trend.
(b) (i) State the trend shown in atomic radius down a group.
   (ii) Explain this trend.
(c) Mendeleev studied periodic data to make predictions for the properties of elements yet to be discovered.

Use the data above to predict the atomic radius of
(i) S
(ii) Ga

[O & C 1997, AS specimen]

2. The diagram below shows the electronic structure of boron.

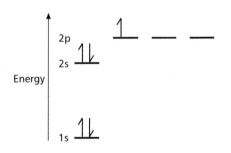

(a) The electrons are represented by arrows. What property of the electrons do these 'up' and 'down' arrows represent?

(b) Suggest why electrons which occupy the 2p sub-levels have a higher energy than electrons in the 2s sub-level.

(c) Complete the following energy level diagram to show the electronic structure of carbon.

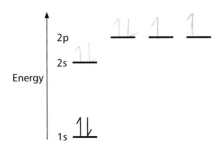

(d) Explain the meaning of the term *first ionisation energy*.

(e) Explain why oxygen has a lower first ionisation energy than nitrogen.

[NEAB 1998]

3. The graph below shows the first and second ionisation energies of the elements lithium to potassium (atomic numbers 3–19).

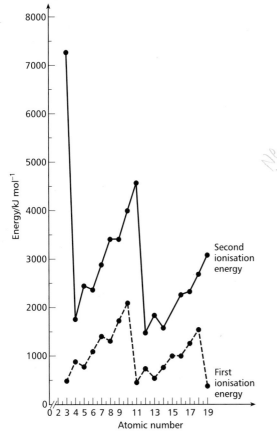

(a) Write equations, including state symbols, to represent the first and second ionisation energy changes for the element neon.

(b) (i) Why is the second ionisation energy greater than the first ionisation energy for every element on the graph?

(ii) Why is the second ionisation energy of lithium so much greater than the second ionisation energy of the other elements?

(c) Estimate values for the first and second ionisation energies of the element with atomic number 2.

(d) Which ion with a single positive charge from the elements 3–19 would you expect to have the smallest ionic radius?
    Justify your answer.

[London 1998]

4. The graph shows the first ionisation energies for the atoms from hydrogen to argon.

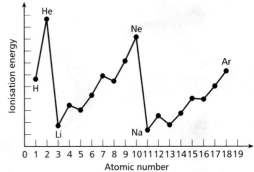

(a) (i) Give the equation which represents the first ionisation energy of oxygen atoms.

(ii) Why is the first ionisation energy of helium the largest of all the atoms?

(iii) Why is the first ionisation energy of oxygen atoms less than that of nitrogen atoms?

(iv) Why do the first ionisation energies of the atoms in Group 1 decrease as the atomic number increases?

(b) (i) Write equations which represent the first and second electron affinities of oxygen atoms.

(ii) The first electron affinity of oxygen atoms is -141 kJ mol^{-1} and the second is $+798 \text{ kJ mol}^{-1}$. Suggest why the first is exothermic and the second endothermic.

(c) Magnesium burns brightly in oxygen to give magnesium oxide, which contains the ions Mg^{2+} and O^{2-}. The formation of both these ions from their elements is strongly endothermic. Why, therefore, should magnesium combine with oxygen?

(d) The table below gives the successive ionisation energies of sodium.

No. of ionisation	1	2	3	4	5	6
Energy/kj mol⁻¹	496	4563	6913	9544	13 352	16 611

No. of ionisation	7	8	9	10	11
Energy/kj mol⁻¹	20 115	25 491	28 934	141 367	159 079

What information about the electronic structure of sodium is provided by this data?

[London (Nuffield) 1998]

16 The s-block elements

C H E M I S T R Y   N O W

A plant operator standing on top of the electrolysis cell, transferring sodium from the two hour tank in front of him to the larger twenty four hour tank to the right of the steps

Sodium is used to make the dye for these jeans, and the drug ibuprofen

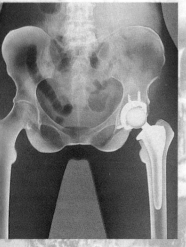

The titanium in replacement hip joints is extracted using sodium

Making sodium

You might be surprised to learn that 20 000 tonnes of sodium is made each year in the UK. It is all made in a single factory in Ellesmere Port, Cheshire, in what must be one of the most dramatic industrial processes. Electrolysis is used to split common salt into sodium and chlorine, turning a very stable compound into two extremely reactive elements.

The salt arrives in tankers and is stored underground before being dried in gas-heated rotary ovens to a moisture content of less than 0.05%. The dried salt is fed into almost 100 electrolysis cells (each about the size of a delivery van) at a rate of 100 kg per minute. The cells are kept hot (about 900 K) by the flow of electric current through them (40 000 A, the same as the consumption of a small town). Even this temperature would not be enough to keep pure sodium chloride molten so that the current can flow; the cells also contain a mixture of calcium and barium chlorides to lower the melting temperature. The process can never stop; if there were a long power cut, the mixture in the cells would solidify and it would be impossible to re-melt it.

The cells contain steel cathodes (where the sodium is formed) and carbon anodes (where the chlorine appears). These are kept apart by a steel mesh; otherwise the sodium and chlorine would react together violently to re-form sodium chloride. Sodium melts at 375 K, so it is formed as a liquid and floats to the top of the cell and into a tank which holds two hours' worth of production. This is regularly emptied into a larger '24 hour' tank which is removed daily by a fork-lift truck. The process is quite labour-intensive and the process workers must wear flameproof clothing (similar to that worn by racing drivers) to protect them from burns. The sodium in the large tanks is kept molten by a gas burner underneath it because the sodium is easier to handle as a liquid. Every so often there is a loud bang from one of the cells caused by moisture in the salt reacting with sodium to produce hydrogen, which ignites.

What happens to the sodium? At the time of writing, most of it is used, on the same site, to make additives for leaded petrol. The rest is used to make a surprising variety of products: indigo (the dye for blue jeans), drugs such as the painkiller ibuprofen and vitamin C, and to extract the metal titanium. And the chlorine? Conveniently the process for making petrol additives also uses chlorine.

Introduction

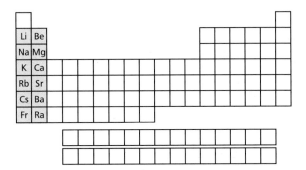

The s-block elements are those in Groups I (the alkali metals) and II (the alkaline earth metals). As the name implies, their outer electrons are in s orbitals. The two groups have considerable similarities: both contain highly reactive metals of unusually low density. The elements are too reactive to be found uncombined and are normally extracted from their compounds by electrolysis. The elements are all good reducing agents. They almost invariably form ionic compounds, which are white unless a transition metal is also present.

16.1 Physical properties of the elements

A summary of some of the physical properties of the s-block elements is given in **Tables 16.1** and **16.2**. Trends in properties are indicated by red arrows, which show the direction of increase.
The trends in Groups I and II are discussed below.

The sizes of the atoms and their ions

In *all* their reactions, elements in Group I lose their one outer electron to form ions with one positive charge.

$$M \longrightarrow M^+ + e^-$$

In *all* their reactions, elements in Group II lose their two outer electrons to form ions with two positive charges.

$$M \longrightarrow M^{2+} + 2e^-$$

The atoms and ions get bigger as we go down the groups. The atomic (metallic) and ionic radii increase because each element has an extra full shell of electrons compared with the one above it. Each element's ionic radius is much smaller than its atomic radius because the whole outer shell has been lost.
The atoms of the elements in Group II are smaller than those in the same period in Group I, because there is one extra proton in the nucleus. This increase in nuclear charge pulls the electrons inwards.

Table 16.1 Properties of Group I elements

	Atomic number, Z	Electron arrange-ment	Metallic radius /nm	Ionic radius M^+/nm	First IE /kJ mol^{-1}	Electro-negativity	Reducing power $E^\ominus$ for $M^+(aq) + e^- \rightleftharpoons M(s)$ /V	$\Delta H^\ominus_{hyd}$ /kJ mol^{-1}	Oxidation number in compounds	T_m/K	T_b/K	Density ρ/ g cm^{-3}
Li lithium	3	[He]2s^1	0.157	0.074	520	1.0	−3.03*	−519	+I	454	1615	0.53
Na sodium	11	[Ne]3s^1	0.191	0.102	496	0.9	−2.71	−407	+I	371	1156	0.97
K potassium	19	[Ar]4s^1	0.235	0.138	419	0.8	−2.92	−322	+I	336	1033	0.86
Rb rubidium	37	[Kr]5s^1	0.250	0.149	403	0.8	−2.93	−301	+I	312	959	1.53
Cs caesium	55	[Xe]6s^1	0.272	0.170	376	0.7	−3.02	−276	+I	302	942	1.88
Fr francium	87	[Rn]7s^1	—	—	—	—	—	—	+I	—	—	—

* See Reducing power, page 193, for an explanation of this anomalous value.

Table 16.2 Properties of Group II elements

	Atomic number, Z	Electron arrange-ment	Metallic radius /nm	Ionic radius M^{2+}/nm	First + second IEs /kJ mol^{-1}	Electro-negativity	Reducing power* $E^\ominus$ for $M^{2+}(aq) + e^- \rightleftharpoons M(s)$ /V	$\Delta H^\ominus_{hyd}$ /kJ mol^{-1}	Oxidation number in compounds	T_m/K	T_b/K	Density ρ/ g cm^{-3}
Be beryllium	4	[He]2s^2	0.112	0.027	900+ 1757 =2657	1.5	−1.85	−2981	+II	1551	3423	1.85
Mg magnesium	12	[Ne]3s^2	0.160	0.072	738+ 1451 =2189	1.2	−2.37	−2082	+II	922	1380	1.74
Ca calcium	20	[Ar]4s^2	0.197	0.100	590+ 1145 =1735	1.0	−2.87	−1760	+II	1112	1757	1.54
Sr strontium	38	[Kr]5s^2	0.215	0.113	550+ 1064 =1614	1.0	−2.89	−1600	+II	1042	1657	2.60
Ba barium	56	[Xe]6s^2	0.224	0.136	503+ 965 =1468	0.9	−2.90	−1450	+II	998	1913	3.51
Ra radium	88	[Rn]7s^2	—	—	—	—	—	—	+II	—	—	—

* The more negative the value of the reducing power, the better the metal is as a reducing agent – see Chapter 25 for a fuller explanation of $E^\ominus$.

Hint: Both francium and radium are radioactive elements and many of their properties are not known with precision.

Did you know? It has been estimated that there are no more than 17 atoms of francium in the whole of the Earth at any moment in time.

Ionisation energies

The first ionisation energy is the energy required for $E(g) \longrightarrow E^+(g) + e^-$, where E represents the element. The lower the ionisation energy, the easier it is to lose the electron.

Ionisation energies decrease on descending Group I because the outer electron gets further from the nucleus, while the outer electron in each element feels the same effective nuclear charge (which takes into account the shielding of the inner electrons). This partly explains why the metals get more reactive on going down the group.

The first ionisation energy of a Group II metal is greater than that of the Group I element in the same period owing to its increased nuclear charge. For Group II elements, which invariably form M^{2+} ions, the sum of the first *two* ionisation energies is the important

Q What is the shielded nuclear charge for the elements in (a) Group I, (b) Group II?

Hint: The terms effective nuclear charge and shielded nuclear charge mean the same thing.

factor. So, on two counts, more energy is required to form these ions. This is part of the reason why Group II elements are less reactive than Group I elements in the same period.

Electronegativity

This is the ability of an atom to attract electrons towards itself. Because of their low effective nuclear charges, s-block elements have *low* electronegativity values, i.e they are very electropositive. This means they tend to lose their outer electrons rather than attract ones from elsewhere. As we go down the groups the elements become more electropositive, i.e. the elements tend to lose electrons more readily. This is because the outer shell is further from the nucleus as we go down the groups.

Group II elements are more electronegative (less electropositive) than their Group I partners in the same period, as the nuclear charge (which attracts electrons) has increased by one. This means that they do not lose electrons as readily as the Group I metals in the same period.

Reducing power

Reducing agents tend to give away electrons. So all the s-block metals are good reducing agents. The effectiveness of a reducing agent can be measured by the $E^\ominus$ values for its half cell reaction. For example:

$$M^+(aq) + e^- \longrightarrow M(s) \text{ in Group I}$$

or $\qquad M^{2+}(aq) + 2e^- \longrightarrow M(s)$ in Group II

These are discussed fully in section Chapter 25 but the essential point is that the more negative is the value of $E^\ominus$, the more easily the metal will lose electrons (which means the better it is as a reducing agent). As we go down the groups, the elements get better as reducing agents. This would be expected, because, as we have seen, the ionisation energy decreases as we go down the group, which means that the metals lose electrons more easily.

In aqueous solutions lithium is a much better reducing agent than expected. This is because of the unusually large enthalpy change of hydration of the Li$^+$ ion (see below).

The enthalpy change of hydration, $\Delta H^\ominus_{hyd}$

This is the amount of energy given out when water molecules cluster round a lone metal ion (**Figure 16.1**):

$$M^+(g) + (aq) \longrightarrow M^+(aq)$$

Hint: '+(aq)' means dissolving in an unspecified amount of water (rather than reacting with water which is represented as '+H$_2$O').

The trend is for $\Delta H^\ominus_{hyd}$ to become less negative on descending the groups. This is because the ions get larger and their charge density is less, so they attract the $O^{\delta-}$ end of water molecules less strongly. In Group I, lithium therefore has the highest $\Delta H^\ominus_{hyd}$. This is why it is the best reducing agent in the group. When lithium acts as a reducing agent:

$$Li(s) + (aq) \longrightarrow Li^+(aq) + e^-$$

The high *negative* value of $\Delta H^\ominus_{hyd}$ of lithium, which means a lot of heat energy is given out, favours the formation of Li$^+$(aq) and this helps the release of the electrons for reduction.

Trends are also apparent in the melting and boiling temperatures of Group I elements and the densities of all s-block metals. There are

Answer: (a) 1+ for all elements in Group I, (b) 2+ for all elements in Group II

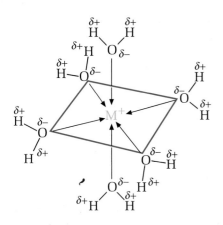

Figure 16.1 Water molecules clustering around a metal ion

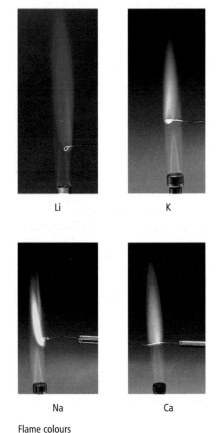

Flame colours

Table 16.3 Flame colours of s-block elements

Li	scarlet	Be	none
Na	yellow	Mg	
K	lilac	Ca	brick-red
Rb	red	Sr	crimson
Cs	blue	Ba	apple-green

some irregularities in the densities, as these depend on three factors: atomic mass, metallic radius and how closely the atoms are packed together.

Flame colours

We saw in section 7.2 that each element produces a unique pattern of lines in its spectrum. This pattern is related to the electronic energy levels in the atom. Most of the s-block elements have spectra with lines in the visible region. This means that when the elements or their compounds are heated in a flame, they produce characteristic colours. This is the basis of atomic emission spectroscopy. However, for the s-block elements the colours themselves are often distinctive enough to identify the element. A list of flame colours is given in **Table 16.3** and examples are shown in the photographs.

16.2 Chemical reactions of the elements

Group I

These metals react very readily to form positive ions, as we could expect from their low ionisation energies, low electronegativities and high negative values of $E^{\ominus}$.

Reaction with halogens

The Group I metals all react readily with the halogens to produce solid ionic halides ($M^+ + X^-$), where M represents any Group I metal. For example:

$$2Na(s) + Cl_2(g) \longrightarrow 2NaCl(s)$$

Reaction with water

All the Group I metals react with cold water to produce a solution of the metal hydroxide and hydrogen. The vigour of the reaction increases rapidly on descending the group, the reaction of caesium being explosive. For example:

$$2K(s) + 2H_2O(l) \longrightarrow 2KOH(aq) + H_2(g)$$

The solutions of the hydroxides are strongly alkaline, since they are completely dissociated into $M^+(aq)$ and $OH^-(aq)$ ions.

Reaction with oxygen

Here there is a difference in behaviour on descending the group. Lithium forms the 'normal' oxide – Li_2O ($2Li^+ + O^{2-}$) – which would be predicted using a simple ionic model.

$$4Li(s) + O_2(g) \longrightarrow 2Li_2O(s)$$
$$\text{lithium oxide}$$

Sodium forms a mixture of the normal oxide, Na_2O ($2Na^+ + O^{2-}$), and the peroxide, Na_2O_2 ($2Na^+ + O_2^{2-}$). The O_2^{2-} ion is called the

Q What is the oxidation number of oxygen in Na_2O_2?

Did you know? There is an O—O *single* bond in the peroxide ion. The dot-cross diagram is:

Q What is the oxidation number of oxygen in KO_2?

Q What is the balanced symbol equation for the reaction of calcium with chlorine?

Hint: The untypical behaviour of lithium and beryllium is discussed in section 15.3.

Q What is the formula of barium peroxide?

peroxide ion. The amounts of each depend on the amount of oxygen available. The peroxide is favoured in excess oxygen.

$$2Na(s) + O_2(g) \longrightarrow Na_2O_2(s)$$
sodium peroxide

The other alkali metals all form the superoxide, MO_2 ($M^+ + O_2^-$). The O_2^- ion is called the superoxide ion. For example:

$$K(s) + O_2(g) \longrightarrow KO_2(s)$$
potassium superoxide

Superoxides are coloured which is untypical for compounds of s-block metals.

The reason that there are different types of oxides is related to the sizes of the ions: O_2^- is larger than O_2^{2-}, which is larger than O^{2-}. Li^+ is too small for enough peroxide or superoxide ions to cluster round it to form a stable crystal lattice.

The reactions with oxygen occur rapidly. When the metals are exposed to air they begin to tarnish after a few seconds, becoming coated with oxides. To prevent this, lithium, sodium and potassium are normally stored under oil. Rubidium and caesium are even more reactive and are normally stored in sealed containers.

Group II
Reaction with halogens

The halides MX_2 are formed. These are ionic ($M^{2+} + 2X^-$), except for beryllium chloride which is covalent.

Reaction with water

The Group II metals are less reactive than those in Group I. Beryllium does not react directly with water at all. Magnesium reacts rapidly with steam and slowly with cold water to form the hydroxide and hydrogen. The rest of the Group II metals react with increasing rapidity on descending the group. For example:

$$Ca(s) + 2H_2O(l) \longrightarrow Ca(OH)_2(aq) + H_2(g)$$

Reaction with oxygen

The 'normal' oxide, MO ($M^{2+} + O^{2-}$), is formed when the metals are heated in oxygen. Strontium and barium also form peroxides. As the M^{2+} ions are smaller than the M^+ ions in Group I, peroxides do not form until lower down the group than in Group I.

16.3 Compounds of the s-block elements

Generally the compounds are typically ionic. They have high melting and boiling temperatures and dissolve better in water than in non-polar solvents. The compounds of lithium and especially beryllium are exceptions and show a good deal of covalency. This occurs because the atoms are very small and the outer electrons very near to the nucleus and thus difficult to remove (they have high ionisation energies). Their small size means that Li^+ and Be^{2+} are highly polarising (see section 9.1), which makes the bonding in their

Answer: $-I$

Answer: $-\frac{1}{2}$

Answer: $Ca(s) + Cl_2(g) \longrightarrow CaCl_2(s)$

Answer: BaO_2

compounds significantly covalent. Some magnesium compounds also show a tendency to covalency and there is a noticeable diagonal relationship (see section 15.3) between lithium and magnesium compounds.

Thermal stability of compounds

Thermal stability describes how easily or otherwise a compound will decompose on heating. Increased thermal stability means a higher temperature is needed to decompose the compound. When we say a compound is thermally stable, we usually mean that it is not decomposed at the temperature of a normal Bunsen flame (approximately 1300 K). **Table 16.4** summarises the patterns.

Beryllium compounds have not been included as they are quite covalent and not typical of the rest.

Some clear trends can be seen:

- Lithium often follows the pattern of Group II rather than Group I. This is an example of the diagonal relationship.
- Nitrates decompose in two distinct ways: Group II metal (and lithium) nitrates give the metal oxide and a mixture of nitrogen dioxide (a brown gas) and oxygen. Group I metal nitrates (except for lithium) decompose less and give the nitrite and oxygen.
- The overall pattern is that:
  1. Compounds of Group I metals are as a whole more stable than those of Group II.
  2. Stability increases on descending Group II.

     These trends can be explained in terms of the **charge density** of the cations. This measures the concentration of charge on the cation.

Hint: The systematic names of nitrate and nitrite are nitrate(v) and nitrite(III) respectively.

Table 16.4 Effect of heat on compounds of s-block elements

	Group I		Group II	
carbonates, CO_3^{2-}	Li	$LiCO_3 \longrightarrow Li_2O + CO_2$		
	Na	stable	Mg	$MgCO_3 \longrightarrow MgO + CO_2$
	K	stable	Ca	same pattern but higher
	Rb	stable	Sr	temperatures needed
	Cs	stable	Ba ↓	for decomposition
hydroxides, OH^-	Li	$2LiOH \longrightarrow Li_2O + H_2O$		
	Na	stable	Mg	$Mg(OH)_2 \longrightarrow MgO + H_2O$
	K	stable	Ca	same pattern but higher
	Rb	stable	Sr	temperatures needed
	Cs	stable	Ba ↓	for decomposition
hydrogencarbonates, HCO_3^-	Li ⎫	All decompose at	Mg	Do not exist as solids –
	Na	below 373 K	Ca	stable only
	K ⎬	$2MHCO_3 \longrightarrow M_2O + H_2O + CO_2$	Sr	in
	Rb		Ba	solution
	Cs ⎭			
nitrates, NO_3^-	Li	$2LiNO_3 \longrightarrow Li_2O + 2NO_2 + \frac{1}{2}O_2$	Mg ⎫	All decompose
	Na ⎫	The rest decompose	Ca	$M(NO_3)_2 \longrightarrow MO$
	K ⎬	$MNO_3 \longrightarrow MNO_2 + \frac{1}{2}O_2$	Sr ⎬	$+ 2NO_2 + \frac{1}{2}O_2$
	Rb		Ba ⎭	
	Cs ⎭			
sulphates, SO_4^{2-} and halides	all thermally stable		all thermally stable	

- The smaller the ion the higher the charge density.
- The greater the charge on the ion the higher the charge density.

Lithium, with its small ion has a large charge density, more typical of Group II.

Solubilities of the salts of s-block metals

Virtually all salts of Group I metals are soluble in water except lithium fluoride, which has a very high lattice energy so that the ions are difficult to separate. Nitrates of Group II metals are all soluble. With anions of charge 2− there is a distinct pattern of solubility as shown in **Table 16.5**.

Table 16.5 The solubility of some Group II metal compounds in mmol dm^{-3} (1 mmol dm^{-3} = 10^{-3} mol dm^{-3})

		CO_3^{2-}	SO_4^{2-}	CrO_4^{2-}	$C_2O_4^{2-}$
Mg^{2+}		1.5	1830	8500	5.7
Ca^{2+}	Increasing size of cation	0.13	47	870	0.05
Sr^{2+}		0.07	0.71	5.9	0.29
Ba^{2+}		0.09	0.009	0.01	0.52

Note:
CO_3^{2-} = carbonate
SO_4^{2-} = sulphate
CrO_4^{2-} = chromate
$C_2O_4^{2-}$ = ethanedioate (oxalate)

Hint: Such a clear-cut pattern of solubilities is unexpected because the solubility of ionic salts depends on several factors.

This shows clearly that the larger the cation, the less soluble the salt.

Figure 16.2 shows what happens when an ionic compound dissolves in water. The lattice breaks up, then the ions are hydrated by water molecules. Both these processes involve enthalpy changes:

- The lattice energy is *put in* to break apart the ions.
- The hydration enthalpies of both the positive and the negative ions are *given out*.

Figure 16.3 shows this on enthalpy diagrams.

Both the lattice energy and the enthalpy changes of hydration depend on the size and charge of the ions in the same sort of way. Highly charged ions have high lattice energies and high $\Delta H^{\ominus}_{hyd}$'s. Large ions have low lattice energies and low $\Delta H^{\ominus}_{hyd}$'s. So, changes in size and charge tend to cancel out their effects on $\Delta H^{\ominus}_{soln}$.

Reactions of the oxides of s-block elements

These all react with water to form hydroxides. Normal oxides give the metal hydroxide only. For example:

$$Li_2O(s) + H_2O(l) \longrightarrow 2LiOH(aq)$$

Peroxides give the metal hydroxide and hydrogen peroxide. For example:

$$Na_2O_2(s) + 2H_2O(l) \longrightarrow 2NaOH(aq) + H_2O_2(aq)$$

Superoxides give the metal hydroxide, hydrogen peroxide and oxygen. For example:

$$2KO_2(s) + 2H_2O(l) \longrightarrow 2KOH(aq) + H_2O_2(aq) + O_2(g)$$

Both peroxides and superoxides are oxidising agents.

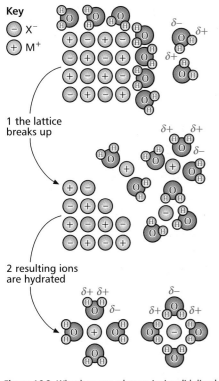

Key
⊖ X$^-$
⊕ M$^+$

1 the lattice breaks up

2 resulting ions are hydrated

Figure 16.2 What happens when an ionic solid dissolves

Did you know? Metal peroxides are used as bleaches because they form hydrogen peroxide when dissolved in water.

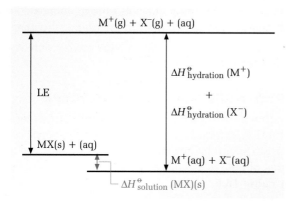 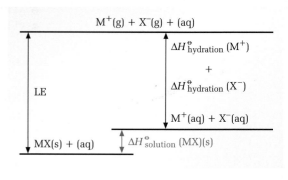

Figure 16.3 (a) and (b) Enthalpy changes when an ionic solid dissolves. In (a) the sum of the hydration enthalpies is greater than the lattice energy, so the process of dissolving is exothermic. In (b) the sum of the hydration enthalpies is less than the lattice energy, so the process of dissolving is endothermic

The metal hydroxides of both Group I and Group II dissolve in water to give $OH^-(aq)$ and are thus alkaline. For example:

$$MOH(s) + (aq) \longrightarrow M^+(aq) + OH^-(aq)$$

Group II hydroxides are less soluble than those of Group I and are therefore weaker alkalis.

Beryllium oxide, BeO, is an exception to the above in that it is amphoteric, and in solution can show either acidic or basic properties, depending on what it is reacting with. In this it resembles aluminium oxide – another example of the diagonal relationship between these elements.

Occurrence of the s-block elements

Both sodium and potassium are relatively abundant elements, each comprising around 2.5% of the Earth's crust and occurring in deposits of their chlorides, which have resulted from the evaporation of seawater. In the UK there are large underground deposits of sodium chloride in Cheshire, around which many chemical industries have grown up. Compounds of the other Group I elements are less common.

In Group II, calcium is found in limestone, $CaCO_3$, and magnesium in dolomite, $CaCO_3.MgCO_3$. Seawater is an important source of both sodium and magnesium salts, especially in hot countries where the heat of the sun can be used to evaporate the water.

Uses of s-block elements and compounds

20 000 tonnes of sodium is used per year in the UK in the manufacture of tetraethyllead (a petrol additive), as a reducing agent in the manufacture of titanium and as a coolant for nuclear reactors. Sodium carbonate is used in the manufacture of glass, and sodium hydroxide is used for making paper, soap and man-made fibres. Magnesium oxide is used as a refractory (heat-resistant) lining for various types of furnaces because of its high thermal stability.

Lithium salts are used to treat certain types of mental depression and the metal itself finds application in some alloys because of its lightness. Magnesium too is used in alloys and castings because it is cheap to cast. In large volumes it is not as reactive as in ribbon form, where it has a high surface area. Metal pencil sharpeners are often made of magnesium. Calcium carbonate (limestone) is used to make

Did you know? The phasing out of leaded petrol will cause a drop in the demand for sodium.

calcium oxide, which is used for neutralising soils, making glass and as a constituent of cement.

Extraction of s-block elements

As they themselves are such powerful reducing agents, the metals cannot be extracted from their compounds by chemical reduction of their ores. So, the s-block elements are normally produced from their ores by electrolysis. The extraction of sodium is described in 'Chemistry Now' in this chapter.

FURTHER FOCUS

Manufacture of sodium hydroxide

Sodium hydroxide is manufactured from brine (sodium chloride solution) in different types of electrolysis cell – the mercury cell is described here and the membrane and diaphragm cells are described in the box in section 17.3. Mercury cells cost more to build, but produce sodium hydroxide that is both purer than that produced in a membrane cell and also at the concentration required by the customers.

The electrolysis takes place in a cell approximately $2\,m \times 15\,m$ with a slightly sloping base like a swimming pool. Mercury flows down the floor of the cell, forming the cathode. The titanium anodes are adjusted so that they are no more than 2 mm away from the mercury. Saturated brine flows through the cell. At the anode:

$$2Cl^-(aq) \longrightarrow Cl_2(g) + 2e^-$$

At the cathode, sodium is discharged at the mercury electrode, dissolves in it and is carried away before it can react with the water. The sodium/mercury mixture, called an amalgam, flows into a tank called a denuder, packed with graphite spheres. Here the sodium/mercury amalgam meets a current of water. The sodium reacts with the water forming sodium hydroxide solution and hydrogen. The reaction is catalysed by the graphite spheres.

$$2Na(amalgam) + 2H_2O(l) \longrightarrow 2NaOH(aq) + H_2(g)$$

The mercury is pumped back up to the electrolysis cell and cycles round continuously. All three products – sodium hydroxide, chlorine and hydrogen – are useful.

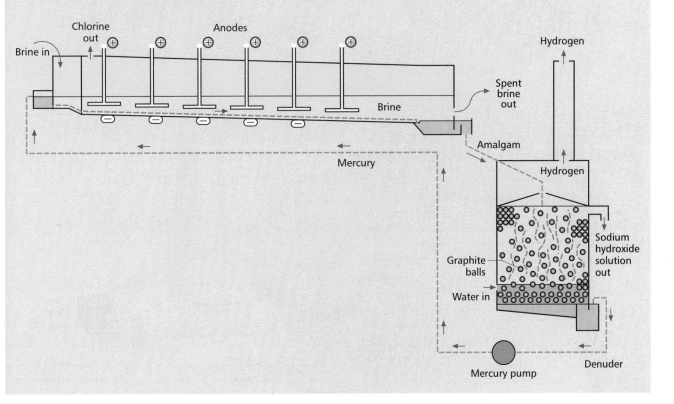

CHEMISTRY AROUND US

Hardness of water

Tap water is taken from rivers, reservoirs and wells and treated to kill any bacteria. It still contains substances which dissolved in rainwater while it percolated through soil and rocks, etc. Hard water contains calcium and magnesium ions, which can cause problems. These ions dissolve when rainwater, which is naturally slightly acidic because of dissolved carbon dioxide, has soaked through limestone rocks which contain calcium and/or magnesium carbonates:

$$CaCO_3(s) + H_2O(l) + CO_2(g) \longrightarrow Ca(HCO_3)_2(aq)$$

calcium   water   carbon   calcium
carbonate   dioxide   hydrogencarbonate

This reaction is reversed by heating and leads to deposits of insoluble calcium (and magnesium) carbonate in hot water pipes, kettles, etc. which may cause blockages and reduce the efficiency of heating elements. The hardness caused by calcium and magnesium hydrogencarbonates is called 'temporary hardness' because it is removed by heating. Hardness caused by calcium and magnesium sulphates or chlorides is unaffected by heat and is called 'permanent hardness'.

Hard water deposit in hot water pipe

Both types of hardness cause scum when soap is used. Soap is a mixture of salts such as sodium octadecanoate (sodium stearate), $C_{17}H_{35}CO_2Na$. Sodium stearate is soluble, but calcium and magnesium stearates are not. These insoluble salts form the scum. Scum is unpleasant and can damage fabrics. Scum formation means that more soap is needed than in soft water.

A number of methods can be used for softening water:

● Boiling removes temporary hardness, but is expensive.
● Calcium hydroxide (slaked lime) is cheap and can be added to precipitate out temporary hardness as calcium carbonate.

$$Ca(HCO_3)_2(aq) + Ca(OH)_2(s) \longrightarrow 2CaCO_3(s) + 2H_2O(l)$$

calcium   calcium   calcium   water
hydrogencarbonate hydroxide   carbonate

Too much slaked lime must not be added or more hardness will be produced.

● Sodium carbonate may be added to precipitate out *any* calcium or magnesium ions:

$$Mg^{2+}(aq) + Na_2CO_3(aq) \longrightarrow MgCO_3(s) + 2Na^+(aq)$$

magnesium   sodium   magnesium   sodium
ions   carbonate   carbonate   ions

Sodium compounds do not cause hardness. Bath salts are simply coloured and perfumed sodium carbonate (washing soda) which soften the water.

● Some homes have water softeners which contain ion exchange resins: plastic beads which contain sodium ions. These are exchanged for calcium or magnesium ions as the hard water passes over the beads. The resin is automatically regenerated each night by pumping sodium chloride through the resin to reverse the process.

Hard water causes scum with soap

Domestic water softener

16.4 Summary

Trends

On descending both Group I and
Group II we see the following trends:

Metallic radius	increase
Ionic radius	increase
First ionisation energy	decrease
Chemical reactivity	increase
Electronegativity	decrease
Thermal stability of compounds	increase
Reducing power	increase
Solubilities of compounds	decrease

As we move from Group I to Group II,
we see the following trends:

Metallic radius	decrease
Ionic radius	decrease
First ionisation energy	increase
Chemical reactivity	decrease
Electronegativity	increase
Thermal stability of compounds	decrease
Reducing power	decrease
Solubilities of compounds	decrease

Reactions

Those of Group I are summarised in **Figure 16.4**.

Those of Group II are summarised in **Figure 16.5**.

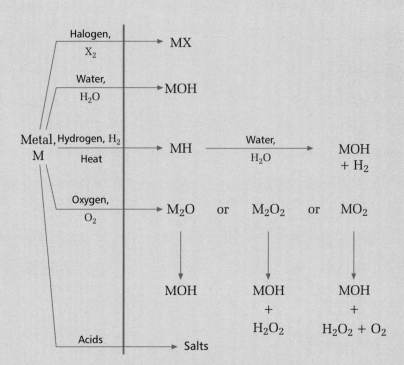

Figure 16.4 Reactions of Group I elements

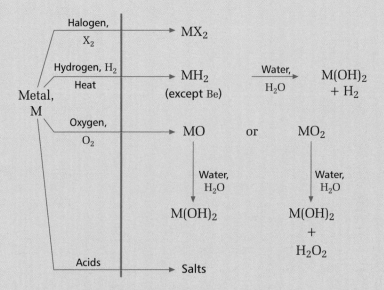

Figure 16.5 Reactions of Group II elements

16.5 Practice questions

1. The following table gives the radii of four isoelectronic species:

Species	Radius/mm
S^{2-}	0.185
Cl^-	0.180
K^+	0.138
Ca^{2+}	0.100

(a) Write the electronic structures of these species in the form $1s^2$ etc.

(b) Explain what is meant by the term *isoelectronic*.

(c) Explain why the ionic radii differ in the way they do.

2. (a) This question concerns a white solid compound of an s-block metal. For each statement below, say what conclusions you can draw at that stage.

(i) On heating it produced a brown gas and a white solid.

(ii) The resulting white solid was sparingly soluble in water to give an alkaline solution.

(iii) A flame test on the original solid gave an apple-green colour.

(b) Write equations for the reactions in (i) and (ii).

3. A white solid compound of an s-block metal was heated and a white solid and a colourless gas were produced. The gas turned limewater (calcium hydroxide solution) milky. The original white solid was soluble in water. What was the original compound? Explain your answer and suggest a test to confirm the metal involved.

16.6 Examination questions

1. The plot below is of the logarithm of successive ionisation energies (I.E.) for all the electrons in a gaseous potassium atom.

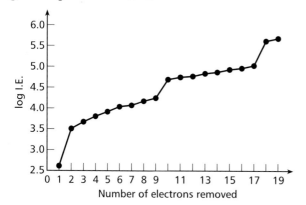

(a) Explain why
(i) the first ionisation energy has such a low value,
(ii) the plot shows a general increase in the values of these ionisation energies.

(b) (i) Give a reason for the change in ionisation energies between the 1st and 2nd ionisations.
(ii) Name the orbital from which the 10th electron is removed.

(c) State why the 18th and 19th ionisations are so high.

(d) Describe by means of a sketch, or otherwise, how the graph for calcium would differ from that for potassium.

(e) A small piece of pure calcium metal was allowed to react with a large volume of water. It was found that 50 cm³ of aqueous hydrochloric acid of concentration 0.2 mol dm⁻³ had to be added to the mixture to produce a neutral solution.
(i) Write a balanced equation for the reaction between calcium and water.
(ii) Calculate the mass of calcium used.
(iii) State the volume of the same hydrochloric acid which would have been required if the same number of moles of pure sodium had been used in place of the calcium. Explain your answer.

[WJEC 1997]

2. (a) (i) Write an equation for the reaction of barium with water.
(ii) Would the reaction in (a)(i) occur more vigorously or less vigorously than the reaction of calcium with water? Identify one contributory factor and use it to justify your answer.
(iii) Write an equation for the action of heat on solid barium carbonate.
(iv) At a given high temperature which of the two carbonates, barium carbonate or calcium carbonate, would decompose more easily?
(v) How would you distinguish between solutions of barium chloride and calcium

chloride? State in each case what you would see as a result of the test on each solution.

(b) 1.71 g of barium reacts with oxygen to form 2.11 g of an oxide **X**.
- (i) Calculate the formula of **X**.
- (ii) Give the formula of the anion present in **X**.
- (iii) What is the oxidation number of oxygen in this anion?
- (iv) Sodium forms an oxide, **Y**, which contains this same anion. Give the formula of **Y**.

(c) Treatment of either **X** or **Y** with dilute sulphuric acid leads to the formation of the sulphate of the metal, together with an aqueous solution of hydrogen peroxide, H_2O_2.
- (i) Write an equation for the reaction of **Y** with dilute sulphuric acid.
- (ii) The hydrogen peroxide solution produced may be separated from the other reaction product. Explain briefly why this is easier to achieve if **X** is used as the initial reagent rather than **Y**.

[London (Nuffield) 1998]

3. Magnesium chloride is an ionic solid. Insert the appropriate enthalpy values on the Born–Haber cycle shown at the top of the next column and calculate the value for the standard enthalpy of formation of one mole of magnesium chloride.

$$Mg(s) + Cl_2(g) \longrightarrow MgCl_2(s)$$

(b) A solution of magnesium chloride can be used to distinguish between carbonate and hydrogencarbonate ions. Describe, with experimental observations, how this is done.

(c) When heated, hydrated magnesium chloride, $MgCl_2.6H_2O$, decomposes with the evolution of hydrogen chloride and the formation of the oxide.

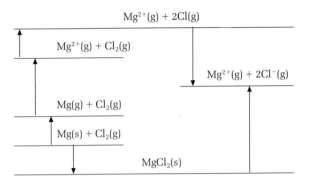

	kJ mol^{-1}
Electron affinity of chlorine	= − 349
First ionisation energy of magnesium	= + 738
Second ionisation energy of magnesium	= +1451
Standard bond dissociation energy of chlorine	= + 243
Standard enthalpy of atomisation of magnesium	= + 148
Standard lattice enthalpy of magnesium chloride	= +2526

Magnesium oxide dissolves slightly in water to give a solution of pH 9. This solution can be titrated with standard hydrochloric acid.
- (i) Using a balanced equation explain why a solution of magnesium oxide is alkaline.
- (ii) Draw the labelled titration curve expected and name an appropriate indicator.

(d) Magnesium oxide may be prepared by heating magnesium carbonate. Comment on the trend in thermal stability of the Group II carbonates.

(e) Magnesium oxide reacts with acids to form salts. For example, magnesium oxide reacts with sulphuric acid to form the sulphate. Comment on the solubility of magnesium sulphate compared to other Group II sulphates.

[NI 1997]

17 The Group VII elements – the halogens

C H E M I S T R Y   N O W

To fluoridate or not to fluoridate?

The outer part of a healthy tooth is made of a mineral called hydroxyapatite, $Ca_5(PO_4)_3OH$. This is a very hard substance but it is attacked by acids. Acids can build up in the mouth when sugary foods break down into lactic acid. This is brought about by the bacteria that coat our teeth. Food and bacteria can build up a layer of plaque, especially on teeth which are not cleaned regularly. Plaque holds the acids in contact with the tooth so that they cannot simply be washed away by rinsing the mouth with water. If these acids erode holes in the enamel, bacteria can pass through into the interior of the teeth and cause dental caries – what most people call tooth decay.

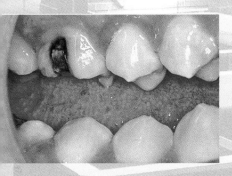

Fluoride ions have been found to inhibit tooth decay. This seems to happen in two ways. Firstly, fluoride ions replace some of the hydroxide ions in hydroxyapatite to form fluoroapatite, an even harder mineral which is more resistant to acid attack. Secondly, fluoride ions inhibit the growth of the bacteria in the plaque which cause acidity.

This has led to the use of fluoride-containing compounds in toothpaste and, in some areas, the addition of fluorides to tap water. Fluorides in toothpaste include tin(II) fluoride (usually called stannous fluoride on the packet), sodium monofluorophosphate (Na_2PO_3F) and sodium fluoride. Tap water is treated by adding sodium fluoride, sodium silicofluoride or hydrofluorosilicic acid to bring the fluoride content up to 1 part per million (ppm). Concentrations of fluoride of greater than 1.5 ppm may cause mottled teeth.

Many studies have shown that fluoridated water reduces tooth decay in children especially and that it is quite safe. So much so that some dentists have talked about tooth decay becoming a thing of the past. Despite this, many people have strongly opposed fluoridation on the grounds of possible long-term health risks, 'tampering with nature' and on civil liberties grounds: once your tap water is treated you have little choice but to drink it. This is despite the fact that natural water supplies usually contain some fluoride ions. The debate continues.

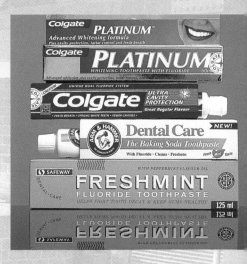

Some foods are unexpectedly high in sugar

In this chapter we will be looking at:
- the physical properties of the elements that underlie their chemical properties: atomic radii, ionisation energies, electronegativity, bond energies
- some of the reactions of the elements
- compounds of the elements with metals, hydrogen, oxygen and other halogens
- extraction of the elements
- uses of the elements

Introduction

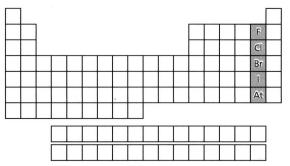

The members of Group VII are called the halogens, which is derived from the Greek for 'salt-formers'. They are all reactive non-metals and have the outer shell arrangement ns^2np^5, which makes them one electron short of having the full outer shell of a noble gas structure.

CONCEPT CHECKPOINTS

The following basic ideas are used in this chapter. You may revise some of these topics elsewhere in the book.
- arrangement of electrons in atoms (sections 2.1 and 7.2)
- formation of ions (sections 2.2, 7.2 and 9.1)
- enthalpy changes (Chapter 8)
- bond energies (bond enthalpies) (section 8.4)

Hint: X is often used as a symbol to refer to any halogen atom.

Hint: 'Volatile' means 'evaporating easily' or 'having a low boiling temperature'.

17.1 The elements

All the elements exist as diatomic molecules with an X—X single bond. They all tend to react by forming ions with one negative charge because the atoms are each one electron short of attaining a full outer shell (see **Figure 17.1**). At room temperature (293 K) fluorine is a pale yellow gas, chlorine a greenish gas, bromine a volatile red-brown liquid and iodine a shiny black solid which gives off a purple vapour on gentle heating. Astatine is both rare and radioactive, and its chemistry has been little studied. **Table 17.1** gives some physical properties of the elements.

The volatility of all the elements is due to the fact that the intermolecular forces are weak van der Waals forces.

There is a clear reactivity trend in the group. Reactivity decreases on descending the group, partly because of the increasing size of the atoms. The electron which is added to form the X^- ion goes into a shell further from, and therefore less strongly attracted to, the nucleus, i.e. the elements have a less negative electron affinity as we go down the group.

The elements are too reactive to be found uncombined. The main sources of the elements are halide salts. All the elements have a

Table 17.1 Some properties of the halogens

Atomic number, Z		Electron arrangement	Electro-negativity	Atomic (covalent) radius/nm	Ionic radius X^-/nm	T_m/K	T_b/K	X—X bond energy/ kJ mol^{-1}	$E^\ominus$ for $\frac{1}{2}X_2(aq) + e^- \rightleftharpoons X^-(aq)$
F	9	$1s^22s^22p^5$	4.0	0.071	0.133	53	85	158*	+2.87†
Cl	17	[Ne]$3s^23p^5$	3.0	0.099	0.180	172	238	243	+1.36
Br	35	[Ar]$3d^{10}4s^24p^5$	2.8	0.114	0.195	266	332	193	+1.07
I	53	[Kr]$4d^{10}5s^25p^5$	2.5	0.133	0.215	387	457	151	+0.54
At	85	[Xe]$4f^{14}5d^{10}6s^26p^5$				575	610		

*see text   †The value for $\frac{1}{2}F_2(g) + e^- \longrightarrow F^-(aq)$

Hint: A halide is a compound containing X⁻ ions, where X is any halogen.

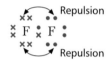

$$:\overset{\cdot\cdot}{\underset{\cdot\cdot}{X}}\cdot \;+e^- \longrightarrow \left[:\overset{\cdot\cdot}{\underset{\cdot\cdot}{X}}{}_{\times}^{\times}\right]^-$$

Figure 17.1 The atom gains an electron to become a negatively charged ion

---

characteristic 'bleachy' smell. There are considerable similarities in the chemistry of the halogens but fluorine, like other elements in the Li–Ne period, is untypical in many ways. Its chemistry is described separately.

17.2 Fluorine and its compounds

Fluorine is the most electronegative element and can therefore attract electrons to itself more effectively than any other element. Thus in all its compounds, both ionic and covalent, fluorine has an oxidation number of $-I$.

Table 17.1 shows that the fluorine molecule has an unexpectedly low bond energy compared with the other halogens. This is due to the small size of the atom, leading to a short intermolecular distance in F_2 and consequently repulsion between non-bonding electrons. This weakens the bond:

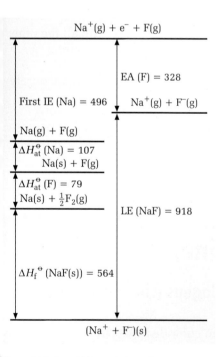

Q Does a low value of $\Delta H^{\ominus}_{at}$ contribute to a lower or higher reactivity of the halogen?

Since the E—F bond energies of fluorine with other elements are generally high (see **Table 17.2**), this means that the formation of covalent fluorides (involving breaking of F—F and making of E—F bonds) is usually strongly exothermic.

Table 17.2 Comparison of E—X tabulated bond energies for the halogens with hydrogen and with carbon/kJ mol⁻¹

Element E	Halogen X			
	F	Cl	Br	I
H	568	432	366	298
C	467	346	290	228

Similar considerations apply to the formation of ionic fluorides. Fluorine has a low value of $\Delta H^{\ominus}_{at}$ due to the weak F—F bond. Ionic fluorides have high lattice energies due to the small size of the F^- ion (see **Table 17.3**). Both factors lead to large exothermic values for $\Delta H^{\ominus}_f$ of ionic fluorides such as sodium flouride, NaF (see **Figure 17.2**).

Table 17.3 Comparison of lattice energies for some ionic halides $(M^+ + X^-)/kJ$ mol⁻¹

Metal M	Halogen X			
	F	Cl	Br	I
Li	1031	848	803	759
Na	918	780	742	705
K	817	711	679	651

Figure 17.2 Born–Haber cycle for sodium fluoride. All values in kJ mol⁻¹

Answer: It makes the halogen more reactive.

Extraction of fluorine

Almost no chemical oxidising agent is strong enough to oxidise F^- to F_2, so the element is produced electrolytically from a mixture of potassium fluoride and hydrogen fluoride. At the anode:

$$F^- \longrightarrow \tfrac{1}{2}F_2 + e^-$$

Fluorine as an oxidising agent

Fluorine is an excellent oxidising agent and will oxidise other elements to their highest oxidation states. For example, sulphur forms sulphur hexafluoride, SF_6, (Ox(S) = + VI) and oxygen forms oxygen difluoride, OF_2. Fluorine will oxidise water to oxygen:

$$2F_2(g) + 2H_2O(l) \longrightarrow 4HF(aq) + O_2(g)$$

> **Q** What is the oxidation number for oxygen in OF_2?

Hydrogen fluoride, HF

This is a liquid which boils at 293 K. It has the highest boiling temperature of the hydrogen halides owing to the formation of strong hydrogen bonds. In fact the F—H – – – F—H hydrogen bond is the strongest known, having a bond energy of 125 kJ mol^{-1}, which approaches the strength of some covalent bonds.

Hydrogen fluoride dissolved in water is a *weak* acid:

$$HF(aq) + H_2O(l) \rightleftharpoons F^-(aq) + H_3O^+(aq)$$

This is due to the very strong H—F bond. Solutions of hydrofluoric acid will dissolve glass (they are used to etch glass) and are therefore stored in polythene containers.

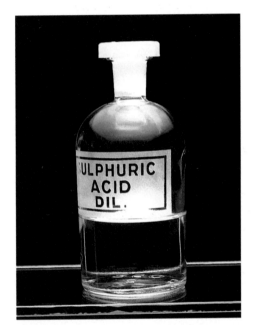

Glassware that has been etched using hydrogen fluoride.

Fluorides

Fluorine is so reactive that it will combine directly with all the other elements (except helium, neon, krypton and nitrogen) to form fluorides.

The fluorides of the s-block elements (and aluminium) are purely ionic. Beryllium fluoride is an exception: it is covalent.

Some transition metals in lower oxidation states form ionic fluorides. Those in higher oxidation states form covalent fluorides: for example, uranium hexafluoride. Such fluorides may be quite volatile: uranium hexafluoride boils at 329 K.

17.3 The other halogens (chlorine, bromine and iodine)

Extraction of the other halogens (chlorine, bromine and iodine)

Chlorine is extracted from sodium chloride by electrolysis (see the box on page 209 and also the box on page 199), while bromine is made from seawater, which contains Br^- ions, by oxidation with chlorine.

$$Cl_2(aq) + 2Br^-(aq) \longrightarrow Br_2(aq) + 2Cl^-(aq)$$

This is an example of a displacement reaction: halogens can displace from their salts halide ions from lower down the group in the

Plant for extracting bromine from seawater at Anglesey

Q What are the oxidation numbers of sulphur and iodine on both sides of the equation?

Periodic Table. Bromine will oxidise $I^-(aq)$ to $I_2(aq)$, as will chlorine. The latter reaction can be used to extract iodine from seawater, which also contains iodide ions. A more important source of iodine is from deposits in Chile containing sodium iodate(V) ($NaIO_3$), from which it is extracted by reduction with sulphur dioxide:

$$5SO_2(aq) + 4H_2O(l) + 2IO_3^-(aq) \longrightarrow 5SO_4^{2-}(aq) + 8H^+(aq) + I_2(aq)$$

Laboratory preparations of the halogens

Chlorine is prepared in the laboratory by oxidation of concentrated hydrochloric acid with potassium manganate(VII).

The apparatus is shown in **Figure 17.3**.

$$2KMnO_4(s) + 16HCl(aq) \rightarrow 2KCl(aq) + 2MnCl_2(aq) + 8H_2O(l) + 5Cl_2(g)$$

The gas is bubbled through water to remove any unreacted hydrochloric acid and dried by bubbling through concentrated sulphuric acid. Being denser than air, it can be collected by downward delivery.

Answer: On the left: S(+IV), I(+V). On the right S(+VI), I(0)

FURTHER FOCUS

The manufacture of chlorine by the diaphragm and membrane cells

Chlorine is manufactured by electrolysis of sodium chloride solution (brine) in the flowing mercury cathode cell (see the box in Chapter 16) and also from molten sodium chloride by the Downs process. The diaphragm cell is another method for electrolysis of brine which competes with the mercury cell.

Level in anode compartment higher than level in cathode compartment

Saturated brine in — Chlorine gas — Hydrogen gas — Steel cathode

Titanium + anode — Asbestos diaphragm — Sodium hydroxide and sodium chloride solution

At the anode: $2Cl^-(aq) \longrightarrow Cl_2(g) + 2e^-$

At the cathode: $2H_2O(l) + 2e^- \longrightarrow H_2(g) + 2OH^-(aq)$

Brine enters the anode compartment where Cl^- ions are discharged as chlorine. The resulting solution, rich in Na^+ ions, and also containing some Cl^-ions, seeps through the asbestos diaphragm into the cathode compartment. Here hydrogen is discharged, resulting in a solution containing both sodium hydroxide and unchanged sodium chloride. The electrolyte level in the cathode compartment is kept higher than in the cathode compartment and this prevents $OH^-(aq)$ ions moving into the cathode compartment where they would be discharged in preference to chlorine. The solution from the anode cell is evaporated to about one-fifth of its original volume, when most of the less soluble sodium chloride crystallises out. The resulting solution contains 50% sodium hydroxide and 1% sodium chloride and this is sufficiently pure for many purposes. Usually several diaphragm cells are run together connected in series.

An improvement of this cell is the membrane cell where a fluorocarbon membrane replaces the diaphragm. This membrane is permeable to cations but not anions, thus allowing $Na^+(aq)$ through but not $OH^-(aq)$ or $Cl^-(aq)$, so the resulting sodium hydroxide contains no sodium chloride impurity. Membrane cells are cheaper to build than mercury cells (which give the same product) but produce less-pure sodium hydroxide. They do not use toxic mercury. It is unlikely that any new diaphragm or mercury cells will be built in the future.

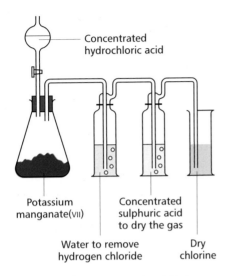

Potassium
manganate(VII)

Concentrated
sulphuric acid
to dry the gas

Water to remove
hydrogen chloride

Dry
chlorine

Figure 17.3 Laboratory preparation of chlorine

Hint: A disproportionation reaction is one in which the oxidation number of some atoms of an element from an entity increases and that of other atoms of the same element from the same entity decreases.

Q Write a balanced symbol equation for the oxidation of water by fluorine, and put in the oxidation numbers of fluorine and oxygen on both sides of the equation.

Bromine and iodine can be prepared by the reaction of a halide salt with sulphuric acid. This produces the hydrogen halide. Oxidation of the hydrogen halide by manganese(IV) oxide produces the halogen

Oxidising power of the halogens

Oxidising agents tend to accept electrons. All the halogens are good oxidising agents. The effectiveness of an oxidising agent can be measured by the $E^{\ominus}$ values for the half cell reactions. For example:

$$\tfrac{1}{2}X_2(aq) + e^- \longrightarrow X^-(aq)$$

These are discussed fully in Chapter 25 but the essential point is that the more positive is the value of $E^{\ominus}$ the better the element is as an oxidising agent. As we go up the group, the elements get better as oxidising agents. This would be expected, because the electronegativity increases as we go up the group (see Table 17.1) which means that the elements gain electrons more easily.

Fluorine is a strong enough oxidising agent to oxidise water to oxygen and hydrogen fluoride but chlorine just slowly disproportionates in water forming hydrochloric acid and chloric(I) acid.

$$\underset{0}{Cl_2(aq)} + H_2O(l) \longrightarrow \underset{+I}{HClO(aq)} + \underset{-I}{HCl(aq)}$$

$$\qquad\qquad\qquad\qquad\qquad\text{chloric(I) acid}\quad\text{hydrochloric acid}$$

17.4 Compounds of chlorine, bromine and iodine

Chlorine, bromine and iodine all form halides with Ox = −I but also form compounds with positive oxidation states up to +VII, the odd numbers being the most common.

Hydrogen halides

Hydrogen fluoride does not fit the pattern of the other hydrogen halides. Hydrogen chloride, HCl, hydrogen bromide, HBr, and hydrogen iodide, HI, are all gases at room temperature but hydrogen fluoride, HF, is a liquid owing to its strong hydrogen bonding. Hydrogen chloride, hydrogen bromide and hydrogen iodide are very soluble in water, forming strong acids called hydrochloric, hydrobromic and hydriodic acids respectively. By contrast, hydrogen fluoride forms weak hydrofluoric acid, because the strong H—F bond must be broken to release H$^+$.

The hydrogen halides can be prepared in the laboratory by the action of phosphoric(v) acid on alkali metal halides:

$$\underset{\substack{\text{sodium}\\\text{halide}}}{NaX(s)} + \underset{\substack{\text{phosphoric(v)}\\\text{acid}}}{H_3PO_4(s)} \longrightarrow \underset{\substack{\text{hydrogen}\\\text{halide}}}{HX(g)} + \underset{\substack{\text{sodium dihydrogen-}\\\text{phosphate}}}{NaH_2PO_4(s)}$$

Answer: $\underset{0}{F_2(g)} + \underset{-II}{H_2O(l)} \longrightarrow \underset{-I}{2HF(aq)} + \underset{0}{\tfrac{1}{2}O_2(g)}$

Table 17.4 Ease of oxidation of halide ions

	Half reaction	$E^{\ominus}$/V
X⁻ more easily oxidised	$\frac{1}{2}I_2 + e^- \rightleftharpoons I^-$	+0.54
	$\frac{1}{2}Br_2 + e^- \rightleftharpoons Br^-$	+1.09
	$\frac{1}{2}Cl_2 + e^- \rightleftharpoons Cl^-$	+1.36

Q Compare the oxidation numbers of sulphur in H_2SO_4, SO_2 and H_2S as shown in the above equations.

Table 17.5 H—X bond energies for the hydrogen halides

	Bond	Tabulated bond energy /kJ mol⁻¹
stronger bond – less easily decomposed	H—F	568
	H—Cl	432
	H—Br	366
	H—I	298

Hydrogen chloride can also be made by the similar reaction of concentrated sulphuric acid on sodium chloride:

$$NaCl(s) + H_2SO_4(l) \longrightarrow NaHSO_4(s) + HCl(g)$$

However, hydrogen bromide and hydrogen iodide are oxidised by sulphuric acid to bromine and iodine respectively, and so they cannot be prepared by this method.

$$2HBr(g) + H_2SO_4(l) \longrightarrow SO_2(g) + 2H_2O(l) + Br_2(l)$$
$$8HI(g) + H_2SO_4(l) \longrightarrow H_2S(g) + 4H_2O(l) + 4I_2(s)$$

Notice that one molecule of sulphuric acid can oxidise two of hydrogen bromide but eight of hydrogen iodide, thus illustrating that I^- is easier to oxidise than Br^- and Br^- easier than Cl^-. The ease of oxidation of X^- is shown by the $E^{\ominus}$ values for the half reactions in Table 17.4.

Thermal stability

The hydrogen halides show a trend in thermal stability:

$$2HX(g) \longrightarrow H_2(g) + X_2(g,l,s)$$

Hydrogen iodide is easily decomposed into its elements by plunging a red-hot wire into a test tube of the gas. Hydrogen bromide may or may not decompose, depending on the exact temperature of the wire. Hydrogen chloride is not decomposed. This trend in the ease of decomposition reflects the strength of the H—X bond (**Table 17.5**).

Metal halides

All the halogens form metal halides. The increasing size of the halide ions from F^- to Cl^- to Br^- to I^- means that the ions become more easily polarised and the properties of the halides less typically ionic. The aluminium halides are a good example. AlF_3 is purely ionic, $AlCl_3$ has some ionic and some covalent character while $AlBr_3$ and AlI_3 exist as covalent dimers.

Tests for halide ions

The presence of Cl^-, Br^- and I^- in aqueous solution can be confirmed by adding a few drops of silver nitrate solution and looking for the formation of a precipitate:

$$AgNO_3(aq) + X^-(aq) \longrightarrow AgX(s) + NO_3^-(aq)$$

Silver chloride is white, silver bromide cream and silver iodide yellow. The last two can be hard to tell apart by eye but adding a little concentrated aqueous ammonia to the precipitate will distinguish them. Silver bromide dissolves but silver iodide does not.

Fluorides do not form a precipitate with silver nitrate because silver fluoride is soluble: a reflection of its pure ionic character.

Oxygen compounds of the halogens

Oxygen has an oxidation number of −II in its compounds (except with fluorine), so the halogen atom must have positive oxidation states in oxygen compounds. Chlorate(I) ions are formed by the

CHEMISTRY AROUND US

Photography

It has long been known that silver salts are darkened on exposure to light. That is why silver nitrate solution is normally stored in bottles of brown glass.

In black and white photography, silver bromide or silver iodide is used in an emulsion with gelatine to form the film. When a photo is taken the film is exposed to light. Halide ions actually absorb the light energy, releasing electrons which are picked up by the silver ions, reducing them to metallic silver.

$$Br^- \longrightarrow Br + e^-$$
$$Ag^+ + e^- \longrightarrow Ag$$

benzene-1,4-diol

When the film is developed, a reducing agent like benzene-1,4-diol (more familiarly called hydroquinone or quinol) is used. The silver atoms act as a catalyst for the reduction of further silver ions around them. These produce silver grains, which form the image. The remaining silver halide must be removed before the film can be safely exposed to light. This is done with a solution of sodium thiosulphate in which the silver ions dissolve as the complex $[Ag(S_2O_3)_2]^{3-}$. Photographers call sodium thiosulphate 'hypo' and this stage 'fixing'.

At this stage the film is a 'negative': black silver is deposited where the light was strongest. To produce a positive photograph, light is shone through the negative onto a further piece of film, which is then processed as before.

Developing a photo

Why is this is a disproportionation reaction?

reaction of chlorine with water (see above) or with cold dilute alkalis.

$$\overset{0}{Cl_2}(aq) + 2OH^-(aq) \longrightarrow \overset{-I}{Cl^-}(aq) + \overset{+I}{ClO^-}(aq) + H_2O(l)$$

With hot concentrated alkali, chlorate(V) ions are formed: also a disproportionation reaction:

$$\overset{0}{3Cl_2}(aq) + 6OH^-(aq) \longrightarrow \overset{+V}{ClO_3^-}(aq) + 5\overset{-I}{Cl^-}(aq) + 3H_2O(l)$$

chlorine   hydroxide ion   chlorate(V) ion   chloride ion   water

Chlorate(V) ions also disproportionate when solid sodium chlorate(V) is heated at its melting point, sodium chlorate(VII) forms:

$$\overset{+V}{4KClO_3}(s) \longrightarrow \overset{+VII}{3KClO_4}(s) + \overset{-I}{KCl}(s)$$

potassium chlorate(V)   potassium chlorate(VII)   potassium chloride

Chlorate(I) ions are stable only in solution. Solutions of chlorate(I) ions are used commercially as household bleach, which also has disinfectant properties. Sodium chlorate(V) is used in weedkillers but, as the chlorate(V) ion is a powerful oxidising agent, it assists burning and these weedkillers are being used less because of the fire risk. Sodium chlorate decomposes on heating to give oxygen:

$$NaClO_3(s) \longrightarrow NaCl(s) + 1\tfrac{1}{2}O_2(g)$$

sodium chlorate(V)   sodium chloride   oxygen

Answer: The oxidation number of one of the chlorine atoms has increased and that of one of the chlorine atoms has decreased after reaction.

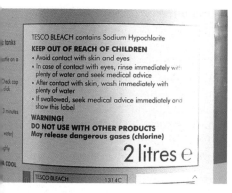

sodium hypochlorite is the non-systematic name for sodium chlorate(I)

Hint: Chlorate(I), chlorate(V) and chlorate(VII) were previously known as hypochlorite, chlorate and perchlorate respectively.

Hint: These acids are called oxoacids for obvious reasons.

Did you know? Different halogens can bond with one another to form so-called interhalogen compounds such as iodine monochloride (ICl) and iodine trichloride (ICl$_3$).

The reaction is catalysed by manganese(IV) oxide and a mixture of these used to be called 'oxygen mixture', and was used in the laboratory to prepare oxygen.

Chlorate(VII) salts are extremely powerful oxidants and are used in explosive detonators and as oxidising agents for rocket fuels. Similar series of compounds are formed by bromine and iodine.

The bonding in the chlorate(I), chlorate(V) and chlorate(VII) ions is shown in **Figure 17.4**.

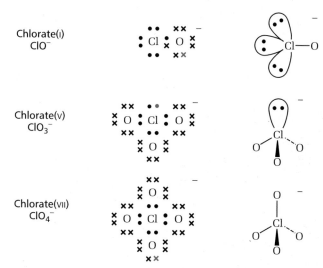

Figure 17.4 Bonding in chlorate ions. The electron (in red) comes from the cation.

The parent acids chloric(I) acid, HClO, chloric(V) acid, HClO$_3$, and chloric(VII) acid, HClO$_4$, show a trend of increasing acidity:

$$HClO_4 > HClO_3 > HClO$$

This is because the negative ion left after the loss of H$^+$ is more stable when there are more electronegative oxygen atoms to spread out the charge.

The halogens form a number of oxides which are thermally unstable, many of them explosively so. They are covalently bonded acidic oxides. Those of formulae Cl$_2$O, ClO$_2$, Cl$_2$O$_6$ and Cl$_2$O$_7$ are known. Chlorine dioxide, ClO$_2$, is a useful industrial oxidising agent. In one of its uses it is a flour additive which both bleaches flour and improves its properties for bread making.

17.5 Economic importance of Group VII

Fluorine is used in the manufacture of fluorocarbons (see Chapter 21) which have many uses including non-stick coatings for saucepans, aerosol propellants and refrigerator coolants. The element is also used to manufacture uranium hexafluoride, one of the few volatile uranium compounds, which is used to separate uranium isotopes by gaseous diffusion. (Uranium enriched in ^{235}U is used in nuclear reactors.)

Chlorine is largely used in the manufacture of organochlorine compounds (which are used as solvents for dry cleaning and degreasing), plastics (for example, PVC) and insecticides. See Chapter 21 for more details. It is also used for treatment of water for drinking and swimming baths and in household bleach.

At present about a quarter of the 30 000 tonnes of bromine manufactured annually in the UK is used to make 1,2-dibromoethane. This is added to leaded petrol to help reduce the build-up of lead oxide inside the engine. This market will decrease as leaded petrol is phased out. Bromine is also used to make pesticides, flame retardants and photographic chemicals.

No iodine is made in the UK. However, 10 000 tonnes of it are extracted annually world-wide. It has a number of uses, the largest being in the pharmaceutical industry and the most familiar being in the manufacture of photographic film.

17.6 Summary

● All the halogens have the outer electron configuration	$ns^2\,np^5$.
● They all form ions of the form	X^-.
● Except for fluorine, they all also form compounds with	positive oxidation states.
● Fluorine is an extremely good	oxidising agent.
● Oxidising power decreases	as we descend the group.
● Fluorine's high reactivity is enhanced by	the weak F—F bond.
● This is caused by	repulsion of the non-bonding electrons.
● Fluorine forms strong covalent bonds with	most other non-metals.
● Ionic fluorides have	high lattice energies.
● Hydrogen fluoride is a weak acid owing to	the strength of the H—F bond.
● In aqueous solution the other hydrogen halides are	strong acids.
● Hydrogen fluoride is a liquid at room temperature owing to	strong hydrogen bonding.
● The other hydrogen halides are	gases.
● Halide ions can be identified by	the formation of precipitates with silver nitrate.

17.7 Practice questions

1. (a) Draw diagrams to show the electronic structure ('dot-cross' diagrams) of the following interhalogens (only the outer-shell electrons need be shown).
   (i) iodine monochloride, ICl
   (ii) bromine pentafluoride, BrF_5
   (b) Draw $\delta+$ and $\delta-$ to show the dipole on the ICl molecule.
   (c) Draw a diagram to show the shape you would expect for a molecule of bromine pentafluoride, BrF_5.

2. When chlorine reacts with hot aqueous sodium hydroxide, disproportionation occurs.
   (a) What is meant by the term disproportionation?
   (b) Write an equation for the reaction and give the oxidation states of chlorine in the reactants and products.

3. (a) Briefly explain the following general trends as we descend the group of halogen elements.
   (i)   The boiling temperatures increase.
   (ii) The X—X bond energies decrease.
   (iii) Their oxidising power decreases.
   (b) Which of these trends has an important exception? Try to explain it.

4. What is the oxidation number of chlorine in the following.
   (a) HCl, Cl_2, $HClO$, $HClO_3$, $HClO_4$?
   (b) Which three of these species are oxoacids?
   (c) Arrange the oxoacids in order of increasing acid strength and explain the trend.

17.8 Examination questions

1. A bottle of bleach bears the slogan 'Contains sodium hypochlorite. This decays into common salt and water after it has killed germs... Do not use with lavatory cleaners containing acid'.
   (a) Some lavatory cleaners contain hydrochloric acid.
      (i)   Hydrochloric acid is a solution of hydrogen chloride, HCl, in water. Write the equation *including state symbols* for the reaction of HCl gas with water.
      (ii) Explain how this shows that hydrogen chloride is behaving as an acid.
      (iii) Hydrochloric acid reacts with sodium hypochlorite to give chlorine gas and sodium chloride.
         Write an equation for this reaction. Sodium hypochlorite has the formula NaClO.
      (iv) State why the instructions say 'Do not use with lavatory cleaners containing acid'.
   (b) On standing (or on warming), a solution of sodium hypochlorite decomposes as follows:

   $$2NaClO \longrightarrow 2NaCl + O_2$$

      (i) Write oxidation states under all the chemical symbols in this equation.
      (ii) Is the label on the bottle accurate about what happens to the sodium hypochlorite? Explain your answer.

   (c) The concentration of sodium hypochlorite in a bleach can be measured by warming the solution and measuring the volume of oxygen collected.

   $100 \, cm^3$ of a bleach solution gave $24 \, cm^3$ of oxygen when warmed. Calculate the mass of NaClO in $1.0 \, dm^3$ of the bleach.
      (A_r: Na = 23; O = 16; Cl = 35.5; 1.0 mol of oxygen molecules occupies $24 \, dm^3$ under the conditions of the experiment.)

   (d) Another method for determining the concentration of bleach is to add an excess of potassium iodide solution and titrate the liberated iodine with sodium thiosulphate solution. The solution goes colourless when all the iodine has reacted with sodium thiosulphate.
      (i) What colour is a solution of iodine in water?
      (ii) Describe how you would proceed to determine accurately the volume of sodium thiosulphate solution needed to react with a certain amount of iodine in solution. Assume you have available several flasks containing equal amounts of iodine in solution and a burette containing sodium thiosulphate solution.
         [O & C Salters 1997]

2. (a) The reaction of chlorine with heated metals can be used to prepare anhydrous metal chlorides such as aluminium chloride.

   (i) Name suitable reagents for a preparation of chlorine.

   (ii) Design and draw an appratus suitable for the preparation of a pure dry sample of a **liquid** chloride, by reaction of dry chlorine with a solid element, X. State what you would include in the risk assessment for this reaction.

(b) Chlorine can form several oxides.

   (i) ClO_2 disproportionates in water. By use of oxidation numbers or otherwise, complete and balance the equation below and use it to explain the meaning of *disproportionation*.

   $$2ClO_2 + H_2O \longrightarrow HClO + \underline{\hspace{1.5cm}}$$

   (ii) Give the formula of **one** other oxide of chlorine. State the oxidation number of chlorine in your chosen oxide.

                                    [Oxford 1996]

3. (a) (i) Complete the table to show the formula of the product formed by direct reaction of the element with excess chlorine:

Element	Sodium	Silicon	Sulphur
Formula			

   (ii) Write equations to represent the reaction with excess water of each of the chlorides in the table.

(b) The table below shows the formulae of some compounds containing halogens. Write the oxidation number (valency) of the halogen in each case.

Formula	Oxidation number
HF	
HCl	
HIO_4	
HClO	

(c) Give **one** example of a way in which fluorine differs from the other members of Group 7.

                                    [AEB 1996]

18 Fundamentals of organic chemistry

CHEMISTRY NOW

The name game

There are over 10 million organic (carbon-based) compounds known. Each needs a name so that chemists can refer to it in conversations and reports and so that information about the compound can be retrieved from databases. Every organic compound has a systematic name related to its structure. This is called its IUPAC name. (IUPAC stands for the International Union of Pure and Applied Chemistry.) The principles behind this naming system are described in this chapter. IUPAC names are unambiguous but are often very long: you would feel odd asking for a bottle of 2-ethanoyloxybenzenecarboxylic acid tablets in the chemist or a shirt made of poly(ethane-1,2-diylbenzene-1,4-dicarboxylate) in a clothes shop.

So most organic compounds also have so-called trivial names, which are easier to say and remember. The trivial names of the two compounds above are aspirin and Terylene respectively.

Chemists can let their imaginations run riot to give compounds trivial names. Sometimes they can be inspired by skeletal formulae, a shorthand described in this chapter, where bonds rather than atoms are shown.

The IUPAC name of compound [1] is tricyclo[2.1.0]pentane but has been dubbed 'houseane'. Derivatives with a methyl group instead of one of the hydrogen atoms have been made. Compound [2] is called roof-methylhouseane.

What do you think the structures of floor-methylhousane and eave-methylhouseane are?

Following the same logic, it is not surprising that [3] is called cubane and [4] basketane but you will need to know a little Latin to know why [5] is called fenestrane (*fenestra* is the Latin for 'window'). The chemist who called [6] 'broken window' was a bit more down to Earth as was the person who named [7] 'squaric acid'.

Notice that some echoes of systematic naming remain; the compounds above that have no carbon–carbon double or triple bonds have names that end in -ane. Compound [8] does have carbon–carbon double bonds and is called propellahex*ene*. Notice also the 'hex' bit which refers to the six-membered rings.

Finally, what about compound [9] – called 'lepidopterene' after its resemblance to a butterfly?

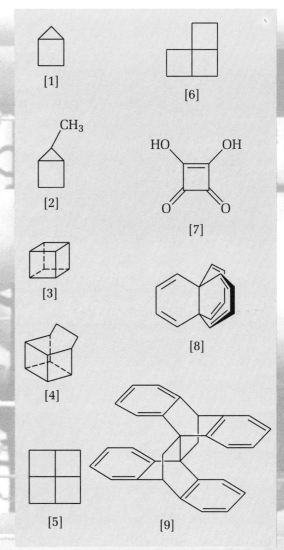

In this chapter we will be looking at:
- the variety of carbon compounds
- bonding and formulae of carbon compounds
- ways of writing formulae of organic compounds
- naming organic compounds
- isomers: compounds with the same molecular formula but different structures
- factors that affect how organic compounds react
- classifying organic reactions

Introduction

Carbon is quite remarkable in the number and variety of compounds that it forms. While most elements have perhaps a few dozen compounds, carbon forms literally millions. All the large and complex molecules that make up life on our planet are carbon-based and there seems to be no limit to the number that can be made or discovered in nature. Many of these compounds have become vital to our present way of life. Plastics, fuels and lubricants, natural and man-made fibres, and many drugs are all carbon compounds.

The vast number of compounds of carbon is due to the ability of the element to form stable chains and rings of carbon atoms. The name 'organic' chemistry is derived from the time when it was thought that such compounds could be synthesised only by living organisms. The idea has long been disproved but the name has continued.

CONCEPT CHECKPOINTS

The following basic ideas are used in this chapter. You may revise some of these topics elsewhere in the book.
- the idea of formula (section 4.5)
- covalent bonding, including polar bonds (section 9.1)
- intermolecular forces (section 10.1)
- bond energies (section 8.4)
- electronegativity (section 9.1)

Hint: Sulphur, in Group VI, also shows some ability to form chains. However, since sulphur normally forms only two covalent bonds there is no possibility of branching, and therefore less variety.

18.1 Reasons for the variety of carbon chemistry

A carbon atom has the electron arrangement $1s^2\ 2s^2\ 2p^2$, i.e. it has four electrons in its outer shell, so it forms four covalent bonds. The carbon–carbon bonds are relatively strong (see **Table 18.1**). These two factors explain why carbon forms chains (which can have branches) and rings.

The carbon–hydrogen bond is also strong ($413\ kJ\ mol^{-1}$) and hydrocarbon chains, with or without branches, form the skeleton of most organic compounds (see **Figures 18.1** and **18.2**).

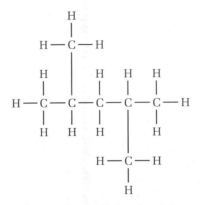

Figure 18.2 A branched hydrocarbon chain

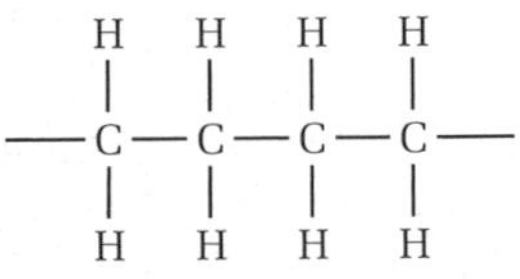

Since we exist in a sea of oxygen, for a compound to be stable, it must not react with oxygen at room temperature. In fact, the reactions of most organic compounds with oxygen are exothermic,

Figure 18.1 Part of a hydrocarbon chain

which means that organic compounds are not *thermodynamically* stable in the presence of oxygen. For example:

$$H-\underset{\underset{H}{|}}{\overset{\overset{H}{|}}{C}}-\underset{\underset{H}{|}}{\overset{\overset{H}{|}}{C}}-\underset{\underset{H}{|}}{\overset{\overset{H}{|}}{C}}-H(g) \ + \ 5O_2(g) \longrightarrow 3CO_2 \ + \ 4H_2O$$

propane   oxygen   carbon   water
                                     dioxide

$$\Delta H^{\ominus} = -2219 \text{ kJ mol}^{-1}$$

However, at room temperature the reactions with oxygen are so slow that organic compounds are *kinetically* stable (see section 8.5). This is because of the large activation energies needed for the reactions with oxygen.

As a comparison, chain molecules based on silicon and hydrogen (called silanes) react immediately on exposure to air, as do hydrides of the other Group IV elements.

Table 18.1 The bond energy of the carbon–carbon bond compared with other elements

Bond	Bond energy/kJ mol^{-1}
C—C	347
N—N	158
O—O	144
Si—Si	226

Anaesthetics

Anaesthetics are substances that induce loss of sensation so that pain cannot be felt. Many fairly unreactive gases have anaesthetic properties. They are believed to work by being absorbed into the fatty tissue that surrounds nerve endings and interfering with the transmission of sensations by the nerves. Early anaesthetics included dinitrogen oxide (nitrous oxide or 'laughing gas'), trichloromethane (chloroform) and ethoxyethane (ether). Each had a major disadvantage for surgical use. Dinitrogen oxide produces only light anaesthesia, making it suitable for minor operations only. It is still used sometimes by dentists during tooth extractions. Trichloromethane is rather toxic and ethoxyethane is explosive. Chlorinated derivatives of methane show an interesting pattern in effectiveness and toxicity.

$$CH_2Cl_2 \quad CHCl_3 \quad CCl_4$$

— better anaesthetics →

— more toxic →

This led chemists in the 1950s to investigate other halogenated hydrocarbons as possible anaesthetics. The ideal product had to be potent, non-toxic, non-flammable and volatile enough to be administered to patients by the usual breathing apparatus used in operating theatres.

Eventually the compound 1-bromo-1-chloro-2,2,2-trifluoroethane was found to have an ideal combination of properties. Its trade name is Fluothane and it is now used

in around three-quarters of the operations carried out in the U.K.

$$Cl-\underset{\underset{Br}{|}}{\overset{\overset{H}{|}}{C}}-\underset{\underset{F}{|}}{\overset{\overset{F}{|}}{C}}-F$$

fluothane

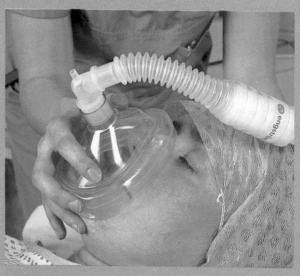

Using fluothane anaesthetic in an operation

18.2 Bonding in carbon compounds

Carbon can form four single covalent bonds as in methane:

$$
\begin{array}{cc}
H & H \\
\overset{\bullet\times}{H \overset{\bullet}{\underset{\times}{\cdot}} C \overset{\bullet}{\underset{\times}{\cdot}} H} & H-\overset{|}{\underset{|}{C}}-H \\
\overset{\bullet\times}{H} & H
\end{array}
$$

or two single bonds and one double bond as in ethene:

or one single bond and one triple bond as in ethyne:

$$
H \overset{\times}{\underset{\times}{\cdot}} C \overset{\times}{\underset{\times}{\cdot}} C \overset{\bullet}{\underset{\times}{\cdot}} H \qquad\qquad H-C\equiv C-H
$$

Hint: In *all* stable compounds, carbon forms the equivalent of four covalent bonds, i.e. it has eight electrons in its outer shell.

Overlap of orbitals

It is worth looking back to section 9.1 about molecular orbitals to remind yourself of how atomic orbitals overlap to form two types of molecular orbitals, σ and π. σ orbitals can be formed by:

- Overlap of two p orbitals along the line joining the nuclei (see **Figure 18.3**). This is how a carbon—carbon single bond is formed

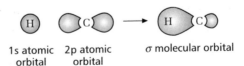

2p atomic orbital σ molecular orbital

Figure 18.3 One way of forming a σ orbital

- Overlap of a p orbital with an s orbital (see **Figure 18.4**). This is how a carbon–hydrogen bond is formed.

1s atomic   2p atomic σ molecular orbital
orbital   orbital

Figure 18.4 Another way of forming a σ orbital

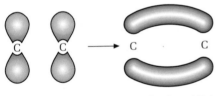

2p atomic orbitals π molecular orbital

Figure 18.5 Forming a π orbital

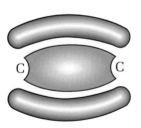

Figure 18.6 The orbitals in C=C

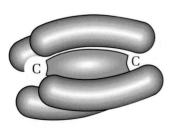

Figure 18.7 The orbitals in C≡C

p orbitals can also overlap to give a π orbital (see **Figure 18.5**): one in which the electron density is on either side of the line joining the nuclei. A carbon–carbon double bond consists of a σ orbital and a π orbital (see **Figure 18.6**), while a carbon–carbon triple bond is formed from a σ and two π orbitals (see **Figure 18.7**). Remember that this is what the signs C=C and C≡C really mean.

The box on the next page gives an even more sophisticated picture of bonding in carbon compounds. Usually we try to use the simplest model that will work for a particular purpose.

FURTHER FOCUS

A more sophisticated picture

Carbon has an outer shell electron arrangement of $2s^2\,2p^2$. However, as 2s and 2p are close in energy the one 2s and three 2p orbitals can hybridise (see the box 'Hybridisation' in section 9.1) to form either four sp^3 orbitals, three sp^2 and one p orbital or two sp orbitals and two p orbitals, as shown below.

sp^3
sp^3 sp^3 $4 \times sp^3$
4 single bonds can be formed
sp^3 109.5°

sp^2 sp^2 $3 \times sp^2$ and $1 \times p$
3 single bonds can be formed via the sp^2 orbitals and $1\,\pi$ bond
sp^2 120°   via the p orbital
p

sp   sp $2 \times sp$ and $2 \times p$
2 single bonds can be formed via the sp orbitals and $2\,\pi$ bonds
p   180°   via the p orbitals
p

Different types of hybridisation lead to the formation of different types of bond: single (σ), double ($\sigma + \pi$) and triple ($\sigma + 2\pi$). The shapes of the molecules are as predicted by electron pair repulsion theory (see section 9.2).

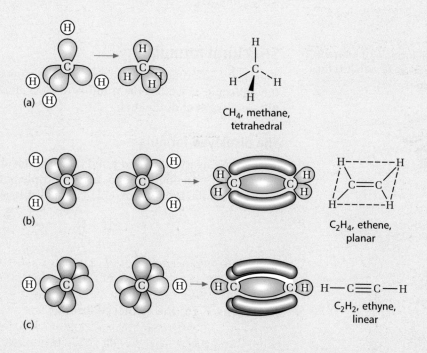

(a)

CH_4, methane, tetrahedral

(b)

C_2H_4, ethene, planar

(c)

C_2H_2, ethyne, linear

18.3 Formulae of carbon compounds

Because many organic compounds are more complex structurally than inorganic compounds, several different types of formulae are used, depending on the amount of information required.

The empirical formula

This formula shows the simplest ratio of the atoms present. For example, ethene:

> 2.8 g of ethene is found to contain: 2.4 g of carbon; 0.4 g of hydrogen.
> 2.4 g of carbon is $2.4/12 = 0.2$ mol of carbon.
> 0.4 g of hydrogen is $0.4/1 = 0.4$ mol of hydrogen.
> Dividing through by the smallest gives C : H as 1 : 2.
> So the empirical formula of ethene is CH_2.

Hint: Look back at section 4.5 if you are not sure about this calculation.

The molecular formula

This shows the number of each type of atom in the molecule. To find the molecular formula we need to know the empirical formula and the relative molecular mass. For example, ethene has an empirical formula CH_2. This could represent molecular formulae such as CH_2, C_2H_4, C_3H_6, etc.: in fact any multiple of the empirical formula. The relative molecular mass (M_r) of ethene is 28. The relative molecular mass of the empirical formula, CH_2, is $12 + (2 \times 1) = 14$, so the molecular formula must contain two empirical formula units, so it is $(CH_2)_2$ or C_2H_4.

Hint: To find the molecular formula, divide the relative molecular mass of the compound by the relative molecular mass of the empirical formula. This will tell you the number of empirical formula units in the molecular formula.

Q The empirical formula of benzene is CH and its M_r is 78. What is the molecular formula?

Structural formulae

These give information about the way the atoms are arranged within the molecule as well as the number of each atom present. There are different ways of doing this:

The displayed formula

This shows every atom and bond in the molecule. — represents a single bond, $=$ a double bond and $\equiv$ a triple bond.

For example, for ethanol, C_2H_6O, the displayed formula is:

$$
\begin{array}{c c}
\text{H} & \text{H} \\
| & | \\
\text{H}-\text{C}-\text{C}-\text{O}-\text{H} \\
| & | \\
\text{H} & \text{H}
\end{array}
$$

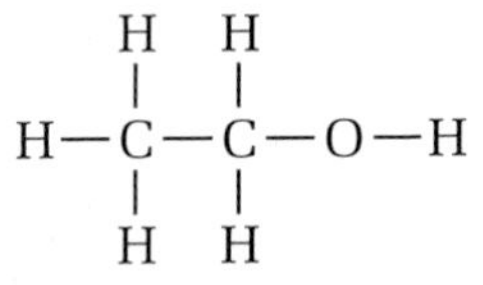

For ethene, C_2H_4, the displayed formula is:

$$
\begin{array}{c}
\text{H} \quad\quad \text{H} \\
\backslash \quad\quad / \\
\text{C}=\text{C} \\
/ \quad\quad \backslash \\
\text{H} \quad\quad \text{H}
\end{array}
$$

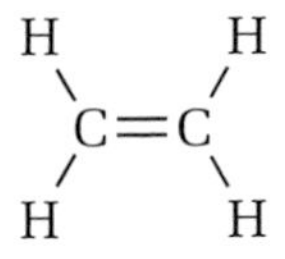

Answer: $(CH)_6 = C_6H_6$

The shorthand structural formula

A shorthand form of structural formula is often used:

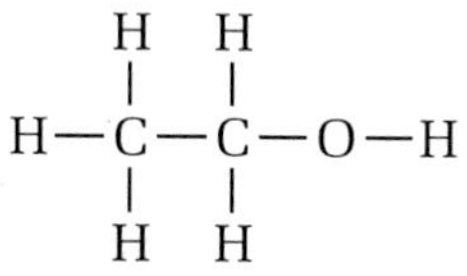

$$
\begin{array}{c}
\quad\;\; H \quad H \\
\quad\;\; | \quad\;\; | \\
H-C-C-O-H \\
\quad\;\; | \quad\;\; | \\
\quad\;\; H \quad H
\end{array}
\qquad \text{may be written } CH_2CH_2OH.
$$

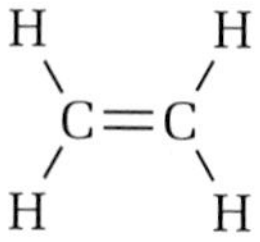

$$
\begin{array}{c}
H \qquad\quad H \\
\;\backslash \qquad\quad / \\
\quad C=C \\
/ \qquad\quad \backslash \\
H \qquad\quad H
\end{array}
\qquad \text{may be written } CH_2CH_2.
$$

In this shorthand, each carbon is written separately, along with the atoms or groups attached to it. Branches in the carbon chains are indicated in brackets:

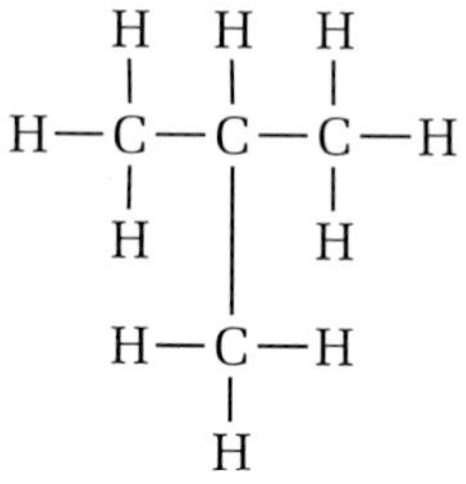

$$
\begin{array}{c}
\quad\;\; H \quad H \quad H \\
\quad\;\; | \quad\;\; | \quad\;\; | \\
H-C-C-C-H \\
\quad\;\; | \quad\;\; | \quad\;\; | \\
\quad\;\; H \quad | \quad H \\
\qquad\;\; H-C-H \\
\qquad\qquad | \\
\qquad\qquad H
\end{array}
\qquad \text{may be written } CH_3CH(CH_3)CH_3.
$$

The three-dimensional structural formula

This attempts to show the three-dimensional structure of the molecule. Bonds coming out of the paper are indicated ◢ and going into the paper by ⋰ .

So ethanol could be written:

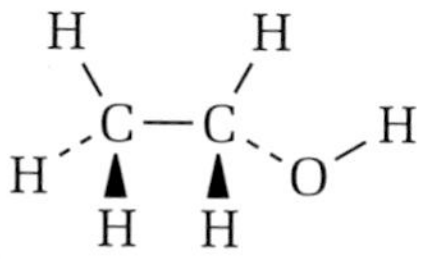

$$
\begin{array}{c}
H \qquad H \\
\backslash \qquad / \\
\quad C-C \\
\;\; H \quad ▲ \quad ▲ \quad O^{-H} \\
\qquad H \quad H
\end{array}
$$

Skeletal notation

With more complex molecules, displayed structural formulae become rather cumbersome. In this notation the carbon atoms are not drawn at all. Straight lines represent carbon–carbon bonds and carbon atoms are assumed to be where the bonds meet. Neither hydrogen atoms nor C—H bonds are drawn. Each carbon is assumed to form enough C—H bonds to make a total of four bonds.

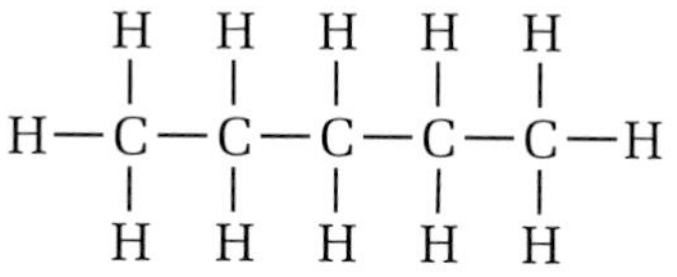

$$
\begin{array}{c}
\quad\;\; H \quad H \quad H \quad H \quad H \\
\quad\;\; | \quad\;\; | \quad\;\; | \quad\;\; | \quad\;\; | \\
H-C-C-C-C-C-H \\
\quad\;\; | \quad\;\; | \quad\;\; | \quad\;\; | \quad\;\; | \\
\quad\;\; H \quad H \quad H \quad H \quad H
\end{array}
\quad \text{would be written: } \sim\!\!\sim
$$

Q Write propane, $CH_3CH_2CH_3$, in skeletal notation.

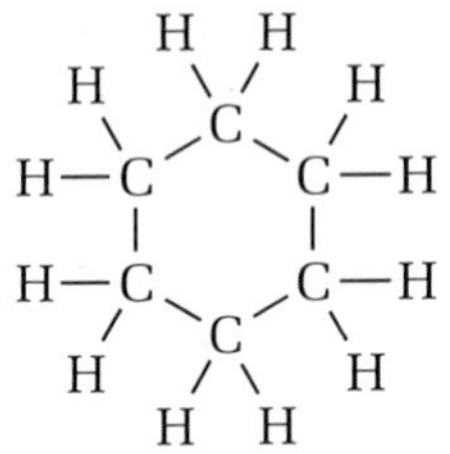

would be written:

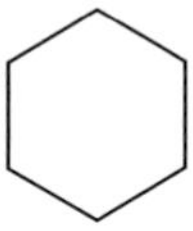

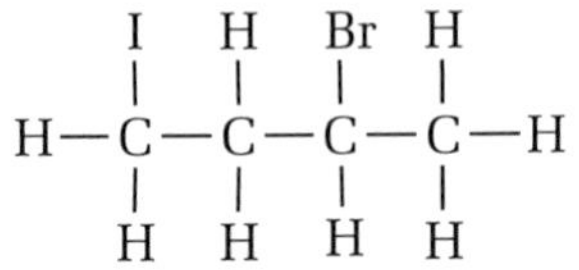

would be written:

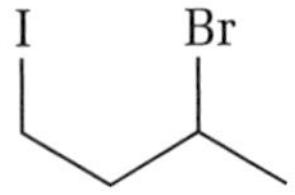

The choice of type of formula to use depends on the circumstances and the type of information you need to give. Notice that skeletal formulae give a rough idea of the bond angles. In an unbranched carbon chain these are 109.5°. Some examples are given in **Table 18.2**.

Table 18.2 Examples of types of formulae found in organic chemistry

Emperical formula	Molecular formula/name	Structural formula			
		Shorthand	Displayed	Skeletal	Three-dimensional
CH_2	C_6H_{12} hex-1-ene	$CH_2CHCH_2CH_2CH_2CH_3$	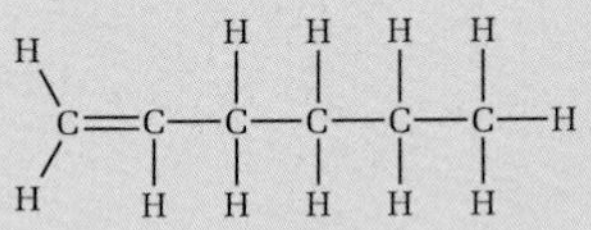	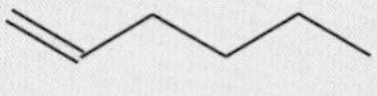	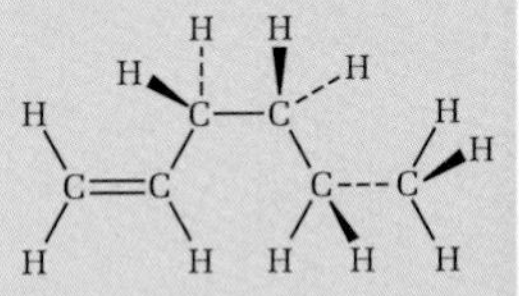
C_2H_6O	C_2H_6O ethanol	CH_3CH_2OH (or C_2H_5OH)	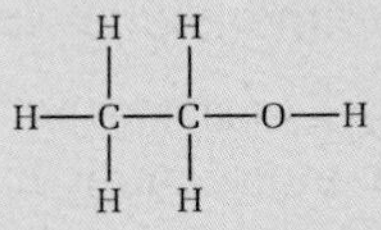	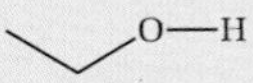	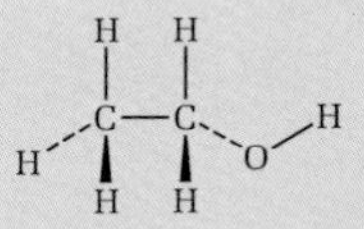
C_2H_6O	C_2H_6O methoxymethane	CH_3OCH_3	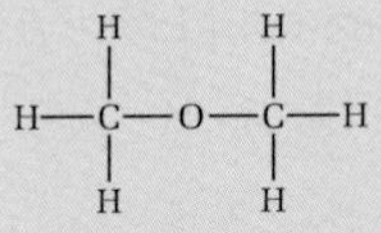	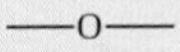	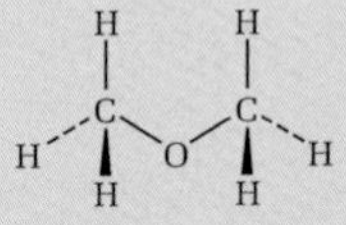
C_3H_7Cl	C_3H_7Cl 2-chloropropane	$CH_3CHClCH_3$	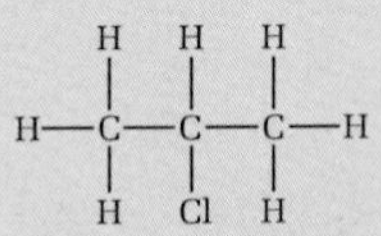	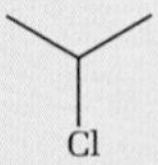	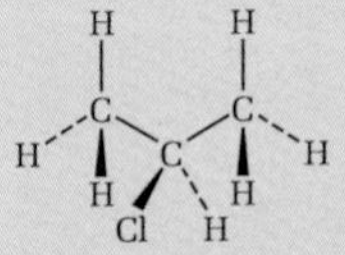
C_3H_6O	C_3H_6O propanone	CH_3COCH_3	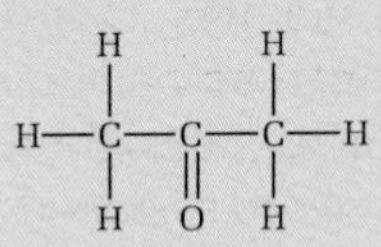	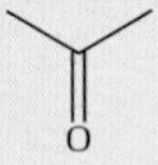	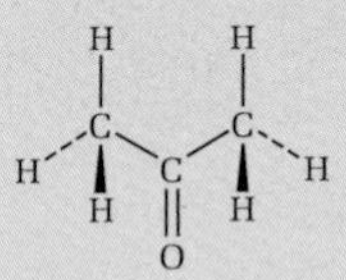

Molecular models

The best way of understanding the three-dimensional shapes of molecules is by building a model. This can be done with molecular modelling kits (see the photograph). Increasingly, computer modelling is being used. Two types of model are most commonly used: ball and

Answer:

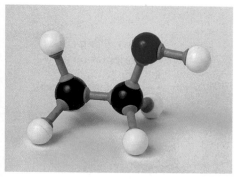

A ball and stick model of ethanol

stick, and space-filling. Ball and stick models are most helpful for visualising the bonds. Space-filling models emphasise the overlap of electron clouds and probably most closely represent the appearance of an actual molecule if it could be seen. **Table 18.3** shows these representations of the molecules in Table 18.2. The CD-ROM which accompanies this book allows you to view some molecules from any angle.

18.4 Naming organic compounds

Did you know? IUPAC stands for International Union of Pure and Applied Chemistry.

There is a systematic scheme for naming compounds developed by IUPAC. Systematic names are related to the structures of the compounds. The complete IUPAC rules are extremely complex and we can do no more than cover the basic principles here.

A systematic name consists of a root, which describes the overall geometry of the molecule by relating it to the longest unbranched hydrocarbon chain or ring. The ending of the root name tells us whether there are any double or triple bonds:

-ane means no double or triple bonds, for example propane

-ene means there is a double bond, for example propene

-yne means there is a triple bond, for example propyne

To this root are added one suffix (ending to a word) and as many prefixes (beginnings of a word) as necessary. Prefixes and suffixes describe what changes have been made to the root molecule. Some common roots, suffixes and prefixes are given in **Table 18.4**. The names of the roots are related to those of saturated hydrocarbons.

Hint: The word 'saturated' is used to mean having no double or triple bonds.

Side chains are indicated by a prefix, whose name is related to the number of carbons:

Methyl, CH_3—
Ethyl, C_2H_5—
Propyl, C_3H_7—
Cyclopropyl, C_3H_5—
Cyclobutyl, C_4H_7—

but benzene as a side group is called phenyl, C_6H_5—.

Table 18.3 Computer generated three-dimensional models

Shorthand structural	Ball and stick representation	Space-filling representation
$CH_2CHCH_2CH_2CH_2CH_3$ hex-1-ene		
CH_3CH_2OH ethanol		
CH_3OCH_3 methoxymethane		
$CH_3CHClCH_3$ 2-chloropropane		
CH_3COCH_3 propanone		

Table 18.4 The hydrocarbons on which the roots used in naming organic compounds are based

Unbranched chains	Rings	Other
methane, CH_4		benzene, C_6H_6
ethane, C_2H_6		
propane, C_3H_8	cyclopropane, C_3H_6	
butane, C_4H_{10}	cyclobutane, C_4H_8	
pentane, C_5H_{12}	etc.	
hexane, C_6H_{14}		
heptane, C_7H_{16}		
octane, C_8H_{18}		
nonane, C_9H_{20}		
decane, $C_{10}H_{22}$		
undecane, $C_{11}H_{24}$		
dodecane, $C_{12}H_{26}$		

For example,

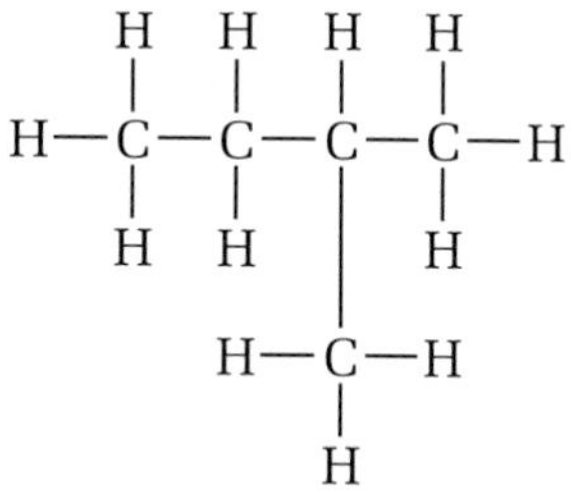

$$H-\underset{\underset{H}{|}}{\overset{\overset{H}{|}}{C}}-\underset{\underset{H}{|}}{\overset{\overset{H}{|}}{C}}-\underset{|}{\overset{\overset{H}{|}}{C}}-\underset{\underset{H}{|}}{\overset{\overset{H}{|}}{C}}-H$$

is called methylbutane.

The longest unbranched chain is four carbons long and there is a side chain of one carbon.

Other groups are indicated by a suffix or prefix as shown in **Table 18.5**. The order in the list is important. If there is more than one group, the higher in the list is called the principal group and is named by a *suffix*, while other groups are named by *prefixes*.

For example,

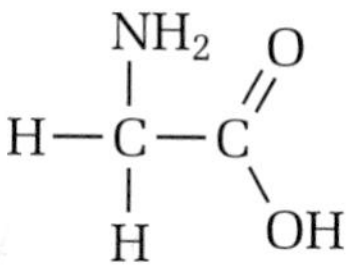

is called aminoethanoic acid

as

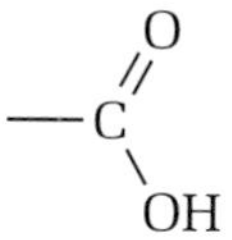

is the principal group rather than —NH_2.

Note that some carbon-containing groups have two names, depending on whether the carbon is counted as part of the root or not.

So $H-\underset{\underset{H}{|}}{\overset{\overset{H}{|}}{C}}-\underset{\underset{H}{|}}{\overset{\overset{H}{|}}{C}}-C\equiv N$ is propanenitrile but

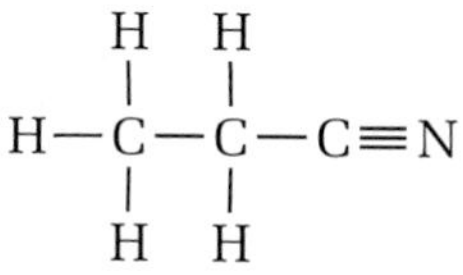

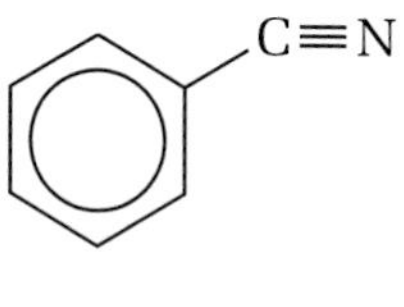

is benzenecarbonitrile.

Table 18.5 The names of groups as suffixes and prefixes

Formula	Suffix	Prefix
(ammonium ion structure: NH_4^+)	-ammonium	
*—COOH	-carboxylic acid (i.e. when hydrogen is replaced by —COOH)	carboxy-
† —(C)(=O)OH	-oic acid	
*—COO⁻	-carboxylate (ion)	
† —(C)(=O)O⁻	-oate (ion)	
*—COOR	alkyl -carboxylate	alkoxycarbonyl-
† —(C)(=O)OR	alkyl -oate	
—CO—Hal	-carbonyl halide	halogenocarbonyl-
† —(C)(=O)Hal	-oyl halide	
—CONH₂	-carboxamide	carbamoyl-
† —(C)(=O)NH₂	-amide	
—CN	-carbonitrile	cyano-
† —(C)≡N	-nitrile	
—CHO	-carbaldehyde	methanoyl-
† —(C)(=O)H	-al	oxo-
† —(C)(=O) (ketone)	-one	oxo-
—OH	-ol	hydroxy-
—SH	-thiol	
—NH₂	-amine	amino-
—NO₂		nitro-
—Hal		halo- (fluoro-, chloro-, bromo-, iodo-)

*COOH, COO⁻ and COOR are often written CO_2H, CO_2^- and CO_2R respectively.
†When the C atom in brackets is counted in the carbon chain which forms the root. (Adapted from *Chemical Nomenclature, Symbols and Terminology for use in School Science*, ASE 1985)

Examples

Chloroethane:

eth indicates that the molecule has a chain of two carbon atoms, **ane** that it has no multiple bonds and **chloro** that one of the hydrogen atoms of ethane is replaced by a chlorine atom.

Propene:

$$H-\overset{\overset{\displaystyle H}{|}}{\underset{\underset{\displaystyle H}{|}}{C}}-\overset{\overset{\displaystyle H}{|}}{C}=C\overset{\displaystyle H}{\underset{\displaystyle H}{}}$$

prop indicates a chain of three carbon atoms and **ene** that there is a C=C (double bond).

Methanol:

$$H-\overset{\overset{\displaystyle H}{|}}{\underset{\underset{\displaystyle H}{|}}{C}}-OH$$

meth indicates a single carbon and **ol** an OH group (an alcohol).

Locants

Ambiguities soon arise, though. Bromopropane could refer to:

$$H-\overset{\overset{\displaystyle H}{|}}{\underset{\underset{\displaystyle H}{|}}{C}}-\overset{\overset{\displaystyle H}{|}}{\underset{\underset{\displaystyle H}{|}}{C}}-\overset{\overset{\displaystyle Br}{|}}{\underset{\underset{\displaystyle H}{|}}{C}}-H \quad \text{or} \quad H-\overset{\overset{\displaystyle H}{|}}{\underset{\underset{\displaystyle H}{|}}{C}}-\overset{\overset{\displaystyle Br}{|}}{\underset{\underset{\displaystyle H}{|}}{C}}-\overset{\overset{\displaystyle H}{|}}{\underset{\underset{\displaystyle H}{|}}{C}}-H$$

A number, called a **locant**, tells us where the bromine atom is on the chain: the first example is 1-bromopropane the second 2-bromopropane.

Note that:

$$H-\overset{\overset{\displaystyle H}{|}}{\underset{\underset{\displaystyle H}{|}}{C}}-\overset{\overset{\displaystyle H}{|}}{\underset{\underset{\displaystyle H}{|}}{C}}-\overset{\overset{\displaystyle Br}{|}}{\underset{\underset{\displaystyle H}{|}}{C}}-H \quad\quad H-\overset{\overset{\displaystyle H}{|}}{\underset{\underset{\displaystyle H}{|}}{C}}-\overset{\overset{\displaystyle H}{|}}{\underset{\underset{\displaystyle H}{|}}{C}}-\overset{\overset{\displaystyle H}{|}}{\underset{\underset{\displaystyle H}{|}}{C}}-Br \quad\quad H-\overset{\overset{\displaystyle H}{|}}{\underset{\underset{\displaystyle H}{|}}{C}}-\overset{\overset{\displaystyle H}{|}}{\underset{\underset{\displaystyle H}{|}}{C}}-\overset{\overset{\displaystyle H}{|}}{\underset{\underset{\displaystyle Br}{|}}{C}}-H$$

are identical, which is more obvious from the ball and stick model.

The apparent difference is due to the fact that we are trying to represent a three-dimensional molecule on flat paper.

More than one locant may be needed:

$$H-\overset{\overset{\displaystyle I}{|}}{\underset{\underset{\displaystyle H}{|}}{C}}-\overset{\overset{\displaystyle Br}{|}}{\underset{\underset{\displaystyle H}{|}}{C}}-\overset{\overset{\displaystyle H}{|}}{\underset{\underset{\displaystyle H}{|}}{C}}-H$$

2-bromo-1-iodopropane

Note that 'bromo' is written before 'iodo', because the rule is **alphabetical** order of the substituting groups, rather than numerical order of the locants.

Hint: Take care.
$$H-\overset{\overset{\displaystyle Br}{|}}{\underset{\underset{\displaystyle H}{|}}{C}}-\overset{\overset{\displaystyle H}{|}}{\underset{\underset{\displaystyle H}{|}}{C}}-\overset{\overset{\displaystyle H}{|}}{\underset{\underset{\displaystyle H}{|}}{C}}-H$$
is not 3-bromopropane. We have merely turned the molecule round. We always use the lowest number possible (1- rather than 3- in this case).

Hint: If there are more than one of the same substituent, each will need a locant to place it on the chain, even if the substituents are on the same carbon atom. For example 1,1-dibromopropane means that both bromines are on the first carbon.

Hint: In chemical names, strings of numbers are separated by commas. A hyphen is placed between words and numbers.

Q Try covering up the names or the formulae in Table 18.6 to test yourself.

The extra prefixes di-, tri-, tetra- are used to indicate two, three, four respectively of the substituent group. Do not get these mixed up with the locants. Di-, tri-, tetra-, tell you *how many* substituents; 1, 2, 3, etc. tell you *where* they are located.

Further examples are given in **Table 18.6**.

Take heart!

Except for fairly simple molecules, working out the correct name can be a difficult task. Fortunately at this stage it is much more important to be able to work out the structure of a molecule from its name, which is a much easier task, than to name a given molecule correctly. Further suffixes and prefixes will be introduced in the appropriate chapters, where examples will be given of their use. Naming organic compounds is best learned by practice: try to see how the name of each compound you come across is related to its structure.

Table 18.6 Examples of systematic naming of organic compounds. Try covering up the name to test youself

Structural formula	Name	Notes
	2,2-dibromopropane	
	2-bromobutan-1-ol	The suffix -ol defines the end of the chain we count from
	butan-2-ol	
	but-1-ene	Not but-2-ene, but-3-ene or but-4-ene as we use the smallest locant possible
	cyclohexane	Cyclo- is used to indicate a ring

Table 18.6 (cont.)

Structural formula	Name	Notes
	2-methylbutane	
	3-methylpentane	This is not 2-ethylbutane. The rule is to base the name on the longest unbranched chain, in this case pentane (picked out in red). Remember the bond angles are 109.5° not 90°
	2,3-dimethylpentane	Again remember the root is based on the longest unbranched chain

18.5 Families of organic compounds

Functional groups

Many organic compounds consist of a hydrocarbon chain with one or more reactive groups attached. These reactive groups are called **functional groups**. Examples include alcohol, —OH, carboxylic acid,

$$-C\overset{\displaystyle O}{\underset{\displaystyle OH}{\big\backslash}}$$, and amine, —NH$_2$. Often the functional

group reacts in the same way, whatever the details of the rest of the molecule.

This means that organic chemistry is usually divided up into chemical families that have the same functional group. The reactions of the group are relatively unaffected by the details of the rest of the molecule to which it is attached. So, it is possible to learn the general reactions of, for example, alcohols and apply this knowledge to any alcohol.

Homologous series

> **Hint:** Members of a homologous series have a general formula. For example the alkanes can be represented by C_nH_{2n+2}

A homologous series is a series of organic compounds, with the same functional group, varying only in the length of the carbon chain to which the functional group is attached. Successive members of the series are called **homologues**. While the length of carbon chain has little effect on the chemical reactivity of the functional group, it does affect physical properties, like melting temperature, boiling temperature and solubility. For example, butane (four carbons) is a gas and hexane (six carbons) a liquid at room temperature. Ethanol (two carbons) is much more soluble in water than hexanol (six carbons).

> **Q** What is the general formula of the alcohols, where one of the hydrogens in an alkane is replaced with an —OH group?

Because members of a homologous series react in the same way, we often want a way to indicate in equations any member of the series. This may be done by using the symbol R to indicate the rest of the molecule. For example R—OH could be used to indicate any alcohol.

18.6 Isomers

Isomers are compounds with the same molecular formula but a different arrangement of atoms in space. Organic chemistry provides many examples of isomerism.

Structural isomerism

This is where the structural formulae differ. The isomers either have different functional groups or the functional groups are attached to the main chain at different points.

Examples

The molecular formula C_2H_6O could represent:

ethanol (an alcohol)   methoxymethane (an ether)

These isomers have different functional groups.
The molecular formula C_3H_6O could represent:

propan-1-ol   propan-2-ol

Answer: $C_nH_{2n+1}OH$ (or $C_nH_{2n+2}O$)

In these isomers, the functional group is attached to a different part of the carbon chain. These are called positional isomers.

The molecular formula C_4H_{10} could represent:

butane   2-methylpropane

These isomers are called chain branching isomers.

Stereoisomerism

This is where two (or more) compounds have the same molecular formula and the same functional groups. They differ in the arrangement of the groups in space. There are two types: *cis–trans* (or geometrical) isomerism and optical isomerism.

Cis–trans isomerism

This involves two groups attached to the atom at either side of a double bond. These may either be on the same side of the bond (*cis*) or on opposite sides (*trans*).

cis-1,2-dichloroethene   *trans*-1,2-dichloroethene

While groups joined by a single bond can rotate, rotation about double bonds is not possible (as this would prevent the overlap of the p orbitals forming the π part of the double bond), so *cis*- and *trans*- isomers are distinct compounds and are not easily interconvertible.

Optical isomerism

Hint: It is difficult to appreciate optical isomerism fully without using models. Even matchsticks and plasticine will do.

Here the two molecules are non-identical mirror images of one another. For example bromochlorofluoromethane exists as two mirror image forms (see **Figure 18.8**).

These two are not identical as **Figure 18.9** shows. Imagine rotating one of the molecules about the C—Cl bond (pointing upwards) until the two bromine, Br, atoms are in the same position (see Figure 18.9).

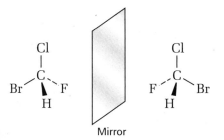

Figure 18.8 The optical isomers of bromochlorofluoromethane

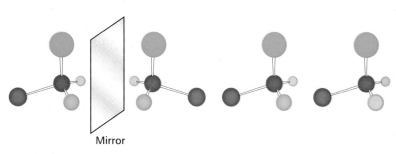

Figure 18.9 Bromochlorofluoromethane has a pair of mirror image isomers ...   ... which are not identical.

FURTHER FOCUS

Optical activity

Light consists of vibrating electric and magnetic fields. We can think of it as vibrating waves like the skipping rope below, except that in the case of light, vibrations occur in all directions at right angles to the direction of motion of the light wave.

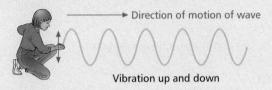

→ Direction of motion of wave

Vibration up and down

If the light passes through a special filter, called a **polaroid** (as in polaroid sunglasses) all the vibrations are cut out except those in one plane, for example the vertical plane.

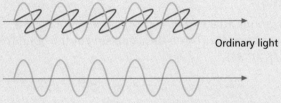

Ordinary light

Vertically polarised light

The light is now vertically polarised. If polarised light passes through a solution containing one enantiomer of an optical isomer, the plane of polarisation is rotated. So vertically polarised light enters the solution and emerges polarised at, say, 60° to the vertical. If one enantiomer rotates the plane of polarisation *clockwise* a solution of the other enantiomer of the same concentration would rotate it by the same angle in the *anticlockwise* direction. The two enantiomers are labelled '+' and '−', the + isomer rotating the plane of polarisation clockwise (as viewed by an observer looking towards the light source) and the − isomer rotating it anticlockwise.

Optical rotation can be measured using a **polarimeter**. If there is no sample in the cell, and the second polaroid is rotated until it is at right angles to the first, the observer

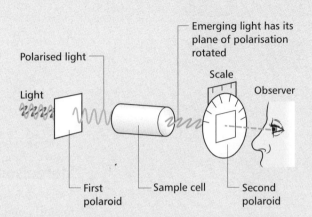

Polarised light

Light

Emerging light has its plane of polarisation rotated

Scale

Observer

First polaroid

Sample cell

Second polaroid

will see no light. This is because the first polaroid will cut out all but the vertical vibrations and the second will remove these too. (Many polaroid sunglasses are supplied with a small extra piece of polaroid to demonstrate this effect.) If the sample rotates the plane of polarisation by 60° clockwise then the second polaroid will have to be rotated through this angle clockwise for the observer to see no light.

Molecules that rotate the plane of polarisation of polarised light are called **optically active** compounds. They are often synthesised by methods that produce equal amounts of both + and − isomers. Such mixtures are not optically active and are called **racemates** (pronounced rass-em-ates) or racemic mixtures.

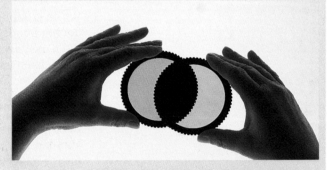

When two pieces of polaroid are at right angles, no light passes through

Did you know? The drug thalidomide used in the 1950s and 1960s to treat morning sickness in pregnant women was a mixture of two optical isomers. One is a safe and effective drug, the other caused some children to have birth defects.

The positions of the hydrogen, H, and fluorine, F, atoms will not match: the two molecules are not superimposable.

Molecules like this have no plane of symmetry. They can easily be identified by the fact that the molecule contains at least one carbon atom attached to four different groups. Optical isomers are said to be chiral (pronounced kiral) meaning 'handed' as in left- and right-handed. The carbon bonded to the four different groups is called the **chiral centre** or the **asymmetric carbon atom** and is often indicated by *.

The two isomers are called a pair of **enantiomers**. They are also called **optical isomers** because they differ in the way they rotate the plane of polarisation of polarised light (see the box 'Optical activity').

Hint: Some objects are identical to their mirror images, for example a sphere or a cube. In other cases the object and its mirror image are not the same. For example, a left shoe and a right shoe are mirror images but they are not identical, i.e. they cannot be superimposed – try it.

Q What is the chiral centre of

$$H-\overset{\overset{\displaystyle H}{|}}{\underset{\underset{\displaystyle H}{|}}{C}}-\overset{\overset{\displaystyle NH_2}{|}}{\underset{\underset{\displaystyle H}{|}}{C}}-\overset{\displaystyle O}{C}\overset{\displaystyle \diagup}{\underset{\displaystyle OH}{\diagdown}}\quad ?$$

2-hydroxypropanoic acid

2-Hydroxypropanoic acid (non-systematic name lactic acid) is also chiral. Although the chiral carbon is bonded to two other carbon atoms, these carbons are part of different groups.

Note that optical isomerism results from the three-dimensional structures of the molecule, and isomers can only be distinguished by three-dimensional representations or, better, by models.

18.7 The physical properties of organic compounds

Physical properties include melting temperatures (T_m), boiling temperatures (T_b) and solubility in water and other solvents. These are determined largely by the intermolecular forces between the molecules (see section 10.1).

Boiling temperatures

Boiling occurs when, on average, molecules have enough energy to overcome the intermolecular forces between them. Two factors are important: the type of intermolecular forces operating and the size of the molecule.

Type of intermolecular force

Hydrogen bonding is stronger than dipole–dipole forces, which are stronger than van der Waals forces. So, other things being equal, hydrogen bonded liquids will have higher boiling temperatures than dipole–dipole bonded liquids, and these in turn will have higher boiling temperatures than liquids in which only van der Waals forces operate. This can be illustrated by the liquids propan-1-ol, propanal and butane, all of which have approximately the same relative molecular mass (see **Table 18.7**).

Figure 18.10 The effect of relative molecular mass on boiling temperature for the alkanes

Size of molecule

In any series of similar compounds where the same type of intermolecular forces operate, the van der Waals forces will increase with the total number of electrons in the molecule and hence with increasing relative molecular mass. So in general a homologous series will show an increase of boiling temperature with relative molecular mass (see **Figure 18.10**).

The substitution of a heavier atom such as chlorine ($A_r = 35.5$) for hydrogen in a hydrocarbon will increase the boiling temperature for two reasons. Not only does it increase the relative molecular mass

Answer: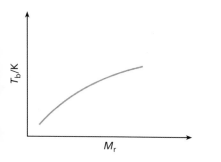

Table 18.7 The effect of different types of intermolecular forces on boiling temperatures

Compound	Structure	Bonding and boiling temperature
propan-1-ol $M_r = 60$	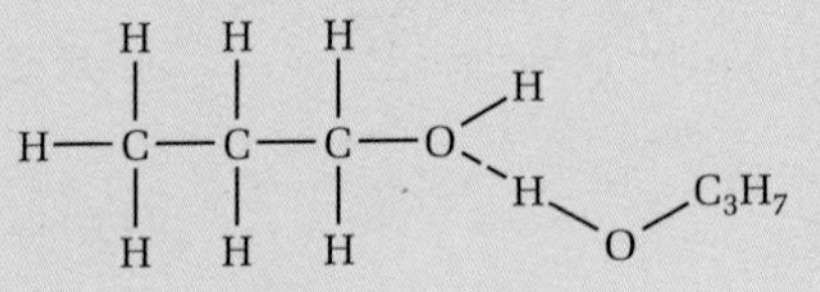	hydrogen bonding $T_b = 371$ K
propanal $M_r = 58$	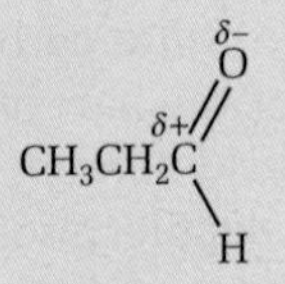	dipole–dipole bonding $T_b = 322$ K
butane $M_r = 58$	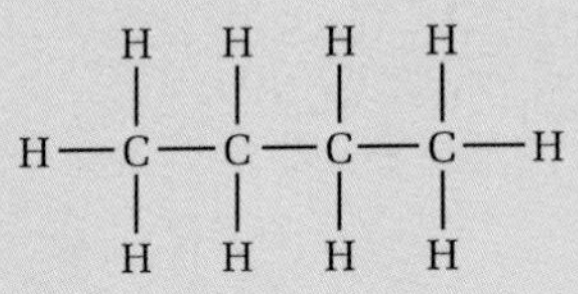	van der Waals bonding $T_b = 135$ K

increasing T_b

but it also makes the molecule more polar and more able to form dipole–dipole bonds.

For example, methane has $T_b = 109$ K and chloromethane has $T_b = 249$ K.

Melting temperatures

These are affected by the same factors as boiling temperature: type of intermolecular force and relative molecular mass. However, a further factor is the shape of the molecule, as this affects the way the molecules can pack together in the solid state. Those that can pack well together have higher melting temperatures than molecules that pack poorly (see **Figure 18.11**). This is because the closer the molecules are, the more effective are the intermolecular forces. Of the two isomers butane and 2-methylpropane, the unbranched butane has the higher melting temperature because its molecules can pack together more closely and are therefore harder to separate.

> **Q** Why are butane and 2-methylpropane sensible molecules to compare, to see the effect of shape on boiling temperatures?

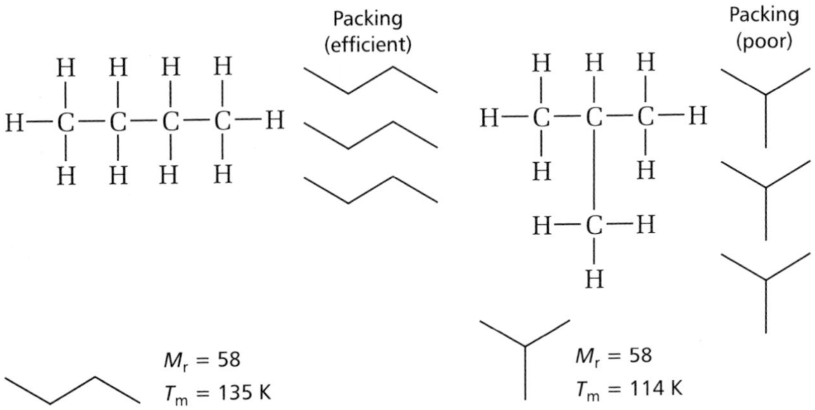

Figure 18.11 Butane molecules pack more closely than those of 2-methylpropane

Answer: They have the same value of M_r and they have van der Waals forces only.

Solubility

The rule that 'like dissolves like' introduced in section 10.2 applies. In particular, molecules with a functional group that can form hydrogen bonds will dissolve well in water, while non-polar molecules, like hydrocarbons will not.

For example, alcohols R—OH, amines R—NH$_2$ and carboxylic

acids R—C⟨$_{OH}^{O}$ will all dissolve well in water provided the

hydrocarbon chain of R is less than about four carbon atoms long. With longer carbon chains, the compounds gradually become less soluble, as the insoluble hydrocarbon begins to dominate the molecule's properties. However, a second hydrogen bonding group increases the solubility again.

Polar, but non-hydrogen bonding groups can also confer water

solubility, so propanone (a ketone), $CH_3{-}\overset{\delta+}{C}{\overset{\overset{\delta-}{O}}{\diagdown}}_{CH_3}$, is very water

soluble. As you might predict, ketones with longer hydrocarbon chains are less water soluble.

Non-polar compounds will dissolve well in non-polar solvents like hydrocarbons. A liquid of intermediate properties can often be used to get two otherwise **immiscible** (un-mixable) substances to mix. For example, water and 1-iodobutane do not mix, but both water and 1-iodobutane will dissolve in ethanol. The ethanol is acting as a **co-solvent**.

18.8 The reactivity of organic compounds

This section looks at some general principles which govern the reactivity of organic compounds. Details about the reactions of the different functional groups are given in the appropriate chapters.

Bond energies

Bond energies tell us the amount of energy required to break a particular bond – they represent the strength of that bond. We might expect that the weakest bond in a molecule would be the most likely to break. This is true up to a point, but there are a number of other factors. However, bond strength may give some pointers. For example, ethanol (with its bond energies in kJ mol^{-1} marked):

$$H\overset{\displaystyle \overset{H}{\underset{413}{|}}}{\underset{\underset{\displaystyle H}{413|}}{\overset{413}{-}C}}\overset{\displaystyle \overset{H}{\underset{413}{|}}}{\underset{\underset{\displaystyle H}{413|}}{\overset{347}{-}C}}\overset{336}{-}O\overset{464}{-}H$$

Table 18.8 Some tabulated bond energies

Bond	Bond energy/kJ mol^{-1}
C—H	413
C—C	347
C—O	358
O—H	464
C—F	467
C—Cl	346
C—Br	290
C—I	228
C=C	612
C≡C	838
C=O	743
C—N	286
C=N	615
C≡N	887
N—H	391
N—O	214
O—O	144

The C—O bond is the weakest and we might predict that it would be the most likely to break. This is the case in many of the reactions of ethanol. However, there are reactions in which the O—H bond breaks even though this is stronger, so bond strength cannot be the only factor. **Table 18.8** lists some of the more common bond energies.

Multiple bonds

At first sight, multiple bonds seem to be stronger than single bonds, but remember that a double bond consists of a σ bond and a π bond, and a triple bond consists of a σ bond and two π bonds.

If we take the C—C value (347 kJ mol^{-1}) to represent the σ bond, then this means that the π bond's contribution to C=C is $612 - 347 = 265$ kJ mol^{-1}, so the π bond is considerably weaker than the σ bond. Similarly the energy of the second π bond in C≡C is given by $838 - 612 = 226$ kJ mol^{-1}, even weaker. So it is possible to break the π component(s) of a multiple bond and leave the σ part intact. This usually occurs in the reactions of double bonds. The carbon chain rarely breaks at the position of the double bond.

Polarity

This is the second major factor that governs the reactivity of organic molecules. Except for bonds between two atoms of the same element, one of the atoms in the bond will always be more electronegative than the other (see **Table 18.9**). It will attract the shared electrons more strongly and the bond will be polar (see section 9.1). This is indicated by the signs $\delta+$ and $\delta-$, showing the partial charges on each atom. For example, in propanone, the C=O bond is far more polar than the C—H bonds, as the difference in electronegativity between C and O is much greater than that between C and H (**Figure 18.12**). So we might expect negatively charged reagents (called nucleophiles – see below) to attack the C atom which is bonded to the oxygen, and positively charged ones (called electrophiles – see below) to attack the oxygen atom. Either way we would get a reaction involving the C=O rather than the C—C or C—H bonds. This is observed in practice in most of the reactions of propanone.

Sometimes the bond energy and polarity approaches give conflicting results and so we cannot make a clear-cut prediction. For example, look at the data for the carbon–halogen bonds in **Table 18.10**.

The carbon–halogen bonds get weaker (and therefore easier to break) as we go from fluorine to iodine but the bonds also get less polar and therefore the carbon becomes less easily attacked by negatively charged reagents. So the two factors, bond energy and polarity, predict different outcomes. Bond energies predict C—F to be the *least* reactive; polarity predicts C—F to be the most reactive. In fact in the reaction with OH$^-$ ions CH$_3$I reacts the fastest and CH$_3$F not at all, so in this case bond energy is the more important factor.

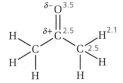

Figure 18.12 Propanone, with electronegativities in red

Hydrocarbon chains

A look at the bond energies in Table 18.8 shows that C—C and C—H bonds are among the strongest single bonds. Table 18.9 shows that the C—C bond is non-polar and the C—H bond relatively non-polar. Both these factors mean that the hydrocarbon skeleton of an organic molecule tends to stay intact during reactions. So organic reactions involve the functional group rather than the carbon chain.

Table 18.9 Electronegativities of elements encountered in organic chemistry

Element	Electronegativity
C	2.5
H	2.1
O	3.5
F	4.0
Cl	3.0
Br	2.8
I	2.5
N	3.0

Table 18.10 Electronegativities and bond energies in carbon–halogen bonds

Electronegativity		Bond energy/kJ mol^{-1}
2.5 4.0 C — F		467
2.5 3.0 C — Cl		346
2.5 2.8 C — Br		290
2.5 2.5 C — I		228

Hint: Dative covalent bonds are also represented by an arrow. To avoid confusion draw a dative bond ⟶ and an inductive effect ⟶

The inductive effect

Another way of representing the polarity of a bond involving two atoms with different negativities is to draw an arrow on the bond in the direction in which the electrons are attracted. So a carbon–halogen bond could be represented:

$$
\begin{array}{cc}
\text{H} & \text{H} \\
| & | \quad \delta+ \;\; \delta- \\
\text{H}-\text{C}\!\!\rightarrow\!\!\text{X} \;\; \text{rather than} \;\; \text{H}-\text{C}-\text{X} \\
| & | \\
\text{H} & \text{H}
\end{array}
$$

showing that the halogen draws electrons towards itself. This is sometimes called an **inductive effect**, and halogens are said to have a **negative inductive effect**.

Alkyl groups like methyl-, ethyl-, etc. have the opposite effect. They tend to release electrons and have a **positive inductive effect**, as shown by the direction of the arrow.

$$
\begin{array}{cc}
\text{H} & \text{H} \\
| & | \\
\text{H}-\text{C}\!\!\rightarrow\!\!\text{C}- \\
| & | \\
\text{H} & \text{H}
\end{array}
$$

The effect is increased if more than one alkyl group is attached to the same carbon:

$$
\begin{array}{c}
\text{CH}_3 \\
\downarrow \\
\text{H}_3\text{C}\!\!\rightarrow\!\!\text{C}- \\
\uparrow \\
\text{CH}_3
\end{array}
$$

The effect is relatively small but can be important. For example, a carbon atom carrying a positive charge is more stable if it is bonded to one or more alkyl groups rather than to hydrogen atoms.

Electron-rich areas

In carbon–carbon double and triple bonds, there is a higher than normal concentration of electrons: four and six respectively per bond, compared with two in a single bond. The electrons are equally shared between the two carbon atoms. These areas of high electron density (electron-rich areas) make these bonds susceptible to attack by positively charged reagents (electrophiles) such as the hydrogen ion, H^+.

Types of reagent

Unless we try to classify organic reactions we will end up with a mass of facts which simply have to be learned. One way of classifying reactions is in terms of the type of reagent which attacks the organic molecule. These may be divided into **nucleophiles**, **electrophiles** and **radicals** (sometimes called free radicals).

Nucleophiles

Nucleophiles are ions or molecules which have electron-rich areas. They are either negatively charged ions or have an atom with a $\delta-$ charge. They attack positively charged carbon atoms in organic molecules. The nucleophile must have a lone pair of electrons with

Hint: The symbol :Nu or :Nu⁻ is often used to indicate any nucleophile. Note that some are negatively charged overall while some are neutral overall.

Q Predict where a nucleophile will attack the ethanoic acid molecule

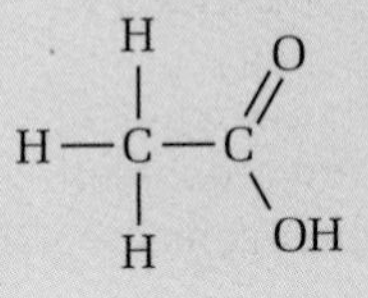

which it can form a dative bond with the positively charged atom in the organic molecule. Since they donate electron pairs, nucleophiles are also Lewis bases (see the box 'Lewis acids' in Chapter 12). Examples of nucleophiles include:

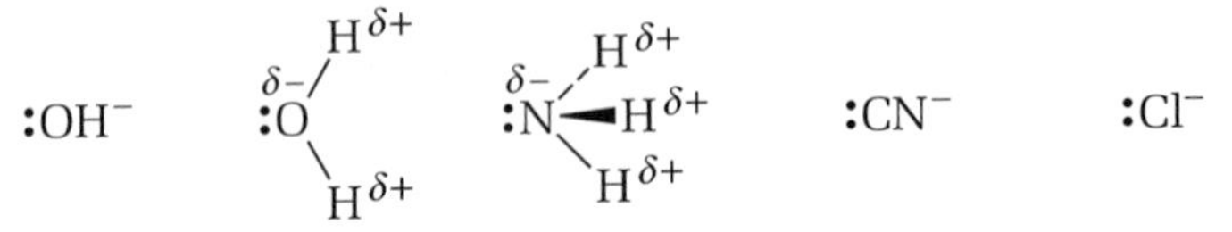

hydroxide ion, water, ammonia, cyanide ion, chloride ion

The first step of a reaction with a nucleophile involves the nucleophile using its lone pair of electrons to form a bond with the electron-deficient (positively charged) carbon atom. Movement of electron pairs in organic reactions is usually shown by 'curly arrows'. Do not confuse them with a straight arrow representing a dative bond (or an inductive effect).

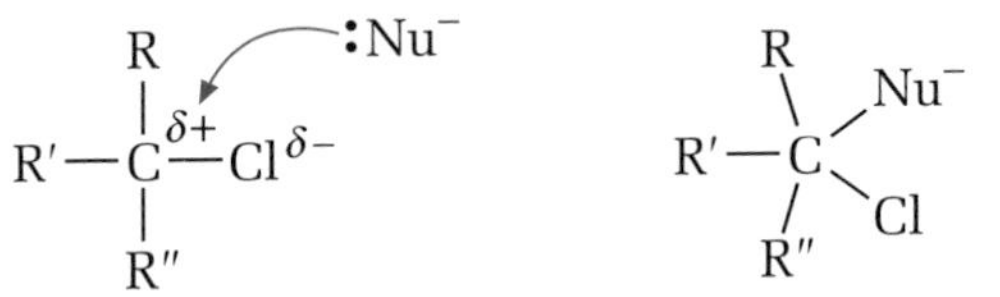

starting material with $C^{\delta+}$ — intermediate

In the intermediate, the carbon is forming five bonds (has ten electrons in its outer shell) so needs to 'shed' a pair of electrons. One possibility is shown.

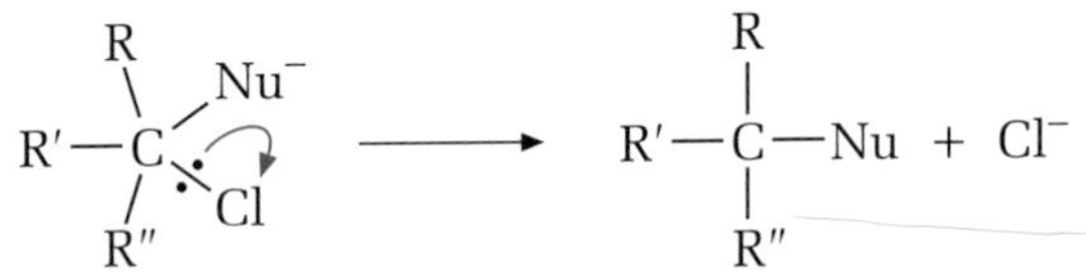

The extra electrons are taken away by an atom or group of atoms called the **leaving group** (in this case a Cl^- ion). Remember that each single bond represents a pair of shared electrons.

Electrophiles

Electrophiles are ions or molecules which are electron-deficient (positively charged) or have an electron-deficient atom (shown by $\delta+$). They tend to attack electron-rich areas of organic molecules such as double bonds.

Some examples of electrophiles include:

Hint: The symbol El^+ or El is used to indicate any electrophile. Note that some are positively charged overall and some neutral overall.

H^+	NO_2^+	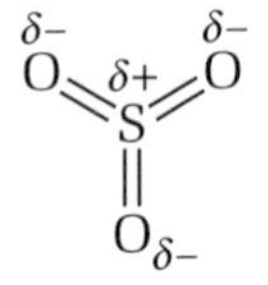
hydrogen ion (proton)	nitryl cation	sulphur trioxide

Electrophiles can accept an electron pair and are therefore Lewis acids (see the box 'Lewis acids' in Chapter 12).

The first step of the reaction of an electrophile with an organic compound involves the electrophile being attracted to an electron-rich area of the molecule, such as a double bond, and then accepting an electron pair from it to form a bond with a carbon atom:

Answer: The carbon atom which is bonded to the two electronegative oxygen atoms

$$R \overset{El^+}{\underset{R'}{C}} = \overset{R''}{\underset{R'''}{C}} \longrightarrow R - \overset{El}{\underset{R'}{C}} - \overset{+}{\underset{R'''}{C}} - R''$$

In this case the electrophile might bond to either carbon atom, although which one depends on the nature of R, R′, R″ and R‴. Notice that in the intermediate the carbon not bonded to the electrophile is forming only three bonds (has only six electrons in its outer shell) and is thus positively charged). The resulting positive ion (sometimes called a **carbocation**) may then be attacked by a negative ion. For example:

$$H - \overset{El}{\underset{R'}{C}} - \overset{+}{\underset{R''}{C}} - R''' + X^- \longrightarrow R - \overset{El}{\underset{R'}{C}} - \overset{X}{\underset{R''}{C}} - R'''$$

Radicals

Radicals, sometimes called **free radicals**, are species with an unpaired electron. They can be formed by the breaking of a single bond in such a way that one of the shared electrons goes to each new species. For example:

$$Br \overset{\cdot}{\underset{\cdot}{}} Br \longrightarrow Br\cdot + Br\cdot$$

This reaction can be brought about by ultraviolet light. Another example is:

$$R - O \overset{\cdot}{\underset{\cdot}{}} O - R \longrightarrow RO\cdot + RO\cdot$$

This reaction occurs with gentle heating.

Such bond breaking, where one electron of the bond goes to each fragment, is called **homolysis** (equal breaking).

Most radicals are extremely reactive and will attack other molecules indiscriminately in order to gain another electron. For example:

$$Br\cdot + CH_4 \longrightarrow \cdot CH_3 + HBr$$

Unless the reaction is between two radicals, a new radical is always formed.

Types of reaction

We can classify organic reactions as **addition**, **elimination** or **substitution**. For example:

Addition:

$$\overset{H}{\underset{H}{}}C = C\overset{H}{\underset{H}{}} + Br_2 \longrightarrow H - \overset{Br}{\underset{H}{C}} - \overset{Br}{\underset{H}{C}} - H$$

Elimination:

$$H - \overset{H}{\underset{H}{C}} - \overset{OH}{\underset{H}{C}} - H \longrightarrow \overset{H}{\underset{H}{}}C = C\overset{H}{\underset{H}{}} + H_2O$$

The setting of fibreglass resin is started off by radicals

Hint: Another way in which a bond can break is called **heterolysis**. Both shared electrons go to one species and none to the other, so ions are formed rather than radicals. For example:

$$H - Cl \longrightarrow H^+ + :Cl^-$$

The electrons both go to the chlorine atom as it is more electronegative than hydrogen.

Q Would you expect the bond in the molecule I—F to break homolytically?

Answer: No. Fluorine is much more electronegative than iodine and the ions F⁻ and I⁺ would be more likely than radicals.

Substitution:

$$\text{H–C(H)(H)–C(OH)(H)–H} + Cl^- \longrightarrow \text{H–C(H)(H)–C(Cl)(H)–H} + OH^-$$

As the names imply, addition involves two molecules joining together, elimination a molecule being ejected, and substitution a replacement of one atom or group by another.

Combining this with the three types of reagent described above, leads to **Table 18.11**, which predicts nine types of organic reaction (combinations of reagent type and reaction type).

Table 18.11 Types of organic reaction

Reagent type	Reaction type		
	Addition	Elimination	Substitution
Nucleophile	✓	✓*	✓
Electrophile	✓		✓
Radical			✓

*In nucleophilic elimination reactions, the nucleophile is often considered to be behaving as a base.

These reactions are usually referred to as a nucleophilic addition or electrophilic substitution and so on. The types which are most important at this level are indicated with a ✓. Not all reactions fit easily into this scheme. Oxidation reactions, particularly, are often considered separately.

Substitution and elimination reactions are almost always possible. Addition reactions are not possible in a compound in which all of the carbon atoms are already forming four single bonds. Such compounds are called **saturated**. Compounds with multiple bonds (where addition reactions are possible) are called **unsaturated**. For example:

$$\text{H–C(H)(H)–C(H)(H)–H}$$

ethane, saturated, so no addition reactions are possible.

$$\text{C}_2\text{H}_4 (C=C) + H_2 \longrightarrow \text{H–C(H)(H)–C(H)(H)–H}$$

ethene unsaturated, addition is possible.

$$H–C\equiv C–H + 2H_2 \longrightarrow \text{H–C(H)(H)–C(H)(H)–H}$$

ethyne, unsaturated, addition is possible.

18.9 Equations in organic chemistry

In inorganic chemistry it is usual to write balanced symbol equations for reactions. This is sometimes done in organic chemistry but reactions are often written in other forms. For example, it is common simply to write the organic starting material and organic product with the reagent and conditions above the arrow rather than a fully balanced equation.

For example:

$$CH_3CH_2Br \xrightarrow[\text{reflux}]{\text{NaOH}} \underset{\text{ethene}}{\overset{\displaystyle H\;\;\;\;\;H}{\underset{\displaystyle H\;\;\;\;\;H}{C=C}}} \quad \text{(an elimination reaction)}$$

bromoethane   ethene

This is partly because organic chemists are usually most interested in the organic product and partly because organic reactions frequently give a mixture of products, and so a balanced equation is not really appropriate. In the example above, some ethanol, CH_3CH_2OH, is also produced.

Another short cut is sometimes used in representing oxidation (addition of oxygen) and reduction (addition of hydrogen) reactions. Rather than specifying the oxidising reagent or the reducing reagent, we sometimes use [O] to represent a source of oxygen and [H] to represent a source of hydrogen.

For example:

$$CH_3C\overset{\displaystyle O}{\underset{\displaystyle H}{\big\langle}} \xrightarrow{\text{[O]}} CH_3C\overset{\displaystyle O}{\underset{\displaystyle OH}{\big\langle}}$$

or

$$CH_3-\overset{\displaystyle O}{\overset{\displaystyle \|}{C}}-CH_3 \xrightarrow{\text{2[H]}} CH_3-\overset{\displaystyle OH}{\underset{\displaystyle H}{C}}-CH_3$$

18.10 Summary

- Carbon forms four   covalent bonds.

- At room temperature, carbon compounds are kinetically stable with respect to   reactions with air and water.

- C—C and C—H bonds are not easily attacked by either positively or negatively charged reagents because   they are not very polar.

- The empirical formula is   the simplest ratio of atoms present in the compound.

- The molecular formula shows | the number and type of atoms present in one molecule of the compound.

- The number of empirical formula units is found by | dividing the relative molecular mass by the relative molecular mass of one empirical formula unit.

- Different types of structural formulae can be used.

$CH_3CH(CH_3)CH_2OH$ is called | shorthand.

is called | displayed.

is called | three-dimensional.

is called | skeletal.

- A homologous series is | a family of organic compounds which vary only in the length of their carbon chains.

- Functional groups are | reactive groups of organic compounds.

- Isomers are molecules with | the same molecular formula but different spatial arrangements of atoms.

- *Cis–trans* isomerism can only occur in molecules with | a double bond.

- The *cis* isomer has two substituents on | the same side of the double bond.

- The *trans* isomer has two substituents on | opposite sides of the double bond.

- Optical isomers are molecues which exist as pairs of | non-superimposable mirror images.

- An atom which has four different groups attached to it is a | chiral centre.

- Melting and boiling temperatures of organic compounds increase with the size and | the polarity of the molecule.

- Molecules which form hydrogen bonds have | the highest melting temperatures.

- Solubility of organic compounds is governed by the rule | 'like dissolves like'.

- Carbon atoms with a $\delta+$ charge can be attacked by | nucleophiles.

- Areas of high electron density in organic compounds can be attacked by | electrophiles.
- A radical has | an unpaired electron.
- Radicals are generated by | homolytic breaking of a covalent bond.
- The three main types of organic reaction are | addition, elimination and substitution.

18.11 Practice questions

1. Name the following compounds.

a)
$$
\begin{array}{c}
H \\
\diagdown \\
C=C-C-H \\
\diagup \quad | \quad | \\
H \quad H \quad H
\end{array}
$$

(d)
$$
HO-\overset{\displaystyle H}{\underset{\displaystyle H}{C}}-\overset{\displaystyle H}{\underset{\displaystyle H}{C}}-\overset{\displaystyle OH}{\underset{\displaystyle H}{C}}-\overset{\displaystyle H}{\underset{\displaystyle H}{C}}-H
$$

b)
$$
H-\overset{\displaystyle H}{\underset{\displaystyle H}{C}}-\overset{\displaystyle H}{C}=\overset{\displaystyle H}{C}-\overset{\displaystyle H}{\underset{\displaystyle H}{C}}-H
$$

(e)
$$
H-\overset{\displaystyle H}{\underset{\displaystyle H}{C}}-\overset{\displaystyle H}{\underset{\displaystyle H}{C}}-\overset{\displaystyle Cl}{\underset{\displaystyle Cl}{C}}-Cl
$$

c)
$$
\begin{array}{c}
H \quad \quad H \quad H \quad \quad H \\
\diagdown \quad | \quad | \quad \diagup \\
C=C-C=C \\
\diagup \quad \quad \quad \quad \diagdown \\
H \quad \quad \quad \quad \quad H
\end{array}
$$

2. Draw the displayed formula of:
(a) 2,2-dichloropropane, (b) butan-2-ol,
(c) 2-methylpropan-2-ol, (d) cyclopropane,
(e) propene.
Which are a pair of isomers?

3. There are four structural isomers with the molecular formula C_4H_9Br. Draw their displayed formulae. One of these can exist as a pair of optical isomers. Which one is this?

4. The substance
$$
H-\overset{\displaystyle H}{\underset{\displaystyle H}{C}}-\overset{\displaystyle H}{\underset{\displaystyle O}{C}}-\overset{\displaystyle H}{\underset{\displaystyle H}{C}}-\overset{\displaystyle H}{\underset{\displaystyle H}{C}}-H
$$
displays

optical isomerism. Indicate the chiral carbon atom with a *. Draw three-dimensional representations of the two enantiomers. Give the compound's systematic name.

5. Copy the formulae and insert $\delta +$ and $\delta -$ signs to indicate the polarity of the following molecules.

(a)
$$
H-\overset{\displaystyle H}{\underset{\displaystyle H}{C}}-\overset{\displaystyle H}{\underset{\displaystyle H}{C}}-O-H
$$

(d)
$$
H-\overset{\displaystyle H}{\underset{\displaystyle H}{C}}-Br
$$

(b)
$$
H-\overset{\displaystyle H}{\underset{\displaystyle H}{C}}-\overset{\displaystyle O}{\overset{\diagup\!\diagup}{C}}\diagdown_{H}
$$

(e)
$$
H-\overset{\displaystyle H}{\underset{\displaystyle H}{C}}-Cl
$$

(c)
$$
H-\overset{\displaystyle H}{\underset{\displaystyle H}{C}}-\overset{\displaystyle O}{\overset{\diagup\!\diagup}{C}}\diagdown_{NH_2}
$$

(f)
$$
H-\overset{\displaystyle H}{\underset{\displaystyle H}{C}}-F
$$

Put d), (e) and (f) in order of increasing $\delta +$ character of the carbon atoms.

6. Use the list of bond energies in Table 18.8 to predict the weakest bond in each of the following compounds.

(a)
$$
H-\overset{\displaystyle H}{\underset{\displaystyle H}{C}}-O-O-\overset{\displaystyle H}{\underset{\displaystyle H}{C}}-H
$$

(c)
$$
H-\overset{\displaystyle H}{\underset{\displaystyle H}{C}}-O-\overset{\displaystyle H}{\underset{\displaystyle H}{C}}-H
$$

(b)
$$
H-\overset{\displaystyle H}{\underset{\displaystyle H}{C}}-\overset{\displaystyle H}{\underset{\displaystyle H}{C}}-I
$$

(d)
$$
Cl-\overset{\displaystyle F}{\underset{\displaystyle Br}{C}}-I
$$

7. Classify the following reagents as nucleophiles, electrophiles or radicals.

H^+, H^-, CH_3NH_2, Cl^-, H_2O, HSO_3^+, $H\bullet$

8. Draw a displayed formula of 'houseane' (see 'Chemistry Now' at the start of this chapter).

18.12 Examination questions

1. (a) Explain what is meant by the term *stereoisomerism*.

(b) Draw three-dimensional representations of each of the four stereoisomers of structural formula **A**.

$$CH_3CH(OH)CH=CHCH_3$$
$$A$$

Number the structures you have drawn 1 to 4.

(c) With reference to the structures you have drawn, or using other examples of your own choice, explain the meaning of, and structural requirements for:
  (i) optical isomerism;
  (ii) *cis-* and *trans-* isomers.

(d) State which of the compounds 1–4 in part (b) will have the same boiling points, explaining the reason for your choice.
[Oxford 1997]

2. (a) There are both cyclic and non-cyclic isomers of hydrocarbons with a given molecular formula.
  (i) Draw full structural formulae for cyclopropane, **A**, and cyclopropene, **B**.
  (ii) Draw **two** non-cyclic structural isomers of **A** and **B**; state the class of compound to which each belongs.
  (iii) A common polymer has the same empirical formula as **A**. Give the empirical formula, and the name of the polymer.

(b) 0.54 g of a hydrocarbon, **C**, were burnt in excess oxygen. The water produced was absorbed by passing through calcium chloride tubes, which gained 0.54 g in mass. The carbon dioxide was absorbed by potassium hydroxide, which gained 1.76 g.

  (i) Show that the empirical formula of **C** is C_2H_3.
  (ii) Given that 0.01 mol of **C** was used, derive the molecular formula of **C**. Show your working.
  (iii) Draw the structural formula of **one** possible isomer of **C** and comment on its shape around any multiple bond(s), or on other points of interest in its structure.
[Oxford 1997]

3. (a) Give the formulae of the three *structural* isomers of C_4H_8 which are non-cyclic.

(b) One of these isomers shows a type of stereoisomerism.
  (i) Give the structures of the stereoisomers and name them.
  (ii) Suggest how these stereoismers might be distinguished.

(c) One of the isomers of C_4H_8 in (a) reacts with HBr to give two different products, the major one of which is a chiral molecule.
  (i) Identify this isomer of C_4H_8.
  (ii) Give the mechanism for the reaction of this isomer with HBr.
  (iii) Why is the major product chiral but the minor one not so?
  (iv) Why is the chiral product the major one, and the none-chiral product the minor one?
  (v) The major product of this addition reaction is found to be optically inactive. Explain why this is so.
[London 1997]

19

Alkanes

C H E M I S T R Y   N O W

Finding and exploiting oil

For many years, predictions have been made about the date at which the Earth's oil and gas resources will be used up. However, over the last ten years the world's proved oil resources (ones from which we know oil can be extracted under current conditions) have actually gone up. This is because new reserves are being discovered and new technology makes it possible to extract oil more efficiently and from previously uneconomic sources.

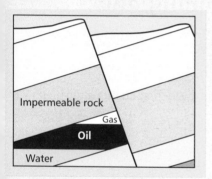

The geology of a typical oil and gas deposit

Discovering oil and gas deposits

Oil and gas were formed millions of years ago when the remains of microscopic plants and animals settled on the sea bed and were buried by sediments such as clay and sand. So geologists look for oil in areas of sedimentary rock such as limestone or sandstone. To trap the oil or gas, a layer of impermeable rock must also be present. Sometimes the oil is present as an underground liquid 'lake' but it may exist soaked into the rock itself.

When looking for new deposits of oil, geologists first use aerial surveys to locate areas with the right rock types to hold oil deposits. They then do a ground survey, looking at rock types, vegetation and fossils which can help date the rocks. A seismic survey will also be done by recording the shock waves from small explosive charges as they are reflected from rock layers. This can give a three-dimensional picture of the rocks below.

Getting the oil out

Once found, the oil has to be extracted – this means drilling. Today it is possible to recover up to 45% of the oil in a typical deposit – 50% more than was possible twenty years ago – and technology is improving all the time. Sometimes the oil in the deposit is found under pressure and this forces it to the surface. In other deposits the oil has to be pumped. Most oil wells are between 1 and 5 km deep but recently wells up to 8 km deep

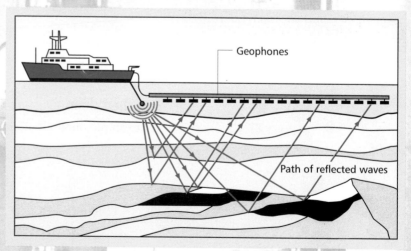

A seismic survey

have become possible. One useful technique is directional drilling. An oil well can be drilled vertically downwards and then the hole can be turned to the horizontal so that more of a deposit can be reached from a single 'parent' well.

In this chapter we will be looking at:
- formulae, naming and isomerism of alkanes
- physical properties of alkanes
- chemical reactions of alkanes
- sources and uses of alkanes

Introduction

Alkanes are saturated hydrocarbons, i.e. they contain only carbon–hydrogen and carbon–carbon single bonds. They may occur as unbranched chains, branched chains and rings. They are among the least reactive organic compounds. Alkanes are the major constituents of both crude oil and natural gas. They are used as fuels, lubricants and as starting materials for a vast range of other compounds and are thus compounds of enormous economic importance. The ups and downs in the price of crude oil have significant economic and political impact.

CONCEPT CHECKPOINTS

The following basic ideas are used in this chapter. You may revise some of these topics elsewhere in the book.
- different types of formulae used in organic chemistry (section 18.3)
- the IUPAC naming system (section 18.4)
- bond energy and polarity (section 18.8)
- radicals as reactive species with unpaired electrons (18.8)

Hint: Unbranched chains are often called 'straight' chains. That is a misnomer: the 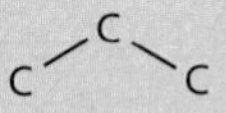

angle is 109.5°, so the chains are far from straight. Also, as there is free rotation about C—C bonds the chains can twist (see Figure 19.1).

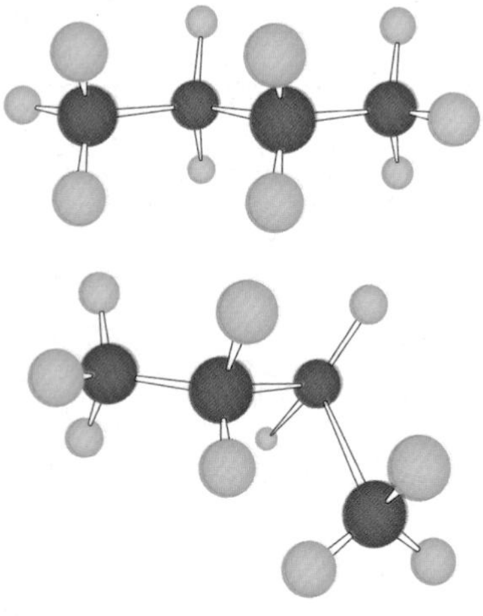

Figure 19.1 A butane molecule can twist. The different forms are called **conformations**

19.1 Formulae, naming and structure

Formulae

Alkanes exist as unbranched chains, branched chains and rings.

Unbranched chain

For example, butane:

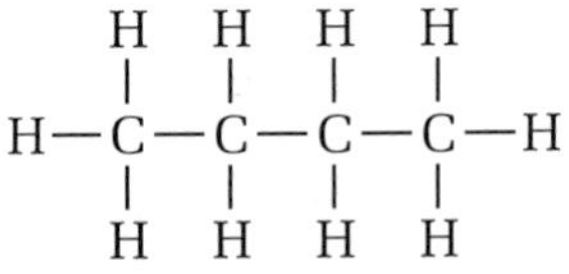

displayed

$CH_3CH_2CH_2CH_3$

shorthand

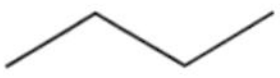

skeletal

Branched chain

For example, methylbutane:

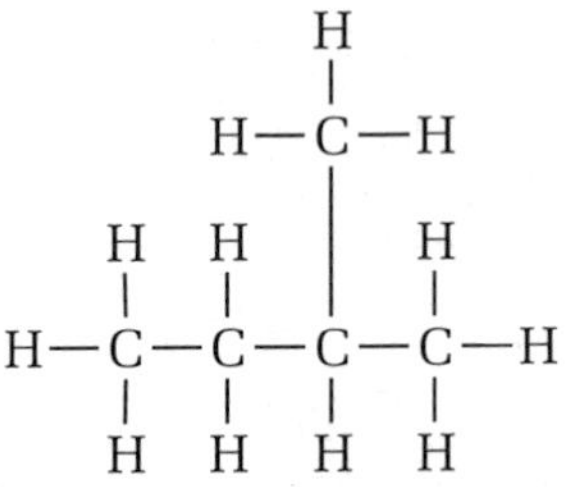

displayed

$CH_3CH_2CH(CH_3)CH_3$

shorthand

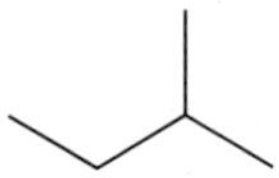

skeletal

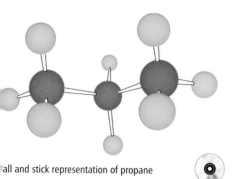

all and stick representation of propane

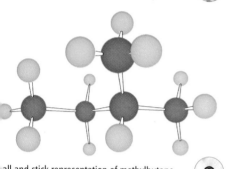

all and stick representation of methylbutane

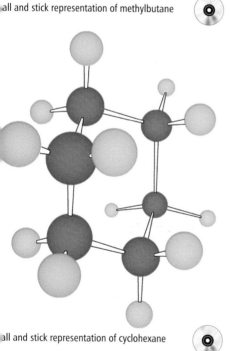

all and stick representation of cyclohexane

able 19.1 Names of the first twelve alkanes

Name	Formula
methane	CH_4
ethane	C_2H_6
propane	C_3H_8
butane	C_4H_{10}
pentane	C_5H_{12}
hexane	C_6H_{14}
heptane	C_7H_{16}
octane	C_8H_{18}
nonane	C_9H_{20}
decane	$C_{10}H_{22}$
undecane	$C_{11}H_{24}$
dodecane	$C_{12}H_{26}$

Rings

For example, cyclohexane:

C_6H_{12}

shorthand

displayed

skeletal

The general molecular formula of chain alkanes, both branched and unbranched, is C_nH_{2n+2}, as each carbon has two hydrogens, except the two end ones which have three. A branch has an extra end hydrogen atom but one less at the branch point. Ring alkanes have the general molecular formula C_nH_{2n} as the 'end' hydrogens are not required.

Naming

The names of the first twelve unbranched alkanes are given in **Table 19.1**. Their names are derived from the root, indicating the number of carbon atoms, and the suffix -ane, denoting an alkane.

When naming branched chains, first identify the longest unbranched chain. This gives the root name. Then the branches or **side chains** are named as prefixes according to their length, e.g. methyl-, ethyl-, propyl-, etc.

Examples

1.

The longest unbranched chain (in red) is five carbons, so the molecule is named as a derivative of pentane. The only side chain has one carbon, so it is methyl-. It is attached at carbon number 3, so the full name is 3-methylpentane. The number 3 is the **locant**.

2.

At first sight, you might be tempted to call this molecule 2-ethylbutane, because of the way the two-dimensional displayed formula has been drawn, but the longest unbranched chain (in

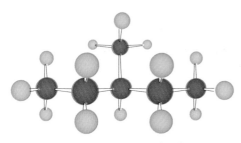

Figure 19.2 Ball and stick representation of 3-methylpentane

red) is five carbons, so the root is pentane. A one-carbon chain is attached at the third carbon, so it too is 3-methylpentane. **Figure 19.2** is a better representation of the molecule.

3.

is 4-ethyl-3-methyloctane as the side chains are listed in alphabetical order rather than in numerical order of their locants.

Rings

Rings are given the prefix cyclo-, so:

cyclopropane

or

cyclobutane

methylcyclohexane

or

1,2-dimethylcyclohexane

or

Hexane has five isomers. Can you name them?

19.2 Isomerism

Methane, ethane and propane have no isomers but butane and longer-chain alkanes have chain branching isomers.

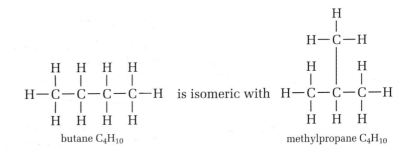

is isomeric with

butane C_4H_{10}

methylpropane C_4H_{10}

Answer: Hexane, 2-methylpentane, 3-methylpentane, 2,3-dimethylbutane, 2,2-dimethylbutane

$$
\begin{array}{c}
\;\;\;\;\text{H}\;\;\;\text{H}\;\;\;\text{H}\;\;\;\text{H}\;\;\;\text{H}\\
\;\;\;\;|\;\;\;\;\;|\;\;\;\;\;|\;\;\;\;\;|\;\;\;\;\;|\\
\text{H}-\text{C}-\text{C}-\text{C}-\text{C}-\text{C}-\text{H}\\
\;\;\;\;|\;\;\;\;\;|\;\;\;\;\;|\;\;\;\;\;|\;\;\;\;\;|\\
\;\;\;\;\text{H}\;\;\;\text{H}\;\;\;\text{H}\;\;\;\text{H}\;\;\;\text{H}
\end{array}
$$

pentane   has three isomers:

methylbutane   and   2,2-dimethylpropane

19.3 Physical properties

Alkanes are essentially non-polar so that the intermolecular forces between them are van der Waals forces only. Thus the shorter chains are gases at room temperature. Pentane is a volatile liquid $(T_b = 309\ \text{K})$. At a chain length of around 18 carbons, the alkanes become solids at room temperature. The solids have a waxy feel. Candle wax is a mixture of moderately long-chain alkanes, and polythene (despite its name) is a very long-chain *alkane*.

Alkanes are insoluble in water but mix with other relatively non-polar liquids.

Camping gas is a mixture of propane and butane. Polar expeditions use special gas mixtures with a higher proportion of propane, because butane liquefies at 273 K (−1 °C)

19.4 Reactions of alkanes

Alkanes are relatively inert, and do not react with acids, bases, oxidising and reducing agents, nucleophiles, electrophiles or polar reagents in general. In fact, alkanes have only three significant reactions.

Combustion

Alkanes will burn in a plentiful supply of oxygen to give carbon dioxide and water.

For example, propane:

$$
\text{C}_3\text{H}_8(\text{g}) + 5\text{O}_2(\text{g}) \longrightarrow 3\text{CO}_2(\text{g}) + 4\text{H}_2\text{O}(\text{l}) \qquad \Delta H = -2219\ \text{kJ}\,\text{mol}^{-1}
$$

The enthalpies of combustion are important, because most of the shorter-chain alkanes are used as fuels: for example, methane

The effect of increasing chain length on the physical properties of alkanes

The air in this balloon is kept hot by the combustion of short-chain hydrocarbon gases

(natural or 'North Sea' gas), propane ('camping' gas), butane ('Calor' gas), petrol (a mixture of hydrocarbons of approximate chain length C_8), paraffin (a mixture of hydrocarbons of chain lengths C_{10} to C_{18}).

In a limited supply of oxygen, carbon monoxide is formed. For example:

$$C_3H_8(g) + 3\tfrac{1}{2}O_2(g) \longrightarrow 3CO(g) + 4H_2O(l)$$

As carbon monoxide is poisonous, care must be taken in the design of gas burners to ensure complete combustion. For the same reason, all gas-burning appliances should be adequately ventilated.

With even less oxygen available, carbon is deposited as soot. You will notice this if you heat a test tube using a Bunsen with its air-hole closed. Soot is also formed in the exhaust pipes of cars whose engines have been running on an over-rich mixture, for example with the choke left out.

Although combustion reactions are important economically, they are of no use for making new carbon compounds because they result in the destruction of the entire carbon chain.

Cracking

This reaction involves heating alkanes to a high temperature (often with a catalyst – 'cat'cracking). Carbon–carbon bonds are broken and two or more shorter chains are produced. As there are insufficient hydrogen atoms to produce two alkanes, one of the new chains must have a carbon–carbon double bond. For example:

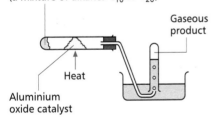

Mineral wool soaked in light paraffin (a mixture of alkanes C_{10} to C_{20})

Gaseous product

Heat

Aluminium oxide catalyst

Figure 19.3 Laboratory cracking of alkanes

Any number of carbon–carbon bonds may break and the chain does not necessarily break in the middle. In the laboratory, cracking may be carried out in the apparatus shown in **Figure 19.3**, using lumps of aluminium oxide as a catalyst.

The products are mostly gases, showing that they have chain lengths of less than C_5 and the mixture decolourises bromine solution, showing that it contains alkenes.

Reaction with halogens

Alkanes do not react with halogens in the dark at room temperature, but react when irradiated with ultraviolet light. For example, a mixture of hexane and a little liquid bromine retains the colour of bromine in the dark, but the bromine colour is rapidly lost if the mixture is exposed to bright sunlight or a photoflood lamp. Fumes of hydrogen bromide are produced, suggesting that a substitution reaction has taken place: the hydrogen in the hydrogen bromide must have come from the alkane.

Hint: The test for hydrogen bromide is to blow the fumes from a bottle of ammonia over the mouth of the test tube. White fumes of ammonium bromide are formed. This test would also give a positive result for other hydrogen halides.

The overall reaction is:

$$C_6H_{14}(l) \quad + \quad Br_2(l) \quad \longrightarrow \quad C_6H_{13}Br(l) \quad + \quad HBr(g)$$

hexane   bromine   bromohexane   hydrogen bromide

It is called a **radical substitution** and the bromohexane is one of a class of compounds called haloalkanes.

Chain reactions

Hint: There are several possible isomers of bromohexane

The mechanism of the above reaction is of considerable interest. It is an example of a **chain reaction** and takes place in three stages: **initiation**, **propagation** and **termination**. We will look at the similar reaction of bromine and methane for simplicity.

The first step involves the absorption of a single quantum of ultraviolet light (of frequency approximately 1×10^{15} s^{-1}) by a bromine molecule. The energy of such a quantum is greater than the Br—Br bond energy of 193 kJ mol^{-1}, so the bond will break. As the two atoms in the bond are identical, it will break homolytically, i.e. one electron going to each bromine, resulting in two separate bromine atoms. These each have an unpaired electron and are called **radicals.** They are written Br• to stress the unpaired electron.

Hint: The symbol $h\nu$ is often used above the reaction arrow to indicate the absorption of light. For example:

$$\text{Br—Br} \xrightarrow{h\nu} 2\text{Br•}$$

Initiation

The first or **initiation** step of the reaction is:

$$\text{Br—Br} \xrightarrow{\text{UV light}} 2\text{Br•}$$

Propagation

Radicals (sometimes called free radicals) are highly reactive and remove a hydrogen atom from methane forming hydrogen bromide and a methyl radical.

$$\text{Br•} + \text{CH}_4 \longrightarrow \text{HBr} + \text{•CH}_3$$

The resulting methyl radical is also reactive and can react with a bromine molecule.

$$\text{•CH}_3 + \text{Br}_2 \longrightarrow \text{CH}_3\text{Br} + \text{Br•}$$

FURTHER FOCUS

The energy of light quanta

The energy of a quantum of electromagnetic radiation is given by:

$$E = h\nu$$

where h is the Planck constant, 6.6×10^{-34} J s, and ν the frequency of the radiation.

For a typical quantum of ultraviolet light $\nu = 1 \times 10^{15}$ s^{-1}, so

$$E = 6.6 \times 10^{-34} \times 10^{15} = 6.6 \times 10^{-19} \text{ J}$$

Hint: Hint: 6×10^{23} (the Avogadro constant) is the number of entities in a mole.

For 1 mole of quanta the total energy is:

$$6.6 \times 10^{-19} \times 6 \times 10^{23} = 396\,000 \text{ J mol}^{-1}$$
$$= 396 \text{ kJ mol}^{-1}$$

i.e. about 400 kJ mol^{-1}

For comparison, visible light has a typical frequency of 1×10^{14} s^{-1} and infra-red (heat) radiation 1×10^{13} s^{-1}. So the energy of their quanta are respectively 40 and 4 kJ mol^{-1}. Typical covalent bond energies are around 300 kJ mol^{-1}, so visible and infra-red radiations are unable to break covalent bonds while ultraviolet light can.

Each of the above steps results in a stable product and a reactive radical. After the two steps the original Br• radical remains. The steps can be repeated over and over again and are therefore called **propagation** steps. It is believed that such steps take place thousands of times before the radicals are destroyed.

Termination

This can happen in the following ways:

$$Br\cdot + Br\cdot \longrightarrow Br_2$$
$$\cdot CH_3 + \cdot CH_3 \longrightarrow C_2H_6$$
$$Br\cdot + \cdot CH_3 \longrightarrow CH_3Br$$

These are collectively called **termination** steps.

Other products are possible as well as the main ones, bromomethane and hydrogen bromide. The equations above show that some ethane is produced at the termination stage.

Another possible propagation step is that a bromine radical can react with some bromomethane which has already been formed:

$$CH_3Br + Br\cdot \longrightarrow \cdot CH_2Br + HBr$$

followed by

$$\cdot CH_2Br + Br_2 \longrightarrow CH_2Br_2 + Br\cdot$$

With more complex alkanes such as hexane, many isomers may be produced because the Br• radical is equally likely to remove any of the hydrogen atoms. Similar reactions occur without light at high temperatures. Chain reactions are of relatively little practical importance because they tend to produce a complex mixture of products.

> **Q** Which of the following are possible products: CHBr₃, CBr₄, CH₃CH₂Br?

19.5 Sources of alkanes

Although a number of methods exist for preparing alkanes in the laboratory, they are rarely used as alkanes are readily available from the distillation of crude oil.

Crude oil and natural gas

Both these valuable sources of organic chemicals have been produced by the breakdown of plant and animal remains, brought about over many years by high pressures and temperatures. In general, plant remains produce gas and animal (plankton) remains give oil.

Crude oil varies considerably in composition depending on its source. As well as alkanes, both unbranched and branched, it may contain aromatic compounds (see Chapter 32), and also oxygen-, nitrogen- and sulphur-containing compounds. The last mentioned are particularly troublesome, producing acidic sulphur dioxide when burned.

Crude oil is first separated into fractions by fractional distillation. The composition of a typical North Sea crude oil is given in **Table 19.2**.

Answer: All of them

Table 19.2 The composition of a typical North Sea crude oil

Product	Gases	Petrol	Naphtha	Kerosene	Gas oil	Fuel oil and wax
Approximate boiling temperature/K	310	310–450	400–490	430–523	590–620	above 620
Chain length	1–5	5–10	8–12	11–16	16–24	25+
Percentage present	2	8	10	14	21	45

19.6 Economic importance of alkanes

Fractional distillation of crude oil

Crude oil is separated into fractions by distillation in cylindrical towers typically 8 m in diameter and 40 m high

Crude oil is little use as it is. The first step to converting it into useful products is fractional distillation, which separates the mixture into fractions: groups of hydrocarbons of similar chain length and therefore similar properties. This is done by heating the crude oil in a furnace so that it vaporises. The vapours pass into a tower, which is cooler at the top than at the bottom. They pass up the tower via a series of trays containing bubble caps and eventually condense to liquid when they arrive at a tray that is sufficiently cool. The liquid that condenses on each tray is piped off separately. Shorter-chain hydrocarbons have lower boiling temperatures so the higher the tray is up the tower, the shorter the chain lengths that collect there (see **Figure 19.4**).

A very high boiling temperature fraction called the **residue** collects at the base of the column while gases are taken from the very top. Different fractions have different uses. The residue can be used for road tar or can be redistilled at reduced pressure, while the refinery gases are often used as fuel in the plant for heating the furnace.

Industrial cracking

Crude oils from different sources have different percentages of each fraction. Unfortunately, the availability of each fraction rarely meets the demand. The major demand is for the petrol and naphtha fractions while longer-chain fractions are used less.

To rectify this mismatch, many of the longer-chain fractions are **cracked**. This has two useful results. Firstly, shorter chains are produced, and secondly, some of the products are alkenes. These are more reactive than alkanes and therefore more suitable for use as **chemical feedstock** for conversion to other compounds.

Different cracking processes can be used. In **steam cracking** the naphtha or gas oil is mixed with steam and passed through a furnace at 1100 K for 0.2 seconds. A typical mixture obtained from the steam cracking of naphtha is shown in **Table 19.3**.

Catalytic cracking takes place at a lower temperature (approximately 800 K) using a surface catalyst consisting of silicon dioxide and aluminium oxide.

Table 19.3 A typical composition of the mixture obtained from the steam cracking of naphtha

Component	Percentage
hydrogen	1
methane	15
ethane	25
propane	16
butane	5
buta-1,3-diene	5
petrol	28
fuel oil	4

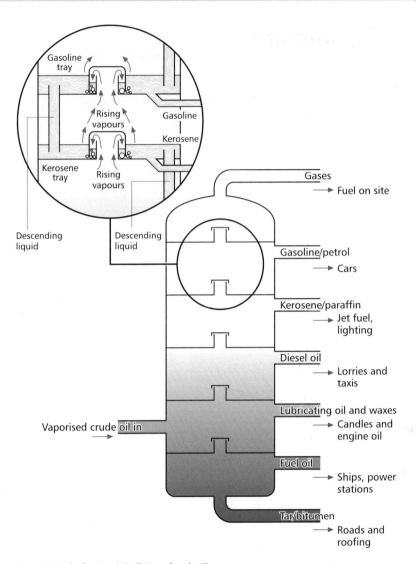

Figure 19.4 The fractional distillation of crude oil

Reforming

Straight chain alkanes are relatively poor motor fuels. They cause knocking in the engine by detonating rapidly rather than burning steadily. Branched chains are much better in this respect. **Reforming** is a process where straight chain alkanes are heated under pressure with a platinum catalyst. The chains break up and reform as branched chain molecules. For example:

octane   2,2,4-trimethylpentane
                          (iso-octane)

19.7 Summary

- Alkanes are saturated hydrocarbons of general formula C_nH_{2n+2}.

- Alkanes may exist as unbranched chains, branched chains or rings.

- Alkanes are insoluble in water and polar solvents.

- At room temperature the C_1–C_4 alkanes are gases.

- At room temperature the C_5–C_{17} alkanes are liquids.

- At room temperature the C_{18} and upward alkanes are solids.

- Alkanes have only three significant reactions: combustion, cracking and radical substitution.

- Complete combustion produces carbon dioxide and water.

- Incomplete combustion produces carbon monoxide or carbon and water.

- Cracking produces shorter-chain alkanes and alkenes.

- Radical substitution reactions with halogens are initiated by ultraviolet light.

- They produce haloalkanes.

- Radical substitution reactions have three stages:
  - initiation where radicals are formed
  - propagation where products are formed and the radicals are regenerated
  - termination where radicals are removed.

- Mixtures of alkanes are found in natural gas and crude oil.

- To separate useful components, crude oil is fractionally distilled.

- To reduce the chain lengths and produce alkenes, longer-chain fractions are cracked.

- To produce branched chains which are more suitable for petrol, straight-chain alkanes may be reformed.

19.8 Practice questions

1. Name the following:

(a) 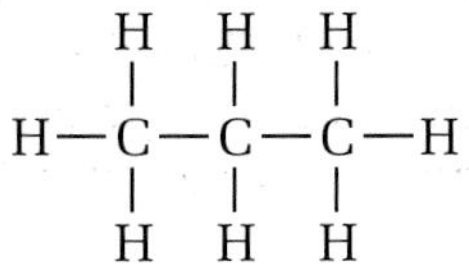
```
      H   H   H
      |   |   |
  H — C — C — C — H
      |   |   |
      H   H   H
```

(c) [pentagon shape]

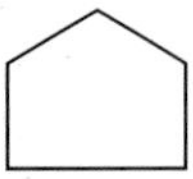

(b) 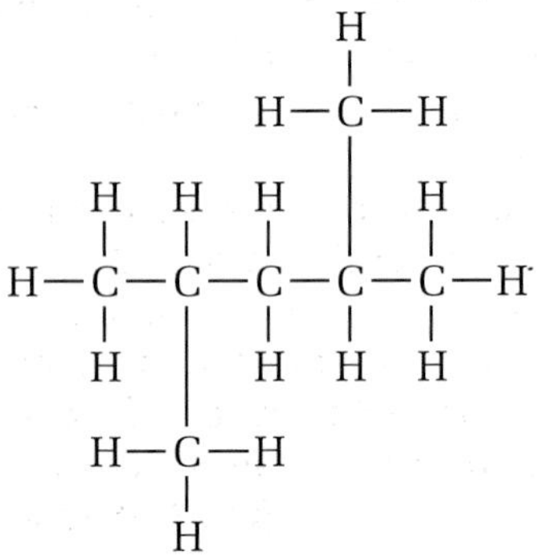
```
                  H
                  |
              H — C — H
                  |
  H   H   H       H
  |   |   |       |
H—C — C — C — C — C — H
  |   |   |   |   |
  H   |   H   H   H
      |
      H — C — H
          |
          H
```

(d)  [hexagon shape]

2. Draw the displayed structural formula of:
   (a) 2-methylpentane,
   (b) 1,1-dimethylcyclohexane,
   (c) 3-ethyl-4-methylheptane,
   (d) cyclooctane

3. Write a balanced equation for the complete combustion of hexane.

4. Which of the following is not a likely product of the reaction of chlorine with hexane in ultraviolet light: 1-chlorohexane, 2-chlorohexane, 2,2-dichlorohexane, dodecane, hex-1-ene?

5. Calculate the lowest frequency of ultraviolet light which has enough energy to break a Cl—Cl bond (bond energy = 243 kJ mol^{-1}).

6. A sample of hexane was cracked in the apparatus shown in Figure 19.3. A sample of 50 cm^3 of gas was produced. The gas decolourised 4 cm^3 of a 0.25 mol dm^{-3} solution of bromine. What percentage of alkene was produced?

7. A hydrocarbon contains 85.7% carbon and 14.3% hydrogen and has a relative molecular mass of 56.
   (a) What is the empirical formula?
   (b) What is its molecular formula?
   (c) The hydrocarbon does not decolourise bromine water. What is its structure?

19.9 Examination questions

1. Butane, C_4H_{10}, can be used as a fuel. Here are some data about butane:

   Boiling point, 0 °C;
   Standard enthalpy change of combustion,
   $\Delta H^{\ominus}_{c,298} = -2880$ kJ mol^{-1}.

   (a) To what homologous series does butane belong?
   (b) Butane has one structural isomer.
       (i) Say what you understand by the term *structural isomer*.
       (ii) Draw the full structural formula of the structural isomer of butane and name it.
   (c) All the H—C—H bonds in butane have the same angle in the three-dimensional molecule. State, and explain, the value of this angle.
   (d) 'The standard enthalpy change of combustion of the isomer in part (b) will be very similar to that of butane itself as all the bonds are the same.'
       Say whether or not this statement is correct and explain why.

   [O & C (Salters) 1997, part specimen]

2. (a) Butane reacts with chlorine, in a free radical chain reaction, to form 1-chlorobutane as one of the products. The reaction takes place in a number of steps:

   Step 1 Cl—Cl $\longrightarrow$ Cl• + Cl•   Initiation
   Step 2 Cl• + CH$_3$CH$_2$CH$_2$CH$_3$
               $\longrightarrow$ CH$_3$CH$_2$CH$_2$ĊH$_2$ + HCl
   Step 3 CH$_3$CH$_2$CH$_2$ĊH$_2$ + Cl$_2$
               $\longrightarrow$ CH$_3$CH$_2$CH$_2$CH$_2$Cl + Cl•
   Step 4 CH$_3$CH$_2$CH$_2$ĊH$_2$ + Cl•
               $\longrightarrow$ CH$_3$CH$_2$CH$_2$CH$_2$Cl   Termination

       (i) What condition is needed to promote **Step 1**?
       (ii) What type of bond breaking occurs in **Step 1**?
       (iii) Classify the type of reaction step occurring in **Steps 2** and **3**.
       (iv) Suggest an equation for another possible chain termination step.
       (v) Give one other example of a reaction with a free radical chain mechanism.

   [London (Nuffield) 1997, part question]

3. The main processes which are used in oil refineries to make petrol are:

isomerisation

e.g. $CH_3CH_2CH_2CH_2CH_3 \longrightarrow CH_3CH(CH_3)CH_2CH_3$
       A   B

cracking

e.g. $CH_3(CH_2)_{10}CH_3$
       C

   $\longrightarrow CH_3CH(CH_3)CH_2CH(CH_3)CH_3 +$
                    D

   $CH_2{=}C(CH_3)CH_2CH_3$
              E

reforming

e.g. $C_6H_{12} \longrightarrow C_6H_6$
       F   G

(a) One of these equations does not balance. Rewrite the full balanced equation.

(b) (i) Name compound **B**.
    (ii) Draw the full structural formula for compound **D**.

(iii) Draw the skeletal formula for compound **E**.

(c) Compound **C** would not be at all efficient as an ingredient of petrol. Suggest why this is so.

(d) Explain, in terms of the structures of the molecules involved, why the isomerisation reaction shown above results in petrol which is better for high compression engines.

(e) Thermal cracking can be carried out in the laboratory.
    (i) Draw a labelled diagram of an apparatus you would use to crack a sample of a liquid hydrocarbon and collect (separately) the two products of the reaction.
    (ii) The apparatus you have designed would probably not crack compound **C** specifically to compounds **D** and **E**. Suggest **two** ways in which industrial chemists attempt to control the cracking reaction to make it more specific.

[O & C (Salters) 1997]

20 Alkenes

Chance favours the prepared mind

Serendipity is the art of making happy discoveries by chance. It can certainly be applied to the discovery of poly(tetrafluoroethene), better known as PTFE or Teflon, by Roy Plunkett in the 1930s. Plunkett and his research team worked for the American chemical giant Du Pont investigating refrigerants, the liquids used for cooling fridges. He was working with a cylinder of the gas tetrafluoroethene when, for no apparent reason, the gas flow stopped. Plunkett did as most of us would do and poked the pipework to remove any blockage but to no avail. He then weighed the cylinder – the weight was unchanged – and shook it: it rattled. So nothing had escaped and the cylinder now contained a solid. Eventually he had to saw the cylinder open to examine its contents which turned out to be a whitish solid. He eventually reasoned that the small molecules of tetrafluoroethene gas must have linked together – polymerised – to form a much bigger molecule of a solid.

Unknowingly, Plunkett had caught a big fish. Teflon, to give it its trade name, is one of the most important polymeric materials. It is chemically very inert, an excellent electrical insulator, slippery and can withstand extremes of temperature – both high and low. It is probably best known as the coating for non-stick pans but it has many other uses and it has been said that without it, the US manned space program would have failed. It was used for everything from spacesuits to the bags used to hold moon rock.

It is interesting to contrast the accidental discovery of Teflon with the well-planned and costly programme which resulted in the discovery of Nylon (see Chapter 35). Both materials were discovered at about the same time and in the same company but in very different ways.

Roy Plunkett – discoverer of Teflon

A Teflon-coated pan

Teflon shears

Introduction

Alkenes are **unsaturated** hydrocarbons. They have one or more carbon–carbon double bonds. This makes them more reactive than alkanes and makes their chemistry more interesting and varied. The reactivity of the alkenes and their availability from cracking makes them attractive to industrial chemists. Ethene, the simplest alkene, is the basic building block for a large range of products, including the polymers polythene, PVC and polystyrene, as well as products like antifreeze, paints and Terylene fabrics.

CONCEPT CHECKPOINTS

The following basic ideas are used in this chapter. You may revise some of these topics elsewhere in the book.
- different types of formulae used in organic chemistry (section 18.3)
- the IUPAC naming system (section 18.4)
- bond energy and polarity (section 18.8)
- electrophiles: reagents that attack electron-rich areas (18.8)

Q What is the general formula for the homologous series of alkenes containing two double bonds?

20.1 Formulae, naming and structure of alkenes

Formulae

Alkenes contain at least one carbon–carbon double bond. There is therefore no alkene with only one carbon atom. The homologous series of alkenes with one double bond has the general formula C_nH_{2n}.

Naming

The simplest alkene is ethene,

$$\begin{array}{c} H \\ \diagdown \\ C=C \\ \diagup \quad \diagdown \\ H \quad\quad H \end{array}$$

, followed by

propene,

$$H-\underset{\underset{H}{|}}{\overset{\overset{H}{|}}{C}}-C=\underset{H}{\overset{H}{C}}$$

Longer chains than propene can form three different types of isomers:

- those with different positioning of the double bond
- *cis–trans*-isomers
- chain-branching isomers

In

$$\begin{array}{c} H \\ \diagdown \\ C=C-\underset{\underset{H}{|}}{\overset{\overset{H}{|}}{C}}-\underset{\underset{H}{|}}{\overset{\overset{H}{|}}{C}}-H \\ \diagup \\ H \end{array}$$

, the double bond is between carbons

1 and 2. It is named but-1-ene rather than but-2-ene. The smaller number is always used.

$$H-\underset{\underset{H}{|}}{\overset{\overset{H}{|}}{C}}-C=C-\underset{\underset{H}{|}}{\overset{\overset{H}{|}}{C}}-H$$

is but-2-ene.

Answer: C_nH_{2n-2}

Hint: The geometry of carbon atoms forming a double and two single bonds is trigonal planar, as there are three groups of electrons around them (see section 9.2).

But-2-ene itself exists as two different isomers. We can see that if the molecule is drawn out with the correct bond angles, there are *cis*- and *trans*- isomers.

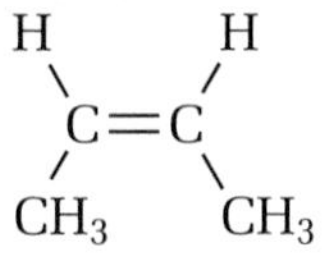

cis-but-2-ene

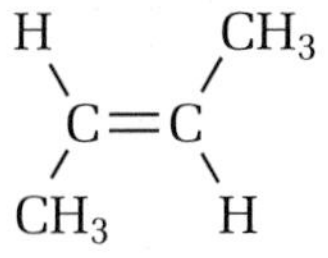

trans-but-2-ene

When naming branched chain alkenes we need to locate the position of the double bond and of the side chains.

So

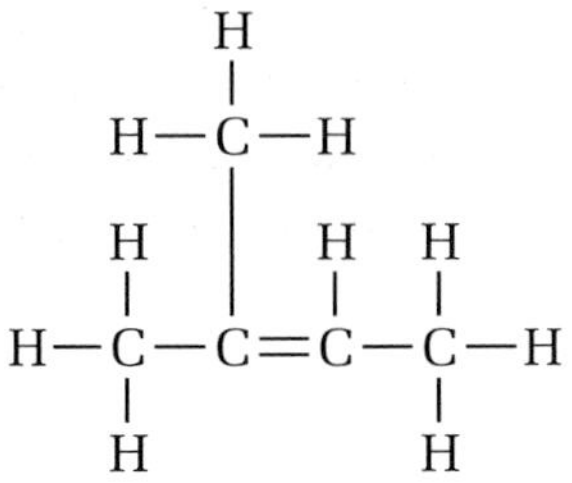

is 2-methylbut-2-ene

and

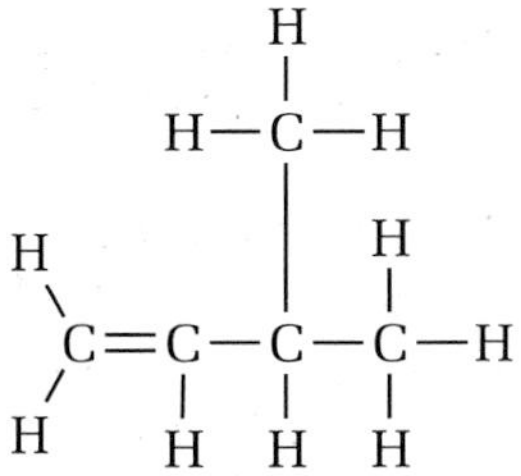

is 3-methylbut-1-ene.

Compounds with more than one double bond are named using di-, tri-, etc. to indicate the number of double bonds as well as locants to show where they are.

So

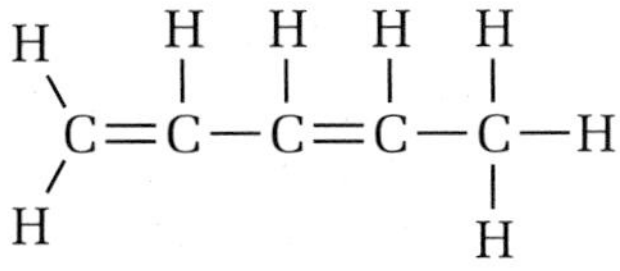

is penta-1,3-diene

Q Work out whether penta-1,3-diene has *cis*- and *trans*- isomers

The shape of alkenes

The carbon atoms that form the double bond in ethene and the four hydrogen atoms to which they are bonded are all in the same plane. There are three groups of electrons around each carbon atom and so the geometry around each carbon atom is trigonal planar. The H—C—H bond angles are about 118°, less than 120°, because the four electrons in the carbon–carbon double bond repel more than the pairs of electrons in the carbon–hydrogen single bonds.

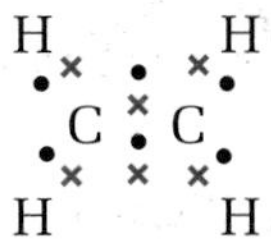

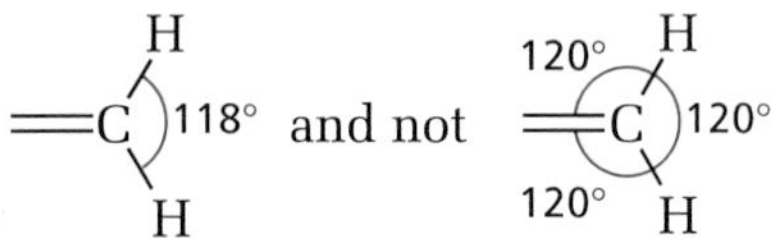

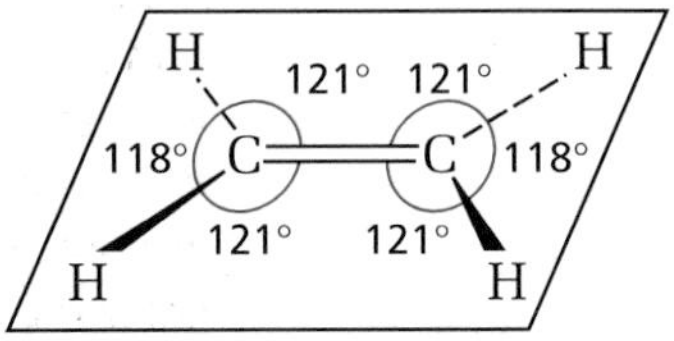

Answer: Yes it does. The substituents on either side of the double bond between carbon 3 and carbon 4 may be *cis* or *trans*.

No rotation is possible about the double bond. This is made clear if we consider the orbitals that make up the double bond: a σ and a π. Rotation of the carbons would break the σ bond. An orbital picture of the bonding is shown in **Figure 20.1** and the photograph.

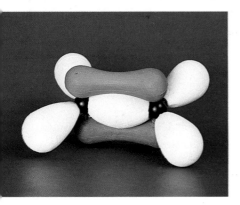

Model of ethene showing the orbitals
In fact, the two carbon atoms are sp² hybridised, see the box 'A more sophisticated picture', Chapter 19

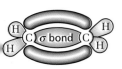

π bond

Figure 20.1 The bonding of ethene

Table 20.1 Melting and boiling temperatures of some alkenes

Alkene	T_m/K	T_b/K
ethene	104	169
propene	88	226
but-1-ene	88	268
cyclohexene	170	357

20.2 Physical properties of alkenes

The double bond has little effect on the intermolecular forces which act *between* the molecules, so their physical properties are very similar to those of the alkanes in terms of melting and boiling temperatures and poor solubility in water. **Table 20.1** shows the melting and boiling temperatures of some alkenes.

20.3 Reactivity of alkenes

The difference between alkenes and alkanes is that alkenes have a carbon–carbon double bond. The bond energies for C—C and C=C are respectively 347 kJ mol^{-1} and 612 kJ mol^{-1} so that at first sight we might expect alkenes to be less reactive than alkanes. This is not so for three reasons:

Firstly, a double bond consists of a σ bond plus a π bond (see section 18.8). The σ bond is the same as in C—C, so the π bond must have an energy of 612 − 347 = 265 kJ mol^{-1}. So it is relatively easy to break the π part of carbon–carbon double bonds, while the σ part remains intact. This happens in most reactions of C=C and it is rare for the carbon chain to actually break in two when alkenes react.

Secondly, the C=C forms an electron-rich area in a molecule, which can be easily attacked by positively charged reagents (**electrophiles**, see section 18.8).

Thirdly, if the π part of the double bond is broken, each of the carbon atoms is left capable of forming a new bond. This allows addition reactions to take place.

So the dominant feature of the chemistry of alkenes is **electrophilic addition** reactions.

20.4 Reactions of alkenes

Combustion

All alkenes will burn in air. Alkenes with more than one double bond produce a noticeably sooty flame. This is because they have a greater percentage of carbon than alkanes and there may be insufficient air to burn all the carbon. Unburnt carbon is left behind as soot. Unlike alkanes, alkenes are not normally burnt as fuels as their reactivity makes them too useful for other purposes.

Q Write the balanced equation for the complete combustion of propene.

You should be able to construct balanced equations for complete combustion of any of the alkenes.

$$\underset{\substack{\text{ethene}}}{\overset{\substack{H \\ \diagdown \\ C=C \\ \diagup \quad \diagdown \\ H \qquad H}}{}} \text{(g)} + \underset{\substack{\text{oxygen}}}{3O_2\text{(g)}} \longrightarrow \underset{\substack{\text{carbon} \\ \text{dioxide}}}{2CO_2\text{(g)}} + \underset{\substack{\text{water}}}{2H_2O\text{(l)}}$$

Reaction of alkenes with halogens

Alkenes react rapidly with chlorine gas or with solutions of bromine or iodine, in an organic solvent, to give dihaloalkanes. Unlike the reaction of alkanes with halogens, ultraviolet light is not required.

$$\overset{\substack{H \qquad H \\ \diagdown \qquad \diagup \\ C=C \\ \diagup \qquad \diagdown \\ H \qquad H}}{} + X_2 \longrightarrow \overset{\substack{H \quad H \\ | \quad | \\ H-C-C-H \\ | \quad | \\ X \quad X}}{}$$

This is an addition reaction. The decolourising of a bromine solution is often used as a test for the presence of carbon–carbon multiple bonds. Both alkenes and alkynes will decolourise bromine solutions.

The fact that the reaction can take place in the dark rules out a radical mechanism such as occurs in the reaction of halogens with alkanes. Further clues to the mechanism are:

● if bromine dissolved in water is reacted with ethene, some 2-bromoethan-1-ol is formed
● if the bromine is dissolved in sodium chloride solution some 1-bromo-2-chloroethane is produced.

Hint: Remember that substituents are listed in alphabetical order.

$$\underset{\substack{\text{2-bromoethan-1-ol}}}{\overset{\substack{H \quad H \\ | \quad | \\ H-C-C-H \\ | \quad | \\ OH \quad Br}}{}} \qquad\qquad \underset{\substack{\text{1-bromo-2-chloroethane}}}{\overset{\substack{H \quad H \\ | \quad | \\ H-C-C-H \\ | \quad | \\ Br \quad Cl}}{}}$$

The mechanism is as follows. At any instant, a bromine molecule is likely to have an instantaneous dipole: $Br^{\delta+}$—$Br^{\delta-}$. This is because the electrons are in constant motion and at any moment are unlikely to be distributed exactly symmetrically. An instant later, the dipole could be reversed.

The $\delta+$ end of this dipole is attracted to the electron-rich π bond in the alkene. The π bond attracts the $Br^{\delta+}$ and repels the electrons shared by the two bromine atoms, thus strengthening the dipole.

$$\overset{\substack{H \qquad\qquad H \\ \diagdown \qquad\quad \diagup \\ C=C \\ \diagup \qquad\quad \diagdown \\ H \quad Br_{\delta+} \quad H \\ \quad\; | \; \delta- \\ \quad\; Br}}{}$$

Answer: $C_3H_6\text{(g)} + 4\tfrac{1}{2}O_2\text{(g)} \longrightarrow 3CO_2\text{(g)} + 3H_2O\text{(l)}$

Eventually, two of the electrons from the π bond form a bond with the $Br^{\delta+}$ and the electrons shared by the bromine atoms are repelled away with the $Br^{\delta-}$ to form a Br^- ion. This leaves a positively charged species which is called a **carbocation**. The positive charge on the carbocation is localised on the carbon atom that is not bonded to the bromine because this carbon atom is forming only three bonds (has *six* electrons in its outer shell) and is therefore electron-deficient.

$$H-\underset{\underset{H}{|}}{\overset{\overset{H}{|}}{C}}-\overset{\overset{H}{\diagup}}{\underset{\diagdown}{C}}^{+}\ +\ Br^-$$

a carbocation

The carbocation is rapidly attacked by any negative ion. The only negative ion present in a non-aqueous solution will be the Br^- but in aqueous solution OH^- will be present, as will Cl^- in a solution of sodium chloride.

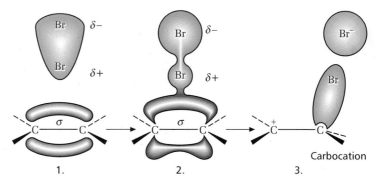

So the addition takes place in two steps:

1. Formation of the carbocation, followed by
2. Rapid reaction with a negative ion.

As the $Br^{\delta+}$—$Br^{\delta-}$ attacks the electron-rich π bond, it is acting as an **electrophile**, so the whole reaction is an **electrophilic addition** reaction. **Figure 20.2** shows the same mechanism in terms of electronic orbitals.

Figure 20.2 Orbitals involved in the reaction of ethene with bromine

Reaction with hydrogen halides

Hydrogen halides, HCl, HBr and HI, add on across the double bond to form haloalkanes. For example:

Q Predict a further product which might be produced if the bromine is dissolved in a solution of sodium iodide.

Answer: 1-Bromo-2-iodoethane

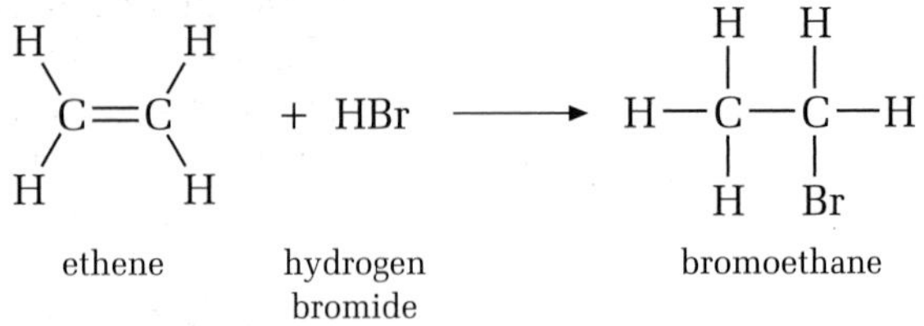

ethene · hydrogen bromide · bromoethane

The reaction is an electrophilic addition and the mechanism is similar to the addition of halogens. In this case the hydrogen halide has a permanent dipole:

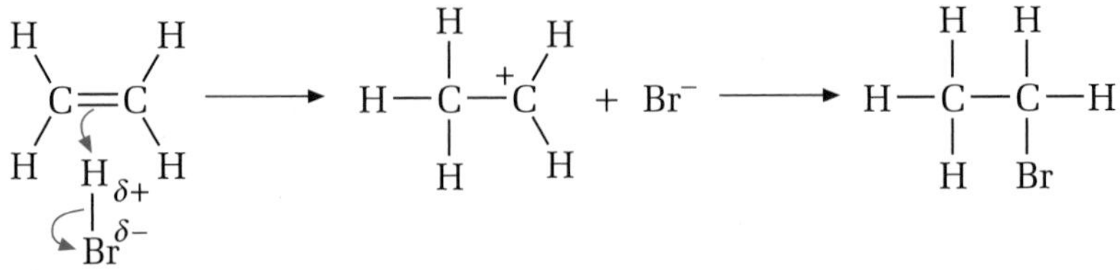

Markovnikov's rule

If hydrogen bromide adds on to ethene, then only one product is possible, bromoethane. With, say, propene there are two possible products, depending on which of the two carbon atoms of the double bond the bromine bonds to:

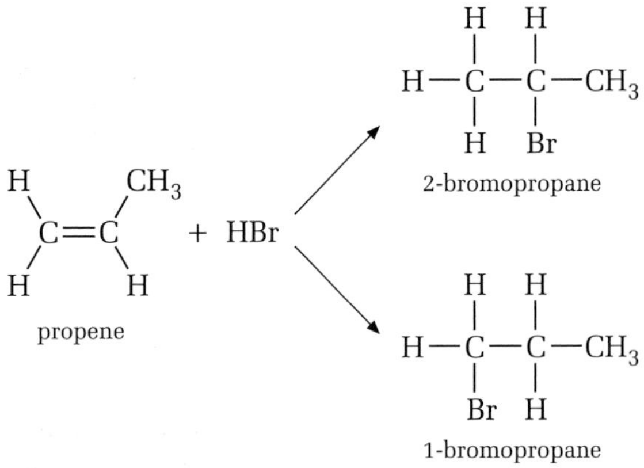

propene · 2-bromopropane · 1-bromopropane

Hint: Markovnikov's rule is sometimes paraphrased 'the rich get richer'.

In fact the product is almost entirely 2-bromopropane. This is an example of **Markovnikov's rule,** which states that when hydrogen halides add onto alkenes the hydrogen adds onto the carbon atom that already has most hydrogens. The reason for this is found in the stability of the intermediate carbocation. Two are possible:

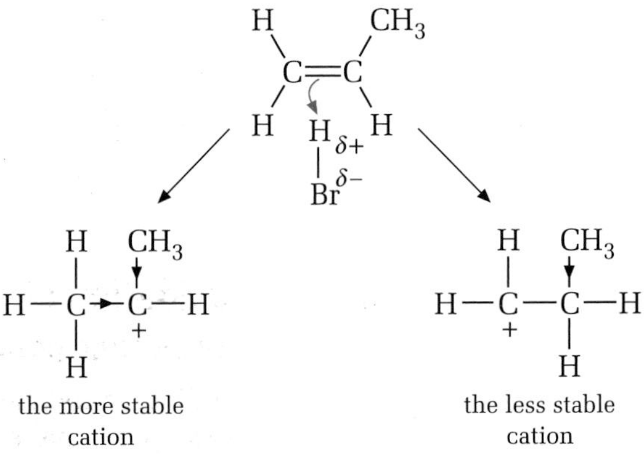

the more stable cation · the less stable cation

In the first of these, the positive charge is stabilised by the tendency of CH_3— to release electrons (the inductive effect, see section 18.8) so this carbocation is favoured and the product we get is the one formed from this, i.e. 2-bromopropane. Other alkyl groups like ethyl-, propyl-, etc. also release electrons.

Reaction with concentrated sulphuric acid

Concentrated sulphuric acid also adds on across the double bond. The reaction occurs at room temperature and is exothermic.

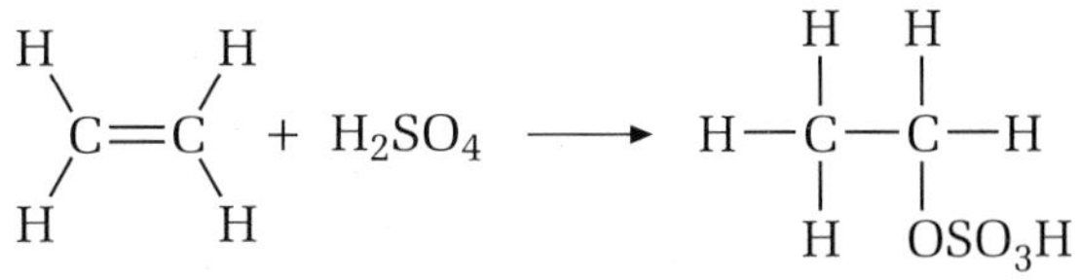

ethene   ethyl hydrogensulphate

On addition of water to the product, an alcohol is formed.

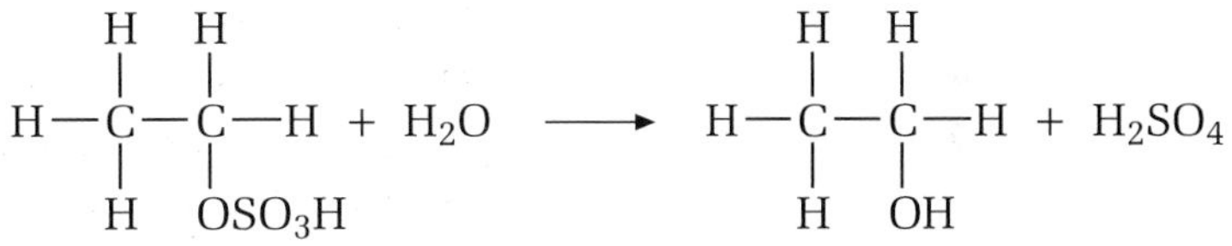

ethyl hydrogensulphate   ethanol

so that the overall effect is to add water across the double bond.

The original reaction with sulphuric acid is another electrophilic addition, the electrophile being the H^+ ion.

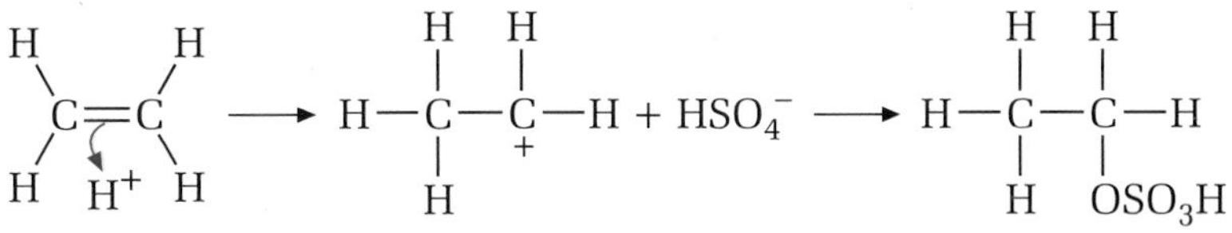

The carbocation formed then reacts rapidly with the negatively charged hydrogensulphate ion.

With an unsymmetrical alkene, such as propene, the carbocation is exactly the same as that found in the reaction with hydrogen bromide, so Markovnikov's rule applies.

In general Markovnikov's rule states that when an unsymmetrical reagent HZ adds across a carbon–carbon double bond, the hydrogen bonds to the carbon atom which already has more hydrogens.

So:

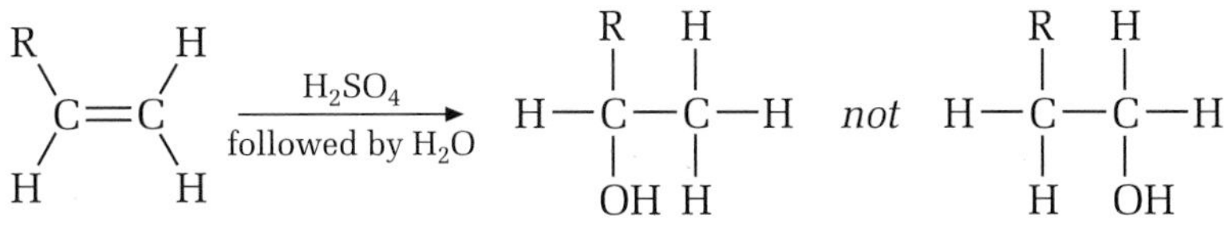

Oxidation of alkenes

By alkaline potassium manganate(VII)

A diol is produced rapidly, the purple colour of the MnO_4^- ion disappears and a precipitate of brown manganese(IV) oxide appears.

This reaction is used as an alternative to the bromine test for multiple bonds. The reaction is believed to proceed through the intermediate shown.

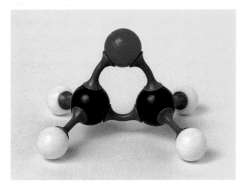

ethene → [intermediate with Mn] → ethane-1,2-diol

Ethane-1,2-diol is also known as ethylene glycol.

By hot, concentrated manganate(VII) ions

By contrast these reagents break the double bond, splitting the alkene into two. By identifying the chain length of the two fragments, it is possible to work out the position of the double bond in a long-chain alkene.

By oxygen

Reaction of ethene with oxygen using a silver catalyst produces epoxyethane.

$$\text{ethane} \xrightarrow[\text{450 K}]{\text{O}_2, \text{Ag catalyst}} \text{epoxyethane}$$

The product is unstable, and therefore very reactive, owing to **ring strain**. The C—C—O bond and C—O—C bond angle *must* both be approximately 60° whereas the normal bond angle would be 109.5°. Epoxyethane reacts with water to form ethane-1,2-diol and this is the industrial method of preparation of this compound, which is used to make polyesters (such as Terylene) and antifreeze.

Epoxyethane can also be made to polymerise forming a polymer

$$-CH_2CH_2-O-CH_2CH_2-O- \text{ etc}$$

This is used in manufacturing detergents, and in plasticisers which are used to improve the flexibility of plastics.

By ozone (trioxygen)

If ozone-enriched oxygen is bubbled through a solution of an alkene, an unstable ozonide is first produced. This then reacts with water to give two carbonyl compounds (these have a C=O, see Chapter 33).

$$C=C + O_3 \longrightarrow \text{an ozonide} \xrightarrow{H_2O} R-C + R'-C$$

an ozonide

If the two carbonyl compounds are identified (by formation of derivatives with Brady's reagent, see section 33.4), then the position

Molecular model of epoxyethane showing bond strain

Q | Write the equation for the reaction of epoxyethane with water.

Answer:

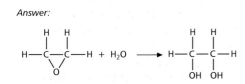

epoxyethane + H₂O → ethane-1,2-diol

of the double bond in the carbon chain of the original alkene can be deduced.

This reaction, called **ozonolysis**, is unusual in that the C=C is completely broken. In the majority of reactions of alkenes, only the π part is broken and the σ bond remains intact.

Addition of hydrogen

Hydrogen is added across double bonds at room conditions using a highly porous nickel catalyst called Raney nickel. Alkanes are produced.

$$\underset{H}{\overset{H}{>}}C=C\underset{H}{\overset{H}{<}} + H_2 \xrightarrow[\text{Ni cat.}]{\text{Raney}} H-\underset{\underset{H}{|}}{\overset{\overset{H}{|}}{C}}-\underset{\underset{H}{|}}{\overset{\overset{H}{|}}{C}}-H$$

Industrially this reaction is used in the manufacture of margarines, **Figure 20.3**. Vegetable oils are compounds that contain hydrocarbon chains which may be unsaturated. They are 'hardened' by reducing the number of double bonds. Saturated oils have somewhat higher melting points than unsaturated ones because their molecules are more regularly shaped and pack together better, making them harder to separate. Industrially the reaction is carried out at around 420 K and 500 kPa pressure with a powdered nickel catalyst. Under these conditions not all the double bonds are hydrogenated, only enough to harden the oil to the required extent.

Figure 20.3 A typical unsaturated vegetable oil before reaction with hydrogen

Vegetable oils are hydrogenated to produce a spreadable solid product

Hint: Polymers are named after the monomer from which they are made.

Polymerisation

Alkenes can polymerise, joining together to form long chains of very high relative molecular mass (up to 1×10^6):

$$\underset{H}{\overset{H}{>}}C=C\underset{H}{\overset{H}{<}} + \underset{H}{\overset{H}{>}}C=C\underset{H}{\overset{H}{<}} + \underset{H}{\overset{H}{>}}C=C\underset{H}{\overset{H}{<}} —$$

ethene

$$-\underset{\underset{H}{|}}{\overset{\overset{H}{|}}{C}}-\underset{\underset{H}{|}}{\overset{\overset{H}{|}}{C}}-\underset{\underset{H}{|}}{\overset{\overset{H}{|}}{C}}-\underset{\underset{H}{|}}{\overset{\overset{H}{|}}{C}}-\underset{\underset{H}{|}}{\overset{\overset{H}{|}}{C}}-\underset{\underset{H}{|}}{\overset{\overset{H}{|}}{C}}-$$

poly(ethene)

This type of reaction is called **addition polymerisation** as no molecule is eliminated. The polymer is named poly(eth*ene*) even though it is actually an alk*ane* and is unreactive, as we would expect of an alkane. The mechanism of the reaction is either radical or ionic, depending on the conditions.

Poly(ethene), usually called polythene, was originally all made by a high temperature (around 600 K) and high pressure (around 300×10^3 kPa) process with traces of peroxide. These initiated a radical polymerisation which produced a product with side chains and a relatively low molecular mass (around 1×10^5). This is called low density polythene and is used for making plastic bags, for example.

High density polythene, with no chain branching and a higher molecular mass, is produced by using Ziegler–Natta catalysts (mixtures of triethyl aluminium and titanium(IV) chloride, see section 36.2). These catalysts also allow for milder conditions: around 5×10^3 kPa and 350 K. The polymerisation proceeds via an ionic mechanism. High density polythene has both a higher density and a higher softening temperature than the low density form – properties which result from the closer packing of the polymer chains. It is used for making washing-up bowls, for example.

CHEMISTRY AROUND US

Addition polymers

Many other addition polymers are in everyday use apart from poly(ethene). They are summarised in the table.

Monomer	Polymer	Systematic chemical name	Common name or trade name (in capitals)	Typical uses
$CH_2{=}CH_2$	$-[CH-CH_2]_n-$	poly(ethene)	polythene or polyethylene ALKATHENE	washing-up bowls, plastic bags
CH_3 $\|$ $CH{=}CH_2$	$[CH(CH_3)-CH_2]_n$	poly(propene)	polypropylene	rope
Cl $\|$ $CH{=}CH_2$	$[CH(Cl)-CH_2]_n$	poly(chloroethene)	polyvinylchloride PVC	vinyl records
CN $\|$ $CH{=}CH_2$	$[CH(CN)-CH_2]_n$	poly(propenenitrile)	polyacrylonitrile acrylic fibre COURTELLE	clothing
(phenyl ring) $CH{=}CH_2$	$[CH(phenyl)-CH_2]_n$	poly(phenylethene)	polystyrene	plastic models ceiling tiles
CH_3 $\|$ $C{=}CH_2$ $\|$ CO_2CH_3	$[C(CH_3)(CO_2CH_3)-CH_2]_n$	poly(methyl 2-methylpropenoate)	polymethylmethacrylate acrylic PERSPEX	cockpit canopies in aircraft, false teeth

20.5 Preparation of alkenes

Industrially alkenes are obtained by cracking alkane fractions obtained from crude oil. In the laboratory there are two main methods of preparing alkenes.

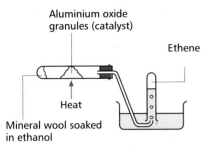

Figure 20.4 Laboratory preparation of ethene by dehydration of ethanol

> ## Q
> Dehydrating more complex alcohols can result in more than one possible alkene. What products are possible from butan-2-ol?

Answer: But-1-ene, *cis*-but-2-ene and *trans*-but-2-ene

Dehydration of alcohols

This may be done by passing alcohol vapour over a heated aluminium oxide catalyst as shown in **Figure 20.4**.

$$\underset{\begin{array}{c}\;\end{array}}{H-\overset{\displaystyle H}{\underset{\displaystyle H}{C}}-\overset{\displaystyle H}{\underset{\displaystyle OH}{C}}-H} \xrightarrow[\text{Al}_2\text{O}_3 \text{ catalyst}]{\text{heat}} \quad \overset{H}{\underset{H}{}}C{=}C\overset{H}{\underset{H}{}} + H_2O$$

$$\longrightarrow H_2O$$

Alternatively, excess concentrated sulphuric acid can be used as a dehydrating agent.

$$\underset{\begin{array}{c}\;\end{array}}{H-\overset{\displaystyle H}{\underset{\displaystyle H}{C}}-\overset{\displaystyle H}{\underset{\displaystyle OH}{C}}-H} \xrightarrow[\substack{(\text{conc. } H_2SO_4) \\ 440 \text{ K}}]{} \quad \overset{H}{\underset{H}{}}C{=}C\overset{H}{\underset{H}{}} + H_2O$$

$$\longrightarrow H_2O$$

(Excess alcohol leads to the formation of an ether, a compound with the functional group R—O—R.)

From haloalkanes

Haloalkanes refluxed (see box), with a strong base dissolved in alcohol lose hydrogen halide to form alkenes:

FURTHER FOCUS

Refluxing

Many organic reactions take some time to go to completion and also need fairly high temperatures. Under these conditions, it is probable that one or more of the reactants, products or solvents would boil away. An added hazard is that many organic vapours are flammable and/or toxic. All these problems can be solved by using the technique of **refluxing**. A water-cooled Liebig condenser is fitted vertically to the reaction flask. Vapours that escape from the reaction mixture condense on the walls of the condenser and drip back into the flask. Thus no volatile liquid should be lost. If required, a drying tube can be fitted to the top of the condenser. This tube contains granules of a suitable drying agent, e.g. calcium chloride, and prevents water vapour entering the flask. The top of the condenser must *not* be stoppered!

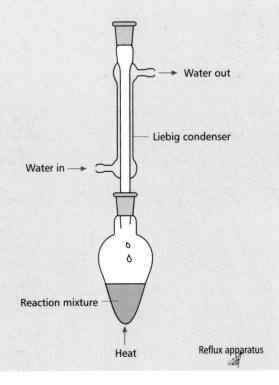

Reflux apparatus

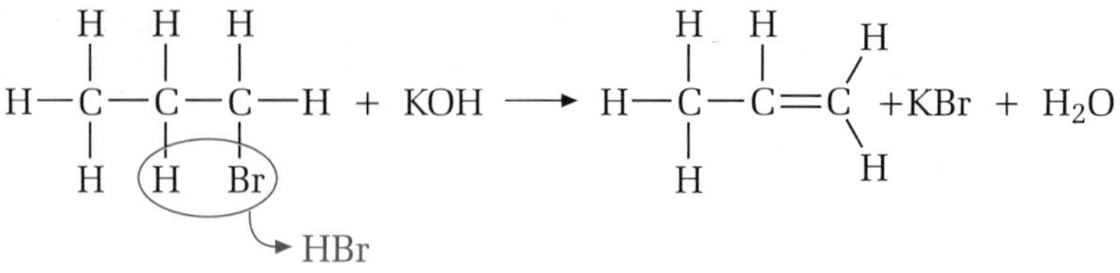

The mechanism is discussed in section 21.4.

Ethene cannot be made by this reaction. A reaction with the solvent occurs (and an ether forms).

1-Bromobutane gives but-1-ene:

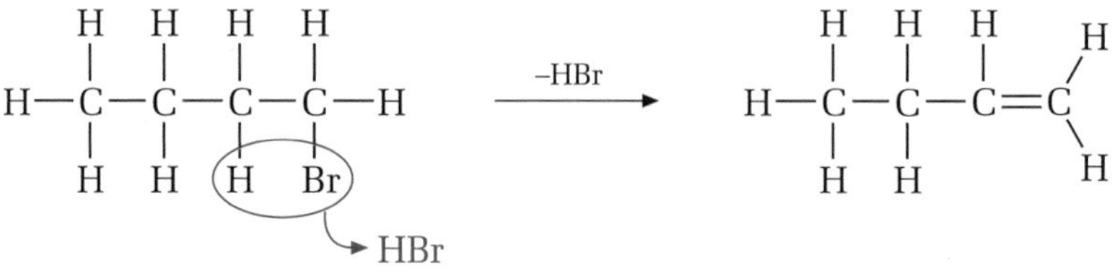

but 2-bromopropane gives a mixture of but-1-ene and but-2-ene (both *cis-* and *trans-*isomers) depending on which hydrogen is eliminated along with the bromine:

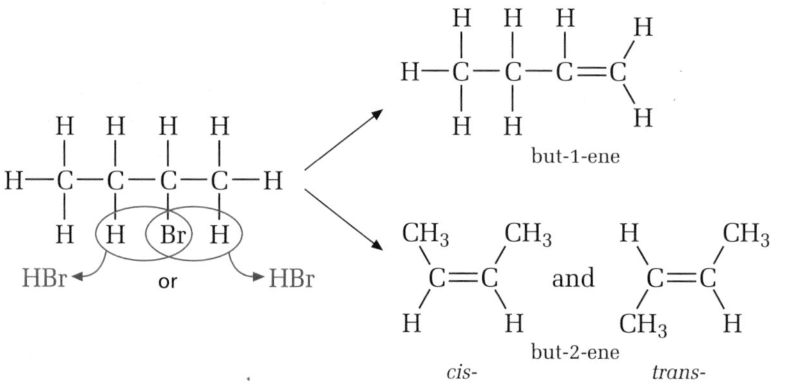

20.6 Economic importance of alkenes

Alkenes are very important industrially. The chemistry of the two most important, ethene and propene, is summarised in **Figures 20.5** and **20.6**. Both alkenes are obtained from naphtha (a crude oil hydrocarbon fraction of chain length C_8 to C_{12}) by cracking. Note the variety of materials that is produced and try to imagine the world without them.

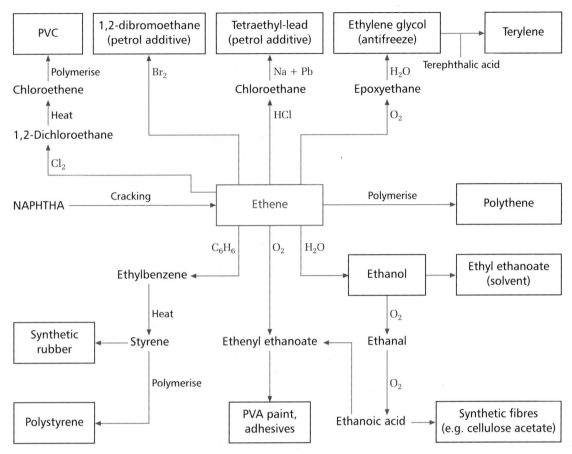

Figure 20.5 Industrial uses of ethene. Note its importance in the manufacture of plastics and synthetic fibres. The products are boxed and given their everyday (rather than systematic) names

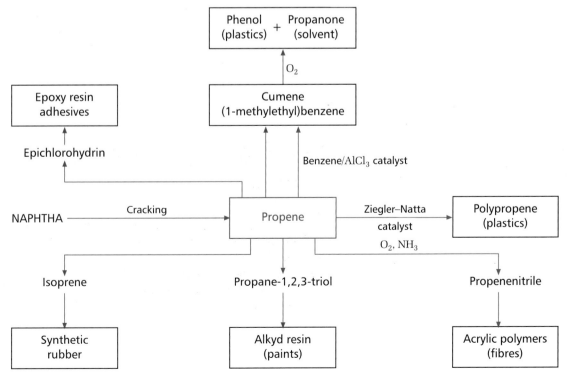

Figure 20.6 Industrial uses of propene

20.7 Summary

- Alkenes are hydrocarbons with   one or more double bonds.

- Alkenes are therefore   unsaturated compounds.

- The general formula of a chain alkene with one double bond is C_nH_{2n}.

- The ethene molecule is flat because   no rotation is possible about double bonds.

- The main intermolecular interactions are   van der Waals forces.

- The double bonds of alkenes are readily attacked by   electrophiles.

- This is because the C=C provides   an electron-rich area in the molecule.

- The typical reactions of alkenes are   electrophilic additions.

- The addition of unsymmetrical reagents, HZ, follows   Markovnikov's rule.

- Markovnikov's rule predicts that the hydrogen atom adds to the   carbon atom which already has most hydrogens.

- Alkenes can be prepared in the laboratory by   dehydration of alcohols

- or   by elimination of hydrogen halides from haloalkanes.

- Industrially alkenes are obtained from   the cracking of naphtha.

The reactions of alkenes are summarised in **Figure 20.7**.

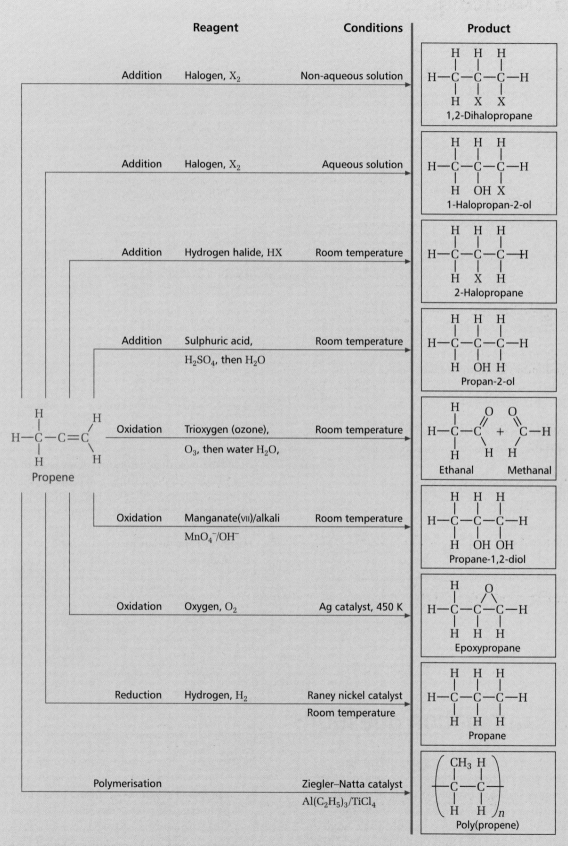

Figure 20.7 Summary of the reactions of alkenes using propene as an example – cover up the right-hand side to test yourself

20.8 Practice questions

1. Name the following.

(a) 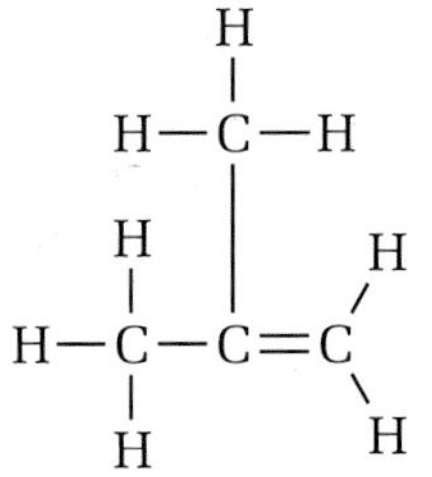
```
         H
         |
     H—C—H
  H      |       H
  |      |      /
H—C——C==C
  |            \
  H             H
```

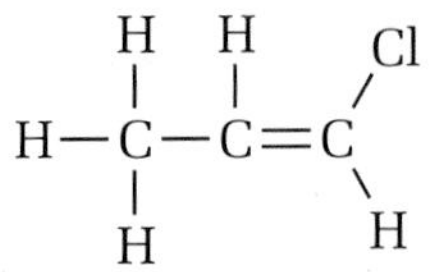

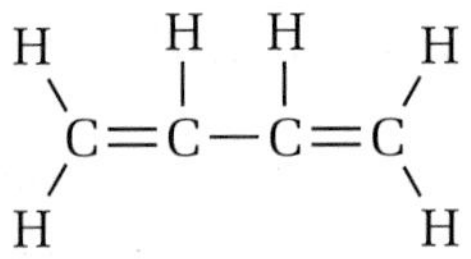

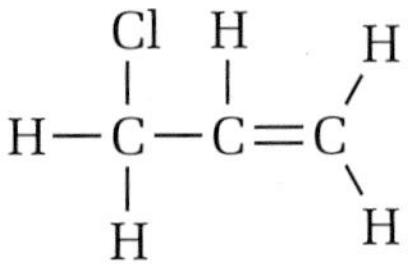

(b)
```
  H   H  H      H
   \  |  |     /
    C=C—C==C
   /          \
  H            H
```

(c)
```
       H  Cl    H
       |  |    /
  H—C—C==C
       |       \
       H        H
```

(d)
```
      H  H   Cl
      |  |   /
  H—C—C==C
      |       \
      H        H
```

(e)
```
      Cl  H    H
      |   |   /
  H—C—C==C
      |       \
      H        H
```

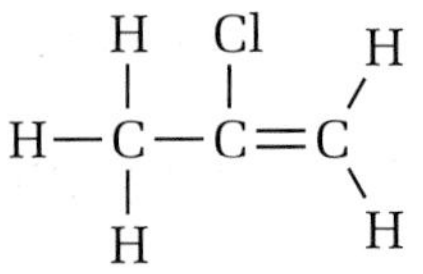

(f) 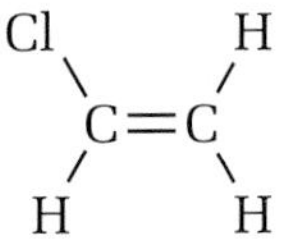
```
  Cl        H
   \       /
    C==C
   /       \
  H         H
```

2. Write displayed formulae for:
(a) but-1-ene, (b) but-2-ene, (c) 2-bromobuta-1,3-diene, (d) cyclohexene

3. (a) Write displayed formulae for the main products of the following reactions.

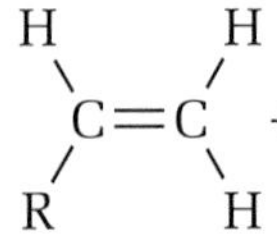

(i) 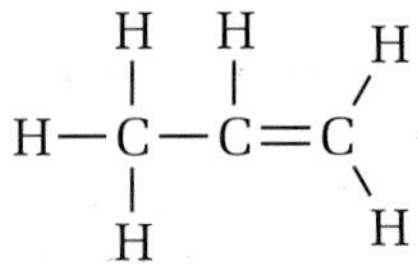
```
     H  H    H
     |  |   /
 H—C—C==C      +   Cl₂
     |      \
     H       H
```

(ii) 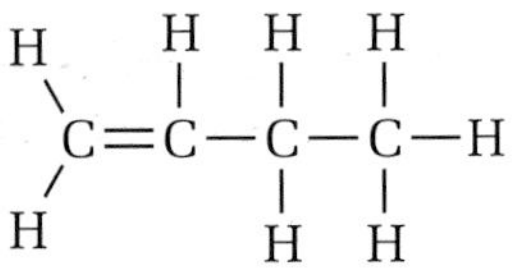
```
  H      H  H  H
   \     |  |  |
    C=C—C—C—H   +   HBr
   /     |  |
  H      H  H
```

(iii) 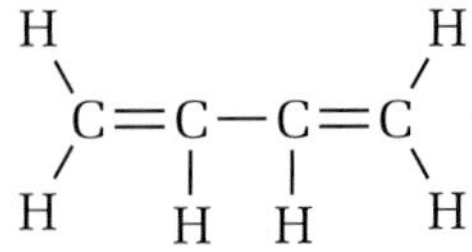
```
  H              H
   \            /
    C=C—C==C      +   HBr
   /    |  |    \
  H     H  H     H
```

(iv)
```
  H      H
   \    /
    C=C      +   H₂SO₄ followed by H₂O
   /    \
  R      H
```

(b) What minor product(s) is/are possible in (ii), (iii) and iv)?

4. Starting from propan-1-ol, how would you produce propan-2-ol in two steps?

5. The compound

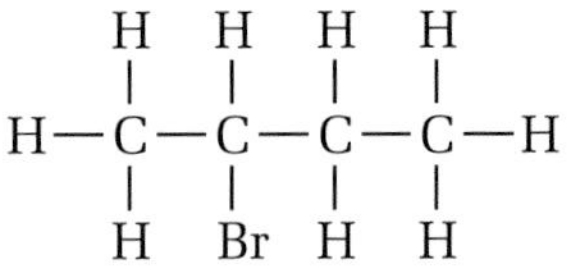

```
      H  H   H  H
      |  |   |  |
  H—C—C—C—C—H
      |  |   |  |
      H  Br  H  H
```

is refluxed with potassium hydroxide in ethanol. What three alkenes might be formed? Each of the products is reacted separately with hydrogen bromide. One will produce two isomeric products; the other two will produce only one product. Give structural formulae for all the products and explain.

20.9 Examination questions

1. (a) Give the structural formulae of the four isomeric alkenes of molecular formula C_4H_8.
   (b) Name the only branched C_4H_8 isomer and outline a mechanism to show how this molecule is protonated by sulphuric acid.
   (c) Give the structure and name of the organic product obtained when the reaction mixture in part (b) is poured into an excess of water.
                                              [NEAB 1998]

2. (a) Myrcene has a molecular formula, $C_{10}H_{16}$ ($M_r = 136$), and its structure is shown as **A** at the top of the next column. This compound is produced by pine trees in North America. Unfortunately, it attracts females of the beetle *Dendroctonus brevicomins*, which lays eggs in the tree. The drilling of the tree injects a pathogenic fungus, causing the tree's death.

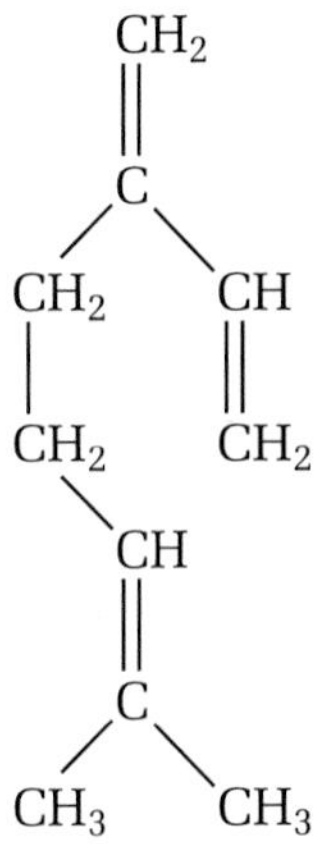

A

(i) State what you would see when bromine dissolved in an inert organic solvent is added to myrcene.

(ii) A sample of myrcene weighing 2.72 g is reacted with a 1.00 mol dm^{-3} solution of bromine; 60.0 cm^3 was required. Show that this is consistent with the structure of myrcene.

(b) Myrcene reacts with hydrogen bromide to give **B**:

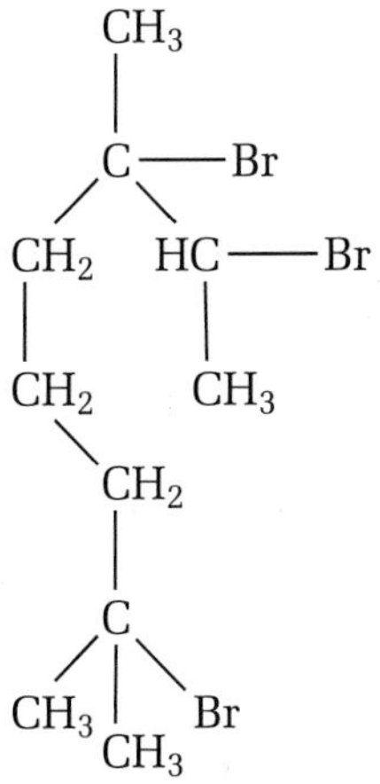

The double bonds can be regenerated by an elimination reaction; one elimination product among many is **C**:

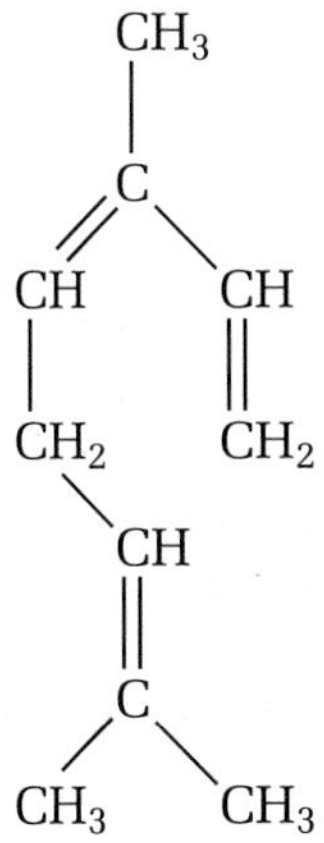

(i) State the reagents and conditions required to form **C** from **B**.

(ii) Explain why products other than myrcene itself are produced in this elimination reaction

(iv) What type of isomerism is shown by the bromo compound **B** which is not shown by myrcene itself? Give a reason.

[London (Nuffield) 1998, AS]

3. (a) Ethene reacts readily with chlorine, forming **A** ($C_2H_4Cl_2$).
   (i) Draw the displayed formula of **A**.
   (ii) Draw the displayed formula of a structural isomer of **A**.

(b) Some alkenes display *cis–trans* isomerism.
   (i) Draw and label a pair of *cis–trans* isomers.
   (ii) Explain the origin of *cis–trans* isomerism.

(c) Describe how you would show that ethene contains a double bond.

[O & C 1997, specimen]

4. (a) Hydrocarbon **B** contains 85.71% carbon.
   (i) Show that the empirical formula of **B** is CH_2.
   (ii) Given that the relative molecular mass of **B** is 56, derive its molecular formula. Show your working.
   (iii) Draw the structural formula of one possible isomer of **B**.

(b) There are a number of hydrocarbons containing five carbon atoms.
   (i) State the molecular formula of an alkane, **C**, and an alkene, **D**, containing 5 carbon atoms.
   (ii) Draw and name **two** structural isomers of **C**.

[O & C 1997, specimen]

21

Haloalkanes

CHEMISTRY NOW

Chlorofluorocarbons in the atmosphere

In 1922, Thomas Midgley carried out a striking demonstration in front of the American Chemical Society. He inhaled a sample of the gas dichlorodifluoromethane and used it to blow out a candle. Midgley had developed the gas as a replacement for ammonia as the working fluid in fridges, and his demonstration was designed to show that the gas was both inert (it did not react in the flame) and non-toxic (it was safe to breathe). Later, dichlorodifluoromethane and similar gases were used extensively as aerosol propellants as well as in fridges.

Since the mid-1970s, we have come to realise that dichlorodifluoromethane and other chlorofluorocarbons (CFCs) are not as innocuous as was thought. High in the atmosphere they break down to release chlorine atoms, which catalyse the breakdown of the gas ozone. This causes holes in the layer of ozone that exists normally in the stratosphere (the layer of the atmosphere between about 10 and 50 km above sea level). Ozone normally absorbs much of the ultraviolet radiation shining on the Earth. The increase in ultraviolet resulting from the holes has caused problems including skin cancers, cataracts in people's eyes, the death of plankton (part of the food chain in the oceans) and damage to plastics and paints.

The chemistry of the problem is now well known. CFCs are *too* inert: they remain in the atmosphere for many tens of years without being broken down. Eventually they reach the stratosphere where the ultraviolet radiation decomposes them to chlorine atoms.

Recently, many countries have signed the Montreal Protocol, an international agreement to phase out CFCs by the year 2000. But the CFCs are so inert that it will be many years before the level in the atmosphere begins to decline significantly.

Many aerosols are now operated by gases such as butane, but this is flammable. One non-flammable replacement for CFCs is a related group of compounds called hydrochlorofluorocarbons (HCFCs), such as $C_2H_3Cl_2F$, which are more easily oxidised in the lower atmosphere.

Computer-generated image of the ozone hole over the North Pole

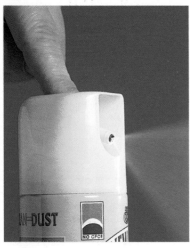

Nowadays most aerosols use ozone-friendly propellants

Introduction

Haloalkanes, sometimes called halogenoalkanes have one or more halogen atoms replacing hydrogens in an alkane skeleton. There are not many naturally occurring haloalkanes, but they are among the most important groups of synthetic compounds. Examples include the plastic PVC (used to make records, electrical cable insulation and drainpipes), Teflon (the non-stick coating on pans) and a number of anaesthetics.

21.1 Formulae, naming and structure

Formulae

Haloalkanes have one or more halogen (fluorine, chlorine, bromine or iodine) atoms replacing hydrogen atoms in an alkane. The general formula of a haloalkane with n carbons is $C_nH_{2n+1}X$ where X is the halogen. This is often shortened to R—X.

Naming

The prefixes fluoro-, chloro-, bromo- and iodo- are used, together with locants where necessary, to indicate the position of the halogen atoms or atoms on the chain or ring.

The prefixes di-, tri-, tetra-, etc. are used as usual to indicate how many atoms of each halogen are present.

Examples

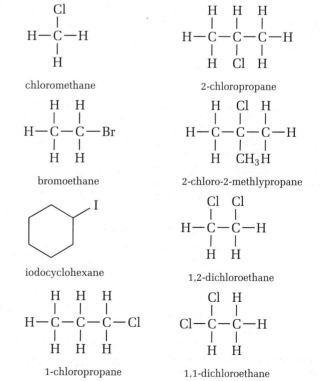

Structure

Haloalkanes may be:

primary, with a halogen at the end of the chain:

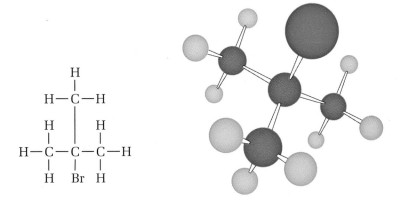

secondary, with a halogen in the body of the chain:

tertiary, with a halogen at a branch in the chain:

Q Try naming the compounds above

The three compounds above all have the molecular formula C_4H_9Br, so they are isomers.

When a compound contains two or more different halogens the substituents are given in alphabetical order, not numerical order. So:

Hint: When writing the formulae of halogen compounds, the symbol X is used to represent any halogen.

is 3-chloro-2-iodohexane *not* 2-iodo-3-chlorohexane.

Answer: 1-Bromobutane, 2-bromobutane, 2-bromo-2-methylpropane

Table 21.1   Boiling temperatures of 1-haloalkanes/K

Parent alkane	Halogen			
	F	Cl	Br	I
methane	195	249	277	316
ethane	235	285	312	345
propane	276	320	344	376
butane	306	351	374	403

Increasing T_b →

Increasing T_b ↓

Q Predict the effect of chain branching on boiling temperature.

21.2 Physical properties of haloalkanes

Although C—X bonds are polar, $C^{\delta+}$—$X^{\delta-}$, they are not polar enough to make the haloalkanes soluble in water. Even those with the shortest hydrocarbon chains are immiscible. The main intermolecular interaction is dipole–dipole bonding. They will, however, dissolve readily in alcohols. They mix well with hydrocarbons hence their use as degreasing agents and dry-cleaning fluids (grease is a hydrocarbon and stains are often greasy in nature).

Boiling temperatures depend on the number and type of halogen atoms in the molecule. Haloalkanes have higher boiling temperatures than the corresponding alkanes owing to their higher relative molecular masses as well as their polarity (see **Table 21.1**). Note the trends:

- increasing T_b with increased chain length
- increasing T_b as we go down the halogen group

21.3 Reactivity of haloalkanes

Two important factors governing the reactivity of the C—X bond are the C—X bond energy and the C—X bond polarity.

Bond energies

These are listed in **Table 21.2**. The trend is due to the shared electrons being closer to the nucleus in fluorine than in iodine.

So bond energies alone would predict that iodo-compounds, with the weakest bonds, would be the most reactive, and fluoro-compounds, with the strongest, would be the least reactive.

Bond polarities

Electronegativities are listed in **Table 21.3**. The halogens are generally more electronegative than carbon so the bond polarity will be $C^{\delta+}$—$X^{\delta-}$. The greater the difference between C and the halogen, the greater the $\delta+$ character of C. The $C^{\delta+}$ will be open to attack by **nucleophiles**.

Electronegativity would predict that fluoro-compounds, which have the greatest polarity, would be the most reactive, and iodo-compounds, with the least polarity, would be the least reactive.

So the two factors predict different outcomes. Which is the more important has been decided by experiment: it is the bond strength that governs the reaction rate. Iodoalkanes are more reactive than fluoroalkanes. But the polarity of the bonds will still predict the nature of the reagent that will attack. Haloalkanes are likely to be attacked by **nucleophiles**, at the $C^{\delta+}$. As they are saturated, addition reactions are not possible. So we would expect **nucleophilic substitution** or **elimination** reactions and these are what actually occur.

Table 21.2   Carbon–halogen bond energies

Bond	Tabulated BE/kJ mol⁻¹
C—F	467
[C—H	413]
C—Cl	346
C—Br	290
C—I	228

stronger ↑

Table 21.3   The electronegativities of the halogens

Halogen	Electronegativity
F	4.0
Cl	3.0
Br	2.8
I	2.5
[C	2.5]
[H	2.1]

Answer: Decreasing T_b as the chains get more branched: branched chains pack less efficiently.

21.4 Reactions of haloalkanes

Nucleophilic substitution

:Nu$^-$ is used to represent any negatively charged nucleophile. This will be the overall reaction:

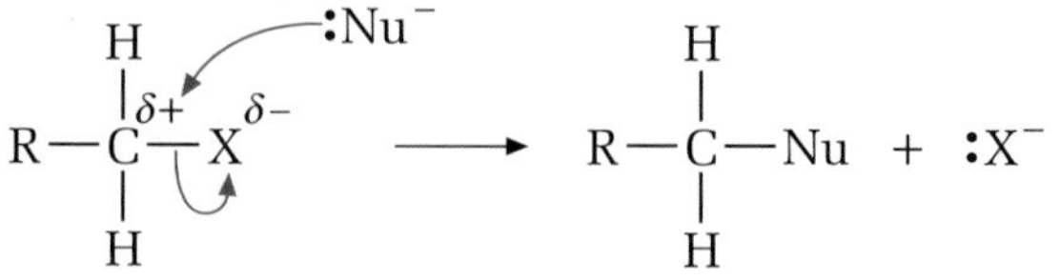

However there are two ways this can happen, called S_N2 and S_N1.

S_N2

Here the nucleophile attaches itself to the $C^{\delta+}$ atom *at the same time* as the halogen leaves. There is a charged species, which we can imagine as an intermediate called an **activated complex**.

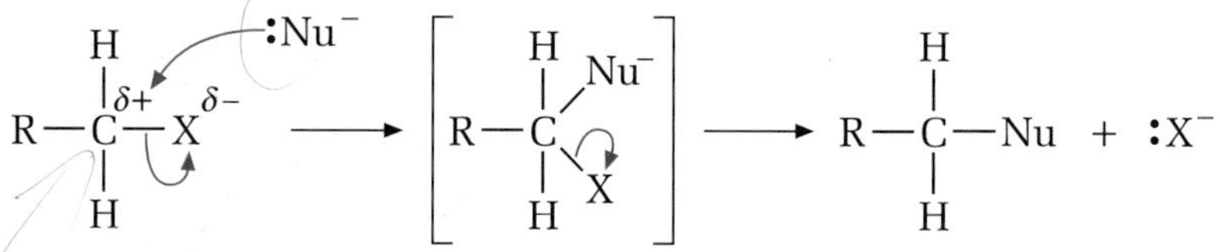

activated complex

The halogen leaves as a halide ion (taking the electrons of the C—X bond with it) and is often called the **leaving group**.

With this mechanism, the rate of reaction depends on the concentration of the nucleophile *and* the concentration of the haloalkane.

It is a **substitution** by a **nucleophile** whose rate is determined by the concentrations of *two* molecules: in short, S_N2.

S_N1

The halogen pulls the electrons from the C—X bond towards it, as it is more electronegative than carbon. In this case, it then leaves the haloalkane, taking the electrons with it and leaving behind a positive ion (a **carbocation**) which is then attacked by the nucleophile.

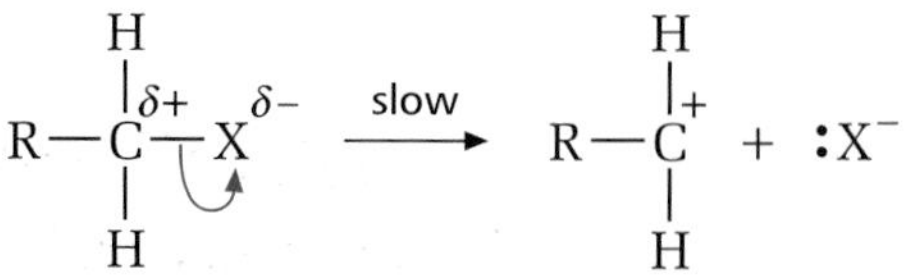

a carbocation

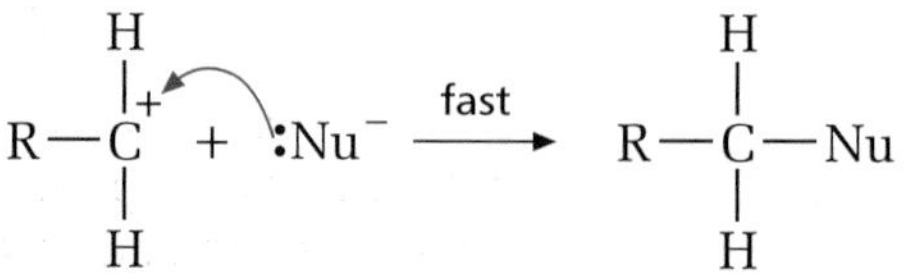

In this two-step mechanism, how fast the reaction occurs will depend on the rate of the slower step, which is the first. We have **substitution** by a **nucleophile** whose rate is determined by the concentration of *one* molecule: in short, S_N1.

Increasing the concentration of the nucleophile will not increase the rate of an S_N1 reaction but increasing the concentration of the haloalkane will.

Predicting the mechanism

Can we predict which sorts of haloalkanes will react by S_N1 or S_N2 or perhaps both?

For the S_N1 mechanism to be the most important, the carbocation has to be relatively stable.

Look at the different haloalkanes:

primary   secondary   tertiary

Remember that alkyl groups release electrons (the inductive effect, see section 18.8). This means that tertiary haloalkanes, which have three alkyl groups, give the most stable ion after loss of X^-, owing to the inductive effect of the three R groups stabilising the positive charge. This allows time for the ion to be attacked by the nucleophile. The next most stable ion would be the secondary and then the primary (which would not be very stable at all).

This is in fact the case. Tertiary haloalkanes react via the S_N1, secondary by both the S_N1 and the S_N2, and primary by the S_N2 mechanism.

Also, the rate will depend on the halogen. Iodo-compounds react more quickly than bromo-compounds, which in turn react more quickly than chloro-compounds because of the C—X bond strengths. Fluoro-compounds are unreactive because of the great strength of the C—F bond.

Examples of nucleophilic substitution reactions
The reaction of halobutanes with aqueous sodium hydroxide

The overall reaction is:

$$R{-}X + OH^- \longrightarrow ROH + X^-$$

What is the experimental evidence for this? We need to show that X^- (a halide ion) is produced. The test for the presence of a halide ion is the formation of a precipitate with silver nitrate solution:

$$AgNO_3(aq) + X^-(aq) \longrightarrow AgX(s) + NO_3^-(aq)$$

However, hydroxide ions also form a precipitate (of silver hydroxide) with silver nitrate, so before adding the silver nitrate, we must neutralise any remaining hydroxide ions.

Hint: The carbocations formed by loss of X^-:

- A few drops of sodium hydroxide solution are added to a halobutane dissolved in ethanol (a co-solvent in which both mix).
- After about a minute, nitric acid is added to neutralise any remaining sodium hydroxide.
- Siver nitrate solution is added.
- A precipitate forms, confirming the halogen has been released as a halide ion.

The results can be interpreted as follows. The OH^- ion is a good nucleophile. The precipitate shows that halide ions are present. The halogen in the halobutane is covalently bonded to the carbon, so the C—X bond must have broken heterolytically. It is reasonable to suppose that the other product is an alcohol and we could test for this (see Chapter 38) The carbon has bonded to the OH^- so a substitution reaction has occurred

The reaction may go via S_N1, S_N2 or both, depending on the haloalkane. The only way to determine this is to find out how the rate depends on the concentrations of the haloalkane and the hydroxide ions.

Water is a poorer nucleophile than the OH^- ion but it will still react slowly:

The resulting ion must lose a proton (H^+) to form an alcohol:

> **Hint:** Heterolytic bond breaking produces a positive and a negative ion.

Other nucleophilic substitution reactions

Haloalkanes can react with a variety of nucleophiles, for example $H_2O:$, $:OH^-$ (as above), $:NH_3$, $RO:^-$, $:CN^-$, $RCO_2:^-$.

Ammonia (concentrated solution, under pressure)

a primary amine
(also a nucleophile)

Ammonia is a nucleophile owing to its lone pair of electrons. Note the similarity of the reaction with the one with water above. Because ammonia is a neutral nucleophile, a proton must be lost to form the neutral product, which is called a primary amine.

This primary amine also has a lone pair and is therefore also a nucleophile. If the haloalkane is in excess, secondary and tertiary amines can be formed and also quarternary ammonium salts (see section 35.1).

$$R-\overset{\overset{\displaystyle H}{|}}{\underset{\underset{\displaystyle H}{|}}{C}}\!-\!X^{\delta-}\overset{\delta+}{} + H\!-\!\overset{\displaystyle \ddot{N}}{\underset{\underset{\displaystyle H}{|}}{\underset{|}{}}}\!-\!\overset{\overset{\displaystyle H}{|}}{\underset{\underset{\displaystyle H}{|}}{C}}\!-\!R \longrightarrow R\!-\!\overset{\overset{\displaystyle H}{|}}{\underset{\underset{\displaystyle H}{|}}{C}}\!-\!\overset{\displaystyle \ddot{N}}{\underset{\underset{\displaystyle H}{|}}{}}\!-\!\overset{\overset{\displaystyle H}{|}}{\underset{\underset{\displaystyle H}{|}}{C}}\!-\!R + X^- + H^+$$

a secondary amine (also a nucleophile)

$$R-\overset{H}{\underset{H}{C}}-X^{\delta-} + H-\overset{\ddot N}{\underset{CH_2R}{|}}-\overset{H}{\underset{H}{C}}-R \longrightarrow R-\overset{H}{\underset{H}{C}}-\overset{\ddot N}{\underset{CH_2R}{|}}-\overset{H}{\underset{H}{C}}-R + X^- + H^+$$

a tertiary amine (also a nucleophile)

$$R-\overset{H}{\underset{H}{C}}-X^{\delta-} \quad R-\overset{H}{\underset{H}{C}}-\overset{\ddot N}{\underset{CH_2R}{|}}-\overset{H}{\underset{H}{C}}-R \longrightarrow R-\overset{H}{\underset{H}{C}}-\overset{CH_2R}{\underset{CH_2R}{\overset{|}{N^+}}}-\overset{H}{\underset{H}{C}}-R + X^-$$

a quaternary ammonium salt:
no lone pair so not a nucleophile

Because of the possibility of forming several products, the reaction of haloalkanes with ammonia is not a very efficient way of preparing specific amines.

Cyanide ions (heat under reflux with potassium cyanide in ethanol)

$$R-\overset{H}{\underset{H}{C}}-X^{\delta-}\;\; {}^-{:}C\!\equiv\!N \longrightarrow R-\overset{H}{\underset{H}{C}}-C\!\equiv\!N + X^-$$

a nitrile

Note that the length of the carbon chain increases by one. For example, if we had started with bromo*ethane* we would have produced *propane*nitrile. For this reason this is an important reaction in synthesis (see Chapter 37). Nitriles can easily be converted into other compounds: for example, they can be hydrolysed to carboxylic acids and reduced to amines (see section 35.2).

Hint: If you are trying to make a target molecule which has one more carbon atom than the starting molecule, this reaction is almost certain to be involved.

Ethoxide ion CH₃CH₂O⁻ (a solution of sodium ethoxide in ethanol)

$$R-\overset{H}{\underset{H}{C}}-X^{\delta-}\;\; {:}OC_2H_5^- \longrightarrow R-\overset{H}{\underset{H}{C}}-OC_2H_5 + X^-$$

an ether

Hint: All these reactions are essentially similar and you will almost certainly find it easier to remember the basic pattern and work out the product with a particular nucleophile rather than trying to recall a list of separate reactions.

The same reaction takes place with ethanol instead of sodium ethoxide, but more slowly because ethanol, having no negative charge, is a poorer nucleophile than the ethoxide ion, in the same way that water is a poorer nucleophile than the hydroxide ion.

Elimination reactions

Earlier we saw the OH^- ion acting as a nucleophile (the lone pair forming a new bond with $C^{\delta+}$). Under different conditions it can act as a base (the lone pair forming a new bond with H^+). In this case we have an elimination reaction rather than a substitution. Here is an example:

2-chloro-2-methylpropane,

$$H-\overset{\overset{\displaystyle H}{|}}{\underset{\underset{\displaystyle H}{|}}{C}}-\overset{\overset{\displaystyle Cl}{|}}{\underset{\underset{\displaystyle \overset{|}{H-C-H}}{|}}{C}}-\overset{\overset{\displaystyle H}{|}}{\underset{\underset{\displaystyle H}{|}}{C}}-H$$, reacts with

potassium hydroxide in ethanol (with no water present) at high temperature to form 2-methylpropene. A molecule of hydrogen chloride, HCl, is eliminated in the process.

$$H-C-C-C-H + KOH \longrightarrow H-C-C=C + KCl + H_2O$$

2-methylpropene

What is the experimental evidence for this?

- A mixture of 2-chloro-2-methylpropane and a solution of potassium hydroxide in ethanol is soaked in mineral wool and heated as shown in **Figure 21.1**.
- The product is gaseous.
- It is found to burn and also to decolourise bromine solution. This suggests it is an alkene: the only likely one is 2-methylpropene.

The mechanism is as follows:

$$H-C-C-C-H + :OH^- \longrightarrow H-C-C=C + H_2O + Cl^-$$

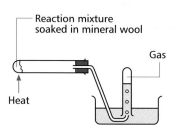

Figure 21.1 Elimination of hydrogen chloride from 2-chloro-2-methylpropane

Reaction mixture soaked in mineral wool

Gas

Heat

Hint: This reaction is a useful way of introducing double bonds into a molecule.

The OH⁻ ion uses its lone pair to form a bond with one of the hydrogen atoms. The electron pair from the C-H bond now forms part of a carbon–carbon double bond. The carbon bonded to the chlorine now has ten electrons in its outer shell. It 'sheds' a pair of electrons which are taken away by the electronegative chlorine atom which becomes a chloride ion (the leaving group).

Since the reagents are the same, there is competition between substitution and elimination.

$$
\begin{array}{c}
\quad\ \text{H}\quad\ \text{H}\quad\ \text{H}\quad\ \text{H} \\
\quad\ |\quad\ \ |\quad\ \ |\quad\ \ | \\
\text{H}-\text{C}-\text{C}-\text{C}-\text{C}-\text{Cl} \\
\quad\ |\quad\ \ |\quad\ \ |\quad\ \ | \\
\quad\ \text{H}\quad\ \text{H}\quad\ \text{H}\quad\ \text{H}
\end{array}
$$

(cold OH⁻ in water) substitution   1-chlorobutane   (hot OH⁻ in ethanol) elimination

$$
\begin{array}{c}
\quad\ \text{H}\quad\ \text{H}\quad\ \text{H}\quad\ \text{H} \\
\quad\ |\quad\ \ |\quad\ \ |\quad\ \ | \\
\text{H}-\text{C}-\text{C}-\text{C}-\text{C}-\text{OH} \\
\quad\ |\quad\ \ |\quad\ \ |\quad\ \ | \\
\quad\ \text{H}\quad\ \text{H}\quad\ \text{H}\quad\ \text{H}
\end{array}
\qquad
\begin{array}{c}
\quad\ \text{H}\quad\ \text{H}\quad\ \text{H}\quad\quad\text{H} \\
\quad\ |\quad\ \ |\quad\ \ |\quad\ / \\
\text{H}-\text{C}-\text{C}-\text{C}=\text{C} \\
\quad\ |\quad\ \ |\quad\quad\quad\backslash \\
\quad\ \text{H}\quad\ \text{H}\quad\quad\quad\ \text{H}
\end{array}
$$

butan-1-ol   but-1-ene

Which type of reaction predominates depends on two factors: the reaction conditions and the type of haloalkane.

Conditions

Aqueous hydroxide ions at room temperature favour substitution. Hydroxide ions dissolved in ethanol at high temperature favour elimination.

Type of haloalkane

Primary haloalkanes tend to undergo substitution and tertiary ones elimination:

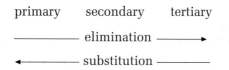

primary   secondary   tertiary

————————— elimination ————→

←————— substitution ————

FURTHER FOCUS

Bases and nucleophiles

The term nucleophile is used in organic chemistry for a species which attacks and forms a bond with an electron-deficient carbon atom, $C^{\delta+}$. Thus a nucleophile must have a lone pair of electrons.

A base, by the Lowry–Brønsted theory (see section 12.2), reacts with a proton, H^+, so it too needs a lone pair of electrons. In fact the Lewis definition of a base (see section 12.2) is that it is a lone pair donor, so really

nucleophiles and bases are very similar. Both are electron pair donors; they differ only in what they donate their lone pair to. Not surprisingly, good bases are generally good nucleophiles.

In inorganic chemistry the idea of a ligand is used. This is a species that donates a lone pair to form a bond with a transition metal ion. Good ligands tend also to be good bases and good nucleophiles. Ammonia is an example.

In some cases a mixture of isomeric elimination products is possible.

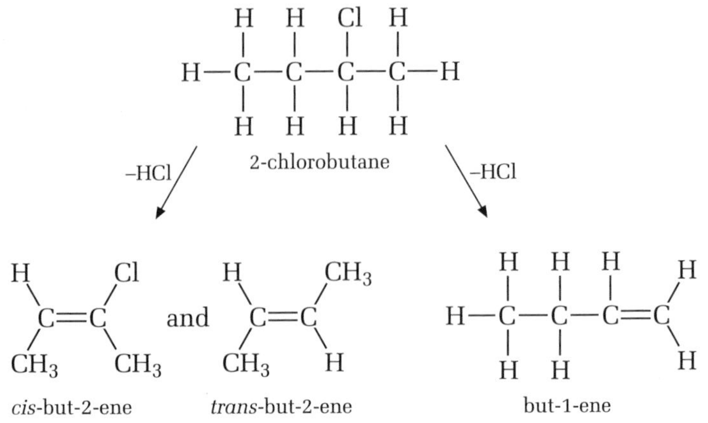

2-chlorobutane

–HCl

–HCl

cis-but-2-ene   *trans*-but-2-ene   but-1-ene

21.5 Preparation of haloalkanes

By addition of H—X across a carbon–carbon double bond

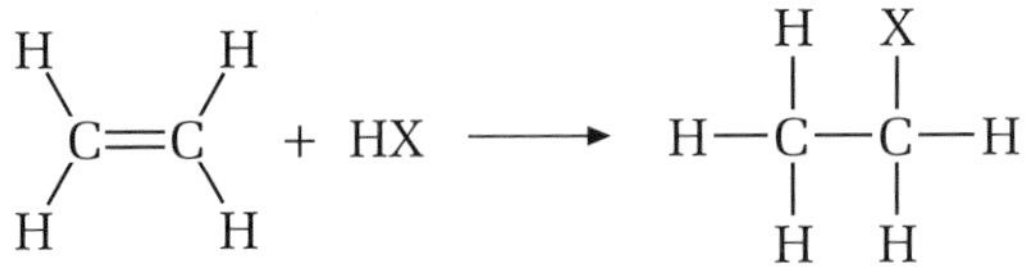

Addition of X—X produces dihaloalkanes (see section 20.4):

Hint: The dihaloalkanes produced by this reaction must have the two halogen atoms on adjacent carbons.

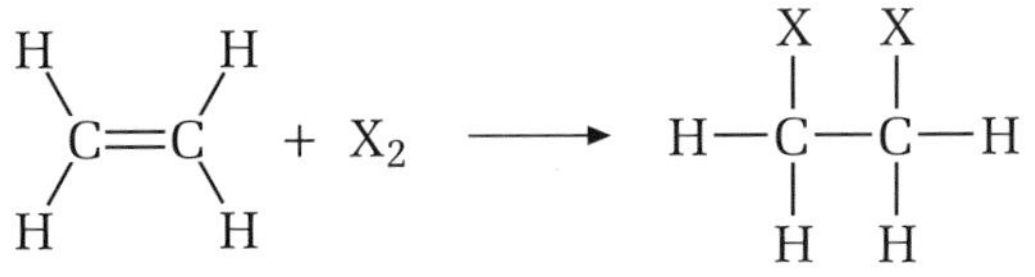

From alcohols

We can use:

1. A hydrogen halide (H—X) or

2. A phosphorus halide (PX_3 or PX_5) or

3. Sulphur dichloride oxide (thionyl chloride, $SOCl_2$: see section 22.4) to replace the —OH group of an alcohol with a halogen atom.

Q In order to be separated by distillation, the haloalkane must have a lower boiling temperature than the alcohol from which it is made. Can you explain the difference in boiling temperatures?

1.
$$R—OH + \begin{Bmatrix} HCl \\ HBr \end{Bmatrix} \longrightarrow \begin{Bmatrix} R—Cl \\ R—Br \end{Bmatrix} + H_2O$$

Hydrogen chloride or hydrogen bromide is usually generated in the reaction vessel by the reaction of concentrated sulphuric acid with sodium chloride or sodium bromide. For example:

$$H_2SO_4(l) + 2NaBr(s) \longrightarrow Na_2SO_4(s) + 2HBr(g)$$

Answer: Alcohols are hydrogen bonded, but haloalkanes have weaker dipole–dipole forces only.

So the alcohol is refluxed with $NaBr/H_2SO_4$, and the haloalkane separated by distillation.

2.
$$ROH + PCl_5 \longrightarrow RCl + POCl_3 + HCl$$

or

$$3ROH + PI_3 \longrightarrow 3RI + H_3PO_3$$

(Phosphorus triiodide is usually made in the reaction vessel by mixing iodine and red phosphorus.)

3.
$$ROH(l) + SOCl_2(l) \longrightarrow RCl(l) + SO_2(g) + HCl(g)$$

Here, as both the other products are gases, the problem of separating the chloroalkane, RCl, is simplified.

21.6 Haloalkenes

These contain both a carbon–carbon double bond and a halogen atom. There are two possibilities:

1. The halogen may be bonded to a carbon *not* involved in the double bond:

Cl H   H
| | /
H—C—C=C
| \
H   H

1-chloroprop-2-ene

2. The halogen may be bonded to one of the carbon atoms which *is* involved in the double bond:

H H   Cl
| | /
H—C—C=C
| \
H   H

1-chloroprop-1-ene

If the halogen atom is bonded to a carbon atom not involved in the double bond, the reactions are similar to those of the haloalkanes *plus* those of alkenes.

If the halogen is attached to one of the carbon atoms in the double bond, the carbon–halogen bond is less reactive. This is due to overlap of full p orbitals on the halogen with the π orbitals of the carbon–carbon double bond (see **Figure 21.2**). The carbon–halogen bond thus acquires some double bond character. This results in increased C—X bond strength and reduced $\delta+$ character of the carbon. Both tend to reduce reactivity.

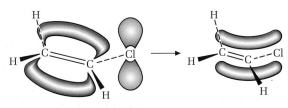

Figure 21.2 Bonding in chloroethene

Answer: The bond length. Stronger bonds (between the same pairs of atoms) are shorter.

Products made from PVC

F   Cl
| |
F—C—C—Br
| |
F   H

Figure 21.3 Fluothane. Can you see how the systematic name fits the rules?

21.7 Economic importance of haloalkanes

Haloalkanes have a number of industrial uses, many of which directly affect our everyday lives and our environment.

Chlorofluorocarbons (also called 'freons') had many uses, for example as aerosol propellants, refrigerants and blowing agents for foams like expanded polystyrene. Freons made for all these uses eventually ended up in the atmosphere, ultimately decomposing to give chlorine atoms. The effects of these on the decomposition of stratospheric ozone are described in the box 'Atmospheric chemistry' in section 27.4 and 'Chemistry Now' in this chapter). Freons are now being phased out but a vast reservoir of them remains in the atmosphere.

Another important haloalkane is fluothane, 1-bromo-1-chloro-2,2,2-trifluoroethane (**Figure 21.3**), which is an anaesthetic gas that has been used in over 500 million operations, see the box 'Anaesthetics' in Chapter 18.

PVC is one of the most widely used plastics and also one of the most versatile, in that its properties can be modified by various additives, so that it can be made flexible enough for rainwear and rigid enough for drainpipes. The plastic is made by polymerising chlorethene, which is made from ethene, a product of cracking petroleum, as follows:

$$
\underset{\text{ethene}}{\overset{\displaystyle H \quad\quad H}{\underset{\displaystyle H \quad\quad H}{C=C}}} \;+\; \underset{\text{chlorine}}{Cl_2} \;\longrightarrow\; \underset{\text{1,2-dichlorethane}}{\overset{\displaystyle Cl \;\; Cl}{\underset{\displaystyle H \;\; H}{H-C-C-H}}}
$$

$$
\underset{\text{1,2-dichlorethane}}{\overset{\displaystyle Cl \;\; Cl}{\underset{\displaystyle H \;\; H}{H-C-C-H}}} \;\xrightarrow{\text{heat}}\; \underset{\text{chloroethene}}{\overset{\displaystyle H \quad\quad Cl}{\underset{\displaystyle H \quad\quad H}{C=C}}} \;+\; \underset{\substack{\text{hydrogen}\\\text{chloride}}}{HCl}
$$

Hint: PVC stands for 'polyvinyl chloride'. Vinyl chloride is the non-systematic name for chloroethene. The systematic name for PVC is poly(chloroethene).

Halogen-containing organic compounds (usually chloro-compounds since chlorine is the cheapest halogen) are used industrially as solvents. They are also involved as intermediates in reactions. This is because they are both easily made and easily converted into other materials.

21.8 Summary

- Haloalkanes have | a halogen atom attached to an alkyl group.

- Haloalkanes may be classified as | primary, secondary or tertiary.

- Primary haloalkanes have | one R group attached to the carbon to which the halogen is bonded.

- Secondary haloalkanes have | two R groups attached to the carbon to which the halogen is bonded.

- Tertiary haloalkanes have | three R groups attached to the carbon to which the halogen is bonded.

- Haloalkanes have higher boiling temperatures than their parent alkane owing to | their increased relative molecular mass and increased polarity.

- Haloalkanes do not mix with | water.

- Haloalkanes mix with | alkanes and other non-polar solvents.

- The C—X bond is polarised | $C^{\delta+}—X^{\delta-}$.

- The $C^{\delta+}$ is attacked by | nucleophiles.

- The typical reactions of haloalkanes are | nucleophilic substitutions.

- These may occur by two mechanisms: | S_N1 or S_N2.

- Primary haloalkanes react by | S_N2.

- Tertiary haloalkanes react by | S_N1.

- Elimination reactions can also occur. The products are | alkenes.

The reactions of haloalkanes are summarised in **Figure 21.4**.

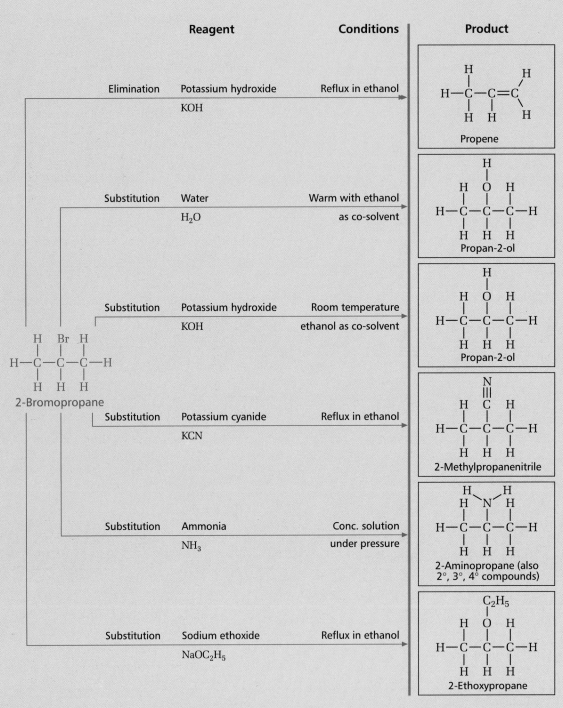

Figure 21.4 Summary of the reactions of haloalkanes using 2-bromopropane as an example – cover up the right-hand side to test yourself

21.9 Practice questions

1. Give the systematic name of each of the following compounds.

(a)
$$\text{H}-\overset{\text{H}}{\underset{\text{H}}{\text{C}}}-\overset{\text{F}}{\underset{\text{H}}{\text{C}}}-\overset{\text{H}}{\underset{\text{H}}{\text{C}}}-\overset{\text{H}}{\underset{\text{H}}{\text{C}}}-\text{H}$$

(b)
$$\text{H}-\overset{\text{H}}{\underset{\text{H}}{\text{C}}}-\overset{\text{F}}{\underset{\text{H}}{\text{C}}}-\overset{\text{H}}{\underset{\text{I}}{\text{C}}}-\overset{\text{Cl}}{\underset{\text{H}}{\text{C}}}-\overset{\text{H}}{\underset{\text{H}}{\text{C}}}-\text{H}$$

(c)
$$\text{H}-\overset{\text{H}}{\underset{\text{H}}{\text{C}}}-\overset{\text{Cl}}{\text{C}}=\text{C}\overset{\text{H}}{\underset{\text{H}}{{}}}$$

2. Write displayed structural formulae for:
   (a) 1,1-dichloropropane
   (b) 2-bromo-1-chlorobutane
   (c) 1,4-dichlorocyclohexane
   (d) 1-bromo-2-methylhexane

3. (a) Classify the following reactions as addition, elimination or substitution.

(i) + HO⁻ ⟶ + Cl⁻

(ii) + HO⁻ ⟶ + H₂O + Cl⁻

(iii)
$$\overset{\text{H}}{\underset{\text{H}}{{}}}\text{C}=\text{C}\overset{\text{Cl}}{\underset{\text{H}}{{}}} + \text{Br}_2 \longrightarrow \text{H}-\overset{\text{H}}{\underset{\text{Br}}{\text{C}}}-\overset{\text{Cl}}{\underset{\text{H}}{\text{C}}}-\text{Br}$$

(b) (i) and (ii) use the same reagents. Describe the conditions required for each.

4. List the following compounds in order of their rate of reaction with aqueous OH⁻, explaining your choice.

(a)
$$\text{H}-\overset{\text{H}}{\underset{\text{H}}{\text{C}}}-\overset{\text{H}}{\underset{\text{H}}{\text{C}}}-\text{Cl}$$

(b)
$$\text{H}-\overset{\text{H}}{\underset{\text{H}}{\text{C}}}-\overset{\text{H}}{\underset{\text{H}}{\text{C}}}-\text{Br}$$

(c)
$$\text{H}-\overset{\text{H}}{\underset{\text{H}}{\text{C}}}-\overset{\text{H}}{\underset{\text{H}}{\text{C}}}-\text{I}$$

5. Mark the polarity δ+ and δ− on the following molecules.

(a)
$$\text{H}-\overset{\text{H}}{\underset{\text{H}}{\text{C}}}-\overset{\text{H}}{\underset{\text{H}}{\text{C}}}-\text{Cl}$$

(c)
$$\text{Cl}-\overset{\text{Cl}}{\underset{\text{H}}{\text{C}}}-\overset{\text{H}}{\underset{\text{H}}{\text{C}}}-\text{H}$$

(b)
$$\text{H}-\overset{\text{H}}{\underset{\text{H}}{\text{C}}}-\overset{\text{H}}{\underset{\text{H}}{\text{C}}}-\text{Br}$$

(d)
$$\overset{\text{H}}{\underset{\text{H}}{{}}}\text{C}=\text{C}\overset{\text{Cl}}{\underset{\text{H}}{{}}}$$

Which carbon atom would have the greatest δ+ character? Explain your answer.

6. (a) What substitution products are produced when 1-bromobutane reacts with the following nucleophiles?
   (i) OH⁻, (ii) NH₃, (iii) C₂H₅OH, (iv) C₂H₅O⁻
   (b) Which reaction, (iii) or (iv), would go faster? Explain your answer.
   (c) Would you expect a different rate if the isomer 2-bromo-2-methylpropane rather than 1-bromobutane reacted with C₂H₅OH and C₂H₅O⁻? Explain your answer

7. When 2-chlorohexane is reacted with a strong base dissolved in ethanol at high temperature, a mixture of products containing two different alkenes is formed. Chlorocyclohexane under the same conditions produces only one.
   (a) Draw structures for the products of each reaction.
   (b) Explain why the first reaction gives two products and the second only one.
   (c) How many products would 3-chloropentane produce under the same conditions?

8. If you were given a sample of bromoethane, how would you convert it to 1,2-dibromoethane in two steps?

9. You are asked to prepare propanoic acid from ethanol. What reaction is likely to be involved at some stage? Try to outline the compounds that might be involved. (Do not give reagents or conditions.)

21.10 Examination questions

1. (a) The graphical formulae of **two** of the **four** structural isomers of C_4H_9Br are:

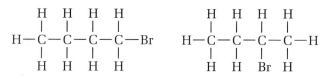

Isomer 1   **Isomer 2**

   (i) Draw the graphical formulae of the other **two** structural isomers.
   (ii) Which **one** of these four isomers reacts most readily with aqueous sodium hydroxide?

   (b) When **Isomer 1** reacts with aqueous sodium hydroxide, a reaction takes place in which the molecule is attacked by the hydroxide ion.

$$C_4H_9Br + NaOH \longrightarrow C_4H_9OH + NaBr$$

   (i) What feature of the C_4H_9Br molecule makes it liable to attack by the hydroxide ion?
   (ii) Give the name of the type of mechanism in this reaction.

   (c) When **Isomer 2** reacts with sodium hydroxide in an alcohol solvent, a reaction represented by the following equation takes place.

$$C_4H_9Br + NaOH \longrightarrow C_4H_8 + NaBr + H_2O$$

   (i) State the type of reaction taking place.
   (ii) Draw graphical formulae to show **two** of the isomers of C_4H_8 which are formed in this reaction.

   (d) A compound **Y** has the composition by mass $C = 29.76\%$, $H = 4.18\%$, $Br = 66.06\%$ and a relative molecular mass of 241.90.
   (i) Calculate the molecular formula of **Y**.
   (ii) **Y** is formed in an addition reaction between an alkene and bromine. Draw the structural formula of the alkene.

[AEB 1995]

2. (a) There are four **structural** isomers of molecular formula C_4H_9Br. The formulae of two of these isomers are given.

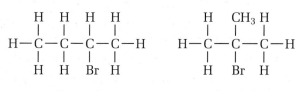

Isomer 1   **Isomer 2**

   (i) Draw the remaining **two** structural isomers.
   (ii) Give the name of **Isomer 2**.

   (b) All four structural isomers of C_4H_9Br undergo similar reactions with ammonia.
   (i) Give the name of the mechanism involved in these reactions.
   (ii) Draw the structural formula of the product formed by the reaction of **Isomer 1** with ammonia.
   (iii) Select the isomer of molecular formula C_4H_9Br that would be the most reactive with ammonia. State the structural feature of your chosen isomer that makes it the most reactive of the four isomers.

   (c) The elimination of HBr from **Isomer 1** produces two structural isomers, compounds **A** and **B**.
   (i) Give the reagent and conditions required for this elimination reaction.
   (ii) Give the structural formulae of the two isomers, **A** and **B**, formed by elimination of HBr from **Isomer 1**.

   (d) Ethene, C_2H_4, reacts with bromine to give 1,2-dibromoethane.
   (i) Give the name of the mechanism involved.
   (ii) Show the mechanism for this reaction.

[AEB 1998]

3. This questions concerns 2-bromo-2-methylbutane.

$$CH_3-CH_2-\underset{\underset{CH_3}{|}}{\overset{\overset{CH_3}{|}}{C}}-Br \text{, which reacts with aqueous}$$

potassium hydroxide solution via an S_N1 mechanism.
   (a) Show this mechanism and identify the rate determining step.
   (b) If the conditions are altered potassium hydroxide will react to give an elimination reaction with the same haloalkane. Draw the structural formula and give the name of an organic product of this elimination reaction, showing all the covalent bonds.
   (c) The rate equation for the substitution reaction in part (a) is

   rate = k[2-bromo-2-methylbutane]

   (i) State the order of the reaction.
   (ii) If the same haloalkane is reacted with cyanide ions instead of hydroxide ions, and all other conditions remain the same, state with reasons whether the rate of the reaction would alter.

[London (Nuffield) 1998, part]

22 Alcohols

CHEMISTRY NOW

◀ Drinking alcohol

Everyone who parties knows about alcohol. It is a social drug which may, in moderation, promote a feeling of well-being and reduce normal inhibitions. It is a nervous system depressant (i.e. it interferes with the transmission of nerve impulses). In larger amounts it leads to loss of balance, poor hand–eye co-ordination, impaired vision and inability to judge speed. Large amounts can be fatal. Excessive long-term use can lead to addiction – alcoholism.

▶ Hangovers

Everyone who parties also knows about hangovers! After drinking, ethanol is absorbed through the walls of the stomach and small intestine into the bloodstream. Some is eliminated unchanged in urine and in the breath. The rest is broken down by the liver. The combined effect of these processes is that an average person can eliminate about $10\ cm^3$ of alcohol per hour. This is approximately the amount of alcohol in half a pint of beer, a glass of wine or a 'short'. So some simple arithmetic should enable you to work out how long it will take to sober up – if you are clear headed enough to do it!

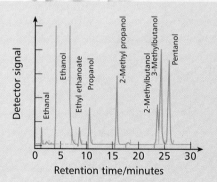

A gas chromatogram of a malt whisky, showing peaks caused by congeners

◀ Congeners

In the body, ethanol is oxidised to ethanal, which is thought to be largely responsible for the symptoms of a hangover. However, all alcoholic drinks contain a complex mixture of small amounts of other organic compounds called congeners. These include aldehydes and esters. They affect the flavour of the drink. They and their breakdown products may also be involved in the hangover. Some congeners are also responsible for the colour of alcoholic drinks and these may be behind the belief that darker-coloured drinks (such as red wine, port and sherry) cause worse hangovers.

Introduction

Alcohols are a family of organic compounds (an 'homologous series') in which the —OH functional group is attached to a hydrocarbon chain.

CONCEPT CHECKPOINTS

The following basic ideas are used in this chapter. You may revise some of these topics elsewhere in the book.
- carbon atoms forming four covalent bonds (section 18.1)
- bonding pairs and lone pairs (section 9.1)
- oxygen being more electronegative than both carbon and hydrogen (section 9.1)
- acidity caused by the H^+ ion (section 12.2)
- redox reactions (Chapter 13)
- nucleophiles (section 18.8)
- substitution and elimination reactions (section 18.8)

22.1 Formulae, naming and structure

The general formula of an alcohol with n carbon atoms is $C_nH_{2n+1}OH$. This is often shortened to ROH.

Naming

Look back at section 18.4 if you need to remind yourself of the general principles of naming organic molecules.

Like all organic compounds, alcohols have two parts to their names:

- the stem, which tells us how many carbon atoms there are in the longest unbranched chain
- the name of the functional group

For alcohols, the name of the functional group (the —OH group) is given by:

- the suffix -ol if the alcohol is the **principal group** (see section 18.4)
- the prefix hydroxy- if it is not the principal group

Hint: no locant is needed with only two carbons: the —OH *must* be on the end of the chain.

So
```
    H
    |
H — C — OH
    |
    H
```
is methanol and
```
    H   H
    |   |
H — C — C — OH
    |   |
    H   H
```
is ethanol.

Ethanol, C_2H_5OH, is the alcohol we drink.

With longer unbranched chains, a locant is needed to tell us *where* on the chain the —OH group is situated, so
```
    H   H   H
    |   |   |
H — C — C — C — OH
    |   |   |
    H   H   H
```

Hint: Remember that locants tell you *where* functional groups are and di-, tri, tetra-, etc. tell you *how many* there are in total.

is propan-1-ol, and
```
    H   H   H
    |   |   |
H — C — C — C — H
    |   |   |
    H   OH  H
```
is propan-2-ol.

If there is more than one —OH group we use di-, tri-, tetra-, etc. to say *how many* —OH groups there are. We will also need locants to say *where* they are.

So

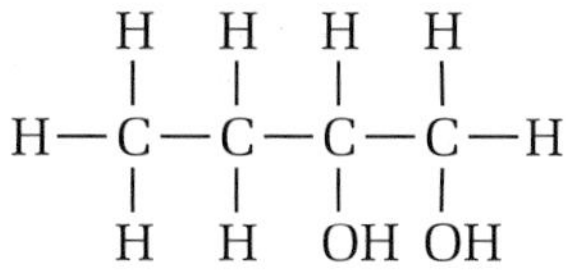

$$\begin{array}{ccccccccc} & H & & H & & H & & H & \\ & | & & | & & | & & | & \\ H- & C & - & C & - & C & - & C & -H \\ & | & & | & & | & & | & \\ & H & & H & & OH & & OH & \end{array}$$

is butane-1,2-diol and

$$\begin{array}{ccccccc} & H & & H & & H & \\ & | & & | & & | & \\ H- & C & - & C & - & C & -H \\ & | & & | & & | & \\ & OH & & OH & & OH & \end{array}$$

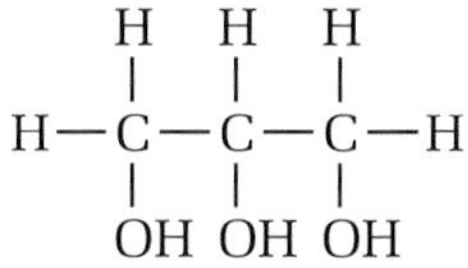

is propane-1,2,3-triol.

A common mistake is to forget that if there are two functional groups on the same carbon, you still need two locants,

so

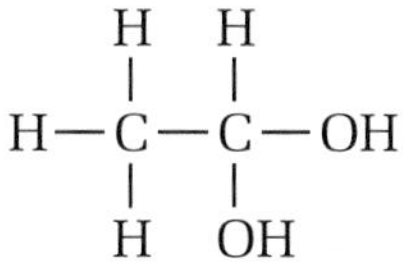

$$\begin{array}{ccccc} & H & & H & \\ & | & & | & \\ H- & C & - & C & -OH \\ & | & & | & \\ & H & & OH & \end{array}$$

would be called ethane-1,1-diol, *not*

ethane-1-diol (though this compound is not stable).

In

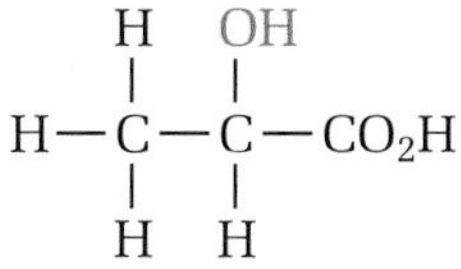

$$\begin{array}{ccccc} & H & & OH & \\ & | & & | & \\ H- & C & - & C & -CO_2H \\ & | & & | & \\ & H & & H & \end{array}$$

the —OH is *not* the principal group, the

—CO_2H group is, so this compound is called 2-hydroxypropanoic acid.

Structure

Classification of alcohols

Alcohols are classified as **primary** (1°), **secondary** (2°) or **tertiary** (3°) according to how many other groups (R) are bonded to the carbon that has the —OH group.

In a primary alcohol, this carbon has one R group.

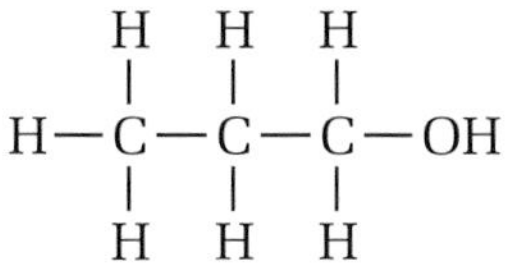

$$\begin{array}{ccccccc} & H & & H & & H & \\ & | & & | & & | & \\ H- & C & - & C & - & C & -OH \\ & | & & | & & | & \\ & H & & H & & H & \end{array}$$

is a primary alcohol.

$$\begin{array}{c} H \\ | \\ H- C -OH \\ | \\ H \end{array}$$

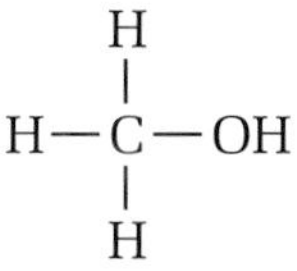

, where the carbon has no R groups, is also considered

to be a primary alcohol.

In a secondary alcohol, the —OH group is attached to a carbon with two R groups.

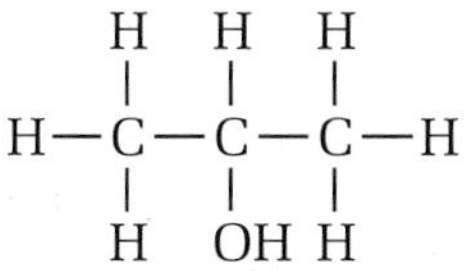

$$\begin{array}{ccccccc} & H & & H & & H & \\ & | & & | & & | & \\ H- & C & - & C & - & C & -H \\ & | & & | & & | & \\ & H & & OH & & H & \end{array}$$

, propan-2-ol, is a secondary alcohol.

Q

$$\begin{array}{ccccc} & H & & H & \\ & | & & | & \\ H- & C & - & C & -H \\ & | & & | & \\ & OH & & OH & \end{array}$$

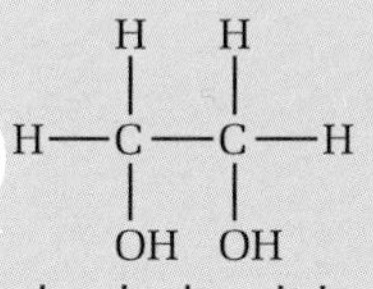

is called ethylene glycol when it is used in anti-freeze. What is its systematic name?

Answer: Ethane-1,2-diol

Tertiary alcohols have three R groups attached to the carbon which is bonded to the —OH.

$$
\begin{array}{c}
\text{H} \\
| \\
\text{H}-\text{C}-\text{H} \\
\text{H} \quad | \quad \text{H} \\
| \quad | \quad | \\
\text{H}-\text{C}-\text{C}-\text{C}-\text{H} \\
| \quad | \quad | \\
\text{H} \quad \text{OH} \quad \text{H}
\end{array}
\quad \text{is a tertiary alcohol.}
$$

Another way of looking at this is:

● A primary alcohol has two hydrogens attached to the carbon bearing the —OH group (or three in the case of methanol).
● A secondary alcohol has one hydrogen attached to the carbon bearing the —OH group.
● A tertiary alcohol has no hydrogens attached to the carbon bearing the —OH group.

Yet another way of thinking of this is that:

● A primary alcohol has the —OH group at the end of the chain.
● A secondary alcohol has the —OH group in the body of the chain.
● A tertiary alcohol has the —OH group at a branch in the chain.

Look at the structures above and convince yourself that this is so. We shall see that primary, secondary and tertiary alcohols have some significant differences in their reactions.

Shape

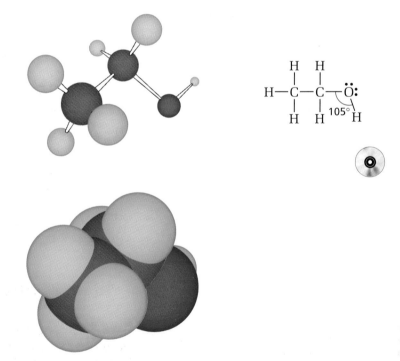

In alcohols, the oxygen atom has two bonding pairs and two lone pairs. So the C—O—H angle is about 105° because the 109.5° angle of a perfect tetrahedron is 'squeezed down' by the presence of the lone

Hint: These three terms are used in exactly the same way for haloalkanes, but slightly differently for amines, so take care.

Q Classify cyclohexanol,

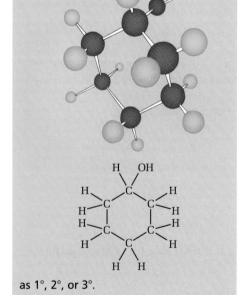

as 1°, 2°, or 3°.

Answer: 2°, because it has only one hydrogen attached to the carbon bearing the —OH group.

pairs (see section 9.1). The important thing is to remember that the C—O—H group is *not* linear, even though the conventional way of drawing displayed formulae makes it seem as though it is. The 3D ball and stick and space-filling models give a better representation of the shape of the molecule.

22.2 Physical properties

The presence of the —OH group means that hydrogen bonding occurs between the molecules of alcohols and also between alcohols and water (see **Figure 22.1**).

The hydrogen bonding has two consequences:

Firstly it leads to boiling temperatures (and melting temperatures) being much higher than those of alkanes of comparable relative molecular mass. For example, butan-1-ol ($M_r = 74$) boils at 390 K compared with pentane ($M_r = 72$) which boils at 309 K. The shorter-chain alcohols are all liquids at room temperature. Decanol is the first solid.

Secondly, alcohols with relatively short carbon chains dissolve well in water. All the alcohols up to C_3 mix completely with water. From this point, the solubility in water gradually decreases with increasing carbon chain length.

A second —OH group in the molecule increases the solubility: pentane-1,5-diol is considerably more soluble in water than pentan-1-ol.

Alcohols mix well with less polar solvents such as hydrocarbons, but there is no hydrogen bonding involved in this case.

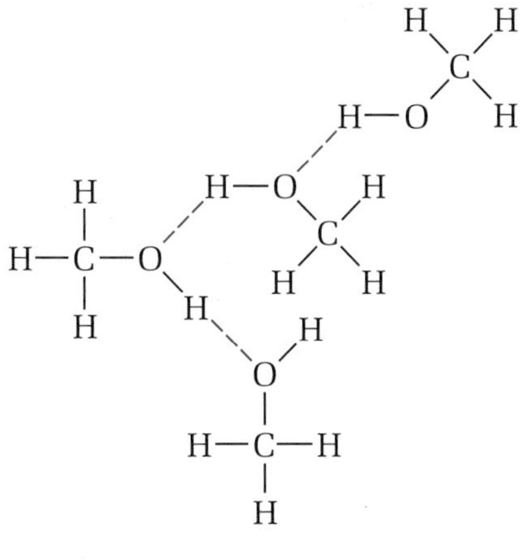

Figure 22.1 Hydrogen bonding in methanol

22.3 Reactivity of alcohols

Let us look at a typical alcohol molecule, propan-1-ol.

Figure 22.2 shows the average bond energies and electronegativities.

The hydrocarbon chain has fairly strong bonds and, more importantly, they are relatively non-polar bonds. The C—C bond is, of course, completely non-polar and the difference in electronegativity between C and H is only 0.4 units. This does not

Hint: Remember the condition for hydrogen bonding: it takes place between an electronegative ('big three' – see section 10.1) atom and a hydrogen atom covalently bonded to an electronegative atom.

Q Why is it important to compare molecules of similar M_r when discussing hydrogen bonding?

Did you know? A person with a lot of body fat contains less water than a muscular person of the same weight. As alcohol is more soluble in water than in fat, the fatter person's blood will contain more alcohol for a given amount consumed.

Q Suggest why propane-1,2,3-triol (glycerine) is a very viscous (treacly) liquid.

Answer: Molecules with similar M_r's will have comparable van der Waals forces, so any differences in melting and boiling temperatures will be caused by differences in hydrogen bonding only.

Answer: With three —OH groups, there is considerable hydrogen bonding between the molecules, which makes them difficult to separate.

Hint: We *do* need a locant in propan–1-ol as the —OH group could be at the end of the chain or in the middle, as in propan-2-ol.

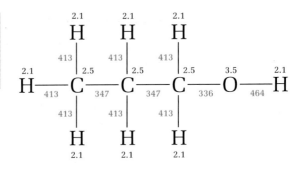

Figure 22.2 Propan-1-ol showing the average bond energies and electronegativities

give much of a 'handle' for charged reagents and we would expect this part of the molecule to remain unaffected in most chemical environments.

By contrast, if we consider C—OH, both the C—O and O—H bonds are strongly polar, $C^{\delta+}$—$O^{\delta-}$—$H^{\delta+}$. So nucleophiles can attack the $C^{\delta+}$. The $O^{\delta-}$ will be susceptible to attack by positively charged species (electrophiles) such as H^+. So, despite the relatively strong C—O and O—H bonds, all the reactions in alcohol molecules will take place around the C—O—H group.

We can also predict *how* the C—O and O—H bonds are likely to break. Because oxygen is so electronegative, it will capture both the shared electrons when either of these bonds breaks.

So if the O—H bond breaks we will get the ions:
$C_3H_7O:^-$ and H^+, *not* the ions $C_3H_7O^+$ and $H:^-$, *nor* the radicals $C_3H_7O\cdot$ and $H\cdot$.

This formation of H^+, a proton, when the O—H bond breaks means that we would predict alcohols to be acidic. As we shall see, alcohols *are* somewhat acidic.

If the C—O bond breaks we will get the ions:
$C_3H_7^+$ and $:OH^-$, *not* the ions $C_3H_7:^-$ and OH^+ *nor* the radicals $C_3H_7\cdot$ and $OH\cdot$.

So another possibility is that alcohols might react by loss of OH^- as the **leaving group**. This is in fact the case in many reactions of alcohols.

Hint: Remember, this is called **heterolytic** bond breaking.

Q What is the name for bond breaking where one electron from the bond goes to each fragment? What are the fragments called?

Q Write a balanced equation for the complete combustion of propanol.

22.4 Reactions of alcohols

Combustion

Alcohols burn readily to carbon dioxide and water in a plentiful supply of oxygen for example:

$$C_2H_5OH(l) + 3O_2(g) \longrightarrow 2CO_2(g) + 3H_2O(l)$$

Ethanol is often used as a fuel, for example, in picnic stoves which burn methylated spirits. This is ethanol with a small percentage of poisonous methanol added to make it unfit to drink so that it can be sold without the tax which is levied on alcoholic drinks. A blue dye is also added to show that it cannot be drunk.

Alcohol-burning stove

Answer: Homolytic, radicals

Answer: $C_3H_7OH + 4\frac{1}{2}O_2 \longrightarrow 3CO_2 + 4H_2O$

Selective oxidation

Combustion is, of course, oxidation but alcohols can be oxidised more selectively by oxidising agents such as sodium or potassium dichromate(VI) in acid solution or potassium manganate(VII).

Primary alcohols are oxidised to **aldehydes** which can themselves be further oxidised to **carboxylic acids.**

For example:

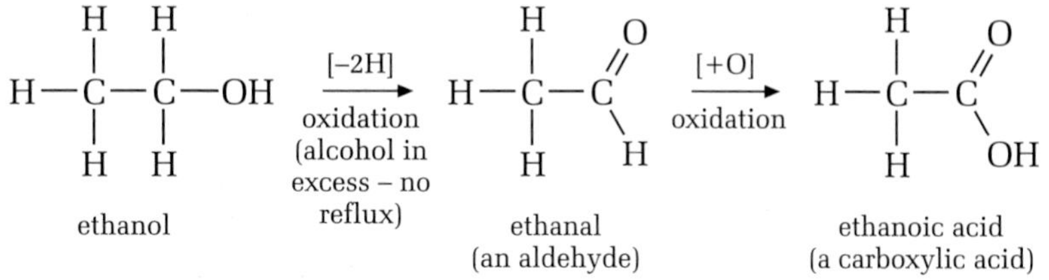

ethanol   [−2H] oxidation (alcohol in excess − no reflux)   ethanal (an aldehyde)   [+O] oxidation   ethanoic acid (a carboxylic acid)

Average Ox(C)   −II   −I   0

Secondary alcohols are oxidised to **ketones**, which are not oxidised further.

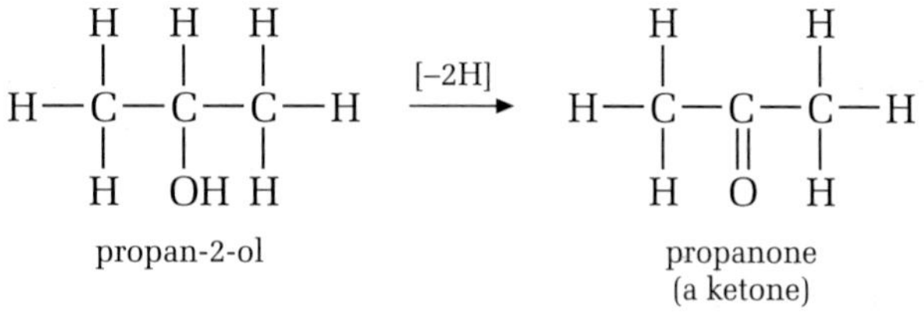

propan-2-ol   [−2H]   propanone (a ketone)

Tertiary alcohols are not easily oxidised at all. Vigorous oxidation results in the breaking of the carbon chain and two carboxylic acids are produced.

We can use this difference in behaviour to distinguish between 1°, 2° and 3° alcohols. The reason for the failure of ketones to oxidise further, or 3° alcohols to oxidise at all, is because in each case, oxidation would require the breaking of the carbon chain, rather than breaking of a C—H bond (which is what happens when an aldehyde is oxidised).

A solution of acidified dichromate ions is often used as the oxidising agent. In the reaction the orange dichromate(VI) ions are reduced to green chromium(III) ions:

$$\overset{+VI}{Cr_2O_7{}^{2-}} + 14H^+ + 6e^- \longrightarrow \overset{+III}{2Cr^{3+}} + 7H_2O$$

down $3 \times 2 = 6$

Bearing in mind the average oxidation number changes,

$$\overset{-II}{C_2H_5OH} \longrightarrow \overset{-I}{C_2H_4O} + 2H^+ + 2e^-$$

up $1 \times 2 = 2$

ethanol   ethanal

we can work out a balanced equation for the reaction of ethanol and acidified dichromate ions. To balance the oxidation number changes, ethanol and dichromate ions must react together in a 3 : 1 ratio to give ethanal.

CHEMISTRY AROUND US

Metabolising ethanol

In the liver, enzymes catalyse the oxidation of ethanol to carbon dioxide and water via ethanal and ethanoic acid.

$$C_2H_5OH \longrightarrow CH_3CHO \longrightarrow CH_3CO_2H \longrightarrow CO_2 + H_2O$$

ethanol   ethanal   ethanoic   carbon   water
                             acid   dioxide

Q Can you see why each of the steps above is an oxidation? (*Hint*: Work out what has been added or taken away at each stage. You could also use oxidation numbers but this is harder.)

Answer: ethanol ⟶ ethanal: two atoms of hydrogen have been removed

ethanal ⟶ ethanoic acid: an atom of oxygen has been added

ethanoic acid ⟶ carbon dioxide and water: oxygen added

or, using oxidation numbers (*Hint*: remember the oxidation number becomes more positive when a species is oxidised):

In ethanol, the *average* oxidation number of the carbon atoms is −II.

In ethanal, the *average* oxidation number of the carbon atoms is −I.

In ethanoic acid, the *average* oxidation number of the carbon atoms is 0.

In carbon dioxide, the oxidation number of the carbon atom is +IV.

Hint: Check that the equation is **chemically** balanced, i.e. that there are the same number of atoms of each element on both sides of the equation.

If we multiply the second half-equation above by three and add the two resulting equations we get:

$$Cr_2O_7^{2-}(aq) + 3C_2H_5OH(l) + 8H^+(aq)$$
ethanol

$$\longrightarrow 2Cr^{3+}(aq) + 3CH_3CHO(g) + 2Cr^{3+}(aq) + 7H_2O(l)$$
ethanal

Notice that the electrons on either side cancel out (this shows that we have got the two equations in the correct ratio) and that six of the H$^+$ ions also cancel.

For the overall reaction to ethanoic acid, the average oxidation number changes are:

$$\overset{-II}{C_2H_5OH} + H_2O \longrightarrow \overset{0}{C_2H_4O_2} + 4H^+ +$$
up 2 × 2 = 4

Hint: Check that you can get this equation by multiplying and adding the two half equations as in the case of oxidation to ethanal above. The arithmetic is a little more complicated.

so in this case a 3 : 2 ethanol : dichromate ion ratio is required. This gives the overall equation:

$$2Cr_2O_7^{2-}(aq) + 3C_2H_5OH(l) + 16H^+(aq)$$
$$\longrightarrow 4Cr^{3+}(aq) + 3CH_3CO_2H(aq) + 11H_2O(l)$$

This reaction was the basis of chemical breathalysers used by the police when drink driving limits were first introduced in the late 1960s (see the box 'Measuring alcohol in the blood').

Making new compounds by oxidation

Ethanal

To prepare ethanal from ethanol, fairly gentle oxidising conditions are used. We use less dichromate than the required ratio of dichromate to ethanol with dilute acid, and heat gently in the apparatus shown in **Figure 22.3**. Ethanal ($T_b = 294$ K) vaporises as soon as it is formed and distils over, thus avoiding further oxidation to ethanoic acid.

Hint: Excess dichromate means more than two moles of dichromate ions to every three moles of ethanol (see the equation above).

Ethanoic acid

To prepare ethanoic acid, an excess of dichromate is used and the mixture refluxed (**Figure 22.4**).

Any ethanol or ethanal will condense and drip back into the flask until it is all eventually oxidised to the acid. After refluxing for around 20 minutes, the ethanoic acid ($T_b = 391$ K) can be distilled off (along with any water) by rearranging the apparatus to that of **Figure 22.5**.

Q Why does ethanal have a lower T_b than both ethanol and ethanoic acid?

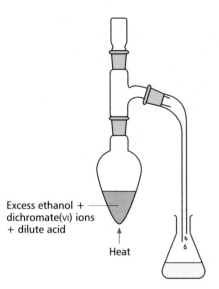

Excess ethanol + dichromate(VI) ions + dilute acid

Heat

Figure 22.3 Apparatus for the oxidation of ethanol to ethanal

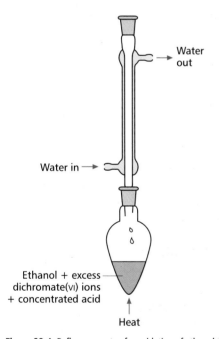

Ethanol + excess dichromate(VI) ions + concentrated acid

Water out

Water in →

Heat

Figure 22.4 Reflux apparatus for oxidation of ethanol to ethanoic and

Answer: Both ethanol and ethanoic acid form hydrogen bonds. Ethanal does not.

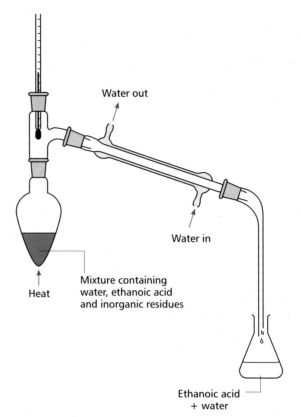

Water out

Water in

Heat

Mixture containing water, ethanoic acid and inorganic residues

Ethanoic acid + water

Figure 22.5 Apparatus for distilling ethanoic acid from the reaction mixture

Alcohols as acids and bases

acting as acid

acting as base

Like water (see section 12.2), an alcohol is capable of donating a proton or accepting one.

As acids

If an alcohol donates a proton to some other species, B, it is acting as an acid. To do this, the O—H bond must break heterolytically leaving a carbon-containing negative ion called an alkoxide ion.

an alkoxide ion

Alcohols are weaker acids than water. The only reactions which they undergo which show evidence of acidity are those with alkali metals. These are less vigorous than the reactions of the same metal with water.

For example:

$$Na(s) + C_2H_5OH(l) \longrightarrow C_2H_5O^-Na^+(s) + \tfrac{1}{2}H_2(g)$$

sodium ethoxide

Sodium ethoxide is a white, ionic solid which can be isolated by evaporating away any excess ethanol. Alkoxide ions are strong bases and good nucleophiles because of the negative charge on the oxygen atom. The evolution of hydrogen when sodium is added, is a useful test for the presence of an —OH group in an organic compound.

As bases

Because of the lone pairs of electrons on the oxygen atom, an alcohol can accept a proton from an acid, HA, thus acting as a base:

The alcohol is said to be **protonated**. Protonation is an important first step in a number of reactions of alcohols.

Formation of haloalkanes

Alcohols react with hydrogen halides (HCl, HBr, HI) to give the corresponding haloalkane. The rate of reaction is in the order HI>HBr>HCl. Strong acids catalyse the reaction, so the hydrogen halide is often generated in the reaction flask by the reaction of an alkali metal halide with concentrated sulphuric acid. (Not in the case of HI as sulphuric acid oxidises hydrogen iodide to iodine – see section 17.4). For example:

$$2KBr(s) + H_2SO_4(l) \longrightarrow K_2SO_4(s) + 2HBr(g)$$

and:

$$C_2H_5OH(l) + HBr(g) \xrightarrow{\text{H}^+ \text{ catalyst}} C_2H_5Br(l) + H_2O(l)$$

The first step in the reaction is the rapid protonation of the —OH group to give a positively charged ion (a carbocation).

Some of the positive charge of the ion resides on the carbon to which the —OH_2 group is attached. This increases its $C^{\delta+}$ character. (It is already somewhat $\delta+$ because it is attached to an electronegative oxygen atom.)

The reaction then continues in one of two ways:

- The $C^{\delta+}$ is attacked by the nucleophile X^- and loses H_2O. This is an S_N2 mechanism, as the rate of this step depends on the concentration of both $C_2H_5OH_2^+$ and X^-. In this case protonation speeds up the reaction by increasing the $\delta+$ character of the carbon atom attached to the —OH group, making it more susceptible to attack by a nucleophile (a 'positive-seeking' reagent) and by improving the leaving group (water, rather than the OH^- ion).

Answer: $Na(s) + HOH(l) \longrightarrow HO^-Na^+(aq) + \tfrac{1}{2}H_2(g)$

Q What do the terms S_N1 and S_N2 stand for?

$$H{-}C{-}C{-}O^+ \xrightarrow{\text{slow}} H{-}C{-}C{-}X + H_2O$$

- Alternatively the protonated alcohol loses H_2O leaving a carbocation which is rapidly attacked by the nucleophile X^-. This is an S_N1 mechanism, as the rate of the slow step depends only on the concentration of $C_2H_5OH_2{}^+$. In this case, protonation speeds the reaction by improving the leaving group; water is a better leaving group than the OH^- ion.

$$H{-}C{-}C{-}O^+ \xrightarrow{\text{slow}} H{-}C{-}C^+ + H_2O \xrightarrow[X^-]{\text{fast}} H{-}C{-}C{-}X$$

carbocation

The S_N1 mechanism involves a carbocation. This is more stable the more alkyl groups there are attached to it, since they release electrons via the inductive effect – see section 18.8 – and stabilise the positive charge. So tertiary alcohols tend to react by S_N1 and primary alcohols by S_N2. This is the same pattern we found for the reaction of haloalkanes with OH^- ions to form alcohols – the reverse of this reaction (see section 21.4).

Alternatively, the conversion of alcohols to haloalkanes can be brought about by using phosphorus halides – PCl_3, PCl_5, PBr_3 or PI_3 (for the last two the phosphorus trihalide is made in the reaction flask by mixing red phosphorus and the halogen). The equations for these reactions are:

$$3ROH + PX_3 \longrightarrow 3RX + H_3PO_3$$
phosphonic acid

$$ROH + PCl_5 \longrightarrow RCl + POCl_3 + HCl$$
phosphorus trichloride oxide

For preparing chloroalkanes, a further reagent can be used, sulphur dichloride oxide, $SOCl_2$ (also called thionyl chloride). This reagent has the advantage that all the products other than the haloalkane are gases and so there is no problem separating them from the haloalkane. For example:

$$CH_3CH_2OH(l) + SOCl_2(l) \longrightarrow CH_3CH_2Cl(l) + SO_2(g) + HCl(g)$$

Dehydration of alcohols

This is an **elimination** reaction. Alcohols can be dehydrated by passing their vapours over heated aluminium oxide. For example:

$$H{-}C{-}C{-}C{-}H \xrightarrow[600\text{ K}]{Al_2O_3} H{-}C{-}C{=}C + H_2O$$

propan-1-ol   propene

H_2O

The apparatus used is shown in **Figure 22.6**.

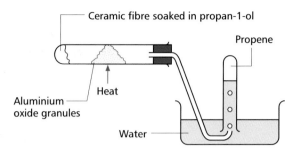

Figure 22.6 Dehydration of an alcohol

With longer-chain, or branched-chain alcohols, there may be more than one possible product and both *cis*- and *trans*- isomers may be found.

butan-2-ol

Al_2O_3
600 K

but-1-ene

H_2O

Al_2O_3
600 K

H_2O

cis-but-2-ene   +   *trans*-but-2-ene

Saytzeff's rule predicts that the predominant product is the isomer in which the double bond of the alkene has the most alkyl groups attached. So but-2-ene (two alkyl groups) is the main product in the example above, because in but-1-ene, the double bond has only one alkyl group.

Phosphoric(v) acid is an alternative dehydrating agent.

Sulphuric acid can also be used to dehydrate alcohols if used in excess. For example:

$$C_2H_5OH \xrightarrow[440\ K]{H_2SO_4} \quad C{=}C \quad + H_2O$$

This reaction is believed to occur in steps as follows:

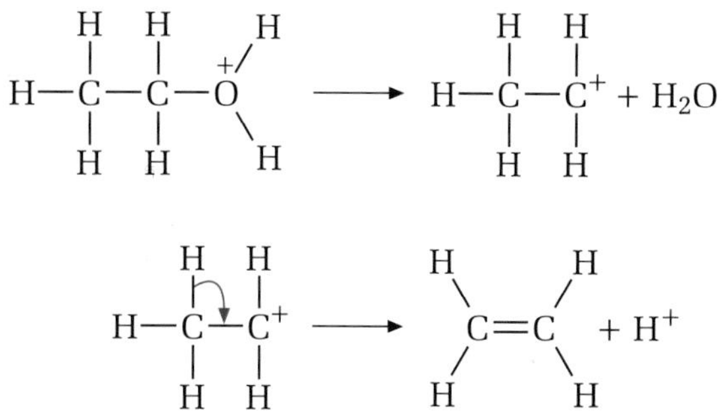

However, if an excess of alcohol is used, the result is the formation of an ether (a compound with the formula R—O—R):

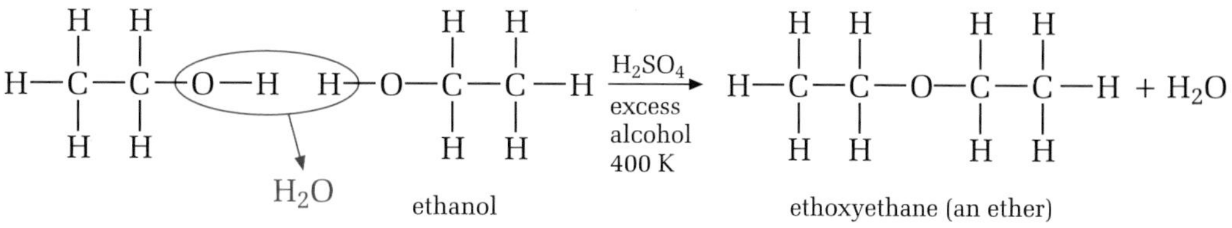

This reaction is known as **Williamson's continuous ether synthesis**.

Formation of esters

Alcohols react with carboxylic acids, RCO_2H (Chapter 34). A molecule of water is eliminated and an ester is produced. For example:

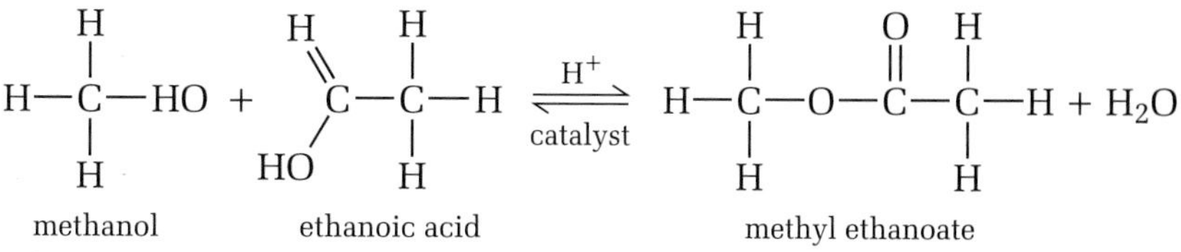

The reaction is catalysed by a strong acid such as sulphuric acid and does not go to completion. An equilibrium mixture containing a good deal of all four components is formed. The overall reaction:

$$acid + alcohol \rightleftharpoons ester + water$$

is rather similar to:

$$acid + base \longrightarrow salt + water$$

and suggests that the alcohol is behaving in some sense as a base.

> **Q** The boiling point of ethoxyethane is 308 K. Suggest how you might separate it from the reaction mixture containing ethanol, sulphuric acid and water. How does this explain the name continuous ether synthesis?
>
> *Answer:* It could be distilled off because it has the lowest boiling point. This could be done continuously as the reaction proceeds.

FURTHER FOCUS

Investigating the mechanism of esterification

Tracer experiments with alcohols containing the ^{18}O isotope show that all the ^{18}O is found in the organic product and none in the water.

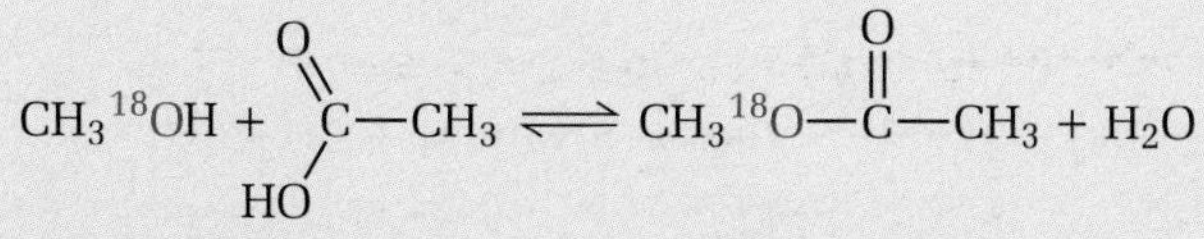

A mass spectrometer can easily detect the difference in mass between methyl ethanoate containing ^{18}O ($M_r = 74$) and that containing ^{16}O ($M_r = 76$).

This indicates that a new bond is formed between the oxygen of the alcohol and the carbon of the carboxylic acid followed by loss of a molecule of water containing the oxygen from the —OH group of the acid. It rules out the possibility that the new bond is formed between the oxygen of the —OH group of the acid and the carbon atom of the alcohol.

The reaction is called an addition–elimination, the overall effect being substitution of —OH on the acid by —O—R.

The detailed mechanism of esterification is discussed in section 14.6. It is a nucleophilic substitution reaction. The reaction takes place more readily with acid chlorides, RCOCl, (Chapter 34) than with carboxylic acids:

$$H-\overset{\delta+}{\underset{Cl^{\delta-}}{C}}\overset{O^{\delta-}}{\diagup}\quad H\ddot{O}-R' \xrightarrow{-Cl^-} R-\overset{O}{\underset{\underset{H}{|}}{\overset{||}{C}}}-\overset{+}{O}-R' \longrightarrow R-\overset{O}{\overset{||}{C}}-O-R' + H^+$$

The overall reaction is as follows:

$$R-\overset{O}{\overset{||}{C}}-Cl + H-O-R' \longrightarrow R-\overset{O}{\overset{||}{C}}-O-R' + HCl$$

an ester

The —Cl atom makes the carbon of the $-\overset{O^{\delta-}}{\underset{Cl^{\delta-}}{\overset{\diagup\!\!\!/}{C^{\delta+}}}}$ group

strongly $\delta+$, as it is attached to *two* electronegative atoms, Cl and O. This allows even a weak nucleophile, such as an alcohol, to attack the $C^{\delta+}$ of the acid chloride.

The esterification reaction with an acid chloride has two advantages over that with an acid: it occurs more quickly and it goes to completion.

The triiodomethane (iodoform) reaction

The reaction occurs only with alcohols containing the group

$$H-\overset{\overset{\displaystyle H}{|}}{\underset{\underset{\displaystyle H}{|}}{C}}-\overset{\overset{\displaystyle OH}{|}}{\underset{\underset{\displaystyle H}{|}}{C}}-$$

So it will work with ethanol and propan-2-ol but not methanol or propan-1-ol.

The alcohol is warmed with a solution of sodium hydroxide and iodine. Alcohols with the above group will form a yellow precipitate of triiodomethane by the reaction:

$$H-\overset{\overset{\displaystyle H}{|}}{\underset{\underset{\displaystyle H}{|}}{C}}-\overset{\overset{\displaystyle OH}{|}}{\underset{\underset{\displaystyle H}{|}}{C}}-R(l) + 4I_2(aq) + 6NaOH(aq) \longrightarrow$$

$$H-\overset{\overset{\displaystyle I}{|}}{\underset{\underset{\displaystyle I}{|}}{C}}-I(s) + R-\overset{O}{\overset{\diagup\!\!\!/}{C}}\underset{O^-Na^+}{}(aq) + 5NaI(aq) + 5H_2O(l)$$

Q What molecule is eliminated when an ester is formed from an acid chloride and an alcohol? How does this help the reaction go to completion?

The reaction can be used as a test for the presence of the above structural group in an organic compound. As the first step involves

Answer: Hydrogen chloride (a gas) is formed. This is easy to remove from the reaction mixture, thus forcing the equilibrium over to the right.

oxidation of the alcohol to a ketone (or aldehyde if R = H), it follows that compounds containing the group

$$H-\underset{\underset{H}{|}}{\overset{\overset{H}{|}}{C}}-\overset{\overset{O}{||}}{C}-$$

will also give a positive result with the test.

22.5 Preparation of alcohols

The main methods of preparing alcohols in the laboratory are summarised below. The reactions are discussed in more detail in the chapters about the starting materials.

From alkenes

$$\underset{H}{\overset{R}{\diagdown}}C=C\underset{H}{\overset{H}{\diagup}} \quad \xrightarrow[\text{then } H_2O]{H_2SO_4} \quad H-\underset{\underset{OH}{|}}{\overset{\overset{R}{|}}{C}}-\underset{\underset{H}{|}}{\overset{\overset{H}{|}}{C}}-H$$

Hint: You could remember the rule by the phrase 'The rich get richer' (in hydrogen).

With unsymmetrical alkenes (those with more alkyl groups on one carbon than the other, the H adds onto the carbon atom which already has most hydrogens. This is a further example of **Markovnikov's rule** (see section 20.4).

From haloalkanes

Boiling haloalkanes with aqueous alkali produces alcohols.

$$R-X + OH^- \xrightarrow[\text{aqueous solution}]{\text{reflux}} R-OH + X^-$$

Reduction of aldehydes, ketones, carboxylic acids and esters

Aldehydes, carboxylic acids and esters are reduced to primary alcohols, while ketones give secondary alcohols. (This is the reverse of the oxidation of alcohols to aldehydes to carboxylic acids.) A number of reducing agents can be used as shown in the summary below.

$$\text{aldehyde} \left.\begin{matrix} \\ \\ \\ \end{matrix}\right\} \quad \xrightarrow{\text{Na/C}_2\text{H}_5\text{OH}} \text{or} \quad \xrightarrow{\text{NaBH}_4 \text{ (aq)}} \text{or} \quad \left\{\begin{matrix} 1° \text{ alcohol} \\ \\ 2° \text{ alcohol} \end{matrix}\right.$$

ketone

$$\xrightarrow{\substack{\text{LiAlH}_4 \text{ in} \\ \text{ethoxyethane}}}$$

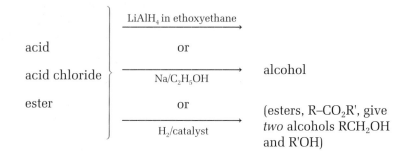

LiAlH$_4$ is called lithium tetrahydridoaluminate(III) or lithium aluminium hydride. NaBH$_4$ is called sodium tetrahydridoborate(III) or sodium borohydride.

> **Hint:** Hydrolysis means reaction with water. An acidic or basic catalyst is often used.

Hydrolysis of esters

Esters can be hydrolysed in either acidic or alkaline conditions to produce alcohols and carboxylic acids (salts of the acids in alkaline conditions).

$$R-\underset{\displaystyle \underset{O}{\|}}{C}-OR' \xrightarrow{\text{H}_2\text{O, H}^+ \text{ or OH}^-} R-\underset{\displaystyle \underset{O}{\|}}{C}-OH + R'OH$$

The alcohol is made from sugars. The fermentation locks prevent oxidation of ethanol to ethanoic acid – vinegar!

22.6 Chemistry of economic importance of alcohols

You are unlikely to buy pure (or almost pure) alcohol for any reason, except, perhaps, methylated spirits, which is ethanol made undrinkable by the addition of a little methanol. 'Meths' is used as a

The strength of alcoholic drinks

Some alcoholic drinks contain a high enough percentage of alcohol to be flammable. This was the basis of an early method of measuring their concentration or 'strength'. 100° proof spirit was the weakest mixture of alcohol and water which, when poured onto gunpowder, would not stop it igniting. Nowadays 100° proof is defined as having a density of 0.92 g cm^{-3} at 51 °F (approximately 282 K). This corresponds to about 50% alcohol.

Some alcoholic drinks and their percentage alcohol content

camping stove fuel and for cleaning. However about a quarter of a million tonnes of ethanol is produced annually in the UK for a variety of uses including the following:

●   alcoholic drinks
●   as a solvent
●   in cosmetics manufacture
●   as an intermediate in the manufacture of many other chemicals.

The use of alcohols as intermediates is due to their reactivity: they can be easily made and are easily converted into other compounds.

Fermentation

Ethanol is the alcohol present in all alcoholic drinks. It is made by fermentation, in which carbohydrates like starch are first broken down into sugars, and then into ethanol, by the action of enzymes obtained from yeast. The key step is:

$$C_6H_{12}O_6(aq) \xrightarrow{\text{enzymes}} 2C_2H_5OH(aq) + 2CO_2(g)$$

glucose (a sugar)   ethanol   carbon dioxide

Fermentation was once a major source of ethanol for industrial use. Now ethanol is made mostly by catalytic hydration of ethene obtained from cracking of crude oil derivatives.

However, in the future, fermentation may again become a significant source of ethanol as stocks of crude oil eventually become depleted. Brazil produces alcohol by fermentation for use as a motor fuel.

The industrial chemistry of some important alcohols is summarised in **Figures 22.7–9**.

Sampling at a fermentation plant in Brazil

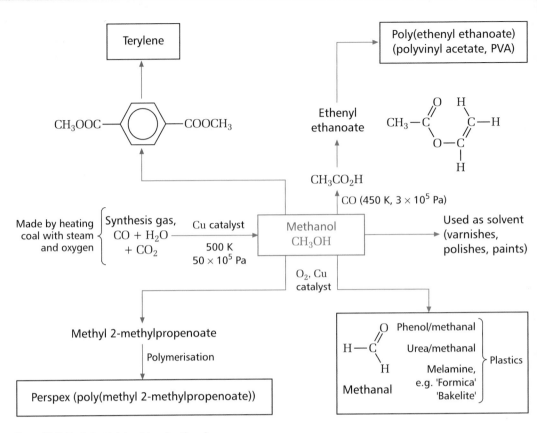

Figure 22.7 The industrial chemistry of methanol

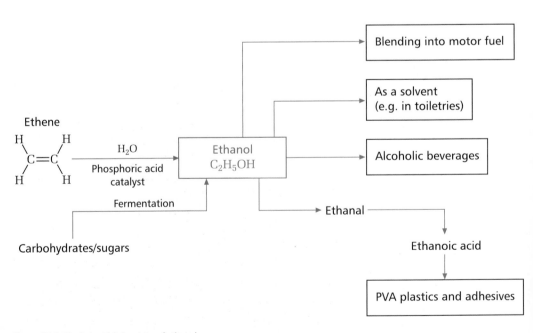

Figure 22.8 The industrial chemistry of ethanol

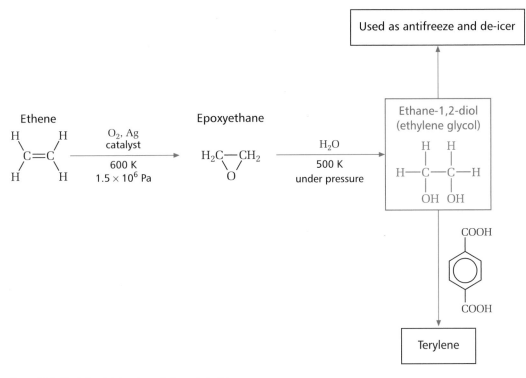

Figure 22.9 The industrial chemistry of ethane-1, 2-diol

CHEMISTRY AROUND US

The use of alcohols in cosmetics

Ethanol is an ingredient in many cosmetics. It comprises around 70% of a typical after-shave lotion. Ethanol is quite volatile and its function is to evaporate, absorbing its enthalpy change of vaporisation and cooling the skin. This closes the pores in the skin which have been opened by the hot water used in shaving. The ethanol also acts as a mild antiseptic preventing infection in any shaving nicks.

Ethanol is also an ingredient in many types of nail varnish. It acts as a solvent for the lacquer. When the solution is applied to the nails, the ethanol evaporates leaving a layer of lacquer on the nail. Nail varnish remover may also contain ethanol but more frequently contains propanone or ethyl ethanoate to dissolve the lacquer.

Polyols (alcohols with more than one —OH group) are found in moisturising creams where they act as humectants (they attract water vapour from the air).

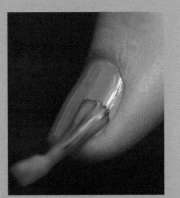 

Water vapour molecules from the air are attracted by the —OH groups of the alcohols in the moisturising cream and are 'trapped' by hydrogen bonding. Alcohols used in this way are propane-1,2,3-triol (glycerine), propane-1,2-diol and hexane-1,3,4,6-tetraol (sorbitol).

Chemistry Around Us

Measuring alcohol in the blood

Since 1967 it has been illegal to drive in the UK with a blood ethanol concentration of greater than 80 mg of alcohol per 100 cm³ of blood.

When the law was first introduced, levels of alcohol in the breath were measured by chemical breathalysers in which a breath sample was blown over orange, acidified potassium dichromate crystals. These oxidised any ethanol in the breath and were themselves reduced to green chromium(III). The more ethanol, the more green crystals were formed. In the lungs there is an equilibrium set up between alcohol dissolved in blood and that in the breath. So breath alcohol levels are proportional to those in blood. (This is an example of Henry's law – see the box 'Solubility of gases – from soft drinks to driving' in section 27.6).

The legal limit of ethanol in the breath is $35\ \mu\mathrm{g\ cm^{-3}}$. (1 μg is one millionth of a gram.)

Modern roadside breathalysers also work by oxidation of ethanol, but in a fuel cell, so that the oxidation generates an electrical voltage which is related to the alcohol concentration.

If a driver fails a roadside test, a more accurate breath alcohol measurement is done at the police station. A beam of infra-red radiation of the wavelength absorbed by a C—H bond stretch (about 2950 cm⁻¹ – see section 38.2) is shone through the breath sample. This is absorbed by the alcohol; the more alcohol, the more infra-red is absorbed. As a further check, blood samples can be tested for alcohol by gas chromatography (see section 23.1). The area of the peak corresponding to ethanol is proportional to its concentration.

> **Q** Work out the blood concentration of ethanol corresponding to the legal limit in the normal chemist's unit of mol dm⁻³.

A modern breathalyser in use

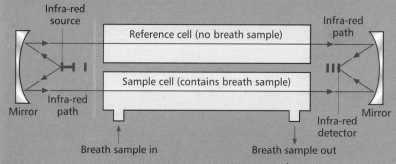

IR analysis of breath alcohol

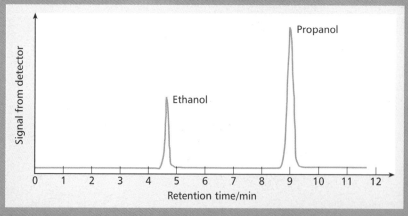

Alcohol in blood can be measured by gas chromatography. A known amount of propan-1-ol is added and the area of the ethanol peak compared with the propanol one

Answer: 0.0174 mol dm⁻³

22.7 Summary

- Alcohols contain the functional group   —OH.

- Alcohols are classified as   primary, secondary or tertiary.

- Primary alcohols have   one R groups attached to the carbon bearing the —OH group.

- Secondary alcohols have   two R groups attached to the carbon bearing the —OH group.

- Tertiary alcohols have   three R groups attached to the carbon bearing the —OH group.

- Alcohols have significantly higher melting and boiling temperatures than alkanes of comparable relative molecular mass because of   hydrogen bonding between the molecules.

- Alcohols with chains of four carbons or fewer mix well with   water.

- All alcohols mix well with   non-polar solvents.

- The C—O—H group is polar. The $C^{\delta+}$ can be attacked by   nucleophiles.

● The reactions of alcohols are summarised below in **Figure 22.10**.

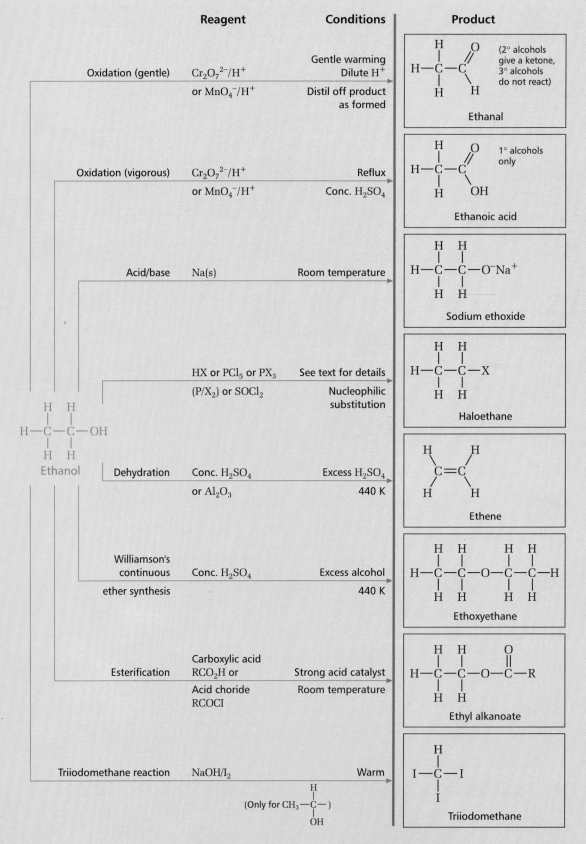

Figure 22.10 Reactions of alcohols using ethanol as an example – cover up the right-hand side to test yourself

- The methods of preparation are summarised in **Figure 22.11**.

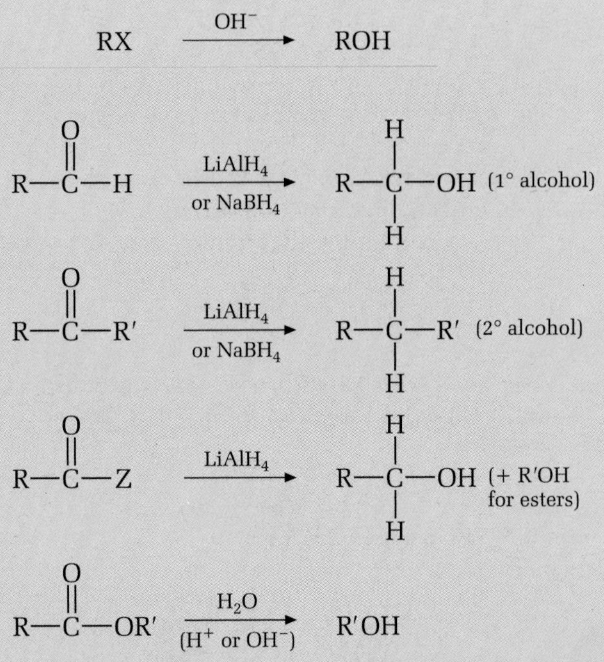

$$RX \xrightarrow{\quad OH^- \quad} ROH$$

$$R-\overset{\displaystyle O}{\overset{\displaystyle \|}{C}}-H \xrightarrow[\text{or } NaBH_4]{LiAlH_4} R-\overset{\displaystyle H}{\underset{\displaystyle H}{\overset{|}{\underset{|}{C}}}}-OH \quad (1° \text{ alcohol})$$

$$R-\overset{\displaystyle O}{\overset{\displaystyle \|}{C}}-R' \xrightarrow[\text{or } NaBH_4]{LiAlH_4} R-\overset{\displaystyle H}{\underset{\displaystyle H}{\overset{|}{\underset{|}{C}}}}-R' \quad (2° \text{ alcohol})$$

$$R-\overset{\displaystyle O}{\overset{\displaystyle \|}{C}}-Z \xrightarrow{\quad LiAlH_4 \quad} R-\overset{\displaystyle H}{\underset{\displaystyle H}{\overset{|}{\underset{|}{C}}}}-OH \quad \substack{(+ \text{ R'OH} \\ \text{for esters})}$$

$$R-\overset{\displaystyle O}{\overset{\displaystyle \|}{C}}-OR' \xrightarrow[(H^+ \text{ or } OH^-)]{H_2O} R'OH$$

Figure 22.11 Methods of preparation of alcohols

22.8 Practice questions

1. Name the following.

(a) 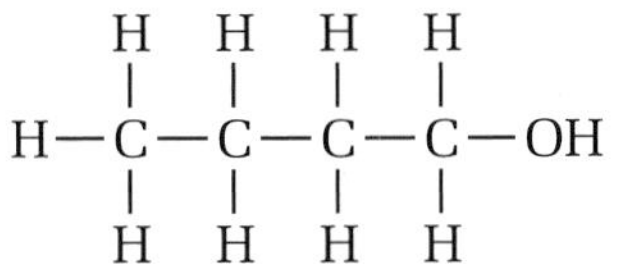
$$H-\overset{H}{\underset{H}{\overset{|}{\underset{|}{C}}}}-\overset{H}{\underset{H}{\overset{|}{\underset{|}{C}}}}-\overset{H}{\underset{H}{\overset{|}{\underset{|}{C}}}}-\overset{H}{\underset{H}{\overset{|}{\underset{|}{C}}}}-OH$$

(b) 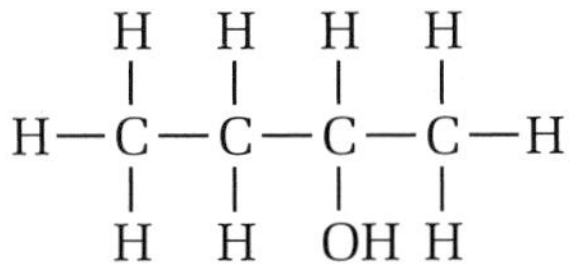
$$H-\overset{H}{\underset{H}{\overset{|}{\underset{|}{C}}}}-\overset{H}{\underset{H}{\overset{|}{\underset{|}{C}}}}-\overset{H}{\underset{OH}{\overset{|}{\underset{|}{C}}}}-\overset{H}{\underset{H}{\overset{|}{\underset{|}{C}}}}-H$$

2. Give the structural formula of:
(a) 2-chloropropan-1-ol
(b) 2-methylpropan-2-ol
(c) pentane-1,3-diol

3. Classify the following as primary, secondary or tertiary alcohols.

(a) 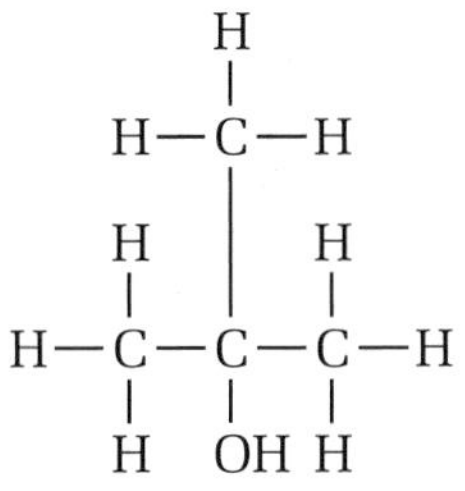
$$H-\overset{H}{\underset{H}{\overset{|}{\underset{|}{C}}}}-\overset{\overset{\displaystyle H}{\underset{\displaystyle |}{\overset{|}{C}-H}}}{\underset{OH}{\overset{|}{\underset{|}{C}}}}-\overset{H}{\underset{H}{\overset{|}{\underset{|}{C}}}}-H$$

(b) 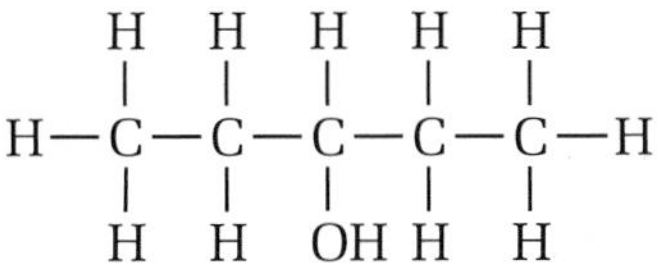
$$H-\overset{H}{\underset{H}{\overset{|}{\underset{|}{C}}}}-\overset{H}{\underset{H}{\overset{|}{\underset{|}{C}}}}-\overset{H}{\underset{OH}{\overset{|}{\underset{|}{C}}}}-\overset{H}{\underset{H}{\overset{|}{\underset{|}{C}}}}-\overset{H}{\underset{H}{\overset{|}{\underset{|}{C}}}}-H$$

4. Write an equation for an alcohol R—OH reacting with (a) an acid (H^+), (b) a base (B^-).

22.9 Examination questions

1. (a) Write an equation for the oxidation of pentan-2-ol by acidified potassium dichromate(VI) showing clearly the structure of the organic product. You may use the symbol [O] for the oxidising agent.
   (b) Pent-2-ene can be formed by the dehydration of pentan-2-ol. Give the reagent and conditions used. Outline a mechanism for this reaction.
   (c) Alcohols **E**, **F** and **G** are branched-chain isomers of pentanol.
   E cannot be oxidised by acidified potassium dichromate(VI).
   F can be oxidised by acidified potassium dichromate(VI) but cannot be dehydrated.
   G can be oxidised by acidified potassium dichromate(VI) and can also be dehydrated. Draw a possible structure for each of the three alcohols.
   (d) Draw and name the isomer of pentene which has three peaks in its low-resolution proton NMR spectrum and give the relative areas under the peaks.

   [NEAB 1998]

2. (a) (i)   Give the structure of 3-methylbutan-2-ol.
       (ii) Name and outline the mechanism for the reaction taking place when 3-methylbutan-2-ol is converted into 2-methylbut-2-ene in the presence of a strong acid.
       (iii) Explain why 3-methylbut-1-ene is also formed in this reaction.
   (b) (i)   Give the structure of the product obtained when 3-methylbutan-2-ol is treated with acidified potassium dichromate(VI).
       (ii) The mass spectrum of this product has dominant peaks at m/z values of 43 and 71. Give the structures of the species responsible for these two peaks.

   [NEAB 1998]

3. Three different reactions of propan-2-ol are shown below.

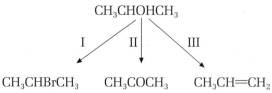

   (a) For each of the reactions I, II and III, give suitable reagents and conditions.
   (b) If 2-methylpropan-2-ol, $(CH_3)_3COH$, was used as the starting material in (a) instead of propan-2-ol, identify the organic products, if any, of reactions I, II and III. You should indicate if no reaction occurs.

   [London (Nuffield) 1998, part question]

4. Methanol may be oxidised catalytically using the following apparatus:

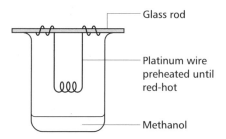

   When placed in position, the wire continues to glow and the pungent odour of methanal is noticed.
   (a) Draw the displayed formula for the pungent-smelling product, methanal.
   (b) (i)   What is the oxidising agent in this reaction?
       (ii) What can be deduced from the fact that the wire continues to glow?
   (c) The reaction can be carried out by an alternative method.
       (i)   What oxidising mixture might be used in an alternative method?
       (ii) When an alternative method is used a possible problem is that the methanal might be oxidised further to methanoic acid.
             Suggest **two** ways of minimising this problem.
   (d) What colour change is expected when methanal is warmed with Benedict's solution (with added sodium hydroxide if necessary)?

   [London (Nuffield) 1997]

Further equilibrium

C H E M I S T R Y   N O W

Equilibria in the blood: bones and stones

Most of the systems in our bodies are controlled by hormones. These are chemical messengers that are released by the glands, travel through the blood and affect the chemistry that occurs in our organs. The chemical reactions in our body are in fine balance. If this balance goes wrong, the consequences are far-reaching. In the rare condition of hyperparathyroidism, the patients literally excrete their own bones in their urine.

It is all to do with this equilibrium:

$$Ca_3(PO_4)_2(s) \rightleftharpoons 3Ca^{2+}(aq) + 2PO_4^{3-}(aq)$$

calcium phosphate   calcium ions   phosphate ions

Cross-section of bone. The calcium phosphate is present in the ring structures

Bone is a complex composite material consisting of an insoluble, fibrous protein called collagen, which is impregnated with inorganic salts, mostly calcium phosphate, $Ca_3(PO_4)_3$. This solid calcium phosphate is in equilibium with its constituent ions dissolved in the blood. Normally this equilibrium is well over to the left, so bones do not dissolve.

We all have four parathyroid glands in the throat, which secrete a hormone called parathormone. This controls the metabolism of calcium salts in the body, via its effect on phosphate ions. If these glands produce too much parathormone (a condition called hyperparathyroidism), the kidneys remove phosphate ions from the blood. Le Châtelier's principle predicts that the above equilibrium position will move to the right to minimise the effect of this disturbance. So calcium phosphate (from the bones) dissolves and the effect of this is to free phosphate ions and calcium ions. The overall result is that the concentration of calcium ions in the blood is higher than normal (and that of phosphate lower than normal).

This has a number of effects. The kidneys (whose function is to maintain a constant composition of the blood) respond by continually removing the excess calcium ions. This can cause precipitation of solid calcium phosphate in the kidneys, producing kidney stones. These can be excruciatingly painful. Other symptoms caused by the raised level of Ca^{2+} in the blood are: headaches, nausea, loss of appetite, constipation, excessive thirst and excessive urination. Without treatment, bone destruction can occur.

Often the problem is caused by a tumour of one of the parathyroid glands, in which case surgery to remove the affected gland usually cures the condition. While awaiting surgery, the patient can be treated to force the equilibrium back to the left and prevent the bones dissolving. The temporary solution is to prescribe tablets which contain sodium dihydrogenphosphate. This has the effect of forcing the equilibrium to the left, reducing the concentration of Ca^{2+} in the blood and keeping the calcium phosphate as solid bone. Patients are also given a diet low in calcium to keep the concentration of Ca^{2+} in the blood low, and alleviate the symptoms.

Introduction

This chapter builds on the ideas introduced in Chapter 11. It looks more closely at the equilibria that operate between different phases (parts of a system that are physically separated, such as liquids and their vapours) and also equilibria that take place in the gas phase. It develops the application of the equilibrium law to these systems.

CONCEPT CHECKPOINTS

The following basic ideas are used in this chapter. You may revise some of these topics elsewhere in the book.
- ☐ how to recognise when equilibrium has been set up (section 11.1)
- ☐ the equilibrium law (section 11.2)
- ☐ partial pressures (section 27.3)
- ☐ vapour pressures (section 11.1)

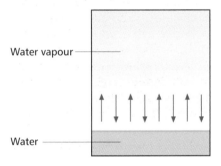

Water vapour

Water

Figure 23.1 The equilibrium between water and its vapour, which can be set up only in a closed system

Bubbles form in the body of the liquid when it boils

23.1 Phase equilibria

The **phases** of a system are parts of it which are separated by a distinct boundary, such as solid, liquid and gas. So phase equilibria are equilibria between different phases of the same substance, and we will take as an example water and its vapour, **Figure 23.1**.

$$\text{water(l)} \rightleftharpoons \text{water(g)}$$

This is a *dynamic* equilibrium. When it is established, water is evaporating at the same rate that vapour is condensing. External conditions may change the equilibrium. For example, if we increase the temperature, the average speed of the liquid molecules will increase and more of them will be able to escape from the liquid. For a moment, evaporation will be proceeding faster than condensation and the system will not be at equilibrium. However, this will lead to more molecules in the vapour and thus the rate of condensation will increase until the two are again equal. The new equilibrium position will have a higher vapour pressure.

The pressure of the vapour when in contact with the liquid phase is called the **saturated vapour pressure** (SVP). If we plot this against temperature we get the graph in **Figure 23.2**.

This is called a **phase diagram** for water and shows that the vapour pressure increases with temperature. The line shows the set of values of pressure and temperature at which water and water vapour can exist at equilibrium. To the left of the line (high pressure, low temperature) liquid is the stable phase, while to the right (high temperature, low pressure) it is vapour that exists.

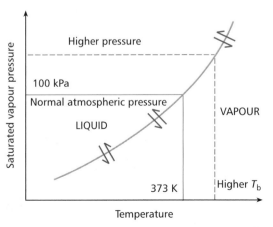

Figure 23.2 The saturated vapour pressure–temperature curve for water

Water boils at lower temperature when the atmospheric pressure is lower

Did you know? At the summit of Mount Everest (8848 m), the boiling temperature of water is approximately 71 °C (344 K). At the summit of Mont Blanc (4807 m) it is 85 °C (358 K) and on top of Ben Nevis (1392 m) 95 °C (368 K).

Q The water in a car radiator does not boil even though the temperature may exceed 100 °C. Can you explain this?

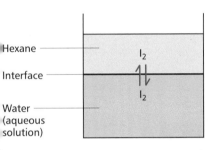

Figure 23.3 Partition of iodine between water and hexane

Hint: The square brackets represent the concentration (in mol dm^{-3}) of the species inside. The subscript 'eqm' shows that we have allowed the system to come to equilibrium before measuring the concentrations.

Q Why does iodine dissolve better in hexane than in water?

Answer: The water is kept under pressure in the sealed cooling system.

Answer: Iodine and hexane are both non-polar, while water is polar: the 'like dissolves like' rule (see section 10.2) applies.

Boiling

Liquids *evaporate* at all temperatures. Even at low temperatures there will always be a few molecules with enough energy to escape. Boiling is different. The *boiling* temperature, T_b, is the temperature at which the vapour pressure of the liquid is equal to atmospheric pressure. This means the vapour pressure is high enough to form bubbles of vapour in the body of the liquid. At lower vapour pressures than this, the pressure of the atmosphere would prevent bubbles forming. Bubble formation means that molecules can escape as vapour from anywhere in the liquid, not just at the surface.

The normal boiling temperature is the temperature at which the saturated vapour pressure is equal to standard atmospheric pressure, 100 kPa. This is marked on Figure 23.2. The graph shows that if the pressure increases, the boiling temperature will also increase and if the pressure decreases, the boiling temperature will decrease too. This lowering of the boiling temperature at low pressures explains why it is hard to make a good cup of tea high on a mountainside where the air pressure is lower than at sea level and water boils at a lower temperature.

Partition

Let us now look at a different example of equilibrium. If we take two liquids which do not mix (are immiscible) such as water and hexane, hexane which is the less dense, will float on top, so that two layers will be formed. If we now add a solute such as a crystal of iodine, I_2, and shake the mixture, the iodine will dissolve – some in each layer. (We actually use potassium iodide solution instead of water, to help the iodine to dissolve, but this is a detail.) Iodine can be seen in the layers because of its colour, pink in hexane and yellow in the aqueous layer. After shaking several times, the colours of the layers will not change, showing that an equilibrium has been set up. (See **Figure 23.3**.) We say the iodine is partitioned between the two layers.

$$I_2(aq) \rightleftharpoons I_2(hexane)$$

At the interface (the point where the two layers meet), some iodine will be moving 'up' and some 'down', but at equal rates: a dynamic equilibrium. If we measure the concentration in mol dm^{-3} of the solute in each layer, we find that there is a constant ratio between them, irrespective of the total amount of iodine used or the volume of solvent in each layer (provided the temperature remains constant). This is sometimes referred to as the Distribution Law.

So
$$\frac{[I_2 (hexane)]_{eqm}}{[I_2(aq)]_{eqm}} = \text{constant}$$

The constant is called the **partition coefficient** or **distribution ratio**, and is a particular example of a more general constant, the **equilibrium constant** (see Chapter 11). Its value (much greater than 1 at room temperature) shows that iodine has a much greater tendency to dissolve in hexane than water. In other words, the position of the equilibrium

$$I_2(aq) \rightleftharpoons I_2(hexane)$$

is well over to the right.

Further Focus

The phase diagram

Solids, as well as liquids and gases, have vapour pressures. This is obvious in the case of a solid like naphthalene (moth balls) which has a distinctive smell, showing that molecules must be escaping into the air as vapour. Solid water (ice), too, has a vapour pressure and its variation with temperature can be added to Figure 23.2. The change directly from solid to vapour is called **sublimation**. Finally, if the variation of melting temperature with pressure is added, we get the complete **phase diagram** for water (see below).

The phase diagram for water is not typical – the melting temperature line, T–B, slopes to the *left*, i.e. the melting temperature decreases with pressure. This is connected with the fact that ice is less dense than water, while most solids are denser than their liquids.

The phase diagram of carbon dioxide (see below), is more typical, showing a *rightward* sloping melting temperature line. (Solid carbon dioxide is denser than liquid carbon dioxide.) The triple point is above atmospheric pressure, so that at atmospheric pressure carbon dioxide sublimes. So 'dry ice', which is solid carbon dioxide, changes directly from solid to gas.

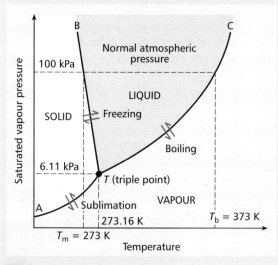

The phase diagram for water (not to scale)

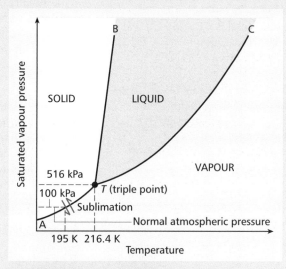

The phase diagram for carbon dioxide

T–C represents the variation of boiling temperature with pressure.

T–B represents the variation of melting temperature with pressure.

T–A represents the variation of sublimation temperature with pressure.

Each line represents the set of pressures and temperatures at which the two phases on either side of it can exist in equilibrium.

T is a unique point, the only temperature and pressure where all three phases are in equilibrium. It is called the **triple point** and for water is 273.16 K and 611 Pa. Moving to the right along a horizontal line (increasing temperature and constant pressure) at a pressure above the triple point, we pass in succession from solid to liquid to vapour, but below the triple point we pass directly from solid to vapour, i.e. the solid will sublime.

Dry ice is used to form mists at concerts. It sublimes at −78 °C. The mist is caused by water vapour in the air condensing at this temperature

Solvent extraction and chromatography make practical use of partition.

Solvent extraction

This is a method of separating one component from a mixture. It is based on finding a solvent which dissolves the desired component much better than it does any of the others. For example, in many

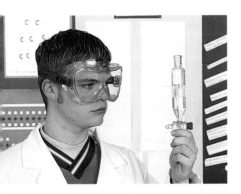

Separating an organic compound by solvent extraction

Hint: A partition coefficient of 20 means that X is twenty times more soluble in ethoxyethane than in water.

Did you know? Decaffeinated coffee is made by extracting the caffeine into liquid carbon dioxide. You can find the conditions under which carbon dioxide is a liquid from the phase diagram (see the figure in the box 'The phase diagram'). This solvent is used because it does not affect the flavour and aroma of the coffee. The extracted caffeine is used in 'cola' drinks and medicines.

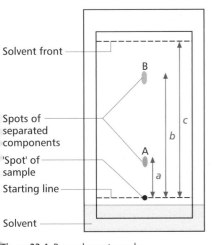

Figure 23.4 Paper chromatography

organic preparations the organic product is formed dissolved in water, mixed with some inorganic compounds.

Ethoxyethane is a solvent often used for extraction because:

- Most organic compounds dissolve well in it, while inorganic compounds tend to dissolve better in water.
- Ethoxyethane does not mix with water.

So, to separate the organic product we shake the aqueous solution with ethoxyethane and allow the two layers to separate. Most of the organic product will be dissolved in the ethoxyethane, while the inorganic ones will remain in the water.

If, for example, the partition coefficient of the organic compound between ethoxyethane and water is 20, i.e.

$$\frac{[X(ethoxyethane)]_{eqm}}{[X(aq)]_{eqm}} = \frac{20}{1}$$

and we use equal volumes of ethoxyethane and water, then $\frac{20}{21}$sts of the original compound will be extracted into ethoxyethane. This can then be distilled off to leave the organic product.

The technique is even more efficient if the ethoxyethane is used in several small portions rather than all at once .

Chromatography

Chromatography describes a whole family of separation techniques, all of which depend on the principle of partition. In each case a solvent, called the **mobile phase** (or **eluant**), moves over a second solvent which does not move, called the **stationary phase**. Each component of the mixture being separated is partitioned between the two solvents. The mobile phase carries the soluble components of the mixture with it. The more soluble the component in the mobile phase, the faster it moves. As well as separating the mixture, chromatography can be used to help identify the components of a mixture.

Paper chromatography

The most familiar chromatographic technique is paper chromatography (**Figure 23.4**), often used for separating dye mixtures, such as those in inks, where a solvent moves up a piece of filter paper by capillary action.

The cellulose of which the paper is made holds many trapped water molecules. These form the stationary phase. As the mobile phase moves past the sample spot, the substances in the spot become partitioned between the mobile and stationary phases (solvent and water). Dyes which are more soluble in the eluant than the water are carried along rapidly with the mobile phase, while those more soluble in water tend to remain where they are. Fresh eluant is constantly moving past the spot and the situation is rather like an enormous number of successive solvent extractions. The speed at which the spots move is proportional to the partition coefficient. When the solvent has moved a convenient distance, it is stopped by removing the paper from the solvent. For each spot, the R_f value (retardation factor) can be calculated from:

$$R_f = \frac{\text{distance moved by spot}}{\text{distance moved by solvent}}$$

Notice that the R_f value must always be less than 1, as the spot cannot move further than the solvent. If an unknown component has the same R_f value as that of a known compound, using the same solvent, it is highly probable that it is the same substance. The R_f value of any substance will differ for different solvents. An elaboration of this technique is **two-way chromatography**.

Two-way chromatography

A square of paper is used and a spot placed in one corner (see **Figure 23.5**).

The chromatograph is run as normal, vertically, using one solvent then the paper is turned through 90° and the chromatogram run again in another solvent. Two different R_f values are obtained for each component. If both R_f's of a spot match those of a known compound, then the two are almost certainly the same.

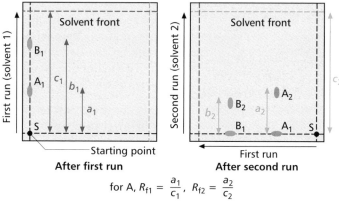

$$\text{for A, } R_{f1} = \frac{a_1}{c_1}, \ R_{f2} = \frac{a_2}{c_2}$$

Figure 23.5 Two-way paper chromatography

Thin layer chromatography (TLC)

This is a variation on paper chromatography in which the paper is replaced by a thin layer of powder such as silica or alumina on a glass or plastic backing. It is used to determine amino acids in blood samples and in analysis of food dyes.

Column chromatography

This is essentially a scaled-up version of thin layer chromatography. The mixture to be separated is placed at the top of a column – a tube packed with an inert material. Solvent is added at the top. Each component moves down the column at a different rate and can be collected separately in a flask at the bottom (see **Figure 23.6**). This method has the advantage that fairly large amounts can be separated and therefore it can be used for separation of mixtures of compounds rather than just for analysis.

Gas–liquid chromatography (GLC)

This technique, sometimes called simply gas chromatography, GC, is one of the most important modern analytical techniques. The apparatus is shown in **Figure 23.7**. The stationary phase is a powder coated with oil. It is either packed into or coated onto the inside of a long glass capillary tube, up to 100 m long and less than $\frac{1}{2}$ mm in diameter. The mobile phase is usually an unreactive gas, such as nitrogen. The sample is partitioned between the oil and the gas, and the components leave the column at different times (the retention times) after injection. Various types of detectors are used, including

Did you know? Frank Spedding used a variation of this technique – ion exchange chromatography – to separate the series of very similar elements called the rare earth elements, previously almost inseparable. In so doing he discovered the element promethium (atomic number 61), previously missing from the Periodic Table.

Did you know? The word 'chromatography' means 'colour writing'.

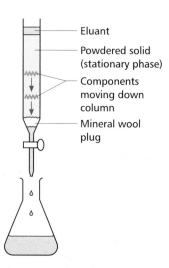

Figure 23.6 Column chromatography

Analysing pesticide residues using gas chromatography. The picture below shows the column

ones that measure the thermal conductivity of the emerging gas. The results are usually presented on a graph (**Figure 23.8**). The area under each peak is proportional to the amount of that component. In some instruments the emerging components are fed directly into a mass spectrometer for identification (see section 7.4). This combined technique is called gas chromatography–mass spectrometry, GCMS. As an analytical method for separating mixtures, GC is extremely sensitive. It can separate minute traces of substances in foodstuffs, and even link crude oil pollution found on beaches with its tanker of origin by comparing oil samples. Perhaps its best-known use is for testing athletes for drug taking.

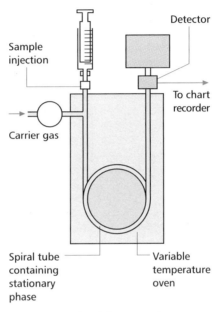

Figure 23.7 Gas–liquid chromatography

Did you know? HPLC can even be used to separate optical isomers (see section 18.6).

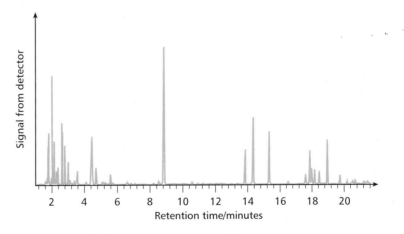

Figure 23.8 Typical GC trace. Each peak represents a different component

High performance liquid chromatography (HPLC)

This is a development of column chromatography. A pump is used to force the solvent over specially designed materials which form the stationary phase. The use of pressure to force the liquid phase through the column speeds up the separation. It also means that there is less time for components to spread (diffuse) into one another, so compounds with quite similar R_f values can be separated. A stainless steel column is needed to withstand the pressure.

FURTHER FOCUS

Fractional distillation

Fractional distillation allows the separation of two components differing only slightly in volatility. For all mixtures of liquids, the vapour above the mixture will contain a greater percentage of the more volatile component than will the liquid. This is shown below on the composition–boiling temperature curve for two liquids, A and B (where B is more volatile than A). This difference is used as a method of separating mixtures, called **fractional distillation**.

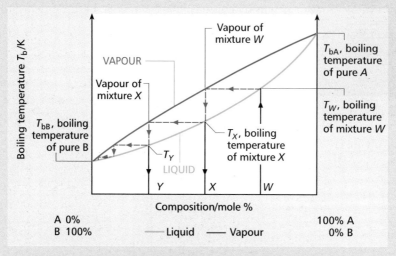

Composition–boiling temperature curve for two liquids, A and B (B more volatile than A)

Imagine starting with a liquid of composition W. This will boil at temperature T_W and give a vapour of composition X, which has more B and less A. If this vapour of composition X is condensed it will form a liquid which also has a composition of X. So, by boiling and condensing, we have ended up with a liquid which is richer in B. This new liquid will boil at temperature T_X (lower than T_W) to give a vapour of composition Y, which condenses to give a liquid of composition Y (with even more B and even less A). We could continue this process with more boiling/condensation cycles until we reached a vapour consisting entirely of pure B. A would all be liquid.

A **fractionating column** produces the effect of many successive boiling/condensation cycles automatically. The column sides have a large surface area (see figure at right). The mixture of A and B boils and the vapour rises up the column. As the temperature drops, the vapour condenses, the liquid (richer in A) drops back into the boiling flask and the vapour (richer in B) moves up the column. The same thing happens many times as the vapour rises up the tube. A long enough column will result in a vapour of pure B at the top of the column and eventually pure A left in the boiling flask.

Some liquids decompose before reaching their boiling temperatures. In this case, distillation can be done under reduced pressure. Since boiling occurs when the vapour pressure of the liquid reaches the external pressure, boiling then occurs at a lower temperature.

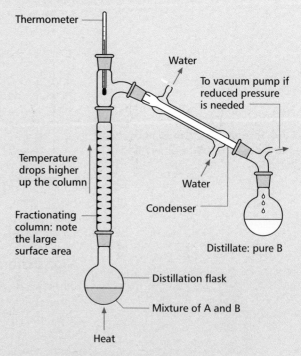

Separating two liquids by fractional distillation

23.2 Gaseous equilibria

Equilibrium reactions which take place in the gas phase also obey the equilibrium law (see Chapter 11), although their concentrations are usually expressed in a different way, using **partial pressures**.

Hint: Both concentration and pressure measure the number of molecules in 1 dm³.

Partial pressure

In a mixture of gases, each gas can be thought of as contributing to the total pressure. This contribution is called the partial pressure. The sum of all the partial pressures of the gases in the mixture is equal to the total pressure. This is called Dalton's law (see section 27.3). The partial pressure of one gas in a mixture is the pressure it would exert if it occupied the container on its own. The symbol p is used for partial pressure. For example, air is a mixture of approximately one-fifth oxygen and four-fifths nitrogen. If the total pressure is atmospheric, 100 kPa:

Hint: Whenever we can smell a solid or a liquid, particles from it have entered our nose and chemically stimulated some nerve endings.

> the partial pressure of oxygen, $p(O_2) = 1/5 \times 100$ kPa $= 20$ kPa
> the partial pressure of nitrogen, $p(N_2) = 4/5 \times 100$ kPa $= 80$ kPa
> which when added together give the total pressure 100 kPa

More precisely, the partial pressure of any gas in a mixture is given by its mole fraction multiplied by the total pressure.

The mole fraction of a gas A

$$= \frac{\text{number of moles of gas A}}{\text{total number of moles of gases in the mixture}}$$

Particles escape from the surfaces of solids (and liquids) so these phases have partial pressures even though the values are usually quite small. The partial pressures of solids and liquids are often called vapour pressures. The size of the partial pressure of a particular liquid or solid depends only on the temperature. It cannot be changed by having more or less of the substance.

Applying the equilibrium law to gaseous equilibria

When dealing with gases it is usual to work in partial pressures rather than concentrations. Then equilibrium constants are given the symbol K_p.

For the reaction

$$aA(g) + bB(g) \rightleftharpoons yY(g) + zZ(g)$$

Q Predict the effect of an increase in temperature on the partial pressure of a solid or liquid.

$$K_p = \frac{p^y Y(g)_{eqm}\, p^z Z(g)_{eqm}}{p^a A(g)_{eqm}\, p^b B(g)_{eqm}}$$

Notice the similarity with the equilibrium law expression for K_c given in section 11.2.

Example 1

For the equilibrium:

$$H_2(g) + I_2(g) \rightleftharpoons 2HI(g)$$

$$K_p = \frac{p^2 HI(g)_{eqm}}{pH_2(g)_{eqm}\, pI_2(g)_{eqm}}$$

Answer: Partial pressure will increase because molecules move faster at higher temperatures and more will escape into the gas phase.

This particular K_p has no units because they cancel.

Hint: K_p may or may not have units depending on the expression from which it derives, just like K_c (Chapter 11). You will need to work out the units for each one.

However, the equation could equally well have been written:

$$2HI(g) \rightleftharpoons H_2(g) + I_2(g)$$

in which case:

$$K_p = \frac{pH_2(g)_{eqm}\, pI_2(g)_{eqm}}{p^2HI(g)_{eqm}}$$

and K_p will have a different value, so it is *vital* when writing expressions for equilibrium constants that the equation is written. Furthermore, the same equation could also have been written:

$$HI(g) \rightleftharpoons \tfrac{1}{2}H_2(g) + \tfrac{1}{2}I_2(g)$$

> **Q** What is the mathematical relationship between the three values of K_p above?

for which

$$K_p = \frac{p^{1/2}H_2(g)_{eqm}\, p^{1/2}I_2(g)_{eqm}}{pHI(g)_{eqm}}$$

or

$$K_p = \frac{\sqrt{pH_2(g)_{eqm}}\,\sqrt{pI_2(g)_{eqm}}}{pHI(g)_{eqm}}$$

> **Q** What is the industrial importance of this reaction?

Example 2

$$3H_2(g) + N_2(g) \rightleftharpoons 2NH_3(g)$$

> **Q** Work out the units for this equilibrium constant.

$$K_p = \frac{p^2NH_3(g)_{eqm}}{p^3H_2(g)_{eqm}\, pN_2(g)_{eqm}}$$

Example 3

This shows how we can use the expression for K_p.
   K_p is 0.020 at 700 K for the reaction:

$$2HI(g) \rightleftharpoons H_2(g) + I_2(g)$$

If the reaction started with pure HI and the initial pressure of HI was 100 kPa, what will be the partial pressure of the hydrogen when equilibrium is reached?
   Set out the calculation in the same way as when using K_c (see section 11.2).
   Let the partial pressure of hydrogen at equilibrium ($pH_{2,eqm}$) be x.

	2HI(g)	$\rightleftharpoons$	H_2(g)	+	I_2(g)
Start	100 kPa		0 kPa		0 kPa
At equilibrium	$(100 - 2x)$ kPa		x kPa		x kPa

The chemical equation tells us:

- that there will be the same number of moles of hydrogen and iodine at equilibrium, therefore if $pH_{2,eqm} = x$, then $pI_{2,eqm} = x$ as well.
- that for each mole of hydrogen or (iodine) produced, *two* moles of hydrogen iodide are *used up*, therefore if $pH_{2,eqm}$ is x, pHI_{eqm} must be $(100 - 2x)$.

Answer: The second is the reciprocal of the first (1 divided by it) and the third is the square root of the second.

$$K_p = \frac{pH_2(g)_{eqm} \times pI_2(g)_{eqm}}{p^2HI(g)}$$

Putting in the figures gives:

Answer: It is the key step in the Haber process for the manufacture of ammonia.

Answer: kPa^{-2}

$$0.020 = \frac{x \times x}{(100 - 2x)^2} = \frac{x^2}{(100 - 2x)^2}$$

Q What will be the partial pressures of iodine and hydrogen iodide at equilibrium?

Taking the square root of each side gives:

$$0.141 = \frac{x}{100 - 2x}$$

$$0.141(100 - 2x) = x$$

$$14.1 - 0.282x = x$$

$$14.1 = 1.282x$$

$$x = \frac{14.1}{1.282}$$

$$x = 10.99$$

$$pH_2(g)_{eqm} = 11 \text{ kPa (to 2 s.f.)}$$

Heterogeneous equilibria

In all the examples of equilibrium that we have considered so far, each of the reactants and products has been in the same phase; they have been **homogeneous.** For example, they have been all gases or all aqueous solutions. Often there will be more than one phase involved in an equilibrium, such as a solid and an aqueous solution, or a solid and a gas. These are called **heterogeneous equilibria.**

A key difference is that the concentrations of pure solids and of pure liquids cannot be changed, unlike those of gases and solutions. It is impossible to squeeze more of a solid or a liquid into the same volume. Compare this to a solution, where more solute can be added to the same amount of solvent, or to a gas, where more molecules can be squeezed into the same volume. The concentration of a solid or a liquid is governed by its density and can be worked out from it. To calculate the concentration we need to know the number of moles in 1 dm^3.

For example, for the solid, silver chloride, AgCl, ($M_r = 143.3$, density 5.56 g cm^{-3})

Q Work out the concentration of mercury; $A_r = 201$, $\rho = 13.6$ g cm^{-3}.

$$\text{density}, \rho = \text{mass} / \text{volume}$$
$$\text{mass} = \text{volume} \times \rho$$

So 1 dm^3 of silver chloride has a mass of $1000 \times 5.56 = 5560$ g
This is $5560/143.3$ mol $= 38.8$ mol and [AgCl(s)] $= 38.8$ mol dm^{-3} and cannot be varied from this value.

Sparingly soluble salts

When excess of the sparingly soluble salt silver chloride is placed in water, the following equilibrium is set up:

$$AgCl(s) \rightleftharpoons Ag^+(aq) + Cl^-(aq)$$

The equilibrium law expression is

Hint: As long as some solid silver chloride is present, changing its *amount* has no effect at all on the equilibrium position. It is *concentration* that appears in the expression for K_c.

$$K_c = \frac{[Ag^+(aq)]_{eqm} \, [Cl^-(aq)]_{eqm}}{[AgCl(s)]_{eqm}}$$

However, as we have seen, the term [AgCl(s)] is constant because it is not possible to change the concentration of the solid.

If we rearrange the equilibrium law expression

$$K_c[AgCl(s)]_{eqm} = [Ag^+(aq)]_{eqm}[Cl^-(aq)]_{eqm}$$

and define a modified equilibrium constant $K_c' = K_c[AgCl(s)]_{eqm}$, then:

$$K_c' = [Ag^+(aq)]_{eqm}[Cl^-(aq)]_{eqm}$$

Answer: $pI_2(g)_{eqm} = 11$ kPa, $pHI(g)_{eqm} = 79$ kPa

Answer: 67.7 mol dm^{-3}

and the units of K_c' are mol^2 dm^{-6}.

Did you know? The concentration of water is 55.6 mol dm^{-3}. See if you can confirm this using a calculation like the one for silver chloride. Use the density of water = 1.00 g cm^{-3} and M_r for water = 18.0.

Did you know? Even 'insoluble' substances such as glass are very slightly soluble.

Equilibrium law expressions are *always* treated like this, so that they incorporate all constant terms into a modified equilibrium constant. Constant terms arise whenever there is a solid or a pure liquid. Some examples are given in the box 'Examples of equilibrium expressions'.

Solubility product

In the particular case of equilibrium between sparingly soluble salts and their ions in solution, as in the example above, the modified equilibrium constant K_c' is called the **solubility product** and given the symbol K_{sp}.

Another example:

$$PbI_2(s) \rightleftharpoons Pb^{2+}(aq) + 2I^-(aq)$$

$$K_{sp} = [Pb^{2+}(aq)]_{eqm}[I^-(aq)]^2_{eqm} \qquad \text{units: mol}^3 \text{ dm}^{-9}$$

The value of K_{sp} in this case is 7.0×10^{-9} mol^3 dm^{-9}. This very small value means that there are very few ions in solution: lead iodide is a virtually insoluble salt.

If we mix two solutions of soluble salts, and the concentrations of ions after mixing are such that a solubility product is exceeded, precipitation of the less soluble salt will occur.

For example, if we mix a 1.0×10^{-3} mol dm^{-3} solution of sodium chloride, NaCl, with a 1.0×10^{-5} mol dm^{-3} solution of silver nitrate, AgNO$_3$, will a precipitate form? The two possible precipitates are silver chloride and sodium nitrate. Silver chloride is the less soluble (all nitrates are soluble).

K_{sp} for silver chloride is:

$$2.0 \times 10^{-10} \text{ mol}^2 \text{ dm}^{-6} = [Ag^+(aq)]_{eqm}[Cl^-(aq)]_{eqm}$$

Hint: If you mix equal volumes of two solutions, the total volume is doubled and the concentrations of each component are halved.

When the solutions are mixed;

$$[Ag^+(aq)] = 5.0 \times 10^{-6} \text{ mol dm}^{-3}, [Cl^-(aq)] = 5.0 \times 10^{-4} \text{ mol dm}^{-3}$$

So

$$[Ag^+(aq)][Cl^-(aq)] = 5.0 \times 10^{-6} \times 5 \times 10^{-4} = 2.5 \times 10^{-9} \text{ mol}^2 \text{ dm}^{-6}$$

This exceeds the solubility product of silver chloride and so a precipitate will form.

The ionisation of water

This is another example of heterogeneous equilibrium:

$$H_2O(l) \rightleftharpoons H^+(aq) + OH^-(aq)$$

$$K_c = \frac{[H^+(aq)]_{eqm} [OH^-(aq)]_{eqm}}{[H_2O(l)]_{eqm}}$$

As with a solid, the concentration of a pure liquid cannot be varied and so $H_2O(l)_{eqm}$ is incorporated into a modified equilibrium constant

$$K_c' = [H^+(aq)]_{eqm}[OH^-(aq)]_{eqm}$$

This is given the special symbol K_w and named the **ionic product** of water. Its value is 1×10^{-14} mol^2 dm^{-6} at 298 K. This is very important in acid–base chemistry (see Chapter 12).

FURTHER FOCUS

Solubility product and solubility

These two terms are often confused. Solubility product, K_{sp} is defined in section 23.2. **Solubility** is the concentration of a saturated solution of the substance in question. They are linked, however.

For example, for silver iodide, AgI, $K_{sp} = 8.0 \times 10^{-17} \, mol^2 \, dm^{-6}$.

$$AgI(s) \rightleftharpoons Ag^+(aq) + I^-(aq)$$

$$K_{sp} = [Ag^+(aq)]_{eqm}[I^-(aq)]_{eqm} = 8.0 \times 10^{-17} \, mol^2 \, dm^{-6}$$

In a saturated solution:

$$[Ag^+(aq)] = [I^-(aq)]$$

Let this equal x.

So $\qquad x^2 = 8.0 \times 10^{-17} \, mol^2 \, dm^{-6}$

and $\qquad x = 8.9 \times 10^{-9} \, mol \, dm^{-3}$

So the concentration of a saturated solution of AgI would be $8.9 \times 10^{-9} \, mol \, dm^{-3}$, as 1 mole of Ag^+ is produced by 1 mole of AgI. This is the solubility of AgI.

Another example is calcium fluoride, CaF_2, $K_{sp} = 4.0 \times 10^{-11} \, mol^3 \, dm^9$. This is a little more complex:

$$CaF_2(s) \rightleftharpoons Ca^{2+}(aq) + 2F^-(aq)$$

$$K_{sp} = [Ca^{2+}(aq)]_{eqm}[F^-(aq)]_{eqm}^2 = 4.0 \times 10^{-11} \, mol^3 \, dm^{-9}$$

In a saturated solution $[F^-(aq)]_{eqm} = 2[Ca^{2+}(aq)]_{eqm}$ as the chemical equation tells us that each mole of CaF_2 which dissociates produces 1 mole of Ca^{2+} (aq) and 2 moles of $F^-(aq)$.

Let $\qquad [Ca^{2+}(aq)]_{eqm} = x$; then $F^-(aq)]_{eqm} = 2x$

Substituting in the above expression for K_{sp} gives:

$$x \times (2x)^2 = 4.0 \times 10^{-11}$$
$$4x^3 = 4.0 \times 10^{-11}$$
$$x^3 = 1.0 \times 10^{-11}$$
$$x = 2.15 \times 10^{-4} \, mol \, dm^{-3}$$
$$[Ca^{2+}(aq)]_{eqm} = 2.2 \times 10^{-4} \, mol \, dm^{-3} \text{ (to 2 s.f.)}$$

Since 1 mole of Ca^{2+}(aq) is produced by 1 mole of CaF_2, this is the solubility of CaF_2.

Table 23.1 Values of K_p at different temperatures for two reactions

$N_2(g) + 3H_2(g) \rightleftharpoons 2NH_3(g)$

T/K	K_p/10^{-10} Pa^{-2}	
298	6.76×10^5	
500	3.55×10^{-2}	decrease
700	7.76×10^{-5}	
900	1.00×10^{-6}	

$H_2(g) + CO_2(g) \rightleftharpoons H_2O(g) + CO(g)$

T/K	K_p (no units)	
298	1.00×10^{-5}	
500	7.55×10^{-3}	increase
700	1.23×10^{-1}	
900	6.01×10^{-1}	

Hint: When the value for $\Delta H^\ominus$ is given for a reversible reaction, it is taken to refer to the forward reaction, i.e. left to right.

Dissociation of solids to gases

Consider the reaction:

$$CaCO_3(s) \rightleftharpoons CaO(s) + CO_2(g)$$

We could write:

$$K_p = \frac{pCaO(s)_{eqm} \, pCO_2(g)_{eqm}}{pCaCO_3(s)_{eqm}}$$

but as the partial pressures produced by solids are constant (at constant temperature) these are incorporated into a modified equilibrium constant, K_p', sometimes called the dissociation pressure of calcium carbonate.

So: $\qquad K_p' = pCO_2(g)_{eqm}$

23.3 The effect of changing conditions on gas-phase equilibria

In Chapter 11 we saw that we can predict the effect of changing conditions using Le Chatelier's principle.

The effect of changing temperature

Changing the temperature results in a new value of the equilibrium constant, K_p. This is shown by the data for the following reactions (**Table 23.1**).

$$N_2(g) + 3H_2(g) \rightleftharpoons 2NH_3(g) \qquad H_2(g) + CO_2(g) \rightleftharpoons H_2O(g) + CO(g)$$
$$\Delta H^\ominus = -92 \, kJ \, mol^{-1} \qquad\qquad \Delta H^\ominus = +41 \, kJ \, mol^{-1}$$

> **Hint:** The larger K_p, the more products and the less reactants.

The general rule is that:

- For an exothermic reaction (ΔH is negative) increasing the temperature decreases the equilibrium constant.
- For an endothermic reaction (ΔH is positive) increasing the temperature increases the equilibrium constant.

So for an exothermic reaction, increasing the temperature will move the equilibrium to the left and for an endothermic reaction, increasing the temperature will move the equilibrium to the right.

We can show this simply for the following reaction:

$$N_2O_4(g) \rightleftharpoons 2NO_2(g) \qquad \Delta H^\ominus = +58\ \text{kJ mol}^{-1}$$

If a syringe containing a mixture of the two gases at equilibrium is placed into a beaker of hot water (see **Figure 23.9**), the volume of the

FURTHER FOCUS

Examples of equilibrium constant expressions

1. $Fe^{3+}(aq) + SCN^-(aq) \rightleftharpoons FeSCN^{2+}(aq)$

$$K_c = \frac{[FeSCN^{2+}](aq)_{eqm}}{[Fe^{3+}(aq)]_{eqm}[SCN^-(aq)]_{eqm}}$$

Units are $dm^3\ mol^{-1}$.

2. $BiCl_3(aq) + H_2O(l) \rightleftharpoons BiOCl(s) + 2HCl(aq)$

$$K_c = \frac{[HCl(aq)]_{eqm}^{\ 2}}{[BiCl(aq)]_{eqm}}$$

Units are $mol\ dm^{-3}$.

[BiOCl(s)] does not appear, as the value of its concentration has been incorporated into the value of K_c. For the same reason [$H_2O(l)$] does not appear either. As the reaction is carried out in aqueous solution [$H_2O(l)$] will not vary at all. Therefore in dilute aqueous solutions it is incorporated into the value of K_c.

3. $Ag_2CrO_4(s) \rightleftharpoons 2Ag^+(aq) + CrO_4^{2-}(aq)$

$$K_{sp} = [Ag^+(aq)]_{eqm}^{\ 2}[CrO_4^{2-}(aq)]_{eqm}$$

Units are $mol^3\ dm^{-9}$.

[$Ag_2CrO_4(s)$] is constant and is therefore incorporated into the value of the equilibrium constant, which is called K_{sp} because this is a case of a sparingly soluble salt in equilibrium with its own ions.

4. $CH_3CO_2H(aq) + H_2O(l) \rightleftharpoons CH_3CO_2^-(aq) + H_3O^+(aq)$

$$K_a = \frac{[CH_3CO_2^-(aq)]_{eqm}\ [H_3O^+(aq)]_{eqm}}{[CH_3CO_2H(aq)]_{eqm}}$$

Units are $mol\ dm^{-3}$.

The concentration of water, [$H_2O(aq)]_{eqm}$, is effectively constant for the same reasons as in the bismuth chloride equilibrium above. It is therefore incorporated into the value of the equilibrium constant. The equilibrium constant is called K_a because this is the dissociation of a weak acid (see section 12.3).

5. $H_2O(l) \rightleftharpoons H^+(aq) + OH^-(aq)$

$$K_w = [H_2O(aq)]_{eqm}[OH^-(aq)]_{eqm}$$

Units are $mol^2\ dm^{-6}$.

The concentration of water is effectively constant, so it is incorporated into the value of K_w. The equilibrium constant is called K_w because it represents the dissociation of water (see section 12.3).

6. $PCl_5(g) \rightleftharpoons PCl_3(g) + Cl_2(g)$

$$K_p = \frac{pPCl_3(g)_{eqm}\ pCl_2(g)_{eqm}}{pPCl_5(g)_{eqm}}$$

Units are kPa.

As this is a gaseous reaction we normally use K_p and use the values of the partial pressures of the reactants and the products. It is quite possible to use K_c but the units will be different.

$$K_c = \frac{[PCl_3(g)]_{eqm}\ [Cl_2(g)]_{eqm}}{[PCl_5(g)]_{eqm}}$$

Units are $mol\ dm^{-3}$.

7. $3Fe(s) + 4H_2O(g) \rightleftharpoons Fe_3O_4(s) + 4H_2(g)$

$$K_p = \frac{p^4H_2(g)_{eqm}}{p^4H_2O(g)_{eqm}}$$

No units.

The solids Fe and Fe_3O_4 each have a constant partial pressure (at a fixed temperature) and so the values of these have been incorporated into K_p. We could also write

$$K_c = \frac{[H_2(g)]_{eqm}^{\ 4}}{[H_2O(g)]_{eqm}^{\ 4}}$$

No units.

Note that in this example water is in the gaseous state (steam), so its pressure and concentration *can* be changed.

mixture increases. This would be predicted anyway since all gases expand on heating, but the volume increase is greater than would be predicted, as shown on the graph (**Figure 23.10**) This shows that the equilibrium has moved to the right (producing more moles of gas).

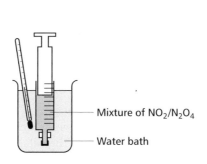

Mixture of NO_2/N_2O_4

Water bath

Figure 23.9 Apparatus for investigating the position of the equilibrium $N_2O_4(g)$ $\rightleftharpoons$ $2NO_2(g)$

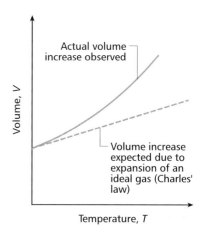

Actual volume increase observed

Volume increase expected due to expansion of an ideal gas (Charles' law)

Volume, V

Temperature, T

Figure 23.10 The effect of increasing the temperature of a mixture of NO_2 and N_2O_4

The effect of changing pressure

As we saw in Chapter 11:

- Changing the pressure at constant temperature will only affect reactions involving gases.
- The equilibrium position will only be changed when there is a different total number of moles on each side of the equation.

So in the reaction $\underbrace{H_2(g) + I_2(g)}_{2 \text{ moles}} \rightleftharpoons \underset{2 \text{ moles}}{2HI(g)}$

the equilibrium position *will not change* when the pressure is increased: the proportions of H_2, I_2 and HI will stay the same.

But in the equilibrium:

$$N_2O_4(g) \rightleftharpoons 2NO_2(g)$$

dinitrogen tetraoxide   nitrogen dioxide
(colourless)   (brown)
1 mole   2 moles

increasing the pressure *will* change the composition of the equilibrium mixture. We can use Le Châtelier's principle to predict the effect of pressure. If we increase the pressure, the equilibrium will move in the direction that reduces the pressure, i.e. to the left where there are fewer molecules of gas.

In this case we can use the colour of the mixture to judge roughly the equilibrium position. If the plunger of a syringe, containing an equilibrium mixture of the gases, is quickly pressed to increase the pressure, the following is seen. First the mixture gets darker, as the concentration of brown nitrogen dioxide momentarily increases (the same amount is squeezed into a smaller space). Then the mixture goes paler than it was at the beginning, as the new equilibrium is established, which results in more dinitrogen tetraoxide and less nitrogen dioxide. The contribution of pN_2O_4 to the total pressure increases and that of pNO_2 decreases in such a way that the value of

$$K_p = \frac{p^2NO_2(g)_{eqm}}{p\,N_2O_4(g)_{eqm}} \text{ remains constant.}$$

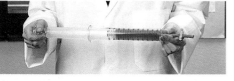

Investigating the effect of pressure on the NO_2/N_2O_4 equilibrium

23.4 Measuring K_p

The basic principles of measuring K_p are the same as for K_c: we need to measure the proportions of the components of the equilibrium mixture without disturbing the equilibrium. There is no direct method of measuring the partial pressure of just one component, so indirect methods have to be used, such as the one described below.

The average relative molecular mass method

Hint: A weighted average takes into account not only the relative molecular masses of the components of a mixture but also the proportions in which they are present.

If a gas mixture is kept in a syringe, its volume can be easily measured under known conditions of temperature and pressure and used to calculate the relative molecular mass of the contents (see section 27.2). This will be the **weighted average** of the relative molecular masses of all the gases present. This can be used to calculate K_p as shown in the following example:

$$N_2O_4(g) \rightleftharpoons 2NO_2(g)$$

At 60 °C (333 K) and atmospheric pressure, 100 kPa, the equilibrium mixture was found to have an average M_r of 60.0. The M_r can vary from 46 (NO_2 only) to 92 (N_2O_4 only). A simple way of working out the proportions of each gas present is as shown.

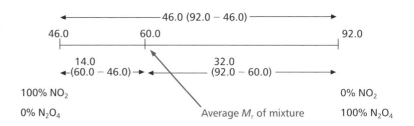

$M_r = 60$ represents a mixture consisting of:

$$\tfrac{14}{46} \times 100\% \ N_2O_4 = 30.4\% \ N_2O_4$$
$$\tfrac{32}{46} \times 100\% \ NO_2 = 69.6\% \ NO_2$$

Since the total pressure is 100 kPa,

$$pN_2O_4 = 30.4\% \text{ of } 100 \text{ kPa} = 30.4 \text{ kPa}$$
$$pNO_2 = 69.6\% \text{ of } 100 \text{ kPa} = 69.6 \text{ kPa}$$
$$K_p = \frac{p^2NO_2(g)_{eqm}}{pN_2O_4(g)_{eqm}}$$
$$K_p = \frac{(69.6)^2}{30.4} \text{ kPa}$$
$$K_p = 160 \text{ kPa at 333 K (to 2 s.f.)}$$

23.5 Summary

● Solutes partition themselves between	two immiscible solvents.
● An equilibrium exists	across the interface between the two solvents.
● The partition cefficient =	$\dfrac{\text{concentration of solute in solvent 1}}{\text{concentration of solute in solvent 2}}$
● A solute may be extracted into a second solvent if: (a) (b)	the two solvents are immiscible. it is more soluble in the second solvent.
● The extraction is more efficient if	the available solvent is used in many small portions rather than one large one.
● In chromatography	a moving solvent phase extracts components from a stationary phase.
● Types of chromatography include	paper, thin layer, column and gas-liquid.
● Components of mixtures are identified by	their R_f values.
● Phase equilibria are equilibria between	different phases (gas, liquid and solid) of the same substance.
● The partial pressure of a gas in a mixture of gases is	the pressure it would exert if it occupied the same volume on its own.
● For the reaction $aA(g) + bB(g) \rightleftharpoons yY(g) + zZ(g)$, $$K_p = \frac{p^y Y(g)_{eqm}\, p^z Z(g)_{eqm}}{p^a A(g)_{eqm}\, p^b B(g)_{eqm}}$$	
● The concentrations (or partial pressure) of pure solids and liquids	cannot vary.
● These concentrations are incorporated into	a modified equilibrium constant.
● These concentrations do not appear in	the expression for K_c or K_p.
● Solubility products are modified equilibrium constants for	equilibria between relatively insoluble salts and their ions in solution.
● If two solutions are mixed, such that a solubility product is exceeded	precipitation will occur.
● For an exothermic reaction, increasing the temperature will move the equilibrium	to the left.
● For an endothermic reaction, increasing the temperature will move the equilibrium	to the right.
● Increasing the pressure will move the equilibrium towards	the side with fewer molecules.

23.6 Practice questions

1. Write down the expression for K_p for the following gaseous equilibria. State the units of K_p.
   (a) $N_2(g) + 3H_2(g) \rightleftharpoons 2NH_3(g)$
   (b) $2SO_2(g) + O_2(g) \rightleftharpoons 2SO_3(g)$
   (c) $PCl_5(g) \rightleftharpoons PCl_3(g) + Cl_2(g)$
   (d) $CO_2(g) + H_2(g) \rightleftharpoons CO(g) + H_2O(g)$
   (e) $N_2(g) + O_2(g) \rightleftharpoons 2NO(g)$
   (f) $2NO(g) \rightleftharpoons N_2(g) + O_2(g)$
   (g) $COCl_2(g) \rightleftharpoons CO(g) + Cl_2(g)$
   (h) What mathematical relationship exists between K_p in (e) and that in (f)?

2. Write down the expression for the modified equilibrium constant for the following heterogeneous equilibria. Give K_c or K_p as appropriate and state the units.
   (a) $BiCl_3(aq) + H_2O(l) \rightleftharpoons BiOCl(s) + 2HCl(aq)$
   (b) $AgBr(s) \rightleftharpoons Ag^+(aq) + Br^-(aq)$
   (c) $PbCl_2(s) \rightleftharpoons Pb^{2+}(aq) + 2Cl^-(aq)$
   (d) $3Fe(s) + 4H_2O(g) \rightleftharpoons Fe_3O_4(s) + 4H_2(g)$
   (e) $H_2O(g) + C(s) \rightleftharpoons H_2(g) + CO(g)$
   (f) $Ag_2CO_3(s) \rightleftharpoons Ag_2O(s) + CO_2(g)$
   (g) $Ca^{2+}(aq) + CO_3^{2-}(aq) \rightleftharpoons CaCO_3(s)$
   (h) $H_2O(l) \rightleftharpoons H_2O(g)$
   (i) Which two of these are solubility products?

3. $$H_2(g) + I_2(g) \rightleftharpoons 2HI(g)$$
   1.9 mol of H and 1.9 mol of I were allowed to reach equilibrium at 710 K. The equilibrium mixture contained 3.0 mol of HI. What is the equilibrium constant? What would be the effect on the equilibrium position of increasing the total pressure? Explain.
   Suggest a method of analysing the equilibrium mixture to show that 3.0 mol of HI was present.

4.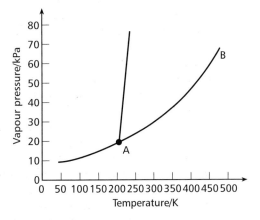

   Look at the phase diagram.
   (a) Mark the areas representing vapour, liquid and solid.

(b) What are the boiling temperatures and melting temperatures of this substance at 60 kPa pressure?
(c) What does line AB represent?
(d) Below what pressure does the substance sublime (turn directly from solid to vapour)?

5. The average M_r of an equilibrium mixture of NO_2 and N_2O_4 was 74.0 at 304 K. Calculate the value of K_p for
   $$N_2O_4(g) \rightleftharpoons 2NO_2(g)$$
   at atmospheric pressure (100 kPa).
   What could you say about the equilibrium position in a mixture whose average M_r was 92.0?

6. The partition coefficient of compound X between ethoxyethane and water is 10.
   i.e. $$\frac{[\text{X in ethoxyethane}]_{eqm}}{[\text{X in water}]_{eqm}} = 10$$
   1 g of X is dissolved in 100 cm³ of water. How much X can be extracted using 100 cm³ of ethoxyethane:
   (a) in one extraction, using all the ethoxyethane?
   (b) in two extractions, using 50 cm³ of ethoxyethane each?

7.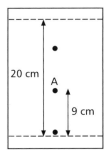

   Calculate the R_f value of spot A.

8.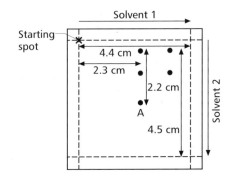

   Calculate the R_f values of spot A in solvent 1 and solvent 2.

9. Given the solubility products:

$PbSO_4$ $1.6 \times 10^{-8} \, mol \, dm^{-6}$
$MgCO_3$ $1.0 \times 10^{-5} \, mol \, dm^{-6}$

which of the following mixtures will produce a precipitate? Equal volumes of the two solutions were mixed in each case.

(a) $1.0 \times 10^{-3} \, mol \, dm^{-3} \, Pb(NO_3)_2$ and
     $1.0 \times 10^{-3} \, mol \, dm^{-3} \, Na_2SO_4$.
(b) $1.0 \, mol \, dm^{-3} \, Mg(NO_3)_2$ and
     $1.0 \times 10^{-4} \, mol \, dm^{-3} \, Na_2CO_3$.
(c) $1.0 \times 10^{-2} \, mol \, dm^{-3} \, MgCl_2$
     and $1.0 \times 10^{-2} \, mol \, dm^{-3} \, Na_2CO_3$

(d) $1.0 \times 10^{-5} \, mol \, dm^{-3} \, Pb(NO_3)_2$
     and $1.0 \, mol \, dm^{-3} \, K_2SO_4$.

10. $H_2(g) + I_2(g) \rightleftharpoons 2HI(g)$

In an equilibrium mixture the partial pressures were:

H_2	$2.20 \times 10^4 \, Pa$
I_2	$0.50 \times 10^4 \, Pa$
HI	$7.30 \times 10^4 \, Pa$

(a) What is the total pressure of the mixture?
(b) What is the equilibrium constant at the temperature of the experiment?

23.7 Examination questions

1. Phosphorus(v) chloride dissociates at high temperatures according to the equation

$$PCl_5(g) \rightleftharpoons PCl_3(g) + Cl_2(g)$$

83.4 g of phosphorus(v) chloride are placed in a vessel of volume 9.23 dm³. At equilibrium at a certain temperature, 11.1 g of chlorine are produced at a total pressure of 250 kPa. Use these data, where relevant, to answer the questions that follow.

(a) Calculate the number of moles of each of the gases in the vessel at equilibrium.
(b) (i)   Write an expression for the equilibrium constant, K_c, for the above equilibrium.
     (ii) Calculate the value of the equilibrium constant, K_c, and state its units.
(c) (i)   Write an expression for the equilibrium constant, K_p, for the above equilibrium.
     (ii) Calculate the mole fraction of chlorine present in the equilibrium mixture.
     (iii) Calculate the partial pressure of PCl_5 present in the equilibrium mixture.
     (iv) Calculate the value of the equilibrium constant, K_p, and state its units.
                                              [NEAB 1998]

2. Hydrogen and iodine react together to give an equilibrium:

$$H_2(g) + I_2(g) \rightleftharpoons 2HI(g)$$

(a) Write an expression for K_p for this equilibrium, giving consideration to its units.
(b) When 0.05 mol of I_2 and 0.50 mol of H_2 were mixed in a closed container at 723 K and 2 atm pressure, 0.11 mol of I_2 were found to be present when equilibrium was established.
     (i)   Calculate the partial pressures of I_2, H_2 and HI in the equilibrium mixture.
     (ii) Hence calculate the value of K_p at 723 K.
(c) In an experiment to establish the equilibrium concentrations in (b), the reaction was allowed to reach equilibrium at 723 K and then quenched by addition to a known, large volume of water. The concentration of iodine in this solution was then determined by titration with standard sodium thiosulphate solution.
     (i)   Explain what is meant by the word **quench** and why quenching is necessary.
     (ii) Write an equation for the reaction between sodium thiosulphate and iodine.
     (iii) What indicator would you use? Give the colour change at the end point.
     (iv) In this titration and in titrations involving potassium manganate(VII), a colour change occurs during reaction. Why is an indicator usually added in iodine/thiosulphate titrations but not in titrations involving potassium manganate(VII)?
                                              [London 1997]

24 More on acids and bases

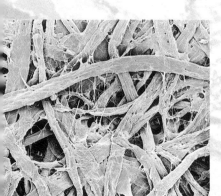

A micrograph showing paper fibres

Severe acid damage to an old book

Treating and acid-damaged book

Chemistry in the library

Lots of librarians are worried about losing their books: not people failing to return their loans but the destruction of the books themselves caused by acids eating away the paper. One estimate suggests that the problem could affect 40 million books world-wide, including many irreplaceable old volumes. You will have seen the problem yourself if you have ever picked up a newspaper that has been lining a drawer for some years: it will have become brittle and fragile.

The problem is caused by acids, which attack the cellulose from which the fibres of the paper are made. Cellulose is a polymer made from long chains of sugar molecules linked together. The acid breaks these links.

Acid in paper comes from two sources: from the paper-making process itself and from acids in polluted air (the same ones that cause acid rain).

During paper-making, paper is treated with size to make it waterproof. Without this it would be as absorbent as blotting paper. The size can contain acidic salts such as aluminium sulphate, which reacts with moisture to form sulphuric acid. Sulphuric and nitric acids are present in the air in most areas.

Book conservationists have developed a number of ways to treat valuable books to stop the rot. One is to neutralise the acids by treating the paper with aqueous alkaline solutions such as calcium hydroxide or magnesium hydrogencarbonate. However, this is not suitable for treating whole books since the water can damage the binding. Alkalis dissolved in non-aqueous solvents can be used but may cause some types of ink to run.

One alternative is to use the gas diethyl zinc. This reacts with acid and also moisture as shown below

$$(C_2H_5)_2Zn(g) + H_2SO_4(aq) \longrightarrow ZnSO_4(s) + 2C_2H_6(g)$$
$$(C_2H_5)_2Zn(g) + H_2O(l) \longrightarrow ZnO(s) + 2C_2H_6(g)$$

The products of the reaction are:

- ethane gas, which simply diffuses away from the book
- zinc sulphate, a colourless, neutral salt
- zinc oxide, an alkali which will help to protect the treated book from further acid attack

This method is still experimental but looks promising.

Introduction

Chapter 12 introduced the ideas of (a) strong acids and bases which in aqueous solution are fully dissociated into ions and (b) weak acids and bases which are only partly dissociated. In this chapter we use some of the ideas about equilibria to calculate the pH of solutions of weak acids and bases. We will also see how these ideas apply to indicators and buffers – solutions which resist changes of pH.

CONCEPT CHECKPOINTS

The following basic ideas are used in this chapter. You may revise some of these topics elsewhere in the book.

☐ acids as proton donors and bases as proton acceptors (Chapter 12)
☐ the pH scale (Chapter 12)
☐ equilibrium between reactants and products in reversible reactions (Chapter 11)
☐ the equilibrium law expression (Chapter 11)
☐ $K_w = [H^+(aq)][OH^-(aq)] = 1.0 \times 10^{-14}$ $mol^2\,dm^{-6}$ (Chapter 12)

Hint: This could equally well be written:

$$HA(aq) + H_2O(l)$$
$$\rightleftharpoons H_3O^+(aq) + A^-(aq)$$

$$K'_c = \frac{[H_3O^+(aq)]_{eqm}[A^-(aq)]_{eqm}}{[HA(aq)]_{eqm}[H_2O(l)]_{eqm}}$$

Since the concentration of $H_2O(l)$ is effectively constant, it is incorporated into the value of K_c so that as before:

$$K_c = \frac{[H_3O^+(aq)]_{eqm}[A^-(aq)]_{eqm}}{[HA(aq)]_{eqm}}$$

What is the value of K_a for a strong acid (one that is *completely* dissociated)?

answer: Infinity. Since the acid is fully dissociated, there are no molecules of HA and the bottom line of the expression for K_a is 0. (1/0 = ∞)

24.1 The dissociation of weak acids and bases

Weak acids

Imagine a weak acid HA which dissociates:

$$HA(aq) \rightleftharpoons H^+(aq) + A^-(aq)$$

The equilibrium constant is given by:

$$K_c = \frac{[H^+(aq)]_{eqm}\,[A^-(aq)]_{eqm}}{[HA(aq)]_{eqm}}$$

For a weak acid, this is usually given the symbol K_a and called the **acid dissociation constant.**

The larger the value of K_a, the further the equilibrium is to the right, the more the acid is dissociated and the stronger it is. Acid dissociation constants for some acids are given in **Table 24.1**.

Calculating the pH of weak acids

In Chapter 12 we calculated the pH of solutions of strong acids (relatively) simply, by assuming that they are fully dissociated. For example, in '1 mol dm^{-3} nitric acid' $[H^+] = 1$ mol dm^{-3}. In weak acids this is no longer true and we must use the equilibrium law to calculate $[H^+]$.

Example: calculating the pH of 1 mol dm^{-3} ethanoic acid

Using the same method as in Chapter 11 for equilibrium calculations, the concentrations in mol dm^{-3} are:

$$CH_3CO_2H(aq) \rightleftharpoons CH_3CO_2^-(aq) + H^+(aq)$$

Before dissociation: 1   0   0

At equilibrium: $1 - [CH_3CO_2^-(aq)]$ $[CH_3CO_2^-(aq)]$ $[H^+(aq)]$

$$K_a = \frac{[CH_3CO_2^-(aq)]_{eqm}\,[H^+(aq)]_{eqm}}{[CH_3CO_2H(aq)]_{eqm}}$$

But as each CH_3CO_2H molecule which dissociates produces one $CH_3CO_2^-$ ion and one H^+ ion.

Table 24.1 Values of K_a for some weak acids

Acid	K_a/mol dm^{-3}
chloroethanoic	1.3×10^{-3}
benzoic	6.3×10^{-5}
ethanoic	1.7×10^{-5}
hydrocyanic	4.9×10^{-10}

Q Which is the strongest acid in Table 24.1?

$$[CH_3CO_2{}^-(aq)]_{eqm} = [H^+(aq)]_{eqm}$$

$$K_a = \frac{[H^+(aq)]_{eqm}{}^2}{1 - [H^+(aq)]_{eqm}}$$

Since the degree of dissociation of ethanoic acid is so small (it is a weak acid), $[H^+(aq)]_{eqm}$ is very small and to a good approximation, $1 - [H^+(aq)]_{eqm} \approx 1$.

so
$$K_a = \frac{[H^+(aq)]_{eqm}{}^2}{1}$$

From Table 24.1
$$K_a = 1.7 \times 10^{-5} \, \text{mol dm}^{-3}$$

so
$$1.7 \times 10^{-5} = [H^+(aq)]_{eqm}{}^2$$
$$[H^+(aq)]_{eqm} = \sqrt{1.7 \times 10^{-5}}$$
$$[H^+(aq)]_{eqm} = 4.12 \times 10^{-3} \, \text{mol dm}^{-3}$$

Taking logs: $\log [H^+(aq)]_{eqm} = -2.384$

So $pH = 2.4$

Example: calculating the pH of 0.1 mol dm^{-3} ethanoic acid

Using the same method, we get:

$$K_a = \frac{[H^+(aq)]_{eqm}{}^2}{0.1 - [H^+(aq)]_{eqm}}$$

Again, $0.1 - [H^+(aq)]_{eqm} \approx 0.1$.

so
$$1.7 \times 10^{-5} = \frac{[H^+(aq)]_{eqm}{}^2}{0.1}$$
$$1.7 \times 10^{-6} = [H^+(aq)]_{eqm}{}^2$$
$$[H^+(aq)]_{eqm} = 1.3 \times 10^3 \, \text{mol dm}^{-3}$$
$$pH = 2.9$$

Weak bases

The dissociation of a weak base B, in aqueous solution may be represented:

$$B(aq) + H_2O(l) \rightleftharpoons BH^+(aq) + OH^-(aq)$$

$$K_c = \frac{[BH^+(aq)]_{eqm} \, [OH^-(aq)]_{eqm}}{[B(aq)]_{eqm}[H_2O(l)]_{eqm}}$$

The concentration of $H_2O(l)$ is effectively constant and is incorporated into the equilibrium constant to give K_b, the **base dissociation constant**.

$$K_b = \frac{[BH^+(aq)]_{eqm} \, [OH^-(aq)]_{eqm}}{[B(aq)]_{eqm}}$$

The larger the value of K_b, the stronger the base. **Table 24.2** lists K_b's for some weak bases.

Table 24.2 Values of K_b for some weak bases

Base	K_b/mol dm^{-3}
ethylamine	5.6×10^{-4}
ammonia	1.7×10^{-5}
phenylamine	4.3×10^{-10}

Q Which is the strongest base in Table 24.2?

Calculating the pH of weak bases

In Chapter 12 we calculated the pH of solutions of strong bases (relatively) simply, by assuming that they are fully dissociated. For example, in '1 mol dm^{-3} sodium hydroxide', $[OH^-] = 1$ mol dm^{-3}. In weak bases this is no longer true and we must use the equilibrium law to calculate $[OH^-]$. We also need to use the expression for K_w, to calculate the corresponding $[H^+]$ and hence the pH.

Answer: Chloroethanoic: it has the largest value of K_a.

Answer: Ethylamine: it has the largest value for K_b.

Example: the pH of 1 mol dm^{-3} ammonia

In aqueous solution, ammonia molecules accept protons from water molecules to produce a solution containing OH^- ions. The concentrations in mol dm^{-3} are:

$$NH_3(aq) + H_2O(l) \rightleftharpoons NH_4^+(aq) + OH^-(aq)$$

Before dissociation: 1   0   0

At equilibrium: $1 - [OH^-(aq)]_{eqm}$ $[NH_4(aq)]_{eqm}$ $[OH^-(aq)]_{eqm}$

$$K_b = \frac{[NH_4^+(aq)]_{eqm}\,[OH^-(aq)]_{eqm}}{[NH_3(aq)]_{eqm}}$$

$[NH_4^+(aq)]_{eqm} = [OH^-(aq)]_{eqm}$, as each NH_3 involved produces one of each ion.

$$1.7 \times 10^{-5} = \frac{[OH^-(aq)]_{eqm}{}^2}{1 - [OH^-(aq)]_{eqm}}$$

Since $[OH^-(aq)]_{eqm}$ is small, $1 - [OH^-(aq)]_{eqm} \approx 1$.

$$1.7 \times 10^{-5} = [OH^-(aq)]_{eqm}{}^2$$
$$[OH^-(aq)]_{eqm} = 4.12 \times 10^{-3}\ \text{mol dm}^{-3}$$

Now we must calculate $[H^+(aq)]_{eqm}$ using:

$$K_w = [H^+(aq)]_{eqm}[OH^-(aq)]_{eqm} = 1.0 \times 10^{-14}\ \text{mol}^2\,\text{dm}^{-6}$$
$$1.0 \times 10^{-14} = [H^+(aq)]_{eqm} \times 4.12 \times 10^{-3}$$

$$[H^+(aq)]_{eqm} = \frac{1.0 \times 10^{-14}}{4.12 \times 10^{-3}}$$

$$[H^+(aq)]_{eqm} = 2.4 \times 10^{-12}\ \text{mol dm}^{-3}\ \text{(to 2 s.f.)}$$

Taking logs:

$$\log[H^+(aq)]_{eqm} = -11.6$$
$$pH = 11.6$$

Q Calculate the pH of 0.1 mol dm^{-3} ammonia in the same way.

An acid–base titration to find the concentration of a base. A **pipette** is used to deliver an accurately measured volume of base of unknown concentration into the flask. The acid of known concentration is in the **burette**

Answer: 11.1

24.2 pH changes during acid–base titrations

Acid–base titrations

In general, a titration is used to find the concentration of a solution by gradually adding to it a second solution that reacts with it. In an acid–base titration, an acid of known concentration is added from a burette to a measured amount of a solution of a base (an alkali) until an indicator shows that the base has been neutralised (or the alkali may be in the burette and the acid in the flask).

We can follow a neutralisation reaction by measuring the pH with a pH electrode. This produces a voltage related to the $[H^+(aq)]$ in the solution. Section 25.2 describes how it works.

pH values of solutions can be accurately displayed:

- on a meter
- on a chart recorder
- on a data logger
- on a computer to produce a graphical output directly

Using a pH meter to measure the acidity of soil

Figure 24.2 shows the results obtained for four cases.

The first thing to notice about these curves is that the pH does *not* change in a regular manner as the alkali is added. Each curve has almost horizontal sections where a lot of alkali can be added without changing the pH much. There is also a very steep portion of each curve where a single drop of alkali changes the pH by several units.

In a titration, the **equivalence point** is the point at which there are exactly the same number of moles of hydrogen ions as there are moles of hydroxide ions. In each of the titrations in Figure 24.2 the equivalence point is reached after 25.0 cm³ of alkali has been added. However, the pH at the equivalence point is not always seven. Notice that in each case, except the weak acid/ weak base titration, there is a large and rapid change of pH at the equivalence point (i.e. the curve is almost vertical) even though this may not be centred on pH 7. This is relevant to the choice of indicator for a particular titration.

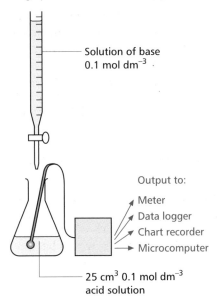

Figure 24.1 Apparatus to investigate pH changes during a titration

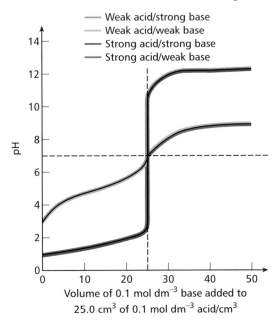

Figure 24.2 Graphs of pH changes for titrations of different acids and bases. In each case, we start with 25.0 cm³ of the acid in the flask and add the base from a burette

FURTHER FOCUS

Indicators

There is a range of indicators available. Some are shown below with their approximate colour changes. None of them changes colour at exactly pH 7.

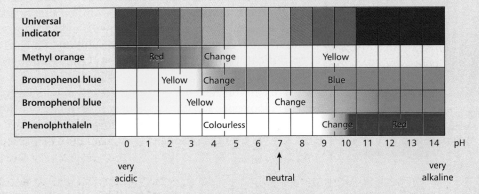

Universal indicator is a mixture of several indicators, chosen to produce a range of colours at different pHs.

Choice of indicators for titrations

When we do a titration to find the concentration of an unknown solution of an acid or alkali, using an indicator, **the end point** is the volume of acid (or alkali) added when the indicator changes colour.

It is important to pick an indicator such that:

Hint: Titrations can be done by adding the base to the acid, or vice versa.

● The colour change is sharp rather than gradual, i.e. no more than one drop of acid or alkali is needed to give a complete colour change. An indicator which changes colour gradually over several cubic centimetres would be of no use.
● The end point of the titration given by the indicator is the same as the equivalence point. Otherwise the titration will give us the wrong answer.

It is also desirable that an indicator gives a distinct colour change. For example, the colourless to red change of phenolphthalein is easier to see than the red to yellow of methyl orange.

Hint: An alkali is a base that is soluble in water.

Some common indicators are given in the box 'Indicators'. Notice that the colour change of most indicators takes place over a pH range of around 2 units, centred around different pHs. For this reason not all indicators are suitable for all titrations.

The following examples compare the suitability of two common indicators, phenolphthalein, which changes between pH 8.2 and 10.0, and methyl orange, which changes between pH 3.2 and 4.2, for four different types of acid/base titrations.

Strong acid/strong base, e.g. hydrochloric acid and sodium hydroxide

Figure 24.3 is the graph of pH against volume of base added. The pH ranges over which the two indicators change colour are shown. To fulfil the two criteria above, the indicator must change within the vertical portion of the pH curve. Here either indicator would be suitable but phenolphthalein is usually preferred because of its more easily seen colour change.

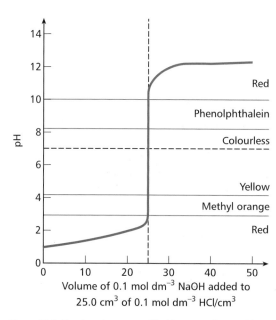

Figure 24.3 Titration of a strong acid with a strong base: adding 0.1 mol dm⁻³ NaOH to 25.0 cm³ of 0.1 mol dm⁻³ HCl

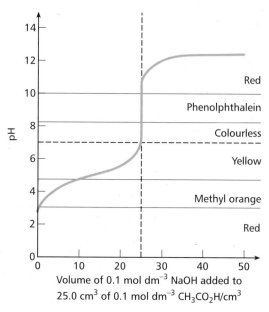

Figure 24.4 Titration of a weak acid with a strong base: adding 0.1 mol dm⁻³ NaOH to 25.0 cm³ of 0.1 mol dm⁻³ CH₃CO₂H

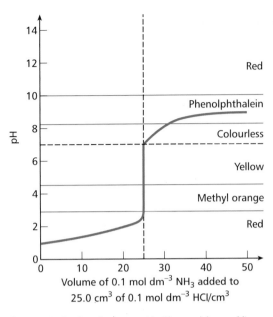

Figure 24.5 Titration of a strong acid with a weak base: adding 0.1 mol dm^{-3} NH$_3$ to 25.0 cm^3 of 0.1 mol dm^{-3} HCl

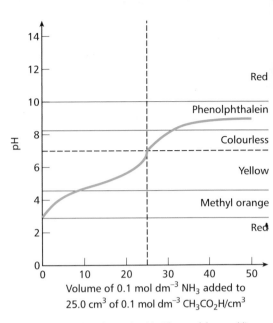

Figure 24.6 Titration of a weak acid with a weak base: adding 0.1 mol dm^{-3} NH$_3$ to 25.0 cm^3 of 0.1 mol dm^{-3} CH$_3$CO$_2$H

Weak acid/strong base titration, e.g. ethanoic acid and sodium hydroxide

See Figure 24.4. Methyl orange is not suitable. It does not change within the vertical portion of the curve. Phenolphthalein will change sharply at exactly 25.0 cm³, the equivalence point, and would therefore be a good choice.

Strong acid/weak base titration, e.g. hydrochloric acid and ammonia

See Figure 24.5. Here methyl orange will change sharply at the equivalence point but phenolphthalein would be of no use.

Weak acid/weak base, e.g. ethanoic acid and ammonia

See Figure 24.6. Here neither indicator is suitable. In fact no indicator could be suitable because an indicator requires a vertical portion of the curve over about two pH units at the equivalence point to give a sharp change.

The pH value at the equivalence point

A closer look at the titration curves for weak acid/strong base and strong acid/weak base shows that in neither curve is the pH at the equivalence point *exactly* equal to 7 (see **Figure 24.7**). This is because the salts that are produced in the reactions are themselves not neutral.

This phenomenon is sometimes called **salt hydrolysis** (hydrolysis means reaction with water). Whenever we have a salt of a weak base and strong acid (e.g. ammonium chloride, a salt of ammonia and hydrochloric acid) or a strong base and weak acid (e.g. sodium ethanoate, a salt of sodium hydroxide and ethanoic acid), the salt solution will not be neutral. An easy to remember rule is that the pH is governed by the 'strong part' of the salt, so:

> Strong acid/weak base gives an acidic salt.
> Weak acid/strong base gives an alkaline salt.

So ammonium chloride is acidic and sodium ethanoate is alkaline.

Q Would you expect a solution of ammonium nitrate to be acidic, alkaline or neutral?

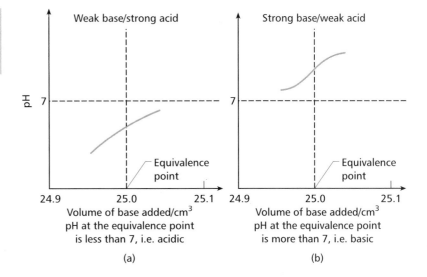

At the equivalence point:

$$NH_3 + HCl \longrightarrow NH_4^+ + Cl^-$$

The only ionic compound left is $NH_4^+Cl^-$. But NH_4^+ is itself a weak acid, as it can dissociate:

$$NH_4^+ \rightleftharpoons NH_3 + H^+$$

This produces H^+ ions in solution and gives a pH of less than 7 (i.e. acidic).

At the equivalence point:

$$NaOH + CH_3CO_2H \longrightarrow CH_3CO_2^- + Na^+ + H_2O$$

The only ionic compound is $CH_3CO_2^-Na^+$. But $CH_3CO_2^-$ is itself a base, as it can remove a proton from water:

$$CH_3CO_2^- + H_2O \rightleftharpoons CH_3CO_2H + OH^-$$

This produces OH^- ions in solution and gives a pH of more than 7 (i.e. alkaline).

Figure 24.7 pH values at the equivalence points of (a) weak base/strong acid, (b) strong base/weak acid

A salt of a weak acid and a weak base may be acidic, alkaline or neutral depending on the relative strengths of the acid and base concerned.

Titration with diprotic acids

A diprotic acid such as maleic acid (*cis*-butenedioic acid) has two protons which can be successively replaced in what are essentially two separate acid–base reactions. So the titration curve has two 'kinks' (see **Figure 24.8**). It may be possible to select indicators so that the two reactions may be titrated separately. With indicator 1, an end point of 25 cm³ is observed and with indicator 2 an end point of 50 cm³ is obtained.

The first end point represents:

$$\underset{\text{maleic acid}}{\overset{\displaystyle H \qquad H}{\underset{\displaystyle CO_2H \quad CO_2H}{C=C}}} \ (aq) \ + \ NaOH(aq) \longrightarrow \underset{\text{monosodium maleate}}{\overset{\displaystyle H \qquad H}{\underset{\displaystyle CO_2H \quad CO_2Na}{C=C}}} \ (aq) \ + \ H_2O \ (l)$$

and the second:

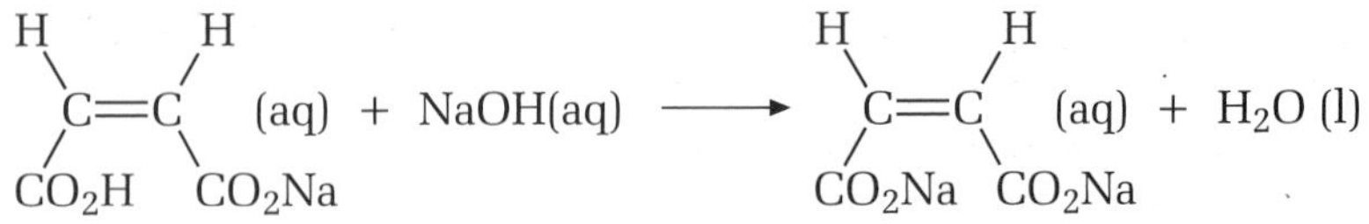

$$\underset{\substack{\text{monosodium maleate}}}{\overset{\displaystyle \underset{\text{CO}_2\text{H} \quad \text{CO}_2\text{Na}}{\overset{\text{H} \qquad \text{H}}{\text{C}=\text{C}}}}{}} \text{(aq)} + \text{NaOH(aq)} \longrightarrow \underset{\substack{\text{disodium maleate}}}{\overset{\displaystyle \underset{\text{CO}_2\text{Na} \quad \text{CO}_2\text{Na}}{\overset{\text{H} \qquad \text{H}}{\text{C}=\text{C}}}}{}} \text{(aq)} + \text{H}_2\text{O (l)}$$

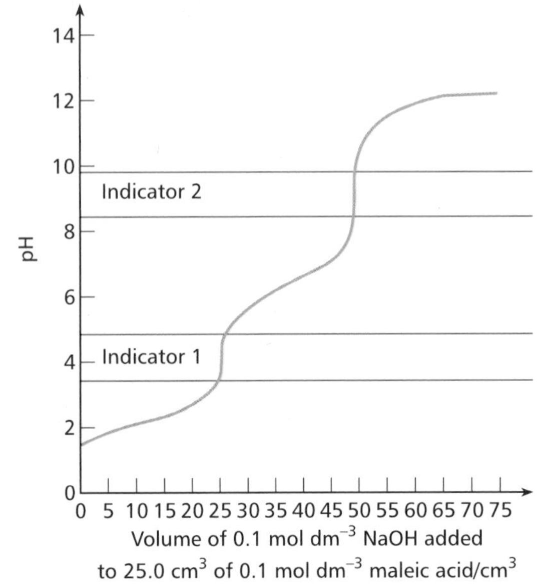

Figure 24.8 Titration of a diprotic acid: adding 0.1 mol dm^{-3} NaOH to 25.0 cm^3 of 0.1 mol dm^{-3} maleic acid

Indicators

How do indicators work? Why do different indicators change colour over different pH ranges? Why do indicators change colour over a pH range of about 2 units?

Indicators are weak acids which dissociate in aqueous solution. Imagine a weak acid HIn:

$$\underset{\text{red}}{\text{HIn(aq)}} \rightleftharpoons \text{H}^+\text{(aq)} + \underset{\text{blue}}{\text{In}^-\text{(aq)}}$$

If HIn and In$^-$ are different colours, say red and blue respectively, the HIn acts as an indicator. In a solution with a high concentration of H$^+$ (an acid) the equilibrium will be forced to the left as predicted by Le Châtelier's principle (see section 11.3). Almost all the indicator will exist as HIn and the solution will be red. In an alkaline solution where the concentration of OH$^-$ is high, H$^+$ ions will be removed as H$_2$O.

$$\text{HIn(aq)} \rightleftharpoons \text{H}^+\text{(aq)} + \text{In}^-\text{(aq)}$$
$$\downarrow + \text{OH}^-$$
$$\text{H}_2\text{O}$$

Hint: In$^-$ is the conjugate base of HIn.

As Le Châtelier's principle predicts, the equilibrium moves to the right, most of the indicator exists as In$^-$, and the solution is blue.

Putting in some numbers

As we have seen, different indicators change colour at different pHs. To understand this we can use the expression:

Hint: K_{In} is a special symbol for K_a and is used where the weak acid is an indicator.

$$K_{\text{In}} = \frac{[\text{H}^+\text{(aq)}]\,[\text{In}^-\text{(aq)}]}{[\text{HIn(aq)}]}$$

where K_{In} is the acid dissociation constant for the indicator.

Note: Throughout this calculation we will assume that all concentrations are measured at equilibrium (which is in fact reached almost instantaneously).

This can be rearranged:

$$K_{In} = [H^+(aq)] \times \frac{[In^-(aq)]}{[HIn(aq)]}$$

Taking logs and remembering that *multiplication* of numbers is achieved by *adding* logs:

$$\log K_{In} = \log[H^+(aq)] + \log\left(\frac{[In^-(aq)]}{[HIn(aq)]}\right)$$

Multiplying both sides by -1:

$$-\log K_{In} = -\log[H^+(aq)] - \log\left(\frac{[In^-(aq)]}{[HIn(aq)]}\right)$$

$-\log[H^+(aq)]$ is, of course, the pH of the solution and $-\log K_{In}$ can be called pK_{In}.

Hint: Think of 'p' as meaning '$-\log_{10}$'.

So

$$pK_{In} = pH - \log\left(\frac{[In^-(aq)]}{[HIn(aq)]}\right)$$

or

$$pH = pK_{In} + \log\left(\frac{[In^-(aq)]}{[HIn(aq)]}\right)$$

or

$$pH = pK_{In} - \log\left(\frac{[HIn(aq)]}{[In^-(aq)]}\right)$$

which is equivalent.

This is called the **Henderson equation.** Values of pK_{In} are given in data books along with the values of K_{In} (see **Table 24.3**). The Henderson equation lets us calculate the ratio $\frac{[HIn(aq)]}{[In^-(aq)]}$ in a solution of a given pH. If $\frac{[HIn(aq)]}{[In^-(aq)]}$ is large then $[HIn(aq)]$ is much greater than $[In^-(aq)]$ and the solution will look red. This is what happens in an acid. If $\frac{[HIn(aq)]}{[In^-(aq)]}$ is much less than 1 then $[HIn(aq)]$ is much less than $[In^-(aq)]$ and the solution will look blue. This is what happens in a base.

In a mixture of two colours of about the same intensity, the human eye sees only the colour of the more concentrated if it is present in a ratio of more than about 10 : 1. So if $\frac{[HIn(aq)]}{[In^-(aq)]} > 10$, the solution will appear red with no trace of blue. If $\frac{[HIn(aq)]}{[In^-(aq)]} < 1/10$, the eye will see blue only, with no trace of red. Between these limits, the eye will see a range of purple colours.

Putting this in the Henderson equation, the pH when the eye just sees red is given by:

$$pH = pK_{In} - \log\left(\frac{[HIn(aq)]}{[In^-(aq)]}\right)$$

$$pH = pK_{In} - \log\frac{10}{1}$$

As $\log 10 = 1$, $\qquad pH = pK_{In} - 1$

Table 24.3 pK_{In} for some common indicators

Indicator	pK_{In}
methyl orange	3.7
methyl red	5.1
phenolphthalein	9.3
bromothymol blue	7.0

Similarly the pH when the eye just sees blue is:

$$pH = pK_{In} - \log \frac{10}{1}$$

As $\log 1/10 = -1$,

$$pH = pK - (-1)$$
$$pH = pK_{In} + 1$$

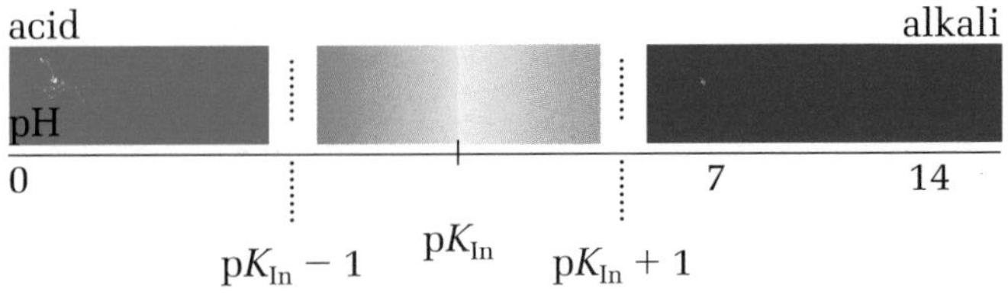

So the indicator will begin to change visibly from red to reddish-purple at $pK_{In} - 1$ and be completely blue by $pK_{In} + 1$: a range of 2 pH units centred on pK_{In}. This will be approximate as the 10 : 1 ratio is just a rule of thumb based on the average human eye and it also assumes that both colours are equally intense.

Figure 24.9 shows the structures of two indicators. The acidic hydrogen is marked in red.

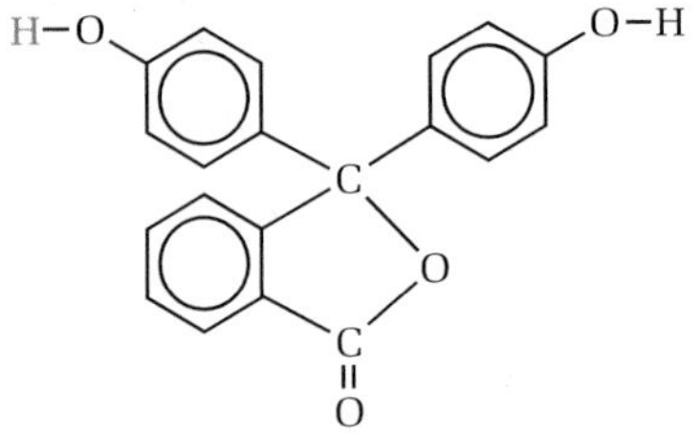

Hint: As indicators are weak acids, they produce H^+ ions when they dissociate. They should always be used in small amounts so that these H^+ ions do not significantly affect the pH of the solution they are placed in.

phenolphthalein

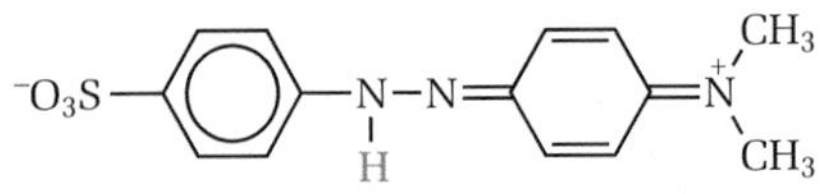

methyl orange

Figure 24.9 The structures of phenolphthalein and methyl orange. The acidic hydrogens are marked in red

Buffer solutions

Buffers are solutions which have the ability to resist changes of acidity or alkalinity, their pH remaining almost constant when small amounts of acid or alkali are added. One example of a system involving a buffer is blood, whose pH is maintained at approximately 7.4. A change of as little as 0.5 of a pH unit is likely to be fatal. Buffers work via the dissociation of weak acids. Imagine a weak acid HA. It will dissociate in solution.

$$HA(aq) \rightleftharpoons H^+(aq) + A^-(aq)$$

As it is a weak acid $[H^+(aq)] = [A^-(aq)]$ and is small.

If a little alkali is added, the OH^- ions will react with H^+ ions to remove them as water molecules:

$$HA(aq) \rightleftharpoons H^+(aq) + A^-(aq)$$
$$\downarrow OH^-(aq)$$
$$H_2O$$

This disturbs the equilibrium and as predicted by Le Châtelier's principle more HA will dissociate to restore the situation, so the pH tends to remain the same. If more H^+ is added, again the equilibrium shifts, this time to the left, H^+ ions combining with A^- ions to produce undissociated HA.

However, since $[A^-]$ is small, the supply of A^- soon runs out and there is no A^- left to 'mop up' the added H^+. So we have half a buffer! However, we can add to the solution a supply of extra A^- by adding a soluble salt of HA such as Na^+A^-. This increases the supply of A^- so that more H^+ can be used up. So there is a way in which both added H^+ and OH^- can be removed. **A buffer can therefore be made from a mixture of a weak acid and a soluble salt of that acid.**

Putting in some numbers

Different buffers can be made which will maintain different pHs.
We can use the Henderson equation:

$$pH = pK_a - \log\left(\frac{[HA(aq)]}{[A^-(aq)]}\right)$$

For example, we could make a buffer from a mixture of 0.1 mol dm^{-3} ethanoic acid and 0.1 mol dm^{-3} sodium ethanoate. pK_a for ethanoic acid is 4.8.

So the pH of the buffer

$$= 4.8 - \log\frac{(0.1)}{(0.1)}$$

$$= 4.8 - \log 1$$
$$pH = 4.8 - 0 = 4.8$$

Changing the concentration of HA or A$^-$ will affect the pH of the buffer. If we use 0.2 mol dm^{-3} ethanoic acid and 0.1 mol dm^{-3} sodium ethanoate, the pH will be given by:

$$pH = 4.8 - \log\frac{(0.2)}{(0.1)}$$

$$= 4.8 - \log 2$$
$$pH = 4.8 - 0.3 = 4.5$$

Making a buffer for a specified pH

Suppose we require a buffer of pH 5, again using ethanoic acid and sodium ethanoate. What concentrations are required?

$$pH = pK_a - \log\left(\frac{[HA(aq)]}{[A^-(aq)]}\right)$$

$$5 = 4.8 - \log\left(\frac{[HA(aq)]}{[A^-(aq)]}\right)$$

$$0.2 = -\log\left(\frac{[HA(aq)]}{[A^-(aq)]}\right)$$

Antilogging both sides of the equation:

$$0.63 = \frac{[HA(aq)]}{[A^-(aq)]}$$

So, for example, a solution which is 0.63 mol dm^{-3} in ethanoic acid and 1 mol dm^{-3} in sodium ethanoate would give a buffer of pH 5.0. When making a buffer to a specified pH, select a weak acid whose pK_a is approximately the same as the required pH, then calculate the required ratio of concentrations of HA and A$^-$. Notice that it is the *ratio* of HA to A$^-$ which is important, not the actual concentrations. However, if more concentrated solutions are used, the buffer can 'mop up' more added acid or alkali before becoming saturated.

Buffers, however, are not perfect. Addition of acid or alkali will change the pH slightly but by far less than the change caused by adding the same amount to a non-buffer. It is also possible to 'saturate' a buffer, i.e. to add so much acid or alkali that all of the available H$^+$ or A$^-$ is used up.

Buffers correspond to the almost horizontal sections of titration curves (see **Figure 24.2**). During any acid–base titration, a mixture of an acid and the salt is produced which therefore acts as a buffer. A useful rule is that a weak acid which is half neutralised by a strong base forms a buffer of pH = pK_a.

Q Find the pH of this buffer using [HA] = 0.1 mol dm^{-3}, [A$^-$] = 0.2 mol dm^{-3}.

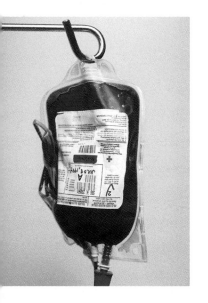

Blood is buffered to a pH of 7.4 by a number of mechanisms. The most important is:

$$H^+(aq) + HCO_3^-(aq) \rightleftharpoons CO_2(aq) + H_2O(l)$$

Addition of extra H$^+$ ions moves this equilibrium to the right, thus removing the added H$^+$. Addition of extra OH$^-$ ions removes H$^+$ by reacting to form water. The equilibrium above moves to the left releasing more H$^+$ ions. The same equilibrium helps to buffer the acidity of soils

Hint: To half neutralise an acid we add half as many moles of base as there are of acid.

Answer: 5.1

FURTHER FOCUS

Buffers and indicators

It is interesting to note that buffers and indicators are very similar, both involving the dissociation of a weak acid. The difference lies in the way they are used. Indicators are used in very small quantities and their equilibria react to the pH of the solution they are placed in. Buffers are used in large quantities and their dissociation dominates the pH, overwhelming the effect of small quantities of added acid or alkali.

24.3 Summary

• The acid dissociation constant, K_a of a weak acid HA is defined by	$K_a = \dfrac{[\text{H}^+(\text{aq})]_{eqm}[\text{A}^-(\text{aq})]_{eqm}}{[\text{HA}(\text{aq})]_{eqm}}$
• The base dissociation constant K_b of a weak base B is defined by	$K_c = \dfrac{[\text{BH}^+(\text{aq})]_{eqm}\,[\text{OH}^-(\text{aq})]_{eqm}}{[\text{B}(\text{aq})]_{eqm}}$
• The equivalence point of a titration is the point at which	the correct amount of acid has been added to react with all the base.
• The end point is the	volume of acid added when the indicator changes.
• Correct choice of indicator makes	the equivalence point and the end point the same.
• Indicators change over a pH range of about	2 units.
• The indicator must change	in the vertical portion of the titration curve.
• For an indicator to be used there must be a	vertical portion of the titration curve of at least 2 pH units.
• Indicators are weak acids in which	the acid and its conjugate base are different colours.
• Buffers are mixtures of	a weak acid and one of its salts.
• Buffers can absorb small quantities of added acid and base without	significant pH change.
• The Henderson equation can be applied to	both buffers and indicators:
• It is	$\text{pH} = pK_a - \log\left(\dfrac{[\text{HA}(\text{aq})]}{[\text{A}^-(\text{aq})]}\right)$

24.4 Practice questions

1. Calculate the pH of the following.
   (a) benzenecarboxylic acid (benzoic acid) (a weak acid, $K_a = 6.3 \times 10^{-5}\ mol\ dm^{-3}$) of concentration:
       (i) $1\ mol\ dm^{-3}$
       (ii) $0.1\ mol\ dm^{-3}$
       (iii) $0.01\ mol\ dm^{-3}$
   (b) phenylamine (a weak base, $K_b = 4.3 \times 10^{-10}\ mol\ dm^{-3}$) of concentration:
       (i) $0.001\ mol\ dm^{-3}$
       (ii) $0.01\ mol\ dm^{-3}$

2. A $0.1\ mol\ dm^{-3}$ solution of a weak acid has a pH of 2.8.
   (a) What is K_a for the acid?
   (b) What is its pK_a?

3. A buffer is made which is $0.1\ mol\ dm^{-3}$ in propanoic acid of $pK_a = 4.9$ and $0.05\ mol\ dm^{-3}$ in sodium propanoate. What is its pH?

4. Methanoic acid has a pK_a of 3.8. What ratio of concentrations of methanoic acid and sodium methanoate would give a buffer of pH 4?

5. Given the following values of pK_a:

   methanoic acid 3.8
   ethanoic acid 4.8
   propanoic acid 4.9

   how would you prepare a buffer of pH 4.6?

6. Which of the following indicators would be suitable for the titration of a strong acid with a weak base? (See Figure 24.5.)

   methyl yellow $\quad pK_{In} = 3.5$
   congo red $\quad pK_{In} = 4.0$
   bromothymol blue $\ pK_{In} = 7.0$

24.5 Examination questions

1. (a) The acid dissociation constant, K_a, of propanoic acid at room temperature is $1.3 \times 10^{-5}\ mol\ dm^{-3}$.
       Calculate the pH of each of the following aqueous solutions at room temperature:
       (i) Propanoic acid of concentration $0.05\ mol\ dm^{-3}$.
       (ii) A solution containing $0.05\ mol\ dm^{-3}$ propanoic acid and $0.05\ mol\ dm^{-3}$ sodium propanoate.
   (b) The experimentally determined graphs at the top of the next column show the changes in pH when aqueous sodium hydroxide of concentration $0.1\ mol\ dm^{-3}$ is added **separately** to 25 cm³ of aqueous hydrochloric acid and 25 cm³ of aqueous propanoic acid both of concentration $0.1\ mol\ dm^{-3}$. The ranges of two indicators are also shown.
       The pH ranges of two common indicators are
       methyl orange $\quad$ 3.2 to 4.4
       phenolphthalein $\quad$ 8.2 to 10
       (i) State, giving a reason, which indicator or indicators would be suitable for the titration of each acid with aqueous sodium hydroxide:
       hydrochloric acid
       propanoic acid

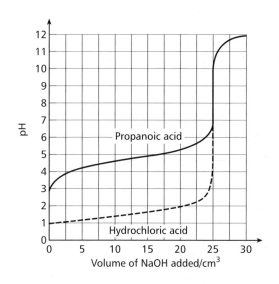

   (ii) What is the value of the pH when the propanoic acid is half-neutralised?
   (iii) What is the significance of this value?
   [WJEC 1997]

2. (a) (i) Aqueous ammonia is said to be a *weak* base. Explain what is meant by the term *weak*.

   (ii) The expression for K_b for aqueous ammonia, $NH_3(aq)$, may be written as

   $$K_b = \frac{[OH^-(aq)][NH_4^+(aq)]}{[NH_3(aq)]}$$

   Write an expression for K_a for the aqueous ammonium ion, $NH_4^+(aq)$, given the equation

   $$NH_4^+(aq) \rightleftharpoons NH_3(aq) + H^+(aq)$$

   (iii) Hence write down an expression for the product $K_b \cdot K_a$.

   (b) (i) Write down an expression for the ionic product of water, K_w, and give its units.

   (ii) I. At 313 K, the numerical value of K_w is 2.91×10^{-14}.
   Calculate the pH of pure water at this temperature.

   II. The numerical value of K_w at 298 K is 1.01×10^{-14}.
   Using Le Chatelier's principle, and the value of K_w at 313 K given in (b)(ii) I., deduce the sign of ΔH for the ionic dissociation of water.

   (c) In the reaction

   $$H_2O + H_2O \rightleftharpoons H_3O^+ + OH^-$$

   explain the rôle of the water molecules in terms of the Lowry–Brønsted theory of acids and bases.

   [WJEC 1997]

3. (a) When ethanoic acid is dissolved in water, the following equilibrium is established:

   $$CH_3CO_2H + H_2O \rightleftharpoons CH_3CO_2^- + H_3O^+ \qquad I$$

   When hydrogen chloride dissolves in ethanoic acid, the equilibrium established is:

   $$CH_3CO_2H + HCl \rightleftharpoons CH_3CO_2H_2^+ + Cl^- \qquad II$$

   Comment on the role of the ethanoic acid in:
   (i) equilibrium I;
   (ii) equilibrium II.

   (b) What is the relationship between the species $CH_3CO_2H_2^+$ and CH_3CO_2H?

   (c) The value of K_a for ethanoic acid at 298 K is 1.74×10^{-5} mol dm^{-3} and for methanoic acid,

HCO$_2$H, it is 1.60×10^{-4} mol dm^{-3} at the same temperature.
   (i) Write an expression for K_a for CH_3CO_2H.
   (ii) Hence calculate the pH of a 0.100 mol dm^{-3} solution of CH_3CO_2H at 298 K.

   (d) The pH of a 0.050 mol dm^{-3} solution of HCO$_2$H is 2.55.
   Using this, together with the data in (c) and your answer to (c)(ii):
   (i) state which of the two acids is the stronger;
   (ii) comment on the relative pH values of the two acids.

   (e) (i) Sketch with reasonable accuracy, on graph paper, how the pH changes during the titration of 20.0 cm^3 of a 0.100 mol dm^{-3} solution of methanoic acid with 0.050 mol dm^{-3} sodium hydroxide solution.

   (ii) Select using the data below a suitable indicator for this titration. Give a brief reason for your choice based on the curve drawn in (e)(i).

Indicator	pH Range
Bromocresol green	3.5–5.4
Bromothymol blue	6.0–7.6
Phenol red	6.8–8.4

   [London 1997]

4. The pH of a solution **A**, a 0.15 mol dm^{-3} solution of a weak monoprotic acid HX, is 2.69.
   (a) Calculate $[H^+]$ in solution **A** and hence determine the value of the acid dissociation constant, K_a, of HX.

   (b) (i) A 25 cm^3 sample of **A** is titrated with 0.25 mol dm^{-3} sodium hydroxide. Calculate the volume of sodium hydroxide needed to reach equivalence in the titration. Give the best estimate you can of the pH of the neutralised solution, stating a reason.

   (ii) Calculate the pH of the titration solution when HX is exactly half-neutralised and $[HX] = [X^-]$.

   (iii) Calculate the pH of the titration solution when a total of 25 cm^3 of 0.25 mol dm^{-3} sodium hydroxide has been added.

   [NEAB 1998]

25 Further redox: electrochemical cells

C H E M I S T R Y N O W

Electricity on the move

Batteries are vital for a whole variety of portable electric and electronic gadgets: laptop computers, mobile phones, personal stereos and camcorders, for example. Many medical advances require small, light batteries: artificial limbs and even artificial hearts are technologically possible but are not yet practicable because present day batteries are still heavy and bulky. Electric cars, too, are still unpopular because their heavy batteries store little electricity, giving them limited range and speed.

Portable electronic technology depends on batteries

section through a lithium ion battery

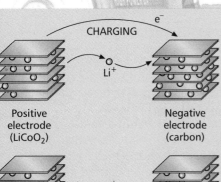

charging and discharging a lithium ion battery

The current leader in mobile battery technology is the lithium ion system used in the latest laptops. This battery is light because it contains lithium rather than a heavy metal such as zinc, nickel, cadmium or lead. It contains a solid polymer-based electrolyte rather than a liquid or paste so that it cannot leak. It can be bent or even cut in half and still work. Weight for weight, lithium batteries have three times the output of the nickel–cadmium (NiCad) batteries they are replacing. Also, they do not suffer from the memory effect, which means that NiCad batteries should be fully discharged before recharging. The charge of a lithium battery can be topped up at any time.

The positive electrode is made of lithium cobalt oxide ($LiCoO_2$) and the negative electrode of carbon rather like graphite. These are arranged in layers with a sandwich of solid electrolyte in between. On charging, electrons are forced through the external circuit from the positive electrode to the negative and at the same time lithium ions move through the solid electrolyte to maintain the balance of charge. On discharging, this process is reversed. A single cell gives a voltage of 3.5–4 V compared with 1.5 V for more typical cells.

Although lithium batteries are relatively new, chemists are already developing the next generation of batteries based on manganese oxides, which promise to be cheaper, safer and less toxic.

In this chapter we will be looking at:
- the use of redox reactions (electron transfer reactions) to generate electrical energy
- half cells, in which the oxidation and reduction parts of a redox reaction are considered separately
- predicting which redox reactions are feasible

Introduction

This chapter builds on the ideas about redox (reduction–oxidation) reactions developed in Chapter 13. It shows how we can carry out the reduction and oxidation parts of redox reactions separately (these are called half cells) so that electrons flow from one to the other through an external circuit. We can therefore measure the potential difference between the two half cells and build up a list (the electrochemical series) which shows how readily they take place. This can be used to predict the feasibility of redox reactions: whether or not they might take place of their own accord. We also look at the practical applications of redox reactions to batteries for generation and storage of electricity.

CONCEPT CHECKPOINTS

The following basic ideas are used in this chapter. You may revise some of these topics elsewhere in the book.
- electrical potential difference ('voltage') (section 6.3)
- redox reactions as electron transfer reactions (Chapter 13)
- the use of oxidation numbers (Chapter 13)

Hint: This is *not* the same as the ionisation of gaseous zinc atoms to form gaseous ions:

$$Zn(g) \longrightarrow Zn^{2+}(g) + 2e^-$$

25.1 Electrochemical cells

One redox reaction that has considerable practical application and is of theoretical interest is that of a metal dissolving and forming a solution of its own aqueous ions.

For example: $\quad Zn(s) + (aq) \longrightarrow Zn^{2+}(aq) + 2e^-$

The zinc is oxidised, since it has lost electrons and its oxidation number has therefore increased.

Reactions like this are interesting because they are the basis of electrical batteries and because they enable us to predict which redox reactions might occur (are feasible) and which cannot take place.

Half cells

If we dip a rod of metal, say zinc, into a solution of its own ions, for example, zinc sulphate solution, then an equilibrium is set up.

$$Zn(s) + (aq) \rightleftharpoons Zn^{2+}(aq) + 2e^-$$

If some zinc dissolves, i.e. the reaction above goes from left to right, then the electrons left behind on the rod build up a negative electrical charge. We say the rod gains a negative electrical potential. This arrangement is called a **half cell** (see Figure 25.1).

If we could determine this potential, it would give us a measure of how readily electrons are released by the metal concerned. This would tell us how good a reducing agent the metal was, because reducing agents release electrons. However, we cannot measure electrical potential, only potential *difference* (often called voltage). What we *can* do is to connect together two different half cells and measure the **potential difference** between them with a voltmeter, as shown in **Figure 25.2** for copper and zinc half cells.

The circuit is completed by a **salt bridge,** the simplest form of which is a piece of filter paper soaked in a solution of a salt (usually

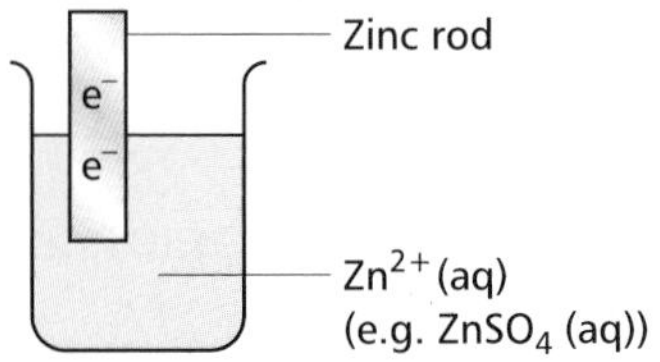

Figure 25.1 Solid zinc in equilibrium with its aqueous ions

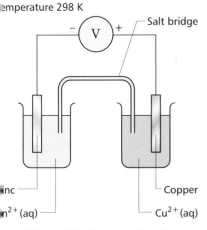

Temperature 298 K

Salt bridge

V   − +

Zinc

Copper

Zn²⁺ (aq)

Cu²⁺ (aq)

Figure 25.2 Two half cells connected together

Hint: A perfect voltmeter does not allow any current to flow: it merely measures the electrical 'push' or pressure that tends to make current flow.

Hint: We know that the zinc half cell is the more negative one because this is where we must connect the negative terminal of the voltmeter.

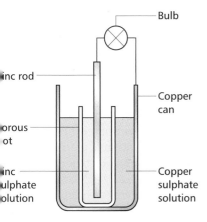

Bulb

Zinc rod

Copper can

Porous pot

Zinc sulphate solution

Copper sulphate solution

Figure 25.3 A Daniell cell lighting a bulb. The porous pot acts like a salt bridge

saturated potassium nitrate). This is used, rather than a piece of wire, to avoid further metal/ion potentials in the circuit. The salt chosen for the salt bridge must not react with either of the salt solutions in the half cells.

If we connect the two half cells shown, we get a potential difference (voltage) of 1.1 V with the zinc half cell being the more negative (if the solutions are 1 mol dm⁻³ and temperature 298 K).

The fact that the zinc half cell is negative tells us that zinc loses its electrons more readily than does copper. If the voltmeter were removed and electrons allowed to flow, they would do so from zinc to copper. The following changes would take place:

1. Zinc would dissolve to form $Zn^{2+}(aq)$, increasing the concentration of $Zn^{2+}(aq)$.
2. The electrons would flow through the wire to the copper rod where they would combine with $Cu^{2+}(aq)$ ions (from the copper sulphate solution) so depositing fresh copper on the rod and decreasing the concentration of $Cu^{2+}(aq)$.

That is, the following two **half reactions** would take place:

$$Zn(s) \longrightarrow Zn^{2+}(aq) + 2e^-$$

and

$$Cu^{2+}(aq) + 2e^- \longrightarrow Cu(s)$$

adding: $Zn(s) + Cu^{2+}(aq) + 2\!\!\!/e^- \longrightarrow Zn^{2+}(aq) + Cu(s) + 2\!\!\!/e^-$

When we add the two half reactions, the electrons cancel out and we get the overall reaction shown, which is exactly the reaction we get on putting zinc directly into a solution of copper ions. It is, of course, a redox reaction with zinc being oxidised and copper ions reduced. The system of two half cells could be used to generate electricity and is, in fact, the basis of an electrical cell called the Daniell cell (see **Figure 25.3**).

The hydrogen electrode

If we want to compare the tendency of different metals to release electrons, we must agree on a standard half cell to which any other half cell can be connected for comparison. The half cell chosen is called the hydrogen electrode, see Figure 25.4.

You might expect this to consist of a rod of hydrogen dipping into a solution of $H^+(aq)$ ions but since hydrogen is a gas, and this is not

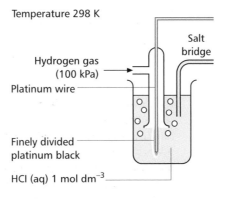

Temperature 298 K

Salt bridge

Hydrogen gas (100 kPa)

Platinum wire

Finely divided platinum black

HCl (aq) 1 mol dm⁻³

Figure 25.4 The hydrogen electrode

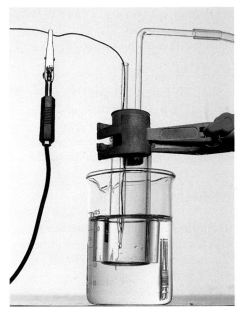

A hydrogen electrode

Table 25.1 Some $E^\ominus$ values. Good reducing agents appear top right, e.g. Li(s). Good oxidising agents appear bottom left, e.g Ag$^+$(aq)

Half reaction	$E^\ominus$/V
Li$^+$(aq) + e$^-$ $\rightleftharpoons$ Li(s)	−3.03
Ca^{2+}(aq) + 2e$^-$ $\rightleftharpoons$ Ca(s)	−2.87
Al^{3+}(aq) + 3e$^-$ $\rightleftharpoons$ Al(s)	−1.66
Zn^{2+}(aq) + 2e$^-$ $\rightleftharpoons$ Zn(s)	−0.76
Pb^{2+}(aq) + 2e$^-$ $\rightleftharpoons$ Pb(s)	−0.13
2H$^+$(aq) + 2e $\rightleftharpoons$ H$_2$(g)|Pt	0.00
Cu^{2+}(aq) + 2e$^-$ $\rightleftharpoons$ Cu(s)	+0.34
Ag$^+$(aq) + e$^-$ $\rightleftharpoons$ Ag(s)	+0.80

Q What would be $E^\ominus$ for the half reaction 2Li$^+$(aq) + 2e$^-$ $\rightleftharpoons$ 2Li(s)?

Q What will be the value of $E^\ominus$ for a Al^{3+}(aq)/Al(s) half cell connected to a Zn^{2+}(aq)/Zn(s) half cell?

Hint: Always state which half cell is the more negative when asked for the value of $E^\ominus$.

Answer: −3.03 V because the number of electrons makes no difference

Answer: 0.90 V, Al negative

possible, we bubble hydrogen into the solution. Hydrogen doesn't conduct, so we make electrical contact via a piece of the unreactive metal platinum, coated with finely divided platinum (to increase the surface area and allow any reaction to proceed rapidly). The electrode is used under standard conditions of [H$^+$(aq)] = 1 mol dm^{-3}, pressure 100 kPa and temperature 298 K.

The potential of the hydrogen electrode is *defined* as zero, so if it is connected to another half cell (see **Figure 25.5**), the measured voltage, called the electromotive force (e.m.f., E), is the electrode potential of that cell. If the second cell is at standard conditions [ions] = 1 mol dm^{-3}, temperature = 298 K), then this is given the symbol $E^\ominus$ (298 K), usually abbreviated to $E^\ominus$ and pronounced 'E standard'. Half cells with negative values of $E^\ominus$ are better at releasing electrons (better reducing agents) than hydrogen.

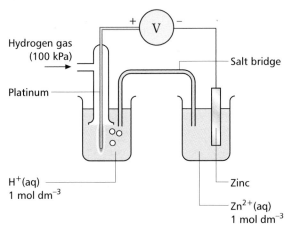

If the zinc is connected to the negative terminal of the voltmeter then $E^\ominus$ is negative

Figure 25.5 Measuring $E^\ominus$ for a zinc half cell

The electrochemical series

A list of some $E^\ominus$ values for metal/metal ion half cells is given in **Table 25.1**.

By convention the equilibria are written with the electrons on the left of the arrow, i.e. as a reduction, so these are sometimes called **reduction potentials.** (Remember RIG – 'Reduction is gain'.) The most commonly used names for $E^\ominus$ are **standard electrode potential** or **redox potential**.

Arranged in this order with the most negative values at the top this list is called the **electrochemical series.** Notice that the number of electrons involved has no effect on the value of $E^\ominus$.

The voltage obtained by connecting two half cells together is found by the difference between the two $E^\ominus$ values. So connecting an Al^{3+}(aq)/Al(s) half cell to a Cu^{2+}(aq)/Cu(s) half cell would give a voltage of 2.00 V (see **Figure 25.6**).

If we connect an Al^{3+}(aq)/Al(s) half cell to a Pb^{2+}(aq)/Pb(s) half cell, the e.m.f. will be 1.53 V and the Al^{3+}(aq)/Al(s) half cell will be negative.

It is well worth sketching diagrams like the ones shown in Figure 25.6. It will prevent you getting muddled with signs. Remember that more negative values are listed at the top.

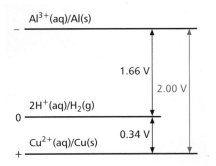

If we connect an $Al^{3+}(aq)/Al(s)$ half cell to a $Cu^{2+}(aq)/Cu(s)$ half cell the e.m.f. will be 2.00 V and the $Al^{3+}(aq)/Al(s)$ half cell will be negative

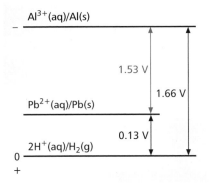

If we connect an $Al^{3+}(aq)/Al(s)$ half cell to a $Pb^{2+}(aq)/Pb(s)$ half cell the e.m.f. will be 1.53 V and the $Al^{3+}(aq)/Al(s)$ half cell will be negative

Figure 25.6 Calculating the value of the voltage when two half cells are connected

---

Q Write the cell diagram for the pair of half cells in Figure 25.2 and work out the value of $E^{\ominus}$ from Table 25.1

Q Write the cell diagram for measuring $E^{\ominus}$ for the system: $Br_2(aq)/2Br^-(aq)$, i.e. $Br_2(aq) + 2e^- \rightleftharpoons 2Br^-(aq)$

Answer: $Zn(s)|Zn^{2+}(aq) \;\vdots\; Cu^{2+}(aq)|Cu(s)$
             $E^{\ominus} = +1.1$ V

Answer: $Pt|H_2(g)|2H^+(aq) \;\vdots\; Br_2(aq), 2Br^-(aq)|Pt$
Note the more reduced form ($Br^-(aq)$) is closest to the platinum electrode.

Cell diagrams

These are a shorthand for writing down the cell formed by connecting two half cells. The usual apparatus diagram is shown in **Figure 25.7** and the cell diagram is written as follows:

$$Al(s)|Al^{3+}(aq) \;\vdots\; Cu^{2+}(aq)|Cu(s) \qquad E^{\ominus} = +2.00 \text{ V}$$

A vertical solid line indicates a **phase boundary**, e.g. between a solid and a solution, and a double vertical dotted line a **salt bridge.**

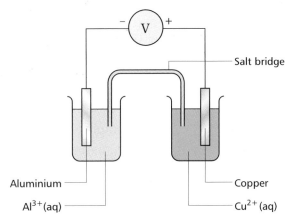

Figure 25.7 A pair of half cells

By convention, we give the polarity (i.e. whether it is positive or negative) of the right-hand electrode, *as the cell diagram is written*. In this case the copper half cell is positive (it is connected to the positive terminal of the voltmeter) and, if allowed to flow, electrons would go from aluminium to copper.

We could equally well have written the cell:

$$Cu(s)|Cu^{2+}(aq) \;\vdots\; Al^{3+}(aq)|Al(s) \qquad E^{\ominus} = -2.00 \text{ V}$$

as we always give the polarity of the right-hand cell.
The cell diagram for a silver electrode connected to a $Pb^{2+}(aq)/Pb(s)$ half cell would be:

$$Ag(s)|Ag^+(aq) \;\vdots\; Pb^{2+}(aq)|Pb(s) \qquad E^{\ominus} = -0.93 \text{ V}$$

Extension to systems of other than metal/metal ion

Cells can also be set up to measure $E^{\ominus}$ values for redox reactions which are not metal/metal ion systems. The problem is tackled in the same way as the hydrogen electrode. We ensure that both the species that we are interested in are present in the solution and make electrical contact with the solution via a piece of platinum.

For example, **Figure 25.8** shows how to measure $E^{\ominus}$ for $Fe^{3+}(aq)/Fe^{2+}(aq)$, i.e.

$$Fe^{3+}(aq) + e^- \rightleftharpoons Fe^{2+}(aq).$$

The cell diagram is written:

$$Pt|H_2(g)|2H^+(aq) \;\vdots\; Fe^{3+}(aq), Fe^{2+}(aq)|Pt \qquad E^{\ominus} = +0.77 \text{ V}$$

In the cell diagram, the two aqueous species are separated by a comma and the one with the lower oxidation number (the more reduced form) goes nearest the platinum electrode.

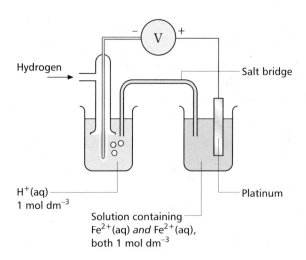

Figure 25.8 Measuring $E^{\ominus}$ for the $Fe^{3+}(aq)/Fe^{2+}(aq)$ system

More complex systems

More complicated systems are possible. For example, manganate(VII) ions ($MnO_4^-(aq)$) can be reduced to $Mn^{2+}(aq)$ but only in the presence of $H^+(aq)$ ions:

$$MnO_4^-(aq) + 8H^+(aq) + 5e^- \rightleftharpoons Mn^{2+}(aq) + 4H_2O(l)$$

The $E^{\ominus}$ values for this half reaction can be measured provided all four species $MnO_4^-(aq)$, $H^+(aq)$, $Mn^{2+}(aq)$ and $H_2O(l)$ are present. Again, a platinum electrode is used, to make electrical contact.

In the cell diagram, the two pairs of reactants, $[MnO_4^-(aq) + 8H^+(aq)]$ and $[Mn^{2+}(aq) + 4H_2O(l)]$, are bracketed together and separated by a comma. The rule that the most reduced species is written nearest the electrode still applies.

$$Pt\,|\,H_2(g)\,|\,2H^+(aq)\;\vdots\;[MnO_4^-(aq) + 8H^+(aq)],[Mn^{2+}(aq)$$
$$+ 4H_2O(l)]\,|\,Pt \qquad E^{\ominus} = +1.51\ V$$

Table 25.2 is an extension of Table 25.1 and includes some systems other than metal/metal ion.

Table 25.2 $E^{\ominus}$ values

Half reaction	$E^{\ominus}/V$
$Li^+(aq) + e^- \rightleftharpoons Li(s)$	−3.03
$Ca^{2+}(aq) + 2e^- \rightleftharpoons Ca(s)$	−2.87
$Al^{3+}(aq) + 3e^- \rightleftharpoons Al(s)$	−1.66
$Zn^{2+}(aq) + 2e^- \rightleftharpoons Zn(s)$	−0.76
$Cr^{3+}(aq) + e^- \rightleftharpoons Cr^{2+}(aq)\,|\,Pt$	−0.41
$Pb^{2+}(aq) + 2e^- \rightleftharpoons Pb(s)$	−0.13
$2H^+(aq) + 2e \rightleftharpoons H_2(g)\,|\,Pt$	0.00
$Cu^{2+} + e^- \rightleftharpoons Cu^+(aq)\,|\,Pt$	+0.15
$Cu^{2+}(aq) + 2e^- \rightleftharpoons Cu(s)$	+0.34
$I_2(aq) + 2e^- \rightleftharpoons 2I^-(aq)\,|\,Pt$	+0.54
$Fe^{3+}(aq) + e^- \rightleftharpoons Fe^{2+}(aq)\,|\,Pt$	+0.77
$Ag^+(aq) + e^- \rightleftharpoons Ag(s)$	+0.80
$Br_2(aq) + 2e^- \rightleftharpoons 2Br^-(aq)\,|\,Pt$	+1.07
$Cl_2(aq) + 2e^- \rightleftharpoons 2Cl^-(aq)\,|\,Pt$	+1.36
$[MnO_4^- + 8H^+(aq)] + 5e^- \rightleftharpoons [Mn^{2+}(aq) + 4H_2O(l)]\,|\,Pt$	+1.51
$Ce^{4+}(aq) + e^- \rightleftharpoons Ce^{3+}(aq)\,|\,Pt$	+1.70

CHEMISTRY AROUND US

Batteries

Batteries for torches, radios, calculators, etc. are the most familiar applications of electrochemical cells. Each man, woman and child in the UK buys on average five batteries per year. Nowadays there is a bewildering variety of types and brands advertised with slogans like 'long life' and 'high power'.

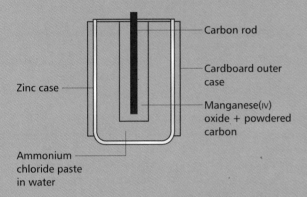

Leclanché cell

The majority of batteries for household use are based on the zinc–carbon system with a variety of different electrolytes. The most common is the Leclanché cell, named after its inventor. It consists of a zinc canister filled with a paste of ammonium chloride (NH_4Cl) and water, the electrolyte. In the centre is a carbon rod, which acts as an inert electrode. It is surrounded by a mixture of manganese(IV) oxide and powdered carbon to make it conduct.

The reactions are:

$$Zn(s) \longrightarrow Zn^{2+}(aq) + 2e^-$$

At the carbon rod:

$$2NH_4^+(aq) + 2e^- \longrightarrow 2NH_3(g) + H_2(g)$$

The hydrogen gas is oxidised to water by the manganese(IV) oxide (preventing a build-up of pressure) while the ammonia dissolves in the water of the paste. The cell diagram is:

$$Zn(s)|Zn^{2+}(aq) \,\vdots\, 2NH_4^+(aq), [2NH_3(g) + H_2(g)]|C(gr)$$
$$E = 1.5\,V$$

As the cell discharges, the zinc is used up and the walls of the zinc canister become thin and prone to leakage. The ammonium chloride electrolyte is acidic (being the salt of a strong acid and a weak base: see section 24.2), and can be corrosive. That is why you should remove spent batteries from equipment. This cell is ideal for, say, doorbells, which need a small current intermittently.

A variant of this cell is the zinc chloride cell. It is similar to the Leclanché but uses zinc chloride as the

electrolyte. Such cells are better at supplying high currents than the Leclanché and are marketed as 'extra life' batteries for radios, torches and shavers.

Long life alkaline batteries are also based on the zinc–carbon–manganese(IV) oxide electrode system with an electrolyte of potassium hydroxide. Powdered zinc is used, whose greater surface area allows the battery to supply high currents. The cell is enclosed in a steel container to prevent leakage. These cells are suitable for equipment taking continuous high currents such as personal stereos. In this situation they can last up to sixteen times as long as ordinary zinc–carbon batteries, but they are more expensive.

Many other electrode systems are in use especially for miniature batteries such as those used in watches, hearing aids, cameras and electronic equipment. These include zinc–air, mercury(II)oxide–zinc, silver oxide–zinc, and lithium–manganese(IV) oxide. Which is used for which application depends on the precise requirements of voltage, current, size and cost.

Rechargeable batteries

These are now available in standard sizes to replace traditional zinc–carbon batteries. Although more expensive to buy, they can be recharged up to 500 times, reducing the effective cost significantly. These cells are called nickel–cadmium and have an alkaline electrolyte. The reaction that occurs is:

$$2NiOOH + Cd + 2H_2O \rightleftharpoons 2Ni(OH)_2 + Cd(OH)_2$$

The reaction goes from left to right on discharge (electrons flowing from Cd to Ni) and right to left on charging.

Types of batteries

FURTHER FOCUS

Electrolysis

Much of this chapter has been about chemical reactions that occur at electrodes and generate an e.m.f. capable of driving a current through a circuit. The opposite process, where an electric current passes through a liquid (or solution) containing ions, and causes chemical changes at the electrodes is called **electrolysis** – the ending '-lysis' means splitting.

The conduction of electricity by ionic compounds

Covalent compounds do not conduct at all. When metals conduct, the current is carried by the electrons in their delocalised 'sea' (see section 9.1). No chemical change occurs: the metal is left completely unaltered. Metals conduct both in the solid and liquid states.

By contrast, ionic compounds conduct only when liquid – either molten or in solution. The current is carried by positive and negative ions, which move through the liquid electrolyte. In the solid state the ions are held in a lattice.

The process is called **electrolysis**:

- Positive ions, called **cations**, migrate towards the **cathode** (the negative electrode).
- Negative ions, called **anions**, migrate towards the **anode** (the positive electrode).
- Chemical reactions occur at the electrodes, so that after passage of electricity the electrolyte has been chemically changed.

For example, when a current is passed through molten lead(II) bromide, $Pb^{2+}\ 2Br^-$, the Pb^{2+} ions migrate towards the cathode and Br^- ions migrate towards the anode, as shown in the diagram below.

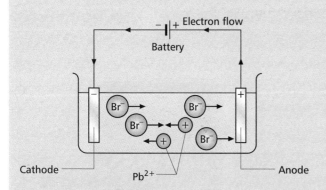

The electrolysis of molten lead bromide

Reactions at the electrodes

> **Q** The power supply must be direct current (DC). Why is alternating current (AC) not suitable?

The cathode gives away electrons which are supplied by the external power supply. These are accepted by the cations (Pb^{2+} in the above example) and the following reaction occurs represented by a half equation:

$$Pb^{2+} + 2e^- \longrightarrow Pb$$

The oxidation number (see section 13.2) of the lead has gone down from +II to 0, so it has been reduced. Cathode reactions are always reductions.

The anode accepts electrons from the anions (Br^- in the above example) and the following reaction occurs, represented by the half equation:

$$Br^- \longrightarrow Br + e^-$$

immediately followed by:

$$2Br \longrightarrow Br_2$$

Overall these may be written:

$$2Br^- \longrightarrow Br_2 + 2e^-$$

The oxidation number of the bromine has increased from −I to 0, so it has been oxidised.

All anode reactions are oxidations.

The overall reaction is found by adding the two half reactions:

$$
\begin{array}{rcl}
Pb^{2+} + 2e^- &\longrightarrow& Pb \\
2Br^- &\longrightarrow& Br_2 + 2e^- \\
\hline
Pb^{2+} + 2Br^- &\longrightarrow& Pb + Br_2
\end{array}
$$

or

$$PbBr_2 \longrightarrow Pb + Br_2$$

The lead bromide has been decomposed into its elements.

Notice that the electrons cancel out. The battery simply moves them from the anode to the cathode through the external circuit.

Electrolysis is the basis of several important industries. A typical industrialised country uses 5–10% of its electricity on electrolytic processes. These include the Down's cell for producing sodium (see page 190) and the mercury and diaphragm/membrane cells for producing chlorine (see pages 199 and 209). Perhaps the most important is the electrolytic extraction of aluminium from aluminium oxide.

Answer: With AC, the polarity of the electrodes changes continuously.

The extraction of aluminium

Aluminium is extracted by the Hall–Héroult process. We extract 300 000 tonnes of it every year in the UK alone.

The raw material for aluminium manufacture is bauxite, which contains aluminium oxide, Al_2O_3, (alumina). The main impurities are oxides, particularly iron(III) oxide and silicon dioxide (sand), so bauxite is first purified. Powdered bauxite is dissolved in hot sodium hydroxide solution and the insoluble impurities are filtered off. The solution is cooled and pure alumina precipitates.

Did you know? The American Charles Hall and Frenchman Paul Héroult discovered the process for extraction of aluminium independently on the same week of the same year while both were aged 23. They both died at the age of 50!

A bauxite mine

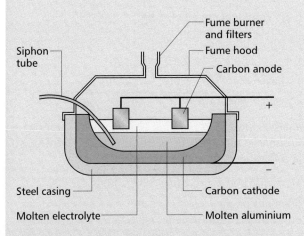

Electrolysis cell for aluminium extraction

Alumina dissolves in molten cryolite, Na_3AlF_6, at approximately 1200 K and this is used as the electrolyte in cells with a carbon anode and cathode (see the diagram). (The melting temperature of pure alumina is 2345 K, so dissolving the alumina in cryolite is preferable to melting it.)

At the cathode:

$$4Al^{3+} + 12e^- \longrightarrow 4Al(s)$$

At the anode:

$$6O^{2-} \longrightarrow 3O_2(g) + 12e^-$$

(We have balanced the number of electrons to show that the same number of electrons is involved at each electrode.)

At the high temperature used, the carbon anode burns away in the oxygen and must be replaced frequently. Apart from replacement of the anode, the process is continuous, alumina being regularly added to the cell and the molten aluminium being siphoned off (the melting temperature of aluminium is 932 K).

> **Q** What is formed from the burning carbon anodes?

The Faraday constant

From the above process:

$$\underset{\text{1 mol}}{Al^{3+}} + \underset{\text{3 mol}}{3e^-} \longrightarrow \underset{\text{1 mol}}{Al}$$

we know that three electrons (of total charge $3 \times 1.6 \times 10^{-19}$ coulombs = 4.8×10^{-19} coulombs) are needed to produce one atom of aluminium. So, three moles of electrons are needed to produce 1 mole (27 g) of aluminium. Since there are approximately 6×10^{23} (the Avogadro constant) electrons in a mole, this is a charge of $4.8 \times 10^{-19} \times 6 \times 10^{23} = 288\,000$ C for three moles of electrons. The charge on one mole of electrons is called the Faraday constant, F. The accurate value of F is $96\,485$ C mol^{-1} but it is often rounded to $96\,500$ C mol^{-1} or $96\,000$ C mol^{-1}.

Answer: Carbon dioxide

25.2 Predicting whether a redox reaction could take place (the feasibility of the reaction)

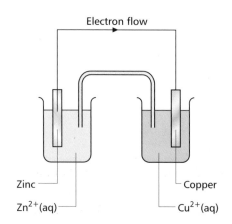

Figure 25.9 Connecting Zn^{2+}(aq)/Zn(s) and Cu^{2+}(aq)/Cu(s)

It is possible to use half cell e.m.f.s to decide on the feasibility of a redox reaction. When we connect a pair of half cells, the electrons will flow from the more negative to the more positive and not in the opposite direction.

Think of the following half cells:

$$Zn^{2+}(aq)/Zn(s) \qquad E^{\ominus} = -0.76\ V \text{ and}$$
$$Cu^{2+}(aq)/Cu(s) \qquad E^{\ominus} = +0.34\ V$$

Figure 25.9 shows these two half cells connected together. Electrons will flow from zinc (the more negative) to copper (the more positive).

So the equilibrium

$$Zn^{2+}(aq) + 2e^{-} \rightleftharpoons Zn(s)$$

actually moves to the left (Zn(s) releases electrons) and the equilibrium

$$Cu^{2+}(aq) + 2e^{-} \rightleftharpoons Cu(s)$$

moves to the right (Cu^{2+}(aq) accepts electrons).

The overall effect is:

$$Zn(s) \longrightarrow Zn^{2+}(aq) + 2e^{-}$$

Adding: $$Cu^{2+}(aq) + 2e^{-} \longrightarrow Cu(s)$$
_____
$$Cu^{2+}(aq) + Zn(s) + \cancel{2e^{-}} \longrightarrow Cu(s) + Zn(s) + \cancel{2e^{-}}$$

So this reaction is feasible and is the reaction that actually happens, either by connecting the two half cells or more directly by adding Zn to Cu^{2+}(aq) ions in a test tube. The reverse reaction:

$$Cu(s) + Zn^{2+}(aq) \longrightarrow Zn(s) + Cu^{2+}(aq)$$

is *not* feasible and does not occur.

We could go through this mental process each time we wished to predict the outcome of a redox reaction. However, there are two short cuts which we can use, one diagrammatic (the 'anticlockwise rule') and the other arithmetical (calculating $E^{\ominus}_{reaction}$).

$E^{\ominus}$–oxidation number diagrams: the anticlockwise rule

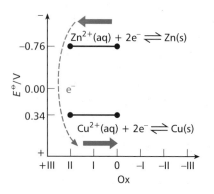

Figure 25.10 $E^{\ominus}$–Ox diagram. Note that the most negative $E^{\ominus}$ value is at the top, as in the electrochemical series, and the values of oxidation numbers are most positive on the left

We plot each half reaction on a diagram of $E^{\ominus}$ against the oxidation number of the oxidised and reduced form in each half cell (**Figure 25.10**).

In redox reactions electrons are transferred from the more negative to the more positive half cell, i.e. on such a diagram they will move downwards. Electrons will flow from Zn^{2+}(aq)/Zn(s) to Cu^{2+}(aq)/Cu(s).

For this to happen, the two equilibria must move in the directions shown by the red arrows. Zn^{2+}(aq)/Zn(s) releases electrons and Cu^{2+}(aq)/Cu(s) accepts them, i.e. the top equilibrium moves from *right* to *left* and the bottom one from *left* to *right*, hence the term 'anticlockwise rule'.

$$Zn(s) \longrightarrow Zn^{2+}(aq) + 2e^{-}$$

Adding: $$Cu^{2+}(aq) + 2e^{-} \longrightarrow Cu(s)$$
_____
$$Zn(s) + Cu^{2+}(aq) + \cancel{2e^{-}} \longrightarrow Zn^{2+}(aq) + Cu(s) + \cancel{2e^{-}}$$

Hint: On $E^{\ominus}$–Ox diagrams, the values on both axes are the 'wrong way round'.

Calculation of $E^{\ominus}_{reaction}$

Taking the same example of the $Zn^{2+}(aq)/Zn(s)$ and $Cu^{2+}(aq)/Cu(s)$ half cells, which are written as equilibria with electrons on the left:

$$Zn^{2+}(aq) + 2e^- \rightleftharpoons Zn(s) \qquad E^{\ominus} = -0.76 \text{ V}$$
$$Cu^{2+}(aq) + 2e^- \rightleftharpoons Cu(s) \qquad E^{\ominus} = +0.34 \text{ V}$$

By convention we take the sign of $E^{\ominus}$ to refer to the forward reaction, so:

$$Zn^{2+}(aq) + 2e^- \longrightarrow Zn(s) \qquad E^{\ominus} = -0.76 \text{ V}$$

For the reverse reaction $E^{\ominus}$ has the opposite sign:

$$Zn(s) \longrightarrow Zn^{2+}(aq) + 2e^- \qquad E^{\ominus} = +0.76 \text{ V}$$

Similarly:

$$Cu^{2+}(aq) + 2e^- \longrightarrow Cu(s) \qquad E^{\ominus} = +0.34 \text{ V}$$

and $\qquad Cu(s) \longrightarrow Cu^{2+}(aq) + 2e^- \qquad E^{\ominus} = -0.34 \text{ V}$

There are two possibilities for adding the half equations, so that the electrons cancel out:

A.
$$Zn^{2+}(aq) + 2e^- \longrightarrow Zn(s) \qquad E^{\ominus} = -0.76 \text{ V}$$
$$Cu(s) \longrightarrow Cu^{2+}(aq) + 2e^- \qquad E^{\ominus} = +0.34 \text{ V}$$

adding: $Zn^{2+}(aq) + 2e^- + Cu(s) \longrightarrow Zn(s) + Cu^{2+}(aq) + 2e^-$
$$E^{\ominus}_{reaction} = -1.10 \text{ V}$$

> **Hint:** In order for the electrons to cancel out, one of the half reactions must be reversed (and the sign for $E^{\ominus}$ changed).

B.
$$Zn(s) \longrightarrow Zn^{2+}(aq) + 2e^- \qquad E^{\ominus} = +0.76 \text{ V}$$
$$Cu^{2+}(aq) + 2e^- \longrightarrow Cu(s) \qquad E^{\ominus} = +0.34 \text{ V}$$

adding: $Zn(s) + Cu^{2+}(aq) + 2e^- \longrightarrow Zn^{2+}(aq) + Cu(s) + 2e^-$
$$E^{\ominus}_{reaction} = +1.10 \text{ V}$$

$E^{\ominus}$ for each of the two possible reactions is found by adding $E^{\ominus}$ for the two relevant half reactions.

We know that in fact reaction B takes place and A does not. Reaction B has a positive value of $E^{\ominus}_{reaction}$. This is a general rule. **Reactions which have a positive value of $E^{\ominus}_{reaction}$ are feasible.** Those with negative values are not feasible. Notice that values of $E^{\ominus}_{reaction}$ refer to a particular direction of the reaction.

Any of these three techniques will of course give the same answer. Note that a prediction of feasibility does *not* necessarily mean that a reaction *will* occur. It could be that under the conditions of the experiment the reaction is too slow. So the only safe predictions are ones that say a reaction *cannot* occur. They also refer only to standard conditions, i.e. 1 mol dm^{-3} solutions, 298 K and 100 kPa. This technique is only useful for electron transfer (redox) reactions.

> **Hint:** The Faraday constant is the amount of charge carried by a mole of electrons.

FURTHER FOCUS

$E^{\ominus}_{reaction}$ and equilibrium constants

We can be rather more precise than just saying that a reaction is feasible or not because $E^{\ominus}_{reaction}$ is actually related to the equilibrium constant for the reaction. As a rule of thumb, if $E^{\ominus}$ is greater than +0.6 V, the reaction goes to completion. If $E^{\ominus}$ is more negative than −0.6 V the reaction does not 'go' at all. Between these values, we would usually regard the system as being in equilibrium.

The actual relationship between E and K is:

$$E^{\ominus}_{reaction} = \frac{RT}{zF} \ln K_c$$

where R is the gas constant (8.31 J K^{-1} mol^{-1})

T is the temperature in K

z is the number of electrons transferred in the half cell reactions

F is the Faraday constant (96 500 C mol^{-1})

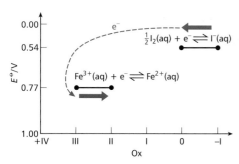

Figure 25.11 $E^{\ominus}$–Ox diagram. Note that the number of electrons makes no difference to $E^{\ominus}$. So we can write

$\frac{1}{2}I_2(aq)+e^- \rightleftharpoons I^-(aq)$ or $I_2(aq)+2e^- \rightleftharpoons 2I^-(aq)$.

Both have the same $E^{\ominus}$ value

Further examples of predicting feasibility

$$Fe^{3+}(aq) + I^-(aq) \longrightarrow Fe^{2+}(aq) + \tfrac{1}{2}I_2(aq)$$

Will the reaction above occur or not?

1. Via the anticlockwise rule.
   Look up the values of $E^{\ominus}$ in Table 25.2, for:

   $$Fe^{3+}(aq) + e^- \rightleftharpoons Fe^{2+}(aq) \quad \text{and} \quad \tfrac{1}{2}I_2(aq) + e^- \rightleftharpoons I^-(aq)$$

   and place on the diagram (see **Figure 25.11**). (Remember that all reactions in the table are written with the electrons on the left). The anticlockwise rule tells us that:

   $$I^-(aq) \longrightarrow \tfrac{1}{2}I_2(aq) + e^-$$

   and will provide an electron for:

   $$Fe^{3+}(aq) + e^- \longrightarrow Fe^{2+}(aq)$$

   Adding the two half equations gives:

   $$Fe^{3+}(aq) + I^-(aq) \longrightarrow Fe^{2+}(aq) + \tfrac{1}{2}I_2(aq)$$

   So this reaction, rather than the reverse, is feasible.

2. Via the calculation of $E^{\ominus}_{reaction}$.
   To construct the required reaction we need to add:

   $$Fe^{3+}(aq) + e^- \longrightarrow Fe^{2+}(aq) \qquad E^{\ominus} = +0.77\ \text{V (Table 25.2)}$$

   and $\quad I^-(aq) \longrightarrow \tfrac{1}{2}I_2(aq) + e^- \qquad E^{\ominus} = -0.54\ \text{V}$

   The second half reaction is the reverse of the reaction in the table, so we have changed the sign of $E^{\ominus}$.

   Adding the two half reactions:

   $$Fe^{3+}(aq) + I^-(aq) \longrightarrow Fe^{2+}(aq) + \tfrac{1}{2}I_2(aq) \qquad E^{\ominus}_{reaction} = +0.23\ \text{V}$$

   The value of $E^{\ominus}_{reaction}$ is positive, so the reaction is feasible.

Hint: $E^{\ominus}_{reaction}$ is less positive that 0.6 V (see the box '$E^{\ominus}$ and equilibrium constants', so this reaction will not go to completion.

Another example:

Is the reaction:

$$Fe^{3+}(aq) + Br^-(aq) \longrightarrow Fe^{2+}(aq) + \tfrac{1}{2}Br_2(aq)$$

feasible?

1. Via the anticlockwise rule (see **Figure 25.12**).

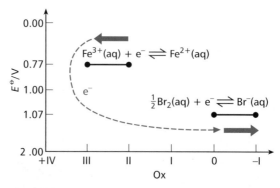

Figure 25.12 E–Ox diagram

Here the anticlockwise rule predicts that:

$$Fe^{2+}(aq) \longrightarrow Fe^{3+}(aq) + e^-$$

will provide an electron for:

$$\tfrac{1}{2}Br_2(aq) + e^- \longrightarrow Br^-(aq)$$

adding $Fe^{2+}(aq) + \tfrac{1}{2}Br_2(aq) \longrightarrow Fe^{3+}(aq) + Br^-(aq)$

This is the reverse reaction to the one we required so our reaction is *not* feasible.

2. Via the calculation of $E^{\ominus}_{reaction}$.
To construct the required reaction we must add:

$$Fe^{3+}(aq) + e^- \longrightarrow Fe^{2+}(aq) \qquad E^{\ominus} = +0.77\ V$$

as in Table 25.2, and

$$Br^-(aq) \longrightarrow \tfrac{1}{2}Br_2(aq) + e^- \qquad E^{\ominus} = -1.07\ V$$

(This half reaction is the reverse of the half reaction in Table 25.2, therefore we change the sign of $E^{\ominus}$).
Adding the two half reactions gives:

$$Fe^{3+}(aq) + Br^-(aq) \longrightarrow Fe^{2+}(aq) + \tfrac{1}{2}Br_2(aq) \qquad E^{\ominus}_{reaction} = -0.3\ V$$

so the reaction is not feasible.

So, $Fe^{3+}(aq)$ is a good enough oxidising agent to oxidise $I^-(aq)$ $\longrightarrow \tfrac{1}{2}I_2(aq)$, but not good enough to oxidise $Br^-(aq) \longrightarrow \tfrac{1}{2}Br_2(aq)$.

FURTHER FOCUS

The pH meter

The hydrogen electrode (see section 25.1) has an $E^{\ominus}$ of zero under standard conditions, i.e. 1 mol dm^{-3} solutions, 100 kPa pressure and 298 K temperature. Its e.m.f. actually depends on concentration of hydrogen ions in which it is immersed:

$$E = E^{\ominus} + \frac{0.026}{z} \ln [H^+(aq)]$$

This is an example of a more general expression called the Nernst equation (see the box 'The effect of concentration on $E^{\ominus}$ values: the Nernst equation', which links cell e.m.f. with concentration of ions in solution).
For the hydrogen electrode $E^{\ominus} = 0$ and as z is the number of electrons transferred in the cell reaction:

$$H^+(aq) + e^- \longrightarrow \tfrac{1}{2}H_2(g)$$

$z = 1$ in this case

and $E = 0.026 \ln [H^+(aq)]$

To convert ln into log we multiply by 2.303 (see section 6.5):

$$E = 0.026 \times 2.303 \ln [H^+(aq)]$$
$$E = -0.059\ pH.$$

So we can use the hydrogen electrode to measure pH.
However, a hydrogen electrode is both cumbersome and in some situations potentially dangerous because it

produces explosive hydrogen gas. Another, more convenient, electrode system whose potential depends on the pH is the glass electrode. This consists of a platinum wire sealed into a very thin-walled glass tube which contains a buffer solution (a solution of fixed hydrogen ion concentration).
The e.m.f. of this electrode depends on the pH of the solution in which it is placed. This electrode coupled with a reference electrode comprises a pH electrode. The voltage difference is measured on a high resistance voltmeter calibrated directly in pH units. The main drawback is that the thin wall of the glass electrode is rather delicate.

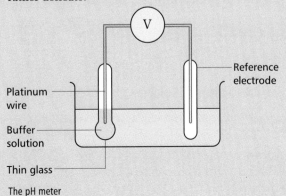

The pH meter

FURTHER FOCUS

The effect of concentration on E values: the Nernst equation

How is the e.m.f. of a half cell affected by changing the concentration of the solution? This can be investigated as follows:

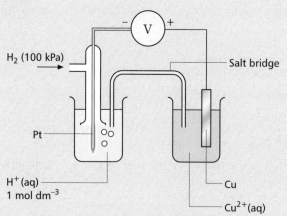

A $Cu^{2+}(aq)/Cu(s)$ half cell is connected to a hydrogen electrode and the voltage recorded for various different concentrations of $Cu^{2+}(aq)$ ions. The results show that the value of the e.m.f. is proportional to $\ln[Cu^{2+}(aq)]$ as shown by the graph.

We can find $E^{\ominus}$ from this graph. For a standard half cell $[Cu^{2+}(aq)] = 1\ mol\ dm^{-3}$. Therefore $\ln[Cu^{2+}(aq)] = 0$.

From the graph, when $\ln[Cu^{2+}(aq)] = 0$, $E^{\ominus} = 0.34\ V$. This agrees with the value of $E^{\ominus}$ from Table 25.1. The gradient of this graph is 0.013 V. The equation of this graph is therefore:

$$E = E^{\ominus} + 0.013\ \ln[Cu^{2+}(aq)]$$

which is an example of a more general expression which may be written:

$$E = E^{\ominus} + \frac{0.026}{z}\ \ln[ion]$$

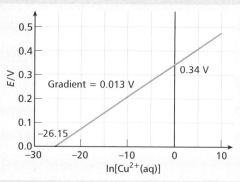

Graph to show the variation of E for $Cu^{2+}(aq)/Cu(s)$ with $[Cu^{2+}(aq)]$

or $$E = E^{\ominus} + \frac{RT}{zF}\ \ln[ion]$$

where R is the gas constant ($8.31\ J\ K^{-1}\ mol^{-1}$)
   T is the temperature in K (298 K)
   F is the value of the Faraday constant – this is the amount of charge carried by a mole of electrons ($96\,500\ C\ mol^{-1}$)
   z is the number of electrons transferred in the half cell reaction (2 in the above case)

This expression is called the **Nernst equation.**

It is also worth noting that the results on the graph are consistent with the predictions of Le Chatelier's principle. In the $Cu^{2+}(aq)/Cu(s)$ half cell we have the equilibrium:

$$Cu^{2+}(aq) + 2e^{-} \rightleftharpoons Cu(s)$$

If the concentration of $Cu^{2+}(aq)$ is reduced, then Le Chatelier's principle would predict that the equilibrium would move to the left giving more $Cu^{2+}(aq)$ and more electrons. In other words, the $E^{\ominus}$ value of the half cell would become more negative (less positive), which is what occurs (see graph)

25.3 Summary

● A half cell consists of	a metal in contact with a solution of its own ions.
● Half cells develop electrical potential because of	the tendency of all metals to give away electrons.
● If two half cells are connected by a voltmeter and salt bridge	their potential difference (e.m.f.) can be measured.
● If the other half cell is a standard hydrogen electrode, the measured e.m.f. is called	$E^{\ominus}$ ('E standard').
● $E^{\ominus}$ values are measured at standard conditions which are:	$1\ mol\ dm^{-3}$ solutions, 100 kPa pressure and 298 K temperature.
● $E^{\ominus}$ values for half cells are listed in order, with the most negative (the best electron releasers) at the top, to give:	the electrochemical series.

- The electrochemical series can be extended to systems other than metal/metal ion by | making electrical contact with a platinum electrode.
- Half cells high in the electrochemical series can transfer electrons to | half cells lower in the list.
- The feasibility of reactions can be predicted by | the 'anticlockwise rule'.
- The feasibility of reactions can also be predicted by | calculating $E^{\ominus}_{reaction}$.
- This is done by | adding together two half reactions and their $E^{\ominus}$ values.
- In order for the electrons in the half reactions to cancel out | one of the half reactions must be reversed (and thus the sign of its $E^{\ominus}$ value changed).
- If the reaction is feasible | $E^{\ominus}_{reaction}$ is positive.
- In a cell diagram | represents   and   ‖ represents | a phase boundary   a salt bridge.
- When we write a cell diagram we give the polaritiy of | the right-hand electrode.

25.4 Practice questions

1. Use the values of $E^{\ominus}$ in Table 25.2 to calculate $E^{\ominus}_{reaction}$ for the following.
   - (a) $Ce^{4+}(aq) + Fe^{2+}(aq) \longrightarrow Ce^{3+}(aq) + Fe^{3+}(aq)$
   - (b) $I_2(aq) + 2Br^-(aq) \longrightarrow Br_2(aq) + 2I^-(aq)$
   - (c) $MnO_4^-(aq) + 8H^+(aq) + 5I^-(aq) \longrightarrow$ $Mn^{2+}(aq) + 4H_2O(l) + 2\frac{1}{2}I_2(aq)$
   - (d) $2H^+(aq) + Pb(s) \longrightarrow Pb^{2+}(aq) + H_2(g)$

2. (a) Represent the following on conventional cell diagrams:

   (i)

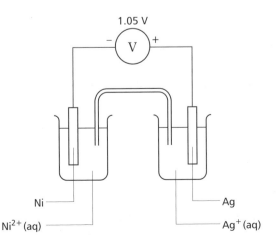

   (ii)

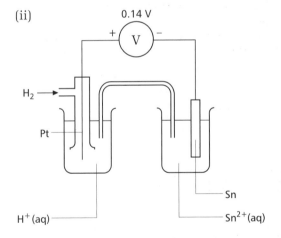

   (iii)

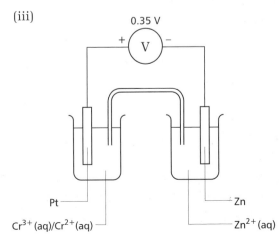

(iv)

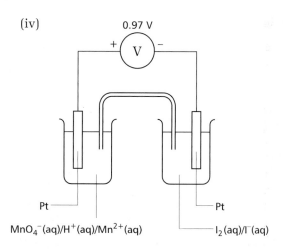

0.97 V

Pt ——

MnO$_4^-$(aq)/H$^+$(aq)/Mn^{2+}(aq)   I$_2$(aq)/I$^-$(aq)

(b) What reaction would take place if each of
these cells were short-circuited (i.e. the
voltmeter were replaced with a piece of wire
so that electrons could flow)?

3. (a) Using the data in Table 25.2, insert the
following half cells on a diagram of $E^\ominus$ against
Ox:
I$_2$(aq)/2I$^-$(aq),
Cl$_2$(aq)/2Cl$^-$(aq),
Br$_2$(aq)/2Br$^-$(aq),
Ag$^+$(aq)/Ag(s)

(b) Which of the halogens could possibly oxidise
Ag(s) to Ag$^+$(aq) ions?

(c) Is the reaction: Br$_2$(aq) + 2Cl$^-$(aq) $\longrightarrow$ Cl$_2$(aq)
+ 2Br$^-$(aq) feasible?

25.5 Examination questions

1. (b) The table shows some values for standard
electrode potentials.

Electrode reaction	$E^\ominus$/V
Fe^{2+}(aq) + 2e$^-$ $\rightleftharpoons$ Fe(s)	−0.44
H$^+$(aq) + e$^-$ $\rightleftharpoons$ $\frac{1}{2}$H$_2$(g)	0.00

An electrochemical cell was set up by
connecting the two electrode systems whose
standard electrode potential values are given
in the table.
(i)   Give the e.m.f. of the cell.
(ii) State which would be the positive
electrode.
(iii) Write an equation to show the overall
reaction in the cell.
(iv) Write down the cell diagram that
represents the overall reaction in the cell.
(v)   Give the name of an instrument that could
be used to measure the e.m.f. of the cell.
[AEB 1998]

2. (a) The diagram at the top of the next column
shows a simple cell.
(i)   Explain what is meant by the term
standard electrode potential of the
Ag$^+$(aq)/Ag(s) couple.

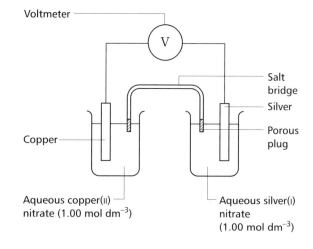

Voltmeter

V

Salt
bridge

Silver

Porous
plug

Copper

Aqueous copper(II)
nitrate (1.00 mol dm^{-3})

Aqueous silver(I)
nitrate
(1.00 mol dm^{-3})

(ii) The standard electrode potentials of the
Ag$^+$(aq)/Ag(s) and Cu^{2+}(aq)/Cu(s) couples
are +0.800 V and +0.340 V respectively.
On a copy of the diagram, label clearly:
(1) the positive electrode;
(2) the direction of the **electron** flow in
the external circuit.
(iii) Give equations for the reactions which are
taking place at each electrode, under
standard conditions.
[Oxford 1997]

26 Further kinetics

C H E M I S T R Y   N O W

'Damn fast reactions indeed'

The following exchange is reputed to have taken place between the German chemist Manfred Eigen and a British colleague, Ron Bell, at a meeting in the 1950s about the study of fast reactions:

Eigen: How would the English language describe reactions faster than fast?

Bell: 'Damn fast reactions', and if they get faster than that, the English language will not fail you, you can call them 'damn fast reactions indeed'.

In the 1950s, the study of fast reactions (ones over in a few microseconds) developed dramatically thanks to a technique called flash photolysis developed by the British Nobel Prize winners George Porter and Ronald Norrish. We can now study reactions such as those that occur in the exploding of petrol in a car engine and we can even observe short-lived transition states.

The method involves firing an intense pulse of light at the reaction mixture. Some of this is absorbed by the reactants, which form excited states. These then react rapidly in a variety of ways to form many species, some of which have very short lifetimes. The concentrations of these species can be followed by a second flash of light a fraction of a second after the first. The short-lived species, such as transition states, absorb particular wavelengths of this light and their concentrations can be measured from the amount of light they absorb. This works on the same principle as a colorimeter. The delay between the first flash, which starts the reaction, and the second, which monitors it, can be varied so that a graph of concentration of each species against time can be plotted and interpreted.

One of the first reactions to be invesigated by flash photolysis was the decomposition of chlorine dioxide radicals to chlorine monoxide and oxygen atoms.

$$ClO_2\bullet \longrightarrow ClO\bullet + O$$

Some 30 years later it was realised that this reaction played an important part in the reactions in the atmosphere by which chlorofluorocarbons (from aerosol propellants) destroy ozone in the upper atmosphere.

Measuring ozone levels in Antarctica

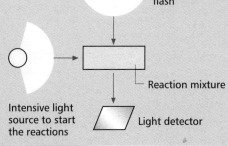

Light source for monitoring flash

Reaction mixture

Intensive light source to start the reactions

Light detector

The principle of flash photolysis

In this chapter we will be looking at:
- how we work out the rate expression from experimental data
- using the rate expression to predict how fast reactions will go under certain conditions
- why relatively small increases in temperature make reactions go much faster
- reaction mechanisms: the series of steps by which we get from reactants to products

Introduction

This chapter builds on the ideas introduced in Chapter 14 and develops them in a more mathematical way so that we can:

- understand how to make a reaction go as fast (or as slowly) as we wish
- work out the steps by which reactions take place

CONCEPT CHECKPOINTS

The following basic ideas are used in this chapter. You may revise some of these topics elsewhere in the book.
- the factors which affect the rates of reactions (section 14.1)
- the rate expression and order of reaction (section 14.4)
- the collision theory of reaction (section 14.5)
- the idea of activation energy (section 14.5)
- the gradient (or slope) of a graph used to measure the rate at which something takes place (section 6.5)

26.1 Determination of the order of a reaction from experimental data

The rate expression

This tells us how the rate of a reaction depends on the concentration of the species involved.

If the rate is not affected by the concentration of a species, we say that the reaction is **zero order** with respect to that species. We do not normally include this species in the rate expression.

If the rate is directly proportional to the concentration of the species, we say that the reaction is **first order** with respect to that species.

If the rate is proportional to square of the concentration of the species, we say that the reaction is **second order** with respect to that species, and so on.

The usual outcome from a reaction rate experiment will be a series of readings of concentration, at different times, of one of the species involved in the reaction. The first step in finding the order with respect to the species is usually to plot these readings on a concentration–time graph.

To help interpretation of the experiment, it is usual to make sure that the concentrations of all the reactants, other than the one being measured, stay the same. This can be done by making their concentrations so large compared with the reactant being investigated, that any change is negligible. For example:

$$R \quad + \quad B \quad \longrightarrow \quad products$$
reactant R   reactant B

If $[R] = 0.01 \, mol \, dm^{-3}$ at the start

and $[B] = 1.00 \, mol \, dm^{-3}$ at the start

At the end of the reaction, $[R] = 0$ (all used up)

and $[B] = 1.00 - 0.01 = 0.99 \, mol \, dm^{-3}$

So during the whole reaction [B] is practically constant.

The graph of [R] plotted against time might look like one of those in **Figure 26.1**.

Notice that in every case the concentration of R decreases with time. This is because R is a reactant, and is therefore being used up.

The rate of the reaction at a particular time and therefore at a

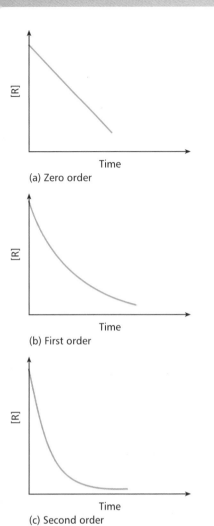

(a) Zero order

(b) First order

(c) Second order

Figure 26.1 Concentration–time graphs for zero, first, and second order reactions.

Hint: If we plotted the concentration of a *product* against time, its concentration would increase.

Hint: You will probably have met half-life in the context of radioactive decay.

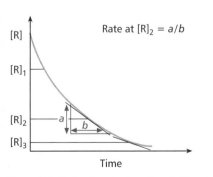

Figure 26.3 Finding the rate of reaction at different values of [R]

particular concentration of R is the **gradient** of the graph at that concentration.

Sometimes it is possible to tell the order with respect to the species measured simply by looking at the graph. If the graph is a straight line, as in Figure 26.8(a), the gradient of the graph is the same whatever the concentration of R. The order with respect to R is therefore zero.

First and second order reactions both give curves but the second order curve is deeper than the first order one: Figure 26.8((b) and (c)). However, you cannot distinguish between them reliably by eye. To do this you have to look at **half-lives**.

Successive half-lives

The half-life of a reaction, $t_{1/2}$, is the time taken for [R] to fall from any chosen value to half that value. The first half-life is often taken from the start of the reaction. The second half-life is from the end of the first and so on (see **Figure 26.2**).

In first order reactions, all the successive half-lives will be the same (within experimental error).

A second order curve will have half-lives which get successively larger.

Do not worry about why this is the case: it arises from mathematical manipulation of the rate expression. However, it makes sense because in a second order reaction, the rate is more strongly dependent on the concentration of R, so as [R] decreases the rate decreases considerably, making the half-life longer.

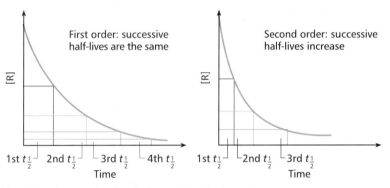

Figure 26.2 Successive half-lives for first and second order reactions

Rate–concentration graphs

A second method of determining the order of a reaction with respect to a particular species is by plotting a graph of **rate** against **concentration** (rather than concentration against time).

On the original graph of [R] against time, draw tangents at different values of [R]. The gradient of these tangents is the rate of change of [R] with time: the reaction rate, $d[R]/dt$, at different concentrations (**Figure 26.3**). These rates can be used to construct a second graph of rate ($d[R]/dt$) against concentration (see Figure 26.3).

If this graph is a horizontal straight line (**Figure 26.4(a)**), this means that the rate is unaffected by [R], so the order is zero.

If the graph is a sloping straight line (Figure 26.4(b)) then rate $\propto [R]^1$ so the order is 1.

If the graph is not a straight line (Figure 26.4(c)) we cannot find the order directly: try plotting rate against $[R]^2$. If this is a straight line (Figure 26.4(d)) then the order is 2, and so on.

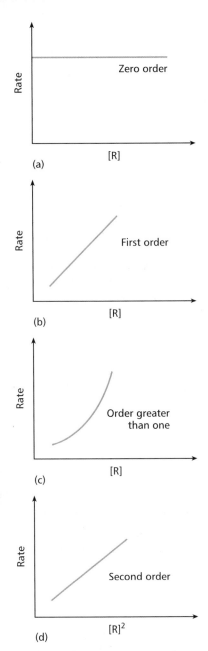

Figure 26.4 Determining the order of a reaction

The initial rate method

The methods above only enable you to find the order with respect to the *one* reactant whose concentration has been measured. The **initial rate** method allows you to find the order with respect to any species in the reaction mixture.

A series of experiments is planned with different initial concentrations of reactants, catalysts, etc. The experiments must be planned so that only one concentration changes between any pair of experiments. The concentration of one reactant is followed and a concentration–time graph plotted as before (**Figure 26.5**). The tangent to the graph at time = 0 is drawn. The gradient of this tangent is the initial rate. The beauty of measuring the *initial* rate is that the concentrations of all substances in the reaction are known *exactly* at this time.

Comparing the initial concentration and the initial rates for pairs of experiments allows the order with respect to each reactant to be found. For example, for the reaction:

$$2NO(g) \quad + \quad O_2(g) \quad \longrightarrow \quad 2NO_2(s)$$

$$\text{nitrogen monoxide} \qquad \text{oxygen} \qquad \text{nitrogen dioxide}$$

the initial rates found are shown in **Table 26.1**.

Table 26.1 Experimental results obtained for the reaction $2NO(g) + O_2(g) \longrightarrow 2NO_2(s)$

Experimental number	Initial [NO]/10^{-3} mol dm^{-3}	Initial [O_2]/10^{-3} mol dm^{-3}	Initial rate $-d[NO]/dt/10^{-4}$ mol dm^{-3} s^{-1}
1	1	1	7
2	2	1	28
3	3	1	63
4	2	2	56
5	3	3	189

On going from experiment 1 to experiment 2, [NO] is doubled while [O_2] stays the same. The rate quadruples (from 7 to 28) suggesting rate $\propto[NO]^2$. This is confirmed by considering experiments 1 and 3 where [NO] is trebled while [O_2] stays the same. Here the rate is increased ninefold as would be expected if rate $\propto[NO]^2$. So the order with respect to NO is 2.

Now take experiments 2 and 4. Here [NO] is constant but [O_2] doubles from mixture 2 to mixture 4. The rate doubles so it looks as if rate $\propto[O_2]$. This is confirmed by considering experiments 3 and 5. Again [NO] is constant, but [O_2] triples. The rate triples too, confirming that the order with respect to O_2 is 1.

So   rate $\propto[NO]^2$

                                  rate $\propto[O_2]^1$

i.e.   rate $\propto[NO]^2[O_2]^1$

Provided that no other species affect the reaction rate, the overall order is 3 and the rate expression is:

$$\text{rate} = k[NO]^2[O_2]^1$$

To find the **rate constant**, k, we simply substitute any set of values of rate, [NO] and [O_2] in the equation.

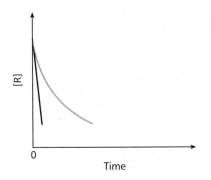

Figure 26.5 Finding the initial rate of a reaction

Find out if you get the same answer for k by substituting the set of results from a different experiment.

Hint: You will probably find the techniques easier to apply to problems than to read about.

Hint: We would get a similar-shaped graph if we plotted, for example, the percentage of people who take a certain shoe size against the shoe size.

Taking the values for experiment 2:

$$28 \times 10^{-4} \text{ mol dm}^{-3} \text{ s}^{-1} = k(2 \times 10^{-3})^2 (\text{mol dm}^{-3})^2 \times 1 \times 10^{-3} \text{ mol dm}^{-3}$$
$$28 \times 10^{-4} \text{ mol dm}^{-3} \text{ s}^{-1} = k(4 \times 10^{-6}) \times 1 \times 10^{-3} \text{ mol}^3 \text{ dm}^{-9}$$
$$28 \times 10^{-4} = k \times 4 \times 10^{-9} \text{ mol}^2 \text{ dm}^{-6} \text{ s}^{-1}$$
$$k = \tfrac{28}{4} \times 10^5 \text{ dm}^6 \text{ mol}^{-2} \text{ s}^{-1}$$
$$k = 7 \times 10^5 \text{ dm}^6 \text{ mol}^{-2} \text{ s}^{-1}$$

The effect of temperature on reaction rate

Small changes in temperature produce large changes in rate. A rule of thumb is that for every 10 K rise in temperature, the rate of a reaction doubles. Temperature is a measure of the average speed of molecules. Molecules in a gas (or in a solution) do not all have the same speed. Their speeds, and therefore energies, are distributed according to the **Maxwell–Boltzmann distribution:** a few having low speeds, a few having high speeds and most somewhere in the middle. This can be shown on a graph (see **Figure 26.6(a)**).

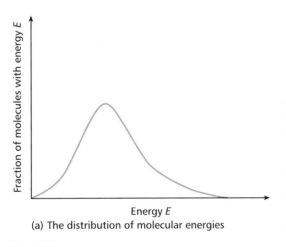

(a) The distribution of molecular energies

(b) Only molecules with energy greater than E_A can react

Figure 26.6

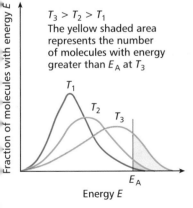

$T_3 > T_2 > T_1$
The yellow shaded area represents the number of molecules with energy greater than E_A at T_3

Figure 26.7 The Maxwell–Boltzmann distribution of molecular energies at three temperatures. Notice that at higher temperatures the peak moves towards a higher energy value and the curve broadens out. Note: The area under each curve is the same because it represents the total number of molecules

Reactions can only take place if collisions between molecules of reactants have enough energy to start bond-breaking. This energy is called the **activation energy,** E_A. If we mark E_A on the Maxwell–Boltzmann distribution graph (Figure 26.6(b)), the area under the graph to the right of the line represents the number of molecules with sufficient energy to react.

The shape of the graph changes with temperature. At higher temperatures there are more molecules with higher energies, so the peak of the graph moves to the right as does the number of molecules with very high energies (see **Figure 26.7**). You can see from the graph that as the temperature increases a greater proportion of molecules has enough energy to react. This is the main reason for the increase in reaction rate with temperature. The total *number* of collisions also increases as the molecules move faster but this is much less significant than the number of *effective* collisions (those with energy greater than E_A).

Collisions also have to have the right orientation: this is called the **steric factor.**

So the rate of reaction depends on three factors:

- the total number of collisions
- the fraction of these which have the right orientation
- the fraction which have energy greater than E_A: this is the shaded area on the appropriate graph of Figure 26.7

and the actual rate of reaction is the product of all three.

The Maxwell–Boltzmann distribution is such that the fraction of molecules with energy greater than E_A is given by $e^{-E_A/RT}$, where R is the gas constant and T the temperature in kelvin. This type of relationship is called an **exponential** relationship and means that a small rise in temperature results in a large increase in the fraction of molecules with energy greater than E_A. This is shown by the shaded areas on Figure 26.7. You can see that the fraction of molecules with energy greater than E_A increases rapidly as the temperature increases.

This leads us to the **Arrhenius equation.** The reaction rate is the product of three factors: the **collision rate, z** (the number of collisions per unit volume per second), is multiplied by the **steric factor, p** (the fraction of molecules which collide in the right orientation), multiplied by the fraction of collisions with sufficient energy to react (E_A or greater).

It is usually written:

$$k = pz[e^{-E_A/RT}]$$

Rate constant which   Steric   Collision   Fraction of molecules
is proportional to   factor   rate   with energy to react
the actual rate

$p \times z$ is often given the symbol A and called the **pre-exponential factor**, so:

$$k = Ae^{-E_A/RT}$$

The mathematics is easier if we take logs of both sides:

$$\ln k = \ln A - E_A/RT$$

(Taking logs to the base e, i.e. ln, of $e^{-E_A/RT}$ gives $-E_A/RT$, because the log of a number is the power to which it is raised. Taking logs of the product of two numbers means we must *add* their logs (see section 6.5). Rearranging:

$$\ln k = \ln A - (E_A/R) \times 1/T$$

This is of the form $y = c + mx$, where $x = 1/T$, so a graph of $\ln k$ against $1/T$ will give a straight line of gradient $-E_A/R$ enabling E_A to be found (see section 6.5), as in **Figure 26.8**.

The intercept on the $\ln k$ axis is $\ln A$ (the pre-exponential factor), i.e. the log of the number of collisions of correct orientation. E_A can be found from the gradient of the graph.

> **Hint:** e is the number 2.718. It is used as the base for natural logs (see section 6.5).

> **Hint:** If you enter R as $8.3\,J\,K^{-1}\,mol^{-1}$ the value of E_A will be in *joules* mol^{-1}, not in *kilojoules* mol^{-1}. Don't forget to convert it to kilojoules by dividing by 1000. It is a very common mistake to forget this factor.

Example

For the reaction: $2HI(g) \longrightarrow I_2(g) + H_2(g)$

the values of k at different temperatures shown in **Table 26.2** are obtained. From these we calculate $\ln k$ and $1/T$ (in red).

Next we plot a graph and calculate the gradient (**Figure 26.9**). From the gradient we can calculate E_A. Activation energies are usually of approximately the same order of size as bond energies. This is because bond breaking occurs in forming the transition state. Typical values of activation energies are between 40 and $400\,kJ\,mol^{-1}$.

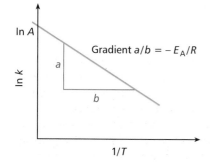

Gradient $a/b = -E_A/R$

Figure 26.8 An Arrhenius plot

Using the Arrhenius equation

Imagine a reaction with an activation energy of $50\,kJ\,mol^{-1}$, a fairly typical value.

$$50\,kJ\,mol^{-1} = 50\,000\,J\,mol^{-1}$$

At a temperature of 300 K (that of a warm room):

the fraction of molecules with energy greater than

$$50\,kJ\,mol^{-1} = e^{-50\,000/(8.3\times300)} = e^{-20.08}$$
$$= 1.9\times10^{-9}$$
$$= 19\times10^{-10}$$

This means that only 19 out of every 10^{10} molecules have enough energy to react.

At a temperature of 310 K:
the fraction of molecules with energy $> 50\,kJ\,mol^{-1}$

$$= e^{-50\,000/(8.3\times310)} = e^{-19.43}$$
$$= 3.6\times10^{-9}$$
$$= 36\times10^{-10}$$

Now 36 out of every 10^{10} molecules can react. Notice how the 10 K rise in temperature has almost doubled the number of molecules able to react and therefore the rate will almost double. This is the rule of thumb mentioned earlier. Beware, though: it is only applicable for reactions with $E_A \approx 50\,kJ\,mol^{-1}$ and at about room temperature.

Hint: Don't be frightened of $e^{-E_A/RT}$; just press the right buttons on your calculator.

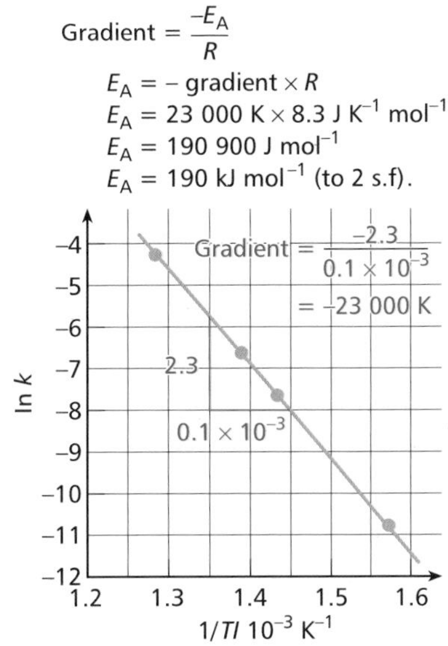

$$\text{Gradient} = \frac{-E_A}{R}$$
$$E_A = -\text{gradient}\times R$$
$$E_A = 23\,000\,K\times8.3\,J\,K^{-1}\,mol^{-1}$$
$$E_A = 190\,900\,J\,mol^{-1}$$
$$E_A = 190\,kJ\,mol^{-1} \text{ (to 2 s.f.)}.$$

Figure 26.9 An Arrhenius plot for the reaction $2HI(g) \longrightarrow I_2(g)+H_2(g)$

Table 26.2 The values of the rate constant, k, at different temperatures for the reaction $2HI(g) \longrightarrow I_2(g)+H_2(g)$

T/K	$1/T/10^{-3}\,K^{-1}$	$k/dm^3\,mol^{-1}\,s^{-1}$	$\ln k$
633	1.579	1.78×10^{-5}	-10.936
666	1.501	1.07×10^{-4}	-9.142
697	1.434	5.01×10^{-4}	-7.599
715	1.398	1.05×10^{-3}	-6.858
781	1.280	1.51×10^{-2}	-4.193

26.2 Reaction mechanisms

The great majority of reactions have more than one step. The separate steps that lead from reactants to products are collectively called the **reaction mechanism**. For example:

$$BrO_3^-(aq) + 6H^+(aq) + 5Br^-(aq) \longrightarrow 3Br_2(aq) + 3H_2O(l)$$

This reaction *must* involve several steps with short-lived intermediate species, as a simultaneous collision of the twelve ions of the reactants is immensely improbable.

Mechanisms usually have to be pieced together by detective work, using several pieces of evidence, as it is rare that any intermediate species can be isolated and identified.

The rate determining step

In a multi-step reaction, the steps are almost always sequential, that is the product(s) of one step is/are the starting material for the next. Therefore the rate of the slowest step governs the rate of the whole process. The slowest step forms a 'bottleneck', called the **rate determining step**. Imagine a canteen where main course, vegetables and potatoes are served by three different people. The rate of getting your meal will be equal to the rate of the slowest server no matter how rapidly the other two work.

Q What is the rate determining step in making a cup of instant coffee?

Answer: Waiting for the kettle to boil.

In a chemical reaction, any step which occurs *after* the rate determining step will not affect the rate. So species which are involved in the mechanism after the rate determining step will not appear in the rate expression. For example, the reaction:

$$A + B + C \longrightarrow Y + Z$$

might occur in the following steps:

Hint: D and E are intermediates.

1. $\qquad\qquad\qquad A + B \xrightarrow{\text{fast}} D$

2. $\qquad\qquad\qquad\qquad D \xrightarrow{\text{slow}} E$

3. $\qquad\qquad\qquad E + C \xrightarrow{\text{fast}} Y + Z$

Step two is the slowest step and so determines the rate. As soon as some E is produced, it rapidly reacts with C to produce Y and Z. However, the concentration of D will depend on the rate of step 1 and so the rate of step 1 could affect the overall rate. Thus any species involved in or *before* the rate determining step could affect the rate and hence appear in the rate expression.

The reaction between iodine and propanone illustrates this, although you would not be expected to recall details for an examination.

The overall reaction is:

$$CH_3-\overset{\overset{O}{\|}}{C}-CH_3(aq) + I_2(aq) \xrightarrow[\text{catalyst}]{H^+} CH_2ICCH_3(aq) + HI(aq)$$

propanone   iodine

Why is there a minus sign before $\dfrac{d[I_2]}{dt}$?

and the rate expression is found to be:

$$\frac{-d[I_2]}{dt} = [CH_3OCCH_3][H^+]$$

The mechanism is:

Answer: The iodine is a reactant and so its concentration is decreasing.

$$
\underset{\substack{\text{I} \quad\quad \text{I}}}{\overset{\substack{\text{H} \quad\quad \text{O}^{\diagup \text{H}}}}{\text{H}-\text{C}-\text{C}-\text{CH}_3}} \xrightarrow{\text{fast}} \underset{\substack{\text{I}}}{\overset{\substack{\text{H} \quad\quad \text{O}}}{\text{H}-\text{C}-\text{C}-\text{CH}_3}} + \text{H}^+ + \text{I}^-
$$

The rate determining step is the first one, which explains why $[\text{I}_2]$ does *not* appear in the rate expression.

Kinetic evidence for reaction mechanisms

It is rarely possible to deduce a reaction mechanism from a single piece of evidence but kinetic evidence can be useful. The reaction of the three isomeric compounds of formula C_4H_9Br with alkalis is a simple example. The overall reaction is:

$$C_4H_9Br + OH^- \longrightarrow C_4H_9OH + Br^-$$

Two mechanisms are possible:

(a) A two-step mechanism:

    Step 1: $C_4H_9Br \xrightarrow{\text{slow}} C_4H_9{}^+ + Br^-$

    followed by, step 2: $C_4H_9{}^+ + OH^- \xrightarrow{\text{fast}} C_4H_9OH$

The slow step involves breaking the C—Br bond while the second (fast) step is a reaction between oppositely charged ions.

(b) A one-step mechanism:

$$C_4H_9Br + OH^- \longrightarrow C_4H_9OH + Br^-$$

The C—Br bond breaks at the same time as the C-OH bond is forming.

There are three compounds of formula C_4H_9Br:

$$
\underset{\substack{\text{H} \quad \text{H} \quad \text{H} \quad \text{H}}}{\overset{\substack{\text{H} \quad \text{H} \quad \text{H} \quad \text{H}}}{\text{H}-\text{C}-\text{C}-\text{C}-\text{C}-\text{Br}}}
\qquad\qquad
\underset{\substack{\text{H} \quad \text{H} \quad \text{Br} \quad \text{H}}}{\overset{\substack{\text{H} \quad \text{H} \quad \text{H} \quad \text{H}}}{\text{H}-\text{C}-\text{C}-\text{C}-\text{C}-\text{H}}}
$$

          1-bromobutane   2-bromobutane

$$
\underset{\substack{\text{H} \quad \text{Br} \quad \text{H}}}{\overset{\substack{\text{H} \quad \text{CH}_3 \; \text{H}}}{\text{H}-\text{C}-\text{C}-\text{C}-\text{H}}}
$$

                 2-bromo-2-methylpropane

These are a set of isomers: they have the same formula but different structures (see section 18.6).

Experiments show that 1-bromobutane reacts by a second order mechanism:

$$\text{rate} = k[C_4H_9Br][OH^-]$$

The rate depends on the concentration of *both* the bomobutane *and* the OH^- ions, suggesting mechanism (b).

Some dental cements can be set using ultraviolet light

Experiments show that 2-bromo-2-methylpropane reacts by a first order mechanism:

$$\text{rate} = k[C_4H_9Br]$$

This suggests mechanism a). Further discussion of these reactions appears in section 21.4.

Photochemical reactions

A mixture of hydrogen and chlorine gases is stable in the dark but reacts explosively to form hydrogen chloride if exposed to sunlight.

$$H_2(g) + Cl_2(g) \xrightarrow{\text{sunlight}} 2HCl(g)$$

The reaction starts when a chlorine molecule absorbs a quantum of ultraviolet light which breaks the Cl—Cl bond, forming two chlorine atoms. These each have an unpaired electron. Such species are called radicals or sometimes free radicals. They are very reactive and start a **chain reaction.** Chain reactions are discussed more fully in section 19.4.

26.3 Summary

● The rate constant, k, is	the constant of proportionality in the rate expression.
● Order with respect to a particular species may be determined from	a concentration–time graph:
● Zero order processes give a	straight line.
● First order processes have	constant half-lives.
● Second order processes, have	successively increasing half-lives.

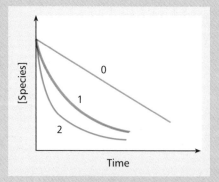

Figure 26.10 Concentration–time graphs showing reactions with different orders

● Order of reaction can also be determined from a graph of	rate against concentration raised to some power:
● **Figure 26.11** represents	zero order.
● **Figure 26.12** represents	first order.

- **Figure 26.13** represents

second order.

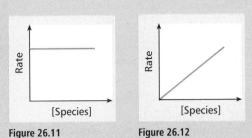 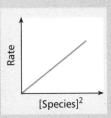

Figure 26.11   Figure 26.12   Figure 26.13

- Order of reaction can also be determined by

the initial rate method.

- If the rate is unchanged when the concentration of a species is doubled, the order of reaction with respect to that species is

0

- If the rate doubles when the concentration of a species is doubled, the order of reaction with respect to that species is

1

- If the rate increases fourfold when the concentration of a species is doubled, the order of reaction with respect to that species is

2

- If the rate increases eightfold when the concentration of a species is doubled, the order of reaction with respect to that species is

3

- The Arrhenius equation is
  where:

$k = A e^{-E_A/RT}$

  - k is

the rate constant

  - E_A is

the activation energy

  - T is

the temperature in kelvin

  - R is

the gas constant

  - A is

the pre-exponential factor, which represents the number of correctly oriented collisions

The Arrhenius equation may also be written

$\ln k = \ln A - E_A/RT$

- E_A can be found from

the gradient of a graph of $\ln k$ against $1/T$.

- Most reactions take place via

a sequential set of simple steps.

- The overall rate is governed by that of

the slowest step.

- This is called

the rate determining step.

- The only species which appear in the rate expression are

those which take part in the mechanism in or before the rate determining step.

- Photochemical reactions start by the absorption of

one quantum of light.

- This breaks

a covalent bond.

- This starts a

chain reaction.

26.4 Practice questions

1. This question is about the following reaction:

$$Br_2(aq) + HCO_2H(aq) \xrightarrow{\text{H}^+ \text{ catalyst}} 2Br^-(aq) + 2H^+(aq) + CO_2(g)$$

Time/min	$[Br_2]$/mol dm^{-3}
0.0	0.0100
0.5	0.0900
1.0	0.0081
1.5	0.0073
2.0	0.0066
3.0	0.0053
4.0	0.0044
6.0	0.0028
8.0	0.0020
10.0	0.0013
12.0	0.0007

(a) These figures were obtained using a colorimeter to measure $[Br_2]$. Give another way by which the rate of reaction could have been followed.

(b) Plot a graph of $[Br_2]$ vertically versus time. Determine the order of the reaction with respect to Br_2 by the following procedures:
   (i) Determine the first three half-lives of the reaction.
   (ii) Find the rate of the reaction (gradient of the graph) for at least 5 different values of $[Br_2]$ and plot a graph of rate against $[Br_2]$.

(c) In this experiment the $[HCO_2H]$ was kept constant. How could this be achieved in practice?

(d) Is it possible to determine the rate with respect to HCO_2H from these figures? Explain your answer.

2. In the reaction:

$$A + B \longrightarrow C$$

The following data were obtained:

Initial [A]	Initial [B]	Initial rate
1	1	3
1	2	12
2	2	24

(a) What is the order of the reaction with respect to: (i) A; (ii) B?

(b) What is the overall order?

3. The decomposition of N_2O_5 in the gas phase:

$$N_2O_5(g) \longrightarrow 2NO_2(g) + \tfrac{1}{2}O_2(g)$$

was investigated at different temperatures with the following results:

Temperature/K	Rate constant, $k/10^3$ s^{-1}
338	48 700
328	15 000
318	4980
308	1350
298	346

Work out the values of $1/T$ and $\ln k$ and plot a graph of $\ln k$ versus $1/T$.
Use the gradient of the graph to calculate the activation energy of the reaction.

4. Which one of the following graphs would confirm that the decomposition of hydrogen peroxide was first order with respect to the concentration of hydrogen peroxide?

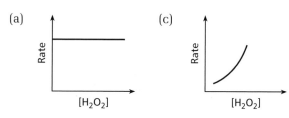

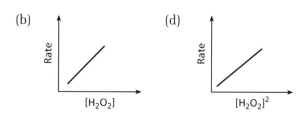

5. The example on page 372 calculates the activation energy for the reaction:

$$2HI(g) \longrightarrow H_2(g) + I_2(g)$$

without a catalyst. The reaction is catalysed by a number of metals. With one metal, the following data were recorded:

Temperature/K	Rate constant, $k/\text{mol}^{-1}\,\text{dm}^3\,\text{s}^{-1}$
625	2.27
667	7.56
727	24.87
769	91.18
833	334.59

(a) Plot a graph of $\ln k$ against $1/T$ and find the activation energy with this catalyst.

(b) Suggest how the metal might operate as a catalyst.

26.5 Examination questions

. (a) (i) Sketch on a copy of the axes below the distributions of molecular energies for a given mass of a gas at two temperatures, T_1 and T_2, where T_1 is higher than T_2.

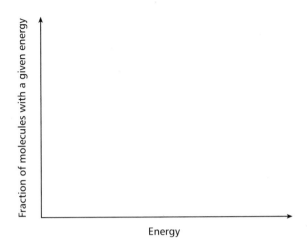

Energy

(ii) State how the areas under your curves are related to each other.

(iii) Using the curves explain why the rates of reactions increase with temperature.

(b) The decomposition of gaseous dinitrogen pentoxide is represented by

$$2N_2O_5(g) \longrightarrow 4NO_2(g) + O_2(g)$$

and is first order with respect to dinitrogen pentoxide.

(i) Write down the rate equation for the decomposition.

(ii) A proposed mechanism for the reaction is made up of the following steps:

$$N_2O_5 \longrightarrow N_2O_3 + O_2 \qquad \text{I}$$
$$N_2O_3 \longrightarrow NO + NO_2 \qquad \text{II}$$
$$NO + 2N_2O_5 \longrightarrow 3NO_2 + N_2O_5 \qquad \text{III}$$

From your rate equation in (b)(i), write down which of the steps would be expected to be the rate determining step.

(iii) Data for the decomposition of dinitrogen pentoxide at 333 K are shown below.

Pressure of dinitrogen pentoxide remaining/Pa	Rate of reaction/Pa per second
1200	1.04
1000	0.88
800	0.69
400	0.34

Plot these data on graph paper and hence calculate the value of the rate constant at 333 K, giving the appropriate unit.

[WJEC 1997]

2. (a) The graph below represents the Maxwell–Boltzman distribution of molecular energies at temperature T_1 K.

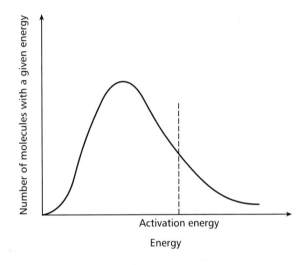

Activation energy

Energy

(i) Sketch on the same axes, the curve which shows the distribution of molecular energies at a higher temperature T_2 K. T_2 is approximately 20 K greater than T_1.

(ii) Use these graphs to explain how the rate of a gas phase reaction changes with increasing temperature.

(b) For a gaseous reaction, state and explain what effect the addition of a catalyst would have on:

(i) the energy distribution of the gas molecules;

(ii) the activation energy for the reaction;

(iii) the rate of reaction.

(c) Thioethanamide reacts with sodium hydroxide as follows:

$$CH_3CSNH_2 + 2OH^- \longrightarrow CH_3CO_2^- + HS^- + NH_3$$

The reaction is first order with respect to both thioethanamide and hydroxide ions.

(i) Write the rate equation for this reaction.

(ii) What is the overall order of the reaction?

(iii) Given that the reaction occurs in two stages and the rate determining step is:

$$CH_3CSNH_2 + OH^- \longrightarrow CH_3CONH_2 + HS^-$$

write an equation for the second step in the reaction.

[London 1997]

27 Gases

Airships: gases for lifting

It is hard to push a balloon below the surface of water in a bath – try it and see. This is because you have to push away the water from where the balloon goes. The water trying to get back to where it was causes an **upthrust** on the balloon. Archimedes' principle tells us that the upthrust is equal to the weight of water displaced by the balloon. The same thing happens in the atmosphere and is the principle on which balloons and airships work.

A hydrogen-filled balloon has an upthrust on it due to the air it displaces. Since hydrogen molecules are lighter than air molecules (the relative molecular masses are hydrogen = 2, oxygen = 32, nitrogen = 28) and the same number of molecules of any gas have the same volume, the upthrust on a hydrogen balloon is greater than the weight of the hydrogen and the balloon will rise and be able to lift a load.

Hydrogen is the best lifting gas for balloons and airships as it has the lightest molecules. It was used in airships for commercial aviation, including passenger services across the Atlantic, until the 1930s. During this decade, explosions destroyed the British R101 and the German Hindenberg (German airships were called Zeppelins) and signalled the end of the airship era.

More recently, airships have been making a comeback – filled with helium. They are used for coastal anti-smuggling patrols, for airborne early warning over naval vessels and to televise sporting events such as the London marathon. As they need no fuel to keep aloft, they have the advantage of long endurance and are cheap to run. They are also much quieter than conventional aircraft or helicopters.

Although safer because of its inertness, helium is not such a good lifting gas as hydrogen. Helium's relative molecular mass is 4, twice that of hydrogen, so a given volume of helium weighs twice as much as the same volume of hydrogen and this reduces the lift available.

Hot air balloons work on a slightly different principle. Hot gas molecules are more spread out than cold gas molecules. So a given volume of hot gas contains fewer molecules (and therefore weighs less) than the same volume of cold air. So the upthrust (equivalent to the weight of *cold* air) is greater than the weight of the *hot* air.

The Breitling Orbiter balloon circumnavigated the globe in 1999

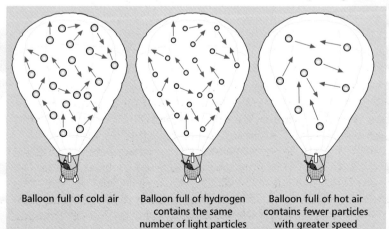

Balloon full of cold air

Balloon full of hydrogen contains the same number of light particles

Balloon full of hot air contains fewer particles with greater speed

Introduction

Gases are the least dense phase of matter. They fill the whole of any container in which they are placed and exert pressure on the walls of that container. Gases consist of well-spaced-out particles moving rapidly at random, whose collisions with the walls of the container cause their pressure. The behaviour of gases at moderate temperatures and pressures is described by the ideal gas equation.

Since many industrial reactions take place in the gas phase an understanding of the behaviour of gases is of considerable economic importance.

27.1 The gas laws

Gay-Lussac's law

Gases are not easy to handle experimentally, simply because they will only stay put in closed containers. Despite this, they were quite well studied even 200 years ago and, in the early 1800s, the Frenchman Joseph Gay-Lussac put forward the law named after him. This said that **gases always react in volumes that are in simple whole number relationships to one another – both reactants and products**. The volumes had to be measured under the same conditions of temperature and pressure. This law was simply a generalisation of many measurements made on gas reactions over many years.

Some examples of gas reactions which illustrate Gay-Lussac's law are:

$$\text{hydrogen} + \text{iodine} \longrightarrow \text{hydrogen iodide}$$
1 volume   1 volume   2 volumes

$$\text{hydrogen} + \text{oxygen} \longrightarrow \text{water}$$
2 volumes   1 volume   2 volumes (if over 373 K, i.e. the water exists as a gas) or 0 volume (if below 373 K)

Hint: The *masses* of equal volumes of different gases will be different.

Avogadro's law

Gay-Lussac's law was explained by the Italian Amedeo Avogadro who stated that **equal volumes of any gas measured at the same temperature and pressure contain the same numbers of particles (atoms or molecules)**. This implies that in any gas, the spaces between the gas molecules are so large compared with the size of the molecules, that the volume the gas occupies is unaffected by the volume of the molecules themselves. This idea is illustrated in **Figure 27.1**. So if we had a second gas with molecules of double the volume, only a tiny extra volume would result, provided the spacing between the molecules remained the same.

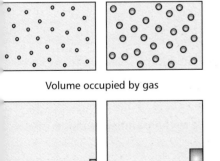

Volume occupied by gas

Actual volume of molecules themselves

Figure 27.1 The actual volume of gas molecules is very small compared with the volume occupied by the gas

Avogadro's law provided a means of comparing the masses of gas molecules directly. Equal numbers of different atoms or molecules could be measured out simply by measuring out the same volume of their different gases (at the same temperature and pressure).

For example at room temperature and pressure:

100 cm^3 of oxygen has a mass of 0.133 g.

100 cm^3 of hydrogen has a mass of 0.0083 g

Since, according to Avogadro's law, the number of particles in each is the same, an oxygen particle must weigh $0.133/0.0083 = 16$ times as much as a hydrogen particle. This formed the basis of the scale of relative atomic and molecular masses.

A consequence of Avogadro's law is that the ratio of the *volumes* of gases which react is the same as the ratio of *moles* of reacting gases.

For example: hydrogen + chlorine ⟶ hydrogen chloride

1 volume   1 volume   2 volumes

$$H_2(g) + Cl_2(g) \longrightarrow 2HCl(g)$$

In order for volumes of gases to be comparable, they must be measured under the same conditions of temperature and pressure. Alternatively, the volumes at the required temperature and pressure can be worked out using **the ideal gas equation**. A number of simple relationships between the pressure, temperature and volumes of gases led to the formulation of this equation.

The ideal gas equation

We find that for a sample of gas of volume V, pressure P, and temperature T,

$$\frac{PV}{T} = \text{constant (for a fixed mass of gas)}$$

If we take 1 mole of gas the constant is given the symbol R and is called the **gas constant**, and for n moles of gas we have

$$\frac{PV}{T} = nR \quad \begin{array}{l} \text{The value of } R \text{ is } 8.314\,\text{J K}^{-1}\,\text{mol}^{-1}, \\ \text{often rounded to } 8.3\,\text{J K}^{-1}\,\text{mol}^{-1} \end{array}$$

This is called the **ideal gas equation**. No gases obey it exactly but it holds quite well for many gases at around normal room conditions. An **ideal gas** would be one that obeys this equation perfectly.

Note on units of *P*, *V* and *T*

When using the ideal gas equation, temperatures must be measured in kelvin. To convert gas volumes to different conditions, as in the box 'Converting gas volumes', any units for volume or pressure may be used as long as they are the same on both sides of the equation.

However, **if you want to calculate *n*, the number of moles of gas**, then :

P must be in Pa

V must be in m^3

T must be in K

R must be in J K^{-1} mol^{-1}

Hint: We now know that hydrogen exists as H_2 molecules not H atoms, so it makes sense to base the scale on hydrogen gas having a relative mass of 2.

Q Write the equation from the following reacting volumes:

nitrogen + hydrogen ⟶ ammonia

1 volume   3 volumes   2 volumes

Hint: The ideal gas equation is derived from:

- Boyle's law:

  $PV = $ constant

  (at constant temperature)
- Charles' law:

  $\dfrac{V}{T} = $ constant

  (at constant pressure) It is often written:

  $PV = nRT$

Hint: The higher the temperature and the lower the pressure, the more nearly real gases obey the ideal gas equation.

Answer: $N_2(g) + 3H_2(g) \longrightarrow 2NH_3(g)$

Other units are often encountered. Most volumes will be measured in cm^3 or dm^3:

$$1 \, m^3 = 10^6 \, cm^3 = 10^3 \, dm^3$$

Industrial chemists often measure pressures in atmospheres:

$$1 \text{ atmosphere} = 10^5 \, Pa \text{ or } 100 \, kPa$$

Many laboratory measurements of pressure are made using a mercury manometer which may give a reading in millimetres of mercury (mmHg or torr).

$$760 \, mmHg = 100 \, kPa.$$

Weather forecasters use millibars:

$$1000 \text{ millibars} = 100 \, kPa$$

But temperatures must *always* be in kelvin, never °C or any other units.

FURTHER FOCUS

Converting gas volumes

We can use the ideal gas equation to calculate the volume a gas would occupy at temperatures and pressures other than those at which it was actually measured.

If a gas has a volume V_1 measured at pressure P_1 and temperature T_1, then:

$$\frac{P_1 V_1}{T_1} = nR$$

If the same gas's volume, V_2, is now measured at a new pressure P_2 and temperature T_2:

$$\frac{P_2 V_2}{T_2} = nR$$

So

$$\frac{P_1 V_1}{T_1} = \frac{P_2 V_2}{T_2}$$

For consistency, chemists often convert gas volumes to **standard temperature and pressure, −273 K and 100 kPa, usually called STP**.

Hint: Don't confuse the temperature of STP (273 K) with the standard conditions for enthalpy changes (298 K).

Example

A sample of gas had a volume of 50.0 cm^3 measured at 20.0 °C and 101 328 Pa. What is its volume at STP?

$$V_1 = 50.0 \, cm^3; \qquad V_2 = ?$$
$$P_1 = 101 \, 328 \, Pa; \qquad P_2 = 100 \, 000 \, Pa$$
$$T_1 = 20.0 \, °C = 293.0 \, K; \qquad T_2 = 273.0 \, K$$

Hint: Remember to convert the temperature to kelvin.

$$\frac{101 \, 328 \times 50.0}{293.0} = \frac{100 \, 000 \times V_2}{273.0}$$

$$V_2 = \frac{101 \, 328 \times 50.0 \times 273.0}{293.0 \times 100 \, 000}$$

Hint: It is easy to make arithmetic mistakes, so look to see if the answer is reasonable. Small changes in pressure and temperature won't make a very large difference to the volume.

$$= 47.2 \, cm^3 \text{ (to 3 s.f.)}$$

It is possible to convert to any set of conditions, not just STP.

The volume of a mole of gas

Avogadro's law states that the same volume of all gases contains the same number of molecules. Thus 1 mole of all gases should have the same volume. This is confirmed by the ideal gas equation from which the volume of 1 mole of gas can be calculated under any conditions.

$$PV = nRT$$

So
$$V = \frac{nRT}{P}$$

At standard temperature and pressure, see box 'Converting gas volumes', $n = 1$, $R = 8.31\,\mathrm{J\,K^{-1}\,mol^{-1}}$, $T = 273\,\mathrm{K}$, $P = 100\,000\,\mathrm{Pa}$

so
$$V = \frac{1 \times 8.31 \times 273}{100\,000} = 0.0227\,\mathrm{m^3}\ \text{(note the units)}.$$

$$1\,\mathrm{m^3} = 10^3\,\mathrm{dm^3} \text{ so } V = 22.7\,\mathrm{dm^3}$$

The volume of 1 mole of any gas = 22 700 cm³ at STP.

27.2 Measurement of relative molecular mass

The relative molecular mass of a gas

The ideal gas equation allows us to measure easily the relative molecular masses of gases:

$$PV = nRT$$

So
$$n = \frac{PV}{RT}$$

So we can calculate the number of moles in a sample of gas if we can measure its pressure, volume and temperature. If we can find the mass of the gas, we know the mass of a known number of moles and can therefore calculate the mass of one mole. This is numerically equal to the relative molecular mass.

The experimental method varies with the method of production of the gas and the apparatus used. One example is when the gas is stored in a pressurised container.

We can find the relative molecular mass of the gas sold for filling cigarette lighters. The apparatus is shown in **Figure 27.2**. The gas container is weighed and then, say, 1.0 dm³ of gas is dispersed into a measuring cylinder, keeping the levels of water inside and outside the measuring cylinder the same, to ensure that the pressure of the gas is the same as atmospheric pressure. The pressure can then be measured with a barometer and room temperature found. The gas container is then reweighed.

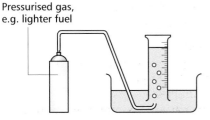

Pressurised gas, e.g. lighter fuel

Figure 27.2 Measuring the relative molecular mass for lighter fuel

Q Lighter fuel is an impure alkane hydrocarbon. Suggest from the M_r which alkane is most likely to be used for it.

Hint: The least accurate measurement is to two significant figures.

For example:

$$\text{loss of mass of the can} = 2.29\text{ g}$$
$$\text{temperature} = 14\,°\text{C (287 K)}$$
$$\text{volume of gas} = 1.0\text{ dm}^3\ (10^{-3}\text{ m}^3)$$
$$\text{atmospheric pressure} = 100\,100\text{ Pa (measured with a barometer)}$$

$$n = \frac{PV}{RT}$$

$$n = \frac{100\,100 \times 10^{-3}}{287 \times 8.3}$$

$$n = 0.042\text{ mol}$$

So 2.29 g is the mass of 0.042 mol

and   1 mol has a mass of $\dfrac{2.29}{0.042} = 54.5$ g

$$M_r = 55\text{ (to 2 s.f.)}$$

The relative molecular masses of volatile liquids

The same type of method can be applied to volatile liquids simply by vaporising them and measuring the volume of the vapour. Suitable apparatus is shown in **Figure 27.3**. The method uses a steam jacket and can be used with liquids of boiling point up to about 80 °C (353 K)

The liquid is injected from a hypodermic syringe and the mass of the liquid used is found from the difference in mass of the syringe before and after injection.

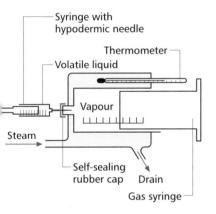

Figure 27.3 Apparatus for measuring the relative molecular mass for a volatile liquid

27.3 Dalton's law of partial pressures

This law, already encountered in section 23.2, is about mixtures of gases. The **partial pressure** of a gas in a mixture is the pressure that gas would exert if it were in the container alone. Dalton's law states that the total pressure of a mixture of gases is the sum of the partial pressures of all the components. This is simply saying that the different gases do not affect each other's behaviour, so their pressures add up.

27.4 Kinetic theory

Kinetic theory is an attempt to explain the observed properties of gases on the basis that gases are made up of small particles, well spaced-out, moving rapidly at random. More formally, kinetic theory makes five assumptions about gas molecules:

1. The particles are moving randomly.
2. We can neglect the volume of the particles themselves in comparison with the total volume of the gas.
3. The particles do not attract one another.
4. The average kinetic energy of the particles is proportional to the temperature of the gas.
5. No energy is lost in collisions between particles.

Answer: Butane (M_r 56) is the most likely with some shorter chain impurities which bring down the average relative molecular mass.

CHEMISTRY AROUND US

Atmospheric chemistry

The greenhouse effect

Greenhouses get hot inside because glass is transparent to visible light, which can thus enter the greenhouse and be absorbed by objects inside it. These objects get hot and radiate their heat as infra-red radiation. But glass does not allow infra-red (heat) radiation through: it remains trapped inside.

Carbon dioxide gas molecules in the atmosphere behave in a similar way to glass, letting in light from the sun, but not letting heat out. Burning fossil fuels produces large quantities of carbon dioxide and there is concern that increasing concentrations of this gas in the atmosphere are leading to a rise in the average temperature of the Earth. Even a small rise in temperature could have far-reaching effects. For example, melting part of the Antarctic ice caps would lead to a rise in sea level and flooding of low-lying areas. It is also likely that it would lead to changes in climate which are difficult to predict in detail.

There are mechanisms for removing carbon dioxide from the atmosphere: plants use it in photosynthesis and large amounts dissolve in the sea. However, there is evidence of raised atmospheric carbon dioxide levels and also of a gradual raising of the Earth's temperature.

> **Did you know?** Methane, emitted in large quantities from the digestive system of cows, is 30 times more effective than carbon dioxide as a greenhouse gas?

Ozone

Advice from Australia: **slip** on a vest, **slop** on some cream, **slap** on a hat

The Earth is bathed in high-energy (short-wavelength), ultraviolet (UV) light from the Sun. Most of this is filtered out before it reaches the Earth's surface, being absorbed by the small concentration (0.25 parts per million) of ozone in the stratosphere, the layer of the atmosphere about 25 km above the Earth's surface. Ozone (trioxygen) is an allotrope of oxygen of formula O_3 and it is formed by photochemical reactions in the atmosphere:

$$O_2(g) \longrightarrow 2O(g)$$

oxygen molecule   oxygen atoms

$$O(g) \quad + \quad O_2(g) \longrightarrow O_3(g)$$

oxygen atom   oxygen molecule   ozone

Ozone is removed by the following reactions with dinitrogen oxide, a gas present in the atmosphere in small amounts owing to the action of bacteria on nitrogen in the soil.

1. $\quad\quad\quad\quad O(g) + N_2O(g) \longrightarrow 2NO(g)$
2. $\quad\quad\quad\quad O_3(g) + NO(g) \longrightarrow NO_2(g) + O_2(g)$
3. $\quad\quad\quad\quad O(g) + NO_2(g) \longrightarrow NO(g) + O_2(g)$

The overall effect of reactions 2 and 3 is:

$$O_3(g) + O(g) \longrightarrow 2O_2(g)$$

and the NO is regenerated, thus acting as a catalyst.

Normally the generation of ozone balances its destruction and the concentration of the gas remains steady. However, in recent years, the amount of nitrogen monoxide, NO, in the atmosphere has increased owing to its production in motor vehicle exhausts. Chlorine atoms, originating in chlorofluorocarbons (CFCs) used as an aerosol propellant among other things, can also act in the same way as NO in the ozone destruction reactions and their concentration has increased.

$$O_3(g) + Cl(g) \longrightarrow ClO(g) + O_2(g)$$
$$O(g) + ClO(g) \longrightarrow Cl(g) + O_2(g)$$

overall $\quad\quad\quad O_3(g) + O(g) \longrightarrow 2O_2(g)$

and the chlorine is regenerated.

The net result of this is that the rate of loss of ozone is greater than its rate of production. The UV filtering effect is reduced and more high-energy UV is reaching the Earth's surface. This may well result in increased incidence of skin cancer as well as affecting marine plankton. This latter effect could have far-reaching consequences because plankton are at the base of the marine food chain.

Recent international agreements have restricted the use and manufacture of chlorofluorocarbons but it is predicted to take several years before the reservoir of CFCs already present is used up.

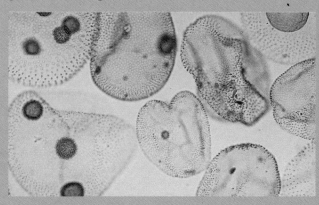

Plankton are under threat from increased UV

CHEMISTRY AROUND US

Solubility of gases: from soft drinks to diving

Gases dissolve in liquids in proportion to their partial pressure. This is called Henry's law. Carbon dioxide is dissolved in fizzy drinks under pressure during manufacture. When we open the bottle or can, the pressure is reduced and the gas comes out of solution and the drink fizzes.

Henry's law is very important to divers who breathe air at high pressure when working at depths down to about 50 metres. The high pressure causes nitrogen to dissolve in the blood to a larger extent than at atmospheric pressure. This leads to two problems. Firstly, the large quantities of nitrogen cause a condition called nitrogen narcosis whose symptoms are rather like drunkenness – not the best conditions for intricate work in a dangerous situation! The second problem occurs when the diver ascends back to atmospheric pressure. The dissolved nitrogen comes out of the blood and bubbles can collect in the joints causing excruciating pain called 'the bends'. The

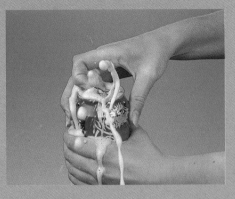

bends can be avoided by ascending slowly to allow the nitrogen to come out of solution gradually. Divers at depths of greater than 50 metres breathe mixtures of helium and oxygen to avoid nitrogen narcosis.

Without going into the mathematics, these assumptions explain the properties of gases as follows:

● Bombardment of the walls of the container explains pressure.
● Increasing kinetic energy with increasing temperature means that molecules will bombard the walls harder and more often at increased temperature, thus increasing the pressure.
● The random motion of well-spaced-out molecules explains diffusion: the process by which gases mix of their own accord.

The distribution of molecular speeds

In any gas, some molecules are moving slowly, some fast and the majority have speeds in between: there is a distribution of speeds. This can be shown on a graph (**Figure 27.4**).

Notice that the distribution is not symmetrical. At higher temperatures, the peak of the graph, which represents the most probable speed, moves to the right (towards higher speed) but the *height* of the peak is reduced. So as the temperature increases, the most probable speed gets faster and there is a wider spread of speeds. This helps to explain why reactions go faster at higher temperatures.

This distribution is referred to as the Maxwell–Boltzmann distribution, which we have already met in section 26.1.

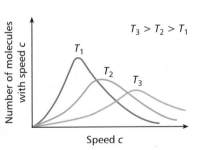

Figure 27.4 The distribution of speeds of gas molecules at different temperatures, T_1, T_2 and T_3

Hint: The curve always starts at the origin. The area under each curve is the same because it represents the total number of molecules.

27.5 Real gases: deviations from the ideal gas equation

No real gas actually obeys the ideal gas equation in its entirety. All real gases become liquid when they are cooled and/or compressed enough. The volume of a liquid hardly changes when the pressure or temperature changes. The ideal gas equation predicts a gradual decrease in volume with decreasing temperature until the volume becomes zero at 0 K.

The reason for this failure to obey the ideal gas equation at high pressure and low temperature is that two of the assumptions of the kinetic theory are no longer valid under these conditions. Once the molecules get close together, as they do at high pressures and low temperatures, then we can no longer ignore the attraction between them. Eventually, the attraction pulls the molecules together and the liquid state results. Also, when the volume of gas is small, it is no longer possible to ignore the volume of the actual molecules in comparison with the volume of the whole gas.

27.6 Summary

● Gay-Lussac's law states that (measured under the same conditions of temperature and pressure)	gases react in volumes that are in simple whole number ratios.
● Avogadro's law states that	equal volumes of all gases (measured at the same temperature and pressure) contain the same number of particles.
● The ideal gas equation is	$\dfrac{PV}{T} = nR$
$P =$	pressure
$V =$	volume
$n =$	number of moles
$T =$	temperature (in K)
$R =$	gas constant ($8.3\,\mathrm{J\,K^{-1}\,mol^{-1}}$)
● The ideal gas equation is obeyed fairly closely by most gases at	room temperature and pressure.
● To change a volume of a gas to standard temperature and pressure (STP), 273 K and 100 kPa use the equation	$\dfrac{P_1 V_1}{T_1} = \dfrac{P_2 V_2}{T_2}$
● One mole of an ideal gas has a volume of	$22\,700\,\mathrm{cm^3}$ at STP (approximately $24\,000\,\mathrm{cm^3}$ at room temperature and pressure).
● The partial pressure of a gas in a mixture of gases is	the pressure that the gas would exert if it alone occupied the container.
● Dalton's law states that the total pressure of a mixture of gases is	the sum of the partial pressures of all the components.

27.7 Practice questions

1. Convert the following gas volumes to STP (273 K and 100 000 Pa or 760 mmHg or 1 atmosphere). Answer in the same volume units as the question.
   (a) 100 cm³ at 290 K and 100 060 Pa;
   (b) 80 cm³ at 373 K and 90 040 Pa;
   (c) 1.00 dm³ at 200 K and 100 000 Pa;
   (d) 100 m³ at 20 °C and 750 mmHg;
   (e) 1.00 pint at 50 °C and 2 atmospheres.

2. The gas hydrogen chloride can be decomposed into its elements, hydrogen, H_2, and chlorine, Cl_2, by heating it over a suitable catalyst. 80 cm³ of hydrogen chloride gives 80 cm³ of the mixture of hydrogen and chlorine. On removing the hydrogen, 40 cm³ of the gas remained.
   (a) What is the formula of hydrogen chloride? (You probably know this already, so make sure you can explain your reasoning. What law or laws did you assume to get the answer?)
   (b) Briefly describe how you might remove the hydrogen.

   (c) Can you think of a way of removing the chlorine instead?
   (d) Sketch a suitable arrangement of gas syringes for the experiment described above.

3. In an experiment it was found that 1.013 g of a hydrocarbon occupied a volume of 227 cm³ at 0 °C and 1 atmosphere. What is the relative molecular mass of the hydrocarbon used? (Take the molar volume at 0 °C and 1 atmosphere to be 22.7 dm³ mol⁻¹.)

4. The results below are from an experiment to determine the relative molecular mass of methanol, using the apparatus described in Figure 27.3 on page 385.

   Change in mass of the hypodermic syringe = 0.083 g
   Increase in volume of the gas syringe = 80.0 cm³
   Temperature of the steam jacket = 100.0 °C
   Atmospheric pressure = 99 950 Pa
   Calculate the relative molecular mass, M_r, of methanol.

27.8 Examination questions

1. The equation $pV = nRT$ may be used in the determination of the relative molecular mass of a volatile liquid.
   The diagram shows the apparatus that could be used in this determination. A known mass of a volatile liquid is injected through the self-sealing rubber cap into the gas syringe, which is then heated in a boiling water bath for several minutes before the volume of the vapour in the syringe is noted.

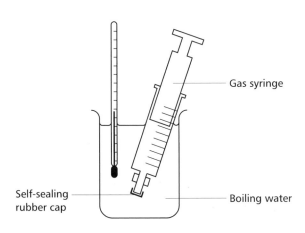

Self-sealing rubber cap
Gas syringe
Boiling water

   (a) (i)   State what is meant by the term *volatile liquid*. Give the name of the equation, $pV = nRT$, and state what the symbols n and R represent in this equation.
       (ii) Suggest why it is essential to leave the syringe in the boiling water bath for several minutes before reading the volume of the vapour.
       (iii) State **three** of the basic assumptions made in the kinetic theory of gases regarding the behaviour of gaseous molecules.
   (b) Using apparatus similar to that shown in the diagram, 0.167 g of ethanol, C_2H_5OH, was injected into a gas syringe and the syringe was then placed in a boiling water bath for several minutes. The atmospheric pressure was 101 300 Pa and the temperature of the bath was 100 °C.
       (i) Calculate the volume, in cm³, of ethanol vapour that would have been produced under these conditions.
            $$R = 8.314 \, J \, K^{-1} \, mol^{-1}$$
       (ii) Explain why a gas syringe of 100 cm³ capacity was found to be unsuitable.
                                                    [AEB 1998]

2. Neon is a monatomic gas of relative atomic mass
    20.2. Calculate the volume occupied by 3.03 g of
    neon at 298 K and 1.01×10^5 Pa pressure.
    [1 mole of ideal gas occupies 22.4 dm^3 at 273 K
    and 1.01×10^5 Pa.]

                            [WJEC 1996, part question]

3. (a) Real gases do not behave ideally.
         (i)   State the **two** major assumptions which
               are made for ideal gas behaviour.
         (ii) I. State the *physical conditions* under
                   which real gases approach ideal gas
                   behaviour, and
               II. explain these conditions in terms of
                   the two assumptions in (a)(i).
                            [WJEC 1996, part question]

4. On a copy of the diagram at the top of the next
    column, where the curve shows the distribution of
    molecular energies at temperature T, sketch

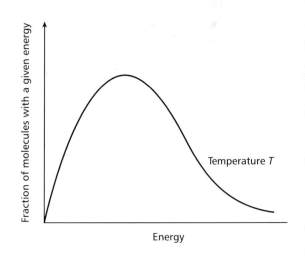

(i)   a curve to represent the distribution of
      molecular energies at a temperature T_1, where
      T_1 is greater than T;
(ii) a curve to represent the distribution of
      molecular energies at a temperature T_2, where
      T_2 is less than T.

                                            [WJEC 1997]

28 Thermodynamics: enthalpy, entropy and free energy

C H E M I S T R Y   N O W

Entropy and the arrow of time

We all know that time flows in one direction only – no-one rises from the dead, gets younger and returns to the womb, for example. But what is it that defines the direction in which time flows? This question has puzzled philosophers but, perhaps surprisingly, the idea of entropy used in this chapter can help to answer the question 'which way does time flow?' Entropy is a mathematical measure of disorder or randomness. Time's arrow always seems to flow in the direction of increasing disorder rather than increasing order – you have probably noticed this effect operating in your room!

This idea helps to explain how we can almost always tell if a film is running backwards. An obvious example is a bomb exploding; the fragments of the bomb fly all over the place and land in random positions. The reverse of this, where the fragments fly from their random positions and assemble themselves into a bomb, simply does not happen. This is the case even though no physical laws have been broken in the 'unexplosion': all the fragments have obeyed Newton's laws of motion and the laws of conservation of energy and momentum. We can still tell that the film is running backwards because order appears spontaneously out of disorder. In the same way, if we open a container of carbon dioxide gas, the gas molecules escape and mix with the air in the room. The reverse 'unmixing' in which carbon dioxide molecules separated themselves from the air and filled a container would be, literally, incredible.

We can, however, 'buy' increases in orderliness by expending energy. The fragments of the bomb could be laboriously picked up and reassembled, the gas could be pumped back into the container and your rooom can be tidied. Chemical reactions in which order is formed do occur, but they require the input of energy. One example is photosynthesis, in which complex, ordered, solid carbohydrates are formed from randomly arranged molecules of carbon dioxide and water. In this case, the driving force is the input of energy from the Sun.

How we can manipulate this driving force towards increasing randomness is one of the themes of this chapter.

An egg hit by a bullet – do you have any difficulty putting these pictures in the right order?

In this chapter we will be looking at:
- how the entropy, *S*, or randomness, of a system is related to the number of ways of arranging the particles in it
- how the entropy, *S*, or randomness, of a system is related to the number of ways of arranging the energy quanta in it
- how changes in entropy and enthalpy (heat energy) are related
- exchange of entropy and enthalpy between the reacting system and its surroundings
- how the feasibility of a reaction is related to its total entropy change
- the idea of free energy change, ΔG
- the relationships between ΔG, *E*⁰ and the equilibrium constant K
- how temperature affects the feasibility of reactions

H i n t : The enthalpy change of a reaction is the heat change at constant pressure and temperature.

Introduction

Thermodynamics is the study of heat and other related changes that occur in chemical reactions. This chapter tackles the most basic problem in chemistry, which is: why do some changes take place of their own accord and others do not? For example, gases mix and do not 'unmix', zinc reacts with copper sulphate to give zinc sulphate and copper but the reverse of this will not happen, and so on.

In section 8.5 we discussed some clues to this and found that the enthalpy and entropy changes of a reaction seemed to be involved. Reactions which give out enthalpy (their ΔH's are negative) are more favoured. Entropy, S, is a measure of randomness of the system and reactions with a positive entropy change (their ΔS's are positive) are more favoured. We built up a diagram:

+ΔH can't	−ΔH might
−ΔS 'go'	−ΔS 'go'
+ΔH might	−ΔH must
+ΔS 'go'	+ΔS 'go'

('go' means be feasible)

We were left with two problems:
1. **How do we measure or calculate entropies?**
2. **What is the relative importance of entropy and enthalpy changes when they are opposed?**

CONCEPT CHECKPOINTS

The following basic ideas are used in this chapter. You may revise some of these topics elsewhere in the book.
- the idea of enthalpy as energy measured under certain conditions (section 8.1)
- the idea of entropy as a measure of disorder (section 8.5)
- energy exists in discrete amounts called quanta (section 7.2)
- *E*⁰ as a measure of the feasibility of redox reactions (section 25.2)
- the equilibrium constant as a measure of the position of equilibrium of a reversible reaction (section 11.2 and Chapter 23)
- Hess's law cycles (section 8.3)

28.1 Entropy

The arrangement of molecules

Scientists believe that molecules move at random and cannot 'know' where they should go. This suggests that reactions happen by chance alone, which in turn means that the *most probable* thing tends to happen. The most probable thing is disorder.

An analogy might be dealing out a hand of 13 from a well-shuffled pack of 52 cards. It is overwhelmingly probable that you will get a haphazard arrangement of cards rather than, say, all of one suit. There is a vast number of haphazard arrangements of 13 cards but only a very few corresponding to getting all the cards in one suit. In chemical reactions, as in cards, the most probable things happen and these involve randomness rather than order. The quantity we call entropy (*S*) is a measure of randomness and is related to the number of possible molecular arrangements that lead to a given outcome. This can be worked out mathematically (see the box 'Why do gases mix?') and in all but the simplest systems, involves numbers of unimaginable size.

Hint: Chemists often use the word 'system' to mean to the chemicals they are dealing with: for example '10 g of water', 'a mixture of oxygen and nitrogen' or 'a mixture of reactants and products in the course of reacting'.

Hint: The greater the number of objects involved in a random process, the more predictable the outcome – the gender of one baby is unpredictable but the population of the world contains half males and half females.

In fact the mathematical relationship is:

$$S = k \ln W$$

where S is entropy

W is the number of ways of arranging the molecules

k is a constant called Boltzmann's constant (1.38×10^{-23} J K^{-1})

and for any *change* in the system:

$$\Delta S = k \, \Delta \ln W$$

where ΔS is the entropy change and $\Delta \ln W$ is the change in the log (to base e) of the number of ways of arranging the molecules in the system brought about by the change in the system.

As $\ln W$ is a pure number with no units, the units for entropy are therefore the same as the units of k (J K^{-1}).

Notice that the mathematical manipulation has the effect of converting W, a vast number, into a much smaller one which is easier to handle. The log of a number is much smaller than the number itself ($\ln 1\,000\,000 = 13.8$) and multiplying by Boltzmann's constant (a very small number) also scales the number down.

To give a feel for the numbers, the entropy of a mole of carbon dioxide is 213.6 J K^{-1} mol^{-1} and the entropy *change* on allowing a mole of a gas to expand into double its volume is $+6$ J K^{-1} mol^{-1}.

The arrangement of energy

We have just seen that entropy and entropy changes are related to the number of ways of arranging the molecules (or atoms or ions) in the system. A further contribution comes from the number of ways

FURTHER FOCUS

Why do gases mix?

It may seem odd to suggest that chemical processes, which have predictable outcomes, are governed by chance alone, but it easy to show that this could be the case. If you tossed 1000 coins, you could bet with confidence that there would be between 450 and 550 heads. Such an outcome could be predicted with near certainty. (It would however be unwise to bet on *exactly* 500 heads.) That chance can lead to predictable outcomes is also true of chemical systems.

Let us take a very simple example, that of gases mixing. Imagine a gas in box 1. A similar-sized box 2 is empty (a vacuum).

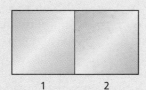

If we remove the partition, we know that a few moments later the gas molecules will be distributed evenly between boxes 1 and 2. We call this diffusion. The gas molecules cannot 'know' that there is a vacuum in the other container or that they are 'supposed' to spread out. They behave randomly. Could diffusion happen by chance alone?

We will start with the simplest possible case. Imagine there were only two molecules, A and B. These could be distributed as shown:

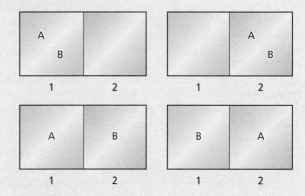

This gives 4 arrangements, i.e. 2^n (where n is the number of particles). There is a 2 in 4 chance of all the molecules being either in box 1 or box 2, and 2 out of 4 of the arrangements correspond to spreading out.

For three molecules, A, B and C:

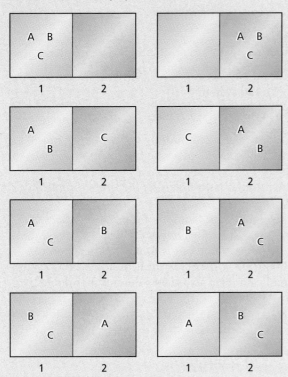

There are 8 arrangements (2^3). There is a 2 in 8 chance of all the molecules being in either box 1 or box 2. Here 6 out of 8 arrangements correspond to spreading out.

For six molecules we get 64 arrangements, and with this number it gets too laborious to draw the possibilities out in full, so we just put the number of ways of getting each arrangement. For example, there is just 1 way of getting all six in box 1, and 6 ways of getting 5 in box 1 and 1 in box 2.

These are ABCDE/F, ABCDF/E, ABCEF/D, ABDEF/C, ACDEF/B and BCDEF/A.

Box	1 2	1 2	1 2	1 2	1 2	1 2	1 2
Number of molecules	6 0	5 1	4 2	3 3	2 4	1 5	0 6
Number of ways	1	6	15	20	15	6	1

83%

Total = 64, 50 of which (83%) correspond to considerable mixing.

The more molecules we have, the more probable spreading out becomes.

With 50 molecules there are 2^{50} (approx 10^{15}) arrangements, only 2 of which represent all the molecules in only one box.

As we consider even greater numbers of molecules, so it becomes overwhelmingly likely that we will get an approximately even distribution of molecules solely by chance.

So we have shown that the diffusion of gases can be accounted for just by probability.

If we double the volume of a gas, we allow many more ways for the molecules to arrange themselves. There was a vast number of possible arrangements in the single container. Now there is a large *extra* number because molecules can now be in box 1 *or* box 2. The system is now more random. There has been an increase in entropy and the change has happened of its own accord, by chance alone.

Entropy is related to the number of ways W, in which the system can be arranged. The more ways, the greater the entropy.

that the **energy** can be arranged between molecules. We saw in section 7.2 that atoms have separate energy levels for their electrons and that energy comes in 'packets' of different sizes called quanta. The same is true of electronic energy levels in molecules, and in fact quantisation applies to *all* the types of energy that a molecule can have. These include the energy that makes it vibrate, rotate and translate (move from place to place). See **Figure 28.1**.

Energy levels in a molecule

These are shown schematically in **Figure 28.2** on page 396.

The higher the temperature of a sample of a substance, the more quanta of energy there are in the molecules which make up the sample, and the more ways there are of arranging the quanta between the energy levels (see the box 'Distribution of quanta of energy'). For example, the quanta could be fairly evenly distributed or just a few of the molecules could possess most of the quanta. This aspect of randomness is taken into account when the entropies of substances and entropy changes in reactions are calculated using:

$$S = k \ln W$$

or

$$\Delta S = k \, \Delta \ln W$$

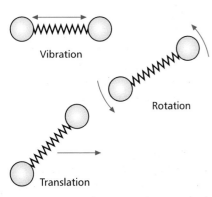

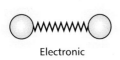

Figure 28.1 Types of energy in a diatomic molecule

FURTHER FOCUS

Distribution of quanta of energy

Let us take a very simple example. Suppose we have just two molecules and four quanta of vibrational energy (which corresponds to heat energy) to share between them (see the diagram).

In how many ways can it be done? One arrangement is all four quanta in molecule 1 and none in molecule 2. Another is three quanta in molecule 1 and one in

molecule 2, and so on. Table 1 shows all the possibilities. There are five. With five quanta there are six arrangements, see Table 2 and so on. So, the more quanta of energy (i.e. the hotter), the more ways in which they can be arranged and the more random the system. This means that heating up the system leads to an increase in entropy.

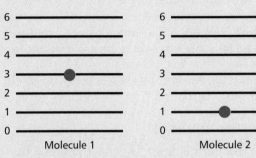

Vibrational energy levels in two molecules showing one possible arrangement of four quanta

Table 1

Molecule 1	Molecule 2
4	0
3	1
2	2
1	3
0	4

Table 2

Molecule 1	Molecule 2
5	0
4	1
3	2
2	3
1	4
0	5

Entropy values

Entropies can be calculated for all substances. They depend on conditions such as temperature, and the standard conditions are 298 K and 100 kPa, as for enthalpies.

$S^{\ominus}$ is the entropy of 1 mole of substance in its standard state under standard conditions.

Some values are given in **Table 28.1**.

Hint: Unlike enthalpies, the entropies of elements in their standard states are not zero. Because of the distribution of energy quanta, entropies could only be zero at 0 K when there are no quanta to be distributed.

Table 28.1 Some values of standard entropies

Substance		$S^{\ominus}/\text{J K}^{-1}\text{mol}^{-1}$
Carbon (diamond)	(s)	2.4
Carbon (graphite)	(s)	5.7
Copper	(s)	33.2
Water	(l)	69.9
Water (steam)	(g)	188.7
Ethanol	(l)	160.7
Carbon dioxide	(g)	213.6
Chlorine	(g)	223.0

Notice that in general the entropies of solids are small, those of liquids larger and those of gases larger still. This reflects the randomness of these states. Notice also the entropy increase when water turns to steam. This is due to the increase in volume.

Entropy and enthalpy

We have seen that heating something up (giving it more quanta of heat energy) results in an increase in entropy. There is a relationship between the amount of enthalpy given to a system and the resulting entropy increase:

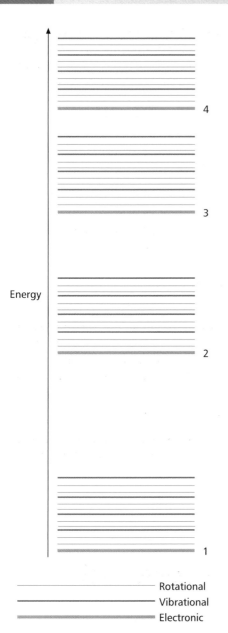

Figure 28.2 Energy levels in a molecule. Translational levels are even more closely spaced than rotational ones and are not shown

Hint: The entropy values are

$S^{\ominus}$ (NH_3) 192 J K^{-1} mol^{-1}
$S^{\ominus}$ (HCl) 187 J K^{-1} mol^{-1}
$S^{\ominus}$ (NH_4Cl) 95 J K^{-1} mol^{-1}

(As expected solid ammonium chloride has a lower value of $S^{\ominus}$ than either ammonia or hydrogen chloride gases)

$$\Delta S^{\ominus} = S^{\ominus}_{products} - S^{\ominus}_{reactants}$$
$$= 95 - (192 + 187)$$
$$= -284 \text{ J K}^{-1} \text{ mol}^{-1}$$

$$\Delta S = \frac{\Delta H}{T}$$

This makes sense because:

- The more heat (more quanta) we transfer, the more arrangements of quanta are possible and the more entropy will be gained, which suggests that $\Delta S \propto \Delta H$.
- If we give a certain number of quanta to a system which has very few (i.e. at a low temperature) it produces a large increase in entropy. If we give the same number of quanta to a system which already has many quanta (i.e. at a high temperature) the difference is less significant. So, if we add a fixed amount of heat energy when T is large, the change in entropy, ΔS, is small and if we add the same amount when T is small, ΔS is large. The argument is rather like saying that a £50 wage increase is more important to a person earning £100 a week than to a person earning £1000 a week. This is consistent with the entropy change being inversely proportional to temperature, i.e. $\Delta S \propto 1/T$.

The system and the surroundings

If we accept the idea that reactions happen by chance and that this leads to disorder, it follows that reactions will go of their own accord if ΔS is positive, because chance alone makes it overwhelmingly likely. But what about a reaction like:

$$NH_3(g) \quad + \quad HCl(g) \quad \longrightarrow \quad NH_4Cl(s)$$
ammonia   hydrogen chloride   ammonium chloride

This is spontaneous, even though we are going from gases (disorder) to solid (order) so that the entropy change is clearly negative.

In fact $\Delta S^{\ominus} = -284 \text{ J K}^{-1} \text{ mol}^{-1}$

So at first sight the reaction should not take place at all.

The problem is that we have not considered *all* the entropy changes, only those of the reactants and products (the **system**). The reaction is exothermic: $\Delta H^{\ominus} = -176 \text{ kJ mol}^{-1}$. This energy is dumped into the surroundings and increases its entropy (see **Figure 28.3**). We need to calculate the *total* entropy change: that of system *and* surroundings and find out whether this is positive. Using the relation:

$$\Delta S = \frac{\Delta H}{T}$$

we can calculate ΔS for the surroundings.

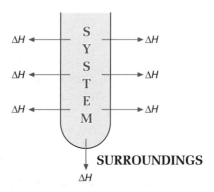

Figure 28.3 The reaction transfers enthalpy from system to surroundings

Ammonium chloride forms spontaneously from hydrogen chloride and ammonia

Hint: Take care with units. Entropies are usually given in $J\,K^{-1}\,mol^{-1}$, enthalpies in $kJ\,mol^{-1}$.

Hint: We must always consider the *total* entropy change in a reaction including system and surroundings.

Q In an explosion what can you say about the change in entropy of (a) the system and (b) the surroundings?

We do need to take care with signs. The ΔS we are calculating is the entropy change of the *surroundings*, while the ΔH is that of the *system*. A negative value of ΔH means energy is being transferred *to* the surroundings and so the entropy *increase* of the surroundings is:

$$\Delta S_{\text{surroundings}} = \frac{-\Delta H_{\text{system}}}{T}$$

$$\Delta S_{\text{surroundings}} = \frac{-(-176)}{T}$$

At room temperature, 298 K $\Delta S_{\text{surroundings}} = \frac{+176}{298}$

$$= 0.59\,kJ\,K^{-1}\,mol^{-1}$$
$$= 590\,J\,K^{-1}\,mol^{-1}$$

The total entropy change $\Delta S_{\text{tot}} = \Delta S_{\text{system}} + \Delta S_{\text{surroundings}}$
$$\Delta S_{\text{tot}} = -284 + 590$$
$$= +306\,J\,K^{-1}\,mol^{-1}$$

So the entropy *increase* of the *surroundings* more than compensates for the entropy *decrease* of the *system* and the total entropy change of the reaction is positive, which is why it takes place spontaneously.

We now have what we were looking for: an indication of reaction feasibility.

If ΔS_{tot} is positive, the reaction can go.

This is an illustration of the **second law of thermodynamics**, which states that the total entropy change of the universe always increases in any change.

28.2 Free energy change, ΔG

We have seen that $\Delta S_{\text{tot}} = \Delta S_{\text{system}} + \Delta S_{\text{surroundings}}$

and $$\Delta S_{\text{surroundings}} = \frac{-\Delta H_{\text{system}}}{T}$$

So for a chemical reaction:

$$\Delta S_{\text{tot}} = \Delta S_{\text{system}} - \frac{\Delta H_{\text{reaction}}}{T}$$

Multiplying by $-T$ gives:

$$-T\Delta S_{\text{tot}} = -T\Delta S_{\text{system}} + \Delta H_{\text{reaction}}$$

Note that $-T\Delta S$ has units of energy per mole ($J\,K^{-1}\,mol^{-1} \times K = J\,mol^{-1}$). We call this energy change the **Gibbs free energy change, ΔG.**

$$\Delta G = -T\Delta S_{\text{tot}}$$

So $$\Delta G = \Delta H_{\text{reaction}} - T\Delta S_{\text{system}}$$

Since we have changed signs (multiplying by $-T$), if ΔG is *negative* the reaction will go.

Answer: They are both positive.

Did you know? The Gibbs free energy is named after the American chemist Josiah Willard Gibbs. He was quite versatile: as well as his chemistry research, he taught Latin at Yale University and invented a railway braking system!

ΔG has the advantage that it refers solely to the reacting system rather than to the system and the surroundings. ΔG's of formation of compounds can be found in tables and can be used to calculate $\Delta G_{reaction}$ using Hess's law cycles in the same way as for ΔH's (see Chapter 8).

As a rule of thumb, we can often use the sign of ΔH alone as a guide to whether a reaction is feasible because in the equation

$$\Delta G = \Delta H_{reaction} - T\Delta S_{system}$$

if T is small, the term $-T\Delta S$ will be small, and $\Delta G \approx \Delta H_{reaction}$.

So at low temperature, if ΔH is negative, ΔG will be too, unless the entropy change of the system is very large and negative. Since many chemical observations are made at room temperature, where T is quite small in absolute terms, ΔG is often approximately equal to ΔH.

Why do we use the term 'free' energy?

Q What do we call ions, such as the nitrate ions in the equation, which take no part in the reaction?

Consider the reaction of copper with silver nitrate solution:

$$2Ag^+(aq) + Cu(s) \longrightarrow Cu^{2+}(aq) + 2Ag(s) \qquad \Delta H^{\ominus} = -146.3 \text{ kJ mol}^{-1}$$

taking place in a test tube (the system).

We would predict that $\Delta S^{\ominus}_{system}$ will be negative, since there are two mobile ions on the left and one on the right. In fact this is so, as we can see from the following values of $S^{\ominus}$:

Entropies of ions in solution are calculated relative to an arbitrary standard, $S^{\ominus}(H^+(aq)) = 0$. Hence negative values are possible.

$$S^{\ominus}(Ag^+(aq)) = 73.0 \text{ J K}^{-1} \text{ mol}^{-1}$$
$$S^{\ominus}(Cu(s)) = 33.0 \text{ J K}^{-1} \text{mol}^{-1}$$
$$S^{\ominus}(Cu^{2+}(aq)) = -100.0 \text{ J K}^{-1} \text{mol}^{-1}$$
$$S^{\ominus}(Ag(s)) = 43.0 \text{ J K}^{-1} \text{mol}^{-1}$$

$$\Delta S^{\ominus}_{system} = \text{total } S^{\ominus}_{products} - \text{total } S^{\ominus}_{reactants}$$
$$\Delta S^{\ominus}_{system} = ((2 \times 43.0) + -100.0) - ((2 \times 73.0) + 33.0)$$
$$\Delta S^{\ominus}_{system} = -193 \text{ J K}^{-1} \text{ mol}^{-1}$$

So *inside the test tube* entropy has decreased by 193 J K^{-1} mol^{-1}. The reaction can only become feasible if the total entropy change, $\Delta S^{\ominus}_{tot}$, is positive. This means that the entropy of the surroundings must increase by at least 193 J K^{-1} mol^{-1}, so that $\Delta S^{\ominus}_{tot}$ is positive and the reaction is feasible.

Since
$$\Delta S_{surroundings} = \frac{\Delta H_{reaction}}{T}$$

$$\Delta H_{reaction} = T\Delta S_{surroundings}$$

We can find the amount of heat ΔH which must be transferred to the surroundings, in order to make ΔS_{tot} positive.

At standard temperature, 298 K:

$$\Delta H^{\ominus} = 298 \times 193 \text{ J mol}^{-1}$$
$$= 57\,514 \text{ J mol}^{-1}$$
$$= 57.5 \text{ kJ mol}^{-1}$$

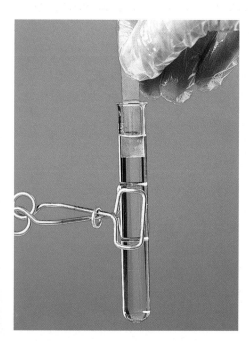

The reaction of copper with silver nitrate solution

So of the 146.3 kJ mol^{-1} (ΔH for the original reaction), 57.5 kJ mol^{-1} *must be transferred to the surroundings as heat* in order for the total entropy change of system plus surroundings to be positive.

The rest (146.3 − 57.5 = 88.8 kJ mol^{-1}) is **free** energy which is available in any form and for any purpose. It need not necessarily be

Answer: They are spectator ions.

given out as heat. The 57.5 kJ mol^{-1} *must* be given out as heat, to provide an entropy increase of the surroundings to balance the entropy decrease of the system.

The free energy of this reaction could be given out as, for example, electricity by making the reaction an electrochemical cell (see the box '$\Delta G^{\ominus}$ and $E^{\ominus}$').

$$\Delta G^{\ominus} = \Delta H^{\ominus} - T\Delta S^{\ominus}$$
$$\Delta G^{\ominus} = -146.3 - \frac{298 \times -193}{1000}$$
$$\Delta G^{\ominus} = -146.3 + 57.5$$
$$\Delta G^{\ominus} = -88.8 \text{ kJ mol}^{-1}$$

FURTHER FOCUS

$\Delta G^{\ominus}$ and $E^{\ominus}$

The free energy, calculated above for the reaction:

$$2Ag^{+}(aq) + Cu(s) \longrightarrow 2Ag(s) + Cu^{2+}(aq)$$

could, for example, be produced as electricity and used, say, to lift a load by powering a motor. This can be done if the reaction is carried out in an electrochemical cell (see the diagram below). $E^{\ominus}$ for this cell = 0.46 V. How much electrical energy can it produce?

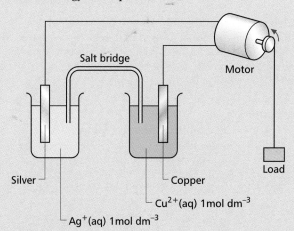

Using the free energy from a cell to lift a load

$E^{\ominus}$, the e.m.f., which is measured in volts, is equal to the number of joules of energy per coulomb of electric charge produced (see section 6.3).

In other words: $E^{\ominus} = \dfrac{\text{joules of energy}}{\text{coulombs}}$

Rearranging this, joules of energy = $E^{\ominus} \times$ coulombs

How do we find the number of coulombs?

$$2Ag^{+}(aq) + Cu(s) \longrightarrow 2Ag(s) + Cu^{2+}(aq)$$

2 electrons transferred (top) / 2 electrons transferred (bottom)

For this reaction to take place, 2 moles of electrons must be transferred.

1 mole of electrons caries a charge of 96 500 coulombs (called 1 faraday).

2 moles of electrons = 2 faradays = 2 × 96 500 coulombs
energy (in joules) = $E^{\ominus} \times 2 \times 96\ 500$
energy = $0.46 \times 2 \times 96\ 500$ J
= 88 780 J per mole of reaction
= 88.8 kJ mol^{-1}

Notice that this is exactly the same as the value for $\Delta G^{\ominus}$ calculated earlier. This is the energy available (free) to do work, i.e. it is $\Delta G^{\ominus}$, and since 'available' implies it is given out (as opposed to taking in), it has a *negative* value.

In general we can write the following relationship:

$$\Delta G^{\ominus} = -zFE^{\ominus},$$

where z = number of moles of electrons transferred in the reaction. This fits in with what we found in section 25.2, that if $E^{\ominus}$ is positive the reaction is feasible. $\Delta G^{\ominus}$ must be negative for the reaction to be feasible and from the equation $E^{\ominus}$ must be positive for this to be so.

Example

What is the free energy change of the reaction:

$$Zn(s) + Cu^{2+}(aq) \longrightarrow Zn^{2+}(aq) + Cu(s)$$

$E^{\ominus}$ for this reaction is + 1.1 V.

$$\Delta G^{\ominus} = -zFE$$

When one mole of reaction occurs, two electrons are transferred from zinc to copper, so $z = 2$.

$$\Delta G^{\ominus} = -2 \times 96\ 500 \times 1.1$$
$$\Delta G^{\ominus} = -212\ 300 \text{ J mol}^{-1}$$
$$\Delta G^{\ominus} = -210 \text{ kJ mol}^{-1} \text{ to 2 s.f.}$$

Hint: The least accurate measurement is to two significant figures.

FURTHER FOCUS

$\Delta G^{\ominus}$ and the equilibrium constant

All reactions can be treated as reversible ones which reach equilibrium. In reactions that seem to go to completion, we can consider that the amounts of reactants remaining at equilibrium are so small that they can be ignored. $\Delta G^{\ominus}$ tells us whether a reaction is feasible or not. The equilibrium constant K tells us whether reactants or products predominate. Both are essentially telling us the same thing. If $\Delta G^{\ominus}$ is negative, products will predominate over reactants and if $\Delta G^{\ominus}$ is positive reactants will predominate over products. If $\Delta G^{\ominus}$ is zero we will have an equilibrium where products and reactants are equally likely. Is there a mathematical relationship between $\Delta G^{\ominus}$ and K? The table summarises the situation.

K	$\Delta G^{\ominus}$
large	negative
1	0
small	positive

The fact that when $\Delta G^{\ominus} = 0$, $K = 1$ suggests a logarithmic relationship ($\ln 1 = 0$). The fact that negative values of $\Delta G^{\ominus}$ give large values of K suggests:

$$-\Delta G^{\ominus} \propto \ln K$$

Both $\Delta G^{\ominus}$ and K are temperature dependent, so not surprisingly temperature appears in the relationship.

The relationship is in fact:

$$\Delta G^{\ominus} = -RT\ln K$$

where R is the gas constant, which frequently turns up in expressions involving molecular collisions.

Hint: The units are consistent: R has units $J\,K^{-1}\,mol^{-1}$, T has units K, so $\Delta G^{\ominus}$ has units $J\,K^{-1}\,mol^{-1} \times K = J\,mol^{-1}$

We now have three parameters that tell us about reaction feasibility. They are $\Delta G^{\ominus}$, $E^{\ominus}$ and K, the equilibrium constant.

They are linked by these equations, which allow us to find values for $\Delta G^{\ominus}$:

$$\Delta G^{\ominus} = -RT\ln K$$
$$\Delta G^{\ominus} = -zFE$$

The table compares them.

As a rule of thumb, we often take take it that reactions where $K > 10^{10}$ are complete and reactions where $K < 10^{-10}$ do not occur. Between these values we think of the reaction as an equilibrium between products and reactants. The values of $E^{\ominus}$ and $\Delta G^{\ominus}$ which correspond to $K = 10^{10}$ are 0.59 V and $-57\,kJ\,mol^{-1}$. Since this is only a rule of thumb, we often remember $K = 10^{10}$, $E^{\ominus} = 0.6\,V$ and $\Delta G^{\ominus} = -60\,kJ\,mol^{-1}$.

	'Does not occur'	'Borderline'	Reactants predominate	'Equilibrium'	Products predominate	'Borderline'	'Complete'
$\Delta G^{\ominus}/kJ\,mol^{-1}$	+85.5	+57	+28.5	0	−28.5	−57	−85.5
$E^{\ominus}/V$	−0.885	−0.59	−0.295	0	+0.295	+0.59	+0.885
K/units depend on reaction	10^{-15}	10^{-10}	10^{-5}	1	10^{5}	10^{10}	10^{15}

28.3 Reaction feasibility and temperature

Since temperature appears in the equation:

$$\Delta G^{\ominus} = \Delta H^{\ominus} - T\Delta S^{\ominus}$$

some reactions may be feasible at some temperatures and not at others. Take the reaction:

$$CaCO_3(s) \longrightarrow CaO(s) + CO_2(g) \qquad \Delta H^{\ominus} = +178\,kJ\,mol^{-1}$$

Here a solid produces a solid and a gas, so the entropy change of the system will be positive. The enthalpy change is positive. Will this reaction go or not? The values of the relevant standard entropies are given below.

$$S/J\,K^{-1}\,mol^{-1}$$

$CaCO_3(s)$	93
$CaO(s)$	40
$CO_2(g)$	214

$$\Delta S^\ominus = S^\ominus{}_{products} - S^\ominus{}_{reactants}$$
$$= (40 + 214) - 93$$
$$= +161\,J\,K^{-1}\,mol^{-1}$$

At 298 K
$$\Delta G^\ominus = \Delta H^\ominus - T\Delta S^\ominus$$
$$= +178 - \frac{298 \times 161}{1000}$$
$$= +178 - 48\,kJ\,mol^{-1}$$
$$= +128\,kJ\,mol^{-1}$$

so the reaction is *not* feasible.

At 2000 K
$$\Delta G^\ominus = +178 - \frac{2000 \times 161}{1000}$$
$$= +178 - 322\,kJ\,mol^{-1}$$
$$= -144\,kJ\,mol^{-1}$$

so the reaction is feasible.

At what temperature does this reaction become feasible?

The borderline between feasible and not feasible is when $\Delta G = 0$. Substituting this into our equation:

$$0 = +178 - \frac{T \times 161}{1000}$$
$$0.161\,T = 178$$
$$T = 1106\,K$$

The reaction is not feasible below 1106 K and is feasible above 1106 K. In fact the reaction does not 'jump' between being feasible or not. An equilibrium will exist around this temperature.

Calculating $\Delta G^\ominus$ values from thermochemical cycles

It is possible to calculate $\Delta G^\ominus$ using thermochemical cycles, in just the same way as for enthalpy changes. For example, in:

$$Cu(s) + ZnO(s) \longrightarrow CuO(s) + Zn(s)$$

is the reaction feasible under standard conditions?

$$\Delta G_f^\ominus(ZnO) = -318\,kJ\,mol^{-1}$$
$$\Delta G_f^\ominus(CuO) = -128\,kJ\,mol^{-1}$$

$$Cu(s) + ZnO(s) \longrightarrow CuO(s) + Zn(s)$$

-318 kJ mol⁻¹   -128 kJ mol⁻¹

+318 kJ mol⁻¹ $Cu(s) + Zn(s) + \frac{1}{2}O_2(g)$ -128 kJ mol⁻¹

$$\Delta G^\ominus = +318 + -128 = +190\,kJ\,mol^{-1}$$

So the reaction is not feasible at 298 K.

Hint: $\Delta G_f^\ominus$ of all elements in their standard states = 0. Values for $\Delta G_f^\ominus$ can be found in data tables.

Q What is $\Delta G^\ominus$ for the reaction $CuO(s) + Zn(s) \longrightarrow Cu(s) + ZnO(s)$?

Answer: $-190\,kJ\,mol^{-1}$: this is the reverse of the previous reaction, so the sign of $\Delta G^\ominus$ is reversed.

Rates

We must always remember that if we predict that a reaction is feasible (i.e. that $\Delta G^\ominus$ is negative), the reaction may not actually occur at a measurable rate. Thermodynamics tells us only about the initial and final states of a reaction and nothing else. It may well be that there is a large activation energy barrier which prevents the reaction taking place at a reasonable speed (see **Figure 28.4**). $\Delta G^\ominus$ tells us *nothing* about the height of the activation energy 'barrier'. However, if $\Delta G^\ominus$ is negative but the reaction is too slow, we might look for a catalyst to speed it up. If $\Delta G^\ominus$ is positive, there is no point in looking for a catalyst because the reaction is not feasible.

Increasing the temperature will always increase the rate of a reaction. In some cases, as in the example about the decomposition of calcium carbonate above, changing the temperature may make the value of ΔG negative and therefore make the reaction feasible. These two effects are quite independent.

For example, as we saw earlier, calcium carbonate needs to be heated above 1106 K before $\Delta G^\ominus$ is negative and the breakdown to calcium oxide and carbon dioxide is possible. At higher temperatures still the rate of breakdown will increase, but these two effects of temperature are quite separate.

> **Hint:** Thermodynamics tells us about the reactants and the products, while kinetics tells us about the reaction mechanism.

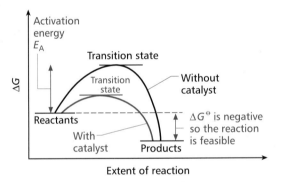

Figure 28.4 A reaction profile for a reaction where $\Delta G^\ominus$ is negative

FURTHER FOCUS

Applications of $\Delta G^\ominus$: Ellingham diagrams

An important industrial problem is extracting metals from their ores. Ores are usually metal oxides or compounds like sulphides and carbonates which can easily be converted to oxides by heating them in air (roasting). The problem is to find a suitable reducing agent which will convert the oxide to the metal. The reducing agent should ideally be cheap and do the reduction at as low a temperature as possible to reduce fuel costs. We can predict which reducing agents are suitable for a particular application by plotting ΔG against T for a variety of relevant reactions. All the reactions are written so that they involve 1 mole of oxygen molecules (2 moles of oxygen atoms). Such a diagram is called an Ellingham diagram.

For example, can carbon be used to reduce zinc oxide to zinc at (a) 1000 K, (b) 1500 K?
The reaction we require is:

$$2C + 2ZnO \longrightarrow 2CO + 2Zn$$

The graph shows that at 1000 K we have the following ΔG values:

1. $\quad 2C + O_2 \longrightarrow 2CO \qquad \Delta G = -400 \text{ kJ mol}^{-1}$
2. $\quad 2Zn + O_2 \longrightarrow 2ZnO \qquad \Delta G = -550 \text{ kJ mol}^{-1}$

So reversing reaction 2:

3. $\quad 2ZnO \longrightarrow 2Zn + O_2 \qquad \Delta G = +550 \text{ kJ mol}^{-1}$

> **Hint:** Reversing the reaction reverses the sign of ΔG.

Adding 1. and 3. we get:

$$2C + 2ZnO \longrightarrow 2CO + 2Zn$$

and $\qquad \Delta G = -400 + 550 = +150 \text{ kJ mol}^{-1}$

so at 1000 K the reaction is **not** feasible.

At 1500 K we have the following ΔG values:

4. $\qquad 2C + O_2 \longrightarrow 2CO \qquad \Delta G = -500 \text{ kJ mol}^{-1}$

5. $\qquad 2Zn + O_2 \longrightarrow 2ZnO \qquad \Delta G = -250 \text{ kJ mol}^{-1}$

So:

6. $\qquad 2ZnO \longrightarrow 2Zn + O_2 \qquad \Delta G = +250 \text{ kJ mol}^{-1}$

Adding 4. and 6.:

$\qquad 2ZnO + 2C \longrightarrow 2CO + 2Zn \qquad \Delta G = -250 \text{ kJ mol}^{-1}$

At 1500 K the reaction **is** feasible.

You can probably see from the graph that where the two lines cross, $\Delta G = 0$. Thus the reaction above is feasible at temperatures above 1200 K.

It is possible to short-circuit the above procedure: at any temperature, the reaction represented by the **lower** line will go **forwards** and the reaction represented by the **upper** line will go **in reverse**. So carbon will only reduce magnesium oxide at temperatures above 2000 K.

Carbon, in the form of coke, is used as a reducing agent in a number of industrial processes, most notably in the production of iron, where iron oxide is reduced to iron in the blast furnace.

Answer: 2300 K

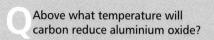
Above what temperature will carbon reduce aluminium oxide?

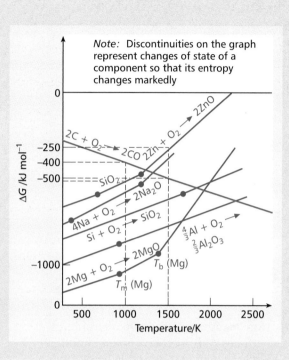

Note: Discontinuities on the graph represent changes of state of a component so that its entropy changes markedly

28.4 Summary

● Since molecules move at random, reactions occur	by chance alone, i.e. the most probable outcome occurs.
● Chance predicts that reactions will go in the direction of	increased randomness.
● The randomness of a system is measured by	entropy, S.
● Entropy is related to the number of ways (W) of arranging	both the molecules and energy quanta in the system.
● $S =$	$k \ln W$, where k is Boltzmann's constant.
● Reactions can occur spontaneously when	they involve an overall increase in entropy.
● This increase in entropy must be the	total change of both the system (reactants and products) and the surroundings (everything else).
● If enthalpy is transferred to the surroundings, the entropy of the surroundings will	increase.
● $\Delta S_{\text{surroundings}} =$	$-\dfrac{\Delta H_{\text{reaction}}}{T}$
● For a spontaneous reaction ΔS_{total}	is positive.

- $\Delta S_{total} =$ $\Delta S_{system} + \Delta S_{surroundings}$

- $\Delta G^{\ominus} =$ $-T\Delta S_{tot}$

- $\Delta G^{\ominus} =$ $\Delta H_{reaction} - T\Delta S_{system}$

- Reactions are only spontaneous if $\Delta G^{\ominus}$ is negative.

- $\Delta G^{\ominus}$ tells us nothing about   the rate of reaction.

- $\Delta G^{\ominus} =$ $-zFE^{\ominus}$, where $E^{\ominus}$ is the e.m.f. of the cell reaction, z is the number of electrons transferred and F the Faraday constant.

- $\Delta G^{\ominus} =$ $-RT \ln K$, where K is the equilibrium constant, R is the gas constant and T the temperature.

- $\Delta G^{\ominus}$ values can be calculated using   Hess's law cycles in the same way as $\Delta H^{\ominus}$'s.

- $\Delta S^{\ominus}$ values can be calculated using $\Delta S^{\ominus} = S^{\ominus}_{products} - S^{\ominus}_{reactants}$.

28.5 Practice questions

1. (a) How many ways are there of arranging 4 particles A, B, C, D in 2 boxes, 1 and 2? Write them down in a table beginning :

1	2
A B C D	0
A B C	D

   (b) What is the probability of finding all the particles in box 2?
   (c) What percentage of the arrangements is the sum of the 3 : 1 and 2 : 2 arrangements?

2. (a) Predict whether the entropy change for the following reactions will be significantly positive, significantly negative or approximately zero and explain your reasoning.
   (i) $Mg(s) + ZnO(s) \longrightarrow MgO(s) + Zn(s)$
   (ii) $2Pb(NO_3)_2(s) \longrightarrow 2PbO(s) + 4NO_2(g) + O_2(g)$
   (iii) $MgO(s) + CO_2(g) \longrightarrow MgCO_3(s)$
   (iv) $H_2O(l) \longrightarrow H_2O(g)$
   (b) Calculate $\Delta S^{\ominus}_{system}$ for each reaction using data below. Comment on your answers.

	$S/J\,K^{-1}\,mol^{-1}$
$Mg(s)$	32.7
$MgO(s)$	26.9
$MgCO_3$	65.7
$Zn(s)$	41.6
$ZnO(s)$	43.6
$Pb(NO_3)_2(s)$	213.0
$PbO(s)$	68.7
$NO_2(g)$	240.0
$O_2(g)$	205.0
$CO_2(g)$	213.6
$H_2O(l)$	69.7
$H_2O(g)$	188.7

3. For the reaction:

$$MgO(s) \longrightarrow Mg(s) + \tfrac{1}{2}O_2(g)$$
$$\Delta H^{\ominus} = +602\ kJ\,mol^{-1}$$
$$\Delta S^{\ominus}_{system} = +109\ J\,K^{-1}\,mol^{-1}$$

   (a) Without doing a calculation, is it possible to predict whether the reaction is feasible or not? Explain your reasoning.
   (b) Using the equation $\Delta G = \Delta H - T\Delta S$ calculate ΔG at
   (i) 1000 K
   (ii) 6000 K
   At which temperature is the reaction feasible?
   (c) Calculate the temperature when $\Delta G = 0$.

4. For the following reactions:

   1. $N_2(g) + 3H_2(g) \longrightarrow 2NH_3(g)$
      $\Delta H^{\ominus} = -92\ kJ\,mol^{-1}$
   2. $2C(gr) + SiO_2(s) \longrightarrow 2CO(g) + Si(s)$
      $\Delta H^{\ominus} = +344\ kJ\,mol^{-1}$

   Calculate:
   (a) $\Delta S^{\ominus}_{system}$
   (b) $\Delta S^{\ominus}_{surroundings}$ at (i) 298 K, (ii) 2000 K
   (c) $\Delta S^{\ominus}_{tot}$ at (i) 298 K, (ii) 2000 K

	$S^{\ominus}/J\,K^{-1}\,mol^{-1}$
$N_2(g)$	191.6
$H_2(g)$	130.6
$NH_3(g)$	192.3
$C(gr)$	5.7
$SiO_2(s$	41.8
$CO(g)$	197.6
$Si(s)$	18.8

5. (a) Use a thermochemical cycle using $\Delta G_f^{\ominus}$ values to find $\Delta G^{\ominus}$ for the reaction:

$$Mg(s) + Cu^{2+}(aq) \longrightarrow Mg^{2+}(aq) + Cu(s)$$

$E^{\ominus}$ for the reaction is $+ 2.71$ V.

(b) Calculate $\Delta G^{\ominus}$ using $\Delta G^{\ominus} = -zFE^{\ominus}$.

	$\Delta G^{\ominus}$/kJ mol^{-1}
$Mg^{2+}(aq)$	-455
$Cu^{2+}(aq)$	$+66$

28.6 Examination questions

1. (a) In the following equation, T represents temperature

$$\Delta G = \Delta H - T\Delta S$$

Give the names of the other terms.

(b) (i) Calculate the value, stating units, of ΔS for the following reaction at 25 °C:

$$CaO(s) + H_2O(l) \longrightarrow Ca(OH)_2(s)$$

($\Delta G = -55.2$ kJ mol^{-1}, $\Delta H = -65.2$ kJ mol^{-1})

(ii) Explain the significance of the signs of the values for each of the following terms in the above reaction:

(iii) Calculate the amount of calcium hydroxide produced when 100 g of calcium oxide are treated with water and the yield is 84%.

2. Phosphorus pentachloride, PCl$_5$, is prepared by passing chlorine gas through phosphorus trichloride, PCl$_3$.

$$PCl_3(l) + Cl_2(g) \rightleftharpoons PCl_5(s)$$

(a) Use the following data to calculate the enthalpy change at 298 K for the production of 1 mole of phosphorus pentachloride from the trichloride. Your answer should include a sign and units.

Compound	$\Delta H_f^{\ominus}$/kJ mol^{-1}
PCl$_3$	-319.7
PCl$_5$	-443.5

(b) Use your answer from (a) to calculate the entropy change in the surroundings at 298 K. Your answer should include a sign and units.

(c) The standard entropy change of the system for this reaction is -215.6 J mol^{-1} K^{-1}.

(i) Suggest **two** reasons why $\Delta S^{\ominus}_{system}$ has a negative value.

(ii) Calculate the total entropy change, $\Delta S^{\ominus}_{total}$, for the reaction.

(iii) Will the reaction proceed spontaneously at 298 K? Explain your answer.

(d) The apparatus used in this reaction is ice-cooled. How does the yield of phosphorus pentachloride change when the temperature is allowed to rise?

[London (Nuffield) 1997]

3. The Ellingham diagram below shows how the free energy change, ΔG, for each of the reactions shown varies with temperature.

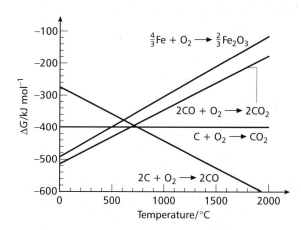

(a) The lines for reactions involving carbon and its oxides cross at about 710 °C. Write the equation for the reaction between carbon and carbon dioxide at this temperature and state its free energy change.

(b) Using the information in the diagram, write the equation for the most likely reaction which leads to the reduction of iron(III) oxide at

(i) 400 °C

(ii) 1000 °C

[NEAB 1998]

29 Structure determination

C H E M I S T R Y   N O W

The structure of sweetness

In the last century, it was not uncommon to taste small quantities of newly synthesised chemicals, and research papers often reported taste along with data such as colour, solubility and melting temperature.

Saccharin was discovered in 1879 by Ira Remsen, Professor of Chemistry at Johns Hopkins University in the USA, and his student Constantine Fahlberg. While eating dinner after a day's work in the lab, Fahlberg noticed that his bread tasted unusually sweet. He guessed that this must have been caused by chemicals he had been working on that day. He returned to the lab, tasted all the substances he had used and eventually picked out the one we now call saccharin (named from the Greek and Latin words for sugar – as in saccharides).

A taste panel in action. The only way to find out if a compound is sweet is to taste it

Sixty years later, the sweetener cyclamate was discovered by Michael Sveda. He was smoking in the lab and the chemical had become transferred to the butt of his cigarette.

Other sweet compounds have been discovered reputedly by a chemist licking his fingers to turn over the page of a book and by a non-English-speaking chemist who interpreted a request to *test* a chemical as an instruction to *taste* it.

Although nowadays these would be considered the result of poor laboratory practice, they had fortunate results. Ultimately there is no way to tell whether a compound is sweet or not without humans tasting it. It is a long and expensive process to test for toxicity (long- and short-term) which is essential before tasting can be done safely. Until recently there was no theory to explain why some compounds are sweet and to predict structures of new sweet-tasting compounds. Nowadays theories such as the 'triangle of sweetness' – see the box 'Sweeteners: the triangle of sweetness' in Chapter 33 – mean that a systematic search for new, sweet molecules can be undertaken and toxicity tests need only be done for molecules which show some probability of being sweet-tasting. In order to apply this theory, chemists need to be able to determine the structures of new compounds they have made. The proof of the pudding, however, remains in the eating.

All these foods contain either saccharin or aspartame as sweeteners

Introduction

The structure of a substance is the way that its atoms are arranged in space. Determining structure involves finding which atoms are connected to each other, measuring the distances between them and finding the angles between them – in fact obtaining enough information to build a scale model. It is important to realise that this is a three-dimensional problem.

One major difficulty is obvious: atoms are too small to be seen. If atoms were visible, structure determination would be easy. As it is, we have to use indirect methods, often several of them, and deduce the arrangement by detective work.

Many of the methods involve probing substances with electromagnetic radiation of different wavelengths. Table 29.1 shows some of the methods used and the type of information that each provides.

Table 29.1 Using electromagnetic radiation to probe structures

Wavelength/m	10^{-10}	10^{-9}	10^{-8}	10^{-7}	10^{-6}	10^{-5}	10^{-4}	10^{-3}	10^{-2}	10^{-1}	10^{0}	10^{1}	10^{2}	10^{3}
Frequency/s^{-1}			3×10^{16}		3×10^{14}		3×10^{12}		3×10^{10}		3×10^{8}		3×10^{6}	
Radiation type	X-rays		Ultraviolet		Visible		Infra-red						Radio waves	
Name of technique	X-ray diffraction		UV/visible spectrophotometry				IR spectro-photometry						Nuclear magnetic resonance	
Summary	Arrangement and spacing of atoms in solids		Electrons moving between different energy levels – identifies different elements and also special groups called chromophores				Vibrations of bonds – identifies the types of bonds present in a molecule						'Flipping' of nuclei in a magnetic field – identifies the number and type of hydrogen (and other) atoms in molecules	

29.1 Structure determination of solids with giant structures

The starting point for any structure determination is the formula of the substance concerned. This means we must know what elements are present and in what proportions. We may know this from the way we made or obtained the substance, or we may have to use a variety of analytical techniques. Some of these are described in Chapter 7 and in the box 'Flame emission spectroscopy' in section 7.2.

X-ray diffraction

This is an important method of determining the structure of solids. It depends on the fact that X-rays have wavelengths of about the same size as the distances between the nuclei of atoms which are bonded together – around 0.1 nm (10^{-10} m, as 1 nm = 10^{-9} m). Atoms have no solid exteriors so we use the nuclei as the fixed points.

The reason we cannot see atoms is that the wavelength of visible light is too large. It is around 5×10^{-7} m = 500 nm which is about

'Seeing' atoms: scanning tunnelling electron microscopy (STEM)

We cannot see atoms directly because the wavelength of visible light is too long. However, STEM is a good second best and allows us to detect individual atoms on a surface.

A metal probe, with a tip sharpened to a single atom, is scanned across very close to the surface. A voltage is applied between the probe and the surface so that a current of electrons flows between them. The effect is called 'tunnelling'. The size of the current varies with the distance between the surface and the probe. The narrower the gap, the bigger the current.

As the probe scans across the surface it is moved up and down under electronic control in such a way that the

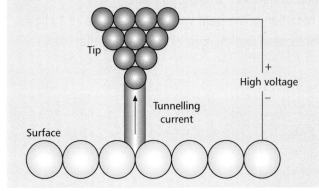

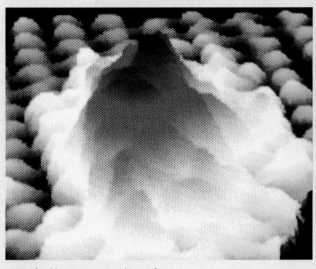

STEM of gold atoms on a graphite surface

current is kept constant, i.e. the gap remains the same. This means that it rises over the surface of each atom and drops into the hollows between them. A computer records the probe's movement and uses it to generate an image of the surface on which individual atoms can be picked out.

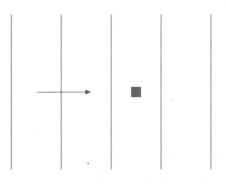

Figure 29.1 Water waves pass undisturbed an object much smaller than their wavelength

Max von Laue, pioneer of X-ray diffraction

5000 times the size of an atom. So light waves are not affected by atoms, in the same way that the water waves in **Figure 29.1** are unaffected by the small obstacle. This is a fundamental limitation, not merely that microscopes that are powerful enough have not yet been built. It takes an object of around the same size as the wavelength to affect the passage of waves significantly.

So, to 'observe' atoms we need radiation of wavelength approximately the same size as atoms: hence the use of X-rays. This was first realised by Max von Laue in 1912.

In section 6.2 we saw how waves are **diffracted** when they pass through small gaps, of size comparable to their wavelength, and also how they can interfere constructively and destructively. The photograph in section 6.2 shows a diffraction pattern produced by water waves interfering after being diffracted through small gaps. A similar sort of pattern is observed when X-rays are directed at a crystal, which is a regularly spaced array of atoms or ions. Analysis of such a pattern enables the spacing between the atoms to be calculated. The basis of this calculation is shown in the next section.

The Bragg condition

Figure 29.2 shows what happens when a beam of X-rays is shone on the surface of a crystal that is composed of a regular array of atoms or ions. The X-rays behave as though they are reflected by the atoms or ions. (They are actually absorbed and re-emitted by them.) Those reflected by atoms in the second layer travel a distance ABC further than those reflected from the surface atoms, so they 'lag behind'. We say they have a 'path difference'. Unless they are in phase with the X-rays reflected from the first layer, they will cancel out (destructive

William Bragg and his son Lawrence, who together won a Nobel prize in 1915 for their work on X-rays and crystals

Hint: 'In phase' means that the peaks and troughs of two waves exactly coincide.

Hint: The angle θ, between the face of the crystal and the X-ray beam is called the grazing angle.

interference) and no X-rays will be detected. Only if the second layer X-rays lag behind by a *whole number of wavelengths* does constructive interference occur and significant amounts of X-rays can be detected. If we start with the X-rays beam parallel to the surface of the crystal and gradually increase the angle, the X-rays reflected from the second layer of atoms lag further and further behind those reflected from the surface layer until they are in phase again but one wavelength behind (see **Figure 29.3**). The two waves will also be in phase again when the second wave is two wavelengths behind the first, and so on.

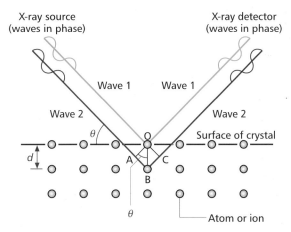

Figure 29.2 The Bragg condition

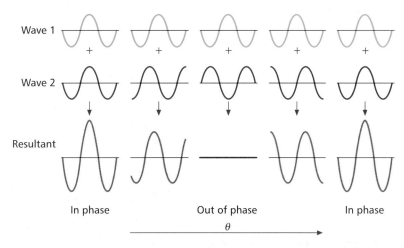

Figure 29.3 As we increase θ, wave 2 (reflected from the second layer of atoms) lags further and further behind wave 1 (reflected from the surface) until it is in phase with wave 1 again but one wavelength behind

So the X-rays are in phase when the path difference ABC $= n\lambda$, where n is a whole number and λ the wavelength of the X-rays.

In **Figure 29.4**, which shows triangles OAB and OBC from Figure 29.2:

$$\frac{AB}{OB} = \sin \theta$$

so

$$AB = OB \sin \theta$$
$$AB = d \sin \theta$$

where d is the spacing between the atoms

As triangles OBC and OAB are congruent (they have the same shape and size):

$$\text{distance ABC} = 2d \sin \theta$$

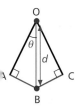

Figure 29.4 Triangles OAB and OBC, redrawn from Figure 29.2

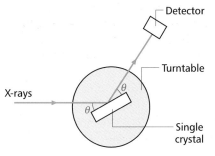

Figure 29.5 Apparatus for single crystal X-ray diffraction

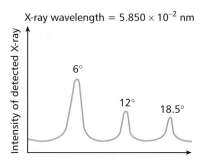

Figure 29.6 Trace obtained from single crystal X-ray diffraction of sodium chloride

Q Calculate the interionic distance, *d*, for *n* = 3.

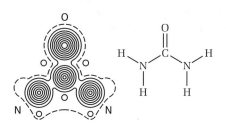

Figure 29.7 Electron density contour map of urea (carbamide), compared with its formula. The positions of the carbon, nitrogen and oxygen atoms (but not the hydrogens) can be clearly seen

Answer: *d* = 0.277 nm

And for the X-rays to be in phase:

$$n\lambda = 2d \sin \theta$$

This relationship is called the **Bragg condition** after the father and son who pioneered X-ray diffraction. It means that if we know the wavelength of the X-rays we are using and can measure the angle at which we get the maximum X-ray signal, we can calculate *d*, the distance between the atoms in the crystal. We may get more than one angle where constructive interference occurs when the 'lag' is 1, 2, or 3 wavelengths, i.e. *n* = 1, 2 or 3.

The X-rays are produced by bombarding a metal target with electrons as described in the box 'Atomic number' in Chapter 7. Detectors include photographic film or a Geiger–Müller tube.

The single crystal method

In this method a single crystal is mounted on a rotating stand, as shown in **Figure 29.5**, and a beam of X-rays is directed at its face. The crystal is rotated along with the detector and the intensity of the reflected beam is measured at different angles.

A trace is obtained like the one shown in **Figure 29.6** for sodium chloride. The three peaks correspond to *n* = 1, *n* = 2, *n* = 3.

$$n\lambda = 2d \sin \theta$$

$$d = \frac{n\lambda}{2 \sin \theta}$$

For *n* = 1, $$d = \frac{1 \times 5.850 \times 10^{-2}}{2 \times 0.1045}$$

$$d = 0.280 \text{ nm}$$

Similarly for *n* = 2, we find:

$$d = 0.281 \text{ nm}$$

The average of the three gives the distance between the ions as 0.279 nm. This is the distance between the centres of the ions, their nuclei.

Electron density maps

More complex techniques than the single crystal method allow us to find the positions of atoms in molecular structures. X-rays are actually diffracted by the *electrons* in atoms. So, one way of presenting the results is as an electron density map, where contours joining positions of equal electron density (electrons per cubic nanometre) represent the electron distribution. An example is shown in **Figure 29.7**.

Electron diffraction

Since hydrogen atoms have only one electron, they are not pinpointed very well by X-ray diffraction. However, a complementary technique – electron diffraction, which uses a beam of electrons rather than X-rays, can locate hydrogen atoms more accurately. It is used with molecules in the gas phase while X-ray diffraction requires solid samples.

Sizes of atoms and ions

X-ray diffraction can measure the distance between the centres of adjacent atoms in a structure. It cannot measure from the centre of an atom to its edge as it not obvious where the atom stops. Look

ngle crystal X-ray diffraction apparatus

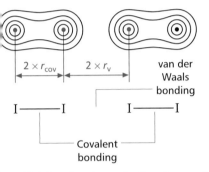

$2 \times r_{cov}$ $2 \times r_v$ van der Waals bonding

I———I   I———I

Covalent bonding

gure 29.8 Part of an electron density contour map for lid iodine

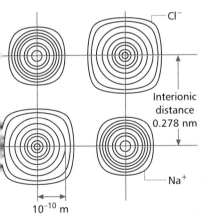

Cl⁻

Interionic distance 0.278 nm

Na⁺

10^{-10} m

gure 29.9 Electron density contour map for sodium loride

again at the electron density map of urea, Figure 29.7. It is clear where the centres of the atoms are but not where their edges are. In this respect atoms are more like party balloons than billiard balls. They are squashy rather than hard. This has implications for the measurement of the radii of atoms and ions.

Metallic radius, r_m

The metallic radius is defined as half the distance between the centres of adjacent atoms in a metallic giant structure.

Covalent radius, r_{cov}

This is defined as half the distance between the centres of adjacent atoms which are held together by a single covalent bond.

The van der Waals radius, r_v

In the electron density map of solid iodine (**Figure 29.8**), there are two I–I distances. The smaller is between a pair of covalently bonded atoms and represents twice the covalent radius. The larger is between two iodine atoms in different molecules. These are not covalently bonded but held close together by van der Waals forces (see section 10.1). Half this distance is called the van der Waals radius. Since van der Waals bonding is weaker than covalent bonding, the atoms are less closely held together and the van der Waals radius is larger than the covalent radius, e.g. for iodine:

$$r_{cov} = 0.128 \text{ nm}$$
$$r_v = 0.177 \text{ nm}$$

Ionic radius, r_i

Here the situation is trickier. Look at the electron density map for sodium chloride (**Figure 29.9**). It is easy to measure the interionic distance (from the centre of Na^+ to the centre of Cl^-), but it is not easy to see where the Na^+ stops and the Cl^- starts. Since the two ions are different, we cannot just halve the interionic distance. The procedure is to make an intelligent guess at the radius of one ion, and then this effectively fixes all the other ionic radii. For example, if we give K^+ the value of 0.137 nm then, since the interionic distance in K^+Cl^- is 0.314 nm, the radius of Cl^- must be 0.177 nm. Then, since the interionic distance in Na^+Cl^- is 0.278 nm, the ionic radius of Na^+ must be 0.101 nm and so on. Because of this element of guesswork there is often discrepancy between ionic radii given in different data books.

29.2 Structure determination of molecular substances

X-ray diffraction can be used to find the structures of molecular substances in the solid state. For example, we have seen the electron density maps of urea, $CO(NH_2)_2$, and iodine, I_2, in the previous section. It is the best method of finding the shape, bond lengths and bond angles of molecules. However, we can often deduce a good deal about a molecule's structure without resorting to X-ray diffraction.

Some values of atomic and ionic sizes

(All radii in nm)

	r_v	r_{cov}	r_i	r_m
I	0.195	0.133	0.215	–
Br	0.190	0.114	0.195	–
Cl	0.180	0.099	0.180	–
Li	0.180	0.134	0.074	0.157
Na	0.230	0.154	0.102	0.191
K	0.280	0.196	0.138	0.235

Note:

- The size increases on going down a group.
- The van der Waals radius is greater than the covalent radius or the metallic radius.
- Forming negative ions *increases* the size of the atom.
- Forming positive ions *decreases* the size of the atom.

> Propene also has the empirical formula CH_2 and has a relative molecular mass of 42. What is its molecular formula?

Formulae

First we need to know the formula of the substance under investigation. This requires **qualitative analysis** to find what elements are present and **quantitative analysis** to find the masses of each. This will give us the simplest ratio of the number of moles of each element present – the **empirical formula**. For example, ethene has an empirical formula of CH_2.

However, this could represent several different molecules: CH_2, C_2H_4, C_3H_6 ...$(CH_2)_n$. To decide which is correct, we need to know the relative molecular mass, M_r. A variety of techniques is available for this, including gas volume measurement (section 27.2), and mass spectrometry (section 7.4). The best technique is mass spectrometry because it is the most accurate. Ethene is found to have a relative molecular mass of 28, twice that of the empirical formula CH_2, so the molecule must contain two units, i.e. it is C_2H_4. This is called the **molecular formula.** It shows the number and type of atoms in the actual molecule. It is always a multiple of the empirical formula.

Chemical reactivity

This may give clues to the structure. For example, ethene decolourises a solution of bromine. This test reveals that ethene has a carbon–carbon double bond (C=C). You may have used Benedict's test to identify a reducing sugar like glucose. In fact the test specifically indicates

the present of an aldehyde group $\left(-C \begin{smallmatrix} \displaystyle // O \\ \displaystyle \backslash \\ H \end{smallmatrix} \right)$ in the molecule

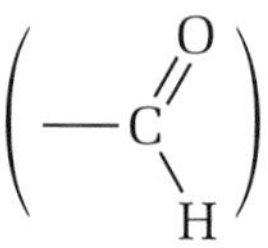

(see section 33.4). There are many examples of specific reactions that show the presence of particular features in molecules, many of which are described in Chapter 38. Other simple clues include acidity, and solubility in water, which may indicate whether or not there are polar groups.

Infra-red (IR) spectroscopy

This is an instrumental method that can be used to identify particular groups of atoms. It depends on the fact that molecules or parts of molecules can vibrate. In fact a molecule behaves as though the atoms were masses connected by springs (representing the bonds). For example, a water molecule can vibrate in three ways (**Figure 29.10**).

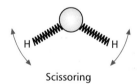

Scissoring

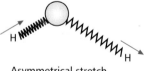

Asymmetrical stretch

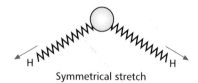

Symmetrical stretch

Figure 29.10 The three types of vibration of a water molecule

Answer: C_3H_6

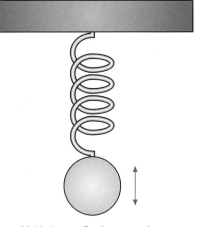

Molecules with many atoms can have very complex vibrations. We will concentrate on vibrations involving just two atoms. The frequency of vibration (number of vibrations per second) depends on the masses of the atoms and the strength of the bond.

Imagine a ball of Plasticine vibrating on a spring (**Figure 29.11**). The more massive the Plasticine, the lower the frequency, and the stiffer the spring the higher the frequency. The same is true of atoms: stronger bonds behave like stiffer springs. So a particular type of bond between a certain pair of atoms will have a characteristic frequency of vibration. Like all molecular energy, this vibration is **quantised** (its amplitude can only have discrete values). A particular bond can only absorb quanta of energy of its own characteristic frequency. When it has done so it vibrates with a greater amplitude (the atoms move more). This is like a child on a swing being pushed by its mother (see the photograph). The child can only pick up energy and swing further if the mother times her pushes at exactly the frequency of the swing – always pushing as the swing is moving away from her.

The frequencies of molecular vibrations fall in the region of the electromagnetic spectrum called **infra-red**, which we feel as heat radiation. If we shine a beam of infra-red radiation through a substance, only those frequencies which correspond to the frequencies of bonds in the substance will be absorbed. The rest will pass through. The beam will then have less energy, at those frequencies, than it started with. Only vibrations which result in a change in dipole moment will actually absorb infra-red energy. So we can find the bonds present in a particular substance by comparing the infra-red frequencies that are absorbed with the known frequencies of particular bonds (see **Figure 29.12**).

There are two types of infra-red spectrophotometer: double beam ones and the more modern Fourier transfer instruments.

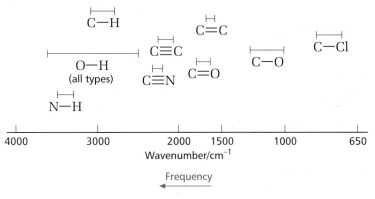

Figure 29.12 The frequencies (wavenumbers) at which some bonds absorb infra-red. The exact frequency depends on a number of factors including the details of the rest of the molecule

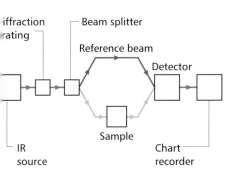

The double beam infra-red spectrophotometer

The principle of the double beam instrument is shown in **Figure 29.13**. A source of infra-red radiation (rather like a tiny electric bar heater) produces infra-red of a spread of frequencies. The diffraction grating splits this up into separate frequencies, just as a prism separates light into its separate colours. By rotating the grating, infra-red of different frequencies passes into the beam splitter. This produces two beams, one of which passes through the sample while

FURTHER FOCUS

Infra-red active and inactive vibrations

Not all vibrations of molecules will absorb infra-red radiation. To absorb infra-red, a molecule must first have a dipole (see section 9.1), because this allows it to interact with the electromagnetic radiation. So, molecules such as CO (C≡O) and HF (H—F), which have a dipole, absorb infra-red radiation, whereas N_2 and H_2, which have no dipole (because both atoms are the same), do not.

$$N\equiv N \quad H-H \quad \overset{\delta+}{C}\equiv\overset{\delta-}{O} \quad \overset{\delta+}{H}-\overset{\delta-}{F}$$

Secondly, only vibrations in which the dipole moment *changes* will absorb infra-red. Think about the symmetrical stretching vibrations of the molecules carbon dioxide, CO_2, which is linear, and sulphur dioxide, SO_2, which is angular.

This particular vibration does not change the dipole moment of the CO_2 molecule, since both the dipoles cancel, so this vibration of CO_2 does not absorb infra-red. In the case of SO_2, the symmetrical stretching vibration *does* change the dipole moment because the S atom gets further away from the two O atoms and the two dipoles do not cancel.

The asymmetrical stretching and bending vibrations of CO_2 *do* absorb infra-red as the dipole moment does change in each case.

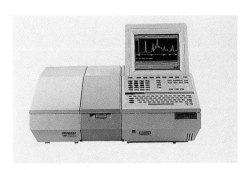

Asymmetrical stretch   Bending

> **Q** What is the purpose of the reference beam?

Answer: As a control, to allow for infra-red which may be absorbed by molecules in the air and by the sample cell.

An infra-red spectrophotometer

the other is a reference beam. The detector compares the intensities of the two beams and sends a signal proportional to the difference between them to a chart recorder. This produces a graph of **transmission** (the percentage of radiation that passes through the sample) against **frequency** of the radiation. In practice, a quantity called **wavenumber** is plotted on this axis in cm^{-1}. Wavenumber is proportional to frequency, ν. In fact wavenumber is the reciprocal of the wavelength, λ.

$$\text{wavenumber} = 1/\lambda$$

Fourier transform infra-red

An alternative to scanning through the wavelengths is to shine a beam of infra-red radiation containing all of the relevant wavelengths through the sample. This is then compared with a reference beam, and a computer constructs the spectrum from the differences between the two beams. This method is much quicker than conventional scanning.

A typical infra-red spectrum is shown in **Figure 29.14**.

High values of transmission of, say, over 90%, mean that the sample is absorbing little or no energy. *Dips* in the graph mean that energy is being absorbed. Confusingly these dips are often referred to as 'peaks'. The wavenumbers at which particular bonds absorb are given in Figure 29.12. Notice that C—Cl absorbs at a lower frequency than C—O, as the chlorine atom is more massive than oxygen, but C=O absorbs at a higher frequency than C—O because the bond is stiffer. The absorptions are given as *bands* of frequencies, as the same bond will absorb at a slightly different frequency in different molecules. It is rarely possible to correlate every peak in an infra-red spectrum with a particular molecular vibration, but usually specific bonds can be identified.

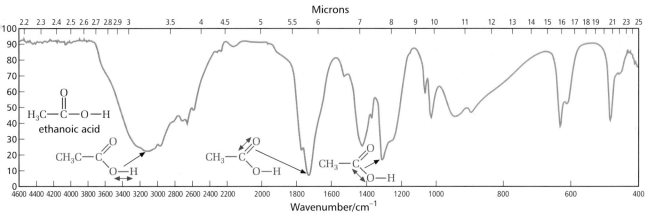

Figure 29.14 The infra-red spectrum of ethanoic acid

Hint: It is worth learning a few IR wavenumbers. $C{=}O \approx 1700$ cm^{-1}, $O{-}H \approx 3100$ cm^{-1}, $C{-}O \approx 1200$ cm^{-1}.

If Figure 29.14 was a spectrum of an unknown compound, we could say that it had $C{=}O$, $C{-}O$ and $O{-}H$ bonds present in it – valuable clues to its structure.

The fingerprint region

The area of an infra-red spectrum between about 1400 cm^{-1} and 900 cm^{-1} usually has many peaks. These often correspond to complex vibrations of the whole molecule and cannot easily be assigned to any particular vibration. However, the shape of this region is unique for any particular substance and can be used to identify it by comparison with a known spectrum, just as people can be identified by their fingerprints. This region is therefore called the fingerprint region.

Mass spectrometry

The principles of this technique were described in section 7.4, where we saw how it was used to measure relative atomic masses of isotopes. When used with compounds, it can give much more information than just the relative molecular mass.

Fragmentation

During their time of flight through the mass spectrometer, many of the ionised molecules will break up, i.e. **fragment**, as their bonds have been weakened by the loss of an electron and they have been given extra energy in the collision which generated the ion. These fragments give clues to the structure of the original molecules. Usually a few molecules remain intact to give a peak at the relative molecular mass of the compound. This is called the **molecular ion** or **parent ion**.

Hint: Don't confuse the *molecular ion peak* (the one of highest mass) with the tallest peak in the spectrum, often called the *base peak*.

An example of the information provided by mass spectra is illustrated by the spectra of butane and its isomer methylpropane (same molecular formular C_4H_{10}, but different structure). See **Figure 29.15**.

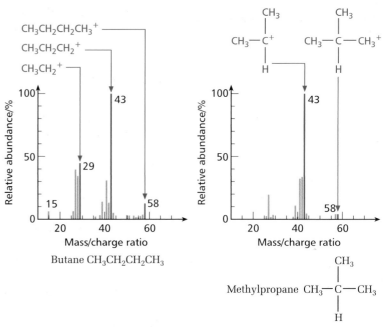

Figure 29.15 Mass spectra of butane and methylpropane

In $CH_3CH_2CH_2CH_3^+$, would it make any difference if the blue bond broke?

Butane,

H—C—C—C—C—H , shows the following main peaks:

$M_r = 58$ molecular ion, $CH_3CH_2CH_2CH_3^+$ and

$M_r = 43$ $CH_3CH_2CH_2^+$ H—C—C—C—C—H formed when the

red bond breaks, and

$M_r = 29$ $CH_3CH_2^+$ H—C—C—C—C—H   formed when the

green bond breaks.

Methylpropane, CH_3—C—CH_3 , shows the following main peaks:

$M_r = 58$ molecular ion, $CH_3CH(CH_3)CH_3^+$, and

$M_r = 43$ H—C—C—C—H   formed when any one of the red bonds breaks.

Answer: No, because the same two fragments are formed.

Hint: It is often difficult to assign all the peaks in a mass spectrum.

Hint: It is the mass peak at lower mass that is three times taller than the other isotope peak.

Q What parent ions would be present in the molecule dichloromethane, CH_2Cl_2?

Hint: The parent ion from chloroethane does *not* have mass 64.5!

But there is **no** peak at $M_r = 29$, as it is not possible to get a fragment of $M_r = 29$ by breaking just one bond in this molecule. So we can distinguish between two very similar molecules.

Isotope peaks

The mass spectrometer is able to detect isotopes separately, so, if an element with more than one common isotope is present, these will be detected. For example, chlorine has two isotopes, ^{35}Cl and ^{37}Cl, which are present in the ratio $^{35}Cl : {}^{37}Cl = 3 : 1$. So any molecule or fragments containing chlorine will give rise to two peaks, separated by two mass numbers and with heights in the ratio $3 : 1$. If you spot this feature in a mass spectrum, it is almost certain that chlorine is present.

The spectrum of chloroethane (**Figure 29.16**) illustrates this. The peaks at mass 64 and 66 are both molecular ion peaks: $CH_3CH_2{}^{35}Cl^+$ and $CH_3CH_2{}^{37}Cl^+$ respectively. The peaks at mass 49 and mass 51 are also in an approximate 3 : 1 ratio. These represent loss of a CH_3 group (mass = 15), leaving $CH_2{}^{35}Cl^+$ and $CH_2{}^{37}Cl^+$.

Satellite peaks

Most elements have more than one isotope, although often one is by far the most abundant. Carbon, for example, has ^{12}C (abundance 98.9%) and tiny amounts of others, mostly ^{13}C. Thus each mass spectrum peak for a carbon compound will have smaller peaks of higher mass close to it. These are often called **satellite peaks.** For example, ethane C_2H_6 will have peaks at 30 corresponding to $^{12}CH_3{}^{12}CH_3$, 31 corresponding to $^{12}CH_3{}^{13}CH_3$ and even 32 corresponding to $^{13}CH_3{}^{13}CH_3$. As there are also isotopes of hydrogen to consider, many combinations are possible. It is usually best to ignore these for simple interpretation of spectra.

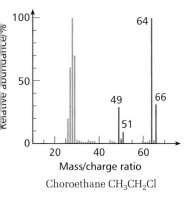

Figure 29.16 The mass spectrum of chloroethane. The chlorine-containing peaks are marked in red

High resolution mass spectra

The mass spectra we have seen so far have given masses to the nearest whole number and are called low resolution. High resolution mass spectrometry measures masses to four or five decimal places. This enables us to distinguish between different combinations of atoms which could make up the same approximate relative atomic mass. Some accurate values of relative atomic masses are:

$$^{12}C = 12.000\ 00 \text{ (by definition)}$$
$$^{1}H = 1.007\ 82$$
$$^{14}N = 14.003\ 07$$
$$^{16}O = 15.994\ 92$$

A compound whose relative molecular mass = 123 (low resolution, to the nearest whole number) could have the formula $C_6H_5NO_2$ or $C_7H_7O_2$, or a number of other possibilities. The accurate values of relative molecular masses of these two possibilities are:

$$C_6H_5NO_2 = 123.0320$$
$$C_7H_7O_2 = 123.0446$$

High resolution mass spectrometry could easily decide between these possibilities.

To save time, tables of relative molecular masses are available, which give all the possible formulae that give rise to any whole number value of relative molecular mass. The exact value of relative molecular mass for each formula is given. So if we know the exact relative molecular mass we can find the formula.

Answer: 84 ($CH_3{}^{35}Cl{}^{35}Cl$), 86 ($CH_3{}^{35}Cl{}^{37}Cl$) and 88 ($CH_3{}^{37}Cl{}^{37}Cl$).

FURTHER FOCUS

'*M* + 1' peaks

In any sample of naturally occurring carbon, about 1% of the atoms will be ^{13}C. This means that in the mass spectrum of, say, methane, CH_4, there will be a parent ion at mass 16 corresponding to $^{12}CH_4$ and another at mass 17 corresponding to $^{13}CH_4$. The second peak, called the $M + 1$ peak, will be 1% of the height of the former. In a molecule containing two carbon atoms, there are two chances of the

molecule containing one ^{13}C atom, so the $M + 1$ peak will be twice as high, 2% of the height of the main parent ion peak. In general if a molecule has n carbon atoms, there will be an $M + 1$ peak of height n% of the height of the main parent ion peak. This is a useful way to find the number of carbon atoms in a molecule.

> **Q** The mass spectrum of an unknown carbon compound has a parent ion at mass 72, height 48 units and an $M + 1$ peak of height 2.9 units. How many carbons does it have?
>
> *Answer:*　6

Nuclear magnetic resonance (NMR) spectroscopy

Many nuclei with odd mass numbers, such as ^1H, ^{13}C, ^{15}N, ^{19}F and ^{31}P have the property of *spin* (as do electrons). This gives them a magnetic field like that of a bar magnet.

If magnets are placed in a magnetic field, they will line up parallel to the field as shown in **Figure 29.17(a)**.

It is also possible that they could line up anti-parallel to the field, as in **Figure 29.17(b)**, but this has a higher energy, as the magnets have to be forced into that position against the repulsion of the field. They can only stay in that position if undisturbed.

The same applies to nuclei with spin, such as hydrogen. They will line up in a magnetic field in the low energy position. However, if energy quanta just equal to the difference between the two positions (ΔE in **Figure 29.18**) are supplied, a few nuclei will 'flip' into the higher energy position. The size of the energy gap, ΔE, depends on the magnetic field strength and corresponds to electromagnetic radiation in the radio region of the spectrum. This is the basis of NMR spectroscopy.

Different magnetic nuclei have different energy gaps for the same magnetic field. Here we will discuss only ^1H (or proton) NMR.

Hint: ^1H NMR is often called proton NMR as it is the hydrogen nuclei (protons) which are involved.

Hint: Remember that frequency, ν, and energy are linked by the equation $\Delta E = h\nu$

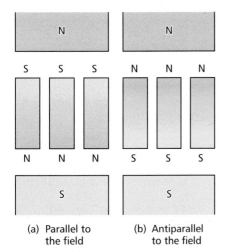

(a) Parallel to the field

(b) Antiparallel to the field

Figure 29.17 The two possible orientations of bar magnets in a magnetic field

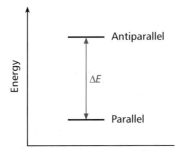

Figure 29.18 Energy level diagram of the two orientations of bar magnets in a magnetic field

The apparatus is shown in **Figure 29.19**. The sample containing hydrogen atoms is placed in a magnetic field, and radio waves are directed at it. When the frequency corresponds to quanta of energy ΔE, the sample absorbs some of the radio waves. In modern instruments we direct pulses containing a range of frequencies and the detector records the changes in the signal.

If all the hydrogen nuclei were identical, we should get only one position of absorption. However, nuclei are **shielded** from the external magnetic field by their electrons. Nuclei with more electrons around them are better shielded, so hydrogen atoms in different chemical environments will absorb the radio waves at different magnetic fields. The greater the electron density around a hydrogen atom, the higher the field that is required for the nucleus to 'flip'. So for methanol we get the NMR spectrum shown in **Figure 29.20**.

The single hydrogen atom attached to the oxygen has a low electron density around it because it is attached directly to an electronegative atom. It has little shielding and therefore needs a relatively low field to 'flip'. The three hydrogens attached to the less electronegative carbon atom are shielded better by their electrons and need a higher field to 'flip'. The areas under the peaks are proportional to the number of hydrogen atoms of each type. The magnetic field at which the peak representing each type of proton appears tells us about its environment.

The NMR spectrum of ethanol is shown in **Figure 29.21**.

This shows hydrogen atoms in *three* environments with different shielding. The single one at low magnetic field (with little shielding) represents the O—H hydrogen, the pair at a somewhat higher magnetic field (with somewhat more shielding) represent the —CH$_2$— hydrogens and the three at the highest magnetic field (with most shielding) are the —CH$_3$ hydrogens, which are furthest away from the electronegative oxygen.

NMR can therefore give information about the numbers of different types of hydrogen atoms in the molecule and where they are with respect to electronegative atoms.

For example we could predict that the NMR spectrum of propan-2-ol would have *three* peaks with areas in the ratios $1:1:6$ representing the hydrogen atoms labelled A, B and C. Hydrogen A attached to the oxygen, would have least shielding and therefore absorb energy at the lowest magnetic field, followed by hydrogen B and then the six equivalent hydrogens labelled C as they get further from the electronegative oxygen atom.

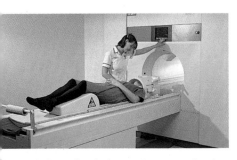

NMR is the basis of medical magnetic resonance imaging (MRI) scanners

Hint: Electronegative atoms pull electrons towards them.

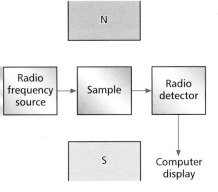

Figure 29.19 Schematic diagram of an NMR spectrometer

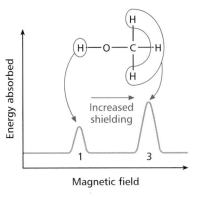

Figure 29.20 NMR spectrum of methanol (low resolution). Peak areas are in the ratio 1 : 3

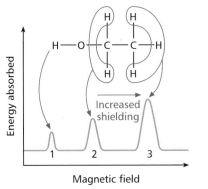

Figure 29.21 NMR spectrum of ethanol (low resolution)

(Propan-2-ol structure, centre right)

Chemical shift

In practice, the positions of the peaks in an NMR spectrum are always measured relative to the signal from a reference compound called tetramethylsilane (TMS) (see **Figure 29.22**). This is added to the sample before the spectrum is run. It has 12 identical hydrogens and produces a strong signal at a high magnetic field. The TMS

Table 29.2 Chemical shift values

Type of proton	Chemical shift/ppm
R—CH$_3$	0.9
R—CH$_2$—R	1.3
R$_3$CH	2.0
CH$_3$—C(=O)	2.0
OR R—C(=O)—CH$_3$	2.1
C$_6$H$_5$—CH$_3$	2.3
R—C≡C—H	2.6
R—CH$_2$—Hal	3.2–3.7
R—O—CH$_3$	3.8
R—O—H	4.5
RHC=CH$_2$	4.9
RHC=CH$_2$	5.9
C$_6$H$_5$—OH	7
C$_6$H$_5$—H	7.3
R—C(=O)—H	9.7
R—C(=O)—O—H	11.5

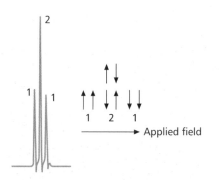

Figure 29.24 Spin–spin splitting by a pair of protons, which can line up as shown

signal is given a value of 0.0 and all the peaks in a normal spectrum are downfield (to the left) of TMS (see **Figure 29.23**). The distance of a peak from this signal is called its **chemical shift, δ**, and is measured in units of parts per million (ppm) of the applied field. Chemical shift values can be used to identify types of proton (see **Table 29.2**).

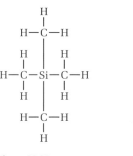

Figure 29.22
Tetramethylsilane (TMS) is added to NMR samples as an **internal standard**

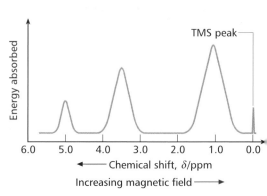

Figure 29.23 Low resolution NMR spectrum of ethanol

Spin–spin splitting.

If we run an NMR spectrum at a high resolution, we find that the peaks are often split into groups. The splitting is caused by the magnetic fields of other protons, close to the protons represented by the peak. This effect allows us to get more information about the environment of each proton in the molecule. The ethyl group, CH$_3$CH$_2$—, in bromoethane is a good example.

The CH$_3$— protons in an ethyl group will experience the magnetic field applied by the NMR spectrometer shielded by their electrons and therefore give a peak at about δ = 1.0 (see Table 29.2). However, this magnetic field will also be modified by the nearby protons of the —CH$_2$— group. Both these protons can line up *with* the applied field, strengthening it slightly, or both can line up *against* it, weakening it slightly or one can line up with and one against it, cancelling out their effects. This last possibility can come about in two ways (proton 1 with the applied field, proton 2 against and vice versa and so is twice as likely as either of the others (see **Figure 29.24**).

This has the effect of splitting the CH$_3$— peak into three smaller peaks (called a triplet) with areas in the ratio 1 : 2 : 1.

The —CH$_2$— protons in the ethyl group will experience the magnetic field applied by the NMR spectrometer shielded by their electrons. In bromoethane, the δ value is about 3.4. The field will also be affected by the nearby protons of the CH$_3$— group. These will add to or cancel part of the applied field depending on whether each CH$_3$— proton lines up with or against the applied field. There are four possibilities illustrated in **Figure 29.25**. The —CH$_2$— peak is therefore split into a quartet of peaks with areas in the ratio 1 : 3 : 3 : 1.

The high resolution spectrum of the ethyl group would look like **Figure 29.26**.

Splitting is caused by the protons adjacent to the one(s) causing the peak:

● One adjacent proton can line up with or against the field splitting a peak into two equal parts of the same height called a doublet.

Q Use the pattern to predict the height ratio of a peak split into a quintet? How many identical protons would you need to cause this?

Hint: For narrow peaks their heights are proportional to their areas.

- Two adjacent protons cause a threefold splitting of a peak to give a triplet of height ratio 1: 2 :1.
- Three adjacent protons split a peak into four to give a quartet of height ratio 1:3:3:1.

The rule is that n protons split an adjacent peak into $n + 1$.

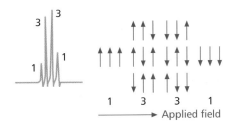

Figure 29.25 Spin–spin splitting by a trio of protons, which can line up as shown

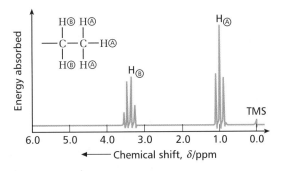

Figure 29.26 High resolution NMR spectrum of an ethyl group

Dipole moments

A chemical bond is polar if the two atoms concerned differ in electronegativity (see section 9.1). A molecule as a whole may have a dipole moment if the individual bond dipoles do not cancel out.

Dipole moments can give information about the shape of a molecule. For example, carbon dioxide, CO_2, has no dipole moment but sulphur dioxide, SO_2, has. This tells us that CO_2 must be linear so that the dipoles of each bond cancel out, while SO_2 must be angular.

Answer: 1:4:6:4:1. Four

Magnetic resonance imaging (MRI): seeing inside the body

Nuclear magnetic resonance is the basis of one of the latest types of body scanner. Magnetic nuclei inside different sorts of tissue will give different NMR signals. A computer is used to build up a picture of the part of the body the doctor is interested in. As it does not use potentially damaging X-rays, this technique has advantages over conventional scanners.

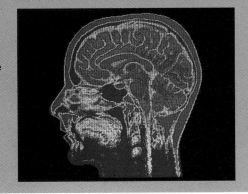

MRI of a patient's brain. The term NMR has been dropped because patients associate the word 'nuclear' with radioactivity

carbon dioxide   sulphur dioxide

Linear: the   Angular: the
dipoles of each   dipoles of each
bond cancel   bond do not cancel

Water, H_2O, has a dipole moment and so must be angular. Ammonia, NH_3, has a dipole moment and so cannot be a flat trigonal molecule or else the dipoles of the individual bonds would cancel. It must therefore be pyramidal.

Measurement of the values of dipole moments is not easy but it can be easy to find out if a molecule has a resultant dipole. A stream of a liquid whose molecules have a dipole will be deflected by a charged rod (see section 9.1 and the photograph on page 95).

CHEMISTRY AROUND US

The structure and activity of drugs

The first drugs were discovered more or less by chance, and theories as to how they operated would be regarded as fanciful today. For example, aspirin was first extracted from willow bark. It was thought that the cure to a condition would be found close to the cause of the condition. So willow trees, which are found in damp places, were expected to hold a cure for rheumatism, a condition associated with cold and damp. In this case the theory worked: aspirin is good at relieving the pain and inflammation of rheumatism.

Nowadays some drugs are still discovered by chance, but increasingly we are able to relate their activity to their structure and thus carry out research much more systematically. A good example is provided by the sulphonamides, a group of antibacterial drugs. These are all related to the compound sulphanilamide:

sulphanilamide

The molecule *para*-aminobenzoic acid (PABA) is vital to most bacteria.

para-aminobenzoic acid (PABA)

They use it to synthesise folic acid, which is necessary for their metabolism. Sulphanilamide has a very similar structure to PABA so it competes with PABA in the process for making folic acid, but it cannot form folic acid because it is the wrong molecule. The bacterial cells thus stop growing and eventually die. Folic acid is equally important to human metabolism, but we absorb it from our food, rather than synthesise it, so sulphanilamide does not harm us.

A number of variations on the basic sulphanilamide, called sulphonamides, have been produced. For example:

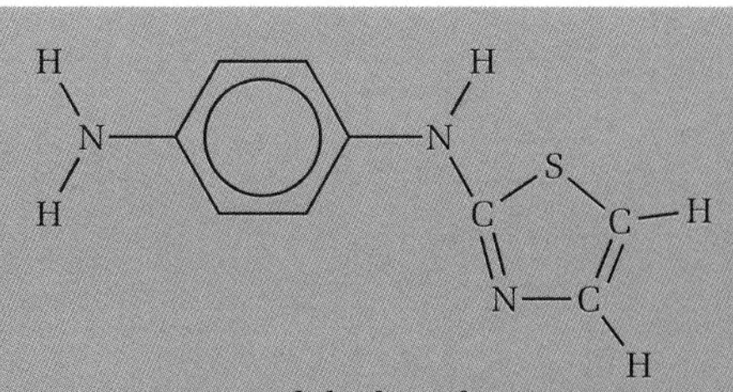

sulphathiazole

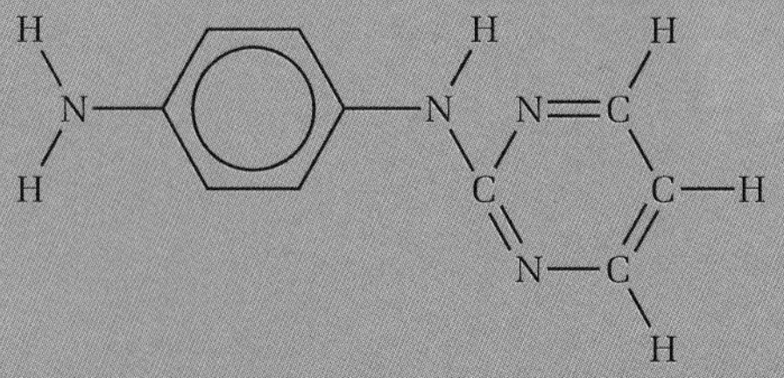

sulphadiazine

These all work in the same way because of their similarity in structure to PABA, but have different rates of absorption and excretion by the body, and different side effects. Over 5000 chemical variations of sulphonamides have been synthesised and tested.

This method, of synthesising closely related compounds to a substance which is known to have a therapeutic effect, is often used to discover new drugs. A good example is the group of narcotic pain relievers based on morphine. Morphine is probably the most effective painkiller known, but it is strongly addictive so that it must be used with great care. However, replacing the marked H atom by a CH_3— group produces codeine, a less potent drug but one safe enough to be bought without prescription. Heroin, even more addictive than morphine, also retains the same basic structure.

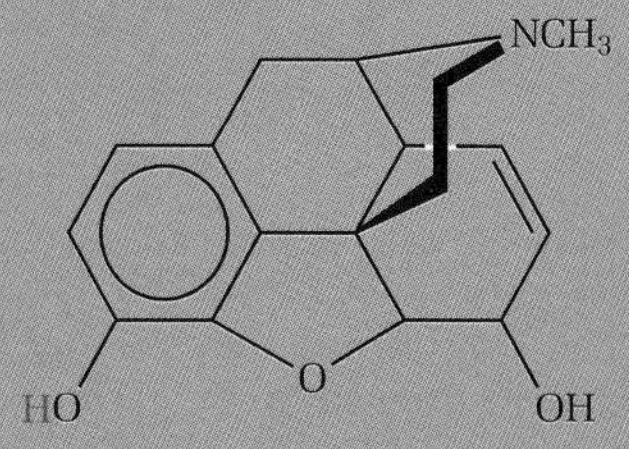

morphine

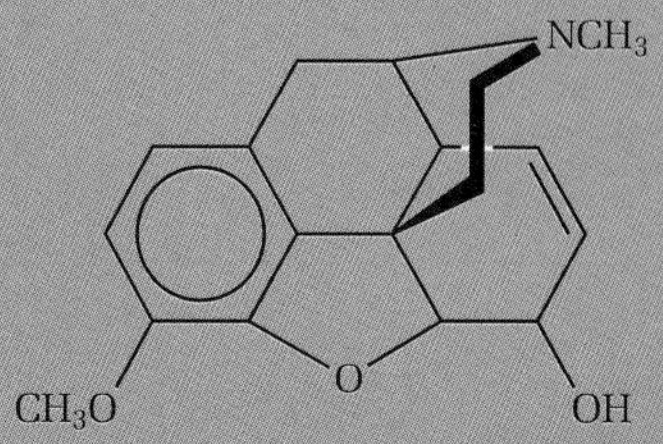

codeine

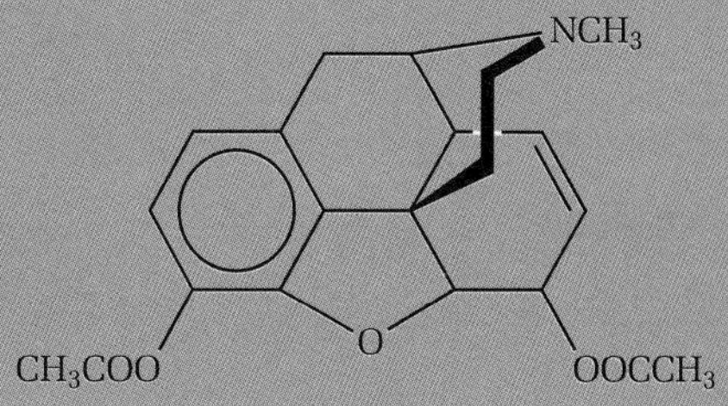

heroin

29.3 Summary

- X-rays have approximately the same wavelength as the spacing between atoms.

- The Bragg condition is $n\lambda = 2d \sin \theta$

  θ is the angle between the X-ray beam and the face of the crystal

  λ is the wavelength of the X-rays

  n is a whole number

  d is the spacing between the atoms

- **Figure 29.27** summarises the information obtained from a variety of techniques and how they contribute to the determination of the structure.

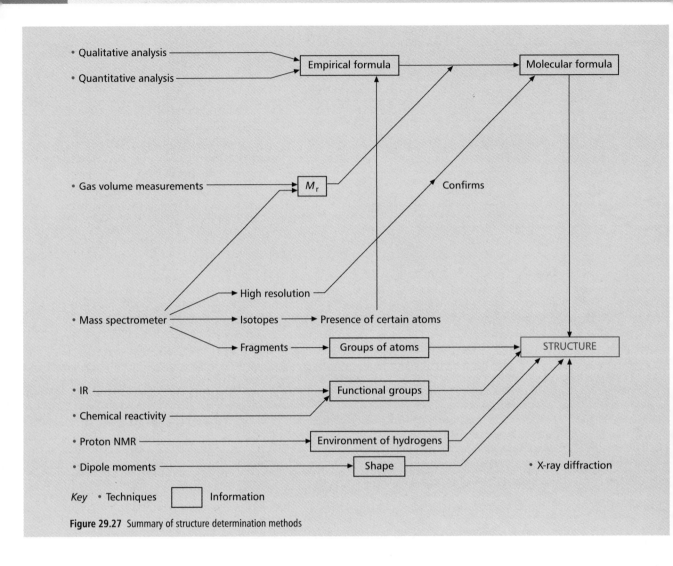

Figure 29.27 Summary of structure determination methods

29.4 Practice questions

1. Using the single crystal method of X-ray diffraction with potassium chloride, a strong X-ray signal was found at any angle of $5.25°$ to the surface of the crystal. If the wavelength of the X-rays was 0.0586 nm, what is the interionic distance in potassium chloride? At what angle would you expect to find the next strong X-ray signal? (Hint $n = 2$.)

2. The mass spectrum of a molecule X gives a molecular ion of $M_r = 60$ at low resolution. The following molecular formulae are possible.

$$C_3H_8O \qquad C_2H_8N_2 \qquad C_2H_4O_2$$

   (a) High resolution mass spectrometry gave M_r of X as 60.057. Use the list of exact A_r's below to calculate the exact masses of the molecular formulae above and then decide which one is X.

$$H = 1.007\ 82$$
$$C = 12.000\ 00$$
$$N = 14.003\ 07$$
$$O = 15.994\ 92$$

   (b) Can you find another molecular formula (using C, H, N and O only) which gives $M = 60$?

3. Explain the following in terms of molecular shape.
   (a) $BeCl_2$ has no dipole moment, but SCl_2 has.
   (b) BCl_3 has no dipole moment, but PCl_3 has.

4. The infra-red spectra of propane, propanal and propan-1-ol are given on the next page:
   (a) Using Figure 29.12 and the structures shown, suggest which bonds are causing the peaks at around 3000 cm^{-1} and 1600 cm^{-1}.

(b) Sketch the likely appearance of the IR spectrum of propanoic acid,

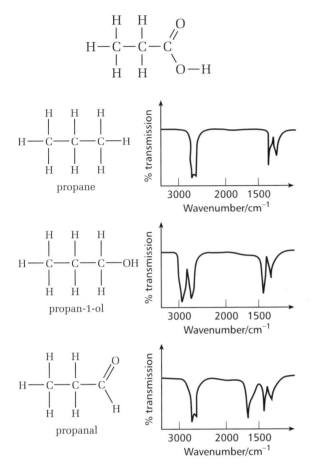

propane

propan-1-ol

propanal

(c) Sketch the probable low resolution NMR spectrum of each of the compounds above.

5. A compound Z contains carbon, hydrogen and oxygen only in the following percentages: C 54.5%, H 9.1%, O 36.4%. It gives a brick-red precipitate when heated with Benedict's solution.
(a) What is the empirical formula?
The mass, IR and NMR spectra are given below.

(b) Look at the mass spectrum. What is the most likely mass of the molecular ion? What formula does this give?
(c) 0.1 g of Z produced 51.3 cm³ of vapour converted to STP. Does this confirm the value of M_r given by the mass spectrum?
(d) Look at the IR spectrum. What does the peak at approx. 1700 cm^{-1} suggest? Is this confirmed by the result of the Benedict's test?
(e) Write down the probable structural formula of Z from the information used so far.
(f) How many types of protons does this structural formula have? Does this fit the observed NMR spectrum?
(g) Would you expect Z to have a dipole moment?

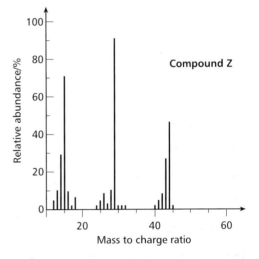

Compound Z

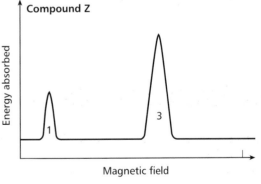

Compound Z

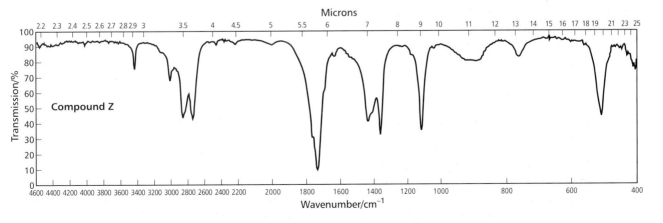

29.5 Examination questions

1. The mass spectrum of of 2-chloropropane is shown below.

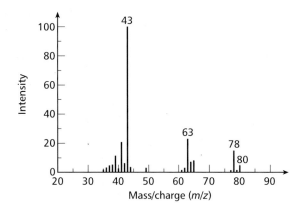

   (i) Why does the spectrum contain several peaks?
   (ii) Identify the species responsible for the peaks at m/z ratios 43, 63, 78, and 80.
   (ii) What information can be deduced from the relative intensity of the two peaks at m/z ratios 78 and 80?

   [Oxford 1997, part]

2. An organic compound **X** contains 82.75% carbon and 17.25% hydrogen by mass.
   (a) (i) Calculate the empirical formula of **X**.
       (ii) Deduce from the mass spectrum below the relative molecular mass of **X**, giving a reason for your choice. Hence show that the molecular formula of **X** is C_4H_{10}.

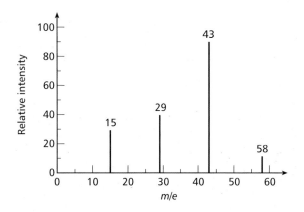

   (b) There are two possible structures **A** and **B** for this molecule:

   | A | B |

   (i) Identify the species responsible for the peaks in the mass spectrum at 43, 29 and 15.
   (ii) Hence deduce which of the structures **A** or **B** is present, giving a reason for your answer.
   (c) Complete combustion of **X** in oxygen gives carbon dioxide and water only.
   (i) Write an equation for this combustion reaction.
   (ii) Calculate the total volume of the gaseous mixture produced when 2 cm^3 of gaseous C_4H_{10} is mixed with 15 cm^3 of oxygen and completely burned. All volumes are measured at room temperature and pressure.

   [London 1997]

3. (a) A proton, a neutron and an electron all travelling at the same velocity enter a magnetic field. State which particle is deflected the most and explain your answer.
   (b) Give two reasons why particles must be ionised before being analysed in a mass spectrometer.
   (c) A sample of boron with a relative atomic mass of 10.8 gives a mass spectrum with two peaks, one at $m/z = 10$ and one at $m/z = 11$. Calculate the ratio of the heights of the two peaks.
   (d) Compound **X** contains only boron and hydrogen. The percentage by mass of boron in **X** is 81.2%. In the mass spectrum of **X** the peak at the largest value of m/z occurs at 54.
   (i) Use the percentage by mass data to calculate the empirical formula of **X**.
   (ii) Deduce the molecular formula of **X**.

   [NEAB 1998]

30

The p-block elements

C H E M I S T R Y   N O W

What's in a name: silicon, silicone, silica and silicates?

Silicon and its compounds have a large variety of uses and often come up in newspaper and magazine articles – about everything from computer chips to polish to breast implants. However, their names are often confused: one often reads of silic*on* breast implants, for example, when these are actually filled with silic*ones*. This may seem unimportant except for the fact that silic*on* is a hard, shiny, fairly brittle solid. Silicones, on the other hand, are a family of compounds which are colourless, viscous relatively unreactive liquids.

The chemical difference is that silic*on* is an element while silic*ones* are long chain molecules consisting of chains of silicon atoms and oxygen atoms each silicon having two side chains.

The compounds vary by having different chain lengths and different side chains.

A breast implant filled with silic*ones* …

Part of a silicone molecule

Silicon (the element) is the basis of the semiconductor chips that are at the heart of computer processors and other electronic devices. The silicones in breast implants are causing concern as a potential health risk.

Silica and silicates also contain both silicon and oxygen. Silica is an alternative name for silicon dioxide, SiO_2, while silicates are a family of ions containing silicon and oxygen (see the box 'Silicones' in this chapter). Silica is the major constituent of sand, and in glass making it is reacted with sodium carbonate to form sodium silicate.

… glass is made from silic*ates* …

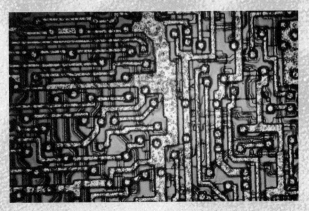
… and a chip made of silic*on*

Introduction

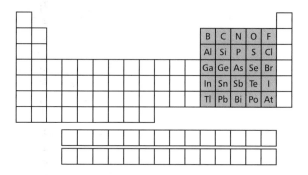

The p-block elements have relatively little in common except that their outer electrons are in p-orbitals (Figure 30.1). This contrasts with the considerable similarities in properties of the elements of the s-block and also between those of the d-block. The p-block is more notable for *trends* which are broadly as shown in Figure 30.2.

You may find it useful to relate the chemistry of each element to these trends.

We have covered the halogens in Chapter 17 and this chapter will concentrate on Groups IV, V and VI. The p-block contains several elements of great social and economic importance as well as chemical interest. Examples include the importance of silicon and germanium as semiconductors, and the use of sulphur, phosphorus and nitrogen in fertilisers.

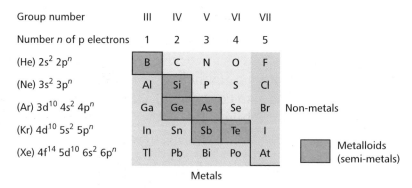

Figure 30.1 The p-block elements, showing electronic structures and the positions of metals, metalloids and non-metals

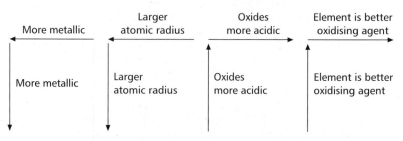

Figure 30.2 Some trends in properties within the p-block of the Periodic Table

30.1 Group IV

Introduction

The Group IV elements show very clearly the trend from non-metals through metalloids to metals on descending the group. The ionisation energies are so large that M^{4+} ions hardly ever form (only in lead fluorides) and the chemistry of the compounds is essentially covalent in the +IV oxidation state although there are some Sn^{2+} and Pb^{2+} compounds – a consequence of the **inert pair** effect in which the outer s electrons do not take part in bonding (see below). Carbon, of course, has the most extensive chemistry of any element. The details of this will be found in the organic chemistry section of this book. **Table 30.1** summarises some important properties.

Table 30.1 Properties of the elements in Group IV

	Atomic number, Z	Electron arrangement	Electro-negativity	Atomic (covalent) radius/nm	Density /g cm^{-3}	T_m/K	T_b/K
C	6	$1s^2 2s^2 2p^2$	2.5	0.077	2.25 (diamond)	3930	(sublimes)
					3.51 (graphite)		
Si	14	[Ne] $3s^2 3p^2$	1.8	0.118	2.33	1683	2628
Ge	32	[Ar] $3d^{10} 4s^2 4p^2$	1.8	0.122	5.35	1210	3103
Sn	50	[Kr] $4d^{10} 5s^2 5p^2$	1.8	0.140	7.28 (white)	505	2533
					5.79 (grey)		
Pb	82	[Xe] $4f^{14} 5d^{10} 6s^2 6p^2$	1.8	0.154	11.34	601	2013

CHEMISTRY AROUND US

Artificial diamonds

Both diamond and graphite are allotropes of carbon – the atoms are simply arranged differently. This raises the tantalising possibility of converting cheap graphite into valuable diamond. The phase diagram for carbon shows the conditions of temperature and pressure under which the different allotropes are stable. The line AB shows the conditions under which it might be possible to convert graphite into diamond. This conversion was first brought about in 1955 at around 2000 K and 5.5×10^9 Pa, and industrial diamonds used for drill bits are now made under conditions like these, using metal catalysts to speed up the conversion.

More recently chemists have tried another approach: growing diamonds by deposition of carbon atoms from the gas phase or from a solution of carbon in molten metals. A small seed crystal is used in the same way that, for example, large crystals of copper sulphate can be grown from a saturated solution. It is now possible to coat objects with diamond film. The potential applications of this are enormous: just some examples could be virtually

everlasting cutting surfaces on tools, totally scratch-resistant glass and wear-resistant bearings.

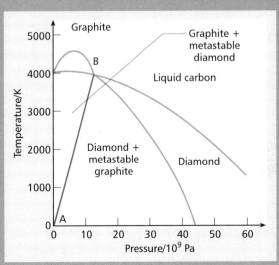

The physical properties of the elements

Carbon has two well-known allotropes – diamond and graphite – as well as some more recently discovered ones such as buckminsterfullerene (see 'Balls of carbon', Chapter 9). Diamond, silicon and germanium all have similar covalently bonded giant structures. As the atoms get larger, the E-E bonds (where E represents any of the elements in the group) become weaker, making the structure less hard and giving a lower melting point. (The bond energies are $C—C = 347\,kJ\,mol^{-1}$, $Si—Si = 226\,kJ\,mol^{-1}$, $Ge—Ge = 167\,kJ\,mol^{-1}$.) Both white tin and lead have giant metallic structures. Diamond is an electrical insulator, silicon and germanium are semiconductors while tin and lead are metallic conductors. Graphite's layer structure is described in 'Balls of carbon', Chapter 9. It conducts electricity to some extent.

Chemical reactivity of the elements

In general the elements are not particularly reactive. Overall, reactivity increases on descending the group. All the elements react directly with oxygen to form EO_2 except lead, which forms PbO. A similar pattern is found in the reaction with chlorine, ECl_4 being formed in every case except for lead which forms $PbCl_2$. These examples illustrate the general trend that the stability of the $+IV$ oxidation state decreases on descending the group while that of the $+II$ state increases.

In carbon, the $+II$ state is very unstable, carbon monoxide, ^{II}CO, reacting rapidly to form carbon dioxide, $^{IV}CO_2$, for example:

$$3CO(g) + Fe_2O_3(s) \longrightarrow 2Fe(s) + 3CO_2(g)$$

So carbon monoxide is a good reducing agent.

> **Q** How can you tell that carbon monoxide is acting as a reducing agent in this reaction?

Answer: The oxidation number of iron is reduced from $+III$ to 0, (or oxygen is removed from the iron).

Conduction of electricity by graphite

The layer structure of graphite is described in 'Balls of carbon', Chapter 9. Each carbon forms σ bonds in a plane at 120° to one another. The 'spare' p orbitals overlap above and below this to form a π orbital which spreads over the whole layer. Electrons can move freely within this orbital and so graphite conducts electricity well in the directions along the planes. Recently a number of electrically conducting polymers have been made. One of the simplest is poly(ethyne). This, like graphite, has a π orbital which spreads along the whole molecule, so making it conduct. Here the orbital is linear rather than a two-dimensional plane, so the molecule conducts along its length.

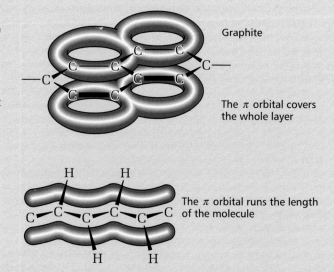

Graphite

The π orbital covers the whole layer

The π orbital runs the length of the molecule

poly(ethyne)

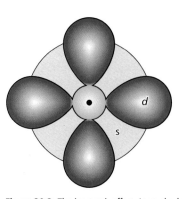

Figure 30.3 The inert pair effect. Inner d orbitals (and f orbitals) do not shield the outer s electrons very effectively. These outer s electrons ('the inert pair') are therefore more strongly attracted to the nucleus and are less available to take part in bonding

Table 30.2 Bond energies in compounds of carbon and silicon

Bond	energy/kJ mol^{-1}	Bond	energy/kJ mol^{-1}
C—C	347	Si—Si	226
C—H	413	Si—H	318
C—O	358	Si—O	466

In the case of lead, PbO is more stable that PbO_2, so that PbO_2 is a good oxidising agent, oxidising Cl^- to Cl_2, for example:

$$PbO_2(s) + 4HCl(aq) \longrightarrow PbCl_2(aq) + Cl_2(g) + 2H_2O(l)$$

The increased stability of the +II oxidation state lower down the group is a consequence of the **inert pair** effect. The two s electrons are less likely to be involved in bonding lower down the group. This effect also occurs in Groups III and IV. The reason is that inner d and f orbitals, because of their shape, do not shield outer electrons as effectively as s and p orbitals. Therefore in atoms with such inner electrons (those in Periods 4, 5 and 6), the outer s electrons are pulled more strongly towards the nucleus and are less available to take part in bonding, as shown in **Figure 30.3**.

The uniqueness of carbon

Carbon has a unique ability to form compounds. At present over ten million are known. The main reason for this is carbon's ability to form chains and rings of atoms. This property is sometimes called **catenation**. This ability is unparalleled, even among the other members of Group IV. Silicon and germanium form chains, but only to a very limited extent. Why? Part of the answer lies in bond energies (**Table 30.2**).

Notice that the bond energies of C—C and C—O are of comparable value, while for silicon, the Si—Si bond is much weaker than Si—O, so that thermodynamically, Si—Si bonds will not be stable in the presence of oxygen, and Si—O bonds will be more favoured than Si—Si bonds. Silicon forms many compounds with —Si—O—Si—O— chains as in silicon dioxide and silicone polymers.

The second factor is kinetic. Part of the reason for the kinetic stability of carbon compounds is that all the low energy orbitals of the carbon atoms are filled once the compound is formed, so that they are not available to form bonds with attacking molecules. The first step in the formation of a new compound is often the temporary filling of an unoccupied orbital. In carbon there is a large energy gap between the highest-energy filled orbital (2p) and the next unfilled orbital (3s). This energy must be supplied if an attacking molecule is to form a bond. By contrast, in silicon, empty 3d orbitals are available at only a slightly higher energy than the filled orbitals (3p), so carbon compounds would have a higher activation energy than comparable silicon compounds for oxidation or reaction with, for example, water. This explains their kinetic stability. **Figure 30.4** shows the situation for CH_4 and SiH_4, but it is the same for more complex hydrides.

Thirdly, carbon forms many compounds with multiple bonds – C=C and C≡C. These involve overlap of p orbitals to form π bonds. Silicon atoms are larger than carbon and cannot approach closely enough to allow efficient overlap of p orbitals to form a π bond. So carbon can form stable chains and rings held together by strong carbon–carbon bonds, both single and multiple. Such molecules are kinetically stable.

Group IV compounds
Hydrides

Carbon forms a vast number of hydrides with rings, chains of unlimited length and varying degrees of branching. They are called alkanes if they have no multiple bonds, alkenes if they have one or

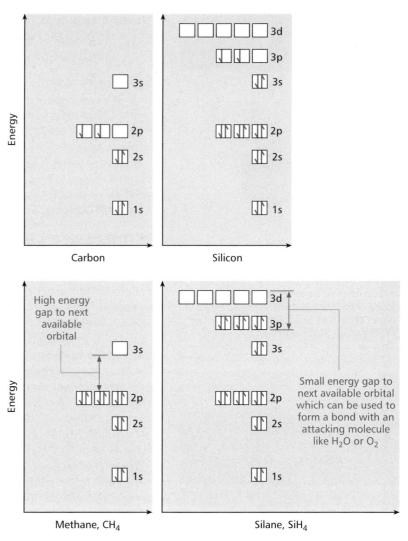

Figure 30.4 Energy levels of orbitals in carbon, silicon, methane (CH_4) and silane (SiH_4)

more double bonds and alkynes if they have a triple bond, C≡C. They are considered in detail in Chapters 19 and 20. They are stable in air except at high temperatures and do not react with water, acids or alkalis. They are gases, liquids or solids at room temperature depending on the chain length.

Silicon forms a series of hydrides called silanes of chain length up to ten silicon atoms, including some with branched chains. They are gases or volatile liquids. They burn on contact with air and are rapidly hydrolysed by water for the reasons discussed above. For example:

$$SiH_4(g) + 2O_2(g) \longrightarrow SiO_2(s) + 2H_2O(l)$$
monosilane   oxygen   silicon dioxide   water

$$Si_2H_6(g) + 4H_2O(g) \longrightarrow 2SiO_2(s) + 7H_2(g)$$
disilane   water   silicon dioxide   hydrogen

Germanium forms hydrides called germanes of chain length up to six. They behave in the same way as the silanes. Tin and lead form only a single hydride each, stannane, SnH_4, and plumbane, PbH_4. Both are unstable. The tendency to shorter chains reflects the decreasing E—E bond strength on descending the group.

Answer: The shared electrons of the bond are further
from the nuclei of the bonded atoms.

Halides

Carbon forms halides, CX_4, with all the halogens, and chain halides can also form. They are all stable in air and water, especially the fluorocarbons such as poly(tetrafluoroethene), ptfe, trade name Teflon,

$$
\begin{array}{ccccc}
 & F & F & F & F \\
 & | & | & | & | \\
-\!\!\!\! & C & \!\!\!-\!\!\! C & \!\!\!-\!\!\! C & \!\!\!-\!\!\! C \!\!\!\!-\!\!\!\! \\
 & | & | & | & | \\
 & F & F & F & F \\
\end{array}
$$

whose inertness is a property which makes it useful for non-stick coatings on saucepans etc.

Silicon forms halides, SiX_4, as well as some chain halides. They are all rapidly hydrolysed, fumes of hydrogen halide being given off even in moist air, for example:

> Q Why should you be careful when you open a bottle of silicon tetrachloride that has been opened before?

$$SiCl_4(l) \quad + \quad 2H_2O(l) \longrightarrow \quad SiO_2(aq) \quad + \quad 4HCl(g)$$

silicon tetrachloride   water   silicon dioxide   hydrogen chloride

Germanium and tin form halides, EX_4, and Ge_2Cl_6 is also known. These halides hydrolyse in the same way as the silicon compounds. $GeCl_2$ and $SnCl_2$ exist but readily oxidise to the tetrachlorides. SnF_4 is ionic ($Sn^{4+} + 4F^-$).

With lead, the +II oxidation state is more stable and lead(IV) chloride easily decomposes into lead(II) chloride and chlorine. In other words, Pb^{2+} ions are reducing agents and Pb^{4+} ions are oxidising agents. The dihalides have an appreciable ionic character in their bonds and PbF_2 is definitely ionic.

The patterns are clear:

- On descending the group, the halides have less of a tendency to form chains owing to the decreasing strength of the E—E bond.
- The dichloride becomes more stable because of the inert pair effect.
- All the tetrahalides hydrolyse easily except for those of carbon, which has no available orbital to accept a lone pair from water as the first step of the reaction.

Oxygen compounds

Here again, there is a considerable contrast between carbon and the rest of the group. Carbon forms carbon dioxide, CO_2 (carbon(IV) oxide), a linear molecule with two carbon–oxygen double bonds. It also forms carbon monoxide (carbon(II) oxide), which is easily oxidised to the dioxide.

$$O\!\!=\!\!C\!\!=\!\!O \qquad\qquad C\overline{\!\!\equiv\!\!}O$$

carbon dioxide   carbon monoxide

Answer: The silicon tetrachloride could have reacted with moisture in the air to build up a pressure of acidic hydrogen chloride gas in the bottle.

It is surprising to find the +II oxidation state at all in the first member of the group.

Table 30.3 Bond energies for carbon–oxygen and silicon–oxygen bonds

	Bond energy/kJ mol^{-1}
C—O	358
C=O	805 (in CO_2)
Si—O	466
Si=O	638

By complete contrast, silicon dioxide has a giant structure bonded by Si—O single bonds. The structure is based on silicon atoms surrounded tetrahedrally by four oxygens. Each oxygen is shared by two silicon atoms. The geometry of the structure is similar to those of diamond and silicon but with an oxygen atom between each of the silicon atoms (see **Figure 30.5**). The resulting structure, quartz, is hard and has a high melting temperature. This difference between carbon dioxide and silicon dioxide can be explained by looking at the bond energies (**Table 30.3**).

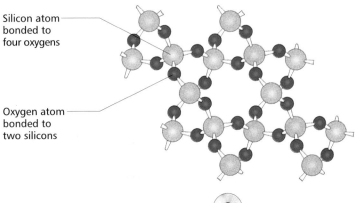

Silicon atom bonded to four oxygens

Oxygen atom bonded to two silicons

Figure 30.5 The giant structure of silicon dioxide

The C=O bond energy is more than twice as great as that for C—O. Thus more energy is given out if carbon forms two C=O bonds (1610 kJ mol^{-1}) than four C—O bonds (1432 kJ mol^{-1}). The Si=O bond is *less* than twice as strong as the Si—O bond, so, for silicon more energy is given out forming four Si—O bonds (1864 kJ mol^{-1}) than two Si=O bonds (1276 kJ mol^{-1}).

GeO_2, SnO_2 and PbO_2 all have giant structures, the last two being ionic. On descending the group, there is the expected trend from acidic to basic: CO_2 and SiO_2 are acidic, GeO_2 and SnO_2 amphoteric.

SnO and PbO exist, lead(II) oxide being more stable than lead(IV) oxide. Pb_3O_4 is a **mixed oxide** which may be thought of as a mixture of PbO and PbO_2 in the ratio 2 : 1. Hence its name is dilead(II)lead(IV)oxide.

Carbonates and silicates

When carbon dioxide is dissolved in water the solution is acidic as the following equilibria occur:

$$CO_2(aq) + H_2O(l) \rightleftharpoons H_2CO_3(aq) \rightleftharpoons HCO_3^-(aq) + H^+(aq)$$

carbon ion   water dioxide   carbonic acid   hydrogencarbonate ion   hydrogen ion

$$\rightleftharpoons 2H^+ + CO_3^-$$

hydrogen ion   carbonate ion

Hint: Hydrogencarbonate is correctly written as one word. It is often written (incorrectly) as two words or hyphenated.

Carbonic acid itself cannot be isolated but metal carbonates and hydrogencarbonates are common.

Silicon dioxide is also acidic. It reacts with molten bases to form silicates. The simplest of these is the tetrahedral orthosilicate ion, SiO_4^{4-}. Ring and chain silicates can also form. (See **Figure 30.6**.)

orthosilicate ion   pyrosilicate ion

Figure 30.6 Structures of some silicate ions

Economic importance of Group IV elements and compounds

Carbon

Carbon compounds have enormous economic importance. Their industrial chemistry is discussed in the organic chemistry sections of this book. Coal and crude oil are the most important sources of carbon compounds. Diamonds are used in cutting tools as well as gemstones, and graphite is used as a lubricant, in batteries, as the bushes of electric motors and baked with clay to form the 'lead' in pencils. Coke, an impure form of carbon obtained by heating coal in the absence of air, is used in the blast furnace to form carbon monoxide, which reduces iron ore to iron.

ndustrial diamond-tipped drill

CHEMISTRY AROUND US

The carbon cycle

The atmosphere contains about 0.03% carbon dioxide and this forms a vast reservoir of carbon which is continually being removed and returned by a variety of processes. These are summarised on the diagram. The system is normally at equilibrium, i.e. the rate of removal of atmospheric carbon dioxide is equal to its rate of return. At present, because of the large amount of fossil fuels being burned, the amount of atmospheric carbon dioxide is increasing. The carbon dioxide acts like the glass in a greenhouse, keeping in heat. There are fears that increased amounts of carbon dioxide in the atmosphere are causing global warming.

The carbon cycle

The brown colouration of sand is due to iron oxide impurities. Silicon dioxide is white

Silicon

Silicon forms almost 30% of the Earth's crust, being found in the form of silicates in many rocks and minerals, including granite and clays, and also as impure silicon dioxide in sand.

Both silicon and germanium are semiconductors and are used to make transistors and 'microchips' which are circuits containing thousands of transistors and other solid state devices on a single wafer of silicon. Silicon for this purpose is made as follows.

- Impure silica (sand) is reduced to impure silicon by carbon.
- The impure silicon is reacted with chlorine to give silicon tetrachloride, a liquid.
- This is purified by distillation and is then reduced back to solid silicon by reaction with hydrogen.
- The silicon is finally purified by zone refining. A heater is passed along a rod of silicon which melts and then resolidifies as the heater moves along. The impurities dissolve better in molten silicon than in the solid and so are swept along to the end of the rod (**Figure 30.7**).

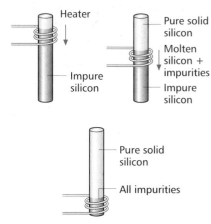

Figure 30.7 Zone refining

Lead

325 000 tonnes of lead are produced each year in the UK. Over half goes into the manufacture of car batteries. The rest goes into pipes, cable sheathing, and in the manufacture of pigments and petrol

---

CHEMISTRY AROUND US

Glass

A major use of silicon compounds is in making glass. The cheapest glass – soda glass – is made by melting together sand (SiO_2), sodium carbonate (Na_2CO_3) and limestone ($CaCO_3$) at 1800 K. A transparent mixture of sodium and calcium silicates is formed:

$$Na_2CO_3 + SiO_2 \longrightarrow CO_2 + NaSiO_3$$
$$CaCO_3 + SiO_2 \longrightarrow CO_2 + CaSiO_3$$

Addition of boron oxide gives borosilicate glasses which withstand high temperatures, while small added amounts of transition metal ions give coloured glasses.

Thin fibres of glass can be used to carry information. Many telephone links now use this method. A laser is used to shine light along a glass fibre no thicker than a human hair.

These 'light pipes' have many advantages over conventional copper wires. In particular a single fibre can carry more information than a wire. This technology is called fibre optics.

Glass fibres are also important for insulation and are embedded in resins used for building canoes, repairing vehicles bodies, etc.

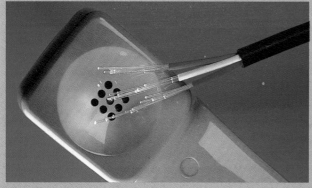

Many modern telephone links use optical fibres

Glass can be coloured, often by adding small amounts of transition metal compounds

CHEMISTRY AROUND US

Semiconductors

Silicon is itself a semiconductor. Its conduction properties can be modified by **doping** it with atoms of elements from the same period in Group III (aluminium) or Group V (phosphorus). Phosphorus has one electron more than silicon and the 'spare' electrons in phosphorus-doped silicon improve the conduction. This is called an n-type semiconductor ('n' for negative, the charge on the electron).

Aluminium has one electron fewer than silicon. The missing electron produces a *hole* which acts like a positive charge. The holes can carry a current as electrons 'hop' into the holes from the next silicon atoms. This has the same effect as the hole moving in the opposite direction. This is called a p-type semiconductor ('p' for positive, the charge of the hole). At a junction between two types of semiconductors electrons can flow from n to p as they are moving from a negatively charged area to a positively charged one, but they will not move in the other direction. The junction acts like a turnstile, allowing the current to flow in one direction only. This is called a rectifier and can be used to convert alternating to direct current.

'Spare' electron

$$Si \bullet Si \bullet Si$$
$$Si \bullet P \bullet Si$$
$$Si \bullet Si \bullet Si$$

n-type
semiconductor

'Hole'

$$Si \bullet Si \bullet Si$$
$$Si \bullet Al \bullet Si$$
$$Si \bullet Si \bullet Si$$

p-type
semiconductor

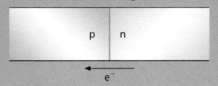

FURTHER FOCUS

The structure of glass

Glass has a giant structure based on negatively charged silicate ions, (see Figure 30.6). In soda glass the positive ions are Na^+ and Ca^{2+}. There is covalent bonding within the silicate ions and ionic bonding between the negative silicate ions and the positive sodium and calcium ions. The diagram is a two-dimensional representation of the three-dimensional structure of glass. Notice that the atoms and ions are not regularly arranged, unlike the particles in most giant structures. In fact at a molecular level glass has many of the features of a liquid. You can think of it as a liquid that has been cooled so quickly that the particles have not had time to arrange themselves in a regular, ordered array.

Glasses are often referred to as supercooled liquids. They are non-crystalline. The glass transition temperature, T_g, is the temperature below which the particles become locked in position and lose their freedom to move. It is possible for a glass to crystallise or devitrify (the word 'vitreous' means glassy). If it does so, it loses its transparency, because light reflects off the boundaries between the crystals rather than going straight through. However, some of the other properties of devitrified glasses (which are called glass ceramics) are better than those of normal glasses. They become unbreakable and some of them do not expand on heating.

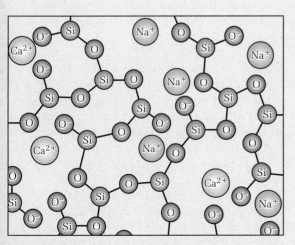

A 2D representation of soda glass. Note the lack of order

Optically flat glass is made by floating molten glass on a bath of molten tin

Moulding glass

The fact that glass does not melt at a single temperature, but gradually gets softer as it is heated and harder as it cools, is important for making glass objects. Optically flat glass sheets for windows are made by floating the glass on molten tin as it sets.

You may have seen a glass blower at work. This skill would be impossible if glass melted suddenly as does ice. Glass bottles and jars are made by blow moulding, where a gob of molten glass is first placed in a mould and shaped by roughly pressing it with a mandrel. The still-soft glass is then transferred to a mould, and compressed air is used to force the glass against the side of the mould. Bowls and similarly shaped objects are made by using a shaped plunger to press a gob of hot glass into a mould.

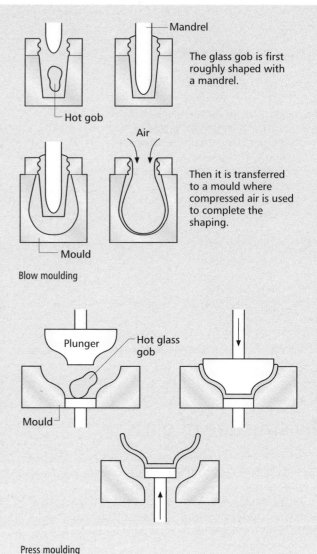

The glass gob is first roughly shaped with a mandrel.

Then it is transferred to a mould where compressed air is used to complete the shaping.

Blow moulding

Press moulding

A glass blower at work

additives although their market is in decline. Over 40% of lead is recycled which is why it is normal to trade in car batteries.

To extract lead, lead ores, such as galena (lead sulphide), are roasted in air to convert them into lead(II) oxide. This is then reduced by coke in a blast furnace.

Environmental lead is a major problem because lead is toxic and it accumulates in the body, where it can cause mental retardation, especially in children. Some historians have tried to link the decline of the Roman Empire to lead poisoning, as the Romans used lead a great deal in plumbing and drinking vessels etc. Certainly analysis of the bones of some Roman rulers has shown high levels of lead. Nowadays, much environmental lead can be attributed to petrol additives. This should be gradually reduced as vehicles that use leaded fuel are phased out. Some older houses still have lead plumbing. Lead may dissolve slightly in the drinking water, especially in soft water areas. In such houses it is wise to run off a certain amount of water before drinking in the morning because the water will have been standing in the pipe all night and may have had time to dissolve a significant quantity of lead.

CHEMISTRY AROUND US

Silicones

These are polymers based on chains.

$$-Si-O-Si-O-Si-$$

They are made by polymerising compounds of the formula:

$$HO-Si-OH$$

where R represents an organic group like CH_3- or C_2H_5-. During polymerisation, water molecules are eliminated:

$$-Si-OH \quad H-O-Si-OH \quad H-O-Si- \longrightarrow$$

$$O-Si-O-Si-O-Si-$$

Small amounts of $R-Si-OH$ are added to the mixture

to act as 'endstop' for the chain:

$$R-Si-O-Si-$$

The more 'endstops' the shorter the average chain length.

Molecules like $R-Si-OH$ can be added to cross-link two chains.

$$-Si-O-Si-O-Si-$$

Both chain length and cross-linking affect the properties of the polymer. The silicones are liquids – the longer the chains the thicker the liquid. They have a large variety of useful properties:

- Lubricants, especially for high temperature applications.
- They are added to polishes to reduce the elbow grease of polishing.
- They are water-repellent and are used to waterproof cloth for tents, anoraks, etc.
- They do not stick and are used to coat the backing papers of elastoplast, stick-on labels, etc.
- They have antifoaming properties – small traces added to stirred vats in industrial processes can reduce troublesome foaming.

Household polish and waterproofer contain silicones

CHEMISTRY AROUND US

Zeolites

In the three-dimensional structure of silica some of the silicon atoms may be replaced by aluminium. Essentially Si^{4+} has been replaced by Al^{3+} and so other positive ions such as Na^+ are required to balance the charges. These aluminosilicates are found in many minerals. They have empirical formulae like $NaAlSi_2O_6$ and are called **zeolites**. The open mesh structures of zeolites contain many

cavities. Zeolites have a number of important uses.

- They are used as ion exchange resins to soften hard water (see the box 'Hardness of water', Chapter 16). They exchange their sodium ions for calcium ions (two Na^+ for each Ca^{2+} to balance the charges).
- They are used to selectively absorb molecules of a certain size from mixtures. Small molecules penetrate

into their cavities and are trapped there, held by van der Waals forces. Used like this they are called molecular sieves. Artificial zeolite can be tailored with cavities of the right size to absorb only certain molecules. For example straight-chain hydrocarbons may be absorbed while branched chains and rings are not.

Silica gel, a drying agent, has a similar structure which absorbs water molecules very well. It is used in the laboratory in dessicators and in the home to

prevent condensation in between the panes of double glazing. You may have come across silica gel in the packaging of cameras or binoculars to keep them dry. It is also sold as anti-damp crystals.

- They act as catalysts – for the cracking of petroleum fractions, for example. The many cavities in the zeolite structures give them an enormous surface area – up to 500 m² per gram – and it is on this surface that catalysis occurs.

> **Did you know?** 'Zeolite' means literally 'boiling stone'. When heated, natural zeolites give off steam – water which has been absorbed in their cavities.

Silica gel is used as a drying agent in packaging

Computer graphic showing a cavity in a zeolite

Summary (Group IV)

- Group IV elements have the outer electron arrangement ns^2np^2.

- On descending the group, Group IV shows clearly the trend from — non-metal to metal.

- The inert pair effect operates. As we descend the group — the +II oxidation state gets more stable and the +IV state less stable.

- Except for the fluorides of tin and lead, all the compounds are — covalent.

- Carbon compounds are very different from those of the rest of the group owing to: — the greater relative strength of C—C bonds compared with the other elements, the unavailability of low energy d orbitals and carbon's small size, which favours bond formation.

- The structure of both oxides of carbon is — molecular.

- The structures of the oxides of the other elements are — giant.

- At room temperature carbon halides and hydrides are stable to both   air and water.

- The halides and hydrides of the other members of the group react with   air and water.

- Carbon forms a vast number of compounds owing to   its ability to form chains (catenation).

- Catenation occurs much less as we descend the group, because   the E—E bond gets weaker.

- Silicon and germanium are both of commercial importance as   semiconductors.

- Silicates are also important for making   glass.

- Lead is of economic importance for making   car batteries, solder and petrol additives.

Practice questions (Group IV)

1. On p. 436 there is a series of reactions for producing pure silicon from impure silica. Write balanced equations for each of the chemical steps.

2. State how the following vary on descending Group IV (C, Si, Ge, Sn, Pb).

   (a) chain forming ability (catenation)
   (b) stability of the +IV oxidation state compared with the +II oxidation state
   (c) electrical conductivity
   (d) type of bonding in the chlorides.
   Try to explain any trends you note.

30.2 Group V

Introduction

Did you know? Both nitrogen and phosphorus are important in fertilisers.

We will only look at the top two members of this group – nitrogen and phosphorus – in any detail. These are both non-metals. Arsenic and antimony are metalloids while bismuth is metallic. We have seen in other groups that the first member is untypical and this occurs in Group V.

Some properties are given in **Table 30.4**

Table 30.4 Properties of Group V elements

	Atomic number, Z	Electron arrangement	Electro-negativity	Atomic (covalent) radius/nm	T_m/K	T_b/K
N	7	$1s^2 2s^2 2p^3$	3.0	0.075	63	77
P (white)	15	$[Ne]\, 3s^2 3p^3$	2.1	0.110	317	553
As (grey)	33	$[Ar]\, 3d^{10} 4s^2 4p^3$	2.0	0.122		886 sublimes
Sb	51	$[Kr]\, 4d^{10} 5s^2 5p^3$	1.9	0.143	904	2023
Bi	83	$[Xe]\, 4f^{14} 5d^{10} 6s^2 6p^3$	1.9		544	1833

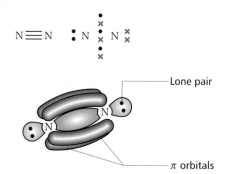

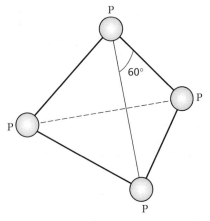

Figure 30.8 Bonding in the nitrogen molecule, N_2

> **Hint:** Allotropes are different forms of the same element which differ in the arrangement of the atoms.

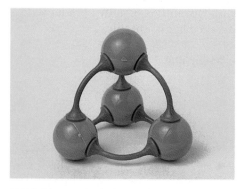

Figure 30.9 The phosphorus molecule, P_4

Model of the P_4 molecule showing the bond strain

The elements

Nitrogen is a gas which makes up approximately 78% of the atmosphere. It exists as diatomic N_2 molecules held together by a triple covalent bond (**Figure 30.8**). The bond energy is high, $945 \, kJ \, mol^{-1}$, which goes some way to explaining nitrogen's lack of reactivity.

Phosphorus has three **allotropes** – white, black and red. White phosphorus exists as P_4 molecules (**Figure 30.9**). Arsenic and antimony also form this structure. To obtain a full outer shell of electrons, Group V elements would need to lose five electrons to form E^{5+}, or gain three to form E^{3-}. No E^{5+} ions form, owing to the large amounts of energy this would require for ionisation, although Sb^{3+} and Bi^{3+} ions exist – the inert pair effect operates again. N^{3-} exists in the nitrides of the s-block elements but otherwise the bonding is covalent.

In white phosphorus, each atom forms three covalent bonds, which give it a full outer shell. $P \equiv P$ does not occur because, like silicon, the phosphorus atom is too large for p-orbitals to overlap efficiently to give π bonds. Black and red phosphorus have giant covalent structures. White phosphorus is more reactive than the other two allotropes (it will ignite in air at only just above room temperature) owing to **bond strain** (see the photograph). The molecule has a tendency to 'spring apart' because the shape of the molecule means the P—P—P bond angle is less than it would otherwise be.

Chemical reactivity of the elements

Nitrogen has few reactions. It will combine with s-block metals to form nitrides containing the N^{3-} ion. For example:

$$3Mg(s) + N_2(g) \longrightarrow Mg_3N_2(s)$$
$$(3Mg^{2+} + 2N^{3-})(s)$$

magnesium   nitrogen   magnesium nitride

This reaction occurs when magnesium is burned in air. Although the main product is white magnesium oxide, magnesium nitride is formed in small amounts and is responsible for the greyish colour of the product.

At high temperatures nitrogen will combine with oxygen to give nitrogen oxides. For example:

$$N_2(g) + O_2(g) \rightleftharpoons 2NO(g)$$

nitrogen   oxygen   nitrogen monoxide

Other oxides of nitrogen, dinitrogen oxide, N_2O, and nitrogen dioxide, NO_2, are also formed. Nitrogen and oxygen react in car engines, where the resulting mixture of oxides is called NO_x, and also in lightning flashes.

Nitrogen will also combine with hydrogen to form ammonia:

$$N_2(g) + 3H_2(g) \rightleftharpoons 2NH_3(g)$$

This is the basis of the Haber process.

Nitrogen can also be 'fixed' (i.e. chemically combined) by bacteria in the roots of certain plants such as clover. The bacteria convert the nitrogen into nitrates, which the plant uses to make proteins.

Phosphorus is much more reactive than nitrogen, owing to the bond strain in the P_4 molecule and because P—P bonds (bond energy

298 kJ mol^{-1}) are much weaker than N≡N bonds (bond energy 945 kJ mol^{-1}).

Phosphorus will react with metals to form phosphides although these are not ionic.

It will burn easily in air to form a mixture of phosphorus(III) oxide (phosphorus trioxide, P_2O_3) and phosphorus(V) oxide (phosphorus pentoxide, P_2O_5).

With halogens tri- or pentahalides, PX_3 and PX_5, are formed depending on which element is in excess.

Compounds of Group V elements

Hydrides

All the Group V elements form hydrides of formula EH_3. These become less stable to heat on descending the group as the E—H bond gets weaker.

Ammonia, NH_3

This is a gas at room temperature ($T_b = 240$ K) consisting of pyramid-shaped molecules of bond angle approximately 107° (see section 9.2) and **Figure 30.10**. Because of its lone pair of electrons, it acts as a weak base by accepting a proton and its solution in water is sometimes called ammonium hydroxide:

$$NH_3(g) + H_2O(l) \rightleftharpoons NH_4^+(aq) + OH^-(aq)$$

The high electronegativity of nitrogen means that ammonia can form hydrogen bonds and is therefore very soluble in water.

In the laboratory, ammonia is prepared by the action of strong bases on ammonium salts:

$$OH^-(aq) + NH_4^+(aq) \longrightarrow NH_3(g) + H_2O(l)$$

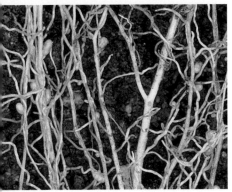

Industrially it is prepared in large quantities by the Haber process which involves direct reaction of nitrogen and hydrogen (see section 11.5).

$$N_2(g) + 3H_2(g) \rightleftharpoons 2NH_3(g)$$

Three ways of 'fixing' nitrogen

Ammonia burns in oxygen:

$$\underset{\text{ammonia}}{4NH_3(g)} + \underset{\text{oxygen}}{3O_2(g)} \longrightarrow \underset{\text{nitrogen}}{2N_2(g)} + \underset{\text{water}}{6H_2O(l)}$$

With a catalyst such as platinum, an alternative oxidation is favoured:

$$\underset{\text{ammonia}}{4NH_3(g)} + \underset{\text{oxygen}}{5O_2(g)} \xrightarrow{\text{platinum}} \underset{\substack{\text{nitrogen}\\\text{monoxide}}}{4NO(g)} + \underset{\text{water}}{6H_2O(l)}$$

Figure 30.10 The ammonia molecule

This reaction is the basis of the industrial process for the manufacture of nitric acid (see the box 'Nitric acid manufacture').

Another hydride of nitrogen exists, hydrazine, N_2H_4. It burns vigorously in air to form steam and nitrogen with the evolution of much heat.

 Write the equation for the combustion of hydrazine.

Oxygen compounds

Table 30.5 shows the oxides of nitrogen and phosphorus. The more important ones are marked with an asterisk.

Answer: $N_2H_4(l) + O_2(g) \longrightarrow N_2(g) + 2H_2O(g)$

FURTHER FOCUS

Nitric acid manufacture (the Ostwald process)

The annual UK production of nitric acid is some 3.5×10^6 tonnes, around 80% of which is used in the manufacture of ammonium nitrate for fertilisers (such as 'Nitram') and explosives for quarrying. Other uses of the acid include the production of fibres like nylon and polyester and making silver nitrate for photography.

The raw materials are liquid ammonia (produced by the Haber process) and air. The air oxidises the ammonia to nitrogen monoxide if a catalyst of platinum/rhodium gauze is used.

$$4NH_3 + 5O_2 \rightleftharpoons 4NO + 6H_2O \qquad \Delta H^{\ominus} = -909 \text{ kJ mol}^{-1}$$

The conditions used are typically 1100 K and a pressure of 4–10 atmospheres (400–1000 kPa). This gives a conversion of about 96%. Too high a temperature results in the ammonia being oxidised to nitrogen rather than nitrogen monoxide.

The hot gas mixture is cooled almost to room temperature. This process has two purposes:

- The heat extracted is used to raise steam which can be used to generate electricity or power the compressor of the first stage.
- The equilibria in the second stage move to the right at low temperature.

These equilibria are:

$$2NO + O_2 \rightleftharpoons 2NO_2 \qquad \Delta H^{\ominus} = -115 \text{ kJ mol}^{-1}$$

and

$$2NO_2 \rightleftharpoons N_2O_4 \qquad \Delta H^{\ominus} = -58 \text{ kJ mol}^{-1}$$

so that nitrogen monoxide reacts with more oxygen to form dinitrogen tetraoxide. This gas then reacts with water in a tower where the rising stream of gas meets a downward flow of water.

$$3N_2O_4(g) + 2H_2O(l) \rightleftharpoons 4HNO_3(aq) + 2NO(g)$$

Nitric acid of approximately 60% concentration is produced. This is the concentration required for fertiliser manufacture. 99% nitric acid for explosives manufacture is obtained by using concentrated sulphuric acid as a drying agent to remove the water.

The Messerschmitt Me-163 which ran on hydrazine

Table 30.5 The oxides of nitrogen and phosphorus

Oxidation number of Group V element	Nitrogen	Phosphorus
+I	*$N_2O(g)$	–
+II	*$NO(g)$	–
+III	$N_2O_3(g)$	*$P_4O_6(s)$
+IV	$NO_2(g)$, $N_2O_4(g)$	$PO_2(g)$
+V	$N_2O_5(s)$	$P_4O_{10}(s)$

Oxides of nitrogen

Dinitrogen oxide (nitrogen(I) oxide, N_2O)

This is a sweet-smelling, colourless gas which is used as an anaesthetic, commonly known as 'laughing gas'. It is sometimes used as an aerosol propellant gas, especially in whipped cream.

It is slightly soluble in water giving a neutral solution. Although it is relatively unreactive, it decomposes to its elements on heating. The heat of a glowing taper is sufficient to do this and the oxygen produced will relight the taper, so the gas can be mistaken for oxygen.

Dinitrogen oxide is prepared by heating a mixture of sodium nitrate and ammonium sulphate. These react to give ammonium nitrate which immediately decomposes to dinitrogen oxide and water:

$$(NH_4)_2SO_4(s) + 2NaNO_3(s) \longrightarrow Na_2SO_4(s) + 2NH_4NO_3(s)$$
$$NH_4NO_3(s) \longrightarrow N_2O(g) + 2H_2O(l)$$

Heating solid ammonium nitrate (as opposed to a mixture of two salts) is not advised because it can explode if the heating is not carefully controlled.

The molecule is unsymmetrical, N—N—O rather than N—O—N, and linear, indicating that the central nitrogen has no lone pairs. Two structures can be written:

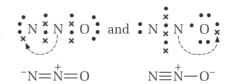

Both involve the central nitrogen giving an electron away, hence the charges. The actual molecule has an N—N bond length halfway

Whipped cream aerosols use dinitrogen oxide as a propellant

Did you know? Humphry Davy discovered the anaesthetic effect of dinitrogen oxide by trying it on himself.

Hint: A dimer is a pair of molecules bonded together.

between that expected for N≡N and N=N and an N—O bond length halfway betwen that for N=O and N—O. So it is often represented as N≡N≡O, a sort of average of the two structures.

Nitrogen monoxide (nitrogen(II) oxide, NO)

This is a colourless gas which is insoluble in water. It can be prepared by the reaction of copper with 50% nitric acid.

$$8HNO_3(aq) + 3Cu(s) \longrightarrow 3Cu(NO_3)_2(aq) + 4H_2O(l) + 2NO(g)$$

nitric acid   copper   copper nitrate   water   nitrogen monoxide

Nitrogen monoxide reacts immediately on exposure to air to give nitrogen dioxide.

$$2NO(g) + O_2(g) \longrightarrow 2NO_2(g)$$

The nitrogen monoxide molecule has an unpaired electron:

$$N=O \qquad or \qquad N\rightleftharpoons O$$

Loss of this electron produces the NO^+ ion, which has the same electron arrangement as nitrogen.

Nitrogen dioxide (nitrogen(IV) oxide, NO₂)

This is a brown gas. It is formed as part of a complex series of reactions in photochemical smogs and it is responsible for their colour.

Nitrogen dioxide exists in equilibrium with its colourless dimer dinitrogen tetraoxide.

$$2NO_2(g) \rightleftharpoons N_2O_4(g) \qquad \Delta H = -58 \, kJ \, mol^{-1}$$

Since the reaction is endothermic, lowering the temperature moves the equilibrium to the right.

Nitrogen dioxide can be prepared by heating lead nitrate:

$$2Pb(NO_3)_2(s) \longrightarrow 2PbO(s) + 4NO_2(g) + O_2(g)$$

lead nitrate   lead(II) oxide   nitrogen dioxide   oxygen

The nitrogen dioxide can be separated out by cooling the gas mixture in an ice/salt freezing mixture. The nitrogen dioxide condenses to a liquid at 262 K (−11 °C).

An alternative preparation is from copper and concentrated nitric acid:

$$Cu(s) + 4HNO_3(aq) \longrightarrow Cu(NO_3)_2 + 2NO_2(g) + O_2(g)$$

copper   nitric acid   copper nitrate   nitrogen dioxide   oxygen

Nitrogen dioxide dissolves in water to give a mixture of nitric(V) acid (nitric acid) and nitric(III) acid (nitrous acid).

$$2NO_2(g) + H_2O(l) \longrightarrow HNO_3(aq) + HNO_2(aq)$$

nitrogen dioxide   water   nitric(V)acid   nitric(III) acid

The molecule is angular with bond angle 134°:

$$\overset{\displaystyle N}{\underset{134°}{O \diagdown O}}$$

Again, as in N_2O, two structures can be written:

The nitrogen has a single non-bonding electron which repels the groups of bonded electrons less than a lone pair would. Thus the O—N—O angle is greater than 120°. An alternative description of the bonding is to imagine a delocalised π orbital spreading over all three atoms but containing just two electrons.

It may be written

On dimerising to N_2O_4, the unpaired electrons on each NO_2 form the bond:

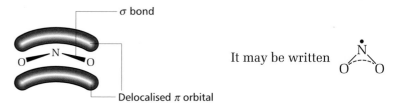

Oxoacids of nitrogen

Nitrogen has two important oxoacids, nitric(III) acid, HNO_2 (nitrous acid), and nitric(V) acid, HNO_3 (nitric acid).

Nitric(III) acid, HNO_2 (nitrous acid)

This is a weak acid, $pK_a = 3.3$.

Hint: Remember, the *larger* the value of pK_a, the weaker the acid.

$$HNO_2(aq) \rightleftharpoons H^+(aq) + NO_2^-(aq)$$
nitric(III) acid   hydrogen ion   nitrate(III) ion
(nitrite ion)

It cannot be isolated pure, because it disproportionates to nitric(V)acid and nitrogen monoxide.

$$\begin{array}{cccc} +III & +V & +II \\ 3HNO_2(aq) & \longrightarrow & HNO_3(aq) + & 2NO(g) + & H_2O(l) \end{array}$$
nitric(III) acid   nitric(V) acid   nitrogen monoxide   water

It is therefore prepared, as required, by the reaction of hydrochloric acid with sodium nitrate(III) (sodium nitrite):

$$HCl(aq) + NaNO_2(aq) \longrightarrow HNO_2(aq) + NaCl(aq)$$

Nitric(III) acid and the nitrate(III)(nitrite) ion, NO_2^-, are oxidising agents, oxidising, for example, iodide ions to iodine and Fe^{2+} ions to Fe^{3+}.

$$\begin{array}{cccc} -I & +III & 0 & +II \\ 2I^-(aq) + 4H^+(aq) + 2NO_2^-(aq) & \longrightarrow & I_2(aq) + 2H_2O(l) + 2NO(g) \end{array}$$

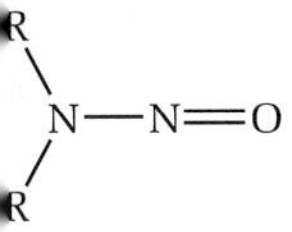

igure 30.11 A nitrosamine

$$\overset{+II}{Fe^{2+}}(aq) + 2\overset{+III}{H^+}(aq) + \overset{+III}{NO_2^-}(aq) \longrightarrow \overset{+III}{Fe^{3+}}(aq) + H_2O(l) + \overset{+II}{NO}(g)$$

Nitric(III) acid is used to form diazonium salts for manufacturing dyes (see the box 'Dyes', Chapter 35). Nitrate(III) salts (nitrites) are added to cooked meats as a preservative (sodium nitrite is E250) although some adverse affects have been reported. Nitrites can produce traces of nitrosamines (**Figure 30.11**) in the stomach and these have been shown to cause cancer in some animals, though not humans.

Nitric(v)acid, HNO_3 (nitric acid)

This is a strong acid. The dissociation:

$$HNO_3(aq) \longrightarrow H^+(aq) + NO_3^-(aq)$$
$$\text{nitric(v) acid} \qquad \text{hydrogen ion} \qquad \text{nitrate ion}$$

is practically complete in aqueous solution. Dilute nitric acid reacts with magnesium to give a salt and hydrogen as would be expected for an acid.

$$Mg(s) + 2HNO_3(aq) \longrightarrow Mg(NO_3)_2(aq) + H_2(g)$$

Nitric acid is also a good oxidising agent. This factor complicates its reactions with metals. In more concentrated acid and with less reactive metals, such as copper, some of the nitrate ions are reduced as the metal is oxidised. For example, with 50% acid (approximately 10 mol dm^{-3}):

$$\overset{0}{3Cu}(s) + 8\overset{+V}{HNO_3}(aq) \longrightarrow 3\overset{+II}{Cu}\overset{+V}{(NO_3)_2}(aq) + 4H_2O(l) + 2\overset{+II}{NO}(g)$$
$$\text{copper} \quad \text{nitric(v) acid} \qquad\qquad \text{copper nitrate(v)} \quad \text{water} \quad \text{nitrogen} \atop \text{monoxide}$$

With concentrated acid:

$$\overset{0}{Cu}(s) + 2\overset{+V}{HNO_3}(aq \longrightarrow \overset{+II}{Cu}\overset{+V}{(NO_3)_2}(aq) + H_2O(l) + \overset{+IV}{NO_2}(g)$$
$$\text{copper} \quad \text{nitric(v) acid} \qquad \text{copper nitrate(v)} \quad \text{water} \quad \text{nitrogen} \atop \text{dioxide}$$

Metal nitrates are all soluble in water because they have low lattice energies owing to the large size and single charge of the nitrate ion.

Two tests are available for the nitrate ion. Firstly, it is reduced to ammonia by **Devarda's alloy** (45% Al, 5% Zn, 50% Cu) in alkaline solution:

$$4Zn(s) + NO_3^-(aq) + 7OH^-(aq) + 6H_2O(l) \longrightarrow 4Zn(OH)_4^{2-}(aq) + NH_3(g)$$

Secondly, in the **brown ring test**, iron(II) sulphate solution is added to the nitrate solution followed by careful addition of concentrated sulphuric acid which forms a separate lower layer. At the junction, a brown ring appears caused by the ion $[(Fe(H_2O)_5NO)]^{2+}$.

In the laboratory, nitric acid can be made by the action of concentrated sulphuric acid on a nitrate salt:

$$NO_3^- + H_2SO_4 \longrightarrow HNO_3 + HSO_4^-$$

followed by distilling off the fairly volatile nitric acid ($T_b = 356 \text{ K}$). Industrially the acid is made by oxidation of ammonia (see the box 'Nitric acid manufacture').

The bonding in nitric acid and the nitrate ion is discussed in section 9.1.

Q What is reduced in the reaction of nitric(v) acid with magnesium?

Q What happens to the oxidation number of the hydrogen in this reaction?

Answer: H^+ ions (to H_2)

Answer: It remains unchanged at +I.

CHEMISTRY AROUND US

Explosives

What is an explosion and why do things explode? An explosion is essentially a rapid exothermic reaction producing large quantities of gases. A good example of an explosive is nitroglycerine (propane-1,2,3-triyl trinitrate).

Hint: Remember, energy is given out when a covalent bond is formed.

TNT

$$4 \ \text{nitroglycerine (s)} \longrightarrow$$

$$12CO_2(g) + 10H_2O(g) + 6N_2(g) + O_2(g)$$

$$\Delta H^{\ominus} = -28\,000 \ \text{kJ mol}^{-1}$$

The large entropy increase associated with the production of 29 moles of gas coupled with the negative value of $\Delta H^{\ominus}$ means $\Delta G^{\ominus}$ is negative. The large amount of heat given off speeds up the reaction and also means the gases expand. Notice also that no oxygen is needed for the explosion of nitroglycerine. The molecule itself has more than enough. Most other explosives need oxygen from the air or from oxidising agents such as sodium chlorate(v), $NaClO_3$. Nitroglycerine is so sensitive that a small shock will detonate it. This makes it too dangerous for routine use, but if it is absorbed in a porous form of silica called kieselguhr, it becomes much safer to handle. Alfred Nobel made this discovery in 1867 and he called the mixture 'dynamite'. Dynamite was the basis of Nobel's fortune which enabled him to establish the Nobel prizes. With sad irony, shortly before his discovery of dynamite, Nobel's factory, which manufactured nitroglycerine, exploded, killing Nobel's younger brother.

Another common explosive is trinitrotoluene, TNT (1-methyl-2,4,6-trinitrobenzene). The combustion of TNT produces nitrogen. It is a rapid exothermic gas-producing reaction and therefore explosive.

In fact, many nitrogen-containing compounds are explosives. One factor is the large bond energy of $N\equiv N$, so reactions which produce nitrogen gas tend to give out energy.

Demolishing a tower block

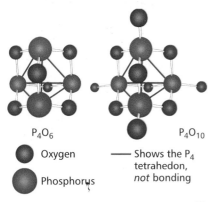

P_4O_6

● Oxygen

● Phosphorus

— Shows the P_4 tetrahedon, *not* bonding

P_4O_{10}

Figure 30.12 Structures of phosphorus(III) oxide and phosphorus(V) oxide

Oxygen compounds of phosphorus

Phosphorus forms two important oxides: phosphorus(III) oxide and phosphorus(V) oxide. The names phosphorus trioxide and phosphorus pentoxide are not appropriate as the molecular formulae are P_4O_6 and P_4O_{10} respectively. The gas phase molecules have the structures shown in **Figure 30.12**.

Each has a tetrahedron of phosphorus atoms, bridged by oxygen atoms.

In P_4O_6 each phosphorus atom forms three single covalent bonds.

In P_4O_{10} each phosphorus atom forms three single covalent bonds and also a double bond to the extra non-bridging oxygen, i.e. it has 10 electrons in its outer shell. This is possible because the presence of 3d orbitals, which are only a little higher in energy than 3p orbitals, means that an electron can be promoted from the 3s orbital into the 3d orbital. This leaves five unpaired electrons for sharing with the other atoms to form bonds. The energy required for promotion is 1320 kJ mol^{-1}.

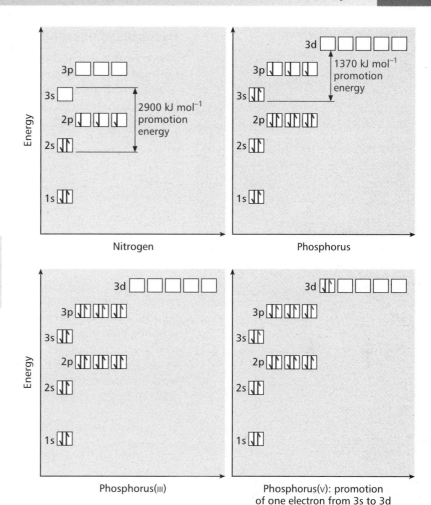

Figure 30.13 The electron arrangements in nitrogen, phosphorus and phosphorus in the +III and +V oxidation states in which phosphorus forms three and five covalent bonds respectively

Hint: The electrons in red are those of the nitrogen or phosphorus atom. The electrons in blue come from the atoms with which it is bonding.

By contrast, in nitrogen, promotion of an electron to the lowest energy unoccupied orbitals (in this case 3s) requires 2900 kJ mol^{-1} and is therefore much less likely (**Figure 30.13**). Nitrogen forms no compounds with five covalent bonds, whereas phosphorus forms several.

The oxides can be formed by burning phosphorus either in a limited supply of oxygen when phosphorus(III) oxide is formed:

$$P_4(s) + 3O_2(g) \longrightarrow P_4O_6(s)$$
phosphorus   oxygen   phosphorus(III) oxide

or in excess oxygen when phosphorus(V) oxide is formed

$$P_4(s) + 5O_2(g) \longrightarrow P_4O_{10}(s)$$
phosphorus(V) oxide

One use of phosphorus(V) oxide is as a drying agent. It will react with water to form one or more of the phosphoric acids depending on the amount of water. Not only will it remove water from mixtures but it will also remove water from compounds, dehydrating, for example, amides to nitriles (see section 34.6).

$$CH_3C \overset{O}{\underset{NH_2}{\big\langle}} \xrightarrow[\text{[P}_4\text{O}_{10}]}{-H_2O} CH_3-C\equiv N$$

ethanamide   ethanenitrile

Table 30.6 Oxoacids of phosphorus

phosphinic acid	H_3PO_2 monoprotic	![structure: O double bond P, HO and H and H attached]
phosphonic acid	H_3PO_3 diprotic	![structure: O double bond P, HO and H and OH attached]
phosphoric(v) acid (orthophosphoric acid)	H_3PO_4 triprotic	![structure: O double bond P, HO and OH and OH attached]

Oxo-acids of phosphorus

There are several of these summarised in **Table 30.6**. The acidic hydrogens are shown in red.

Polymeric phosphoric acids are also formed, such as diphosphoric(v) acid, which may be thought of as two phosphoric(v) acid molecules joined via an oxygen, after a molecule of water has been eliminated.

diphosphoric(V) acid

These are not unlike the silicates in structure. The most important oxoacid is phosphoric(v) acid, a crystalline solid which forms syrupy solutions in water owing to the large amount of hydrogen bonding possible between the acid and water.

The acid is triprotic. The salt sodium dihydrogenphosphate(v) can be made with the same number of moles of sodium hydroxide as acid, and disodium hydrogenphosphate by reaction of two moles of sodium hydroxide with one mole of acid.

$$H_3PO_4(aq) + NaOH(aq) \longrightarrow NaH_2PO_4(s) + H_2O(l)$$

phosphoric(v) acid   sodium hydroxide   sodium dihydrogen phosphate(v)   water

$$H_3PO_4(aq) + 2NaOH(aq) \longrightarrow Na_2HPO_4(s) + 2H_2O(l)$$

disodium hydrogenphosphate(v)

Trisodium phosphate cannot be formed this way because the PO_4^{3-} ion is a strong base and can remove an H^+ ion from water:

$$PO_4^{3-} + H_2O \longrightarrow HPO_4^{2-} + OH^-$$

phosphate ion   water   hydrogenphosphate(v) ion   hydroxide ion

Phosphoric(v) acid can be made in the laboratory by the reaction of phosphorus(v) oxide with water.

$$P_4O_{10}(s) + 6H_2O(l) \longrightarrow 4H_3PO_4(s)$$

phosphorus(v) oxide   water   phosphoric(v) acid

Industrially it is made by the reaction of phosphate rock (calcium phosphate) with sulphuric acid.

$$Ca_3(PO_4)_2 + 3H_2SO_4 \longrightarrow 2H_3PO_4 + 3CaSO_4$$

90% of phosphoric acid manufactured is used to make fertilisers like diammonium hydrogenphosphate(v):

$$2NH_3 + H_3PO_4 \longrightarrow (NH_4)_2HPO_4$$

ammonia   phosphoric acid   diammonium hydrogenphosphate

Another use of phosphoric acid is the rustproofing of iron and steel, in which a coating of insoluble iron phosphate is formed on the surface of the metal.

Anti-rust jelly contains phosphoric(v) acid

Table 30.7 Oxidation number chart for compounds of nitrogen and phosphorus

Nitrogen	Ox	Phosphorus
HNO_3, MNO_3	V	P_4O_{10}, H_3PO_4, PCl_5
N_2O_4, NO_2	IV	
HNO_2, MNO_2	III	P_4O_6, H_3PO_3, PCl_3
	II	
N_2O	I	
N_2	0	P_4
	−I	
N_2H_4	−II	
NH_3, MN	−III	PH_3, MP

Table 30.8 Fertilisers containing nitrogen and/or phosphorus

Trade name	Formula
Nitram (ammonium nitrate)	NH_4NO_3
Superphosphate of lime	$Ca(H_2PO_4)_2 + CaSO_4$
Triple superphosphate	$Ca(H_2PO_4)_2$
Nitrophos	$Ca(H_2PO_4)_2 + Ca(NO_3)_2$
Urea	$CO(NH_2)_2$
Ammonium sulphate	$(NH_4)_2SO_4$
Nitrochalk	$NH_4NO_3 + CaCO_3$

Oxidation number charts

Both nitrogen and phosphorus display a variety of oxidation numbers in their compounds. This is in contrast to the s-block elements and those of Groups III and IV.

An oxidation number chart is shown in **Table 30.7** for nitrogen and phosphorus compounds. Only a few compounds are listed and the most important of these are shown in red.

Economic importance of Group V elements and compounds

Both nitrogen and phosphorus are elements vital for plant growth. The major use for compounds of these elements is fertiliser manufacture. Ammonia, nitric acid and nitrates are all used for making fertilisers. Some of the more important fertilisers are listed in **Table 30.8**.

● Nitric(v) acid is used in the maufacture of explosives such as nitroglycerine, dynamite and TNT.

● Nitric(v) acid is also used to manufacture synthetic fibres such as nylon and polyester.

● Phosphoric acid is used as an anti-rust treatment for iron and steel.

● Phosphates are used in toothpastes as abrasives (calcium hydrogenphosphate) and a source of fluoride (sodium monofluorophosphate).

CHEMISTRY AROUND US

The nitrogen cycle

This is a summary of how nitrogen is fixed (converted into compounds) and subsequently returns to the atmosphere as molecular nitrogen. Nitrogen is fixed by bacteria in the root nodules of plants such as legumes and clover. It is also fixed by conversion to nitrogen oxides (and thence nitric acid) in lightning flashes, by the Haber process and in combustion reactions in vehicle engines and power stations. The nitric acid then produces nitrates which may be converted back to nitrogen by soil bacteria or converted to organic nitrogen compounds directly by plants or plants and animals.

Ammonia may be produced from these organic compounds by decay of their waste products or by decay of the animals and plants themselves on their deaths. Other bacteria convert ammonia back to nitrogen or (via nitrites) to nitrates. The whole system is in equilibrium, the amount of atmospheric nitrogen remaining constant.

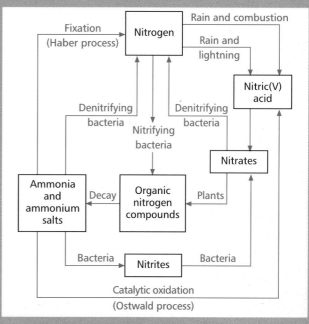

The nitrogen cycle

Summary (Group V)

- The Group V elements have the outer electron arrangement ns^2np^3.

- On descending the group there is a clear trend from   non-metals to metals.

- Nitrogen exists as molecules with the formula N_2

- The large $N\equiv N$ bond energy makes the N_2 molecule   unreactive.

- White phosphorus exists as molecules with the formula P_4

- Red and black phosphorus allotropes have   giant structures.

- Phosphorus atoms are too large to form effective π bonds by   overlap of p orbitals.

- Nitrogen can form three normal covalent bonds plus one   dative covalent bond.

- Phosphorus can form five covalent bonds by   promotion of an electron from a 3s orbital to a 3d orbital.

- With the more reactive s-block elements, nitrogen forms ionic nitrides containing the ion N^{3-}.

- There are no phosphorus compounds containing the ion P^{3-}.

- The hydrides become less stable on descending the group because   the E—H bond gets weaker.

- Both ammonia (NH_3) and phosphine (PH_3) molecules are shaped   tetrahedrally, with a lone pair.

- Ammonia readily accepts a proton so   it is a good base.

- Nitrogen forms three important oxides: dinitrogen oxide, N_2O, nitrogen monoxide, NO, and nitrogen dioxide NO_2.

- Nitrogen dioxide, NO_2, can dimerise to form   dinitrogen tetraoxide, N_2O_4.

- Nitrogen forms two important oxoacids   nitric(III) acid (HNO_2) and nitric(V) acid (HNO_3).

- Nitric(V) acid is both an acid and   an oxidising agent.

- All metal nitrates are   soluble.

- Phosphorus forms two acidic oxides   phosphorus(III) oxide, P_4O_6 and phosphorus(V) oxide, P_4O_{10}.

- Phosphorus(V) oxide is used as a   dehydrating agent.

- Phosphorus(V) acid, H_3PO_4, can donate all three protons and therefore is   a triprotic acid.

Practice questions Group V

3. Nitrogen forms N_2 ($N\equiv N$) and phosphorus P_4 (see Figure 30.9).
   (a) How many P—P bonds are there in a phosphorus molecule?
   (b) Use bond energies to calculate $\Delta H^\ominus$ for:

$$2N_2 \longrightarrow N_4$$

   Assume the hypothetical N_4 molecule has the same structure as P_4.
   (c) Use your answer to explain why N_4 does not exist.
   (d) Use a similar strategy to explain why P_2 ($P\equiv P$) does not exist.

Bond energies/kJ mol^{-1}			
$N\equiv N$	945	N—N	158
$P\equiv P$	485	P—P	198

4. Nitrogen forms only one chloride, NCl_3, while phosphorus forms two, PCl_3 and PCl_5. Describe the bonding in each of these compounds by means of dot-cross diagrams and predict the shape of each molecule. Explain carefully why phosphorus can form PCl_5 while NCl_5 is unknown.

5. In compounds with the s-block elements, nitrides containing the N^{3-} ion exist. Why do not compounds form containing P^{3-} ions even though the sum of the first three ionisation energies of phosphorus is less than the sum of the first three ionisation energies for nitrogen?

30.3 Group VI

Introduction

We will only look at the top two members of the group – oxygen and sulphur – in any detail. We can see the usual trend from non-metals to metals on descending the group. Oxygen and sulphur are clearly non-metals, selenium and tellurium show some properties of both metals and non-metals while polonium is metallic. Typically, the elements either form E^{2-} ions or bond covalently, although there is some evidence for Te^{4+} and Po^{4+} (not 6+, the inert pair effect operates).

Some physical properties are listed in **Table 30.9**.

The elements

Oxygen, O_2 (dioxygen) exists as a diatomic gas which makes up approximately 20% of the Earth's atmosphere. The atoms are held together by a double bond of bond energy 498 kJ mol^{-1}. Oxygen has an allotrope, trioxygen, O_3, usually called ozone (see the box 'Ozone').

Table 30.9 Properties of Group VI elements

	Atomic number, Z	Electron arrangement	Electro-negativity	Atomic (covalent) radius/nm	Ionic radius E^{2-}/nm	T_m/K	T_b/K
O	8	$1s^2 2s^2 2p^4$	3.5	0.073	0.140	55	90
S*	16	[Ne] $3s^2 3p^4$	2.5	0.102	0.185	386 (rh) 392 (mon)	718
Se	34	[Ar] $3d^{10}4s^2 4p^4$	2.4	0.117	0.195	490	958
Te	52	[Kr] $4d^{10}5s^2 5p^4$	2.0	0.135	0.220	723	1263
Po	84	[Xe] $4f^{14}5d^{10}6s^2 6p^4$				527	1235

*Sulphur has two allotropes: rh = rhombic, mon = monoclinic

FURTHER FOCUS

Ozone

Oxygen has an allotrope called ozone (trioxygen), O_3. This is an angular molecule with bond angle 117°. It has delocalised π bonding. Ozone is unstable with respect to oxygen. It can be prepared by passing oxygen through an electric discharge and its characteristic smell can often be detected near high-voltage electrical apparatus such as some early models of photocopier. Contrary to the old fashioned idea that ozone contributed to the bracing atmosphere of some seaside resorts, the gas is poisonous. Paradoxically it is also vital to life on Earth. A layer of the atmosphere at about 25 kilometres above the Earth's surface contains ozone made by photochemical reactions. This layer absorbs damaging ultraviolet radiation and prevents it reaching the Earth's surface. There is concern

that pollutants are reducing the amount of ozone in this layer with far-reaching effects (see the box 'Atmospheric chemistry' in Chapter 27). Ironically car exhaust fumes can lead to too much ozone at low levels in the atmosphere. This causes breathing difficulties for some people. It also damages plants and causes plastics, paints and dyes to deteriorate.

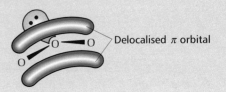

Delocalised π orbital

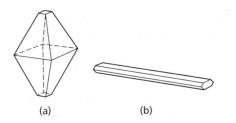

(a)   (b)

Figure 30.14 Crystals of (a) rhombic and (b) monoclinic sulphur

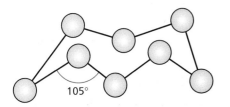

105°

Figure 30.15 The structure of the S_8 molecule, a 'crown-shaped' ring

Sulphur, too, has allotropes described by their crystal shapes as rhombic and monoclinic (needles) (**Figure 30.14**). Both allotropes are made up of different arrangements of S_8 molecules. These are eight-membered puckered rings with S—S single bonds and a bond angle of 105° (**Figure 30.15**) – just what would be predicted as each sulphur forms two covalent bonds and has two lone pairs.

This is similar to the situation in Group V where nitrogen forms triply bonded N_2 and phosphorus singly bonded P_4 units.

Rhombic sulphur is the stable allotrope below 369 K, monoclinic is stable above this temperature.

Chemical reactivity of the elements

Oxygen forms compounds with all elements, except some of the noble gases, and combines with most of them directly. Since it is the most electronegative element except for fluorine, it always has a negative oxidation number in compounds other than those with fluorine.

In most compounds, the oxidation number of oxygen is $-II$ but in peroxides (containing O_2^{2-}), it has Ox $= -I$ and in superoxides (containing the O_2^{-} ion), it has Ox $= -\frac{1}{2}$. Oxygen forms ionic oxides containing O^{2-} as well as covalent oxides.

Sulphur combines directly with most metals to form ionic sulphides containing the S^{2-} ion. Sulphur will also combine with many non-metals and can form positive oxidation states up to $+VI$. This is made possible by the promotion of electrons from 3p to 3d and 3s to 3d, allowing a maximum of six covalent bonds to be formed (see **Figure 30.16**).

Compounds of Group VI elements
Hydrides

Oxygen forms two hydrides: water, H_2O, and hydrogen peroxide, H_2O_2. Both are molecular with the shapes and structures shown in **Figure 30.17**. The angles are approximately as predicted by electron pair repulsion theory.

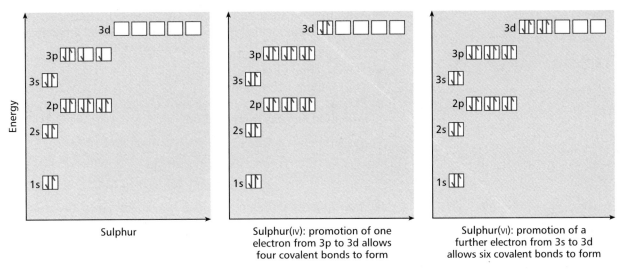

Figure 30.16 Promotion of electrons in sulphur allows up to six covalent bonds to form. (The electrons in red are those of sulphur)

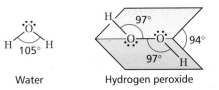

Water   Hydrogen peroxide

Figure 30.17 The structures of water and hydrogen peroxide

Q What other unexpected properties of water result from hydrogen bonding?

Q When ammonium nitrate is dissolved in water, the temperature of the solution falls. What does this tell you?

Water

Many of the physical properties are unexpected. For example, its melting and boiling temperatures are unusually high (273 K and 373 K respectively compared with 188 K and 212 K for hydrogen sulphide, H_2S, which has a larger relative molecular mass). These and other discrepancies can be explained by hydrogen bonding resulting from the high electronegativity of the oxygen atom (see section 10.1).

Water is able both to donate and to accept a proton and thus show both acidic and basic properties so it may be called an **amphoteric** oxide. Water donates a proton to, for example, ammonia and therefore acts as an acid:

$$H_2O + :NH_3 \longrightarrow OH^- + NH_4^+$$
$$\text{acid} \quad \text{base}$$

Water accepts a proton from, for example, hydrogen chloride and therefore acts as a base.

$$H_2O: + HCl \longrightarrow H_3O^+ + Cl^-$$

Water is a good solvent for ionic and polar compounds because of its polarity:

$$\delta+ \overset{\delta-}{\underset{H \quad H}{O}} \delta+$$

and ability to form hydrogen bonds.

Water hydrates ions (see section 10.2). This is an exothermic process. When an ionic compound dissolves, energy is needed to break the lattice. For many ionic compounds, the hydration energy is of the same order as the lattice energy, so the energy change of each is approximately cancelled out.

Hydrogen peroxide

Hydrogen peroxide is weakly acidic. The pure compound is a pale blue liquid. It readily decomposes into water and oxygen:

$$2H_2O_2(l) \longrightarrow 2H_2O(l) + O_2(g)$$

Answer: The fact that ice is less dense than water; the high surface tension of water.

Answer: The lattice energy (endothermic) is larger than the hydration energy (exothermic).

The reaction is catalysed by many substances, including manganese(IV) oxide, lead(IV) oxide, iron filings and enzymes present in blood, potato, etc. The reaction occurs readily because:

- The O—O bond is weak (144 kJ mol^{-1}).
- The reaction is exothermic.
- The reaction has a positive entropy change because it involves the formation of a gas from a liquid.

The reaction is a disproportionation (see section 13.3).

$$\overset{-\text{I}}{2H_2O_2(l)} \longrightarrow \overset{-\text{II}}{2H_2O(l)} + \overset{0}{O_2(g)}$$

Hydrogen peroxide can be made in the laboratory by the reaction of barium peroxide with dilute sulphuric acid.

$$BaO_2(s) + H_2SO_4(aq) \longrightarrow H_2O_2(aq) + BaSO_4(s)$$

Hydrogen sulphide (H_2S)

This is the only important hydride of sulphur. It is well known as a gas with a powerful smell of bad eggs. It is extremely toxic. The hydrogen sulphide molecule has the same bonding and structure as water although the bond angle is less. It is prepared in the laboratory by the reaction of metal sulphides with acids. For example:

$$FeS(s) + 2HCl(aq) \longrightarrow H_2S(g) + FeCl_2(aq)$$

| iron(II) sulphide | hydrochloric acid | hydrogen sulphide | iron(II) chloride |

In aqueous solution, hydrogen sulphide is weakly acidic.

$$H_2S(aq) \rightleftharpoons H^+(aq) + HS^-(aq) \qquad pK_a = 7.1$$

hydrogen sulphide / hydrogensulphide ion

$$HS^-(aq) \rightleftharpoons H^+(aq) + S^{2-}(aq) \qquad pK_a = 12.9$$

hydrogensulphide ion / sulphide ion

Q Why is HS⁻ a weaker acid than H_2S?

Aqueous hydrogen sulphide forms precipitates of sulphides, with metal ions. For example:

$$Pb^{2+}(aq) + H_2S(aq) \longrightarrow PbS(s) + 2H^+(aq)$$

lead ion / hydrogen sulphide / lead sulphide / hydrogen ion

Hydrogen sulphide is a good reducing agent. For example:

$$\overset{-\text{II}}{H_2S(aq)} + \overset{0}{Br_2(aq)} \longrightarrow \overset{0}{S(s)} + \overset{-\text{I}}{2HBr(aq)}$$

Oxides and oxoacids of sulphur

Sulphur forms two oxides: sulphur dioxide, SO_2, and sulphur trioxide, SO_3.

Sulphur dioxide

Sulphur dioxide can be prepared in the laboratory by burning sulphur in air or oxygen:

$$S(s) + O_2(g) \longrightarrow SO_2(g)$$

sulphur   oxygen   sulphur dioxide

Answer: Because dissociation of HS⁻ involves loss of H⁺ from a negative ion.

Did you know? Sulphur dioxide is used as a food preservative, and home brewers use an aqueous solution of it (made from 'Campden tablets') to sterilise their equipment.

or by the action of dilute acids on sulphate(IV) (sulphite) salts:

$$SO_3^{2-}(aq) + 2H^+(aq) \longrightarrow SO_2(g) + H_2O(l)$$

sulphite(IV) ion

The sulphur dioxide molecule is angular with a bond angle of 120°:

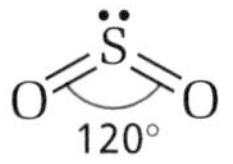

The sulphur oxygen bonds are double, S = O, so that the sulphur has ten electrons in its outer shell. This is possible due to promotion of electrons from the 3s and 3p orbitals into the empty 3d orbitals (see Figure 30.16).

Hint: Sulphuric(IV) acid, the hydrogensulphate(IV) ion and the sulphate(IV) ion are still frequently referred to by their non-systematic names, sulphurous acid, the hydrogensulphite ion and the sulphite ion respectively.

The gas dissolves in water when the following equilibria are set up:

$$\underset{\text{sulphur dioxide}}{H_2O(l) + SO_2(g)} \rightleftharpoons \underset{\text{sulphuric(IV) acid}}{H_2SO_3(aq)} \rightleftharpoons H^+(aq) + \underset{\text{hydrogensulphate(IV) ions}}{HSO_3^-(aq)}$$

$$\rightleftharpoons 2H^+(aq) + \underset{\text{sulphate(IV) ions}}{SO_3^{2-}(aq)}$$

The sulphate(IV) ion is a good reducing agent, being oxidised to sulphate(VI) ions. For example:

$$\overset{0}{Cl_2}(aq) + \overset{+IV}{SO_3^{2-}}(aq) + H_2O(l) \longrightarrow 2\overset{-I}{Cl^-}(aq) + \overset{+VI}{SO_4^{2-}}(aq) + 2H^+(aq)$$

Sulphur trioxide

Sulphur trioxide can be prepared in the laboratory by passing a dried mixture of sulphur dioxide and oxygen over a heated platinum catalyst.

$$SO_2(g) + \tfrac{1}{2}O_2(g) \xrightleftharpoons{\text{Pt catalyst}} SO_3(g)$$

The product can be collected as a solid in a receiver cooled in ice, as its melting point is 290 K. Sulphur trioxide exists as a trigonal planar molecule in the gas phase. Sulphur trioxide reacts violently with water forming sulphuric acid:

$$SO_3(g) + H_2O(l) \longrightarrow H_2SO_4(l)$$

which reacts with more sulphur trioxide to give oleum (fuming sulphuric acid):

$$\underset{\text{sulphur trioxide}}{SO_3(g)} + \underset{\text{sulphuric acid}}{H_2SO_4(l)} \longrightarrow \underset{\text{oleum}}{H_2S_2O_7(l)}$$

This is the basis of the Contact process for manufacturing sulphuric acid.

Sulphuric acid

Sulphuric acid is a vital industrial chemical and it has been claimed that it is involved at some stage in the production of virtually all manufactured goods. The manufacture of sulphuric acid is described in section 11.5. Its wide use is due to the fact that it is cheap and can

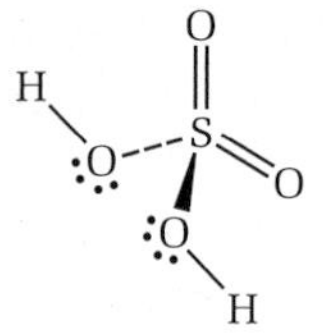

Figure 30.18 The sulphuric acid molecule

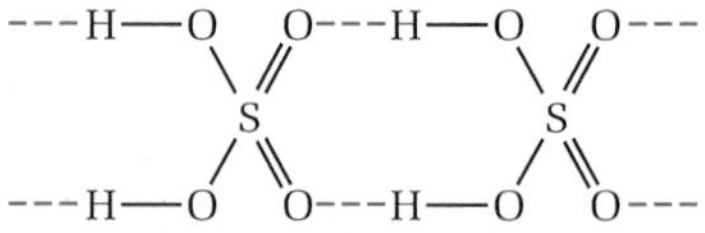

Figure 30.19 Hydrogen bonding in sulphuric acid

> **Hint:** When diluting sulphuric acid, it is safer to add acid to water (rather than the reverse). The reaction $H_2SO_4(l) \longrightarrow H_2SO_4(aq)$ is exothermic and the (relatively) small amount of water would boil as it was added.
>
> 'Always remember that you oughta
> Add the acid to the water'

> **Did you know?** Solid sodium hydrogensulphate is used in lavatory cleaners to help dissolve limescale.

behave chemically in three distinct ways: as an acid, as an oxidising agent and as a dehydrating agent.

The sulphuric acid molecule is approximately tetrahedral (**Figure 30.18**). Sulphuric acid is a viscous liquid due to hydrogen bonding (**Figure 30.19**), which also accounts for its relatively high boiling temperature (611 K).

It is a strong acid. The ionisation:

$$H_2SO_4(l) \xrightarrow{H_2O} H^+(aq) + HSO_4^-(aq)$$

goes to completion but the second proton is lost less easily as H^+ is being removed from a negative ion.

$$HSO_4^-(aq) \rightleftharpoons H^+(aq) + SO_4^{2-}(aq) \qquad pK_a = 2$$

The acid can form two types of salts. Reaction with sodium hydroxide in a 1 : 1 molar ratio produces the salt sodium hydrogensulphate:

$$NaOH(aq) + H_2SO_4(aq) \longrightarrow NaHSO_4(aq) + H_2O(l)$$

This salt contains the hydrogensulphate ion HSO_4^- and is therefore acidic.

Reaction of sulphuric acid and sodium hydroxide in a 1 : 2 molar ratio produces the salt sodium sulphate which is neutral, being the salt of a strong acid and a strong base.

$$2NaOH(aq) + H_2SO_4(aq) \longrightarrow Na_2SO_4(aq) + 2H_2O(l)$$

Sulphuric acid undergoes the normal reactions of an acid with metals, metal oxides and carbonates.

Sulphuric acid as a dehydrating agent

Concentrated (almost pure) sulphuric acid reacts violently with water. It can therefore be used as a drying agent, removing traces of water from gases that are bubbled through it. It will also remove water from compounds. For example, it will remove the water of crystallisation from hydrated copper(II) sulphate.

> **Hint:** Concentrated sulphuric acid will dehydrate skin and eye tissue and should be treated with great care.

$$CuSO_4.5H_2O(s) \xrightarrow[(H_2SO_4)]{-5H_2O} CuSO_4(s)$$
$$\text{blue} \qquad\qquad\qquad \text{white}$$

and it will also remove the elements of water from sucrose.

$$C_{12}H_{22}O_{11}(s) \xrightarrow[(H_2SO_4)]{-H_2O} 12C(s)$$

It has important uses in organic chemistry as a dehydrating agent.

Sulphuric acid as an oxidising agent

Concentrated sulphuric acid acts as an oxidising agent. The reactions with halide ions are interesting examples.

● Hydrogen iodide is easily oxidised:

$$\overset{-I}{8HI(g)} + \overset{+VI}{H_2SO_4(l)} \longrightarrow 4H_2O(l) + \overset{-II}{H_2S(g)} + \overset{0}{4I_2(s)}$$

The oxidation number of the sulphur atom drops from +VI to −II enabling eight I^- ions to be oxidised to iodine.

CHEMISTRY AROUND US

Vulcanisation of rubber

Disulphur dichloride, S_2Cl_2, is used in the rubber industry in the process of **vulcanisation**. Here sulphur atoms link hydrocarbon chains which are thus prevented from being pulled apart when the rubber is stretched. Vulcanised rubber is much harder and more elastic than untreated rubber and is suitable for applications such as car tyres. Vulcanisation was discovered by chance in 1839 by Charles Goodyear, founder of the tyre firm.

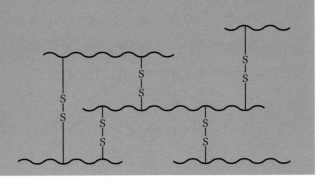

Table 30.10 Oxidation number chart for compounds of sulphur and oxygen

Sulphur	Ox	Oxygen
SO_3, SO_4^{2-}, SF_6	+VI	
	+V	
SO_2, SO_3^{2-}, SF_4	+IV	
	+III	
SCl_2	+II	OF_2
S_2Cl_2	+I	
S_8	0	O_2
	$-\frac{1}{2}$	KO_2 and other superoxides
	−I	H_2O_2 and other peroxides
H_2S, Na_2S and other metallic sulphides	−II	H_2O, Na_2O and other metallic oxides

- Hydrogen bromide is less easily oxidised:

$$\overset{-I}{2HBr(g)} + \overset{+VI}{H_2SO_4(l)} \longrightarrow 2H_2O(l) + \overset{+IV}{SO_2(g)} + \overset{0}{Br_2(g)}$$

Here the oxidation number of the sulphur atoms only drops from +VI to +IV allowing only two Br^- ions to be oxidised to bromine.

- Hydrogen chloride and hydrogen fluoride cannot be oxidised by sulphuric acid.

Oxidation number charts

Sulphur and oxygen both display several oxidation numbers in their compounds. This is illustrated in **Table 30.10**.

Oxygen has a positive oxidation number only in compounds with fluorine (the only element more electronegative than oxygen). Sulphur forms higher oxidation states than oxygen because it can use all six of its outer electrons in bonding by promoting some of them into its 3d orbitals. This does not occur in oxygen because its next empty orbital is 3s, which is of considerably higher energy than the highest occupied orbital, 2p.

Summary (Group VI)

- Group VI elements have an outer electron arrangement of — ns^2np^4.

- As we descend the group there is a clear trend from — non-metals to metals.

- Oxygen molecules have the formula — O_2.

- Sulphur molecules form ring-shaped molecules of formula — S_8

- Oxygen has an allotrope — ozone, O_3.

- Sulphur has allotropes — rhombic and monoclinic sulphur.

- In most of its compounds Oxygen has Ox = — −II

- In peroxides Ox(O) = — −I

- In superoxides Ox (O) = — $-\frac{1}{2}$

- In oxygen fluoride Ox(O) = — +II

● In sulphides Ox(S) =	$-II$
● Sulphur also forms compounds in which it has positive oxidation numbers up to	$+VI$
● Sulphur can form this increased variety of compounds by	promotion of electrons into the 3d orbitals.
● Many anomalous properties of water are caused by	hydrogen bonding.
● These include	high melting and boiling temperatures low density of ice its ability to dissolve ionic compounds.
● Hydrogen sulphide is a gas because	it does not form hydrogen bonds.
● Hydrogen sulphide has the properties of being	weakly acidic and a reducing agent.
● Sulphur dioxide reacts with water to form	sulphurous acid (sulphuric(IV) acid).
● Sulphur trioxide reacts with water to form	sulphuric acid (sulphuric(VI) acid).
● Sulphuric acid is	a strong acid a dehydrating agent an oxidising agent.

Practice questions (Group VI)

6. Sulphuric acid is manufactured from sulphur in four stages.

$$S(s) + O_2(g) \longrightarrow SO_2(g)$$
$$2SO_2(g) + O_2(g) \rightleftharpoons 2SO_3(g)$$
$$SO_3(g) + H_2SO_4(l) \longrightarrow H_2S_2O_7(l)$$
$$H_2S_2O_7(l) + H_2O(l) \longrightarrow 2H_2SO_4(l)$$

(a) Give the oxidation number of sulphur in each species.
(b) Which two steps are redox reactions?

7. The atomic number of sulphur is 16.
(a) Write down the ground-state electron configuration for an isolated sulphur atom.
(b) In sulphuric acid, sulphur forms six covalent bonds, two doubles and two singles.
  (i) Which electrons are promoted to make this possible?
  (ii) Draw a diagram to show the electronic structure ('dot-cross' diagram) of sulphuric acid (only the outer-shell electrons need be shown).

30.4 Examination questions on s- and p-block elements in general

1. The figure below shows part of the Periodic Table. Using only the elements shown answer the questions below.

Be	B	C
Mg	Al	Si
		Ge
		Sn
		Pb

(a) (i) Write down the formulae of the chlorides of B and C.
  (ii) Write down the formulae of **two** chlorides which are electron deficient.
  (iii) Give an explanation, in terms of electronic structure, why the chloride of silicon is rapidly hydrolysed by water whereas the chloride of carbon is not.
(b) Explain the *inert pair effect* by reference to the elements of Group IV.

[WJEC 1997, part question]

2. (a) Answer the following questions, choosing your answers from the elements in Group IV of the Periodic Table (carbon to lead).

   (i) Which element forms a gaseous oxide which is neutral and highly toxic?

   (ii) Which element forms an amphoteric oxide?

   (iii) Which element forms an oxide with a macromolecular structure and a very high melting point?

   (iv) Of which element is buckminsterfullerene an allotrope?

   (v) Which element has outer shell electron configuration $4s^2 4p^2$?

   (vi) Which element forms a tetraethyl compound which is added to petrol to increase the octane number?

   (b) Lead(II) sulphate is an insoluble compound which has been used as a white pigment.

   (i) Using dilute sulphuric acid as one of the reagents, describe the preparation of a pure, dry sample of lead(II) sulphate.

   (ii) Give the **ionic** equation for this reaction.

   [Oxford 1997]

3. The substance hydrazine, N_2H_4, is used as a rocket fuel because it reacts very exothermically with oxygen. Hydrazine can be stored as a liquid at low temperatures.

   (a) The full structural formula of hydrazine is

   Draw a dot-cross diagram for hydrazine, showing the outer electron shells only.

   (b) Hydrazine reacts with oxygen according to the equation:

   $$N_2H_4(g) + O_2(g) \longrightarrow N_2(g) + 2H_2O(g)$$

   Calculate a value for the enthalpy change of combustion of hydrazine, using these bond enthalpies in kJ mol^{-1}.

N—N	+158
N—H	+391
O=O	+498
O—H	+464
N≡N	+945

   (c) At the high temperature of the rocket engine, a reaction might take place between nitrogen gas and oxygen gas to produce a polluting gas.

   (i) Write an equation for this reaction.

   (ii) State how the product causes pollution.

   (d) Which has the greater entropy, one mole of liquid hydrazine or one mole of gaseous hydrazine? Explain your answer.

   [O & C (Salters) 1997]

4. The path of a lightning flash has a peak temperature of 30 000 K and produces shock waves which trigger reactions such as:

   $$N_2 + 4O_2 \longrightarrow 2NO + 2O_3 \qquad \text{\textit{Equation 1}}$$

   This is followed by

   $$NO + O_3 \longrightarrow NO_2 + O_2 \qquad \text{\textit{Equation 2}}$$
   $$NO_2 + OH \longrightarrow HNO_3 \qquad \text{\textit{Equation 3}}$$

   Reactions 2 and 3 proceed slowly (taking about a day) so very little of the nitrogen monoxide, NO, produced in a thunderstorm is rained out by the same storm.

   (a) (i) Which of the substances in this list are *radicals*?

   N_2 NO   OH HNO_3

   (ii) Explain your choice.

   (iii) What name is given to the type of radical reaction illustrated by *Equation 3*?

   (b) Reactions 2 and 3 have low activation enthalpies. Suggest why, despite this, they still occur slowly in the atmosphere.

   (c) The HNO_3 formed in *Equation 3* dissolves in rainwater to give an acidic solution (nitric acid).

   (i) Write an equation for the reaction of HNO_3 with water.

   (ii) Is nitric acid a *strong* or a *weak* acid?

   (iii) Explain what is meant by the terms *strong acid* and *weak acid*.

   (d) Lightning is just one way in which the element nitrogen is converted into its compounds.

   (i) N_2 is an unreactive gas. Suggest a feature of its molecular structure which could be responsible for its lack of reactivity.

   (ii) Describe another way (apart from lightning flashes) by which nitrogen in the air is changed to nitrogen monoxide.

   (e) Large quantities of nitrogen are converted to ammonia in the Haber process.

   (i) Write an equation for the main Haber process reaction.

   (ii) Suggest a technical reason why ammonia was not made this way until 1913.

   [O & C (Salters) 1997]

31 The d-block elements

Chemistry in the blacksmith's shop

Why do blacksmiths spend so long hammering iron when they make it into horseshoes or other products (collectively called wrought iron)? One obvious answer is to shape it, but in fact there is a lot of interesting chemistry going on as well.

Iron straight from the blast furnace – called cast iron – is only about 96% pure. It contains dissolved carbon, the compound iron carbide (Fe_3C) and some slag. When the iron solidifies, crystals of these form and make the iron brittle. Cast iron will easily shatter with a firm blow, so it is no use for horseshoes.

When the blacksmith heats iron to about 1100 K, firstly some of the carbon in it reacts with oxygen in the air and is burnt off as carbon dioxide or carbon monoxide. Secondly, a layer of iron(II) oxide (FeO) forms on the surface. As the iron is hammered and folded over on itself, this iron oxide reacts with iron carbide to form iron.

$$Fe_3C(s) + FeO(s) \longrightarrow 4Fe(s) + CO(g)$$

Thirdly, the slag is mechanically squeezed out of the iron. The combined effect of these three processes is to leave the iron purer, less brittle and more malleable (more easily shaped by hammering) – a much more useful material than cast iron.

Sometimes, iron needs to be hard rather than malleable – the sharp blade of a sword, for example. Once a blacksmith has shaped a sword blade, it is then **case hardened** by being heated in a coal- or coke-fired furnace. This transfers some carbon from the coal or coke back into the surface layer of the iron, making it hard.

Of course, blacksmiths have been carrying out this process for hundreds of years as an art, long before the chemistry was understood.

The Blacksmith by Jefferson David Chalfant

Introduction

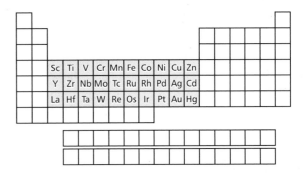

The d-block elements are sometimes called the transition elements (see section 31.1). We have seen that elements in the s- and p-blocks tend to have strong similarities to other members of their group and that there are noticeable trends as we move along a period. In the d-block, the elements show considerable *similarities* to one another even as we move across a period.

There are four main facets of the chemistry of d-block elements: their redox chemistry, the colours of their compounds, their catalytic activity and their ability to form complexes – compounds in which the metal ion is surrounded by other atoms or ions. The elements themselves are particularly useful to us because they are relatively unreactive, mostly strong, metals.

Hint: The first d-series is the elements between scandium and zinc, whose highest energy electrons are in 3d orbitals. The second d-series is the elements between yttrium and cadmium, whose highest energy electrons are in 4d orbitals, and so on.

31.1 Similarities between the d-block elements

Some of these are shown in **Figures 31.1** and **31.2**. The elements in each d-series are remarkably similar to one another in size and also in first ionisation energy. These similarities can be explained by looking at their electronic structures.

Figure 31.3 shows the energy levels of the first few orbitals drawn so as to show their distance from the nucleus. The electron arrangement of calcium is shown. The next level to be filled is 3d, which is where the first d-series starts with scandium.

Notice that although the 3d orbital is slightly higher in energy, it is closer to the nucleus than 4s. So the next ten electrons will go into the 3d orbitals, but the outer electrons will still be in 4s. This explains the similarities of the d-block elements. They all have the outer electron arrangement $4s^2$ (see **Figure 31.4**). (This is not quite true as we shall see later, but it is a good approximation.)

The first d-block element (scandium) has the electron arrangement $[Ar]3d^14s^2$, the next, (titanium) is $[Ar]3d^24s^2$, the next (vanadium) $[Ar]3d^34s^2$ and so on. Each atom has one more nuclear charge than the one before but the extra electron, being in 3d (an inner shell),

Q [Ar] represents the electron arrangement of argon. Write it out in full.

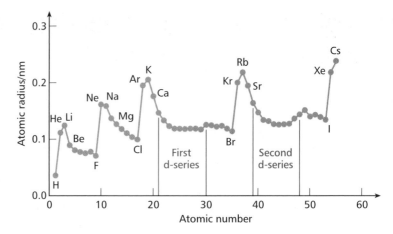

Figure 31.1 A graph of atomic (covalent) radius against atomic number (van der Waals radius is used for the inert gases)

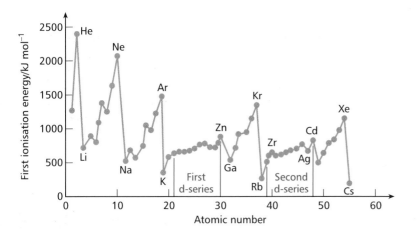

Figure 31.2 A graph of first ionisation energy against atomic number

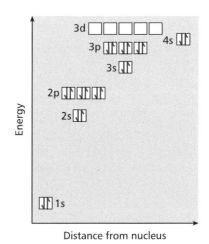

Figure 31.3 The energies of orbitals showing their distances from the nucleus. The electron arrangement of calcium is shown

		3d	4s
Sc	[Ar] $3d^1 4s^2$		
Ti	[Ar] $3d^2 4s^2$		
V	[Ar] $3d^3 4s^2$		
Cr	[Ar] $3d^5 4s^{1*}$		
Mn	[Ar] $3d^5 4s^2$		
Fe	[Ar] $3d^6 4s^2$		
Co	[Ar] $3d^7 4s^2$		
Ni	[Ar] $3d^8 4s^2$		
Cu	[Ar] $3d^{10} 4s^{1*}$		
Zn	[Ar] $3d^{10} 4s^2$		

Figure 31.4 Electronic arrangements of the elements in the first d-series. *See the text opposite

Hint: If you are not confident about the idea of shielded nuclear charge, refer back to section 9.1.

Answer: $1s^2 2s^2 2p^6 3s^2 3p^6$

shields the nucleus quite effectively and the outer electrons 'feel' almost the same shielded nuclear charge. So their sizes and first ionisation energies are quite similar and so are many other properties.

The arrangements of chromium, Cr, and copper, Cu, do not quite fit the pattern. 4s and 3d are very close in energy and electrons can easily move from one to another. Their arrangements occur because there is an extra stability associated with full ($3d^{10}$) or half full ($3d^5$) d-shells. This is rather like the extra stability of full shells in the noble gases.

Transition elements

You will often see the term transition elements used to refer to elements in the d-block of the Periodic Table. The two terms are not quite the same. The formal definition of a transition element is that it is one which forms at least one *compound* with a part full d-shell of electrons. Since Scandium forms Sc^{3+}, which is $3d^0$, in all its compounds, and zinc forms Zn^{2+} ($3d^{10}$) in all its compounds, they are not strictly transition elements. However, they are d-block elements.

31.2 Physical properties of d-block elements

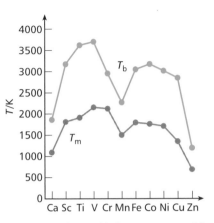

Figure 31.5 Melting and boiling temperatures of the elements in the first d-series

We have seen that physical properties of d-block metals – for example, the first ionisation energy and metallic radius – vary relatively little across a period. The same applies to many other properties like melting temperature, boiling temperature and hardness. The d-block metals can be said to be typical metals, being good conductors of heat and electricity, hard, strong, shiny, having high melting and boiling temperatures. One notable exception is mercury, which is liquid at room temperature ($T_m = 234$ K). No simple explanation exists for this oddity.

These physical properties together with fairly low chemical reactivity make these metals extremely useful. Examples include iron (and its alloy steel) for vehicle bodies and to reinforce concrete, copper for water pipes, and titanium for jet engine parts, which must withstand high temperatures. Melting and boiling temperatures are shown in **Figure 31.5**. The 'dips' at calcium ($3d^0$), manganese ($3d^5$) and zinc ($3d^{10}$) are caused by the extra stability of half full, empty and full d-shells. These electron arrangements make electrons less available for contribution to the 'pool' for metallic bonding, thus weakening the metallic bond and giving low melting and boiling temperatures.

31.3 Chemical properties of d-block elements

The chemistry of d-block metals has four main features which are common to all the elements, except zinc and scandium, which are not typical.

1. **Variable oxidation states**. Typically, the d-block metals show more than one oxidation state in their compounds (**see Table 31.1**). This is in contrast to the s-block metals which have a fixed oxidation number in all their compounds (Ox = +I for Group I and Ox = +II for Group II).

2. **Complex formation**. The d-block elements form **complexes**. A complex is a compound in which molecules or ions called **ligands** form dative covalent bonds to a metal atom or, more usually, a metal ion.

3. **Colour**. The majority of transition metal ions are coloured. Some examples you may be familiar with are: hydrated copper(II) sulphate, blue; nickel(II) carbonate, green, iron(III) chloride, brown. Contrast this with the s-block metals whose ions are colourless. Thus, sodium chloride, potassium nitrate, calcium oxide are all white. Zinc and scandium ions are also colourless.

4. **Catalysis**. Many transition metals and their compounds show catalytic activity. For example, iron in the Haber process, vanadium(v) oxide in the Contact process and manganese(IV) oxide for the decomposition of hydrogen peroxide.

Q Sodium chromate, Na_2CrO_4, is yellow. Explain how this can be the case.

Q What are the products of (a) the Haber process and (b) the Contact process?

Answer: The chromate ion, CrO_4^{2-}, is yellow – it contains a transition metal.

Answer: (a) ammonia, (b) sulphuric acid

Variable oxidation states

A typical d-block element can show a variety of oxidation states in different compounds as shown in **Table 31.1** for the first transition series.

The more commonly encountered states are shown in red, though not all are stable. Some patterns emerge:

● Except for scandium and zinc (which are not transition metals) all the elements show the +I and +II oxidation states which correspond to forming bonds using only the 4s electrons.
● There is an increase in the maximum oxidation number from scandium to manganese. For these metals, the maximum oxidation number corresponds to both 4s electrons and all the 3d electrons being used in bond formation. For example, manganese, $3d^5 4s^2$, forms manganese(VII).
● From manganese to zinc, the maximum oxidation number decreases. This suggests that both 4s electrons and the *unpaired* d electrons can be used to form bonds. For example, cobalt ($3d^7 4s^2$) has three unpaired d electrons, so its maximum oxidation number in compounds is +V (two 4s electrons and three unpaired d electrons).

Note that only the lower oxidation states actually exist as free ions, so that, for example, Mn^{2+} ions exist but Mn^{7+} ions do not. In all Mn(VII) compounds the manganese is covalently bonded (see **Figure 31.6**, for example).

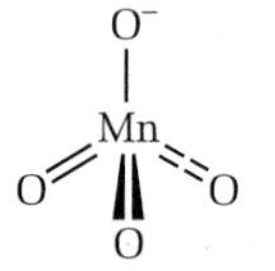

Figure 31.6 Bonding in the MnO_4^- ion

Table 31.1 Oxidation numbers exhibited by the elements of the d-series in their compounds

Sc	Ti	V	Cr	Mn	Fe	Co	Ni	Cu	Zn
	+I	+I	+I	+I	+I	+I	+I	+I	
	+II	+II	+II	+II	+II	+II	+II	+II	+II
+III	+III	+III	+III	+III	+III	+III	+III	+III	
	+IV	+IV	+IV	+IV	+IV	+IV	+IV		
		+V	+V	+V	+V	+V			
			+VI	+VI	+VI				
				+VII					

The anticlockwise rule

Because the oxidation number of the d-block elements can vary in their compounds, they take part in many redox (electron transfer) reactions. The anticlockwise rule (see section 25.2), can help predict what happens in these reactions.

For example, the redox chemistry of iron is fairly straightforward because the only important oxidation numbers are 0 (Fe), +II (Fe^{2+}) and +III (Fe^{3+}).

We can look up the the $E^{\ominus}$ values for the half reactions:

$$Fe^{2+}(aq) + 2e^- \rightleftharpoons Fe(s) \qquad E^{\ominus} = -0.44\ V$$

and

$$Fe^{3+}(aq) + e^- \rightleftharpoons Fe^{2+}(aq) \qquad E^{\ominus} = +0.77\ V$$

and insert them on an $E^{\ominus}$–oxidation number diagram (**Figure 31.7**) with any other half reactions that we are interested in, for example chlorine/chloride ions and hydrogen/hydrogen ions:

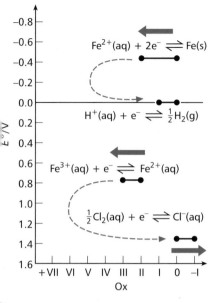

igure 31.7 $E^\ominus$–Ox diagram for iron compounds

Hint: Both the above reactions occur as predicted but you should remember that the anticlockwise rule can only predict that a reaction *could* happen, not that it *must*. The reaction could be so slow as not to occur at all over a reasonable time-scale.

Hint: In this reaction the $H_2(g)$ escapes and therefore the reaction does go to completion, as predicted by Le Chatelier's principle.

Hint: A useful rule of thumb is that a reaction with $E^\ominus_{reaction} \geqslant +0.6$ V will go to completion. See section 25.2.

$$\tfrac{1}{2}Cl_2(aq) + e^- \rightleftharpoons Cl^-(aq) \qquad E^\ominus = +1.36 \text{ V}$$
$$H^+(aq) + e^- \rightleftharpoons \tfrac{1}{2}H_2(g) \qquad E^\ominus = 0.00 \text{ V}$$

The anticlockwise rule tells us that half reactions at the top of the diagram will go from right to left and drive any reactions below them from left to right. So if we look at the reaction between $Fe^{2+}(aq)$ and $Cl^-(aq)$ we can predict that:

$$Fe^{3+}(aq) + e^- \rightleftharpoons Fe^{2+}(aq) \qquad E^\ominus = +0.77 \text{ V}$$

will go from right to left so we change the sign of $E^\ominus$, giving:

$$Fe^{2+}(aq) \longrightarrow Fe^{3+}(aq) + e^- \qquad E^\ominus = -0.77 \text{ V}$$

and

$$\tfrac{1}{2}Cl_2(aq) + e^- \longrightarrow Cl^-(aq) \qquad E^\ominus = +1.36 \text{ V}$$

will go from left to right. Adding gives:

$$Fe^{2+}(aq) + \tfrac{1}{2}Cl_2(aq) \longrightarrow Fe^{3+}(aq) + Cl^-(aq) \qquad E^\ominus_{reaction} = +0.59 \text{ V}$$

$E^\ominus$ for this reaction is positive and almost $+0.6$ V, so the reaction will essentially go to completion.

In the same way we can predict from the diagram that:

$$Fe(s) + 2H^+(aq) \longrightarrow Fe^{2+}(aq) + H_2(g) \qquad E^\ominus_{reaction} = +0.44 \text{ V}$$

Complex formation

A complex is formed when a transition metal ion is surrounded by other molecules or ions which use lone pairs to form dative covalent bonds with the d-block metal. The molecules or ions which form the dative bonds are called **ligands**. Ligands are negative ions or molecules with a dipole, the negative end of which forms the dative bond. Ligands include: $:Cl^-$, $:NH_3$, $:OH^-$, $:OH_2$.

The number of ligands that surround the d-block metal ion is usually four or six. Typical complex ions include $[Co(NH_3)_6]^{3+}$ and $[CoCl_4]^{2-}$:

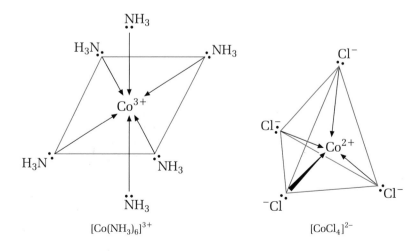

$$[Co(NH_3)_6]^{3+} \qquad\qquad [CoCl_4]^{2-}$$

In $[Co(NH_3)_6]^{3+}$, since the metal ion has a charge of $+3$ and the ligands are all neutral, the complex ion has an overall charge of $+3$. The geometry of the ion is octahedral.

In [CoCl$_4$]$^{2-}$ the metal ion has a charge of +2 and each of the four ligands has a charge of -1. The complex ion has an overall charge of -2. The geometry is tetrahedral.

The number of ligands surrounding the metal ion is called the **coordination number**. Coordination numbers of four and six are the most common. The usual geometries are tetrahedral and octahedral respectively. A few complexes of coordination number four adopt a square planar geometry. For example:

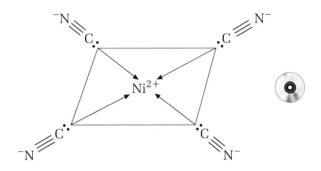

There are also linear complexes, especially of Ag$^+$ ions. These include Ag(CN)$_2^-$, used in electroplating, and Ag(S$_2$O$_3$)$_2^{3-}$ used in photography.

Notice that complex ions may have a positive or negative charge, or less commonly be neutral.

Bonding in complex ions

In transition metal complexes, dative covalent bonds are formed by lone pairs on the ligands donating electrons into the partly empty d orbitals of the d-block metal ion. This contrasts with solvation (or hydration) (see section 10.2) of s-block metal ions, which may be surrounded by polar molecules with the negative ends of their dipoles towards the positive metal ion. In these the bonding is just the electrostatic attraction between the positive ion and the dipoles.

Polydentate ligands: chelation

Some molecules, called **polydentate ligands**, have more than one lone pair that can bond to a transition metal ion. The 'dentate' part o the word comes from the Latin for tooth – the ligands can 'bite' the metal ion more than once.

Bidentate ligands include the following:

● Ethane-1,2-diamine, sometimes called 1,2-diaminoethane or ethylene diamine:

$$
\begin{array}{c}
\overset{\displaystyle H \quad\; H}{\underset{\displaystyle \underset{H}{\overset{\displaystyle \;}{N}} \;\; \underset{H}{\overset{\displaystyle \;}{N}}}{\underset{\displaystyle \;}{H-\underset{H}{\overset{\displaystyle |}{C}}-\underset{H}{\overset{\displaystyle |}{C}}-H}}} \\
M^{n+}
\end{array}
$$

Each nitrogen has a lone pair which can form a dative bond to the metal ion. The name of this ligand is often abbreviated to 'en', e.g. [Cr(en)$_3$]$^{3+}$.

● Benzene-1,2-diol, sometimes called 1,2-dihydroxybenzene:

Both ligand sites of bidentate ions usually bond to the same metal forming a ring. However, they can act as bridges between two metal ions.

An important polydentate ligand is 1,2-bis[bis(carboxymethyl) amino]ethane often still called by its non-systematic name ethylenediaminetetraacetate or edta:

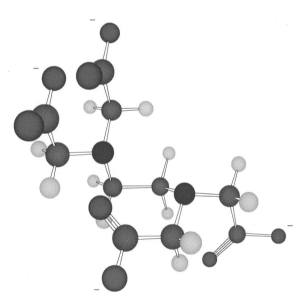

This can act as a hexadentate ligand using lone pairs on each of the four O^- ions and both the nitrogens.

Complex ions with polydentate ligands are called **chelates** (pronounced key-lates) from the Greek word for claw. Chelates can be used to effectively remove d-block metal ions from solution.

Naming d-block metal complexes

Metal complexes are named by placing the name(s) of the ligand(s) (in alphabetical order if there are more than one and ignoring prefixes like di-, tri, etc. in deciding the alphabetical order) before the name of the metal atom. If the overall complex has a negative charge this is indicated by the suffix '-ate'. When the suffix '-ate' is used, the Latin version of the metal name is used (if there is one), so we have 'cuprate' and 'ferrate' rather than 'copperate' and 'ironate'. The oxidation number of the metal is given in brackets at the end. The names used for ligands are given in **Table 31.2**.

Table 31.2 Names of some ligands

Ligand	Formula	Name
ammonia	$:NH_3$	ammine-
carbon monoxide	$:C{\equiv}O$	carbonyl-
chloride ion	$:Cl^-$	chloro-
cyanide ion	$:C{\equiv}N^-$	cyano-
ethane-1, 2-diamine	$H_2NCH_2CH_2NH_2$	ethane-1, 2-diamine-
edta	See above	edta-
hydroxide ion	$:OH^-$	hydroxo-
water	$:OH_2$	aqua-

For example:

$[Cu(H_2O)_6]^{2+}$	hexaaquacopper(II) ion
$[Fe(CN)_6]^{4-}$	hexacyanoferrate(II) ion ('-ate' is used as the ion is negatively charged and called '-ferrate' not '-ironate')
$Ni(CO)_4$	tetracarbonyl nickel(0)
$[CoCl_2(NH_3)_4]^+$	tetraaminedichlorocobalt(III) ion

The oxidation number of the metal is found by subtracting the total charge of the ligands (including their signs) from the charge on the ion:

So in: $[Cu(H_2O)_6]^{2+} + 2 - 0 = +II$ because H_2O has a charge of zero; $[Fe(CN)_6]^{4-} - 4 - (-6) = +II$ because CN^- has a charge of -1; $Ni(CO)_4\ 0 - 0 = 0$ because CO has a charge of zero; $CoCl_2(NH_3)_4]^+ + 1 - (-2) = +III$ because NH_3 has no charge and Cl^- has a charge of -1.

The names of any other ions are given in the usual way so we might have a solution of *potassium* hexacyanoferrate(II) or hexaaquacobalt(II) *chloride*.

Isomerism in complexes

Isomerism occurs when two or more compounds have the same molecular formula but a different arrangement of their atoms in space. Three different types occur in d-block metal complexes:

Ionisation isomerism

Here ligands vary in their bonding. For example, three compounds exist with the overall formula $CrCl_3.6H_2O$. They are:

1. $[Cr(H_2O)_6]^{3+} + 3Cl^-$ violet   hexaaquachromium(III) chloride;

2. $[CrCl(H_2O)_5]^{2+} + 2Cl^- + H_2O$ light green   pentaaquachloro-chromium(III) chloride;

3. $[CrCl_2(H_2O)_4]^+ + Cl^- + 2H_2O$ dark green   tetraaquadichloro-chromium(III)chloride.

Q What is the name of the ion $[FeCl_6]^{3-}$?

Hint: Square brackets are usually used between the formula of a complex ion and its charge.

Q What is the oxidation number of iron in $[FeCl_6]^{4-}$?

Hint: It is more important at this level to be able to work from the name to the correct formula rather than correctly name a given compound.

Did you know? One of the most successful anti-cancer drugs developed in recent years is *cis*-platin.

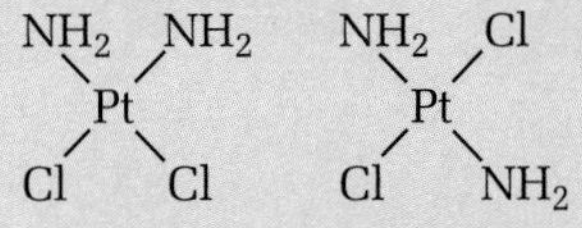

cis-platin   *trans*-platin

This has been most effective in the treatment of testicular cancer. It is believed to work by bonding to DNA so that it prevents the replication of cancerous cells. Interestingly the isomeric compound *trans*-platin has no anti-cancer effect.

Answer: The hexachloroferrate(III) ion

Answer: +II

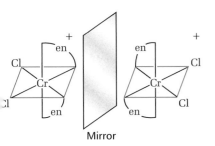

a) *cis*

b) *trans*

gure 31.8 *Cis–trans* isomerism

As well as by their colours, these complexes can be distinguished by addition of silver nitrate. Only the free Cl^- ions will react to form a precipitate with silver nitrate; those bonded to the chromium (as ligands) will not. So 1 mole of compound 1 will react with 3 moles of silver nitrate, 1 mole of compound 2 with 2 moles of silver nitrate and 1 mole of compound 3 with 1 mole of silver nitrate.

Geometrical (*cis–trans*) isomerism

Here ligands differ in their position in space relative to one another. Compound 3 above also illustrates geometrical isomerism. The complex is octahedral and two arrangements of the ligands in space are possible (**Figure 31.8**).

In (a) the chloride ligands are next to one another – this is called the *cis*-form. In (b) the chlorides are on opposite sides of the chromium atom – this is called the *trans*-form. So the full names of the compounds are:

(a) *cis*-tetraaquadichlorochromium(III) chloride;
(b) *trans*-tetraaquadichlorochromium(III) chloride.

You may need to look at models to convince yourself that there are only two possible *cis–trans* isomers of this compound.

Mirror

en is an abbreviation for ethane-1,2-diamine

igure 31.9 Optical isomerism in $CrCl_2en_2^+$

Optical isomerism

Here two isomers are non-identical mirror images of one another. This only occurs when a metal ion is complexed with two or more bidentate ligands. See **Figure 31.9**.

Hint: Mirror images may be identical (such as a cube and its mirror image) or non-identical (such as your left and right hands).

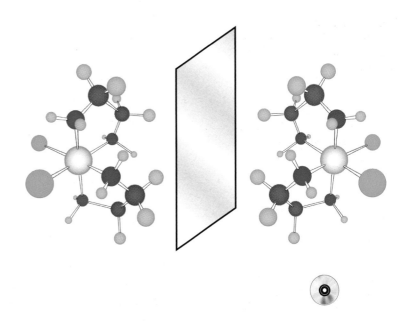

Hint: Pairs of optical isomers can be distinguished by the use of the prefixes *d*- and *l*- to their names.

You may need to look very carefully at the above diagrams to see that the two molecules are not identical. Imagine rotating one of them round its vertical axis until the positions of the chlorines match. If you are still unsure, you may need to look at models.

Optical isomers are said to be **chiral** (pronounced kiy-ral) which means 'handed'. They have identical chemical properties. Their physical properties are also identical except for their effect on polarised light (see the box 'Optical activity' in Chapter 18. A solution of one isomer will rotate the plane of polarisation of polarised light clockwise. A solution of equal concentration of the other isomer will rotate the plane of polarisation of polarised light by the same amount anticlockwise. Optical isomerism is also encountered in organic chemistry (see section 18.6).

Competition between ligands: displacement reactions and stability constants

Some ligands may form stronger bonds than other ligands with a particular metal ion. In this case, the better ligand will displace the poorer one.

For example, copper(II) sulphate dissolved in water forms the tetraaquacopper(II) ion $[Cu(H_2O)_4]^{2+}$, which is responsible for the blue colour of the solution. Addition of chloride ions in high concentrations leads to the replacement of H_2O ligands by Cl^- ligands one at a time ('stepwise'):

1. $[Cu(H_2O)_4]^{2+}$ (aq) $+ Cl^-$(aq) $\rightleftharpoons [Cu(H_2O)_3Cl]^+$(aq) $+ H_2O$(l)
   pale blue
2. $[Cu(H_2O)_3Cl]^+$(aq) $+ Cl^-$(aq) $\rightleftharpoons [Cu(H_2O)_2Cl_2]$(aq) $+ H_2O$(l)
3. $[Cu(H_2O)_2Cl_2]$(aq) $+ Cl^-$(aq) $\rightleftharpoons [Cu(H_2O)Cl_3]^-$(aq) $+ H_2O$(l)
4. $[Cu(H_2O)Cl_3]^-$(aq) $+ Cl^-$(aq) $\rightleftharpoons [CuCl_4]^{2-}$(aq) $+ H_2O$(l)
   yellow

The overall reaction is:

5. $[Cu(H_2O)_4]^{2+}$(aq) $+ 4Cl^-$(aq) $\rightleftharpoons [CuCl_4]^{2-}$(aq) $+ 4H_2O$(l)

Each of the equilibria 1–4 lies somewhat to the right implying that Cl^- is a better ligand than H_2O.

The equilibrium law expression for the overall reaction is:

$$K_c = \frac{[[CuCl_4]^{2-}(aq)]_{eqm}}{[[Cu(H_2O)_4]^{2+}(aq)]_{eqm}\,[Cl^-(aq)]^4_{eqm}} = 3.9 \times 10^5 \; dm^{12} \, mol^{-4}$$

(Remember: pure liquids do not appear in K_c expressions: see section 23.2.) The overall equilibrium is well over to the right and $[CuCl_4]^{2-}$(aq) predominates over $[Cu(H_2O)_4]^{2+}$(aq). If concentrated hydrochloric acid, which contains a high concentration of chloride ions, is added to copper sulphate, the blue colour of $[Cu(H_2O)_4]^{2+}$(aq) is replaced by the yellow-green of $[CuCl_4]^{2-}$(aq). K_c is called the overall stability constant for $[CuCl_4]^{2-}$(aq). The higher K_c is, the more stable the complex.

Ammonia is an even better ligand than the chloride ion, Cl^-. It will displace both water from $[Cu(H_2O)_4]^{2+}$(aq) and Cl^- from $[CuCl_4]^{2-}$(aq) forming the dark blue $[Cu(NH_3)_4]^{2+}$(aq). The equilibrium constant for the overall replacement of water by ammonia is:

$$[Cu(H_2O)_4]^{2+}(aq) + 4NH_3(aq) \rightleftharpoons [Cu(NH_3)_4]^{2+}(aq) + 4H_2O(l)$$

$$K_c = \frac{[[Cu(NH_3)_4]^{2+}(aq)]_{eqm}}{[[Cu(H_2O)_4]^{2+}(aq)]_{eqm}\,[NH_3(aq)]_{eqm}^4} = 1.5 \times 10^{13} \; dm^{12} \, mol^{-4}$$

The overall stability constant for $[Cu(NH_3)_4]^{2+}$(aq) is larger than that for $[CuCl_4]^{2-}$(aq), so NH_3 is a better ligand than either Cl^- or H_2O.

The colours of $[Cu(H_2O)_4]^{2+}$ (left) and $[CuCl_4]^{2-}$ (right)

FURTHER FOCUS

Stepwise and overall stability constants

Each of the ligand replacement steps 1, 2, 3 and 4 in the formation of $CuCl_4^{2-}$ from $Cu(H_2O)_4^{2+}$ has a stability constant K_{C1}, K_{C2}, K_{C3}, K_{C4} respectively.

For step 1,

$$K_{c1} = \frac{[[Cu(H_2O)_3Cl]^+(aq)]_{eqm}}{[[Cu(H_2O)_4]^{2+}(aq)]_{eqm}\ [Cl^-(aq)]_{eqm}}$$

$$K_{c2} = \frac{[[Cu(H_2O)_2Cl_2](aq)]_{eqm}}{[[Cu(H_2O)_3Cl]^+(aq)]_{eqm}\ [Cl^-(aq)]_{eqm}}$$

$$K_{c3} = \frac{[[Cu(H_2O)Cl_3]^-(aq)]_{eqm}}{[[Cu(H_2O)_2Cl_2](aq)]_{eqm}\ [Cl^-(aq)]_{eqm}}$$

$$K_{c4} = \frac{[[CuCl_4]^{2-}(aq)]_{eqm}}{[[Cu(H_2O)Cl_3]^-(aq)]_{eqm}\ [Cl^-(aq)]_{eqm}}$$

Now,

$$K_{c1} \times K_{c2} \times K_{c3} \times K_{c4} = \frac{[[Cu(H_2O)_3Cl]^+(aq)]_{eqm}}{[[Cu(H_2O)_4]^{2+}(aq)]_{eqm}\ [Cl^-(aq)]_{eqm}}$$

$$\times \frac{[[Cu(H_2O)_2Cl_2](aq)]_{eqm}}{[[Cu(H_2O)_3Cl]^+(aq)]_{eqm}\ [Cl^-(aq)]_{eqm}}$$

$$\times \frac{[[Cu(H_2O)Cl_3]^-(aq)]_{eqm}}{[[Cu(H_2O)_2Cl_2](aq)]_{eqm}\ [Cl^-(aq)]_{eqm}}$$

$$\times \frac{[[CuCl_4]^{2-}(aq)]_{eqm}}{[[Cu(H_2O)Cl_3]^-(aq)]_{eqm}\ [Cl^-(aq)]_{eqm}}$$

$$= \frac{[[CuCl_4]^{2-}(aq)]_{eqm}}{[[Cu(H_2O)_4]^{2+}(aq)]_{eqm}\ [Cl^-(aq)]_{eqm}^4}$$

But this expression is just that for K_c – the overall stability constant (see main text).

So

$$K_c = K_{c1} \times K_{c2} \times K_{c3} \times K_{c4}$$

Taking logs: $\log K_c = \log K_{c1} + \log K_{c2} + \log K_{c3} + \log K_{c4}$

This is a general result for any set of stepwise ligand replacement reactions.

The values are:

$$\log K_c = 5.62$$
$$\log K_{c1} = 2.80$$
$$\log K_{c2} = 1.60$$
$$\log K_{c3} = 0.49$$
$$\log K_{c4} = 0.73$$

If $\log K_c$ is positive, the equilibrium is over to the right. This is equivalent to $K_c > 1$.

It is usual to refer to the log (i.e. $\log_{10}$) of stability constants. The larger $\log K_c$, the more stable the complex. Those for some Cu^{2+} complexes are given in **Table 31.3**.

Notice that the polydentate ligands have noticeably larger values of $\log K_c$ than monodentate ones. (Since these are logs, a value of 16.9 represents a K_c of about 5×10^3 larger than does a value of 13.2.)

Table 31.3 Stability constant for some Cu(II) complexes

	Ligand	Complex	$\log K_c$
monodentate	Cl^-	$CuCl_4^{2-}$	5.6
	NH_3	$Cu(NH_3)_4^{2+}$	13.2
bidentate			16.9
			25
tetradentate– in this situation– potentially hexadentate	edta	$Cu(edta)^{2-}$	18.9

This increased stability is mainly due to the entropy change of the reaction. Compare:

$$[Cu(H_2O)_4]^{2+}(aq) + 4Cl^-(aq) \longrightarrow [CuCl_4]^{2-}(aq) + 4H_2O(l)$$

5 entities   5 entities

with $[Cu(H_2O)_4]^{2+}(aq) + edta(aq) \longrightarrow [Cu(edta)]^{2+}(aq) + 4H_2O(l)$

2 entities   5 entities

In the second reaction, *one* molecule of edta releases four of water. The larger number of entities on the right in this reaction means that there is a significant entropy increase as the reaction goes from left to right. This entropy increase favours the formation of chelates (complexes with polydentate ligands).

It is worth noting that ligand exchange reactions in which both ligands are of similar size and charge often occur without a change in coordination number. For example:

$$[Cr(H_2O)_6]^{3+}(aq) + 6NH_3(aq) \longrightarrow [Cr(NH_3)_6]^{3+}(aq) + 6H_2O(l)$$

Water and ammonia are of similar size and neither has a charge.

However, if one ligand is significantly different in size and charge from the other, there may well be a change in coordination number. For example

$$[Co(H_2O)_6]^{2+}(aq) + 4Cl^-(aq) \longrightarrow [CoCl_4]^{2-}(aq) + 6H_2O(l)$$

> **Q** What are the coordination numbers of the metal ions in $[Co(H_2O)_6]^{2+}(aq)$ and $[CoCl_4]^{2-}(aq)$?

Colour of d-block metal compounds

Colours and colour changes are among the most striking aspects of d-block metal chemistry. A good example is the reaction of zinc with a solution containing a vanadium(V) compound. The solution gradually changes from the yellow of vanadium(V) to blue vanadium(IV) to green vanadium(III) to the mauve of vanadium(II) as the zinc gradually reduces the vanadium compounds (see the photograph).

Absorption of light by d-block metal atoms

We have seen in section 7.2 that when electrons in a substance move from one energy level to a higher one, they absorb a quantum of electromagnetic energy equal in energy to the gap between the two levels. The frequency, ν, of this is given by the equation $E = h\nu$ where E is the energy gap and h Planck's constant. If ν is in the visible region of the spectrum, this will result in the substance being coloured. If a substance absorbs, say, green light, it will let through red and blue and thus appear purple (see **Figure 31.10**).

In an isolated atom, all five d orbitals have exactly the same energy. However, when ligands approach the metal atom or ion, they

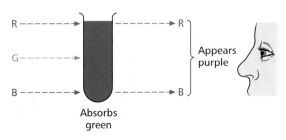

Figure 31.10 The d-block metal complexes look coloured because they absorb light of some colours and let other colours through

Answer: 6, 4

FURTHER FOCUS

Colours of transition metal ions

The shapes of the five d orbitals are shown on an x,y,z coordinate system:

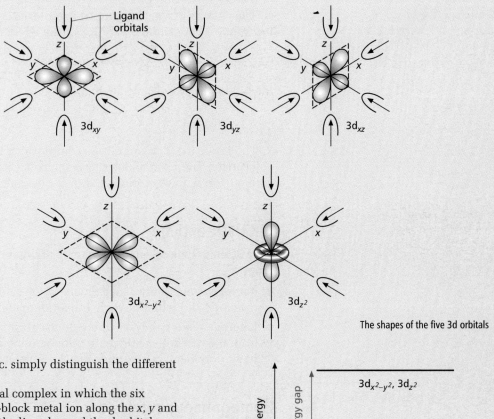

The shapes of the five 3d orbitals

The labels $3d_{xy}$, $3d_{yz}$, etc. simply distinguish the different d orbitals.

Think of an octahedral complex in which the six ligands approach the d-block metal ion along the x, y and z axes. The orbitals on the ligands repel the d orbitals which point along the axes more than those which do not. So the energy of the $3d_{x^2-y^2}$ and $3d_{z^2}$ orbitals are raised compared with the other three orbitals. The resulting energy gap means that movement of electrons between d orbitals absorb quanta of electromagnetic energy and cause colour.

If the ligands are arranged tetrahedrally, the situation is reversed and the $3d_{xy}$, $3d_{yz}$, and $3d_{xz}$, orbitals are of higher energy than $3d_{x^2-y^2}$, and $3d_{z^2}$. The size of the energy gap will also vary. So in a ligand exchange reaction where the

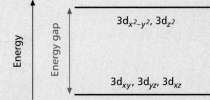

coordination number changes, we will expect to see a change in colour.

$$[Co(H_2O)_6]^{2+}(aq) + 4Cl^-(aq) \rightleftharpoons [CoCl_4]^{2-}(aq) + 6H_2O(l)$$

    pink   blue

is a good example.

affect the energy levels of different d orbitals differently, raising some slightly and lowering some slightly (see the box 'Colours of transition metal ions').

In most cases the resulting energy gap between the d orbitals corresponds to frequencies of electromagnetic radiation in the visible region of the spectrum, so most transition metal compounds are coloured.

Electrons can only move from one d orbital to another if there are spaces in the d orbitals, so Zn^{2+} compounds which have the electron arrangement $3d^{10}$ (i.e. the d orbitals are full) are not coloured. Sc^{3+} compounds ($3d^0$) have no d electrons and are therefore also colourless (as are the compounds of s-block metals). The compound

Did you know? Titanium(IV) oxide is used as a white pigment in paints, because it resists yellowing and is a good scatterer of light.

titanium(IV) oxide, TiO_2, is also colourless. The Ti^{4+} ion is also $3d^0$. Compounds of s-block elements which also contain a transition metal like, say, potassium manganate(VII), $KMnO_4$, may, of course, be coloured because of the presence of the transition metal.

Chemical changes, such as replacing one ligand by another, or oxidising or reducing the metal ion, will slightly affect the energies of the d orbitals and produce a compound with a different colour.

The colours of transition metal complexes can be used in analytical techniques. For example, Fe^{2+} ions form a red complex with

the bidentate ligand 1,10-phenanthroline

The intensity of colour of this complex can be measured using a colorimeter and used to determine the concentration of Fe^{2+} ions by comparison with a solution of known concentration.

Catalytic activity

Transition metals as catalysts may be divided into two distinct groups:

- **homogeneous** catalysts which are in the same phase as the reactants and which involve transition metal compounds
- **heterogeneous** catalysts where the catalyst is in a different phase from the reactants and where transition metal elements or transition metal compounds may be involved

Homogeneous catalysts

We have already discussed in section 14.6 the reaction of peroxodisulphate(VI) ions oxidising iodide ions to iodine and have explained how the reaction is catalysed by either Fe^{2+} or Fe^{3+} ions.

$$S_2O_8^{2-}(aq) + 2I^-(aq) \xrightarrow{Fe^{2+} \text{ or } Fe^{3+}} I_2(aq) + 2SO_4^{2-}(aq)$$

Fe^{2+} ions as catalyst

Peroxodisulphate ions oxidise Fe^{2+} ions to Fe^{3+} ions. These then oxidise I^- to I_2.

Fe³⁺ ions as catalyst

I^- reduces Fe^{3+} to Fe^{2+}, which then reduces peroxodisulphate ions. Note that while the single step reaction occurs between two negatively charged ions (peroxodisulphate and iodide), each of the steps in both of the catalysed reactions occur between oppositely charged ions. This helps to explain the increased rate.

An $E^\ominus$–Ox diagram is useful in explaining the steps in the catalysed reactions (**Figure 31.11**).

The anticlockwise rule shows that:

- iodide ions can reduce Fe^{3+} ions to Fe^{2+} ions
- Fe^{2+} ions can reduce $S_2O_8^{2-}$ to sulphate ions and Fe^{3+} ions are regenerated.

Hint: Remember that on $E^\ominus$–Ox diagrams the ●—● represents the two oxidation states of the species whose oxidation state changes.

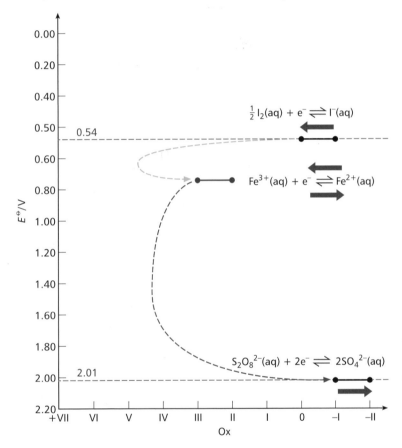

Figure 31.11 $E^\ominus$–Ox diagram for the $S_2O_8^{2-}/I^-$ reaction catalysed by iron ions. N.B. In the reaction:

$$S_2O_8^{2-} + 2e^- \rightleftharpoons 2SO_4^{2-}$$

oxygen is reduced from O(−I) to O(−II). The Ox's of the sulphur atoms remain unchanged

You may be able to see that *any* half cell with $E^\ominus$ between $+0.54$ V and $+2.01$ V is a possible catalyst for the peroxodisulphate/iodide reaction, while those outside this range are not.

Examples of possible catalysts include:

$$Co^{3+}(aq)/Co^{2+}(aq),$$
$$MnO_4^-(aq) + 8H^+(aq)/Mn^{2+}(aq) + 4H_2O(l)$$
$$CrO_4^{2-}(aq) + 8H^+(aq)/Cr^{3+} + 4H_2O(l)$$

These have been entered on **Figure 31.12**.

In practice, only Mn(VII) actually catalyses the reaction, a useful reminder that predictions made by the anticlockwise rule can only *suggest* that a reaction is possible, not that it must take place.

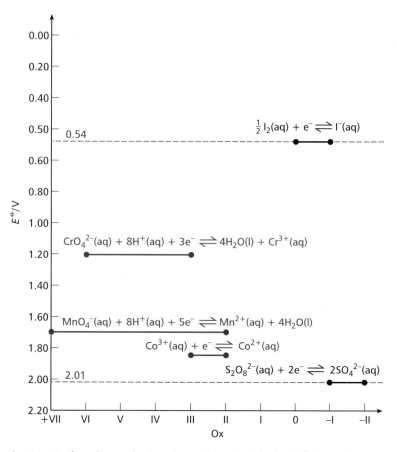

Figure 31.12 $E^{\ominus}$–Ox diagram showing other possible catalysts for the $S_2O_8^{2-}/I^-$ reaction

Heterogeneous catalysts

Hint: Adsorption is not the same as absorption. Adsorption involves the formation of weak bonds, such as van der Waals bonds between the reactant and the surface.

Section 14.6 describes how heterogeneous catalysts work. They adsorb reactants on their surfaces by forming weak chemical bonds with them. This has two effects: weakening bonds within the reactant and holding the reactants close together on the metal surface in the correct orientation for reaction. The d-block metals have partly full d orbitals which can be used to form bonds with adsorbed reactants. Thus they can be effective heterogeneous catalysts.

Examples of d-block elements and compounds used as heterogeneous catalysts are shown in **Table 31.4**.

Table 31.4 Some examples of heterogeneous catalysis involving d-block metals or their compounds

Process	Product	Catalyst
Haber	ammonia	iron
contact	sulphuric acid	vanadium(v) oxide
hydrogenation of oils	margarine	nickel
Ostwald	nitric acid	platinum/rhodium
oxidation of propan-2-ol	propanone	copper

31.4 Examples of the chemistry of some d-block elements

This section discusses the chemistry of selected d-block metals and their compounds.

Scandium

Scandium shows no typical transition metal properties. It forms only one oxidation state, $+III$, apart from $Ox = 0$. The Sc^{3+} ion is colourless because Sc^{3+} has no d electrons. The metal is similar to calcium in its reactivity with water:

$$Sc(s) + 3H_2O(l) \longrightarrow Sc(OH)_3(aq) + 1\tfrac{1}{2}H_2(g)$$

Vanadium

Redox chemistry of vanadium

Vanadium forms four important oxidation states: $+II$, $+III$, $+IV$ and $+V$. All can be obtained in aqueous solution. **Table 31.5** summarises the species present in acidic solution.

Simple aqueous ions $V^{4+}(aq)$ and $V^{5+}(aq)$ do not exist. Covalent bonds with oxygen atoms are formed and the vanadium(IV) state is usually represented as $VO^{2+}(aq)$ and the vanadium(V) state as $VO_2^{+}(aq)$. Similar situations occurs with high oxidation states of other transition metals.

An $E^{\ominus}$–oxidation number diagram helps us to understand the aqueous redox chemistry of vanadium. The one in **Figure 31.13**

Table 31.5 Vanadium species in aqueous solution. The colours are shown in the photographs below, which have been produced by reducing $VO_2^{+}(aq)$ with zinc in acid solution

Ox	Species	Colour
+V	$VO_2^{+}(aq)$	yellow
+IV	$VO^{2+}(aq)$	blue
+III	$V^{3+}(aq)$	green
+II	$V^{2+}(aq)$	violet

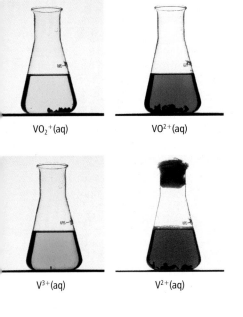

VO$_2$⁺(aq)   VO²⁺(aq)

V³⁺(aq)   V²⁺(aq)

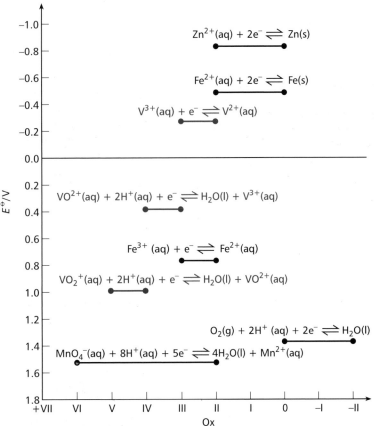

Figure 31.13 $E^{\ominus}$–Ox diagram for some oxidation states of vanadium

Table 31.6 Vanadium oxides

Formula	Name
VO	vanadium(II) oxide
V_2O_3	vanadium(III) oxide
VO_2	vanadium(IV) oxide
V_2O_5	vanadium(V) oxide

The chromate(VI) ion

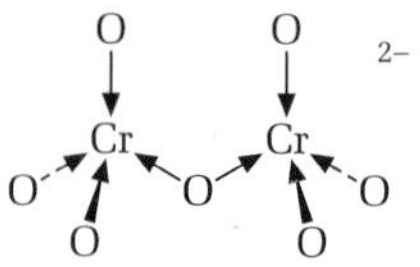

The dichromate(VI) ion

Figure 31.14 The structures of the chromate(VI) and dichromate(VI) ions

Q What happens to this equilibrium if (a) H⁺ ions are added, (b) OH⁻ ions are added?

Did you know? Chromium is the constituent that makes stainless steel stainless.

Answer: (a) It moves to right, (b) It moves to the left.

shows the potentials in acid solution. Half reactions involving vanadium compounds are in red.

From this we can make a number of predictions:

- Zinc could reduce VO_2^+(aq) [+V] to VO_2^{2+}(aq) [+IV], VO^{2+}(aq) [+IV] to V^{3+}(aq) [+III] and V^{3+}(aq) [+III] to V^{2+}(aq) [+II] – a series of reactions that actually occurs.

- Oxygen will oxidise any vanadium species to VO_2^+ [+V]. In fact, V^{2+} [+II] is oxidised to V^{3+} [+III] and V^{3+} [+III] to VO^{2+} [+IV] by oxygen but the oxidation of VO^{2+} [+IV] to VO_2^+ [+V] is very slow, so VO^{2+} [+IV] is the most stable state in aqueous solution.

- Fe^{2+} will reduce VO_2^+ [+V] to VO^{2+} [+IV], another reaction which is observed.

These reactions can be followed by observing the colours of the different vanadium species formed.

Oxides of vanadium

The known oxides of vanadium are shown in **Table 31.6**.

Their properties illustrate a general trend in the d-block where the acidity of the oxides increases with the oxidation number of the metal. Vanadium(II) oxide and vanadium(III) oxide are basic, vanadium(IV) oxide amphoteric and vanadium(V) oxide acidic.

Chromium

Chromium metal is bluish-white. It has a high melting temperature (2130 K) and is quite resistant to chemical attack, hence its most familiar use as a shiny plating on car bumpers, cycle handlebars, etc.

Redox chemistry of chromium

Chromium has an extensive redox chemistry, the most important oxidation states being Cr(II) (blue), Cr(III) (green) and Cr(VI) (yellow/orange). In aqueous solution Cr(VI) exists in two forms, the chromate(VI) ion, CrO_4^{2-}, and the dimeric dichromate(VI) ion $Cr_2O_7^{2-}$. The orange dichromate ion is stable in acid solution and the yellow chromate ion in alkalis, as shown by the equilibrium below.

$$2CrO_4^{2-}(aq) + 2H^+(aq) \rightleftharpoons Cr_2O_7^{2-}(aq) + H_2O(l)$$

The chromate ion is tetrahedral, having a similar structure to the sulphate ion (**Figure 31.14**) while the dichromate ion consists of two tetrahedra linked by a bridging oxygen.

Chromium(III) is the most stable oxidation state in aqueous solution. Chromium(II) is easily oxidised to chromium(III) by oxygen and can only be prepared in the absence of air. If it is prepared by reduction of chromium(VI) by zinc in acid solution, the hydrogen produced can be used to exclude air. The electrode potentials in **Figure 31.15** show that this reaction is feasible.

The chromium(VI) state is powerfully oxidising and $Cr_2O_7^{2-}/H^+$ is often used as an oxidising agent in organic chemistry. The $E^\ominus$–Ox diagram shows that $Cr_2O_7^{2-}$(aq) can oxidise I^- to I_2, Br^- to Br_2, but not Cl^- to Cl_2. The diagram also shows that chromium(II) will reduce all the halogens to halide ions.

different oxidation states of chromium have different colours

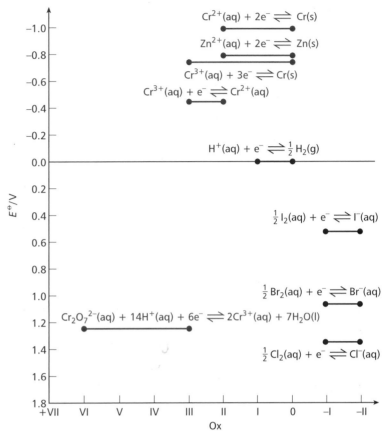

Figure 31.15 $E^\ominus$–Ox diagram for some oxidation states of chromium

Oxides of chromium

The two oxides of chromium, chromium(III) oxide, Cr_2O_3, and chromium(VI) oxide, CrO_3, are typical in that the oxide with the higher oxidation number is more acidic. Chromium(VI) oxide dissolves in water to give chromic acid, H_2CrO_4. Chromium(III) oxide is amphoteric.

Did you know? Chromic acid, which is both an acid and an oxidising agent, is useful for cleaning laboratory glassware

Chromium(III) oxide contains the Cr^{3+} ion while chromium(VI) oxide is covalently bonded.

Manganese

Manganese metal is brittle and fairly reactive and thus has relatively few uses. It is, however, important as a constituent of many alloys. In its compounds, manganese displays more oxidation states than any other metal in the first d-series. All the positive oxidation states up to +VII are known, VII, IV, and III being the most important.

Redox chemistry of manganese compounds

Much of the redox chemistry of manganese compounds can be related to **Figure 31.16**. $E^\ominus$ values show that manganese should react with acids to give manganese(II) salts. The reaction is observed.

Manganese(II), in the form of pale pink hexaaquamanganese(II) ions, $[Mn(H_2O)_6]^{2+}$, is the most stable oxidation state of manganese in aqueous solution, owing partly to its $3d^5$ electron arrangement. It is precipitated out of alkaline solutions as insoluble pale pink manganese(II) hydroxide, $Mn(OH)_2$.

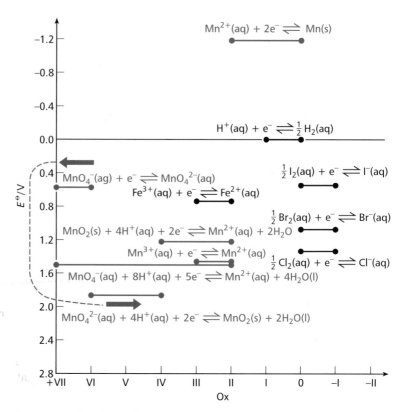

Figure 31.16 $E^\ominus$–Ox diagram for some oxidation states of manganese

Manganese(IV) oxide is a black, insoluble, ionic solid. It is a good oxidising agent, $E^\ominus$ values predicting that it will oxidise Fe^{2+} to Fe^{3+}, I^- to $\frac{1}{2}I_2$ and Br^- to $\frac{1}{2}Br_2$.

Manganese(VII) is an even more powerfully oxidising state. It is usually encountered as the dark purple manganate(VII), MnO_4^-, ion. $E^\ominus$ values show it should oxidise Cl^- to $\frac{1}{2}Cl_2$ and this reaction is often used as a laboratory preparation of chlorine.

$$MnO_4^-(aq) + 8H^+(aq) + 5Cl^-(aq)$$
$$\longrightarrow Mn^{2+}(aq) + 4H_2O(l) + 2\tfrac{1}{2}Cl_2(aq) \qquad E^\ominus_{reaction} = +0.15\ V$$

Hint: The manganate(VII) ion is sometimes called the permanganate ion.

Potassium manganate(VII) can be used in redox titrations to measure the concentration of reducing agents. It needs no indicator as the end point is shown by the disappearance of its purple colour.

The manganese (VI) state is represented in solution by the green manganate(VI) ion, MnO_4^{2-}. In acid solution it disproportionates. This reaction is indicated in red on Figure 31.16 The overall reaction is:

$$3MnO_4^{2-}(aq) + 4H^+(aq)$$
$$\longrightarrow MnO_2(s) + 2MnO_4^{2-}(aq) + 2H_2O(l) \qquad E^\ominus = +0.9\ V$$

This reaction does not occur in alkaline solution.
Manganese(III) in acid solution disproportionates to manganese(II) and manganese(IV).

Oxides of manganese

These are summarised in **Table 31.7**.

Table 31.7 Oxides of manganese.

Formulae	Name	Properties
MnO	manganese(II) oxide	grey–green ionic solid, basic
Mn_2O_3	manganese(III) oxide	brown ionic solid, basic
MnO_2	manganese(IV) oxide	black solid, ionic, amphoteric
Mn_2O_7	manganese(VIII) oxide	explosive dark coloured liquid, covalently bonded, dissolves in water to give manganic(VII) acid, $HMnO_4$

As the oxidation number of the metal increases, the usual trends of increasing acidity and increasing covalency are seen.

Iron

Iron is without doubt the most important metal in present day society. Around 33 000 tonnes are produced daily in the UK, most being used to produce steels – alloys of iron with up to 30% of other elements added to improve their properties. In many ways, iron is not an ideal constructional metal especially as it corrodes quite readily. However, this disadvantage is outweighed by its cheapness, the result of its abundance (it is the second most abundant metal in the Earth's crust) and relative ease of extraction. Also, alloying and heat treatment produce steels with a remarkable range of properties.

Redox chemistry of iron

This is relatively simple because iron shows only two common oxidation states in its compounds, iron(II) and iron(III). An $E^\ominus$–Ox diagram is shown in **Figure 31.17**. Of these two states, Fe^{3+} is the more stable as it has a $3d^5$ electron arrangement. Solutions containing Fe^{2+} are oxidised by air to Fe^{3+}.

The $E^\ominus$–Ox diagram shows that metallic iron could react with acids to form $Fe^{2+}(aq)$ ions and hydrogen, and this reaction does take place. Bromine will oxidise $Fe^{2+}(aq)$ to $Fe^{3+}(aq)$ but $Fe^{3+}(aq)$ will oxidise $I^-(aq)$ to iodine.

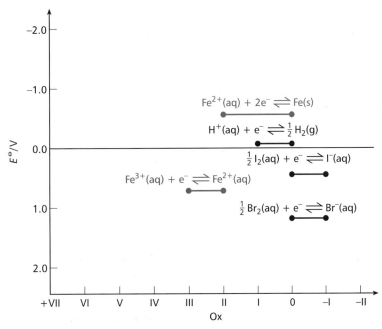

Figure 31.17 $E^\ominus$–Ox diagram for some oxidation states of iron

Rusting

This is probably the most important redox reaction of iron. Metallic iron is converted in the presence of oxygen and water to rust (hydrated iron(III) oxide, $Fe_2O_3.xH_2O$).

The rusting or corrosion of iron is an electrochemical process in which a cell is set up within the metal (**Figure 31.18**).

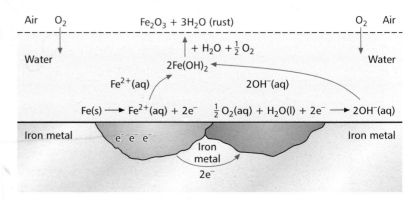

Figure 31.18 The electrochemical rusting of iron

In any piece of iron, some areas will tend to accept electrons and others to give them away. Such areas may be caused by impurities in the iron. A more reactive impurity like zinc would release electrons better than iron, and be negative, while a less reactive impurity like copper would tend to form a positive area. Most iron has impurities but even in very pure iron, positive and negative areas can be produced by less obvious factors such as stress caused by bending the metal and by uneven oxidation of the surface.

If the iron surface is covered with water, which contains dissolved oxygen from the air, the following reactions can take place:

$$Fe(s) \longrightarrow Fe^{2+}(aq) + 2e^-$$
$$\tfrac{1}{2}O_2(aq) + H_2O + 2e^- \longrightarrow 2OH^-(aq)$$

The electrons produced by the first reaction flow through the iron (which, of course, is a good conductor) to take part in the second reaction. The $Fe^{2+}(aq)$ and $OH^-(aq)$ ions diffuse away through the solution and where they meet, they react to give iron(II) hydroxide:

$$Fe^{2+}(aq) + 2OH^-(aq) \longrightarrow Fe(OH)_2(s)$$

This is then oxidised by dissolved oxygen to iron(III) hydroxide which forms hydrated iron(III) oxide, which is rust:

$$2Fe(OH)_2 + H_2O + \tfrac{1}{2}O_2 \longrightarrow Fe_2O_3 + 3H_2O$$

So rusting takes place only in the presence of air and water. It is accelerated by dissolved ionic salts which make the water a better electrical conductor.

Did you know? Rust occupies a larger volume than iron. This is what causes the blistering of paint covering a rusted surface.

The aqueous chemistry of iron ions

Tests for iron ions

Both Fe^{2+} and Fe^{3+} exist in aqueous solution as octahedral hexaaqua ions. $[Fe(H_2O)_6]^{2+}$ is pale green and $[Fe(H_2O)_6]^{3+}$ is pale brown, and dilute solutions are hard to tell apart. A simple test to distinguish the

CHEMISTRY AROUND US

Prevention of corrosion

To prevent corrosion, iron may be coated with grease, paint or another metal to keep away the water and oxygen which are essential for the reaction. Alternatively, blocks of a more reactive metal than iron can be attached to the iron surface. Magnesium is often used. In this case, the reaction:

$$Mg(s) \longrightarrow Mg^{2+}(aq) + 2e^-$$

occurs more readily than

$$Fe(s) \longrightarrow Fe^{2+}(aq) + 2e^-$$

and the magnesium will dissolve away leaving the iron intact. This is called **sacrificial protection**. The magnesium lumps, of course, need regular replacement. This method is used on ships' hulls and pipelines where a paint surface would be unlikely to stay undamaged for long. Zinc plating or galvanising has the same effect, zinc also being more reactive than iron. Once the coating is scratched a cell is set up, but the more reactive zinc dissolves rather than the iron. On tin-plated iron, as used in food cans, the reverse occurs. Tin is less reactive than iron and the iron dissolves leaving behind the tin. You may have noticed how rapidly food cans rust once they are scratched. On an unscratched can, the tin's function is to keep air and water away from the iron.

The magnesium protects the ship's hull

A tin can rusts quickly after being opened

two is to add dilute alkali which precipitates the hydroxides, whose colours are more obviously different.

$$[Fe(H_2O_6)]^{2+}(aq) + 2OH^-(aq) \longrightarrow Fe(OH)_2(s) + 6H_2O(l)$$
iron(II) hydroxide (green)

$$[Fe(H_2O_6)]^{3+}(aq) + 3OH^-(aq) \longrightarrow Fe(OH)_3(s) + 6H_2O(l)$$
iron(III) hydroxide (brown)

Two other colour reactions provide tests to distinguish Fe^{2+} from Fe^{3+} ions.

● Addition of potassium thiocyanate ($K^+ + SCN^-$) to $[Fe(H_2O_6)]^{3+}$ produces the blood-red pentaaquathiocyanate iron(III) ion.

$$[Fe(H_2O)_6]^{3+}(aq) + SCN^-(aq) \longrightarrow [Fe(H_2O)_5SCN]^{2+}(aq) + H_2O(l)$$

The colour of the ion is very intense and can be used to detect very small concentrations of $Fe^{3+}(aq)$.

● The test for $Fe^{2+}(aq)$ is the formation of a deep blue colour, Prussian blue, on addition of potassium hexacyanoferrate(III).

$$[Fe(H_2O)_6]^{2+}(aq) + [Fe(CN)_6]^{3-}(aq) \longrightarrow [Fe[Fe(CN)_6]^- + 6H_2O(l)$$
Prussian blue

The acidity of aqueous iron ions

Solutions of $Fe^{2+}(aq)$ are not appreciably acidic, whereas a solution of $Fe^{3+}(aq)$ ($pK_a = 2.2$) is a stronger acid than ethanoic acid

($pK_a = 4.8$). This is because the Fe^{3+} ion is both smaller and more highly charged than Fe^{2+} making it more strongly polarising. So in the $[Fe(H_2O)_6]^{3+}(aq)$ ion the iron strongly attracts electrons from the oxygen atoms of the water ligands thus weakening the O—H bonds in these water molecules. These will then readily donate H^+ ions making the solution acidic (**Figure 31.19**).

$$[Fe(H_2O)_6]^{3+}(aq) \rightleftharpoons [Fe(H_2O)_6OH]^{2+}(aq) + H^+(aq)$$

Figure 31.19 The acidity of $Fe^{3+}(aq)$ ions

The acidity of the aqueous Fe^{3+} ion explains why iron(III) carbonate does not exist, but iron(II) carbonate does. The Fe^{3+} ion is sufficiently acidic to react with the carbonate ion to form hydrated iron(III) hydroxide.

$$[Fe(H_2O)_6]^{3+}(aq) + 3CO_3^{2-}(aq) \rightleftharpoons [Fe(OH)_3(H_2O)_3](s) + 3HCO_3^{-}(aq)$$

CHEMISTRY AROUND US

Haemoglobin

Haemoglobin is the red pigment in blood. It is responsible for carrying oxygen from the lungs to the cells of the body.

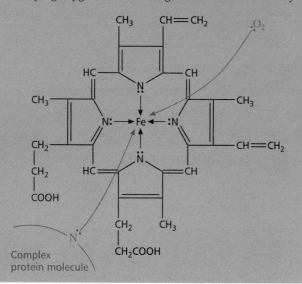

The molecule consists of an Fe^{2+} ion with a coordination number of six. Four of the coordination sites are taken up by a ring system called a porphyrin which acts as a tetradentate ligand. This complex is called 'haem'.

Below the plane of this ring is a fifth nitrogen atom acting as a ligand. This atom is part of a complex protein called globin. The sixth site can accept an oxygen molecule as a ligand. The Fe^{2+}—O_2 bond is weak, allowing the oxygen molecule to be easily given up to cells.

Better ligands than oxygen can bond irreversibly to the iron and thus destroy haemoglobin's oxygen-carrying capacity. This explains the poisonous effect of carbon monoxide and cyanide ions, both of which are very good ligands.

Anaemia is a condition which may be caused by a shortage of haemoglobin. The body suffers from a lack of oxygen and the symptoms include fatigue, breathlessness and a pale skin colour. The causes may be loss of blood or deficiency of iron in the diet. The latter may be treated by taking 'iron' tablets which contain iron(II) sulphate.

Did you know? Brass is an alloy of about 67% copper and 33% zinc.

Copper

Copper is an extensively used metal. UK consumption is almost 400 000 tonnes per year, most of which is obtained from recycling. New copper is extracted from sulphide ores. Copper's lack of chemical reactivity and ease of working makes it suitable for plumbing pipes and fittings, while its main use is as an electrical conductor. It is a constituent of many alloys such as brass, gunmetal and bronze.

Redox chemistry of copper

Copper forms only two stable oxidation states, copper(I) and copper(II), in its compounds (see **Figure 31.20**).

Copper(I) has a $3d^{10}$ electron arrangement and therefore is not transitional. As would be expected, most of its compounds are white although its best known compound, copper(I) oxide, Cu_2O, is red-brown.

Copper(II) ($3d^9$) is transitional and most of its compounds are blue in aqueous solution because of the hydrated copper ion. Copper(II) oxide, CuO, is black.

In aqueous solution $Cu^+(aq)$ will disproportionate to $Cu^{2+}(aq)$ and $Cu(s)$ as shown by the anticlockwise rule (see **Figure 31.20**).

$$2Cu^+(aq) \longrightarrow Cu(s) + Cu^{2+}(aq) \qquad E^{\ominus} = +0.37 \text{ V}$$

Some ligand displacement reactions of copper have been described in section 31.3. That with ammonia is complicated by the precipitation of insoluble, pale blue copper(II) hydroxide. An aqueous solution of ammonia contains $OH^-(aq)$ ions due to the equilibrium:

$$NH_3(aq) + H_2O(l) \rightleftharpoons NH_4^+(aq) + OH^-(aq)$$

These precipitate copper hydroxide:

$$[Cu(H_2O)_4]^{2+}(aq) + 2OH^-(aq) \longrightarrow Cu(OH)_2(s) + 4H_2O(l)$$

On adding excess ammonia, the copper dissolves as the tetraamine copper(II) ion which is a very dark blue:

$$Cu(OH)_2(s) + 4NH_3(aq) \longrightarrow [Cu_3(NH_4)]^{2+}(aq) + 2OH^-(aq)$$

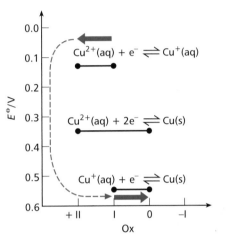

Figure 31.20 $E^{\ominus}$–Ox diagram for some copper compounds

Zinc

Zinc metal has the outer electron arrangement $3d^{10}4s^2$. It forms only one oxidation state, Zn(II) which is $3d^{10}$. The metal is therefore non-transitional, its compounds typically being white. Zinc does, however, form complexes such as the tetrahedral $[Zn(OH)_4]^{2-}(aq)$, $[Zn(NH_3)_4]^{2+}(aq)$, $[ZnCl_4]^{2-}(aq)$.

31.5 Economic importance of the d-block elements

Extraction of d-block metals

A few of the least reactive transition metals such as copper, silver and gold (the coinage metals) are found uncombined. The rest are found in ores, usually as compounds of oxygen or sulphur. The general method of extracting them is to convert the sulphides into oxides by roasting them (heating them in air). Sulphur dioxide is a by-product at this stage – it may be used for sulphuric acid manufacture. The oxide must then be reduced to the metal by a reducing agent. A suitable reducing agent must be able to reduce the oxide and also be cheap. Ellingham diagrams (see the box 'Ellingham diagrams', section 28.3) can be used to help select an appropriate reductant and a minimum temperature. Coke or carbon monoxide is used in many processes, notably in the blast furnace for making iron. Alternatively, a more reactive metal may be used to displace the required metal from its oxide.

When selecting the best reducing agent, a number of other factors must be borne in mind. A reducing agent that works at relatively low temperatures will reduce the energy requirements of the process. The required purity of the metal is also a factor. Some elements such as titanium and tungsten would form carbides if carbon were used as a reducing agent. Tungsten is extracted from its oxide, WO_3, by reduction with hydrogen at high temperature. **Table 31.8** summarises the industrial extraction of the first row d-block metals.

Some of these minerals are quite scarce overall. However, they can all be found as high grade ores (ores containing a high percentage of mineral) at a few locations on the Earth.

Table 31.8 Extraction of some transition metals from their ores

Element	Typical ore	Substance to be reduced	Reductant	Notes
Sc	Not extracted on an industrial scale			
Ti	Rutile, TiO_2	$TiCl_4$	Mg or Na	an inert atmosphere needed
V	carnolite, an ore of K, V, U and O	V_2O_5	Al	
Cr	chromite, $FeCr_2O_4$	$Na_2Cr_2O_7$	C, then Al	
Mn	pyrolusite, MnO_2, and hausmannite, Mn_3O_4	Mn_3O_4	Al	
Fe	haematite, Fe_2O_3, and magnetite, Fe_3O_4	Fe_2O_3	C(CO)	blast furnace
Co	smaltite, $CoAs_2$, and cobaltite, CoAsS	Co_3O_4	Al	
Ni	millerite, NiS	NiO	C	
Cu	copper pyrite, $CuFeS_2$, and copper glance, CuS	Cu_2S	S*	
Zn	zinc blende, ZnS, and calomine, $ZnCO_3$	ZnO	C(CO)	blast furnace

*The reaction:

$$\overset{+I\ \ -II}{Cu_2S(s)} + \overset{0}{O_2} \longrightarrow \overset{0}{2Cu} + \overset{+IV\ -II}{SO_2}$$

is used. Since Ox(S) goes up, it is the reducing agent.

FURTHER FOCUS

The purification of nickel

Nickel is produced by reducing nickel(II) oxide with carbon:

$$NiO(s) + C(s) \longrightarrow Ni(s) + CO(g)$$

Nickel of extremely high purity can be obtained by heating the impure nickel with carbon monoxide at 330 K. Carbon monoxide is a good ligand and the tetrahedral complex tetracarbonyl nickel(0) is formed.

$$Ni(s) + 4CO(g) \longrightarrow Ni(CO)_4(g)$$

This is unusual because the nickel is in oxidation state zero and a neutral complex is formed. The complex is also unusually volatile for a metal compound ($T_b = 316$ K) and it can be separated from impurities by distillation. Heating the tetracarbonylnickel(0) to 473 K decomposes it, leaving very pure nickel:

$$Ni(CO)_4(g) \longrightarrow Ni(s) + 4CO(g)$$

Some uses of d-block elements and their compounds

These are summarised in **Table 31.9**.

In addition, many d-block metal compounds are essential to the body's biochemistry, e.g. iron in haemoglobin in blood, cobalt in vitamin B_{12}, zinc and copper in several enzymes.

Table 31.9 Some uses of d-block elements and their compounds

Metal	Uses
Sc	Virtually no significant uses
Ti	Constructional – high-speed aircraft, nuclear reactors, heart pacemakers. Replacement joints, e.g. hip joints. Construction of chemical plant. TiO_2 is a white pigment in paints. $TiCl_4$ is a catalyst for making poly(alkenes)
V	Alloys – special steels
Cr	Chrome plating. Alloys – special steels. Chrome alum mordants in dyeing, also compounds as pigments
Mn	Alloys – special steels
Fe	Alloy–steel (see the box below), car bodies, reinforcing concrete, ships, bridges, general construction, domestic appliances. Catalyst in Haber process
Co	Alloy – stellite. CoCrW – cutting tools. AlNiCo, constantan, nichrome (see below). ^{60}Co – radioactive source for medical and other uses. Compounds as pigments (blue)
Ni	Alloys – coinage. AlNiCo – magnets, construction. Nichrome – electrical heating elements. Industrial catalysts, hydrogenation of oils to margarine
Cu	Electrical wiring, plumbing pipes. Many alloys, e.g. bronze, brass, gunmetal. Industrial catalyst methanol → methanal. Coinage. Destroying fungi and algae
Zn	Galvanising, alloys, e.g. brass, dry batteries. ZnO white pigments in paints

CHEMISTRY AROUND US

Steel making and alloy steels

Iron straight from the blast furnace contains impurities, such as carbon and silicon, which make it too brittle for most purposes. In steel making, the impurities are removed by blowing a jet of pure oxygen into the molten iron and adding lime, calcium oxide. The oxide impurities, being acidic because they are non-metals, combine with the basic calcium oxide to form a slag containing calcium carbonate, calcium silicate, etc. This molten slag floats on the steel and can be tapped off. In the basic oxygen process, now the most common, a water-cooled lance is used to supply the oxygen. A modern steel furnace can take a charge of 350 tonnes of iron and make it into steel in under an hour.

The composition of the steel is further tailored in the process of secondary steel making.

There are many kinds of steel for particular purposes. All have less than 1.5% carbon. Other metals may be added to give alloy steels whose exact composition can be monitored by examining the emission spectrum of a sample while the steel is still in the converter. On-line computer controlled spectrometers can deliver a print-out of the steel's composition to the furnace operator within minutes of sampling.

The table shows just a few of the thousands of alloy steels produced.

Many alloy steels are made in an electric arc furnace

where scrap steel is recycled. The scrap is melted by the heat of an electric arc struck from the steel to carbon electrodes. Precise quantities of other metals can be added to the molten scrap.

Name	Approximate composition	Special properties	Use
manganese steel	86% Fe, 13% Mn, 1% C	toughness	drill bits
stainless steel	73% Fe, 8% Ni, 18% Cr, 1% C	non-rusting	cutlery, sinks
cobalt steel	90% Fe, 9% Co, 1% C	hardness	ball bearings
tungsten steel	81% Fe, 18% W, 1% C		armour plate

Basic oxygen steel converter

FURTHER FOCUS

The extraction of iron: the blast furnace

Iron is the second most abundant metal in the Earth's crust (5.8%, after aluminium, 8.0%). It is found as the ores haematite, Fe_2O_3 and magnetite, Fe_3O_4, which are obtained by quarrying or open cast mining. British deposits are of low quality and most iron ore is imported from as far afield as Scandinavia, America and the former USSR. The major impurity is silica (SiO_2, sand).

The principle of reducing iron ore to iron with carbon has been known for over 3000 years.

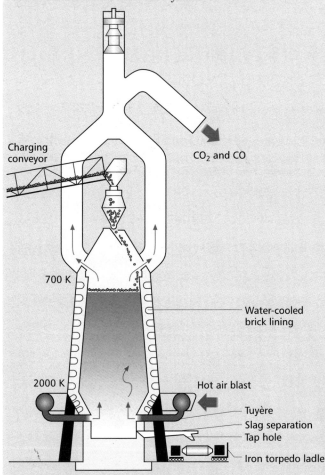

Charging conveyor

CO_2 and CO

700 K

Water-cooled brick lining

2000 K

Hot air blast

Tuyère
Slag separation
Tap hole
Iron torpedo ladle

$$CaCO_3(s) \longrightarrow CaCO(s) + CO_2(g)$$

$$Fe_2O_3(s) + 3CO(g) \longrightarrow 2Fe(l) + 3CO_2(g)$$

$$CaO(s) + SiO_2(s) \longrightarrow CaSiO_3(l)$$

$$C(s) + CO_2(g) \longrightarrow 2CO(g) \quad \Delta H = +172 \text{ kJ mol}^{-1}$$

$$C(s) + O_2(g) \longrightarrow CO_2(g) \quad \Delta H = -394 \text{ kJ mol}^{-1}$$

The furnace is shown above. It is made of steel, lined inside with firebricks.

It is charged at the top with a mixture of iron ore, coke (largely carbon) and limestone (calcium carbonate).

At the base of the furnace, coke burns in a blast of preheated air (which gives the furnace its name). Heat is generated by this exothermic reaction resulting in a temperature of approximately 2000 K (above the melting temperature of iron which is 1808 K).

The carbon dioxide produced reacts with more coke a little higher up to produce carbon monoxide, the reducing agent. This reaction is endothermic so the temperature drops.

Higher up the furnace the carbon monoxide reduces the ore to iron.

Higher still, calcium carbonate is decomposed to calcium oxide, which reacts with silicon dioxide impurities in the ore to form molten calcium silicate (slag).

The molten iron and slag trickle to the base of the furnace. Slag floats on top of the molten iron and the two can be tapped off and separated.

Operation of the furnace is continuous, producing up to 10 000 tonnes of iron per day. About every twenty years, the furnace is shut down for replacement of the brick lining.

The waste slag solidifies and must be disposed of. Nowadays slag is used for road construction and cement manufacture. The iron produced is 90–5% pure, containing silicon, sulphur, and phosphorus impurities as well as around 4% carbon which makes it brittle.

Blast furnace

Blast furnace being tapped

31.6 Summary

- The first row of the d-block elements are those in the series from — scandium to zinc.

- The second row are those in the series from — yttrium to cadmium.

- The third row are those in the series from — lanthanum to mercury.

- The definition of a transition metal is — an element which forms at least one compound in which it has a part-filled d-shell of electrons.

- The 3d shell is an inner shell and d electrons screen — the outer electrons from the nuclear charge.

- The physical properties of d-block elements tend to be — similar to one another.

- The d-block metals have the properties of typical metals: — hard, strong, shiny, good conductors of electricity and heat and fairly high densities.

- Their chemistry is typified by four characteristics: — variable oxidation numbers; complex formation; coloured compounds; catalytic activity.

- Complexes are formed when ligands form — dative covalent bonds with transition metals.

- The charge on a complex may be — neutral, positive or negative.

- A ligand which can form more than one dative bond is called — polydentate (many toothed).

- Complexes with polydentate ligands are called — chelates.

- Isomers are compounds with — the same molecular formula but different spatial arrangements of atoms.

- The three types of isomerism which occur in d-block metal complexes are: — ionisation isomerism; geometrical (*cis-trans*) isomerism; optical (mirror image) isomerism.

- Good ligands may displace — poorer ligands from complexes.

- The stability of a complex is measured by — the log of its stability constant, $\log K$.

- The larger $\log K$ — the more stable the complex.

- Chelates are usually very stable because their formation involves — an increase in entropy in the system.

- The colour of d-block metal compounds is caused by — electrons moving from one d orbital to another (whose energy is slightly different owing to the effect of ligands).

31.7 Practice questions

1. Give the oxidation states of the metal in
    (a) $[Co(NH_3)_6]^{3+}$, (b) $[CoCl_4]^{2-}$, (c) $[Ni(CN_4)]^{2-}$.

2. Explain carefully why scandium and zinc are
    (a) d-block metals but (b) not transition metals.
    (c) Give another d-block ion from the first d-series which is not transitional.

3. Write the formulae of the following ions.
    (a) hexaaquachromium(III),
    (b) tetramminedichlorocobalt(III),
    (c) tetraaquadihydroxoiron(III)

4. This question is about aqueous solutions of copper(II) sulphate. Some stability constants of complex ions are given below.

log K	Complex	
5.6	$[CuCl_4]^{2-}(aq)$	(yellow)
13.1	$[Cu(NH_3)_4]^{2+}(aq)$	(deep blue)
18.8	$[Cuedta]^{2+}$	(pale blue)

    (a) What colour is an aqueous solution of copper(II) sulphate?
    (b) What ion is responsible for this colour?
    (c) Describe and explain what happens when excess concentrated hydrochloric acid is added to the solution.

(d) Describe and explain what would happen if excess ammonia solution is added to the solution remaining after (c).

(e) Describe and explain what would happen if a solution of edta(aq) was added to the solution remaining after (d).

(f) What would happen if ammonia solution is added directly to the original solution? Why is it different to what happened in (d)?

(g)

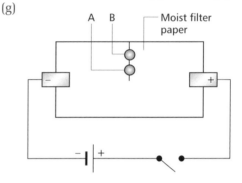

A drop containing $[CuCl_4]^{2-}(aq)$ is placed at A, and a drop containing $[Cu(NH_3)_4]^{2+}(aq)$ at B. What will happen when the current is switched on?

31.8 Examination questions

1. (a) Complete the boxes below to show the electronic configuration of a V^{3+} ion using the convention shown for the V atom.

    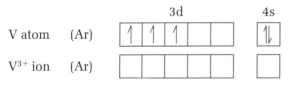

    (b) Vanadium is a transition element. Give two characteristic properties of such a transition element other than the ability to form coloured ions.
    (c) Ammonium vanadate(V) dissolves in sulphuric acid to give a yellow solution, the colour being due to the VO_2^+ ion.
        (i) What is the oxidation number of vanadium in the VO_2^+ ion?
        (ii) Give the systematic name of the VO_2^+ ion.
    (d) Treatment of the yellow solution from (c) with zinc causes the colour to change to green then to blue, followed by green again and finally violet. Give the formulae of the ions responsible for each of these colours.

(e) In the sequence of changes in (d), zinc acts as a reducing agent.
    (i) State the meaning of the term **reducing agent**.
    (ii) Write a half equation showing how zinc acts as a reducing agent.
(f) (i) Write the half equation for the conversion of VO_2^+ to VO^{2+} in acid solution.
    (ii) Hence write the equation for the reduction of VO_2^+ to VO^{2+} by zinc.
                                    [London (Nuffield) 1998]

2. (a) List **three** *chemical* characteristics of the transition elements.
    (b) Give **one** example, of your own choice, of the *chemical* use of a named transition metal of the 3d series **or** one of its compounds in a major industrial process. State the chemical property on which the use depends.
    (c) Complete the boxes at the top of the next column by inserting arrows to show the ground state electronic configuration of

(i) a chromium atom;

	3d					4s
Argon core						

(ii) a Cr^{3+} ion.

	3d					4s
Argon core						

(d) In acidic aqueous solution the dichromate(VI) ion, $Cr_2O_7^{2-}$, is a powerful oxidising agent. The oxidation of iron(II) ions by dichromate(VI) ions may be represented by

$$Cr_2O_7^{2-}(aq) + 14H^+(aq) + 6Fe^{2+}(aq)$$
$$\longrightarrow 2Cr^{3+}(aq) + 6Fe^{3+}(aq) + 7H_2O(l)$$

(i) Deduce the change in the oxidation state of chromium in this reaction.

(ii) Calculate the number of moles of $Fe^{2+}(aq)$ in 25.00 cm³ of acidic aqueous iron(II) sulphate containing 12.15 g dm⁻³ of iron(II) sulphate, $FeSO_4$, ($M_r = 151.91$).

(iii) Calculate the volume of aqueous potassium dichromate(VI) of concentration 0.0200 mol dm⁻³ that will completely oxidise the number of moles of $Fe^{2+}(aq)$ in (d)(ii).

(e) State what you would expect to see if aqueous sodium hydroxide was added slowly to a solution of aqueous chromium(III) sulphate until the alkali is in excess.

[WJEC 1997]

3. (a) Give **two** physical properties of iron metal which show it to be a typical d-block element.

(b) (i) Complete the following ground state electronic configurations, where [Ar] represents the ground state electronic configuration of the argon atom.

    Fe   [Ar] ....
    Fe^{2+} [Ar] ....

(ii) Explain why the Fe^{2+} ion might be expected to be less stable than the Fe^{3+} ion.

(c) (i) State the colour of aqueous solutions of iron(II) salts. Give the formula and shape of the complex ion responsible for the colour.

(ii) What colour change slowly occurs if a solution containing this ion is allowed to stand? Explain your answer.

(d) (i) What would be observed if aqueous potassium iodide were added to an aqueous solution containing Fe^{3+} ions? Explain any observations in terms of the reaction taking place.

(ii) Write an ionic equation for the reaction.

(e) Explain why compounds of d-block elements are often coloured.

[AEB 1998]

4. A solution of cobalt(II) chloride was reacted with ammonia and ammonium chloride while a current of air was blown through the mixture. A red compound, **X**, was produced which contained a complex ion of cobalt. The compound had the following composition:

	% by mass
Co	23.6
N	27.9
H	6.0
Cl	42.5

(a) Use the data to confirm that the empirical formula of **X** is $CoN_5H_{15}Cl_3$.

(b) A sample of **X** with mass 1.00 g reacted with silver nitrate solution and 1.15 g of silver chloride was formed.
Calculate the number of moles of free chloride ions per mole of **X** using the information that the molecular and empirical formulae of **X** are the same. Hence deduce the formula of the complex ion in **X**.
Predict the three dimensional structure of the ion and show this in a sketch indicating the positions of the different ligands.

(c) Explain the role of the air, the ammonia and the ammonium chloride in the formation of **X**, giving equations where appropriate. An overall equation is not required.

(d) A solution of cobalt(II) chloride reacts with concentrated hydrochloric acid forming a complex ion which is tetrahedral. With solutions containing the bidentate ethanedioate ions, $C_2O_4^{2-}$, cobalt forms an octahedral complex ion.
Deduce the formula for these two complexes and suggest why different coordination numbers occur in these complexes.

[London (Nuffield) 1998]

32

Arenes

CHEMISTRY NOW

Kevlar: a polymer five times stronger than steel

One of the most successful polymers of recent years was developed by the Du Pont company and has the trade name Kevlar. It is one of a class of compounds called aramids. Formed into fibres, it is five times stronger than steel on a weight-to-weight basis. It is in fact used as a replacement for steel in the manufacture of car tyres and is also used for boat sails and in making aircraft wings. Its strength is best illustrated by its use in making bullet-proof vests and flak jackets.

Racing drivers wear Kevlar clothing because it is fire-resistant as well as abrasion-resistant

Kevlar has the structure shown below. It is a polyamide, like nylon, held together by the amide group —CONH—. Unlike those in nylon, the amide groups link benzene rings. These rings are described as aromatic, hence the name 'aramids'. The difference in properties between nylon and Kevlar is accounted for by the rigidity of the flat benzene rings as opposed to the flexibility of the alkyl groups which link the amide groups in nylon.

Kevlar

Benzene rings

Kevlar can help protect motor cyclists even in high speed falls

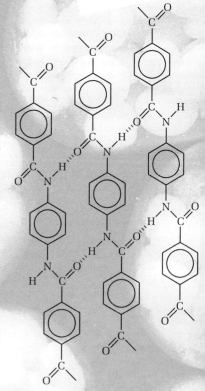

The polymer chains in Kevlar are linked together by hydrogen bonds as shown to form sheets. These sheets pack together well like a pile of sheets of paper.

Although the chemistry of the polymerisation process is similar to that of nylon, the development of Kevlar was not without problems. One of these was that the only suitable solvent for it was concentrated sulphuric acid!

Introduction

Arenes, often called aromatic compounds, are organic compounds which are derivatives of benzene, C_6H_6. The simplest arene is benzene itself. It has a ring structure that is particularly stable because of its unique bonding. Benzene and related compounds have characteristic properties. Such compounds were first isolated from sweet-smelling oils such as balsam, hence the name 'aromatic' which has now been taken over to refer to their structures rather than their aromas.

Benzene is given the special symbol ⬡

Arenes can have substituents attached to a benzene ring or can be based on two or more rings fused together as in the examples below.

naphthalene   anthracene   phenanthrene

32.1 Bonding and structure of benzene

The bonding and structure of benzene and related compounds was a long-standing puzzle to the early organic chemists (see the box 'The structure of benzene').

Benzene consists of a flat, regular hexagon of carbon atoms, each of which is bonded to a single hydrogen. The geometry of benzene is shown in **Figure 32.1**. The benzene molecule is unexpectedly stable.

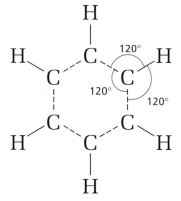

Figure 32.1 The geometry of benzene. The dashed lines show the shape and do not represent single bonds

Table 32.1 Carbon–carbon bond lengths

Bond	Length/nm
C—C	0.154
C≈C (in benzene)	0.140
C=C	0.134
C≡C	0.120

The C—C bond lengths in benzene have been found to be half-way between those expected for a carbon–carbon single bond and a carbon–carbon double bond (see **Table 32.1**). Each bond is intermediate between a single and a double bond. The symbol

is used to represent this. The carbon atoms are bonded by σ bonds and there is a ring of electron density like a doughnut above and below the ring. This is an extended (delocalised) π bond and is responsible for many of benzene's characteristic properties and its unusual stability. The box 'Bonding in benzene' gives a more detailed picture of the bonding using the idea of hybridisation of orbitals (see the boxes 'Hybridisation' in section 9.1 and 'A more sophisticated picture' in section 18.2.

Evidence for the delocalised structure and extra stability of benzene

Bond lengths

There is a relationship between bond length and bond order (single, double, triple, etc.) for bonds between the same pair of atoms (see section 9.1). X-ray diffraction shows that all the C—C bond lengths in benzene are the same and are 0.140 nm (midway between C—C and C=C (see **Figure 32.2**). This is consistent with the p orbitals overlapping the whole molecule.

FURTHER FOCUS

Bonding in benzene

A better picture of the bonding in benzene is given by using the idea of hybridisation. Each carbon is hybridised so that it has three sp² orbitals and one p orbital. A hexagonal skeleton of six σ orbitals is formed by the overlap of sp² orbitals. The other sp² orbital forms a σ bond with hydrogen, see below.

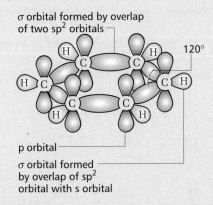

The bonding in benzene

The angles of a regular hexagon are 120°

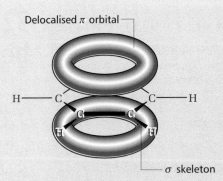

The delocalised π orbital in benzene

The angle between sp² orbitals is 120° and this is the angle of a regular hexagon (see the diagram). So the benzene molecule has no ring strain. The 'spare' p orbitals overlap to give a delocalised π orbital all the way round the hexagon. This results in an orbital consisting of a doughnut-shaped cloud of electron density above and below the plane of the hexagon (see the diagram). Wherever a delocalised structure occurs, the resulting molecule is more stable than would otherwise be expected.

There is a similarity between the bonding in benzene and the bonding in graphite (see section 9.2).

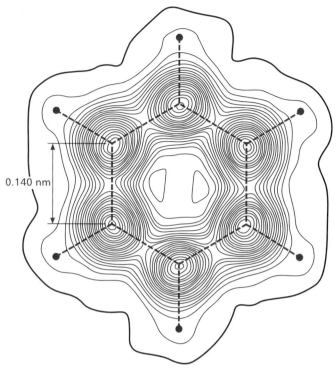

Figure 32.2 An electron density contour map of benzene obtained from X-ray diffraction

Electron density map

The electron density contour map of benzene obtained from X-ray diffraction (Figure 32.2) clearly shows the high electron density equally spread around the whole hexagon.

Thermochemical evidence

Thermochemical cycles can be used to compare the actual benzene molecule with the hypothetical Kekulé-type structure (see the box 'The structure of benzene'). In every case, the real benzene molecule turns out to be much more stable than the Kekulé-type structure.

Enthalpies of hydrogenation

The enthalpy change for hydrogenation of cyclohexene is:

$$\Delta H^{\ominus} = -120 \text{ kJ mol}^{-1}$$

cyclohexene   cyclohexane

Therefore the enthalpy change of hydrogenation of hypothetical Kekulé-type benzene should be three times this:

$$\Delta H^{\ominus} = -360 \text{ kJ mol}^{-1}$$

'Kekulé-type'   cyclohexane
benzene

> **Q** What would be the systematic name for Kekulé-type benzene?

> **Hint:** Remember that in cyclohexane there are two hydrogen atoms at each 'corner'; in benzene there is only one.

Answer: 1,3,5-cyclohexatriene

The structure of benzene

Benzene's formula, C_6H_6, implies a good deal of unsaturation (the chain alkane of length C_6 has the formula C_6H_{14}). Formulae like

$$CH_2{=}C{=}\overset{\overset{\displaystyle H}{|}}{C}{-}\overset{\overset{\displaystyle H}{|}}{C}{=}C{=}CH_2$$

were proposed but benzene rarely undergoes addition reactions, which would be expected of a compound of this structure. In 1865 Friedrich August Kekulé proposed a ring structure following a dream about atoms 'in snake-like motion' where one of the snakes had seized hold of its own tail. Conventional ideas about bonding require this structure to have three double bonds as shown below. This **Kekulé-type** representation is still used in many books.

or   in skeletal notation

However, there are three objections to this proposed structure:

● A cyclic triene should show addition reactions which benzene rarely does.
● This structure should give rise to two isomeric disubstituted compounds as shown:

and

(i.e the two substituents could be separated by a double bond or a single bond).

● The hexagon would not be symmetrical: double bonds are shorter than single bonds.

Kekulé himself suggested a solution to the second dilemma by proposing that benzene consisted of structures in rapid equilibrium

Later this rapid alternation of two structures evolved into the idea of **resonance** between two structures, both of which contribute to the actual structure. The actual structure was thought to be a hybrid (a sort of average) of the two. Such **resonance hybrids** were believed to be more stable than either of the separate structures. Current ideas about the structure of benzene are described in the box 'Bonding and structure in benzene'.

Friedrich August Kekulé

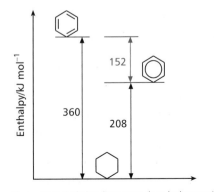

Figure 32.3 Enthalpy diagram to show hydrogenation of benzene and hypothetical Kekulé-type benzene

The enthalpy change of hydrogenation of 'real' benzene is:

$$\Delta H^{\ominus} = -208 \text{ kJ mol}^{-1}$$

We can put both real and Kekulé-type benzene on an enthalpy diagram with cyclohexane as the common point (**Figure 32.3**). This shows that 'real' benzene is 152 kJ mol^{-1} more stable than Kekulé-type benzene.

Enthalpy change of atomisation

We can calculate the enthalpy change of atomisation of 'real' benzene for the thermochemical cycle below. (It is 5561 kJ mol^{-1}.)

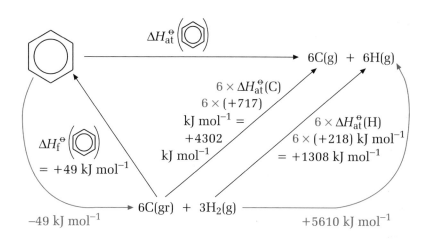

The enthalpy change of atomisation of 'Kekulé-type' benzene can be calculated from bond energies:

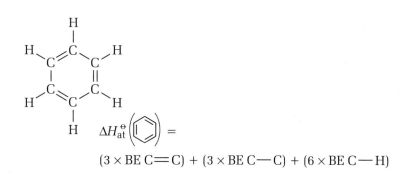

$$\Delta H_{at}^{\ominus}\left(\text{benzene}\right) = (3 \times BE\ C\!=\!C) + (3 \times BE\ C\!-\!C) + (6 \times BE\ C\!-\!H)$$

Using tabulated bond energies:

$$\Delta H_{at}^{\ominus}\left(\text{benzene}\right) = (3 \times 612) + (3 \times 347) + (6 \times 413)$$
$$= 1836 + 1041 + 2478$$
$$= +5355\ \text{kJ mol}^{-1}$$

Again, both values can be put on an enthalpy diagram with the separate atoms as the common factor (**Figure 32.4**).

This calculation shows that 'real' benzene is 206 kJ mol^{-1} more stable than 'Kekulé-type benzene'.

The above two calculations make it clear that benzene is more stable than expected by something like 150 to 200 kJ mol^{-1}. This quantity is called the **aromatic stabilisation energy**. Benzene's stability is due to its bonding of σ bonds plus a delocalised π bond which extends over the whole ring. This produces 'doughnuts' of high electron density above and below the molecule. The resulting bonds may be thought of as having a bond order of around 1.5 – intermediate between double and single. Both the high electron density and the unusual stability, sometimes called the **aromatic stability**, are important in the chemistry of benzene and its derivatives.

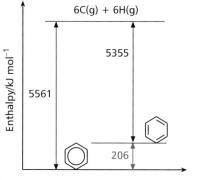

Figure 32.4 Enthalpy diagram to show the atomisation of benzene and hypothetical 'Kekulé-type' benzene

Hint: The discrepancy between the two calculations can be explained by the fact that tabulated bond energies are only averages.

32.2 Naming aromatic compounds

Substituted arenes are generally named as derivatives of benzene, so benzene forms the root of the name.

 is called methylbenzene;

is called chlorobenzene and so on.

With more than one substituent, **locants** are used to show where they are attached. The ring is numbered from where the principal group (see section 18.4) is attached at carbon 1. So:

is 2-aminobenzenecarbaldehyde.

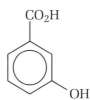 is 3-hydroxybenzenecarboxylic acid.

However,

is still called phenol and not benzeneol (hydroxybenzene is occasionally used)

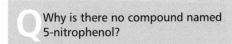

Q Why is there no compound named 5-nitrophenol?

is called 2-nitrophenol.

Benzene rings with two —OH groups are named systematically:

is benzene-1,2-diol

When a benzene ring is regarded as a side chain, 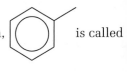 is called

Answer: It is the same as 2-nitrophenol and we always use the smaller number for locants.

the phenyl group. Sometimes a conflict arises:

could be named phenylmethane or methylbenzene. It is usually called methylbenzene because most of its reactions are those of benzene rather than those of methane. The name draws attention to this.

could be named phenylethene or ethenylbenzene.

In this case the main reactions are those of ethene rather than those of benzene, so phenylethene is usually chosen.

As always, it is more important to be able to work from the name to the correct structure than to name a compound correctly whose formula you know.

Examples

You can test yourself by covering the names or the structures.

ethylbenzene

benzene-carboxylic acid

nitrobenzene

1,2-dimethyl-benzene

Hint: Non-systematic names are still used for many derivatives of benzene. In particular benzenecarboxylic acid is nearly always called benzoic acid and benzenecarbaldehyde, benzaldehyde.

32.3 Physical properties of arenes

Benzene is a liquid at room temperature. It boils at 353 K and freezes at 279 K. Its boiling temperature is comparable with that of hexane (342 K) but its melting temperature is much higher than hexane's (178 K). This is because benzene's flat, hexagonal molecules pack together very well in the solid state. They are therefore harder to separate, and this separation is necessary for the solid to melt.

Side chains on the benzene ring increase the boiling temperature by about 30 K per carbon atom of the side chain, because the larger molecules have large van der Waals forces. However, side chains on the benzene ring *decrease* the melting temperature considerably compared with benzene because the side chain reduces the molecules' symmetry and prevents them from packing together efficiently (see **Table 32.2**).

Hint: Remember that the melting temperature is the same as the freezing temperature.

Table 32.2 Melting and boiling temperatures of some aromatic compounds

Compound	T_m/K	T_b/K
benzene	279	353
methylbenzene	178	384
ethylbenzene	178	409
propylbenzene	174	432
1,2-dimethylbenzene	248	418
1,3-dimethylbenzene	225	412
1,4-dimethylbenzene	286	411

Naphthalene is a volatile solid at room temperature

(T_m = 354 K, T_b = 491 K). It is used in mothballs – the smell demonstrating its volatility. The increased melting and boiling temperatures are what would be expected from its relative molecular mass.

Like other hydrocarbons that are non-polar, arenes do not mix wit water, but mix with other hydrocarbons and other non-polar solvents

32.4 Reactivity of arenes

Q What sort of charge does an electrophile have?

Two important factors govern the reactivity of arenes. Firstly the rin has an area of high electron density and is therefore susceptible to attack by electrophiles.

Secondly, although the ring is unsaturated and addition reactions might be expected, the stability of the aromatic ring is such that the system is rarely destroyed and substitution reactions are far more common.

Any reaction which destroys the aromatic system will require an amount of energy to be *put in*, equal to the aromatic stabilisation energy. This tends to make such reactions endothermic.

The above two points mean that the majority of the reactions of aromatic systems are **electrophilic substitution** reactions. Bear in mind that aromatic compounds that have substituents will show the reactions of the substituents as well as those of the aromatic system.

32.5 Reactions of arenes

Combustion

Q Compare the C : H ratio of benzene, C_6H_6, with that of hexane, C_6H_{14}.

Hint: Examiners often use 'burns with a smoky flame' as a hint that a compound is aromatic.

Because of their high carbon : hydrogen ratio, arenes burn in air with flames that are noticeably smoky. This means there is often unburned carbon remaining which produces soot. A smoky flame can be used as a pointer to the presence of an aromatic system in a compound.

Electrophilic substitution reactions

These involve attack by electrophiles, which are attracted by the high electron density of the delocalised system of the aromatic ring. These electrons are similarly attracted towards the electrophile and bond forms with the cloud of π electrons. The species formed is called a π complex. We will use El^+ to represent the electrophile.

Arenes burn with a smoky flame

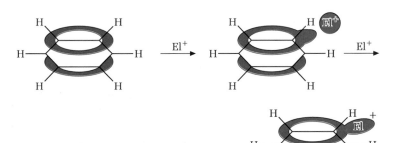

π complex

Answer: Positive – either as a positive ion or the positive end of a dipole

Answer: Benzene 1 : 1; hexane, 6 : 14 (1 : 2.3).

Hint: In organic chemistry, 'curly' arrows are used to indicate the movement of pairs of electrons.

Eventually a bond is formed between one of the carbon atoms and the electrophile. To do this, the carbon must use the electrons that it contributes to the delocalised system. This destroys the aromatic system. To regain the stability of the aromatic system, the carbon ejects a hydrogen ion.

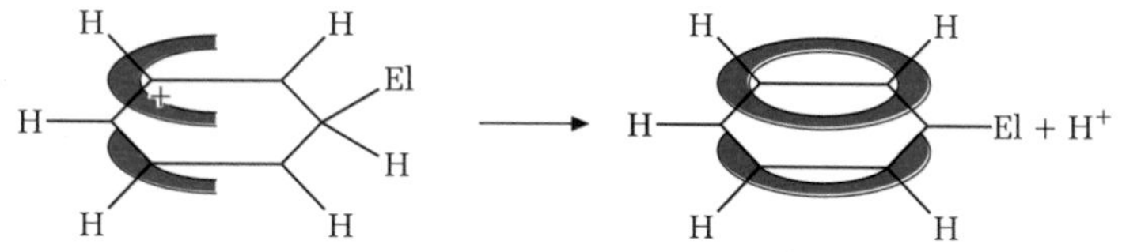

The sum total of this is the replacement or substitution of H^+ by El^+.

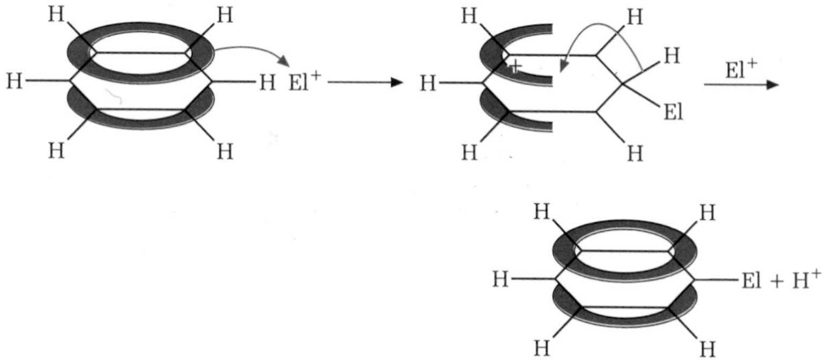

The same overall process occurs in nitration, halogenation, Friedel–Crafts and sulphonation reactions.

Nitration

Nitration is the substitution of an —NO_2 group for one of the hydrogens on the ring.

The electrophile NO_2^+ is generated in the reaction mixture of concentrated nitric and sulphuric acids:

Hint: H_2SO_4 is a stronger acid than HNO_3 and donates a proton (H^+) to HNO_3 which then loses a molecule of water to give NO_2^+.

$$HNO_3 + 2H_2SO_4 \longrightarrow NO_2^+ + H^+ + 2HSO_4^- + H_2O$$

The overall product of the reaction of the NO_2^+ with benzene is nitrobenzene:

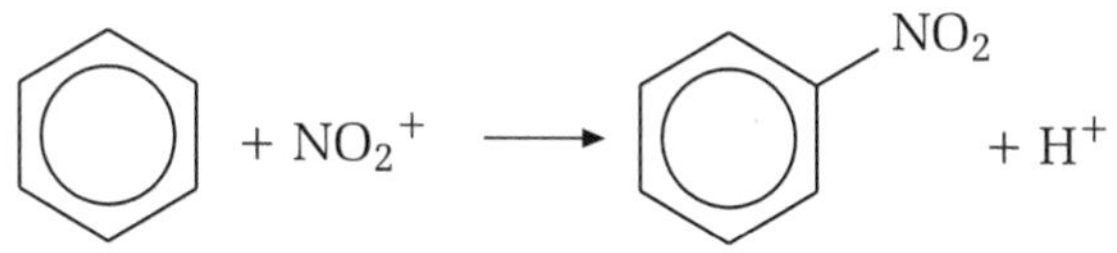

nitrobenzene

However, a little dinitrobenzene may also be formed by the further attack of NO_2^+ on nitrobenzene. In fact, only a small percentage of dinitrobenzene is formed. This is because the nitro- group withdraws electrons from the ring and so nitrobenzene is less susceptible to attack by electrophiles than benzene itself. Like most electron-withdrawing groups, the nitro- group directs further substituents to the 3 position (see below), so the main disubstituted isomer produced is 1,3-dinitrobenzene.

TNT

Methylbenzene, ⟨CH₃ structure⟩, formerly called toluene,

is more susceptible than benzene to attack by electrophiles because the methyl group releases electrons onto the ring. Electron-releasing groups direct further substitution to the 2-,4- and 6- positions (see section 32.5). If nitration of methylbenzene is carried out under sufficiently vigorous conditions (refluxing with a mixture of fuming nitric acid and sulphuric acid) the ring can be made to accept three nitro-substituents and 1-methyl-2,4,6-trinitrobenzene (trinitrotoluene, TNT) is formed. However, there is little danger of forming this product by accident. Nitro groups are electron-withdrawing and each additional one makes the ring less reactive and less likely to react with another NO_2^+ ion. So nitration of methylbenzene under mild conditions is safe enough to be used as a school practical.

TNT is an important high explosive with both military and peaceful applications. It is a solid of low melting point (less than 373 K) and can therefore be melted easily. This property is used both in filling shells etc. and by bomb disposal teams who can melt TNT out of unexploded bombs using steam to heat it.

The explosion of TNT is shown in the following equation:

$$2 \; \text{(1-methyl-2,4,6-trinitrobenzene)} \; (s) + 10\tfrac{1}{2}O_2(g) \longrightarrow$$
$$14\,CO_2(g) + 3N_2(g) + 5H_2O(g)$$

The reaction is strongly exothermic and the rapid formation of a lot of gas as well as heat produces the destructive effect. The water will, of course, be steam at the temperature of an explosion.

1,3,5-trinitrophenol (picric acid) can explode on impact and is therefore useful as a detonator to set off other explosives.

Filling TNT shells (1940)

1,3-dinitrobenzene

To produce nitrobenzene, benzene is refluxed with a mixture of nitric and sulphuric acids at 330 K. The dinitrobenzenes are solids and can be separated from the liquid nitrobenzene by cooling the mixture.

Halogenation

Halogenation is the substitution of a halogen atom for one of the hydrogens on the aromatic ring. Halogens can act as electrophiles by virtue of their instantaneous dipoles $X^{\delta+}$—$X^{\delta-}$ (see section 20.4). However, they are not good enough electrophiles to react with benzene except in the presence of a catalyst. Suitable catalysts are aluminium halides or iron filings (which react with halogens to form iron(III) halides). The catalysts work as shown using bromine and iron filings as an example:

$$\overset{\delta+}{Br}\!-\!\overset{\delta-}{Br}\!: \ + \ \overset{\delta+}{Fe}\!\!\begin{array}{c} \nearrow \overset{\delta-}{Br} \\ -\overset{\delta-}{Br} \\ \searrow \overset{\delta-}{Br} \end{array} \ \rightleftharpoons \ Br^+ \ + \ FeBr_4^-$$

A small concentration of the electrophile Br^+ is formed, which then attacks the benzene ring. The mechanism is as for nitration. First a π complex is formed, followed by the formation of a bond between Br^+ and one of the carbon atoms:

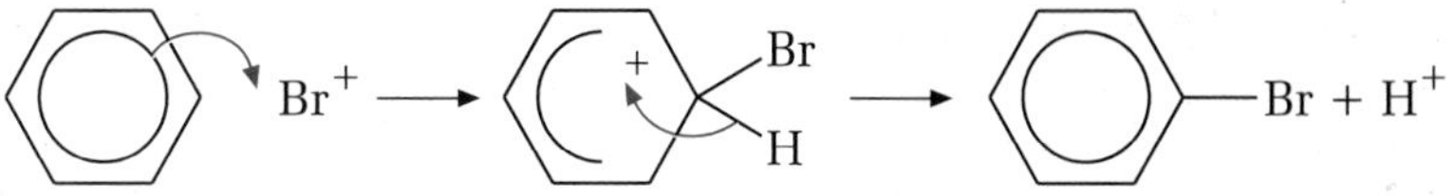

An H^+ ion is then lost.
    The overall reaction is:

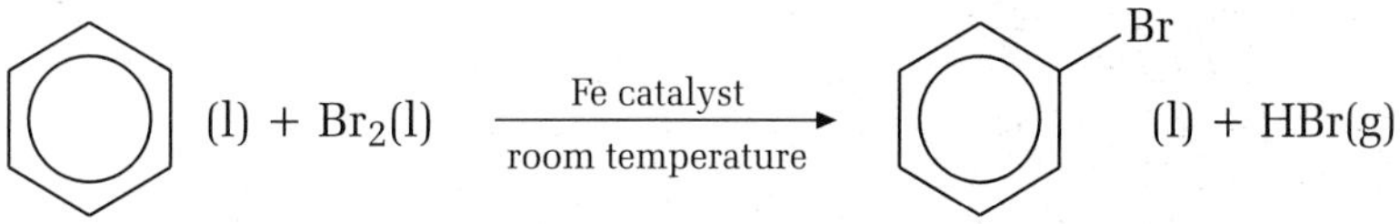

The hydrogen bromide can be detected as it forms white fumes on contact with moist air. Its presence confirms that hydrogen has been removed from the benzene and so the reaction must be *substitution* rather than *addition*. The equivalent reaction works with chlorine, and the aluminium chloride, $AlCl_3$, catalyst works in the same way as iron(III) bromide, $FeBr_3$. Neither reaction needs UV light, although halogens will *add on* to arenes in UV light (see below).
    All the halogens, being electronegative, withdraw electrons from the benzene ring, making it less susceptible to attack by electrophiles, so little disubstituted product is formed. Halogens are exceptions to the general rule that electron-withdrawing substituents direct further substitution to the 3- position. Halogens direct to the 2- and 4- positions, so some 1,2-dihalobenzene and 1,4-dihalobenzene may be formed.
    Interhalogen compounds such as iodine monochloride, ICl, also attack benzene rings. In this case, only iodobenzene is formed. This is because iodine monochloride has a permanent dipole, $I^{\delta+}\!-\!Cl^{\delta-}$, due to the greater electronegativity of chlorine than iodine. The benzene ring is thus attacked only by the $I^{\delta+}$.

> **Hint:** Another test for hydrogen halides is that they form white fumes with ammonia.

> **Q** What would be the product if benzene were reacted with Cl—Br?

> **Hint:** In organic chemistry, R— is used to indicate an unspecified organic group. Here it represents an alkyl group, such as methyl, CH_3—, ethyl, C_2H_5—, etc.

Friedel–Crafts reactions

These reactions substitute an organic group, R, for a hydrogen on an aromatic ring. They also involve the use of aluminium chloride as a catalyst and were discovered by Charles Friedel and James Crafts.

Both chloroalkanes, R—Cl, and acid chlorides, $R\!-\!\overset{\displaystyle O}{\underset{\displaystyle Cl}{\overset{\|}{C}}}$, react

with $AlCl_3$ (which is an electron-deficient compound because the

Answer: Bromobenzene

aluminium atom has only six electrons in its outer shell) to form $AlCl_4^-$ and R^+ or $R-C^+=O$ respectively:

$$R-Cl + AlCl_3 \rightleftharpoons R^+ + AlCl_4^-$$

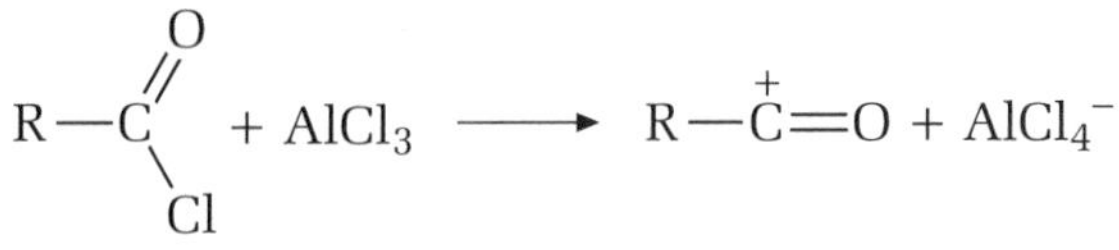

$$R-\overset{\overset{\displaystyle O}{\|}}{\underset{\underset{\displaystyle Cl}{\diagdown}}{C}} + AlCl_3 \longrightarrow R-\overset{+}{C}=O + AlCl_4^-$$

Both R^+ and $R-C^+=O$ are good electrophiles which attack the benzene ring to form substitution products in the same way as other electrophiles.

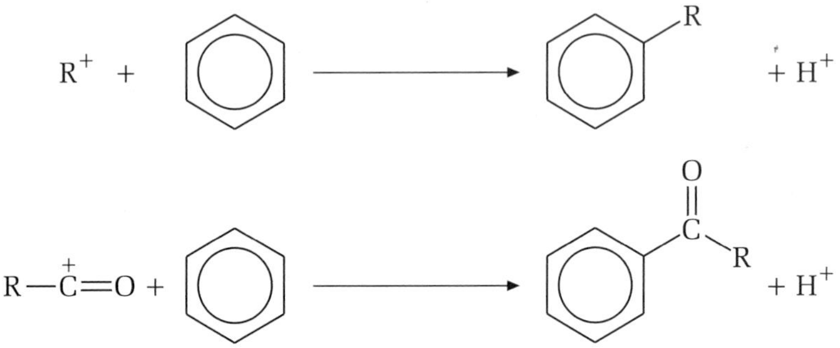

The products are alkyl-substituted arenes or aromatic ketones (see Chapter 33) respectively. The overall reactions are:

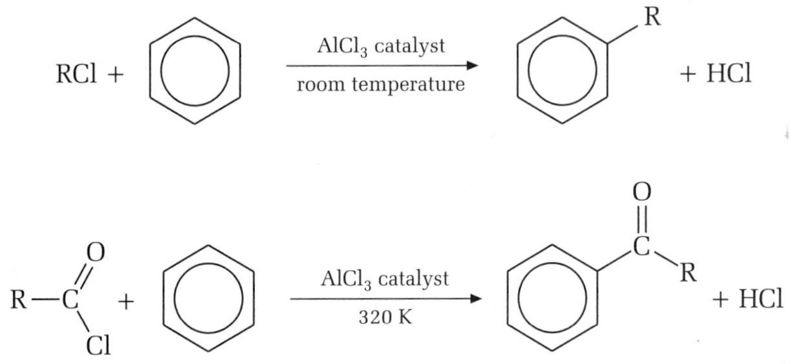

Notice the similarity between the way the aluminium chloride acts as a catalyst and the action of the iron(III) bromide in the halogenation reaction. Both act by generating a good electrophile.

Alkylation can also be achieved by reacting benzene with an alkene in the presence of an acid and an aluminium chloride catalyst. Here the electrophile is produced by the protonation of the alkene by the acid.

An electrophile such as $H-\overset{\overset{\displaystyle H}{|}}{\underset{\underset{\displaystyle H}{|}}{C}}-\overset{\overset{\displaystyle H}{|}}{\underset{+}{C}}-H$ is the attacking species.

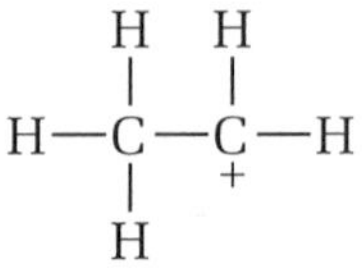

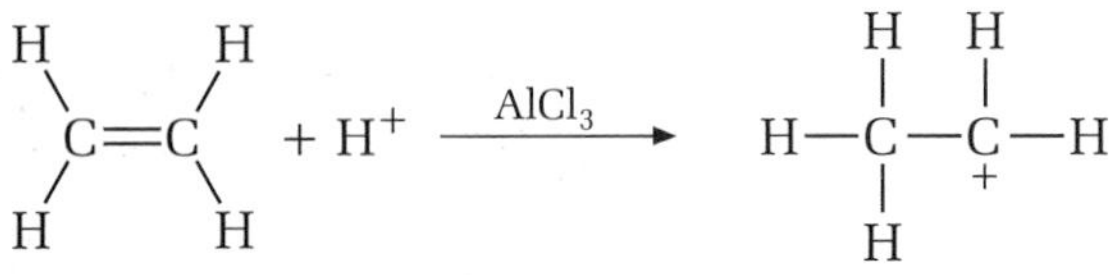

Then:

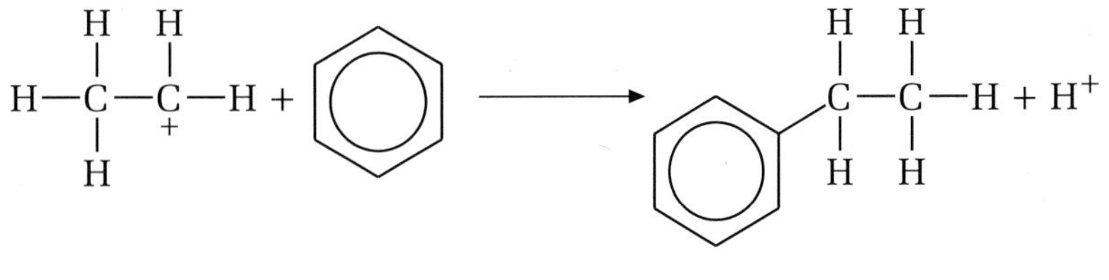

Sulphonation

This involves substitution of an —SO_3H group for a hydrogen on the aromatic ring. When benzene is refluxed with concentrated sulphuric acid or fuming sulphuric acid (a solution of sulphur trioxide in sulphuric acid) benzenesulphonic acid is formed. The electrophile is thought to be the HSO_3^+ ion.

Hint: Notice that the product has a C—S bond unlike that in ethyl hydrogensulphate, $C_2H_5SO_4H$ (see section 20.4), which has a C—O bond.

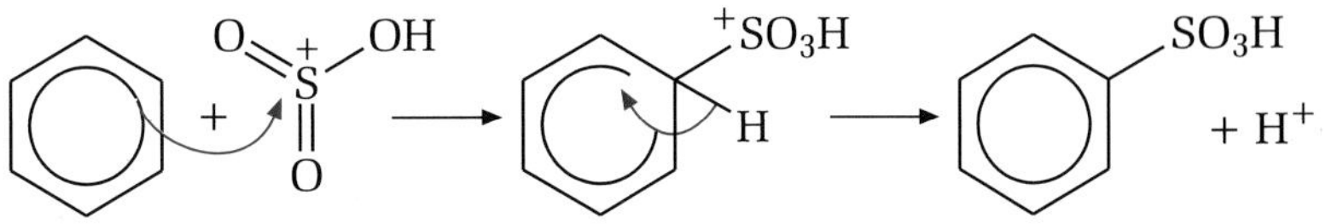

benzenesulphonic acid

The Friedel–Crafts reaction and sulphonation both have industrial uses in making detergents (see the box 'Manufacture of detergents').

FURTHER FOCUS

The cumene process

Phenol is an important intermediate for the manufacturing of many products (see Figure 32.6). Almost all the phenol produced today is made by the **cumene process**.

Benzene and propene are heated together with an aluminium chloride catalyst to produce (1-methylethyl)-benzene which is called cumene.

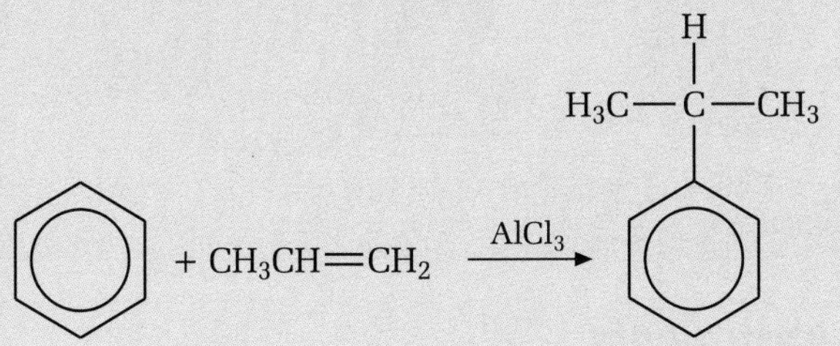

This is then oxidised by air to give a compound called a hydroperoxide which is decomposed in the presence of acid to phenol and propanone.

The economics of this process are very favourable. The raw materials are air, benzene and propene – the last two being plentiful products of the petroleum industry. Another saleable product is produced as well as phenol: propanone is in demand as a solvent and in the manufacture of bisphenol A, which is used to make epoxy and polycarbonate resins. In the manufacture of bisphenol A, phenol is reacted with propanone. The cumene process produces one mole of propanone to every mole of phenol – approximately 6 tonnes of propanone for 10 tonnes of phenol.

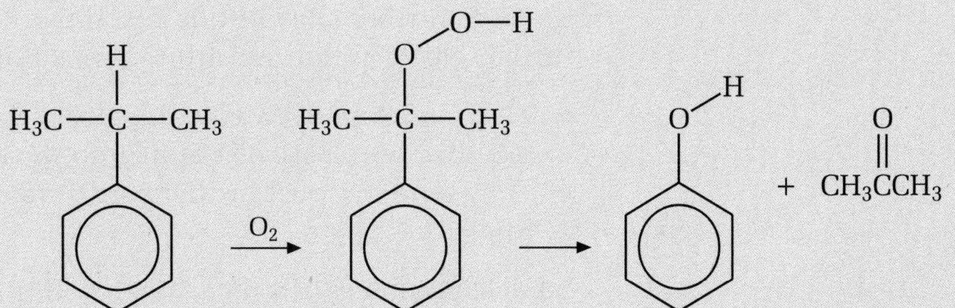

cumene

phenol   propanone

CHEMISTRY AROUND US

Manufacture of detergents

We can now see how some familiar reactions can be strung together to manufacture a useful product, the detergent sodium dodecylbenzenesulphonate. A long-chain alkene such as dodec-1-ene can be obtained from the cracking of crude oil fractions. Dodec-1-ene can be made to add onto a benzene ring in the presence of hydrogen chloride and aluminium chloride catalyst – a variation of the Friedel–Crafts reaction.

$$CH_3(CH_2)_9C\!\!=\!\!C\genfrac{}{}{0pt}{}{H}{H} \quad + \quad \bigcirc \quad + \quad \frac{AlCl_3}{HCl} \quad CH_3(CH_2)_{11}\!\!-\!\!\bigcirc$$

dodecene   dodecylbenzene

The product, dodecylbenzene is then reacted with sulphur trioxide to form 4-dodecylbenzenesulphonic acid.

$$CH_3(CH_2)_{11}\!\!-\!\!\bigcirc \quad + \; SO_3 \quad \longrightarrow \quad CH_3(CH_2)_{11}\!\!-\!\!\bigcirc\!\!-\!\!SO_3H$$

4-dodecylbenzenesulphonic acid

This is neutralised by sodium hydroxide to form the sodium salt, which is the detergent.

$$CH_3(CH_2)_{11}\!\!-\!\!\bigcirc\!\!-\!\!SO_3H \; + \; NaOH \quad \longrightarrow$$

$$CH_3(CH_2)_{11}\!\!-\!\!\bigcirc\!\!-\!\!SO_3^-Na^+ \; + \; H_2O$$

sodium 4-dodecylbenzenesulphonate (a detergent)

Note how the reactions used are essentially those which can be carried out in the laboratory, although the conditions vary somewhat. For example, sulphur trioxide gas (hard to handle in the laboratory) is used rather than sulphuric acid for the sulphonation step. This detergent makes up around 10% by weight of most commercial washing powders.

Household detergents

The effect of substituents

If a benzene ring already has one or more substituents it may undergo further substitution reactions. The substituents affect further electrophilic substitution reactions in two ways:

● They may withdraw electrons from the ring making it less reactive, or release electrons into the ring making it more reactive
● They tend to direct further substituents to certain positions on the ring.

Some common substituents are listed in **Figure 32.5**.

In general, substituents which activate the ring (by releasing electrons and making the ring more easily attacked by electrophiles

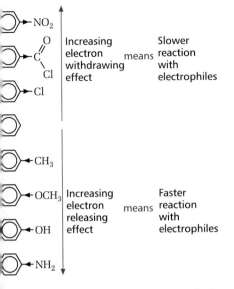

igure 32.5 Electron-withdrawing and electron-releasing substituents

lead to further substitution at the 2-, 4- and 6- positions. This is because the increased electron density tends to occur mainly at these positions, so this is where the electrophile attacks.

Deactivating substituents tend to *withdraw* electrons from the 2-, 4- and 6- positions, so when further substitution does occur, it tends to be at the 3- and 5- positions. Halogens are an exception: they deactivate the ring but direct further substituents to the 2- and 4- positions.

Addition reactions of arenes

While the typical reactions of arenes are substitutions in which the aromatic system remains intact, addition reactions are possible under suitable conditions.

Addition of hydrogen

Hydrogen adds onto benzene rings using a nickel catalyst at 420 K to give cyclohexane.

$$\text{benzene} + 3H_2 \xrightarrow[\text{420 K}]{\text{Ni catalyst}} \text{cyclohexane}$$

Note that addition of hydrogen to an arene needs somewhat more vigorous conditions than addition to an alkene (see section 20.4).

Addition of halogens

Both chlorine and bromine add onto benzene at room temperature when exposed to UV light (strong sunlight is sufficient). Both reactions go via a radical mechanism. For example:

Hint: Don't forget that in 1,2,3,4,5,6-hexachlorocyclohexane each carbon has a hydrogen attached to it as well as a chlorine.

$$\text{benzene} + 3Cl_2 \xrightarrow{\text{UV light}} \text{hexachlorocyclohexane}$$

1,2,3,4,5,6-hexachlorocyclohexane

Note that this reaction is quite different from the substitution reactions with halogens. These take place in the dark, require a catalyst and produce hydrogen halide. The product of chlorine addition, 1,2,3,4,5,6-hexachlorocyclohexane has a number of geometrical isomers, one of which is the insecticide Gammexane.

32.6 Chemical evidence for the bonding and structure of benzene

The reactions we have looked at so far provide confirming evidence that benzene does *not* have a Kekulé-type structure (with three double bonds) and *does* have aromatic stability. The majority of reactions of benzene are **substitutions**, rather than additions. Kekulé-

Over-the-counter painkillers: aspirin and paracetamol

There is an enormous market for non-prescription painkillers. A large number of brands are available but all are formulated from just four active ingredients: aspirin, paracetamol, codeine and ibuprofen. The structures of both aspirin and paracetamol are related to phenol.

aspirin
2-ethanoyloxybenzene-
carboxylic acid

paracetamol
4-(N-ethanoylamino)-
phenol

A number of simple derivatives of aspirin are also useful. The calcium salt is sold as soluble aspirin, the ionic salt being more soluble in water than the covalently bonded acid, while the sodium salt is mixed with a hydrogencarbonate to give effervescent aspirin which fizzes when added to water. The carbon dioxide gas evolved has an agitating effect which helps the tablet to dissolve.

The two drugs are comparable in their ability to relieve mild pain and both have the effect of reducing fever. Aspirin also has anti-inflammatory properties. Neither drug is free from side-effects. Aspirin may cause irritation and bleeding of the stomach while an overdose of paracetamol may cause permanent liver damage. Paracetamol is now sold in smaller packs and it has been suggested that, were aspirin a new drug, it would not be approved for over-the-counter sale without prescription.

All non-prescription painkillers are formulated from a choice of four active ingredients

type benzene would be expected to undergo addition reactions easily because it is an alkene.

The reactions with bromine highlight the differences.

Benzene does not decolourise bromine solution as would an alkene. It reacts only with liquid bromine (much more concentrated) and only with the help of a catalyst.

The reaction is substitution, which leaves the aromatic system unchanged, rather than addition, which would destroy the aromatic system and require input of the aromatic stabilisation energy.

Addition reactions of benzene occur only under rather vigorous conditions compared with those of alkenes (see sections 20.4 and 32.5).

32.7 Reactions of side chains

Groups attached to aromatic rings will undergo their own characteristic reactions, sometimes modified by being attached to the ring. We will deal here only with alkane and alkene side chains. Other functional groups will be considered in the relevant chapters.

Oxidation

Alkyl side chains attached to benzene rings are more easily oxidised than benzene itself. Strong oxidising agents such as acidified manganate(VII) ions or acidified dichromate(VI) ions oxidise alkyl side chains of any lengths to a carboxylic acid group.

For example:

ethylbenzene   benzenecarboxylic acid

Weaker oxidising agents, like manganese(IV) oxide, oxidise the side chains to aldehydes:

methylbenzene   benzenecarbaldehyde

Benzene itself does not react with either of these oxidising agents.

Radical halogenation of the side chain

Radical halogenation of alkyl groups occurs more readily than that of aromatic rings, so when chlorine is bubbled into methylbenzene, and exposed to UV light, substitution of the side chain occurs rather than the benzene ring.

methylbenzene   (chloromethyl)-   (dichloromethyl)- (trichloromethyl)-
                   benzene   benzene   benzene

> **Hint:** Notice the use of brackets to distinguish (chloromethyl)benzene from chloromethylbenzene, which would imply that the chlorine was on the benzene ring.

Hydrogen chloride is also formed.

> Q How many isomers are there of (a) (chloromethyl)benzene, (b) chloromethylbenzene? Name them.

Phenylethene

Phenylethene , has an alkene side chain attached to the

benzene ring. The alkene group is more reactive than benzene and so it is more sensible to refer to it as phenylethene rather than ethenylbenzene. It is more commonly known by its non-systematic name of styrene. The compound undergoes all the reactions typical of alkenes including polymerisation to poly(phenylethene), usually called polystyrene.

Answer: (a) 1 only, (b) 3: 2-chloromethylbenzene, -chloromethylbenzene, 4-chloromethylbenzene

32.8 Preparation of arenes

Industrially, benzene is obtained by the fractional distillation of coal tar and crude oil. Only small amounts are present in crude oil, and the process of reforming makes more. Here alkanes are heated under pressure with a suitable catalyst. Some of the unbranched chain alkanes form rings and then lose hydrogen to form aromatic compounds.

For example, hexane gives benzene, and heptane produces methylbenzene. In the laboratory, alkyl-substituted benzenes can be prepared by the Friedel–Crafts reaction (see section 32.5).

32.9 Economic importance of arenes

Benzene itself has been used as a solvent but it is a mild carcinogen and has largely been replaced for this purpose by the less toxic methylbenzene. Aromatic compounds are added to petrol to improve the octane rating. However, because of the toxicity of benzene and other arenes, there is some debate as to whether these are preferable to lead-based additives.

Benzene is the starting material for a number of other important compounds which lead to a wide variety of finished products – especially plastics and fibres. Some of the most important processes and reactions are summarised in **Figure 32.6**.

32.10 Haloarenes

Haloarenes are aromatic rings in which one or more of the hydrogens of the ring is replaced by a halogen. They still have the aromatic π system.

Reactivity of haloarenes

Compared with the haloalkanes (see Chapter 21), the C—X bond in the haloarenes is shorter and thus stronger. (For example C—Cl in chloromethane is 0.177 nm and C—Cl in chlorobenzene is 0.169 nm.) This is because the p orbitals on the halogen atom overlap with the π system on the aromatic ring. This provides extra bonding of π-type in addition to the C—X σ bond (see **Figure 32.7**). In other words, the C—X bond has some double bond character.

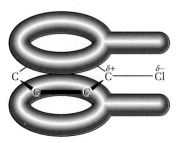

Figure 32.7 Bonding in chlorobenzene

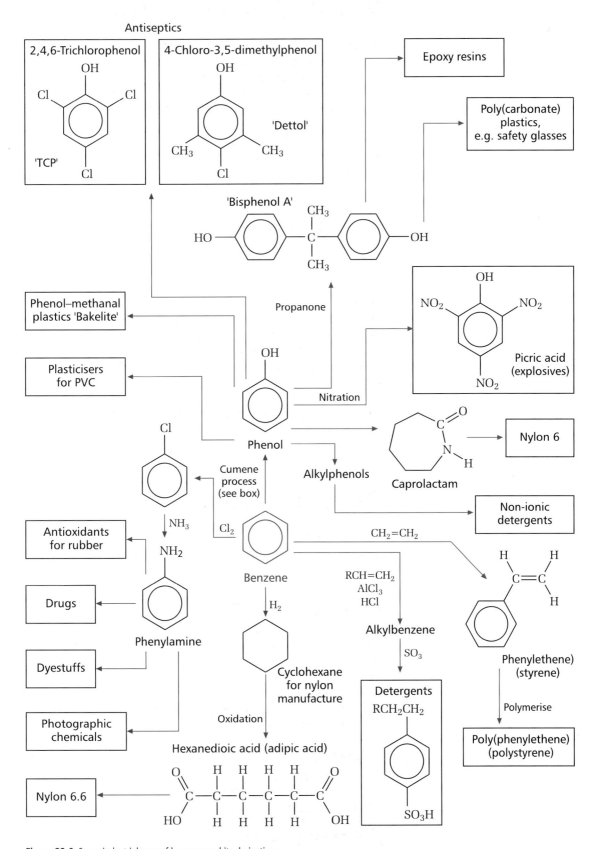

Figure 32.6 Some industrial uses of benzene and its derivatives

Hint: The same thing happens in arylamines and phenols (see sections 35.1 and 32.11).

This overlap of orbitals containing electrons also reduces the $\delta+$ character of the carbon to which the halogen is bonded. So there are two effects:

● a stronger bond
● less positive charge on the carbon

Both effects predict that haloarenes will be less reactive than haloalkanes towards nucleophilic substitution and this is what is found in practice. For example, chlorobenzene will undergo nucleophilic substitution with aqueous sodium hydroxide only at 600 K and 2×10^4 kPa pressure, while the comparable reaction with chloroalkane takes place at room temperature and pressure.

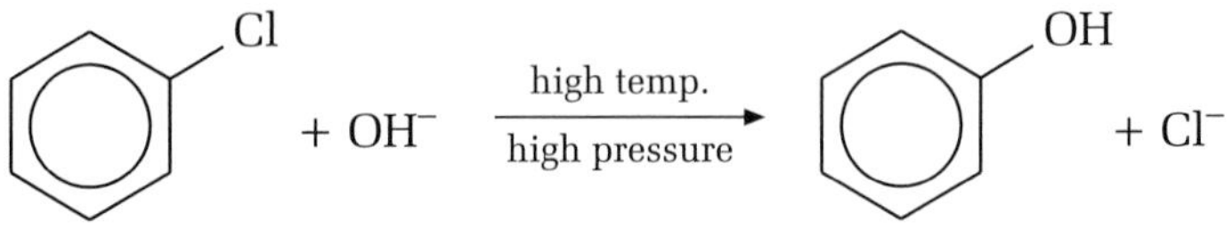

chlorobenzene   phenol

Elimination reactions do not occur: they would involve disruption of the π system of the aromatic ring, which would require a large amount of energy.

The aromatic ring will react in the same way as in benzene itself – typically by electrophilic substitution reactions. However, the attachment of an electronegative halogen atom draws electrons away from the ring and makes it less reactive towards electrophiles.

Unusually for deactivating substituents, the halogens are 2- and 4-directing. For example:

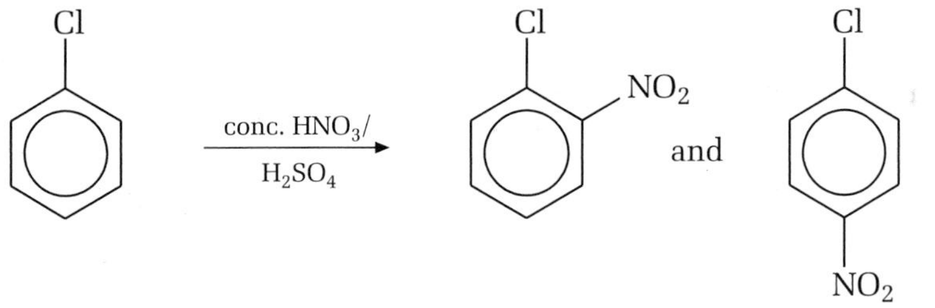

Hint: Nucleophilic substitution reactions involve the C—X bond while electrophilic substitution reactions involve the aromatic ring.

chlorobenzene   1-chloro-   1-chloro-
                         2-nitrobenzene   4-nitrobenzene

Note that compounds like (chloromethyl)benzene behave like halo*alkanes*, not halo*arenes*, because the halogen is not bonded directly to the arene ring. So there is no overlap of electrons from the halogen with the π system of the ring.

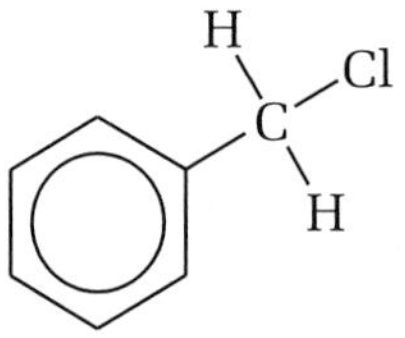

Preparation of haloarenes

There are two main ways of preparing haloarenes:

1. Directly from the arene plus halogen with a catalyst (section 32.5). For example:

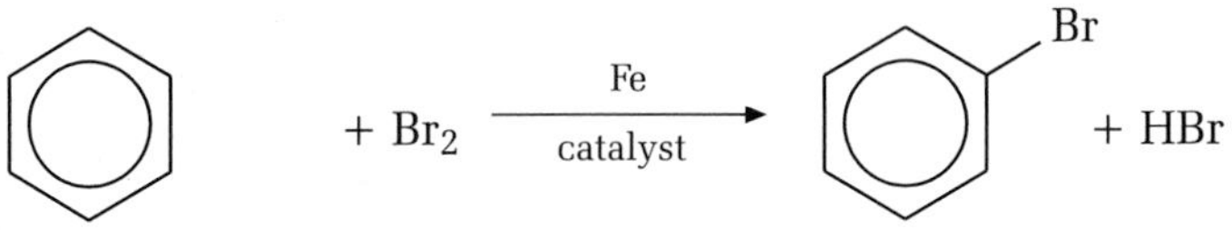

2. From a diazonium salt (section 35.1), by warming with a copper(I) halide:

(benzenediazonium chloride) $N_2^+Cl^-$ →[CuCl / HCl (conc.)] (chlorobenzene) Cl + N_2

or with potassium iodide:

$N_2^+Cl^-$ + KI ⟶ I + KCl + N_2

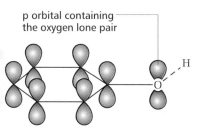

p orbital containing the oxygen lone pair

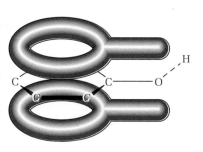

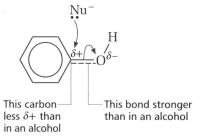

Figure 32.8 Interaction of the oxygen lone pair with the aromatic system in phenol

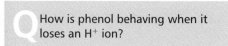

This carbon less $\delta+$ than in an alcohol

This bond stronger than in an alcohol

Figure 32.9 Phenol is less susceptible than alcohols to attack by nucleophiles

How is phenol behaving when it loses an H$^+$ ion?

Answer: As an acid.

32.11 Phenols

Phenols are aromatic rings in which one or more of the hydrogens of the ring is replaced by an —OH group. They still have the aromatic π system.

Reactivity of phenols

You might expect phenols to be very similar to alcohols. However, in phenols, the bonding in the benzene ring interacts with that in the —OH group, so that in many respects their reactivity is quite different from that of alcohols. **Figure 32.8** shows how one of the lone pairs on the oxygen atom in phenol can overlap with the delocalised π system on the benzene ring to form an extended delocalised π orbital.

So, the C—O bond in phenol has some double bond character, making it stronger than the C—O bond in an alcohol. This is confirmed by measurement of bond lengths. The C—O bond in ethanol has a length of 0.143 nm while that in phenol is 0.136 nm. Compare this with a typical C=O bond of length 0.122 nm. The extra strength of the C—O bond in phenol (which could be represented C⚌O to stress its partial double bond character) means that it will be harder to break the C—O bond in phenols than in alcohols.

A second factor caused by this overlapping of p orbitals is that the $\delta+$ charge of the carbon bonded to the oxygen can be spread over the whole delocalised system, thus making this carbon less susceptible to attack by nucleophiles than is the corresponding carbon in alcohols. These two factors combine to make nucleophilic substitution reactions involving loss of the —OH group less likely in phenols than in alcohols (see **Figure 32.9**).

This is very similar to the situation in haloarenes. However, there is a further factor which effects the reactivity of phenols.

The phenoxide ion ⟨O⟩—O$^-$ results from loss of a proton

(H$^+$) ion by phenol. In this ion the p–π overlap means that the negative charge of this ion can be delocalised over the whole

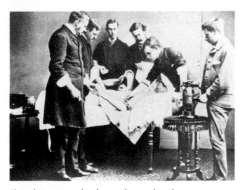

Phenol sprays used to be used as antiseptics

molecule, leading to extra stability of the ion. No such delocalisation (and therefore stability) is possible in alkoxide ions such as ethoxide, $C_2H_5O^-$.

The fact that the —OH group is attached to the benzene ring has two further effects on the reactivity of phenol:

Firstly, elimination reactions are unlikely because they would involve disruption of the aromatic system.

Secondly, oxidation is not likely either, except under vigorous conditions. The carbon to which the —OH group is attached has no hydrogen bonded to it, so phenol is effectively a tertiary alcohol (see section 22.1). In other words, oxidation of phenol would involve breaking C—C bonds *and* destruction of the aromatic system.

As well as reactions of the —OH group, the benzene ring can also react. The —OH group releases electrons onto the benzene ring, making it more reactive towards electrophilic substitution than benzene itself. This may seem odd, as oxygen is more electronegative than carbon and would be expected to attract electrons towards itself. It does in fact attract electrons through the C—O σ bond, but this is outweighed by the release of electrons from oxygen's lone pairs onto the benzene ring through the π overlap. The net effect is an overall release of electrons.

Reactions of phenol

Combustion

Phenol burns in air with the smoky flame characteristic of aromatic compounds.

Redox reactions

Phenol resists oxidation under the conditions that oxidise primary and secondary alcohols. This is because phenol has no hydrogen on the carbon to which the —OH group is attached. So loss of hydrogen, the first step of oxidation, cannot occur.

Phenol can be reduced by heating molten phenol with powdered zinc. Benzene is produced.

$$\text{OH} \quad (l) + Zn(s) \xrightarrow{700\ K} (l) + ZnO(s)$$

Reactions of the —OH group in phenol

Acidity

Phenol is considerably more acidic than alcohols: pK_a for phenol = 9.9, compared with pK_a for ethanol = 16, and for a typical weak acid, ethanoic acid, pK_a = 4.8. This is due to the delocalisation of the negative charge in the phenoxide ion, which stabilises it as described above.

$$\text{OH} + H_2O \rightleftharpoons \text{O}^- + H_3O^+$$

phenoxide ion

> **Q** How would you expect the boiling temperature of phenol to compare with that of an alkane of comparable relative molecular mass?

Answer: Greater, owing to hydrogen bonding between phenol molecules

CHEMISTRY AROUND US

Disinfectants and antiseptics

Antiseptics and disinfectants both kill germs. Antiseptics may be applied to the skin while disinfectants are normally applied only to surfaces because they may irritate the skin. Phenol is a disinfectant but causes blistering of the skin, while some of its derivatives have both better germicidal properties and are safer to use as antiseptics.

The germ-killing properties of phenols were first discovered around the middle of the last century when it was noticed that amputees at sea, whose stumps had been covered with tar, suffered less from post-operative infections. Tar contains phenol and a number of related compounds. The structures of phenol and some other germicides are given below with their germ-killing power compared with that of phenol.

Household disinfectants are aqueous solutions of phenol derivatives. As phenols are not particularly soluble in water, a soap is first made which dissolves the active ingredients. It is usual to add colouring and a perfume – often one smelling of pine. Once a compound is known to have a particular medical effect such as germ-killing, it is usual to synthesise close derivatives of it and test them for the required effect. This process often leads to the discovery of compounds that are more effective or have fewer side-effects.

phenol	2-chloro-phenol	2,4-dichloro-phenol	2,4,6-trichloro-phenol (TCP)	4-chloro-3,5-dimethylphenol (Dettol)⁻
1	4	13	23	280

Increasing germ killing power

> **Q** How would you expect the solubility of 1,4-dihydroxybenzene to compare with that of phenol?

Phenol is only slightly soluble in water but dissolves in aqueous sodium hydroxide solution.

sodium phenoxide

The equilibrium can be displaced to the left by adding concentrated hydrochloric acid, which makes the phenol precipitate out of solution.

Note that *alkoxides* cannot be made by reaction of an alcohol with an alkali metal hydroxide, only by reaction with an alkali metal itself. This is a further illustration of the greater acidity of phenols compared with alcohols.

Alkali metal phenoxides can also be made by direct reaction of molten phenol with the alkali metal. Hydrogen is given off. The phenoxide ion which is generated is a strong nucleophile.

Hint: This is an example of a typical acid reaction:
acid + metal ⟶ salt + hydrogen

Phenol is not a strong enough acid to react with sodium carbonate solution to produce carbon dioxide. This test enables it to be distinguished from carboxylic acids (see section 34.3), which do produce carbon dioxide when added to a carbonate.

Answer: More soluble because it has two hydrogen bonding —OH groups

Phenols with electron-withdrawing substituents like $—NO_2$ are stronger acids than phenol itself. The substituents increase the acid strength by further delocalising the negative charge remaining after the molecule has lost a proton. Phenols with electron-releasing substituents like $—CH_3$ are less acidic than phenol itself.

Phenols, are stronger acids and therefore weaker bases than alcohols, so they are less easily protonated than alcohols.

Did you know? Phenol was once known as carbolic acid. The name is still used in carbolic soaps, which contain small amounts of phenol and derivatives as antiseptics. (Pure phenol is an unpleasantly corrosive substance causing blistering of the skin and it should be treated with respect.)

Substitution of the —OH group by halogens

This reaction takes place much less easily than in alcohols owing to the increased strength of the C—OH bond and the reduced $\delta+$ character of the carbon, which is therefore less easily attacked by nucleophiles. Hydrogen halides do not react at all with phenol and even phosphorus pentachloride produces only a poor yield of chlorobenzene:

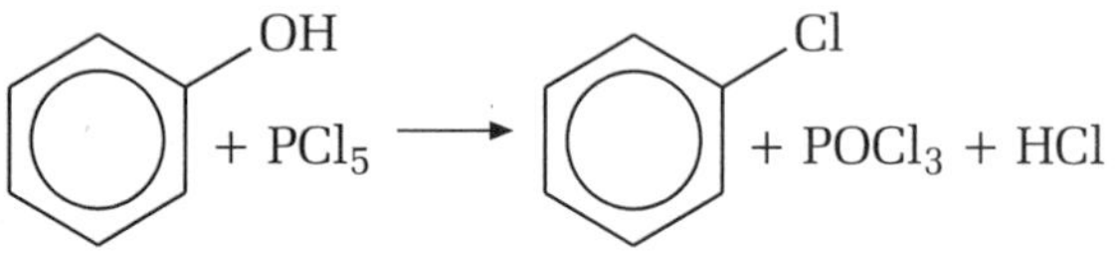

Dehydration

This does not occur because it would involve disruption of the aromatic system.

Ether formation

Reaction of phenoxide ions with haloalkanes produces ethers by a nucleophilic substitution reaction. For example:

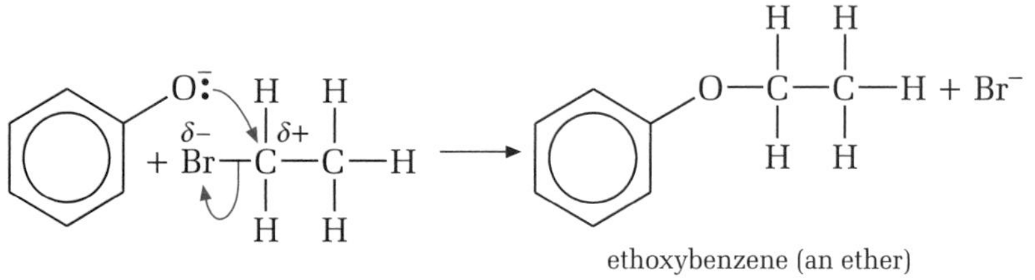

ethoxybenzene (an ether)

This method is called Williamson's synthesis, as distinct from Williamson's continuous synthesis (see section 22.4).

Formation of esters

Phenols are weaker nucleophiles than alcohols because their lone pair electrons are partially delocalised onto the benzene ring. Thus they do not form esters by reaction with carboxylic acids directly.

However, the phenoxide ion, 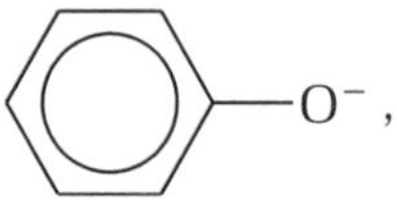 , is a better nucleophile than phenol and it will react with acid derivatives such as acid chlorides or acid anhydrides (see section 34.6), which are themselves more reactive than the parent acid:

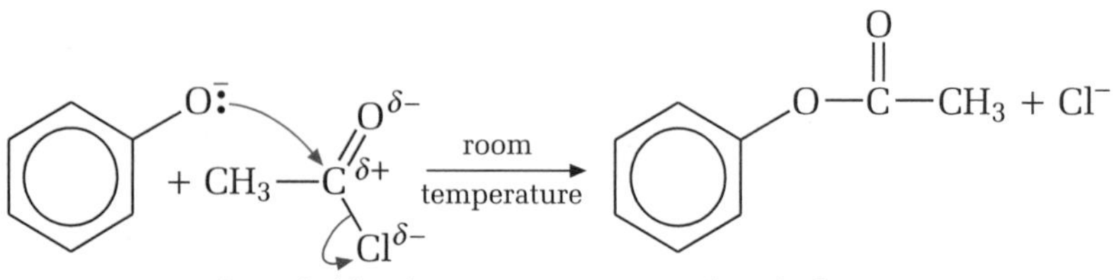

ethanoyl chloride phenyl ethanoate (an ester)

The reaction is carried out by dissolving phenol in sodium hydroxide to generate the phenoxide ion before adding the acid chloride.

Reaction with iron(III) chloride

Phenol produces a purple complex when mixed with iron(III) chloride in which the phenol is acting as a ligand (see section 31.3). This is often used as a test for a phenol or, in fact, any —OH group bonded to an unsaturated system.

Reactions of the benzene ring in phenol

Because of the overall electron-releasing effect of the —OH group the aromatic ring in phenol is much more reactive towards electrophilic substitution than the benzene ring. This may be shown in various ways:

- the same reaction occurring more rapidly
- more substitution taking place under the same conditions
- less vigorous conditions being required for the same reaction

Like most ring activators, the —OH group directs further substituents to the 2-, 4- and 6- positions.

Electrophilic substitution reactions

Nitration

Phenol can be nitrated by dilute nitric acid at room temperature to give a mixture of 2- nitrophenol and 4-nitrophenol.

phenol   2-nitrophenol   4-nitrophenol

Compare this with benzene, where heating with a mixture of concentrated nitric and sulphuric acids is required for nitration. Nitration of phenol under more vigorous conditions yields 2,4,6-trinitrophenol – the explosive picric acid.

2,4,6-trinitrophenol

Halogenation

Phenol will react at room temperature with aqueous bromine or chlorine to give a trisubstituted product. No catalyst is needed.

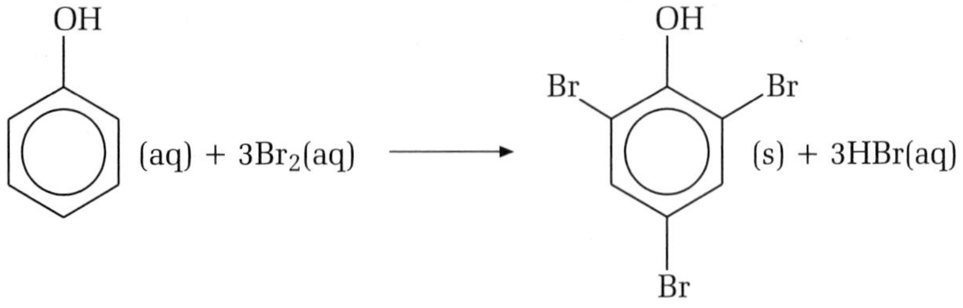

Compare this with benzene, where liquid bromine and a catalyst are required yet produce only a monosubstituted product.

These two examples are enough to show the greatly increased reactivity of the ring towards electrophiles.

Addition reactions

Phenol can be hydrogenated under similar conditions to benzene. Cyclohexanol is produced:

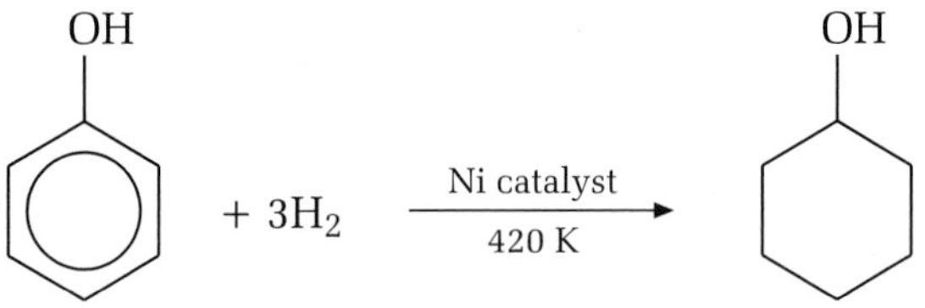

cyclohexanol

Preparation of phenols

Phenol can be prepared from benzenesulphonic acid by heating it with solid sodium hydroxide and acidifying the sodium phenoxide produced.

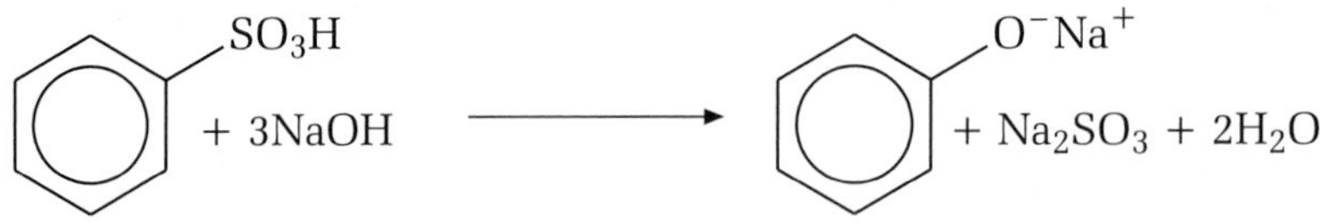

benzenesulphonic acid   sodium phenoxide

phenol

Chemistry of economic importance

The industrial chemistry of phenol is included in **Figure 32.6**.

CHEMISTRY AROUND US

Phenol–methanal plastics

Phenol and methanal react together with either an acid or alkali catalyst to form a polymer. Water is eliminated in the reaction which is therefore called **condensation polymerisation**.

Further reaction produces cross-links between the chains.

This produces a polymer called Bakelite, after its inventor, Leo Bakeland. The plastic sets hard when it forms and cannot be melted again. It is therefore called a **thermosetting polymer**. Bakelite is hard and rather brittle. However, it is cheap and has been used for making electrical sockets, motor engine distributor caps and saucepan handles, where resistance to heat is important.

32.12 Summary

Arenes

- Arenes (or aromatic compounds) are derivatives of   benzene C_6H_6.

- The shape of benzene is   a flat regular hexagon of carbon atoms linked by σ bonds.

- The p orbitals overlap to form   a delocalised π system.

- All the C—C bond lengths in benzene are   the same.

- The bonds are intermediate between   single and double bonds.

- The delocalised π bonds give the ring   a high electron density.

- Thermochemical cycles indicate that benzene is approximately $150\,kJ\,mol^{-1}$ more stable than expected.

- This is called its   aromatic stabilisation energy.

- In their boiling points and solubility, aromatic hydrocarbons are typical of   non-polar molecules.

- Arenes react typically by   electrophilic substitution reactions.

- Substituents on a benzene ring which withdraw electrons make the ring   less reactive.

- Substituents on a benzene ring which release electrons make it   more reactive.

- Electron-releasing groups direct further substituents to   the 2-, 4- and 6- positions.

- Electron withdrawing groups direct further substituents to   the 3- and 5- positions.

- Halogens are exceptions. They withdraw electrons but direct to the   2-, 4- and 6- positions.

- Whether oxidation of alkyl side chains results in the side chain becoming an aldehyde or carboxylic acid group depends on   the strength of the oxidising agent.

The reactions of benzene are summarised in **Figure 32.10**.

Haloarenes

- Haloarenes are less reactive than haloalkanes because
  the C—X bond in haloarenes has some double bond character and the carbon has less $\delta+$ character.

- The halogen atom of a haloarene
  deactivates the aromatic ring

  and directs further substituents to
  the 2- and 4- position.

- Elimination reactions do not occur because
  disruption of the aromatic ring requires too much energy.

Phenols

- Phenols contain the —OH functional group bonded
  directly to a benzene ring.

- Phenols have significantly higher melting and boiling temperatures than alkanes of comparative relative molecular mass because of
  hydrogen bonding between the molecules.

- The —OH group releases electrons onto the ring, making it more reactive to
  electrophilic substitution reactions.

- The —OH group directs further substituents to
  the 2-, 4- and 6- positions.

- The C—OH bond in phenol is strengthened because of
  overlap between the orbital on the ring and the lone pairs of the oxygen.

- The phenoxide ion is stabilised by
  delocalisation of the negative charge.

- Phenols are therefore stronger acids than
  alcohols.

- Phenol is prepared by
  the action of sodium hydroxide on benzenesulphonic acid.

The reactions of phenol are summarised in **Figure 32.11**.

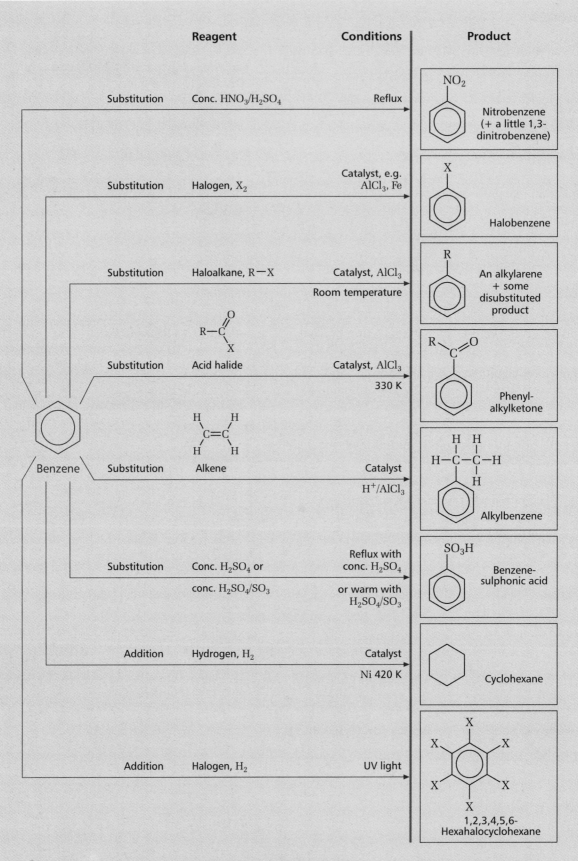

Figure 32.10 The reactions of benzene – cover up the right-hand side to test yourself

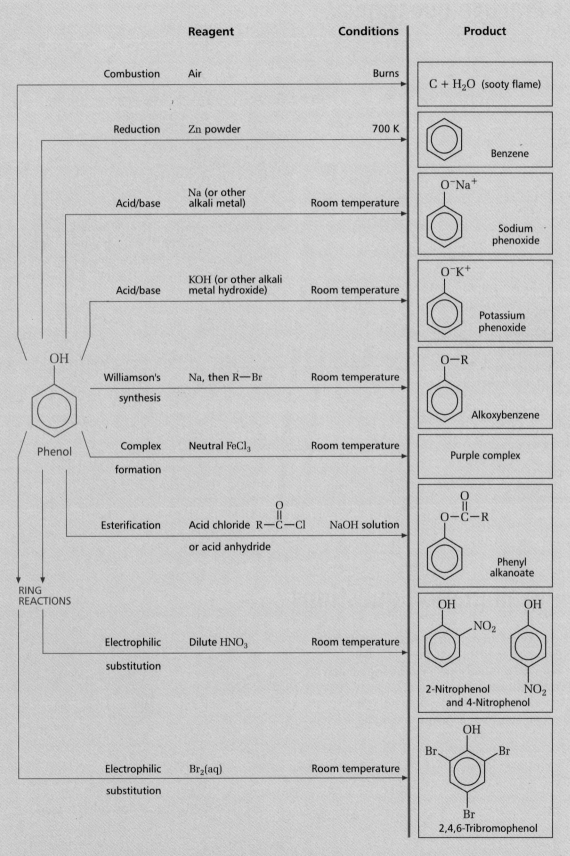

Figure 32.11 The reactions of phenol – cover up the right-hand side to test yourself

32.13 Practice questions

Arenes

1. Name the following.

(a) 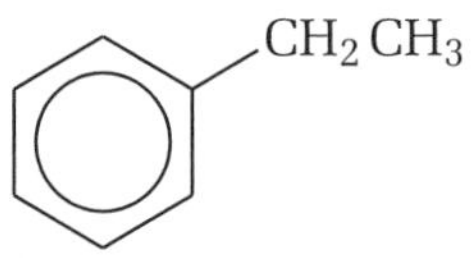 [benzene ring with CH₂CH₃ substituent]

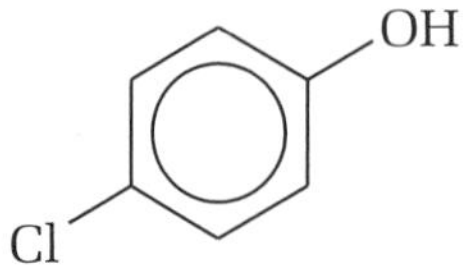

(b) 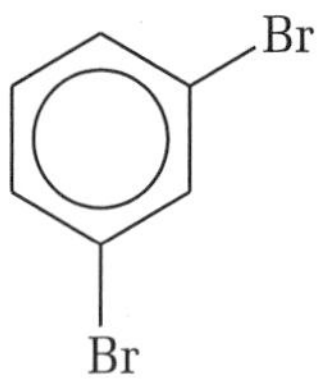 [benzene ring with Br at two positions]

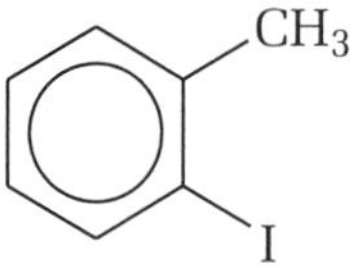

(c) 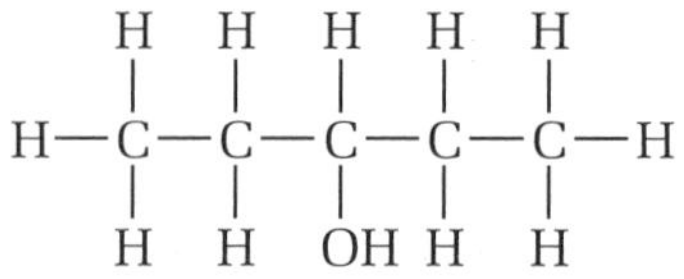 $H-\underset{H}{\overset{H}{C}}-\underset{H}{\overset{H}{C}}-\underset{OH}{\overset{H}{C}}-\underset{H}{\overset{H}{C}}-\underset{H}{\overset{H}{C}}-H$

(d) 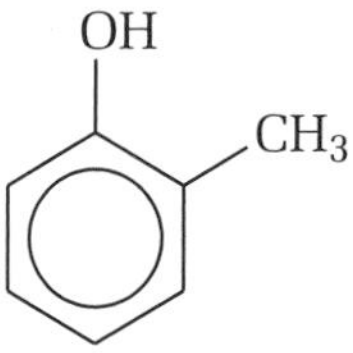 [benzene ring with OH and CH₃ substituents]

(c) [benzene ring with OH and Cl substituents]

(d) [benzene ring with CH₃ and I substituents]

2. Write displayed structural formulae for:
   (a) 2-chloromethylbenzene
   (b) 4-chloromethylbenzene
   (c) benzene-1,4-dicarboxylic acid
   (d) 2-phenylprop-1-ene
   (e) 4-nitrophenol
   (f) 1,4-dihydroxybenzene

3. Classify the following as 1°, 2° or 3° alcohols or phenols:

(a) 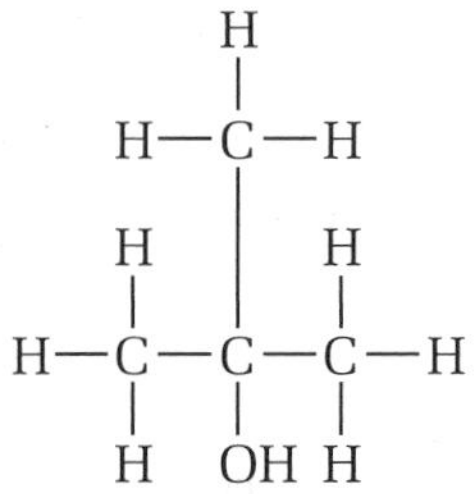 [structure: H−C−H with methyl groups, H−C−C−C−H with OH]

(b) 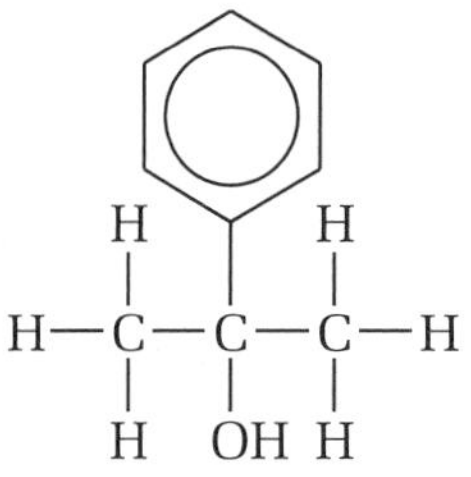 [benzene ring with H−C−C−C−H chain with OH]

4. The nitro group, —NO_2, is an electron-withdrawing group, while the methyl group, —CH_3, releases electrons. Put the following in order of acid strength. Explain your answer.

(a) 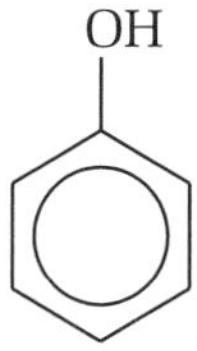 [phenol with OH]

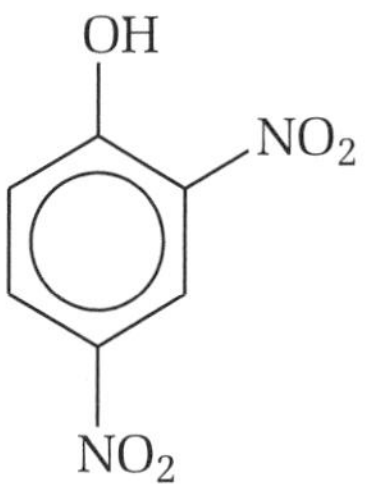

(b) 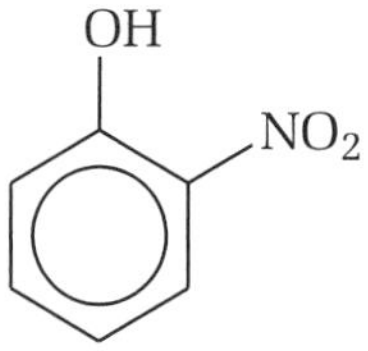 [phenol with OH and NO_2]

(c) [phenol with OH and two NO_2 groups]

(d) 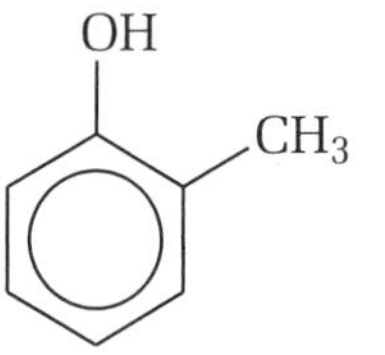 [phenol with OH and CH_3]

32.14 Examination questions

1. (a) The carbon–carbon bond length in benzene is different from that in ethene. State which compound contains the longer bond and give a reason for your answer.
   (b) Write an equation for the preparation of nitrobenzene from benzene and name the type of mechanism involved.
   (c) (i) Calculate the maximum possible yield of nitrobenzene starting from 5.0 g of benzene.
       (ii) If the actual yield obtained was 5.6 g, calculate the percentage yield.
       [NEAB 1998]

2. Three reactions of methylbenzene can be summarised on a flow sheet shown opposite.
   (a) Name substance **A** and the reagents **B** and **C**.

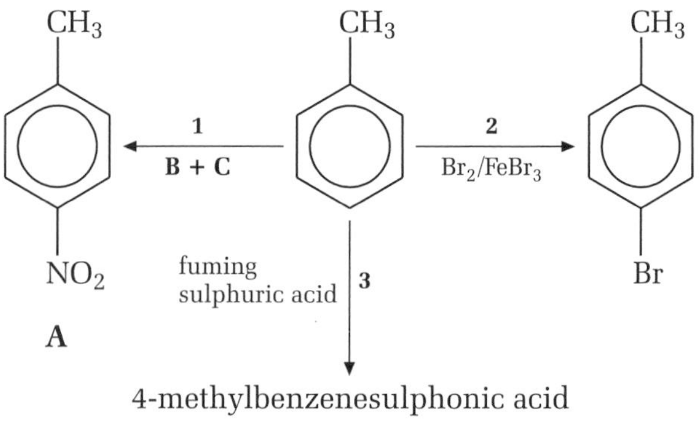

[Flow diagram: central benzene ring with CH₃, converting via reaction 1 (B + C) to left structure with CH₃ and NO₂ (labelled **A**); via reaction 2 (Br₂/FeBr₃) to right structure with CH₃ and Br; via reaction 3 (fuming sulphuric acid) to 4-methylbenzenesulphonic acid]

(b) (i) Draw the structural formula for 4-methylbenzenesulphonic acid.
    (ii) State the formula of the molecule which attacks the benzene ring in reaction **3**.

(iii) Name an important group of industrial products that is made from benzenesulphonic acids.

(c) (i) Write an equation to show how the catalyst iron(III) bromide induces polarisation of a bromine molecule in reaction **2**.

(ii) Classify reaction **2** as fully as possible.

(d) A student tried to make 4-methylcyclohexanol by the following route.

CH$_3$ CH$_3$ CH$_3$

[benzene ring with Br] → Step 1 → [cyclohexane ring with Br] → Step 2 → [cyclohexane ring with OH]

Br   Br   OH

(i) Suggest reagents and conditions for each step.

(ii) The final yield of 4-methylcyclohexanol was rather low. This was thought to be due to the formation of some 4-methylcyclohexene.

Suggest a chemical test and the colour change you would expect to observe for an alkene such as 4-methylcyclohexene.

[London (Nuffield) 1998]

3. This question is about the effects of delocalisation of electrons in elements, compounds and ions.

(a) What is the meaning of the term delocalisation? Show how the data below gives evidence for the delocalised structure of benzene and buta-1,3-diene.

$$\Delta H^\ominus_{reaction}$$

$$C_2H_4 + H_2 \longrightarrow C_2H_6 \qquad -137 \text{ kJ mol}^{-1}$$
$$C_6H_6 + 3H_2 \longrightarrow C_6H_{12} \qquad -208 \text{ kJ mol}^{-1}$$
$$CH_2{=}CH{-}CH{=}CH_2 + 2H_2$$
$$\text{buta-1,3-diene}$$
$$\longrightarrow CH_3CH_2CH_2CH_3 \qquad -236 \text{ kJ mol}^{-1}$$

The compound naphthalene can be represented in two ways:

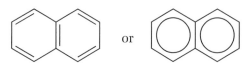

or

Write an equation showing the complete hydrogenation of naphthalene and estimate the enthalpy change which accompanies it (no detailed calculation is expected).

(b) Review the effects of delocalisation in a variety of structures.

You should consider:

● structure and bonding including bond angles in at least two ions;
● delocalisation in organic acids and bases;
● reactions of benzene;
● physical properties of metals.

You should aim to use your knowledge of delocalisation to explain and interpret the examples you discuss.

[London (Nuffield) 1998]

33 Carbonyl compounds

C H E M I S T R Y   N O W

The smell of success

Chanel No. 5 is probably the world's best known perfume – ever since Marilyn Monroe revealed that she wore nothing else in bed. From a chemical point of view, Chanel No. 5 is noted for being the first major perfume to be based on a synthetic ingredient, the aldehyde 2-methylundecanal.

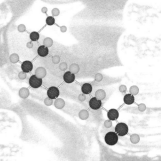

2-methylundecanal

This compound produces the 'top note' of the fragrance – the first part of the aroma that we detect because it is the most volatile component and evaporates first. 'No. 5''s middle note is based on a tropical flower fragrance, ylang ylang, and its bottom note on vetivert, derived from a tropical grass.

Carbonyl compounds (aldehydes and ketones) occur in many aromas, including that of musk. This originally came from a gland found near the anus of the male musk deer which uses the secretion to attract its mate. Chemists have succeeded in synthesising the chemical which causes the smell, 3-methylcyclopentadecanone, also called muscone.

The biochemistry of smell is related to molecular shape. In the nose, there are nerve endings called cilia, tiny hair-like structures. These contain receptor molecules with cavities that fit molecules of certain shapes, and trigger nerve messages to the brain when an appropriately shaped molecule arrives. Some scientists believe that there is a link between the nose and the pituitary gland which controls the sex organs. This may explain the aphrodisiac effect which is claimed for many perfumes.

Marilyn Monroe

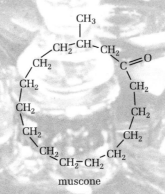

muscone

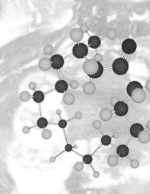

Introduction

The carbonyl group is $\diagdown C{=}O$. The term 'carbonyl compound' includes two types of compounds: aldehydes and ketones.

In aldehydes, the carbon bonded to the oxygen (the carbonyl carbon) has at least one hydrogen atom bonded to it, so the general formula of an aldehyde is:

$$\begin{array}{c} R \\ \diagdown \\ C{=}O \\ \diagup \\ H \end{array}$$ sometimes written as RCHO.

In ketones, the carbonyl carbon has two R groups so the formula of a ketone is:

$$\begin{array}{c} R \\ \diagdown \\ C{=}O \\ \diagup \\ R' \end{array}$$

Hint: 'Alkyl' means based on a saturated hydrocarbon group. 'Aryl' means based on an aromatic system.

The R groups in both aldehydes and ketones may be alkyl or aryl.

Although aldehydes and ketones are not met often in everyday life, they have been described as the backbone of organic chemistry because of their importance in the synthesis of other compounds.

CONCEPT CHECKPOINTS

The following basic ideas are used in this chapter. You may revise some of these topics elsewhere in the book.
- nucleophiles and electrophiles (section 18.8)
- addition reactions (section 18.8)
- redox reactions (Chapter 13)
- the factors which govern the shapes of molecules (section 9.2)

33.1 Formulae, naming and structure

Aldehydes have the general formula $\begin{array}{c} R \\ \diagdown \\ C{=}O \\ \diagup \\ H \end{array}$ where R may be H.

Ketones have the general formula $\begin{array}{c} R \\ \diagdown \\ C{=}O \\ \diagup \\ R' \end{array}$. The two R groups may be the same or different, but neither can be H.

Naming

Aldehydes are named using the suffix -al where the aldehyde is the principal group (see section 18.4) and the prefix oxo- when it is not.

The carbon of the aldehyde functional group is counted as part of the carbon chain of the root. So

H—C—C is ethanal.

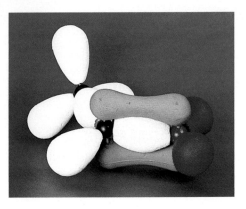

The orbitals in the ethanal molecule. The green ones are a π orbital and the red ones lone pairs on the oxygen atom

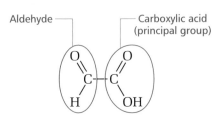

is oxoethanoic acid (as the aldehyde is not the principal group).

The aldehyde group can only occur at the end of a chain, so locants are not needed. When an aldehyde is a substituent on, say, a benzene ring, the suffix -carbaldehyde is used and the carbon is *not* counted as part of the root name.

So: is counted as a derivative of benzene

(not of methylbenzene) and is called benzenecarbaldehyde. It is sometimes still called benzaldehyde.

When the ketone is the principal group ketones are named using the suffix -one. When it is not the principal group, it shares with aldehydes the prefix oxo-. No confusion should occur, because in ketones the carbonyl group must come *within* the chain whereas in aldehydes it must come at the *end*. As with aldehydes, the carbon atom of the ketone functional group is counted as part of the root. So the simplest ketone:

H—C—C—C—H is called propanone.

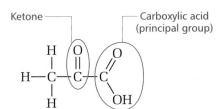

is 2-oxopropanoic acid since the ketone is not the principal group.

No ketone with fewer than three carbon atoms is possible. However:

H—C—H
C=O   is named phenylethanone because the phenyl group is considered to be a substituent.

Locants are not needed in propanone or in butanone:

$$\begin{array}{ccccccc} & H & H & O & H & \\ & | & | & \| & | & \\ H- & C- & C- & C- & C & -H \\ & | & | & & | & \\ & H & H & & H & \end{array}$$

because there is no possible ambiguity about the position of the carbonyl group.

However there are two possible isomeric pentanones:

$$\begin{array}{cccccc} H & H & O & H & H \\ | & | & \| & | & | \\ H-C-C-C-C-C-H \\ | & | & & | & | \\ H & H & & H & H \end{array} \quad \text{and} \quad \begin{array}{cccccc} H & O & H & H & H \\ | & \| & | & | & | \\ H-C-C-C-C-C-H \\ | & & | & | & | \\ H & & H & H & H \end{array}$$

pentan-3-one   pentan-2-one

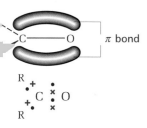

How many isomers are there of hexan-2-one?

π bond

ure 33.1 Bonding in the carbonyl group

H$_3$ 121°

121°

ure 33.2 Approximate bond angles in ethanal

ure 33.3 Hydrogen bonding between propanone and er

id you know? Propanone is ometimes used for quickly drying boratory glassware. The wet glassware rinsed with propanone which then vaporates rapidly as it is much more olatile than water.

wer: 3: hexanal, hexan-2-one, hexan-3-one

Shapes

The bonding between carbon and oxygen in the carbonyl group consists of a σ bond and a π bond. There are three groups of electrons around the carbon atom and the molecule is flat and has a trigonal shape (**Figure 33.1**). (R, R', C and O are all in the same plane.) The R—C—R' angle (or R—C—H angle) is a little less than 120° because the four electrons in the C=O bond repel more than the two electrons in the C—R and C—R' (or C—H) bonds (**Figure 33.2**).

33.2 Physical properties of carbonyl compounds

The carbonyl group is strongly polar, $C^{\delta+}=O^{\delta-}$, so dipole–dipole forces between the molecules are quite significant. This leads to boiling temperatures higher than those of alkanes of comparable relative molecular mass but not as high as those of alcohols, where hydrogen bonding can occur between the molecules:

butane	$CH_3CH_2CH_2CH_3$	$M_r = 60$	$T_b = 273$ K
propanone	CH_3COCH_3	$M_r = 58$	$T_b = 329$ K
propan-1-ol	$CH_3CH_2CH_3OH$	$M_r = 60$	$T_b = 371$ K

The shorter-chain carbonyl compounds are completely miscible with water owing to the formation of hydrogen bonds between the carbonyl compound and water (**Figure 33.3**).

As the length of the carbon chain increases so the solubility in water decreases.

Methanol, HCHO, is a gas at room temperature. It is often encountered as a 40% aqueous solution called 'formalin', which has a fishy, unpleasant smell and is used for preserving biological specimens. Other short-chain aldehydes and ketones are liquids. They have characteristic, fairly pleasant smells (propanone is found in many brands of nail varnish remover). Benzenecarbaldehyde smells of almonds and is used to scent soaps and flavour food.

33.3 The reactivity of carbonyl compounds

The C=O bond in carbonyl compounds is strong (see **Table 33.1**). is stronger than C=C and more than twice as strong as C—O. (C=C is less than twice as strong as C—C), so you might predict that the C=O bond would be the least reactive in an aldehyde or a ketone. However, most reactions of carbonyl compounds do involve the C=O. The reason for this is the big difference in electronegativity between carbon and oxygen, which makes the C=O strongly polar $C^{\delta+}=O^{\delta-}$. This means that nucleophilic reagents can attack the $C^{\delta+}$ while electrophiles like H^+ can attack the $O^{\delta-}$. Also, since they contain a double bond, carbonyl compounds are **unsaturated** and therefore addition reactions are possible. The most typical reaction of the carbonyl group are **nucleophilic additions**.

   Reactions of the rest of the carbon skeleton can take place, especially those of aromatic rings. When attached to an aromatic ri the carbonyl group is a deactivating substituent as, indeed, are mos unsaturated groups.

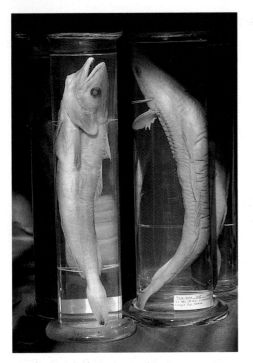

Formalin is used as a preservative

> **Q** Name a deactivating substituent which is not unsaturated.

Table 33.1 Comparison of bond strengths

C=O	740 kJ mol^{-1}
C=C	612 kJ mol^{-1}
C—O	358 kJ mol^{-1}
C—C	347 kJ mol^{-1}

33.4 Reactions of carbonyl compounds

Carbonyl compounds react in a wide variety of ways.

Nucleophilic addition reactions

Hint: Nucleophiles need a lone pair, which they use to form bonds with $C^{\delta+}$.

The general pattern for this reaction is as follows:

$$
\begin{array}{ccc}
\underset{R'}{\overset{R}{\diagdown}}C\!\!=\!\!O \xrightarrow{\;:Nu^-\;} & \underset{R'}{\overset{R}{\diagdown}}\underset{O^-}{\overset{Nu}{C}} \xrightarrow[\text{(from solvent)}]{H^+} & \underset{R'}{\overset{R}{\diagdown}}\underset{O-H}{\overset{Nu}{C}}
\end{array}
$$

Not all nucleophiles are negatively charged (some use the negative end of a dipole to attack $C^{\delta+}$), so the fine details of the reaction ma differ with neutral nucleophiles.

Answer: Halogens

Addition of hydrogensulphite ions

The nucleophile is the hydrogensulphite ion (the hydrogensulphate(IV) ion), SO_3H^-, from a solution of sodium hydrogensulphite:

The overall effect is the addition of $NaHSO_3$ across the C=O bond.

Addition of hydrogen cyanide

Here the nucleophile is $:CN^-$:

> **Hint:** The —CN group is called 'nitrile' in an organic compound and 'cyanide' in an inorganic compound.

a 2-hydroxynitrile

Sodium cyanide is used as a source of cyanide ions. The —CN group is called **nitrile** and it reacts with acids to give a carboxylic acid, so reaction of 2-hydroxynitriles gives 2-hydroxycarboxylic acids.

Addition of alcohols

These also add on across the double bond of aldehydes in the same way, $RO^{\delta-}$—$H^{\delta+}$ being the nucleophile:

This product is called a **hemiacetal**. Further reaction can take place to give an **acetal**

a hemiacetal   an acetal

Hemiacetals and acetals usually cannot be isolated because they are stable only in solution. **Ketals**, analogous compounds made from ketones, are more difficult to prepare.

All these reactions involve addition of $H^{\delta+}Z^{\delta-}$ across the double bond $C^{\delta+}$=$O^{\delta-}$ in such a way that the $H^{\delta+}$ adds onto the $O^{\delta-}$ and $Z^{\delta-}$ to the $C^{\delta+}$.

Addition–elimination (condensation) reactions

As the name implies, these reactions involve first **addition** to form an unstable intermediate, which then rapidly loses (**eliminates**) a molecule of water.

Reaction with hydrazine (H_2N—NH_2).

The reaction occurs as follows:

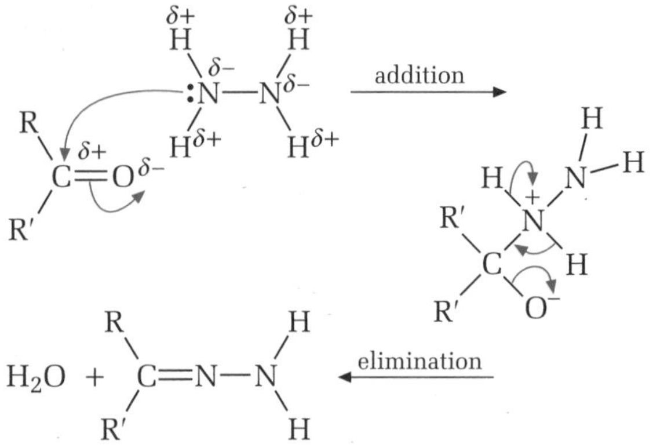

The product is called a **hydrazone.** You may well find it easier to remember the product by concentrating on the elimination step:

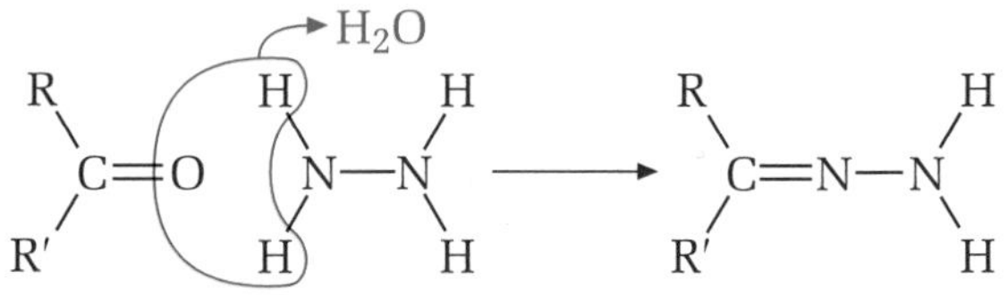

hydrazine   a hydrazone

Other compounds related to ammonia will undergo similar reactions

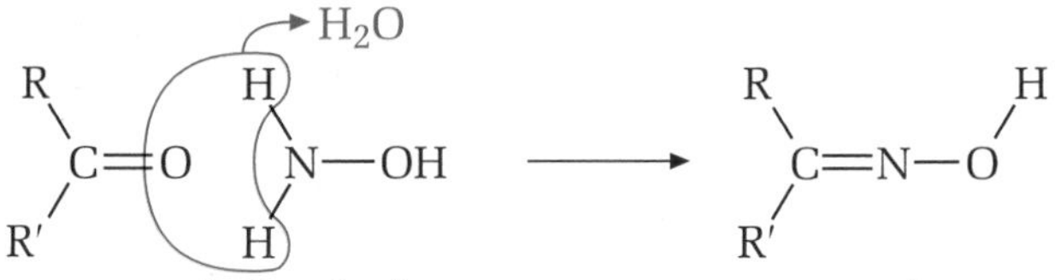

hydroxylamine   an oxime

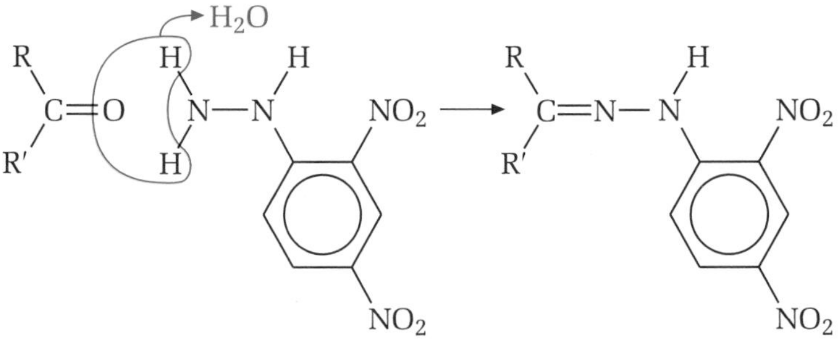

2,4-dinitrophenylhydrazine   a 2,4-dinitrophenylhydrazone
(Brady's reagent)

The derivatives are usually named by reference to the starting material, e.g. 'ethanal oxime' or 'propanone 2,4-dinitrophenylhydrazone'.

Identification of carbonyl compounds

Hint: Carbonyl compounds may also be identified by instrumental methods (see Chapter 38).

The basic method of identification of an unknown carbonyl compound is to (a) make a solid derivative and (b) measure the melting point of the derivative.

The derivatives made from 2,4-dinitrophenylhydrazine, often called Brady's reagent, are orange-coloured crystalline solids. They are easily prepared by mixing the carbonyl compound with an acid solution of Brady's reagent in methanol. The crystals of the 2,4-dinitrophenylhydrazone are filtered off and purified by recrystallisation (see the box 'Recrystallisation'). Their melting temperatures are measured. The original carbonyl compound is then identified by reference to tables of melting temperatures of 2,4-dinitrophenylhydrazone derivatives.

Comparison of reactivity of aldehydes and ketones with nucleophiles

Both nucleophilic addition reactions and addition–elimination reactions involve nucleophilic attack on the carbonyl carbon, $C^{\delta+}$. Aldehydes react more readily than ketones for two reasons. First, in a ketone, the electron-releasing (inductive) effect of *two* alkyl groups reduces the positive charge on the carbonyl carbon making it less easily attacked by nucleophiles.

$$
\begin{array}{cc}
R & R \\
\searrow \delta+ \ \delta- & \searrow \delta+ \ \delta- \\
C = O & C = O \\
\nearrow & / \\
R & H
\end{array}
$$

Secondly, the two alkyl groups of a ketone tend to get in the way of attacking nucleophiles. This is sometimes called **steric hindrance.**

FURTHER FOCUS

Measurement of melting temperatures

The accurate measurement of melting temperatures is a useful indicator of how pure a specimen of a compound is. A pure specimen of the compound should melt over a very small temperature range. Impure compounds will melt gradually over a range of a few degrees. The expected melting temperature of a compound can be found from reference books or databases. One apparatus for measuring melting temperatures is the Thiele tube:

A small sample of the solid is placed in a capillary tube attached to the bulb of a thermometer. This is inserted into a Thiele tube filled with an oil of high boiling temperature. The apparatus is gently heated as shown. Convection currents in the oil heat the capillary tube and thermometer. The melting temperature is noted. On cooling, the temperature at which the sample solidifies can be used to check the first reading.

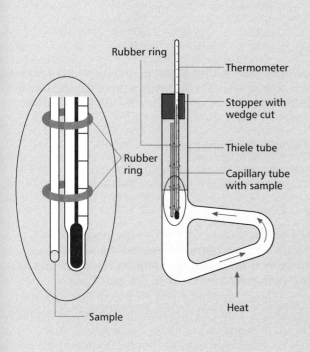

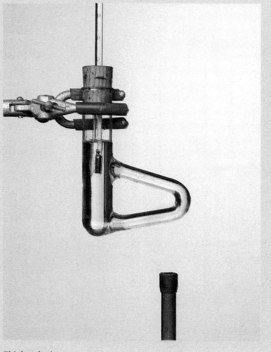

Thiele tube in use

FURTHER FOCUS

Recrystallisation

This is a technique used for purifying solids, by removing traces of unchanged reactants and unwanted side-products from the product of a reaction. A solvent is needed in which the product to be purified is much more soluble at its boiling temperature than at 273 K.

Boiling solvent is added to the impure product until just enough has been added to dissolve it all. If there are any insoluble impurities they can be removed by filtering the hot solution. The solution is then cooled to 273 K in an ice bath. The product is less soluble at this temperature and will precipitate out and can be removed by filtration. Any soluble impurities, which should be present only in fairly small quantities, will remain dissolved in the solvent. The effectiveness of the method depends on the selection of a suitable solvent in which the product is much more soluble at high temperatures than low temperatures.

Redox reactions

Aldehydes can be oxidised to carboxylic acids or reduced to primary alcohols.

$$R{-}\underset{\underset{H}{|}}{\overset{\overset{H}{|}}{C}}{-}O{-}H \xleftarrow{+2[H]} \underset{H}{\overset{R}{\diagdown}}C{=}O \xrightarrow{+[O]} \underset{H{-}O}{\overset{R}{\diagdown}}C{=}O$$

1° alcohol   aldehyde   carboxylic acid

← reduction   oxidation →

Ketones *cannot* be oxidised easily but can be reduced to secondary alcohols.

$$R{-}\underset{\underset{R'}{|}}{\overset{\overset{H}{|}}{C}}{-}O{-}H \xleftarrow{+2[H]} \underset{R'}{\overset{R}{\diagdown}}C{=}O$$

2° alcohol

Oxidation

The usual oxidising agents for conversion of aldehydes to carboxylic acids are acidified dichromate(VI) ions or acidified manganate(VII) ions. Very powerful oxidising conditions are required to oxidise ketones. Such reactions break the carbon chain.

Distinguishing aldehydes from ketones

Weak oxidising agents can oxidise aldehydes but not ketones. This is the basis of the tests to distinguish the two.

Benedict's test

Benedict's reagent is a mixture of copper(II) ions in an alkaline solution containing a complexing agent. An alternative way of making this solution is to mix Fehling's solution A (containing the Cu^{2+}) and Fehling's solution B (containing the alkali and a complexing agent). Warming an aldehyde with Benedict's solution (or a mixture of Fehling's A and B) produces a brick-red precipitate of copper(I) oxide as the copper(II) oxidises the aldehyde to a carboxylic acid and is itself reduced to copper(I). Ketones give no reaction to this test.

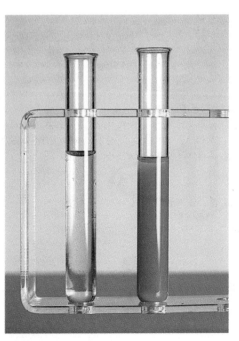

Benedict's test before and after

The silver mirror test

Aldehydes (but not ketones) are oxidised by Ag^+ ions in alkaline solution. The Ag^+ is reduced to metallic silver. When an aldehyde is warmed with Tollens' reagent (a solution of Ag^+ ions in aqueous ammonia), metallic silver is formed. In a spotlessly clean test tube a silver mirror will be formed on the inside of the test tube. Ketones give no reaction to this test.

Reduction

Both aldehydes and ketones can be reduced to alcohols by a variety of reducing agents:

- sodium in ethanol, which generates hydrogen
- hydrogen with a catalyst of nickel, platinum or palladium
- lithium tetrahydridoaluminate(III), $LiAlH_4$, in ethoxyethane solution followed by addition of water
- sodium tetrahydridoborate(III), $NaBH_4$, in aqueous solution.

Both of the last two reducing agents generate the nucleophile H^-, the hydride ion.

$$\begin{array}{c} R \\ \diagdown \\ C=O + H^- \\ \diagup \\ R' \end{array} \longrightarrow \begin{array}{c} R\ \ H \\ \diagdown / \\ C \\ \diagup \diagdown \\ R'\ \ O^- \end{array} \xrightarrow[\text{(from solvent)}]{H^+} \begin{array}{c} R\ \ H \\ \diagdown / \\ C \\ \diagup \diagdown \\ R'\ \ OH \end{array}$$

This reaction could therefore also be classified as a nucleophilic addition reaction.

Reactions of the alkyl groups of carbonyl compounds

Halogens react with both aldehydes and ketones. Substitution of hydrogen atoms in the alkyl group by halogen atoms occurs. For example:

$$\underset{\text{propanone}}{H-\overset{\overset{H}{|}}{\underset{\underset{H}{|}}{C}}-\overset{\overset{O}{||}}{C}-\overset{\overset{H}{|}}{\underset{\underset{H}{|}}{C}}-H} \xrightarrow[\text{catalyst}]{H^+} \underset{\text{iodopropanone}}{H-\overset{\overset{H}{|}}{\underset{\underset{H}{|}}{C}}-\overset{\overset{O}{||}}{C}-\overset{\overset{H}{|}}{\underset{\underset{H}{|}}{C}}-I}$$

The reaction is acid-catalysed. Further substitution can occur, firstly of the same methyl group and then, when that is fully substituted, of the second. The mechanism is discussed in section 26.2.

The triiodomethane reaction

Aldehydes and ketones which contain the group

$$H-\overset{\overset{\displaystyle H}{|}}{\underset{\underset{\displaystyle H}{|}}{C}}-C\overset{\displaystyle O}{\diagup}{\diagdown}$$

give a positive **triiodomethane reaction**. Reaction with iodine and

Hint: Lithium tetrahydridoaluminate(III) is sometimes called lithium aluminium hydride and sodium tetrahydridoborate(III), sodium borohydride.

Q Write an equation for the reaction of sodium and ethanol to produce hydrogen.

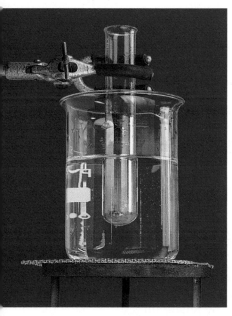

The silver mirror test

Q Why is H^- a nucleophile?

Answer: $Na + C_2H_5OH \longrightarrow C_2H_5ONa + \frac{1}{2}H_2$

Answer: It has a lone pair *and* a negative charge.

Which of the following will give a positive triiodomethane reaction: propanone, ethanal, methanal?

Hint: Alcohols containing the group

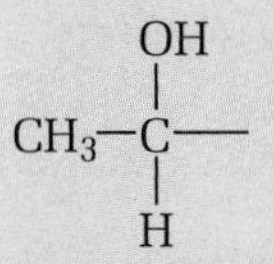

$$CH_3-\underset{\underset{H}{|}}{\overset{\overset{OH}{|}}{C}}-$$

will also give a positive triiodomethane reaction.

sodium hydroxide produces yellow crystals of triiodomethane, for example:

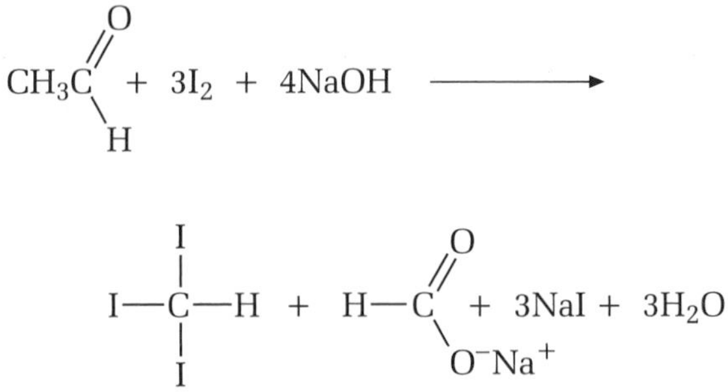

$$CH_3\overset{\overset{O}{\diagup\!\diagup}}{\underset{\diagdown}{C}}_H + 3I_2 + 4NaOH \longrightarrow$$

$$I-\underset{\underset{I}{|}}{\overset{\overset{I}{|}}{C}}-H \;+\; H-\overset{\overset{O}{\diagup\!\diagup}}{\underset{\diagdown}{C}}_{O^-Na^+} + 3NaI + 3H_2O$$

triiodomethane

Triiodomethane was once called iodoform.

33.5 Preparation of carbonyl compounds

Write the equation in displayed formulae for the oxidation of ethanol to ethanal.

Acidified dichromate(VI) ions oxidise primary alcohols to aldehydes and secondary alcohols to ketones. Aldehydes can be further oxidised to carboxylic acids. However, aldehydes have lower boiling temperatures than the corresponding alcohols (since alcohol molecules form hydrogen bonds to one another and aldehydes do not). This means that aldehydes can be distilled off the reaction mixture before they can be further oxidised.

33.6 Carbohydrates

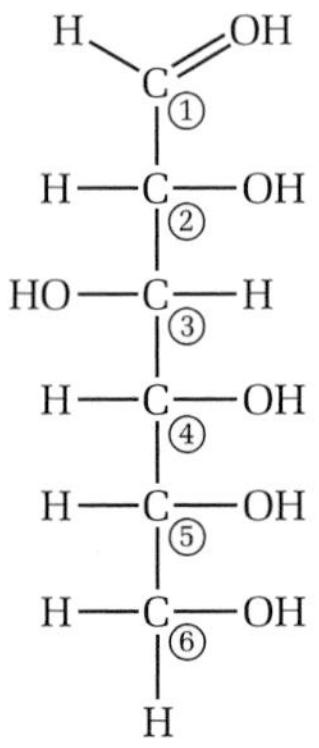

$$H-\underset{①}{\overset{\overset{\displaystyle H}{\diagdown}}{C}}{\overset{\displaystyle OH}{\diagup}}$$
$$H-\underset{②}{C}-OH$$
$$HO-\underset{③}{C}-H$$
$$H-\underset{④}{C}-OH$$
$$H-\underset{⑤}{C}-OH$$
$$H-\underset{⑥}{C}-OH$$
$$H$$

Figure 33.4 Glucose

Carbohydrates are a group of compounds of general formula $C_n(H_2O)_m$, which explains the name. They occur naturally in all plants where they are produced by **photosynthesis**: the endothermic reaction of water and carbon dioxide which is fuelled by light energy.

$$6CO_2 + 6H_2O \xrightarrow[\text{photosynthesis}]{\text{light}} C_6H_{12}O_6 + 6O_2$$

glucose

One of the simplest carbohydrates is the sugar glucose, a sweet-tasting compound.

One way of presenting the formula of glucose is in **Figure 33.4**, which shows that it is an aldehyde. However, most glucose molecules exist in a cyclic form, in which the —OH group or carbon number five has reacted with the aldehyde group. This is just the same as the reaction of an alcohol with the aldehyde to form a hemiacetal (see page 533). In this case, both functional groups are part of the same molecule, so we have an **intramolecular** (within the molecule) reaction:

Answer: propanone, ethanal

Answer: $$H-\underset{\underset{H}{|}}{\overset{\overset{H}{|}}{C}}-\underset{\underset{H}{|}}{\overset{\overset{H}{|}}{C}}-OH \xrightarrow{[-2H]} H-\underset{\underset{H}{|}}{\overset{\overset{H}{|}}{C}}-\overset{\overset{O}{\diagup\!\diagup}}{\underset{\diagdown}{C}}_H$$

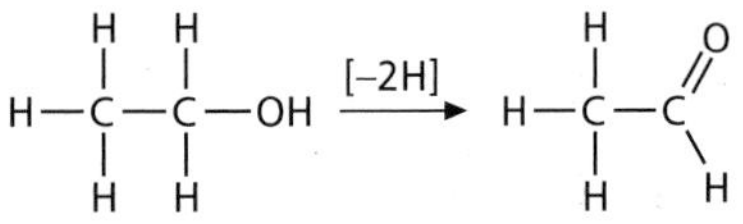

Figure 33.5 The ring form of glucose

the chain form of glucose

the ring form of glucose

Any of the other —OH groups could in principle take part in the same reaction but the six-membered ring which forms is the most stable because it has the least ring strain (it allows the C—C—C bond angles in the ring to be close to 109.5°). The ring is not flat, as shown in **Figure 33.5**. In aqueous solution the ring form is in equilibrium with the chain form.

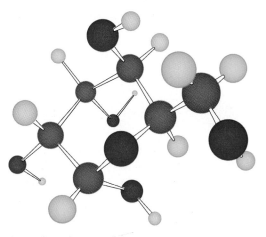

The ring form of glucose

Fructose is an isomer of glucose. It is also a sugar, sweeter than glucose, and is found in fruits and honey. It is now made on a large scale by the action of enzymes on corn – hence it is called corn syrup – and is used extensively in the food industry.

The functional group of fructose is a ketone:

CHEMISTRY AROUND US

Sweeteners: the triangle of sweetness

The sweetness of sugars has been known for thousands of years. The average person in the UK consumes around 750 g of sucrose weekly which provides 12 500 kJ (or about 3000 calories) of energy. Many people try to reduce this energy intake without sacrificing the sweetness by using artificial sweeteners. One of these, lead ethanoate ('sugar of lead'), has been known since Roman times but is no longer used because of the toxicity of lead compounds. The table lists some sweet compounds and compares their sweetness with that of sucrose (table sugar). The values are approximate as they can only be found by using human tasters to find the concentration of a solution which is as sweet as a standard sucrose solution.

Substance	Sweetness	Comments
sucrose	1	natural sugars
glucose	0.5	
fructose	1.5	
cycalamate	30	some evidence suggests a possible link with cancer
saccharin	350	bitter aftertaste
aspartame	200	trade name Nutrasweet. Unstable, therefore short shelf-life in products
sucralose	650	

Most artificial sweeteners have been discovered by accident because it is not normal practice to taste newly synthesised compounds until they have been extensively tested for toxicity – a long and expensive process – and there is no way to measure sweetness without tasting. There does, however, seem to be some link between chemical structure and sweetness. Most sweet compounds seem to have a system AH,B where A and B are electronegative atoms. These are thought to form hydrogen bonds with a protein in the taste buds. To do this effectively, A and B must be around 0.3 nm apart.

The structures of some sweet compounds are shown with the AH,B atoms in red.

aspartame

saccharin

sucrose

glucose

sodium cyclamate

More recently, it has been suggested that a third group, X, is involved, which is non-polar and thus repels hydrogen bonds. This leads to the idea of a 'triangle of sweetness' with the dimensions shown:

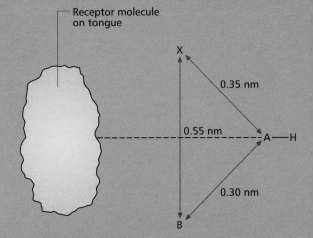

Receptor molecule on tongue

X
0.35 nm
0.55 nm — A — H
0.30 nm
B

These theories lead to the possibility of synthesising new sweeteners by design rather than trial and error.

Fructose can also form a ring in a similar way to glucose. This time the ring can be five-membered.

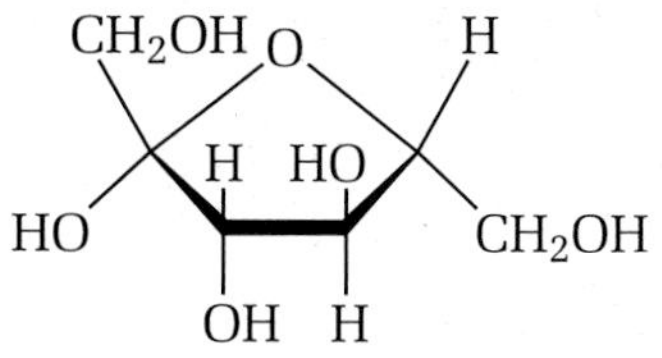

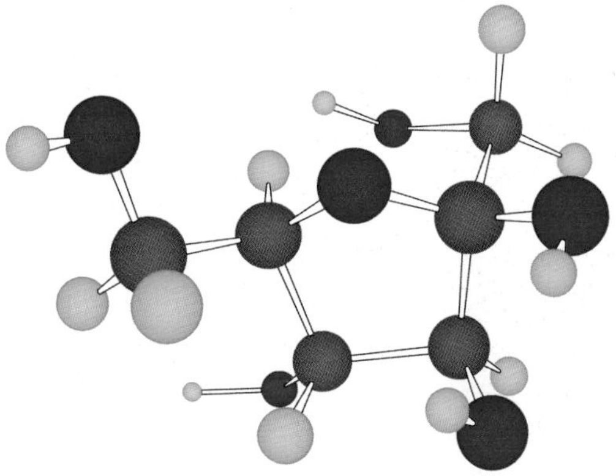

The ring form of fructose

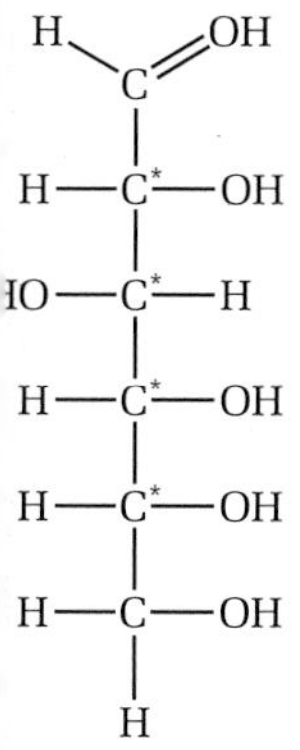

The ring form is in equilibrium with the chain form as in glucose. Both glucose and fructose (as well as other sugars) are called monosaccharides ('single sugars'). Two sugars can link together with the elimination of a molecule of water to form a disaccharide ('double sugar'). The best known example is sucrose in which a glucose molecule is linked to a fructose molecule. Sucrose is ordinary table sugar.

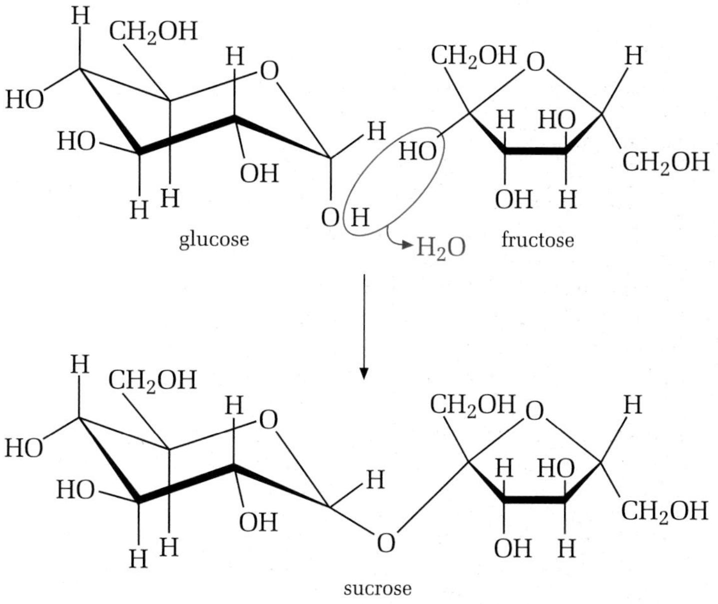

sucrose

Both glucose and fructose have a number of isomers. Glucose has four chiral carbon atoms and so exists in optically active forms (see section 18.6).

The four chiral carbon atoms are marked * in **Figure 33.6**. Each of these carbons is bonded to four different groups. Notice that you

gure 33.6 The chiral carbons of glucose

Why are the top and bottom carbon atoms in Figure 33.6 not chiral?

nswer: The top one is bonded to only three fferent groups. Two of the four groups bonded to the ottom one are the same.

Hint: Hydrolysis means *breaking down* by reaction with water. Do not confuse this with hydration, which means *addition* of water (or hydrogenation which means addition of hydrogen). So

$$AB \xrightarrow{H_2O} A—H + B—OH \text{ is hydrolysis}$$

and $AB \xrightarrow{H_2O} AHBOH$ is hydration.

Foods containing starch

must consider the whole group to which the carbon atom is bonded, not just the first atom.

Polysaccharides

Polysaccharides are polymers of up to a few thousand monosaccharides. Both starch and cellulose are examples of polysaccharides made from glucose. They differ in the geometry of the way in which the glucose molecules are linked. In both cases the bonds between the glucose molecules are each formed with elimination of a water molecule, as in the formation of sucrose (above). The links in starch, also called amylose, can be broken down either by the action of enzymes such as salivary amylase in the digestive system, or by boiling with dilute acid. This reaction is called a **hydrolysis** reaction. Starch is synthesised in plants and forms their main food reserve. Bread, rice and potatoes are foods with an especially high starch content.

Cellulose is responsible for the structure of plant material. Humans cannot digest cellulose, though it is useful in our diets as roughage.

Tests for carbohydrates
Reducing sugars

Sugars like glucose, which have an aldehyde functional group, sometimes called **aldoses**, are oxidised by Benedict's (or Fehling's) solution and produce a brick-red precipitate of copper(I) oxide by reducing the Cu(II) to Cu(I). They are therefore called **reducing sugars**. Benedict's test can therefore be used as a test for reducing sugars.

Although it is a ketone, fructose will also produce a positive result with Benedict's test. This is because of the equilibrium:

$$
\begin{array}{ccc}
& H & \\
& | & \\
H—C—OH & & \\
| & & \\
C{=}O & \rightleftharpoons & \\
| & & \\
HO—C—H & & \\
| & & \\
H—C—OH & & \\
| & & \\
H—C—OH & & \\
| & & \\
H—C—OH & & \\
| & & \\
H & &
\end{array}
$$

Sucrose does not react with Benedict's solution and is therefore not a reducing sugar.

Starch

Starch produces a deep blue-black colour when treated with a solution of iodine in potassium iodide solution. This is used as a test for starch. Cellulose does not give a positive result with this test.

Iodine and starch give a blue-black colour

Reactions of carbohydrates

Dehydration

Addition of concentrated sulphuric acid dehydrates carbohydrates, the main product being carbon:

$$C_n(H_2O)_m \xrightarrow{H_2SO_4} nC + mH_2O$$

Hydrolysis

Polysaccharides can be broken down into monosaccharides by boiling with dilute acid or by the use of a suitable enzyme.

$$\underset{\text{polysaccharide}}{(C_6(H_2O)_5)_n} + nH_2O \xrightarrow[\text{or enzyme catalyst}]{H^+} \underset{\text{monosaccharide}}{nC_6(H_2O)_6}$$

A molecule of water is required to break each link in the polysaccharide, hence the term hydrolysis. For example:

$$\underset{\text{sucrose}}{\text{G} \overset{}{\underset{O}{\frown}} \text{F}} + H_2O \longrightarrow \underset{\text{glucose}}{\text{G}_{OH}} + \underset{\text{fructose}}{HO_{\frown}\text{F}}$$

he dehydration of sucrose by concentrated sulphuric acid

Oxidation

Reducing sugars, including glucose and fructose, are oxidised easily and therefore give a positive result with Benedict's test. Di- and polysaccharides do not. Hydrolysis of di- and polysaccharides produces reducing sugars which can be oxidised.

33.7 Economic importance of carbonyl compounds

Methanal

The major use of methanal is in the manufacture of thermosetting polymers. Bakelite, a polymer of phenol and methanal, has been described (see the box 'Phenol–methanal plastics', Chapter 32). A similar polymer can be made from methanal and urea (NH_2CONH_2). It too is a condensation polymer, a molecule of water being eliminated with each urea–methanal link formed as shown. New bonds are in red.

$$\text{H}-\overset{\overset{\text{H}}{|}}{\text{N}}-\overset{\overset{\text{O}}{||}}{\text{C}}-\overset{\overset{\text{H}}{|}}{\text{N}}-(\text{H} \quad \text{O} \quad \text{H})-\overset{\overset{\text{H}}{|}}{\text{N}}-\overset{\overset{\text{O}}{||}}{\text{C}}-\overset{\overset{\text{H}}{|}}{\text{N}}-(\text{H} \quad \text{O} \quad \text{H})-\overset{\overset{\text{H}}{|}}{\text{N}}-\overset{\overset{\text{O}}{||}}{\text{C}}-\overset{\overset{\text{H}}{|}}{\text{N}}-\text{H} \quad \text{etc.}$$

$$H^+ \text{ catalyst} \downarrow$$

$$\sim\sim\text{N}-\overset{\overset{\text{H}}{|}}{\underset{}{\text{C}}}-\overset{\overset{\text{O}}{||}}{\text{C}}-\overset{\overset{\text{H}}{|}}{\text{N}}-\overset{}{\text{C}}-\overset{\overset{\text{O}}{||}}{\text{C}}-\overset{\overset{}{}}{\text{N}}-\overset{}{\text{C}}-\overset{\overset{\text{O}}{||}}{\text{C}}-\text{N}\sim\sim$$

Cross-links can form:

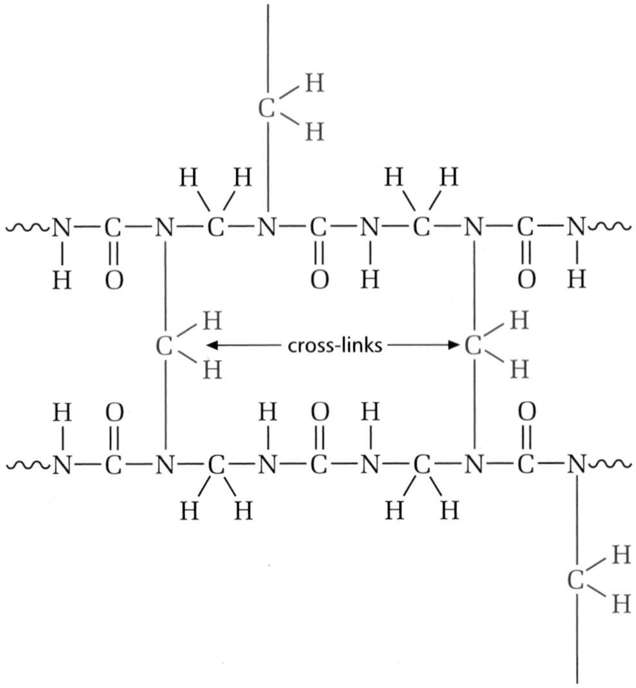

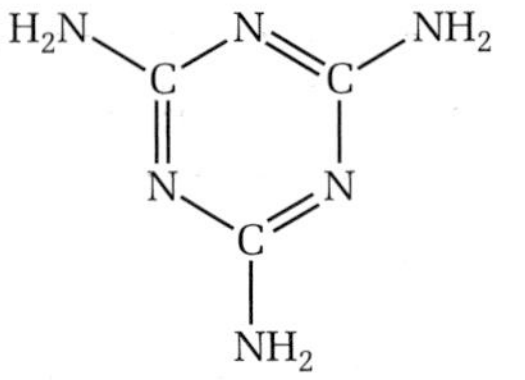

Figure 33.7 Melamine

to produce a rigid thermosetting polymer, which is used as an adhesive to stick the 'chips' together in chipboard and also for moulding electrical sockets. A similar polymer is made from methanal and melamine (**Figure 33.7**): —NH_2 groups on melamine are linked by methanal in the same way as the —NH_2 groups in urea.

'Melamine' is also the trade name for the resulting polymer which is used for making picnic crockery and kitchen worktops, for example. 'Melamine' has a low density, is colourless (but can be coloured if required), electrically insulating and unaffected by light, moderate heat and water.

Methanal is manufactured by the oxidation of methanol by air using a copper catalyst at 800 K.

$$CH_3OH + \tfrac{1}{2}O_2 \longrightarrow HCHO + H_2O$$

Ethanal

Figure 33.8 summarises some of the industrial uses of ethanal. Ethanal is manufactured by the oxidation of ethanol in a similar way to that of methanol above or by the Wacker process in which ethene reacts with oxygen with a catalyst system of aqueous palladium(II) and copper(II) chlorides at 300–330 K.

Hint: A **co-product** of an industrial process is one that is just as saleable as the main product. A **by-product** is one that is in less demand than the main one and in some cases must be disposed of.

Propanone

Most propanone is produced as a co-product of the cumene process by which phenol is made (see the box 'The cumene process', Chapter 32). The rest is made by the oxidation of propan-2-ol by air at 770 K and 300 kPa with a copper catalyst. Hydrogen peroxide is a co-product.

$$\underset{\text{propan-2-ol}}{\underset{\displaystyle \begin{array}{c} \\ H\!-\!\overset{\displaystyle \overset{H}{|}}{\underset{\displaystyle \underset{H}{|}}{C}}\!-\!\overset{\displaystyle \overset{H}{|}}{\underset{\displaystyle \underset{OH}{|}}{C}}\!-\!\overset{\displaystyle \overset{H}{|}}{\underset{\displaystyle \underset{H}{|}}{C}}\!-\!H \end{array}} + O_2} \xrightarrow[\text{Cu catalyst}]{\text{770 K, 300 kPa}}$$

$$\underset{\text{propanone}}{H\!-\!\overset{\displaystyle \overset{H}{|}}{\underset{\displaystyle \underset{H}{|}}{C}}\!-\!\overset{}{\underset{\displaystyle \underset{O}{\|}}{C}}\!-\!\overset{\displaystyle \overset{H}{|}}{\underset{\displaystyle \underset{H}{|}}{C}}\!-\!H} + H_2O_2$$

The uses of propanone are summarised in **Figure 33.9**.

Other uses of carbonyl compounds

- Butanone is used industrially as a solvent.
- A number of carbonyl compounds are used as perfumes and flavourings.
- The chemistry of sugars and starches is of enormous importance in the processed food industry.
- Cellulose is used to make viscose fibres, cellophane and an explosive called guncotton.

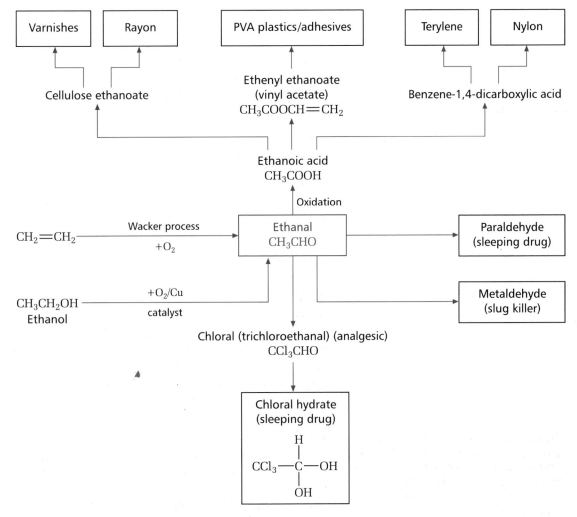

Figure 33.8 Industrial chemistry of ethanal

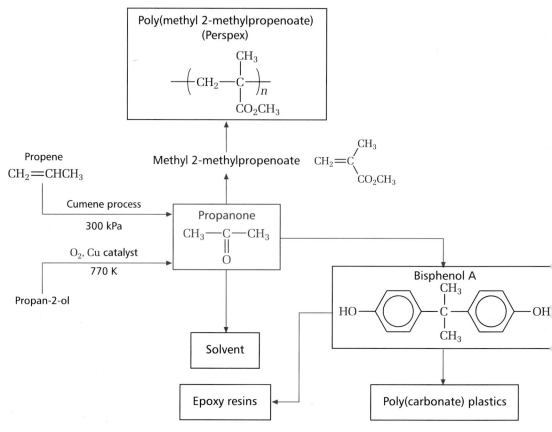

Figure 33.9 Industrial chemistry of propanone

33.8 Summary

- Aldehydes and ketones both contain the carbonyl functional group

$$\diagdown C{=}O$$

- Aldehydes have the general formula

$$\begin{array}{c} R \\ \diagdown \\ C{=}O \\ \diagup \\ H \end{array}$$ where R may be H.

- Ketones have the general formula

$$\begin{array}{c} R \\ \diagdown \\ C{=}O \\ \diagup \\ R' \end{array}$$ where neither R nor R' is H.

- The shape of the carbonyl group is   flat and trigonal.

- The carbonyl group has bond angles of   approximately 120°.

- The carbonyl group is strongly polarised as $C^{\delta+}\!\!=\!\!O^{\delta-}$

- The forces that operate between the molecules are   dipole–dipole.

- The $C^{\delta+}$ may be attacked by   nucleophiles.

- The $O^{\delta-}$ may be attacked by   electrophiles, for example, H^+.

- Aldehydes, but not ketones, give a positive result with   the Benedict's, Fehling's or silver mirror test.

- Aldehydes and ketones can be identified by making   a derivative with 2,4-dinitrophenylhydrazine (Brady's reagent).

- Aldehydes can be prepared in the laboratory by oxidation of   primary alcohols.

- Ketones can be prepared in the laboratory by oxidation of secondary alcohols.

- Carbohydrates have the general formula $C_n(H_2O)_m$.

- Most glucose molecules exist as   six-membered rings.

- The carbonyl group in glucose is   an aldehyde.

- Most fructose molecules exist as   five-membered rings.

- The carbonyl group in fructose is   a ketone.

- Simple sugars (monosaccharides) link together by   the elimination of water.

- Sucrose is a disaccharide consisting of a   molecule of glucose and one of fructose.

- Starch and cellulose are both   polysaccharides.

- Glucose and fructose are   reducing sugars.

- Starch gives a blue-black complex with   iodine.

- The reactions of carbonyl compounds are summarised in **Figure 33.10**.

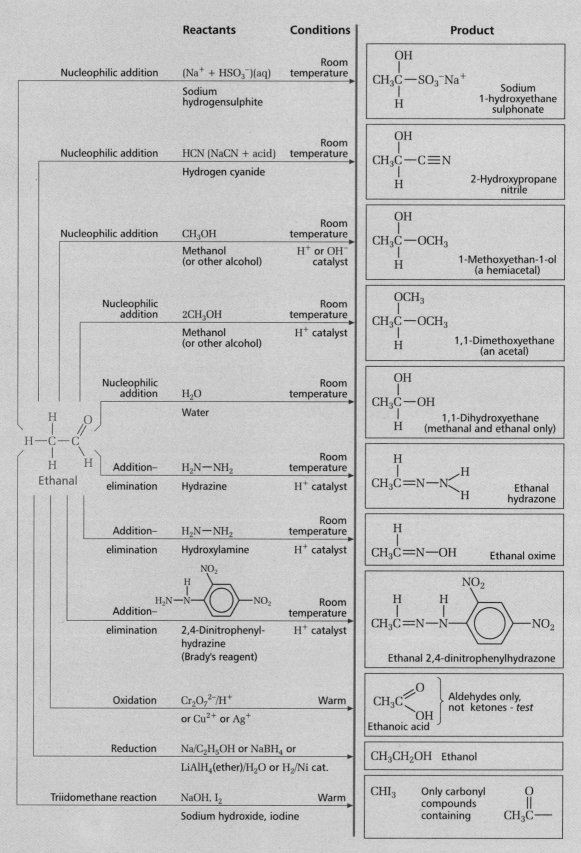

Figure 33.10 The reactions of carbonyl compounds using ethanal as an example – cover up the right-hand side to test yourself.

33.9 Practice questions

1. Name the following compounds.

(a) $H-\overset{\displaystyle H}{\underset{\displaystyle H}{C}}-\overset{\displaystyle H}{\underset{\displaystyle H}{C}}-\overset{\displaystyle H}{\underset{\displaystyle H}{C}}-C\overset{\displaystyle O}{\underset{\displaystyle H}{}}$

(b) $H-\overset{H}{\underset{H}{C}}-\overset{H}{\underset{H}{C}}-\overset{H}{\underset{H}{C}}-\overset{H}{\underset{H}{C}}-\overset{O}{\underset{}{C}}-\overset{H}{\underset{H}{C}}-H$

(c) A cyclohexanone ring structure with =O

(d) $H-\overset{H}{\underset{H}{C}}-\overset{O}{\underset{}{C}}-\overset{H}{\underset{H}{C}}-\overset{O}{\underset{}{C}}-\overset{H}{\underset{H}{C}}-H$

2. Write structural formulae for:
(a) butanal, (b) chloroethanal, (c) butanone,
(d) cyclopentanone.

3. Give the structural formulae of the organic product of the following reactions.

(a) $C_2H_5C\overset{\displaystyle O}{\underset{\displaystyle H}{}} + HCN$

(b) $CH_3-\overset{O}{\underset{}{C}}-CH_3 + Br_2$

(c) $CH_3-\overset{O}{\underset{}{C}}-CH_3 + NaBH_4$

(d) $H-\overset{O}{\underset{}{C}}-H + K_2Cr_2O_7/H^+$

(e) $CH_3-\overset{O}{\underset{}{C}}-CH_3 + I_2$

(f) $CH_3-\overset{O}{\underset{}{C}}-C_2H_5 + H_2N-NH_2$

33.10 Examination questions

1. (a) Name and draw the full structures of **one** ketone **A** and **one** aldehyde **B**, each with formula $C_5H_{10}O$.
   (b) Describe a simple **chemical** test which would enable you to differentiate between samples of **A** and **B**. State the observations you would expect to make for each sample and explain the chemistry involved.
   (c) For the reaction of your aldehyde **B** with HCN, give:
       (i) the equation;
       (ii) the mechanism.
                                    [Oxford 1996]

2. (a) Outline the reaction of propanone with the following reagents. Give the equation for the reaction, the conditions, and the name of the organic product.
       (i) Hydrogen cyanide
       (ii) Sodium tetrahydridoborate(III) (sodium borohydride) (you may represent NaBH₄ as [H])
   (b) (i) Give the mechanism for the reaction in (a)(i).

   (ii) What type of mechanism is this?
   (iii) What feature of the carbonyl group makes this type of mechanism possible? Explain how this feature arises.
   (iv) Explain briefly, by reference to its structure, why ethene would not react with HCN in a similar way.
                          [London (Nuffield) 1998]

3. (a) Give a chemical test by which you could distinguish between ethanal and propanone. State the reagent(s) and conditions for the test, describe what you would observe, and give the name or formula of the organic product.
   (b) Consider the following series of reactions involving ethanal, then answer the questions which follow.

   $S \xleftarrow{\text{HCN(l)}} CH_3CHO \xrightarrow{\text{2,4-Dinitrophenylhydrazine}} T$

   $CH_3CHO \xrightarrow{\quad NaBH_4 \quad} U$

(i) Draw graphical formulae to show the structures of compounds **S**, **T** and **U**.

(ii) Give the name of compound **T** and describe its appearance.

(c) Give the name and an outline of the mechanism for the reaction of ethanal with HCN(l) to produce compound **S**.

[AEB 1996]

4. Propenal, $CH_2{=}CHCHO$, is one of the materials that gives crispy bacon its sharp odour. In the following question assume that the carbon–carbon double bond and the aldehyde group in propenal behave independently.

(a) Give the structural formulae of the compounds formed when propenal reacts with:
   (i) hydrogen bromide;
   (ii) hydrogen cyanide;
   (iii) 2,4-dinitrophenylhydrazine.

(b) (i) Give the mechanism for the reaction between hydrogen cyanide and the aldehyde group. You may represent the aldehyde group as

$$\begin{array}{c} R \\ \diagdown \\ C{=}O \\ \diagup \\ H \end{array}$$

   (ii) The reaction in (i) occurs best in slightly acidic conditions. It is slower if the pH is high or low. Suggest reasons why this is so.

(c) Explain why lithium tetrahydridoaluminate(III) (lithium aluminium hydride), $LiAlH_4$, reacts only with the $\diagup C{=}O$ bond and not with the $\diagup C{=}C\diagdown$ bond, even though these bonds have the same electronic structure.

(d) Suggest reactions, giving equations and conditions, which would convert propenal into a compound which would react with iodine in the presence of sodium hydroxide solution.

[London (Nuffield) 1998]

5. Octan-2-one may be prepared by the oxidation of octan-2-ol using chromic acid which is a mixture of sodium dichromate(VI) and sulphuric acid.

$$CH_3(CH_2)_5CHOHCH_3 + [O] \longrightarrow CH_3(CH_2)_5COCH_3 + H_2O$$

The apparatus used is shown at the top of the next column.

The method is as follows:

Chromic acid is first prepared by dissolving 100 g (0.33 mol) of sodium dichromate(VI) dihydrate in 300 cm³ of water and slowly adding 73 cm³ (1.34 mol) of concentrated sulphuric acid. The solution is cooled and diluted to 500 cm³ with water.

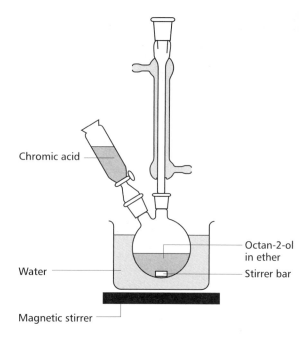

A solution of 32.5 g (0.25 mol) of octan-2-ol in 100 cm³ of ether is placed in the flask and 125 cm³ (0.083 mol) of chromic acid, an excess, is added dropwise to the stirred solution. The temperature is kept between 25 °C and 30 °C using a water bath. The stirring is continued at room temperature for 2 hours and the reaction mixture is then transferred to a separating funnel. The ether layer is separated from the dark green aqueous layer with four 60 cm³ portions of ether. The ether extracts are combined and washed with sodium hydrogencarbonate solution (40 cm³ of a saturated solution). The ether extract is then left over anhydrous sodium sulphate. After filtration the extract is distilled and the octan-2-one collected at 170–172 °C.

(a) (i) Suggest why the mixture needs to be vigorously stirred.

   (ii) Describe how you would use a separating funnel to separate the ether layer from the aqueous layer.

   (iii) Suggest the purpose of the sodium hydrogencarbonate solution.

   (iv) Suggest the purpose of the anhydrous sodium sulphate.

   (v) Name the species which is responsible for the green colour in the aqueous layer.

   (vi) Comment on the range of temperature used to collect the octan-2-one.

(b) (i) If 26.2 g of octan-2-one is obtained calculate the percentage yield.

   (ii) Suggest **two** reasons why the yield is not 100%.

(c) Write balanced equations for the following reactions of octan-2-one:
   (i) octan-2-one + hydroxylamine
   (ii) octan-2-one + 2,4-dinitrophenylhydrazine

(d) Octan-2-one has a cheese-like odour which increases when it is heated. Explain this observation.

[NI 1997]

34 Carboxylic acids and their derivatives

CHEMISTRY NOW

Sour milk, cramp and gout: the role of lactic acid

Lactic acid, systematic name 2-hydroxypropanoic acid, has the molecular formula $C_3H_6O_3$. In effect it is 'half' a molecule of glucose, $C_6H_{12}O_6$, and it is formed from sugars by anaerobic decomposition ('anaerobic' means 'without air'). This happens when milk goes off and it is brought about by bacteria in the milk. The lactic acid produced makes the milk taste sour. It also makes the fat droplets, which are normally dispersed in the milk, coalesce, causing the milk to separate.

Bottle of sour milk, showing separation into layers

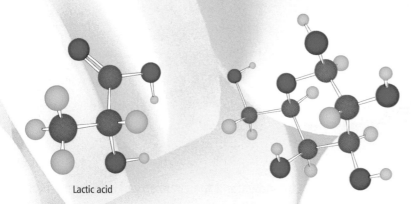

Lactic acid

Lactic acid is half a glucose molecule

100 metre sprinting is an 'oxygen debt' activity

In our muscles, glucose is usually metabolised aerobically, producing carbon dioxide, water and energy. This is the same overall chemical process as burning it in oxygen. However, in 'oxygen debt' activities, such as 100 metre sprinting, the muscles cannot obtain oxygen fast enough to metabolise glucose aerobically at the required rate. Anaerobic metabolism, which produces less energy, takes over, producing lactic acid. This builds up in the muscles, makes them feel tired and causes cramp. On resting, the lactic acid is removed by the bloodstream and decomposed in the liver, and the cramp disappears.

Lactic acid can also cause pain of a different type in heavy drinkers. Here the liver's capacity is saturated by breaking down ethanol, and lactic acid remains in the bloodstream, causing pain and fatigue in the muscles. The acid also promotes the precipitation in the joints of salts of uric acid, which causes the joint pain called gout. Often the first joint affected is in the big toe.

Introduction

This chapter deals with a number of closely related groups of compounds. Carboxylic acids have the functional group:

This is interesting because it includes two arrangements that we have seen before: the carbonyl group, $C=O$, found in aldehydes and ketones and the hydroxy group, OH, found in alcohols. We shall see how the presence of both groups on the same carbon atom leads to considerable changes in the properties of each group. The most obvious is that the OH group in carboxylic acids is significantly acidic while the OH group in alcohols is only very weakly acidic.

In the acid derivatives the OH group of the acid is replaced by different groups as shown:

ester   amide   acid chloride

anhydride

The easiest way to understand the chemistry of acid derivatives is by comparison with that of the parent acids.

The most familiar carboxylic acid is ethanoic acid (acetic acid) which is responsible for the sour taste of vinegar. Short-chain esters are fairly volatile and have pleasant fruity smells, one example being 3-methylbutyl ethanoate which smells of pear drops.

3-methylbutyl ethanoate

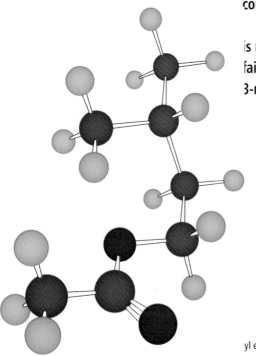

yl ethanoate

Fats and oils are esters with longer carbon chains.

Anhydrides and acid chlorides are more reactive than their 'parent' carboxylic acids and have important uses as industrial intermediates for this reason.

Amides are less reactive. Proteins are poly(amides) and therefore the amide group is closely linked with the chemistry of life. Nylon is also a poly(amide) while Terylene is a poly(ester).

High protein (left) and high fat foods (right). Both proteins and fats are acid derivatives

CONCEPT CHECKPOINTS

The following basic ideas are used in this chapter. You may revise some of these topics elsewhere in the book.
- delocalisation (sections 9.1 and 32.1)
- nucleophiles (section 18.8)
- acids as proton donors (section 12.2)
- substitution reactions (section 18.8)
- redox reactions (Chapter 13)
- hydrogen bonding and dipole–dipole forces (section 10.1)

34.1 Formulae, naming and structure

The carboxylic acid functional group is $-\overset{\displaystyle O}{\underset{\displaystyle OH}{C}}$, sometimes

written as —COOH or as —CO_2H. The carbon of the functional group has only one 'spare' bond, so this group can only occur at the end of a carbon chain.

Naming

Carboxylic acids are named using the suffix -oic acid. The carbon atom of the functional group is counted as part of the carbon chain of the root. So $H-\overset{\displaystyle O}{\underset{\displaystyle OH}{C}}$ is methanoic acid, $H-\overset{\displaystyle H}{\underset{\displaystyle H}{C}}-\overset{\displaystyle O}{\underset{\displaystyle OH}{C}}$ is

ethanoic acid and so on.

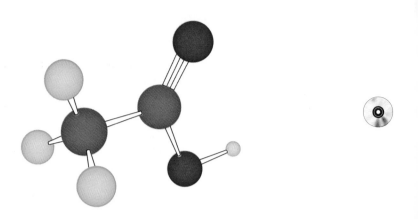

Ethanoic acid

Where there are substituents or side chains on the carbon chain, the
are numbered using locants, counting from the carbon of the
carboxylic acid as carbon number one. So

$$\begin{array}{c} HBr \\ | | \\ H-C-C-C \\ | | \\ HH \end{array}$$ is 2-bromopropanoic acid;

$$\begin{array}{c} HCH_3H \\ ||| \\ H-C-C-C-C \\ ||| \\ HHH \end{array}$$ is 3-methylbutanoic acid.

When the functional group is attached to a benzene ring, the suffix
-carboxylic acid is used and the carbon of the functional group is *no*
counted as part of the root. So

is benzenecarboxylic acid (still
sometimes called benzoic acid).

Acid derivatives

The acid derivatives have the general formula $R-C\overset{O}{\underset{Z}{\big|\big|}}$

If R is an alkyl group, $R-C\overset{O}{\big|\big|}$ is called the acyl group.

Acid chlorides (or acyl chlorides) are $R-C\overset{O}{\underset{Cl}{\big|\big|}}$ and are named

using the suffix -oyl chloride. So $CH_3-C\overset{O}{\underset{Cl}{\big|\big|}}$ is ethanoyl chloride.

Anhydrides have the formula

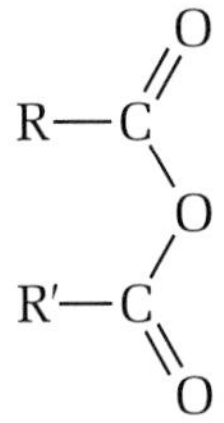

$$R-C \overset{O}{\underset{O}{\big\Vert}} \quad R'-C \overset{O}{\big\Vert}$$

They can be thought of as two molecules of acid from which a molecule of water has been eliminated, for example:

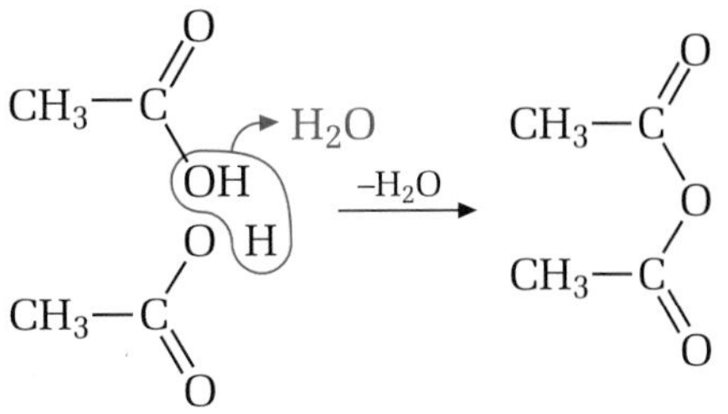

$$CH_3-C \quad H_2O \quad CH_3-C$$
$$-H_2O$$
$$CH_3-C \quad CH_3-C$$

Hint: Take care with the names of esters. It is easy to get them 'the wrong way round'.

Symmetrical anhydrides, derived from two molecules of the same acid, are simply named as the anhydride of the parent acid, so the above compound is called ethanoic anhydride. Mixed anhydrides, derived from two different acids, are named by listing the parent acids in alphabetical order.

$$CH_3-C$$
So $\quad CH_3CH_2-C \quad$ O is named ethanoic propanoic anhydride.

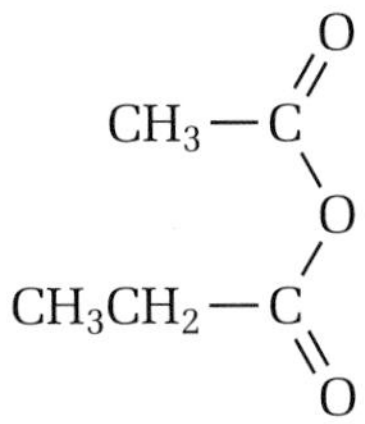

Esters have the general formula $\quad R-C \overset{O}{\big\Vert}_{O-R'} \quad$ and they are named

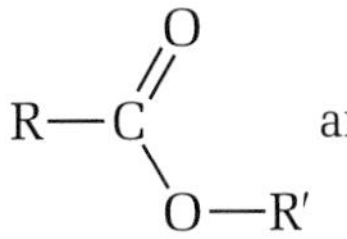

as alkyl or aryl derivatives of the parent acid, so $\quad CH_3-C \overset{O}{\underset{OC_3H_7}{\big\Vert}} \quad$ is

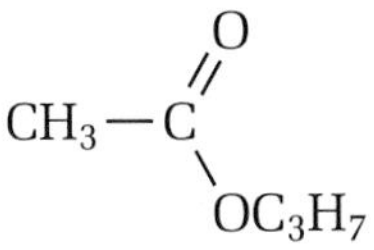

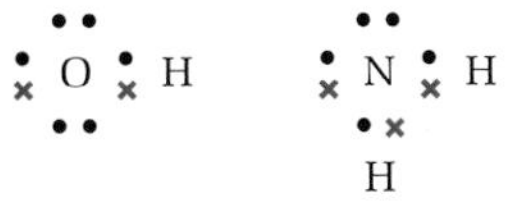

Figure 34.1 Dot-cross diagrams of the —OH and —NH₂ groups

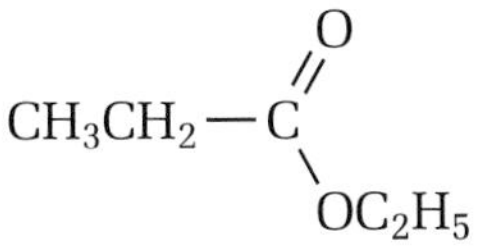

propyl ethanoate; $CH_3CH_2-C \overset{O}{\underset{OC_2H_5}{\big\Vert}}$ is ethyl propanoate.

Hint: Species with the same numbers of electrons are described as isoelectronic.

Amides have the —OH group of the parent carboxylic acid replaced by an —NH₂ group (which has the same number of electrons as the —OH group (**Figure 34.1**). They are named using the suffix -amide.

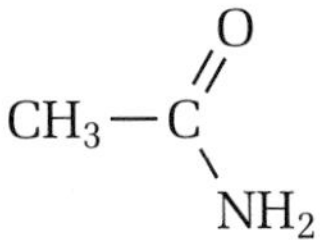

So $\quad CH_3-C \overset{O}{\underset{NH_2}{\big\Vert}} \quad$ is ethanamide.

Shape

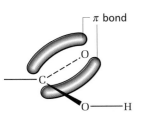

Figure 34.2 Bonding in the carboxylic acid functional group

The C=O double bond consists of a σ bond plus a π bond formed by overlap of p orbitals on each atom (**Figure 34.2**).

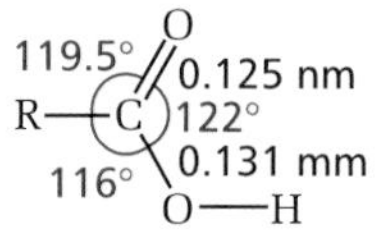

The molecule is not quite flat, so
the angles do not add up to 360°

Figure 34.3 The shape of the carboxylic acid functional
group

Did you know? Pure ethanoic acid is
sometimes called 'glacial' ethanoic acid
because it may freeze in a cold
laboratory. 'Glacial' means 'ice-like'.

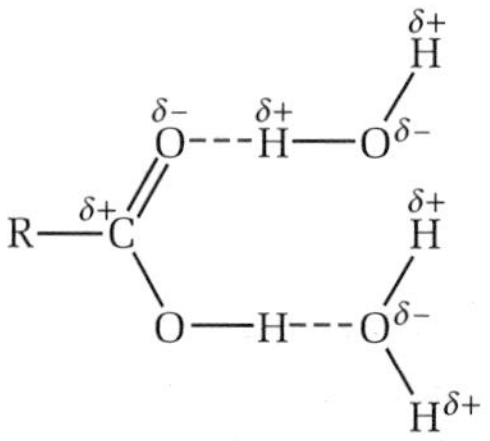

Figure 34.4 A molecule of a carboxylic acid forming
hydrogen bonds with water

> **Q** What would be the relative
> molecular mass of an ethanoic acid
> dimer?

Did you know? The non-systematic
names of hexanoic and octanoic acids
are caproic and caprylic acid
respectively, from the same derivation as
Capricorn the goat. They are present in
goat fat and cause its unpleasant smell.

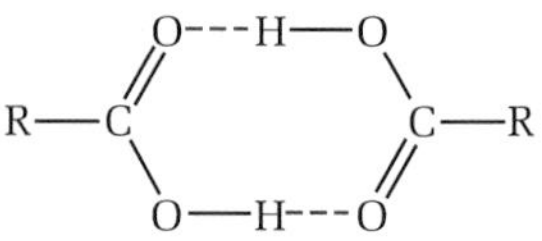

Figure 34.5 A hydrogen bonded dimer of two carboxylic
acid molecules

Answer: 120

The carboxylic acid group is virtually flat and trigonal, with all the
bond angles approximately 120°, as we would expect from electron
pair repulsion theory (**Figure 34.3**).

34.2 Physical properties of carboxylic acids

The carboxylic acid group can form hydrogen bonds with water
molecules (**Figure 34.4**). This results in carboxylic acids dissolving
well in water, provided that their carbon chains are fairly short. The
carboxylic acids up to, and including, C_4 (butanoic acid) are
completely soluble in water.

The acids have much higher melting temperatures than the
alkanes of similar relative molecular mass because they form
hydrogen bonds with one another in the solid state. Ethanoic acid
($M_r = 60$) melts at 290 K while butane ($M_r = 58$) melts at 135 K.
Ethanoic acid's high melting point means that it will freeze in a cool
laboratory.

A carboxylic acid molecule may also form hydrogen bonds with
another carboxylic acid molecule in the liquid or gaseous state to
form a dimer (**Figure 34.5**) (see section 10.1).

As their carbon chain gets longer, carboxylic acids dissolve
increasingly well in non-polar solvents.

The acids have characteristic smells. You will recognise the smell
of ethanoic acid as vinegar, while butanoic acid causes the smell of
rancid butter.

34.3 Reactivity of carboxylic acids

The carboxylic acid group is polarised as shown:

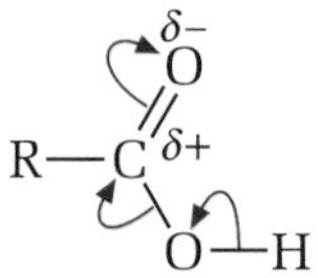

The $C^{\delta+}$ is therefore likely to be attacked by nucleophiles while the
$O^{\delta-}$ may be attacked by positively charged species like H^+. However,
the $C^{\delta+}$ tends to attract electrons from the C—OH bond. This reduces
the $\delta+$ character of this carbon atom and makes it less easily
attacked by nucleophiles than the carbonyl carbon in aldehydes and
ketones. Compare this with the —OH group in phenol, which has a
similar electron-releasing effect. The oxygen of the —OH group in
turn attracts electrons from the OH bond, weakening this bond and
allowing the loss of the hydrogen as an H^+ ion.

So the two important features of the chemistry of carboxylic acids
are:

● the carbonyl carbon is susceptible to nucleophilic attack
● the —OH group easily loses a proton, making it acidic.

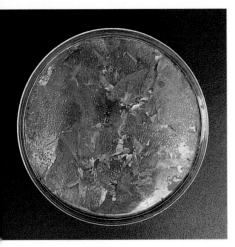

Frozen ethanoic acid

Nucleophilic attack

Nucleophiles attack the $C^{\delta+}$.

This is normally followed by loss of the —OH group as an OH⁻ ion.

Loss of a proton – acidity

If the hydrogen of the —OH group is lost, a negative ion – a **carboxylate ion** – is left. The negative charge is shared over the whole of the carboxylate group, making the resulting ion more stable.

a carboxylate ion

In this ion, the negative charge is delocalised over the atoms shown in red.

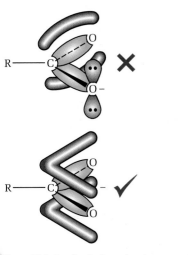

Figure 34.6 Bonding in the carboxylate group. The lone pair on the O⁻ overlaps with the π orbital of the C=O group to form a delocalised system

The double-headed arrow indicates that both forms contribute to the actual structure, which is often represented as:

The bonding can be described as overlap between the π orbitals of the C=O and a lone pair in a p-orbital on the oxygen (**Figure 34.6**).

There is evidence for this delocalisation in the bond lengths in the ethanoate ion in, for example, sodium ethanoate. Both carbon–oxygen bonds are identical in length, 0.127 nm, which is about half-way between C=O (0.122 nm) and C—O (0.136 nm) (**Figure 34.7**).

R—C 0.127 nm
0.127 nm

Figure 34.7 Bond lengths in the ethanoate ion

Kitchen chemistry – ethanoic acid (vinegar) reacts with sodium carbonate (washing soda)

Table 34.1 pK_a's of some carboxylic acids. Remember: larger values of pK_a represent weaker acids

Acid	Formula	pK_a
methanoic	HCO_2H	3.8
ethanoic	CH_3CO_2H	4.8
propanoic	$CH_3CH_2CO_2H$	4.9
butanoic	$CH_3CH_2CH_2CO_2H$	4.8
chloroethanoic	CH_2ClCO_2H	2.9
dichloroethanoic	$CHCl_2CO_2H$	1.3
trichloroethanoic	CCl_3CO_2H	0.7
2-chloropropanoic	$CH_3CHClCO_2H$	2.8
3-chloropropanoic	$CH_2ClCH_2CO_2H$	4.1
bromoethanoic	CH_2BrCO_2H	2.9
fluoroethanoic	CH_2FCO_2H	2.7
benzenecarboxylic	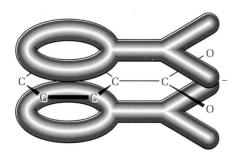 CO_2H	4.2

Figure 34.8 The benzenecarboxylate ion showing interaction between the $—CO_2^-$ group and the benzene ring

Carboxylic acids are weak acids, so the equilibrium:

$$R-C\overset{O}{\underset{OH}{}} \rightleftharpoons R-C\overset{O}{\underset{O^-}{}} + H^+$$

is well over to the left as shown by the pK_a value of 4.8. They are, however, generally stronger acids than phenols (phenol has a pK_a of 9.9) and will displace carbon dioxide from solutions of carbonates – a test which can be used to distinguish unsubstituted carboxylic acids from unsubstituted phenols.

The effect of substituents on acidity

The acidity of a carboxylic acid is affected by the electron-releasing or electron-attracting power of the group attached to the $—CO_2H$ group.

Electron-withdrawing groups increase the acidity by spreading out even further the negative charge on the carboxylate ion formed when H^+ is lost. Conversely, electron-releasing groups such as $—CH_3$ reduce the acid strength. You can see evidence for this in **Table 34.1**. Compared with methanoic acid, ethanoic acid is a weaker acid as it has an electron-*releasing* $—CH_3$ substituent. Compared with ethanoic acid, the chloro-, dichloro- and trichloro- derivatives get successively stronger because they have more electron-*withdrawing* chlorine atoms. You can also see the effect of changing the halogen atom:

$$CH_2BrCO_2H < CH_2ClCO_2H < CH_2FCO_2H$$
$$pK_a \quad\quad 2.90 \quad\quad\quad\quad 2.86 \quad\quad\quad\quad 2.66$$
$$\xrightarrow{\text{stronger acid}}$$

The halogen atom has less effect the further it is from the $—CO_2H$ group.

$$pK_a \quad\quad\quad\quad 4.1 \quad\quad\quad\quad\quad\quad 2.8$$
$$\xrightarrow{\text{stronger acid}}$$

Benzenecarboxylic acid is stronger than ethanoic acid because the negative charge on the carboxylate ion can be delocalised by interaction with the benzene ring as shown in **Figure 34.8**.

34.4 Reactions of carboxylic acids

As acids

Carboxylic acids form ionic salts by reaction with the more reactive metals, alkalis, metal oxides or metal carbonates in the usual way.

Reaction of carboxylic acids with ammonia gives ammonium salts, which can then be dehydrated by strong heating to give **amides**. For example:

ethanoic acid   ammonium ethanoate   ethanamide
(an amide)

Nucleophilic substitution reactions
Reaction with phosphorus pentachloride

Phosphorus pentachloride, PCl_5, and sulphur dichloride oxide, $SOCl_2$, (thionyl chloride) both generate the nucleophile $Cl^{\delta-}$ which replaces the —OH group of the acid to produce an **acid chloride**:

ethanoic acid   ethanoyl chloride

Alcohols react reversibly with carboxylic acids in the presence of a strong acid catalyst to form esters.

ethanoic acid   ethanol   ethyl ethanoate   water

Alcohols are rather weak nucleophiles and will only attack the $C^{\delta+}$ of the acid when the acid has been protonated by the strong acid catalyst, thus increasing the positive charge of the carbonyl carbon. The mechanism is discussed in more detail in section 14.6.

Dehydration

Phosphorus pentoxide will remove a molecule of water from two molecules of carboxylic acid to produce an anhydride.

ethanoic acid   ethanoic anhydride

Reduction

Lithium tetrahydridoaluminate(III), $LiAlH_4$, will reduce carboxylic acids via aldehydes to primary alcohols. For example:

ethanoic acid   ethanol

Aldehydes are more easily reduced than carboxylic acids so it is not practicable to stop at the aldehyde. Less powerful reducing agents than lithium tetrahydridoaluminate(III) will not reduce carboxylic acids.

34.5 Preparation of carboxylic acids

Oxidation of alcohols or aldehydes

Both alcohols and aldehydes can be oxidised to carboxylic acids, by refluxing with excess potassium dichromate and acid (see section 22.4).

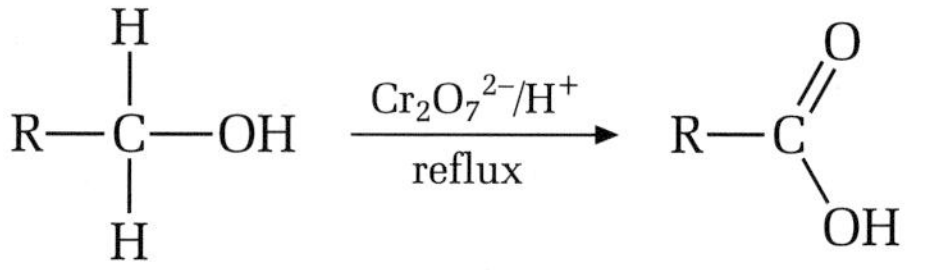

an alcohol   a carboxylic acid

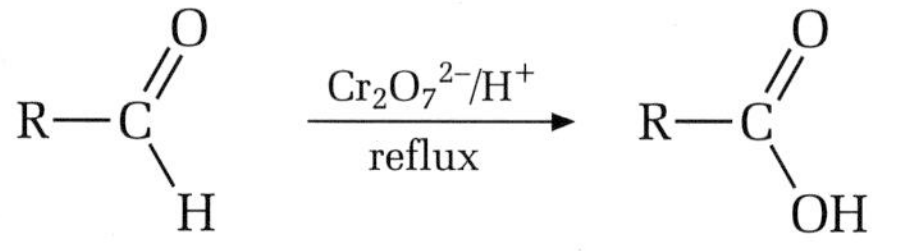

an aldehyde   a carboxylic acid

From acid derivatives

All the acid derivatives can be hydrolysed (reacted with water) to give the parent acid. The basic reaction can be represented:

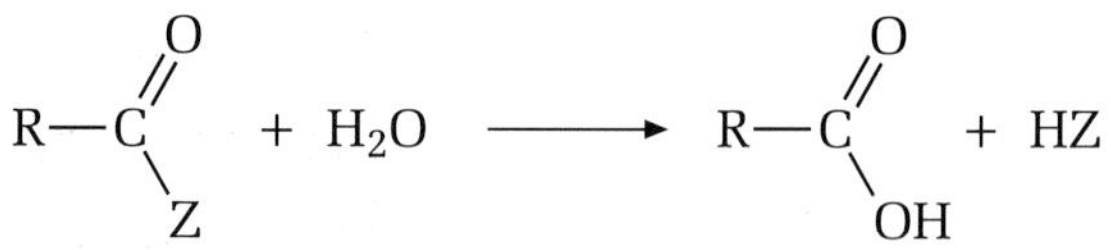

The conditions vary with the acid derivative used. Acid chlorides and anhydrides react rapidly even with moist air. Esters react slowly with water in the presence of an acid catalyst. Amides must be refluxed for some time with an acid. Details can be found in section 34.6.

From nitriles

Nitriles, R—C≡N, are hydrolysed to carboxylic acids by boiling with aqueous solutions of strong acids.

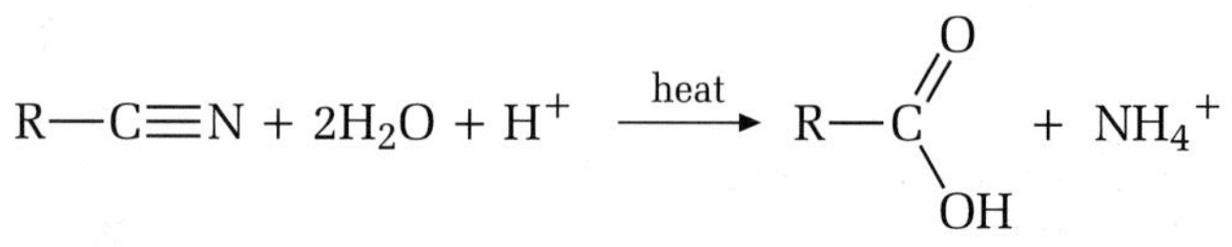

34.6 Acid derivatives

Physical properties

Table 34.2 lists some physical properties of derivatives of ethanoic acid with those of the parent acid for comparison.

Although it is not easy to make comparisons because of the differences in relative molecular mass, some patterns can be seen. The amides have higher melting temperatures than the parent acid while those of the ester, anhydride and chloride are lower. This is because the amide, with two N—H bonds, can form more hydrogen bonds than the acid, while the other three can form none, because they have no hydrogen bonded to an electronegative atom.

The same sort of pattern is seen in the boiling temperatures and for the same reason (except that the anhydride has a slightly higher boiling point than the acid because it has a considerably larger relative molecular mass).

The amide is very soluble in water, as is the parent acid, this time because hydrogen bonds are formed with water. The ester is less soluble because there is less hydrogen bonding. The other two derivatives react rapidly with water, so it is not possible to measure their solubility.

Why does a difference in relative molecular mass affect the comparisons of physical properties of acid derivatives?

Table 34.2 Properties of derivatives of ethanoic acid

Property	Ethanoyl chloride, CH_3COCl	Ethanoic anhydride, $CH_3CO_2COCH_3$	Ethanoic acid, CH_3CO_2H	Methyl ethanoate, $CH_3CO_2CH_3$	Ethanamide, CH_3CONH_2
T_m/K	161	200	290	175	355
T_b/K	324	413	391	330	494
solubility in water	← react →		very soluble	soluble	very soluble
M_r	78.5	102	60	74	59

Reactions of acid derivatives

Acid–base properties

Esters, anhydrides and acid chlorides have no acidic hydrogens. Amides can lose a proton but they are much weaker acids than carboxylic acids. As they have a lone pair on the nitrogen, they can also accept a proton and act as bases. However, this lone pair is involved in delocalisation (see **Figure 34.9**), and is less available to accept a proton than it would be in, for example, ammonia. So amides are weak bases.

Nucleophilic substitution reactions

In all the acid derivatives, the carbonyl carbon atom has a $\delta+$ charge and is therefore attacked by nucleophiles. The general reaction is:

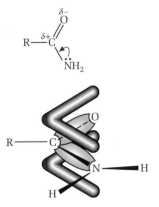

Figure 34.9 Delocalisation of the lone pair on the —NH₂ group

$$R-\overset{\delta-}{\underset{Z}{\overset{\overset{\displaystyle O}{\|}}{C}}}{}^{\delta+} + :Nu^- \longrightarrow R-\overset{\overset{\displaystyle O}{\|}}{\underset{Nu}{C}} + Z^-$$

Answer: Greater relative molecular mass means greater van der Waals forces.

How readily the reaction occurs depends on three factors:

1. How good the nucleophile is;
2. The magnitude of the $\delta+$ charge on the carbonyl carbon, which in turn depends on the electron-releasing or attracting power of Z;
3. The ease of expulsion of Z^- (the leaving group).

Factors 2 and 3 tend to be linked: groups which strongly attract electrons tend to form stable negative ions, Z^-, and are good leaving groups.

Acid derivatives can be listed in order of their reactivity towards nucleophiles:

acid chlorides	anhydrides	acids	esters	amides

- The Z groups of acid chlorides and anhydrides *withdraw* electrons from the carbonyl carbon, making these compounds more reactive than carboxylic acids.
- In esters and amides, the Z group *releases* electrons onto the carbonyl carbon, making these compounds less reactive.
- Acids and esters are very similar in reactivity.

The products of the reactions of some nucleophiles with some acid derivatives are shown in **Table 34.3**. These reactions all involve conversion of one acid derivative into another.

The bottom line of the table, for example, shows that carboxylic acids can be prepared by reaction of any derivative with water (hydrolysis) under suitable conditions.

Other nucleophiles

Alcohols are relatively poor nucleophiles (and phenols are even worse), so alkoxide RO^- or phenoxide $-O^-$ ions may be used instead, since these are better nucleophiles but give the same products.

Sodium salts of carboxylic acids are nucleophiles:

> **Q** What reactants would you need to make ethanoic propanoic anhydride?

Acid chlorides will react with these nucleophiles to form anhydrides. This enables mixed anhydrides to be made.

Answer: Propanoyl chloride and sodium ethanoate or ethanoyl chloride and sodium propanoate

Table 34.3 The products of the reactions of acid derivatives with nucleophiles. All reactions take place at room temperature unless otherwise stated

Acid derivative → Nucleophile ↓	Acid chloride $R\!-\!C(=\!O)Cl$	Anhydride $R\!-\!C(=\!O)\!-\!O\!-\!C(=\!O)\!-\!R$	Carboxylic acid $R\!-\!C(=\!O)OH$	Ester $R\!-\!C(=\!O)OR'$	Amide $R\!-\!C(=\!O)NH_2$
	← Increasing reactivity →				
Ammonia, NH_3	$R\!-\!C(=\!O)NH_2$ amide	$R\!-\!C(=\!O)NH_2$ amide	$R\!-\!C(=\!O)O^-NH_4^+$ ammonium salt $\;\xrightarrow{-H_2O}\;$ $R\!-\!C(=\!O)NH_2$ amide	$R\!-\!C(=\!O)NH_2$ amide	—
Amine, $R''NH_2$	$R\!-\!C(=\!O)\,O\!-\!NHR''$	$R\!-\!C(=\!O)\,O\!-\!NHR''$	$R\!-\!C(=\!O)\,O\!-\!NHR''$	$R\!-\!C(=\!O)\,O\!-\!NHR''$	—
	← N-substituted amides →				
Alcohol, $R''OH$	$R\!-\!C(=\!O)\,O\!-\!R''$ ester	$R\!-\!C(=\!O)\,O\!-\!R''$ ester	$R\!-\!C(=\!O)\,O\!-\!R''$ ester (reflux with H^+ catalyst)	$R\!-\!C(=\!O)\,O\!-\!R''$ different ester (reflux with H^+ catalyst)	—
Water, H_2O	$R\!-\!C(=\!O)OH$ carboxylic acid	$R\!-\!C(=\!O)OH$ carboxylic acid	—	$R\!-\!C(=\!O)\,O\!-\!H$ $R^+\!-\!OH$ carboxylic acid + alcohol (reflux with H^+ catalyst)	$R\!-\!C(=\!O)OH$ carboxylic acid (reflux with H^+ catalyst)

Not all nucleophilic substitution reactions of acid derivatives go to completion. In particular, the hydrolysis (reaction with water) of esters produces an equilibrium mixture containing the ester, water, acid and alcohol. The acid catalyst, of course, affects only the *rate* at which equilibrium is reached, not the composition of the equilibrium mixture.

Bases also catalyse hydrolysis of esters, but in this case the salt of the acid is produced rather than the acid itself. This removes the acid from the reaction mixture and moves the equilibrium over to the right.

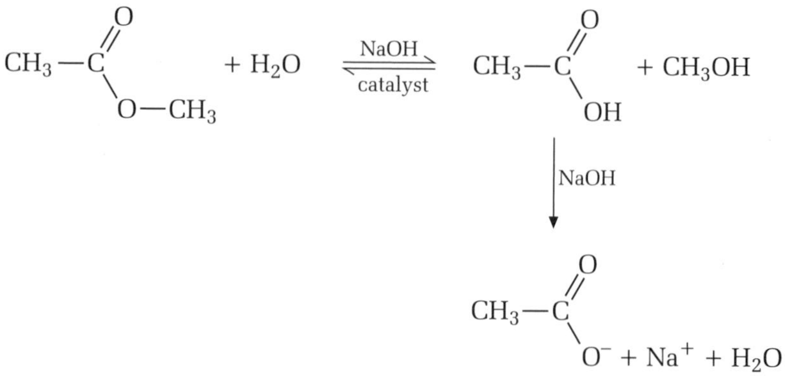

$$CH_3-C\overset{\displaystyle O}{\underset{\displaystyle O-CH_3}{\Big\|}} + H_2O \underset{\text{catalyst}}{\overset{\text{NaOH}}{\rightleftharpoons}} CH_3-C\overset{\displaystyle O}{\underset{\displaystyle OH}{\Big\|}} + CH_3OH$$

$$\Big\downarrow \text{NaOH}$$

$$CH_3-C\overset{\displaystyle O}{\underset{\displaystyle O^-}{\Big\|}} + Na^+ + H_2O$$

sodium ethanoate

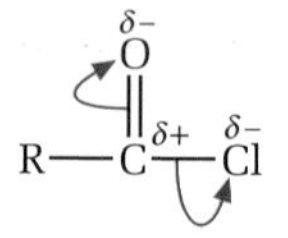

Acid chloride – two
electron-withdrawing atoms

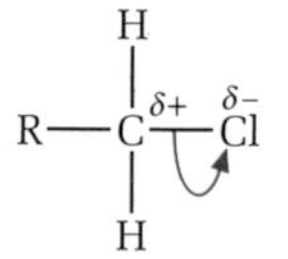

Chloroalkane – only one
electron-withdrawing atom

Figure 34.10 Comparison between an acid chloride and
a chloralkane

Comparison of the reactivity of acid chlorides and chloroalkanes

Acid chlorides are much more reactive towards nucleophiles than
chloroalkanes. For example, a weak nucleophile like water will react
vigorously with an acid chloride but only very slowly indeed with a
chloroalkane. This is because of the presence of the oxygen atom in
the acid chloride. Both this and the chlorine atom withdraw
electrons from the carbon to which the chlorine is attached, so this
carbon has a much greater $\delta+$ charge in an acid chloride than in a
chloroalkane (see **Figure 34.10**).

Reduction of acid derivatives

Acid chlorides

Acid chlorides can be reduced to aldehydes by hydrogen using a
poisoned palladium catalyst to prevent further reduction to alcohols.

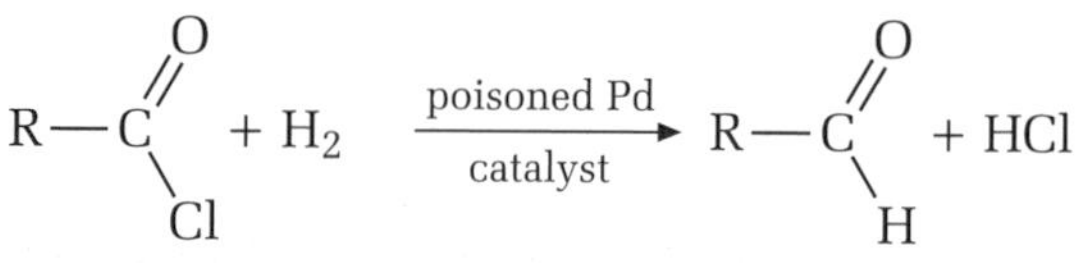

$$R-C\overset{\displaystyle O}{\underset{\displaystyle Cl}{\Big\|}} + H_2 \underset{\text{catalyst}}{\overset{\text{poisoned Pd}}{\longrightarrow}} R-C\overset{\displaystyle O}{\underset{\displaystyle H}{\Big\|}} + HCl$$

aldehyde

With an unpoisoned catalyst, hydrogen will reduce acid chlorides to
primary alcohols.

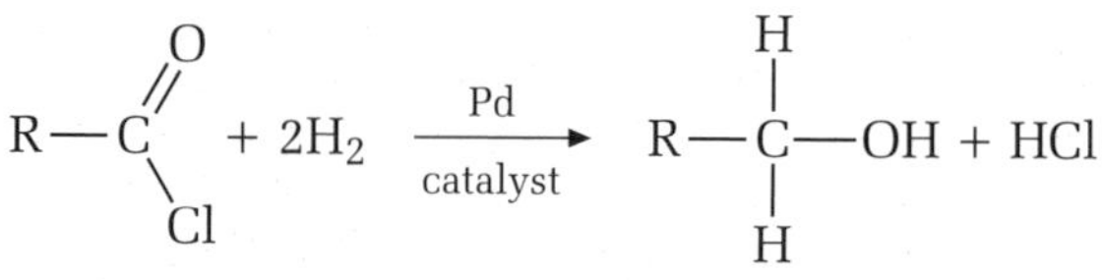

$$R-C\overset{\displaystyle O}{\underset{\displaystyle Cl}{\Big\|}} + 2H_2 \underset{\text{catalyst}}{\overset{\text{Pd}}{\longrightarrow}} R-\overset{\displaystyle H}{\underset{\displaystyle H}{\overset{\displaystyle |}{\underset{\displaystyle |}{C}}}}-OH + HCl$$

1° alcohol

Q Under what conditions is (a) LiAlH$_4$
and (b) NaBH$_4$ used?

This reaction can also be brought about by using lithium
tetrahydridoaluminate(III) or sodium tetrahydridoborate(III).

Anhydrides

These can be reduced in a similar way and with similar reagents to
those used for acid chlorides. Either aldehydes or primary alcohols
are formed.

Answer: (a) In ethoxyethane solution followed by
addition of water, (b) in aqueous solution

R—C(=O)—O—C(=O)—R → (H₂, poisoned Pd catalyst) → 2R—C(=O)—H (aldehyde); or (H₂/Pd or LiAlH₄) → 2R—CH₂—OH (1° alcohol)

Esters

Esters are reduced by either catalytic hydrogenation or lithium tetrahydridoaluminate(III) or sodium in ethanol to give a mixture of two alcohols.

$$R\text{—}C(=O)\text{—}O\text{—}R' \xrightarrow{\text{reduction}} R\text{—}CH_2\text{—}OH + R'OH$$

1° alcohol (may be 1°, 2° or 3° alcohol depending on R')

Amides

Amides are reduced by catalytic hydrogenation or lithium tetrahydridoaluminate(III) or sodium in ethanol to give primary amines.

$$R\text{—}C(=O)\text{—}NH_2 \xrightarrow{\text{reduction}} R\text{—}CH_2\text{—}NH_2$$

1° amine

CHEMISTRY AROUND US

Inks for ink jet printers

Most home computers use ink jet printers. The print head works by squirting minute droplets of ink at the paper. This ink must be liquid before squirting but must not smudge or rub off once on the paper. One of the dyes used is based on a black carboxylic acid, RCO_2H, where R is a complex organic group. It is used as a solution of its sodium salt, $RCO_2^-Na^+$, which, being ionic, is soluble in water. Paper is somewhat acidic (it contains H^+ ions), so when the dye hits the paper, the following equilibrium is set up:

$$RCO_2^- + H^+ \rightleftharpoons RCO_2H$$

As carboxylic acids are weak acids, this equilibrium is well over to the right and the insoluble carboxylic acid is formed. This will not wash out of the paper, so the ink will not smudge.

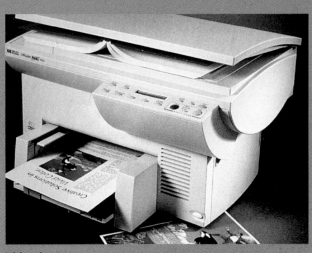

Ink jet printer

Other reactions of acid derivatives

Dehydration of amides

Amides can be dehydrated with phosphorus pentoxide to produce nitriles (compounds containing the —C≡N group).

$$R-\overset{\displaystyle O}{\underset{\displaystyle NH_2}{C}} \quad \xrightarrow[\text{P}_2\text{O}_5]{-\text{H}_2\text{O}} \quad R-C\equiv N$$

Friedel–Crafts acylation

Acid chlorides react with aromatic hydrocarbons in the presence of a catalyst of aluminium chloride. This generates the electrophile

$$R-\overset{+}{C}=O$$

which attacks the benzene ring. An aromatic ketone is produced:

$$\bigcirc \;+\; R-\overset{\displaystyle O}{\underset{\displaystyle Cl}{C}} \quad \xrightarrow{\text{AlCl}_3} \quad \bigcirc\!\!-\overset{\displaystyle O}{\underset{\displaystyle R}{C}} \;+\; HCl$$

Preparation of acid derivatives

Acid derivatives can be produced by nucleophilic substitution reactions from a carboxylic acid or another acid derivative as described in Table 34.3.

Amides can be made by heating the ammonium salts of carboxylic acids to dehydrate them.

$$R-\overset{\displaystyle O}{\overset{\|}{C}}-O^-NH_4^+ \quad \xrightarrow{\text{heat}} \quad R-\overset{\displaystyle O}{\overset{\|}{C}}-NH_2 \;+\; H_2O$$

Anhydrides of dicarboxylic acids can also be made by dehydration.

butane-1,4-dioic acid   butane-1,4-dioic anhydride

Butene-1,4-dioic acid exists in *cis*- and *trans*- forms.

cis-butene-1,4-dioic acid   trans-butene-1,4-dioic acid

Only the *cis*- form forms an anhydride. In the *trans*- form the —OH groups are too far apart. No rotation of a C=C is possible.

34.7 Economic importance of carboxylic acids and their derivatives

Ethanoic acid is an important industrial chemical. It is made by four different processes.

1. Naphtha is oxidised by air at 450 K and a pressure of 5000 kPa. Significant quantities of methanoic and propanoic acids are also formed. These are not in such demand as ethanoic acid and present disposal problems.
2. Butane can be oxidised in similar conditions.
3. Methanol is reacted with carbon monoxide at 450 K and 3000 kPa to give ethanoic acid in 99% yield.
4. Ethanol (produced from ethene by the Wacker process) can be oxidised to ethanoic acid.

Vinegar, a solution of ethanoic acid, is made by fermentation.

The industrial chemistry of ethanoic acid is summarised in **Figure 34.11**.

Dicarboxylic acids are important in the manufacture of poly(esters) and poly(amides) (see section 36.2).

Animal and vegetable oils and fats are esters of the alcohol propane-1,2,3-triol (glycerol).

Edible oils and fats contain three molecules of long chain (around C_{12}–C_{18}) carboxylic acids called fatty acids, combined with propane-1,2,3-triol. As the non-systematic name of this triol is glycerol, fats and oils are referred to as **triglycerides**.

a triglyceride

Traditionally vinegar was made by fermentation of sugars to ethanol followed by oxidation. 'Non-brewed condiment' originates from crude oil

Hint: Naphtha is a short-chain hydrocarbon fraction derived from crude oil.

Hint: Do not confuse animal and vegetable oils with the oils derived from crude oils, which are hydrocarbons.

A typical triglyceride may contain two or three different fatty acids. The only difference between fats and oils is that fats are solid at room temperature while oils are liquids. When eaten, fats and oils are broken down by hydrolysis to give uncombined fatty acids. Some of these cannot be produced by the body and have to be present in the diet. These are called **essential fatty acids**.

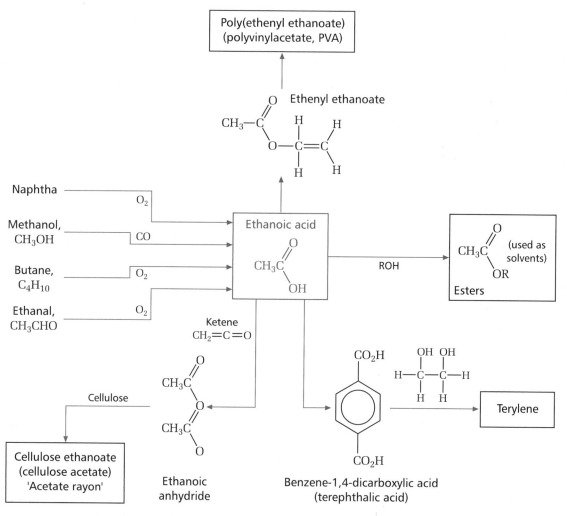

Figure 34.11 The industrial chemistry of ethanoic acid

34.8 Summary

- The functional groups of acid derivatives are:

carboxylic acid

$$R-\overset{\overset{\displaystyle O}{\|}}{C}-OH$$

acid chloride

$$R-\overset{\overset{\displaystyle O}{\|}}{C}-Cl$$

ester

$$R-\overset{\overset{\displaystyle O}{\|}}{C}-OR'$$

anhydride

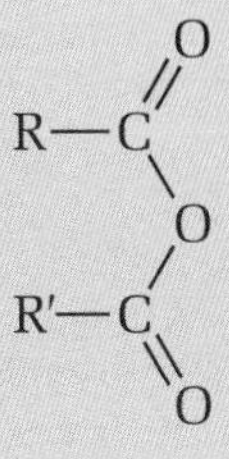

$$
\begin{array}{c}
\text{R}-\text{C} \overset{\displaystyle O}{\underset{\displaystyle O}{\Big\|}} \\
\qquad\qquad \text{R}'-\text{C}\overset{\displaystyle}{\underset{\displaystyle O}{\diagdown}}
\end{array}
$$

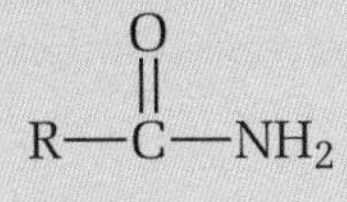

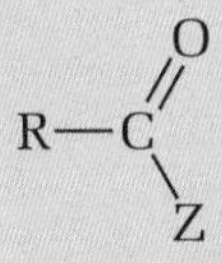

amide

$$
\text{R}-\overset{\displaystyle O}{\overset{\displaystyle \|}{\text{C}}}-\text{NH}_2
$$

- The $\text{R}-\text{C}\overset{\displaystyle O}{\underset{\displaystyle Z}{\diagup\,\diagdown}}$ group is

the flat and trigonal, with all bond angles approximately 120°.

- The group $\overset{\displaystyle \diagdown}{\underset{\displaystyle Z\diagup}{\text{C}}}\overset{\delta+\ \ \delta-}{=}\text{O}$ is polarised as shown. The $\delta+$

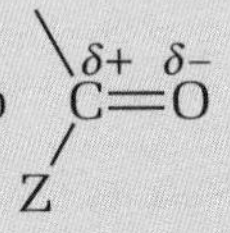

character of the carbon is determined by   the electron-attracting or releasing power of Z.

- The intermolecular forces which operate are:
  hydrogen bonding in   carboxylic acids
  amides

  dipole–dipole forces in   esters
  acid chlorides
  anhydrides

- Carboxylic acids, RCO_2H, are acids which are   weak.

- Electron-withdrawing substituents make the acids   stronger because they delocalise the negative charge of the carboxylate ion.

- In the carboxylate ion the lengths of the two carbon–oxygen bonds are   identical owing to delocalisation.

- Acid derivatives can be converted into one another or the parent acid by   nucleophilic substitution reactions using an appropriate nucleophile.

- The order of reactivity of acid derivatives with nucleophiles is   acid chloride > acid anhydride > carboxylic acid > ester > amide.

- Acid chlorides, anhydrides and esters can be reduced to   1° alcohols.

- By using a suitable reducing agent, acid chlorides and anhydrides can be reduced to   aldehydes.

- Amides can be dehydrated to   nitriles.

- Carboxylic acids can be prepared by   oxidation of alcohols or aldehydes
  or   by hydrolysis of other acid derivatives.

- The reactions of carboxylic acids are summarised in **Figure 34.12**

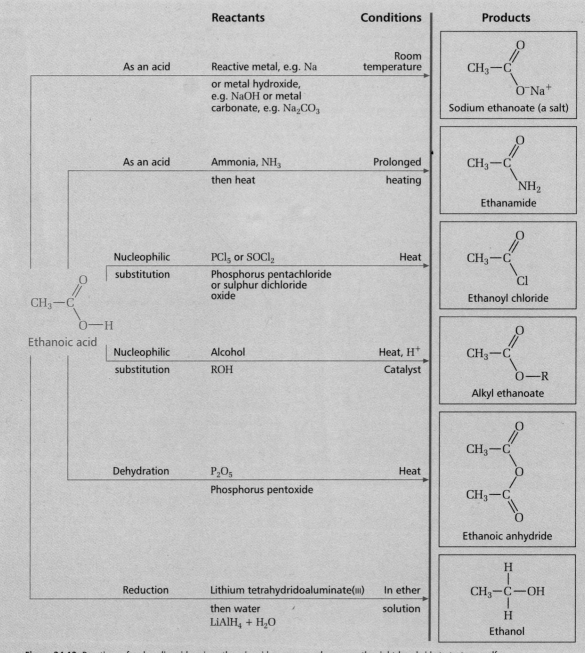

Figure 34.12 Reactions of carboxylic acids using ethanoic acid as an example – cover the right-hand side to test yourself

34.9 Practice questions

1. Name the following.

(a) $CH_3CH_2-C \underset{OH}{\overset{O}{<}}$

(b) $CH_2BrCH_2-C \underset{OH}{\overset{O}{<}}$

(c) $CH_3-C \underset{OC_2H_5}{\overset{O}{<}}$

(d) $CH_3CH_2-C \underset{NH_2}{\overset{O}{<}}$

2. Give the structural formula of:
   (a) 2-chloropropanamide
   (b) methyl propanoate
   (c) ethanoic propanoic anhydride
   (d) propanoyl chloride

3. Give the products of the following reactions.
   (a) propanoic acid and ammonia, followed by heating
   (b) ethanoyl chloride plus methanol

(c) butanoic anhydride plus water
(d) butanoic acid plus phosphorus pentachloride

List the following in order of acid strength.
Explain your reasoning.
(a) CH_2BrCO_2H, (b) CH_2FCO_2H, (c) CH_2ClCO_2H,
(d) CHF_2CO_2H

5. List the following in order of acid strength and
explain your answer.
$CH_3CH_2CH_2CO_2H$
$CH_3CH_2CHClCO_2H$
$CH_3CHClCH_2CO_2H$
$CH_2ClCH_2CH_2CO_2H$

34.10 Examination questions

Consider the reaction scheme below showing
some reactions of propanoic acid.

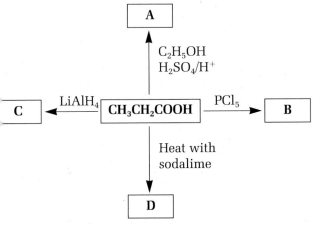

Name and draw the structures of **A**, **B**, **C** and **D**.
[WJEC 1997, part]

. (a) Draw the structural formula for each of the
following compounds **and** state the reagent
and reaction conditions that could be used for
preparing each from propanoic acid,
C_2H_5COOH.
  (i)   Propanoyl chloride
  (ii) Sodium propanoate
(b) (i) Give the name **and** structural formula of
the organic product of the reaction
between propanoyl chloride and sodium
propanoate.
  (ii) State how the product formed in (b)(i)
could be converted into propanoic acid.
Write an equation for the reaction.
(c) Draw a structure to represent the organic
product of the reaction between:
  (i) benzenecarboxylic acid, C_6H_5COOH, and
ethanol, C_2H_5OH;
  (ii) benzene-1,4-dicarboxylic acid,
$HOOCC_6H_4COOH$, and ethane-1,2-diol,
$HOCH_2CH_2OH$.
(d) (i) What is the general name given to the type
of compound formed in (c)(ii)?

(ii) Suggest a use for this type of compound
and state a property of the compound
which makes it suitable for such a use.
[AEB 1995]

3. Consider the following reaction scheme and
answer the questions which follow.

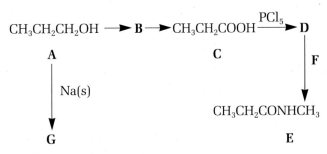

(a) Give the reagent(s) and condition(s) required
for the direct conversion of compound **A** into
compound **C**.
(b) The conversion of **A** into **C** proceeds via
compound **B**. Give the structure of **B** and
describe how the conditions you have given in
(a) could be modified to give **B**, rather than **C**,
as the major product.
(c) Compound **D** may be prepared by the reaction
of compound **C** with PCl_5 under anhydrous
conditions. Write an equation for the reaction,
state what is meant by the term *anhydrous
conditions*, and explain why such conditions
are necessary.
(d) Identify, by name or formula, the reagent **F**, and
draw the graphical formula of compound **E**.
(e) Compound **A** reacts with sodium metal to give
compound **G**.
  (i) Describe **one** observation that you could
make during this reaction.
  (ii) Write an equation for the reaction.
[AEB 1994]

4. A chemist is investigating one of the flavouring
compounds isolated from beer and shows that it is

a liquid ester (X) with the following formula.

$$CH_3CH_2CH_2CH_2CH_2-C\begin{array}{c} \diagup\diagup O \\ \diagdown O-CH_2CH_3 \end{array}$$

ester X

(a) Name ester X.
(b) The chemist then plans to prepare the ester in the laboratory by the following route.

$$CH_3CH_2CH_2CH_2CH_2CH_2Br$$

step 1 ↓

$$CH_3CH_2CH_2CH_2CH_2CH_2OH$$

step 2 ↓

$$CH_3CH_2CH_2CH_2CH_2COOH$$

step 3 ↓

$$CH_3CH_2CH_2CH_2CH_2COOCH_2CH_3$$

(i) In **step 1**, the bromo compound, $CH_3CH_2CH_2CH_2CH_2CH_2Br$, is treated with OH^- ions. Draw a mechanism to show what happens during this reaction and name the *type* of reaction taking place. You may represent the bromo compound by $R-CH_2-Br$ in your mechanism.

(ii) **Step 2** involves heating the alcohol, $CH_3CH_2CH_2CH_2CH_2CH_2OH$, under reflux with an oxidising agent. Draw a labelled diagram of the apparatus you would use to carry out **step 2**.

(iii) **Step 3** involves the reaction of $CH_3CH_2CH_2CH_2CH_2COOH$ with a compound Y to produce the ester. Draw the full structural formula of compound Y.

(c) The ester made by this sequence of reactions is a liquid. Suggest a technique that could be used to show that it is the same as ester X isolated from beer.

[O & C (Salters) 1997]

5. (a) This question is about the preparation of ethyl ethanoate from ethanol and ethanoic acid by the following reaction.

$$C_2H_5OH + CH_3CO_2H \rightleftharpoons CH_3CO_2C_2H_5 + H_2O$$

A student prepared ethyl ethanoate as follows:

- A mixture of ethanol, ethanoic acid and concentrated acid was placed in a distillation flask fitted with a reflux condenser, the flask being immersed in a cold water bath.

- The water in the bath was then heated to boiling and the flask contents boiled under reflux for approximately 20 minutes.

- The flask was then allowed to cool and set up for distillation; ethyl ethanoate was distilled off.

- The ethyl ethanoate was shaken with aqueous sodium carbonate and the lower aqueous layer discarded. The upper ethyl ethanoate layer was then shaken with aqueous calcium chloride to remove unused ethanol, the lower layer being discarded. The ethyl ethanoate was then placed in a flask with anhydrous calcium chloride and allowed to stand for half an hour.

- Finally, the liquid was filtered and re-distilled.

(i) What is meant by the term **reflux** and why is it necessary in this preparation?

(ii) Why was the ethyl ethanoate shaken with aqueous sodium carbonate?

(iii) Why was the ethyl ethanoate allowed to stand in contact with anhydrous calcium chloride?

(iv) The student reacted 21 g of pure ethanoic acid with the exactly calculated amount of ethanol and a small quantity of concentrated sulphuric acid. 20 g of ethyl ethanoate was obtained. What was the percentage yield? Suggest why a higher yield was not obtained.

(v) Identify the products of reaction if ethyl ethanoate is boiled with aqueous sodium hydroxide.

(b) Substance **A**, $C_7H_{14}O_2$, is used as a flavouring and as a solvent; it reacts with aqueous sodium hydroxide to form sodium ethanoate and substance **B**, $C_5H_{12}O$. Substance **B** can be oxidised to an acid **C**, $C_5H_{10}O_2$, by boiling under reflux with acidified potassium dichromate(VI). **C** contains an asymmetric carbon atom.

Write down the structures for **A**, **B** and **C**.

B can also be converted in a single step to a halogenoalkane **D**, $C_5H_{11}Cl$, which also has an asymmetric carbon atom. Treatment of **D** with ethanolic potassium hydroxide gives **E**, C_5H_{10}.

Write down the structures for **D** and **E**.

[London 1997, AS]

35 Organic nitrogen compounds

C H E M I S T R Y   N O W

Wallace Carothers

Wallace Carothers and the discovery of nylon
Nylon accounts for about 10% of all synthetic fibres, a world-wide production of almost 40 million tonnes each year. It is a polyamide containing the linkage —CONH—. It was discovered in 1935 by a team at the Du Pont company in America led by Wallace Carothers. Carothers was a brilliant chemist. From Harvard University, where he started academic research, he was 'head-hunted' by Du Pont. They wanted to find a synthetic material to replace silk (which was expensive) for making stockings. Carothers and his team found unexpected difficulties in making their new synthetic material into silk-like fibres. After seven years of work, they were on the point of giving up when they found the answer in a technique called cold drawing. This involves stretching the material to line up the chain molecules. It is supposed to have been discovered during a challenge in the lab to find out who could make the longest thread out of a ball of polymer.

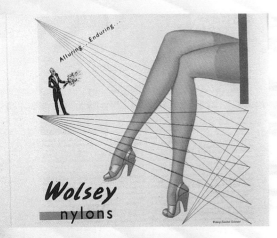

Wolsey
nylons

ontroversy surrounds the origin of the name nylon. Some say it is derived from New York London (Du Pont's headquarters) while others believe it was simply dreaned up by the company's advertising department and made to sound a little like rayon, an earlier synthetic abric

Uses of nylon

Sadly, Carothers did not live to see the success of his discovery. He suffered fron depression and in 1937, before nylon came onto the market, he took his own life.

The first major use for nylon was not in fact for stockings but for parachutes (also previously made from silk) and in this use the material undoubtedly saved many lives during World War II. Nowadays, as well as its use in fabrics, nylon is used to make things as diverse as climbing ropes and engineering components.

Introduction

This chapter deals with two main groups of compounds: amines and nitriles. Amines are best regarded as derivatives of ammonia in which one or more hydrogen atoms in the ammonia molecule have been replaced by organic groups. Nitriles contain the functional group —C≡N. Both amines and nitriles are very reactive groups of compounds and are therefore useful as intermediates in synthesis.

Other nitrogen-containing functional groups are amides, which we have dealt with in the Chapter 34, and hydrazones and oximes, which were mentioned in Chapter 33.

35.1 Amines

Formulae, naming and structure

Primary amines have the general formula RNH_2, where the R can be an alkyl or aryl group. Such amines are named as derivatives of ammonia using the suffix –amine. For example:

CH_3—NH_2 methylamine
C_2H_5—NH_2 ethylamine

phenylamine (often still called aniline, and sometimes aminobenzene)

If the amine is not the principal group, the prefix amino- is used. For example:

is called aminoethanoic acid

This notation may also be used to distinguish between isomers. For example:

1-aminopropane   and   2-aminopropane

Secondary and tertiary amines have the general formulae RR′NH and RR′R″N respectively. They are named as di- and trisubstituted derivatives of ammonia respectively. For example:

Q Give two other isomers of
1-aminopropane and
2-aminopropane.

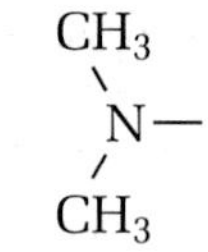

$$CH_3 \text{—} \overset{\displaystyle \ \ }{\underset{\displaystyle CH_3}{N}} \text{—} H$$

dimethylamine

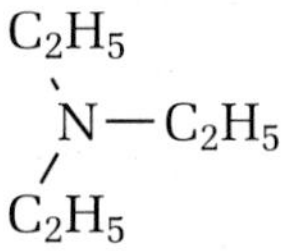

$$C_2H_5 \text{—} \overset{\displaystyle \ \ }{\underset{\displaystyle C_2H_5}{N}} \text{—} C_2H_5$$

triethylamine

$$CH_3 \text{—} \overset{\displaystyle \ \ }{\underset{\displaystyle C_3H_7}{N}} \text{—} H$$

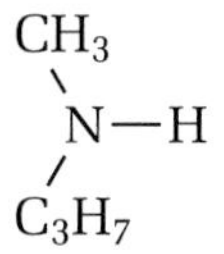

methylpropylamine

When there are two or more substituents they are written in alphabetical order.

Q What is the relationship between
N-methylphenylamine and
(phenylmethyl)amine?

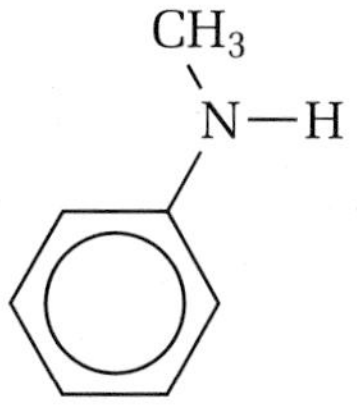

$$CH_3 \text{—} \overset{\displaystyle \ \ }{N} \text{—} H$$

is called *N*-methylphenylamine (the substituents are listed in alphabetical order). *N*- indicates that the methyl group is bonded to the nitrogen, rather than to the benzene ring.

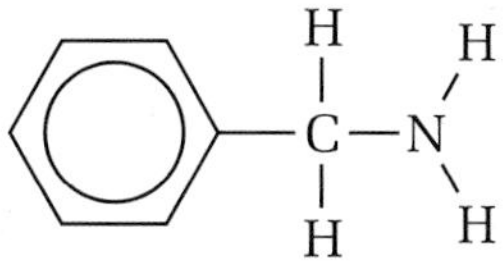

is called (phenylmethyl)amine – an alkyl amine, not an aromatic one. The brackets help to make it clear that the phenyl group is not bonded directly to the nitrogen.

Notice the rather different way in which the terms primary, secondary and tertiary are used with amines compared with alcohols. In amines, 1°, 2° and 3° refer to the number of substituents (R— groups) on the *nitrogen* atom. In alcohols, 1°, 2° and 3° refer to the number of substituents on the *carbon* atom bonded to the —OH group.

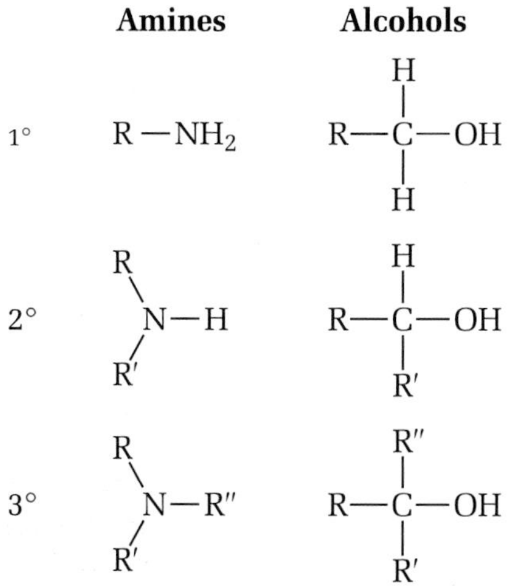

	Amines	**Alcohols**
1°	$R - NH_2$	$R - \overset{H}{\underset{H}{C}} - OH$
2°	$\overset{R}{\underset{R'}{N}} - H$	$R - \overset{H}{\underset{R'}{C}} - OH$
3°	$\overset{R}{\underset{R'}{N}} - R''$	$R - \overset{R''}{\underset{R'}{C}} - OH$

Answer: Trimethylamine and ethylmethylamine

Answer: They are isomers. (There are also three other isomers in which the —CH₃ group is in different positions on the benzene ring).

Lone pair in orbital

H_3C — N — CH_3
CH_3
All angles approximatley 107°

Figure 35.1 The shape of the trimethylamine molecule

Shape

Ammonia is pyramidal with bond angles of approximately 107°. This is because the lone pair repels more than do the bonding pairs of electrons in the N—H bonds (see section 9.2). Amines retain this basic shape (see **Figure 35.1**).

Physical properties of amines
Boiling temperatures

Amines are polar:

$$R—\overset{\overset{H}{|}}{\underset{\underset{H}{|}}{C}}\overset{\delta+}{—}\overset{\delta-}{N}\overset{H}{\underset{H}{\diagdown}}$$

Hint: Lower T_b means the molecules are easier to separate.

Primary and secondary amines can hydrogen bond to one another. However, as nitrogen is less electronegative than oxygen (electronegativities: $O = 3.5$; $N = 3.0$), the hydrogen bonds are not as strong as those in alcohols. This explains why the boiling temperatures of amines are lower than those of comparable alcohols:

methylamine, CH_3NH_2: $M_r = 31$, $T_b = 267\ K$
methanol, CH_3OH: $M_r = 32$, $T_b = 338\ K$

Hint: Isomeric means 'Same molecular formula, different arrangement of atoms in space'.

Shorter-chain amines – methylamine, ethylamine, dimethylamine and trimethylamine – are gases at room temperature, and those with slightly longer chains are volatile liquids. They have characteristic fishy smells; indeed rotting fish and animal flesh smell of di- and triamines produced by the decomposition of proteins.

Disubstituted amines have only one hydrogen bonded to nitrogen and trisubstituted ones none so there is less hydrogen bonding and the boiling temperatures get lower, as illustrated by the three isomeric amines of formula C_3H_9N in **Table 35.1**.

Propan-1-ol, shown for comparison, has the highest boiling temperature because oxygen is more electronegative than nitrogen.

Table 35.1 Boiling temperatures of some isomeric amines compared with those of alcohols

Name	Formula	T_b/K		M_r
1-aminopropane	$C_3H_7—NH_2$	321	lower	59
ethylmethylamine	$C_2H_5—NHCH_3$	310	T_b	59
trimethylamine	$CH_3—N(CH_3)_2$	276	↓	59
propan-1-ol	C_3H_7OH	338		60

Phenylamine has almost the same density as water. Heat from a bulb at the base of the lamp changes the density enough for the phenylamine to float when hot and sink when cool. This is used in decorative lamps as shown in the picture

Solubility

Primary amines with chain lengths up to about C_4 are very soluble in water and alcohols because they form hydrogen bonds with these solvents. Di- and trisubstituted amines are less water-soluble because there is less hydrogen bonding. Most amines are soluble in less polar solvents. Phenylamine is not very soluble in water owing to the benzene ring, which cannot form hydrogen bonds.

The reactivity of amines

One of the main features of the chemistry of amines is the fact that they have a lone pair of electrons. This may be used to form a bond with:

● an H^+ ion, when we say the amine is acting as a **base**
● an electron-deficient carbon atom, when we say it is acting as a a **nucleophile**
● a transition metal ion, when we say it is acting as a **ligand**

However, the three types of behaviour are essentially similar. Nitrogen is less electronegative than oxygen, so the lone pair in amines is less strongly held (and therefore more easily donated) than in alcohols. Therefore, amines are better bases, nucleophiles and ligands than alcohols.

Amines as bases

Amines can accept a proton (an H^+ ion):

$$R\overset{\cdot\cdot}{N}H_2 + H^+ \longrightarrow RNH_3{}^+$$

amine   alkylammonium ion

Their strengths as bases (ability to accept a proton) are governed by the availability of the lone pair of electrons. This is increased by electron-releasing substituents such as alkyl groups. Primary alkylamines are therefore stronger bases than ammonia and secondary alkylamines are stronger bases still (see **Table 35.2**. A *smaller* value of pK_b means the compound is a *stronger* base).

$$R \rightarrow \overset{\cdot\cdot}{N}H_2$$

a primary alkylamine

$$R \rightarrow \overset{\cdot\cdot}{N} - H \\ \qquad \uparrow \\ \qquad R$$

a secondary alkylamine

Table 35.2 Base strengths of some amines

Name	Formula	pK_b	
ammonia	NH_3	4.74	
methylamine	CH_3NH_2	3.36	RNH_2
ethylamine	$C_2H_5NH_2$	3.28	
1-aminopropane	$C_3H_7NH_2$	3.23	1″ amines
dimethylamine	$(CH_3)_2NH$	3.23	R_2NH
diethylamine	$(C_2H_5)_2NH$	3.07	2° amines
trimethylamine	$(CH_3)_3N$	4.20	R_3N
triethylamine	$(C_2H_5)_3N$	3.36	3° amines
phenylamine	⬡—NH_2	9.30	Aryl amine

However, in aqueous solution, tertiary alkylamines are weaker bases than both primary and secondary alkylamines This is because the R_3HN^+ ion, formed when a tertiary alkylamine accepts a proton, cannot hydrogen bond to water molecules as well as can the $R_2NH_2{}^+$ formed by a secondary alkylamine. This makes the R_3NH^+ ion less soluble than the $R_2NH_2{}^+$ ion and counteracts the increased availability of the lone pair in R_3N.

In aqueous solution the order of base strength is therefore :

$$R_2NH > RNH_2 > R_3N > NH_3$$

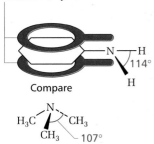

Figure 35.2 The shape of the phenylamine molecule

Table 35.3 C—N bond lengths

Bond	Length/nm
C—N	0.147
C⚌N in phenylamine	0.135
C=N	0.130

Table 35.4 Bond polarities of amines compared with those of alcohols

$$\overset{2.5 \quad\quad 3.5}{\delta+C-O\delta-}$$

$$\overset{2.5 \quad\quad 3.0}{\delta+C-N\delta-}$$

In non–hydrogen bonding solvents the expected order of base strength is observed:

$$R_3N > R_2NH > RNH_2 > NH_3$$

Aryl groups *withdraw* electrons from the nitrogen atom by overlap of the lone pair electrons with the delocalised π system on the benzene ring, so aryl amines are weaker bases than ammonia:

A similar effect is seen with phenol (a weaker acid, hence a stronger base, than alcohols).

To allow more efficient overlap of the lone pair-containing orbital with the π system, phenylamine is a shallower pyramidal shape than alkyl amines, with an H—N—H angle of 114° (**Figure 35.2**). The C—N bond has some double bond character as indicated by the bond lengths in **Table 35.3**.

Bond energies and polarity

The C—N bond in amines is relatively weak and might therefore be expected to break easily, more easily than, say, the C—O bond in alcohols.

$$C-N\ 286\ \text{kJ mol}^{-1};\ \ C-O\ 358\ \text{kJ mol}^{-1};\ \ C-C\ 347\ \text{kJ mol}^{-1}$$

However, the C—N bond is less polar than a C—O bond because nitrogen is less electronegative than oxygen (see **Table 35.4**). This means that the carbon of the C—N bond in amines has less $\delta+$ character than the carbon of the C—O bond in alcohols. So the carbon atom in amines is less susceptible to nucleophilic attack. Thus it is unusual for amines to undergo nucleophilic elimination reactions or substitution reactions. This contrasts with the reactions of alcohols where the OH group is frequently lost.

Reactions of amines

Combustion

Amines will burn in air to form carbon dioxide, water and nitrogen. Arylamines give the characteristic smoky flame of aromatic compounds.

As bases

Amines will react with acids to form salts. For example:

> **Hint:** The salts of amines are sometimes named as the hydrochloride of the parent amine

$$\underset{\text{ethylamine}}{C_2H_5\overset{..}{N}H_2} + H^+ + Cl^- \longrightarrow \underset{\substack{\text{ethylammonium chloride}\\ \text{(ethylamine hydrochloride)}}}{C_2H_5NH_3{}^+ + Cl^-}$$

The products are ionic compounds which can be crystallised.

In the case of a relatively insoluble amine, like phenylamine, the amine will dissolve in excess hydrochloric acid owing to the formation of the soluble ionic salt. Addition of a strong base removes the proton from the salt and regenerates the insoluble amine.

Figure 35.3 Amitriptylene hydrochloride

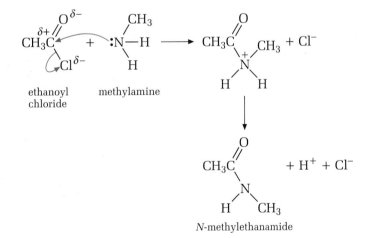

phenylamine

phenylammonium chloride
(phenylamine hydrochloride)
water-soluble ionic salt

phenylamine

The smell of a solution of an amine disappears on addition of acid because of the formation of the ionic, and therefore involatile, salt. The formation of a soluble salt derivative of an amine is a common way of making long-chain amines water-soluble. It is often used to make amines soluble for use as drugs. The antidepressant amitriptylene is an example. The free amine would be insoluble in water but amitriptylene hydrochloride, being ionic, is water soluble (**Figure 35.3**).

Since an equilibrium exists between the amine and its hydrochloride, the action of the drug is unaffected.

$$\text{drug} + \text{H}^+ + \text{Cl}^- \rightleftharpoons \text{drugH}^+ + \text{Cl}^-$$

Formation of amides

Amines react with acid chlorides or anhydrides to form N-substituted amides. This is a nucleophilic substitution reaction in which the amine acts as the nucleophile. For example:

ethanoyl   methylamine
chloride

N-methylethanamide

Garment with polyamide label

Notice that the final step requires the loss of an H$^+$ ion from the

group.

This reaction occurs only with primary and secondary amines.

The reaction is important in the formation of poly(amides) like nylon.

Answer: Starting with a tertiary amine would produce a species which did not have an H$^+$ ion to lose in the final step.

Q What is the displayed formula of the N-substituted amide formed by the reaction of methylamine with benzoyl chloride?

Reaction of amines with benzoyl chloride,

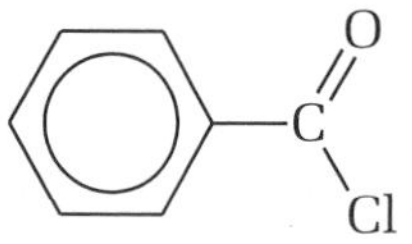

produces solid N-substituted amides which can be purified by recrystallisation. The melting point of these derivatives can be used to identify the original amine.

Reaction with haloalkanes

When an amine is heated with excess haloalkane the reaction occurs as shown:

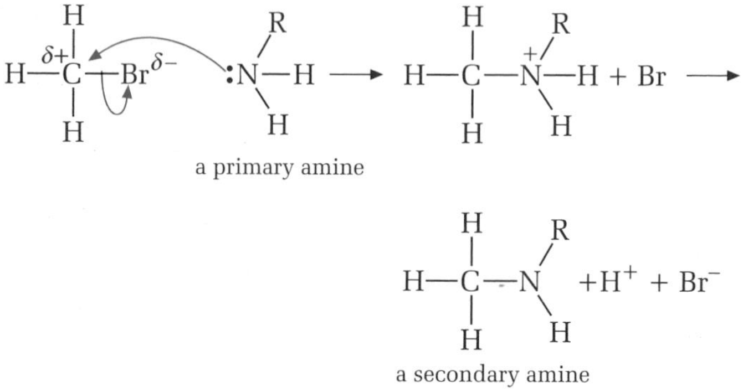

a primary amine

a secondary amine

This is also a nucleophilic substitution reaction.

A secondary amine is produced first but if the haloalkane is in excess, the secondary amine (a better nucleophile than a primary amine) also reacts, forming a tertiary amine:

Hint: Secondary amines are better nucleophiles than primary amines for the same reason that they are better bases.

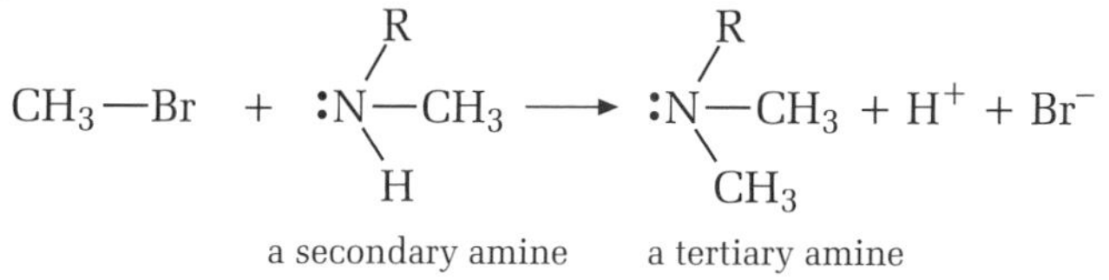

a secondary amine   a tertiary amine

Finally, the tertiary amine can also react producing a **quaternary ammonium salt**:

a quaternary
ammonium salt

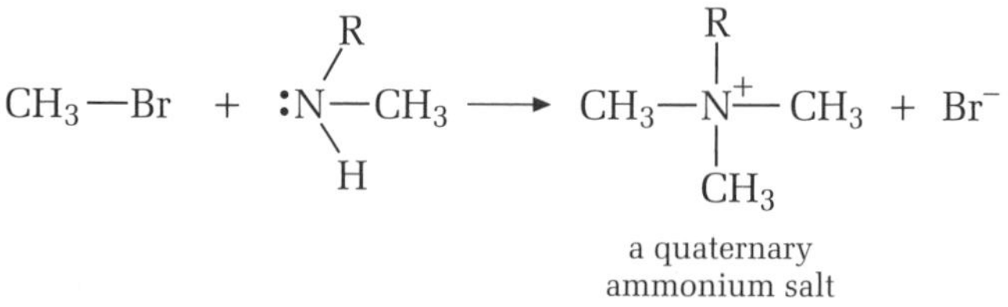

Reaction with nitrous acid (nitric(III) acid)

Nitrous acid is unstable and is produced in the reaction vessel by the reaction of sodium nitrite (sodium nitrate(III)) with dilute hydrochloric acid:

$$NaNO_2(aq) + HCl(aq) \longrightarrow NaCl(aq) + HNO_2(aq)$$

nitrous acid

Nitrous acid reacts with amines to produce the ion $R-N^+\equiv N$, called either an alkyl or aryl diazonium ion depending on the nature of R.

Answer:

$$R-NH_2 \xrightarrow{HNO_2/HCl} R-N^+\equiv N + Cl^-$$

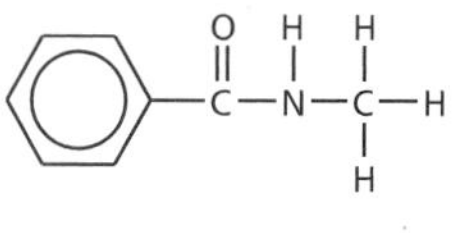

Q What is the equation for the decomposition of R—N$^+$≡N?

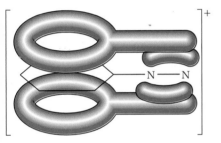

H_2O → ROH   An alcohol

Cl^- → RCl   A chloroalkane

R^+ NO_2^- → RNO_2 A nitroalkane

ROH → R_2O An ether
(from first reaction)

Figure 35.4 Possible reactions of R$^+$

Figure 35.5 Delocalisation in the benzenediazonium ion

Answer: R—N$^+$≡N ⟶ R$^+$ + N$_2$

Alkyldiazonium ions are unstable and rapidly decompose to give a stable nitrogen molecule and a carbocation, R$^+$.

R$^+$ rapidly reacts with any available species in the solution to give a mixture of products. Some possibilities are shown in **Figure 35.4**.

An alkene can also be formed by loss of H$^+$. For example:

$$C_2H_5^+ \longrightarrow \overset{H}{\underset{H}{C}}=\overset{H}{\underset{H}{C}} + H^+$$

Aryldiazonium ions are more stable, provided the solution is kept cold (below about 278 K, 5 °C). They are, however, explosively unstable in the solid state, so that they are always used in solution. This stability is due to delocalisation of the positive charge onto the aromatic ring caused by overlap of p orbitals in the —N$^+$≡N group with the π system of the benzene ring (see **Figure 35.5**).

Aromatic diazonium compounds undergo a number of useful reactions. We shall use benzenediazonium chloride,

⬡—N$^+$≡N + Cl$^-$, produced by the reaction of phenylamine

with nitrous acid, as an example.

Allowing an aqueous solution of benzenediazonium chloride to warm up to room temperature produces phenol and nitrogen. Heating to 373 K with a source of Cl$^-$, Br$^-$, I$^-$ or CN$^-$ and a suitable catalyst produces a halogen-substituted or cyano-substituted benzene. The catalysts are copper(I) compounds (see **Figure 35.6**).

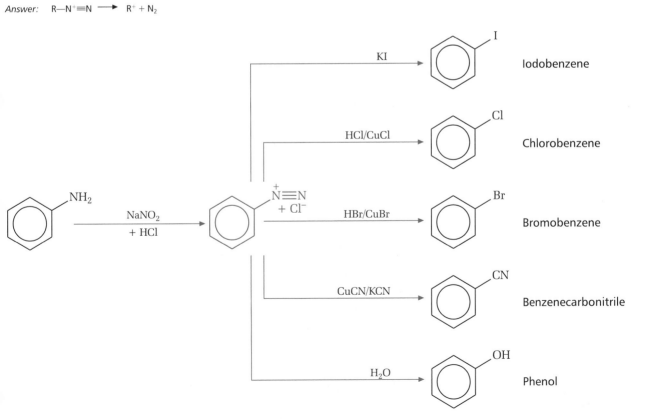

Figure 35.6 Reactions of benzenediazonium chloride

Coupling reactions

Diazonium ions react with phenols or aromatic amines in electrophilic substitution reactions that result in the joining (coupling) of the diazonium compound with the phenol or amine. The reactions are carried out in alkaline conditions.

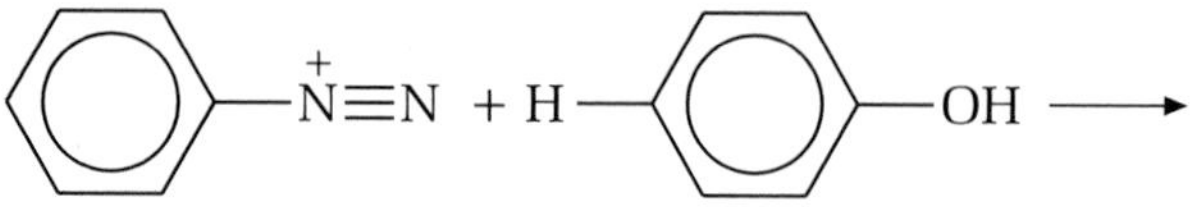

$$\text{(ring)} - \overset{+}{N} \equiv N + H - \text{(ring)} - OH \longrightarrow$$

phenol

$$\text{(ring)} - N = N - \text{(ring)} - OH + H^+$$

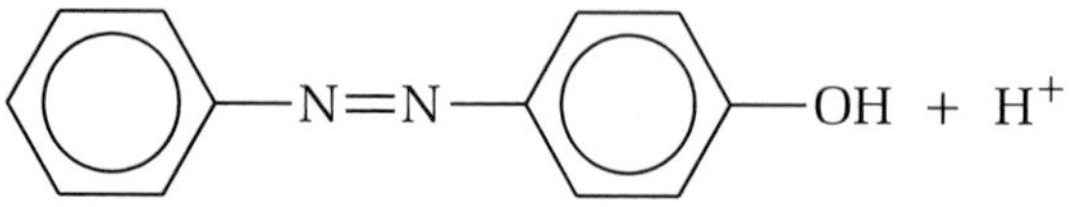

4-(phenylazo)phenol
(yellow)

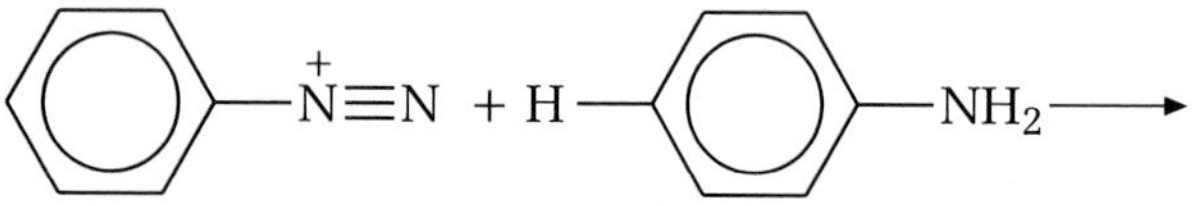

$$\text{(ring)} - \overset{+}{N} \equiv N + H - \text{(ring)} - NH_2 \longrightarrow$$

phenylamine

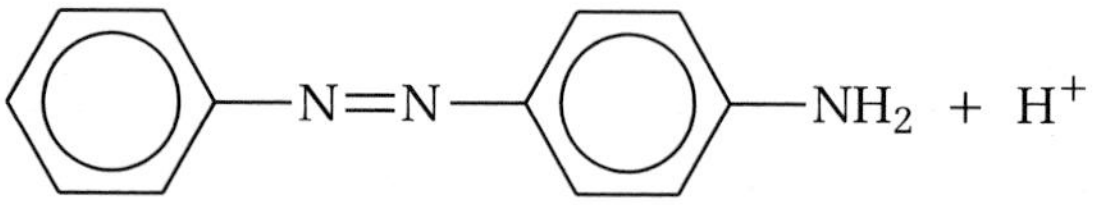

$$\text{(ring)} - N = N - \text{(ring)} - NH_2 + H^+$$

4-(phenylazo)phenylamine
(yellow)

The resulting compounds all contain the unit —N=N—. Remember that nitrogen atoms have a lone pair, so the bond angle around the nitrogen atom will be approximately 120° and the —N=N— unit will be flat. A better representation of the shape of such molecules is shown in **Figure 35.7**.

The compounds with an —N=N— linkage can exist as a pair of cis/trans- isomers, in just the same way that alkenes can be cis- or trans-.

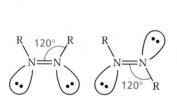

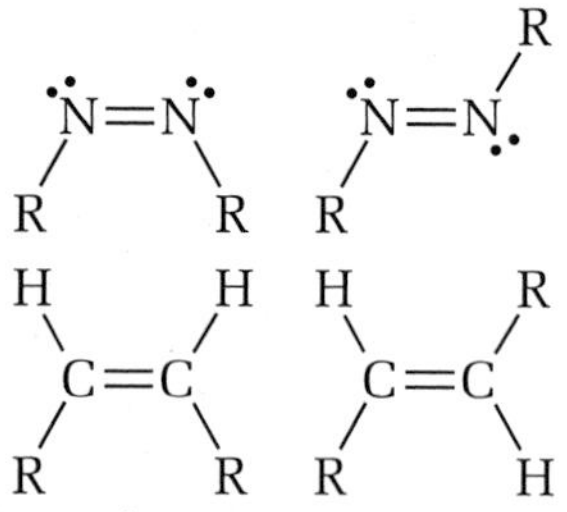

cis-   trans-

Figure 35.7 The structures of diazonium compounds

The products of coupling reactions have intense colours (the two examples given are yellow). Many such compounds are used as dyes. The —N=N— links the π systems of the two aromatic rings to give an extended delocalised system (**Figure 35.8**).

Such extended delocalised systems are described as **conjugated**. Molecules with extended systems of conjugation are frequently coloured. Some of these coloured compounds can act as indicators. Methyl orange is an example:

$$NaO_3S - \text{(ring)} - \overset{..}{N} = \overset{..}{N} - \text{(ring)} - N \overset{CH_3}{\underset{CH_3}{}}$$

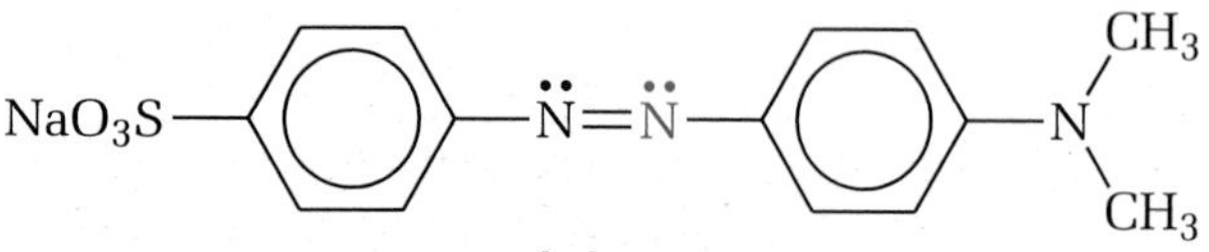

methyl orange

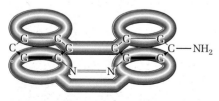

Figure 35.8 The conjugated system in
cis-4-(phenylazo)phenylamine

Indicators are dyes which can accept protons from an acid (see section 24.2). In alkaline solution methyl orange is yellow, but in acid solution, the nitrogen atom marked in red accepts a proton from the acid using its lone pair to form a dative bond. This affects the conjugated system and the protonated form is red.

Reactions of the benzene ring in aromatic amines

The substituents —NH_2, —NHR and —NR_2 release electrons onto the aromatic ring and so make it more reactive towards electrophilic substitution. The 2- and 4- positions are most activated.

CHEMISTRY AROUND US

Dyes

An effective dye must be coloured, must bind efficiently to the cloth so that it does not wash out, and must not fade on exposure to light or to air.

Different dyes bond to fabrics in different ways. **Direct dyes** bond to the fabric by intermolecular forces only: van der Waals, dipole–dipole and hydrogen bonding. These are not particularly strong forces, and direct dyes have a tendency to wash out. The structure of the dye 'direct brown 138' is shown. It has three diazo groups, —N=N—, which form a conjugated system with the four benzene rings. This is responsible for the colour. It also has a number of polar groups, —NH_2. These form hydrogen bonds with the —OH and —NH groups present in some fabrics. The cellulose in cotton has —OH groups, nylon and wool are both poly(amides) which have —NH— groups.

Direct Brown 138

Vat dyes are insoluble in water. They contain ketone groups C = O which, before dyeing, are first reduced to C—OH groups and then converted to soluble sodium salts C—O^- Na^+. When the fabric is added, the dye molecules become trapped in the structure of the fibres. They are then oxidised back to the insoluble ketone form. This prevents them from being washed out. Indigo, used to dye blue jeans, is a vat dye.

indigo

Azoic dyes make use of the coupling reaction of diazonium salts. The fibre is first impregnated with a phenol or naphthol, applied as the soluble salt.

The cloth is then treated with a diazonium salt and the coupling reaction takes place on the material. The dye is thus formed on the cloth. For example:

bonded to cloth

'Pau red' still bonded to cloth

Reactive dyes actually form covalent bonds with fibre molecules and are therefore extremely colour-fast. A dye molecule is first reacted with the molecule trichlorotriazine:

trichlorotriazine

Trichlorotriazine can react with either —OH groups (in cotton) or —NH groups (in wool and nylon), thus covalently bonding the dye to the fabric.

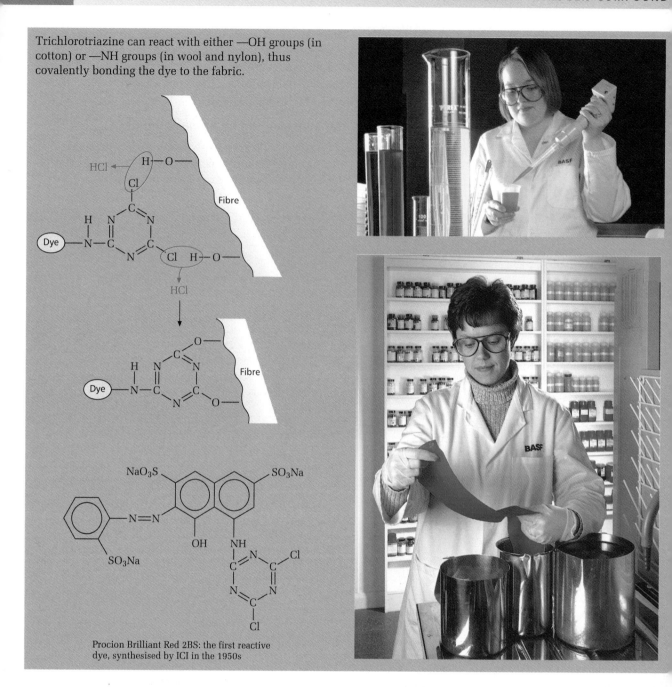

Procion Brilliant Red 2BS: the first reactive dye, synthesised by ICI in the 1950s

Amines as ligands

Hint: Ligands are compounds that form dative covalent bonds with transition metal ions (see section 31.3).

The lone pair of electrons present on the nitrogen atom of amines makes them good ligands. A good example is the reaction of amines with copper(II) ions in which blue coloured complexes of formula $[Cu(H_2O)_2(RNH_2)_2]^{2+}$ are formed.

The compound ethane-1,2-diamine, sometimes called by its non-systematic name ethylene diamine is often encountered as a bidentate ligand.

Colour in organic chemistry

Substances are coloured because they absorb visible light of certain wavelengths and transmit or reflect others. For example, a substance which absorbs light in the violet and red regions of the spectrum will transmit the rest of the light and look green.

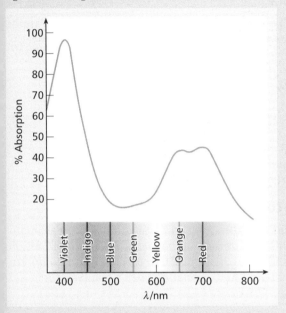

Visible absorption spectrum of a compound, which looks green because it absorbs violet, orange and red, and transmits green

When an atom or molecule absorbs light an electron is promoted from one energy level, or orbital, to a higher one (see section 7.2). So for a substance to absorb visible light, it must have a pair of electron energy levels separated by an energy gap corresponding to the energy of a quantum of visible light. In transition metals, the d orbitals may have suitable energy gaps (see the box 'Colours of transition metal ions' in Chapter 31). In organic chemistry, certain groups called chromophores absorb UV/visible light. Common chromophores include C=C, C=O, C=N and N=N. These groups all have in common the fact that they are unsaturated and therefore have both s and p orbitals (as well as lone pairs in all but C=C).

Whenever two orbitals overlap to form a molecular orbital (see section 9.1) *two* molecular orbitals are always

formed, one of lower energy called a bonding orbital and one of higher energy called an antibonding orbital. The electrons normally go into the lower energy bonding orbital, so we often forget about the antibonding one. However, when we are thinking about absorbing light, the antibonding orbitals become important because electrons can be promoted into them from bonding or non-bonding (lone pair) orbitals.

The diagram shows a typical energy level diagram and the electron transitions that can occur.

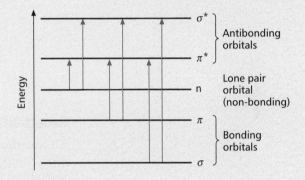

Energy level diagram

We have seen in section 9.1 that delocalisation of p orbitals can affect their energies. This will therefore affect the colour of light that they absorb. For example, ethene, which has one carbon–carbon double bond, is not coloured: it absorbs light in the UV part of the spectrum only. However, carotene, which has a delocalised system of eleven carbon–carbon double bonds, is coloured. It absorbs light in the blue region of the visible spectrum and therefore appears orange.

If you look at the structures of many of the dyes in this chapter, you will see that they have delocalised systems of alternating single and double bonds (or aromatic rings). These systems are described as **conjugated** and they are often responsible for colour. Examples include: 4-(phenylazo)phenylamine (Figure 35.8), methyl orange (p. 582), 'Acid Orange 7' (Figure 35.9) and 'Direct Brown 138' (box 'Dyes', p. 583).

β-carotene

Preparation of amines
Reduction of nitriles

Nitriles are reduced to primary amines by lithium tetrahydridoaluminate(III):

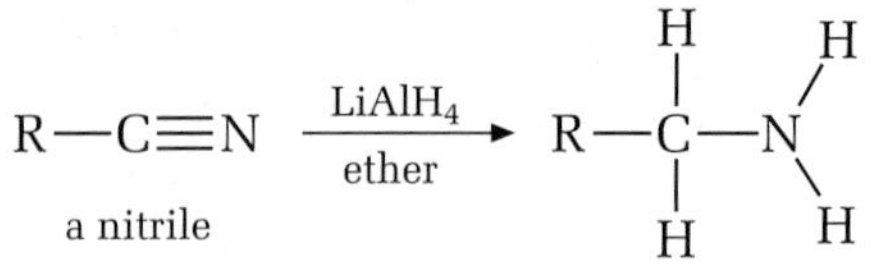

$$R-C\equiv N \xrightarrow[\text{ether}]{\text{LiAlH}_4} R-\underset{\underset{H}{|}}{\overset{\overset{H}{|}}{C}}-N\underset{H}{\overset{H}{\diagdown}}$$

a nitrile

Other reducing agents such as sodium/ethanol or hydrogen with a catalyst can be used.

Reduction of amides

Lithium tetrahydridoaluminate(III) will also reduce amides to amines. N-substituted amides will produce 2° or 3° amines For example:

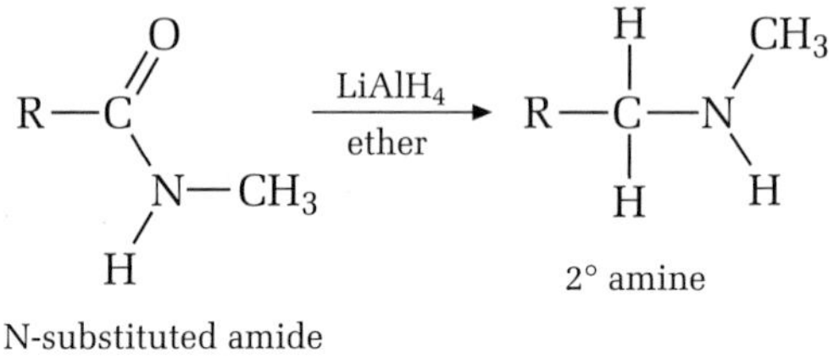

$$R-\overset{\overset{O}{\parallel}}{C}\underset{\underset{H}{|}}{\diagdown}_{N-CH_3} \xrightarrow[\text{ether}]{\text{LiAlH}_4} R-\underset{\underset{H}{|}}{\overset{\overset{H}{|}}{C}}-N\underset{H}{\overset{CH_3}{\diagup}}$$

N-substituted amide   2° amine

Reduction of nitro compounds

This method is useful for producing aromatic amines from aromatic nitro compounds. Only 1° amines can be made. A variety of reducing agents can be used including lithium tetrahydridoaluminate(III), tin and hydrochloric acid, and hydrogenation with a catalyst, for example:

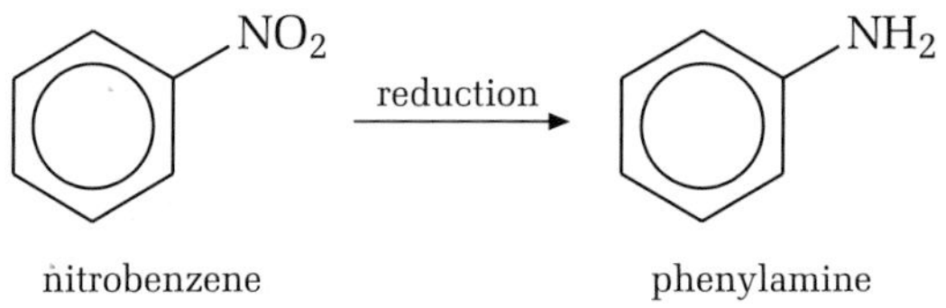

nitrobenzene   phenylamine

Other nitrogen-containing compounds such as oximes and hydrazones can also be reduced to amines.

Reaction of ammonia with haloalkanes

The disadvantage of this method is that a mixture of primary, secondary and tertiary amines is produced as well as quaternary ammonium salts. The required product must then be separated by fractional distillation. The reaction takes place on heating a mixture of ammonia and the haloalkane dissolved in alcohol in a sealed tube.

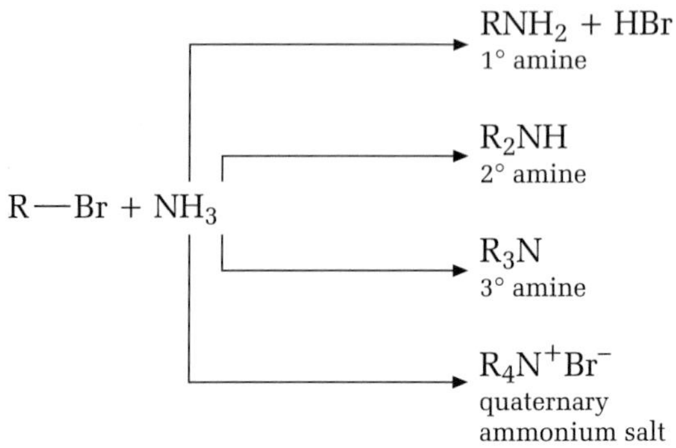

$$R-Br + NH_3$$

$$RNH_2 + HBr$$
1° amine

$$R_2NH$$
2° amine

$$R_3N$$
3° amine

$$R_4N^+Br^-$$
quaternary
ammonium salt

Q How would you convert ethanamide into ethylamine?

The reaction of ammonia with alcohols

A similar reaction takes place between ammonia and alcohols (but not phenols) when they are heated together under pressure with a suitable catalyst such as aluminium oxide. Again, a mixture of 1°, 2° and 3° amines is formed

$$R\!-\!OH + NH_3 \longrightarrow$$
$$RNH_2 + H_2O \quad 1° \text{ amine}$$
$$R_2NH \quad 2° \text{ amine}$$
$$R_3N \quad 3° \text{ amine}$$

This is a nucleophilic substitution reaction. Phenols are less susceptible to nucleophilic attack than alcohols (see section 32.11).

Hofmann degradation of amides

Hint: The Hofmann degradation is useful in planning a synthesis (see Chapter 37) because it is a method of shortening the carbon chain.

This reaction produces a primary amine with one fewer carbon atom than the original amide (hence the term 'degradation'). The amide is reacted with bromine and alkali:

$$R\!-\!\underset{\underset{NH_2}{|}}{\overset{\overset{O}{\|}}{C}} + Br_2 + 4NaOH \longrightarrow$$

$$R\!-\!NH_2 + 2NaBr + Na_2CO_3 + 2H_2O$$

So, ethanamide would be converted into methylamine by this reaction.

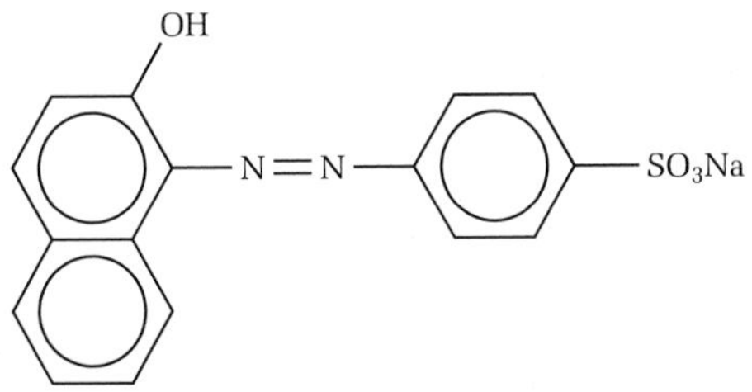

Figure 35.9 'Acid Orange 7', an azo dye

Economic importance of amines

- Aromatic amines are important in the manufacture of azo dyes – those produced from diazonium salts by coupling reactions. An example is shown in **Figure 35.9**. Note the conjugated system of double bond and aromatic rings.
- Diamines such as 1,6-diaminohexane are used in the manufacture of nylon.
- Many drugs of different types have amine functional groups. Some examples are shown in **Table 35.5**. The amine is marked in red.
- Amines are also used industrially in the manufacture of cationic detergents. These are quaternary ammonium compounds with a long hydrocarbon chain and a positively charged organic group.

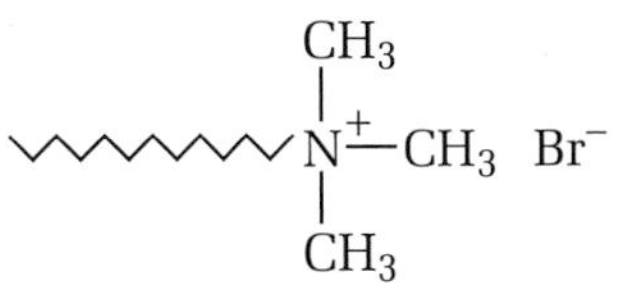

$$\text{wwww}\overset{\overset{\displaystyle CH_3}{|}}{\underset{\underset{\displaystyle CH_3}{|}}{N^+}}\!-\!CH_3 \quad Br^-$$

Answer: By reduction

Lycra swimwear

Hair conditioners contain quaternary ammonium compounds

Car dashboards are filled with polyurethane foam

Such detergents are not particularly good at cleaning, but have germicidal properties and are often an ingredient in nappy washing solutions. They are also used in hair and fabric conditioners. Both wet fabric and wet hair pick up negative charges on their surfaces. These attract positively charged cationic detergent molecules which coat the surfaces of the fabric or hair, lubricating the surfaces and preventing build-up of static electricity, which causes 'flyaway' hair.

- Finally, amines are used in the manufacture of polyurethanes. These are versatile polymers, whose properties can be tailored to meet a great many uses, from foams used in cavity wall insulations and car dashboard padding, to elastomeric fibres such

Table 35.5 Some drugs with amine functional groups

Name	Formula	Type
chlordiazepoxide (Librium)		tranquilliser
sulphanilamide		antibacterial
amphetamine		stimulant
dexchlorpheniramine (Polaramine)		antihistamine
amitriptylene		antidepressant
pethidine		painkiller

Antihistamine drugs

Allergies are abnormal bodily reactions to foreign substances called allergens, usually proteins. Common allergens are pollen, dust and housemites but a number of people are allergic to substances in food such as the yellow dye tartrazine. The symptoms of an allergy, which include skin rashes, runny nose, sore throat, swelling, headache, etc., are caused by the release of a chemical called histamine, which interacts with reactive sites called receptors found in cells in many body tissues.

drugs are available to counteract the effects of histamine. Histamine contains an ethylamine group. Many antihistamine drugs also contain an ethylamine or similar group. Such drugs compete with histamine for receptor sites and thus block the action of histamine. Other drugs which happen to have an ethylamine group also have antihistamine properties as well as their intended mode of action. Examples include some of the so-called tricyclic antidepressants such as imipramine and desipramine.

Ethylamine group

histamine

Imipramine R = CH₃
Desipramine R = H

Histamine may be released locally, for example, at the site of an insect bite, or into the whole bloodstream. Many

Can you see why they are called 'tricyclic'?

Q How would you expect the properties of a polyurethane to change with more cross-linking?

Burning foam may produce toxic gases

Answer: Become more rigid.

as Lycra used for making stretchy fabrics for swimwear and underwear. Polyurethanes are made by a polymerisation process from a diol or polyol (to provide cross-linking) and isocyanate.

$$HO-R-OH + O{=}C{=}N-R'-N{=}C{=}O$$

a diol   a diisocyanate

the urethane linkage

Amines are used in the manufacture of the diisocyanates. One problem with polyurethanes is that, when burned, they give off toxic gases including nitric acid, nitrogen dioxide and hydrogen cyanide. This means that untreated polyurethane is no longer used for furniture foams.

35.2 Nitriles

Formulae, naming and structure

Nitriles contain the functional group —C≡N. As with carboxylic acids, this group can only occur at the end of a carbon chain. The —C≡N group is named using the suffix -nitrile when it is the

Hint: Isonitriles have the functional group —N≡C, rather than —C≡N.

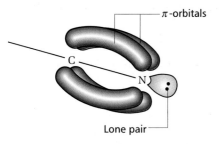

Figure 35.10 Bonding in the nitrile group

principal group and the prefix cyano- when it is not. When the suffix -nitrile is used, the carbon of the functional group is counted as part of the root, so:

$$CH_3C{\equiv}N \text{ is ethanenitrile}$$

and

$$CH_3CH_2C{\equiv}N \text{ is propanenitrile.}$$

Where the —C≡N is attached to a benzene ring, the carbon of the functional group is not counted as part of the root and the suffix -carbonitrile is used. For example:

is called benzenecarbonitrile.

The —C≡N group is formed by a σ bond and two π bonds (**Figure 35.10**). The unit R—C≡N is linear. The nitrogen atom has a lone pair.

Physical properties of nitriles

The —$C^{\delta+}{\equiv}N^{\delta-}$ unit is fairly polar (the electronegativity values are C = 2.5, N = 3.0). Thus the short-chain nitriles are liquids at room temperature and are fairly soluble both in water and in less polar solvents.

Reactivity of nitriles

The most important feature of the reactivity of the nitrile group is its unsaturation which means that addition reactions are possible.

Reactions of nitriles

Reduction

Hint: Lithium tetrahydridoaluminate(III) is normally used as a solution in ethoxyethane (ether) followed by addition of water.

Lithium tetrahydridoaluminate(III) or sodium in ethanol will reduce nitriles to primary amines.

$$R{-}C{\equiv}N \xrightarrow{[+4H]} R{-}\underset{\underset{H}{|}}{\overset{\overset{H}{|}}{C}}{-}N\overset{H}{\underset{H}{\diagdown}}$$

Hydrolysis

Nitriles are hydrolysed by boiling with either acids or alkalis to form first the amide and then the carboxylic acid (or its salt if alkali has been used).

$$R{-}C{\equiv}N \xrightarrow[H^+]{H_2O} R{-}\overset{O}{\underset{NH_2}{\overset{\|}{C}}} \xrightarrow{H_2O} R{-}\overset{O}{\underset{OH}{\overset{\|}{C}}} + NH_4^+$$

nitrile   amide   carboxylic acid

$$R{-}C{\equiv}N \xrightarrow{H_2O, NaOH} R{-}\overset{O}{\underset{O^-Na^+}{\overset{\|}{C}}} + NH_3$$

salt

Q Suggest why this order of reactivity is found.

Preparation of nitriles

From haloalkanes

Potassium cyanide dissolved in alcohol reacts with haloalkanes to yield nitriles by a nucleophilic substitution reaction. For example:

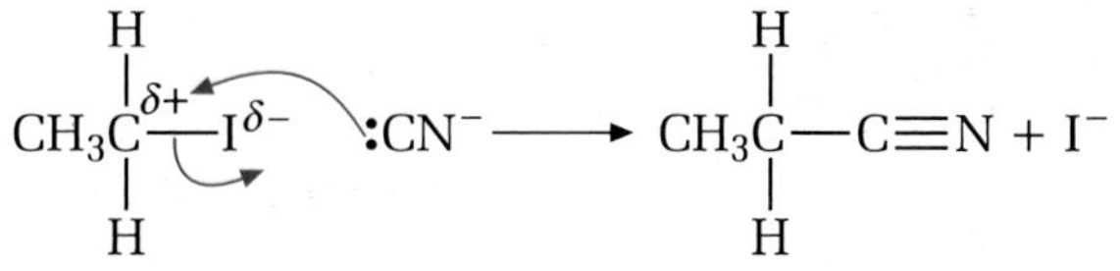

iodoethane propanenitrile

The order of reactivity of different halogens is I > Br > Cl.

This reaction is very important in planning organic syntheses (see Chapter 37) because it enables the length of the carbon chain to be increased by one. In the above example, iodo*ethane* produces *propane*nitrile. Haloarenes are less reactive than haloalkanes and this is not a feasible method for producing aromatic nitriles. They are made from diazonium salts as described below.

From diazonium salts

Diazonium salts are made from aromatic amines by reaction with nitrous acid below 278 K (5 °C). Treatment of these salts with aqueous potassium cyanide in the presence of copper(I) cyanide produces an aromatic nitrile (see page 581). For example:

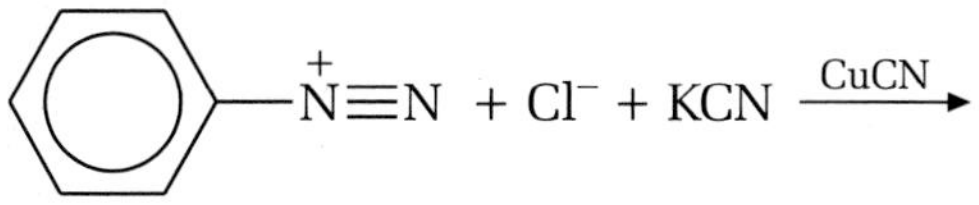

benzenediazonium chloride

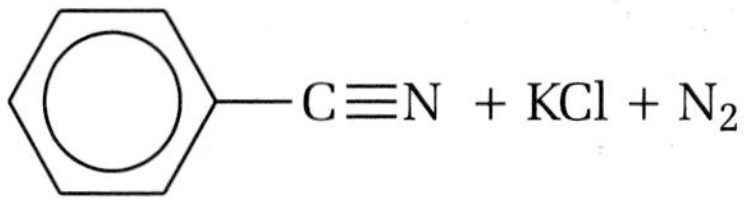

benzenecarbonitrile

By dehydration of amides

Heating with phosphorus pentoxide dehydrates amides to nitriles.

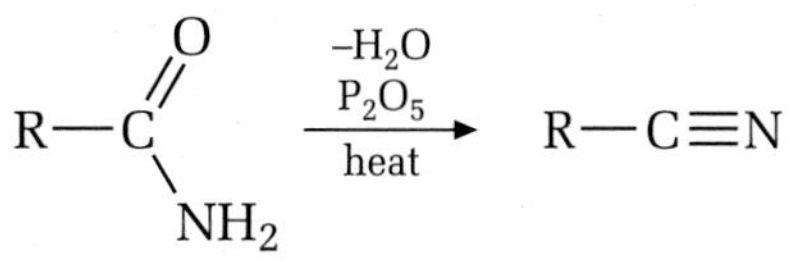

Hydroxynitriles

Hydroxynitriles may be made by the action of CN^- ions on aldehydes or ketones. For example:

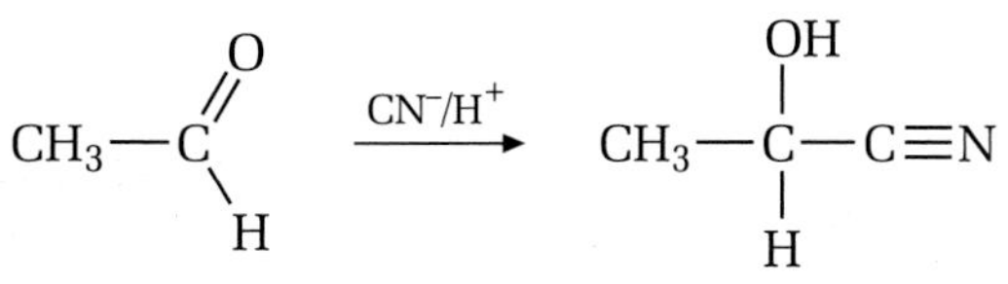

ethanal 2-hydroxypropanenitrile

Answer: The C—I bond is weaker than C—Br which is weaker than C—Cl.

Knitting yarn showing the Courtelle label

Economic importance of nitriles

Probably the most important nitrile industrially is propenenitrile, which has both an alkene and a nitrile functional group:

$$\underset{H}{\overset{H}{}}C=\underset{H}{\overset{H}{C}}-C\equiv N$$

It can be polymerised to poly(propenenitrile) by an addition polymerisation process which starts with an aqueous solution of the monomer from which the insoluble polymer precipitates.

$$\left(\begin{matrix} & N \\ & \|\| \\ H & C \\ | & | \\ -C-C- \\ | & | \\ H & H \end{matrix}\right)_n$$

poly(propenenitrile)

The non-systematic name of propenenitrile is acrylonitrile, which is the origin of the name of the polymer 'acrylic' and one of its trade names Acrilan. Other brand names include Orlon and Courtelle. The main use is as a fibre similar in many ways to wool. The fabrics are stronger and lighter than wool but garments are flammable and do not retain their shape so well. In some acrylic fibres, a small percentage of chloroethene is included in the polymer to make it easier to dye.

Nitriles are also involved in the manufacture of monomers for the production of Perspex and nylon.

35.3 Summary

Amines

● Amines are derived from ammonia, NH_3, by	replacement of one or more hydrogen atoms by alkyl or aryl groups.
● Primary amines have the general formula	$RNH_2.$
● Secondary amines have the general formula	$RR'NH.$
● Tertiary amines have the general formula	$RR'R''N.$
● The shapes of amines are	pyramidal, based on that of ammonia.

• Short-chain amines are soluble in	water, because they are polar.
• Amines have a lone pair of electrons, so they accept	H^+ ions and act as bases.
• In aqueous solution, base strengths of alkyl amines are in the order	2° amine > 1° amine > 3° amine > $NH_3 \gg$ arylamine
• Alkyldiazonium ions rapidly decompose to	R^+ and N_2, giving ROH and other products.
• Aryldiazonium ions are stable below	278 K.
• Aryldiazonium ions form dyes by	coupling reactions.
• The —NH_2 group activates the benzene ring especially at	the 2- and 4- positions.
• Amines can be prepared by or	reduction of nitriles, amides or nitro compounds, by the reaction of ammonia with haloalkanes or alcohols.
• The Hofmann degradation of amides produces an amine with	one carbon atom less than the starting amide.
• Amines are industrially important in the manufacture of	dyes, poly(amides), polyurethanes and a number of types of drugs.

The reactions of amines are summarised in **Figure 35.11**.

Nitriles

• Nitriles contain the functional group	—C≡N.
• Nitriles are fairly polar and those with short chains are	liquids which dissolve quite well in water.
• Nitriles can be made by	dehydration of amides.
• Alkylnitriles can be prepared by	the reaction of haloalkanes with sodium cyanide.
• Arylnitriles can be prepared by	treating diazonium salts with potassium cyanide.
• A nitrile prepared from a haloalkane has	one more carbon than the haloalkane.

The reactions of nitriles are summarised in **Figure 35.12**.

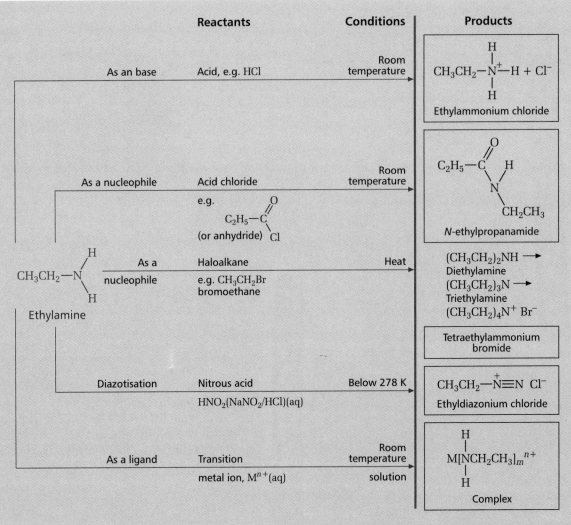

Figure 35.11 The reactions of amines using ethylamine as an example – cover up the right-hand side to test yourself

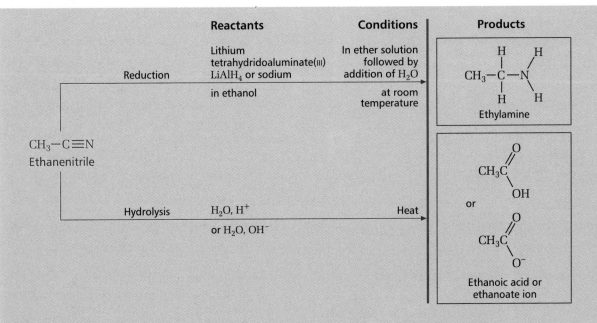

Figure 35.12 Reactions of nitriles using ethanenitrile as an example – cover up the right-hand side to test yourself

5.4 Practice questions

Name the following.

(a)
$$C_3H_7-\overset{\overset{\displaystyle CH_3}{|}}{N}-H$$

(b)
$$C_3H_7-\overset{\overset{\displaystyle C_3H_7}{|}}{N}-C_3H_7$$

(c)

(benzene ring)—C≡N

(d) $C_3H_7-C\equiv N$

(e)
$$C_3H_7-\overset{\overset{\displaystyle C_3H_7}{|}}{\underset{\underset{\displaystyle C_3H_7}{|}}{\overset{+}{N}}}-C_3H_7$$

Give the structures of:
(a) dipropylamine
(b) cyclohexylamine
(c) butanenitrile
(d) the tetramethylammonium ion

3. Arrange the following in order of their strengths as bases, weakest first:
(a) CH_3-NH_2
(b) $(CH_3)_2NH$
(c)

(benzene ring)—NH_2

(d)

(benzene ring with NH_2 and CH_3)

Hint: —CH_3 groups release electrons.

4. Name the organic products of the following reactions.
(a) ethylmethylamine with dilute acid
(b) propylamine plus ethanoyl chloride
(c) methylamine plus bromoethane
(d) ethanenitrile plus lithium tetrahydridoaluminate(III) in ethoxyethane followed by addition of water
(e) propanamide plus phosphorus pentoxide

5.6 Examination questions

(a) Explain why propylamine is classed as a Brønsted–Lowry base.
(b) Explain why propylamine is a stronger base than ammonia.
(c) Propylamine is obtained from the reaction between 1-bromopropane and an excess of ammonia. Name the type of reaction taking place and outline a mechanism.
(d) Propylamine can also be prepared from propanenitrile, CH_3CH_2CN. Name the type of reaction involved and write an equation for this reaction. What advantage does this method of synthesis have over that in part (c)?

[NEAB 1996]

(a) (i)   Write the equations for the reactions between phenylamine, $C_6H_5NH_2$, and
I.   hydrochloric acid,
II. sodium nitrate(III) (sodium nitrite) and hydrochloric acid to form benzenediazonium chloride

(ii) State the temperature range used in the reaction in (a)(i) II. and explain what determines this range.
(b) (i)   Draw the structure of the azo dye formed when benzenediazonium chloride couples in alkaline conditions with 2-naphthol which has the structure shown:

(ii) By reference to the structure in (b)(i) describe the meaning of the term *chromophore*.

[WJEC 1997, part question]

3. (a) The organic compound **A** below has two different nitrogen atoms in its structure.

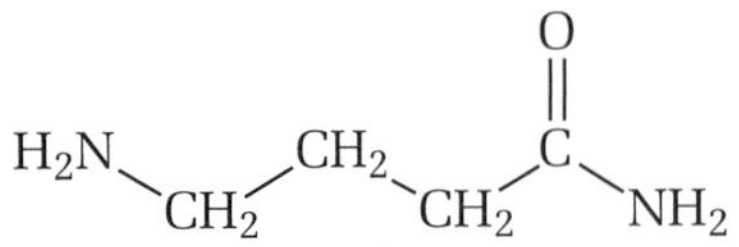

A

  (i)   **Name** the **two** functional groups in **A**.
  (ii) State which functional group you expect to be the more basic, and explain your answer.
  (iii) Draw an isomer of **A** which shows optical isomerism.

[Oxford 1997]

4. 3-Amino-4-methylbenzenesulphonic acid can be obtained from methylbenzene in three steps:

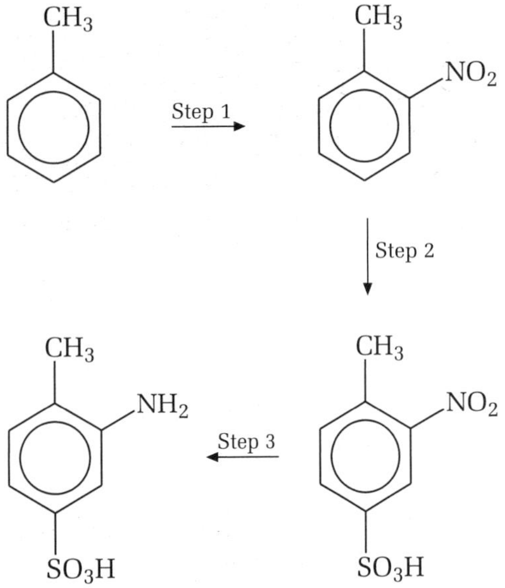

(a) For **each** step, name the type of reaction taking place and suggest a suitable reagent or combination of reagents.
(b) Identify the reactive inorganic species present in Step 2 and outline a mechanism for this reaction.

[NEAB 1998

5. A weakly acid compound **A** ($C_8H_9NO_2$) gives no reaction with a mixture of sodium nitrite and hydrochloric acid at low temperature. On heating **A** under reflux with excess dilute hydrochloric acid hydrolysis occurs giving two compounds **B** (C_6H_8NClO) and **C** ($C_2H_4O_2$). After complete separation from all other components of the mixture, **C** was found to react with sodium carbonate, liberating a colourless gas.

When **B** was cooled to about 3 °C and sodium nitrite solution added at the same temperature, a colourless solution **D** ($C_6H_5ClN_2O$) was formed. Addition of phenol to this solution gave a coloured precipitate **E**.

The mass spectra of **A**, **B** and **D** all show a peak at $m/e = 76$.
(i)   Deduce structures for compounds **A** to **E** inclusive.
(ii) Show how you have used the data to reach your conclusions, writing equations where appropriate.

[London (Nuffield) 1998, part question

36

Polymers

C H E M I S T R Y   N O W

Plastic with a memory

Some polymers can be made to 'remember' a particular shape and return to it when heated. This is done by using β-radiation to produce a degree of cross-linking in a thermoplastic.

One application of memory plastic is to make the sleeving which holds together bunches of wires in the electrical systems of cars.

A length of wide bore tube, made of memory plastic, based on poly(ethene), can be slid over a bunch of wires. It is heated with a hot air gun (like a powerful hairdryer) and shrinks into a narrow bore shape which it has 'remembered'. This holds the bunch of wires tightly together.

Poly(ethene) consists of long hydrocarbon chains which, when heated, can slide past one another, allowing the plastic to be moulded into shape.

Heat shrink material can be used to hold together bunches of wire like this

To make the 'memory plastic' tubing:

The poly(ethene) is heated, moulded into the *final* narrow-bore shape and cooled.

The tube is then exposed to β-radiation. This causes some cross-links to form between the chains but not enough to prevent softening on heating.

Now the tube is heated once more, shaped into a wider bore and cooled. This shaping stretches the cross-links and they remain stretched as the plastic cools.

In the cold plastic, the chains are 'frozen' in place. The tube is now ready for use and can be slipped easily over the wires.

On heating with the hot air gun, the stretched cross-links contract and pull the tube back into the narrow-bore shape it had when it was irradiated.

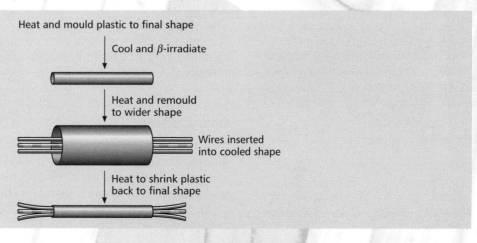

Heat and mould plastic to final shape

Cool and β-irradiate

Heat and remould to wider shape

Wires inserted into cooled shape

Heat to shrink plastic back to final shape

Introduction

Polymers are compounds consisting of giant molecules made up of many smaller molecules (called monomers) linked together. Many materials in everyday life are polymers, including plastics like PVC, Perspex and Bakelite and fibres such as nylon, Terylene and acrylics. Polymers are also closely linked with the chemistry of life.

Proteins are polymers which occur in all living things. They have a wide variety of functions, including structural materials like muscle fibres, hair and cartilage, hormones like insulin which control particular aspects of metabolism and enzymes which catalyse innumerable chemical reactions in the body. DNA (deoxyribonucleic acid), the molecule which stores genetic information and ensures that we resemble our parents, is also a polymer.

Concept Checkpoints

The following basic ideas are used in this chapter. You may revise some of these topics elsewhere in the book.
- the formation of amides from carboxylic acids and amines (section 34.6)
- intermolecular forces (Chapter 10)
- optical activity (section 18.6)
- radicals and chain reactions (sections 18.8 and 19.4)

Hint: Compounds with two functional groups are called bifunctional compounds.

Hint: The test for proteins is the **biuret test**, in which the suspected protein is warmed with alkaline copper sulphate solution. A violet colour indicates the presence of protein.

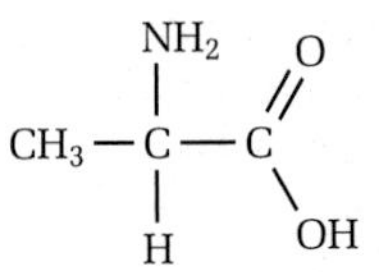

36.1 Proteins

Proteins are polymers built up from monomers called **amino acids**.

Amino acids

These molecules have two functional groups: a carboxylic acid and primary amine. All the important naturally occurring amino acids, of which there are about 20, are 2-amino acids, that is, the amino group is on the carbon next to the $-CO_2H$ group (**Figure 36.1**).

2-Amino acids have the general formula:

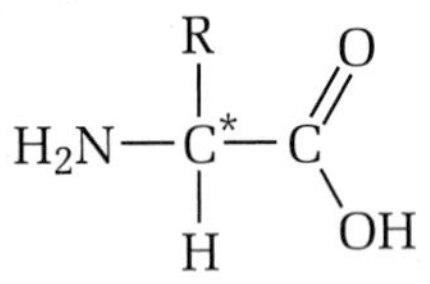

$$H_2N-\underset{\underset{H}{|}}{\overset{\overset{R}{|}}{C^*}}-C\underset{OH}{\overset{O}{\diagup\diagdown}}$$

The twenty naturally occurring amino acids are listed in the box 'Twenty naturally occurring amino acids'. Each has a three-letter symbol, short for its non-systematic name, which is usually used to identify it.

Optical activity

R can be a whole variety of groups, including ones with functional groups. Except for the case when R is H, $-NH_2$ or $-CO_2H$, the carbon marked * in the general formula above has four different groups bonded to it and is therefore **chiral** (or **asymmetric**). Amino acids can therefore exist in two mirror image forms which are optically active (see section 18.6).

$$CH_3-\underset{\underset{H}{|}}{\overset{\overset{NH_2}{|}}{C}}-C\underset{OH}{\overset{O}{\diagup\diagdown}}$$

Figure 36.1 2-aminopropanoic acid: a 2-amino acid, also called alanine

Q What is the systematic name of valine? (See the box 'Twenty naturally occurring acids' for the formula.)

Q The amino acid isoleucine has two chiral carbons. Which are they?

$$H_2NCHCO_2H$$
$$CHC_2H_5$$
$$CH_3$$

isoleucine

nswer: 2-Amino-3-methylbutanoic acid

nswer: $H_2NC^*HCO_2H$
$C^*HC_2H_5$
CH_3

Acid and base properties

Amino acids have both an acidic and a basic functional group. The carboxylic acid group has a tendency to lose a proton (act as an acid).

The amine group has a tendency to accept a proton (act as a base).

Amino acids exist largely as **zwitterions**, in which the carboxylic acid is deprotonated and the amino group protonated, the molecule remaining neutral overall:

a zwitterion

This ionic nature explains the fact that amino acids have high melting temperatures, and that they dissolve well in water and poorly in non-polar solvents. Typically amino acids are white solids at room temperature, resembling ionic salts in many of their properties.

FURTHER FOCUS

Optical activity of amino acids: the 'CORN' law

Since all 2-amino acids (except glycine) have a chiral carbon (one with four different groups attached) they all have two mirror image forms called a pair of **enantiomers**. Solutions of the same concentration of each enantiomer will rotate the plane of polarisation of polarised light through the same angle but in opposite directions. The symbols '+' and '−' are used to indicate this. '+' denotes a clockwise rotation as seen by an observer looking towards the light source and '−' indicates an anticlockwise rotation.

The absolute configuration of an amino acid (the position of all the groups in space) can be found by X-ray diffraction. Amino acids whose absolute configuration is as shown are called L-amino acids. You can remember this by the so-called CORN law. Look along the H—C bond. If the other three groups, going clockwise, are in the order: —CO_2H, —R, —NH_2 then the compound is an L-acid, otherwise it is the mirror image which is given the symbol D. All the naturally occurring amino acids are of the L-configuration.

Perhaps surprisingly, there is no simple relationship between absolute configuration (shown by D or L) and the direction of rotation of the plane of polarised light (shown by + or −). For example, L-glutamic acid is + but L-cysteine is − . What *is* certain, however, is that if the L form is + then the D form *of the same compound* will be − . So the two enantiomers of glutamic acid are L(+) glutamic acid and D(−) glutamic acid. L(−) and D(+) glutamic acids are impossible.

FURTHER FOCUS

Twenty naturally occurring amino acids

Formula	Name	Abbreviation

H_2NCHCO_2H
     $\mid$
     H
	glycine	Gly

H_2NCHCO_2H
     $\mid$
     CH_3
	alanine	Ala

H_2NCHCO_2H
     $\mid$
     $CHCH_3$
     $\mid$
     CH_3
	valine	Val

H_2NCHCO_2H
     $\mid$
     CH_2
     $\mid$
     $CH_3(CH_3)_2$
	leucine	Leu

H_2NCHCO_2H
     $\mid$
     CHC_2H_5
     $\mid$
     CH_3
	isoleucine	Ile

$HN-CHCO_2H$ proline ring (CH_2, CH_2, CH_2)	proline (Note: Proline is a *secondary amine*)	Pro
H_2NCHCO_2H CH_2 / indole ring	tryptophan	Try

H_2NCHCO_2H
     $\mid$
     CH_2
     $\mid$
     CH_2SCH_3
	methionine	Met

H_2NCHCO_2H
     $\mid$
     CH_2—(phenyl ring)
	phenylalanine	Phe

H_2NCHCO_2H
     $\mid$
     CH_2OH
	serine	Ser

Formula	Name	Abbreviation

H_2NCHCO_2H
     $\mid$
     $CHOH$
     $\mid$
     CH_3
	threonine	Thr

H_2NCHCO_2H
     $\mid$
     CH_2SH
	cysteine	Cys

H_2NCHCO_2H
     $\mid$
     CH_2
     $\mid$
     $CONH_2$
	asparagine	Asn

H_2NCHCO_2H
     $\mid$
     CH_2
     $\mid$
     CH_2CONH_2
	glutamine	Gln

H_2NCHCO_2H
     $\mid$
     CH_2—(phenyl ring)—OH
	tyrosine	Tyr

H_2NCHCO_2H
     $\mid$
     CH_2
     $\mid$
 $C=CH$ / HN N / CH (imidazole ring)
	histidine	His

H_2NCHCO_2H
     $\mid$
     $(CH_2)_3$
     $\mid$
     NH
     $\mid$
 $NH=C-NH_2$
	arginine	Arg

H_2NCHCO_2H
     $\mid$
     $(CH_2)_3$
     $\mid$
     CH_2NH_2
	lysine	Lys

H_2NCHCO_2H
     $\mid$
     CH_2CO_2H
	aspartic acid	Asp

H_2NCHCO_2H
     $\mid$
     CH_2
     $\mid$
     CH_2CO_2H
	glutamic acid	Glu

Peptides, polypeptides and proteins

The amino group of one amino acid can react with the carboxylic acid group of another to form an amide (see section 34.4). A molecule of water is eliminated in this nucleophilic substitution reaction. Compounds formed by the linkage of amino acids are called **peptides**, and in this context the amide linkage is often called a peptide linkage.

$$H_2\ddot{N}-\underset{R}{\overset{H}{\underset{|}{\overset{|}{C}}}}-\overset{O^{\delta-}}{C^{\delta+}}\diagdown_{OH} + H_2\ddot{N}-\underset{R'}{\overset{H}{\underset{|}{\overset{|}{C}}}}-C\diagdown_{OH} \longrightarrow$$

$$H_2N-\underset{R}{\overset{H}{\underset{|}{\overset{|}{C}}}}-\overset{O}{\overset{||}{C}}-\underset{R'}{\overset{H}{\underset{|}{\overset{|}{N}}}}-\underset{R'}{\overset{H}{\underset{|}{\overset{|}{C}}}}-C\diagdown_{OH} + H_2O$$

a dipeptide

The amide linkage is shown in red. The resulting molecule is a dimer containing two amino acid units. A peptide with two amino acid units is called a **dipeptide**. The dipeptide still retains $-NH_2$ and $-CO_2H$ groups and can react further to give tri- and tetrapeptides and so on. Molecules containing up to about 50 amino acids are called polypeptides, while molecules with more than 50 amino acid units are called proteins.

The structure of proteins

Proteins have complex structures. At least three levels of structure can be distinguished in proteins.

The primary structure

The primary structure refers to the sequence of different amino acids along the protein chain. As there are around twenty common amino acids which can be in any order, and proteins contain over 50 amino acids, the number of possibilities is enormous. Each protein has a specific sequence of amino acids. Proteins are rather like necklaces made of beads of twenty different shades. Any necklace can be recognised by its particular sequence of shades. In the same way the primary structure of a specific protein can be defined using the three-letter names of the amino acids. For example, just one short sequence of the protein insulin (the hormone controlling sugar metabolism) runs:

—Val—Glu—Ala—Leu—Tyr—

One end of any protein or peptide has a free $-NH_2$ group and the other a free $-CO_2H$ group. These are often referred to as the N-terminal end and the C-terminal end respectively. It is usual to write the N-terminal end on the left.

For example, the sequence Gly—Ala would represent:

$$H_2N-\underset{H}{\overset{H}{\underset{|}{\overset{|}{C}}}}-\overset{O}{\overset{||}{C}}-\underset{H}{\overset{H}{\underset{|}{\overset{|}{N}}}}-\underset{H}{\overset{CH_3}{\underset{|}{\overset{|}{C}}}}-CO_2H$$

$$\underbrace{}_{Gly} \quad \underbrace{}_{Ala}$$

> **Q** Draw displayed formulae of Val—Gly and Gly—Val.

while Ala—Gly would represent:

$$H_2N-\underset{\underset{H}{|}}{\overset{\overset{CH_3}{|}}{C}}-\overset{\overset{O}{\parallel}}{C}-\underset{\underset{H}{|}}{\overset{\overset{H}{|}}{N}}-\underset{\underset{H}{|}}{\overset{\overset{H}{|}}{C}}-CO_2H$$

$\underbrace{\qquad}_{Ala} \quad \underbrace{\qquad}_{Gly}$

The two are different.

The secondary structure

X-ray diffraction studies of protein molecules have shown that many of them have a helical or spiral structure – an idea first proposed by the US chemist Linus Pauling. A typical protein helix has 18 amino acids for every five turns of the helix (see **Figure 36.2**).

The helical structure of proteins is called the secondary structure. The chain is held in its helical shape by hydrogen bonding between N—H and O=C groups (see **Figures 36.3** and **36.4**).

Hint: An alternative secondary structure adopted by some proteins is the *β*-pleated sheet. The protein molecules line up side by side, linked by hydrogen bonds as shown below:

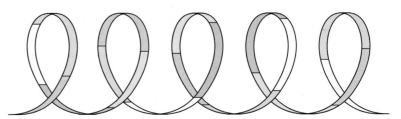

Figure 36.2 The helical structure of a protein. The shaded strips represent amino acid links. 18 amino acid units occupy 5 turns of the helix

Did you know? A working biological molecule may be made up of two or more protein molecules associated together. The arrangement of these is called the **quaternary structure**. Haemoglobin, for example, has four protein sub-units.

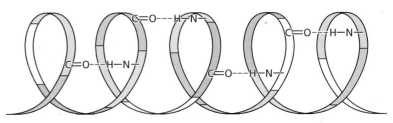

Figure 36.3 The helix of a protein is held by hydrogen bonds

The tertiary structure

Finally, the protein helix may be bent, twisted or folded into a particular shape. This is the tertiary structure.

The easiest way to visualise the primary, secondary and tertiary structure of a protein is to imagine a length of wire representing the protein chain. The wire is painted in strips of different colours, each strip representing an amino acid. The primary structure is the pattern of coloured strips on the wire. If the wire is wound into a spiral, the tightness of the spiral represents the secondary structure. The resulting spiral could then be folded like a coiled telephone lead to represent the tertiary structure.

Determination of protein structure

The secondary and tertiary structures of proteins can only be investigated by X-ray diffraction techniques. The primary structure (the amino acid sequence) can be investigated by normal chemical techniques.

Answer:

How do you find the R$_f$ value?

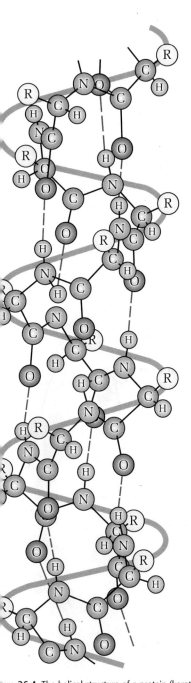

ure 36.4 The helical structure of a protein (keratin). rogen bonds that maintain the shape are shown in k. The brown line traces out the spiral shape

Boiling a protein with hydrochloric acid of concentration 6 mol dm^{-3} for 24 hours hydrolyses all the amide (peptide) linkages and produces a mixture of all the amino acids in the original protein. The mixture can be separated and the amino acids identified by **two-way paper chromatography** (see section 23.1). Amino acids, being colourless, do not give visible spots but can be located by spraying the paper with **ninhydrin**, which reacts with amino acids to give a purple colour. This allows the amino acids present in the original protein to be found by comparing the two R$_f$ values obtained for each spot with R$_f$ values obtained for known amino acids in the same solvents.

A quantitative separation by, for example, column chromatography (see section 23.1) will give the relative numbers of each amino acid. For example, insulin, one of the simplest proteins, has a total of 51 amino acids as shown in **Table 36.1**.

Determining the amino acid sequence is more difficult and a number of methods are used. Only an outline is possible here.

N-terminal and C-terminal analysis

Reagents are available that will react with either the N-terminal end or the C-terminal end of a protein or peptide. If the protein is then hydrolysed, the amino acids that were at the N-terminal and C-terminal ends of the chain can be identified because they are attached to the appropriate reagents.

Partial hydrolysis

Hydrolysis under milder conditions than those used for complete hydrolysis can result in the protein being broken into peptides, each of three or four amino acids. These can be identified by the techniques described above. The amino acid sequence of the original protein can then be deduced from the overlapping peptide fragments. The principle can be seen from the following simple example. Partial hydrolysis of a tetrapeptide yielded three fragments:

$$\text{N-terminal end} \left\{ \begin{array}{l} \text{Gly—Val} \\ \text{Ala—Gly} \\ \text{Val—Gly} \end{array} \right.$$

The original peptide must have had the sequence below to yield the fragments shown:

$$\text{N-terminal end Ala—Gly—Val—Gly}$$

Enzyme-controlled hydrolysis

This is a complementary technique to partial hydrolysis. Certain enzymes will catalyse the hydrolysis of specific peptide bonds only. For example, trypsin will break only the peptide bonds formed by the C-terminal ends of the amino acids Lys and Arg. So partial hydrolysis with this enzyme will produce peptides in which these amino acids are at the C-terminal end.

Frederick Sanger and his co-workers at Cambridge took 10 years in the late 1940s and early 1950s to determine the amino acid sequence of the simple protein insulin. Sanger won a 1958 Nobel prize for this work. Nowadays, many of the procedures can be automated and the process is much faster.

swer: R$_f$ = $\dfrac{\text{distance moved by spot}}{\text{distance moved by solvent}}$

Table 36.1 The 51 amino acids which make up insulin

Phe	3
Val	5
Asn	3
Gln	3
His	2
Leu	6
Cys	6
Glu	4
Ser	3
Ala	3
Tyr	4
Gly	4
Arg	1
Thr	1
Pro	1
Lys	1
Ile	1
	51

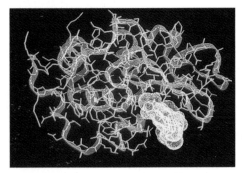

Computer graphic representation of lysozyne (shown in blue) and the substrate (shown in yellow)

The structure of proteins and their properties

Following X-ray diffraction studies, it has been possible to build scale models of the structures of proteins and it has been possible to see how their structures influence their properties. We shall look at just a few examples.

Enzymes

Enzymes are immensely efficient protein-based catalysts that occur in living systems.

They can accelerate reactions by factors of up to 10^{10}. (This mean that a reaction that is complete in 1 second with the enzyme would take *300 years* without it.)

Enzymes are very specific, usually catalysing just one reaction of one compound called the **substrate** of that enzyme.

Enzymes fit closely to the substrate and the molecule with which it is reacting and temporarily hold the two molecules in the correct orientation for them to react. The products are then released by the enzyme. The shape of the enzyme is thus very important. The photograph shows a model of the shape of the enzyme lysozyme, a naturally occurring antibiotic found in tears. It catalyses the breakdown of polysaccharides found in the cell walls of bacteria, thus killing the bacteria. The substrate fits into the deep cavity in th enzyme called the **active site** of the enzyme.

Because the catalytic activity of an enzyme is so dependent on its shape, enzymes are very sensitive to changes in temperature and pH These can disrupt the hydrogen bonds responsible for maintaining secondary and tertiary structures. Most enzymes will rapidly denature (change their shape) at temperatures above about 320 K. This is why enzymes have an optimum temperature as catalysts. Below the optimum temperature, the reaction is slow for the usual reasons. Above this temperature, the enzyme denatures and loses its catalytic effect (**Figure 36.5**).

The uses of enzymes

Part of the 'new' science of biotechnology is concerned with using enzymes to catalyse reactions of economic importance. This is because enzymes are very efficient and work at comparatively low temperatures and pressures.

People have long used enzymes to catalyse the reactions that make alcohol from carbohydrates and yoghurt from milk. More recently biological washing powders have used protease enzymes to dissolve protein-based stains such as blood and egg. Some washing powders now contain lipase enzymes which break down lipids (fats).

Enzymes can now be bound to solid supports so that reactants can be passed over them without the enzyme being washed away.

One medical use of enzymes is in the treatment of slipped discs. A slipped disc occurs when a portion of disc material, between the vertebrae in the spine, bulges out causing painful pressure on a nerve. Conventional treatment requires surgery to remove the bulging portion of the disc. As an alternative, the enzyme chymopapain

can be injected into the bulging disc to denature the protein of the disc, causing it to shrink and relieve the pressure on the nerve. The procedure is much quicker and less painful than surgery. A similar enzyme is sometimes used to 'tenderise' joints of meat by dissolving tough fibres.

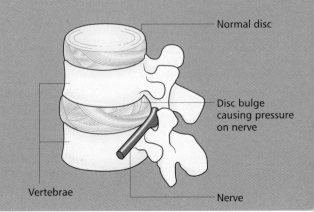

The stretchiness of wool

Wool is a protein fibre where the helix is, as usual, held together by hydrogen bonds (**Figure 36.6**). When wool is gently stretched, the hydrogen bonds stretch (**Figure 36.7**), and the fibre extends. Releasing the tension allows the hydrogen bonds to return to their normal length and the fibre returns to its original shape. However, washing at high temperatures can break the hydrogen bonds and a garment may permanently lose its shape.

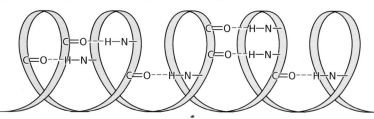

Figure 36.6 Hydrogen bonds in wool

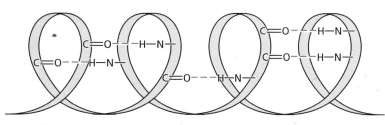

Figure 36.7 The wool is gently stretched

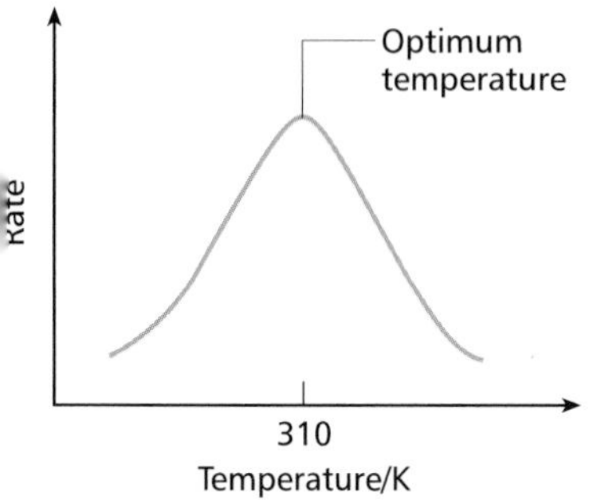

Hair perming and permanent creasing of clothes

As well as hydrogen bonding at least two other types of bond are involved in the secondary and tertiary structures of proteins. One is bonding between the side chains or R-groups of the amino acids. An acidic R-group such as that of aspartic acid can react with a basic side chain on another amino acid, such as lysine (**Figure 36.8**).

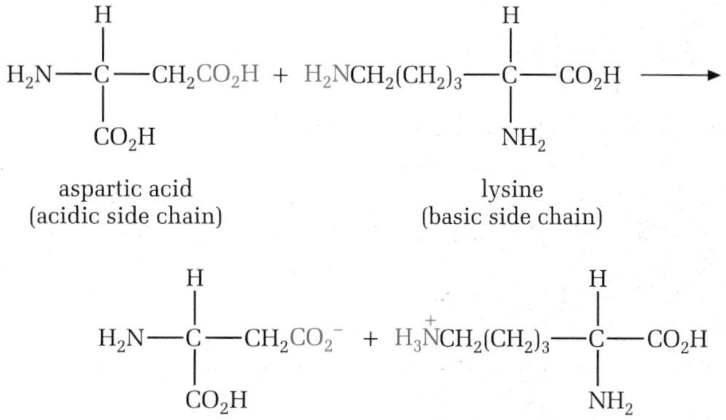

$$H_2N-\underset{\underset{CO_2H}{|}}{\overset{\overset{H}{|}}{C}}-CH_2CO_2H \; + \; H_2NCH_2(CH_2)_3-\underset{\underset{NH_2}{|}}{\overset{\overset{H}{|}}{C}}-CO_2H \; \longrightarrow$$

aspartic acid   lysine
(acidic side chain)   (basic side chain)

$$H_2N-\underset{\underset{CO_2H}{|}}{\overset{\overset{H}{|}}{C}}-CH_2CO_2^- \; + \; H_3\overset{+}{N}CH_2(CH_2)_3-\underset{\underset{NH_2}{|}}{\overset{\overset{H}{|}}{C}}-CO_2H$$

Figure 36.8 Aspartic acid and lysine can react together

The second is bonding between two units of the amino acid cysteine which has the side chain —CH_2SH (**Figure 36.9**). Two cysteine units can be oxidised to form an S—S bond. The resulting 'double' amino acid is called cystine and can link two protein chains as shown in **Figure 36.10**.

Insulin has three S—S bridges (**Figure 36.11**). The S—S bonds in cystine are easily broken by mild reducing agents and reformed by mild oxidising agents.

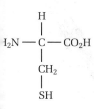

Rate

— Optimum temperature

310
Temperature/K

Figure 36.5 Typical graph of reaction rate against temperature for an enzyme-catalysed reaction

$$H_2N-\underset{\underset{\underset{SH}{|}}{\overset{|}{CH_2}}}{\overset{\overset{H}{|}}{C}}-CO_2H$$

Figure 36.9 Cysteine

Q Explain why the conversion of cystine to cysteine is a reduction

Answer: Hydrogen is added.

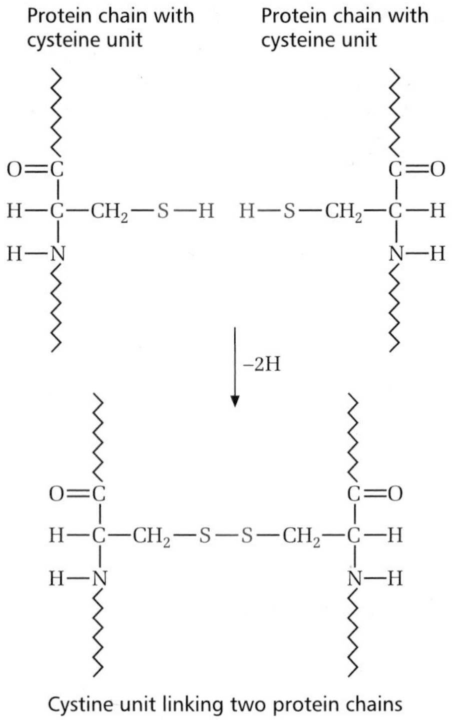

Protein chain with cysteine unit

Protein chain with cysteine unit

$$O=C$$
$$H-C-CH_2-S-H \quad H-S-CH_2-C-H$$
$$H-N \qquad\qquad\qquad\qquad N-H$$

| −2H

$$O=C \qquad\qquad\qquad\qquad C=O$$
$$H-C-CH_2-S-S-CH_2-C-H$$
$$H-N \qquad\qquad\qquad\qquad N-H$$

Cystine unit linking two protein chains

Figure 36.10 Two cysteine molecules can link via a weak S—S bond to form the double amino acid cystine

$$Cys-S-S-Cys \xrightarrow{\text{reduction}} Cys-SH + HS-Cys$$

$$Cys-SH + HS-Cys \xrightarrow{\text{oxidation}} Cys-S-S-Cys$$

This is the basis of both permanent waving of hair and permanent creasing of woollen garments (such as trousers). Both hair and wool contain the protein keratin, which contains a large proportion of cystine with —S—S— bridges.

In perming, a mild reducing agent is used to break the S—S bonds. The hair is then curled using rollers and the S—S bonds reformed by treating the hair with a gentle oxidising agent (usually hydrogen peroxide). This 'locks' the hair in its curled arrangement.

A similar sequence of applying a reducing agent, creasing and then oxidising is used in permanent creasing. Both processes are illustrated schematically in **Figure 36.12**.

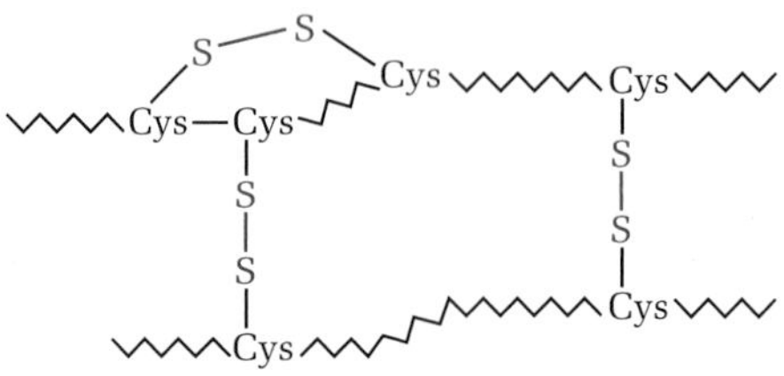

Figure 36.11 Sulphur–sulphur bridges in the insulin molecule

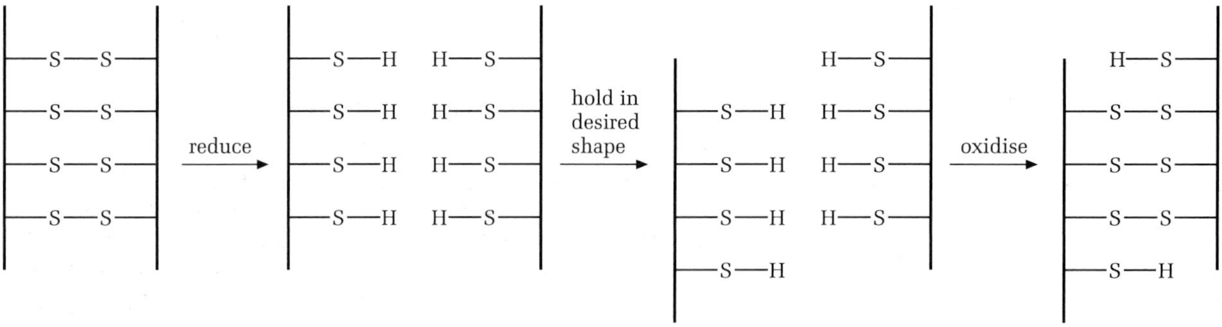

Figure 36.12 Breaking and reforming S—S bridges can produce permanent changes in the shapes of protein molecules

Q Why can't you 'unfry' an egg by cooling it down?

Hint: 'Unsaturated' means 'having a double bond'.

Answer: The protein in the egg white is denatured by high temperature. Once the hydrogen bonds have been broken it is immensely improbable that they will reform in exactly the same way on cooling

36.2 Synthetic polymers

This is a large and varied group of materials, many of which have been discussed in earlier chapters under the relevant functional groups.

The first completely synthetic polymer was Bakelite, which was patented in 1907. Since then, a large number of different types of polymer have been developed with a range of properties to suit them for almost any application (see the photograph).

One way of classifying polymers is by the type of reaction by which they are made.

Addition polymers are made from unsaturated monomers, and the empirical formula of the polymer is the same as that of the monomer. Only one type of monomer is needed. This is called **homopolymerisation**.

Polymers around us

Condensation polymers are made from monomers that have two functional groups. For every bond formed between two monomers, a small molecule, such as water or hydrogen chloride, is expelled. Polymerisation reactions which involve two (or more) different types of monomer are called **copolymerisation** processes.

Addition polymers

Addition polymers are commonly made from monomers that are derivatives of ethene of general formula:

$$\underset{H}{\overset{H}{>}}C=C\underset{R}{\overset{H}{<}}$$

They polymerise as shown:

$$\underset{H}{\overset{H}{>}}C=C\underset{R}{\overset{H}{<}} + \underset{H}{\overset{H}{>}}C=C\underset{R}{\overset{H}{<}} + \underset{H}{\overset{H}{>}}C=C\underset{R}{\overset{H}{<}} \longrightarrow$$

$$-\overset{\overset{\displaystyle H}{|}}{\underset{\underset{\displaystyle H}{|}}{C}}-\overset{\overset{\displaystyle H}{|}}{\underset{\underset{\displaystyle R}{|}}{C}}-\overset{\overset{\displaystyle H}{|}}{\underset{\underset{\displaystyle H}{|}}{C}}-\overset{\overset{\displaystyle H}{|}}{\underset{\underset{\displaystyle R}{|}}{C}}-\overset{\overset{\displaystyle H}{|}}{\underset{\underset{\displaystyle H}{|}}{C}}-\overset{\overset{\displaystyle H}{|}}{\underset{\underset{\displaystyle R}{|}}{C}}-$$

Some examples are given in **Table 36.2**.

A number of methods of polymerisation are used. One of the most common is **radical polymerisation** which requires an **initiator** to supply the initial radicals and continues via the **propagation** and **termination** steps typical of a **chain reaction** (see section 19.4). Radicals are often generated by the decomposition of benzoyl peroxide whose relatively weak O—O bond breaks homolytically:

$$2\bigcirc\hspace{-1em}\cdot + 2CO_2 \longleftarrow 2\bigcirc\hspace{-1em}\begin{array}{c}O\\||\\C\\|\\O\cdot\end{array}$$

Table 36.2 Addition polymers

R	Name of polymer	Common or trade name
—H	poly(ethene)	polythene (Alkathene)
—CH$_3$	poly(propene)	polypropylene
—Cl	poly(chloroethene)	PVC (polyvinyl chloride)
—C≡N	poly(propenenitrile)	acrylic (Acrilan, Courtelle)
⬡	poly(phenylethene)	polystyrene

The radical then attacks the double bond of the monomer CH_2CHX, forming a new radical:

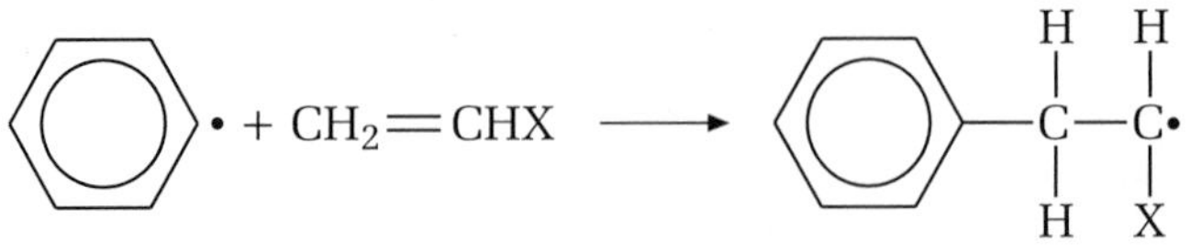

This can then attack a further monomer:

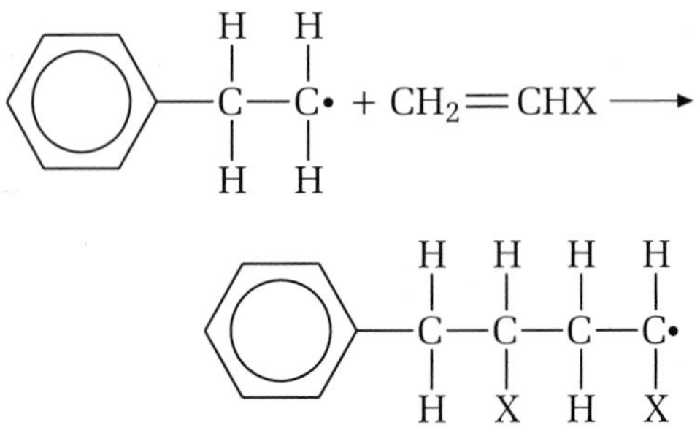

and so on (these are **propagation** steps). **Termination** may occur when two radicals react either as below:

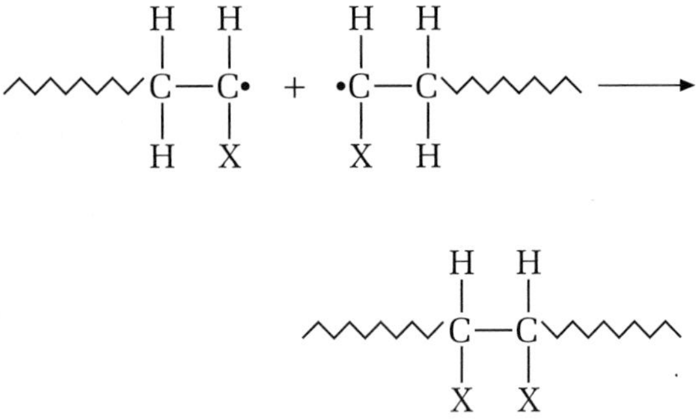

or by transfer of a hydrogen atom:

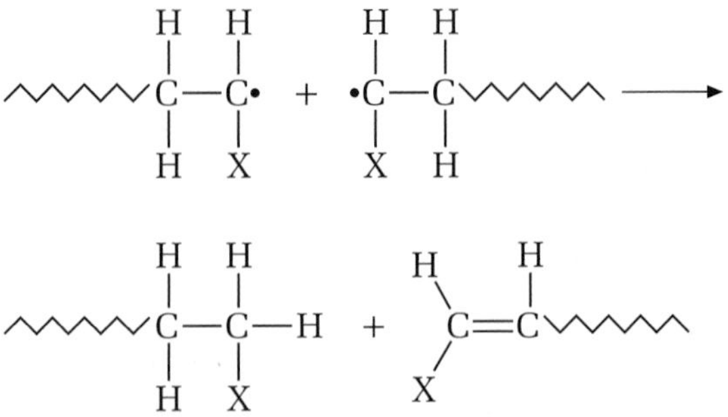

Ziegler–Natta catalysts

Another common method of polymerisation of alkenes is by use of catalysts which include a transition metal. One such catalyst system is triethylaluminium, $Al(C_2H_5)_3$, and titanium(IV) chloride, $TiCl_4$, and is called a **Ziegler–Natta** catalyst after Karl Ziegler and Giulio Natta, who won the 1963 Nobel Prize for chemistry for their work on

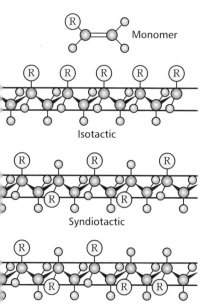

Figure 36.13 Geometries of addition polymers

Hint: Remember that hydrocarbon chains are not straight: the C—C—C bond angle is 109.5°.

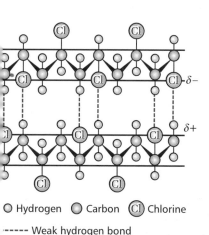

Figure 36.14 Weak bonding between chains in poly(chloroethene)

polymerisation. Ziegler–Natta catalysts have two important attributes:

- They allow polymerisation to take place under relatively mild conditions of temperature and pressure.
- They produce polymers of very regular geometry which has an important effect on their properties.

The geometry of polymer chains

In an addition polymer derived from a substituted ethene:

$$\underset{H}{\overset{H}{C}}{=}\underset{R}{\overset{H}{C}} + \underset{H}{\overset{H}{C}}{=}\underset{R}{\overset{H}{C}} + \underset{H}{\overset{H}{C}}{=}\underset{R}{\overset{H}{C}} \longrightarrow$$

$$-\overset{\underset{|}{H}}{\underset{|}{C}}-\overset{\underset{|}{H}}{\underset{|}{C}}-\overset{\underset{|}{H}}{\underset{|}{C}}-\overset{\underset{|}{H}}{\underset{|}{C}}-\overset{\underset{|}{H}}{\underset{|}{C}}-\overset{\underset{|}{H}}{\underset{|}{C}}-$$

many geometrical arrangements of the product may occur. If we imagine the main carbon chain to be in a horizontal plane, then the substituent (R) may either stick up above or be down below the plane.

- If all the substituents are above the plane, the arrangement is called **isotactic**.
- If substituents are alternately above and below the plane, it is called **syndiotactic**
- If the substituents are randomly arranged above and below the plane, it is described as **atactic** (see **Figure 36.13**).

Polymers made using Ziegler–Natta-type catalysts are more regular than those made by radical polymerisation or other mechanisms.

The regularity or irregularity of polymer chains has considerable bearing on the properties of the finished polymer. For example, in poly(chloroethene) (PVC), there is weak bonding, similar to hydrogen bonding, between the chlorine atoms on one chain and hydrogen atoms on the next, which prevents the chains from sliding over one another and makes the polymer tough and rigid (see **Figure 36.14**). The effect of these forces is greater if the polymer is regular, so that a hydrogen atom on one chain always lines up with a chlorine atom on the other. An irregular arrangement might allow two chlorines to line up, which would lead to repulsion between them.

Polar substituent groups can lead to increased attraction between the chains, while bulky side chains can reduce attraction by forcing the chains apart.

Modification of the properties of polymers

The properties of polymers can be 'tailored' by a number of methods to meet the requirements of a particular application.

A plasticiser can be added. Plasticisers consist of small molecules which get between the polymer chains and reduce the attraction between them, making the plastic more flexible. Their effect is rather like that of a lubricant.

Fillers may be added to make the plastic cheaper.

CHEMISTRY AROUND US

High and low density polythene

Low density poly(ethene) (polythene) is made by polymerising ethene at high pressure and high temperature via a radical mechanism like the one described earlier. This produces a polymer with a certain amount of chain branching – a consequence of the rather random nature of radical reactions. The branched chains do not pack together particularly well and the product is quite flexible, stretches well and has a fairly low density. These properties make it suitable for packaging (plastic bags), sheeting and insulation for electrical cables.

High density polythene is made at temperatures and pressures little higher than room conditions and uses a Ziegler–Natta-type catalyst. This results in a polymer with much less chain branching (around one branch for every 200 carbons on the main chain). The chains can pack together well, so that the polymer is described as highly crystalline. This makes the density of the plastic greater and its melting point higher. Typical uses are milk crates, buckets and bottles for which low density polythene would be insufficiently rigid.

High density polythene

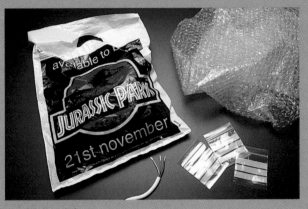

Low density polythene

Other additives may include pigments, flame retardants and stabilisers to prevent decomposition by UV light.

Another way of modifying the properties of polymers is by copolymerising: adding a small quantity of another monomer at the polymerisation stage.

Polymer properties are also affected by the relative molecular mass of the polymer, which can be controlled at the manufacturing stage. Polymers of low relative molecular mass (i.e. having short chains) will have a relatively low viscosity when molten, which may make them easier to process when they are being moulded.

It is also possible to introduce some **cross-linking** (with covalent bonds) into polymers. Cross-links join polymer chains and make the resulting polymer less elastic and more rigid (see **Figure 36.15**).

In general, polymers without cross-links soften on heating as molecular vibration pushes the chains apart and reduces the intermolecular forces between them. Such plastics are described as **thermoplastic** or **thermosoftening**. They can therefore be moulded by heating them, shaping them and allowing them to cool.

Cross-linked polymers do not usually soften on heating and are described as **thermosetting**. They have to be moulded into shape when manufactured. They do nor soften and eventually decompose on strong heating. Thermosetting plastics are useful where resistance to heat is important, for example in saucepan handles.

Elastomers

An important property of many polymers is that they are stretchy: when pulled they stretch and when the pull is released they return to their original shape. Materials which do this are called elastomers.

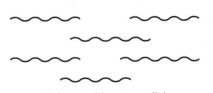

Polymer without cross-links

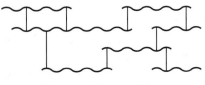

Polymer with cross-links

Figure 36.15 Cross-linking

Hint: The term copolymer is *not* short for condensation polymer. A copolymer is one with more than one monomer. For example, butadiene may be polymerised with about 25% styrene. This gives a polymer called styrene–butadiene rubber (SBR) which is suitable for tyres and shoe soles

They have this property because in the unstretched state the molecular chains are randomly coiled up; pulling them partly straightens out the chains and they return to a randomly coiled arrangement when released. For the substance to be an elastomer, the molecular chains must be free to move. That is, the material must be above its glass temperature, T_g, (see the box 'The Structure of Glass' in Chapter 30).

Condensation polymers

Condensation polymers are normally made from two different monomers, each of which has two functional groups. For example, a diol and a dicarboxylic acid would react together to give a polyester by eliminating molecules of water (**Figure 36.16**). The same polymer could have been produced from a diacid dichloride rather than a dicarboxylic acid, in which case hydrogen chloride would have been eliminated instead of water.

Figure 36.16 Making a polyester

Other common synthetic condensation polymers are given in **Table 36.3**. Manufacture of condensation polymers can usually be achieved simply by mixing the monomers if they are reactive enough.

Cross-linking can be brought about by adding to the reaction mixture a small amount of a compound with *three* functional groups. For example, polyesters can be cross-linked by addition of some propane-1,2,3-triol. The cross-linked resins obtained are called alkyd resins and are used in paints (see the box 'Paint' in this chapter).

Silicones

Silicones are the odd ones out in this chapter in that they are not wholly organic polymers, the backbone of the molecule being an Si—O—Si chain and R an organic group:

$$-\overset{\displaystyle R}{\underset{\displaystyle R}{\overset{|}{\underset{|}{Si}}}}-O-\overset{\displaystyle R}{\underset{\displaystyle R}{\overset{|}{\underset{|}{Si}}}}-O-\overset{\displaystyle R}{\underset{\displaystyle R}{\overset{|}{\underset{|}{Si}}}}-$$

Silicones have a wide range of useful properties:

● They are water-repellent and are used for waterproofing fabrics.
● They are lubricants and are added to polishes.
● They have non-stick ability and are used to coat the backing paper which protects self-adhesive stickers and sticking plasters (see also the box 'Silicones' in Chapter 30).

Silicones have a wide variety of uses

Table 36.3 Condensation polymers

Monomer A	Monomer B	Linkage	Name	Molecule eliminated
dicarboxylic acid	diol	polyester	polyester e.g. Terylene	H_2O
diacid dichloride	diol	polyester	polyester	HCl
dicarboxylic acid	diamine	polyamide	polyamide, e.g. nylon	H_2O
diacid dichloride	diamine	polyamide	polyamide	HCl
urea	methanal	urea–methanal	urea–methanal	H_2O
phenol	methanal	phenol–methanal	phenol–methanal, e.g. Bakelite	H_2O
diisocyanate	diol	polyurethane	polyurethane	none, so strictly polyurethanes are not condensation polymers although they have two different monomers
dialkylsilanediol		silicone	silicone	H_2O

Paint

Paint consists of two main components, a **pigment** which provides the colour and a **vehicle**, the liquid mixture by which the pigment is applied to the surface. The vehicle itself is in two parts: a **binder**, which binds the pigment to the surface, and a **solvent**, a fairly volatile liquid which evaporates after the paint has been applied, leaving the binder and pigment behind on the surface. The volatility of the solvent is important: if it is too great, the paint will dry too quickly and be difficult to apply; if it is not volatile enough, the paint will dry too slowly and tend to form runs on the painted surface. In emulsion paint, the solvent is water, in gloss it is usually a mixture of hydrocarbons, though water-based glosses are also on the market.

The most important white pigment is titanium(IV) oxide (coated with silica and alumina), which scatters light well and is chemically inert so that the paint does not 'yellow'. Colours are provided by organic dyes such as azo dyes (see the box 'Dyes', Chapter 35) or transition metal compounds.

Perhaps the most important component is the binder. In gloss paints, this is usually an alkyd resin: a polyester which is cross-linked by triol groups. As the paint dries, the alkyd resin reacts with oxygen in the air to form a polymer which is insoluble in the solvent. The number of cross-links is critical: too many and the film would be brittle. Some flexibility is required to cope with expansion of the surface caused by temperature changes or absorption of water. Paints also contain additives to control viscosity and to prevent the paint separating in the can during storage.

$$HO-\overset{\overset{\displaystyle O}{\|}}{C}-A-\overset{\overset{\displaystyle O}{\|}}{C}-OH \qquad \text{is a dicarboxylic acid}$$

$$HO-B-OH \qquad \text{is a diol}$$

$$HO-\overset{\overset{\displaystyle OH}{|}}{X}-OH \qquad \text{is a triol}$$

Triol groups

36.3 Summary

• Polymers are	large molecules made of many small molecules (monomers) linked together.
• Amino acids are bifunctional compounds with the groups	$-NH_2$ and $-CO_2H$.
• Their general formula is	$H_2N-CHR-CO_2H$
• Peptides are	poly(amino acids) with fewer than 50 amino acids.
• Proteins are peptides with	more than 50 amino acids.
• The primary structure of a protein refers to	its amino acid sequence.
• The secondary structure refers to	its usually helical shape maintained largely by hydrogen bonding.
• The tertiary structure refers to	the folding of the helix.
• The primary structure of proteins may be investigated by	hydrolysis followed by 2-way paper chromatography to identify the fragments.
• Enzymes are	protein-based catalysts found in biological systems.

● As catalysts, enzymes are both	very efficient and very specific.
● Enzymes are easily denatured by	moderately high temperatures and changes in pH.
● Enzymes work most efficiently at	an optimum temperature and pH.
● Addition polymers are produced by	linking unsaturated monomers.
● The empirical formula of an addition polymer is the same as that of	the monomer.
● Condensation polymers are formed from	monomers with two functional groups.
● In condensation polymerisation reactions, small molecules are	eliminated.
● Ziegler–Natta-type catalysts can produce	geometrically regular addition polymers.
● Thermoplastic plastics are ones which	soften on heating.
● Thermosetting plastics are ones which	do not soften on heating.
● Thermosetting polymers generally have many	cross-links between their chains.

36.4 Practice questions

1. Two polymerisation reactions may be represented by the following equations:

$$nCH_2{=}CHCl \longrightarrow \ {+}CH_2{-}CHCl\ {)}_n$$
$$\text{monomer A} \qquad\qquad \text{polymer A}$$

polymer B

(a) Give the names of:
 (i) monomer A   (ii) polymer A
(b) Name the type of polymerisation involved in the formation of:
 (i) polymer A
 (ii) polymer B
(c) What molecule is eliminated in the formation of polymer B?

2. An octapeptide was partially hydrolysed and produced the following fragments:
Asp-Arg-Val; Ile-His-Pro; Val-Tyr-Ile; Pro-Phe; Arg-Val-Tyr.
  What is the amino acid sequence of the octapeptide?

3. Suggest how you might shorten the average chain length when making a polyester from a diol and a dicarboxylic acid.

36.5 Examination questions

1. This question is concerned with the molecular interactions between the polymer chains in various semi-crystalline plastic materials in common use.

Chain unit of polymer	Melting temperature /°C	Strongest type of bonding *between* chains
—CH₂—CH₂— Poly(ethene) low density	115	....
—CH₂—CH₂— Poly(ethene) high density	138	....
—O—CH₂—O—CH₂— Poly(oxymethylene)	180	Dipole/Dipole
Terylene	265	....
Nylon 66	265	....
Bakelite	—	Covalent

(a) Copy and complete the right-hand column to show the strongest type of bonding present between polymer chains.

(b) (i) Why are the densities of the two types of poly(ethene) different?
(ii) Why is the melting temperature of high density poly(ethene) greater than that of low density poly(ethene)?

(c) Why is the melting temperature of bakelite not given?

(d) Suggest **four** further pieces of data that you would like to see included in the table if you wished to evaluate the suitability of various polymers for use as a rope on board a boat.
[London (Nuffield) 1997]

2. (a) Explain the term *polymerisation*.
(b) Polymers found in natural materials can be formed by the reaction between amino acids.
(i) Draw the graphical formula of the product formed when two molecules of alanine, $CH_3CH(NH_2)COOH$, react together.
(ii) Give the name of the important linkage formed and draw a ring round it on the formula drawn in (b)(i).
(iii) Give the name of the type of naturally occurring polymer containing this linkage.

(c) Poly(ethene) is an example of a synthetic polymer. It is manufactured in two main forms, low density poly(ethene) and high density poly(ethene).
(i) Write an equation to represent the polymerisation of ethene.
(ii) What is the main structural difference between the polymer chains in the two main forms of poly(ethene)? Explain how this difference affects the densities of the polymers.
(iii) Give **one** further physical property that is affected by the structural difference given in (c)(ii).
(iv) Low density poly(ethene) is manufactured via a free radical mechanism. Draw a graphical formula to represent the free radical formed between a free radical, **R•**, and a molecule of ethene in the reaction.
(v) What type of catalyst is used in the manufacture of high density poly(ethene)?

(d) Poly(ethene) is a non-biodegradable plastic.
(i) Explain the term *non-biodegradable*.
(ii) Give **one** environmental benefit of using biodegradable plastics.
(iii) Developing biodegradable plastics involves compromise. Suggest **one** factor that requires careful consideration and explain your choice.
[AEB 1998]

3. (a) Explain, with an example, what is meant by the term *addition polymerisation*.
(b) The structure of two polymers **A** and **B** are shown.
(i) Draw the structures of the monomers required to make both **A** and **B**.

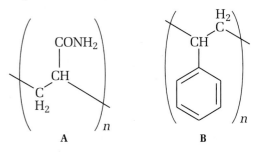

A   B

(ii) Which of the two polymers **A** and **B** is more likely to be suitable for the storage of a concentrated aqueous solution of sodium hydroxide? Give reasons for your choice.
[Oxford 1997]

4. One of the constituents of the fabric Lycra, used in making sports clothing, is a polyether with the formula-type

$$\left[CH_2-CH_2-O\right]_n$$

This constituent gives softness and stretchiness to the fabric whereas another polymer gives Lycra its strength and elasticity. This is a polyurethane constituent with a formula such as

$$\left[\begin{array}{c} C-N-\bigcirc-N-C-O-CH_2-CH_2-O \\ \parallel\ \mid\ \ \ \ \ \ \ \ \ \ \ \mid\ \parallel \\ O\ \ H\ \ \ \ \ \ \ \ \ \ \ H\ \ O \end{array}\right]_n$$

(a) Assuming that the polymer is made by loss of water molecules, give the formula of its monomer.

(b) What name is given to the type of polymerisation illustrated by the polyether example?

[London (Nuffield) 1998]

5. A naturally occurring dipeptide, **X**, has the molecular formula $C_8H_{17}O_3N_3$. It can be broken down into its two constituent amino acids, **A** and **B**, by heating with moderately concentrated hydrochloric acid. The two amino acids can then be separated by paper chromatography using a mixture of butan-1-ol, ethanoic acid and water as the solvent.

Amino acid **A** has an R_f value of 0.26 and amino acid **B** has an R_f value of 0.14.

(a) Draw a labelled diagram **to scale** of the resulting chromatogram marking the positions of the original and final spots and the solvent front.

(b) (i) Only amino acid **B** is optically active. What structural feature must be present in **B** but absent in **A** which causes the plane of plane-polarised light to be rotated?

(ii) Draw the displayed formula of the optically inactive amino acid, **A**.

(iii) Deduce the molecular and a possible structural formula of **B**.

(iv) Suggest a structural formula for the dipeptide **X**.

(c) (i) How soluble would you expect the dipeptide **X** to be in water? Justify your answer.

(ii) Would you expect a solution of **X** in water to be acidic, neutral or alkaline? Justify your answer.

[London (Nuffield) 1997]

6. (a) (i) Give the **general** formula, **A**, for a naturally occurring amino acid.

(ii) Use formula **A** to explain, with the aid of diagrams, the meaning of *chirality*.

(iii) A polyamide forms when **A** is polymerised. In what major way does the structure of this polymer differ from that of a protein.

(b) (i) What is a Brønsted–Lowry base?

(ii) Write an equation to show **A** behaving as a Brønsted–Lowry base.

(c) Kevlar is a very strong, flexible, polymeric, aromatic amide. It is used for reinforcing tyres, and for bullet-proof vests. Part of its polymer chain is shown below.

$$-OC-\bigcirc-CONH-\bigcirc-NHCO-\bigcirc-CO-$$

Draw a diagram, using full structural formula, illustrating the forces between at least three polymer chains in Kevlar, and use it to suggest reasons for the described applications of Kevlar.

[Oxford 1997]

7. The dipeptide isoleucylserine, ile-ser, consists of two amino acid 'residues' joined by a peptide link. In the following incomplete diagram of the dipeptide, the peptide link itself has been omitted.

$$\begin{array}{ccc} H_2N-CH- & & -CH-CO_2H \\ \mid & & \mid \\ CHCH_2CH_3 & & CH_2OH \\ \mid & & \\ CH_3 & & \end{array}$$

(a) Copy and complete the diagram by inserting the peptide link.

(b) On the diagram circle each of the **three** chiral centres.

(c) What procedure could be used to obtain a mixture of the two amino acids from isoleucylserine?

(d) The mixture resulting from (c) may be concentrated and separated by paper chromatography. The resulting chromatogram would approximate to the following:

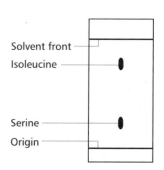

Show, on a copy of the diagram, how you would determine the R_f value for isoleucine.

[London (Nuffield) 1998, part]

Synthetic routes

Robots in the lab

Visit a laboratory belonging to a company which discovers possible new drug substances (called 'new chemical entities' or NCEs in the jargon) and you are likely to find robots doing at least some of the work. These are not androids in lab coats: they are essentially motorised syringes under computer control, but they can take over a lot of routine operations in synthetic organic chemistry.

Drug companies deal in 'libraries' of compounds: sets of related compounds, which they then screen for possible activity as drugs. Thanks to recent advances in methods of rapid screening of compounds for activity, there is a demand for more and more compounds to be made. One method of doing this, called combinatorial chemistry, is to make libraries of compound trays often containing 96 sample tubes in an 8×12 array. With, for example, 8 alcohols and 12 acid chlorides, a set (or library) of 96 different esters can be made simply by mixing all possible combinations of alcohol and acid chloride. The robot can be programmed to do this quite simply and the tray of 96 esters can then be used for screening.

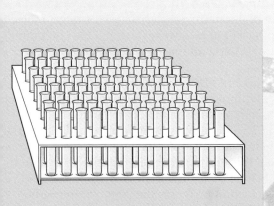

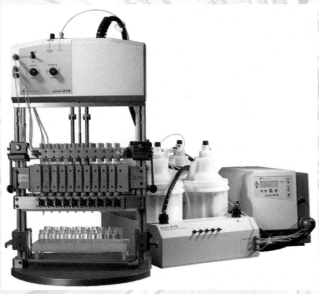

The above technique can be combined with another method called solid phase chemistry. Here, one of the starting materials is chemically bonded to plastic beads while a reagent in solution is added to it. The product remains bonded to the bead which makes purification of the product simple: any unwanted solutions can simply be washed away. If required, further reaction steps can be done with the product still bonded to the beads. When required, the product can be released from the bead by reversing the reaction which bonded it in the first place.

Introduction

This chapter deals with the problem of devising a series of reactions fo making ('synthesising') a given molecule, often called the target molecule. Sometimes (often, in exam questions) you will be told the molecule from which you must start. In real life, the starting molecule will be chosen on the grounds of availability, expense and reactivity along with other considerations like ease of storage, toxicity and so on

Synthesis of a target molecule is a common problem in industries that deal with drug or pesticide manufacture. Frequently a molecule is found to have a particular pharmaceutical effect, for example, as an antibiotic. Drug companies may then synthesise, on a small scale, a number of compounds of similar structures and screen them for possib antibiotic properties. Any promising compounds may then be made in larger quantities for thorough investigation of their effectiveness, side effects and so on. A large scale method of manufacture must then be devised for any commercially viable products.

In this chapter we will be looking at:
- using the organic reactions we have met in earlier chapters to plan how to convert a starting material into a target molecule

---

CONCEPT CHECKPOINTS

The following basic ideas are used in this chapter. You may revise some of these topics elsewhere in the book.

The reactions of the functional groups we have met:
- alkanes (Chapter 19)
- alkenes (Chapter 20)
- haloalkanes (Chapter 21)
- alcohols (Chapter 22)
- arenes, haloarenes and phenols (Chapter 32)
- carbonyl compounds (Chapter 33)
- carboxylic acids and their derivatives (Chapter 34)
- organic nitrogen compounds (Chapter 35)

Hint: Remember that no reaction will ever have a 100% yield and that, say, a three-step synthesis in which each step has an 80% yield will produce an overall yield of $80 \times 80 \times 80\% = 51.2\%$.

Q What will be the yield of a three-step synthesis in which each step has a 50% yield?

Answer: 12.5%

37.1 Basic ideas

If you are given the problem of devising a scheme for making target molecule 'X' from starting material 'A', always start by writing down the displayed formula of the starting material and the target molecu]

Then one way of proceeding is to write down all the compounds which can be made from A and all the ways in which X can be prepared (**Figure 37.1**).

You may then see how B, C, D or E can be converted, in one or more steps to T, U, V, W. It is important to keep the number of step as small as possible to maximise the yield of the target.

Sometimes you will be able to see straight away that a particular reaction will be needed. If, for example, the target molecule has one more carbon atom than the starting material, it is almost certain tha the reaction of cyanide ions with a haloalkane will be needed at some stage, since this reaction increases the length of the carbon chain by one. For example:

$$CH_3Br + CN^- \longrightarrow CH_3CN + Br^-$$
bromomethane　　　　　ethanenitrile

Similarly, if the target molecule has one fewer carbon atom than the starting material, the Hofmann degradation of amides, which reduc the carbon chain length by one, will be required, for example:

$$CH_3C\overset{\displaystyle O}{\underset{\displaystyle NH_2}{\big|}} + Br_2 + 4NaOH \longrightarrow$$
ethanamide

$$CH_3NH_2 + Na_2CO_3 + 2NaBr + 2H_2O$$
methylamine

Hint: It goes without saying that you need to recall the reactions of all the functional groups you have met.

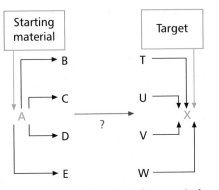

Figure 37.1 Devising a synthesis of compound X from compound A

37.2 Methods of preparation of functional groups

These have been given in the chapter about each functional group but are listed here as a summary (**Table 37.1**). Only the basic reaction has been given here. Fuller details of reagents, conditions, etc. will be found in the appropriate chapter. Remember that some compounds are readily available commercially: for example, alkanes, alkenes and a number of aromatic compounds which are derived from crude oil or coal tar. These rarely need to be made in the laboratory and are not listed here.

The interrelationships between these functional groups are shown in **Figure 37.2**.

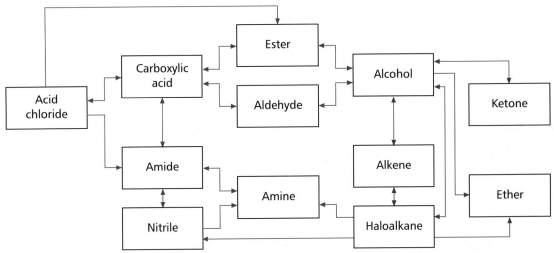

Figure 37.2 Interrelationships between functional groups

Hint: An ether is a compound containing the functional group R—O—R.

37.3 Reagents used in organic chemistry

Oxidising agents

A commonly used oxidising agent is acidified dichromate(VI) ions, $Cr_2O_7^{2-}/H^+$. This will oxidise primary alcohols to aldehydes and aldehydes to carboxylic acids. Secondary alcohols are oxidised to ketones. A similar oxidising agent is a solution of manganate(VII) ions, which may be used in acid, neutral or alkaline solution.

Reducing agents

Different reducing reagents have different capabilities. Lithium tetrahydridoaluminate(III), $LiAlH_4$, will reduce C=O or C≡N, but not C=C. It is used in an ether solution followed by the addition of water.

Sodium tetrahydridoborate(III) is a similar but milder reducing agent. It also reduces C=O but not C=C. It can be used in aqueous solution.

Table 37.1 Summary of methods of synthesising functional groups. The table refers to non-aromatic compounds, i.e. R is an alkyl or substituted alkyl group

1. Alkenes

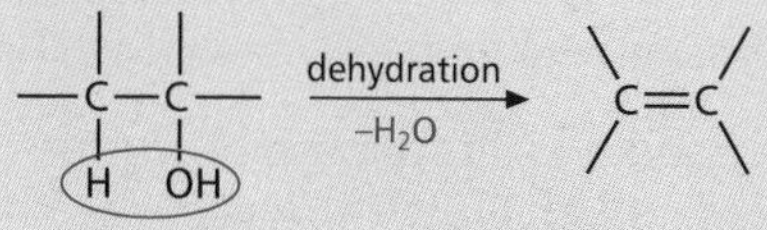

alcohol $\xrightarrow[\text{dehydration} \\ -H_2O]{}$ alkene

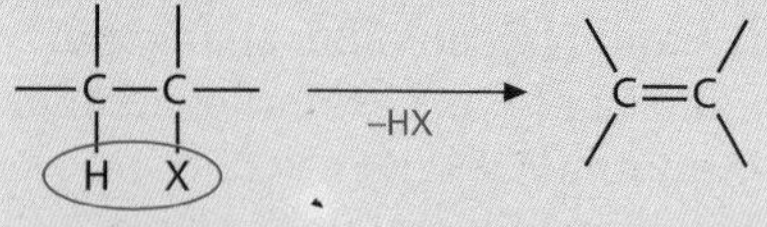

haloalkane $\xrightarrow{-HX}$ alkene

2. Alkynes

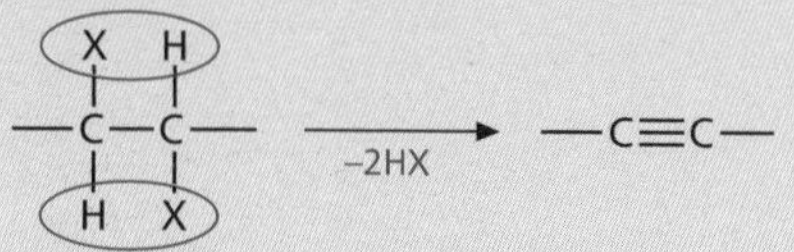

dihaloalkane $\xrightarrow{-2HX}$ $-C\equiv C-$

calcium carbide $Ca^{2+}C\equiv C^{2-} \xrightarrow{H_2O} H-C\equiv C-H$ Ethyne only

3. Haloalkanes

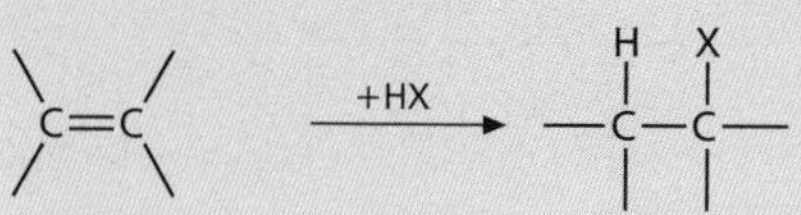

alkene $\xrightarrow{+HX}$ haloalkane   Remember Markovnikov's rule!

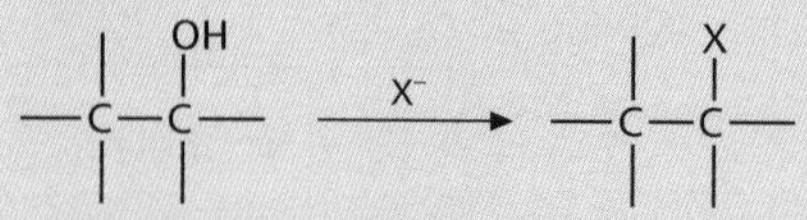

alcohol $\xrightarrow{X^-}$ haloalkane   Many different reagents, e.g. PCl_5, I_2/P, HX, etc.

4. Alcohols

ester $R'-C(=O)-O-R \xrightarrow[\text{hydrolysis}]{H_2O} ROH$ H^+ or OH^- catalyst

haloalkane $\xrightarrow{OH^-}$ alcohol

aldehyde $\xrightarrow{\text{reduction}} R-CH(OH)-H$ 1° alcohol

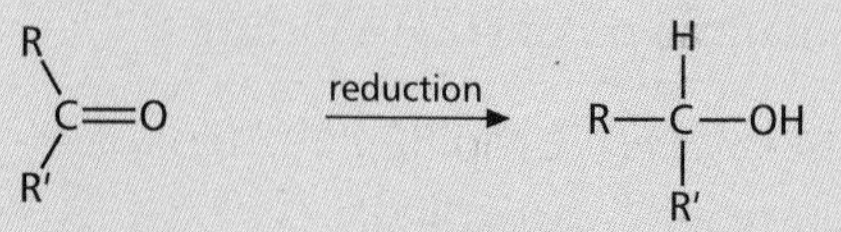

ketone $\xrightarrow{\text{reduction}} R-CH(OH)-R'$ 2° alcohol

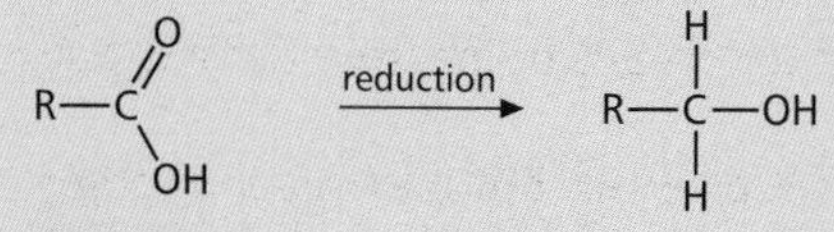

carboxylic acid $R-C(=O)-OH \xrightarrow{\text{reduction}} R-CH_2-OH$ 1° alcohol

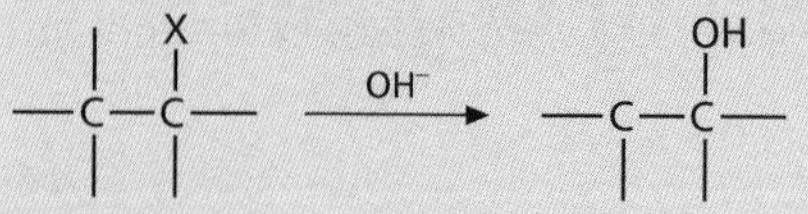

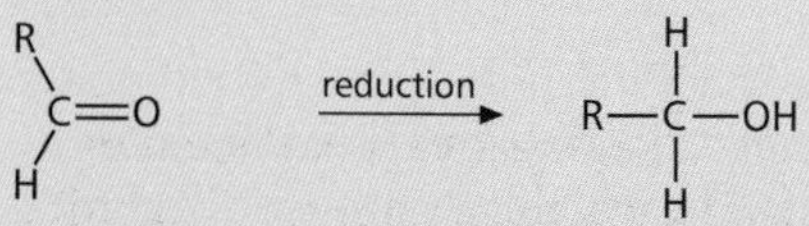

Notes

amine $R-NH_2 \xrightarrow[\text{(NaNO}_2/\text{HCl)}]{HNO_2} R-OH$

5. Aldehydes

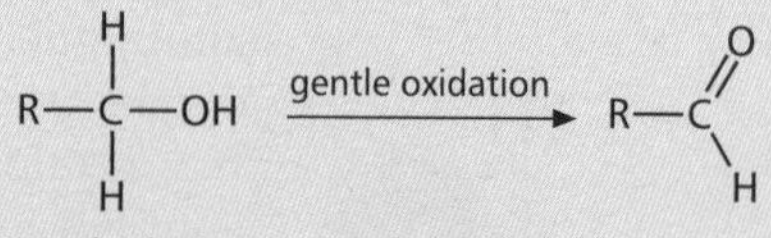

1° alcohol $R-CH_2-OH \xrightarrow{\text{gentle oxidation}} R-CHO$ Distil off product to prevent further oxidation

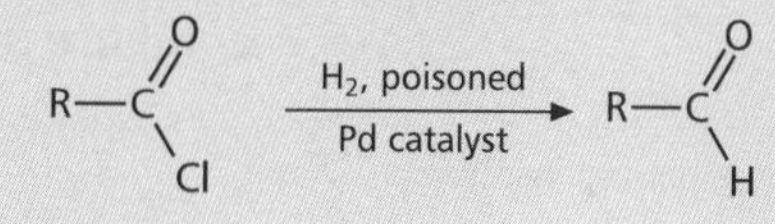

acid chloride $R-C(=O)-Cl \xrightarrow[\text{Pd catalyst}]{H_2, \text{ poisoned}} R-CHO$

6. Ketones

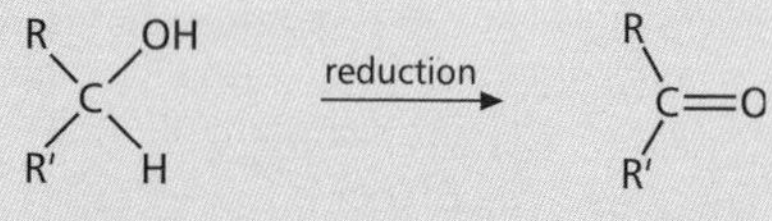

2° alcohol $R-C(OH)(R')-H \xrightarrow{\text{reduction}} R-C(=O)-R'$

7. Carboxylic acids

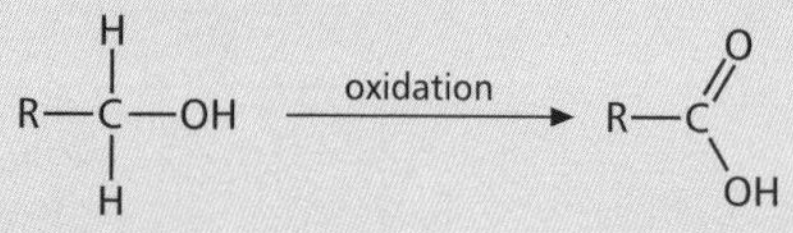

1° alcohol $R-CH_2-OH \xrightarrow{\text{oxidation}} R-COOH$

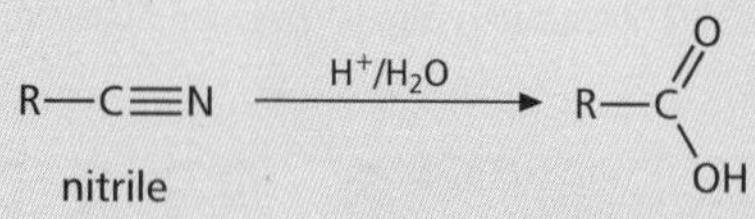

nitrile $R-C\equiv N \xrightarrow{H^+/H_2O} R-COOH$

amide $R-C(=O)-NH_2 \xrightarrow{H^+/H_2O} R-COOH$

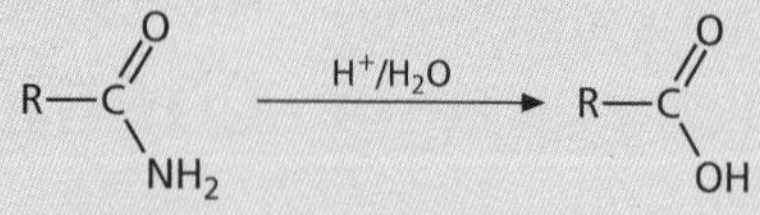

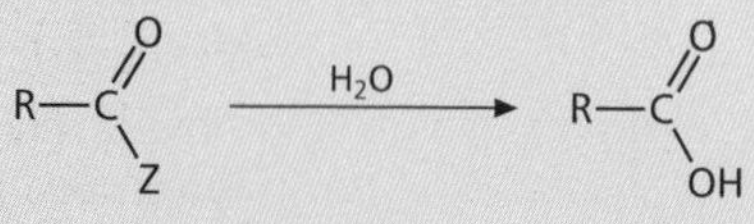

other acid derivative $R-C(=O)-Z \xrightarrow{H_2O} R-COOH$

8. Acid derivatives

These can be interconverted by use of a suitable nucleophile, W^-:

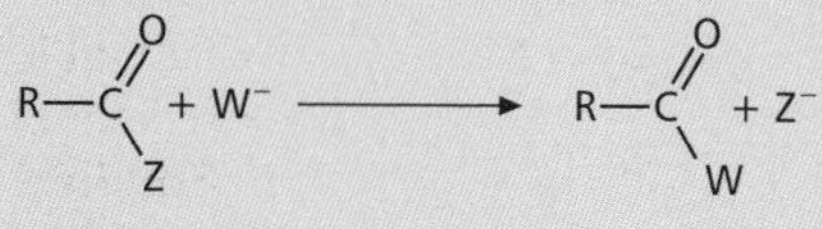

acid derivative $R-C(=O)-Z + W^- \longrightarrow R-C(=O)-W + Z^-$

Notes

9. Amines

			Notes
$R—NO_2$ **nitroalkane**	$\xrightarrow{\text{reduction}}$	$R—NH_2$	

$$R—\overset{\displaystyle O}{\underset{\displaystyle NH_2}{C}} \quad \xrightarrow{\text{reduction}} \quad R—\overset{\displaystyle H}{\underset{\displaystyle H}{C}}—NH_2$$

amide

$$R—C{\equiv}N \quad \xrightarrow{\text{reduction}} \quad R—\overset{\displaystyle H}{\underset{\displaystyle H}{C}}—NH_2$$

nitrile

			Notes
$R—X$ **haloalkane**	$\xrightarrow{NH_3}$	$R—NH_2$	Also 2°, 3°, 4° compounds
$R—OH$ **alcohol**	$\xrightarrow{NH_3}$	$R—NH_2$	Also 2°, 3° compounds

$$R—\overset{\displaystyle O}{\underset{\displaystyle NH_2}{C}} \quad \xrightarrow[\text{degradation}]{\text{Hofmann}} \quad R—NH_2$$

amide

The product has 1 carbon less than the starting material

10. Nitriles

			Notes

$$R—\overset{\displaystyle O}{\underset{\displaystyle N H_2}{C}} \quad \xrightarrow[-H_2O]{\text{dehydration}} \quad R—C{\equiv}N$$

amide

$$R—C{=}N{-}OH \quad \xrightarrow[-H_2O]{\text{dehydration}} \quad R—C{\equiv}N$$

oxime

$R—X$	$\xrightarrow{CN^-}$	$R—C{\equiv}N$	The product has 1 more carbon atom than the starting material

Both these reducing agents will reduce polar unsaturated groups, such as $C^{\delta+}{=}O^{\delta-}$, but not non-polar ones, such as $C{=}C$. This is because both reagents generate the nucleophile H^-, which attacks $C^{\delta+}$ but not the electron-rich $C{=}C$.

To reduce $C{=}C$ but not $C{=}O$, hydrogen with a nickel catalyst is used.

Reducing agents such as iron or tin and hydrochloric acid may be used to reduce $R—NO_2$ to $R—NH_2$.

Dehydrating agents

Phosphorus pentoxide is frequently used to remove a molecule of water from an organic compound, for example, to convert an amide,

$$R—\overset{\displaystyle O}{\underset{\displaystyle NH_2}{C}}$$

, into a nitrile, $R—C{\equiv}N$, or an alcohol to an alkene.

Alcohols can also be converted to alkenes by passing their vapours over heated aluminium oxide.

Sulphuric acid is also a dehydrating agent but may react in other ways (for example, it reacts with alkenes to give alkyl hydrogensulphates) and so phosphorus pentoxide is preferred.

37.4 Examples of reaction schemes

How can we convert 1-bromopropane into propanoic acid?

$$H-\underset{\underset{H}{|}}{\overset{\overset{H}{|}}{C}}-\underset{\underset{H}{|}}{\overset{\overset{H}{|}}{C}}-\underset{\underset{H}{|}}{\overset{\overset{H}{|}}{C}}-Br \xrightarrow{?} H-\underset{\underset{H}{|}}{\overset{\overset{H}{|}}{C}}-\underset{\underset{H}{|}}{\overset{\overset{H}{|}}{C}}-\overset{\overset{\displaystyle O}{\diagup\diagdown}}{C}\underset{O-H}{}$$

> **Q** Cover up the products which can be made from 1-bromopropane. Can you remember them all? Cover up the materials which can be converted into propanoic acid. Can you remember them all?

Both the starting material and the target have the same number of carbon atoms, so no alteration to the carbon skeleton is needed. Now write down all the compounds which can be made in one step from 1-bromopropane and all those from which propanoic acid can be made in one step as shown in **Figure 37.3**.

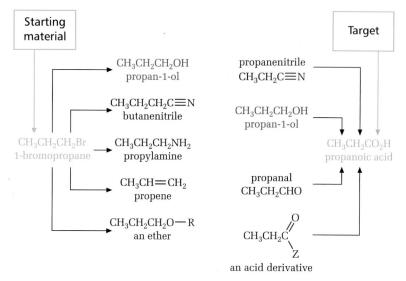

Figure 37.3 Devising a synthesis of propanoic acid from 1-bromopropane

In this case two of the compounds are the same. 1-bromopropane can be converted into propan-1-ol (in red) which can be converted into propanoic acid. So the conversion we require can be done in two steps:

(i) $CH_2CH_2CH_2Br$ $\xrightarrow{\text{reflux with OH}^-(aq)}$ $CH_3CH_2CH_2OH$
        1-bromopropane   propan-1-ol

(ii) $CH_3CH_2CH_2OH$ $\xrightarrow{\text{reflux with Cr}_2O_7^{2-}/H^+}$ $CH_3CH_2CO_2H$
        propan-1-ol   propanoic acid

Both these reactions have a good yield.

How can we convert ethanol into propylamine?

$$H-\underset{\underset{H}{|}}{\overset{\overset{H}{|}}{C}}-\underset{\underset{H}{|}}{\overset{\overset{H}{|}}{C}}-O-H \xrightarrow{?} H-\underset{\underset{H}{|}}{\overset{\overset{H}{|}}{C}}-\underset{\underset{H}{|}}{\overset{\overset{H}{|}}{C}}-\underset{\underset{H}{|}}{\overset{\overset{H}{|}}{C}}-N\underset{\diagdown H}{\overset{\diagup H}{}}$$

Q Cover up the products which can be made from ethanol. Can you remember them all? Cover up the materials which can be converted into propylamine. Can you remember them all?

Propylamine has one more carbon atom than ethanol. This suggests that the formation of a nitrile is involved at some stage.

Write down all the compounds which can be made from ethanol and all the compounds from which the propylamine can be made (**Figure 37.4**). Here, no compound which can be made in one step

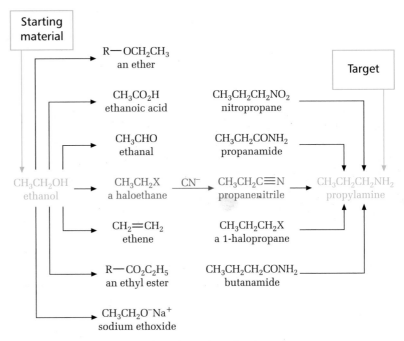

Figure 37.4 Devising a synthesis of propylamine from ethanol

from the starting material can be converted into the product, so more than two steps must be required. But we already know that the formation of a nitrile is required. A haloethane can be converted into propanenitrile, so the synthesis can be completed in three steps:

(i) CH_3CH_2OH $\xrightarrow{\text{reflux with } KBr/H^+}$ CH_3CH_2Br

           ethanol   bromoethane

(ii) CH_3CH_2Br $\xrightarrow{CN^-}$ $CH_3CH_2C{\equiv}N$

         bromoethane   propanenitrile

(iii) $CH_3CH_2C{\equiv}N$ $\xrightarrow{LiAlH_4}$ $CH_3CH_2CH_2NH_2$

       propanenitrile   propylamine

Chloroethane or iodoethane could have been chosen instead of bromoethane.

How can we convert propanoic acid to ethanol?

$$H-\underset{\underset{H}{|}}{\overset{\overset{H}{|}}{C}}-\underset{\underset{H}{|}}{\overset{\overset{H}{|}}{C}}-\overset{\overset{O}{\|}}{C}\diagdown_{O-H} \quad \xrightarrow{?} \quad H-\underset{\underset{H}{|}}{\overset{\overset{H}{|}}{C}}-\underset{\underset{H}{|}}{\overset{\overset{H}{|}}{C}}-O-H$$

Ethanol has one carbon atom less than propanoic acid, so one stage almost certainly involves the Hofmann degradation of an amide. This immediately suggests that the first step should be the conversion of propanoic acid to propanamide and the second should be the

Hofmann degradation of propanamide to ethylamine. Ethylamine can be converted to ethanol by treatment with nitrous acid.

1. $CH_3CH_2CO_2H$ $\xrightarrow[\text{heat}]{NH_3, \text{ then}}$ $CH_3CH_2CONH_2$
      propanoic acid   propanamide

2. $CH_3CH_2CONH_2$ $\xrightarrow{Br_2/NaOH}$ $CH_3CH_2NH_2$
      propanamide   ethylamine

3. $CH_3CH_2NH_2$ $\xrightarrow[(HCl/NaNO_2)]{HNO_2}$ CH_3CH_2OH
      ethylamine   ethanol

How can we convert propan-1-ol into bromopropanone?

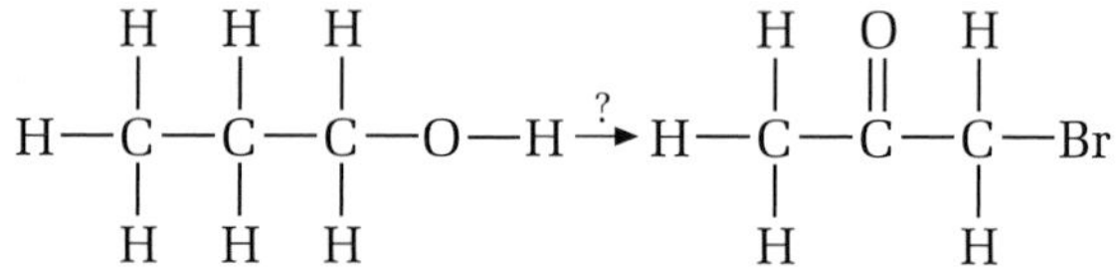

Both propan-1-ol and bromopropanone have the same number of carbon atoms. Write down all the compounds that can be made from propan-1-ol and and all those from which bromopropanone can be made (**Figure 37.5**).

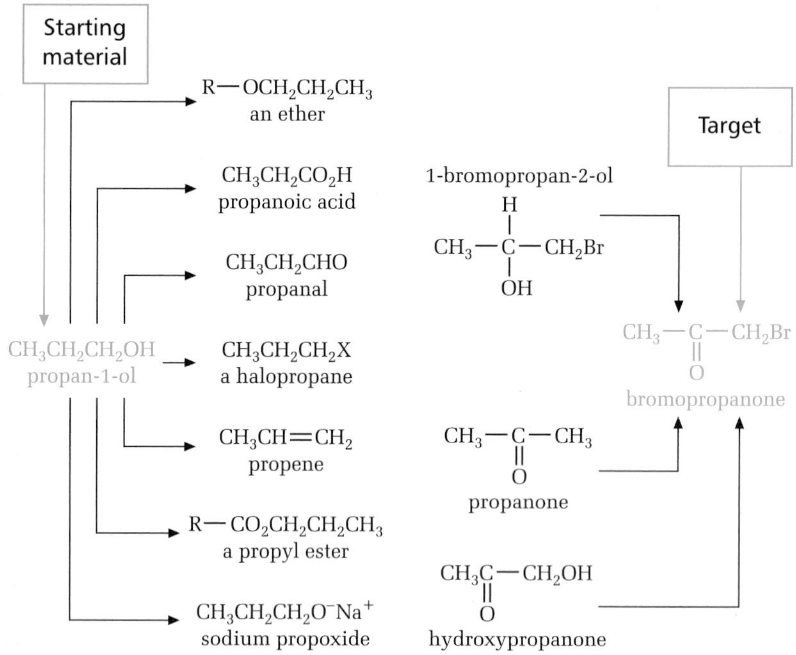

Figure 37.5 Devising a synthesis of bromopropanone from propan-1-ol

No two are the same, so a two-step synthesis is not possible. Notice that all the compounds that can be converted to bromopropanone have an oxygen atom bonded to the second carbon atom. This is the key to this synthesis. How can we get a functional group onto carbon number two when virtually all the substances we can make from the starting material have their functional groups on carbon number one? The exception is propene, $CH_3CH{=}CH_2$. Addition of H—Z to this obeys Markovnikov's rule (section 20.4) so that the functional group will be attached to carbon number two. Addition of sulphuric acid followed by water yields propan-2-ol which can be converted by oxidation into propanone which (from Figure 37.5), can be converted into bromopropanone. So the conversion can be achieved by:

1. $CH_3CH_2CH_2OH$ $\xrightarrow[\text{Al}_2\text{O}_3]{\text{hot vapour}}$ $CH_3{-}CH{=}CH_2$

        propan-1-ol   propene

2. $CH_3{-}CH{=}CH_2$ $\xrightarrow[\text{H}_2\text{O}]{\text{H}_2\text{SO}_4 \text{ then}}$ $CH_3{-}CH(OH){-}CH_3$

         propene   propan-2-ol

3. $CH_3{-}CH(OH){-}CH_3$ $\xrightarrow[\text{heat}]{\text{Cr}_2\text{O}_7^{2-}/\text{H}^+}$ $CH_3{-}CO{-}CH_3$

         propan-2-ol   propanone

4. $CH_3{-}CO{-}CH_3$ $\xrightarrow{\text{Br}_2/\text{H}^+}$ $CH_3{-}CO{-}CH_2Br$

         propanone   bromopropanone

Hint: Dehydration followed by addition of sulphuric acid, then water, is a useful way of converting a primary alcohol to a secondary alcohol.

As an alternative to step 2 we could have added, say, HBr to give 2-bromopropane and then refluxed with aqueous alkali to give propan-2-ol. However, it is generally better to use the minimum number of steps to get the maximum yield.

FURTHER FOCUS

Industrial manufacture compared with laboratory synthesis

It is often the case that the industrial process used for manufacturing a particular chemical is different from that used in the laboratory. Some of the factors to be considered include:

- In the laboratory it is difficult to obtain very high temperatures and pressures.
- Raw material costs are much more important in an industrial process.
- Industrially it is very helpful if a product can be made by a continuous process rather than in small batches.
- The question of by-products is important. In a small-scale preparation they can be thrown away. Industrially this may present a large-scale disposal problem, particularly if any by-products are toxic or otherwise environmentally unacceptable. Ideally, by-products should be saleable too, in which case they are known as co-products. Failing this they should be innocuous and easily disposed of.
- The **energy balance** of an industrial process is important. The energy generated by exothermic processes can be used elsewhere in the plant or to offset energy requirements of endothermic processes. This is rarely a concern in laboratory preparations.
- Generally it is desirable to avoid elaborate purification procedures in large-scale processes.
- Ideally very toxic reactants such as cyanides would be avoided in industrial processes, while these might be acceptable in small quantities and under careful control in the laboratory.

Some of these points are illustrated by the laboratory and industrial preparations of propanone.

The obvious starting material for making propanone is propene. Propene is readily available from the cracking of petroleum fractions and is reactive because of its double bond.

The most likely laboratory synthesis would be:

1. $CH_3{-}\overset{\displaystyle H}{\underset{}{C}}{=}CH_2$ $\xrightarrow[\substack{\text{then H}_2\text{O}\\(\text{hydration})}]{\text{H}_2\text{SO}_4}$ $CH_3{-}\overset{\displaystyle H}{\underset{\displaystyle OH}{C}}{-}CH_3$

      propene   propan-2-ol

2. $CH_3{-}\overset{\displaystyle H}{\underset{\displaystyle OH}{C}}{-}CH_3$ $\xrightarrow[(\text{oxidation})]{\text{Cr}_2\text{O}_7^{2-}/\text{H}^+}$ $CH_3{-}\overset{}{\underset{\displaystyle O}{C}}{-}CH_3$

      propan-2-ol   propanone

In industry, some propanone is made by a similar route but the hydration is done by the direct reaction of steam and propene at 600 K with a catalyst of phosphoric(V) acid and silicon(IV) oxide. The oxidation is carried out using oxygen (obtained from air) as a cheap oxidising agent. At around 600 K and 2000 kPa pressure with a copper catalyst, propanone and hydrogen peroxide (a saleable co-product) are produced.

An alternative industrial process which produces propanone is the cumene process (see the box, 'The cumene process', Chapter 32), which involves reacting ethene with benzene, followed by oxidation, and cleavage of the hydroperoxide which is produced. The advantage of this apparently roundabout process is that phenol is also produced and, indeed, is the main product. Again, air is the source of the oxidising agent, which is much cheaper than dichromate ions. Yields of over 85% are obtained.

37.5 Practice questions

1. How would you convert in one step:
   (a) 1-bromobutane to pentanenitrile?
   (b) ethanol to ethanoic acid?
   (c) propanoic acid to propan-1-ol?
   (d) butene to butan-2-ol?
   (e) cyclohexanol to cyclohexene?

2. How would you convert in two steps:
   (a) ethene to ethanoic acid?
   (b) ethanol to propanenitrile?

   (c) propanoic acid to ethylamine?
   (d) phenylamine to phenol?
   (e) propanone to 2-bromopropane?
   (f) benzene to phenylamine?

3. How would you convert in three steps:
   (a) propan-1-ol to propanone?
   (b) ethene to ethane-1,2-dioyl dichloride?

37.6 Examination questions

1. This question relates to the following reaction scheme.

$$C_2H_5Br \xrightarrow{\text{step 1}} C_2H_5CN \xrightarrow{\text{step 2}} C_2H_5CH_2NH_2$$

$$\xrightarrow{\text{step 3}} C_2H_5CH_2OH$$

   (a) Give the reagents, the conditions required and the equation for step 1 and step 2.
   (b) (i) Give a mechanism for step 1.
       (ii) What type of mechanism is this?
   (c) The conversion of C_2H_5Br to $C_2H_5CH_2OH$ by this method is ineffective, not least because step 3 gives a very poor yield of only 7%. Outline an alternative synthetic route, stating clearly the reagents and conditions of the steps you suggest.

   [London 1997]

2. *Metoclopramide*, **F**, is an antagonist of dopamine receptors and can be used as an emetic.

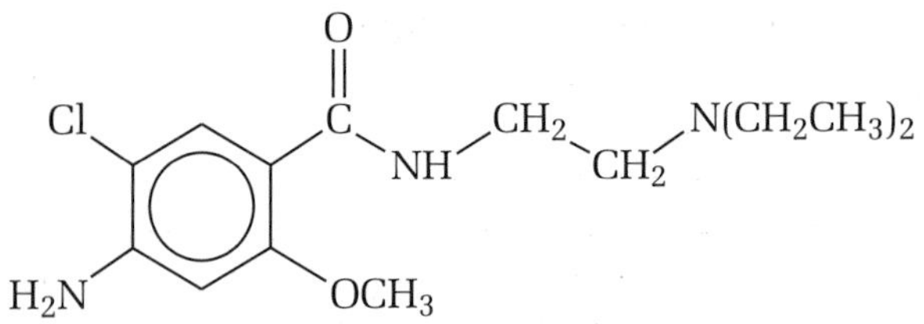

   F

   (a) Name the three nitrogen-containing functional groups in **F**.
   (b) Compound **G** (shown at the top of the next column) is to be assessed as a simple model for metoclopramide.
       Starting with 3-chlorobenzoic acid, aminoethane and standard reagents, suggest a

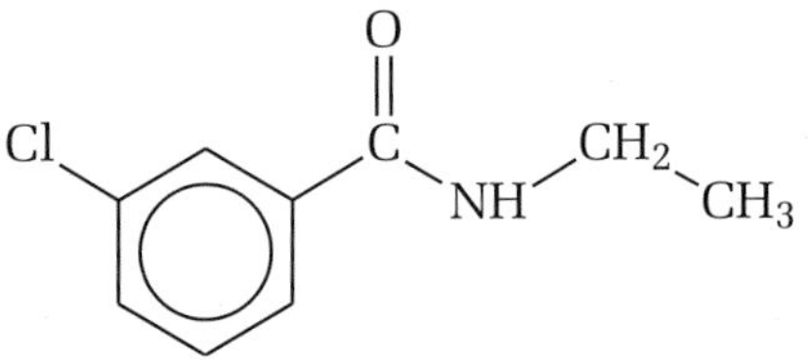

   G

   route by which **G** could be made (more than one stage may be needed). Give equations for your proposed reactions.
   (c) Predict the products of **G** with hot aqueous NaOH, giving your reasoning.
   [O & C (Salters) 1997, specimen]

3. (a) Devise routes for the synthesis of **G** and **H** from the natural product **J**. Your syntheses may involve more than one reaction; for each reaction give the reagent(s), essential conditions and the full structure of the product.

$$CH_3(CH_2)_7COOH$$
$$J$$

$$CH_3(CH_2)_7COOC_2H_5 \qquad\qquad CH_3(CH_2)_7NH_2$$
$$G \qquad\qquad\qquad\qquad H$$

   (b) Compound **G** is hydrolysed when warmed in solution with aqueous NaOH. Draw the mechanism for this reaction.
   [Oxford 1997]

4. Organic compounds which are used as drugs in medicine often have their structures modified in order to make them more hydrophilic (soluble in water) or lipophilic (soluble in fatty tissue). One such drug is chloramphenicol, **A**.

The —**CH₂OH** group in the molecule can be altered in the following ways:

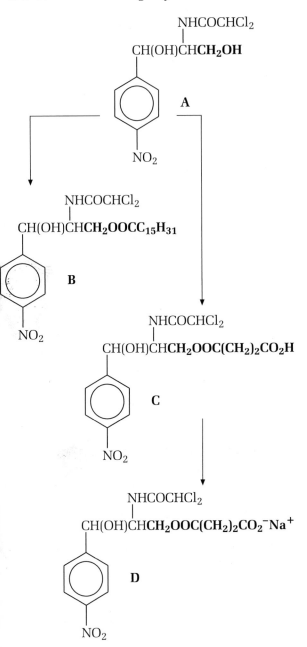

(a) (i)   Suggest which one of the compounds **A**, **B**, **C** or **D** would be most soluble in water and hence suitable for intravenous injection.
    (ii) Explain your reasoning.
(b) (i)   Which one of the compounds **A**, **B**, **C** or **D** would you expect to be least soluble in water and hence suitable to be administered to patients as a suspension in water?
    (ii) Give a reason for your answer.
(c) (i)   The conversion of **A** to **B** and that of **A** to **C** involves the same type of reaction. What type of reaction is this?

(ii)   Under what conditions is this type of reaction often brought about in the laboratory?
(iii) Give the formulae for the reagents required for the conversion of
        A to **B**;
        C to **D**.
(d) (i)   **Outline** a practical procedure by which a solid sample of **D** could be purified in the laboratory.
    (ii) Suggest how the purity of this sample might be checked.
(e) No matter which of the forms **B**, **C** or **D** is taken, the compound **A** is re-formed in the acidic conditions in the stomach by the same type of reaction. What type of reaction is this?
                                              [London (Nuffield) 1998]

5. The flow chart below summarises some of the organic reactions you have studied.

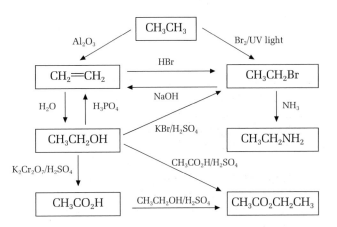

(a) Explain what is meant by the following reaction types. In each case select **one** example from the flow chart to illustrate your answer.
    ● free radical substitution
    ● nucleophilic substitution
    ● elimination
    ● oxidation
    ● esterification
(b) How can ethene be converted to ethane?
(c) An intermediate is sometimes isolated in the conversion of ethanol to ethanoic acid. What is its structural formula?
(d) Using the chart, or otherwise, plan a two-stage synthesis of propylamine, $CH_3CH_2CH_2NH_2$, starting from propan-1-ol. Give the name and formula of the product of the first stage of the synthesis and the reagents you would use for each stage.
                                              [London (Nuffield) 1998]

38 Identifying organic compounds

C H E M I S T R Y   N O W

The benzene mystery updated

The structure of benzene was a mystery to chemists for many years. Today, modern analytical techniques could quickly solve its structure.

The empirical formula, CH, could be found by combustion analysis: burning the compound and determining the amount of carbon dioxide and water produced.

The mass spectrum shows a molecular ion at M_r 78 indicating that the empirical formula is C_6H_6. There is also an $M + 1$ peak of 6% of the height of the parent ion, confirming that th molecule has six carbons.

Compared with the formula of a C_6 alkane (C_6H_{14}), benzene is eight hydrogens short. This implies that benzene has the equivalent of four double bonds or three double bonds and a ring

Next the infra-red (IR) and nuclear magnetic resonance (NMR) spectra would be run. The NMR spectrum shows just one peak, indicating that all the hydrogens are in identical environments, strongly suggesting a ring with one hydrogen attached to each carbon.

The IR spectrum shows no peak at about 1600 cm^{-1}, corresponding to C=C, confirming the result of simple chemical tests such as benzene's failure to decolourise bromine solution

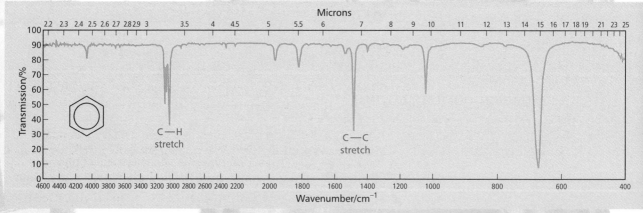

The infra-red spectrum of benzene

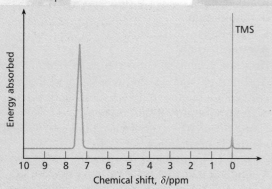

The NMR spectrum of benzene

The mass spectrum of benzene

Finally X-ray diffraction could be used to confirm the actual positions of the atoms.

Introduction

This chapter deals with the problem of how we can determine the structure of an organic compound. That is to say, what atoms are present, what bonds hold them together and how they are arranged in space. This is a tall order when presented with a few milligrams of material. The solution lies through detective work, piecing together evidence of different types from different sources.

In fact it is fairly unusual to have no idea whatever of the identity of a compound. More common is the situation where a chemist believes that he or she has synthesised or extracted a particular compound and all that is needed is confirmation of its identity: a much easier problem.

In a modern organic chemistry laboratory, the three most used techniques are mass spectrometry, infra-red spectroscopy (IR) and nuclear magnetic resonance (NMR). In the first part of this chapter we will see how information from these three techniques and others can be used to find the structures of three unknown compounds X, Y and Z.

38.1 Finding the structure of an unknown compound

Purity

Firstly we need to know if our unknown compound is pure. For a solid we can measure its melting point. A pure solid should have a sharp melting point while a mixture will melt gradually over a range of a few degrees.

If we think we know what a compound is, we can do a **mixed melting point determination**. We mix our unknown with a specimen of the compound we suspect it is. If the mixture melts sharply at the melting temperature of the known compound then the two are the same. If two different compounds have been mixed the melting point will be lower and less sharp.

As a further check on purity, chromatography (see section 23.1) may help. If the substance shows evidence of separation with any type of chromatography such as thin layer, paper or gas–liquid, it cannot be pure.

Qualitative analysis

The aim here is to determine what elements are present in the sample. Instrumental methods are normally used, for example, flame emission spectrophotometry (see the box 'Flame emission spectrophotometry', Chapter 7). Carbon and hydrogen are present in all organic compounds. The other elements likely to be present are oxygen, nitrogen, halogens, sulphur and, occasionally, phosphorus.

The presence of carbon and hydrogen can be shown by burning the substance and testing for the presence of carbon dioxide and water.

Hint: In practice nitrogen is first converted to a mixture of oxides and then reduced back to elemental nitrogen.

Quantitative analysis

This determines the masses of each element present and thus the empirical (simplest) formula. The basic method is **combustion analysis.** It involves burning the unknown compound in excess oxygen and measuring the amounts of water, carbon dioxide, sulphur dioxide and nitrogen produced. This is done by measuring the amount of infra-red radiation they absorb.

The method described determines carbon, hydrogen, sulphur and nitrogen only. Other elements must be determined separately. Oxygen is assumed to represent the difference after the other four elements have been measured.

The sample is placed in a platinum capsule and burned completely in a stream of oxygen diluted with helium as a carrier gas. The final combustion products pass through a series of cells in which the infra-red absorption of the water, sulphur dioxide and carbon dioxide is measured in turn. These are removed from the gas stream to leave the nitrogen which is measured from the thermal conductivity of the remaining gas. The measurements are used to calculate the masses of each gas present and hence the masses of hydrogen, sulphur, carbon and nitrogen in the original sample. Oxygen is found by difference. The process is shown in **Figure 38.1**.

Hint: Traditionally, the amounts of water and carbon dioxide were measured by weighing the absorbents.

From the masses of the combustion products the empirical formula can be found as shown in the example below.

Example: compound X

Hint: We are using compound X to see how structure can be found from a variety of techniques.

0.23 g of a compound X containing carbon, hydrogen and oxygen only, gave 0.44 g of carbon dioxide and 0.27 g of water on complete combustion in oxygen. What is its formula?

Empirical formula

Carbon

0.44 g of CO_2 ($M_r = 44$) is $0.44/44 = 0.01$ mol CO_2

As each mole of CO_2 has 1 mol of C, the sample contained 0.01 mol of C atoms.

Hydrogen

0.27 g of H_2O ($M_r = 18$) is $0.27/18 = 0.015$ mol H_2O

As each mole of H_2O has 2 mol of H, the sample contained 0.03 mol of H atoms.

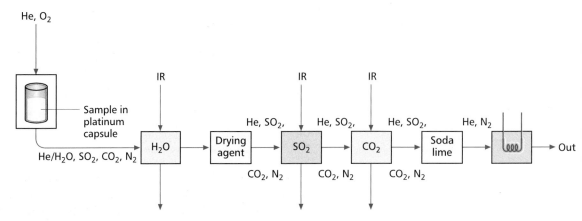

He, O_2

Sample in platinum capsule

He/H_2O, SO_2, CO_2, N_2

IR

H_2O

Drying agent

CO_2, N_2

He, SO_2, CO_2, N_2

IR

SO_2

CO_2, N_2

He, SO_2, CO_2, N_2

IR

CO_2

CO_2, N_2

He, SO_2, CO_2, N_2

Soda lime

He, N_2

Out

Figure 38.1 Combustion analysis

Oxygen

0.01 mole of carbon atoms ($A_r = 12$) has a mass of 0.12 g.
0.03 mole of hydrogen atoms ($A_r = 1$) has a mass of 0.03 g.
Total of C plus H is 0.15 g.

The rest (0.23 − 0.15 g) must be oxygen, so the sample contained 0.08 g of oxygen. 0.08 g of oxygen ($A_r = 16$) is 0.08/16 = 0.005 mol oxygen atoms.

Formula

So the sample contains

      0.01 mol C
      0.03 mol H
      0.005 mol O

Dividing through by the smallest (0.005) gives the ratio:

      C 2
      H 6
      O 1

so the **empirical formula** is C_2H_6O.

Relative molecular mass

The empirical formula of sample X in the example could represent a range of molecular formulae: C_2H_6O ($M_r = 46$), $C_4H_{12}O_2$ ($M_r = 92$), etc., represented by $(C_2H_6O)_n$. To find the value of n we need to know the relative molecular mass, M_r. A variety of methods are available, including gas volume measurements (see section 27.2). However, nowadays mass spectrometry is the main method for determining relative molecular mass, and it can also provide other types of information.

Q **What would the relative molecular mass of X be if its formula were $C_6H_{18}O_3$?**

Mass spectrometry

The principle of this technique has been described in section 7.4 and some of its applications can be found in section 29.2. For organic structure determination it can offer five types of information:

1. Relative molecular mass can be determined from the mass/charge ratio of the parent ion (also called the molecular ion).

2. The presence of certain elements can be deduced from isotope peaks. For example, chlorine-containing compounds will produce pairs of peaks differing by two mass units, whose abundances are in the ratio 3 : 1 because of the isotopes ^{35}Cl and ^{37}Cl.

3. High resolution mass spectrometry, which measures relative molecular masses to four or five decimal places, enables us to distinguish between compounds containing different elements but which have the same relative molecular mass to the nearest whole number.

4. Fragmentation of the ions as they fly through the mass spectrometer can also give clues to the structure, as we shall see in the examples.

5. The $M + 1$ peak tells us how many carbon atoms the molecule has. This is a peak at a mass of one unit greater than the parent ion. It has a height $n\%$ of that of the parent ion where n is the number of carbon atoms in the molecule.

Answer: 138

Q It is impossible to see the $M + 1$ peak in Figure 38.2 without enlarging the spectrum. What percentage of the parent ion peak height would you expect the $M + 1$ peak to have?

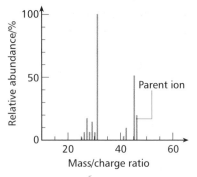

Figure 38.2 The mass spectrum of compound X

Answer: 2% of that of the parent ion (as there are two carbon atoms)

The mass spectrum of compound X is given in **Figure 38.2**. The parent ion gives the value of $M_r = 46$. Thus the molecular formula is the same as the empirical formula in this case: C_2H_6O.

Functional groups

Once we know the molecular formula we need to know the functional groups present. This is done by looking at the chemical reactions of the compound and by infra-red spectroscopy.

Chemical reactions

Some tests are very straightforward.

Is the compound acidic (suggests carboxylic acid or phenol) or basic (suggests an amine)?

Is the compound solid (suggests long carbon chain or ionic bonding), liquid (suggests medium length carbon chain or polar or hydrogen bonding) or gas (suggests short carbon chain, little or no polarity)?

Does the compound dissolve in water (suggests polar groups) or not (suggests no polar groups)?

Does the compound burn with a smoky flame (suggests high C : H ratio, possibly aromatic) or non-smoky flame (suggests low C : H ratio, probably non-aromatic)?

Some specific chemical tests are listed in **Table 38.1**.

Table 38.1 Chemical tests for functional groups

Test	Result	Inference	Notes
Shake with bromine water	Decolourises	C=C present	Br_2 will react with alkanes in strong light, so test must be done in dark
Add Na	H_2 given off	—OH present	Could be carboxylic acid, phenol or alcohol
If —OH present, add Na_2CO_3(aq)	CO_2 produced	—CO_2H present	But could be phenol with strongly electron-withdrawing groups
Add neutral $FeCl_3$(aq)	Purple colour	⬡—OH present	
Add Brady's reagent	Orange precipitate	Aldehyde or ketone present	
Heat with: Benedict's solution or Tollens' reagent	Brick-red precipitate Silver mirror	} Aldehyde present	
Heat with I_2/NaOH(aq)	Yellow precipitate	CH_3—C(OH)(H)— or CH_3—C(=O)— present	Triiodomethane reaction
Add $CuSO_4$(aq) and NaOH(aq) and warm	Lilac colour	Peptide link present —C(=O)—N(H)—	Biuret test
Add ninhydrin solution	Blue colour	Amino acid or peptide present	

Q Write the equation for the reaction of sodium with ethanol.

These tests may give sufficient information to identify the compound. In the example of compound X, the molecular formula was C_2H_6O. This compound gave off hydrogen on adding sodium, and therefore had an —OH group, so the only possibility is ethanol, CH_3CH_2OH. This can be confirmed by a positive triiodomethane test.

Infra-red (IR) spectra

This method has been described in section 29.2. Particular functional groups produce peaks in different areas of the spectrum as summarised in **Figure 38.3**.

Table 38.2 Position of carbonyl (C=O) peaks in the IR spectra of different compounds

Molecule	Wave-number/cm^{-1}
Ketone (R$_2$CO)	1725–1700
Aldehyde (RCHO)	1740–1720
Aromatic ketone (R$_2$CO)	1700–1680
Aromatic aldehyde (RCHO)	1715–1695
Carboxylic acid (RCO$_2$H)	1725–1700
Ester (RCO$_2$R)	1750–1730
Amide (RCONH$_2$)	1680–1640
Acid chloride (RCOCl)	1815–1790

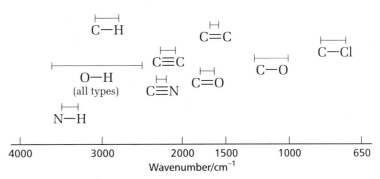

Figure 38.3 Infra-red absorption of some functional groups

Hint: Use common sense. There is no point in deciding that a compound is a carboxylic acid on the basis of a peak at, say, 1720 cm^{-1}, if the compound is not acidic.

Variations in the rest of the molecule can shift the peak slightly as shown in **Table 38.2** for the C=O group, which appears in several functional groups.

The infra-red spectrum of compound X, which we now believe to be ethanol, is shown in **Figure 38.4**.

There are peaks at 3300 cm^{-1} and 1100 cm^{-1} caused by an O—H stretching vibration and a C—O stretching vibration respectively. These confirm our belief that compound X is an alcohol.

Hint: Matching the spectrum of X with the spectrum of a sample known to be ethanol would also confirm that the two were the same.

Nuclear magnetic resonance (NMR) spectra

The method has been described in section 29.2. The simplest method, ^{1}H NMR, gives information about the number and environment of hydrogen atoms in the molecule. Resonance occurs

Q If you suspected that compound X was an aldehyde, what peak would you look for in the infra-red spectrum to confirm or deny this?

Answer: $C_2H_5OH + Na \longrightarrow C_2H_5ONa + \frac{1}{2}H_2$

Answer: A C=O stretching peak at about 1700 cm^{-1}.

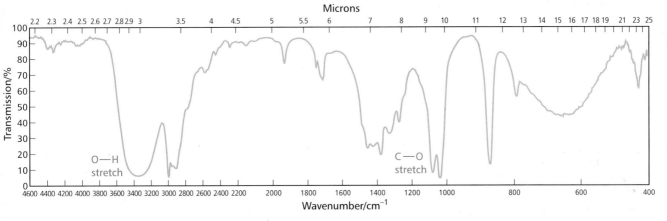

Figure 38.4 Infra-red spectrum of compound X

Q What is the formula of TMS? How many identical hydrogen atoms does it have?

Table 38.3 Typical hydrogen chemical shift values (δ)/ppm

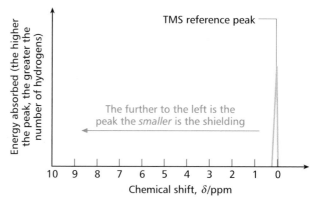

Type of hydrogen atom	Chemical shift
R—CH$_3$	0.9
R—CH$_2$—R	1.3
R$_3$CH	2.0
CH$_3$—C(=O)OR	2.0
R—C(=O)—CH$_3$	2.1
(phenyl)—CH$_3$	2.3
R—C≡C—H	2.6
R—CH$_2$—Hal	3.2–3.7
R—O—CH$_3$	3.8
R—O—H	4.5
RHC=CH$_2$	4.9
RHC=CH$_2$	5.9
(phenyl)—OH	7
(phenyl)—H	7.3
R—C(=O)H	9.7
R—C(=O)O—H	11.5

Q Predict the NMR spectrum of the isomer of ethanol, methoxymethane, CH$_3$—O—CH$_3$.

when the applied magnetic field is of just the right magnitude to allow a hydrogen nucleus to 'flip' from one energy state to another in a magnetic field. However, the hydrogen nucleus is protected from the external field to some extent by the electrons. This is called **shielding**. Hydrogen atoms bonded to electronegative atoms like oxygen are shielded less than ones bonded to, for example, carbon because the oxygen pulls the electrons away. The amount of shielding is measured in NMR spectra by the chemical shift (δ) from a reference compound called tetramethylsilane (TMS). This compound is used because the signal from its hydrogen atoms is well away from those of most other compounds.

The *greater* the chemical shift, the *less* the shielding. Most hydrogen atoms in organic molecules have values of δ between 0 and 10 (see **Figure 38.5**).

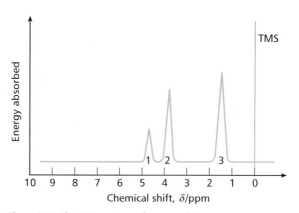

Figure 38.5 NMR spectra use the compound TMS as a reference

The chemical shift values of hydrogen atoms in different environments are shown in **Table 38.3**.

The low resolution NMR spectrum of compound X is shown in **Figure 38.6**.

Figure 38.6 The NMR spectrum of compound X

Answer: Si(CH$_3$)$_4$, 12

Answer: There is only one type of hydrogen (there are six of them) with a shielding approximately the same as the H$_b$ hydrogens in ethanol, because they are bonded to a carbon adjacent to an oxygen. Methoxymethane's NMR spectrum is shown in **Figure 38.7**.

The spectrum shows three types of hydrogen atom present in the ratio 1 : 2 : 3 at δ values of 4.7, 3.8 and 1.5. By reference to Table 38.3, the one at δ = 4.7 could be an O—H hydrogen. The two hydrogens at δ = 3.8 are more shielded and could be the —CH$_2$— hydrogens in ethanol and the three hydrogens at δ = 1.5 are more shielded still and could be the —CH$_3$ hydrogens. So the spectrum is consistent with X being ethanol.

In ethanol, there are three types of hydrogen atom, H_a, H_b and H_c:

The three-dimensional representation makes it clear that all three H_c's are identical. The single hydrogen, H_a, attached to the oxygen atom has little shielding because the oxygen pulls the electrons away from it.

The two hydrogens, H_b, attached to carbon 1 are more shielded because the effect of the oxygen is less, while the three hydrogens, H_c, bonded to carbon 2 are the most shielded as the oxygen is now two atoms away.

Hint: Even more information is available from high resolution NMR (see section 29.2).

Example: compound Y

0.44 g of a compound Y containing carbon, hydrogen and oxygen only gave 0.88 g of carbon dioxide and 0.36 g of water on complete combustion in oxygen. The mass spectrum, NMR spectrum and IR spectrum are given in **Figure 38.8**. Compound Y gave an orange precipitate with Brady's reagent and a brick-red precipitate with Benedict's test.

Empirical formula

Carbon

0.88 g of CO_2 ($M_r = 44$) is $0.88/44 = 0.02$ mol CO_2

As each mole CO_2 has 1 mol of C, the sample contained 0.02 mol of C atoms.

Hydrogen

0.36 g of H_2O ($M_r = 18$) is $0.36/18 = 0.02$ mol H_2O

As each mole of H_2O has 2 mol of H, the sample contained 0.04 mol of H atoms.

Oxygen

0.02 mol of carbon atoms ($A_r = 12$) has a mass of 0.24 g.

0.04 mol of hydrogen atoms ($A_r = 1$) has a mass of 0.04 g.

Total of C plus H is 0.28 g.

The rest ($0.44 - 0.28$) must be oxygen, so the sample contained 0.16 g of oxygen.

0.16 g of oxygen ($A_r = 16$) is $0.16/16 = 0.01$ mol oxygen atoms.

Formula

So the sample contains

	0.02 mol C
	0.04 mol H
	0.01 mol O

Dividing through by the smallest (0.01) gives the ratio:

C	2
H	4
O	1

so the empirical formula of Y is C_2H_4O.

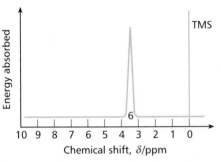

Figure 38.7 The NMR spectrum of methoxymethane

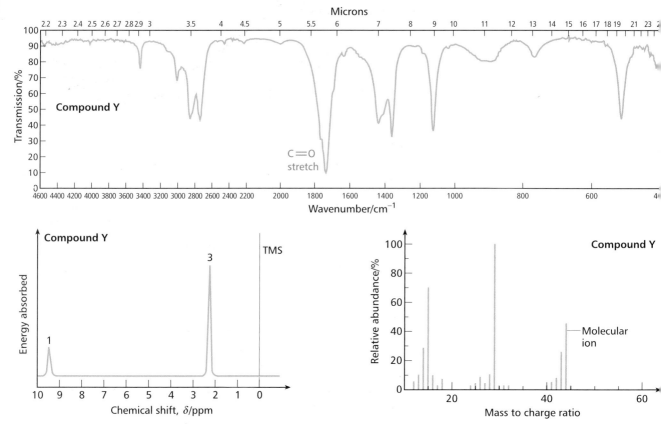

Figure 38.8 IR, NMR and mass spectra for compound Y

Hint: The terms 'molecular ion' and 'parent ion' mean the same thing.

M_r of empirical formula $= (2 \times 12) + (4 \times 1) + (1 \times 16) = 44$

The mass spectrum gives a molecular ion peak at $M_r = 44$.

So Y's molecular formula is C_2H_4O.

A precipitate with Brady's reagent and positive Benedict's test indicates an aldehyde, so the only possibility is ethanal:

$$CH_3 — C{\overset{\displaystyle O}{\underset{\displaystyle H}{\Vert}}}$$

From the IR spectrum, this is confirmed by a peak at approximately $1750 \ cm^{-1}$ due to C=O.

    The NMR shows two types of hydrogen atoms in the ratio $3:1$.

The single proton is very unshielded – this is the $—C{\overset{O}{\underset{H}{\Vert}}}$ – the

δ value fits with the value in Table 38.3 for such a hydrogen. The three hydrogens of $\delta = 2.1$ are the CH_3 group.

    The mass spectrum shows fragments of $M_r = 29$ and $M_r = 15$ corresponding to the C—C bond breaking:

$$H—\overset{\displaystyle H}{\underset{\displaystyle H}{C}}{\Big\{}C{\overset{\displaystyle O}{\underset{\displaystyle H}{\Vert}}}$$

        15   29

Example: compound Z

0.74 g of a compound Z conta
only gave 1.32 g of carbon dioxide
combustion in oxygen. The infra-red
NMR spectrum of Z are shown in **Figure**
acidic, effervescing on addition of sodium ca

Empirical formula

Carbon

1.32 g of CO_2 ($M_r = 44$) is $1.32/44 = 0.03$ mol CO_2

As each mole of CO_2 has 1 mol of C, the sample contained 0.03 mol of C atoms.

Hydrogen

0.54 g of H_2O ($M_r = 18$) is $0.54/18 = 0.03$ mol H_2O

As each mole of H_2O has 2 mol of H, the sample contained 0.06 mol of H atoms.

Oxygen

0.03 mol of carbon atoms ($A_r = 12$) has a mass of 0.36 g.

0.06 mol of hydrogen atoms ($A_r = 1$) has a mass of 0.06 g.

Total of C plus H is 0.42 g.

The rest $(0.74 - 0.42)$ must be oxygen, so the sample contained 0.32 g of oxygen.

0.32 g of oxygen ($A_r = 16$) is $0.32/16 = 0.02$ mol oxygen atoms.

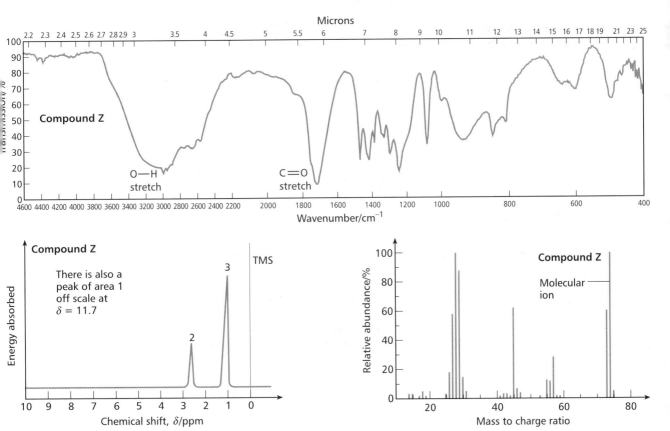

Figure 38.9 IR, NMR and mass spectra for compound Z

contains

0.03 mol C
0.06 mol H
0.02 mol O

Dividing through by the smallest (0.02) gives the ratio:

C 1.5
H 3
O 1

Hint: If dividing through by the number of moles doesn't give a simple number ratio, multiply up to get ...

so the **empirical formula** of Z is $C_3H_6O_2$.

M_r of empirical formula = $(3 \times 12) + (6 \times 1) + (2 \times 16) = 74$. The mass spectrum gives a molecular ion peak at $M_r = 74$, so the molecular formula of Z is $C_3H_6O_2$.

Effervescence with sodium carbonate suggests a carboxylic acid, so the only possibility is propanoic acid:

$$CH_3CH_2 - C \begin{smallmatrix} O \\ \\ OH \end{smallmatrix}$$

From the IR spectrum, this is confirmed by a peak at approximately 1720 cm^{-1} due to C=O and a very broad peak at about 3000 cm^{-1} due to O—H (the broadening is due to hydrogen bonding).

The NMR shows three types of hydrogen atoms in the ratio $1 : 2 : 3$ as the formula of propanoic acid requires. The single hydrogen has a

δ value expected for a $-C \begin{smallmatrix} O \\ \\ O-H \end{smallmatrix}$ hydrogen.

The mass spectrum shows fragments of $M_r = 45$ and $M_r = 29$.

These correspond to $C \begin{smallmatrix} O \\ \\ OH \end{smallmatrix} +$ and $CH_3CH_2{}^+$ caused by the C—C bond

in red breaking:

$$CH_3CH_2 \rightthreetimes C \begin{smallmatrix} O \\ \\ OH \end{smallmatrix}$$

$\quad\quad 29 \quad\quad\quad\quad 45$

Sodium chloride plates used for infra-red spectroscopy

Hint: The spectrum will also contain peaks caused by the nujol.

38.2 Infra-red spectroscopy in organic chemistry

Sample preparation

This is quite simple. The sample has to be held in the infra-red beam.

For liquid samples, a drop is squeezed between a pair of sodium chloride plates to form a thin film. Solids are ground up with a liquid hydrocarbon called nujol to form a thin paste, called a **mull**, which is used to form the thin film. The spectrum is scanned in less than a minute.

An alternative to a mull is to grind solids up with potassium bromide. This eliminates the problem of getting the spectrum of nujol along with that of the sample.

Infra-red spectra of alkanes

The IR spectrum of hexane is shown in **Figure 38.10**. Apart from the fingerprint region (see the box in Chapter 29, page 415), alkanes have little of interest in their IR spectra, because their only bonds, C—C and C—H, are present in most organic compounds. The strong peak at approximately $2950\ cm^{-1}$ is a C—H stretch while those at 1400–$1500\ cm^{-1}$ are H—C—H bending vibrations.

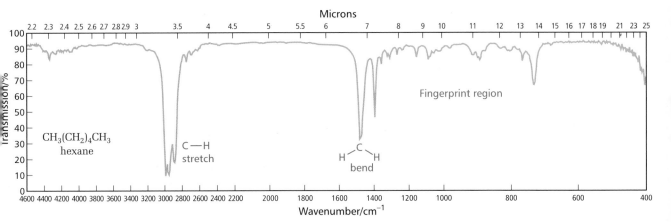

Figure 38.10 The infra-red spectrum of hexane

Infra-red spectra of alkenes

The infra-red spectrum of oct-1-ene is shown in **Figure 38.11**. The main peak characteristic of an alkene is that at $1650\ cm^{-1}$ due to a C=C stretching vibration.

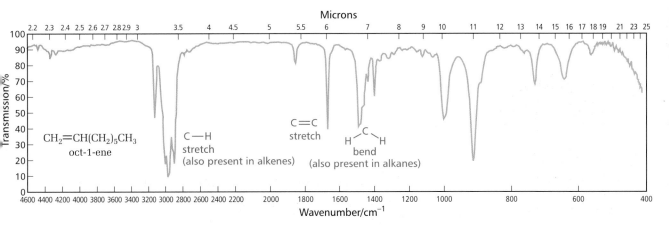

Figure 38.11 The infra-red spectrum of oct-1-ene

Infra-red spectra of haloalkanes

The main feature other than the peaks observed in the alkanes is the C—X stretch. This is seen in the ranges shown in **Table 38.4** for different halogens.

Answer: C—C and C—H

Since most infra-red instruments operate in the range 600–4000 cm^{-1}, only the C—Cl and C—F bonds are usually observed. The infra-red spectrum of 1-chlorobutane is shown in **Figure 38.12**.

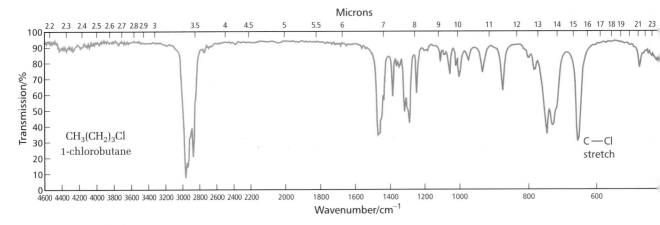

Figure 38.12 The infra-red spectrum of 1-chlorobutane

Table 38.4 Infra-red peaks for carbon–halogen bonds

Bond	Wave number/cm^{-1}
C—F	1400–1000
C—Cl	800–600
C—Br	600–500
C—I	500

Infra-red spectra of alcohols

The infra-red spectra of alcohols show a peak caused by an O—H stretching vibration at between 3300 cm^{-1} and 3600 cm^{-1}. The large range is caused by hydrogen bonding between alcohol molecules.

If the hydrogen is bonded to another molecule by hydrogen bonding, this effectively increases the mass of the hydrogen atom and reduces the frequency of the vibration. So the exact frequency at which the O—H bond vibrates in a particular molecule depends on the amount of hydrogen bonding in which it is involved.

In pure liquid alcohols, the peak is often broad – also because of hydrogen bonding. Hydrogen bonds are constantly breaking and reforming, so that different alcohol molecules may be hydrogen bonded (directly or indirectly) to different numbers of other molecules. This means that in any sample of alcohol molecules, there will be a spread of molecules with different numbers of others bound to them and consequently a spread of vibrational frequencies (see **Figure 38.13**).

A C—O—H bending vibration is seen at around 1350 cm^{-1} and a C—O stretching vibration between 1050 cm^{-1} and 1200 cm^{-1}. The infra-red spectrum of propan-2-ol is shown in **Figure 38.14**.

> **Q** Would you expect the O—H peak to be broadened if the alcohol were dissolved in a non-polar solvent? Explain.

$$\overset{\longleftrightarrow}{—O—H}$$

No hydrogen bonding

$$—O—H—\;—\;—O\diagdown$$

If the hydrogen is bonded to another molecule by hydrogen bonding, this effectively increases the mass of the hydrogen atom and reduces the frequency of vibration

Figure 38.13 The effect of hydrogen bonding on the vibrational frequency of the O—H bond

Answer: No, the peak would not be broad because there would be no hydrogen bonding with the solvent and in a typical solution there are many more solvent molecules than solute molecules, so encounters between two alcohol molecules would be rare.

Infra-red spectra of arenes

The infra-red spectrum of benzene is shown in **Figure 38.15**. The important peaks are at approximately 3030 cm^{-1} due to a C—H stretch and at approximately 1500 cm^{-1} due to a C—C stretch in the aromatic ring. Substituted benzene derivatives would, of course, also show peaks characteristic of their substituents as well.

Infra-red spectra of carbonyl compounds

The infra-red spectrum of propanone is shown in **Figure 38.16**. The carbonyl group shows a prominent peak at around 1700 cm^{-1} due to a C=O stretching vibration. The peak is usually strong and sharp. In aldehydes it is between 1740 and 1720 cm^{-1} while in ketones it is between 1700 and 1680 cm^{-1}.

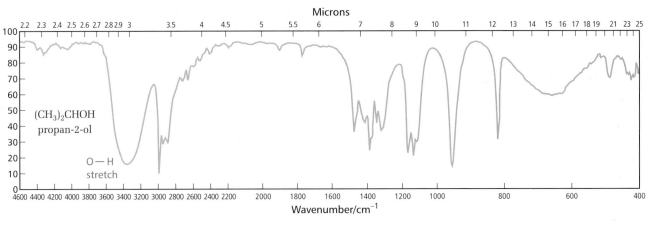

Figure 38.14 The infra-red spectrum of propan-2-ol

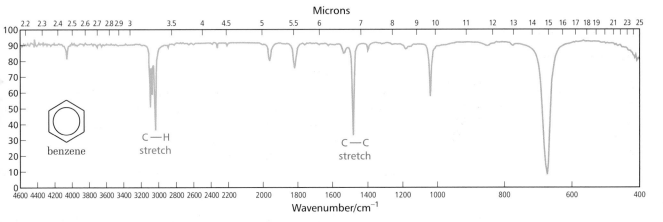

Figure 38.15 The infra-red spectrum of benzene

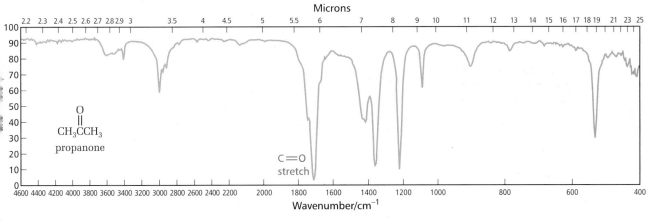

Figure 38.16 The infra-red spectrum of propanone

Infra-red spectra of carboxylic acids and their derivatives

Carboxylic acids

The IR spectrum of ethanoic acid is shown in **Figure 38.17**.

The most important peaks in the spectrum are those at 3100 cm^{-1} due to an —OH stretch and 1700 cm^{-1} due to a C=O stretch. We have met both these before, the former in alcohols and the latter in aldehydes and ketones. The —OH peak is broadened owing to hydrogen bonding as in alcohols. The additive nature of infra-red spectra is shown in **Figure 38.18**.

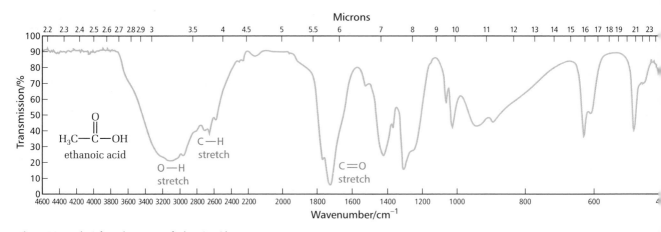

Figure 38.17 The infra-red spectrum of ethanoic acid

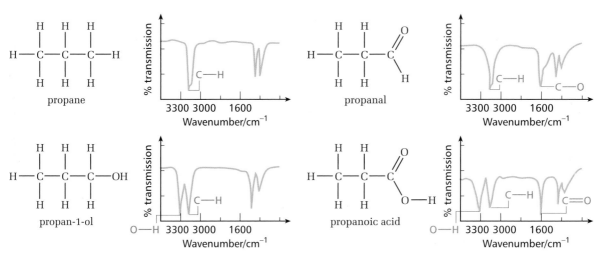

Figure 38.18 The infra-red spectra of propane, propanol, propanal and propanoic acid. Note how the spectrum builds up as each new functional group is added

Acid derivatives

All the acid derivatives contain a carbonyl group and therefore show a strong C=O stretching vibration at around 1750 cm⁻¹ although this may be shifted up or down by as much as 50 cm⁻¹. The O—H stretch present in carboxylic acids is, of course, absent although amides have an N—H stretching vibration at almost the same frequency. This peak is also broadened by hydrogen bonding.

Infra-red spectra of amines

Figure 38.19 shows the infra-red spectrum of diethylamine. The main peak of interest is the N—H stretch which occurs in the range 3300–3500 cm⁻¹. Like the O—H stretch in alcohols, it is broadened by hydrogen bonding. This peak is similar in frequency to the O—H stretch in alcohols because the masses of nitrogen and oxygen atoms are very similar, as are the strengths of the O—H and N—H bonds.

Infra-red spectra of nitriles

The infra-red spectrum of benzenecarbonitrile is shown in **Figure 37.20**. Nitriles have a peak between 2200 cm⁻¹ and 2300 cm⁻¹ due to the C≡N stretching vibration.

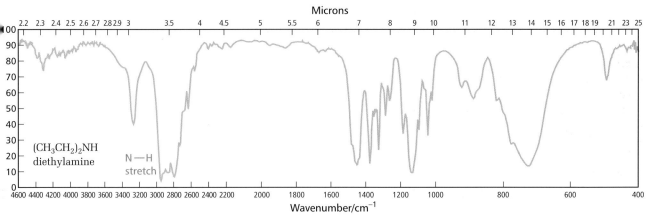

Figure 38.19 The infra-red spectrum of diethylamine

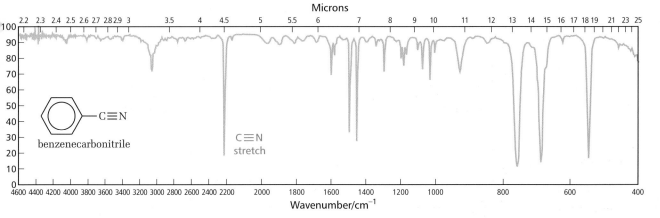

Figure 38.20 The infra-red spectrum of benzenecarbonitrile

38.3 Mass spectrometry in organic chemistry

Low resolution mass spectrometry is used in organic chemistry both as a means of measuring relative molecular mass and to provide other structural information from isotope peaks and fragmentation patterns.

The mass spectra of alkanes

Figure 38.21 shows the mass spectrum of butane. The parent (molecular) ion peak is at $M_r = 58$ and the other major peaks at $M_r = 43$, $M_r = 29$ and $M_r = 15$ are caused by fragments formed when one of the C—C bonds breaks. Minor peaks are caused by loss of hydrogen atoms from the main peaks.

Mass spectra of organohalogen compounds

Part of the mass spectrum of 1-chlorobutane is shown in **Figure 38.22**. Remember that the mass spectrometer separates different isotopes. So the mass of the parent ion is not 92.5 (M_r for 1-chlorobutane, C_4H_9Cl). There are two parent ion peaks. One represents $C_4H_9{}^{35}Cl$ of mass 92 and the other $C_4H_9{}^{37}Cl$ of mass 94. Notice that these peak heights are

What fragments do you think the the peaks at mass 63 and 65 represent in the mass spectrum of chlorobutane?

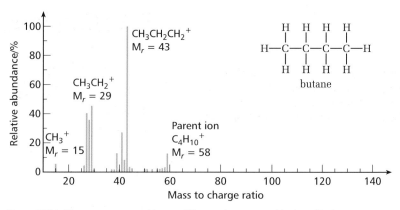

Figure 38.21 The mass spectrum of butane. Minor peaks are caused by loss of hydrogen atoms from the main peaks

in approximate ratio 3 : 1, the abundance ratio of $^{35}Cl : ^{37}Cl$. This feature of twin peaks separated by two mass units with heights in the ratio 3 : 1 is characteristic of the mass spectra of all chlorine-containing compounds.

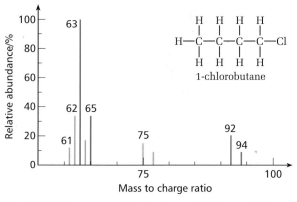

Figure 38.22 Mass spectrum of 1-chlorobutane. (Only the part of the spectrum above mass/charge ratio = 55 is shown. Chlorine-containing peaks are in red)

Mass spectra of arenes

The mass spectrum of phenylethanone,

is shown in **Figure 38.23**.

The parent ion peak is at mass number 120 (the small peak at mass number = 121 is the $M + 1$ peak). The peak at mass number 105 is the parent ion that has lost a —CH_3 group. That at mass number 77 is the phenyl group, $C_6H_5^+$, formed by the loss of CH_3CO. The unit CH_3CO^+ forms the peak at mass number 43. The peak at mass number 51 is less easily assigned: it is $C_4H_3^+$, a fragment of the benzene ring. The $C_6H_5^+$ peak of mass number 77 is found in the mass spectrum of many aromatic compounds. See **Figure 38.24**.

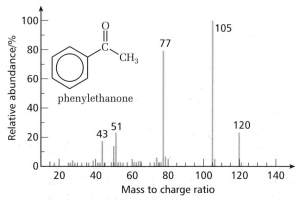

Figure 38.23 The mass spectrum of phenylethanone

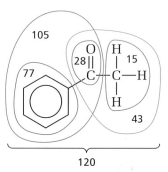

Figure 38.24 Fragments of phenylethanone

Answer: $CH_2CH_2{}^{35}Cl^+$ and $CH_2CH_2{}^{37}Cl^+$

38.4 NMR in organic chemistry

Hint: Re-read section 29.2. Nuclear magnetic resonance (NMR) spectroscopy before you try to follow the interpretations of the NMR spectra below.

Low resolution NMR is not routinely used today, and detailed interpretation of high resolution spectra is beyond the scope of this book. Two simple examples follow to illustrate the use of the proton NMR technique.

Remember that:

- The height (strictly the peak area) which is marked on the spectrum by each peak tells us the number of protons causing the peak.
- The δ value tells us about shielding (put simply, how close these protons are to an electronegative atom).
- The splitting of a peak is caused by the protons adjacent to the hydrogen atoms causing the peak: n protons split the peak into $n + 1$ components.

The NMR spectrum of butanone

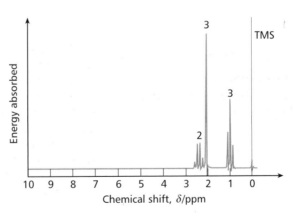

butanone

Figure 38.25 High resolution NMR spectrum of butanone

The spectrum (**Figure 38.25**) shows that there are three types of hydrogen atoms in the ratio $2 : 3 : 3$.

The group of 3 at $\delta = 1$ represents the protons labelled H_a. They are the furthest from the electronegative oxygen atom and are therefore the most shielded. The group is split into a triplet by the adjacent CH_2 protons, labelled H_b. These H_b protons give the peak of height 2 at $\delta = 2.3$. They are less shielded because they are closer to the $C=O$ group. This peak is split into a quartet by the CH_3 protons next to it. The peak of height 3 at $\delta = 2.1$ is caused by the protons labelled H_c. These have almost the same δ value as the CH_2 protons as they are the same distance from $C=O$. This peak is not split because the nearest protons, the CH_2 group are too far away.

The NMR spectrum of 2-bromopropane

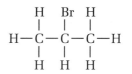

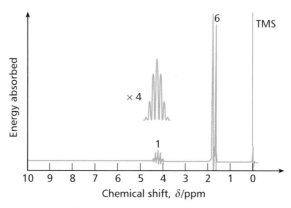

Figure 38.26 High resolution NMR spectrum of 2-bromopropane. The peak at δ 4.2 is shown enlarged four times for clarity

The spectrum (**Figure 38.26**) shows two types of protons in the ratio 6 : 1. The single proton is the one bonded to the C—Br. It is split into a septet (a group of seven) by the six identical protons of the two CH groups. Its δ value of 4.2 shows that it is relatively unshielded because it is close to the electronegative bromine atom. The peak of area 6 is caused by the six protons of the two CH_3 groups and is split into two by the single proton of the C—Br group. These six protons are further from the bromine atom and are well shielded as shown by their δ value of 1.8.

38.5 Summary

• Organic structure determination involves the following stages:	a check on the purity of the substance; qualitative analysis to determine the elements present; quantitative analysis by combustion to determine the empirical formula; determination of the relative molecular mass to find the molecular formula; chemical tests to determine which functional groups are present.
• Mass spectrometry can be used to find:	relative molecular mass from the mass of the parent ion; the presence of certain elements from isotopic abundance ratios; molecular formula (by high resolution mass spectrometry); clues to structure from fragmentation patterns; the number of carbon atoms from the height of the $M + 1$ peak.
• Infra-red spectra can indicate	which functional groups are present.
• NMR spectra can tell us about	the number of hydrogen atoms of different types present in a molecule.

38.6 Practice questions

1. Compound A is a liquid containing C, H and O only. On combustion, 0.36 g gave 0.88 g carbon dioxide and 0.36 g water. Its IR, mass spectrum and low resolution NMR spectrum are shown. The liquid was neutral and mixed with water but did not decolourise bromine solution. It formed an orange precipitate with Brady's reagent but did not react with Benedict's solution.

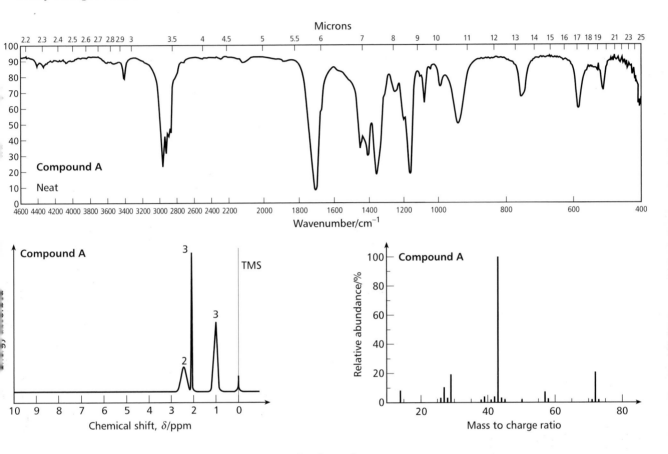

(a) Calculate the empirical formula and molecular formula.
(b) What is the structure of the compound? Explain how the evidence leads to your conclusion and give as much confirming evidence as possible.

2. The IR spectrum, mass spectrum and high resolution NMR spectrum of compound B, which is a haloalkane, are shown. Use the spectra to identify it and explain your reasoning.

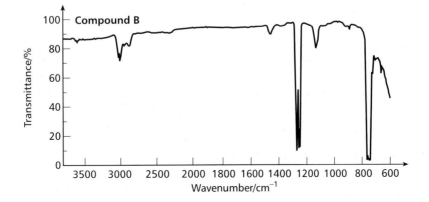

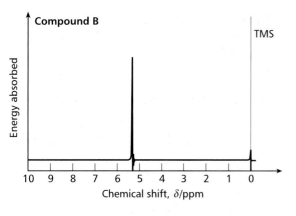

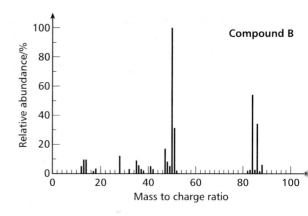

3. The IR spectrum, mass spectrum and NMR spectrum of compound C are shown. C is acidic, fizzing when added to sodium carbonate solution, and soluble in water. Identify C and explain your reasoning.

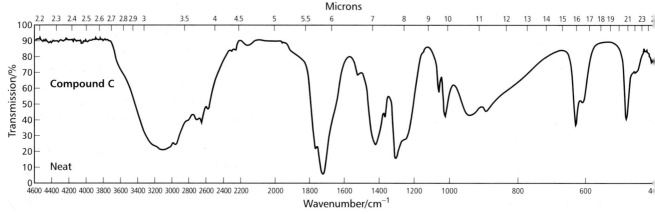

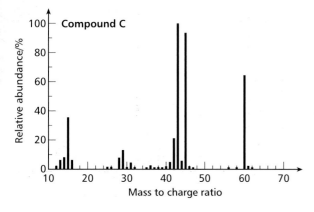

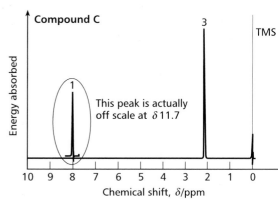

38.7 Examination questions

1. (a) The low resolution ^{1}H NMR spectrum of compound **A**, with the molecular formula C_4H_8O, is shown in **Figure 1**.
   (i)   Use the data given in **Figure 2** to deduce the type of proton responsible for each peak in **Figure 1**.
   (ii) Draw the graphical formula of compound **A**.
   (iii) The ratio of the areas under the peaks **X**, **Y** and **Z** is 2 : 3 : 3. Suggest an explanation for this.

   (b) Butanal is a structural isomer of compound **A**.
   (i)   Explain the term *structural isomerism*.
   (ii) Draw the graphical formula of butanal.
   (iii) State **two** ways in which you would expect the ^{1}H NMR spectrum for butanal to differ from that of compound **A**.

   (c) Compound **A** can be obtained by the oxidation of butan-2-ol, $CH_3CH_2CH(OH)CH_3$, which exists as optical isomers.
   (i)   Explain the term *optical isomers*.

(ii) Draw the graphical formula to show the spatial distribution of the groups in each optical isomer.

(iii) Explain why butan-1-ol, $CH_3CH_2CH_2CH_2OH$, does not exhibit this type of isomerism.

[AEB 1998]

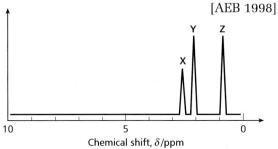

Figure 1

Type of proton	Chemical shift/ppm
R—CH$_3$	0.9
R—CH$_2$—R	1.4
R—CO—CH$_3$	2.1
R—CH$_2$—CO—	2.5
R—CHO	9.7

Figure 2

2. An organic compound **X**, containing only carbon, hydrogen and oxygen, was analysed by combustion. 2.20 g of the compound produced 4.03 g of carbon dioxide and 1.10 g of water.

An aqueous solution of the compound reacted with sodium carbonate producing a gas. The solution also decolourised a solution of bromine.

The principal peaks in the mass spectrum of the compound are shown below.

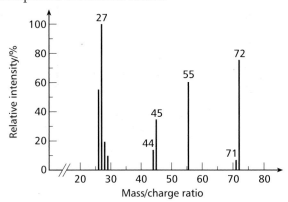

Use the information given above to calculate the empirical and molecular formula of the compound, making your method clear.

Deduce the structure of the compound **X** explaining why it reacts with sodium carbonate and bromine.

Give equations for these two reactions.

Suggest formulae for the species which cause the peaks in the mass spectrum at 27, 44 and 45 and suggest why the peaks at 55 and 71 occur.

(Mass spectrum adapted from 'Modern Chemical Techniques', Royal Society of Chemistry)

[London (Nuffield) 1997]

3. (a) An organic compound **A** has a molar mass of 46 g mol^{-1} and the following elemental composition by mass:

C 52.13%, H 13.15%; O 34.72%

Determine the molecular formula of **A**.

(b) The organic compound **A** has an infra-red spectrum which shows the following features:

Absorption at 2900 cm^{-1}
C—H stretching frequency
Absorption at 3300 cm^{-1}
O—H stretching frequency
Absorption at 1050 cm^{-1}
C—O stretching frequency
Absorption at 1400 cm^{-1}
C—H bending frequency
The shape and position of the —OH peak indicates substantial hydrogen bonding.

(i) Explain, briefly, what is meant by the term *hydrogen bonding*.

(ii) By reference to the infra-red spectrum and your answer to (a) deduce the structure of **A**.

Give **three** reasons in support of your answer.

(c) The mass spectrum of **A** is given below.

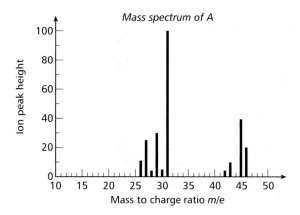

Using the structural formula of **A** deduced above, suggest formulae for the positive ions responsible for *m/e* peaks at 45, 31 and 29.

(d) (i) When **A** is treated with ethanoyl chloride a compound **B** is formed containing 4 carbon atoms.
Give the name and structure of **B** and state to which class of organic compounds it belongs.

(ii) State how your would carry out the addition of ethanoyl chloride to the compound, **A**, paying particular attention to safety.

[WJEC 1997]

Answers

Chapter 7

1. C: $1s^2 2s^2 2p^2$ or 2,4; O: $1s^2 2s^2 2p^4$ or 2,6;
   Al: $1s^2 2s^2 2p^6 3s^2 3p^1$ or 2,8,3; K: $1s^2 2s^2 2p^6 3s^2 3p^6 4s^1$
   or 2, 8, 8, 1

2. (a) V: 20p, 20n, 20e
   W: 6p, 7n, 6e
   X: 20p, 22n, 20e
   Y: 7p, 8n, 7e
   Z: 9p, 10n, 9e
   (b) V and X. (They have the same number of protons but a different number of neutrons.)

3. 63.6. (Did you remember to use the abundances: 30% ^{65}Cu and 70% ^{63}Cu from the graph?)

4. (a) 1.98×10^{-19} J
   6.6×10^{-18} J
   6.6×10^{-20} J
   1.98×10^{-11} J
   (b) 119 kJ mol^{-1}
   3960 kJ mol^{-1}
   39.6 kJ mol^{-1}
   $1.19 \times 10^{10} \text{ kJ mol}^{-1}$

5. (a) 9922 kJ mol^{-1}
   (b) There is a large jump in IE after loss of the first electron for Na and after loss of the second for Mg.
   (c) Electrons are being removed from a more and more positively charged ion.
   (d) The nuclear charge of magnesium is greater than that of sodium.

6. Group III because there is a large jump in IE after loss of the third electron, i.e. there are three electrons in the outer shell.

7. $\nu = 8.05 \times 10^{14} \text{ s}^{-1}$
   (a) 5.3×10^{-19} J per atom
   (b) 319 kJ mol^{-1}
   993 kJ mol^{-1}

8. $1.59 \times 10^{14} \text{ s}^{-1}$ Paschen series

9. $1.7 \times 10^{-39} \text{ m}^3$
   $2.4 \times 10^{14} \text{ kg m}^{-3}$

10. (a) 70, 72, 74
    (b) 35, 37, 70, 72, 74

11. (a) $1.5 \times 10^{13} \text{ s}^{-1}$
    (b) $2 \times 10^{-5} \text{ m}$
    (c) Infra-red

Chapter 8

1. (a) 46 kJ mol^{-1}
   (b) Smaller owing to heat loss
   (c) 46 kJ mol^{-1} The reaction between all strong acids and strong bases has the same enthalpy change of neutralisation because the reaction in every case is $H^+ + OH^- \longrightarrow H_2O$.

2. (a) 6.5×10^{-3}
   (b) 10.30 kJ K^{-1}
   (c) propan-1-ol: (i) 0.0126 (ii) 25.19 kJ
   (iii) $-1999 \text{ kJ mol}^{-1}$
   butan-1-ol: (i) 0.0111 (ii) 29.4 kJ
   (iii) $-2654 \text{ kJ mol}^{-1}$
   pentan-1-ol: (i) 9.499×10^{-3} (ii) 31.51 kJ
   (iii) $-3317 \text{ kJ mol}^{-1}$

3. $+2061 \text{ kJ mol}^{-1}$

4. (a) -70 kJ mol^{-1}. See Figure 8.3 (left), p.59
   (b) -217 kJ mol^{-1}. See Figure 8.3 (left).
   (c) -97 kJ mol^{-1}. See Figure 8.3 (left).
   (d) -195 kJ mol^{-1}. See Figure 8.3 (left).
   (e) $+301 \text{ kJ mol}^{-1}$. See Figure 8.3 (right).

5. (a) Increase (b) Increase (c) Decrease (d) Decrease

6. -62 kJ mol^{-1}

7. (a) -85 kJ mol^{-1} (b) -86 kJ mol^{-1}
   These are virtually the same, as predicted by Hess's law. (The difference is caused by rounding errors in the data.)

Chapter 9

1.

cont.

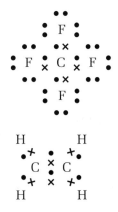

(a) angular (remember 2 lone pairs) (b) linear
(c) pyramidal (1 lone pair) (d) perfect tetrahedron
(e) angular (2 lone pairs) (f) trigonal bipyramidal
(g) pyramidal (1 lone pair) (h) octahedral

(i) perfect tetrahedral (j)

H 121° H
C=C 118° , flat
H 121° H

(k)

H—N...N—H
~107° H ~107°

(l) tetrahedral at both carbon atoms

Each one follows the pattern of the model
compound in the chapter.
NaBr: Figure 9.1, LE=-751.7 kJ mol^{-1};
CaCl$_2$: Figure 9.2, LE=-2255 kJ mol^{-1}; CaO:
Figure 9.3, LE=3454 kJ mol^{-1}; Li$_2$O: Figure 9.4,
LE=2863 kJ mol^{-1}

(a) $\overset{\delta+}{H}—\overset{\delta-}{Cl}$

(b) $\overset{\delta+}{C}\equiv\overset{\delta-}{O}$

(c) $\overset{\delta-}{F}—\overset{\delta+}{Cl}$

(d) H—$\overset{\delta+}{C}$—$\overset{\delta-}{Cl}$ with H above and H below

(e) $\overset{\delta-}{O}=\overset{\delta+}{C}=\overset{\delta-}{O}$

(f)
H
\ $\overset{\delta+}{C}=\overset{\delta-}{O}$
/
H

(g) $\overset{\delta-}{Cl}—\overset{\delta+}{C}—\overset{\delta-}{Cl}$ with $Cl^{\delta-}$ above and $Cl^{\delta-}$ below

(e) and (g) because the individual dipoles cancel
out.

(a) 2, 2, 7, 7, 5, 6, 1
(b) The shared electrons 'feel' a greater nuclear
charge from fluorine than from hydrogen.

The outer electrons 'feel' a shielded nuclear charge
of 7 (the greatest possible). This is true of the outer
electrons in all the halogens but those in fluorine
are closest to the nucleus. Francium.

7.

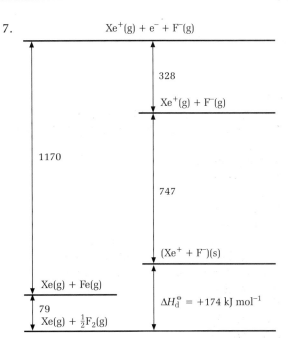

$\Delta H_f^{\ominus}=+174$ kJ mol^{-1}. Xenon is a noble gas and
exists as atoms. The large positive value of $\Delta H_f^{\ominus}$
means that a lot of energy would have to be put in
to form the compound from its elements.
    The Cs$^+$ ions would be expected to be about the
same size as Xe$^+$ because the elements are
adjacent in the Periodic Table. Lattice energies
depend on charge and size of the ions concerned.

8. The bonding is delocalised.

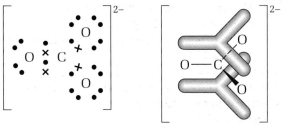

9. As we go from left to right across the Periodic
Table, nuclear charge increases, attracting the
shared electrons in the bond more strongly and
making the bond stronger. As we descend a Group
in the Periodic Table, the shared electrons get
further from the nucleus (as the atoms get larger)
and are less strongly attracted to the nucleus,
making the bond weaker.

10. BeI$_2$. This has the smallest, most highly charged
positive ion and the largest negative ion so that it
is most polarised. These are Fajans' rules.

Chapter 10

1. (a) hydrogen bonding (b) van der Waals (c) van der
Waals (d) dipole–dipole (e) hydrogen bonding
2. butane, propanone, propanol. van der Waals,
dipole–dipole, hydrogen bonding
3. Ethanol and propanoic acid have a high ratio of
hydrogen bonding groups to hydrocarbon chain.
Ethyl propanoate has a lower ratio.

Chapter 11

1. (a) $\dfrac{[Fe^{2+}(aq)]^2_{eqm}[I_2(aq)]_{eqm}}{[Fe^{3+}(aq)]_{eqm}{}^2[I^-(aq)]_{eqm}{}^2}$

   (b) $\dfrac{[CH_3CO_2C_5H_{11}]_{eqm}}{[C_5H_{10}]_{eqm}[CH_3CO_2H]_{eqm}}$

   (c) $\dfrac{[OH^-(aq)]_{eqm}[NH_4{}^+(aq)]_{eqm}}{[NH_4OH(aq)]_{eqm}}$

   (d) $\dfrac{[NH_4{}^+(aq)]_{eqm}}{[NH_3(aq)]_{eqm}[H^+(aq)]_{eqm}}$

   (e) $\dfrac{[Fe^{2+}(aq)]_{eqm}[I_2(aq)]_{eqm}{}^{1/2}}{[Fe^{3+}(aq)]_{eqm}[I^-(aq)]_{eqm}}$

   (f) $\dfrac{[[Cu(NH_3)_4]^{2+}(aq)]_{eqm}}{[NH_3(aq)]_{eqm}{}^4[Cu^{2+}(aq)]_{eqm}}$

   (g) $\dfrac{[[FeNCS]^{2+}(aq)]_{eqm}}{[Fe^{3+}(aq)]_{eqm}[NCS^-(aq)]_{eqm}}$

   (h) $\dfrac{[Sn^{2+}(aq)]_{eqm}[Fe^{3+}(aq)]_{eqm}{}^2}{[Sn^{4+}(aq)]_{eqm}[Fe^{2+}(aq)]_{eqm}{}^2}$

   (i) The value in (e) is the square root of the value in (a)

2. (a) $dm^3\,mol^{-1}$ (b) $dm^3\,mol^{-1}$ (c) $mol\,dm^{-3}$
   (d) $dm^3\,mol^{-1}$ (e) $dm^{3/2}\,mol^{-1/2}$ (f) $dm^{12}\,mol^{-4}$
   (g) $dm^3\,mol^{-1}$ (h) no units

3. (a) 0.033 mol
   (b) $CH_3CO_2H + C_2H_5OH \rightleftharpoons CH_3CO_2C_2H_5 + H_2O$
       0.033 mol   0.033 mol   0.067 mol   0.067 mol
   (c) 4.1
   (d) There are the same number of molecules on each side of the equation.

4. (a) (i) Moves right (ii) Moves left (iii) Moves right
       (iv) Moves right
   (b) (i) Moves left (ii) Moves right (iii) No effect
       (iv) No effect

5. Yes, it is. There will be an equilibrium between ethanoic acid dissolved in hexane and dissolved in water. The ethanoic acid that dissolves in the aqueous solution will be neutralised by the alkali. More acid will then dissolve into the aqueous layer from the hexane. The equilibrium is pulled to the right until all the ethanoic acid is neutralised.

Chapter 12

1. (a) HBr is the conjugate acid and Br^- its conjugate base. H_3O^+ is the conjugate acid and H_2O its conjugate base.
   (b) H_2SO_4 is the conjugate acid and $HSO_4{}^-$ its conjugate base.
       H_2O is the conjugate acid and OH^- its conjugate base.
   (c) $HSO_4{}^-$ is the conjugate acid and $SO_4{}^{2-}$ its conjugate base.

H_3O^+ is the conjugate acid and H_2O its conjugate base.

2. (a) (i) 1.0 (ii) 3 (iii) −0.3
   (b) (i) 1.7 (ii) 2.7 (iii) −0.6
   (c) (i) 12 (ii) 11 (iii) 14.3

Chapter 13

1. (a) +III (b) +IV (c) +IV (d) −I (e) +IV (f) 0
   (g) −I (h) −III (i) +V (j) +III (k) +V (l) +VI
2. (a) oxidised (b) unchanged (c) reduced
   (d) reduced (e) disproportionates
3. (a) cobalt(III) chloride (b) sulphuric(VI) acid (c) sulphuric(IV) acid (d) sodium nitrate(V) (e) lead(II) oxide (f) lead(IV) oxide (g) sodium chlorate(VII) (h) sodium chlorate(V) (i) sodium chlorate(I)
4. (a) $Fe(s)+2Fe^{3+}(aq) \longrightarrow 3Fe^{2+}(aq)$
   (b) $Al(s)+3H^+ \longrightarrow Al^{3+}(aq)+1\frac{1}{2}H_2(g)$
   (c) $Sn(s)+4HNO_3(aq)$
       $\longrightarrow SnO_2(s)+4NO_2(g)+2H_2O(l)$

Chapter 14

1. (a) Collect the carbon dioxide gas given off.
   (b) Use a colorimeter to monitor the colour change from blue to colourless.
   (c) Monitor the decrease in volume of the gas mixture.
   (d) Monitor the decrease in conductivity.
   (e) Monitor the decrease in conductivity or use a colorimeter to measure the colour of the bromine.
   (f) Sample and titrate the sodium hydroxide with acid.
   Other methods may be possible for all the above.
2. (a) $-5 \times 10^{-3}\,mol\,dm^{-3}\,s^{-1}$
   (b) $+3 \times 10^{-3}\,mol\,dm^{-3}\,s^{-1}$
3. (a) (i) 2 (doubling [NO] quadruples the rate)
       (ii) 1 (doubling [H_2] doubles the rate)
       (iii) 3
   (b) Rate $= k[NO]^2[H_2]$
   (c) $8.3 \times 10^4\,dm^6\,mol^{-2}\,s^{-1}$
   (d) $8.3 \times 10^{-5}\,mol\,dm^{-3}\,s^{-1}$

Chapter 15

1. (a) $Cl > Br > I$ because the electron is removed from a shell further from the nucleus in each case. In each case it feels the same shielded nuclear charge.
   (b) $Si > P > S$ because the increased nuclear charge pulls the electrons inwards
2. $133/1.88 = 70.7\,cm^3\,mol^{-1}$
3. (a) 5+ (b) 4+ (c) 7+

Chapter 16

1. (a) $1s^2 2s^2 2p^6 3s^2 3p^6$
   (b) Having the same number of electrons
   (c) The radii decrease because the nuclear charge is increasing.

(a) (i) It is the nitrate of lithium or a Group II metal (the other Group I nitrates decompose to give oxygen).

   (ii) The metal must be in Group II (Group I compounds are all soluble).

   (iii) Barium

(b) $Ba(NO_3)_2(s) \longrightarrow BaO(s) + 2NO_2(g) + \frac{1}{2}O_2(g)$
   $BaO(s) + H_2O(l) \longrightarrow Ba(OH)_2(aq)$

Lithium carbonate. The other Group I metal carbonates are thermally stable and Group II metal carbonates are insoluble in water. A flame test should produce a scarlet colour to confirm the presence of lithium.

Chapter 17

(a) (i) 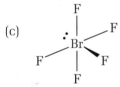   (ii)

(b) $\overset{\delta+}{I}\!-\!\overset{\delta-}{Cl}$

(c)

2. (a)

   (b)

   (c)

   (d)

   (e)

(b) and (c) are isomers. (d) and (e) are also isomers.

3.

2-Bromopropane exists as a pair of optical isomers.

4.

$$CH_3-\overset{\text{H}}{\underset{\text{OH}}{\overset{|}{\underset{|}{C^*}}}}-CH_2CH_3$$

Name: butan-2-ol

(a) A reaction in which Ox of some atoms of an element goes up and Ox of some atoms of the same element from the same compound goes down

(b) $3Cl_2(aq) + 6NaOH(aq)$
   $\longrightarrow 5NaCl(aq) + NaClO_3(aq) + 3H_2O(l)$
   Ox(Cl) in $Cl_2 = 0$, in $NaCl = -I$, in $NaClO_3 = +V$

(a) (i) The molecules have more electrons and therefore the van der Waals forces increase.

   (ii) The shared electrons are further from the nuclei.

   (iii) The elements are less able to accept an electron as the added electron goes into a shell further from the nucleus.

(b) The F—F bond energy is smaller than the Cl—Cl bond energy owing to repulsion between non-bonding electrons in F_2.

(a) $-I, 0, +I, +V, +VII$

(b) $HClO, HClO_3, HClO_4$

(c) $HClO < HClO_3 < HClO_4$. The charge on the anion left after loss of H^+ is spread over the increased number of oxygen atoms.

Chapter 18

(a) Propene (b) But-2-ene (c) Buta-1,3-diene
(d) Butane-1,3 diol (e) 1,1,1 Trichloropropane

5. (a)

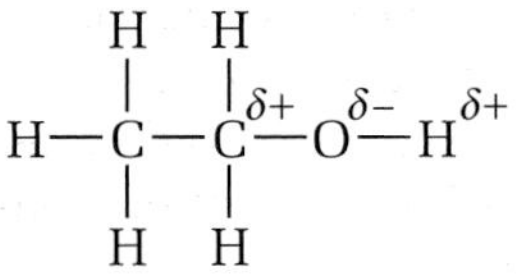

H H
| |
H—C—C—O—H with $\delta+$ on C, $\delta-$ on O, $\delta+$ on H
| |
H H

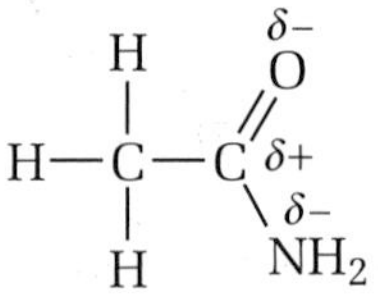

(d)

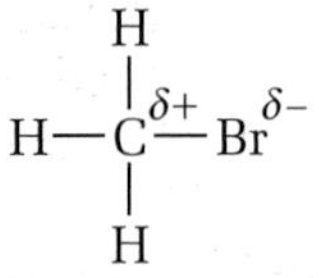

H
|
H—C—Br with $\delta+$ on C, $\delta-$ on Br
|
H

(b)

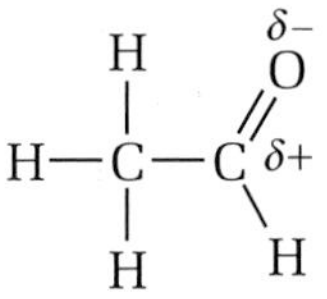

H   O (with $\delta-$)
| ‖
H—C—C ($\delta+$)
| \
H   H

(e)

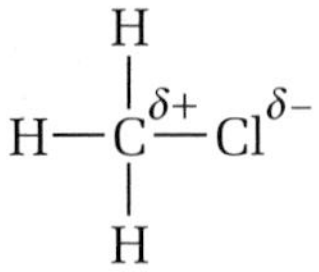

H
|
H—C—Cl with $\delta+$ on C, $\delta-$ on Cl
|
H

(c)

H   O (with $\delta-$)
| ‖
H—C—C ($\delta+$)
| \ ($\delta-$)
H   NH$_2$

(f)

H
|
H—C—F with $\delta+$ on C, $\delta-$ on F
|
H

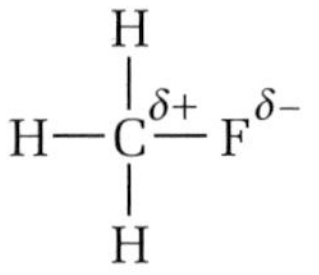

(d), (e), (f)

6. (a) O—O (b) C—I (c) C—O (d) C—I
7. Nucleophiles: H^-, CH_3NH_2, Cl^-, H_2O
    Electrophiles: H^+, HSO_3^+.
    Radical: H•

8.

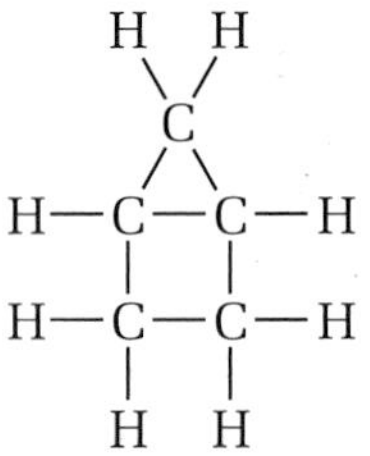

H H
\ /
C
|
H—C—C—H
| |
H—C—C—H
| |
H H

Chapter 19
1. (a) Propane
    (b) 2,4-Dimethylpentane
    (c) Cyclopentane
    (d) Cyclohexane

2. (a)

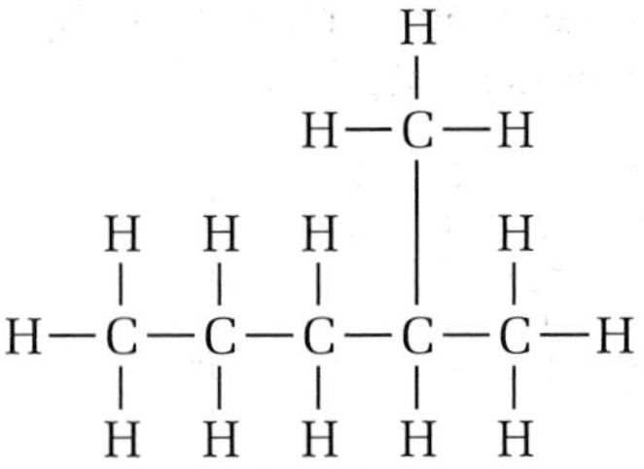

H
|
H—C—H
H H H | H
| | | | |
H—C—C—C—C—C—H
| | | | |
H H H H H

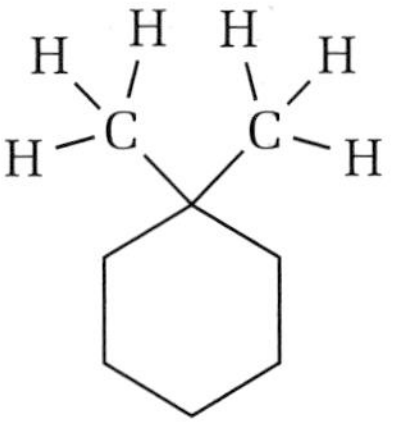

(b)

H H H   H
\ |/ |
H—C   C—H
    \   /
     (cyclohexane ring)

(c)

H
|
H—C—H
|
H—C—H
H H H H | H H H
| | | | | | | |
H—C—C—C—C—C—C—C—H
| | | | | | |
H H H H H H H
|
H—C—H
|
H

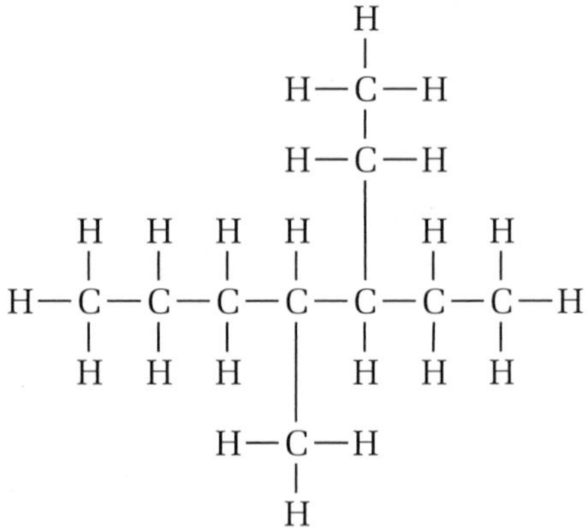

(d)

H H H
H \ | | / H
\   C—C   /
H—C   C—H
| |
H—C   C—H
/   C—C   \
H / | | \ H
   H H H H

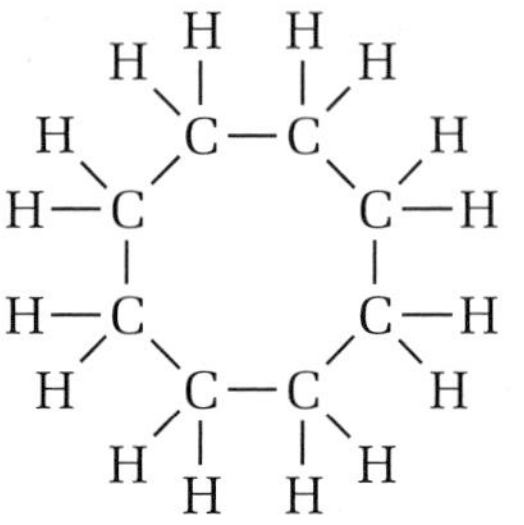

3. $C_6H_{14} + 9\tfrac{1}{2}O_2 \longrightarrow 6CO_2 + 7H_2O$
4. Hex-1-ene
5. $6.14 \times 10^{14}\ s^{-1}$
6. approx. 50% at room temperature
7. (a) CH_2, (b) C_4H_8 (c) It must have a ring: it could b
    cyclobutane or methylcyclopropane.

Chapter 20
1. (a) Methylpropene (b) Buta-1,3-diene
    (c) 2-Chloropropene (d) 1-Chloropro-1-pene
    (e) 3-Chloroprop-1-ene (f) Chloroethene

2. (a)

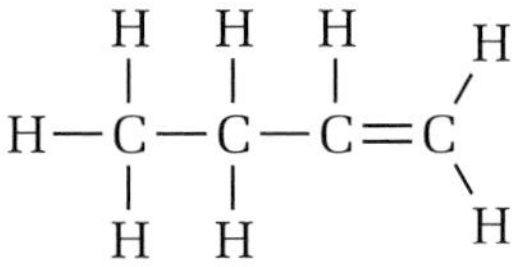

H H H   H
| | | /
H—C—C—C=C
| | \
H H   H

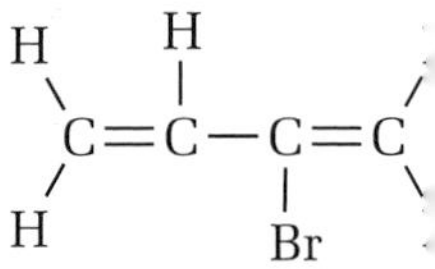

(b)

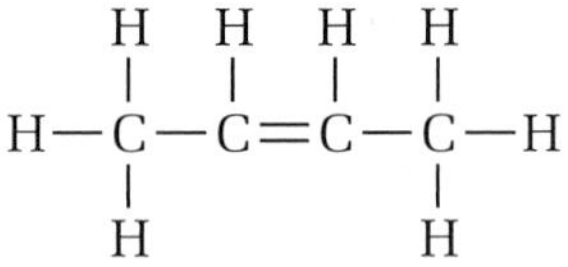

H H H H
| | | |
H—C—C=C—C—H
| |
H   H

(c)

H   H
\ |
C=C—C=C
/ | \
H   H   Br

(d)

(cyclohexene ring)

3. (a) (i)

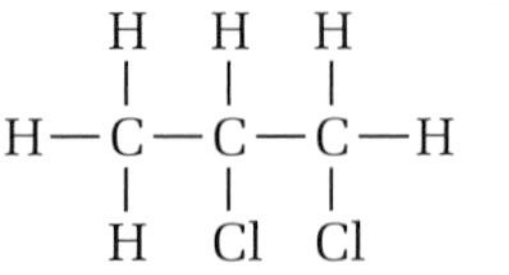

H H H
| | |
H—C—C—C—H
| | |
H Cl Cl

(ii)

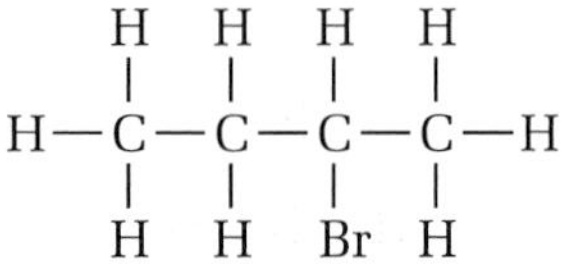

H H H H
| | | |
H—C—C—C—C—H
| | | |
H H Br H

(iii)

H H H H
| | | |
H—C—C—C—C—H
| | | |
H Br Br H

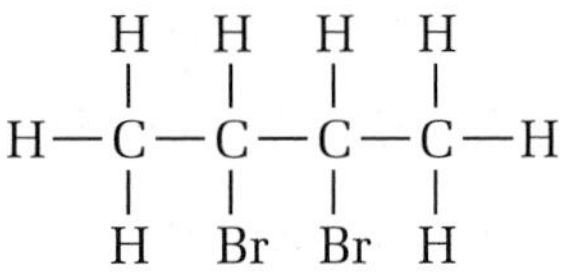

```
        H  H
        |  |
(iv)  R—C—C—H
        |  |
       OH  H
```

(b) (ii) BrCH₂CH₂CH₂CH₃
     (iii) BrCH₂CH₂CH₂CH₂Br, BrCH₂CH₂CHBrCH₃
     (iv) RCH₂CH₂OH

4. 1. Dehydrate to propene.
   2. React with concentrated sulphuric acid and
      then water.

5.
```
     H  H  H      H   H     H  H     H
     |  |  |       \ /        \ /
 H—C—C—C=C          C          C
     |  |    \     / \        / \
     H  H     H   H   C=C     H   H
                      / \
                     H   H
```

```
       H     H
        \   /
         C
        / \        H
   H   /   \      /
    \ /     C=C
     C        \   / H
    / \        C
   H   \      / \
        H    H   H
```

With HBr, but-1-ene will produce 1-bromobutane
and 2-bromobutane.
cis-But-2-ene and *trans*-but-2-ene will both
produce 2-bromobutane.

Chapter 21

1. (a) 2-Fluorobutane
   (b) 2-Chloro-4-fluoro-3-iodopentane
   (c) 2-Chloropropene

2.
```
         H  H  Cl
         |  |  |
(a)  H—C—C—C—Cl
         |  |  |
         H  H  H
```

```
         H  H  H  H
         |  |  |  |
(b)  H—C—C—C—C—H
         |  |  |  |
         H  H  Br Cl
```

(c)
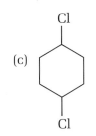

```
                      H
                      |
                   H—C—H
      H  H  H  H    |    H
      |  |  |  |    |    |
(d) H—C—C—C—C—C—C—Br
      |  |  |  |    |    |
      H  H  H  H    H    H
```

3. (a) (i) Substitution (ii) Elimination (iii) Addition
   (b) (i) Cold aqueous hydroxide ions
       (ii) Hot hydroxide ions dissolved in alcohol

4. (c) > (b) > (a). The C—I bond is weakest and the
   C—Cl bond strongest.

5.
```
                                                    δ−
      H   H                             H   Cl
      |   | δ+   δ−                      |   | δ+    δ−
(a) H—C—C—Cl                    (c) H—C—C—Cl
      |   |                              |   |
      H   H                              H   H
```

```
      H   H                             H       Cl
      |   | δ+   δ−                       \      | δ−
(b) H—C—C—Br                    (d)       C=C
      |   |                               / δ+/
      H   H                              H       H
```

(c) because the δ+ carbon has 2 chlorines bonded
   to it.

6.
```
         H  H  H  H
         |  |  |  |
(a) (i) H—C—C—C—C—O—H
         |  |  |  |
         H  H  H  H
```

```
            H  H  H  H     H
            |  |  |  |     /
(ii)   H—C—C—C—C—N
            |  |  |  |     \
            H  H  H  H      H
```

```
            H  H  H  H        H  H
            |  |  |  |        |  |
(iii) H—C—C—C—C—O—C—C—H
            |  |  |  |        |  |
            H  H  H  H        H  H
```

```
            H  H  H  H        H  H
            |  |  |  |        |  |
(iv)  H—C—C—C—C—O—C—C—H
            |  |  |  |        |  |
            H  H  H  H        H  H
```

(b) (iv) would go faster because it uses a
    negatively charged nucleophile.
(c) Yes; this isomer would react via an S_N1
    mechanism rather than S_N2.

7.
```
         H  H  H  H  H      H
         |  |  |  |  |      /
(a) H—C—C—C—C—C=C
         |  |  |  |         \
         H  H  H  H          H
```

```
         H  H  H  H  H  H
         |  |  |  |  |  |
     H—C—C—C—C=C—C—H
         |  |  |        |
         H  H  H        H
```

(hexagon ring figure)

(b) In both cases chlorine is eliminated along with *either* of the hydrogens adjacent to it. In 2-chlorohexene this gives rise to two possible products. In chlorocyclohexane there is only one product possible.

(c) One only

8. 1. Eliminate hydrogen bromide to give ethene by heating with hydroxide ions dissolved in alcohol.

   2. Add bromine across the double bond.

9. Nucleophilic substitution of a haloalkane using cyanide ions to increase the carbon chain length by one.

Ethanol $\longrightarrow$ a haloethane $\longrightarrow$ propanenitrile $\longrightarrow$ propanoic acid

Chapter 22

1. (a) Butan-1-ol (b) Butan-2-ol

2. (a)

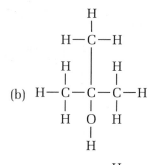

(b)

(c)

3. (a) Tertiary (b) Secondary

4. (a) With an acid: $H^+ + R—OH \longrightarrow ROH_2^+$

   (b) With a base: $R—OH + B^- \longrightarrow RO^- + BH$

Chapter 23

1. (a) $\dfrac{p^2NH_3(g)_{eqm}}{pN_2(g)_{eqm}\, p^3H_2(g)_{eqm}}$

   (b) $\dfrac{p^2SO_3(g)_{eqm}}{p^2SO_2(g)_{eqm}\, pO_2(g)_{eqm}}$

   (c) $\dfrac{pPCl_3(g)_{eqm}\, pCl_2(g)_{eqm}}{pPCl_5(g)}$

   (d) $\dfrac{pCO(g)_{eqm}\, pH_2O(g)_{eqm}}{pCO_2(g)_{eqm}\, pH_2(g)_{eqm}}$

   (e) $\dfrac{p^2NO(g)_{eqm}}{pN_2(g)_{eqm}\, pO_2(g)_{eqm}}$

   (f) $\dfrac{pN_2(g)_{eqm}\, pO_2(g)_{eqm}}{p^2NO(g)_{eqm}}$

   (g) $\dfrac{pCO(g)_{eqm}\, pCl_2(g)_{eqm}}{pCOCl_2(g)_{eqm}}$

   (h) (f) is the reciprocal of (e).

2. (a) $K_c = \dfrac{[HCl(aq)]_{eqm}^{2}}{[BiCl_3(aq)]_{eqm}}$, units: $mol\ dm^{-3}$

   (b) $K_c = [Ag^+(aq)]_{eqm}[Br^-(aq)]_{eqm}$, units: $mol^2\ dm^{-6}$

   (c) $K_c = [Pb^{2+}(aq)]_{eqm}[Cl^-(aq)]_{eqm}^{2}$, units: $mol^3\ dm^{-9}$

   (d) $K_p = \dfrac{p^4H_2(g)_{eqm}}{p^4H_2O(g)_{eqm}}$, no units

   (e) $K_p = \dfrac{pH_2(g)_{eqm}\, pCO(g)_{eqm}}{pH_2O(g)_{eqm}}$, units: Pa

   (f) $K_p = pCO_2(g)_{eqm}$, units: Pa

   (g) $K_c = \dfrac{1}{[Ca^{2+}(aq)]_{eqm}\, [CO_3{}^{2-}(aq)]_{eqm}}$, units: $dm^6\ mol^{-2}$

   (h) $K_p = pH_2O(g)_{eqm}$, units: Pa

   (i) (b) and (c) are solubility products

3. 56.3. No effect: there are the same number of molecules on both sides of the equation. Dissolve the HI in water and titrate with alkali.

4. (a)

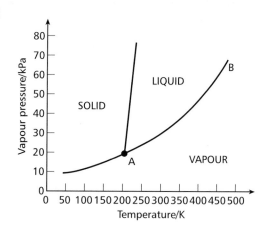

(b) $T_b = 450$ K, T_m 220 K (c) The boiling point/pressure curve, the set of values of pressure and temperature at which liquid and vapour are at equilibrium. (d) 20 kPa

5. 25.2 kPa. It would be completely over to the left.

6. (a) 0.91 g
   (b) 0.97 g

7. 0.45

8. 0.522, 0.49

9. All

10. (a) 10^5 Pa (b) 48.4

Chapter 24

1. (a) (i) 2.1 (ii) 2.6 (iii) 3.1
   (b) (i) 7.8 (ii) 8.4

(a) 2.5×10^{-5} mol dm^{-3} (b) 4.6

4.6

0.63

Mix ethanoic acid and sodium ethanoate so that the ratio of their concentrations is 1.6 : 1.

Methyl yellow, congo red

Chapter 25

(a) +0.93 V

(b) −0.55 V

(c) +0.97 V

(d) +0.13 V

(a) (i) Ni(s)|Ni^{2+}(aq) $\vdots\vdots$ Ag$^+$(aq)|Ag(s)
$E^{\ominus} = +1.05$ V

(ii) Pt|H$_2$(g)|2H$^+$(aq) $\vdots\vdots$ Sn^{2+}(aq)|Sn(s)
$E^{\ominus} = -0.14$ V

(iii) Pt|Cr^{2+}(aq), Cr^{3+}(aq) $\vdots\vdots$ Zn^{2+}(aq)| Zn(s)
$E^{\ominus} = -0.35$ V

(iv) Pt|[Mn^{2+}(aq)+4H$_2$O(l)],
[MnO$_4^-$(aq)+8H$^+$(aq)] $\vdots\vdots$ I$_2$(aq), 2I$^-$(aq)|Pt
$E^{\ominus} = -0.97$ V

(b) (i) Nickel would dissolve and silver be deposited.

(ii) Tin would dissolve and hydrogen gas be produced.

(iii) Zinc would dissolve and Cr^{3+} be converted to Cr^{2+}.

(iv) Iodide ions would be converted to iodine and MnO$_4^-$ ions be converted to Mn^{2+}.

3. (a)

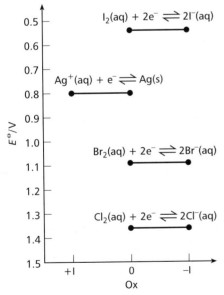

(b) Cl$_2$(aq) and Br$_2$(aq)

(c) No

Chapter 26

1. (a) Collecting the carbon dioxide gas given off

(b) (i) First order: the first three half-lives are approximately the same.

(ii) First order: the graph shows that rate $\propto$[Br$_2$]

(c) By maintaining [HCO$_2$H] much greater than [Br$_2$]

(d) No. We do not know how the rate varies with [HCO$_2$H].

2. (a) (i) 1 (ii) 2 (b) 3

3. 102 kJ mol^{-1}

4. (b)

5. (a) 108 kJ mol^{-1}

(b) HI molecules might be adsorbed onto the surface of the catalyst, thus weakening the H—I bond.

Chapter 27

1. (a) 94 cm^3 (b) 53 cm^3 (c) 1.37 dm^3

(d) 91.9 m^3 (e) 1.7 pints

2. (a) HCl: there are equal volumes of hydrogen and chlorine (Avogadro's law).

(b) Pass it over heated copper oxide, for example.

(c) Pass it over soda-lime, for example.

(d)

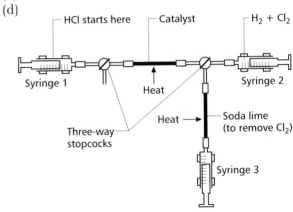

3. 101.3

4. 32

Chapter 28

1. (a) 16 (b) 1/16 (c) 87.5%

2. (a) (i) Approximately zero (ii) Significantly positive (iii) Significantly negative (iv) Significantly positive

(b) (i) −7.8 J K^{-1} mol^{-1}, solid $\longrightarrow$ solid

(ii) +876.4 J K^{-1} mol^{-1}, solid $\longrightarrow$ gases

(iii) −174.8 J K^{-1} mol^{-1}, gas $\longrightarrow$ solid

(iv) +119.0 J K^{-1} mol^{-1}, liquid $\longrightarrow$ gas

3. (a) No, because $\Delta H^{\ominus}$ and $\Delta S^{\ominus}$ have the same sign.

(b) (i) +493 kJ mol^{-1} (ii) −52 kJ mol^{-1}

(c) 5523 K

4. For reaction 1: (a) −199 J K^{-1} mol^{-1}

(b) (i) 309 J K^{-1} mol^{-1} (ii) 46 J K^{-1} mol^{-1}

(c) (i) 110 J K^{-1} mol^{-1} (ii) −153 J K^{-1} mol^{-1}

For reaction 2: (a) 361 J K^{-1} mol^{-1}

(b) (i) −1150 J K^{-1} mol^{-1} (ii) −172 J K^{-1} mol^{-1}

(c) (i) −789 J K^{-1} mol^{-1} (ii) 189 J K^{-1} mol^{-1}

5. (a) −521 kJ mol^{-1} (b) −523 kJ mol^{-1}

The difference is due to rounding errors in the data.

Chapter 29

1. 0.320 nm, 10.6°
2. (a) C_3H_8O, 60.05748; $C_2H_8N_2$, 60.0687; $C_2H_4O_2$, 60.02112; C_3H_8O
   (b) Several answers are possible, including for example C_3NH_{10}.
3. (a) $BeCl_2$ is linear whereas SCl_2 is angular.
   (b) BCl_3 is trigonal planar but PCl_3 is pyramidal.
4. (a) 3000 cm^{-1} is O—H; 1600 cm^{-1} is C=O.
   (b)

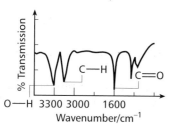

   (c)

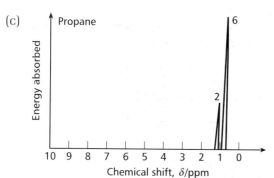

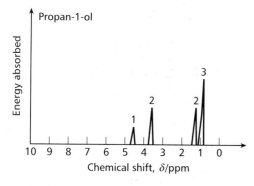

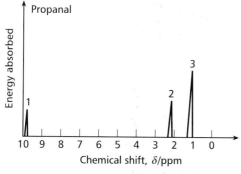

5. (a) C_2H_4O (b) 44, C_2H_4O (c) Yes (d) C = O, yes
   (e) H—C—C (f) 2, yes (g) Yes

Chapter 30

1. $SiO_2 + C \longrightarrow CO_2 + Si$
   $Si + 2Cl_2 \longrightarrow SiCl_4$
   $SiCl_4 + 2H_2 \longrightarrow Si + 2HCl$
2. (a) Decreases because the E—E bond gets weaker.
   (b) +II becomes more stable owing to the inert pair effect.
   (c) Increases: the lower members of the group are metallic.
   (d) Covalent $\longrightarrow$ ionic: the lower members of the group are metallic.
3. (a) 6
   (b) +942 kJ mol^{-1}
   (c) Two N_2 molecules are 942 kJ mol^{-1} more stable than one molecule of N_4.
   (d) Two P_2 molecules are 218 kJ mol^{-1} less stable than one molecule of P_4.
4.

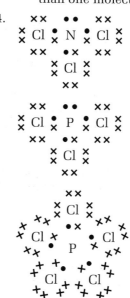

   NCl_3, PCl_3 are pyramidal with bond angles of less than 105°, while PCl_5 is trigonal bipyramidal. In phosphorus an electron can be promoted from 3s to 3d. This is not possible in the case of nitrogen.
5. The P^{3-} ion would be bigger than N^{3-}, so the lattice energy of the resulting compound would be less negative.
6. (a) S, 0; SO_2, IV; SO_3, VI; H_2SO_4, VI; $H_2S_2O_7$, VI
   (b) The first two
7. (a) $1s^2 2s^2 2p^6 3s^2 3p^4$
   (b) (i) A 3s and the paired 3p electron are promoted to 3d.
       (ii)

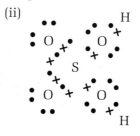

Chapter 31

1. (a) +III (b) +II (c) +II
2. (a) Scandium and zinc atoms both have electrons in the d orbitals.
   (b) Neither have partially filled d orbitals in their compounds. Scandium always forms the 3+ ion, losing both its outer s electrons and its one d electron, whereas zinc always forms Zn^{2+} in which the d orbitals are full.
   (c) Cu^+ ($3d^{10}$), Ti^{4+} ($3d^0$)
3. (a) $[Cr(H_2O)_6]^{3+}$
   (b) $[Co(NH_3)_4Cl_2]^+$
   (c) $Fe[(H_2O)_4(OH)_2]^+$
4. (a) Blue
   (b) $[Cu(H_2O)_4]^{2+}$
   (c) Colour changes from blue to yellow as Cl^- ions displace H_2O because Cl^- is a better ligand.
   (d) Colour changes to deep blue as NH_3 displaces Cl^- because NH_3 is a better ligand.
   (e) Colour changes to pale blue as edta displaces NH_3 because edta is a better ligand.
   (f) A pale blue precipitate of copper hydroxide, $Cu(OH)_2$, would form initially because ammonia solution contains OH^- ions. In (d) these would be neutralised by the hydrochloric acid.
   (g) $[CuCl_4]^{2-}$ (yellow) moves towards the positive anode and $[Cu(NH_3)_4]^{2+}$ (blue) moves towards the negative cathode.

Chapter 32

1. (a) Ethylbenzene (b) 1,3-Dibromobenzene
   (c) 4-Chlorophenol (d) 2-Iodomethylbenzene
2. (a)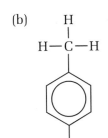

   (c)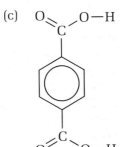

   (b)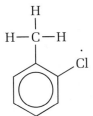

   (d)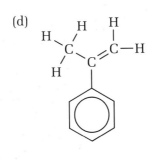

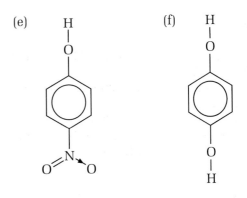

3. (a) 3° alcohol (b) 3° alcohol (c) 2° alcohol
   (d) phenol
4. c > b > a > d. Electron-withdrawing groups stabilise the negative ion formed by loss of H^+.

Chapter 33

1. (a) Butanal (b) Hexan-2-one (c) Cyclohexanone
   (d) Pentane-2,4-dione
2. (a)
3. (a)
   (b)

(c)
```
     H  H  H
     |  |  |
  H— C— C— C —H
     |  |  |
     H  O  H
        |
        H
```

(d)
```
        O
        ‖
  H— C
        \
         O—H
```

(e)
```
     H  O  H
     |  ‖  |
  H— C— C— C —I
     |     |
     H     H
```

(f)
```
           H
           |
        H\ N ⁄H
           ·
     H  H  N  H
     |  |  ‖  |
  H— C— C— C— C —H
     |  |     |
     H  H     H
```

Chapter 34

1. (a) Propanoic acid (b) 3-Bromopropanoic acid
   (c) Ethyl ethanoate (d) Propanamide

2. (a)
```
     H  Cl   O
     |  |   ⁄⁄
  H— C— C— C
     |  |   \
     H  H    N—H
             |
             H
```

(b)
```
     H  H    O
     |  |   ⁄⁄
  H— C— C— C     H
     |  |   \    |
     H  H    O— C —H
                |
                H
```

(c)
```
        H      O
        |     ⁄⁄
   H— C— C
        |      
        H      
        
     H  H      O
     |  |     ⁄
  H— C— C— C
     |  |     \\
     H  H      O
```

(d)
```
     H  H    O
     |  |   ⁄⁄
  H— C— C— C
     |  |   \
     H  H    Cl
```

3. (a) Propanamide (b) Methyl ethanoate
   (c) Butanoic acid (d) Butanoyl chloride
4. (d) > (b) > (c) > (a). The more electronegative
   halogen stabilises the negative charge on the ion
   left after loss of H^+. The two fluorines are better
   than one.
5. $CH_3CH_2CHClCO_2H > CH_3CHClCH_2CO_2H >$
   $CH_2ClCH_2CH_2CO_2H > CH_3CH_2CH_2CO_2H$
   The electron-withdrawing chlorine atom makes
   the acid stronger the nearer it is to the —CO_2H
   group.

Chapter 35

1. (a) Methylpropylamine (b) Tripropylamine
   (c) Benzenecarbonitrile; (d) Butanenitrile
   (e) Tetrapropylammonium ion

2. (a)
```
     H  H  H     H  H  H
     |  |  |     |  |  |
  H— C— C— C— N— C— C— C —H
     |  |  |  |  |  |  |
     H  H  H  H  H  H  H
```

(b)
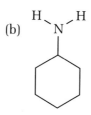

(c)
```
     H  H  H
     |  |  |
  H— C— C— C— C≡N
     |  |  |
     H  H  H
```

(d)
```
              H
              |
           H— C —H
              |
     H        |        H
     |        |        |
  H— C————— N⁺ ————— C —H
     |        |        |
     H        |        H
              |
           H— C —H
              |
              H
```

3. (c) < (d) < (a) < (b).
4. (a) The ethylmethylammonium ion
   (b) *N*-Propylethanamide (c) Ethylmethylamine
   (d) Propylamine (e) Propanenitrile

Chapter 36

1. (a) (i) chloroethene (ii) poly(chloroethene)
   (b) (i) addition (ii) condensation
   (c) water
2. Asp-Arg-Val-Tyr-Ile-His-Pro-Phe
3. Add some monofunctional alcohol or carboxylic
   acid.

Chapter 37

1. (a) React with potassium cyanide.
   (b) Reflux with excess acidified potassium dichromate.
   (c) Reduce with lithium tetrahydridoaluminate(III).
   (d) React with sulphuric acid and then add water.
   (e) Dehydrate by passing over heated aluminium oxide.

2. (a) 1. React with sulphuric acid and then add water.
      2. Reflux with excess acidified potassium dichromate.
   (b) 1. React with potassium bromide and concentrated sulphuric acid.
      2. React with potassium cyanide.
   (c) 1. React with ammonia.
      2. Hofmann degradation
   (d) 1. React with sodium nitrite and hydrochloric acid (cold).
      2. Allow to warm up.
   (e) 1. Reduce with any reducing agent.
      2. React with potassium bromide and concentrated sulphuric acid.
   (f) 1. Nitrate with a mixture of concentrated nitric and sulphuric acids.
      2. Reduce with lithium tetrahydridoaluminate(III) for example.

3. (a) 1. Dehydrate by passing over heated aluminium oxide. 2. React with sulphuric acid and then add water. 3. Reflux with excess acidified potassium dichromate.
   (b) 1. React with alkaline potassium manganate(VII). 2. Reflux with excess acidified potassium dichromate. 3. React with phosphorus pentachloride.

Chapter 38

1. (a) both C_4H_8O (b) Butanone
2. Dichloromethane
3. Ethanoic acid

Further examination questions

Chapter 7

1. (a) Part of the emission spectrum of sodium is shown in the figure below.
The most intense line in the spectrum has a wavelength of 590 nm.
The lines in the spectrum may be identified by their colour and by their wavelength (λ).

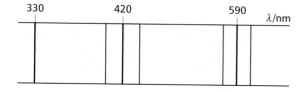

(i) Suggest the colour of the line at 590 nm.
(ii) Give the name of the units of wavelength.
(iii)Describe the process within the sodium atom that leads to the production of these lines.
(iv) State a large-scale use of lamps filled with sodium vapour.

(b) Briefly describe how you would distinguish between solid samples of sodium chloride and potassium chloride in the laboratory.

[AEB 1995]

Chapter 8

2. (a) Define the term *standard enthalpy of formation*.
(b) Tetrachloromethane, CCl_4, is a colourless liquid at room temperature.
Calculate its standard enthalpy of formation, using the data given below.

Process	$\Delta H_f^{\ominus}$/kJ mol^{-1}
$Cl_2(g) \longrightarrow 2Cl(g)$	+242
$C(graphite) \longrightarrow C(g)$	+715
$CCl_4(l) \longrightarrow CCl_4(g)$	+26
$CCl_4(g) \longrightarrow C(g) + 4Cl(g)$	+1308

[Oxford 1997]

3. Ammonia is a covalent molecule.
(i) Describe what is meant by a covalent bond.
(ii) Explain the meaning of *bond enthalpy*.
(iii)Calculate the bond enthalpy of the N—H bond in NH_3 using the data given below. Show your method of working clearly.

$$N_2(g) + 3H_2(g) \longrightarrow 2NH_3(g)$$
$$\Delta H^{\ominus} (298 \text{ K}) = -92 \text{ kJ mol}^{-1}$$

Bond	Bond enthalpy/kJ mol^{-1}
N≡N	946
H—H	436

(iv) The enthalpy of formation of
H H
\ /
N—N (g)
/ \
H H
is 94 kJ mol^{-1}

Using the N—H bond enthalpy derived in (iii), calculate the bond enthalpy of the N—H bond. (If you have not derived the N—H bond enthalpy in (iii), use the value 400 kJ mol^{-1}.)

[Oxford 1997, part question]

Chapter 9

4. An incomplete Born–Haber cycle for the formation of silver oxide, Ag_2O, from its constituent elements is shown below.

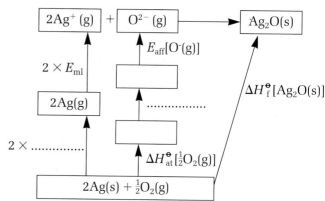

(a) (i) Complete the diagram by entering in the appropriate places the missing symbols for enthalpy changes and the missing formulae with state symbols.

(ii) Using the following data, calculate a value, including sign and units, for the lattice energy of silver oxide. Give your answer to 3 significant figures.

Atomisation energy
of silver, $\Delta H_{at}^{\ominus}[Ag(s)]$ $= +285$ kJ mol^{-1}
Atomisation energy
of oxygen, $\Delta H_{at}^{\ominus}[\frac{1}{2}O_2(g)]$ $= +249$ kJ mol^{-1}
First ionisation energy of silver, E_{ml} $= +731$ kJ mol^{-1}
Electron affinity of oxygen, $E_{aff}[O(g)]$ $= -141$ kJ mol^{-1}
Electron affinity of oxygen ions,
$E_{aff}[O^-(g)]$ $= +798$ kJ mol^{-1}
Enthalpy change of formation
of silver oxide, $\Delta H_f^{\ominus}[Ag_2O(s)]$ $= -31$ kJ mol^{-1}

(b) The silver ion is smaller than the halide ions.
(i) Draw a diagram to show the effect the silver ion has on a halide ion next to it in the lattice of a silver halide.

(ii) State TWO quantities which must be known about the ions in a compound in order to calculate a **theoretical** lattice energy from interionic attraction.

(iii) How would a theoretical lattice energy for a silver halide compare with a Born–Haber cycle value? Give a reason for your answer.

[London Nuffield 1997]

Chapter 10

5. (a) 4.50 g of water is evaporated by 10.0 kJ of electrical energy.
   (i) Calculate the number of moles of water evaporated.
   (ii) Calculate the enthalpy change of vaporisation per mole of water. Your answer should include both sign and units.
   (b) (i) Draw a diagram to show the principal molecular force between two water molecules.
   (ii) Explain why the value for the enthalpy change of vaporisation of water is much greater than that for the other Group 6 hydrides.

[London (Nuffield) 1997, AS]

Chapter 11

6. This question refers to the Haber process for the synthesis of ammonia.
   The equation which represents the reaction is given below.

$$N_2(g) + 3H_2(g) \rightleftharpoons 2NH_3(g)$$
$$\Delta H^\ominus (298 \text{ K}) = -92 \text{ kJ mol}^{-1}$$

(i) Give **one** source each of nitrogen and hydrogen for this process.
(ii) Write the expression for the equilibrium constant, K_p, for the above process. If the pressure is measured in atmospheres what will be the units of K_p?
(iii) State *Le Chatelier's principle*.
(iv) State and explain the effect on the above equilibrium of
   I. increasing the pressure, and
   II. removing ammonia from the mixture of gases.
(v) I. Describe the effect on the equilibrium yield of increasing the operating temperature of an exothermic reaction.
   II. Considering your response to (v) I. above explain why the ammonia synthesis is operated at a temperature of 400 °C.

(vi) Name the catalyst used in the Haber process.
(vii) I. Describe the function of a catalyst.
   II. Describe the effect of a catalyst on the position of equilibrium.

[WJEC 1996]

7. (a) The following equilibrium mixture may be formed, in the presence of a dilute strong acid catalyst, at room temperature over a period of several days.

$$CH_3COOH(l) + CH_3CH_2OH(l)$$
$$\rightleftharpoons CH_3COOCH_2CH_3(l) + H_2O(l)$$

Describe, giving essential practical details, how you would perform a set of experiments to determine an average value for the equilibrium constant, K_c, for the above reaction.
(**No** calculations need to be described).
(b) 6.0 g of ethanoic acid and 4.6 g of ethanol were added to 4.4 g of ethyl ethanoate, and the mixture was allowed to reach equilibrium. It was found that 0.04 mol of ethanoic acid were present in the equilibrium mixture. Calculate the equilibrium constant, K_c, for the reaction.
(c) The experiment in (b) is repeated using a larger amount of ethanol in the initial mixture. State and explain what effect this change would have on:
   (i) the value of K_c
   (ii) the position of the final equilibrium
   (iii) the time taken for the reaction to reach equilibrium.

[AEB 1995]

Chapter 22

8. This question is about ethanol and some of its reactions.
   (a) A 750 cm³ bottle of red wine is labelled as containing 12.4% of ethanol by volume.
   (i) Calculate the volume of ethanol in a glass of this red wine, assuming that there are six glasses of wine in a bottle.
   (ii) Calculate the number of moles of ethanol in one glass of red wine.
   [molar mass of ethanol = 46 g mol⁻¹; density of ethanol = 0.79 g cm⁻³]
   (b) One method of analysing the amount of ethanol is to use acidified potassium dichromate(VI), $K_2Cr_2O_7$, to oxidise the ethanol. The colour change is from orange to green. The equation for the oxidation is:

$$K_2Cr_2O_7(aq) + 3C_2H_5OH(aq) + 4H_2SO_4(aq)$$
$$\longrightarrow K_2SO_4(aq) + Cr_2(SO_4)_3(aq)$$
$$+ 3CH_3CHO(aq) + 7H_2O(l)$$

(i) Which species in the equation is responsible for the green colour?

(ii) Draw the displayed formula of the organic product, ethanal.

(iii) Calculate the minimum mass of potassium dichromate(VI), $K_2Cr_2O_7$, needed to oxidise the ethanol in one glass of red wine. Use the Periodic Table (p. 680) as a source of data.

(c) Further oxidation of the ethanal produces ethanoic acid, CH_3CO_2H.

(i) What is the Brønsted–Lowry definition of an acid?

(ii) Ethanoic acid is considered to be a weak acid. What is meant by the term *weak acid*?

(iii) Write a balanced equation, including state symbols, for the neutralisation of ethanoic acid by sodium hydroxide solution.

(iv) The solution produced by the reaction in (iii) conducts electricity. Give the formula of the organic ion present.

(v) Electrolysis of this solution produces two gases at the anode.
One of the gases turns calcium hydroxide solution cloudy.
The other gas is an alkane.
By considering the formula of the anion, suggest the names and formulae of these two gases.

[London (Nuffield) 1998]

Chapter 25

9. (b) The table below gives *standard electrode potentials, $E^\ominus$*, for some systems for which the ion/electron half equations are given.

Half equation	$E^\ominus$/ V
$\frac{1}{2}Cl_2 + e^- \rightleftharpoons Cl^-$	+1.36
$\frac{1}{2}Br_2 + e^- \rightleftharpoons Br^-$	+1.07
$\frac{1}{2}I_2 + e^- \rightleftharpoons I^-$	+0.54
$MnO_2 + 4H^+ + 2e^- \rightleftharpoons Mn^{2+} + 2H_2O$	+1.23

Using the appropriate information from the table answer the following.

(i) State what is observed, and give an explanation for the reactions that occur, when chlorine is bubbled through aqueous potassium iodide.

(ii) Explain why a black solid is formed when excess liquid bromine is added to aqueous potassium iodide.

(iii) Explain the meaning of the term *standard electrode potential*.

Chlorine gas is liberated when manganese(IV) oxide is heated with concentrated hydrochloric acid. Commen on this reaction in the light of the standard $E^\ominus$ data above.

(c) Give the name and formula of a sodium compound containing chlorine in **each** of the following oxidation states: I and V.
For **each** compound give a large-scale use.

[WJEC 1997, part]

Chapter 26

10. (a) The equation for the reaction between thiosulphate ions and hydrogen ions is

$$S_2O_3^{2-}(aq) + 2H^+(aq) \longrightarrow SO_2(g) + S(s) + H_2O(l$$

(i) What is the oxidation number of sulphur in thiosulphate ions, $S_2O_3^{2-}$; sulphur dioxide, SO_2; sulphur, S?

(ii) State and explain the type of redox reaction represented by the equation.

(b) The effect of temperature on the rate of reaction was investigated.
Solutions of sodium thiosulphate and hydrochloric acid were heated to the same temperature.
The time for the reaction to produce a fixed amount of sulphur was measured, and the reaction repeated at different temperatures.

(i) How could you heat the solutions to ensure that both reactants are at the same temperature?

(ii) How could you measure the time for the reaction to produce a fixed amount of sulphur?

(iii) How could you obtain a measure of the rate of reaction from your measurement of time?

(c) The results obtained from a series of experiments are tabulated below. Most of the measurements have been converted into values of l/temperature and ln rate.

Temperature /K	l/Temperature /K^{-1}	Rate	ln rate
293	3.41×10^{-3}	7.08×10^{-3}	−4.95
303	3.30×10^{-3}	1.23×10^{-2}	−4.40
313	3.19×10^{-3}	2.13×10^{-2}	−3.85
323		3.34×10^{-2}	
333	3.00×10^{-3}	5.50×10^{-2}	−2.90

(i) Complete the table by calculating the missing values.

(ii) Plot a graph of ln rate on the vertical axis, against l/temperature on the horizontal axis.

(iii) Calculate the activation energy, E_A, for the reaction, using your graph and the relationship:

$$\ln \text{rate} = \text{constant} - \frac{E_A}{R}(1/T)$$

where $R = 8.31 \, \text{J K}^{-1} \, \text{mol}^{-1}$.
Remember to include a sign and units in your answer.

[London (Nuffield) 1998]

Chapter 28

1. Use the data in the table below to answer the following questions.
Give chemical equations and calculate numerical values of ΔS wherever possible.

(a) Entropy can be linked to disorder. When H_2O goes from ice to water and then to steam, the value of its standard entropy, $S^\ominus$, alters. Illustrate this alteration by sketching a labelled graph of entropy against temperature from 200 K to 450 K, paying particular attention to the (approximate) relative sizes of all the entropy changes in your graph.

(b) At all temperatures below 100 °C, steam at atmospheric pressure condenses spontaneously to form water. Explain this observation in terms of ΔG and calculate the enthalpy of vaporisation of water at 100 °C.

(c) Explain why the reaction of 1 mol of methane with steam to form carbon monoxide and hydrogen ($\Delta H^\ominus = +210 \, \text{kJ mol}^{-1}$) is spontaneous only at high temperatures.

(d) Explain why the change of 1 mol of diamond to graphite ($\Delta H^\ominus = -2 \, \text{kJ mol}^{-1}$) is feasible at all temperatures yet does not occur at room temperature.

(e) The reaction between 1 mol of calcium oxide and carbon dioxide to form calcium carbonate ($\Delta H^\ominus = -178 \, \text{kJ mol}^{-1}$) ceases to be feasible above a certain temperature, T_s. Determine the value of T_s.

Entropy data

Species	$S^\ominus$/J K^{-1} mol^{-1}	Species	$S^\ominus$/J K^{-1} mol^{-1}
C(graphite)	6	H_2O(g)	189
C(diamond)	3	H_2O(l)	70
H_2(g)	131	CH_4(g)	186
CO(g)	198	CaO(s)	40
CO_2(g)	214	$CaCO_3$(s)	90

[NEAB 1998]

Chapter 30

12. The mass spectrum of a chloride of phosphorus, PCl_x, shows three main groups of lines, the m/e values of which are shown in the table below.

	m/e
I	66, 68
II	101, 103, 105
III	136, 138, 140, 142

There are no lines with m/e greater than 142. Chlorine is present as two isotopes, ^{35}Cl and ^{37}Cl, and Phosphorus is present in one isotopic form only, ^{31}P.

(i) Give the formulae, including isotopic masses and the charge on the species, of the particles responsible for the lines at:
$m/e = 66$;
$m/e = 103$.

(ii) Deduce the value of x in PCl_x.

(iii) Draw a dot and cross diagram to show the bonding in PCl_x.

(iv) State and explain the shape of this molecule.

(v) Write an equation for the reaction of this chloride with water.

[London (Nuffield) 1998, part question]

Chapter 32

13. The reaction scheme below shows a route by which the drug benzedrine may be prepared from benzene.

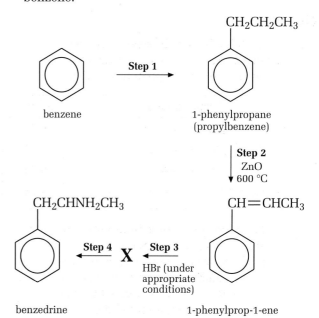

(a) (i) Give the reagents and conditions for the conversion of benzene to 1-phenylpropane in **Step 1**. Write an equation for the reaction.

(ii) Identify the compound **X** and state the reagents and conditions for its conversion to benzedrine.

(b) The yield of benzedrine produced at the end of this route is low as a number of other unwanted reactions occur. Suggest **two** organic products which may be formed as well as benzedrine and show how they might be produced.

(c) What would you predict for the physical properties and solubility of benzedrine? Give reasons for your suggestions.

(d) Benzedrine has an isomer, 4-aminopropylbenzene.

C_3H_7

NH_2

Describe a chemical reaction you could use to distinguish between samples of benzedrine and 4-aminopropylbenzene. You should include the observations you would expect to make with each compound and equations for the reactions involved.

(e) The identity of benzedrine can be confirmed by instrumental methods. Predict the results which benzedrine would give in investigations using **two** different methods, making your reasoning clear.

[London (Nuffield) 1998]

Chapter 37

14. The structural formula of the hormone adrenaline is

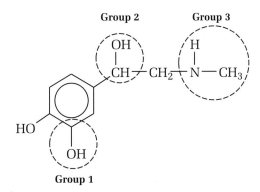

Group 2   Group 3

OH   H
| |
CH—CH₂—N—CH₃

HO

OH

Group 1

(a) What is the molecular formula of adrenaline?

(b) Name the functional groups enclosed within the numbered dotted circles and indicate, where appropriate, whether they are primary, secondary or tertiary.

(c) State whether you think adrenaline is likely to dissolve in water. Justify your answer.

(d) Which functional group reacts with:
   (i) aqueous sodium hydroxide;
   (ii) dilute hydrochloric acid?

(e) Name the reagents you would use to carry ou the following reactions with adrenaline:
   (i) converting functional **Group 1** from —OH into —OCOCH₃;
   (ii) converting functional **Group 3** from —NHCH₃ into —N(CH₃)₂.

(f) Explain how the —NHCH₃ group in adrenaline and the reagent you suggested in (e)(ii) can react together.

[London 1998

Chapter 38

15. (a) Compound **W** can be converted into three different organic compounds as shown by the reaction sequence below. Give the structures of the new compounds **X**, **Y** and **Z**.

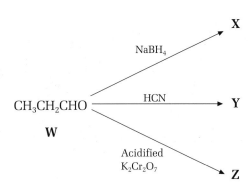

X

NaBH₄

CH₃CH₂CHO   HCN   Y

W

Acidified
K₂Cr₂O₇

Z

(b) Outline a mechanism for the formation of **Y**.

(c) The infra-red spectra shown opposite are those of the four compounds **W**, **X**, **Y** and **Z**.
   (i) Using the table of infra-red absorption data given below, identify which compound would give rise to each spectrum with the letter **W**, **X**, **Y** or **Z**.
   (ii) Suggest the wavenumber of the absorption caused by the C≡N bond. (The wavenumber of this absorption is outside the fingerprint region.)

Table of infra-red absorption data

Bond	Wavenumber/cm^{-1}
C—H	2850–3300
C—C	750–1100
C=C	1620–1680
C=O	1680–1750
C—O	1000–1300
O—H in alcohols	3230–3550
O—H in acids	2500–3000

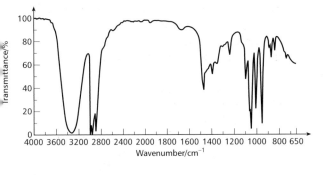

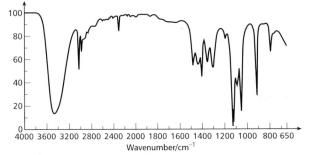

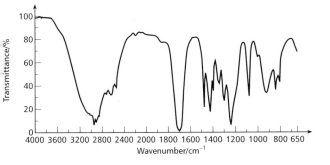

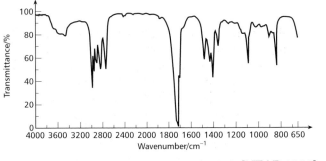

[NEAB 1998]

Index

The Periodic Table

Key

Relative atomic mass
Symbol
Name
Atomic number

Group

Period

s-block

	I	II
1	1.0 **H** Hydrogen 1	
2	6.9 **Li** Lithium 3	9.0 **Be** Beryllium 4
3	23.0 **Na** Sodium 11	24.3 **Mg** Magnesium 12
4	39.1 **K** Potassium 19	40.1 **Ca** Calcium 20
5	85.5 **Rb** Rubidium 37	87.6 **Sr** Strontium 38
6	132.9 **Cs** Caesium 55	137.3 **Ba** Barium 56
7	223.0 **Fr** Francium 87	226.0 **Ra** Radium 88

d-block

45.0 **Sc** Scandium 21	47.9 **Ti** Titanium 22	50.9 **V** Vanadium 23	52.0 **Cr** Chromium 24	54.9 **Mn** Manganese 25	55.9 **Fe** Iron 26	58.9 **Co** Cobalt 27	58.7 **Ni** Nickel 28	63.5 **Cu** Copper 29	65.4 **Zn** Zinc 30
88.9 **Y** Yttrium 39	91.2 **Zr** Zirconium 40	92.9 **Nb** Niobium 41	95.9 **Mo** Molybdenum 42	99.0 **Tc** Technetium 43	101.1 **Ru** Ruthenium 44	102.9 **Rh** Rhodium 45	106.4 **Pd** Palladium 46	107.9 **Ag** Silver 47	112.4 **Cd** Cadmium 48
138.9 **La** * Lanthanum 57	178.5 **Hf** Hafnium 72	180.9 **Ta** Tantalum 73	183.9 **W** Tungsten 74	186.2 **Re** Rhenium 75	190.2 **Os** Osmium 76	192.2 **Ir** Iridium 77	195.1 **Pt** Platinum 78	197.0 **Au** Gold 79	200.6 **Hg** Mercury 80
227.0 **Ac** † Actinium 89	261.1 **Rf** Rutherfordium 104	262.1 **Db** Dubrium 105	263.1 **Sg** Seaborgium 106	262.1 **Bh** Bohrium 107	— **Hs** Hassium 108	— **Mt** Meitnerium 109			

p-block

III	IV	V	VI	VII	0
					4.0 **He** Helium 2
10.8 **B** Boron 5	12.0 **C** Carbon 6	14.0 **N** Nitrogen 7	16.0 **O** Oxygen 8	19.0 **F** Fluorine 9	20.2 **Ne** Neon 10
27.0 **Al** Aluminium 13	28.1 **Si** Silicon 14	31.0 **P** Phosphorus 15	32.1 **S** Sulphur 16	35.5 **Cl** Chlorine 17	40.0 **Ar** Argon 18
69.7 **Ga** Gallium 31	72.6 **Ge** Germanium 32	74.9 **As** Arsenic 33	79.0 **Se** Selenium 34	79.9 **Br** Bromine 35	83.8 **Kr** Krypton 36
114.8 **In** Indium 49	118.7 **Sn** Tin 50	121.8 **Sb** Antimony 51	127.6 **Te** Tellurium 52	126.9 **I** Iodine 53	131.3 **Xe** Xenon 54
204.4 **Tl** Thallium 81	207.2 **Pb** Lead 82	209.0 **Bi** Bismuth 83	210.0 **Po** Polonium 84	210.0 **At** Astatine 85	222.0 **Rn** Radon 86

f-block

*Lanthanides

140.1 **Ce** Cerium 58	140.9 **Pr** Praseodymium 59	144.2 **Nd** Neodymium 60	146.9 **Pm** Promethium 61	150.4 **Sm** Samarium 62	152.0 **Eu** Europium 63	157.3 **Gd** Gadolinium 64	158.9 **Tb** Terbium 65	162.5 **Dy** Dysprosium 66	164.9 **Ho** Holmium 67	167.3 **Er** Erbium 68	168.9 **Tm** Thulium 69	173.0 **Yb** Ytterbium 70	175.0 **Lu** Lutetium 71

†Actinides

232.0 **Th** Thorium 90	231.0 **Pa** Protactinium 91	238.0 **U** Uranium 92	237.1 **Np** Neptunium 93	244.1 **Pu** Plutonium 94	243.1 **Am** Americium 95	247.1 **Cm** Curium 96	247.1 **Bk** Berkelium 97	251.1 **Cf** Californium 98	252.1 **Es** Einsteinium 99	257.1 **Fm** Fermium 100	258.1 **Md** Mendelevium 101	259.1 **No** Nobelium 102	260.1 **Lr** Lawrencium 103